ons

Com Catalogue

Australia

10th Edition 2016

STANLEY GIBBONS LTD
London and Ringwood

By Appointment to
Her Majesty The Queen
Philatelists
Stanley Gibbons Ltd,
London

Published by Stanley Gibbons Ltd
Editorial, Publications Sales Offices
and Distribution Centre:
7 Parkside, Christchurch Road, Ringwood,
Hants BH24 3SH

1st Edition – 2002
2nd Edition – 2004
3rd Edition – 2006
4th Edition – 2007
5th Edition – 2009
6th Edition – 2010
7th Edition – 2012
8th Edition – 2013
9th Edition – 2014
10th Edition – 2016

British Library Cataloguing in Publication Data.
A catalogue record for this book is available from the British Library.

Errors and omissions excepted
the colour reproduction of stamps is only as accurate as the printing process will allow.

ISBN-10: 0-85259-973-0
ISBN-13: 978-0-85259-973-0

Item No. R2871-16
Printed by
Stephens & George

Contents

Stanley Gibbons Holdings Plc

Stanley Gibbons Limited, Stanley Gibbons Auctions
399 Strand, London WC2R 0LX
Tel: +44 (0)207 836 8444
Fax: +44 (0)207 836 7342
E-mail: help@stanleygibbons.com
Website: www.stanleygibbons.com
for all departments, Auction and Specialist Stamp Departments.

Open Monday–Friday 9.30 a.m. to 5 p.m. Shop. Open Monday–Friday 9 a.m. to 5.30 p.m. and Saturday 9.30 a.m. to 5.30 p.m.

Stanley Gibbons Publications Gibbons Stamp Monthly and Philatelic Exporter
7 Parkside, Christchurch Road, Ringwood, Hampshire BH24 3SH.
Tel: +44 (0)1425 472363
Fax: +44 (0)1425 470247
E-mail: help@stanleygibbons.com
Publications Mail Order.
FREEPHONE 0800 611622

Monday–Friday 8.30 a.m. to 5 p.m.

Stanley Gibbons (Guernsey) Limited
18–20 Le Bordage, St Peter Port, Guernsey GY1 1DE.
Tel: +44 (0)1481 708270
Fax: +44 (0)1481 708279
E-mail: investment@stanleygibbons.com

Stanley Gibbons (Jersey) Limited
18 Hill Street, St Helier, Jersey, Channel Islands JE2 4UA.
Tel: +44 (0)1534 766711
Fax: +44 (0)1534 766177
E-mail: investment@stanleygibbons.com

Stanley Gibbons (Asia) Limited
Room 618, 6/F,
100 Queen's Road Central
Central,
Hong Kong
Tel: +852 3180 9370
E-mail: elee@stanleygibbons.com

Stanley Gibbons Publications Overseas Representation
Stanley Gibbons Publications are represented overseas by the following

Australia ***Renniks Publications PTY LTD***
Unit 3 37-39 Green Street, Banksmeadow, NSW 2019, Australia
Tel: +612 9695 7055
Website: www.renniks.com

Canada ***Unitrade Associates***
99 Floral Parkway, Toronto, Ontario M6L 2C4, Canada
Tel: +1 416 242 5900
Website: www.unitradeassoc.com

Germany ***Schaubek Verlag Leipzig***
Am Glaeschen 23, D-04420 Markranstaedt, Germany
Tel: +49 34 205 67823
Website: www.schaubek.de

Italy ***Ernesto Marini S.R.L.***
V. Struppa, 300, Genova, 16165, Italy
Tel: +3901 0247-3530
Website: www.ernestomarini.it

Japan ***Japan Philatelic***
PO Box 2, Suginami-Minami, Tokyo 168-8081, Japan
Tel: +81 3330 41641
Website: www.yushu.co.jp

Netherlands also covers Belgium Denmark, Finland & France
Uitgeverij Davo BV
PO Box 411, Ak Deventer, 7400 Netherlands
Tel: +315 7050 2700
Website: www.davo.nl

New Zealand ***House of Stamps***
PO Box 12, Paraparaumu, New Zealand
Tel: +61 6364 8270
Website: www.houseofstamps.co.nz

New Zealand ***Philatelic Distributors***
PO Box 863
15 Mount Edgecumbe Street
New Plymouth 4615, New Zealand
Tel: +6 46 758 65 68
Website: www.stampcollecta.com

Norway ***SKANFIL A/S***
SPANAV. 52 / BOKS 2030
N-5504 HAUGESUND, Norway
Tel: +47-52703940
E-mail: magne@skanfil.no

Singapore ***C S Philatelic Agency***
Peninsula Shopping Centre #04-29
3 Coleman Street, 179804, Singapore
Tel: +65 6337-1859
Website: www.cs.com.sg

South Africa ***Peter Bale Philatelics***
P O Box 3719, Honeydew, 2040, South Africa
Tel: +27 11 462 2463
Tel: +27 82 330 3925
E-mail: balep@iafrica.com

Sweden ***Chr Winther Sorensen AB***
Box 43, S-310 20 Knaered, Sweden
Tel: +46 43050743
Website: www.collectia.se

USA ***Regency Superior Ltd***
229 North Euclid Avenue
Saint Louis, Missouri 63108, USA

PO Box 8277, St Louis, MO 63156-8277, USA
Toll Free Tel: (800) 782-0066
Tel: (314) 361-5699
Website: www.RegencySuperior.com
Email: info@regencysuperior.com

General Philatelic Information and Guidelines to the Scope of Stanley Gibbons Commonwealth Catalogues

These notes reflect current practice in compiling the Stanley Gibbons Commonwealth Catalogues.

The Stanley Gibbons Stamp Catalogue has a very long history and the vast quantity of information it contains has been carefully built up by successive generations through the work of countless individuals. Philately is never static and the Catalogue has evolved and developed over the years. These notes relate to the current criteria upon which a stamp may be listed or priced. These criteria have developed over time and may have differed somewhat in the early years of this catalogue. These notes are not intended to suggest that we plan to make wholesale changes to the listing of classic issues in order to bring them into line with today's listing policy, they are designed to inform catalogue users as to the policies currently in operation.

PRICES

The prices quoted in this Catalogue are the estimated selling prices of Stanley Gibbons Ltd at the time of publication. They are, unless it is specifically stated otherwise, for examples in fine condition for the issue concerned. Superb examples are worth more; those of a lower quality considerably less.

All prices are subject to change without prior notice and Stanley Gibbons Ltd may from time to time offer stamps below catalogue price. Individual low value stamps sold at 399 Strand are liable to an additional handling charge. Purchasers of new issues should note the prices charged for them contain an element for the service rendered and so may exceed the prices shown when the stamps are subsequently catalogued. Postage and handling charges are extra.

No guarantee is given to supply all stamps priced, since it is not possible to keep every catalogued item in stock. Commemorative issues may, at times, only be available in complete sets and not as individual values.

Quotation of prices. The prices in the left-hand column are for unused stamps and those in the right-hand column are for used.

A dagger (†) denotes that the item listed does not exist in that condition and a blank, or dash, that it exists, or may exist, but we are unable to quote a price. We welcome information concerning items which are currently unpriced; such assistance may lead to them being priced in future editions.

Prices are expressed in pounds and pence sterling. One pound comprises 100 pence (£1 = 100p).

The method of notation is as follows: pence in numerals (e.g. 10 denotes ten pence); pounds and pence, up to £100, in numerals (e.g. 4·25 denotes four pounds and twenty-five pence); prices above £100 are expressed in whole pounds with the '£' sign shown.

Unused stamps. Great Britain and Commonwealth: the prices for unused stamps of Queen Victoria to King George V are for lightly hinged examples. Unused prices for King Edward VIII, King George VI and Queen Elizabeth issues are for unmounted mint.

Some stamps from the King George VI period are often difficult to find in unmounted mint condition. In such instances we would expect that collectors would need to pay a high proportion of the price quoted to obtain mounted mint examples. Generally speaking lightly mounted mint stamps from this reign, issued before 1945, are in considerable demand.

Used stamps. The used prices are normally for fine postally used stamps, but may be for stamps cancelled-to-order where this practice exists.

A pen-cancellation on early issues can sometimes correctly denote postal use. Instances are individually noted in the Catalogue in explanation of the used price given.

Prices quoted for bisects on cover or large piece are for those dated during the period officially authorised.

Stamps not sold unused to the public (e.g. some official stamps) are priced used only.

The use of 'unified' designs, that is stamps inscribed for both postal and fiscal purposes, results in a number of stamps of very high face value. In some instances these may not have been primarily intended for postal purposes, but if they are so inscribed we include them. We only price such items used, however, where there is evidence of normal postal usage.

Cover prices. To assist collectors, cover prices are quoted for issues up to 1945 at the beginning of each country.

The system gives a general guide in the form of a factor by which the corresponding used price of the basic loose stamp should be multiplied when found in fine average condition on cover.

Care is needed in applying the factors and they relate to a cover which bears a single of the denomination listed; if more than one denomination is present the most highly priced attracts the multiplier and the remainder are priced at the simple figure for used singles in arriving at a total.

The cover should be of non-philatelic origin; bearing the correct postal rate for the period and distance involved and cancelled with the markings normal to the offices concerned. Purely philatelic items have a cover value only slightly greater than the catalogue value for the corresponding used stamps. This applies generally to those high-value stamps used philatelically rather than in the normal course of commerce. Low-value stamps, e.g. ¼d. and ½d., are desirable when used as a single rate on cover and merit an increase in 'multiplier' value.

First day covers in the period up to 1945 are not within the scope of the system and the multiplier should not be used. As a special category of philatelic usage, with wide variations in valuation according to scarcity, they require separate treatment.

Oversized covers, difficult to accommodate on an album page, should be reckoned as worth little more than the corresponding value of the used stamps. The condition of a cover also affects its value. Except for 'wreck covers', serious damage or soiling reduce the value where the postal markings and stamps are ordinary ones. Conversely, visual appeal adds to the value and this can include freshness of appearance, important addresses, old-fashioned but legible handwriting, historic town-names, etc.

The multipliers are a base on which further value would be added to take account of the cover's postal historical importance in demonstrating such things as unusual, scarce or emergency cancels, interesting routes, significant postal markings, combination usage, the development of postal rates, and so on.

Minimum price. The minimum catalogue price quoted is 10p. For individual stamps prices between 10p. and 95p. are provided as a guide for catalogue users. The lowest price charged for individual stamps or sets purchased from Stanley Gibbons Ltd is £1

Set prices. Set prices are generally for one of each value, excluding shades and varieties, but including major colour changes. Where there are alternative shades, etc., the cheapest is usually included. The number of stamps in the set is always stated for clarity. The prices for sets containing *se-tenant* pieces are based on the prices quoted for such combinations, and not on those for the individual stamps.

Varieties. Where plate or cylinder varieties are priced in used condition the price quoted is for a fine used example with the cancellation well clear of the listed flaw.

Specimen stamps. The pricing of these items is explained under that heading.

Stamp booklets. Prices are for complete assembled booklets in fine condition with those issued before 1945 showing normal wear and tear. Incomplete booklets and those which have been 'exploded' will, in general, be worth less than the figure quoted.

Repricing. Collectors will be aware that the market factors of supply and demand directly influence the prices quoted in this Catalogue. Whatever the scarcity of a particular stamp, if there is no one in the market who wishes to buy it cannot be expected to achieve a high price. Conversely, the same item actively sought by numerous potential buyers may cause the price to rise.

All the prices in this Catalogue are examined during the preparation of each new edition by the expert staff of Stanley Gibbons and repriced as necessary. They take many factors into account, including supply and demand, and are in close touch with the international stamp market and the auction world.

Commonwealth cover prices and advice on postal history material originally provided by Edward B Proud.

GUARANTEE

All stamps are guaranteed originals in the following terms:

If not as described, and returned by the purchaser, we undertake to refund the price paid to us in the original transaction. If any stamp is certified as genuine by the Expert Committee of the Royal Philatelic Society, London, or by BPA Expertising Ltd, the purchaser shall not be entitled to make any claim against us for any error, omission or mistake in such certificate.

Consumers' statutory rights are not affected by the above guarantee.

The recognised Expert Committees in this country are those of the Royal Philatelic Society, 41 Devonshire Place, London W1G, 6JY, and BPA Expertising Ltd, PO Box 1141, Guildford, Surrey GU5 0WR. They do not undertake valuations under any circumstances and fees are payable for their services.

MARGINS ON IMPERFORATE STAMPS

Superb | Very fine | Fine | Average | Poor

GUM

Unmounted | Very lightly mounted | Lightly mounted | Mounted/ large part original gum (o.g.). | Heavily mounted small part o.g.

CENTRING

Superb | Very fine | Fine | Average | Poor

CANCELLATIONS

Superb | Very fine | Fine | Average | Poor

Superb | Very fine

Fine | Average | Poor

CONDITION GUIDE

To assist collectors in assessing the true value of items they are considering buying or in reviewing stamps already in their collections, we now offer a more detailed guide to the condition of stamps on which this catalogue's prices are based.

For a stamp to be described as 'Fine', it should be sound in all respects, without creases, bends, wrinkles, pin holes, thins or tears. If perforated, all perforation 'teeth' should be intact, it should not suffer from fading, rubbing or toning and it should be of clean, fresh appearance.

Margins on imperforate stamps: These should be even on all sides and should be at least as wide as half the distance between that stamp and the next. To have one or more margins of less than this width, would normally preclude a stamp from being described as 'Fine'. Some early stamps were positioned very close together on the printing plate and in such cases 'Fine' margins would necessarily be narrow. On the other hand, some plates were laid down to give a substantial gap between individual stamps and in such cases margins would be expected to be much wider.

An 'average' four-margin example would have a narrower margin on one or more sides and should be priced accordingly, while a stamp with wider, yet even, margins than 'Fine' would merit the description 'Very Fine' or 'Superb' and, if available, would command a price in excess of that quoted in the catalogue.

Gum: Since the prices for stamps of King Edward VIII, King George VI and Queen Elizabeth are for 'unmounted' or 'never hinged' mint, even stamps from these reigns which have been very lightly mounted should be available at a discount from catalogue price, the more obvious the hinge marks, the greater the discount.

Catalogue prices for stamps issued prior to King Edward VIII's reign are for mounted mint, so unmounted examples would be worth a premium. Hinge marks on 20th-century stamps should not be too obtrusive, and should be at least in the lightly mounted category. For 19th-century stamps more obvious hinging would be acceptable, but stamps should still carry a large part of their original gum—'Large part o.g.'—in order to be described as 'Fine'.

Centring: Ideally, the stamp's image should appear in the exact centre of the perforated area, giving equal margins on all sides. 'Fine' centring would be close to this ideal with any deviation having an effect on the value of the stamp. As in the case of the margins on imperforate stamps, it should be borne in mind that the space between some early stamps was very narrow, so it was very difficult to achieve accurate perforation, especially when the technology was in its infancy. Thus, poor centring would have a less damaging effect on the value of a 19th-century stamp than on a 20th-century example, but the premium put on a perfectly centred specimen would be greater.

Cancellations: Early cancellation devices were designed to 'obliterate' the stamp in order to prevent it being reused and this is still an important objective for today's postal administrations. Stamp collectors, on the other hand, prefer postmarks to be lightly applied, clear, and to leave as much as possible of the design visible. Dated, circular cancellations have long been 'the postmark of choice', but the definition of a 'Fine' cancellation will depend upon the types of cancellation in use at the time a stamp was current—it is clearly illogical to seek a circular datestamp on a Penny Black.

'Fine', by definition, will be superior to 'Average', so, in terms of cancellation quality, if one begins by identifying what 'Average' looks like, then one will be half way to identifying 'Fine'. The illustrations will give some guidance on mid-19th-century and mid-20th-century cancellations of Great Britain, but types of cancellation in general use in each country and in each period will determine the appearance of 'Fine'.

As for the factors discussed above, anything less than 'Fine' will result in a downgrading of the stamp concerned, while a very fine or superb cancellation will be worth a premium.

Combining the factors: To merit the description 'Fine', a stamp should be fine in every respect, but a small deficiency in one area might be made up for in another by a factor meriting an 'Extremely Fine' description.

Some early issues are so seldom found in what would normally be considered to be 'Fine' condition, the catalogue prices are for a slightly lower grade, with 'Fine' examples being worth a premium. In such cases a note to this effect is given in the catalogue, while elsewhere premiums are given for well-centred, lightly cancelled examples.

In the 21st-century many postal administrations seem to feel that there is little need for stamps to be legibly cancelled and ink-jet markings, heavy obliterations and pen cancellations are very much the order of the day, while a large proportion of stamps are left without a postal marking of any kind. Used stamps of this type are of very little value and the prices shown in this catalogue are for clear circular operational date stamps or appropriate commemorative cancellations, although the latter are also frowned upon by many collectors.

Stamps graded at less than fine remain collectable and, in the case of more highly priced stamps, will continue to hold a value. Nevertheless, buyers should always bear condition in mind.

The Catalogue in General

Contents. The Catalogue is confined to adhesive postage stamps, including miniature sheets. For particular categories the rules are:

(a) Revenue (fiscal) stamps are listed only where they have been expressly authorised for postal duty.

(b) Stamps issued only precancelled are included, but normally issued stamps available additionally with precancel have no separate precancel listing unless the face value is changed.

(c) Stamps prepared for use but not issued, hitherto accorded full listing, are nowadays foot-noted with a price (where possible).

(d) Bisects (trisects, etc.) are only listed where such usage was officially authorised.

(e) Stamps issued only on first day covers or in presentation packs and not available separately are not listed but may be priced in a footnote.

(f) New printings are only included in this Catalogue where they show a major philatelic variety, such as a change in shade, watermark or paper. Stamps which exist with or without imprint dates are listed separately; changes in imprint dates are mentioned in footnotes.

(g) Official and unofficial reprints are dealt with by footnote.

(h) Stamps from imperforate printings of modern issues which occur perforated are covered by footnotes, but are listed where widely available for postal use.

Exclusions. The following are excluded:

(a) non-postal revenue or fiscal stamps;

(b) postage stamps used fiscally (although prices are now given for some fiscally used high values);

(c) local carriage labels and private local issues;

(d) bogus or phantom stamps;

(e) railway or airline letter fee stamps, bus or road transport company labels or the stamps of private postal companies operating under licence from the national authority;

(f) cut-outs;

(g) all types of non-postal labels and souvenirs;

(h) documentary labels for the postal service, e.g. registration, recorded delivery, air-mail etiquettes, etc.;

(i) privately applied embellishments to official issues and privately commissioned items generally;

(j) stamps for training postal officers.

Full listing. 'Full listing' confers our recognition and implies allotting a catalogue number and (wherever possible) a price quotation.

In judging status for inclusion in the catalogue broad considerations are applied to stamps. They must be issued by a legitimate postal authority, recognised by the government concerned, and must be adhesives valid for proper postal use in the class of service for which they are inscribed. Stamps, with the exception of such categories as postage dues and officials, must be available to the general public, at face value, in reasonable quantities without any artificial restrictions being imposed on their distribution.

For errors and varieties the criterion is legitimate (albeit inadvertent) sale through a postal administration in the normal course of business. Details of provenance are always important; printers' waste and deliberately manufactured material are excluded.

Certificates. In assessing unlisted items due weight is given to Certificates from recognised Expert Committees and, where appropriate, we will usually ask to see them.

Date of issue. Where local issue dates differ from dates of release by agencies, 'date of issue' is the local date. Fortuitous stray usage before the officially intended date is disregarded in listing.

Catalogue numbers. Stamps of each country are catalogued chronologically by date of issue. Subsidiary classes are placed at the end of the country, as separate lists, with a distinguishing letter prefix to the catalogue number, e.g. D for postage due, O for official and E for express delivery stamps.

The catalogue number appears in the extreme left-column. The boldface Type numbers in the next column are merely cross-references to illustrations.

Once published in the Catalogue, numbers are changed as little as possible; really serious renumbering is reserved for the occasions when a complete country or an entire issue is being rewritten. The edition first affected includes cross-reference tables of old and new numbers.

Our catalogue numbers are universally recognised in specifying stamps and as a hallmark of status.

Illustrations. Stamps are illustrated at three-quarters linear size. Stamps not illustrated are the same size and format as the value shown, unless otherwise indicated. Stamps issued only as miniature sheets have the stamp alone illustrated but sheet size is also quoted. Overprints, surcharges, watermarks and postmarks are normally actual size. Illustrations of varieties are often enlarged to show the detail. Stamp booklet covers are illustrated half-size, unless otherwise indicated.

Designers. Designers' names are quoted where known, though space precludes naming every individual concerned in the production of a set. In particular, photographers supplying material are usually named only where they also make an active contribution in the design stage; posed photographs of reigning monarchs are, however, an exception to this rule.

CONTACTING THE CATALOGUE EDITOR

The editor is always interested in hearing from people who have new information which will improve or correct the Catalogue. As a general rule he must see and examine the actual stamps before they can be considered for listing; photographs or photocopies are insufficient evidence.

Submissions should be made in writing to the Catalogue Editor, Stanley Gibbons Publications at the Ringwood office. The cost of return postage for items submitted is appreciated, and this should include the registration fee if required.

Where information is solicited purely for the benefit of the enquirer, the editor cannot undertake to reply if the answer is already contained in these published notes or if return postage is omitted. Written communications are greatly preferred to enquiries by telephone or e-mail and the editor regrets that he or his staff cannot see personal callers without a prior appointment being made. Correspondence may be subject to delay during the production period of each new edition.

The editor welcomes close contact with study circles and is interested, too, in finding reliable local correspondents who will verify and supplement official information in countries where this is deficient.

We regret we do not give opinions as to the genuineness of stamps, nor do we identify stamps or number them by our Catalogue.

TECHNICAL MATTERS

The meanings of the technical terms used in the catalogue will be found in our *Philatelic Terms Illustrated.*

References below to (more specialised) listings are to be taken to indicate, as appropriate, the Stanley Gibbons *Great Britain Specialised Catalogue* in five volumes or the *Great Britain Concise Catalogue*.

1. Printing

Printing errors. Errors in printing are of major interest to the Catalogue. Authenticated items meriting consideration would include: background, centre or frame inverted or omitted; centre or subject transposed; error of colour; error or omission of value; double prints and impressions; printed both sides; and so on. Designs *tête-bêche*, whether intentionally or by accident, are listable. *Se-tenant* arrangements of stamps are recognised in the listings or footnotes. Gutter pairs (a pair of stamps separated by blank margin) are not included in this volume. Colours only partially omitted are not listed. Stamps with embossing omitted are reserved for our more specialised listings.

Printing varieties. Listing is accorded to major changes in the printing base which lead to completely new types. In recess-printing this could be a design re-engraved; in photogravure or photolithography a screen altered in whole or in part. It can also encompass flat-bed and rotary printing if the results are readily distinguishable.

To be considered at all, varieties must be constant.

Early stamps, produced by primitive methods, were prone to numerous imperfections; the lists reflect this, recognising re-entries, retouches, broken frames, misshapen letters, and so on. Printing technology has, however, radically improved over the years, during which time photogravure and lithography have become predominant. Varieties nowadays are more in the nature of flaws and these, being too specialised for this general catalogue, are almost always outside the scope.

In no catalogue, however, do we list such items as: dry prints, kiss prints, doctor-blade flaws, colour shifts or registration flaws (unless they lead to the complete omission of a colour from an individual stamp), lithographic ring flaws, and so on. Neither do we recognise fortuitous happenings like paper creases or confetti flaws.

Varieties of varieties. We no longer provide individual listings for combinations of two or more varieties; thus a plate variety or overprinting error will not be listed for different watermark orientations.

Overprints (and surcharges). Overprints of different types qualify for separate listing. These include overprints in different colours; overprints from different printing processes such as litho and typo; overprints in totally different typefaces, etc. Major errors in machine-printed overprints are important and listable. They include: overprint inverted or omitted; overprint double (treble, etc.); overprint diagonal; overprint double, one inverted; pairs with one overprint omitted, e.g. from a radical shift to an adjoining stamp; error of colour; error of type fount; letters inverted or omitted, etc. If the overprint is handstamped, few of these would qualify and a distinction is drawn. We continue, however, to list pairs of stamps where one has a handstamped overprint and the other has not.

Albino prints or double prints, one of them being albino (i.e. showing an uninked impression of the printing plate) are listable unless they are particularly common in this form (see the note below Travancore No. 32fa, for example). We do not, however, normally list reversed albino overprints, caused by the accidental or deliberate folding of sheets prior to overprinting (British Levant Nos. 51/8).

Varieties occurring in overprints will often take the form of broken letters, slight differences in spacing, rising spaces, etc. Only the most important would be considered for listing or footnote mention.

Sheet positions. If space permits we quote sheet positions of listed varieties and authenticated data is solicited for this purpose.

De La Rue plates. The Catalogue classifies the general plates used by De La Rue for printing British Colonial stamps as follows:

VICTORIAN KEY TYPE

Die I

1. The ball of decoration on the second point of the crown appears as a dark mass of lines.
2. Dark vertical shading separates the front hair from the bun.
3. The vertical line of colour outlining the front of the throat stops at the sixth line of shading on the neck.
4. The white space in the coil of the hair above the curl is roughly the shape of a pin's head.

Die II

1. There are very few lines of colour in the ball and it appears almost white.
2. A white vertical strand of hair appears in place of the dark shading.
3. The line stops at the eighth line of shading.
4. The white space is oblong, with a line of colour partially dividing it at the left end.

Plates numbered 1 and 2 are both Die I. Plates 3 and 4 are Die II.

GEORGIAN KEY TYPE

Die I

A. The second (thick) line below the name of the country is cut slanting, conforming roughly to the shape of the crown on each side.
B. The labels of solid colour bearing the words "POSTAGE" and "& REVENUE" are square at the inner top corners.
C. There is a projecting "bud" on the outer spiral of the ornament in each of the lower corners.

Die II

A. The second line is cut vertically on each side of the crown.
B. The labels curve inwards at the top.
C. There is no "bud" in this position.

Unless otherwise stated in the lists, all stamps with watermark Multiple Crown CA (w **8**) are Die I while those with watermark Multiple Crown Script CA (w **9**) are Die II. The Georgian Die II was introduced in April 1921 and was used for Plates 10 to 22 and 26 to 28. Plates 23 to 25 were made from Die I by mistake.

2. Paper

All stamps listed are deemed to be on (ordinary) paper of the wove type and white in colour; only departures from this are normally mentioned.

Types. Where classification so requires we distinguish such other types of paper as, for example, vertically and horizontally laid; wove and laid bâtonné; card(board); carton; cartridge; glazed; granite; native; pelure; porous; quadrillé; ribbed; rice; and silk thread.

Wove paper

Laid paper

Granite paper

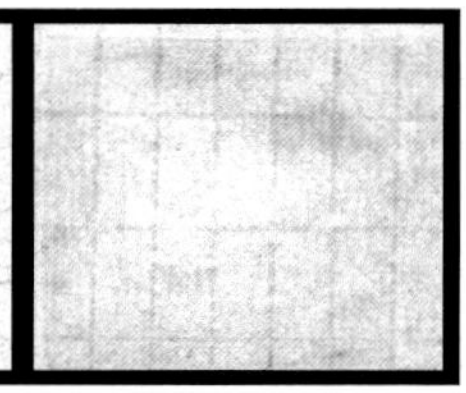

Quadrillé paper

Burelé band

The various makeshifts for normal paper are listed as appropriate. The varieties of double paper and joined paper are recognised. The security device of a printed burelé band on the back of a stamp, as in early Queensland, qualifies for listing.

Descriptive terms. The fact that a paper is handmade (and thus probably of uneven thickness) is mentioned where necessary. Such descriptive terms as "hard" and "soft"; "smooth" and "rough"; "thick", "medium" and "thin" are applied where there is philatelic merit in classifying papers.

Coloured, very white and toned papers. A coloured paper is one that is coloured right through (front and back of the stamp). In the Catalogue the colour of the paper is given in italics, thus:

black/*rose* = black design on rose paper.

Papers have been made specially white in recent years by, for example, a very heavy coating of chalk. We do not classify shades of whiteness of paper as distinct varieties. There does exist, however, a type of paper from early days called toned. This is off-white, often brownish or buffish, but it cannot be assigned any definite colour. A toning effect brought on by climate, incorrect storage or gum staining is disregarded here, as this was not the state of the paper when issued.

"Ordinary" and "Chalk-surfaced" papers. The availability of many postage stamps for revenue purposes made necessary some safeguard against the illegitimate re-use of stamps with removable cancellations. This was at first secured by using fugitive inks and later by printing on paper surfaced by coatings containing either chalk or china clay, both of which made it difficult to remove any form of obliteration without damaging the stamp design.

This catalogue lists these chalk-surfaced paper varieties from their introduction in 1905. Where no indication is given, the paper is "ordinary".

The "traditional" method of indentifying chalk-surfaced papers has been that, when touched with a silver wire, a black mark is left on the paper, and the listings in this catalogue are based on that test. However, the test itself is now largely discredited, for, although the mark can be removed by a soft rubber, some damage to the stamp will result from its use.

The difference between chalk-surfaced and pre-war ordinary papers is fairly clear: chalk-surfaced papers being smoother to the touch and showing a characteristic sheen when light is reflected off their surface. Under good magnification tiny bubbles or pock marks can be seen on the surface of the stamp and at the tips of the perforations the surfacing appears "broken". Traces of paper fibres are evident on the surface of ordinary paper and the ink shows a degree of absorption into it.

Initial chalk-surfaced paper printings by De La Rue had a thinner coating than subsequently became the norm. The characteristics described above are less pronounced in these printings.

During and after the Second World War, substitute papers replaced the chalk-surfaced papers, these do not react to the silver test and are therefore classed as "ordinary", although differentiating them without recourse to it is more difficult, for, although the characteristics of the chalk-surfaced paper remained the same, some of the ordinary papers appear much smoother than earlier papers and many do not show the watermark clearly. Experience is the only solution to identifying these, and comparison with stamps whose paper type is without question will be of great help.

Another type of paper, known as "thin striated" was used only for the Bahamas 1s. and 5s. (Nos. 155a, 156a, 171 and 174) and for several stamps of the Malayan states. Hitherto these have been described as "chalk-surfaced" since they gave some reaction to the silver test, but they are much thinner than usual chalk-surfaced papers, with the watermark showing clearly. Stamps on this paper show a slightly 'ribbed' effect when the stamp is held up to the light. Again, comparison with a known striated paper stamp, such as the 1941 Straits Settlements Die II 2c. orange (No. 294) will prove invaluable in separating these papers.

Glazed paper. In 1969 the Crown Agents introduced a new general-purpose paper for use in conjunction with all current printing processes. It generally has a marked glossy surface but the degree varies according to the process used, being more marked in recess-printing stamps. As it does not respond to the silver test this presents a further test where previous printings were on chalky paper. A change of paper to the glazed variety merits separate listing.

Green and yellow papers. Issues of the First World War and immediate postwar period occur on green and yellow papers and these are given separate Catalogue listing. The original coloured papers (coloured throughout) gave way to surface-coloured papers, the stamps having "white backs"; other stamps show one colour on the front and a different one at the back. Because of the numerous variations a grouping of colours is adopted as follows:

Yellow papers

(1) The original *yellow* paper (throughout), usually bright in colour. The gum is often sparse, of harsh consistency and dull-looking. Used 1912–1920.

(2) The *white-backs*. Used 1913–1914.

(3) A bright lemon paper. The colour must have a pronounced greenish tinge, different from the "yellow" in (1). As a rule, the gum on stamps using this lemon paper is plentiful, smooth and shiny, and the watermark shows distinctly. Care is needed with stamps printed in green on yellow paper (1) as it may appear that the paper is this lemon. Used 1914–1916.

(4) An experimental *orange-buff* paper. The colour must have a distinct brownish tinge. It is not to be confused with a muddy yellow (1) nor the misleading appearance (on the surface) of stamps printed in red on yellow paper where an engraved plate has been insufficiently wiped. Used 1918–1921.

(5) An experimental *buff* paper. This lacks the brownish tinge of (4) and the brightness of the yellow shades. The gum is shiny when compared with the matt type used on (4). Used 1919–1920.

(6) A *pale yellow* paper that has a creamy tone to the yellow. Used from 1920 onwards.

Green papers

(7) The original "green" paper, varying considerably through shades of blue-green and yellow-green, the front and back sometimes differing. Used 1912–1916.

(8) The *white backs*. Used 1913–1914.

(9) A paper blue-green on the surface with *pale olive* back. The back must be markedly paler than the front and this and the pronounced olive tinge to the back distinguish it from (7). Used 1916–1920.

(10) Paper with a vivid green surface, commonly called *emerald-green*; it has the olive back of (9). Used 1920.

(11) Paper with *emerald-green* both back and front. Used from 1920 onwards.

3. Perforation and Rouletting

Perforation gauge. The gauge of a perforation is the number of holes in a length of 2 cm. For correct classification the size of the holes (large or small) may need to be distinguished; in a few cases the actual number of holes on each edge of the stamp needs to be quoted.

Measurement. The Gibbons *Instanta* gauge is the standard for measuring perforations. The stamp is viewed against a dark background with the transparent gauge put on top of it. Though the gauge measures to decimal accuracy, perforations read from it are generally quoted in the Catalogue to the nearest half. For example:

Just over perf 12¾ to just under 13¼ = perf 13
Perf 13¼ exactly, rounded up = perf 13½
Just over perf 13¼ to just under 13¾ = perf 13½
Perf 13¾ exactly, rounded up = perf 14

However, where classification depends on it, actual quarter-perforations are quoted.

Notation. Where no perforation is quoted for an issue it is imperforate. Perforations are usually abbreviated (and spoken) as follows, though sometimes they may be spelled out for clarity. This notation for rectangular stamps (the majority) applies to diamond shapes if "top" is read as the edge to the top right.

P 14: perforated alike on all sides (read: "perf 14").

P 14×15: the first figure refers to top and bottom, the second to left and right sides (read: "perf 14 by 15"). This is a compound perforation. For an upright triangular stamp the first figure refers to the two sloping sides and second to the base. In inverted triangulars the base is first and the second figure to the sloping sides.

P 14–15: perforation measuring anything between 14 and 15: the holes are irregularly spaced, thus the gauge may vary along a single line or even along a single edge of the stamp (read: "perf 14 to 15").

P 14 *irregular*: perforated 14 from a worn perforator, giving badly aligned holes irregularly spaced (read: "irregular perf 14").

P *comp(ound)* 14×15: two gauges in use but not necessarily on opposite sides of the stamp. It could be one side in one gauge and three in the other; or two adjacent sides with the same gauge. (Read: "perf compound of 14 and 15".) For three gauges or more, abbreviated as "P 12, 14½, 15 *or compound*" for example.

P 14, 14½: perforated approximately 14¼ (read: "perf 14 or 14½"). It does *not* mean two stamps, one perf 14 and the other perf 14½. This obsolescent notation is gradually being replaced in the Catalogue.

Imperf: imperforate (not perforated)

Imperf×P 14: imperforate at top ad bottom and perf 14 at sides.

P 14×*imperf*: perf 14 at top and bottom and imperforate at sides.

Such headings as "P 13×14 (*vert*) and P 14×13 (*horiz*)" indicate which perforations apply to which stamp format—vertical or horizontal.

Some stamps are additionally perforated so that a label or tab is detachable; others have been perforated for use as two halves. Listings are normally for whole stamps, unless stated otherwise.

Imperf×perf

Other terms. Perforation almost always gives circular holes; where other shapes have been used they are specified, e.g. square holes; lozenge perf. Interrupted perfs are brought about by the omission of pins at regular intervals. Perforations merely simulated by being printed as part of the design are of course ignored. With few exceptions, privately applied perforations are not listed.

In the 19th-century perforations are often described as clean cut (clean, sharply incised holes), intermediate or rough (rough holes, imperfectly cut, often the result of blunt pins).

Perforation errors and varieties. Authenticated errors, where a stamp normally perforated is accidentally issued imperforate, are listed provided no traces of perforation (blind holes or indentations) remain. They must be provided as pairs, both stamps wholly imperforate, and are only priced in that form.

Stamps imperforate between stamp and sheet margin are not listed in this catalogue, but such errors on Great Britain stamps will be found in the *Great Britain Specialised Catalogue*.

Pairs described as "imperforate between" have the line of perforations between the two stamps omitted.

Imperf between (horiz pair): a horizontal pair of stamps with perfs all around the edges but none between the stamps.

Imperf between (vert pair): a vertical pair of stamps with perfs all around the edges but none between the stamps.

Imperf between (vertical pair)

Imperf horizontally (vertical pair)

Where several of the rows have escaped perforation the resulting varieties are listable. Thus:

Imperf vert (horiz pair): a horizontal pair of stamps perforated top and bottom; all three vertical directions are imperf—the two outer edges and between the stamps.

Imperf horiz (vert pair): a vertical pair perforated at left and right edges; all three horizontal directions are imperf—the top, bottom and between the stamps.

Straight edges. Large sheets cut up before issue to post offices can cause stamps with straight edges, i.e. imperf on one side or on two sides at right angles. They are not usually listable in this condition and are worth less than corresponding stamps properly perforated all round. This does not, however, apply to certain stamps, mainly from coils and booklets, where straight edges on various sides are the manufacturing norm affecting every stamp. The listings and notes make clear which sides are correctly imperf.

Malfunction. Varieties of double, misplaced or partial perforation caused by error or machine malfunction are not listable, neither are freaks, such as perforations placed diagonally from paper folds, nor missing holes caused by broken pins.

Types of perforating. Where necessary for classification, perforation types are distinguished.

These include:

Line perforation from one line of pins punching single rows of holes at a time.

Comb perforation from pins disposed across the sheet in comb formation, punching out holes at three sides of the stamp a row at a time.

Harrow perforation applied to a whole pane or sheet at one stroke.

Rotary perforation from toothed wheels operating across a sheet, then crosswise.

Sewing machine perforation. The resultant condition, clean-cut or rough, is distinguished where required.

Pin-perforation is the commonly applied term for pin-roulette in which, instead of being punched out, round holes are pricked by sharp-pointed pins and no paper is removed.

Mixed perforation occurs when stamps with defective perforations are re-perforated in a different gauge.

Punctured stamps. Perforation holes can be punched into the face of the stamp. Patterns of small holes, often in the shape of initial letters, are privately applied devices against pilferage. These (perfins) are outside the scope except for Australia, Canada, Cape of Good Hope, Papua and Sudan where they were used as official stamps by the national administration. Identification devices, when officially inspired, are listed or noted; they can be shapes, or letters or words formed from holes, sometimes converting one class of stamp into another.

Rouletting. In rouletting the paper is cut, for ease of separation, but none is removed. The gauge is measured, when needed, as for perforations. Traditional French terms descriptive of the type of cut are often used and types include:

Arc roulette (percé en arc). Cuts are minute, spaced arcs, each roughly a semicircle.

Cross roulette (percé en croix). Cuts are tiny diagonal crosses.

Line roulette (percé en ligne or *en ligne droite).* Short straight cuts parallel to the frame of the stamp. The commonest basic roulette. Where not further described, "roulette" means this type.

Rouletted in colour or coloured roulette (percé en lignes colorées or *en lignes de coleur).* Cuts with coloured edges, arising from notched rule inked simultaneously with the printing plate.

Saw-tooth roulette (percé en scie). Cuts applied zigzag fashion to resemble the teeth of a saw.

Serpentine roulette (percé en serpentin). Cuts as sharply wavy lines.

Zigzag roulette (percé en zigzags). Short straight cuts at angles in alternate directions, producing sharp points on separation. US usage favours "serrate(d) roulette" for this type.

Pin-roulette (originally *percé en points* and now *perforés trous d'epingle*) is commonly called pin-perforation in English.

4. Gum

All stamps listed are assumed to have gum of some kind; if they were issued without gum this is stated. Original gum (o.g.) means that which was present on the stamp as issued to the public. Deleterious climates and the presence of certain chemicals can cause gum to crack and, with early stamps, even make the paper deteriorate. Unscrupulous fakers are adept in removing it and regumming the stamp to meet the unreasoning demand often made for "full o.g." in cases where such a thing is virtually impossible.

The gum normally used on stamps has been gum arabic until the late 1960s when synthetic adhesives were introduced. Harrison and Sons Ltd for instance use *polyvinyl alcohol,* known to philatelists as PVA. This is almost invisible except for a slight yellowish tinge which was incorporated to make it possible to see that the stamps have been gummed. It has advantages in hot countries, as stamps do not curl and sheets are less likely to stick together. Gum arabic and PVA are not distinguished in the lists except that where a stamp exists with both forms this is indicated in footnotes. Our more specialised catalogues provide separate listing of gums for Great Britain.

Self-adhesive stamps are issued on backing paper, from which they are peeled before affixing to mail. Unused examples are priced as for backing paper intact, in which condition they are recommended to be kept. Used examples are best collected on cover or on piece.

5. Watermarks

Stamps are on unwatermarked paper except where the heading to the set says otherwise.

Detection. Watermarks are detected for Catalogue description by one of four methods: (1) holding stamps to the light; (2) laying stamps face down on a dark background; (3) adding a few drops of petroleum ether 40/60 to the stamp laid face down in a watermark tray; (4) by use of the Stanley Gibbons Detectamark, or other equipment, which work by revealing the thinning of the paper at the watermark. (Note that petroleum ether is highly inflammable in use and can damage photogravure stamps.)

Listable types. Stamps occurring on both watermarked and unwatermarked papers are different types and both receive full listing.

Single watermarks (devices occurring once on every stamp) can be modified in size and shape as between different issues; the types are noted but not usually separately listed. Fortuitous absence of watermark from a single stamp or its gross displacement would not be listable.

To overcome registration difficulties the device may be repeated at close intervals *(a multiple watermark)*, single stamps thus showing parts of several devices. Similarly, a *large sheet watermark* (or *all-over watermark*) covering numerous stamps can be used. We give informative notes and illustrations for them. The designs may be such that numbers of stamps in the sheet automatically lack watermark: this is not a listable variety. Multiple and all-over watermarks sometimes undergo modifications, but if the various types are difficult to distinguish from single stamps notes are given but not separate listings.

Papermakers' watermarks are noted where known but not listed separately, since most stamps in the sheet will lack them. Sheet watermarks which are nothing more than officially adopted papermakers' watermarks are, however, given normal listing.

Marginal watermarks, falling outside the pane of stamps, are ignored except where misplacement caused the adjoining row to be affected, in which case they may be footnoted.They usually consist of straight or angled lines and double-lined capital letters, they are particularly prevalent on some Crown CC and Crown CA watermarked stamps.

Watermark errors and varieties. Watermark errors are recognised as of major importance. They comprise stamps intended to be on unwatermarked paper but issued watermarked by mistake, or stamps printed on paper with the wrong watermark. Varieties showing letters omitted from the watermark are also included, but broken or deformed bits on the dandy roll are not listed unless they represent repairs.

Watermark positions. The diagram shows how watermark position is described in the Catalogue. Paper has a side intended for printing and watermarks are usually impressed so that they read normally when looked through from that printed side. However, since philatelists customarily detect watermarks by looking at the back of the stamp the watermark diagram also makes clear what is actually seen.

Illustrations in the Catalogue are of watermarks in normal positions (from the front of the stamps) and are actual size where possible.

Differences in watermark position are collectable varieties. This Catalogue now lists inverted, sideways inverted and reversed watermark varieties on Commonwealth stamps from the 1860s onwards except where the watermark position is completely haphazard.

Great Britain inverted and sideways inverted watermarks can be found in the *Great Britain Specialised Catalogue* and the *Great Britain Concise Catalogue*.

Where a watermark comes indiscriminately in various positions our policy is to cover this by a general note: we do not give separate listings because the watermark position in these circumstances has no particular philatelic importance.

As shown in the table, a watermark described as "sideways" will normally show the top of the letters or device (as shown in its illustration), pointing to the left of the stamp, as seen from the front and to the right as seen from the back.

For clarification, or in cases where the "normal" watermark is "sideways inverted", a note is generally provided at the foot of the relevant listing, particularly where sideways and sideways inverted varieties exist.

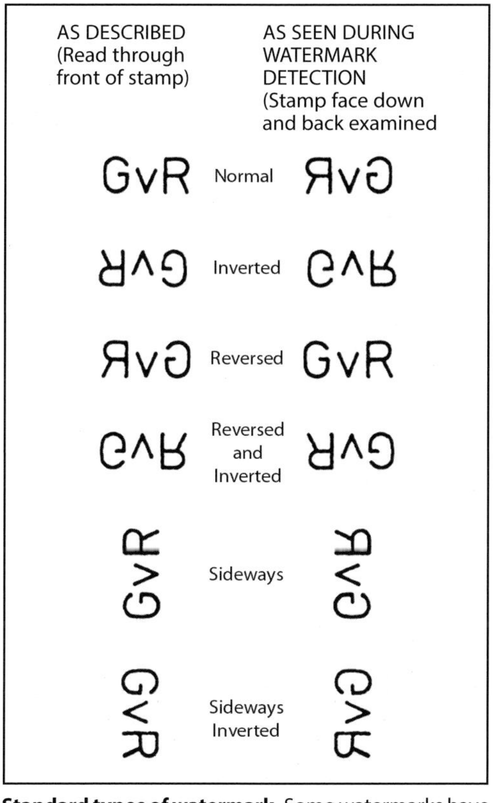

Standard types of watermark. Some watermarks have been used generally for various British possessions rather than exclusively for a single colony. To avoid repetition the Catalogue classifies 11 general types, as under, with references in the headings throughout the listings being given either in words or in the form ("W w **9**") (meaning "watermark type w **9**"). In those cases where watermark illustrations appear in the listings themselves, the respective reference reads, for example, W **153**, thus indicating that the watermark will be found in the normal sequence of illustrations as (type) **153**.

The general types are as follows, with an example of each quoted.

W	*Description*	*Example*
w **1**	Large Star	St. Helena No. 1
w **2**	Small Star	Turks Is. No. 4
w **3**	Broad (pointed) Star	Grenada No. 24
w **4**	Crown (over) CC, small stamp	Antigua No. 13
w **5**	Crown (over) CC, large stamp	Antigua No. 31
w **6**	Crown (over) CA, small stamp	Antigua No. 21
w **7**	Crown CA (CA over Crown), large stamp	Sierra Leone No. 54
w **8**	Multiple Crown CA	Antigua No. 41
w **9**	Multiple Script CA	Seychelles No. 158
w **9***a*	do. Error	Seychelles No. 158a
w **9***b*	do. Error	Seychelles No. 158b
w **10**	V over Crown	N.S.W. No. 327
w **11**	Crown over A	N.S.W. No. 347

CC in these watermarks is an abbreviation for "Crown Colonies" and CA for "Crown Agents". Watermarks w **1**, w **2** and w **3** are on stamps printed by Perkins, Bacon; w **4** onwards on stamps from De La Rue and other printers.

w **1**
Large Star

w **2**
Small Star

w **3**
Broad-pointed Star

Watermark w **1**, *Large Star*, measures 15 to 16 mm across the star from point to point and about 27 mm from centre to centre vertically between stars in the sheet. It was made for long stamps like Ceylon 1857 and St. Helena 1856.

Watermark w **2**, *Small Star* is of similar design but measures 12 to 13½mm from point to point and 24 mm from centre to centre vertically. It was for use with ordinary-size stamps such as Grenada 1863–71.

When the Large Star watermark was used with the smaller stamps it only occasionally comes in the centre of the paper. It is frequently so misplaced as to show portions of two stars above and below and this eccentricity will very often help in determining the watermark.

Watermark w **3**, *Broad-pointed Star*, resembles w **1** but the points are broader.

w **4**
Crown (over) CC

w **5**
Crown (over) CC

Two *Crown (over) CC* watermarks were used: w **4** was for stamps of ordinary size and w **5** for those of larger size.

w **6**
Crown (over) CA

w **7**
CA over Crown

Two watermarks of *Crown CA* type were used, w **6** being for stamps of ordinary size. The other, w **7**, is properly described as *CA over Crown*. It was specially made for paper on which it was intended to print long fiscal stamps: that some were used postally accounts for the appearance of w **7** in the Catalogue. The watermark occupies twice the space of the ordinary Crown CA watermark, w **6**. Stamps of normal size printed on paper with w **7** watermark show it *sideways*; it takes a horizontal pair of stamps to show the entire watermark.

w **8**
Multiple Crown CA

w **9**
Multiple Script CA

Multiple watermarks began in 1904 with w **8**, *Multiple Crown CA,* changed from 1921 to w **9**, *Multiple Script CA*. On stamps of ordinary size portions of two or three watermarks appear and on the large-sized stamps a greater number can be observed. The change to letters in script character with w **9** was accompanied by a Crown of distinctly different shape.

It seems likely that there were at least two dandy rolls for each Crown Agents watermark in use at any one time with a reserve roll being employed when the normal one was withdrawn for maintenance or repair.

Both the Mult Crown CA and the Mult Script CA types exist with one or other of the letters omitted from individual impressions. It is possible that most of these occur from the reserve rolls as they have only been found on certain issues. The MCA watermark experienced such problems during the early 1920s and the Script over a longer period from the early 1940s until 1951.

During the 1920s damage must also have occurred on one of the Crowns as a substituted Crown has been found on certain issues. This is smaller than the normal and consists of an oval base joined to two upright ovals with a circle positioned between their upper ends. The upper line of the Crown's base is omitted, as are the left and right-hand circles at the top and also the cross over the centre circle.

Substituted Crown

The *Multiple Script CA* watermark, w **9**, is known with two errors, recurring among the 1950–52 printings of several territories. In the first a crown has fallen away from the dandy-roll that impresses the watermark into the paper pulp. It gives w **9a**, *Crown missing*, but this omission has been found in both "Crown only" (*illustrated*) and "Crown CA" rows. The resulting faulty paper was used for Bahamas, Johore, Seychelles and the postage due stamps of nine colonies

w **9a**:
Error, Crown missing

w **9b**:
Error, St. Edward's Crown

When the omission was noticed a second mishap occurred, which was to insert a wrong crown in the space, giving w **9b**, St. Edward's Crown. This produced varieties in Bahamas, Perlis, St. Kitts-Nevis and Singapore and the incorrect crown likewise occurs in (Crown only) and (Crown CA) rows.

w **10**
V over Crown

w **11**
Crown over A

Resuming the general types, two watermarks found in issues of several Australian States are: w **10**, *V over Crown*, and w **11**, *Crown over A*.

w **12**
Multiple St. Edward's Crown Block CA

w **13**
Multiple PTM

The *Multiple St. Edward's Crown Block CA* watermark, w **12**, was introduced in 1957 and besides the change in the Crown (from that used in Multiple Crown Script CA, w **9**) the letters reverted to block capitals. The new watermark began to appear sideways in 1966 and these stamps are generally listed as separate sets.

The watermark w **13**, *Multiple PTM*, was introduced for new Malaysian issues in November 1961.

w **14**
Multiple Crown CA Diagonal

By 1974 the two dandy-rolls the "upright" and the "sideways" for w **12** were wearing out; the Crown Agents therefore discontinued using the sideways watermark one and retained the other only as a stand-by. A new dandy-roll with the pattern of w **14**, *Multiple Crown CA Diagonal,* was introduced and first saw use with some Churchill Centenary issues.

The new watermark had the design arranged in gradually spiralling rows. It is improved in design to allow smooth passage over the paper (the gaps between letters and rows had caused jolts in previous dandy-rolls) and the sharp corners and angles, where fibres used to accumulate, have been eliminated by rounding.

This watermark had no "normal" sideways position amongst the different printers using it. To avoid confusion our more specialised listings do not rely on such terms as "sideways inverted" but describe the direction in which the watermark points.

w **15**
Multiple POST OFFICE

During 1981 w **15**, *Multiple POST OFFICE* was introduced for certain issues prepared by Philatelists Ltd, acting for various countries in the Indian Ocean, Pacific and West Indies.

w **16**
Multiple Crown Script CA Diagonal

A new Crown Agents watermark was introduced during 1985, w **16**, *Multiple Crown Script CA Diagonal.* This was very similar to the previous w **14**, but showed "CA" in script rather than block letters. It was first used on the omnibus series of stamps commemorating the Life and Times of Queen Elizabeth the Queen Mother.

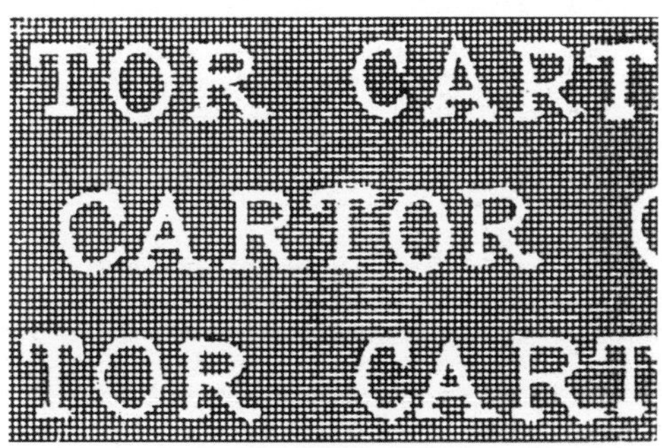

w **17**
Multiple CARTOR

Watermark w **17**, *Multiple CARTOR*, was used from 1985 for issues printed by this French firm for countries which did not normally use the Crown Agents watermark.

w **18**

In 2008, following the closure of the Crown Agents Stamp Bureau, a new Multiple Crowns watermark, w **18** was introduced

In recent years the use of watermarks has, to a small extent, been superseded by fluorescent security markings. These are often more visible from the reverse of the stamp (Cook Islands from 1970 onwards), but have occurred printed over the design (Hong Kong Nos. 415/30). In 1982 the Crown Agents introduced a new stock paper, without watermark, known as "C-Kurity" on which a fluorescent pattern of blue rosettes is visible on the reverse, beneath the gum. This paper was used for issues from Gambia and Norfolk Island.

6. Colours

Stamps in two or three colours have these named in order of appearance, from the centre moving outwards. Four colours or more are usually listed as multicoloured.

In compound colour names the second is the predominant one, thus:

orange-red = a red tending towards orange;
red-orange = an orange containing more red than usual.

Standard colours used. The 200 colours most used for stamp identification are given in the Stanley Gibbons Stamp Colour Key. The Catalogue has used the Stamp Colour Key as standard for describing new issues for some years. The names are also introduced as lists are rewritten, though exceptions are made for those early issues where traditional names have become universally established.

Determining colours. When comparing actual stamps with colour samples in the Stamp Colour Key, view in a good north daylight (or its best substitute; fluorescent "colour matching" light). Sunshine is not recommended. Choose a solid portion of the stamp design; if available, marginal markings such as solid bars of colour or colour check dots are helpful. Shading lines in the design can be misleading as they appear lighter than solid colour. Postmarked portions of a stamp appear darker than normal. If more than one colour is present, mask off the extraneous ones as the eye tends to mix them.

Errors of colour. Major colour errors in stamps or overprints which qualify for listing are: wrong colours; one colour inverted in relation to the rest; albinos (colourless impressions), where these have Expert Committee certificates; colours completely omitted, but only on unused stamps (if found on used stamps the information is footnoted) and with good credentials, missing colours being frequently faked.

Colours only partially omitted are not recognised, Colour shifts, however spectacular, are not listed.

Shades. Shades in philately refer to variations in the intensity of a colour or the presence of differing amounts of other colours. They are particularly significant when they can be linked to specific printings. In general, shades need to be quite marked to fall within the scope of this Catalogue; it does not favour nowadays listing the often numerous shades of a stamp, but chooses a single applicable colour name which will indicate particular groups of outstanding shades. Furthermore, the listings refer to colours as issued; they may deteriorate into something different through the passage of time.

Modern colour printing by lithography is prone to marked differences of shade, even within a single run, and variations can occur within the same sheet. Such shades are not listed.

Aniline colours. An aniline colour meant originally one derived from coal-tar; it now refers more widely to colour of a particular brightness suffused on the surface of a stamp and showing through clearly on the back.

Colours of overprints and surcharges. All overprints and surcharges are in black unless stated otherwise in the heading or after the description of the stamp.

7. Specimen Stamps

Originally, stamps overprinted SPECIMEN were circulated to postmasters or kept in official records, but after the establishment of the Universal Postal Union supplies were sent to Berne for distribution to the postal administrations of member countries.

During the period 1884 to 1928 most of the stamps of British Crown Colonies required for this purpose were overprinted SPECIMEN in various shapes and sizes by their printers from typeset formes. Some locally produced provisionals were handstamped locally, as were sets prepared for presentation. From 1928 stamps were punched with holes forming the word SPECIMEN, each firm of printers using a different machine or machines. From 1948 the stamps supplied for UPU distribution were no longer punctured.

Stamps of some other Commonwealth territories were overprinted or handstamped locally, while stamps of Great Britain and those overprinted for use in overseas postal agencies (mostly of the higher denominations) bore SPECIMEN overprints and handstamps applied by the Inland Revenue or the Post Office.

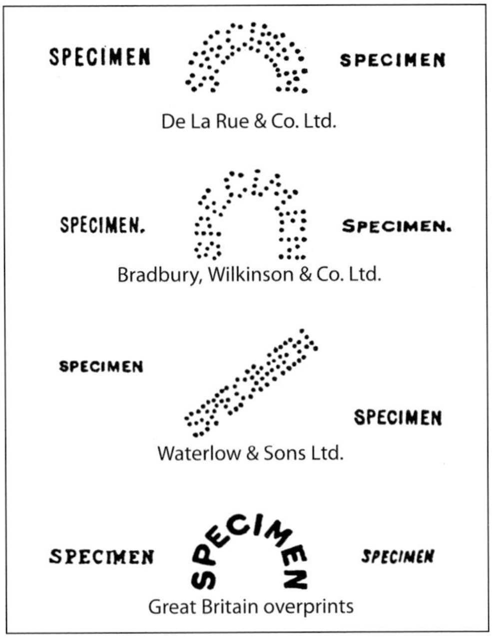

De La Rue & Co. Ltd.

Bradbury, Wilkinson & Co. Ltd.

Waterlow & Sons Ltd.

Great Britain overprints

Some of the commoner types of overprints or punctures are illustrated here. Collectors are warned that dangerous forgeries of the punctured type exist.

The *Stanley Gibbons Commonwealth Catalogues* record those Specimen overprints or perforations intended for distribution by the UPU to member countries. In addition the Specimen overprints of Australia and its dependent territories, which were sold to collectors by the Post Office, are also included.

Various Perkins Bacon issues exist obliterated with a "CANCELLED" within an oval of bars handstamp.

Perkins Bacon "CANCELLED" Handstamp

This was applied to six examples of those issues available in 1861 which were then given to members of Sir Rowland Hill's family. 75 different stamps (including four from Chile) are recorded with this handstamp although others may possibly exist. The unauthorised gift of these "CANCELLED" stamps to the Hill family was a major factor in the loss of the Agent General for the Crown Colonies (the forerunner of the Crown Agents) contracts by Perkins Bacon in the following year. Where examples of these scarce items are known to be in private hands the catalogue provides a price.

For full details of these stamps see *CANCELLED by Perkins Bacon* by Peter Jaffé (published by Spink in 1998).

All other Specimens are outside the scope of this volume.

Specimens are not quoted in Great Britain as they are fully listed in the Stanley Gibbons *Great Britain Specialised Catalogue*.

In specifying type of specimen for individual high-value stamps, "H/S" means handstamped, "Optd" is overprinted and "Perf" is punctured. Some sets occur mixed, e.g. "Optd/Perf". If unspecified, the type is apparent from the date or it is the same as for the lower values quoted as a set.

Prices. Prices for stamps up to £1 are quoted in sets; higher values are priced singly. Where specimens exist in more than one type the price quoted is for the cheapest. Specimen stamps have rarely survived even as pairs; these and strips of three, four or five are worth considerably more than singles.

8. Luminescence

Machines which sort mail electronically have been introduced in recent years. In consequence some countries have issued stamps on fluorescent or phosphorescent papers, while others have marked their stamps with phosphor bands.

The various papers can only be distinguished by ultraviolet lamps emitting particular wavelengths. They are separately listed only when the stamps have some other means of distinguishing them, visible without the use of these lamps. Where this is not so, the papers are recorded in footnotes or headings.

For this catalogue we do not consider it appropriate that collectors be compelled to have the use of an ultraviolet lamp before being able to identify stamps by our listings. Some experience will also be found necessary in interpreting the results given by ultraviolet. Collectors using the lamps, nevertheless, should exercise great care in their use as exposure to their light is potentially dangerous to the eyes.

Phosphor bands are listable, since they are visible to the naked eye (by holding stamps at an angle to the light and looking along them, the bands appear dark). Stamps existing with or without phosphor bands or with differing numbers of bands are given separate listings. Varieties such as double bands, bands omitted, misplaced or printed on the back are not listed.

Detailed descriptions appear at appropriate places in the listings in explanation of luminescent papers; see, for example, Australia above No. 363, Canada above Nos. 472 and 611, Cook Is. above 249, etc.

For Great Britain, where since 1959 phosphors have played a prominent and intricate part in stamp issues, the main notes above Nos. 599 and 723 should be studied, as well as the footnotes to individual listings where appropriate. In general the classification is as follows.

Stamps with phosphor bands are those where a separate cylinder applies the phosphor after the stamps are printed. Issues with "all-over" phosphor have the "band" covering the entire stamp. Parts of the stamp covered by phosphor bands, or the entire surface for "all-over" phosphor versions, appear matt. Stamps on phosphorised paper have the phosphor added to the paper coating before the stamps are printed. Issues on this paper have a completely shiny surface.

Further particularisation of phosphor – their methods of printing and the colours they exhibit under ultraviolet – is outside the scope. The more specialised listings should be consulted for this information.

9. Coil Stamps

Stamps issued only in coil form are given full listing. If stamps are issued in both sheets and coils the coil stamps are listed separately only where there is some feature (e.g. perforation or watermark sideways) by which singles can be distinguished. Coil stamps containing different stamps *se-tenant* are also listed.

Coil join pairs are too random and too easily faked to permit of listing; similarly ignored are coil stamps which have accidentally suffered an extra row of perforations from the claw mechanism in a malfunctioning vending machine.

10. Stamp Booklets

Stamp booklets are now listed in this catalogue.

Single stamps from booklets are listed if they are distinguishable in some way (such as watermark or perforation) from similar sheet stamps.

Booklet panes are listed where they contain stamps of different denominations *se-tenant*, where stamp-size labels are included, or where such panes are otherwise identifiable. Booklet panes are placed in the listing under the lowest denomination present.

Particular perforations (straight edges) are covered by appropriate notes.

The majority of booklets were made up from normal sheets and panes may be bound upright or inverted and booklets may be stapled or stitched at either the left or right-hand side. Unless specifically mentioned in the listings, such variations do not command a price premium.

11. Miniature Sheets and Sheetlets

We distinguish between "miniature sheets" and "sheetlets" and this affects the catalogue numbering. An item in sheet form that is postally valid, containing a single stamp, pair, block or set of stamps, with wide, inscribed and/or decorative margins, is a miniature sheet if it is sold at post offices as an indivisable entity. As such the Catalogue allots a single MS number and describes what stamps make it up. The sheetlet or small sheet differs in that the individual stamps are intended to be purchased separately for postal purposes. For sheetlets, all the component postage stamps are numbered individually and the composition explained in a footnote. Note that the definitions refer to post office sale—not how items may be subsequently offered by stamp dealers.

12. Forgeries and Fakes

Forgeries. Where space permits, notes are considered if they can give a concise description that will permit unequivocal detection of a forgery. Generalised warnings, lacking detail, are not nowadays inserted, since their value to the collector is problematic.

Forged cancellations have also been applied to genuine stamps. This catalogue includes notes regarding those manufactured by "Madame Joseph", together with the cancellation dates known to exist. It should be remembered that these dates also exist as genuine cancellations.

For full details of these see *Madame Joseph Forged Postmarks* by Derek Worboys (published by the Royal Philatelic Society London and the British Philatelic Trust in 1994) or *Madame Joseph Revisited* by Brian Cartwright (published by the Royal Philatelic Society London in 2005).

Fakes. Unwitting fakes are numerous, particularly "new shades" which are colour changelings brought about by exposure to sunlight, soaking in water contaminated with dyes from adherent paper, contact with oil and dirt from a pocketbook, and so on. Fraudulent operators, in addition, can offer to arrange: removal of hinge marks; repairs of thins on white or coloured papers; replacement of missing margins or perforations; reperforating in true or false gauges; removal of fiscal cancellations; rejoining of severed pairs, strips and blocks; and (a major hazard) regumming. Collectors can only be urged to purchase from reputable sources and to insist upon Expert Committee certification where there is any kind of doubt.

The Catalogue can consider footnotes about fakes where these are specific enough to assist in detection.

ACKNOWLEDGEMENTS

We are grateful to individual collectors, members of the philatelic trade and specialist societies and study circles for their assistance in improving and extending the Stanley Gibbons range of catalogues. The addresses of societies and study circles relevant to this volume are:

Australian States Study Circle
Royal Sydney Philatelic Club
Membership Secretary — Mr. P. Brigden RSPC
G.P.O. Box 1751, Sydney
N.S.W. 1043 Australia

British Society of Australian Philately
Secretary — Dr P.G.E. Reid
12 Holly Spring Lane
Bracknell, Berks RG12 2JL

Papuan Philatelic Society
Membership Secretary — Mr M. Robinson
P.O Box 3275, Birkdale,
Queensland 4159, Australia

Western Australia Study Group
Secretary — Mr B. Pope
P.O Box 423, Claremount
Western Australia 6910

Abbreviations

Printers

A.B.N. Co.	American Bank Note Co, New York.
B.A.B.N.	British American Bank Note Co. Ottawa
B.D.T.	B.D.T. International Security Printing Ltd, Dublin, Ireland
B.W.	Bradbury Wilkinson & Co, Ltd.
Cartor	Cartor S.A., La Loupe, France
C.B.N.	Canadian Bank Note Co, Ottawa.
Continental	Continental Bank Note Co. B.N. Co.
Courvoisier	Imprimerie Courvoisier S.A., La-Chaux-de-Fonds, Switzerland.
D.L.R.	De La Rue & Co, Ltd, London.
Enschedé	Joh. Enschedé en Zonen, Haarlem, Netherlands.
Format	Format International Security Printers Ltd., London
Harrison	Harrison & Sons, Ltd. London
J.W.	John Waddington Security Print Ltd., Leeds
P.B.	Perkins Bacon Ltd, London.
Questa	Questa Colour Security Printers Ltd, London
Walsall	Walsall Security Printers Ltd
Waterlow	Waterlow & Sons, Ltd, London.

General Abbreviations

Alph	Alphabet
Anniv	Anniversary
Comp	Compound (perforation)
Des	Designer; designed
Diag	Diagonal; diagonally
Eng	Engraver; engraved
F.C.	Fiscal Cancellation
H/S	Handstamped
Horiz	Horizontal; horizontally
Imp, Imperf	Imperforate
Inscr	Inscribed
L	Left
Litho	Lithographed
mm	Millimetres
MS	Miniature sheet
N.Y.	New York
Opt(d)	Overprint(ed)
P or P-c	Pen-cancelled
P, Pf or Perf	Perforated
Photo	Photogravure
Pl	Plate
Pr	Pair
Ptd	Printed
Ptg	Printing
R	Right
R.	Row
Recess	Recess-printed
Roto	Rotogravure
Roul	Rouletted
S	Specimen (overprint)
Surch	Surcharge(d)
T.C.	Telegraph Cancellation
T	Type
Typo	Typographed
Un	Unused
Us	Used
Vert	Vertical; vertically
W or wmk	Watermark
Wmk s	Watermark sideways

(†) = Does not exist

(–) (or blank price column) = Exists, or may exist, but no market price is known.

/ between colours means "on" and the colour following is that of the paper on which the stamp is printed.

Colours of Stamps

Bl (blue); blk (black); brn (brown); car, carm (carmine); choc (chocolate); clar (claret); emer (emerald); grn (green); ind (indigo); mag (magenta); mar (maroon); mult (multicoloured); mve (mauve); ol (olive); orge (orange); pk (pink); pur (purple); scar (scarlet); sep (sepia); turq (turquoise); ultram (ultramarine); verm (vermilion); vio (violet); yell (yellow).

Colour of Overprints and Surcharges

(B.) = blue, (Blk.) = black, (Br.) = brown, (C.) = carmine, (G.) = green, (Mag.) = magenta, (Mve.) = mauve, (Ol.) = olive, (O.) = orange, (P.) = purple, (Pk.) = pink, (R.) = red, (Sil.) = silver, (V.) = violet, (Vm.) or (Verm.) = vermilion, (W.) = white, (Y.) – yellow.

Arabic Numerals

As in the case of European figures, the details of the Arabic numerals vary in different stamp designs, but they should be readily recognised with the aid of this illustration.

٠	١	٢	٣	٤	٥	٦	٧	٨	٩
0	1	2	3	4	5	6	7	8	9

Features Listing

An at-a-glance guide to what's in the Stanley Gibbons catalogues

Area	Feature	Collect British Stamps	Stamps of the World	Thematic Catalogues	Comprehensive Catalogue, Parts 1-22 (including Commonwealth and British Empire Stamps and country catalogues)	Great Britain Concise	Specialised catalogues
General	SG number	√	√	√	√	√	√
General	Specialised Catalogue number						√
General	Year of issue of first stamp in design	√	√	√	√	√	√
General	Exact date of issue of each design				√	√	√
General	Face value information	√	√	√	√	√	√
General	Historical and geographical information	√	√	√	√	√	√
General	General currency information, including dates used	√	√	√	√	√	√
General	Country name	√	√	√	√	√	√
General	Booklet panes				√	√	√
General	Coil stamps				√		√
General	First Day Covers	√				√	√
General	Brief footnotes on key areas of note	√	√	√	√	√	√
General	Detailed footnotes on key areas of note				√	√	√
General	Extra background information				√	√	√
General	Miniature sheet information (including size in mm)	√	√	√	√	√	√
General	Sheetlets				√		
General	Stamp booklets				√	√	√
General	Perkins Bacon "Cancelled"				√		
General	PHQ Cards	√				√	√
General	Post Office Label Sheets					√	
General	Post Office Yearbooks	√				√	√
General	Presentation and Souvenir Packs	√				√	√
General	*Se-tenant* pairs	√			√	√	√
General	Watermark details - errors, varieties, positions				√	√	√
General	Watermark illustrations	√			√	√	√
General	Watermark types	√			√	√	√
General	Forgeries noted				√		√
General	Surcharges and overprint information	√	√	√	√	√	√
Design and Description	Colour description, simplified		√	√			
Design and Description	Colour description, extended	√			√	√	√
Design and Description	Set design summary information	√	√	√	√	√	√
Design and Description	Designer name				√	√	√
Design and Description	Short design description	√	√	√	√	√	√

Area	Feature	Collect British Stamps	Stamps of the World	Thematic Catalogues	Comprehensive Catalogue, Parts 1-22 (including Commonwealth and British Empire Stamps and country catalogues)	Great Britain Concise	Specialised catalogues
Design and Description	Shade varieties				√	√	√
Design and Description	Type number	√	√		√	√	√
Illustrations	Multiple stamps from set illustrated	√			√	√	√
Illustrations	A Stamp from each set illustrated in full colour (where possible, otherwise mono)	√	√	√	√	√	√
Price	Catalogue used price	√	√	√	√	√	√
Price	Catalogue unused price	√	√	√	√	√	√
Price	Price - booklet panes				√	√	√
Price	Price - shade varieties				√	√	√
Price	On cover and on piece price				√	√	√
Price	Detailed GB pricing breakdown	√			√	√	√
Print and Paper	Basic printing process information	√	√	√	√	√	√
Print and Paper	Detailed printing process information, e.g. Mill sheets				√		√
Print and Paper	Paper information				√		√
Print and Paper	Detailed perforation information	√			√	√	√
Print and Paper	Details of research findings relating to printing processes and history						√
Print and Paper	Paper colour	√	√		√	√	√
Print and Paper	Paper description to aid identification				√	√	√
Print and Paper	Paper type				√	√	√
Print and Paper	Ordinary or chalk-surfaced paper				√	√	√
Print and Paper	Embossing omitted note						√
Print and Paper	Essays, Die Proofs, Plate Descriptions and Proofs, Colour Trials information						√
Print and Paper	Glazed paper				√	√	√
Print and Paper	Gum details				√		√
Print and Paper	Luminescence/Phosphor bands - general coverage	√			√	√	√
Print and Paper	Luminescence/Phosphor bands - specialised coverage						√
Print and Paper	Overprints and surcharges - including colour information	√	√	√	√	√	√
Print and Paper	Perforation/Imperforate information	√	√		√	√	√
Print and Paper	Perforation errors and varieties				√	√	√
Print and Paper	Print quantities						√
Print and Paper	Printing errors				√	√	√
Print and Paper	Printing flaws						√
Print and Paper	Printing varieties				√	√	√
Print and Paper	Punctured stamps - where official				√		
Print and Paper	Sheet positions				√	√	√
Print and Paper	Specialised plate number information						√
Print and Paper	Specimen overprints (only for Commonwealth & GB)				√	√	√
Print and Paper	Underprints					√	√
Print and Paper	Visible Plate numbers	√			√	√	√
Print and Paper	Yellow and Green paper listings				√		√
Index	Design index	√			√	√	

International Philatelic Glossary

English	***French***	***German***	***Spanish***	***Italian***
Agate	Agate	Achat	Agata	Agata
Air stamp	Timbre de la poste aérienne	Flugpostmarke	Sello de correo aéreo	Francobollo per posta aerea
Apple Green	Vert-pomme	Apfelgrün	Verde manzana	Verde mela
Barred	Annulé par barres	Balkenentwertung	Anulado con barras	Sbarrato
Bisected	Timbre coupé	Halbiert	Partido en dos	Frazionato
Bistre	Bistre	Bister	Bistre	Bistro
Bistre-brown	Brun-bistre	Bisterbraun	Castaño bistre	Bruno-bistro
Black	Noir	Schwarz	Negro	Nero
Blackish Brown	Brun-noir	Schwärzlichbraun	Castaño negruzco	Bruno nerastro
Blackish Green	Vert foncé	Schwärzlichgrün	Verde negruzco	Verde nerastro
Blackish Olive	Olive foncé	Schwärzlicholiv	Oliva negruzco	Oliva nerastro
Block of four	Bloc de quatre	Viererblock	Bloque de cuatro	Bloco di quattro
Blue	Bleu	Blau	Azul	Azzurro
Blue-green	Vert-bleu	Blaugrün	Verde azul	Verde azzuro
Bluish Violet	Violet bleuâtre	Bläulichviolett	Violeta azulado	Violtto azzurrastro
Booklet	Carnet	Heft	Cuadernillo	Libretto
Bright Blue	Bleu vif	Lebhaftblau	Azul vivo	Azzurro vivo
Bright Green	Vert vif	Lebhaftgrün	Verde vivo	Verde vivo
Bright Purple	Mauve vif	Lebhaftpurpur	Púrpura vivo	Porpora vivo
Bronze Green	Vert-bronze	Bronzegrün	Verde bronce	Verde bronzo
Brown	Brun	Braun	Castaño	Bruno
Brown-lake	Carmin-brun	Braunlack	Laca castaño	Lacca bruno
Brown-purple	Pourpre-brun	Braunpurpur	Púrpura castaño	Porpora bruno
Brown-red	Rouge-brun	Braunrot	Rojo castaño	Rosso bruno
Buff	Chamois	Sämisch	Anteado	Camoscio
Cancellation	Oblitération	Entwertung	Cancelación	Annullamento
Cancelled	Annulé	Gestempelt	Cancelado	Annullato
Carmine	Carmin	Karmin	Carmín	Carminio
Carmine-red	Rouge-carmin	Karminrot	Rojo carmín	Rosso carminio
Centred	Centré	Zentriert	Centrado	Centrato
Cerise	Rouge-cerise	Kirschrot	Color de ceresa	Color Ciliegia
Chalk-surfaced paper	Papier couché	Kreidepapier	Papel estucado	Carta gessata
Chalky Blue	Bleu terne	Kreideblau	Azul turbio	Azzurro smorto
Charity stamp	Timbre de bienfaisance	Wohltätigkeitsmarke	Sello de beneficenza	Francobollo di beneficenza
Chestnut	Marron	Kastanienbraun	Castaño rojo	Marrone
Chocolate	Chocolat	Schokolade	Chocolate	Cioccolato
Cinnamon	Cannelle	Zimtbraun	Canela	Cannella
Claret	Grenat	Weinrot	Rojo vinoso	Vinaccia
Cobalt	Cobalt	Kobalt	Cobalto	Cobalto
Colour	Couleur	Farbe	Color	Colore
Comb-perforation	Dentelure en peigne	Kammzähnung, Reihenzähnung	Dentado de peine	Dentellatura e pettine
Commemorative stamp	Timbre commémoratif	Gedenkmarke	Sello conmemorativo	Francobollo commemorativo
Crimson	Cramoisi	Karmesin	Carmesí	Cremisi
Deep Blue	Blue foncé	Dunkelblau	Azul oscuro	Azzurro scuro
Deep bluish Green	Vert-bleu foncé	Dunkelbläulichgrün	Verde azulado oscuro	Verde azzurro scuro
Design	Dessin	Markenbild	Diseño	Disegno

English	French	German	Spanish	Italian
Die	Matrice	Urstempel. Type, Platte	Cuño	Conio, Matrice
Double	Double	Doppelt	Doble	Doppio
Drab	Olive terne	Trüboliv	Oliva turbio	Oliva smorto
Dull Green	Vert terne	Trübgrün	Verde turbio	Verde smorto
Dull purple	Mauve terne	Trübpurpur	Púrpura turbio	Porpora smorto
Embossing	Impression en relief	Prägedruck	Impresión en relieve	Impressione a relievo
Emerald	Vert-eméraude	Smaragdgrün	Esmeralda	Smeraldo
Engraved	Gravé	Graviert	Grabado	Inciso
Error	Erreur	Fehler, Fehldruck	Error	Errore
Essay	Essai	Probedruck	Ensayo	Saggio
Express letter stamp	Timbre pour lettres par exprès	Eilmarke	Sello de urgencia	Francobollo per espresso
Fiscal stamp	Timbre fiscal	Stempelmarke	Sello fiscal	Francobollo fiscale
Flesh	Chair	Fleischfarben	Carne	Carnicino
Forgery	Faux, Falsification	Fälschung	Falsificación	Falso, Falsificazione
Frame	Cadre	Rahmen	Marco	Cornice
Granite paper	Papier avec fragments de fils de soie	Faserpapier	Papel con filamentos	Carto con fili di seta
Green	Vert	Grün	Verde	Verde
Greenish Blue	Bleu verdâtre	Grünlichblau	Azul verdoso	Azzurro verdastro
Greenish Yellow	Jaune-vert	Grünlichgelb	Amarillo verdoso	Giallo verdastro
Grey	Gris	Grau	Gris	Grigio
Grey-blue	Bleu-gris	Graublau	Azul gris	Azzurro grigio
Grey-green	Vert gris	Graugrün	Verde gris	Verde grigio
Gum	Gomme	Gummi	Goma	Gomma
Gutter	Interpanneau	Zwischensteg	Espacio blanco entre dos grupos	Ponte
Imperforate	Non-dentelé	Geschnitten	Sin dentar	Non dentellato
Indigo	Indigo	Indigo	Azul indigo	Indaco
Inscription	Inscription	Inschrift	Inscripción	Dicitura
Inverted	Renversé	Kopfstehend	Invertido	Capovolto
Issue	Émission	Ausgabe	Emisión	Emissione
Laid	Vergé	Gestreift	Listado	Vergato
Lake	Lie de vin	Lackfarbe	Laca	Lacca
Lake-brown	Brun-carmin	Lackbraun	Castaño laca	Bruno lacca
Lavender	Bleu-lavande	Lavendel	Color de alhucema	Lavanda
Lemon	Jaune-citron	Zitrongelb	Limón	Limone
Light Blue	Bleu clair	Hellblau	Azul claro	Azzurro chiaro
Lilac	Lilas	Lila	Lila	Lilla
Line perforation	Dentelure en lignes	Linienzähnung	Dentado en linea	Dentellatura lineare
Lithography	Lithographie	Steindruck	Litografía	Litografia
Local	Timbre de poste locale	Lokalpostmarke	Emisión local	Emissione locale
Lozenge roulette	Percé en losanges	Rautenförmiger Durchstich	Picadura en rombos	Perforazione a losanghe
Magenta	Magenta	Magentarot	Magenta	Magenta
Margin	Marge	Rand	Borde	Margine
Maroon	Marron pourpré	Dunkelrotpurpur	Púrpura rojo oscuro	Marrone rossastro
Mauve	Mauve	Malvenfarbe	Malva	Malva
Multicoloured	Polychrome	Mehrfarbig	Multicolores	Policromo
Myrtle Green	Vert myrte	Myrtengrün	Verde mirto	Verde mirto
New Blue	Bleu ciel vif	Neublau	Azul nuevo	Azzurro nuovo
Newspaper stamp	Timbre pour journaux	Zeitungsmarke	Sello para periódicos	Francobollo per giornali
Obliteration	Oblitération	Abstempelung	Matasello	Annullamento
Obsolete	Hors (de) cours	Ausser Kurs	Fuera de curso	Fuori corso

English	*French*	*German*	*Spanish*	*Italian*
Ochre	Ocre	Ocker	Ocre	Ocra
Official stamp	Timbre de service	Dienstmarke	Sello de servicio	Francobollo di
Olive-brown	Brun-olive	Olivbraun	Castaño oliva	Bruno oliva
Olive-green	Vert-olive	Olivgrün	Verde oliva	Verde oliva
Olive-grey	Gris-olive	Olivgrau	Gris oliva	Grigio oliva
Olive-yellow	Jaune-olive	Olivgelb	Amarillo oliva	Giallo oliva
Orange	Orange	Orange	Naranja	Arancio
Orange-brown	Brun-orange	Orangebraun	Castaño naranja	Bruno arancio
Orange-red	Rouge-orange	Orangerot	Rojo naranja	Rosso arancio
Orange-yellow	Jaune-orange	Orangegelb	Amarillo naranja	Giallo arancio
Overprint	Surcharge	Aufdruck	Sobrecarga	Soprastampa
Pair	Paire	Paar	Pareja	Coppia
Pale	Pâle	Blass	Pálido	Pallido
Pane	Panneau	Gruppe	Grupo	Gruppo
Paper	Papier	Papier	Papel	Carta
Parcel post stamp	Timbre pour colis postaux	Paketmarke	Sello para paquete postal	Francobollo per pacchi postali
Pen-cancelled	Oblitéré à plume	Federzugentwertung	Cancelado a pluma	Annullato a penna
Percé en arc	Percé en arc	Bogenförmiger Durchstich	Picadura en forma de arco	Perforazione ad arco
Percé en scie	Percé en scie	Bogenförmiger Durchstich	Picado en sierra	Foratura a sega
Perforated	Dentelé	Gezähnt	Dentado	Dentellato
Perforation	Dentelure	Zähnung	Dentar	Dentellatura
Photogravure	Photogravure, Heliogravure	Rastertiefdruck	Fotograbado	Rotocalco
Pin perforation	Percé en points	In Punkten durchstochen	Horadado con alfileres	Perforato a punti
Plate	Planche	Platte	Plancha	Lastra, Tavola
Plum	Prune	Pflaumenfarbe	Color de ciruela	Prugna
Postage Due stamp	Timbre-taxe	Portomarke	Sello de tasa	Segnatasse
Postage stamp	Timbre-poste	Briefmarke, Freimarke, Postmarke	Sello de correos	Francobollo postale
Postal fiscal stamp	Timbre fiscal-postal	Stempelmarke als Postmarke verwendet	Sello fiscal-postal	Fiscale postale
Postmark	Oblitération postale	Poststempel	Matasello	Bollo
Printing	Impression, Tirage	Druck	Impresión	Stampa, Tiratura
Proof	Épreuve	Druckprobe	Prueba de impresión	Prova
Provisionals	Timbres provisoires	Provisorische Marken. Provisorien	Provisionales	Provvisori
Prussian Blue	Bleu de Prusse	Preussischblau	Azul de Prusia	Azzurro di Prussia
Purple	Pourpre	Purpur	Púrpura	Porpora
Purple-brown	Brun-pourpre	Purpurbraun	Castaño púrpura	Bruno porpora
Recess-printing	Impression en taille douce	Tiefdruck	Grabado	Incisione
Red	Rouge	Rot	Rojo	Rosso
Red-brown	Brun-rouge	Rotbraun	Castaño rojizo	Bruno rosso
Reddish Lilac	Lilas rougeâtre	Rötlichlila	Lila rojizo	Lilla rossastro
Reddish Purple	Poupre-rouge	Rötlichpurpur	Púrpura rojizo	Porpora rossastro
Reddish Violet	Violet rougeâtre	Rötlichviolett	Violeta rojizo	Violetto rossastro
Red-orange	Orange rougeâtre	Rotorange	Naranja rojizo	Arancio rosso
Registration stamp	Timbre pour lettre chargée (recommandée)	Einschreibemarke	Sello de certificado lettere	Francobollo per raccomandate
Reprint	Réimpression	Neudruck	Reimpresión	Ristampa
Reversed	Retourné	Umgekehrt	Invertido	Rovesciato
Rose	Rose	Rosa	Rosa	Rosa
Rose-red	Rouge rosé	Rosarot	Rojo rosado	Rosso rosa
Rosine	Rose vif	Lebhaftrosa	Rosa vivo	Rosa vivo
Roulette	Percage	Durchstich	Picadura	Foratura
Rouletted	Percé	Durchstochen	Picado	Forato
Royal Blue	Bleu-roi	Königblau	Azul real	Azzurro reale

English	*French*	*German*	*Spanish*	*Italian*
Sage green	Vert-sauge	Salbeigrün	Verde salvia	Verde salvia
Salmon	Saumon	Lachs	Salmón	Salmone
Scarlet	Écarlate	Scharlach	Escarlata	Scarlatto
Sepia	Sépia	Sepia	Sepia	Seppia
Serpentine roulette	Percé en serpentin	Schlangenliniger Durchstich	Picado a serpentina	Perforazione a serpentina
Shade	Nuance	Tönung	Tono	Gradazione de colore
Sheet	Feuille	Bogen	Hoja	Foglio
Slate	Ardoise	Schiefer	Pizarra	Ardesia
Slate-blue	Bleu-ardoise	Schieferblau	Azul pizarra	Azzurro ardesia
Slate-green	Vert-ardoise	Schiefergrün	Verde pizarra	Verde ardesia
Slate-lilac	Lilas-gris	Schierferlila	Lila pizarra	Lilla ardesia
Slate-purple	Mauve-gris	Schieferpurpur	Púrpura pizarra	Porpora ardesia
Slate-violet	Violet-gris	Schieferviolett	Violeta pizarra	Violetto ardesia
Special delivery stamp	Timbre pour exprès	Eilmarke	Sello de urgencia	Francobollo per espressi
Specimen	Spécimen	Muster	Muestra	Saggio
Steel Blue	Bleu acier	Stahlblau	Azul acero	Azzurro acciaio
Strip	Bande	Streifen	Tira	Striscia
Surcharge	Surcharge	Aufdruck	Sobrecarga	Soprastampa
Tête-bêche	Tête-bêche	Kehrdruck	Tête-bêche	Tête-bêche
Tinted paper	Papier teinté	Getöntes Papier	Papel coloreado	Carta tinta
Too-late stamp	Timbre pour lettres en retard	Verspätungsmarke	Sello para cartas retardadas	Francobollo per le lettere in ritardo
Turquoise-blue	Bleu-turquoise	Türkisblau	Azul turquesa	Azzurro turchese
Turquoise-green	Vert-turquoise	Türkisgrün	Verde turquesa	Verde turchese
Typography	Typographie	Buchdruck	Tipografia	Tipografia
Ultramarine	Outremer	Ultramarin	Ultramar	Oltremare
Unused	Neuf	Ungebraucht	Nuevo	Nuovo
Used	Oblitéré, Usé	Gebraucht	Usado	Usato
Venetian Red	Rouge-brun terne	Venezianischrot	Rojo veneciano	Rosso veneziano
Vermilion	Vermillon	Zinnober	Cinabrio	Vermiglione
Violet	Violet	Violett	Violeta	Violetto
Violet-blue	Bleu-violet	Violettblau	Azul violeta	Azzurro violetto
Watermark	Filigrane	Wasserzeichen	Filigrana	Filigrana
Watermark sideways	Filigrane couché	Wasserzeichen liegend	Filigrana acostado	Filigrana coricata
Wove paper	Papier ordinaire, Papier uni	Einfaches Papier	Papel avitelado	Carta unita
Yellow	Jaune	Gelb	Amarillo	Giallo
Yellow-brown	Brun-jaune	Gelbbraun	Castaño amarillo	Bruno giallo
Yellow-green	Vert-jaune	Gelbgrün	Verde amarillo	Verde giallo
Yellow-olive	Olive-jaunâtre	Gelboliv	Oliva amarillo	Oliva giallastro
Yellow-orange	Orange jaunâtre	Gelborange	Naranja amarillo	Arancio giallastro
Zig-zag roulette	Percé en zigzag	Sägezahnartiger Durchstich	Picado en zigzag	Perforazione a zigzag

Guide to Entries

A **Country of Issue** – When a country changes its name, the catalogue listing changes to reflect the name change, for example Namibia was formerly known as South West Africa, the stamps in Southern Africa are all listed under Namibia, but split into South West Africa and then Namibia.

B **Country Information** – Brief geographical and historical details for the issuing country.

C **Currency** – Details of the currency, and dates of earliest use where applicable, on the face value of the stamps.

D **Illustration** – Generally, the first stamp in the set. Stamp illustrations are reduced to 75%, with overprints and surcharges shown actual size.

E **Illustration or Type Number** – These numbers are used to help identify stamps, either in the listing, type column, design line or footnote, usually the first value in a set. These type numbers are in a bold type face – **123**; when bracketed (**123**) an overprint or a surcharge is indicated. Some type numbers include a lower-case letter – **123a**, this indicates they have been added to an existing set.

F **Date of issue** – This is the date that the stamp/set of stamps was issued by the post office and was available for purchase. When a set of definitive stamps has been issued over several years the Year Date given is for the earliest issue. Commemorative sets are listed in chronological order. Stamps of the same design, or issue are usually grouped together, for example some of the New Zealand landscapes definitive series were first issued in 2003 but the set includes stamps issued to May 2007.

G **Number Prefix** – Stamps other than definitives and commemoratives have a prefix letter before the catalogue number.
Their use is explained in the text: some examples are A for airmail, D for postage due and O for official stamps.

H **Footnote** – Further information on background or key facts on issues.

I **Stanley Gibbons Catalogue number** – This is a unique number for each stamp to help the collector identify stamps in the listing. The Stanley Gibbons numbering system is universally recognized as definitive.

Where insufficient numbers have been left to provide for additional stamps to a listing, some stamps will have a suffix letter after the catalogue number (for example 214a). If numbers have been left for additions to a set and not used they will be left vacant.

The separate type numbers (in bold) refer to illustrations (see E).

J **Colour** – If a stamp is printed in three or fewer colours then the colours are listed, working from the centre of the stamp outwards (see **R**).

K **Design line** – Further details on design variations

L **Key Type** – Indicates a design type on which the stamp is based. These are the bold figures found below each illustration, for example listed in Cameroon, in the West Africa catalogue, is the Key type A and B showing the ex-Kaiser's yacht *Hohenzollern*. The type numbers are also given in bold in the second column of figures alongside the stamp description to indicate the design of each stamp. Where an issue comprises stamps of similar design, the corresponding type number should be taken as indicating the general design. Where there are blanks in the type number column it means that the type of the corresponding stamp is that shown by the number in the type column of the same issue. A dash (–) in the type column means that the stamp is not illustrated. Where type numbers refer to stamps of another country, e.g. where stamps of one country are overprinted for use in another, this is always made clear in the text.

M **Coloured Papers** – Stamps printed on coloured paper are shown – e.g. "brown/*yellow*" indicates brown printed on yellow paper.

N **Surcharges and Overprints** – Usually described in the headings. Any actual wordings are shown in bold type. Descriptions clarify words and figures used in the overprint. Stamps with the same overprints in different colours are not listed separately. Numbers in brackets after the descriptions are the catalogue numbers of the non-overprinted stamps. The words "inscribed" or "inscription" refer to the wording incorporated in the design of a stamp and not surcharges or overprints.

O **Face value** – This refers to the value of each stamp and is the price it was sold for at the Post Office when issued. Some modern stamps do not have their values in figures but instead it is shown as a letter, for example Great Britain use 1st or 2nd on their stamps as opposed to the actual value.

P **Catalogue Value** – Mint/Unused. Prices quoted for Queen Victoria to King George V stamps are for lightly hinged examples.

Q **Catalogue Value** – Used. Prices generally refer to fine postally used examples. For certain issues they are for cancelled-to-order.

Prices
Prices are given in pence and pounds. Stamps worth £100 and over are shown in whole pounds:

Shown in Catalogue as	Explanation
10	10 pence
1.75	£1.75
15.00	£15
£150	£150
£2300	£2300

Prices assume stamps are in 'fine condition'; we may ask more for superb and less for those of lower quality. The minimum catalogue price quoted is 10p and is intended as a guide for catalogue users. The lowest price for individual stamps purchased from Stanley Gibbons is £1.

Prices quoted are for the cheapest variety of that particular stamp. Differences of watermark, perforation, or other details, often increase the value. Prices quoted for mint issues are for single examples, unless otherwise stated. Those in *se-tenant* pairs, strips, blocks or sheets may be worth more. Where no prices are listed it is either because the stamps are not known to exist (usually shown by a †) in that particular condition, or, more usually, because there is no reliable information on which to base their value.
All prices are subject to change without prior notice and we cannot guarantee to supply all stamps as priced. Prices quoted in advertisements are also subject to change without prior notice.

R **Multicoloured** – Nearly all modern stamps are multicoloured (more than three colours); this is indicated in the heading, with a description of the stamp given in the listing.

S **Perforations** – Please see page xiii for a detailed explanation of perforations.

A Country of issue

Bangladesh

B Country Information

In elections during December 1970 the Awami League party won all but two of the seats in the East Pakistan province and, in consequence, held a majority in the National Assembly. On 1 March 1971 the Federal Government postponed the sitting of the Assembly with the result that unrest spread throughout the eastern province. Pakistan army operations against the dissidents forced the leaders of the League to flee to India from where East Pakistan was proclaimed independent as Bangladesh. In early December the Indian army moved against Pakistan troops in Bangladesh and civilian government was re-established on 22 December 1971.

From 20 December 1971 various Pakistan issues were overprinted by local postmasters, mainly using handstamps. Their use was permitted until 30 April 1973. These are of philatelic interest, but are outside the scope of the catalogue.

C Currency

(Currency. 100 paisa = 1 rupee)

D Illustration

L **17**

E Illustration or Type number

F Date of issue

1978 (8 Mar). No. *L* 57 surch with Type *L* **16**. Chalky paper.

L63	L **14**	25c. on 2½c. ultramarine, green and buff	75	1·75

(Des A. G. Mitchell. Litho Harrison)

G Number prefix

1981 (3 June). P 14½.

L64	L **17**	5c. multicoloured	10	10
L65		10c. multicoloured	10	10
L66		20c. multicoloured	15	15
L67		30c. multicoloured	25	25
L68		40c. multicoloured	30	30
L69		50c. multicoloured	30	45
L64/9 *Set of 6*			1·00	1·25

H Footnote

Issues for the Government Life Insurance Department were withdrawn on 1 December 1989 when it became the privatised Tower Corporation.

(Des G. R. Bull and G. R. Smith. Photo Harrison)

I Stanley Gibbons catalogue number

1959 (2 Mar). Centenary of Marlborough Province. T **198** and similar horiz designs. W **98** (sideways). P 14½×14.

772	2d. green	30	10
773	3d. deep blue	30	10
774	8d. light brown	1·25	2·25
772/4 *Set of 3*		1·60	2·25

J Colour

K Design line

Designs:—3d. Shipping wool, Wairau Bar, 1857; 8d. Salt industry, Grassmere.

1915 (12 July). Stamps of German Kamerun. Types *A* and *B*, surch as T **1** (Nos. B1/9) or **2**. (Nos. B10/13) in black or blue.

L Key type column

B1	A	1½d. on 3pf. (No. k7) (B.)	13·00	42·00
		a. Different fount "d"	£150	£350

340	**41**	2d. purple (1903)	£350	£325
341	**28**	3d. bistre-brown (1906)	£700	£600
342	**37**	4d. blue and chestnut/*bluish* (1904)	£300	£350
		a. Blue and yellow-brown/bluish	£300	£350

M Coloured papers

N Surcharges and overprints

1913 (1 Dec). Auckland Industrial Exhibition. Nos. 387aa, 389, 392 and 405 optd with T **59** by Govt Printer, Wellington.

412	**51**	½d. deep green	20·00	55·00
413	**53**	1d. carmine	25·00	48·00
		a. "Feather" flaw	£225	
414	**52**	3d. chestnut	£130	£250
415		6d. carmine	£160	£300
412/15 *Set of 4*			£300	£600

P Catalogue value – Mint

O Face value

Q Catalogue value – Used

These overprinted stamps were only available for letters in New Zealand and to Australia.

(Des Martin Bailey. Litho Southern Colour Print)

R Multicoloured stamp

2008 (2 July). Olympic Games, Beijing. T **685** and similar diamond-shaped designs. Multicoloured. Phosphorised paper. P 14½.

3056	50c. Type **685**	1·00	85

S Perforations

Australia

The Australian colonies of New South Wales, Queensland, South Australia, Tasmania, Victoria and Western Australia produced their own issues before federation in 1901. Stamps inscribed for the individual states continued in use after federation until the end of December 1912.

WATERMARK VARIETIES. Some stamp printers in the Australian colonies paid little attention to the position of the watermark in the sheets they produced so that some entire printings had the watermark inverted, some 50% upright and 50% inverted while on others the inverted watermarks were restricted to odd sheets. Reversed, inverted and reversed, and on stamps with sideways watermarks, sideways inverted and sideways inverted and reversed watermarks, are frequently encountered, especially on the stamps of New South Wales and the later issues of Tasmania, Victoria and Western Australia. In such circumstances it is impossible to provide adequate prices for such items, so, generally, only those watermark varieties occurring on stamps printed in Great Britain are included in the following listings.

DOUBLE PRINTS. Numerous examples of "double prints," also "printed double, one albino" varieties are found on the locally printed line-engraved stamps of the Australian colonies. These are particularly prevalent in the stamps of South Australia and Tasmania. We no longer list such varieties.

NEW SOUTH WALES

PRICES FOR STAMPS ON COVER

Nos. 1/83	*from* × 2
Nos. 84/7	*from* × 3
No. 88	—
Nos. 89/96	*from* × 2
Nos. 97/8	—
Nos. 99/101	*from* × 2
Nos. 102/13	*from* × 3
No. 114	*from* × 10
Nos. 115/17	*from* × 2
Nos. 118/27	*from* × 3
Nos. 131/53	*from* × 2
Nos. 154/70	*from* × 3
Nos. 171/81	—
Nos. 186/202	*from* × 2
Nos. 203/6	*from* × 10
Nos. 207/21	*from* × 5
Nos. 222/37	*from* × 6
Nos. 238/42	—
Nos. 243/4	*from* × 6
Nos. 253/64	*from* × 10
Nos. 265/8	*from* × 15
Nos. 269/70	*from* × 2
Nos. 271/3	*from* × 10
Nos. 280/1	*from* × 2
Nos. 288/97	*from* × 10
Nos. 298/312	*from* × 12
Nos. 313/31	*from* × 10
No. 332	—
Nos. 333/49	*from* × 12
No. 350	—
Nos. 351/63	*from* × 12
No. O1	—
Nos. O2/12	*from* × 4
Nos. O13/18	—
Nos. O19/34	*from* × 20
Nos. O35/8	—
Nos. O39/47	*from* × 40
Nos. O48/53	—
Nos. O54/8	*from* × 20
No. O59	—
Nos. D1/7	*from* × 50
Nos. D8/10	—
Nos. D11/15	*from* × 50

EMBOSSED LETTER SHEETS AND ENVELOPES. From 1 November 1838 the Sydney G.P.O. supplied letter sheets pre-stamped with an albino embossing, as illustrated, at 1½d. each or 1s.3d. per dozen. From January 1841 the price was reduced to 1s. per dozen. The public were also able to present their own stationery for embossing. The circular design measures approximately 29 mm in diameter, and examples are known on laid or wove paper of varying colours. Embossing continued until 1 May 1852 after which the Post Office refused to carry mail which was not franked with postage stamps. The die was used for reprints in 1870 and 1898 before it was destroyed later the same year.

A **1**

PRINTERS. The early issues of New South Wales were printed on a press supervised by the Inspector of Stamps, Charles Kay. On 1 January 1857 this responsibility passed to the Government printer who produced all subsequent issues, *unless otherwise stated.*

SPECIMEN OVERPRINTS. Those listed are from U.P.U. distributions between 1892 and 1903. Further "Specimen" overprints exist, but these were used for other purposes. From 1891 examples of some of these Specimens, together with cancelled stamps, were sold to collectors by the N.S.W. Post Office.

NEW SOUTH WALES USED IN NEW CALEDONIA. From October 1859 mail for Europe from New Caledonia was routed via Sydney and franked with New South Wales stamps in combination with local issues. Such N.S.W. stamps were cancelled on arrival in Sydney.

1

2

(Eng Robert Clayton, Sydney)

1850 (1 Jan). T **1**. Plate I. No clouds.

(a) Soft yellowish paper

1	1d. crimson-lake	£12000	£550
2	1d. carmine	£12000	£500
3	1d. reddish rose	£11000	£475
4	1d. brownish red	£12000	£500

(b) Hard bluish paper

5	1d. pale red	£11000	£475
6	1d. dull lake	£12000	£500

1850 (Aug). T **2**. Plate I re-engraved by Henry C. Jervis, commonly termed Plate II. With clouds.

(a) Hard toned white to yellowish paper

7	1d. vermilion	£9000	£375
8	1d. dull carmine	£9000	£375
	a. No trees on hill (R. 2/2)	£12000	£750
	b. Hill unshaded (R. 2/3)	£12000	£750
	c. Without clouds (R. 3/5)	£12000	£750

(b) Hard greyish or bluish paper

9	1d. crimson-lake	£9000	£375
10	1d. gooseberry-red	£11000	£550
11	1d. dull carmine	£9000	£375
12	1d. brownish red	£9000	£350
	a. No trees on hill (R. 2/2)	£12000	£750
	b. Hill unshaded (R. 2/3)	£12000	£750
	c. Without clouds (R. 3/5)	£12000	£750

(c) Laid paper

13	1d. carmine	£14000	£700
14	1d. vermilion	£15000	£650
	a. No trees on hill (R. 2/2)	—	£1200
	b. Hill unshaded (R. 2/3)	—	£1200
	c. Without clouds (R. 3/5)	—	£1200

The varieties quoted with the letters "a", "b", "c" of course exist in each shade; the prices quoted are for the commonest shade, and the same applies to the following portions of this list.

Nos. 1/14 were printed in sheets of 25 (5×5).

LAID PAPER. Nos. 13/14, 34/5, 38 and 43*d/e* can be found showing parts of the papermaker's watermark (T. H. SAUNDERS 1847 in double-lined capitals and the figure of Britannia seated in an oval beneath a crown).

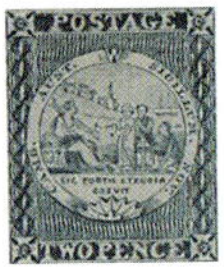

3

4

A (Pl I)

Illustrations A, B, C and D are sketches of the lower part of the inner circular frame, showing the characteristic variations of each plate.

(Eng John Carmichael)

1850 (1 Jan). Plate I. Vertical-lined background. T **3**.

(a) Early impressions, full details of clouds, etc

15	2d. greyish blue	£17000	£550
16	2d. deep blue	—	£650
	a. Double lines on bale (R. 2/7)	—	£1100

(b) Intermediate impressions

16*b*	2d. greyish blue	£9000	£325
16*c*	2d. deep blue	£9500	£400

(c) Later impressions, clouds, etc., mostly gone, T **4**

17	2d. greyish blue	£7000	£190
18	2d. dull blue	£7000	£180

(d) Stamps in the lower row partially retouched (end Jan)

19	2d. greyish blue	£8000	£300
20	2d. dull blue	£8500	£350

5

B (Pl II)

C (Pl III)

(Plate entirely re-engraved by Henry C. Jervis)

1850 (Apr–July). T **5**. Plate II. Horizontal-lined background. Bale on left side supporting the seated figure, dated. Dot in centre of the star In each corner.

(a) Early impressions

21	2d. indigo	£12000	£350
22	2d. lilac-blue	—	£1300
23	2d. grey-blue	£12000	£300
24	2d. bright blue	£12000	£300
	a. Fan as in Pl III, but with shading outside (R. 1/1)	—	£550
	b. Fan as in Pl III, but without shading, and inner circle intersects the fan (R. 1/2)	—	£600
	c. Fan as B, but inner circle intersects fan (R. 1/3)	—	£600
	d. No whip and inner circle intersects fan (R. 1/4)	—	£600
	e. No whip (R. 1/8, 2/8)	—	£475
	f. Pick and shovel omitted (R. 1/10)	—	£600
	g. "CREVIT" omitted (R. 2/1)	—	£950

(b) Worn impressions

25	2d. dull blue	£7000	£170
26	2d. Prussian blue	£7000	£200
	a. Fan as in Pl III, but with shading outside (R. 1/1)	—	£425
	b. Fan as in Pl III, but without shading, and inner circle intersects the fan (R. 1/2)	—	£425
	c. Fan as B, but inner circle intersects fan (R. 1/3)	—	£425
	d. No whip and inner circle intersects fan (R. 1/4)	—	£425
	e. No whip (R. 1/8, 2/8)	£9500	£350
	f. Pick and shovel omitted (R. 1/10)	—	£425
	g. "CREVIT" omitted (R. 2/1)	£12000	£650

(c) Bottom row retouched with dots and dashes in lower spandrels (from July)

27	2d. Prussian blue	£8000	£325
28	2d. dull blue	£8000	£225
	e. No whip (R. 2/8)	—	£375
	g. "CREVIT" omitted (R. 2/1)	—	£550

(Plate re-engraved a second time by Henry C. Jervis)

1850 (Sept). Plate III. Bale not dated and single-lined, except on No. 30c which is doubled-lined. No dots in stars.

29	2d. ultramarine	£8000	£225
30	2d. deep blue	£8000	£225
	a. No whip (R. 2/3, 2/7)	—	£375
	b. Fan with 6 segments (R. 2/8)	—	£500
	c. Double lines on bale (R. 1/7, 1/10, 1/12)	—	£350

(Plate re-engraved a third time by Henry C. Jervis)

1851 (Jan). Plate IV. Double-lined bale, and circle in centre of each star.

(a) Hard bluish grey wove paper

31	2d. ultramarine	£7500	£200
32	2d. Prussian blue	£7500	£170
33	2d. bright blue	£7500	£190
	a. Hill not shaded (R. 1/12)	—	£325
	b. Fan with 6 segments (R. 2/8)	—	£325
	c. No clouds (R. 2/10)	—	£325
	d. Retouch (R. 2/1)	—	£400
	e. No waves (R. 1/9, 2/5)	—	£275

(b) Stout yellowish vertically laid paper

34	2d. ultramarine	£8500	£250
35	2d. Prussian blue	£9500	£275
	a. Hill not shaded (R. 1/12)	—	£425
	b. Fan with 6 segments (R. 2/8)	—	£425
	c. No clouds (R. 2/10)	—	£425
	d. Retouch (R. 2/1)	—	£500
	e. No waves (R. 1/9, 2/5)	—	£375
	f. "PENOE" (R. 1/10, 2/12)	—	£450

The retouch, Nos. 33d and 35d., occurs outside the left margin line on R. 2/1.

6

D (Pl V)

7

(Plate re-engraved a fourth time by Henry C. Jervis)

1851 (Apr). T **6**. Plate V. Pearl in fan.

(a) Hard greyish wove paper

36	2d. ultramarine	£8000	£180
37	2d. dull blue	£8000	£180
	a. Pick and shovel omitted (R. 2/5)	—	£375
	b. Fan with 6 segments (R. 2/8)	—	£375

(b) Stout yellowish vertically laid paper

38	2d. dull ultramarine	£11000	£425
	a. Pick and shovel omitted (R. 2/5)	—	£650
	b. Fan with 6 segments (R. 2/8)	—	£650

Nos. 15/38 were printed in sheets of 24 (12×2), although the existence of an inter-panneau *tête-bêche* pair from Plate II indicates that the printer applied two impressions of the plate to each sheet of paper. The two panes were normally separated before issue. The original Plate I was re-cut four times to form Plates II to V. An interesting variety occurs on R. 1/9-11 and 2/7 in all five plates. It consists of ten loops of the engine-turning on each side of the design instead of the normal nine loops.

(Eng Henry C. Jervis)

1850 (1 Jan)–**51**. T **7**.

(a) Soft yellowish wove paper

39	3d. yellow-green	£9000	£325
40	3d. myrtle green	£19000	£1400
41	3d. emerald-green	£10000	£350
	a. No whip (R. 4/3–4)	—	£500
	b. "SIGIIIUM" for "SIGILLUM" (R. 5/3)	—	£700

(b) Bluish to grey wove paper (July 1850)

42	3d. yellow-green	£9000	£275
43	3d. emerald-green	£9500	£275
	b. No whip (R. 4/3–4)	—	£400
	c. "SIGIIIUM" for "SIGILLUM" (R. 5/3)	—	£600

(c) Yellowish to bluish laid paper (Jan 1851)

43*d*	3d. bright green	£14000	£600
43*e*	3d. yellowish green	£12000	£500
	f. No whip (R. 4/3–4)	—	£850
	g. "SIGIIIUM " for "SIGILLUM" (R. 5/3)	—	£1200

Nos. 39/43*e* were printed in sheets of 25 (5×5).

8

9

(Des A. W. Manning from sketch by W. T. Levinge; eng on steel by John Carmichael, Sydney)

1851 (18 Dec)–**52**. Imperf.

(a) Thick yellowish paper

44	**8**	1d. carmine	£4250	£300
		a. No leaves right of "SOUTH" (R. 1/7, 3/1)	—	£500

No.	Type	Description	Unused	Used
		b. Two leaves right of "SOUTH" (R. 2/5)	—	£750
		c. "WALE" (R. 1/9)	—	£750
		(b) Bluish medium wove paper (1852)		
45	8	1d. carmine	£1900	£160
46		1d. scarlet	£1900	£160
47		1d. vermilion	£1900	£140
48		1d. brick-red	£1900	£140
		a. No leaves right of "SOUTH" (R. 1/7, 3/1)	£3750	£350
		b. Two leaves right of "SOUTH" (R. 2/5)	—	£450
		c. "WALE" (R. 1/9)	—	£450
		(c) Thick vertically laid bluish paper (1852?)		
49	8	1d. orange-brown	£6500	£450
50		1d. claret	£6500	£475
		a. No leaves right of "SOUTH" (R. 1/7, 3/1)	—	£850
		b. Two leaves right of "SOUTH" (R. 2/5)	—	£1100
		c. "WALE" (R. 1/9)	—	£1200

Nos. 44/50 were printed in sheets of 50 (10×5).

(Eng John Carmichael (Nos. 51/9), Henry C. Jervis (Nos. 60/4))

1851 (24 July)–**55**. Imperf.

No.	Type	Description	Unused	Used
		(a) Plate I		
		(i) Thick yellowish wove paper		
51	8	2d. ultramarine	£1800	£120
		(ii) Fine impressions, blue to greyish medium paper		
52	8	2d. ultramarine	£1400	35·00
53		2d. chalky blue	£1300	35·00
54		2d. dark blue	£1300	35·00
55		2d. greyish blue	£1300	35·00
		(iii) Worn plate, blue to greyish medium paper		
56	8	2d. ultramarine	£850	35·00
57		2d. Prussian blue	£850	35·00
		(iv) Worn plate, blue wove medium paper		
58	8	2d. ultramarine	£750	35·00
59		2d. Prussian blue	£750	35·00
		(b) Plate II. Stars in corners (Oct 1853)		
		(i) Bluish medium to thick wove paper		
60	9	2d. deep ultramarine	£2000	£130
61		2d. indigo	£2100	£100
		a. "WAEES" (R. 3/3)	—	£475
		(ii) Worn plate, hard blue wove paper		
62	9	2d. deep Prussian blue	£2000	£120
		a. "WAEES" (R. 3/3)	—	£475
		*(c) Plate III, being Plate I (T **8**) re-engraved by H. C. Jervis. Background of crossed lines (Sept 1855)*		
		(i) Medium bluish wove paper		
63	–	2d. Prussian blue	£1000	75·00
		a. "WALES" partly covered with wavy lines (R. 1/3)	—	£275
		(ii) Stout white wove paper		
64	–	2d. Prussian blue	£1000	75·00
		a. "WALES" partly covered with wavy lines (R. 1/3)	£2750	£275

Nos. 51/64 were printed in sheets of 50 (10×5).

(Eng John Carmichael)

1852 (3 Dec). Imperf.

No.	Type	Description	Unused	Used
		(a) Medium greyish blue wove paper		
65	8	3d. deep green	£3750	£225
66		3d. green	£3250	£160
67		3d. dull yellow-green	£3000	£110
		a. "WAEES" with centre bar of first "E" missing (R. 4/7)	—	£450
		(b) Thick blue wove paper		
69	8	3d. emerald-green	£3750	£250
71		3d. blue-green	£3750	£275
		a. "WAEES" with centre bar of first "E" missing (R. 4/7)	—	£750

Nos. 65/71 were printed in sheets of 50 (10×5).

1852 (Apr)–**53**. Imperf.

No.	Type	Description	Unused	Used
		(a) Plate I		
		(i) Medium white wove paper		
72	8	6d. Vandyke brown	—	£950
		a. "WALLS" (R. 2/3)	—	£1800
		(ii) Medium bluish grey wove paper		
73	8	6d. Vandyke brown	£3750	£250
74		6d. yellow-brown	£4000	£275
75		6d. chocolate-brown	£3750	£250
76		6d. grey-brown	£3750	£250
		a. "WALLS" (R. 2/3)	—	£750
		(b) Plate I re-engraved by H. C. Jervis. Coarse background (June 1853)		
77	–	6d. brown	£4250	£300
78	–	6d. grey-brown	£4000	£300

Examples of the 6d. in Vandyke brown on thick yellowish paper are proofs.

Nos. 72/6 and 77/8 were printed in sheets of 25 (5×5).

(Eng Henry C. Jervis)

1853 (May). Imperf. Medium bluish paper

No.	Type	Description	Unused	Used
79		8d. dull yellow	£13000	£600
80		8d. orange-yellow	£13000	£600
81		8d. orange	£14000	£650
		a. No bow at back of head (R. 1/9)	—	£1800
		b. No leaves right of "SOUTH" (R. 3/1)	—	£1800
		c. No lines in spandrel (R. 2/2, 3/2, 4/2)	—	£1000

Nos. 79/81 were issued in sheets of 50 (10×5).

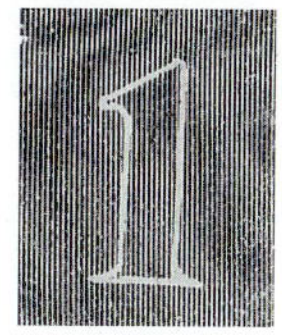

10

NOTE. All watermarked stamps from No. 82 to No. 172 have double-lined figures, as T **10**.

1854 (Jan–Mar). Yellowish wove paper. Wmk double-line "**1**", "**2**", or "**3**" as T **10**, to match face value. Imperf.

No.	Type	Description	Unused	Used
82	8	1d. red-orange (Feb)	£450	35·00
83		1d. orange-vermilion	£450	35·00
		a. No leaves right of "SOUTH" (R. 1/7, 3/1)	£850	£100
		b. Two leaves right of "SOUTH" (R. 2/5)	£1200	£150
		c. "WALE" (R. 1/9)	£1200	£150
84	–	2d. ultramarine (Pl III) (Jan)	£350	15·00
85	–	2d. Prussian blue (Pl III)	£350	15·00
86	–	2d. chalky blue (Pl III)	£350	12·00
		a. "WALES" partly covered by wavy lines (R. 1/3)	£900	65·00
87	8	3d. yellow-green (Mar)	£650	50·00
		a. "WAEES" with centre bar of first "E" missing (R. 4/7)	£1500	£180
		b. Error. Wmk "**2**"	£6500	£1600

Nos. 82/7 were printed in sheets of 50 (10×5).

11

12

13

14

(6d. and 1s. des E. H. Corbould after sketches by W. T. Levinge. Printed by New South Wales Govt Ptg Dept from Perkins Bacon plates)

1854 (1 Feb)–**59**. Wmk double-line "**5**", "**6**", "**8**" or "**12**" to match face value. Imperf.

No.	Type	Description	Unused	Used
88	11	5d. dull green (1.12.55)	£1300	£650
89	12	6d. deep slate	£1800	35·00
		a. Wmk sideways	†	£1200
90		6d. greenish grey	£1600	35·00
91		6d. slate-green	£1600	35·00
92		6d. bluish grey	£1600	55·00
93		6d. fawn	£1700	95·00
		a. Wmk "**8**" (15.8.59)	£4000	£110
94		6d. grey	£1600	55·00
95		6d. olive-grey	£1600	35·00
96		6d. greyish brown	£1600	35·00
		a. Wmk "**8**" (15.8.59)	£4000	£110
		ab. Wmk sideways	—	£500
97	13	8d. golden yellow (1.12.55)	£16000	£1400
98		8d. dull yellow-orange	£15000	£1300
99	14	1s. rosy vermilion (2.54)	£4250	75·00
		a. Wmk "**8**" (20.6.57)	£9000	£180
100		1s. pale red	£3750	70·00
101		1s. brownish red	£4250	80·00

Nos. 93a, 96a and 99a come from printings made when supplies of the correct numeral watermarks were unavailable.

Plate proofs of the 6d. in red-brown and of the 1s. in deep blue on unwatermarked paper exist handstamped "CANCELLED" in oval of bars (see note on Perkins Bacon "CANCELLED" in Catalogue introduction) (*Price £12000 each*).

A single used example of No. 91 exists printed on both sides. It is in the Royal Philatelic Collection.

For further examples of Types **11/14** on different watermarks see Nos. 141/53, 160/70, 215, 218, 231/3, 236 and 329.

15

16

(Eng John Carmichael)

1856 (1 Jan)–**59**. For Registered Letters. No wmk. Imperf.

(a) Soft medium yellowish paper

102	**15**	(6d.) vermilion and Prussian blue	£1700	£170
		a. Frame printed on back	£12000	£5000
103		(6d.) salmon and indigo	£1600	£190
104		(6d.) orange and Prussian blue	£1600	£225
105		(6d.) orange and indigo	£1600	£200

(b) Hard medium bluish wove paper, with manufacturer's wmk in sans-serif, double-lined capitals across sheet and only showing portions of letters on a few stamps in a sheet

106	**15**	(6d.) orange and Prussian blue (4.59)	£2250	£250

For further examples of Type **15** on different watermarks see Nos. 119/27.

2d. Major retouch (Plate I, R. 2/12)

2d. Major retouch (Plate I, R. 9/8)

(Printed by New South Wales Govt Ptg Dept from plates engraved by Perkins, Bacon & Co)

1856 (7 Jan)–**60**. Wmk double-line "**1**", "**2**" or "**3**" to match face value. Imperf.

(a) Recess

107	**16**	1d. orange-vermilion (6.4.56)	£325	24·00
		a. Error. Wmk "**2**"	†	£8500
108		1d. carmine-vermilion	£325	24·00
109		1d. orange-red	£350	24·00
		a. Printed on both sides	£3750	£2500
110		2d. deep turquoise-blue (Pl I)	£300	14·00
111		2d. ultramarine (Pl I)	£275	14·00
112		2d. blue (Pl 1)	£275	14·00
		a. Major retouch (1858)	£2250	£450
		b. Error. Wmk "**1**"	†	£8500
		c. Wmk "**5**" (3.57)	£850	70·00
113		2d. pale blue (Pl I)	£275	14·00
114		2d. blue (Pl II) (1.60)	£850	65·00
115		3d. yellow-green (10.10.56)	£1500	£100
116		3d. bluish green	£1600	£110
117		3d. dull green	£1600	£110
		a. Error, Wmk "**2**"	—	£3750

(b) Lithographic transfer of Plate I

118	**16**	2d. pale blue (3.8.59)	—	£800
		a. Retouched	—	£2500

For further examples of Type **16** on different watermarks see Nos. 131/40, 154/8, 171/2, 211/12, 226/8 and 327/8.

Two plates were used for the 2d. The 2d. Plate I was retouched, on a total of ten positions, Nos. 112a and 133a refer to the third retouch of R. 2/12 and R. 9/8. Earlier retouches of these exist. Stamps from Plate II are wider apart and are more regularly spaced. There is also a white patch between "A" of "WALES" and the back of the Queen's head on later printings from Plate II, but this is not obvious on the early printings.

On the 3d. the value is in block letters on a white background. No. 112c comes from a printing made when supplies of the "2" paper were unavailable. There are only two known of No. 112b one of which is in the Royal Collection. Two used examples are known with "8" watermark, both of which are in museum collections.

The 1d. exists privately rouletted 10, a used pair of which is known postmarked 15 May 1861.

No. 114 was mainly used at post offices in Queensland.

The lithographic retouches (No. 118a) occur on the three stamps at the left of the bottom row of the sheet and consist of strong horizontal lines below "TWO PENCE".

STAMPS WITH STRAIGHT EDGES. Stamps between Nos. 119 and 244 and also Nos. 327/9 can be found with one or two sides imperforate. These come from the outside rows which were not perforated between the stamps and the sheet margins. Being from the edge of the sheet such stamps are often found without watermark or showing portions of the double-lined "NEW SOUTH WALES" marginal watermark.

1860 (Feb)–**63**. For Registered Letters.

(a) P 12

(i) Hard medium bluish wove paper with manufacturer's wmk in sans-serif, double-lined capitals across sheet, showing portions of letters on a few stamps

119	**15**	(6d.) orange and Prussian blue	£900	75·00
120		(6d.) orange and indigo	£900	80·00

(ii) Coarse, yellowish wove paper with manufacturer's wmk in Roman capitals (Feb 1860)

121	**15**	(6d.) rose-red and Prussian blue	£600	50·00
122		(6d.) rose-red and indigo	£700	95·00
123		(6d.) salmon and indigo		

(b) P 13

(i) Coarse, yellowish wove paper with manufacturer's wmk in Roman capitals (1862)

124	**15**	(6d.) rose-red and Prussian blue	£700	65·00

*(ii) Yellowish wove paper. Wmk double-line "**6**" (May 1863)*

125	**15**	(6d.) rose-red and Prussian blue	£275	24·00
126		(6d.) rose-red and indigo	£375	32·00
127		(6d.) rose-red and pale blue	£275	22·00

2d. Major retouch around neck and above "TWO PENCE" (Plate II, R. 5/9)

1860 (14 Feb)–**72**. Wmk double-lined figure of value.

(a) P 12

131	**16**	1d. orange-red	£325	23·00
132		1d. scarlet	£250	23·00
133		2d. pale blue (Pl I)	£650	£140
		a. Retouched	—	£1400
134		2d. greenish blue (Pl II)	£225	13·00
136		2d. Prussian blue (Pl II)	£225	13·00
		a. Error. Wmk "**1**"	—	£3500
		b. Retouched (*shades*)	—	£425
137		2d. Prussian blue (Pl I) (3.61)	£250	14·00
138		2d. dull blue (Pl I)	£225	13·00
139		3d. yellow-green (1860)	£1700	60·00
140		3d. blue-green	£850	48·00
141	**11**	5d. dull green (1863)	£400	£110
142		5d. yellowish green (1863)	£400	£110
143	**12**	6d. grey-brown	£700	65·00

144		6d. olive-brown	£700	75·00
145		6d. greenish grey	£800	60·00
146		6d. fawn	£750	85·00
147		6d. mauve	£700	38·00
148		6d. violet	£600	19·00
149	**13**	8d. lemon yellow	—	£2000
150		8d. orange	£6000	£1200
151		8d. red-orange	£6000	£1200
152	**14**	1s. brownish red	£1400	70·00
153		1s. rose-carmine	£1400	70·00
		(b) P 13		
154	**16**	1d. scarlet (1862)	£150	24·00
155		1d. dull red	£150	24·00
156		3d. blue-green (12.62)	90·00	13·00
157		3d. yellow-green	£100	9·50
		a. Wmk "**6**" (7.72)	£225	15·00
158		3d. dull green	£100	9·00
		a. Wmk "**6**" (7.72)	£250	18·00
160	**11**	5d. bluish green (12.63)	£120	32·00
161		5d. bright yellow-green (8.65)	£225	75·00
162		5d. sea-green (1866)	£140	35·00
162*a*		5d. dark bluish green (11.70)	95·00	25·00
163	**12**	6d. reddish purple (Pl I) (7.62)	£200	6·50
164		6d. mauve	£200	6·50
165		6d. purple (Pl II) (1864)	£150	4·75
		a. Wmk "**5**" (7.66)	£750	28·00
		ab. Wmk "**5**" sideways	†	£1200
		b. Wmk "**12**" (12.66 and 1868)	£700	23·00
166		6d. violet	£160	6·50
		a. Wmk "**5**" (7.66)	—	38·00
167		6d. aniline mauve	£1300	£140
167*a*	**13**	8d. red-orange (1862)	£450	55·00
167*b*		8d. yellow-orange	£475	45·00
		ba. Wmk sideways	†	£1200
167*c*		8d. bright yellow	£450	45·00
168	**14**	1s. rose-carmine (1862)	£300	8·00
169		1s. carmine	£275	8·50
170		1s. crimson-lake	£275	8·50
		(c) Perf compound 12×13		
171	**16**	1d. scarlet (1862)	—	£1700
172		2d. dull blue (1.62)	£2250	£180

No. 133 was made by perforating a small remaining stock of No. 113. Nos. 137/8 were printed from the original plate after its return from London, where it had been repaired.

No. 136b refers to the second retouch on R. 5/9. Other retouches to plate II exist.

Nos. 157a, 158a and 165a/b come from printings made when supplies of paper with the correct face value were unavailable.

The Royal Philatelic Collection contains examples of Nos. 131 and 168 in imperf between pairs.

For later printings in these types, with different watermarks and perforations, see Nos. 195, 211/2, 215, 218, 226/8, 231/3, 236, 269/70 and 327/9.

24

25

(Des E. H. Corbould, R.I.)

1861–88. W **25**. Various perfs.

174	**24**	5s. dull violet, P 12 (1861)	£2000	£325
		a. Perf 13 (1861)	£325	35·00
175		5s. royal purple, P 13 (1872)	£800	70·00
176		5s. deep rose-lilac, P 13 (1875)	£225	35·00
177		5s. deep purple, P 13 (1880)	£275	50·00
		a. Perf 10 (1882)	£300	75·00
178		5s. rose-lilac, P 10 (1883)	£275	55·00
179		5s. purple, P 12 (1885)	—	70·00
		a. Perf 10×12 (1885)	—	£180
180		5s. reddish purple, P 10 (1886)	£275	60·00
		a. Perf 12×10 (1887)	£425	65·00
		b. Mixed perfs 10 and 12	—	†
181		5s. rose-lilac, P 11 (1888)	£325	£140

This value was replaced by Nos. 261, etc. in 1888 but reissued in 1897, *see* Nos. 297*c/e*.

26

27

28

(Printed by De La Rue & Co, Ltd, London and perf at Somerset House, London)

1862–65. Surfaced paper. P 14.

		(i) W **27**		
186	**26**	1d. dull red (Pl I) (1.4.64)	£200	90·00
		(ii) No wmk		
187	**26**	1d. dull red (Pl II) (1.65)	£200	80·00
188	**28**	2d. pale blue (25.3.62)	£200	95·00

(Printed from the De La Rue plates in the Colony)

1862 (12 Apr). Wmk double-lined "**2**" (No. 189) or "**5**" (No. 190). P 13.

189	**28**	2d. blue	£110	32·00
		a. Perf 12	£200	50·00
		b. Perf 12×13	£600	£200
190		2d. dull blue (9.62)	£110	35·00

29

1863–69. W **29**. P 13.

191	**26**	1d. pale red (3.69)	£225	32·00
192	**28**	2d. pale blue (4.63)	55·00	3·00
		a. Perf 12		
193		2d. cobalt-blue	55·00	3·00
194		2d. Prussian blue	60·00	3·75

1864–65. W **27**. P 13.

195	**16**	1d. pale red (6.64)	£110	55·00
196	**26**	1d. dark red-brown (Pl I)	£300	45·00
197		1d. brownish red (Pl II)	80·00	9·00
		a. Imperf between (horiz pair)	†	£2500
198		1d. brick-red (Pl II)	80·00	9·00
		a. Highly surfaced paper (1865)	£300	£180
199	**28**	2d. pale blue	£225	6·00

Plates I and II were made from the same die; they can only be distinguished by the colour or by the marginal inscription.

1865–66. Thin to very thin wove paper. No wmk. P 13.

200	**26**	1d. brick-red	£200	45·00
201		1d. brownish red	£200	45·00
202	**28**	2d. pale blue (11.65)	£130	6·00

32

34

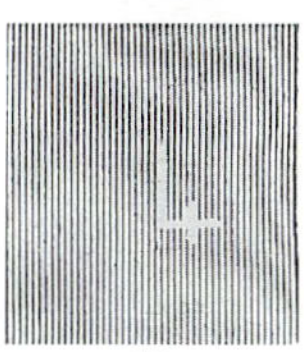

33

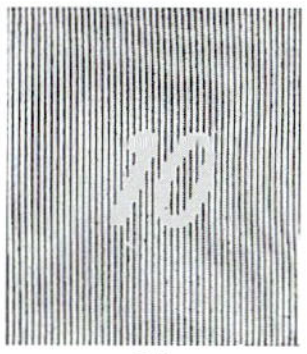

35

1867 (Sept)–**93**. W **33** and **35**.

203	**32**	4d. red-brown, P 13	£120	8·50
204		4d. pale red-brown, P 13	£120	8·50
205	**34**	10d. lilac, P 13	55·00	8·50
		a. Imperf between (horiz pair)	£3000	
		s. Optd "Specimen"	30·00	
206		10d. lilac, P 11 (1893)	18·00	9·00
		a. Perf 10	19·00	11·00
		b. Perf 10×11 or 11×10	27·00	11·00
		c. Perf 12×11	£160	16·00

See also Nos. 269/70.

36

37

38

NINEPENCE

(39)

From 1871 to 1903 the 9d. is formed from the 10d. by a black surch. (T **39**), 15 mm long on Nos. 219 to 220g, and 13½ mm long on subsequent issues.

1871–1902. W **36**.

207	**26**	1d. dull red, P 13 (8.71)	38·00	3·25
		a. Imperf vert (horiz pair)	†	£2750
		b. Imperf between (horiz pair)	†	£2750
208		1d. salmon, P 13 (1878)	38·00	3·50
		a. Perf 10 (6.80)	£250	40·00
		b. Perf 10×13 (6.80)	65·00	8·50
		ba. Perf 13×10	32·00	2·50
		c. *Scarlet*. Perf 10 (4.82)	—	£180
209	**28**	2d. Prussian-blue, P 13 (11.71)	48·00	1·75
		a. Perf 11×12, comb (11.84)	£250	40·00
		c. Imperf between (horiz pair)	†	£3250
210		2d. pale blue, P 13 (1876)	42·00	1·75
		a. Perf 10 (6.80)	£250	23·00
		b. Perf 10×13 (6.80)	£100	16·00
		ba. Perf 13×10	32·00	1·25
		c. Surfaced paper. Perf 13	—	£200
211	**16**	3d. yellow-green, P 13 (3.74)	75·00	5·00
		a. Perf 10 (6.80)	90·00	12·00
		b. Perf 11 (1902)	£160	£100
		c. Perf 12 (5.85)	—	£150
		d. Perf 10×12 or 12×10 (5.85)	£150	40·00
		e. Perf 11×12 (1902)	£130	40·00
212		3d. bright green, P 10 (6.80)	£120	20·00
		a. Perf 13×10 (6.80)	£110	24·00
		b. Perf 13		
213	**32**	4d. pale red-brown, P 13 (8.77)	£120	22·00
214		4d. red-brown, P 13	£120	17·00
		a. Perf 10 (6.80)	£225	60·00
		b. Perf 10×13 (6.80)	£150	24·00
		ba. Perf 13×10	£130	7·00
215	**11**	5d. bluish green, P 10 (8.84)	40·00	42·00
		a. Perf 12 (5.85)	£250	£100
		b. Perf 10×13 or 13×10		
		c. Perf 10×12 (5.85)	£120	65·00
		ca. Perf 12×10	60·00	42·00
216	**37**	6d. bright mauve, P 13 (1.1.72)	£100	2·25
		a. Imperf between (horiz pair)	†	£3000
217		6d. pale lilac, P 13 (1878)	£100	2·25
		a. Perf 10 (6.80)	£200	12·00
		b. Perf 10×13 (6.80)	£140	16·00
		ba. Perf 13×10	£120	2·50
		c. Imperf between (horiz pair). (Perf 13×10)	†	£3000
218	**13**	8d. yellow, P 13 (3.77)	£200	17·00
		a. Wmk sideways	†	—
		b. Perf 10 (6.80)	£325	26·00
		c. Perf 13×10 (6.80)	£225	24·00
219	**34**	9d. on 10d. pale red-brown, P 13 (8.71)	75·00	5·50
220		9d. on 10d. red-brown, P 13 (1878)	75·00	13·00
		a. Perf 10 (6.80)	15·00	10·00
		b. Perf 12 (5.85)	22·00	18·00
		c. Perf 11 (12.85)	60·00	10·00
		d. Perf 12×10 (5.85)	£275	£180
		e. Perf 10×11 or 11×10 (12.85)	70·00	19·00
		g. Perf 12×11, comb (1.84)	18·00	6·00
		ga. Perf 11×12		
		gs. Optd "Specimen"	27·00	
221	**38**	1s. black, P 13 (1.4.76)	£160	12·00
		aa. Imperf horiz (vert pair)	†	£3000
		a. Perf 10 (6.80)	£225	24·00
		b. Perf 10×13 (6.80)	£250	48·00
		ba. Perf 13×10	£180	14·00
		c. Perf 11		
		e. Imperf (pair)	†	£2750

Stamps from this series without watermark are from the edge of the sheet.

A used horizontal pair of the 2d. Prussian-blue imperf vertically, is in the Royal Philatelic Collection.

Nos. 211b and 211e were printed in 1902 on wmk **36** paper, left over when it was superseded by wmk **40**.

Collectors should note that for issues prior to 1888 (other than those specifically described as "Perf 11×12, comb" our classification of perforations follows the long-standing convention whereby "Perf 12" denotes a perforation of 11½, 12 and "Perf 13" denotes one of 12½, 13.

BISECTS. Between 1887 and 1913 various 1d. and 2d. stamps can be found vertically or diagonally bisected. This was unauthorised.

40

1882 (Apr)–**97**. W **40**.

222	**26**	1d. salmon, P 10	40·00	3·00
		a. Perf 13		
		b. Perf 10×13	†	£200
		ba. Perf 13×10	65·00	2·75
223		1d. orange *to* scarlet, P 13	£850	£450
		a. Perf 10	23·00	2·25
		ab. Imperf between (horiz pair)	†	£3750
		b. Perf 10×13	£120	9·50
		c. Perf 10×12 or 12×10 (4.85)	£275	65·00
		d. Perf 11×10 (12.85)	£475	£120
		e. Perf 12×11 (12.85)	—	£120
		f. Perf 11×12, comb (1.84)	10·00	1·25
		h. Perf 11 (12.85)	—	£140
224	**28**	2d. pale blue, P 13	£450	90·00
		a. Perf 10	50·00	1·25
		b. Perf 10×13	£150	7·50
		ba. Perf 13×10	70·00	3·25
225		2d. Prussian blue, P 10	60·00	1·00
		b. Perf 12 (4.85)	—	£225
		c. Perf 11 (12.85)	—	£100
		d. Perf 12×11 (12.85)	£400	£100
		e. Perf 10×12 (4.85)	£225	65·00
		ca. Perf 12×10	£400	£100
		f. Perf 10×11 or 11×10 (12.85)	£450	£150
		g. Perf 11×12, comb (1.84)	13·00	1·00
		ga. Printed double	†	£700
		gb. Imperf three sides (left stamp of horizontal pair)	£2000	
226	**16**	3d. yellow-green, P 10 (1886)	30·00	2·25
		b. Wmk sideways		
		bs. Optd "Specimen"	27·00	
		c. Perf 10×12	£180	42·00
		ca. Perf 12×10	£140	18·00
		d. Perf 11	10·00	1·00
		da. Imperf vert (horiz pair)	£700	
		e. Perf 11×12 or 12×11	6·00	1·00
		f. Perf 12	15·00	2·50
		g. Imperf (pair)	£500	
227		3d. bluish green, P 10	35·00	2·25
		a. Wmk sideways	60·00	11·00
		b. Perf 11	26·00	2·50
		ba. Imperf between (horiz pair)		
		c. Perf 10×11	35·00	3·25
		ca. Perf 11×10	£100	35·00
		d. Perf 11×12 or 12×11	11·00	2·75
		e. Perf 10×12 or 12×10	50·00	4·25
228		3d. emerald-green, P 10 (1893)	65·00	10·00
		a. Wmk sideways	—	22·00
		b. Perf 10×11	65·00	6·50
		ba. Perf 11×10	£120	42·00
		c. Perf 10×12	60·00	6·50
		ca. Perf 12×10	80·00	9·00
		d. Perf 12×11	—	15·00
229	**32**	4d. red-brown, P 10	£120	5·50
		a. Perf 10×12 (4.85)	—	£160
		b. Perf 11×12, comb (1.84)	£120	3·00
230		4d. dark brown, P 10	£120	4·75
		a. Perf 12 (4.85)	£325	£200
		b. Perf 10×12 (4.85)	£225	60·00
		ba. Perf 12×10	£325	£150
		c. Perf 11×12, comb (1.84)	85·00	2·75
231	**11**	5d. dull green, P 10 (1890)	50·00	3·25
		as. Optd. "Specimen"	27·00	
		b. Perf 11×10	70·00	
		c. Perf 12×10 (4.85)	£100	8·00
232		5d. bright green, P 10	75·00	14·00
		b. Perf 10×11 (12.85)	80·00	9·50
		ba. Perf 11×10	80·00	13·00
		c. Perf 10×12 (4.85)	£160	45·00
		ca. Perf 12×10	£110	75·00
233		5d. blue-green, P 10	25·00	1·75
		a. Perf 12 (4.85)	26·00	1·75
		ab. Wmk sideways	80·00	
		aba. Mixed perfs 12 and 13		
		b. Perf 11 (12.85)	11·00	1·25
		c. Perf 10×11 (12.85)	50·00	3·25
		d. Perf 11×12 or 12×11 (12.85)	11·00	1·25
		da. Wmk sideways (P 11×12)	80·00	25·00
		e. Imperf (pair)	£475	
234	**37**	6d. pale lilac, P 10	95·00	1·50
		a. Perf 10×13 or 13×10	—	£300
		b. Perf 10×12 or 12×10 (4.85)	£100	1·75
235		6d. mauve, P 10	95·00	1·50

		a. Perf 12 (4.85)	£130	10·00
		b. Perf 11 (12.85)	£130	8·00
		c. Perf 10×12 (4.85)	£100	8·50
		ca. Perf 12×10	£100	2·50
		cb. Imperf between (horiz pair)	†	£2750
		d. Perf 11×12 (12.85)	£130	14·00
		da. Perf 12×11	£100	2·00
		e. Perf 11×10 or 10×11 (12.85)	£110	2·75
236	**13**	8d. yellow, P 10 (1883)	£200	20·00
		a. Perf 12 (4.85)	£300	30·00
		b. Perf 11 (12.85)	£200	25·00
		c. Perf 10×12 (4.85)	£250	60·00
		ca. Perf 12×10	£200	55·00
236*d*	**34**	9d. on 10d. red-brown, P 11×12 (28.2.97)	18·00	20·00
		das. Optd "Specimen"	27·00	
		db. Perf 12	12·00	20·00
		dc. Perf 11	11·00	21·00
		dca. Surch double	£325	£425
236*e*		10d. violet, P 11×12 (1897)	35·00	25·00
		eas. Optd "Specimen"	30·00	
		eb. Perf 12×11½	12·00	21·00
		ec. Perf 12	23·00	27·00
		ed. Perf 11	27·00	29·00
237	**38**	1s. black, P 10	£140	7·50
		a. Perf 11 (12.85)	£275	19·00
		b. Perf 10×12	—	£250
		c. Perf 10×13		
		ca. Perf 13×10	£275	28·00
		d. Perf 11×12, comb (1.84)	£140	7·50

41

42

1885–86. W **41** (sideways).

(i) Optd "POSTAGE", in black

238	**42**	5s. lilac and green, P 13 (15.10.85)		
		a. Perf 10		
		b. Perf 12×10	£800	£140
239		10s. lilac and claret, P 13 (17.5.86)		
		a. Perf 12	£1600	£225
		ab. Opt double	—	†
240		£1 lilac and claret, P 13 (17.5.86)	—	£8000
		a. Perf 12	£10000	£5000

(ii) Overprinted in blue

241	**42**	10s. mauve and claret, P 10	£1800	£225
		as. Optd "Specimen"	75·00	
		b. Perf 12	£300	70·00
		c. Perf 12×11		
242		£1 rose-lilac and claret, P 12×10	£9000	£5000

1886–87. W **41**.

243	**26**	1d. scarlet, P 10 (12.86)	60·00	15·00
		a. Perf 11×12, comb	18·00	8·50
244	**28**	2d. deep blue, P 10 (12.87)	£100	22·00
		a. Perf 11×12, comb	38·00	7·00
		b. Imperf (pair)	†	£3000

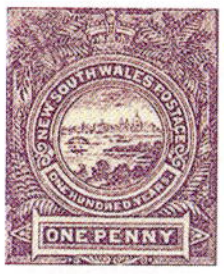

45 View of Sydney

46 Emu

47 Captain Cook

48 Queen Victoria and Arms of Colony

49 Superb Lyrebird

50 Eastern Grey Kangaroo

51 Map of Australia

52 Capt. Arthur Phillip, first Governor and Lord Carrington, Governor in 1888

(Des M. Tannenberg (1d., 6d.), Miss Devine (2d., 8d.), H. Barraclough (4d.), Govt Ptg Office (1s.), C. Turner (5s.), Mrs. F. Stoddard (20s.). Eng W. Bell).

1888 (1 May)–**89**. Centenary of New South Wales.

(a) W **40**. *P 11×12*

253	**45**	1d. lilac (9.7.88)	15·00	1·00
		a. Perf 12×11½	24·00	1·25
		b. Perf 12	16·00	50
		c. Imperf (pair)	£2250	
		d. Mauve	14·00	50
		da. Imperf between (pair)		
		db. Perf 12×11½	17·00	70
		dc. Perf 12	17·00	70
254	**46**	2d. Prussian blue (1.9.88)	22·00	50
		a. Imperf (pair)	£375	£550
		b. Imperf three sides (right stamp of horiz pair)	£1700	
		c. Perf 12×11½	22·00	40
		d. Perf 12	22·00	40
		e. Chalky blue	17·00	40
		ea. Perf 12×11½		
		eb. Perf 12	22·00	60
255	**47**	4d. purple-brown (8.10.88)	27·00	4·25
		a. Perf 12×11½	50·00	8·50
		b. Perf 12	50·00	5·50
		c. Perf 11	£300	95·00
		d. Red-brown	17·00	5·00
		da. Perf 12×11½	20·00	4·50
		db. Perf 12	20·00	4·50
		e. Orange-brown, P 12×11½	38·00	5·00
		f. Yellow-brown, P 12×11½	22·00	5·00
256	**48**	6d. carmine (26.11.88)	35·00	4·50
		a. Perf 12×11½	50·00	5·00
		b. Perf 12	35·00	11·00
257	**49**	8d. lilac-rose (17.1.89)	25·00	9·00
		a. Perf 12×11½	60·00	16·00
		b. Perf 12	25·00	9·50
		c. Magenta	85·00	16·00
		ca. Perf 12×11½	38·00	9·50
		cb. Perf 12	42·00	9·50
258	**50**	1s. maroon (21.2.89)	50·00	2·50
		a. Perf 12×11½	50·00	3·00
		b. Perf 12	55·00	2·50
		c. Violet-brown	50·00	3·00
		ca. Imperf (pair)	£1400	
		cb. Perf 12×11½	80·00	4·75
		cc. Perf 12	80·00	2·75
253s/8s		Optd "Specimen" *Set of 6*	£190	

(b) W **41**. *P 11×12*

259	**45**	1d. lilac (1888)	70·00	
		a. Mauve	45·00	7·00
260	**46**	2d. Prussian blue (1888)	£110	7·00

(c) W **25** *(sideways on 20s.) P 10*

261	**51**	5s. deep purple (13.3.89)	£425	55·00
		a. Deep violet	£425	60·00
262	**52**	20s. cobalt-blue (27.4.88)	£750	£160

Nos. 255c and 261/2 are line perforated, the remainder are comb.

A lithographed postal forgery exists of the 2d. on unwatermarked paper and perforated 11 (*Price* £450, *used*). These were in use in Sydney between March and May 1895.

53

54

1890. W **53** (5s.) or **54** (20s.). P 10.

263	**51**	5s. lilac	£275	32·00
		a. Perf 11	£375	50·00
		ab. Imperf between (horiz pair)		
		b. Perf 12	£450	55·00
		c. Perf 10×11 or 11×10	£375	32·00

		d. Mauve	£375	32·00
		da. Perf 11	£375	50·00
264	**52**	20s. cobalt-blue	£475	£160
		a. Perf 11	£475	90·00
		b. Perf 10×11		
		c. Ultramarine, P 11	£425	90·00
		ca. Perf 12	£450	£150
		cb. Perf 11×12 or 12×11	£375	90·00
263s/4s Optd "SPECIMEN" (5s.) or "Specimen" *Set of 2*			£200	

55 Allegorical figure of Australia

Halfpenny (**56**)

SEVEN-PENCE HALFPENNY (**57**)

1890 (22 Dec). W **40**.

265	**55**	2½d. ultramarine, P 11×12 comb	16·00	60
		as. Optd "Specimen"	27·00	
		b. Perf 12×11½, comb	50·00	50·00
		c. Perf 12, comb	20·00	1·00

WATERMARK VARIETIES: The attention of collectors is drawn to the note on inverted and reversed watermarks on the stamps of the Australian States at the top of the Australia listings.

1891 (5 Jan). Surch as T **56** and **57**. W **40**.

266	**26**	½d. on 1d. grey, P 11×12 comb	4·50	5·50
		b. Surch double	£750	
267	**37**	7½d. on 6d. brown, P 10	5·50	9·50
		a. Perf 11	5·00	3·25
		b. Perf 12	13·00	4·00
		c. Perf 11×12 or 12×11	6·50	3·50
		d. Perf 10×12	7·00	4·25
268	**38**	12½d. on 1s. red, P 10	17·00	30·00
		a. "HALFPENNY" omitted		
		b. Perf 11	14·00	25·00
		c. Perf 11×12, comb	14·00	18·00
		d. Perf 12×11½, comb	15·00	24·00
		e. Perf 12, comb	29·00	19·00
266/8s Optd "SPECIMEN" *Set of 3*			75·00	

1891 (1 July). Wmk "10" as W **35**. P 10.

269	**16**	3d. green	16·00	80·00
270		3d. dark green	6·50	19·00

58

Type I. Narrow "H" in "HALF"

1892 (21 Mar)–**99**. Type I. W **40**.

271	**58**	½d. grey, P 10	65·00	2·50
		a. Perf 11	95·00	8·50
		b. Perf 10×12 or 12×10	90·00	12·00
		c. Perf 11×12	5·50	40
		cs. Optd "SPECIMEN"	22·00	
		d. Perf 12	5·50	1·00
		e. Imperf (pair)		
272		½d. slate, P 11×12 (1897)	4·75	40
		a. Perf 12×11½	4·75	55
		b. Perf 12	4·75	40
		c. Imperf three sides (left stamp of horiz pair). Perf 12×11½	£1700	
273		½d. bluish green, P 11×12 (1.99)	8·00	40
		a. Perf 12×11½	2·00	80
		b. Perf 12	8·00	1·50

The perforations 11×12, 12×11½, 12, are from comb machines.

The die for Type **58** was constructed from an electro taken from the die of the De La Rue 1d., Type **26**, with "ONE" replaced by "HALF" and two "½" plugs added to the bottom corners. These alterations proved to be less hard-wearing than the remainder of the die and defects were visible by the 1905 plate of No. 333. It seems likely that repairs were undertaken before printing from the next plate in late 1907 which produced stamps as Type II.

59

1894–1904. Optd "POSTAGE" in blue. W **59** (sideways).

274	**42**	10s. mauve and claret, P 10	£600	£160
275		10s. violet and claret, P 12	£325	50·00
		a. Perf 11	£500	90·00
		b. Perf 12×11	£350	60·00
276		10s. violet and aniline crimson, P 12×11	£325	55·00
		a. Chalk-surfaced paper (1903)	£375	60·00
		b. Perf 12	£425	85·00
277		10s. violet and rosine (*chalk-surfaced paper*), P 12 (1904)	£375	85·00
		a. Perf 11	£425	90·00
		b. Perf 12×11	£375	55·00
278		10s. violet and claret (*chalk-surfaced paper*), P 12×11 (1904)	£475	95·00
279		£1 violet and claret, P 12×11		

60

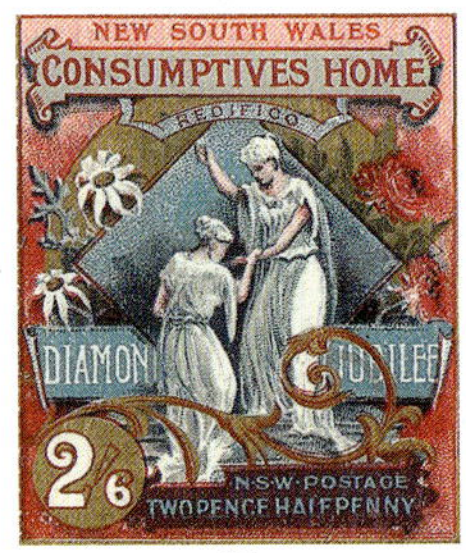

61

(Des C. Turner. Litho Govt Printing Office, Sydney)

1897 (22–28 June). Diamond Jubilee and Hospital Charity. T **60/1**. W **40**. P 12×11 (1d.) or 11 (2½d.).

280	**60**	1d. (1s.) green and brown (22.6)	50·00	50·00
281	**61**	2½d. (2s.6d.) gold, carmine and blue (28.6)	£250	£225
280s/1s Optd "Specimen" *Set of 2*			£300	

These stamps, sold at 1s. and 2s.6d. respectively, paid postage of 1d. and 2½d. only, the difference being given to a Consumptives' Home.

62

63

64

Dies of the 1d.

Die I

Die II

1d. Die I. The first pearl on the crown on the left side is merged into the arch, the shading under the fleur-de-lis is indistinct, the "S" of "WALES" is open.

Die II. The first pearl is circular, the vertical shading under the fleur-de-lis clear, the "S" of "WALES" not so open.

Dies of the 2½d.

Die I

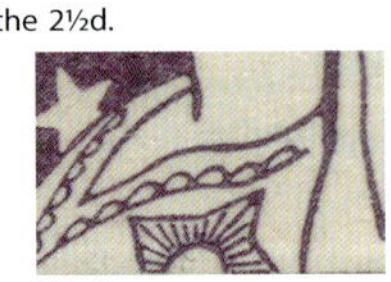

Die II

2½d. Die I. There are 12 radiating lines in the star on the Queen's breast.

Die II. There are 16 radiating lines in the star and the eye is nearly full of colour.

(Des D. Souter (2d., 2½d.). Eng W. Amor)

1897 (22 June)–**99**. W **40** (sideways on 2½d.). P 12×11 (2½d.) or 11×12 (others)

288	**62**	1d. carmine (Die I)	4·75	75
		a. Perf 12×11½	4·75	75
		s. Optd "Specimen"	22·00	
289		1d. scarlet (Die I)	9·50	1·00
		a. Perf 12×11½	9·50	1·25
		b. Perf 12	9·50	1·50
		ba. Imperf horiz (vert pair)	£850	
290		1d. rose-carmine (Die II) (10.97)	4·75	50
		a. Perf 12×11½	4·00	50
		b. Perf 12	7·00	50
		c. Imperf (pair)	£750	†
		d. Imperf between (pair)	£1200	
291		1d. salmon-red (Die II) (P 12×11½)	7·00	1·25
		a. Perf 12	9·00	1·75
292	**63**	2d. deep dull blue	16·00	1·50
		a. Perf 12×11½	8·50	1·50
		b. Perf 12	16·00	1·50
		s. Optd "Specimen"	22·00	
293		2d. cobalt-blue	17·00	1·00
		a. Perf 12×11½	7·00	1·00
		b. Perf 12	14·00	1·00
294		2d. ultramarine (1.12.97)	14·00	50
		a. Perf 12×11½	4·25	50
		b. Perf 12	4·25	50
		s. Optd "Specimen"	23·00	
295	**64**	2½d. purple (Die I)	27·00	2·50
		a. Perf 11½×12	28·00	2·50
		b. Perf 11	28·00	3·75
		s. Optd "Specimen"	22·00	
296		2½d. deep violet (Die II) (11.97)	35·00	2·25
		a. Perf 11½×12	28·00	2·25
		b. Perf 12	29·00	2·25
297		2½d. Prussian blue (17.1.99)	25·00	3·25
		a. Perf 11½×12	7·00	3·50
		b. Perf 12	7·00	4·50

The perforations 11×12, 12×11½ and 12 are from comb machines, the perforation 11 is from a single-line machine.

Nos. 288/96 were originally issued in celebration of Queen Victoria's Diamond Jubilee.

1897–99. Reissue of T **24**. W **25**. P 11.

297*c*	5s. reddish purple (*shades*)	48·00	13·00
	ca. Imperf between (horiz pair)	£9500	
	d. Perf 12	70·00	42·00
	e. Perf 11×12 or 12×11	50·00	19·00

1898–99. W **40**. P 11×12.

297*f*	**48**	6d. emerald-green	32·00	28·00
		fa. Perf 12×11½	32·00	18·00
		fb. Perf 12	26·00	18·00
		fs. Optd "Specimen"	24·00	
297*g*		6d. orange-yellow (1899)	32·00	11·00
		ga. Perf 12×11½	17·00	10·00
		gb. Perf 12	32·00	10·00
		gc. Yellow, P 12×11½	17·00	5·50

1899 (Oct). Chalk-surfaced paper. W **40** (sideways on 2½d.). P 12×11½ or 11½×12 (2½d.), comb.

298	**58**	½d. blue-green (Type I)	3·50	1·50
		a. Imperf (pair)	£250	£350
299	**62**	1d. carmine (Die II)	5·50	70
		a. Imperf horiz (vert pair)	£1000	
300		1d. scarlet (Die II)	5·50	70
		a. Imperf three sides (block of four)	£1200	
		b. Perf 11	†	£1200
		c. Mixed perfs 12×11½ and 11		
301		1d. salmon-red (Die II)	20·00	1·50
		a. Imperf (pair)	£275	£350
		b. Mixed perfs 12×11½ and 11		
302	**63**	2d. cobalt-blue	5·00	1·00
		a. Imperf (pair)	£300	
		b. Imperf horiz (vert pair)	£1800	
303	**64**	2½d. Prussian blue (Die II)	9·00	1·00
		a. Imperf (pair)	£350	
303*b*	**47**	4d. red-brown	30·00	15·00
		c. Imperf (pair)	£600	
304		4d. orange-brown	15·00	7·50
305	**48**	6d. deep orange	45·00	4·75
		a. Imperf (pair)	£600	
306		6d. orange-yellow	14·00	8·50
307		6d. emerald-green	85·00	25·00
		a. Imperf (pair)	£600	
308	**49**	8d. magenta	40·00	5·50
309	**34**	9d. on 10d. dull brown	10·00	20·00
		a. Surcharge double	£275	£600
		b. Albino surcharge	£275	
310		10d. violet	25·00	25·00
311	**50**	1s. maroon	24·00	3·50
312		1s. purple-brown	24·00	4·25
		a. Imperf (pair)	£700	

65 The spacing between the Crown and "NSW" is 1 mm in T **65** as against 2 mm in T **40**

66 Superb Lyrebird

67

1902–03. Chalk-surfaced paper. W **65** (sideways on 2½d.). P 12×11½ or 11½×12 (2½d.), comb

313	**58**	½d. blue-green (Type I)	4·75	40
		a. Perf 12×11	4·75	40
		b. Mixed perfs 12×11½ and 11	£650	
314	**62**	1d. carmine (Die II)	2·75	20
		a. Perf 11	†	£1100
315	**63**	2d. cobalt-blue	7·00	1·50
		a. Imperf (pair)	£400	
		b. Perf 11	—	—
		c. Mixed perfs 12×11½ and 11		
316	**64**	2½d. dark blue (Die II)	14·00	1·00
317	**47**	4d. orange-brown	55·00	13·00
318	**48**	6d. yellow-orange	19·00	8·00
319		6d. orange	28·00	3·25
320		6d. orange-buff	50·00	3·75
321	**49**	8d. magenta	22·00	8·50
322	**34**	9d. on 10d. brownish orange	10·00	4·50
323		10d. violet	25·00	23·00
324	**50**	1s. maroon	70·00	2·75
325		1s. purple-brown	70·00	2·75
326	**66**	2s.6d. green (1903)	45·00	23·00
		s. Optd "SPECIMEN"	75·00	

1903–08. W **65**.

327	**16**	3d. yellow-green, P 11	14·00	1·75
		b. Perf 12	14·00	1·75
		ba. Imperf between (horiz pair)		
		c. Perf 11×12 or 12×11	10·00	1·00
328		3d. dull green, P 12	50·00	5·00
		a. Perf 11×12 or 12×11	23·00	3·75
		b. Perf 11	23·00	3·75
329	**11**	5d. dark blue-green, P 11×12 or 12×11	10·00	1·50
		a. Wmk sideways	35·00	7·00
		b. Perf 11	28·00	1·50
		ba. Wmk sideways	—	65·00
		c. Perf 12	50·00	6·50
		ca. Wmk sideways	£120	65·00
		d. Imperf (pair)	£450	

Stamps from this series without watermark are from the edge of the sheet.

(Typo Victoria Govt Printer, Melbourne)

1903 (18 July). Wmk double-lined V over Crown. W w **10**.

330	**67**	9d. brown and ultramarine, P 12¼×12½, *comb*	16·00	3·25
		s. Optd "SPECIMEN."	48·00	
331		9d. brown and deep blue, P 12¼×12½, *comb*	16·00	3·25
332		9d. brown and blue, P 11	£4500	£1600

Type II. Broad "H" in "HALF"

68

1905 (1 Oct)–**10**. Chalk-surfaced paper. W **68** (sideways on 2½d.). P 12×11½ or 11½×12 (2½d.) comb, unless otherwise stated.

333	**58**	½d. blue-green (Type I)	4·50	1·00
		a. Perf 11½×11	17·00	2·50
		b. Type II (1908)	2·50	1·00
		ba. Type I (substituted cliché) in pair with Die II	85·00	70·00
		bb. Perf 11½×11	3·25	1·00
		bc. Mixed perfs 12×11½ and 11		

334	62	1d. rose-carmine (Die II)	2·75	10
		a. Double impression	£550	£650
		b. Perf 11½×11	10·00	75
335	63	2d. deep ultramarine	2·25	40
		b. Perf 11½×11	2·75	40
		c. Perf 11		
336		2d. milky blue (1910)	4·75	20
		a. Perf 11	60·00	80·00
		b. Perf 11½×11	4·75	30
337	64	2½d. Prussian blue (Die II)	4·00	2·50
338	47	4d. orange-brown	10·00	4·00
339		4d. red-brown	12·00	5·00
340	48	6d. dull yellow	19·00	4·50
		a. Perf 11½×11	23·00	6·50
341		6d. orange-yellow	19·00	2·50
		a. Perf 11½×11	28·00	7·50
342		6d. deep orange	16·00	2·50
		a. Perf 11	£350	
343		6d. orange-buff	23·00	2·75
		a. Perf 11½×11	32·00	6·00
344	49	8d. magenta	26·00	8·00
345		8d. lilac-rose	55·00	8·00
346	34	10d. violet	17·00	9·00
		a. Perf 11½×11	13·00	5·50
		b. Perf 11	13·00	6·50
347	50	1s. maroon	27·00	1·75
348		1s. purple-brown (1908)	42·00	2·75
349	66	2s.6d. blue-green	80·00	45·00
		a. Perf 11½×11	75·00	19·00
		b. Perf 11	45·00	24·00

No. 333ba occurred when a block of four units from the Type II plate (R. 3/5-4/6) were replaced by new clichés, one of which (right pane, R. 4/6) was Type I.

69

1905 (Dec). W **69**. Chalk-surfaced paper. P 11.

350	52	20s. cobalt-blue	£375	80·00
		a. Perf 12	£400	85·00
		b. Perf 11×12 or 12×11	£375	70·00

(Typo Victoria Govt Printer, Melbourne)

1905 (Dec). Wmk double-lined "A" and Crown, W w **11**. P 12×12½ comb.

351	67	9d. brown and ultramarine	26·00	1·75
		a. Perf 11	£110	70·00
		b. Mixed perfs 12×12½ and 11	£1600	
352		9d. yellow-brown and ultramarine	17·00	1·75
		a. Perf 11	£110	70·00

1907 (July–Dec). W w **11** (sideways on 2½d.). P 12×11½ or 11½×12 (2½d.), comb, unless otherwise stated

353	58	½d. blue-green (Type I)	4·75	6·00
354	62	1d. dull rose (Die II)	25·00	4·25
355	63	2d. cobalt-blue	7·50	4·25
		a. Wmk sideways	—	£325
356	64	2½d. Prussian blue (Die II)	70·00	£130
357	47	4d. orange-brown	28·00	30·00
358	48	6d. orange-buff	50·00	48·00
359		6d. dull yellow	50·00	48·00
360	49	8d. magenta	32·00	50·00
361	34	10d. violet, P 11 (12.07)	35·00	60·00
362	50	1s. purple-brown	75·00	12·00
		a. Perf 11	†	£1700
363	66	2s.6d. blue-green	£100	£100

Stamps from this series without watermark are from the edge of the sheet.

STAMP BOOKLETS

There are very few surviving examples of Nos. SB1/4. Listings are provided for those believed to have been issued with prices quoted for those known to still exist.

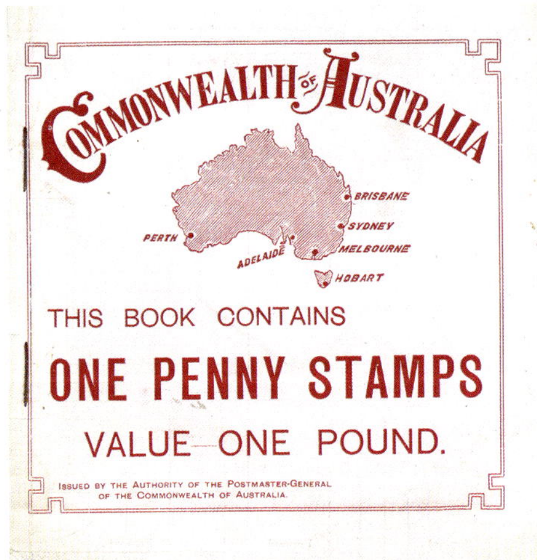

B 1 *(Illustration reduced. Actual size* 150×175 *mm)*

1904 (May)–**09**. Black on red cover as Type B **1** and picture of one of six different State G.P.O's on back. Stapled.

SB1	£1 booklet containing 240×1d. in four blocks of 30 and two blocks of 60	
	a. Red on pink cover (1909)	
	b. Blue on pink cover	

1904 (May). Black on grey cover as No. SB1. Stapled.

SB2	£1 booklet containing 120×2d. in four blocks of 30	

B 2 *(Illustration reduced. Actual size* 85×57 *mm)*

1910 (May). Black on cream. cover 80-85×55-57 mm, as Type B **2**.

SB3	2s. booklet containing 11×½d. (No. 333), either in block of 6 plus block of 5 or block of 11, and 18×1d. (No. 334), either in three blocks of 6 or block of 6 plus block of 12	£7000

Unsold stock of No. SB3 was uprated with one additional ½d. in May 1911.

1911 (Aug). Red on pink cover as No. SB3. Stapled.

SB4	2s. booklet containing 12×½d. (No. 333), either in two blocks of 6 or block of 12, and 18 1d. (No. 334) either in three blocks of 6 or 1 block of 6 plus block of 12	£6000

OFFICIAL STAMPS

O S (O **1**)   O S (O **2**)   O S (O **3**)

The space between the letters is normally 7 mm as illustrated, except on the 5d. and 8d. (11–11½ *mm*), 5s. (12 *mm*) and 20s. (14 *mm*). Later printings of the 3d., W **40**, are 5½ mm, and these are listed. A wide (8.5 *mm*) variety exists at R. 4/4 on all values other than the 3d., 5d., 8d., 5s., 10s. and 20s.

Varieties of Type O **1** exist with "O" sideways.

Nos. O1/35 overprinted with Type O **1**

1879. Wmk double-lined "**6**". P 13.

O1	16	3d. dull green	—	£600

1879 (Oct)–**85**. W **36**. P 13.

O2	26	1d. salmon	48·00	2·75

		a. Perf 10 (5.81)	£180	38·00
		b. Perf 13×10 (1881)	60·00	4·50
O3	**28**	2d. blue	48·00	2·50
		a. Perf 10 (7.81)	£225	35·00
		b. Perf 10×13 (1881)	75·00	25·00
		ba. Perf 13×10	60·00	3·50
		d. Perf 11×12 (11.84?)	—	£225
O4	**16**	3d. dull green (R.) (12.79)	£950	£350
O5		3d. dull green (3.80)	£325	75·00
		a. Perf 10 (1881)	£180	65·00
		b. Yellow-green. Perf 10 (10.81)	£170	30·00
		ba. Perf 13×10 (1881)	£160	30·00
		bb. Perf 12 (4.85)	£225	55·00
		be. Perf 10×12 or 12×10 (4.85)	£225	55·00
O6	**32**	4d. red-brown	£300	9·00
		a. Perf 10 (1881)	—	£225
		b. Perf 10×13 (1881)	£325	90·00
		ba. Perf 13×10	£250	13·00
O7	**11**	5d. green, P 10 (8.84)	25·00	32·00
O8	**37**	6d. pale lilac	£300	7·00
		a. Perf 10 (1881)	£425	42·00
		b. Perf 13×10 (1881)	£250	42·00
O9	**13**	8d. yellow (R.) (12.79)	—	£550
O10		8d. yellow (1880)	—	50·00
		a. Perf 10 (1881)	£500	90·00
O11	**34**	9d. on 10d. brown, P 10 (30.5.80)	£950	£900
		s. Optd "Specimen"	60·00	
O12	**38**	1s. black (R.)	£475	22·00
		a. Perf 10 (1881)	—	35·00
		b. Perf 10×13 (1881)	—	50·00
		ba. Perf 13×10	—	12·00

Other stamps are known with red overprint but their status is in doubt.

1880–88. W **25**.

		(a) P 13		
O13	**24**	5s. deep purple (15.2.80)	£850	£100
		a. Royal purple	—	£300
		b. Deep rose-lilac	£850	£100
		(b) P 10		
O14	**24**	5s. deep purple (9.82)	£850	£170
		a. Opt double	£4250	£1700
		b. Rose-lilac (1883)	£600	£120
		ba. Opt double, one albino		
		(c) P 10×12		
O15	**24**	5s. purple (10.86)		
		(d) P 12×10		
O16	**24**	5s. reddish purple (1886)	£750	£120
		(e) P 12		
O17	**24**	5s. purple	†	£650
		(f) P 11		
O18	**24**	5s. rose-lilac (1888)	£475	95·00

1880 (31 May). W **35**. P 13.

O18*a*	**34**	10d. lilac	£400	£110
		ab. Perf 10 and 11, compound	£425	£200
		ac. Perf 10	£425	
		aca. Opt double, one albino	£475	
		as. Optd "Specimen"	70·00	

1882–85. W **40**. P 10.

O19	**26**	1d. salmon	70·00	4·75
		a. Perf 13×10	—	£130
O20		1d. orange to scarlet	26·00	1·75
		a. Perf 10×13	—	£130
		b. Perf 11×12, comb (1.84)	13·00	1·40
		c. Perf 10×12 or 12×10 (4.85)	—	£110
		d. Perf 12×11 (12.85)		
O21	**28**	2d. blue	40·00	1·00
		a. Perf 10×13 or 13×10	£200	75·00
		c. Perf 11×12, comb (1.84)	9·00	1·00
		ca. Opt double	£950	£400
		e. Perf 12×11 (12.85)		
O22	**16**	3d. yellow-green (7 *mm*)	14·00	5·00
		aa. Opt double, one albino	£160	
		a. Wmk sideways	£225	£110
		b. Perf 12 (4.85)	£120	80·00
		ba. Opt double, one albino	£250	
		c. Perf 12×10 (4.85)	—	7·50
		ca. Opt double	†	£650
		d. Perf 12×11		
O23		3d. bluish green (7 *mm*)	30·00	8·50
		a. Perf 12 (4.85)	£120	80·00
		b. Perf 12×10 (4.85)		
		c. Perf 10×11 (12.85)		
O24		3d. yellow-green (5½ *mm*)	15·00	5·50
		a. Wmk sideways	40·00	38·00
		as. Optd "Specimen"	38·00	
		b. Perf 10×12 or 12×10 (4.85)	28·00	5·50
		c. Perf 10×11 or 11×10 (12.85)	—	7·00
O25		3d. bluish green (5½ *mm*)	12·00	11·00
		a. Wmk sideways		
		b. Perf 10×12 or 12×10 (4.85)	17·00	12·00
		c. Perf 10×11 or 11×10 (12.85)	5·00	4·25
O26	**32**	4d. red-brown	70·00	5·50
		a. Perf 11×12, comb (1.84)	18·00	4·00
		b. Perf 10×12 (4.85)	—	70·00
O27		4d. dark brown	40·00	4·00
		a. Perf 11×12, comb (1.84)	19·00	4·00
		b. Perf 12 (4.85)	£250	£150
		c. Perf 10×12 (4.85)	£250	90·00
O28	**11**	5d. dull green	24·00	25·00
		a. Perf 12×10 (4.85)		
O29		5d. blue-green	25·00	35·00
		a. Perf 12 (4.85)	£100	£120
		as. Optd "Specimen"	38·00	
		b. Perf 10×11	15·00	19·00
		c. Perf 11	†	£150
O30	**37**	6d. pale lilac	22·00	5·50
		a. Perf 11 (12.85)	55·00	8·00
O31		6d. mauve	22·00	7·00
		a. Perf 12 (4.85)	—	45·00
		b. Perf 10×12 or 12×10 (4.85)	22·00	6·50
		d. Perf 11×10 (12.85)	22·00	7·00
		e. Perf 11×12		
		ea. Perf 12×11 (12.85)	85·00	19·00
O32	**13**	8d. yellow	26·00	11·00
		aa. Opt double	—	†
		a. Perf 12 (4.85)	£150	45·00
		b. Perf 10×12 or 12×10 (4.85)	26·00	11·00
		ba. Opt double	†	—
		d. Perf 11 (12.85)	26·00	27·00
		da. Opt double	£850	
		db. Opt treble	†	£1200
O33	**38**	1s. black (R.)	55·00	15·00
		a. Perf 10×13	—	60·00
		b. Perf 11×12, comb (1.84)	29·00	8·00
		ba. Opt double	—	£500

1886–87. W **41**. P 10.

O34	**26**	1d. scarlet	£100	7·50
O35	**28**	2d. deep blue	†	£600
		a. Perf 11×12, comb	†	£600

1887–90. Nos. 241/2 optd in black.

		(a) With Type O **1**		
O36	**42**	10s. mauve and claret, P 12 (1890)	—	£3750
		(b) With Type O **2** *(30 April 1889)*		
O37	**42**	10s. mauve and claret P 12	£6000	£1400
		as. Optd "Specimen"	£100	
		b. Perf 10	£7500	£3000
		(c) With Type O **3** *(7 Jan 1887)*		
O38	**42**	£1 mauve and claret, P 12×10	£38000	£19000

Only nine examples of No. O38 are recorded, three of which are mint. One of the used stamps, in the Royal Collection, shows overprint Type O **3** double.

1888 (17 July)–**90**. Optd as Type O **1**.

		(a) W **40**. *P 11×12*		
O39	**45**	1d. lilac	6·00	75
		a. Perf 12	3·75	75
		b. Mauve	3·25	75
		ba. Perf 12	3·75	75
O40	**46**	2d. Prussian blue (15.10.88)	4·50	40
		aa. Opt double, one albino		
		ab. Opt double	—	†
		a. Perf 12	9·00	2·50
O41	**47**	4d. purple-brown (10.10.89)	11·00	4·25
		a. Perf 12	18·00	6·00
		b. Perf 11		
		c. Red-brown	13·00	3·75
		ca. Opt double	†	£650
		cb. Perf 12	19·00	6·00
O42	**48**	6d. carmine (16.1.89)	9·00	9·50
		a. Perf 12	19·00	9·50
		ab. Opt double	—	†
O43	**49**	8d. lilac-rose (1890)	24·00	12·00
		a. Perf 12	55·00	17·00
O44	**50**	1s. maroon (9.1.90)	40·00	4·00
		a. Perf 12	40·00	4·50
		b. Purple-brown	38·00	4·75
		ba. Opt double		
		bb. Perf 12	40·00	6·00
O39s/44s Optd "Specimen" *Set of 6*			£250	
		(b) W **41**. *P 11×12 (1889)*		
O45	**45**	1d. mauve		
O46	**46**	2d. blue		
		(c) W **25**. *P 10*		
O47	**51**	5s. deep purple (R.) (9.1.90)	£2000	£800
O48	**52**	20s. cobalt-blue (10.3.90)	£18000	£1100

1890 (15 Feb)–**91**. Optd as Type O **1**. W **53** (5s.) or **54** (20s.). P 10.

O49	**51**	5s. lilac	£650	£170
		a. Mauve	£400	£100
		b. Dull lilac, P 12	£800	£170
O50	**52**	20s. cobalt-blue (3.91)	£19000	£1100
O49s/50s Optd "SPECIMEN" *Set of 2*			£250	

The used prices quoted for Nos. O48 and O50 are for cancelled-to-order examples.

1891 (Jan). Optd as Type O **1**. W **40**.

(a) On No. 265. P 11×12

O54	**55**	2½d. ultramarine	12·00	10·00

(b) On Nos. 266/8

O55	**26**	½d. on 1d. grey, P 11×12	70·00	80·00
		a. Opt double	£1500	†
O56	**37**	7½d. on 6d. brown, P 10	50·00	70·00
O57	**38**	12½d. on 1s. red, P 11×12	70·00	£110
O54s/7s Optd "Specimen" *Set of* 4			£150	

1892 (May). No. 271 optd as Type O **1**. P 10.

O58	**58**	½d. grey	14·00	19·00
		a. Perf 11×12	5·50	16·00
		as. Optd "SPECIMEN"	32·00	
		b. Perf 12	10·00	11·00
		c. Perf 12×11½	32·00	17·00

Official stamps were withdrawn from the government departments on 31 December 1894.

POSTAGE DUE STAMPS

D **1**

(Dies eng by A. Collingridge. Typo Govt Printing Office, Sydney)

1891 (1 Jan)–**97**. W **40**. P 10.

D1	D **1**	½d. green (21.1.92)	12·00	6·50
D2		1d. green	30·00	4·00
		a. Imperf vert (horiz pair)	†	£6000
		b. Perf 11 (1896)	20·00	3·50
		c. Perf 12	75·00	40·00
		d. Perf 12×10 (1892)	75·00	40·00
		e. Perf 10×11 (1894)	32·00	8·00
		f. Perf 11×12 or 12×11	22·00	3·50
D3		2d. green	23·00	4·00
		a. Perf 11	23·00	3·50
		b. Perf 12 (1897)	75·00	40·00
		c. Perf 12×10 (1894)	75·00	40·00
		d. Perf 10×11 (1894)	30·00	11·00
		e. Perf 11×12 or 12×11	23·00	4·00
		f. Wmk sideways	65·00	20·00
D4		3d. green	65·00	12·00
		a. Perf 10×11 (1893)	65·00	12·00
D5		4d. green	60·00	3·75
		a. Perf 11		
		b. Perf 10×11 (1893)	50·00	3·75
		c. Perf 10×12	†	£1000
D6		6d. green	60·00	15·00
D7		8d. green	£120	27·00
D8		5s. green	£275	50·00
		a. Perf 11	£650	£150
		b. Perf 11×12	—	£325
D9		10s. green	£750	70·00
		a. Perf 12×10	£550	
D10		20s. green	£850	£100
		a. Perf 12	£1400	
		b. Perf 12×10	£650	
D1s/10s Optd "SPECIMEN" *Set of* 10 (incl D3fs)			£225	

Used prices for 10s. and 20s. are for cancelled-to-order stamps. Postally used examples are rare.

1900. Chalk-surfaced paper. W **40**. P 11.

D12	D **1**	1d. emerald-green	25·00	4·75
		a. Perf 12	50·00	13·00
		b. Perf 11×12 or 12×11	27·00	4·25
D13		2d. emerald-green	30·00	6·50
		a. Perf 12	—	£100
		b. Perf 11×12 or 12×11	24·00	6·50
D14		3d. emerald-green, P 11×12 or 12×11	80·00	25·00
D15		4d. emerald-green (7.00)	48·00	13·00

TELEGRAPH STAMPS

T **1**

(Des of vignette H. T. Glover. Vignette litho, frame typo Govt Printer)

1871 (1 Feb). W **41** (sideways). Bluish paper. P 13.

T1	1d. black and brownish red	£180	
T2	2d. black and blue	£275	
T3	6d. black and Indian red	£275	
T4	1s. black and bright blue	£400	
T5	2s. black and brown	£750	
T6	4s. black and mauve	£950	
T7	6s. black and carmine	£1400	
T8	8s. black and lilac	£1700	
	a. Perf 10	£1500	

New South Wales became part of the Commonwealth of Australia on 1 January 1901.

QUEENSLAND

The area which later became Queensland was previously part of New South Wales known as the Moreton Bay District. The first post office, at Brisbane, was opened in 1834 and the use of New South Wales stamps from the District became compulsory from 1 May 1854.

Queensland was proclaimed a separate colony on 10 December 1859, but continued to use New South Wales issues until 1 November 1860.

Post Offices opened in the Moreton Bay District before 10 December 1859, and using New South Wales stamps, were

Office	*Opened*	*Numeral Cancellation*
Brisbane	1834	95
Burnett's Inn/Goode's Inn/Nanango	1850	108
Callandoon	1850	74
Condamine	1856	151
Dalby	1854	133
Drayton	1846	85
Gayndah	1850	86
Gladstone	1854	131
Goode's Inn	1858	108
Ipswich	1846	87
Maryborough	1849	96
Rockhampton	1858	201
Surat	1852	110
Taroom	1856	152
Toowoomba	1858	214
Warwick	1848	81

PRICES FOR STAMPS ON COVER

Nos. 1/3	*from* × 2
Nos. 4/56	*from* × 3
Nos. 57/8	—
Nos. 59/73	*from* × 4
Nos. 74/82	*from* × 2
Nos. 83/109	*from* × 3
Nos. 110/13	*from* × 2
Nos. 116/17	*from* × 3
Nos. 118/27	—
Nos. 128/50	*from* × 4
Nos. 151/65	—
Nos. 166/78	*from* × 10
Nos. 179/83	*from* × 4
Nos. 184/206	*from* × 15
No. 207	—
Nos. 208/28	*from* × 15
No. 229	*from* × 100
No. 230	—
Nos. 231/54	*from* × 15
Nos. 256/62*c*	*from* × 10
Nos. 264*a*/*b*	*from* × 2
Nos. 265/6	*from* × 20
Nos. 270/4	—
Nos. 281/5	*from* × 10
Nos. 286/308	*from* × 12
Nos. 309/13	—
Nos. F1/37	—

PERKINS BACON "CANCELLED". For notes on these handstamps, showing "CANCELLED" between horizontal bars forming an oval, see Catalogue Introduction.

1

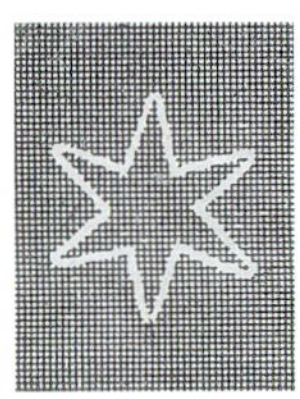

2 Large Star

3 Small Star

(Dies eng W. Humphrys. Recess P.B.)

1860. W **2**

(a) Imperf

1	**1**	1d. carmine-rose	£6500	£800
2		2d. blue	£16000	£1800
3		6d. green	£10000	£800

(b) Clean-cut perf 14–16

4	**1**	1d. carmine-rose	£2750	£300
5		2d. blue	£1400	£110
		a. Imperf between (horiz pair)	†	—
6		6d. green (15 Nov)	£1400	70·00

3d. re-entry

3d. retouch (R.2/8)

The 3d. re-entry which occurs on one stamp in the second row, shows doubling of the left-hand arabesque and the retouch has redrawn spandrel dots under "EN" of "PENCE", a single dot in the centre of the circle under "E" and the bottom outer frame line closer to the spandrel's frame line.

1860–61. W **3**.

(a) Clean-cut perf 14–16

7	**1**	2d. blue	£950	£110
		a. Imperf between (horiz pair)	†	£11000
8		3d. brown (15.4.61)	£750	75·00
		a. Re-entry	—	£275
		b. Retouch	—	£275
9		6d. green	£1300	75·00
10		1s. violet (15.11.60) (H/S "CANCELLED" in oval £10000)	£1400	£110
11		"REGISTERED" (6d.) olive-yellow (1.61) (H/S "CANCELLED" in oval £10000)	£950	£100
		a. Imperf between (pair)	£13000	

(b) Clean-cut perf 14 at Somerset House (7.61)

12	**1**	1d. carmine-rose (H/S "CANCELLED" in oval £9500)	£375	60·00
13		2d. blue (H/S "CANCELLED" in oval £9500)	£850	65·00

(c) Rough perf 14–16 (9.61)

14	**1**	1d. carmine-rose	£100	50·00
15		2d. blue	£300	28·00
		a. Imperf between (horiz pair)	£10000	
16		3d. brown (H/S "CANCELLED" in oval £11000)	85·00	32·00
		a. Imperf vert (horiz pair)	£10000	
		b. Re-entry	£400	£140
		c. Retouch (R. 2/8)	—	£140
17		6d. deep green (H/S "CANCELLED" in oval £10000)	£550	30·00
18		6d. yellow-green	£650	30·00
19		1s. violet	£1100	90·00
20		"REGISTERED" (6d.) orange-yellow	£110	40·00

The perforation of No. 8 is that known as "intermediate between clean-cut and rough", No. 20 can also be found with a similar perforation.

Line through design

(Printed and perforated by Thomas Ham, Brisbane)

1862–67. Thick toned paper. No wmk.

(a) P 13 rough perforations (1862–63)

21	**1**	1d. Indian red (16.12.62)	£500	75·00
22		1d. orange-vermilion (2.63)	£110	17·00
		a. Imperf (pair)	—	£2750
23		2d. pale blue (16.12.62)	£140	27·00
24		2d. blue	85·00	9·00
		a. Imperf (pair)	—	£2500
		b. Imperf between (horiz pair)	†	£15000
		c. Imperf between (vert pair)	£5000	
25		3d. brown	£120	45·00
		a. Re-entry	—	£140
		b. Retouch (R. 2/8)	—	£140
26		6d. apple green (17.4.63)	£180	15·00
		a. Line through design at right	—	£130
		b. Line through design at left	—	£130
27		6d. yellow-green	£170	12·00
		a. Imperf between (horiz pair)	†	£16000
		b. Line through design at right	—	£110
		c. Line through design at left	—	£110
28		6d. pale bluish green	£275	45·00
		a. Imperf (pair)	—	£2750
		b. Line through design at right	—	£225
		c. Line through design at left	—	£225
29		1s. grey (14.7.63)	£350	24·00
		a. Imperf between (horiz pair)	†	£17000
		b. Imperf between (vert pair)	†	—
		s. Handstamped "SPECIMEN"	50·00	

The top or bottom row of perforations was sometimes omitted from the sheet, resulting in stamps perforated on three sides only.

Prior to the plates being printed from in Brisbane, damage occurred to the 6d. plate in the form of a scratch across two adjoining stamps. The position of the pair in the plate is not yet recorded. One joined pair is known.

This flaw was not corrected until around 1869 when, after plate cleaning, only faint traces remain. These are hard to see.

The Royal Philatelic Collection contains an example of No. 22 imperf between (horizontal pair), used.

(b) P 12½×13 rough (1863–67)

30	**1**	1d. orange-vermilion	£120	32·00
31		2d. blue	£110	20·00
32		3d. brown	£130	26·00
		a. Re-entry	—	£130
		b. Retouch (R. 2/8)	—	£130
33		6d. apple green	£225	50·00
		a. Line through design at right	—	£300
		b. Line through design at left	—	£300
34		6d. yellow-green	£225	50·00
		a. Line through design at right	—	£300
		b. Line through design at left	—	£300
35		6d. pale bluish green		
		a. Line through design at right		
		b. Line through design at left		
36		1s. grey	£550	45·00
		a. Imperf between (horiz pair)		

This paper was used again for a very limited printing in 1867 which can be properly regarded as the First Government Printing. The perforations were now clean-cut. The designs and the background to the head are very well defined, the plates having been cleaned when transferred to the Government Printing Office.

(c) P 13 Clean-cut (1867)

37		1d. orange-vermilion	£120	28·00
38		2d. blue	90·00	11·00
40		6d. apple green	£225	19·00
41		6d. yellow-green	£225	23·00
42		6d. deep green		

Previously listed and then removed, the significance of this issue has been reassessed and it is now re-listed under this paper.

Copies of the 3d. and 1s. have been identified with these characteristics but there are no records of them being printed at this time.

1864–65. W **3**.

(a) P 13

44	**1**	1d. orange-vermilion (1.65)	£120	60·00
		a. Imperf between (horiz pair)	£5500	
45		2d. pale blue (1.65)	£120	17·00
46		2d. deep blue	£120	17·00
		a. Imperf between (vert pair)	£8500	
		b. Imperf between (horiz pair)	†	£13000
		c. Bisected (1d.) (on cover)	†	£4000
47		6d. yellow-green (1.65)	£225	22·00
		a. Line through design at right	—	£160
		b. Line through design at left	—	£160
48		6d. deep green	£275	22·00
		a. Line through design at right	—	£160
		b. Line through design at left	—	£160
49		"REGISTERED" (6d.) orange-yellow (21.6.64)	£170	35·00
		b. Imperf		

(b) P 12½×13

50	**1**	1d. orange-vermilion	£160	80·00
50*a*		2d. deep blue	£275	80·00

The "REGISTERED" stamp was reprinted in 1895. See note below No. 82.

1866 (24 Jan). Wmk "QUEENSLAND/POSTAGE — POSTAGE/STAMPS — STAMPS" in three lines in script capitals with double wavy lines above and below the wmk and single wavy lines with projecting sprays between each line of words. There are ornaments ("fleurons") between "POSTAGE" "POSTAGE" and between "STAMPS" "STAMPS". Single stamps only show a portion of one or two letters of this wmk.

(a) P 13

51	**1**	1d. orange-vermilion	£200	45·00
52		2d. blue	£100	17·00

(b) P 12½×13

52*a*	**1**	1d. orange-vermilion	£275	75·00
52*b*		2d. blue	£275	75·00

First transfer

Double transfer

1866–67. Lithographed on thick paper. No wmk. P 13.

(a) First Transfer (Sept 1866) "FOUR" in taller thin letters

53		4d. reddish lilac (*shades*)	£425	29·00
		a. Re-entry	—	£130
		b. Double transfer	£5500	£2500
54		4d. grey-lilac (*shades*)	£425	29·00
		a. Re-entry	—	£130
		b. Double transfer	—	£2500

Second transfer

(b) Second Transfer (Feb 1867) "FOUR" in shorter letters

55		4d. lilac (*shades*)	£425	22·00
		a. Retouch (R. 2/8)	—	£120
		b. "FOUR" missing	—	£550
56		4d. grey-lilac (*shades*)	£425	22·00
		a. Retouch (R. 2/8)	—	£120
		b. "FOUR" missing	—	£600
		s. Handstamped "SPECIMEN"	55·00	
57		5s. bright rose	£1300	£180
58		5s. pale rose	£1200	£140
		a. Imperf between (vert pair)	†	£8500
		s. Handstamped "SPECIMEN"	70·00	

The 4d. was lithographed from two separate transfers from the 3d. plate and the 5s. was taken from the 1s. plate.

The alterations in values were made by hand on the stones and there are minor varieties in the shape and position of the letters.

4

2d. Pl II. Dot by "U"

2d. Pl II. Dots near arabesque

1868–74. Wmk small truncated Star, W **4** on each stamp, and the word "QUEENSLAND" in single-lined Roman capitals four times in each sheet. P 13.

59	**1**	1d. orange-vermilion (18.1.71)	95·00	7·50
60		2d. pale blue (3.4.68) (Pl I)	80·00	5·00
61		2d. blue (18.1.71) (Pl I)	75·00	3·50
62		2d. bright blue (Pl I)	85·00	2·75
63		2d. greenish blue (Pl I)	£150	2·75
64		2d. dark blue (Pl I)	85·00	2·75
65		3d. olive-green (27.2.71)	£200	7·00
		a. Re-entry	—	65·00
		b. Retouch (R. 2/8)	—	65·00
66		3d. greenish grey	£225	6·50
		a. Re-entry	—	60·00
		b. Retouch (R. 2/8)	—	60·00
67		3d. brown	£120	5·50
		a. Re-entry	—	55·00
		b. Retouch (R. 2/8)	—	55·00
68		6d. yellow-green (10.11.71)	£250	7·50
69		6d. green	£225	10·00
70		6d. deep green	£300	17·00
71		1s. greenish grey (13.11.72)	£800	50·00
72		1s. brownish grey	£800	50·00
73		1s. mauve (19.2.74)	£400	23·00
59s/73s		H/S "SPECIMEN" *Set of 5*	£250	

(b) P 12 (about Feb 1874)

74	**1**	1d. orange-vermilion	£500	29·00
75		2d. blue (Pl II)	£950	75·00
76		3d. greenish grey	—	£225
		a. Re-entry		
		b. Retouch (R. 2/8)		
77		3d. brown	£750	£225
		a. Re-entry		
		b. Retouch (R. 2/8)		
78		6d. green	£1800	50·00
79		1s. mauve	£850	55·00

(c) P 13×12

80	**1**	1d. orange-vermilion	—	£200
81		2d. blue (Pl II)	£1600	45·00
82		3d. greenish grey	—	£350

A second plate of the 2d. denomination was sent by Perkins, Bacon to the Colony in 1872 and it was first printed from in August of that year. The new plate is helpful in separating many of the 2d. printings up to 1879.

Plate II of the 2d. may be identified by a smudged dot to the left of "U" in "QUEEN" and tiny dots near the lower curl of the right arabesque.

Reprints were made in 1895 of all five values on Wmk W **4**, and perforated 13; the colours are:—1d. orange and brownish orange, 2d. deep dull blue (Pl II), 3d. brown, 6d green, 1s. red-violet and dull violet. The "Registered" was also reprinted with these on the same paper, but perforated 12. One sheet of the 2d. reprint is known to have had the perforations missing between the fourth and fifth vertical rows.

5

6

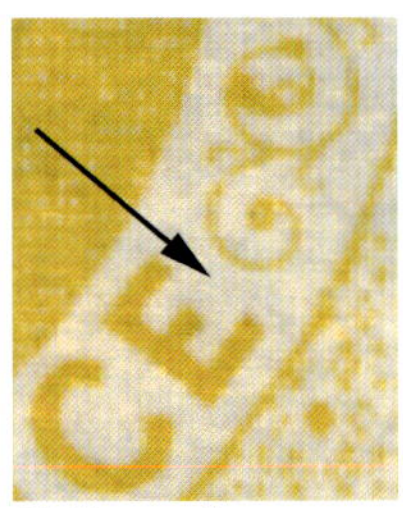
4d. First transfer

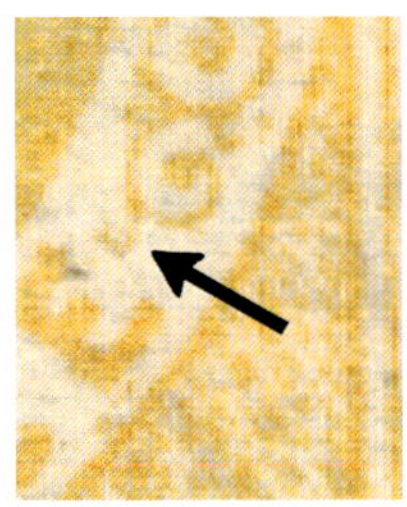
4d. Second transfer

The first transfer of the 4d. was taken from the 3d. plate, identified by the lack of the curl at the foot of the arabesque, the second was from Plate II of the 2d. On the first transfer the "P" of "POSTAGE" is to the right of the centre of the Queen's necklace, on the second transfer it is to the left of it.

(4d., litho. Other values recess)

1868–78. Wmk Crown and Q. W **5**.

(a) P 13 (1868–75)

83	**1**	1d. orange-vermilion (10.11.68)	£110	6·00
		a. Imperf (pair)	£800	
84		1d. pale rose-red (4.11.74)	90·00	16·00
85		1d. deep rose-red	£160	16·00
86		2d. pale blue (20.11.68) (Pl I)	85·00	2·00
87		2d. deep blue (4.11.74) (Pl II)	80·00	4·50
88		3d. brown (11.6.75)	£130	14·00
		a. Re-entry	—	85·00
		b. Retouch (R. 2/8)	—	85·00
89		4d. yellow (*shades*) (1st transfer) (1.1.75)	£2000	£110

		s. Handstamped "SPECIMEN"	£100	
90		6d. deep green (9.4.69)	£200	9·00
91		6d. yellow-green	£190	6·50
92		6d. pale apple-green (1.1.75)	£225	9·00
		a. Imperf (pair)	£700	
93		1s. mauve	£375	65·00
		(b) P 12 (1876–78)		
94	1	1d. deep orange-vermilion	75·00	6·00
95		1d. pale orange-vermilion	85·00	6·00
96		1d. rose-red	85·00	11·00
97		1d. flesh	£120	13·00
98		2d. pale blue (Pl II)	£130	15·00
99		2d. bright blue (Pl II)	70·00	1·75
100		2d. deep blue (Pl II)	70·00	2·00
101		3d. brown	£120	9·50
		a. Re-entry	—	70·00
		b. Retouch (R. 2/8)	—	70·00
102		4d. yellow (*shades*) (1st transfer)	£1600	45·00
103		4d. buff-yellow (*shades*) (2nd transfer)	£1600	45·00
104		6d. deep green	£250	10·00
105		6d. green	£225	4·25
106		6d. yellow-green	£250	4·50
107		6d. apple-green	£275	7·00
108		1s. mauve	£100	9·00
109		1s. purple	£250	5·00
		a. Imperf between (vert pair)	†	—
		(c) P 13×12 or 12×13		
110	1	1d. orange-vermilion	—	£150
110*a*		1d. rose-red	—	£180
111		2d. deep blue (Pl II)	£1400	£250
112		4d. yellow	—	£375
113		6d. deep green	—	£300
		(d) P 12½×13 (1868)		
114	1	1d. orange-vermilion	—	£350
115		2d. deep blue (Pl I)	—	£350
115*a*		6d. yellow-green	†	£1200
		(e) P 12½ (1868)		
115*b*	1	2d. deep blue (Pl I)	†	£1000
115*c*	1	2d. deep blue (Pl II)	†	£750

Reprints of the above were made in 1895 on thicker paper, Wmk. W **6**, perf 12. The colours are:—1d. vermilion-red, 2d. deep dull blue and pale ultramarine, 3d. brown, 6d. dull yellow-green and 1s. lilac-grey.

The Royal Philatelic Collection contains an example of No. 95 imperf between (vert pair), used.

1879. No wmk. P 12.

116	1	6d. pale emerald-green	£400	27·00
117		1s. mauve (*fiscal cancel £5*)	£225	£100

No. 117 has a very indistinct lilac *burelé* band at back.

Nos. 116/17 can be found showing portions of a papermaker's watermark, either T. H. Saunders & Co or A. Pirie & Sons.

1880. Lithographed from transfers from the 1s. die. Wmk Crown and Q. W **6**. P 12.

118	1	2s. pale blue	£160	60·00
119		2s. blue (*fiscal cancel £4*)	£160	60·00
		a. Imperf vert (horiz pair)	£8500	
120		2s. deep blue (*fiscal cancel £4*)	£190	60·00
121		2s.6d. dull scarlet	£325	80·00
122		2s.6d. bright scarlet (*fiscal cancel £4*)	£325	80·00
123		5s. pale yellow-ochre	£475	£120
124		5s. yellow-ochre (*fiscal cancel £5*)	£475	£120
125		10s. reddish brown	£850	£200
126		10s. bistre brown	£850	£200
127		20s. rose (*fiscal cancel £7*)	£1800	£250

Of the 2s. and 20s. stamps there are five types of each, and of the other values ten types of each.

Beware of fiscally used copies that have been cleaned and provided with forged postmarks.

7

Die I

Die II

Dies I and II often occur in the same sheet.

Die I. The white horizontal inner line of the triangle in the upper right-hand corner merges into the outer white line of the oval above the "L".

Die II. The same line is short and does not touch the inner oval.

1879–81. Typo. P 12.

		(a) Wmk Crown and Q. W **5**		
128	7	1d. reddish brown (Die I) (15.5.79)	£150	45·00
		a. Die II	£225	45·00
		ab. Imperf between (horiz pair)	†	£2250
		ac. "QOEENSLAND"	£1700	£275
129		1d. orange-brown (Die I)	£200	45·00
130		2d. blue (Die I) (10.4.79)	£140	13·00
		a. "PENGE" (R. 12/6)	£950	£130
		b. "QUEENSbAND" (R. 5/6)	—	£130
		c. "QU" joined	—	£130
131		4d. orange-yellow (6.6.79)	£1300	£100
		(b) No wmk, with lilac burelé band on back		
132	7	1d. reddish brown (Die I) (21.10.79)	£750	£120
		a. Die II	£850	£140
		ab. "QOEENSLAND"	—	£1900
133		2d. blue (Die I) (21.10.79)	£750	60·00
		a. "PENGE" (R. 12/6)	£3750	£700
		b. "QUEENSbAND" (R. 5/6)		
		(c) Wmk Crown and Q. W **6**		
134	7	1d. reddish brown (Die I) (31.10.79)	85·00	9·50
		b. Die II	£120	9·50
		ba. "QOEENSLAND"	£500	60·00
135		1d. dull orange (Die I)	65·00	11·00
		a. Die II	70·00	12·00
		ab. "QOEENSLAND"	£250	45·00
		ac. Imperf between (horiz pair)	†	—
136		1d. scarlet (Die I) (7.3.81)	60·00	9·50
		aa. Imperf vert (horiz pair)	†	£2250
		a. Die II	65·00	9·50
		ab. "QOEENSLAND"	£275	38·00
137		2d. blue (Die I) (10.4.79)	85·00	4·00
		a. "PENGE"	£350	50·00
		b. "QUEENSbAND"	£350	50·00
		c. Die II	95·00	6·50
138		2d. grey-blue (Die I)	85·00	3·25
		a. "PENGE"	£350	50·00
		b. "QUEENSbAND"	£350	50·00
		c. Die II	85·00	6·50
139		2d. bright blue (Die I)	90·00	3·00
		a. "PENGE"	£350	50·00
		b. "QUEENSbAND"	£350	50·00
		c. Imperf between (horiz pair)	£2250	£2250
		d. Die II	90·00	6·50
140		2d. deep blue (Die I)	90·00	3·25
		a. "PENGE"	£350	50·00
		b. "QUEENSbAND"	£350	50·00
		c. Die II	80·00	8·50
141		4d. orange-yellow	£375	20·00
		a. Imperf vert (horiz pair)	£12000	
142		6d. deep green	£170	7·50
143		6d. yellow-green	£180	7·00
		a. Imperf vertically (horiz pair)		
144		1s. deep violet (3.80)	£170	10·00
145		1s. pale lilac	£160	15·00

The variety "QO" is No. 48 in the first arrangement, and No. 44 in a later arrangement on the sheets.

All these values have been seen imperf and unused, but we have no evidence that any of them were used in this condition.

The above were printed in sheets of 120, from plates made up of 30 groups of four electrotypes. There are four different types in each group, and two such groups of four are known of the 1d. and 2d., thus giving eight varieties of these two values. There was some resetting of the first plate of the 1d., and there are several plates of the 2d.; the value in the first plate of the latter value is in thinner letters, and in the last plate three types in each group of four have the "TW" of "TWO" joined, the letters of "PENCE" are larger and therefore much closer together, and in one type the "O" of "TWO" is oval, that letter being circular in the other types.

(8)

9

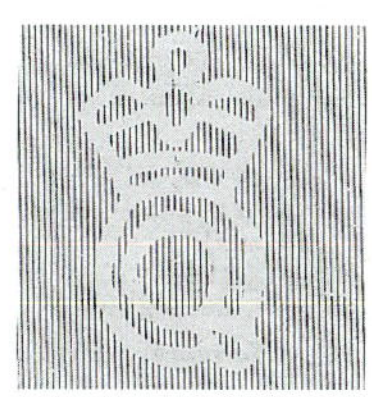

10

1880 (21 Feb). Surch with T **8**.

151	7	½d. on 1d. (No. 134) (Die I)	£325	£180
		a. Die II	£800	£475
		ab. "QOEENSLAND"	£1900	£1300

Examples with "Half-penny" reading downwards are forged surcharges.

£1 Re-entry (R. 1/2)

£1 Retouch (R. 6/4)

(Eng H. Bourne. Recess Govt Printing Office, Brisbane, from plates made by B.W.)

1882 (13 Apr)–**95**. P 12.

		*(a) W **5** (twice sideways). Thin paper*		
152	**9**	2s. bright blue (14.4.82)	£275	65·00
153		2s.6d. vermilion (12.7.82)	£130	26·00
154		5s. rose	£130	27·00
155		10s. brown (12.7.82)	£250	50·00
156		£1 deep green (30.5.83)	£550	£140
		a. Re-entry (R. 1/2)	—	£325
		b. Retouch (R. 6/4)	—	£325
152s/6s (*ex* 2s. 6d.) H/S "SPECIMEN" *Set of* 4			£275	
		*(b) W **10**. Thick paper (10.11.86)*		
157	**9**	2s. bright blue	£300	65·00
158		2s.6d. vermilion	55·00	27·00
159		5s. rose	55·00	42·00
160	**9**	10s. brown	£130	50·00
161		£1 deep green	£325	85·00
		a. Re-entry (R. 1/2)	£850	£200
		b. Retouch (R. 6/4)	£850	£200
		*(c) W **6** (twice sideways). Thin paper (1895)*		
162	**9**	2s.6d. vermilion	85·00	45·00
163		5s. rose	90·00	26·00
164		10s. brown	£475	£110
165		£1 deep green	£375	£100
		a. Re-entry (R. 1/2)	£900	£250
		b. Retouch (R. 6/4)	£900	£250

The re-entry on the £1 shows as a double bottom frame line and the retouch occurs alongside the bottom right numeral.

See also Nos. 270/1, 272/4 and 309/12.

11

12

In T **12** the shading lines do not extend entirely across, as in T **11**, thus leaving a white line down the front of the throat and point of the bust.

4d. "PENGE" for "PENCE" (R. 9/1)

4d. "EN" joined in "PENCE" (R. 4/6)

1882 (1 Aug)–**91**. W **6**.

		(a) P 12		
166	**11**	1d. pale vermilion-red (23.11.82)	11·00	1·00
		a. Double impression		
167		1d. deep vermilion-red	11·00	1·00
168		2d. blue	23·00	1·00
		a. Imperf between (horiz pair)	†	£3000
169		4d. pale yellow (18.4.83)	45·00	3·25
		a. "PENGE" for "PENCE"	£275	50·00
		b. "EN" joined in "PENCE"	£225	35·00
		c. Imperf (11.91)	†	£475
170		6d. green (6.11.82)	30·00	2·00
171		1s. violet (6.2.83)	55·00	11·00
172		1s. lilac	27·00	7·00
173		1s. deep mauve	24·00	7·00
174		1s. pale mauve	13·00	7·00
		a. Imperf	†	—
		(b) P 9½×12 (1884)		
176	**11**	1d. pale red	£160	65·00
177		2d. blue	£550	85·00
178		1s. mauve	£275	80·00

The above were printed from plates made up of groups of four electrotypes as previously. In the 1d. the words of value are followed by a full stop. There are four types of the 4d., 6d. and 1s., eight types of the 1d., and 12 types of the 2d.

No. 169c is from a sheet used at Roma post office and comes cancelled with the "46" numeral postmark.

1887 (5 May)–**89**. W **6**.

		(a) P 12		
179	**12**	1d. vermilion-red	17·00	1·00
180		2d. blue	17·00	1·00
		a. Oval white flaw on Queen's head behind diadem (R. 12/5)	70·00	9·00
181		2s. deep brown (12.3.89)	80·00	75·00
182		2s. pale brown	70·00	65·00
		(b) P 9½×12		
183	**12**	2d. blue	£425	80·00

These are from new plates; four types of each value grouped as before. The 1d. is without stop. In all values No. 2 in each group of four has the "L" and "A" of "QUEENSLAND" joined at the foot, and No. 3 of the 2d. has "P" of word "PENCE" with a long downstroke.

The 2d. is known bisected and used as a 1d. value.

13

14

1890. W **6** (sideways on ½d.). P 12½, 13 (comb machine).

184	**13**	½d. pale green	19·00	2·00
185		½d. deep green	14·00	2·00
186		½d. deep blue-green	7·50	2·00
187	**12**	1d. vermilion-red	8·00	50
		a. Imperf (pair)	£300	£325
		b. Oval broken by tip of bust (R. 10/3)	45·00	5·00
		c. Double impression	†	£650
188		2d. blue (old plate)	9·00	50
189		2d. pale blue (old plate)	9·00	50
190		2d. pale blue (retouched plate)	11·00	1·00
		a. "FWO" for "TWO" (R. 8/7)	—	25·00
191	**14**	2½d. carmine	16·00	2·50
192	**12**	3d. brown	9·00	4·00
193	**11**	4d. yellow	18·00	4·00
		a. "PENGE" for "PENCE"	£100	28·00
		b. "EN" joined in "PENCE"	80·00	24·00
194		4d. orange	27·00	4·00
		a. "PENGE" for "PENCE"	£140	28·00
		b. "EN" joined in "PENCE"	£110	24·00
195		4d. lemon	29·00	7·50
		a. "PENGE" for "PENCE"	£150	38·00
		b. "EN" joined in "PENCE"	£120	30·00
196		6d. green	11·00	2·00
197	**12**	2s. red-brown	45·00	55·00
198		2s. pale brown	55·00	60·00

This issue is perforated by a new vertical comb machine, gauging about 12¾×12¾. The 3d. is from a plate similar to those of the last issue, No. 2 in each group of four types having "L" and "A" joined at the foot. The ½d. and 2½d. are likewise in groups of four types, but the differences are very minute. In the retouched plate of the 2d. the letters "L" and "A" no longer touch in No. 2 of each group and the "P" in No. 3 is normal.

1895. W **10**.

		A. Thick paper		
		(a) P 12½, 13		
202	**12**	1d. vermilion-red (16.1.95)	4·75	60
		a. Oval broken by tip of bust (R. 10/3)	42·00	6·50
203		1d. red-orange	4·75	60
		a. Oval broken by tip of bust (R. 10/3)	42·00	6·50
204		2d. blue (retouched plate) (16.1.95)	6·50	60
		a. "FWO" for "TWO" (R. 8/7)	80·00	22·00
		(b) P 12		
205	**11**	1s. mauve (8.95)	40·00	25·00
		B. Unwmkd paper; with blue burelé band at back. P 12½, 13		
206	**12**	1d. vermilion-red (19.2.95)	2·50	2·50
		a. Oval broken by tip of bust (R. 10/3)	22·00	22·00
		b. "PE" of "PENNY" omitted (R. 1/2)	£300	£325
206*c*		1d. red-orange	2·50	2·50
		C. Thin paper. Crown and Q faintly impressed. P 12½, 13		
207	**12**	2d. blue (retouched plate) (6.95)	13·00	£160
		a. "FWO" for "TWO" (R. 8/7)	£140	

15

16

17

18

1895–96.

*A. W **6** (sideways on ½d.)*

(a) P 12½, 13

208	**15**	½d. green (11.5.95)	3·25	1·75
		a. Double impression	£2000	£2000
209		½d. deep green	3·25	1·75
		a. Printed both sides	£275	
210	**16**	1d. orange-red (28.2.95)	3·50	50
211		1d. pale red	8·00	65
212		2d. blue (19.6.95)	35·00	50
213	**17**	2½d. carmine (8.95)	24·00	5·50
214		2½d. rose	24·00	5·50
215	**18**	5d. purple-brown (10.95)	27·00	5·00

(b) P 12

217	**16**	1d. red (8.95)	90·00	50·00
218		2d. blue (8.95)	80·00	30·00

*B. Thick paper. W **10** (sideways) (part only on each stamp)*

(a) P 12½, 13

219	**15**	½d. green (6.8.95)	2·75	6·00
220		½d. deep green	2·75	6·00

(b) P 12

221	**15**	½d. green	42·00	
222		½d. deep green	42·00	

C. No wmk; with blue burelé band at back

(a) P 12½, 13

223	**15**	½d. green (1.8.95)	10·00	7·00
		a. Without *burelé* band	75·00	
224		½d. deep green	10·00	

(b) P 12

225	**15**	½d. green	22·00	
		a. Without *burelé* band	£140	

Nos. 223a and 225a are from the margins of the sheet.

D. Thin paper, with Crown and Q faintly impressed. P 12½, 13.

227	**15**	½d. green	2·00	6·00
228	**16**	1d. orange-red	3·25	2·00

19

1896–1902. W **6**. P 12½, 13.

229	**19**	1d. vermilion	20·00	70
230		6d. green (1902)	†	£16000

Only used examples of No. 230 are known, mostly with readable postmarks from 1902. It is suggested that electrotypes of this unissued design were inadvertently entered in a plate of No. 249.

20

21

22

23

24

25

"Cracked plate"

Die I

Die II

Two Dies of 4d.:

Die I. Serif of horizontal bar on lower right 4d. is clear of vertical frame line.

Die II. Serif joins vertical frame line.

1897–1908. Figures in all corners. W **6** (sideways on ½d.). P 12½, 13 (comb).

231	**20**	½d. deep green	5·00	8·00
		a. Perf 12	—	£150
232	**21**	1d. orange-vermilion	2·50	40
233		1d. vermilion	2·50	40
		a. Perf 12 (1899)	8·00	3·50
234		2d. blue	8·00	40
		a. Cracked plate	£190	35·00
		b. Perf 12 (1905)	£1000	7·00
		ba. Cracked plate	£2750	£250
235		2d. deep blue	7·00	40
		a. Cracked plate	£170	35·00
236	**22**	2½d. rose (10.98)	17·00	28·00
237		2½d. purple/*blue* (20.1.99)	9·50	3·25
238		2½d. brown-purple/*blue*	9·50	3·25
239		2½d. slate/*blue* (5.08)	9·00	9·00
240	**21**	3d. brown (10.98)	10·00	3·00
241		3d. deep brown	8·00	3·00
242		3d. reddish brown (1906)	13·00	4·25
243		3d. grey-brown (1907)	24·00	4·75
244		4d. yellow (Die I) (10.98)	13·00	3·25
		a. Die II	32·00	11·00
245		4d. yellow-buff (Die I)	11·00	3·25
		a. Die II	26·00	11·00
246	**23**	5d. purple-brown	8·50	3·00
247		5d. dull brown (1906)	9·50	9·00
248		5d. black-brown (1907)	15·00	6·00
249	**21**	6d. green (1.4.98)	8·50	2·75
250		6d. yellow-green	7·00	3·50
251	**24**	1s. pale mauve (1.7.99)	14·00	3·75
252		1s. dull mauve	14·00	3·75
253		1s. bright mauve	19·00	5·00
254	**25**	2s. turquoise-green	35·00	50·00

Stamps of this issue also exist with the irregular line perforation 12½, 13.

The 1d. perf 12×9½ exists used and unused but their status has not yet been established (*price £120 unused*).

The cracked plate variety on the 2d. developed during 1901 and shows as a white break on the Queen's head and neck. The electro was later replaced.

1897–98. W **6**

(a) Zigzag roulette in black

(ab) Zigzag roulette in green

(b) The same but plain

(c) Roulette (a) and also (b)

(d) Roulette (b) and perf 12½, 13

(e) Roulette (a) and perf 12½, 13

(f) Compound of (a), (b), and perf 12½, 13

256	**21**	1d. vermilion (*a*)	17·00	13·00
		a. Zigzag roulette in green (*ab*)	£250	
257		1d. vermilion (*b*)	18·00	7·50
258		1d. vermilion (*c*)	19·00	26·00
259		1d. vermilion (*d*)	9·50	6·50
260		1d. vermilion (*e*)	75·00	95·00
261		1d. vermilion (*f*)	95·00	£100

26

(Des M. Kellar)

1899 (Sept)–**1906**. W **6**. P 12½, 13 (comb).

262	**26**	½d. deep green	3·25	2·50
		a. Grey-green	2·50	2·50
		b. Green (P 12) (1905)	£110	60·00
		c. Pale green (1906)	10·00	4·00

Stamps of T **26** without wmk, are proofs.

Stamps of this issue also exist with the irregular line perforation 12½, 12.

27

27a

(Des F. Elliott)

1900 (19 Jun). Anglo-Boer War Patriotic Fund. W **6**. P 12.

263	**27**	1d. (6d.) claret	£140	£120
264	**27a**	2d. (1s.) violet	£350	£275

These stamps, sold at 6d. and 1s. respectively, paid postage of 1d. and 2d. only, the difference being contributed to The Anglo–Boer War Patriotic Fund.

28

QUEENSLAND — A

QUEENSLAND — B

TWO TYPES OF "QUEENSLAND". Three different duty plates, each 120 (12 x 10), were produced for Type **28**. The first contained country inscriptions as Type A and was only used for No. 265. The second duty plate used for Nos. 265/6 and 282/4 contained 117 examples as Type B and three as Type A occurring on R. 1/6, R. 2/6 and R. 3/6. The third plate, used for Nos. 266, 283, 284 and 285 had all inscriptions as Type B.

(Typo Victoria Govt Printer, Melbourne)

1903 (4 July)–**05**. W w **10**. P 12½.

265	**28**	9d. brown and ultramarine (A)	55·00	8·00
266		9d. brown and ultramarine (B) (1905)	38·00	8·00

1903 (Oct). As Nos. 162 and 165. W **6** (twice sideways). P 12½, 13 (irregular line).

270	**9**	2s.6d. vermilion	£200	55·00
271		£1 deep green	£2000	£700
		a. Re-entry (R. 1/2)	£4000	£1400
		b. Retouch (R. 6/4)	£4000	£1400

(Litho Govt Ptg Office, Brisbane, from transfers of the recess plates)

1905 (Nov)–**06**. W **6** (twice sideways).

(a) P 12½, 13 (irregular line)

272	**9**	£1 deep green	£1000	£170
		a. Re-entry (R. 1/2)	£2000	£375
		b. Retouch (R. 6/4)	£2000	£375

(b) P 12

273	**9**	5s. rose (7.06)	£150	£100
274		£1 deep green (7.06)	£550	£130
		a. Re-entry (R. 1/2)	£1000	£300
		b. Retouch (R. 6/4)	£1000	£300

30

32

Redrawn types of T **21**

T **30**. The head is redrawn, the top of the crown is higher and touches the frame, as do also the back of the chignon and the point of the bust. The forehead is filled in with lines of shading, and the figures in the corners appear to have been redrawn also.

T **32**. The forehead is plain (white instead of shaded), and though the top of the crown is made higher, it does not touch the frame; but the point of the bust and the chignon still touch. The figure in the right lower corner does not touch the line below, and has not the battered appearance of that in the first redrawn type. The stamps are very clearly printed, the lines of shading being distinct.

1906 (Sept). W **6**. P 12½, 13 (comb).

281	**30**	2d. dull blue (*shades*)	10·00	5·50

(Typo Victoria Govt Printer, Melbourne)

1906 (Sept)–**10**. Wmk Crown and double-lined A, W w **11**.

(a) P 12×12½

282	**28**	9d. brown and ultramarine (A)	75·00	7·50
283		9d. brown and ultramarine (B)	23·00	4·50
283*a*		9d. pale brown and blue (A)	70·00	7·50
284		9d. pale brown and blue (B)	14·00	4·50

(b) P 11 (1910)

285	**28**	9d. brown and blue (B)	£5000	£800

(c) Compound perf 12×12½ and 11

285*a*		9d. brown and ultramarine (B)	†	£1600

33

1907–**11**. W **33**.

(a) P 12½, 13 (comb)

286	**26**	½d. deep green	2·00	4·50
287		½d. deep blue-green	2·00	4·50
288	**21**	1d. vermilion	3·00	30
		a. Imperf (pair)	£400	
289	**30**	2d. dull blue	32·00	3·50
289*a*		2d. bright blue (3.08)	27·00	18·00
290	**32**	2d. bright blue (4.08)	4·25	30
291	**21**	3d. pale brown (8.08)	22·00	2·75
292		3d. bistre-brown	12·00	3·75
293		4d. yellow (Die I)	12·00	4·50
		a. Die II	42·00	14·00
294		4d. grey-black (Die I) (4.09)	25·00	6·50
		a. Die II	50·00	15·00
295	**23**	5d. dull brown	35·00	20·00
295*a*		5d. sepia (12.09)	20·00	24·00
296	**21**	6d. yellow-green	22·00	4·25
297		6d. bright green	19·00	8·00
298	**24**	1s. violet (1908)	22·00	3·50
299		1s. bright mauve	20·00	3·50
300	**25**	2s. turquoise-green (8.08)	38·00	45·00

Stamps of this issue also exist with the irregular line perforation 12½, 13. This was used when the comb perforation was under repair.

(b) P 13×11 to 12½ (May 1911)

301	**26**	½d. deep green	7·00	13·00
302	**21**	1d. vermilion	7·50	7·00
303	**32**	2d. blue	10·00	9·00
304	**21**	3d. bistre-brown	18·00	26·00
305		4d. grey-black	70·00	90·00
		a. Die II	£140	£160
306	**23**	5d. dull brown	26·00	70·00
307	**21**	6d. yellow-green	38·00	55·00
308	**23**	1s. violet	60·00	85·00

The perforation (*b*) is from a machine introduced to help cope with the demands caused by the introduction of penny postage. The three rows at top (or bottom) of the sheet show varieties gauging 13×11½, 13×11, and 13×12, respectively, these are obtainable in strips of three showing the three variations.

(Litho Govt Ptg Office, Brisbane)

1907 (Oct)–**11**. W **33** (twice sideways). P 12½, 13 (irregular line).

309	**9**	2s.6d. vermilion	42·00	50·00
		a. Dull orange (1910)	75·00	90·00
		b. Reddish orange (1911)	£180	£225
310		5s. rose (12.07)	80·00	65·00
		a. Deep rose (1910)	£100	90·00
		b. Carmine-red (1911)	£250	£275
311		10s. blackish brown	£150	75·00
		a. Sepia (1911)	£425	£300
312		£1 bluish green	£400	£130
		a. Re-entry (R. 1/2)	£800	£300
		b. Retouch (R. 6/4)	£800	£300
		c. Deep bluish green (1910)	£550	£350
		ca. Re-entry (R. 1/2)	£1200	£700
		cb. Retouch (R. 6/4)	£1200	£700
		d. Deep yellowish green (1911)	£1800	£1400
		da. Re-entry (R. 1/2)	£4250	£2750
		db. Retouch (R. 6/4)	£4250	£2750

The 1911 printings are on thinner, whiter paper.

The lithographic stones used for Nos. 272/4 and 309/12 took the full sheet of 30 so the varieties on the £1 recess-printed version also appear on the stamps printed by lithography.

1911. W **33**. Perf irregular compound, 10½ to 12½.

313	**21**	1d. vermilion	£1500	£700

This was from another converted machine, formerly used for perforating Railway stamps. The perforation was very unsatisfactory.

STAMP BOOKLETS

There are very few surviving examples of Nos. SB1/4. Listings are provided for those believed to have been issued with prices quoted for those known to still exist.

1904 (1 Jan)–**09**. Black on a red cover as Type B **1** of New South Wales. Stapled.

SB1	£1 booklet containing 240 1d. in four blocks of 30 and two blocks of 60	
	a. Red on pink cover (1909)	
	b. Blue on pink cover	£15000

1904 (1 Jan). Black on grey cover as No. SB1. Stapled.

SB2	£1 booklet containing 120 2d. in four blocks of 30

1910 (May). Black on cream cover as Type B **2** of New South Wales. Stapled.

SB3	2s. booklet containing 11 ½d. (No. 301), either in block of 6 plus block of 5 or block of 11 and 18 1d. (No 302), either in three blocks of 6 or block of 6 plus block of 12	

Unsold stock of No. SB3 was uprated with one additional ½d. in May 1911.

1911 (Aug). Red on pink cover as No. SB3. Stapled.

SB4	2s. booklet containing 12 ½d. (No. 301), either in two blocks of 6 or block of 12, and 18 1d. (No. 302), either in three blocks of 6 or block of 6 plus block of 12	£6000
	a. Red on white cover	£5500

POSTAL FISCALS

Authorised for use from 1 January 1880 until 1 July 1892

CANCELLATIONS. Beware of stamps which have had pen-cancellations cleaned off and then had faked postmarks applied. Used prices quoted are for postally used examples between the above dates.

F **1**

F **2**

1866–68. Litho, Govt Ptg Office.

A. No wmk. P 13

F1	F **1**	1d. blue	£120	27·00
F2		6d. deep violet	£200	£120
F3		1s. blue-green	£190	85·00
F4		2s. brown	£350	£200
F5		2s.6d. dull red	£425	£170
F6		5s. yellow	£1100	£400
F6*a*		6s. light brown	£1700	
F7		10s. green	£1300	£550
F8		20s. rose	£2000	£900

B. Wmk F **2**. *P 13*

F9	F **1**	1d. blue	65·00	65·00
F10		6d. deep violet	£200	£140
F11		6d. blue	£600	£375
F12		1s. blue-green	£180	90·00
F13		2s. brown	£350	£160
F13*a*		5s. yellow	£1100	£375
F14		10s. green	£1300	£550
F15		20s. rose	£2000	£1000

F **3**

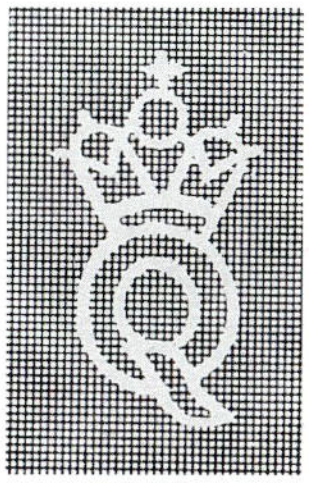
F **3a**

1871–72. Litho, Govt Ptg Office. P 12 or 13.

A. Wmk Large Crown and Q, Wmk F **3a**

F16	F **3**	1d. mauve	55·00	22·00
F17		6d. red-brown	£100	45·00
		a. Imperf vert (horiz pair)		
F18		1s. green	£130	45·00
F19		2s. blue	£190	70·00
F20		2s.6d. brick-red	£350	£140
F21		5s. orange-brown	£450	£200
F22		10s. brown	£900	£400
F23		20s. rose	£1800	£600

B. No wmk. Blue burelé band at back

F24	F **3**	1d. mauve	65·00	24·00
F25		6d. red-brown	£100	48·00
F26		6d. mauve	£425	£150
F27		1s. green	£150	48·00
F28		2s. blue	£250	£160
F29		2s.6d. vermilion	£450	£170
F30		5s. yellow-brown	£600	£200
F31		10s. brown	£1000	£400
F32		20s. rose	£1800	£600

No. F19 is known imperforate horizontally (vert pair), with fiscal cancellation.

F **4**

F **5**

1878–79. Typo.

A. No wmk. Lilac burelé band at back. P 12

F33	F **4**	1d. violet	£190	95·00

B. Wmk Crown and Q, W **5**. *P 12*

F34	F **4**	1d. violet	£110	65·00
		d. Imperf between (horiz pair)		

Stamps as Type F **5** may not have been issued until after 1 July 1892 when the proper use of duty stamps for postal service was terminated but there are several examples which appear to have genuinely passed through the post during the 1890's. Unless they are dated during 1892 their postal use was certainly unauthorised although they may have been accepted.

Queensland became part of the Commonwealth of Australia on 1 January 1901.

SOUTH AUSTRALIA

PRICES FOR STAMPS ON COVER

Nos. 1/3	*from* × 3
No. 4	†
Nos. 5/12	*from* × 2
Nos. 13/18	*from* × 3
Nos. 19/43	*from* × 4
Nos. 44/9*b*	—
Nos. 50/110	*from* × 3
No. 111	—
Nos. 112/34	*from* × 6
Nos. 135/45	*from* × 3
Nos. 146/66	*from* × 5
Nos. 167/70*a*	*from* × 10
Nos. 171/2*a*	—
Nos. 173/94*a*	*from* × 12
Nos. 195/208	—
Nos. 229/31	*from* × 12
No. 232	—
Nos. 233/42	*from* × 12
Nos. 268/75	*from* × 30
Nos. 276/9	—
Nos. 280/8	*from* × 30
Nos. 289/92	—
Nos. 293/304	*from* × 15
No. 305	—
Nos. O1/13	—
Nos. O14/36	*from* × 20
Nos. O37/42	*from* × 5
Nos. O43/4	*from* × 50
Nos. O45/7	—
Nos. O48/52	*from* × 30
No. O53	—
Nos. O54/85	*from* × 50
Nos. O86/7	—

SPECIMEN OVERPRINTS. Those listed are from U.P.U. distributions between 1889 and 1895. Further "Specimen" overprints exist, but these were used for other purposes.

PERKINS BACON "CANCELLED". For notes on these handstamps, showing "CANCELLED" between horizontal bars forming an oval, see Catalogue Introduction.

1

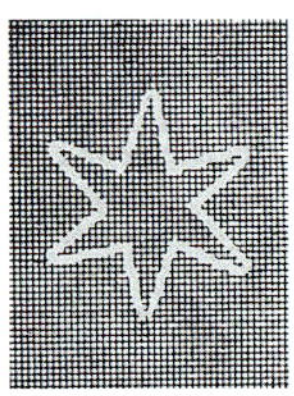
2 Large Star

(Eng Wm Humphrys. Recess P.B.)

1855 (1 Jan–Oct). Printed in London. W **2**. Imperf.

1	**1**	1d. dark green (Oct 1855) (H/S "CANCELLED" in oval £12000)	£10000	£500
2		2d. rose-carmine (*shades*) (H/S "CANCELLED" in oval £11000)	£800	85·00
3		6d. deep blue (Oct 1855) (H/S "CANCELLED" in oval £10000)	£4500	£170

Prepared and sent to the Colony, but not issued

4	**1**	1s. violet (H/S "CANCELLED" in oval £20000)	£26000	

A printing of 500,000 of these 1s. stamps was delivered, but, as the colour was liable to be confused with that of the 6d. stamp, this stock was destroyed on 5 June 1857. It is believed that surviving examples of No. 4 come from Perkins Bacon remainders which came on to the market in the late 1890s.

Proofs of the 1d. and 6d. without wmk exist, and these are found with forged star watermarks added, and are sometimes offered as originals.

For reprints of the above and later issues, see note after No. 194.

1856–58. Printed by Printer of Stamps, Adelaide, from Perkins, Bacon plates. W **2**. Imperf.

5	**1**	1d. deep yellow-green (15.6.58)	£9500	£550
6		1d. yellow-green (11.10.58)	£8500	£650
7		2d. orange-red (4.58)	£2250	80·00
8		2d. blood-red (14.11.56)	£3000	60·00
		a. Printed on both sides	†	£1300
9		2d. red (*shades*) (23.4.56)	£750	40·00
		a. Printed on both sides	†	£850
10		6d. slate-blue (7.57)	£4500	£200
11		1s. red-orange (8.7.57)	—	£750
12		1s. orange (11.6.58)	£11000	£475

1858–59. Rouletted. (This first rouletted issue has the same colours as the local imperf issue). W **2**.

13	**1**	1d. yellow-green (8.1.59)	£1000	65·00
14		1d. light yellow-green (18.3.59)	£1000	70·00
		a. Imperf between (pair)		
15		2d. red (17.2.59)	£350	22·00
		a. Printed on both sides	†	£850
17		6d. slate-blue (12.12.58)	£850	65·00
18		1s. orange (18.3.59)	£1900	50·00
		a. Printed on both sides	†	£1900

3

4

(5)

The "TEN PENCE" surcharge (T **5**) was produced from a setting of six (3×2). There are noticable differences between the six types.

1860–69. Second rouletted issue, printed (with the exception of No. 24) in colours only found rouletted or perforated. Surch with T **5** (Nos. 35/7). W **2**.

19	**1**	1d. bright yellow-green (22.4.61)	£130	50·00
20		1d. dull blue-green (17.12.63)	£140	50·00
21		1d. sage-green	£150	50·00
		a. Imperf between (horiz pair)		
22		1d. pale sage-green (27.5.65)	£130	
23		1d. deep green (1864)	£550	85·00
24		1d. deep yellow-green (1869)	£275	
24*a*		2d. pale red	£250	4·00
		b. Printed on both sides	†	£550
25		2d. pale vermilion (3.2.63)	£150	4·75
26		2d. bright vermilion (19.8.64)	£150	3·75
		a. Imperf between (horiz pair)	£3750	£750
27	**3**	4d. dull violet (24.1.67)	£160	45·00
28	**1**	6d. violet-blue (19.3.60)	£450	8·00
29		6d. greenish blue (11.2.63)	£275	4·50
30		6d. dull ultramarine (25.4.64)	£225	4·50
		a. Imperf between (horiz pair)	†	£2250
31		6d. violet-ultramarine (11.4.68)	£425	7·00
32		6d. dull blue (26.8.65)	£350	7·50
		a. Imperf between (pair)	†	£3000
33		6d. Prussian blue (7.9.69)	£1000	50·00
33*a*		6d. indigo	—	70·00
34	**4**	9d. grey-lilac (24.12.60)	£150	9·00
		a. Imperf between (horiz pair)	†	£4000
35		10d. on 9d. orange-red (B.) (20.7.66)	£500	48·00
36		10d. on 9d. yellow (B.) (29.7.67)	£700	30·00
37		10d. on 9d. yellow (Blk.) (14.8.69)	£3750	80·00
		a. Surch inverted at the top	†	£7000
		c. Roul×perf 10	†	—
38	**1**	1s. yellow (25.10.61)	£1300	32·00
		a. Imperf horiz (vert pair)	†	£5500
39		1s. grey-brown (10.4.63)	£425	32·00
40		1s. dark grey-brown (26.5.63)	£400	32·00
41		1s. chestnut (25.8.63)	£350	11·00
42		1s. lake-brown (27.3.65)	£325	12·00
		a. Imperf between (horiz pair)	†	£2250
43	**3**	2s. rose-carmine (24.1.67)	£500	32·00
		a. Imperf between (vert pair)	†	£2500

1868–71. Remainders of old stock subsequently perforated by the 11½–12½ machine.

(a) Imperf stamps. P 11½–12½

44	**1**	2d. pale vermilion (Feb 1868)	—	£1300
45		2d. vermilion (18.3.68)	—	£1400

(b) Rouletted stamps. P 11½–12½

46	**1**	1d. bright green (9.11.69)	—	£750
47		2d. pale vermilion (15.8.68)	£2500	£650
48		6d. Prussian blue (8.11.69)	—	£400
		aa. Horiz pair perf all round, roul between		
48*a*		6d. indigo	—	£500
49	**4**	9d. grey-lilac (29.3.71)	£2750	£250
		a. Perf×roulette	—	£275
49*b*	**1**	1s. lake-brown (23.5.70)		

1867–70. W **2**. P 11½–12½×roulette.

50	**1**	1d. pale bright green (2.11.67)	£375	29·00
51		1d. bright green (1868)	£350	24·00
52		1d. grey-green (26.1.70)	£400	29·00
		a. Imperf between (horiz pair)		
53		1d. blue-green (29.11.67)	£550	65·00
54	**3**	4d. dull violet (7.68)	£3000	£160
55		4d. dull purple (1869)	—	£130
56	**1**	6d. bright pale blue (29.5.67)	£950	19·00
57		6d. Prussian blue (30.7.67)	£900	19·00
		a. Printed on both sides		
58		6d. indigo (1.8.69)	£1000	26·00
59	**4**	10d. on 9d. yellow (B.) (2.2.69)	£1400	35·00
		a. Printed on both sides	—	£1200

60	1	1s. chestnut (4.68)	£475	20·00
61		1s. lake-brown (3.3.69)	£475	20·00

NOTE. The stamps perf 11½, 12½, or compound of the two, are here combined in one list, as both perforations are on the one machine, and all the varieties may be found in each sheet of stamps. This method of classifying the perforations by the machines is by far the most simple and convenient.

(6)

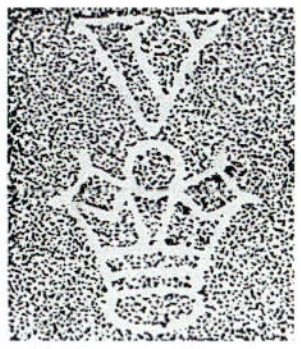
7 (=Victoria W **19**)

1868–79. Surch with T **6** (Nos. 66/8). W **2**. P 11½–12½.

62	1	1d. pale bright green (8.2.68)	£375	70·00
63		1d. grey-green (18.2.68)	£325	70·00
64		1d. dark green (20.3.68)	£180	22·00
		a. Printed on both sides	†	£1100
65		1d. deep yellow-green (28.6.72)	£170	22·00
		a. Imperf between (horiz pair)	†	£3250
66	3	3d. on 4d. Prussian blue (Blk.) (7.2.71)	—	£850
67		3d. on 4d. sky-blue (Blk.) (12.8.70)	£600	18·00
		a. Imperf		
		b. Rouletted	—	£1400
68		3d. on 4d. deep ultramarine (Blk.) (9.72)	£160	9·00
		a. Surch double	†	£3750
		b. Additional surch on back	—	£3000
		c. Surch omitted	£40000	£20000
70		4d. dull purple (1.2.68)	£110	15·00
71		4d. dull violet (1868)	£100	8·00
72	1	6d. bright pale blue (23.2.68)	£600	11·00
73		6d. Prussian blue (29.9.69)	£325	7·00
		a. Perf 11½×imperf (horiz pair)	†	£2250
74		6d. indigo (1869)	£325	17·00
75	4	9d. claret (7.72)	£200	8·00
76		9d. bright mauve (1.11.72)	£200	8·00
		a. Printed on both sides	†	£900
77		9d. red-purple (15.1.74)	£110	8·00
78		10d. on 9d. yellow (B.) (15.8.68)	£2000	50·00
		a. Wmk Crown and S A (W **10**) (1868)	—	£1700
79		10d. on 9d. yellow (Blk.) (13.9.69)	£450	65·00
80	1	1s. lake-brown (9.68)	£225	18·00
81		1s. chestnut (8.10.72)	£200	20·00
82		1s. dark red-brown	£170	12·00
83		1s. red-brown (6.1.69)	£180	12·00
84	3	2s. pale rose-pink (10.10.69)	£2000	£180
85		2s. deep rose-pink (8.69)	—	£120
86		2s. crimson-carmine (16.10.69)	£170	21·00
87		2s. carmine (1869)	£160	13·00
		a. Printed on both sides	†	£750

No. 68c comes from two sheets on which, it is believed, some stamps showed the surcharge omitted and others the surcharge double. One of the used examples of No. 68c is known postmarked in 1875 and many of the others in 1879.

No. 78a was a trial printing made to test the perforating machine on the new D.L.R. paper.

A used example of No. 70 in imperf between horiz pair is in the Royal Philatelic Collection.

1870–71. W **2**. P 10.

88	1	1d. grey-green (6.70)	£325	24·00
89		1d. pale bright green (9.8.70)	£325	21·00
90		1d. bright green (1871)	£275	21·00
91	3	3d. on 4d dull ultramarine (R.) (6.8.70)	£1400	£110
92		3d. on 4d pale ultramarine (Blk.) (14.2.71)	£500	35·00
93		3d. on 4d ultramarine (Blk.) (14.8.71)	£325	40·00
93*a*		3d. on 4d. Prussian blue (Blk.) (16.12.71)	—	£1000
94		4d. dull lilac (1870)	£190	11·00
95		4d. dull purple (1871)	£180	11·00
96	1	6d. bright blue (19.6.70)	£350	17·00
97		6d. indigo (11.10.71)	£500	16·00
98		1s. chestnut (4.1.71)	£325	40·00

NOTE. Stamps perf 10 all round were produced by a new rotary machine, introduced early in 1870. This machine was not large enough to perforate entire sheets, and perforation therefore had to be completed with the perf 11½-12½ line machine, giving rise to the compound perforations listed as Nos. 99/110.

1870–73. W **2**. P 10×11½–12½, 11½–12½×10, or compound.

99	1	1d. pale bright green (11.10.70)	£325	23·00
		a. Printed on both sides		
100		1d. grey-green	£300	18·00
101		1d. deep green (19.6.71)	£190	11·00
102	3	3d. on 4d. pale ultramarine (Blk.) (9.11.70)	£550	80·00
103		4d. dull lilac (11.5.72)	—	20·00
104		4d. slate-lilac (5.3.73)	£200	20·00
105	1	6d. Prussian blue (2.3.70)	£275	8·00
106		6d. bright Prussian blue (26.10.70)	£300	10·00
107	4	10d. on 9d. yellow (Blk.) (1.70)	£300	60·00
108	1	1s. chestnut (17.6.71)	£375	80·00
109	3	2s. rose-pink (24.4.71)	—	£225
110		2s. carmine (2.3.72)	£325	65·00

1871 (17 July). W **7**. P 10.

111	3	4d. dull lilac	£5500	£325
		a. Printed on both sides	†	£4250

8 Broad Star

(**9**)

1876–1900. Surch with T **9** (Nos. 118/21). W **8**.

(a) P 11½–12½

112	3	3d. on 4d. ultramarine (1.6.79)	£160	30·00
		a. Surch double	†	£1800
113		4d. violet-slate (15.3.79)	£160	16·00
114		4d. plum (16.4.80)	90·00	7·50
115		4d. deep mauve (8.6.82)	90·00	6·00
116	1	6d. indigo (2.12.76)	£190	5·00
		a. Imperf between (horiz pair)	†	—
117		6d. Prussian blue (7.78)	£150	4·50
118	4	8d. on 9d. brown-orange (7.76)	£200	9·00
119		8d. on 9d. burnt umber (1880)	£200	10·00
		a. Surch double	†	—
120		8d. on 9d. brown (9.3.80)	£200	10·00
		a. Imperf between (vert pair)	£3000	
121		8d. on 9d. grey-brown (10.5.81)	£180	7·00
		a. Surch double	†	£2500
122		9d. purple (9.3.80)	95·00	10·00
		a. Printed on both sides	—	£650
123		9d. rose-lilac (21.8.80)	27·00	4·50
		a. Printed on both sides	†	£600
124		9d. rose-lilac (*large holes*) (26.5.00)	16·00	4·50
125	1	1s. red-brown (3.11.77)	85·00	2·75
		a. Imperf between (horiz pair)	†	£900
126		1s. reddish lake-brown (1880)	85·00	3·75
127		1s. lake-brown (9.1.83)	90·00	3·00
128		1s. Vandyke brown (1891)	95·00	8·50
129		1s. dull brown (1891)	85·00	3·25
130		1s. chocolate (*large holes*) (6.5.97)	27·00	3·50
		a. Imperf vert (horiz pair)	£450	
131		1s. sepia (*large holes*) (22.5.00)	27·00	6·00
		a. Imperf between (vert pair)	£600	
132	3	2s. carmine (15.2.77)	48·00	7·50
		a. Imperf between (horiz pair)	†	£2750
133		2s. rose-carmine (1885)	60·00	8·00
134		2s. rose-carmine (*large holes*) (6.12.98)	40·00	8·00

The perforation with larger, clean-cut holes resulted from the fitting of new pins to the machine.

No. 123a is known with the impression on the back either sideways or inverted. The Royal Philatelic Collection contains an unused marginal pair of the former.

(b) P 10

135	1	6d. Prussian blue (11.11.79)	£190	24·00
136		6d. bright blue (1879)	£200	19·00
136*a*		1s. reddish lake-brown	£475	

(c) P 10×11½–12½, 11½–12½×10, or compound

137	3	4d. violet-slate (21.5.79)	£170	24·00
138		4d. dull purple (4.10.79)	80·00	2·75
139	1	6d. Prussian blue (29.12.77)	£130	2·75
140		6d. bright blue	£160	6·00
141		6d. bright ultramarine	£110	2·75
142		1s. reddish lake-brown (9.2.85)	£130	11·00
143		1s. dull brown (29.6.86)	£170	14·00
144	3	2s. carmine (27.12.77)	90·00	6·50
145		2s. rose-carmine (1887)	85·00	6·00
		a. Imperf between (horiz pair)	†	£1800

10

11

12

1901–02. Wmk Crown SA (wide). W **10**. P 11½–12½ (large holes).

146	**4**	9d. claret (1.2.02)	20·00	24·00
147	**1**	1s. dark brown (12.6.01)	22·00	16·00
148		1s. dark reddish brown (1902)	25·00	18·00
		a. Imperf horiz (vert pair)	£2750	£2750
149		1s. red-brown (aniline) (18.7.02)	25·00	35·00
150	**3**	2s. crimson (29.8.01)	45·00	16·00
151		2s. carmine	27·00	12·00

(Plates and electrotypes by D.L.R. Printed in Adelaide)

1868–76. W **10**.

		(a) Rouletted		
152	**12**	2d. deep brick-red (8.68)	£150	7·00
153		2d. pale orange-red (5.10.68)	£140	2·75
		a. Printed on both sides	†	£700
		b. Imperf between (horiz pair)	†	£1300
		c. Imperf horiz (vert pair)	†	£1700
		(b) P 11½–12½		
154	**11**	1d. blue-green (10.1.75)	£170	42·00
155	**12**	2d. pale orange-red (5.5.69)	£1400	£250
		(c) P 11½–12½×roulette		
156	**12**	2d. pale orange-red (20.8.69)	—	£170
		(d) P 10×roulette		
157	**12**	2d. pale orange-red (7.5.70)	£500	40·00
		(e) P 10		
158	**11**	1d. blue-green (4.75)	£100	8·00
159	**12**	2d. brick-red (4.70)	60·00	3·75
160		2d. orange-red (1.7.70)	22·00	1·00
		a. Printed on both sides	†	£425
		(f) P 10×11½–12½, 11½–12½×10, or compound		
161	**11**	1d. blue-green (27.8.75)	£190	42·00
162	**12**	2d. brick-red (19.1.71)	£750	35·00
163		2d. orange-red (3.2.71)	£200	35·00
		a. Imperf (8.76)	£1200	£1100

1869. Wmk Large Star W **2**.

		(a) Rouletted		
164	**12**	2d. orange-red (13.3.69)	£170	24·00
		(b) P 11½–12½×roulette		
165	**12**	2d. orange-red (1.8.69)	£2000	£120
		(c) P 11½–12½		
165*a*	**12**	2d. orange-red (7.69)	—	£1200

1871 (15 July). Wmk V and Crown, W **7**. P 10.

166	**12**	2d. brick-red	£180	50·00

13

(14)

1876–1904. Wmk Crown SA (close). W **13**.

		(a) P 10 (1876–85)		
167	**11**	1d. blue-green (9.2.76)	38·00	1·50
		a. Yellowish green (11.78)	50·00	1·75
		b. Deep green (11.79)	27·00	30
		bb. Printed double	†	—
168	**12**	2d. orange-red (8.76)	48·00	50
		a. Dull brick-red (21.5.77)	55·00	1·00
		b. Blood-red (31.10.79)	£300	4·25
		c. Pale red (4.85)	17·00	40
		(b) P 10×11½–12½, 11½–12½×10 or compound (1877–80)		
169	**11**	1d. deep green (11.2.80)	80·00	13·00
		a. Blue-green (2.3.80)	35·00	7·50
170	**12**	2d. orange-red (4.9.77)	£180	13·00
		a. Dull brick-red (6.80)	£180	13·00
		(c) P 11½–12½ (1877–84)		
171	**11**	1d. blue-green (2.84)	—	£160
172	**12**	2d. orange-red (14.9.77)	—	£160
		a. Blood-red (1.4.80)	—	£160
		(d) P 15 (1893)		
173	**11**	1d. green (8.5.93)	45·00	1·00
174	**12**	2d. pale orange (9.2.93)	27·00	1·00
		a. Orange-red	26·00	1·00
		b. Imperf between (vert pair)	£950	
		(e) P 13 (1895–1903)		
175	**11**	1d. pale green (11.1.95)	12·00	1·00
		a. Green	12·00	20
		b. Imperf between (vert pair)	£1800	
176		1d. rosine (8.8.99)	12·00	65
		a. Scarlet (23.12.03)	8·00	1·25
		b. Deep red	9·50	1·50
177	**12**	2d. pale orange (19.1.95)	16·00	10
		a. *Orange-red* (9.5.95)	22·00	10
178		2d. bright violet (10.10.99)	6·50	10
		(f) P 12×11½ (comb) (1904)		
179	**11**	1d. rosine (2.2.04)	14·00	1·75
		a. Scarlet (25.7.04)	8·50	1·00
180	**12**	2d. bright violet (11.10.04)	14·00	1·00

Examples of the 1d. pale green with thicker lettering come from a worn plate.

1882 (1 Jan). No. 167 surch with T **14**.

181	**11**	½d. on 1d. blue-green	14·00	12·00

15 16 17 18

1883–99. W **13** (sideways on ½d.).

		(a) P 10 (1883–95)		
182	**15**	½d. chocolate (1.3.83)	17·00	2·25
		a. Imperf between (horiz pair)	†	£1500
		b. Red-brown (4.4.89)	9·50	2·25
		c. Brown (1895)	5·50	4·00
183	**16**	3d. sage-green (12.86)	35·00	2·75
		a. Olive-green (6.6.90)	24·00	5·00
		b. Deep green (12.4.93)	22·00	5·00
		s. Optd "SPECIMEN"	40·00	
184	**17**	4d. pale violet (3.90)	55·00	3·00
		a. Aniline violet (3.1.93)	50·00	7·50
		s. Optd "SPECIMEN"	40·00	
185	**18**	6d. pale blue (4.87)	65·00	3·75
		a. Blue (5.5.87)	50·00	1·25
		s. Optd "SPECIMEN"	40·00	
		(b) P 10×11½–12½, 11½–12½×10 or compound (1891)		
186	**15**	½d. red-brown (25.9.91)	32·00	11·00
		a. Imperf between (horiz pair)	£375	
		(c) P 11½–12½ (1890)		
187	**15**	½d. red-brown (12.10.90)	42·00	9·00
		(d) P 15 (1893–94)		
188	**15**	½d. pale brown (1.93)	11·00	1·50
		aa. Imperf between (horiz pair)		
		a. Deep brown	11·00	1·50
		b. Imperf between (horiz pair)	£375	
		c. Perf 12½ between (pair)	£325	80·00
189	**17**	4d. purple (1.1.94)	45·00	4·00
		a. Slate-violet	45·00	4·25
190	**18**	6d. blue (20.11.93)	65·00	4·00
		(e) P 13 (1895–99)		
191	**15**	½d. pale brown (9.95)	5·00	45
		a. Imperf between (horiz pair)		
		b. Deep brown (19.3.97)	6·00	30
192	**16**	3d. pale olive-green (26.7.97)	15·00	3·25
		a. Deep olive-green (27.11.99)	6·00	3·25
193	**17**	4d. violet (21.1.96)	6·00	1·00
194	**18**	6d. pale blue (3.96)	12·00	1·50
		a. Blue	11·00	1·50

REPRINTS. In 1884, and in later years, reprints on paper wmkd Crown SA, W **10**, were made of Nos. 1, 2, 3, 4, 12, 13, 14, 15, 19, 24, 27, 28, 32, 33, 34, 35, 36, 37, 38, 40, 43, 44, 49a, 53, 65, 67, 67 with surcharge in red, 70, 71, 72, 73, 78, 79, 81, 83, 86, 90, 118, 119, 120, 121, 122, 155, 158, 159, 164, 181, 182. They are overprinted "REPRINT".

In 1889 examples of the reprints for Nos. 1/3, 12, 15, 19, 27, 32/8, 44, 67, 67 surcharged in red, 70/1, 73, 83, 86, 118, 121/2, 158/9, 164 and 181/2, together with No. 141 overprinted "SPECIMEN", were supplied to the U.P.U. for distribution.

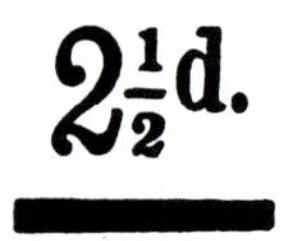

19 (20) (21)

(Plates and electrotypes by D.L.R. Printed in Adelaide)

1886 (20 Dec)–**96**. T **19** (inscr "POSTAGE & REVENUE"). W **13**. Parts of two or more wmks, on each stamp, sometimes sideways. P 10.

195	2s.6d. mauve	£120	16·00
	a. Perf 11½–12½. *Dull violet*	90·00	9·00

		bb. Bright aniline violet	95·00	9·00
196		5s. rose-pink	£140	19·00
		a. Perf 11½–12½	£110	19·00
		ab. Rose-carmine	£110	22·00
197		10s. green	£275	75·00
		a. Perf 11½–12½	£250	70·00
198		15s. brownish yellow	£750	£375
		a. Perf 11½–12½	£800	£250
199		£1 blue	£550	£180
		a. Perf 11½–12½	£500	£170
200		£2 Venetian red	£4000	£550
		a. Perf 11½–12½	£3750	£500
201		50s. dull pink	£4750	£750
		a. Perf 11½–12½	£4500	£650
202		£3 sage green	£5500	£700
		a. Perf 11½–12½	£5250	£600
203		£4 lemon	£10000	
		a. Perf 11½–12½	£8500	£1400
204		£5 grey	£8500	
		a. Perf 11½–12½	£8500	
205		£5 brown (P 11½–12½) (1896)	£5500	£1000
206		£10 bronze	£9000	£1800
		a. Perf 11½–12½	£8500	£1400
207		£15 silver	£32000	
		a. Perf 11½–12½	£30000	£2250
208		£20 claret	£40000	
		a. Perf 11½–12½	£38000	£2500
195s/208s Optd "SPECIMEN" *Set of 14**			£1300	

Variations exist in the length of the words and shape of the letters of the value inscription.

The 2s.6d. dull violet, 5s. rose-pink, 10s., £1 and £5 brown exist perf 11½–12½ with either large or small holes; the 2s.6d. aniline, 5s. rose-carmine, 15s., £2 and 50s. with large holes only and the remainder only with small holes.

Stamps perforated 11½–12½ small holes, are, generally speaking, rather rarer than those with the 1895 (large holes) gauge.

Stamps perf 10 were issued on 20 Dec 1886. Stamps perf 11½–12½ (small holes) are known with earliest dates covering the period from June 1890 to Feb 1896. Earliest dates of stamps with large holes range from July 1896 to May 1902.

*The listing of the "SPECIMEN" set distributed by the UPU comprises stamps with W **13**, perf 10, with an overprint 12¼ mm long, except No. 205 which is perf 11½–12½, with an overprint 15¼ mm long. These should not be confused with the same values with other "SPECIMEN" overprints, usually on stamps perf 11½–12½, and often with W **10**, which were prepared for presentation purposes and for inclusion in sets for sale to collectors.

1891 (1 Jan)–**93**. T **17/18** surch with T **20/1**. W **13**.

		(a) P 10		
229	**17**	2½d. on 4d. pale green (Br.)	8·00	2·50
		a. Fraction bar omitted	£110	80·00
		b. Deep green	8·00	1·75
		ba. Fraction bar omitted	£110	75·00
		bb. "2" and "½" closer together	26·00	18·00
		bc. Imperf between (horiz pair)		
		bd. Imperf between (vert pair)	†	£3250
		s. Optd "SPECIMEN"	32·00	
230	**18**	5d. on 6d. pale brown (C.)	19·00	7·50
		a. Deep brown	19·00	7·00
		b. No stop after "5D"	£170	
		s. Optd "SPECIMEN"	32·00	
		(b) P 10×11½–12½ or 11½–12½×10		
231	**17**	2½d. on 4d. pale green (Br.)	60·00	6·50
		a. Deep green	60·00	6·50
		(c) P 11½–12½		
232	**17**	2½d. on 4d. deep green	75·00	85·00
		(d) P 15		
233	**17**	2½d. on 4d. green (14.10.93)	50·00	2·75
		a. Fraction bar omitted		
		b. "2" and "½d." closer	£120	22·00

On Nos. 229bb and 233b the base of the "1" of "½" and the back of the large "2" are 0.5 mm apart. On normal stamps the spacing is 1 mm.

22 Red Kangaroo

23

24 G.P.O., Adelaide

(Des M. Tannenberg, plates by D.L.R.)

1894 (1 Mar)–**1906**. W **13**.

		(a) P 15		
234	**22**	2½d. violet-blue	45·00	7·00
235	**23**	5d. brown-purple	42·00	3·75
234s/5s Optd "SPECIMEN" *Set of 2*			70·00	
		(b) P 13		
236	**22**	2½d. violet-blue (11.2.95)	32·00	1·75
237		2½d. indigo (25.3.98)	10·00	2·00
238	**23**	5d. Brown-purple (1.96)	10·00	1·75
		a. Purple	10·00	1·75
		(c) P 12×11½ (comb)		
239	**22**	2½d. indigo (4.7.06)	15·00	5·00
240	**23**	5d. dull purple (1.05)	20·00	2·50

(Typo D.L.R.)

1899 (27 Dec)–**1905**. W **13**.

		(a) P 13		
241	**24**	½d. yellow-green	7·50	1·50
		(b) P 12×11½ (comb)		
242	**24**	½d. yellow-green (7.05)	8·00	2·50

25

The measurements given indicate the length of the value inscription in the bottom label. The dates are those of the earliest known postmarks.

1902–04. As T **19**, but top tablet as T **25** (thin "POSTAGE"). W **13**.

	(a) P 11½–12½		
268	3d. olive-green (18½ *mm*) (1.8.02)	17·00	3·00
	a. Wmk sideways	†	£1700
269	4d. red-orange (17 *mm*) (29.11.02)	30·00	4·75
270	6d. blue-green (16–16½ *mm*) (29.11.02)	12·00	3·00
271	8d. ultramarine (19 *mm*) (25.4.02)	8·50	17·00
272	8d. ultramarine (16½ *mm*) (22.3.04)	12·00	17·00
	a. "EIGNT" (R.2/9)	£2500	£3000
273	9d. rosy lake (19.9.02)	15·00	11·00
	a. Imperf between (vert pair)	£2500	
274	10d. dull yellow (29.11.02)	18·00	18·00
275	1s. brown (18.8.02)	26·00	8·00
	a. Imperf between (horiz pair)		
	b. Imperf between (vert pair)	£2500	
	c. "POSTAGE" and value in red-brown	£1200	£1100
276	2s.6d. pale violet (19.9.02)	80·00	48·00
	a. Bright violet (2.2.03)	40·00	15·00
277	5s. rose (17.10.02)	£120	75·00
278	10s. green (1.11.02)	£200	90·00
279	£1 blue (1.11.02)	£500	£250
	(b) P 12		
280	3d. olive-green (20 *mm*) (15.4.04)	32·00	3·50
	a. "POSTAGE" omitted; value below "AUSTRALIA"	£4250	
281	4d. orange-red (17½–18 *mm*) (18.2.03)	25·00	3·00
282	6d. blue-green (15 *mm*) (14.11.03)	26·00	16·00
283	9d. rosy lake (2.12.03)	£120	30·00

No. 280a comes from the bottom row of the sheet. Other stamps show the value below "AUSTRALIA" with "POSTAGE" over the bottom frame (*Price £950, unused*).

A used example of No. 273 in imperf between horiz pair is in the Royal Philatelic Collection.

PRINTER. Stamp printing in Adelaide ceased in 1909 when the Printer of Stamps, J. B. Cooke, was appointed head of the Commonwealth Stamp Printing Branch in Melbourne. From 9 March 1909 further printings of current South Australia stamps were made in Melbourne.

26

V

X

In Type X the letters in the bottom line are slightly larger than in Type V, especially the "A", "S" and "P".

Y

Z

In Type Z the letters "S" and "G" are more open than in Type Y.

Nos. 196/a and 277 are similar to Type Y with all letters thick and regular and the last "S" has the top curve rounded instead of being slightly flattened.

1904–11. As T **19**, but top tablet as T **26** (thick "POSTAGE"). W **13**. P 12.

284	6d. blue-green (27.4.04)	40·00	3·00
	a. Imperf between (vert pair)	£4750	
285	8d. bright ultramarine (4.7.05)	18·00	8·50
	a. Value closer (15¼ *mm*)	70·00	28·00
	b. Dull ultramarine (2.4.08)	26·00	6·50
	ba. Ditto. Value closer (15¼ *mm*)	£110	20·00

286	9d. rosy lake (17–17¼ *mm*) (18.7.04)	24·00	6·50
	a. Value 16½–16¾ mm (2.06)	65·00	7·50
	b. Brown-lake. Perf 12½ small holes (11.3.11)	17·00	25·00
287	10d. dull yellow (8.07)	18·00	24·00
	a. Imperf between (horiz pair)	£2750	£3000
	b. Imperf between (vert pair)	£4000	
288	1s. brown (12.4.04)	32·00	4·00
	a. Imperf between (vert pair)	£2500	
	b. Imperf between (horiz pair)	£2750	
289	2s.6d. bright violet (V.) (14.7.05)	75·00	40·00
	a. Dull violet (X) (8.06)	75·00	27·00
290	5s. rose-scarlet (Y) (13.7.04)	75·00	48·00
	a. Scarlet (Z) (8.06)	75·00	48·00
	b. Pale rose. Perf 12½ (small holes) (Z) (6.10)	£120	70·00
291	10s. green (26.8.08)	£200	£150
292	£1 blue (29.12.04)	£325	£170
	a. Perf 12½ (small holes) (6.10)	£250	£160

The "value closer" variety on the 8d. occurs six times in the sheet of 60. The value normally measures 16½ mm but in the variety it is 15¼ mm.

The 9d., 5s. and £1, perf 12½ (small holes), are late printings made in 1910–11 to use up the Crown SA paper.

No. 286*b* has the value as Type C of the 9d. on Crown over A paper.

27

1905–12. W **27**. P 12×11½ (new comb machine).

293	**24**	½d. pale green (4.07)	16·00	1·25
		a. Yellow-green	8·50	1·25
		b. Thin ready gummed paper (1912)	6·00	8·00
		ba. Mixed perf 12×11½ and 12½	£850	
294	**11**	1d. rosine (2.12.05)	7·00	20
		a. Scarlet (4.11)	4·00	1·25
295	**12**	2d. bright violet (2.2.06)	26·00	30
		aa. Imperf three sides (horiz pair)	£3000	
		a. Mauve (4.08)	7·50	30
296	**22**	2½d. indigo-blue (14.9.10)	9·00	14·00
297	**23**	5d. brown-purple (11.3.08)	30·00	6·50

No. 295aa is perforated at foot.

Three types of the 9d., perf 12½, distinguishable by the distance between "NINE" and "PENCE".

A. Distance 1¾ mm. B. Distance 2¼ mm. C. Distance 2½ mm.

1906–12. T **19** ("POSTAGE" thick as T **26**). W **27**. P 12 or 12½ (small holes).

298	3d. sage-green (19 *mm*) (26.6.06)	16·00	5·50
	a. Imperf between (horiz pair)	†	£5500
	b. Perf 12½. *Sage-green* (17 *mm*) (9.12.09)	17·00	11·00
	c. Perf 12½. *Deep olive* (20 *mm*) (7.10)	75·00	11·00
	d. Perf 12½. *Yellow-olive* (19 *mm*) (16.12.11)	80·00	60·00
	da. Perf 12½. *Bright olive-green* (19–19¾ *mm*) Thin ready gummed paper (8.9.11)	12·00	24·00
	e. Perf 11 (17 *mm*) (1910)	£1000	£700
299	4d. orange-red (10.9.06)	12·00	3·00
	a. Orange	12·00	3·00
	b. Perf 12½. *Orange*	25·00	8·50
	c. Thin ready gummed paper (19.8.12)	25·00	30·00
300	6d. blue-green (1.9.06)	17·00	2·50
	a. Perf 12½ (21.4.10)	8·00	9·00
	ab. Perf 12½. Imperf between (vert pair)	£2250	£2500
	b. Thin ready gummed paper (3.12)	10·00	18·00
301	8d. bright ultramarine (P 12½) (8.09)	10·00	22·00
	a. Value closer (8.09)	45·00	85·00
302	9d. brown-lake (3.2.06)	23·00	5·50
	aa. Imperf between (horiz strip of three)	£4750	
	a. Imperf between (vert pair)	£2000	
	b. Deep lake (9.5.08)	50·00	9·00
	c. Perf 12½. *Lake* (A) (5.9.09)	11·00	10·00
	d. Perf 12½. *Lake* (B) (7.09)	42·00	10·00
	e. Perf 12½. *Brown-lake*	42·00	10·00
	ea. Perf 12½. *Deep lake*. Thin paper (C)	35·00	10·00
	f. Perf 11 (1909)	†	£1500
303	1s. brown (30.5.06)	12·00	5·00
	aa. Imperf between (vert pair)	£3250	
	a. Imperf between (horiz pair)	£3500	
	b. Perf 12½ (10.3.10)	10·00	7·50
	c. Thin ready gummed paper (4.8.11)	14·00	15·00
304	2s.6d. bright violet (X) (10.6.09)	75·00	30·00
	a. Perf 12½. *Pale violet* (X) (6.10)	75·00	35·00
	ab. Perf 12½. *Deep purple* (X) Thin ready gummed paper (15.11.12)	£120	£110
305	5s. bright rose (P 12½) (Z) Thin ready gummed paper (24.4.11)	£130	£130

The "value closer" variety of the 8d. occurred 11 times in the sheet of 60 in the later printing only. On No. 301 the value measures 16½ mm while on No. 301a it is 15¼ mm.

The 1s. brown, perf compound of 11½ and 12½, formerly listed is now omitted, as it must have been perforated by the 12 machine, which in places varied from 11½ to 13. The 4d. has also been reported with a similar perforation.

STAMP BOOKLETS

There are very few surviving examples of Nos. SB1/4. Listings are provided for those believed to have been issued with prices quoted for those known still to exist.

1904 (1 Jan)–**09**. Black on red cover as Type B **1** of New South Wales. Stapled.

SB1	£1 booklet containing 240 1d. in four blocks of 30 and two blocks of 60	
	a. Red on pink cover (1909)	
	b. Blue on pink cover	£15000

1904 (1 Jan). Black on grey cover as No. SB1. Stapled.

SB2	£1 booklet containing 120 2d. in four blocks of 30	

1910 (May). Black on cream cover as Type B **2** of New South Wales. Stapled.

SB3	2s. booklet containing 11 ½d. (No. 241), either in block of 6 plus block of 5 or block of 11, and 18 1d. (No. 176*a*), either in three blocks of 6 or block of 6 plus block of 12	

Unsold stock of No. SB3 was uprated with one additional ½d. in May 1911.

1911 (Aug). Red on pink cover as No. SB3. Stapled.

SB4	2s. booklet containing 12 ½d. (No. 241), either in two blocks of 6 or block of 12, and 18 1d. (No. 176*a*), either in three blocks of 6 or block of 6 plus block of 12	£7000

OFFICIAL STAMPS

A. Departmentals

Following suspected abuses involving stamps supplied for official use it was decided by the South Australian authorities that such supplies were to be overprinted with a letter, or letters, indicating the department of the administration to which the stamps had been invoiced.

The system was introduced on 1 April 1868 using overprints struck in red. Later in the same year the colour of the overprints was amended blue, and, during the latter months of 1869, to black.

In 1874 the Postmaster-General recommended that this somewhat cumbersome system be replaced by a general series of "O.S." overprints with the result that the separate accounting for the Departmentals ceased on 30 June of that year. Existing stocks continued to be used, however, and it is believed that much of the residue was passed to the Government Printer to pay postage on copies of the *Government Gazette*.

We are now able to provide a check list of these most interesting issues based on the definitive work. *The Departmental Stamps of South Australia* by A. R. Butler, FRPSL, RDP, published by the Royal Philatelic Society, London in 1978.

No attempt has been made to assign the various overprints to the catalogue numbers of the basic stamps, but each is clearly identified by both watermark and perforation. the colours are similar to those of the contemporary postage stamps, but there can be shade variations. Errors of overprint are recorded in footnotes, but not errors occurring on the basic stamps used.

Most departmental overprints are considered to be scarce to rare in used condition, with unused examples, used multiples and covers being regarded as considerable rarities.

Forgeries of a few items do exist, but most can be readily identified by comparison with genuine examples. A number of forged overprints on stamps not used for the genuine issues also occur.

A. (Architect)

Optd in red with stop. W **2**. 2d. (Roul), 4d. (P 11½–12½), 6d. (Roul), 1s. (Roul)
Optd in red without stop W **2**. Roul. 1d., 2d., 6d., 1s.
Optd in black. (*a*) W **2**. 4d. (P 10×11½–12½), 6d. (P 11½–12½), 2s. (Roul)
(*b*) W **10**. 2d. D.L.R. (Roul), 2d. D.L.R. (P 10)

A.G. (Attorney-General)

Optd in red. W **2**. Roul. 1d., 2d., 6d., 1s.
Optd in blue. (*a*) W **2**. Roul. 6d.
(*b*) W **10**. Roul. 2d. D.L.R.
Optd in black. (*a*) W **2**. 1d (P 11½–12½×Roul), 4d. (P 11½–12½), 4d. (P 10), 6d. (P 11½–12½×Roul), 6d. (P 11½–12½), 1s. (P 11½–12½×Roul), 1s. (P 11½–12½) 1s. (P 10)
(*b*) W **10**. 2d. D.L.R. (Roul), 2d. D.L.R. (P 10)

A.O. (Audit Office)

Optd in red. W **2**. 2d. (Roul), 4d. (P 11½–12½), 6d. (Roul)
Optd in blue. (*a*) W **2**. P 11½–12½. 1d., 6d.
(*b*) W **10**. Roul. 2d. D.L.R.
Optd in black. (*a*) W **2**. 1d. (P 11½–12½), 1d. (P 10), 2d. D.L.R. (Roul), 4d. (P 11½–12½) 4d. (P 10), 4d. (P 10×11½–12½), 6d. (Roul), 6d. (P 11½–12½), 1s. (P 11½–12½), 1s. (P 11½–12½×Roul)
(*b*) W **7**. P 10. 4d.
(*c*) W **10**. 2d. D.L.R. (Roul), 2d. D.L.R. (P 10)

B.D. (Barracks Department)

Optd in red. W **2**. Roul. 2d., 6d., 1s.

B.G. (Botanic Garden)

Optd in black. (*a*) W **2**. 1d. (P 11½–12½×R), 1d. (P 11½–12½), 1d. (P 10×11½–12½), 2d. D.L.R. (Roul), 6d. (Roul), 6d. (P 11½–12½×Roul), 6d. (P 11½–12½), 1s. (P 11½–12½×Roul), 1s. (P 11½–12½), 1s. (P 10), 1s. (P 10×11½–12½)
(*b*) W **7**. P 10, 2d. D.L.R.
(*c*) W **10**. 2d. D.L.R. (Roul), 2d. D.L.R. (P 10)
The 6d. (W **2**. Roul) is known without stop after "B".

B.M. (Bench of Magistrates)

Optd in red. W **2**. Roul. 2d.
Optd in black. W **10**. Roul. 2d. D.L.R.

C. (Customs)

Optd in red. W **2**. 1d. (Roul), 2d. (Roul), 4d. (P 11½–12½), 6d. (Roul), 1s. (Roul)
Optd in blue (*a*) W **2**. Roul. 1d., 4d., 6d., 1s., 2s.
(*b*) W **10**. Roul. 2d. D.L.R.
Optd in black. (*a*) W **2**. 1d. (Roul), 1d. (P 10), 1d. (P 10×11½–12½), 4d. (P 11½–12½), 4d. (P 10), 4d. (P 10×11½–12½), 6d. (Roul), 6d. (P 11½–12½), 6d. (P 10), 1s. (P 11½–12½×Roul), 1s. (P 11½–12½), 2s. (Roul)
(*b*) W **7**. P 10. 2d. D.L.R.
(*c*) W **10**. 2d. D.L.R. (Roul), 2d. D.L.R. (P 10×Roul), 2d. D.L.R. (P 10), 2d. D.L.R. (P 10×11½–12½)
The 2d. (W **10**. (Roul) with black overprint is known showing the error "G" for "C".

C.D. (Convict Department)

Optd in red. W **2**. 2d. (Roul), 4d. (P 11½–12½), 6d. (Roul), 1s. (Roul)
Optd in black. (*a*) W **2**. 1d. (P 11½–12½×Roul), 2d. D.L.R. (Roul), 4d. (P 11½–12½), 6d. (Roul), 6d. (P 11½–12½×Roul, 1s. (P 11½–12½×Roul)
(*b*) W **10**. 2d. D.L.R. (Roul), 2d. D.L.R. (P 11½–12½), 2d. D.L.R. (P 11½–12½×Roul)

C.L. (Crown Lands)

Optd in red. W **2**. 2d. (Roul), 4d. (P 11½–12½), 6d. (Roul), 1s. (Roul)
Optd in blue. (*a*) W **2**. Roul. 4d., 6d.
(*b*) W **10**. Roul. 2d. D.L.R.
Optd in black. (*a*) W **2**. 2d. D.L.R. (Roul), 4d. (P 11½–12½), 4d. (P 10), 4d. (P 10×11½–12½), 6d. (Roul), 6d. (P 11½–12½), 1s. (P 11½–12½×Roul), 2s. (Roul), 2s. (P 11½–12½)
(*b*) W **7**. P 10. 2d. D.L.R., 4d.
(*c*) W **10**. 2d. D.L.R. (Roul), 2d. D.L.R. (P 10), 2d. D.L.R. (P 10×11½–12½)
The 2s. (W **2**. P 11½–12½) with black overprint is known showing the stop omitted after "L".

C.O. (Commissariat Office)

Optd in red. W **2**. (Roul), 4d. (P 11½–12½) 6d. (Roul), 1s. (Roul)
Optd in black. (*a*) W **2**. 4d. (P 10), 4d. (P 10×11½–12½), 6d. (P 11½–12½), 1s. (P 11½–12½), 2s. (Roul), 2s. (P 11½–12½)
(*b*) W **10**. 2d. D.L.R. (Roul), 2d. D.L.R. (P 10)
The 6d. (W **2**. Roul) with red overprint is known showing the error "O" for "C", and the 2s. (W **2**. P 11½–12½) with black overprint with the stop omitted after "O".

C.P. (Commissioner of Police)

Optd in red. W **2**. 2d. (Roul). 4d. (P 11½–12½), 6d. (Roul)

C.S. (Chief Secretary)

Optd in red. W **2**. 2d. (Roul), 4d. (P 11½–12½), 6d. (Roul), 1s. (Roul)
Optd in blue. (*a*) W **2**. Roul. 4d., 6d.
(*b*) W **10**. Roul. 2d. D.L.R.
Optd in black. (*a*) W **2**. 2d. D.L.R. (Roul), 4d. (Roul), 4d. (P 11½–12½×Roul), 4d. (P 11½–12½), 4d. (P 10), 4d. (P 10×11½–12½), 6d. (P 11½–12½×Roul), 6d. (P 11½–12½), 6d. (P 10), 6d. (P 10×11½–12½), 1s. (P 11½–12½×Roul), 1s. (P 11½–12½), 1s. (P 10), 1s. (P 10×11½–12½), 2s. (P 10×11½–12½)
(*b*) W **7**. P 10. 2d.
(*c*) W **10**. 2d. D.L.R. (Roul), 2d. D.L.R. (P 10)
The 6d. and 1s. (W **2**. Roul) with red overprint are known showing the error "G" for "C".

C.Sgn. (Colonial Surgeon)

Optd in red. W **2**. 2d. (Roul), 4d. (P 11½–12½), 6d. (Roul)
Optd in black. (*a*) W **2**. 2d. D.L.R. (Roul), 4d. (P 10), 4d. (P 10×11½–12½), 6d. (Roul), 6d. (P 11½–12½×Roul) 6d. (P 11½–12½)
(*b*) W **10**. 2d. D.L.R. (Roul), 2d. D.L.R. (P 11½–12½×Roul), 2d. (P 10×Roul), 2d. D.L.R. (P 10)
Two types of overprint exist on the 2d. D.L.R., the second type having block capitals instead of the serifed type used for the other values.

D.B. (Destitute Board)

Optd in red. W **2**. 1d. (Roul), 2d. (Roul), 4d. (P 11½–12½), 6d. (Roul), 1s. (Roul)
Optd in blue. (*a*) W **2**. 2d. D.L.R. (Roul), 4d. (P 11½–12½), 6d. (Roul)
(*b*) W **10**. Roul. 2d. D.L.R.
Optd in black. (*a*) W **2**. 1d. (P 11½–12½), 4d. (P 11½–12½), 4d. (P 10), 6d. (P 10×11½–12½) 1s (P 10)
(*b*) W **10**. 2d. D.L.R. (Roul), 2d. D.L.R. (P 11½–12½), 2d. D.L.R. (P 10), 2d. D.L.R. (P 10×11½–12½)
The 2d. D.L.R. (W **10**. P 10) with black overprint is known showing the stop omitted after "D".

D.R. (Deeds Registration)

Optd in red. W **2**. Roul, 2d., 6d.

E. (Engineer)

Optd in red. W **2**. 2d. (Roul), 4d. (P 11½–12½), 6d. (Roul), 1s. (Roul)
Optd in blue. (*a*) W **2**. Roul. 1s.
(*b*) W **10**. Roul. 2d. D.L.R.
Optd in black. (*a*) W **2**. 4d. (P 11½–12½), 4d. (P 10), 4d. (P 10×11½–12½), 6d. (P 11½–12½), 1s. (P 11½–12½×Roul), 1s. (P 11½–12½), 1s. (P 10×11½–12½)
(*b*) W **7**. P 10. 4d.
(*c*) W **10**. P 10. 2d. D.L.R.

E.B. (Education Board)

Optd in red. W **2**. 2d. (Roul), 4d. (P 11½–12½), 6d. (Roul)
Optd in blue. (*a*) W **2**. Roul. 4d., 6d.
(b) W 10. Roul. 2d. D.L.R.
Optd in black. (*a*) W **2**. 2d. D.L.R. (Roul), 4d (Roul), 4d. (P 11½–12½), 4d. (P 10), 6d. (P 11½–12½×Roul), 6d. (P 11½×12½)
(*b*) W **7**. P 10. 2d. D.L.R.
(*c*) W **10**. 2d. D.L.R. (Roul), 2d. D.L.R. (P 10), 2d. D.L.R. (P 10×11½–12½)

G.F. (Gold Fields)

Optd in black. (*a*) W **2**. Roul. 6d.
(*b*) W **10**. 2d. D.L.R. (P 10×Roul), 2d. D.L.R. (P 10)

G.P. (Government Printer)

Optd in red. W **2**. Roul. 1d., 2d., 6d., 1s.
Optd in blue. (*a*) W **2**. Roul. 1d., 6d., 1s., 2s.
(*b*) W **10**. Roul. 2d. D.L.R.
Optd in black. (a) W 2. 1d. (Roul), 1d. (P 11½–12½×Roul), 1d. (P 11½–12½) 1d. (P 10) 1d. (P 10×11½–12½), 6d. (P 11½–12½×Roul), 1s. (P 10×11½–12½), 2s. (Roul), 2s. (P 11½–12½) 2s. (P 10×11½–12½)
(*b*) W 10. 2d. D.L.R. (Roul), 2d. D.L.R. (P 10)
The 1d. and 1s. (W **2**. Roul) with red overprint are known showing "C.P." instead of "G.P.".

G.S. (Government Storekeeper)

Optd in red. W **2**. Roul. 2d.

G.T. (Goolwa Tramway)

Optd in red. W **2**. 1d. (Roul), 2d. (Roul), 4d. (P 11½–12½), 6d. (Roul), 1s. (Roul)
Optd in black. (*a*) W **2**. 2d. D.L.R. (Roul), 4d. (P 11½–12½)
(*b*) W **10**. Roul. 2d. D.L.R.
The 2d. and 6d. (both W **2**. Roul) with red overprint are known showing the stop omitted after "T". The 6d, and 1s. (W **2**. Roul) with red overprint are known showing "C.T.", instead of "G.T.".

H. (Hospitals)

Optd in black. (*a*) W **2**. P 10×11½–12½. 4d.
(*b*) W **7**. P 10. 2d. D.L.R.
(*c*) W **10**. 2d. D.L.R. (P 10), 2d. D.L.R. (P 10×11½–12½)

H.A. (House of Assembly)

Optd in red. W **2**. 1d. (Roul), 2d. (Roul), 4d. (P 11½–12½), 6d. (Roul), 1s. (Roul)
Optd in black. (*a*) W **2**. 1d. (P 11½–12½), 1d. (P 10) 1d. (P 10×11½–12½), 4d. (P 11½–12½), 4d. (P 10) 6d. (Roul), 6d. (P 11½–12½) 1s. (P 11½–12½×Roul), 1s. (P 11½–12½)
(*b*) W **10**. 2d. D.L.R. (Roul), 2d. D.L.R. (P 10)

I.A. (Immigration Agent)

Optd in red. W **2**. 1d. (Roul), 2d. (Roul), 4d. (P 11½–12½), 6d. (Roul)

I.E. (Intestate Estates)

Optd in black. W **10**. P 10. 2d. D.L.R.

I.S. (Inspector of Sheep)

Optd in red. W **2**. Roul. 2d., 6d.
Optd in blue. W **2**. P 11½–12½. 6d.
Optd in black. (*a*) W **2**. 2d. D.L.R. (Roul), 6d. (P 11½–12½×Roul)
(*b*) W **10**. 2d. D.L.R. (Roul). 2d. D.L.R. (P 10)

L.A. (Lunatic Asylum)

Optd in red. W **2**. 1d. (Roul), 2d. (Roul), 4d. (P 11½–12½), 6d. (Roul), 1s. (Roul)
Optd in black. (*a*) W **2**. 4d. (P 11½–12½), 4d. (P 10), 4d. (P 10×11½–12½), 6d. (P 11½–12½), 1s. (P 11½–12½), 2s. (Roul)
(*b*) W **10**. 2d. D.L.R. (Roul), 2d. D.L.R. (P 10)

L.C. (Legislative Council)

Optd in red. W **2**. Roul. 2d., 6d.
Optd in black. (*a*) W **2**. Roul. 6d.
(*b*) W **10**. 2d. D.L.R. (Roul), 2d. D.L.R. (P 10×Roul)

The 2d. and 6d. (both W **2**. Roul) with red overprint are known showing the stop omitted after "C".

L.L. (Legislative Librarian)

Optd in red. W **2**. 2d. (Roul), 4d. (P 11½–12½), 6d. (Roul)
Optd in black. (*a*) W **2**. P 11½–12½. 6d.
(*b*) W **10**. P 10. 2d. D.L.R.

The 2d. and 6d. (both W **2**. Roul) with red overprint are known showing the stop omitted from between the two letters.

L.T. (Land Titles)

Optd in red. W **2**. 2d. (Roul), 4d. (P 11½–12½), 6d. (Roul), 1s. (Roul)
Optd in blue. W **10**. Roul. 2d. D.L.R.
Optd in black. (*a*) W **2**. 4d. (P 11½–12½), 4d. (P 10), 4d. (P 10×11½–12½), 6d. (P 11½–12½×Roul), 6d. (P 11½–12½), 6d. (P 10), 6d. (P 10×11½–12½)
(*b*) W **7**. P 10. 2d. D.L.R.
(*c*) W **10**. 2d. D.L.R. (Roul), 2d. D.L.R. (P 10)

The 2d. and 6d. (both W **2**. Roul) with red overprint are known showing the stop omitted after "T".

M. (Military)

Optd in red. W **2**. Roul. 2d., 6d., 1s.
Optd in black. W **2**. 6d. (P 11½–12½×Roul), 1s. (P 11½–12½×Roul), 2s. (Roul)

M.B. (Marine Board)

Optd in red. W **2**. 1d. (Roul), 2d. (Roul), 4d. (Roul), 4d. (P 11½–12½), 6d. (Roul), 1s. (Roul)
Optd in black. (*a*) W **2**. 1d. (Roul), 1d. (P 11½–12½), 2d. D.L.R. (Roul), 4d. (P 11½–12½×Roul), 4d. (P 11½–12½), 4d. (P 10), 4d. (P 10×11½–12½), 6d. (Roul), 6d. (P 11½–12½), 6d. (P 10), 6d. (P 10×11½–12½), 1s. (P 11½–12½×Roul), 1s. (P 11½–12½) 1s. (P 10), 1s. (P 10×11½–12½)
(*b*) W **7**. P 10. 4d.
(*c*) W **10**. Roul. 2d. D.L.R.

M.R. (Manager of Railways)

Optd in red. W **2**. Roul. 2d., 6d.
Optd in black. (*a*) W **2**. 1d. (P 11½–12½), 1d. (P 10), 2d. D.L.R. (Roul), 4d. (Roul), 4d. (P 11½–12½), 6d. (P 11½–12½×Roul), 1s. (P 11½–12½×Roul), 2s. (P 11½–12½ 1, 2s. (P 10×11½–12½)
(*b*) W **10**. 2d. D.L.R. (Roul), 2d. D.L.R. (P 10), 2d. D.L.R. (P 10×11½–12½)

M.R.G. (Main Roads Gambierton)

Optd in red without stops. W **2**. Roul. 2d., 6d.
Optd in blue without stops. W **10**. Roul. 2d. D.L.R.
Optd in black without stops. W **10**. 2d. D.L.R. (Roul), 2d. D.L.R. (Roul 10)
Optd in black with stops. W **10**. 2d. D.L.R. (Roul), 2d. D.L.R. (Roul 10)

The 2d. D.L.R. (W **10**. P 10) with black overprint is known showing the stops omitted after "M" and "R".

N.T. (Northern Territory)

Optd in black (*a*) W **2**. P 11½–12½. 1d., 3d. on 4d., 6d., 1s.
(*b*) W **10**. 2d. D.L.R. (Roul), 2d. D.L.R. (P 10)

O.A. (Official Assignee)

Optd in red. W **2**. 2d. (Roul), 4d. (P 11½–12½)
Optd in blue. W **10**. Roul. 2d. D.L.R.
Optd in black. (*a*) W **2**. P 10. 4d.
(*b*) W **7**. P 10. 2d. D.L.R.
(*c*) W **10**. 2d. D.L.R. (Roul), 2d. D.L.R. (P 10×roul), 2d. D.L.R. (P 10)

P. (Police)

Optd in blue. (*a*) W **2**. Roul. 6d.
(*b*) W **10**. Roul. 2d. D.L.R.
Optd in black. (*a*) W **2**. 6d. (P 11½–12½×Roul), 6d. (P 11½–12½), 6d. (P 10)
(*b*) W **7**. P 10. 2d. D.L.R.
(*c*) W **10**. 2d. D.L.R. (Roul), 2d. D.L.R. (P 11½–12½), 2d. D.L.R. (P 11½–12½×Roul), 2d. D.L.R. (P 10×Roul), 2d. D.L.R. (P 10), 2d. D.L.R. (P 10×11½–12½)

P.A. (Protector of Aborigines)

Optd in red. W **2**. Roul. 2d., 6d.
Optd in black. (*a*) W **2**. P. 2d. D.L.R., 6d.
(*b*) W **10**. 2d. D.L.R. (Roul), 2d. D.L.R. (P 10)

P.O. (Post Office)

Optd in red. W **2**. Roul. 1d., 2d., 6d., 1s.
Optd in blue. (*a*) W **2**. Roul. 2d.
(*b*) W **10**. Roul. 2d. D.L.R.
Optd in black. (*a*) W **2**. 1d. (P 10×11½–12½), 2d. D.L.R. (Roul), 2d. D.L.R. (P 11½–12½×Roul), 4d. (P 11½–12½), 6d. (Roul), 6d. (P 11½×12½), 1s. (P 11½–12½×Roul), 1s. (P 11½×12½) 1s. (P 11½–12½), 1s. (P 10) 1s. (P 10×11½–12½)
(*b*) W **10**. 2d. D.L.R. (Roul), 2d. (P 11½–12½×Roul), 2d. D.L.R. (P 10×Roul), 2d. D.L.R. (P 10)

The 4d. (W **2**. P 11½–12½) with black overprint is known showing the stop omitted after "O".

P.S. (Private Secretary)

Optd in red. W **2**. 1d. (Roul), 2d. (Roul), 4d. (P 11½–12½), 6d. (Roul), 1s. (Roul)
Optd in black. (*a*) W **2**. 1d. (P 11½–12½×Roul), 1d. (P 11½–12½), 1d. (P 10), 2d. (Roul), 3d. (in black) on 4d. (P 11½–12½), 3d. (in red) on 4d. (P 10), 3d. (in black) on 4d. (P 10), 4d. (P 11½–12½), 4d. (P 10), 4d. (P 10×11½–12½) 6d. (Roul), 6d. (P 11½–12½×Roul), 6d. (P 11½–12½), 6d. (P 10), 9d. (Roul), 9d. (P 11½–12½) 10d. on 9d. (P 10), 10d. on 9d. (P 10×11½–12½), 1s. (P 11½–12½×Roul)
(*b*) W **7**. P 10. 2d. D.L.R.
(*c*) W **10**. 2d. D.L.R. (Roul), 2d. D.L.R. (P 10)

P.W. (Public Works)

Optd in red without stop after "W". W **2**. Roul. 2d., 6d., 1s.
Optd in black. (*a*) W **2**. 2d. D.L.R. (Roul), 4d. (P 10), 6d. (Roul), 6d. (P 11½–12½), 1s. (P 11½–12½×Roul)
(*b*) W **10**. 2d. D.L.R. (Roul), 2d. D.L.R. (P 10)

R.B. (Road Board)

Optd in red. W **2**. 1d. (Roul), 2d. (Roul), 4d. (P 11½–12½), 6d. (Roul), 1s. (Roul)
Optd in blue without stops. W **10**. Roul. 2d D.L.R
Optd in black. (*a*) W **2**. 1d. (P 11½–12½×Roul), 1d. (P 10), 4d. (Roul), 4d. (P 10), 6d. (P 10), 2s. (Roul)
(*b*) W **7**. P 10. 2d. D.L.R.
(*c*) W **10**. 2d. D.L.R. (Roul), 2d. D.L.R. (P 10×Roul), 2d. D.L.R. (P 10)

The 6d. (W **2**. Roul) with red overprint is known showing the stop omitted after "B".

R.G. (Registrar-General)

Optd in red. W **2**. Roul. 2d., 6d., 1s.
Optd in blue. (*a*) W **2**. P 11½–12½×Roul. 6d.
(*b*) W **10**. 2d. D.L.R. (Roul), 2d. D.L.R. (P 11½–12½×Roul)
Optd in black. (*a*) W **2**. 2d. D.L.R. (Roul), 6d. (P 10), 6d. (P 10×11½–12½), 1s. (P 11½–12½×Roul), 1s. (P 10)
(*b*) W **7**. P 10. 2d. D.L.R.
(*c*) W **10**. 2d. D.L.R. (Roul), 2d. D.L.R. (P 10×Roul), 2d. D.L.R. (P 10), 2d. D.L.R. (P 10×11½–12½)

The 2d. (W **2**. Roul) with red overprint is known showing "C" for "G".

S. (Sheriff)

Optd in red. W **2**. Roul. 2d., 6d.
Optd in blue. W **10**. Roul. 2d. D.L.R.
Optd in black. (*a*) W **2**. 6d. (Roul), 6d. (P 11½–12½×Roul), 6d. (P 11½–12½), 6d. (P 10)
(*b*) W **10**. 2d. D.L.R. (Roul), 2d. D.L.R. (P 10×Roul), 2d. D.L.R. (P 10)

S.C. (Supreme Court)

Optd in red. W **2**. Roul. 2d. 6d.
Optd in black. W **10**. P 10. 2d. D.L.R.

S.G. (Surveyor-General)

Optd in red. W **2**. 2d. (Roul), 4d. (P 11½–12½), 6d. (Roul)
Optd in blue. (*a*) W **2**. Roul. 4d.
(*b*) W **10**. Roul. 2d. D.L.R.
Optd in black. (*a*) W **2**. 2d. D.L.R. (Roul), 4d. (P 11½–12½), 4d. (P 10) 4d. (P 10×11½–12½), 6d. (P 11½–12½×Roul), 6d. (P 11½–12½), 6d. (P 10), 6d. (P 10×11½–12½)

(*b*) W **7**. P 10. 2d. D.L.R.
(*c*) W **10**. 2d. D.L.R. (Roul), 2d. D.L.R. (P 11½–12½), 2d. D.L.R. (P 10×Roul), 2d. D.L R (P 10)
The 2d. (W **7** and W **10**. P 10) with black overprint are known showing "C" for "G".

S.M. (Stipendiary Magistrate)

Optd in red. W **2**. Roul. 1d., 2d., 4d., 6d., 1s.
Optd in blue. (*a*) W **2**. Roul. 2d., 4d., 6d.
(*b*) W **10**. Roul. 2d. D.L.R.
Optd in black. (*a*) W **2**. 1d. (P 11½–12½), 1d. (P 10), 2d. D.L.R. (Roul), 4d. (Roul), 4d. (P 11½–12½×Roul), 4d. (P 11½–12½), 4d. (P 10), 4d. (P 10×11½–12½), 6d. (P 11½–12½×Roul), 6d. (P 11½–12½), 6d. (P 10), 6d. (P 10×11½–12½), 1s. (P 11½–12½×Roul)
(*b*) W **7**. P 10. 2d. D.L.R.
(*c*) W **10**. 2d. D.L.R. (Roul), 2d. D.L.R. (P 11½–12½), 2d. D.L.R. (P 10×Roul) 2d. D.L.R. (P 10), 2d D.L.R. (P 10×11½–12½)
The 2d. and 4d. (both W **2**. Roul) with red overprint are known showing the stop omitted after "M".

S.T. (Superintendent of Telegraphs)

Optd in red. W **2**. Roul. 2d., 6d.
Optd in blue. W **10**. Roul. 2d. D.L.R.
Optd in black. (*a*) W **2**. Roul. 2d. D.L.R., 6d.
(*b*) W **7**. P 10. 2d. D.L.R.
(*c*) W **10**. 2d. D.L.R. (Roul), 2d. D.L.R. (P 10×Roul), 2d. D.L.R. (P 10)
The 2d. and 6d. (both W **2**. Roul) with red overprint are known showing the stop omitted after "T".

T. (Treasury)

Optd in red. W **2**. 1d. (Roul), 2d. (Roul), 4d. (P 11½–12½×Roul), 6d. (Roul), 1s. (Roul)
Optd in blue. (*a*) W **2**. Roul. 1d., 4d., 6d.
(*b*) W **10**. Roul. 2d. D.L.R.
Optd in black. (*a*) W **2**. 1d. (P 10), 2d. D.L.R. (Roul), 4d. (Roul), 4d. (P 11½–12½), 4d. (P 10), 6d. (Roul), 6d. (P 11½–12½), 1s. (P 11½–12½×Roul), 1s. (P 10×11½–12½), 2s. (Roul), 2s. (P 11½–12½), 2s. (P 10×11½–12½)
(*b*) W **7**. P 10. 2d. D.L.R.
(*c*) W **10**. 2d. D.L.R. (Roul), 2d. D.L.R. (P 10)

T.R. (Titles Registration)

Optd in black. (*a*) W **2**. 4d. (P 11½–12½), 4d. (P 10×11½–12½), 6d. (P 11½–12½), 1s. (P 11½–12½)
(*b*) W **10**. P 10. 2d. D.L.R.

V. (Volunteers)

Optd in black. (*a*) W **2**. 4d. (P 10×11½–12½), 6d. (P 11½–12½), 1s. (P 11½–12½)
(*b*) W **10**. P 10. 2d. D.L.R.
(*c*) W **10**. 2d. D.L.R. (Roul), 2d. D.L.R. (P 10×Roul), 2d. D.L.R. (P 10)
The 2d. (W **10**. P 10×Roul) overprinted in black is only known showing the stop omitted after "V".

VA. (Valuator of Runs)

Optd in black without stop after "V". (*a*) W **2**. Roul. 4d.
(*b*) W **10**. P 10. 2d. D.L.R.

VN. (Vaccination)

Optd in black without stop after "V". W **2**. 4d. (P 10), 4d. (P 10×11½–12½)

W. (Waterworks)

Optd in red. W **2**. Roul. 2d.
Optd in black. W **10**. 2d. D.L.R. (Roul), 2d. D.L.R. (P 10)
The 2d. (W **2**. Roul) with red overprint is known showing the stop omitted after "W".

B. General

O.S. (O **1**)   **O.S.** (O **2**)

1874–77. Optd with Type O **1**. W **2**.

(a) P 10

O1	3	4d. dull purple (18.2.74)	£2750	£550

(b) P 11½–12½×10

O2	1	1d. green (2.1.74)	—	£475
O3	3	4d. dull violet (12.2.75)	£120	6·50
O4	1	6d. Prussian blue (20.10.75)	£170	11·00
O4*a*	3	2s. rose-pink		
O5		2s. carmine (3.12.76)	—	£150

(c) P 11½–12½

O6	1	1d. deep yellow-green (30.1.74)	£3500	£400
		a. Printed on both sides	—	£1300
O7	3	3d. on 4d. ultramarine (26.6.77)	£8000	£3000
		a. No stop after "S"	—	£4000
O8		4d. dull violet (13.7.74)	85·00	9·00
		a. No stop after "S"	—	75·00
O9	1	6d. bright blue (31.8.75)	£250	22·00
		a. "O.S." double	—	£350
O10		6d. Prussian blue (27.3.74)	£225	9·50
		a. No stop after "S"	—	£100
O11	4	9d. red-purple (22.3.76)	£4000	£1600
		a. No stop after "S"	£4500	£2250
O12	1	1s. red-brown (5.8.74)	£110	6·50
		a. "O.S." double	—	£325
		b. No stop after "S"	£375	80·00
O13	3	2s. crimson-carmine (13.7.75)	£325	32·00
		a. No stop after "S"	—	£150
		b. No stops	—	£180
		c. Stops at top of letters		

1876–85. Optd with Type O **1**. W **8**.

(a) P 10

O14	1	6d. bright blue (1879)	£170	20·00

(b) P 10×11½–12½, 11½–12½×10, or compound

O15	3	4d. violet-slate (24.1.78)	£110	8·50
O16		4d. plum (29.11.81)	70·00	2·75
O17		4d. deep mauve	70·00	2·50
		a. No stop after "S"	£225	50·00
		b. No stop after "O"		
		c. "O.S." double		
		d. "O.S." inverted	—	£275
		e. Imperf between (horiz pair)		
O18	1	6d. bright blue (1877)	£140	5·50
		a. "O.S." inverted		
		b. No stop after "O"		
		c. Mixed perfs 10 and 11½–12½	—	†
O19		6d. bright ultramarine (27.3.85)	£140	5·50
		a. "O.S." inverted		
		b. "O.S." double		
		c. "O.S." double, one inverted	—	£550
		d. No stop after "S"	£550	75·00
		e. No stops after "O" and "S"		
O20		1s. red-brown (27.3.83)	95·00	7·00
		a. "O.S." inverted		
		b. No stop after "O"		
		c. No stop after "S"	—	80·00
O21	3	2s. carmine (16.3.81)	£275	9·00
		a. "O.S." inverted	—	£475
		b. No stop after "S"	—	£110

(c) P 11½–12½

O22	3	3d. on 4d. ultramarine	£7500	
O23		4d. violet-slate (14.3.76)	£200	26·00
O24		4d. deep mauve (19.8.79)	90·00	12·00
		a. "O.S." inverted	†	£800
		b. "O.S." double, one inverted		
		c. No stop after "S"	—	80·00
O25	1	6d. Prussian blue (6.77)	£130	7·50
		a. "O.S." double	—	£170
		b. "O.S." inverted		
O26	4	8d. on 9d. brown (9.11.76)	£5500	£2750
		a. "O.S." double	£6500	
		b. "O" only	—	£3000
O26*c*		9d. purple	£8500	
O27	1	1s. red-brown (12.2.78)	55·00	8·50
		a. "O.S." inverted	£700	£250
		b. No stop after "S"	£350	85·00
O28		1s. lake-brown (8.11.83)	70·00	4·00
O29	3	2s. rose-carmine (12.8.85)	£225	8·50
		a. "O.S." double	—	£250
		b. "O.S." inverted	—	£300
		c. No stop after "S"	—	90·00

1891–1902. Optd with Type O **2**.

*(a) W **8**. P 11½–12½*

O30	1	1s. lake-brown (18.4.91)	85·00	11·00
O31		1s. Vandyke brown	95·00	8·50
O32		1s. dull brown (2.7.96)	75·00	5·50
		a. No stop after "S"	—	90·00
O33		1s. sepia (*large holes*) (4.1.02)	70·00	5·50
		a. "O.S." double	—	£425
		b. No stop after "S"		
O34	3	2s. carmine (26.6.00)	£140	15·00
		a. No stop after "S"		

*(b) W **8**. P 10×11½–12½*

O35	3	2s. rose-carmine (9.11.95)	£140	10·00
		a. No stop after "S"	£425	
		b. "O.S." double		

*(c) W **10**. P 11½–12½*

O36	1	1s. dull brown (1902)	95·00	45·00

1874–76. Optd with Type O **1**. W **10**.

(a) P 10

O37	11	1d. blue-green (30.9.75)	£225	38·00
		a. "O.S." inverted		
		b. No stop after "S"		

O38	**12**	2d. orange-red (18.2.74)	55·00	6·50
		a. No stop after "S"	—	50·00
		b. "O.S." double		
		(b) P 10×11½–12½, 11½–12½×10, or compound		
O39	**11**	1d. blue-green (16.9.75)		
		a. No stop after "S"		
O40	**12**	2d. orange-red (27.9.76)	—	29·00
		(c) P 11½–12½		
O41	**11**	1d. blue-green (13.8.75)	—	60·00
		a. "O.S." inverted		
		b. No stop after "S"		
O42	**12**	2d. orange-red (20.5.74)	—	£150

1876–80. Optd with Type O **1**. W **13**.

		(a) P 10		
O43	**11**	1d. blue-green (2.10.76)	32·00	1·75
		a. "O.S." inverted	—	£110
		b. "O.S." double	£225	£110
		c. "O.S." double, one inverted		
		d. No stops	—	60·00
		e. No stop after "O"		
		f. No stop after "S"	—	21·00
		g. Deep green	50·00	1·00
		ga. "O.S." double	—	£140
O44	**12**	2d. orange-red (21.9.77)	15·00	1·00
		a. "O.S." inverted	—	65·00
		b. "O.S." double	£225	£120
		c. "O.S." double, one inverted		
		d. "O.S." double, both inverted	—	£350
		e. No stops	—	£110
		f. No stop after "O"	—	28·00
		g. No stop after "S"		
		h. Dull brick-red	75·00	1·00
		(b) P 10×11½–12½, 11½–12½×10 or compound		
O45	**11**	1d. deep green (14.8.80)	—	60·00
		a. "O.S." double		
O46	**12**	2d. orange-red (6.4.78)	£100	28·00
		a. "O.S." inverted	—	£300
		b. No stop after "S"	—	£130
		(c) P 11½–12½		
O47	**12**	2d. orange-red (15.7.80)	—	90·00

1882 (20 Feb). No. 181 optd with Type O **1**.

O48	**11**	½d. on 1d. blue-green	£110	25·00
		a. "O.S." inverted		

1888 (15 Nov)–**91**. Nos. 184 and 185*a* optd with Type O **1**. P 10.

O49	**17**	4d. pale violet (24.1.91)	£120	10·00
O50	**18**	6d. blue	55·00	1·50
		a. "O.S." double		
		b. No stop after "S"		

1891. Nos. 229*b* and 231*a*/2 optd with Type O **1**.

		(a) P 10		
O51	**17**	2½d. on 4d. deep green (Br.) (1.8)	£130	14·00
		a. "2" and "½" closer together	—	50·00
		b. "O.S." inverted		
		c. "O.S." double		
		d. "OS." omitted (in vert pair with normal)		
		e. No stop after "S"		
		(b) P 10×11½–12½ or 11½–12½×10.		
O52	**17**	2½d. on 4d. deep green (Br.) (1.10)	£140	29·00
		(c) P 11½–12½		
O53	**17**	2½d. on 4d. deep green (Br.) (1.6)	£250	85·00

1891–96. Optd with Type O **2**. W **13**.

		(a) P 10		
O54	**11**	1d. deep green (22.4.91)	70·00	2·00
		a. "OS." double	£190	85·00
		b. "O.S." double, one inverted		
		c. No stop after "S"	£110	13·00
		d. Blackish blue opt	£250	4·50
O55	**12**	2d. orange-red (22.4.91)	60·00	3·50
		a. "O.S." double		
		b. "O.S." double, both inverted		
		c. No stop after "S"	—	26·00
		(b) P 15		
O56	**11**	1d. green (8.9.94)	30·00	1·25
		a. "O.S." double		
		b. No stop after "S"		
		c. "O.S." inverted		
O57	**12**	2d. orange-red (16.6.94)	28·00	60
		a. "O.S." double	—	90·00
		b. "O.S." inverted	—	60·00
		(c) P 13		
O58	**11**	1d. green (20.5.95)	40·00	1·25
		a. No stop after "S"	£150	10·00
O59	**12**	2d. orange-red (11.2.96)	45·00	50
		a. "O.S." double	£325	
		b. No stop after "S"	£140	10·00
		c. "O.S." inverted		

1891–99. Optd with Type O **2**. W **13** (sideways on ½d.).

		(a) P 10		
O60	**15**	½d. brown (2.5.94)	55·00	11·00
		a. "O.S." inverted	£250	
		b. No stop after "S"	£140	50·00
O61	**17**	4d. pale violet (13.2.91)	70·00	5·00
		a. "O.S." double		
		b. "S." omitted	—	£160
		c. No stop after "S"		
		d. Aniline violet (31.8.93)	70·00	11·00
		da. "O.S." double		
		dc. No stop after "S"		
O62	**18**	6d. blue (4.4.93)	45·00	2·50
		a. No stop after "S"		
		b. Blackish blue opt		
		(b) P 10×11½–12½		
O63	**15**	½d. brown (26.3.95)	48·00	8·00
		(c) P 11½–12½		
O64	**15**	½d. red-brown (13.6.91)	80·00	15·00
		(d) P 15		
O65	**15**	½d. pale brown (8.6.95)	75·00	20·00
O66	**17**	4d. slate-violet (4.4.95)	95·00	5·50
		a. "O.S." double	£475	£130
O67	**18**	6d. blue (20.9.93)	60·00	4·25
		(e) P 13		
O68	**15**	½d. deep brown (17.5.98)	65·00	6·00
		a. Opt triple, twice sideways	£375	
		b. "O.S." inverted		
O69	**17**	4d. violet (12.96)	£120	3·00
		a. "O.S." double	£450	£110
		b. No stop after "S"	£350	55·00
O70	**18**	6d. blue (13.9.99)	70·00	2·75
		a. No stop after "S"	£225	80·00

1891–95. Nos. 229*b*, 230*a* and 231*a* optd with Type O **2**.

		(a) P 10		
O71	**17**	2½d. on 4d. deep green (Br.) (18.8.94)	50·00	27·00
		a. Fraction bar omitted		
		b. "2" and "½" closer together	£120	55·00
		c. "O.S." inverted	£550	
		d. No stop after "S"	—	85·00
O72	**18**	5d. on 6d. deep brown (C.) (2.12.91)	55·00	18·00
		a. No stop after "5D"	£250	
		b. No stop after "S"	£190	70·00
		(b) P 10×11½–12½		
O73	**17**	2½d. on 4d. deep green (Br.) (17.9.95)	—	85·00
		a. "O.S." double		

1897–1901. Nos. 235/6 and 238*a* optd with Type O **2**.

		(a) P 15		
O74	**23**	5d. brown-purple (29.3.01)	£110	20·00
		(b) P 13		
O75	**22**	2½d. violet-blue (12.5.97)	£100	7·50
		a. No stop after "S"	—	65·00
O76	**23**	5d. purple (29.9.01)	£110	27·00
		a. No stop after "S"		

O. S.

(O **3**)

1899–1901. Optd with Type O **3**. W **13**. P 13.

O80	**24**	½d. yellow-green (12.2.00)	21·00	8·00
		a. "O.S." inverted	£140	
		b. No stop after "S"	85·00	
O81	**11**	1d. rosine (22.9.99)	27·00	1·60
		a. "O.S." inverted	£140	90·00
		b. "O.S." double	†	£475
		c. No stop after "S"	£100	18·00
O82	**12**	2d. bright violet (1.6.00)	32·00	80
		a. "O.S." inverted	£140	65·00
		b. "O.S." double		
		c. No stop after "S"	90·00	18·00
O83	**22**	2½d. indigo (2.10.01)	80·00	19·00
		a. "O.S." inverted	£450	£170
		b. No stop after "S"	£300	
O84	**17**	4d. violet (18.11.00)	80·00	5·50
		a. "O.S." inverted	£475	
		b. No stop after "S"	£250	
O85	**18**	6d. blue (8.10.00)	45·00	5·50
		a. No stop after "S"	£140	

1891 (May). Optd as Type O **3** but wider. W **13**. P 10.

O86	**19**	2s.6d. pale violet	£7500	£5500
O87		5s. pale rose	£8000	£6000

Only one sheet (60) of each of these stamps was printed.

The use of stamps overprinted "O S" was made invalid by the Posts and Telegraph Act of 1 November 1902.

South Australia became part of the Commonwealth of Australia on 1 January 1901.

TASMANIA

PRICES FOR STAMPS ON COVER

Nos. 1/4	*from* × 6
Nos. 5/12	*from* × 5
Nos. 14/24	*from* × 3
Nos. 25/56	*from* × 5
Nos. 57/77	*from* × 6
Nos. 78/9	—
Nos. 80/90	*from* × 3
No. 91	—
Nos. 92/109	*from* × 3
No. 110	—
Nos. 111/23	*from* × 3
Nos. 124/6	—
Nos. 127/34	*from* × 5
Nos. 135/55	*from* × 4
Nos. 156/8	*from* × 20
Nos. 159/66	*from* × 10
Nos. 167/9	*from* × 15
Nos. 170/4	*from* × 6
Nos. 216/22	*from* × 15
Nos. 223/5	—
Nos. 226/7	*from* × 15
Nos. 229/36	*from* × 20
Nos. 237/57	*from* × 10
No. 258	—
Nos. 259/62	*from* × 10
Nos. F1/25	—
Nos. F26/9	*from* × 15
Nos. F30/9	—

SPECIMEN OVERPRINTS. Those listed are from U.P.U. distributions between 1892 and 1904. Further "Specimen" overprints exist, but these were used for other purposes.

1

2

3

(Eng C.W. Coard. Recess H. and C. Best at the *Courier* newspaper, Hobart)

1853 (1 Nov). 24 varieties in four rows of six each. No wmk. Imperf.

(a) Medium soft yellowish paper with all lines clear and distinct

1	1	1d. pale blue	£12000	£1500
2		1d. blue	£12000	£1500

(b) Thin hard white paper with lines of the engraving blurred and worn

3	1	1d. pale blue	£11000	£1300
4		1d. blue	£11000	£1300

1853 (1 Nov). No wmk. Imperf. In each plate there are 24 varieties in four rows of six each.

(a) Plate I. Finely engraved. All lines in network and background thin, clear, and well defined

(i) First state of the plate, brilliant colours

5	2	4d. bright red-orange	£8500	£1000
6		4d. bright brownish orange	—	£1300

(ii) Second state of plate, with blurred lines and worn condition of the central background

7	2	4d. red-orange	£6000	£475
8		4d. orange	£5500	£450
9		4d. pale orange	—	£450

(b) Plate II. Coarse engraving, lines in network and background thicker and blurred

10	2	4d. orange	£5500	£425
11		4d. dull orange	£5500	£375
12		4d. yellowish orange	£5500	£375

In the 4d. Plate I, the outer frame-line is thin all round. In Plate II it is, by comparison with other parts, thicker in the lower left angle.

The 4d. is known on vertically laid paper from proof sheets. Examples from Plate I have the lines close together and those from Plate II wide apart (Price £10,000 *unused*).

In 1879 reprints were made of the 1d. in blue and the 4d., Plate I, in brownish yellow, on thin, tough, white wove paper, and perforated 11½. In 1887, a reprint from the other plate of the 4d. was made in reddish brown and black on thick white paper, imperforate, and in 1889 of the 1d. in blue and in black, and of the 4d. (both plates) in yellow and in black on white card, imperforate. As these three plates were defaced after the stamps had been superseded, all these reprints show two, or three thick strokes across the Queen's head.

All three plates were destroyed in July 1950.

PERKINS BACON "CANCELLED". For notes on these handstamps, showing "CANCELLED" between horizontal bars forming an oval, see Catalogue Introduction.

(Eng W. Humphrys, after water-colour sketch by E. Corbould. Recess P.B.)

1855 (17 Aug–16 Sept). Wmk Large Star. W w **1**. Imperf.

14	3	1d. carmine (16.9) (H/S "CANCELLED" in oval £12000)	£10000	£900
15		2d. deep green (16.9)	£5500	£550
16		2d. green (16.9) (H/S "CANCELLED" in oval £13000)	£5500	£450
17		4d. deep blue	£5000	£130
18		4d. blue (H/S "CANCELLED" in oval £12000)	£5000	£130

Proofs of the 1d. and 4d. on thick paper, *without watermark*, are sometimes offered as the issued stamps. The 6d. dull lilac on this watermark was prepared, but not issued. Examples exist from a creased proof sheet (*Price* £750 *unused*).

(Recess H. and C. Best, Hobart, from P.B. plates)

1856 (Apr)–**57**. No wmk. Imperf.

(a) Thin white paper

19	3	1d. pale brick-red (4.56)	£13000	£650
20		2d. dull emerald-green (1.57)	£16000	£950
21		4d. deep blue (5.57)	£2750	£130
22		4d. blue (5.57)	£2750	£130
23		4d. pale blue (5.57)	—	£170

(b) Pelure paper

24	3	1d. deep red-brown (11.56)	£8500	£750

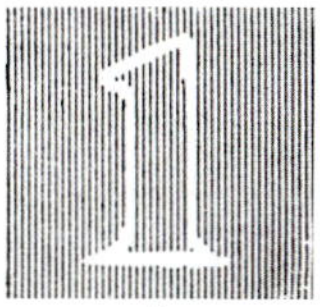
4

7

8

(Recess H. Best (August 1857–May 1859), J. Davies (August 1859–March 1862), J. Birchall (March 1863), M. Hood (October 1863–April 1864), Govt Printer (from July 1864), all from P.B. plates)

1857 (Aug)–**67**. Wmk double-lined numerals "1", "2" or "4" as W **4** on appropriate value. Imperf.

25	3	1d. deep red-brown	£1000	50·00
26		1d. pale red-brown	£600	40·00
27		1d. brick-red (1863)	£425	40·00
28		1d. dull vermilion (1865)	£350	35·00
29		1d. carmine (1867)	£350	30·00
30		2d. dull emerald-green	—	£130
31		2d. green	—	60·00
32		2d. yellow-green	£900	£110
33		2d. deep green (1858)	£850	70·00
34		2d. slate-green (1860)	£400	85·00
35		4d. deep blue	—	85·00
36		4d. pale blue	£450	26·00
37		4d. blue	£450	28·00
38		4d. bright blue	£450	28·00
		a. Printed on both sides	†	—
39		4d. cobalt-blue	—	90·00

Printings before July 1864 were all carried out at the *Courier* printing works which changed hands several times during this period.

CANCELLATIONS. Beware of early Tasmanian stamps with pen-cancellations cleaned off and faked postmarks applied.

(Recess P.B.)

1858. Wmk double-lined numerals "6" or "12" as W **4**. Imperf.

40	7	6d. dull lilac (H/S "CANCELLED" in oval £13000)	£1200	90·00
41	8	1s. vermilion (*shades*) (H/S "CANCELLED" in oval £12000)	£800	80·00

(Recess J. Davies (March 1860), J. Birchall (April 1863), Govt Printer (from February 1865), all from P.B. plates)

1860 (Mar)–**67**. Wmk double-lined "6" as W **4**. Imperf.

44	7	6d. dull slate-grey	£850	85·00
45		6d. grey	—	90·00
46		6d. grey-violet (4.63)	£750	85·00
47		6d. dull cobalt (2.65)	£1200	£140
48		6d. slate-violet (2.65)	£850	75·00
49		6d. reddish mauve (4.67)	£1100	£180

In 1871 reprints were made of the 6d. (in mauve) and the 1s. on white wove paper, and perforated 11½. They are found with or without "REPRINT". In 1889 they were again reprinted on white card, imperforate. These later impressions are also found overprinted "REPRINT" and perforated 11½.

PERFORATED ISSUES. From 1 October 1857 the Tasmania Post Office only supplied purchasers requiring five or more complete sheets of stamps. The public obtained their requirements, at face value, from licensed stamp vendors, who obtained their stocks at a discount from the Post Office.

> From 1863 onwards a number of stamp vendors applied their own roulettes or perforations. The Hobart firm of J. Walch & Sons achieved this so successfully that they were given an official contract in July 1869 to perforate sheets for the Post Office. The Government did not obtain a perforating machine until late 1871

1863–71. Double-lined numeral watermarks. Various unofficial roulettes and perforations.

(a) By J. Walch & Sons, Hobart

(i) Roulette about 8, often imperf×roul (1863–68)

50	**3**	1d. brick-red	—	£475
51		1d. carmine	£900	£300
52		2d. yellow-green	—	£1200
53		2d. slate green		
54		4d. pale blue	—	£450
55	**7**	6d. dull lilac	—	£500
56	**8**	1s. vermilion	—	£1300

(ii) P 10 (1864–69)

57	**3**	1d. brick-red	£180	60·00
58		1d. dull vermilion	£180	50·00
59		1d. carmine	£140	50·00
60		2d. yellow-green	£800	£150
61		2d. slate-green	£800	£200
62		4d. pale blue	£375	20·00
63		4d. blue	£375	20·00
64	**7**	6d. grey-violet	£550	25·00
65		6d. dull cobalt	£750	£100
66		6d. slate-violet	—	50·00
67		6d. reddish mauve	£800	£100
68	**8**	1s. vermilion	£600	55·00
		a. Imperf vert (horiz pair)		

(iii) P 12 (1865–71—from July 1869 under contract to the Post Office)

69	**3**	1d. dull vermilion	£150	
70		1d. carmine	£110	22·00
		a. Error. Wmkd "2" (*pen cancel* £300)	—	£2750
71		2d. yellow-green	£600	95·00
72		4d. deep blue	£325	21·00
73		4d. blue	£325	23·00
74		4d. cobalt-blue	—	60·00
75	**7**	6d. slate-violet	£400	29·00
		a. Imperf between (vert pair)		
76		6d. reddish mauve	£170	42·00
		a. Imperf between (vert or horiz pair) (*pen cancel* £200)		
77	**8**	1s. vermilion	£425	70·00
		b. Imperf between (horiz pair) (*pen cancel* £275)	—	£3250

(iv) Perf compound 10×12 (1865–69)

78	**3**	1d. carmine	£3000	
79		4d. blue	—	£2500

(b) P 12½ by R. Harris, Launceston (1864–68)

80	**3**	1d. brick-red	£160	50·00
81		1d. dull vermilion	£150	50·00
82		1d. carmine	95·00	24·00
83		2d. yellow-green	£750	£170
84		2d. slate-green	£650	£180
85		4d. blue	£425	55·00
86		4d. bright blue	£425	55·00
87	**7**	6d. dull cobalt	£750	£100
88		6d. slate-violet	£550	60·00
89		6d. reddish mauve	£800	£130
90	**8**	1s. vermilion	£650	£130
		a. Imperf between (horiz pair) (*pen cancel* £300)		

(c) Imperf×oblique roulette 11½ at Oatlands (1866)

91	**3**	4d. blue	—	£800
91*a*	**7**	6d. dull cobalt	†	—

(d) Oblique roulette 10–10½, possibly at Deloraine (1867)

92	**3**	1d. brick-red	—	£750
93		1d. carmine	£2500	£650
94		2d. yellow-green	—	£1100
95		4d. bright blue	—	£850
96	**7**	6d. grey-violet	—	£1500

(e) Oblique roulette 14–15, probably at Cleveland (1867–69)

97	**3**	1d. brick-red	—	£1000
98		1d. dull vermilion	—	£1000
99		1d. carmine	—	£1000
100		2d. yellow-green	—	£1400
101		4d. pale blue	—	£1000
102	**7**	6d. grey-violet	—	£1800
103	**8**	1s. vermilion	—	£2250

(f) Pin-perf 5½ to 9½ at Longford (1867)

104	**3**	1d. carmine	£1000	£300
105		2d. yellow-green		
106		4d. bright blue	—	£550
107	**7**	6d. grey-violet	—	£550
108		6d. reddish mauve	—	£1200
109	**8**	1s. vermilion		

(g) Pin-perf 12 at Oatlands (1867)

110	**3**	4d. blue		

(h) Pin-perf 13½ to 14½ (1867)

111	**3**	1d. brick-red	—	£700
112		1d. dull vermilion	—	£700
113		1d. carmine		
114		2d. yellow-green	—	£1200
115		4d. pale blue	—	£600
116	**7**	6d. grey-violet	—	£1200
117	**8**	1s. vermilion		

(j) Serrated perf 19 at Hobart (1868–69)

118	**3**	1d. carmine (*pen-cancel* £20)	£750	£225
119		2d. yellow-green	—	£750
120		4d. deep blue	£1700	£225
121		4d. cobalt-blue	—	£225
122	**7**	6d. slate-violet	—	£1000
123	**8**	1s. vermilion		

(k) Roul 4½, possibly at Macquarie River (1868)

124	**3**	4d. blue		
125	**7**	6d. reddish mauve		
126	**8**	1s. vermilion		

An example of the 1d. carmine is known perforated 10 on three sides and serrated 19 on the fourth.

These local separations (Nos. 91/126) were sometimes applied only between the horizontal rows or vertical columns of sheets, so that pairs can be found 'imperforate vertically' or 'imperforate horizontally'.

For stamps perforated 11½ or 12 by the Post Office see Nos. 134*a*/43.

11

12

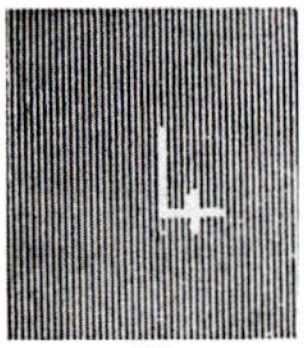

13

14

(Typo Govt Printer, Hobart, from plates made by D.L.R.)

1870 (1 Nov)–**71**. Wmk single-lined numerals W **12** (2d.), **13** (1d., 4d.) or **14** (1d., 10d.).

(a) P 12 by J. Walch & Sons

127	**11**	1d. rose-red (wmk "10")	£120	20·00
		b. Deep rose-red	£130	15·00
128		1d. rose-red (wmk "4") (3.71)	£140	60·00
		a. Imperf (pair)	†	—
129		2d. yellow-green	£180	11·00
		b. Blue-green	£190	11·00
		ba. Double print		
130		4d. blue	£1200	£475
131		10d. black	24·00	50·00
		a. Imperf (pair)	£700	

(b) P 11½ by the Post Office (1871)

132	**11**	1d. rose-red (wmk "10")	£1100	
133		2d. yellow-green	£300	18·00
		a. Blue-green	£180	9·50
		ab. Double print	£5000	£1800
134		10d. black	50·00	50·00
		aa. Imperf vert (horiz pair)		

The above were printed on paper obtained from New South Wales.

See also Nos. 144/55, 156/8, 159/66, 170/4, 226/7, 242 and 255/6.

(Recess P.B.)

1871. Wmk double-lined numeral "**12**". P 11½ by the Post Office.

134*a*	**8**	1s. vermilion		

(Recess Govt Printer, Hobart)

1871–91. Double-lined numeral watermarks as W **4**. Perforated by the Post Office.

(a) P 11½

135	**7**	6d. dull lilac	£225	22·00
136		6d. lilac	£200	22·00
		a. Imperf between (vert pair)	—	£1700
		b. Imperf between (horiz pair)		
137		6d. deep slate-lilac (3.75)	£200	22·00
		a. Imperf (pair)	—	£1300
138		6d. bright violet (5.78)	£225	35·00
		b. Imperf between (horiz pair)	£3500	
139		6d. dull reddish lilac (10.79)	£200	40·00
140	**8**	1s. brown-red (1.73)	£300	65·00
		a. Imperf between (horiz pair)		
141		1s. orange-red (3.75)	£275	65·00
141*a*		1s. orange (5.78)		

(b) P 12

142	**7**	6d. reddish purple (1884)	£160	20·00
		a. Imperf between (horiz pair)	£2000	
143		6d. dull claret (7.91)	50·00	14·00

The perforation machine used on Nos. 142/3 was previously owned by J. Walch and Sons and passed to the ownership of the Government in 1884. It may have been used to perforate leftover sheets of previous printings.

15

16

"Wedge" flaw (Right pane R. 10/6)

Plate scratch (Left pane R. 10/1)

(Typo Govt Printer, Hobart, from plates made by D.L.R.)

1871 (25 Mar)–**78**. W **15**.

(a) P 11½

144	**11**	1d. rose (5.71)	15·00	2·25
		a. Imperf (pair) (*pen cancel £150*)	—	£1300
		b. Bright rose	14·00	2·25
		c. Carmine	20·00	3·25
		d. Pink	20·00	3·25
		e. Vermilion (4.75)	£275	75·00
		f. Wedge flaw	£300	45·00
145		2d. deep green (11.72)	75·00	2·50
		a. Blue-green	50·00	2·50
		b. Yellow-green (12.75)	£250	4·50
146		3d. pale red-brown	70·00	4·25
		a. Imperf (pair)	£600	£1000
		b. Imperf horiz (vert pair)	£3500	
		c. Deep red-brown	75·00	4·50
		d. Purple-brown (1.78)	75·00	4·25
		da. Plate scratch	£475	75·00
		e. Brownish purple	65·00	4·25
147		4d. pale yellow (8.8.76)	£150	45·00
		a. Ochre (7.78)	90·00	9·00
		b. Buff	75·00	11·00
148		9d. blue (2.10.71)	29·00	8·00
		a. Imperf (pair)	£550	
		b. Double print	†	£3250
149		5s. purple (*pen cancel £3.75*)	£350	80·00
		b. Mauve	£325	80·00

(b) P 12

150	**11**	1d. rose	£140	28·00
		a. Carmine	£150	30·00
		b. Wedge flaw	—	£140
151		2d. green	£650	£140
152		3d. red-brown	£130	21·00
		a. Deep red-brown	£130	21·00
153		4d. buff	£350	23·00
154		9d. pale blue	55·00	
		a. Imperf between (horiz pair)	£3750	
155		5s. purple	£550	
		a. Mauve	£450	

(Typo D.L.R.)

1878 (28 Oct). W **16**. P 14.

156	**11**	1d. carmine	11·00	1·00
		a. Rose-carmine	6·50	1·00
		b. Scarlet	18·00	1·25
157		2d. pale green	11·00	1·00
		a. Green	11·00	1·00
158		8d. dull purple-brown	14·00	10·00

(Typo Govt Printer, Hobart (some printings of 1d. in 1891 by *Mercury Press*) from plates made by Victoria Govt Printer, Melbourne (½d.) or D.L.R. (others))

1880 (Apr)–**91**. W **16**.

(a) P 11½

159	**11**	½d. orange (8.3.89)	3·00	3·25
		a. Deep orange	3·00	3·25
160		1d. dull red (14.2.89)	14·00	3·25
		a. Vermilion-red	10·00	2·50
		b. Wedge flaw	£120	35·00
161		3d. red-brown	23·00	5·00
		a. Imperf (pair)	£450	
		b. Plate scratch	£225	75·00
162		4d. deep yellow (1.83)	80·00	18·00
		a. Chrome-yellow	80·00	20·00
		b. Olive-yellow	£140	27·00
		c. Buff	40·00	9·50

(b) P 12

163	**11**	½d. orange	5·50	6·50
		a. Deep orange	5·50	6·50
		ab. Wmk sideways		
164		1d. pink (1891)	38·00	15·00
		a. Imperf (pair)	£400	£425
		b. Rosine	35·00	11·00
		c. Dull rosine	35·00	12·00
		ca. Imperf (pair)	£375	
		d. Wedge flaw	£200	65·00
165		3d. red-brown	8·00	8·50
		a. Imperf between (horiz pair)	£2250	
		b. Plate scratch	95·00	80·00
166		4d. deep yellow	£140	32·00
		a. Chrome-yellow	£160	25·00
		ab. Printed both sides	£1500	

SPECIMEN AND PRESENTATION REPRINTS OF TYPE 11. In 1871 the 1d., 2d., 3d., 4d. blue, 9d., 10d. and 5s. were reprinted on soft white wove paper to be followed, in 1879, by the 4d. yellow and 8d. on rough white wove. Both these reprintings were perforated 11½. In 1886 it was decided to overprint remaining stocks with the word "REPRINT".

In 1889 Tasmania commenced sending sample stamps to the U.P.U. in Berne and a further printing of the 4d. blue was made, imperforate, on white card. This, together with the 5s. in mauve on white card, both perforated 11½ and overprinted "REPRINT", were included in presentation sets supplied to members of the states' legislatures in 1901.

(**17**)

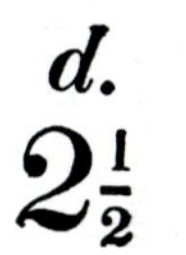

(**18**) (2¼ *mm* between "d", and "2")

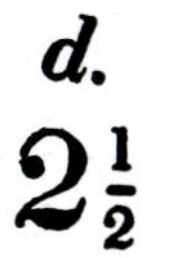

(**19**) (3½ *mm* between "d" and "2")

1889 (1 Jan). No. 156*b* surch locally with T **17**.

167	**11**	½d. on 1d. scarlet	10·00	24·00
		a. "al" in "Half" printed sideways (R. 1/2)	£1900	£1700

No. 167a occurred in a second printing and was later corrected.

A reprint on white card, perforated 11½ or imperforate, overprinted "REPRINT" was produced in 1901.

1891 (1 Jan–June). Surch locally. W **16**.

(a) With T **18**. *P 11½*

168	**11**	2½d. on 9d. pale blue	21·00	4·25
		a. Surch double, one inverted	£700	£800
		b. Deep blue (May)	12·00	7·50

(b) With T **19**. *P 12*

169	**11**	2½d. on 9d. pale blue (June)	5·00	3·50
		a. Blue surch		

A reprint, using a third setting, perforated 11½ and overprinted "REPRINT" was produced in 1901.

(Typo Govt Printer, Hobart)

1891 (Apr–Aug). W **15**.

(a) P 11½

170	**11**	½d. orange	75·00	50·00
		a. Brown-orange	50·00	45·00
171		1d. rosine	23·00	10·00
		a. Wedge flaw	£225	90·00

(b) P 12

172	**11**	½d. orange	65·00	45·00
		a. Imperf (pair)	£300	
173		1d. dull rosine	42·00	40·00
		a. Rosine	55·00	40·00
		b. Wedge flaw	£325	£225
174		4d. bistre (Aug)	23·00	32·00

20

21

21a

(Typo D.L.R.)

1892 (12 Feb)–**99**. W **16**. P 14.

216	**20**	½d. orange and mauve (11.92)	2·75	1·25
217	**21**	2½d. purple	2·75	1·75
218	**20**	5d. pale blue and brown	7·00	3·75
219		6d. violet and black (11.92)	15·00	4·75
220	**21a**	10d. purple-lake and deep green (30.1.99)	11·00	14·00
221	**20**	1s. rose and green (11.92)	12·00	3·00
222		2s.6d. brown and blue (11.92)	32·00	32·00
223		5s. lilac and red (3.2.97)	90·00	27·00
224		10s. mauve and brown (11.92)	£190	£120
225		£1 green and yellow (2.97)	£500	£475
216/25 *Set of* 10			£750	£600
216s/25s Optd "SPECIMEN" *Set of* 10			£650	

See also Nos. 243 and 257/8.

(Typo Govt Printer, Hobart)

1896. W **16**. P 12.

226	**11**	4d. pale bistre	15·00	7·00
227		9d. pale blue	9·50	3·00
		a. Blue	9·50	3·75

22 Lake Marion

23 Mount Wellington

24 Hobart

25 Tasman's Arch

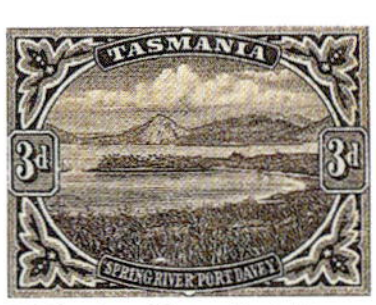

26 Spring River, Port Davey

27 Russell Falls

28 Mount Gould, Lake St. Clair

29 Dilston Falls

30

(Eng L. Phillips. Recess D.L.R.)

1899 (Dec)–**1900**. W **30** (sideways on vert designs). P 14.

229	**22**	½d. deep green (31.3.00)	8·50	6·50
230	**23**	1d. bright lake (13.12.99)*	5·50	1·75
231	**24**	2d. deep violet (15.12.99)*	22·00	1·75
232	**25**	2½d. indigo (1900)	22·00	3·75
233	**26**	3d. sepia (1900)	20·00	6·00
234	**27**	4d. deep orange-buff (1900)	24·00	9·00
235	**28**	5d. bright blue (31.3.00)	38·00	11·00
236	**29**	6d. lake (31.3.00)	32·00	35·00
229/36 *Set of* 8			£150	65·00
229s/36s Optd "Specimen" *Set of* 8			£550	

*Earliest known postmark dates.

See also Nos. 237/9, 240/1, 245/8, 249/54, 259, 260 and 261/2.

DIFFERENCES BETWEEN LITHOGRAPHED AND TYPOGRAPHED PRINTINGS OF TYPES 22/9

LITHOGRAPHED	TYPOGRAPHED
General appearance fine.	*Comparatively crude and coarse appearance.*
½d. All "V over Crown" wmk.	All "Crown over A" wmk.
1d. The shading on the path on the right bank of the river consists of very fine dots. In printings from worn stones the dots hardly show.	The shading on the path is coarser, consisting of large dots and small patches of colour.
The shading on the white mountain is fine (or almost absent in many stamps).	The shading on the mountain is coarse, and clearly defined.
2d. Three rows of windows in large building on shore, at extreme left, against inner frame.	Two rows of windows.
3d. Clouds very white.	Clouds dark.
Stars in corner ornaments have long points.	Stars have short points.
Shading of corner ornaments is defined by a coloured outer line.	Shading of ornaments terminates against white background.
4d. Lithographed only.	—
6d. No coloured dots at base of waterfall.	Coloured dots at base of waterfall.
Outer frame of value tablets is formed by outer line of design.	Thick line of colour between value tablets and outer line.
	Small break in inner frame below second "A" of "TASMANIA".

(Litho, using transfers from D.L.R. plates, Victoria Government Printing Office, Melbourne)

1902 (Jan)–**05**. Wmk V over Crown, W w **10** (sideways on ½d., 2d.). P 12½.

237	**22**	½d. green (2.03)	4·75	1·50
		a. Wmk upright	28·00	27·00
		b. Perf 11 (1904)	6·50	15·00
		c. Perf comp of 12½ and 11	£200	£140
		d. Perf comp of 12½ and 12	£600	
		s. Optd "SPECIMEN"	£120	
238	**23**	1d. carmine-red	20·00	1·75
239	**24**	2d. deep reddish violet	13·00	70
		a. Perf 11	13·00	9·00
		b. Perf comp of 12½ and 11	£180	90·00
		c. Wmk upright (2.04)	90·00	17·00
		d. Deep rose-lilac (4.05)	18·00	1·75
		da. Perf 11	11·00	2·50
		db. Perf comp of 12½ and 11	£225	£100
		s. Optd "SPECIMEN"	£130	

As the V and Crown paper was originally prepared for stamps of smaller size, portions of two or more watermarks appear on each stamp.

We only list the main groups of shades in this and the following issues. There are variations of shade in all values, particularly in the 2d. where there is a wide range, also in the 1d. in some issues.

(Typo, using electrotyped plates, Victoria Govt Ptg Office, Melbourne)

1902 (Oct)–**04**. Wmk V over Crown, W w **10**. P 12½.

240	**23**	1d. pale red (wmk sideways)	17·00	4·25
		a. Perf 11	50·00	12·00
		b. Perf comp of 12½ and 11	£500	£100
		c. Wmk upright (1.03)	27·00	12·00
		ca. Perf 11	65·00	15·00
		d. Rose-red (wmk upright) (4.03)	14·00	4·00
		da. Perf 11	26·00	4·00
		db. Perf comp of 12½ and 11	£475	£100
		ds. Optd "SPECIMEN"	£120	
241		1d. scarlet (wmk upright) (9.03)	19·00	3·50
		a. Perf 11	24·00	3·75
		b. Perf comp of 12½ and 11	—	55·00
		c. Rose-scarlet (1904)	18·00	3·50
		ca. Perf 11	9·00	4·00
		cb. Perf comp of 12½ and 11	£180	55·00

The 1d. scarlet of September 1903 was from new electrotyped plates which show less intense shading.

(Typo Victoria Govt Ptg Office, Melbourne)

1903 (Apr–Dec). Wmk V over Crown, W w **10**. P 12½.

242	**11**	9d. blue (Apr)	20·00	3·75
		a. Perf 11	8·50	18·00
		b. Perf comp of 12½ and 11	£950	£950
		c. Wmk sideways	£350	£160
		d. Pale blue	20·00	10·00
		e. Bright blue	21·00	12·00
		f. Ultramarine	£425	
		g. Indigo	£225	
243	**20**	1s. rose and green (Dec)	50·00	8·00
		a. Perf 11	90·00	80·00
242s/3s		Optd "SPECIMEN" *Set of 2*	£225	

1½d. (**31**)

ONE PENNY (**32**)

1904 (29 Dec). No. 218 surch with T **31**.

244	**20**	1½d. on 5d. pale blue and brown	1·50	1·75
		s. Optd "SPECIMEN"	70·00	

Stamps with inverted surcharge or without surcharge *se-tenant* with stamps with normal surcharge were obtained irregularly and were not issued for postal use.

> **PRINTER.** The Victoria Govt Ptg Office became the Commonwealth Stamp Printing Branch in March 1909.

(Litho, using transfers from D.L.R. plates, Victoria Govt Ptg Office, Melbourne)

1905 (Sep)–**12**. Wmk Crown over A, W w **11** (sideways on horiz stamps). P 12½.

245	**24**	2d. deep purple	18·00	1·00
		a. Perf 11	50·00	2·50
		b. Perf comp of 12½ and 11	30·00	9·00
		c. Perf comp of 12½ and 12	£190	£120
		d. Perf comp of 11 and 12	£350	£200
		e. Slate-lilac (1906)	25·00	1·25
		ea. Perf 11	60·00	2·75
		eb. Perf comp of 12½ and 11		
		ed. Perf comp of 11 and 12	£325	£200
		ee. Perf comp of 12½ and 12		
		f. Reddish lilac (1907)	42·00	3·50
		fa. Perf 11	50·00	6·50
		fb. Perf comp of 12½ and 11	£160	
246	**26**	3d. brown (1906)	12·00	4·75
		a. Perf 11 (9.05)	32·00	38·00
		b. Perf comp of 12½ and 11	£275	£275
247	**27**	4d. pale yellow-brown (3.07)	21·00	4·75
		a. Perf 11	65·00	20·00
		b. Orange-buff (5.09)	65·00	5·50
		ba. Perf 11	65·00	29·00
		bb. Perf comp of 12½ and 11	£475	£475
		c. Brown-ochre (wmk sideways). Perf 11 (6.11)	30·00	55·00
		ca. Perf comp of 12½ and 11	—	£700
		d. Orange-yellow (3.12)	16·00	38·00
		da. Perf 11	48·00	65·00
		db. Perf comp of 12½ and 11	£475	£475
248	**29**	6d. lake (7.08)	80·00	9·00
		a. Perf 11	95·00	9·00
		b. Perf comp of 12½ and 11	£500	£500

Stamps with perf compound of 12½ and 12 or 11 and 12 are found on sheets which were sent from Melbourne incompletely perforated along the outside edge of the pane or sheet. The missing perforations were applied in Hobart using a line machine measuring 12 (11.8 is the exact gauge). This perforation can only occur on one side of a stamp.

(Typo, using electrotyped plates, Victoria Govt Ptg Office, Melbourne).

1905 (Aug)–**11**. Wmk Crown over A, W w **11** (sideways on horiz designs). P 12½.

249	**22**	½d. yellow-green (10.12.08)	2·50	75
		a. Perf 11	2·50	75
		b. Perf comp of 12½ and 11	£130	32·00
		c. Perf comp of 11 and 12	£300	
		d. Wmk upright (1909)	25·00	8·50
		da. Perf 11	£110	
250	**23**	1d. rose-red	7·00	30
		a. Perf 11	6·50	30
		b. Perf comp of 12½ and 11	5·50	7·00
		c. Perf comp of 12½ and 12	£170	60·00
		d. Perf comp of 11 and 12	£200	60·00
		e. Wmk sideways (1907)	24·00	3·00
		ea. Perf 11	25·00	4·00
		eb. Perf comp of 12½ and 11	95·00	23·00
		f. Imperf (pair)	£700	£750
250*g*		1d. carmine-red (3.10)	14·00	3·25
		ga. Perf 11	14·00	3·25
		gb. Perf comp of 12½ and 11	21·00	9·50
		gc. Perf comp of 12½ and 12	£170	55·00
		gd. Perf comp of 11 and 12	£200	60·00
		gf. Wmk sideways	14·00	3·00
		gg. Perf 11	15·00	3·00
		gh. Perf comp of 12½ and 11	19·00	9·00
		h. Carmine-vermilion (1911)	18·00	12·00
		ha. Perf 11	21·00	11·00
		hb. Perf comp of 12½ and 11	65·00	14·00
		hc. Perf comp of 12½ and 12		
		hd. Perf comp of 11 and 12		
251	**24**	2d. plum (8.07)	38·00	70
		a. Wmk upright	45·00	5·50
		b. Perf 11	6·50	30
		ba. Wmk upright (12.07)	45·00	5·50
		c. Perf comp of 12½ and 11	42·00	18·00
		d. Perf comp of 12½ and 12	£425	£140
		e. Perf comp of 11 and 12	£250	£110
		f. Bright reddish violet (1910)	13·00	4·25
		fa. Perf 11	12·00	2·25
		fb. Perf comp of 12½ and 11	55·00	22·00
		fc. Perf comp of 12½ and 12	£425	£130
253	**26**	3d. brown (3.09)	22·00	11·00
		a. Wmk upright		
		b. Perf 11	30·00	14·00
		c. Perf comp of 12½ and 11	£425	£450
254	**29**	6d. carmine-lake (12.10)	24·00	45·00
		a. Perf 11	24·00	55·00
		b. Perf comp of 12½ and 11	£450	
		c. Dull carmine-red (3.11)	25·00	55·00
		ca. Wmk upright	60·00	65·00
		cb. Perf 11	27·00	65·00
		cc. Perf comp of 12½ and 11	£475	£500

The note after No. 248 re perfs compound with perf 12 also applies here.

Nos. 250/f were printed from the same plates as Nos. 241/cb. Nos. 250*g*/hd are from a further pair of new plates and the images are sharper.

(Typo Victoria Govt Printing Office, Melbourne).

1906–09. Wmk Crown over A, W w **11**. P 12½.

255	**11**	8d. purple-brown (1907)	27·00	23·00
		a. Perf 11	19·00	7·50
256		9d. blue (1907)	7·50	5·50
		a. Perf 11	7·50	9·00
		b. Perf comp of 12½ and 11 (1909)	£110	
		c. Perf comp of 12½ and 12 (1909)	£400	
		d. Perf comp of 11 and 12	£500	
257	**20**	1s. rose and green (1907)	13·00	9·00
		a. Perf 11 (1907)	29·00	45·00
		b. Perf comp of 12½ and 11	23·00	50·00
		c. Perf comp of 12½ and 12	£250	
258		10s. mauve and brown (1906)	£275	£275
		a. Perf 11	£475	£475
		b. Perf comp of 12½ and 12	£800	

The note after No. 248 re perfs compound with perf 12, also applies here.

(Typo, using stereotyped plates, Commonwealth Stamp Ptg Branch, Melbourne)

1911 (Jan). Wmk Crown over A, W w **11** (sideways). P 12½.

259	**24**	2d. bright violet	20·00	7·00
		a. Wmk upright	48·00	13·00
		b. Perf 11	9·50	5·50
		ba. Wmk upright	40·00	11·00
		c. Perf comp of 12½ and 11	£130	38·00
		d. Perf comp of 12½ and 12	£475	

Stamps from this stereotyped plate differ from No. 251 in the width of the design (33 to 33¾ *mm*, against just over 32 *mm*), in the taller, bolder letters of "TASMANIA", in the slope of the mountain in the left background, which is clearly outlined in white, and in the outer vertical frame-line at left, which appears "wavy". Compare Nos. 260, etc, which are always from this plate.

1912 (Oct). No. 259 surch with T **32**. P 12½.

260	**24**	1d. on 2d. bright violet (R.)	1·00	1·00
		a. Perf 11	1·50	3·50
		b. Perf comp of 12½ and 11	£275	£300

(Typo, using electrotyped plates, Commonwealth Stamp Ptg Branch, Melbourne).

1912 (Dec). Thin ready gummed paper, white gum (as Victoria, 1912)*. W w **11** (sideways on 3d.). P 12½.

261	**23**	1d. carmine-vermilion	26·00	18·00
		a. Perf 11	21·00	18·00
		b. Perf comp of 12½ and 11	†	£600
262	**26**	3d. brown	70·00	£100

*See note below Victoria No. 455.

STAMP BOOKLETS

There are very few surviving examples of Nos. SB1/4. Listings are provided for those believed to have been issued with prices quoted for those known to still exist.

1904 (1 Jan)–**09**. Black on red cover as Type B **1** of New South Wales. Stapled.

SB1 £1 booklet containing 240 1d. in 12 blocks of 20 (5×4)

a. Red on pink cover (1909)
b. Blue on pink cover

1904 (1 Jan). Black on grey cover No. SB1. Stapled.

SB2 £1 booklet containing 120 2d. in four blocks of 30

1910 (1 May). Black on white cover as Type B **2** of New South Wales. Stapled.

SB3 2s. booklet containing 11 ½d. (No. 249), either in block of 6 plus block of 5 or block of 11, and 18 1d. (No. 250), either in three blocks of 6 or block of 6 plus block of 12 .... £7500

Unsold stock No. SB3 was uprated with one additional ½d. in May 1911.

1911 (Aug). Red on pink cover as No. SB3. Stapled.

SB4 2s. booklet containing 12 ½d. (No. 249), either in two blocks of 6 or block of 12, and 18 1d. (No. 250), either in three blocks of 6 or block of 6 plus block of 12 .... £6500

POSTAL FISCAL STAMPS

VALIDITY. Nos. F1/29 were authorised for postal purposes on 1 November 1882.

CLEANED STAMPS. Beware of postal fiscal stamps with pen-cancellations removed.

F **1**

F **2**

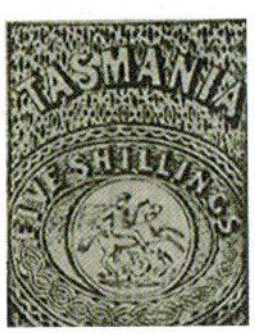

F **3**

F **4**

(Recess Alfred Bock, Hobart)

1863–80. Wmk double-lined "1". W **4**.

		(a) Imperf		
F1	F **1**	3d. green (1.65)	£650	£225
F2	F **2**	2s.6d. carmine (11.63)	£650	£225
F3		2s.6d. lake (5.80)		
F4	F **3**	5s. brown (1.64)	£1300	£750
F5		5s. sage-green (1880)	£850	£375
F6	F **4**	10s. orange (1.64)	£1600	£750
F7		10s. salmon (5.80)	£1300	£750
		(b) P 10		
F8	F **1**	3d. green	£400	£140
F9	F **2**	2s.6d. carmine	£350	
F10	F **3**	5s. brown	£550	
F11	F **4**	10s. orange	£500	
		(c) P 12		
F12	F **1**	3d. green	£375	£170
F13	F **2**	2s.6d. carmine	£325	£160
F14	F **3**	5s. brown	£550	
F15		5s. sage-green	£400	£160
F16	F **4**	10s. orange	£475	£225
F17		10s. salmon	£450	£180
		(d) P 12½		
F18	F **1**	3d. green	£600	
F19	F **2**	2s.6d. carmine	£550	
F20	F **3**	5s. brown	£850	
F21	F **4**	10s. orange-brown	£650	
		(e) P 11½		
F22	F **1**	3d. green	£750	
F23	F **2**	2s.6d. lake	£325	£180
F24	F **3**	5s. sage-green	£425	£170
F25	F **4**	10s. salmon	£550	£325

See also No. F30.

In 1879, the 3d., 2s.6d., 5s. (brown), and 10s. (orange) were reprinted on thin, tough, white paper, and are found with or without "REPRINT". In 1889 another reprint was made on white card, imperforate and perforated 12. These are also found with or without "REPRINT".

F **5** Duck-billed Platypus

REVENUE
(F **6**)

(Typo D.L.R.)

1880 (19 Apr). W **16** (sideways). P 14.

F26	F **5**	1d. slate	42·00	9·00
F27		3d. chestnut	25·00	4·75
F28		6d. mauve	95·00	2·50
F29		1s. rose-pink	£140	30·00
		a. Perf comp of 14 and 11		

All values are known imperf, but not used.

Reprints are known of the 1d. in deep blue and the 6d. in lilac. The former is on yellowish white, the latter on white card. Both values also exist on wove paper, perf 12, with the word "REPRINT".

1888. W **16**. P 12.

F30	F **2**	2s.6d. lake	£130	85·00
		a. Imperf between (horiz pair)	£2000	

1900 (15 Nov). Optd with Type F **6**.

		*(a) On Types F **2** and F **4***		
F32	F **2**	2s.6d. lake (No. F30)	£500	£500
		a. "REVFNUE"	£800	
		b. Opt inverted	£1600	
		c. Imperf (pair)	£1300	
F33	F **4**	10s. salmon (No. F17)	£800	£750
		a. "REVFNUE"		
		(b) On Nos. F27 and F29		
F34	F **5**	3d. chestnut	42·00	35·00
		a. Double opt, one vertical	£225	£250
F35		1s. rose-pink		
		*(c) On stamps as Nos. F26/9, but typo locally. W **16**. P 12*		
F36	F **5**	1d. blue	25·00	30·00
		b. Imperf vert (horiz pair)	£550	
		c. "REVENUE" inverted	£200	
		d. "REVENUE" double	£325	£325
		e. Pale blue	25·00	
F37		6d. mauve	£120	
		a. Double print	£750	
F38		1s. pink	£300	£275
		(d) On No. 225		
F39	**20**	£1 green and yellow	£275	£225
		a. Opt double, one vertical	£475	£450

It was not intended that stamps overprinted with Type F **6** should be used for postal purposes, but an ambiguity in regulations permitted such usage until all postal fiscal stamps were invalidated for postal purposes on 30 November 1900.

F38 is known with "REVENUE" inverted, fiscally used.

Printings of some of the above with different watermarks, together with a 2d. as Nos. F36/8, did not appear until after the stamps had become invalid for postal purposes.

Tasmania became part of the Commonwealth of Australia on 1 January 1901.

VICTORIA

PRICES FOR STAMPS ON COVER

Nos. 1/17	*from* × 2
Nos. 18/22	*from* × 4
Nos. 23/4	*from* × 2
No. 25	*from* × 3
Nos. 26/32	*from* × 2
No. 33	*from* × 6
No. 34	*from* × 8
Nos. 35/9	*from* × 4
No. 40	*from* × 3
Nos. 41/53	*from* × 2
No. 54	*from* × 3
No. 55	—
No. 56	*from* × 4
Nos. 57/72	*from* × 2
No. 73	*from* × 3
Nos. 74/80	*from* × 2
No. 81	*from* × 3
Nos. 82/7	*from* × 4
Nos. 88/200	*from* × 3
Nos. 201/6	*from* × 5
Nos. 207/8	*from* × 10
Nos. 209/14	*from* × 5
Nos. 215/19	—
Nos. 220/6	*from* × 20
Nos. 227/33	—
Nos. 234/7	*from* × 20
Nos. 238/52	—
Nos. 253/6	*from* × 20
No. 257	*from* × 10

PRICES FOR STAMPS ON COVER

No.	258	*from* × 20
No.	259	*from* × 10
Nos.	260/4	—
Nos.	265/6	*from* × 20
Nos.	267/73	*from* × 10
Nos.	274/91	—
Nos.	292/304	*from* × 10
Nos.	305/9	*from* × 5
Nos.	310/23	*from* × 10
Nos.	324/8	—
No.	329	*from* × 12
Nos.	330/50	*from* × 8
Nos.	351/2	—
Nos.	353/4	*from* × 4
No.	355	*from* × 10
Nos.	356/73	*from* × 15
Nos.	374/5	*from* × 3
Nos.	376/98	*from* × 10
Nos.	399/400	—
Nos.	401/6	*from* × 10
Nos.	407/15	—
Nos.	416/30	*from* × 10
Nos.	431/2	—
Nos.	433/43	*from* × 4
Nos.	444/53	—
Nos.	454/5	*from* × 10
Nos.	456/63	*from* × 6
No.	464	—
Nos.	D1/8	*from* × 30
Nos.	D9/10	—
Nos.	D11/37	*from* × 30

During the expansion of the Australian settlements in the fourth decade of the 19th century the growing population of the Port Phillip District in the south of New South Wales led to a movement for its creation as a separate colony. This aspiration received the approval of the British Government in 1849, but the colony of Victoria, as it was to be called, was not to be created until 1 July 1851.

In the meantime the New South Wales Legislative Council voted for the introduction of postal reforms, including the use of postage stamps, from 1 January 1850, and this act was also to apply to the Port Phillip District where stamps inscribed "VICTORIA" would predate the creation of that colony by eighteen months.

Until the end of 1859 the stamps of Victoria, with the exception of Nos. 40 and 73, were produced by local contractors working under the supervision of the colonial administration.

SPECIMEN OVERPRINTS. Those listed are from U.P.U. distributions in 1892 and 1897. Further "Specimen" overprints exist, but these were used for other purposes.

HAM PRINTINGS. The first contractor was Thomas Ham of Melbourne. He was responsible for the initial printings of the "Half-Length" 1d., 2d. and 3d., together with the replacement "Queen-on-Throne" 2d. The first printings were produced from small sheets of 30 (5×6) laid down directly from the engraved die which showed a single example of each value. Subsequent printings, of which No. 4*a* was the first, were in sheets of 120 (two panes of 60) laid down using intermediate stones of various sizes. Impressions from the first printings were fine and clear, but the quality deteriorated when intermediate stones were used.

1 Queen Victoria ("Half Length")

(Lithographed by Thomas Ham, Melbourne)

1850 (3 Jan)–**53**. Imperf.

1d. Thin line at top

2d. Fine border and background

3d. White area to left of orb

(a) Original state of dies: 1d. (tops of letters of "VICTORIA" reach to top of stamp); 2d. (fine border and background); 3d. (thicker white outline around left of orb, central band of orb does not protrude at left). No frame-lines on dies

1	**1**	1d. orange-vermilion	£32000	£10000
		a. Orange-brown	†	£2250
		b. Dull chocolate-brown	£20000	£2500
2		2d. lilac-mauve (*shades*) (Stone A)	£15000	£1000
3		2d. brown-lilac (*shades*) (Stone B)	£13000	£500
		a. Grey-lilac	—	£550
4		3d. bright blue (*shades*)	£8000	£600
		a. Blue (*shades*)	£7000	£450
		ab. Retouched (between Queen's head and right border) (No. 11 in transfer group) (8 varieties)	—	£600
		ac. Retouched (under "V") (No. 10 in transfer group)	£14000	£1000

With the exception of No. 4*a* the above were printed from small stones of 30 (5×6) laid down directly from the engraved die which showed a single example of each value. There were two stones of the 2d. and one for each of the other values. No. 4*a* is the second printing of the 3d. for which the sheet size was increased to 120, the printing stone being constructed from an intermediate stone of 15 (5×3).

1d. Thick line at top

2d. Coarse background

3d. White area small and band protruding to left of orb

(b) Second state of dies: 1d. (more colour over top of letters of "VICTORIA"); 2d. (fine border as (a) but with coarse background); 3d. (thinner white outline around left of orb, central band of orb protrudes at left)

5	**1**	1d. red-brown (*shades*) (2.50)	£9500	£450
		a. Pale dull red-brown	£8000	£450
6		2d. grey-lilac (*shades*) (1.50)	£7000	£200
		a. Dull grey	£13000	£225
7		3d. blue (*shades*) (6.51)	£4750	£190
		a. Retouched (22 varieties) *from*	£6000	£350

Printed in sheets of 120 (10×12) with the printing stones constructed from intermediate stones of 30 (5×6) for the 1d. and 2d. or 10 (5×2) for the 3d. It is believed that the use of the smaller intermediate stone for the latter resulted in the many retouches.

Frame-lines added

(c) Third state of dies: As in (b) but with frame-lines added, very close up, on all four sides

8	**1**	1d. dull orange-vermilion (11.50)	£5500	£650
		a. Dull red (*shades*)	£4750	£200
9		1d. deep red-brown (5.51)	£12000	£1200
		a. Brownish red (*shades*)	£4500	£180
		b. Dull rose (*shades*)	£4500	£180
10		2d. grey (*shades*) (8.50)	£8000	£200
		a. Olive-grey (*shades*)	£8500	£200
11		3d. blue (*shades*) (12.52)	£2750	90·00
		a. Deep blue (*shades*)	£3250	90·00
		b. Pale greenish blue (*shades*)	£4000	£170

Printed in sheets of 120 (12×10) produced from intermediate stones of 30 (6×5) for No. 8 and 12 (6×2) for the others.

White veil

(d) As (c) but altered to give, for the 1d. and 3d., the so-called "white veils", and for the 2d., the effect of vertical drapes to the veil

12	1	1d. reddish brown (6.51)	£7000	£170
		a. Bright pinky red (shades)	£2250	£170
13		2d. drab (1.51)	£8000	£190
		a. Grey-drab	£8000	£180
		b. Lilac-drab	£8000	£180
		c. Red-lilac	—	£1300
		d. Void lower left corner	†	£22000
14		3d. blue (*shades*) (1.53)	£1200	80·00
		a. Deep blue (shades)	£1300	80·00
		b. Greenish blue (shades)	£1600	85·00
		c. Retouched (9 varieties)	£2750	£180

Printed in sheets of 120 (12×10) produced from intermediate stones of 12 (6×2) on which the details of the veil were amended as described above.

The "void corner" error occurred on the printing stone. It is believed that only four examples still exist.

2d. Coarse border and background

(e) Fourth state of 2d. die only: Coarse border and background. Veil details as in original die

15	1	2d. red-lilac (*shades*) (5.50)	£7500	£325
		a. Lilac	£7500	£350
		b. Grey	£9500	£425
		c. Dull brownish lilac	£7500	£180
		d. Retouched lower label—value omitted *from*	†	£15000
		e. Other retouches (17 varieties) *from*	£9500	£350

Printed in sheets of 120 (12×10) produced from an intermediate stone of 30 (6×5).

(f) 2d. as (e), but with veils altered to give effect of vertical drapes

16	1	2d. lilac-grey (1.51)	£5500	£170
		a. Deep grey	£6500	£170
		b. Brown-lilac (shades)	£5000	£110
17		2d. cinnamon (*shades*) (2.51)	£3500	£170
		a. Drab (shades)	£3750	95·00
		b. Pale dull brown (shades)	£3500	£120
		c. Greenish grey	£3500	£110
		d. Olive-drab (shades)	£3750	£190
		e. Buff	£12000	£250

Printed in sheets of 120 (12×10) produced from two successive intermediate stones of 30 (6×5) on which the details of the veil were amended as described above.

This was the final printing of the 2d. "Half Length" as the die for this value had been damaged. A replacement 2d. design was ordered from Thomas Ham.

For the later printings of the 1d. and 3d. in this design see Nos. 23/4, 26/31, 48/9 and 78/9.

2 Queen-on-Throne

3

(Recess-printed by Thomas Ham)

1852 (27 Dec). Imperf.

18	2	2d. reddish brown	£600	28·00
		a. Chestnut	—	£140
		b. Purple-brown	£700	28·00

Printed in sheets of 50 (10×5) from a hand-engraved plate of the same size. Each stamp in the sheet had individual corner letters made-up of various combinations, none of which contained the letter "J".

Reprints were made in 1891 using the original plate, on paper wmk V over Crown, both imperf and perf 12½.

For later printings of this design see Nos. 19/22 and 36/9.

CAMPBELL & CO PRINTINGS. In May 1853 the Victoria postal authorities placed an order for 1d. and 6d. stamps in the "Queen-on-Throne" design with Perkins, Bacon in London. These would not arrive for some time, however, and supplies of Ham's printings were rapidly becoming exhausted. Local tenders were, therefore, solicited for further supplies of the 1d. and 3d. "Half Lengths" and the 2d. "Queen-on-Throne". That received from J. S. Campbell & Co was accepted. The stamps were produced by lithography, using transfers from either the "Half Length" engraved die or the 2d. "Queen-on-Throne" engraved plate of 50. Stamps from the Campbell & Co printings can be distinguished from later printings in lithography by the good quality paper used.

(Lithographed by J. S. Campbell & Co, Melbourne, using transfers taken from Ham's engraved plate)

1854 (Jan–July). Good quality white or toned paper. Imperf.

(a) Clear impressions with details around back of throne generally complete

19	2	2d. brownish purple	£550	38·00
		a. Grey-brown	£700	38·00
		b. Purple-black	—	38·00
		c. Dull lilac-brown (toned paper only)	£750	50·00

(b) Poor impressions with details around back of throne not fully defined

20	2	2d. violet-black (2.54)	£700	45·00
		a. Grey-black	£750	45·00
		b. Grey-lilac	£700	45·00
		c. Dull brown (on toned)	£700	45·00
		ca. Substituted transfer (in pair)	—	£3000

(c) Weak impressions with background generally white without details. Toned paper only

21	2	2d. grey-purple (7.54)	£475	35·00
		a. Purple-black	£475	35·00

(d) Printings using an intermediate stone. Impression flat and blurred. Background details usually complete. Toned paper only

22	2	2d. grey-drab (*shades*) (5.54)	£650	38·00
		a. Black	—	£140

Nos. 19/21 were produced using transfers taken directly from the original Ham engraved plate. It is believed that the different strengths of the impressions were caused by the amount of pressure exerted when the transfers were taken. The stamps were printed in sheets of 100 (2 panes 10×5). On one stone a block of four at bottom left, lettered "FL GM" over "QV RW", was damaged and the stone was repaired by using a block of four substituted transfers. These were lettered "VZ WA" over "FL GM". No. 20ca covers any one of these substituted transfers in pair with normal. As horizontal pairs these are lettered "WA HN" or "GM SX" and as vertical "VZ" over "VZ" or "WA" over "WA".

For No. 22 an intermediate stone was used to produce a printing stone of 300 (6 panes 10×5). The insertion of a further stage into the process caused the blurred appearance of stamps from this printing. No. 22*a* is believed to come from proof sheets issued to post offices for normal use. Examples are usually cancelled with Barred Oval 108 and Barred Numerals 1 and 2.

(Lithographed by J.S. Campbell & Co, Melbourne)

1854 (Feb–June). Good quality wove paper. Imperf.

23	1	1d. orange-red (*shades*)	£3000	£140
		a. Rose	£6500	£750
24		3d. blue (*shades*) (6.54)	£1100	50·00
		a. Retouched under "C" of "VICTORIA"	—	£150

The 1d. was produced in sheets of 192 (two panes of 96 (12×8)) and the 3d. in sheets of 320 (two panes of 160 (18×9)). Both printing stones were constructed from transfers taken from intermediate stones of 24 (6×4). The spacing between stamps is far wider than on the Ham printings. The 3d. panes of 160 were constructed using six complete transfers of 24 and three of 6 with the final impression in the bottom two rows removed.

The 1d. Campbell printings have the frame lines almost completely absent due to lack of pressure when taking transfers.

The 3d. retouch, No. 24a, occurs on R. 3/5 of the intermediate stone.

CAMPBELL & FERGUSSON PRINTINGS. Increased postal rates in early 1854 led to a requirement for a 1s. value and in April a contract for this stamp was awarded to Campbell & Fergusson (the new corporate style of J. S. Campbell & Co). Further contracts to print the 1d. and 3d. "Half Lengths" and the 2d. "Queen-on-Throne" followed. All were produced by lithography with the two "Half Lengths" using transfers from the original engraved die and the 2d. "Queen-on-Throne" transfers from Ham's original engraved plate.

All Campbell & Fergusson printings were on paper of a poorer quality than that used for the earlier contract.

(Lithographed by Campbell & Fergusson)

1854 (6 July). Poorer quality paper. Imperf.

25	3	1s. blue (*shades*)	£1000	40·00
		a. Greenish blue	£1200	40·00
		b. Indigo-blue	—	£190

No. 25 was produced in sheets of 100 (8×12 with an additional stamp appearing at the end of rows 6 to 9). The printing stones used each contained four such sheets. They were constructed from an intermediate stone of 40 (8×5) taken from a single engraved die. Each pane of 100 showed two complete transfers of 40, one of 20, and one of a vertical strip of 4.

For this stamp rouletted or perforated see Nos. 54 and 81.

(Lithographed by Campbell & Fergusson)

1854 (July)–**57**. Poorer quality paper. Imperf.

26	**1**	1d. brown (*shades*)	£3000	£130
		a. Brick-red (shades)	£3250	£110
		b. Dull red (shades)	£3500	£110
27		1d. *Orange-brown (shades)* (8.55)	£3250	£140
		a. Dull rose-red (shades)	£3750	80·00
		b. Bright rose-pink	£6000	£160
		c. Retouched (6 varieties)	£6000	£450
28		1d. pink (*shades*) (2.55)	£1400	48·00
		a. Rose (shades)	£1400	48·00
		b. Lilac-rose (shades)	£1500	48·00
		c. Dull brown-red (shades)	£1700	£140
		d. Retouched (8 varieties)	£2500	£325
29		3d. bright blue (*shades*) (7.57)	£2250	70·00
		a. Greenish blue (shades)	£1900	55·00
		b. Retouch under "C" of "VICTORIA"	£3000	£130
30		3d. *Prussian blue (shades)* (11.56)	£3000	95·00
		a. Milky blue	£3750	£150
		b. Retouch under "C" of "VICTORIA"	—	£275
31		3d. steel-blue (*shades*) (heavier impression) (5.55)	—	65·00
		a. Greenish blue (shades)	£1900	48·00
		b. Blue (shades)	£1900	48·00
		c. Deep blue (shades)	£1600	48·00
		d. Indigo (shades)	—	55·00

The 1d. was produced in sheets of 400 (2 panes 20×10) constructed from transfers originating from the J. S. Campbell & Co intermediate stone. Each pane contained six complete transfers of 24, three of 12, two of 8 and one of 4.

The 3d. was produced in sheets of 320 (2 panes of 160) (No. 29), 200 (No. 30) or 400 (2 panes of 200) (No. 31.) The stone for No. 29 was constructed from transfers taken from the J. S. Campbell intermediate stone with the retouch on R. 3/5 still present. The panes of 160 contained six transfers of 24 and three of 6 with the last impression in both rows 8 and 9 removed. Quality of impression is generally poor. The stone for No. 30, once again taken from the Campbell intermediate stone, was laid down in the same combination of transfers as the 1d. value. Impressions from it were, however, so poor that transfers from a new intermediate stone were used for No. 31. Impressions from this stone, on which the panes of 200 were in a similar layout to the 1d. were much further apart than those on the stones used to produce Nos. 29/30.

The Campbell & Fergusson printings of the "Half Lengths" are listed in the order in which they were printed.

CALVERT PRINTINGS. Contracts for the provision of other values required by the postal rate changes in 1853 were placed with Samuel Calvert of Melbourne who used typography as the printing process. Calvert continued to print, and later roulette, stamps for the Victoria Post Office until March 1858 when it was discovered that he had placed some of the stock in pawn.

4

5

6

(Typographed from woodblocks by Samuel Calvert)

1854 (1 Sept)–**55**. Imperf.

32	**4**	6d. reddish brown (13.9.54)	£1000	75·00
		a. Dull orange	£550	19·00
		b. Orange-yellow	£550	19·00
33	**5**	6d. ("TOO LATE") lilac and green (1.1.55)	£2750	£250
34	**6**	1s. ("REGISTERED") rose-pink and blue (1.12.54)	£3500	£200
35	**4**	2s. dull bluish green/*pale yellow*	£3750	£200

No. 33 was provided to pay the additional fee on letters posted after the normal closure of the mails. This service was only available in the larger towns; examples are usually postmarked Castlemaine, Geelong or Melbourne. The service was withdrawn on 30 June 1857 and remaining stocks of the "TOO LATE" stamps were used for normal postal purposes.

No. 34 was issued to pay the registration fee and was so used until 5 January 1858 after which remaining stocks were used for normal postage.

These four values were produced from individually-engraved boxwood woodblocks. The 6d. was in sheets of 100 printed by two impressions from two plates of 25. The 2s. was in sheets of 50 from a single plate of 25. The bicoloured "TOO LATE" and "REGISTERED" stamps are unusual in that Calvert used a common woodblock "key" plate of 25 for both values combined with "duty" plates made up from metal stereos. Both values were originally in sheets of 50, but the "REGISTERED" later appeared in sheets of 100 for which a second "key" plate of 25 was utilised.

For these stamps rouletted or perforated see Nos. 53, 55/8, 60/1 and 82.

(Lithographed by Campbell & Fergusson)

1855 (Mar)–**56**. Poorer quality paper. Imperf.

(a) Printings from stones which were not over-used; background around top of throne generally full and detail good

36	**2**	2d. lilac (*shades*) (7.55)	£475	32·00
		a. Purple (shades)	£475	32·00
		b. "TVO" for "TWO"	£9000	£1300

(b) Early printings from stones which were over-used. Similar characteristics to those above, though detail is not quite so full. Distinctive shades

37	**2**	2d. brown	—	80·00
		a. Brown-purple	£500	27·00
		b. Warm purple	—	27·00
		c. Rose-lilac	—	27·00
		d. Substituted transfer (pair)	—	£750

(c) Later printings from the same stones used for No. 37 when in a worn condition. Impressions heavy, coarse and overcoloured; details blurred; generally white background around top of throne

38	**2**	2d. dull lilac-mauve (1856)	£500	50·00
		a. Dull mauve	£500	50·00
		b. Grey-violet	—	50·00
		c. Red-lilac	—	50·00
		d. Substituted transfer (pair)	—	£750

(d) Printings from a stone giving blotchy and unpleasing results, with poor definition. Mainly shows in extra colour patches found on most stamps

39	**2**	2d. dull purple (7.55)	—	70·00
		a. Dull grey-lilac	£500	70·00
		b. On thick card paper	—	£650

The Campbell & Fergusson 2d. "Queen-on-Throne" printings were in sheets of 200 (4 panes 10×5) constructed from transfers taken from the original Ham engraved plate.

Four separate stones were used. On Stone A a creased transfer running through R. 4/8, 4/9 and 5/8 caused the "TVO" variety on the stamp from the bottom row of one pane. On Stone C the impression in the first vertical row of one pane were found to be so faulty that they were replaced by substituted transfers taken from elsewhere on the sheet causing abnormal horizontal pairs lettered "UY BF", "TX MQ", "DI WA", "SW GM" and "CH RW". The vertical pairs from the substituted transfers are lettered "UY" over "TX" and "DI" over "SW".

PERKINS BACON "CANCELLED". For notes on this handstamp, showing "CANCELLED" between horizontal bars forming an oval, see Catalogue Introduction.

7 Queen-on-Throne

8 "Emblems"

(Recess Perkins, Bacon & Co, London)

1856 (23 Oct). Wmk Large Star. Imperf.

40	**7**	1d. yellow-green (H/S "CANCELLED" in oval £12000)	£300	42·00

Supplies of this stamp, and the accompanying 6d. which was only issued rouletted (see No. 73), arrived in the colony at the end of 1854, but the 1d. was not placed on sale until almost two years later.

No. 40 was reprinted from the original plate in 1891. Examples, in either dull yellow-green or bright blue-green, are imperforate and on V over Crown watermarked paper.

(Typographed from electrotypes by Calvert)

1857 (26 Jan–6 Sept). Imperf.

(a) Wmk Large Star, W w **1**

41	**8**	1d. yellow-green (18 Feb)	£225	27·00
		a. Deep green	£325	40·00
		b. Printed on both sides	†	£2750
42		4d. vermilion	£500	11·00
		a. Brown-vermilion	£475	9·50
		b. Printed on both sides	†	£2750
43		4d. dull red (20 July)	£375	8·50
44		4d. dull rose (6 Sept)	£475	8·50

(b) No wmk. Good quality medium wove paper

45	**8**	2d. pale lilac (25 May)	£600	11·00
		a. Grey-lilac	£600	11·00

Nos. 41/5 were produced in sheets of 120, arranged as four panes of 30 (6×5) (1d. and 4d.) or twelve panes of 10 (2×5) (2d.), using electrotypes taken from a single engraved die of each value.

The setting of the 4d. was rearranged before the printing of Nos. 43/4.

Only two examples of No. 41b and No. 42b have been recorded.

For this printing rouletted or perforated see Nos. 46/7, 50/2, 59, 74 and 77.

ROULETTES AND PERFORATIONS. In August 1857 a rouletting machine was provided at the G.P.O., Melbourne, to enable the counter clerks to separate stamp stocks before sale to the public. This machine produced roulettes of 7½–9 in one direction across six rows at a time. There was also a single wheel device which gauged 7–7½. Both were in use between the earliest known date of 12 August and the end of 1857.

Calvert was granted a separate contract in October 1857 to roulette the stamps he printed, but only Nos. 57/61 had been produced when it was found, in April 1858, that he had pawned a quantity of the sheets. His contracts were terminated and his successor, F. W. Robinson, used a roulette machine of a different gauge before switching to a gauge 12 perforating machine in January 1859.

1857 (12 Aug–Sept). Rouletted 7–9 by counter clerks at G.P.O., Melbourne.

46	**8**	1d. yellow-green (No. 41)	£650	£110
47		2d. pale lilac (No. 45)	—	50·00
		a. Grey-lilac	—	50·00
48	**1**	3d. blue (*shades*) (No. 24)	£3250	£250
		a. Retouch under "C" of "VICTORIA"	†	£475
49		3d. bright blue (*shades*) (No. 29)	—	£250
		a. Greenish blue (*shades*)	£3250	£225
		b. Retouch under "C" of "VICTORIA"	†	£600
50	**8**	4d. vermilion (No. 42)	—	£100
51		4d. dull red (No. 43)	—	42·00
52		4d. dull rose (No. 44) (Sept)	—	28·00
53	**4**	6d. reddish brown (No. 32)	—	£100
		a. Dull orange	—	60·00
		b. Orange-yellow	—	70·00
54	**3**	1s. blue (*shades*) (No. 25)	—	£110
		a. Greenish blue	—	£110
55	**6**	1s. ("REGISTERED") rose-pink and blue (No. 34)	£10000	£400
56	**4**	2s. dull bluish green/*pale yellow* (No. 35)	£8500	£650

With the exception of the 1s., Nos. 54/*a*, these stamps are normally found rouletted on one or two sides only.

1857 (Oct). Rouletted by Calvert.

(a) Rouletted 7–9 on all four sides and with finer points than No. 53b

57	**4**	6d. orange-yellow (No. 32*b*)	—	£100

(b) Serpentine roulette 10–10½

58	**4**	6d. orange-yellow (No. 32*b*)	£3250	£180

(c) Serrated 18–19

59	**8**	2d. grey-lilac (No. 45*a*)	£1400	£600
60	**4**	6d. orange-yellow (No. 32*b*)	£4500	£160

(d) Compound of serrated 18–19 and serpentine 10–10½

61	**4**	6d. orange-yellow (No. 32*b*)	—	£600

No. 59 was not covered by the contract given to Calvert, but it is believed to be a test run for the rouletting machine. No. 61 always shows serrated 18–19 on three sides and the serpentine roulette at the top or bottom of the stamp.

(Typo from electrotypes by Calvert)

1858 (14 Jan–Apr). Good quality white wove paper. No wmk.

(a) Rouletted 7–9 on all four sides

62	**8**	1d. pale emerald	£550	29·00
		a. Emerald-green	£550	29·00
63		4d. rose-pink (18 Jan)	£425	6·50
		a. Bright rose	£425	6·50
		b. Reddish pink	—	11·00
		c. Imperf horiz (vert pair)	†	£650

(b) Imperf (Apr)

64	**8**	1d. pale emerald	£425	21·00
		a. Emerald-green	—	24·00
65		4d. rose-pink	£500	23·00
		a. Bright rose	—	23·00
		b. Reddish pink	—	30·00

Nos. 62/5 were produced in sheets of 120, arranged as four panes of 30 (6×5).

The Royal Collection contains a used horizontal pair of the 4d. showing the vertical roulettes omitted.

The majority of Nos. 64/5 were issued in April after Calvert's contracts had been terminated, although there is some evidence that imperforate sheets of the 4d., at least, were issued earlier.

For the 1d. of this issue perforated see No. 75.

ROBINSON PRINTINGS. Calvert's contracts were cancelled in April 1858 and the work was then placed with F. W. Robinson, who had unsuccessfully tendered in 1856. The same electrotypes were used, but a perforating machine was introduced from January 1859. Robinson continued to print and perforate stamps under contract until the end of 1859 when the Victoria Post Office purchased his equipment to set up a Stamp Printing Branch and appointed him Printer of Postage Stamps.

(Typo from electrotypes by Robinson)

1858 (May–Dec).

(a) Imperf

(i) Coarse quality wove paper

66	**8**	4d. dull rose (*oily ink*)	—	80·00

(ii) Smooth vertically-laid paper

67	**8**	4d. dull rose (*oily ink*)	—	55·00
		a. Dull rose-red	—	55·00
68		4d. dull rose-red (*normal ink*) (20.5)	£650	30·00

(b) Rouletted 5½–6½

(i) Smooth-laid paper

69	**8**	2d. brown-lilac (*shades*) (*horiz laid*) (June)	£275	10·00
		a. Vert laid paper (21.4)	£425	13·00
70		2d. violet (*horiz laid*) (27.11)	£350	6·50
		a. Dull violet	£400	18·00
71		4d. pale dull rose (*vert laid*) (1.6)	£325	3·75
		a. Horiz laid paper	†	£900
		b. Dull rose-red	£275	3·75
		c. Rose-red	£275	3·75
		ca. Serrated 19	†	£550

(ii) Good quality wove paper

72	**8**	1d. yellow-green (24.12)	£475	40·00

Nos. 66/72 were produced in sheets of 120, arranged as four panes of 30 (6×5).

For stamps of this issue perforated see Nos. 76 and 80.

(Recess Perkins, Bacon & Co, London)

1858 (1 Nov). Wmk Large Star, W w **1**. Rouletted 5½–6½.

73	**7**	6d. bright blue	£475	18·00
		a. Light blue	£500	28·00

No. 73 was received from London at the same time as the 1d., No. 40, but was kept in store until November 1858 when the stock was rouletted by Robinson. When issued the gum was in a poor state.

Imperforate examples exist from Perkins Bacon remainders. Examples are known handstamped "CANCELLED" in oval of bars. *Price* £11000.

Imperforate reprints, in shades of indigo, were made from the original plate in 1891 on V over Crown watermarked paper.

1859 (Jan–May). P 12 by Robinson.

74	**8**	1d. yellow-green (No. 41)	—	£500
75		1d. emerald-green (No. 64*a*)	—	£500
		a. Imperf between (horiz pair)		
76		1d. yellow-green (as No. 72) (11.1)	£425	18·00
		a. Imperf horiz (vert pair)	—	£450
		b. Thin, glazed ("Bordeaux") paper	†	£160
77		2d. pale lilac (No. 45)	—	£450
		a. Grey-lilac	—	£550
78	**1**	3d. blue (*shades*) (No. 24) (2.2)	£2500	£140
		a. Retouch under "C" of "VICTORIA"	—	£400
79		3d. greenish blue (*shades*) (No. 29*a*)	†	£425
		a. Retouch under "C" of "VICTORIA"	†	£1200
80	**8**	4d. dull rose-red (No. 68)	—	£325
81	**3**	1s. blue (*shades*) (No. 25) (4.2)	£375	16·00
		a. Greenish blue	£400	13·00
		b. Indigo-blue	—	45·00
		c. Retouched (shading omitted at left)		
82	**4**	2s. dull bluish green/*pale yellow* (No. 35) (5.59)	£600	55·00

The 1s. was reprinted in 1891 using transfers taken from the original die. These reprints were on V over Crown watermarked paper and perforated 12½.

For perforated 6d. black and 2s. blue both as Type **4** see Nos. 102 and 129/30.

(Typo from electrotypes by Robinson)

1859 (17 May–23 Dec). P 12.

(a) Good quality wove paper

83	**8**	4d. dull rose	£325	6·50
		a. Roul 5½–6½	†	£850

(b) Poorer quality wove paper

84	**8**	1d. dull green (7.59)	£275	28·00
		a. Green (11.11)	£275	28·00
85		4d. rose-carmine (16.7)	£325	7·00
		a. *Rose-pink* (*thick paper*) (30.11)	—	15·00

(c) Horizontally laid paper with the lines wide apart

86	**8**	1d. dull green (18.7)	£400	
		a. Laid lines close together	—	50·00
		b. Green (*shades*) (10.59)	£300	28·00
87		4d. rose-pink (*shades*) (23.12)	£275	7·50
		a. Laid lines close together	—	10·00

STAMP PRINTING BRANCH. On 1 January 1860 F. W. Robinson was appointed Printer of Postage Stamps and his equipment purchased by the Post Office to establish the Stamp Printing Branch. All later Victoria issues were printed by the Branch which became part of the Victoria Government Printing Office in December 1885. In 1909 the Commonwealth Stamp Printing Office under J. B. Cooke was established in Melbourne and produced stamps for both the states and Commonwealth until 1918.

9

10

11

(Des and eng F. Grosse. Typo from electrotypes)

1860 (31 Jan)–**66**. P 12.

(a) No wmk

88 **9** 3d. deep blue (*horiz laid paper*) .... £600 70·00
a. Light blue ....
89 4d. rose-pink (*thin glazed Bordeaux paper*) (21.4.60) .... — 35·00
a. Rose .... £550 35·00
ab. Thicker coarser paper (7.60) .... £550 35·00

(b) On paper made by T. H. Saunders of London wmkd with the appropriate value in words as W **10**

90 **9** 3d. pale blue (1.61) .... £275 7·00
a. Bright blue (10.61) .... £275 8·50
b. Blue (4.63) .... £275 6·00
c. Deep blue (4.64) .... £300 6·00
d. "TRREE" for "THREE" in wmk .... — £700
91 3d. maroon (13.2.66) .... £350 30·00
a. Perf 13 .... £350 32·00
92 4d. rose-pink (1.8.60) .... — 9·50
a. Rose-red .... £170 4·75
b. Rose-carmine .... — 9·50
c. Dull rose .... £170 4·75
d. Printed on "FIVE SHILLINGS" diagonal wmk paper (11.9.62) .... £3500 23·00
93 6d. orange (25.10.60) £8000 £450
94 6d. black (20.8.61) .... £400 8·50
a. Grey-black .... £400 8·50

(c) On paper made by De La Rue wmkd with the appropriate value as a single-lined numeral as W **11**

95 **9** 4d. dull rose-pink (9.10.62) .... £190 6·00
a. Dull rose .... £200 6·50
b. Rose-red .... — 6·00
c. Roul 8 (28.7.63) £2250 £250
d. Imperf (14.7.63) .... — 75·00
e. Perf 12½×12 ....
f. Perf 12½ ....

All three values were produced in sheets of 120, initially as four panes of 30 (6×5). Printings of the 3d. from 1864 were in a changed format of six panes of 20 (4×5).

The "TRREE" watermark error comes from early printings of No. 90 on R. 10/7.

Two examples of the 4d. on Saunders paper are known bisected in 1863, but such use was unauthorised.

Nos. 95c/d were issued during July and August 1863 when the normal perforating machine had broken down. They are best collected used on piece and cancelled within the period (July-September 1863).

Nos. 95e/f were perforated or part-perforated with a machine gauging 12¼-12½, borrowed from the Government Printer in 1863, while the perf 12 machine was being repaired.

Reprints, from new plates, were made of the 3d. and 4d. in 1891 on "V over Crown" paper and perforated 12½.

1860 (Apr)–**63**. P 12.

(a) No wmk

96 **8** 1d. bright green (*horiz laid paper*) ....
97 1d. bright green (*thin, glazed Bordeaux paper*) (25.5.60) .... — 75·00

(b) On paper made by T. H. Saunders of London wmkd with the appropriate value in words as W **10**

98 **8** 1d. pale yellowish green (8.7.60) .... £130 8·00
a. Yellow-green .... £150 8·00
b. Error. Wmkd "FOUR PENCE" .... † £8500
99 2d. brown-lilac (7.7.61) .... — 60·00
100 2d. bluish slate (8.61) .... £200 6·00
a. Greyish lilac (9.61) .... £225 6·50
b. Slate-grey (1.62) .... — 6·00
c. Printed on "THREE PENCE" wmkd paper. *Pale slate* (27.12.62) .... £225 28·00
ca. Bluish grey (2.63) .... £250 28·00

(c) On paper made by De La Rue wmkd single-lined "2", W **11**

101 **8** 2d. dull reddish lilac (24.4.63) .... £325 15·00
a. Grey-lilac (10.63) .... £325 30·00
ab. Error. Wmkd "6" .... † £6500
b. Grey-violet (11.63) .... £250 28·00
c. Slate (12.63) .... £325 40·00

Only two examples of No. 98b have been recorded, one of which is in the Royal Collection.

1861 (22 June). On paper made by T. H. Saunders of London wmkd "SIX PENCE" as W **10**. P 12.

102 **4** 6d. black .... £425 75·00

No. 102 was produced as an emergency measure after the decision had been taken to change the colour of the current 6d. from orange (No. 93) to black (No. 94). During the changeover the old Calvert "woodblock" plates were pressed into service to provide two months' supply.

12

13

(Des, eng and electrotyped De Gruchy & Leigh, Melbourne. Typo)

1861 (1 Oct)–**64**. P 12.

(a) On paper made by T. H. Saunders of London. Wmk "ONE PENNY" as W **10**

103 **12** 1d. pale green .... £170 23·00
a. Olive-green .... — 24·00

(b) On paper made by De La Rue. Wmk single-lined "1" as W **11**

104 **12** 1d. olive-green (1.2.63) .... £130 26·00
a. Pale green (9.63) .... £130 18·00
b. Apple-green (4.64) .... £130 17·00

(c) On paper supplied to Tasmania by Perkins, Bacon. Wmk double-lined "1", W **4** *of Tasmania*

105 **12** 1d. yellow-green (10.12.63) .... £225 24·00
a. Dull green .... — 24·00
b. Imperf between (pair) .... † —

All printings were in sheets of 120 containing four panes of 30 (6×5).

Reprints from new plates were made in 1891 on paper watermarked "V over Crown" and perforated 12½.

(Frame die eng F. Grosse. Typo from electrotypes)

1862 (26 Apr)–**64**. Centre vignette cut from T **9** with a new frame as T **13**.

(a) On paper made by T. H. Saunders of London. Wmk "SIX PENCE" as W **10**. *P 12*

106 **13** 6d. grey .... £200 19·00
a. Grey-black .... £200 21·00
b. Jet-black .... £225 23·00

(b) On paper made by De La Rue. Wmk single-lined "6" as W **11**

107 **13** 6d. grey (p 12) (18.6.63) .... £170 7·00
a. Jet-black .... — 9·00
b. Grey-black .... £170 7·50
c. Perf 13. *Jet-black* .... £180 9·00
ca. Grey-black .... £180 9·00

Printings before August 1863 were in sheets of 120 containing four panes of 30 (6×5). For subsequent printings of No. 107 the format was changed to six panes of 20 (4×5).

Reprints from new plates were made in 1891 on paper watermarked "V over Crown" and perforated 12½.

SINGLE-LINED NUMERAL WATERMARK PAPERS. The first consignment of this paper, showing watermarks as W **11**, arrived in Victoria during October 1862. Five further consignments followed, all but the last supplied by De La Rue.

The complexity of the scheme for different watermarks for each value, together with the time required to obtain further supplies from Great Britain, resulted in the emergency use of paper obtained from Tasmania and of the wrong numeral watermark on certain printings.

The final order for this paper was placed, in error with the firm of T. H. Saunders of London. Although the actual watermarks are the same (the dandy rolls were the property of the Victoria Government and supplied to each firm in turn) there are considerable differences between the two types of paper. That manufactured by Saunders is of a more even quality and is smoother, thicker, less brittle and less white than the De La Rue type.

De La Rue supplied white paper watermarked "1", "2", "4", "6" and "8", blue paper watermarked "1" and green paper watermarked "2". The Saunders consignment of October 1865 contained white paper watermarked "1", "4" and "6", blue paper watermarked "1", green paper watermarked "2" and pink paper watermarked "10".

It is helpful for comparison purposes to note that all white paper watermarked "2" or "8" can only be De La Rue and all pink paper watermarked "10" can only be Saunders.

14

15

16

17

18

(Des and eng F. Grosse. Typo from electrotypes)

1863–73. "Laureated" series.

(a) On paper made by De La Rue wmkd with the appropriate value in single-lined numerals as W **11**

108	**14**	1d. pale green (P 12) (9.9.64)	£110	14·00
		a. Perf 12½×12 (9.64)		
		b. Perf 13 (10.10.64)	£100	8·00
		c. *Bluish green* (P 13)	95·00	6·00
		ca. Printed double	†	£1500
		d. *Green* (P 12) (7.65)	£100	6·00
		da. Perf 13	95·00	6·50
		e. *Deep green* (P 12) (12.65)	£130	6·50
		ea. Perf 13	—	6·50
		eb. Perf 12×13	—	12·00
		f. *Bright yellow-green* (P 13)	—	22·00
109		2d. violet (P 12) (1.4.64)	£140	12·00
		a. *Dull violet* (P 12) (10.64)	£150	12·00
		ab. Perf 12½×12	£750	
		ac. Perf 12½		
		ad. Perf 13	£140	9·00
		b. *Dull lilac* (P 13) (4.65)	£120	9·00
		ba. Perf 12 (7.66)	—	18·00
		bb. Perf 12×13 (7.66)	—	19·00
		c. *Reddish mauve* (P 13) (11.65)	£130	19·00
		d. *Rose-lilac* (P 13) (1.66)	£120	11·00
		da. Perf 12×13 or 13×12	£110	11·00
		e. *Grey* (P 12) (7.66)	£170	14·00
		ea. Perf 13	£110	5·50
110		4d. deep rose (P 12) (11.9.63)	£225	5·50
		a. Printed double	†	£1500
		b. *Rose-pink* (P 12) (9.63)	£180	2·75
		c. *Pink* (P 12) (7.5.64)	£180	2·75
		ca. Error. Wmkd single-lined "8"	†	£8000
		cb. Perf 12½×12 (9.64)		
		d. *Dull rose* (P 13) (10.64)	£160	2·75
		e. *Dull rose-red* (P 13)	£160	2·75
		ea. Perf 12 (8.65)	£225	75·00
111	**16**	6d. blue (P 12) (13.2.66)	£120	10·00
		a. Perf 13	£120	4·50
		b. Perf 12×13	£110	10·00
112	**14**	8d. orange (P 13) (22.2.65)	£750	£110
113	**17**	1s. blue/*blue* (P 13) (10.4.65)	£250	5·50
		a. Perf 12×13 (4.66)	£250	5·50
		ab. Imperf between (vert pair)	†	£6500
		b. *Bright blue/blue* (P 13) (6.67)	£200	6·00
		c. *Indigo-blue/blue* (P 13) (3.68)	—	4·00
		d. *Dull blue/blue* (P 12) (6.74)	—	3·75

(b) Emergency printings on Perkins, Bacon paper borrowed from Tasmania. Wmk double-lined "4" as W **4** *of Tasmania*

114	**14**	4d. deep rose (P 12) (7.1.64)	£225	10·00
		a. *Pale rose* (P 12)	—	10·00
		b. *Dull reddish rose* (P 13) (11.8.65)	£225	10·00
		ba. Perf 12	—	10·00
		bb. Perf 12×13	—	21·00
		c. *Red* (P 13) (4.12.65)	£225	10·00

(c) Emergency printings on De La Rue paper as W **11***, but showing incorrect single-lined numeral. P 13*

115	**14**	1d. bright yellow-green (wmkd "8") (27.12.66)	£275	27·00
116		1d. bright yellow-green (wmkd "6") (6.67)	—	65·00
117		2d. grey (wmkd "8") (18.1.67)	£250	6·00
118	**15**	3d. lilac (wmkd "8") (29.9.66)	£250	50·00
119	**16**	10d. grey (wmkd "8") (21.10.65)	£950	£150
		a. *Grey-black*	£950	£160

(d) On paper made by T. H. Saunders wmkd with the appropriate value in single-lined numerals as W **11**

120	**14**	1d. deep yellow-green (P 12×13) (1.66)	£190	28·00
		a. Perf 13 (3.66)	£110	13·00
		b. Perf 12 (7.66)	—	28·00
121		4d. rose-red (P 13) (12.12.65)	£140	4·25
		aa. Wmk sideways	†	—
		a. Perf 12×13 or 13×12 (2.66)	£200	9·00
		b. Perf 12 (4.66)	—	9·00
122	**16**	6d. blue (P 13) (28.5.66)	£120	3·25
		a. Perf 12	£120	6·50
		b. Perf 12×13	£120	4·25
123		10d. dull purple/*pink* (P 13) (22.3.66)	£275	7·00
		a. Perf 12×13	£325	8·00
		b. *Blackish brown/pink* (P 13) (12.69)	£275	7·00
		c. *Purple-brown/pink* (P 13) (11.70)		
124	**17**	1s. bright blue/*blue* (P 13) (5.12.70)	£150	4·50
		a. *Pale dull blue/blue* (P 12) (1.73)	£250	8·50
		ab. Perf 13	—	18·00
		b. *Indigo-blue/blue* (P 12) (9.73)	—	13·00
		ba. Perf 13	£150	6·50

(e) Emergency printings on Saunders paper as W **11***, but showing incorrect single-lined numeral. P 13*

125	**14**	1d. bright yellow-green (wmkd "4") (6.3.67)	£200	48·00
126		1d. bright yellow-green (wmkd "6") (6.67)	£300	60·00
127		2d. grey (wmkd "4") (21.2.67)	£225	8·50
128		2d. grey (wmkd "6") (13.5.67)	£350	9·00

The 1d., 2d., 4d. and 8d. were originally produced in sheets of 120 containing eight panes of 15 (3×5). The 3d. and 6d. were in sheets of 120 (12×10) and the 1d. (from February 1866), 2d. (from July 1866) and 4d. (from April 1866) subsequently changed to this format. The 10d. was in sheets of 120 containing twenty panes of 6 (2×3). The 1s. was originally in sheets of 60 containing three panes of 20 (4×5), but this changed to 120 (12×10) in April 1866.

Nos. 108a, 109ab/ac and 110cb were perforated or part-perforated with a machine gauging 12½, borrowed from the Government Printer in September 1864, while the perf 12 machine was being repaired.

Only single examples are thought to exist of Nos. 110a, 110ca and 113ab and two of No. 108ca.

For later emergency printings on these papers see Nos. 153/66.

(Typo from composite woodblock and electrotype plate)

1864–80. Wmk single-lined "2" as W **11**.

(a) On De La Rue paper.

129	**4**	2s. light blue/*green* (P 13) (22.11.64)	£425	12·00
		a. *Dark blue/green* (P 12) (9.65)	£450	20·00
		ab. Perf 13 (6.66)	£425	9·50
		b. *Blue/green* (P 13) (6.68)	£375	7·00
		c. *Greenish blue/green* (P 13) (7.73)	£375	9·50
		ca. Perf 12	£400	11·00
		d. *Deep greenish blue/green* (P 12½) (7.80)	£375	9·50

(b) On Saunders paper.

130	**4**	2s. dark blue/*green* (P 13) (23.11.67)	£425	8·50
		a. *Blue/green* (P 13) (10.71)	£425	8·50
		ab. Perf 12 (8.74)	£450	9·00
		c. *Deep greenish blue/green* (P 12½) (5.80)	£400	7·00

Nos. 129/30 were produced in sheets of 30 containing two panes of 15 (3×5). The plate contained eighteen of the original woodblock impressions and twelve electrotypes taken from them.

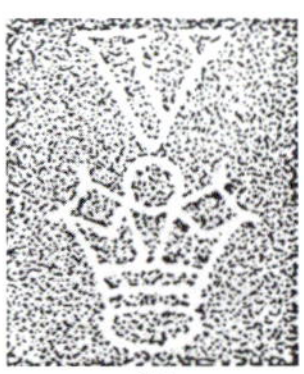

19

20

V OVER CROWN WATERMARKS. The changeover from the numeral watermarks to a general type to be used for all values was first suggested at the end of 1865, but the first supplies did not reach Melbourne until April 1867. Five different versions were used before the V over Crown watermark was superseded by the Commonwealth type in 1905. The five versions are listed as follows:

Type **19** De La Rue paper supplied 1867 to 1882. Shows four points at the top of the crown with the left and right ornaments diamond-shaped

Type **33** De La Rue paper supplied 1882 to 1895. No points at the top of the crown with the left and right ornaments oval-shaped

Type **82** Waterlow paper supplied 1896 to 1899. Wide base to crown

Type **85** Waterlow paper used for postal issues 1899 to 1905. Wide top to crown

Type **104** James Spicer and Sons paper used for postal issues August and September 1912. Narrow crown

(Typo from electrotypes)

1867–81. Wmk. V over Crown. W **19**.

(a) P 13

131	**14**	1d. bright yellow-green (10.8.67)	£100	3·75
		a. *Bright olive-green* (1.69)	£160	23·00
		b. *Yellow-green* (4.69)	£110	3·75
		c. *Dull green* (3.70)	£110	3·50
		d. *Pale green* (10.70)	£100	3·50
		e. *Grass-green* (1871)	£100	3·75
		f. *Bluish green (shades)* (7.72)	£100	4·25
		fa. Wmk sideways	†	—
		g. *Green (shades)* (9.72)	£100	3·25
		ga. Wmk sideways	†	—
132		2d. slate-grey (*shades*) (26.8.67)	£120	3·50
		a. *Grey-lilac* (29.1.68)	£120	5·00
		b. *Lilac* (26.8.68)	95·00	3·25
		ba. Wmk sideways	†	—
		c. *Dull mauve (shades)* (10.68)	95·00	3·50
		d. *Lilac-grey* (1.69)	—	3·75

No.	Type	Description	Unused	Used
		e. Lilac-rose (2.69)	£100	3·25
		f. Mauve (4.69)	£120	3·50
		g. Red-lilac (5.69)	£100	3·00
		h. Dull lilac (6.69)	£100	2·50
		i. Silver-grey (9.69)	£190	9·50
133	15	3d. lilac (28.8.67)	£450	55·00
		a. Grey-lilac (6.68)	£475	60·00
134		3d. yellow-orange (12.6.69)	80·00	15·00
		aa. Wmk sideways	†	—
		a. Dull orange (6.70)	65·00	9·00
		ab. Wmk sideways	†	—
		b. Orange (3.73)	—	9·00
		c. Bright orange (3.73)	80·00	9·00
		d. Orange-brown (*glazed paper*) (10.78)	55·00	25·00
135	14	4d. dull rose (28.11.67)	£120	7·50
		a. Wmk sideways	†	70·00
		b. Aniline red (*shades*) (21.4.69)	—	11·00
		c. Rose-pink (11.69)	—	7·00
		d. Rose (*shades*) (8.71)	£120	3·50
		e. Dull rose (*glazed paper*) (5.3.79)	£120	6·00
		f. Dull rose-red (*glazed paper*) (11.79)	—	9·50
		g. Bright lilac-rose (*aniline*) (*glazed paper*) (2.80)	£130	5·50
		h. Rosine (*aniline*) (*glazed paper*) (9.80)	£350	9·00
136	16	6d. deep blue (15.1.68)	—	7·00
		a. Blue (21.12.68)	85·00	5·00
		ab. Wmk sideways	†	—
		b. Indigo-blue (10.69)	85·00	5·00
		c. Prussian blue (9.72)	85·00	6·00
		d. Indigo (4.73)	85·00	6·00
		e. Dull blue (*worn plate*) (3.74)	—	6·50
		f. Dull ultramarine (2.12.75)	95·00	6·50
		g. Light Prussian blue (12.75)	£130	6·50
		h. Dull violet-blue (7.77)	—	16·00
		i. Blue (*glazed paper*) (6.78)	£100	6·50
		j. Dull milky-blue (*glazed paper*) (9.79)	£100	7·00
		k. Prussian blue (*glazed paper*) (4.80)	—	7·00
		l. Light blue (*glazed paper*) (4.81)	£100	7·50
		m. Deep blue (*glazed paper*) (10.81)	£100	7·00
137	14	8d. lilac-brown/*pink* (24.1.77)	£200	5·50
		a. Purple-brown/pink (2.78)	£200	5·50
		b. Chocolate/pink (8.78)	£225	10·00
		ba. Compound perf 13×12	†	£325
		c. Red-brown/pink (12.78)	90·00	5·00
		d. Wmk sideways	†	£400
138	17	1s. light blue/*blue* (11.5.75)	£225	21·00
139	18	5s. blue/*yellow* (26.12.67)	£3750	£425
		a. Wmk reversed	—	£500
140		5s. indigo-blue and carmine (I) (8.10.68)	£650	55·00
		a. Blue and carmine (4.69)	£600	24·00
		b. Pale bright blue and carmine (*glazed paper*) (24.7.77)	£750	55·00
		c. Grey-blue and carmine (*glazed paper*) (4.78)	£600	28·00
		d. Wmk sideways. *Deep lavender-blue and carmine* (4.6.80)	£600	48·00
141		5s. bright blue and red (II) (*glazed paper*) (12.5.81)	£550	28·00
		a. Indigo-blue and red (*glazed paper*)	—	50·00

(b) P 12

No.	Type	Description	Unused	Used
142	14	1d. pale green (10.71)	£120	9·00
		a. Grass-green (1871)	£100	9·00
		b. Bluish green (*shades*) (7.72)	—	13·00
		c. Green (*shades*) (9.72)	£100	7·00
143	15	3d. dull orange (5.72)	70·00	7·00
		a. Orange (3.73)	—	2·50
		b. Bright orange (3.73)	—	2·50
		c. Dull orange-yellow (*glazed paper*) (12.80)		
144	14	4d. rose (*shades*) (8.71)	£120	3·00
		a. Compound perf 12×13	—	£400
		b. Dull rose (*glazed paper*) (3.79)	—	3·25
		c. Dull rose-red (*glazed paper*) (11.79)	—	6·50
		d. Bright lilac-rose (*aniline*) (*glazed paper*) (2.80)	£250	17·00
		e. Rosine (*aniline*) (*glazed paper*) (9.80)	£140	14·00
145	16	6d. deep blue (2.2.72)		
		a. Prussian blue (9.72)	90·00	8·50
		b. Indigo (4.73)	95·00	9·00
		c. Dull blue (*worn plate*)		
		d. Blue (*glazed paper*) (6.78)	—	8·50
		e. Dull milky-blue (*glazed paper*)	—	8·50
		f. Light blue (*glazed paper*) (4.81)	—	9·00
146	14	8d. red-brown/*pink* (*glazed paper*) (11.80)	£200	23·00
147	17	1s. light blue/*blue* (5.75)	—	13·00
148	18	5s. bright blue and red (II) (*glazed paper*) (5.81)	£550	15·00
		a. Indigo-blue and red	£650	19·00

(c) P 12½

No.	Type	Description	Unused	Used
149	15	3d. dull orange-yellow (*glazed paper*) (12.80)	£100	15·00
150	14	4d. rosine (*aniline*) (*glazed paper*) (9.80)		
151	16	6d. Prussian blue (*glazed paper*) (4.80)		
		a. Light blue (*glazed paper*) (4.81)		
		b. Deep blue (*glazed paper*) (10.81)	95·00	9·00
152	14	8d. lilac-brown/*pink* (8.77)	£200	23·00
		a. Red-brown/pink (*glazed paper*) (11.80)	†	£500

The same electrotypes as the previous issues were used for this series with the exception of the 5s. which was a new value. The 1d., 2d., 3d., 4d., 6d. and 1s. plates were arranged to print sheets of 120 (12×10) and the 8d. conformed to this when reintroduced in 1877. New plates for the 1d. (1868), 2d. (1869) and 6d. (1875) were constructed by Robinson's successor, J. P. Atkinson, using the improved facilities then available.

Atkinson was also responsible for the printing of the 5s. value. The original printings in blue on yellow paper were produced in sheets of 25, or possibly 50, using a vertical strip of five electrotypes. Due to its size the 5s. did not exactly fit the watermarked paper and, to avoid a preprinted sheet number, a proportion of the printing was made on the back of the paper creating the reversed watermark variety, No. 139a. These varieties occur in the first printing only as Atkinson created a plate of 25 for the second printing in March 1868.

Two Types of the 5s.: Printings of the 5s. bicoloured to April 1880 were made from electrotypes taken from the monocoloured plate. These showed a blue line beneath the crown (Type I). In early 1881 this plate was found to be too worn for further use and a new die was made from which a plate of 100 was constructed. Stamps from this plate are without the blue line beneath the crown (Type II).

PERFORATIONS 1859-1883. Collectors should note that our descriptions of perforations follow a longstanding convention.

"Perf 12" (1859 to mid–1866 and mid–1871 to 1883)–line perf machines perforating between 11½ and 12.

"Perf 13" (1864 to 1881)–line perf machines generally gauging between 12½ and 12¾, two of which were converted to comb perforation in 1871. It should be noted that, following a repair in 1879, one of these machines produced an irregular gauge varying between 12¼ and13½.

"Perf 12½" (1863 and 1864)–a line perforating machine borrowed from the Government Printer while the perf 12 machine was being repaired. Stamps perforated (or part–perforated) on this machine were Nos. 95e/f, 108a, 109ab/ac and 110cb. All are rare.

"Perf 12½" (late 1879 onwards)–line or comb machines gauging exactly 12½.

"Mixed perforations"–this description covers stamps where both gauges are present on the same side or sides of the stamp, as a result of reperforation.

(Typo from electrotypes)

1867–70. Emergency printings on various papers due to shortages of V over Crown paper. P 13.

(a) Perkins, Bacon paper borrowed from Tasmania. Wmkd double-lined numerals as W **4** *of Tasmania*

No.	Type	Description	Unused	Used
153	14	1d. pale yellowish green (wmkd "1") (24.9.67)	£130	12·00
		a. Deep yellow-green (10.67)	£130	12·00
154		1d. pale yellow-green (wmkd "4") (27.5.68)	£2750	£130
155		2d. grey-lilac (wmkd "4") (3.2.68)	£250	5·00
		a. Slate (4.68)	£250	3·50
		b. Mauve (7.68)	—	4·50
		c. Imperf (pair)	†	£5500
156		2d. mauve (wmkd "1") (30.6.68)	£250	5·50
157	15	3d. grey-lilac (wmkd "1") (8.68)	£350	80·00
158	14	4d. dull rose-red (wmkd "4") (5.68)	£250	5·00
159	16	6d. blue (wmkd "4") (20.6.68)	£325	40·00
		a. Indigo-blue	—	42·00
160		6d. blue (wmkd "1") (28.7.68)	£180	12·00
161		6d. dull blue (wmkd "2") (1870)	†	£3750

(b) Saunders paper. Wmkd in words as W **10**

No.	Type	Description	Unused	Used
162	14	1d. pale yellow-green (wmkd "SIX PENCE") (23.3.68)	£950	75·00
		a. Wmk sideways	†	—
164	16	6d. blue (wmkd "SIX PENCE") (20.5.68)	£750	60·00
		a. Indigo-blue	—	60·00
165		6d. dull blue (wmkd "THREE PENCE") (6.12.69)	£475	30·00
		a. Deep blue	—	35·00
166		6d. dull blue (wmkd "FOUR PENCE") (21.5.70)	£750	50·00
		a. Deep blue	—	55·00

(c) V over Crown, W **19**, *coloured paper*

No.	Type	Description	Unused	Used
167	14	2d. mauve/*lilac* (7.68)	£180	6·50
		a. Lilac/lilac	£180	6·50

(d) Saunders single-lined numeral "4" as W **11**

No.	Type	Description	Unused	Used
168	16	6d. dull blue (21.5.70)	†	£2250

The supply of paper was so short during 1868 that many odds and ends were utilised. Nos. 161 (five known) and 168 (ten known) are the rarest of these emergency printings.

The 2d. slate-grey is known watermarked "SIX PENCE". The single example is in the Royal Philatelic Collection,

(Printed in Melbourne from a double electrotyped plate of 240 supplied by D.L.R.)

1870 (28 Jan)–**73**. Wmk V over Crown. W **19**

169	**20**	2d. brown-lilac (P 13)	£110	3·00
		a. Dull lilac-mauve (9.70)	£100	1·25
		b. Mauve (*worn plate*) (3.73)	£100	1·25
170		2d. dull lilac-mauve (P 12) (28.7.71)	£100	2·50
		a. Mauve (*worn plate*) (3.73)	£100	2·25

9 9

NINEPENCE

(**21**)

1871 (22 Apr). No. 123*c* surch with T **21** in blue.

171	**16**	9d. on 10d. purple-brown/*pink*	£750	12·00
		a. Blackish brown/pink	£800	14·00
		b. Surch double	†	£2750
		c. Wmk sideways	†	—

22 **23** **24**

25 **26** **27**

(Des and eng W. Bell. Typo from electrotyped plates)

1873 (25 Mar)–**74**. Saunders paper. Wmk single-lined "10" as W **11**.

172	**25**	9d. pale brown/*pink* (P 13)	£190	40·00
		a. Red-brown/pink (7.74)	£180	38·00
173		9d. pale brown/*pink* (P 12)	£200	40·00

½ ½

HALF

(**28**)

1873 (25 Jun). No. 131*g* surch with T **28** in red.

174	**14**	½d. on 1d. green (P 13)	85·00	19·00
		a. Grass-green	90·00	19·00
		b. Short "1" at right (R. 1/3)	—	£100
		c. Mixed perf 13 and 12	†	—
175		½d. on 1d. green (P 12)	£110	19·00
		a. Grass-green	£110	19·00
		b. Short "1" at right (R. 1/3)	—	£100

Die I

Die II

Two Dies of 2d.:
Die I. Single-lined outer oval
Die II. Double-lined outer oval

(Des and eng W. Bell. Typo from electrotyped plates)

1873–**87**. Wmk V over Crown, W **19** (sideways on ½d.).

(a) P 13

176	**22**	½d. rose-red (10.2.74)	32·00	3·00
		a. Lilac-rose (1874)	32·00	3·25
		b. Rosine (*shades*) (*glazed paper*)	30·00	3·00
		c. Pale red (*glazed paper*) (1882)	32·00	3·00
		d. Mixed perf 13 and 12	†	£400
		e. Perf 12×13		
177	**23**	1d. *dull bluish green* (14.12.75)	65·00	2·50
		a. Green (*shades*) (1877)	65·00	2·50
		b. Yellow-green (*glazed paper*)	75·00	2·25
		c. Mixed perf 13 and 12		
178	**24**	2d. deep lilac-mauve (I) (1.10.73)	90·00	1·00
		a. Dull violet-mauve	90·00	1·00
		b. Dull mauve	90·00	1·00
		c. Pale mauve (*worn plate*) (*glazed paper*) (1.79)	90·00	1·25
		d. Mixed perf 13 and 12	£600	£375
179		2d. lilac-mauve (II) (*glazed paper*) (17.12.78)	85·00	1·25
		a. Grey-mauve (1.80)	—	2·75
		b. Pale mauve (6.80)	£110	2·75
		c. Vert pair, lower stamp imperf horiz	†	£3250
180	**26**	1s. indigo-blue/*blue* (16.8.76)	£140	4·50
		a. Wmk sideways	†	£750
		b. Deep blue/blue (7.77)	£150	3·75
		c. Pale blue/blue (3.80)	£150	4·50
		ca. Wmk sideways	†	£750
		d. Bright blue/blue (9.80)	£170	7·50
		e. Bright blue/blue (*glazed paper*) (21.11.83)	£170	5·00
		f. Pale blue/blue (*glazed paper*)		
		g. Mixed perf 13 and 12	†	—

(b) P 12

181	**22**	½d. rose-red (1874)	32·00	6·00
		a. Lilac-rose (1874)	32·00	6·00
		b. Rosine (*shades*) (*glazed paper*)	32·00	6·00
		c. Pale red (*glazed paper*) (1882)	32·00	6·00
182	**23**	1d. dull bluish green (1875)	75·00	9·00
		a. Green (*shades*) (1877)	70·00	11·00
		b. Yellow-green (*glazed paper*)	—	10·00
183	**24**	2d. deep lilac-mauve (I) (1873)	—	13·00
		a. Dull violet-mauve	—	13·00
		b. Dull mauve	£110	5·50
		c. Pale mauve (*worn plate*) (*glazed paper*) (1879)	£120	6·50
184		2d. lilac-mauve (II) (*glazed paper*) (1878)	£120	5·50
		a. Grey-mauve (*glazed paper*) (1880)	—	6·50
		b. Pale mauve (*glazed paper*) (1880)	—	8·00
185	**25**	9d. lilac-brown/*pink* (1.12.75)	£250	18·00
186	**26**	1s. deep blue/*blue* (1880)	—	7·50
		a. Bright blue/blue (1880)	—	7·50

(c) P 12½

187	**22**	½d. rosine (*shades*) (*glazed paper*) (1880)		
		a. Pale red (*glazed paper*) (1882)		
188	**23**	1d. yellow-green (*glazed paper*) (1880)		
189	**24**	2d. grey-mauve (II) (*glazed paper*) (1880)		
		a. Pale mauve (1880)		
190	**27**	2s. deep blue/*green* (*glazed paper*) (8.7.81)	£250	24·00
		a. Light blue/green (*glazed paper*) (4.83)		
		ab. Wmk sideways	£250	24·00
		b. Ultramarine/green (*glazed paper*) (6.84)	—	28·00
		ba. Wmk sideways	—	60·00

8d 8d

EIGHTPENCE

(**29**)

1876 (1 July). No. 185 surch with T **29** in blue.

191	**25**	8d. on 9d. lilac-brown/*pink*	£500	35·00
		a. "F.IGHTPENCE"	—	£500

No. 191a was caused by a broken "E" and it occurred once in each sheet of 120.

1877–79. Saunders paper. Wmk "10" as W **11**.

192	**14**	8d. lilac-brown/*pink* (P 13)	—	£500
		a. Purple-brown/pink (2.78)	£225	18·00
		b. Chocolate/pink (8.78)	†	£600
		c. Red-brown/pink (8.79)	£190	7·50
193		8d. red-brown/*pink* (P 12) (8.79)	£350	26·00
194		8d. red-brown/*pink* (P 12½) (8.79)	—	60·00

Nos. 192/4 occur amongst the V over Crown printings, the two types of pink paper having become mixed.

1878 (21 Feb–5 Apr). Emergency printings on coloured papers. Wmk V over Crown, W **19** (sideways on ½d.). P 13.

195	**22**	½d. rose-red/*pink* (1.3.78)	85·00	45·00
196	**23**	1d. yellow-green/*yellow* (5.3.78)	£150	35·00
197		1d. yellow-green/*drab* (5.4.78)	£275	70·00
198	**24**	2d. dull violet-mauve/*lilac* (21.2.78)	—	£1000
199		2d. dull violet-mauve/*green* (23.2.78)	£350	45·00
		a. Mixed perfs 12 and 13		
200		2d. dull violet-mauve/*brown* (21.3.78)	£325	45·00

There was a shortage of white V over Crown, W **19**, watermarked paper in the early months of 1878 and various coloured papers were used for printings of the ½d., 1d. and 2d. values until fresh stocks of white paper were received.

No. 198 is often misidentified. It can be confused with discoloured examples of Nos. 178/*b*, and has often been faked.

30

31

32

(Des and eng C. Naish. Typo from electrotyped plates)

1880 (3 Nov)–**84**. Wmk V over Crown. W **19**.

201	**30**	1d. green (P 12½) (2.84)	£170	25·00
202	**31**	2d. sepia (P 12½)	70·00	2·50
		a. Sepia-brown (2.81)	70·00	2·50
		b. Brown (aniline) (5.81)	70·00	2·50
		c. Dull black-brown (10.81)	—	2·50
		d. Dull grey-brown (3.82)	65·00	2·50
203		2d. sepia (P 13)		
		a. Mixed perf 13 and 12	†	£650
204		2d. sepia (P 12)	—	£150
		a. Sepia-brown (2.81)	—	£150
		b. Brown (aniline) (5.81)	—	£150
205		2d. mauve (*worn plate*) (P 12½) (2.84)	£375	15·00
206	**32**	4d. rose-carmine (P 12½) (10.81)	£110	8·00
		aa. Wmk sideways	†	—
		a. Rosine (7.82)	£110	7·50

Nos. 201 and 205 are subsequent printings of stamps first produced on watermark W **33**.

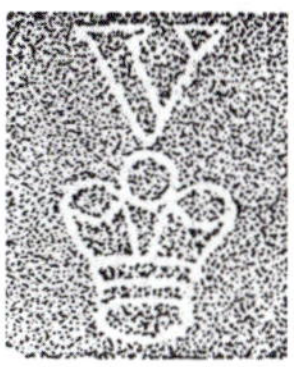
33

1882–84. Wmk V over Crown W **33** (sideways on ½d.). P 12½.

207	**22**	½d. rosine (3.83)	60·00	19·00
		a. Perf 12	—	40·00
208	**23**	1d. yellow-green (9.82)	75·00	6·50
		a. Perf 12		
209	**30**	1d. yellow-green (29.10.83)	75·00	4·75
		a. Green (1.84)	70·00	4·75
		b. Pale green (5.84)	70·00	3·00
210	**31**	2d. dull grey-brown (15.8.82)	55·00	2·25
		a. Chocolate (3.83)	55·00	2·25
		ab. Perf 12	†	£425
211		2d. mauve (20.12.83)	70·00	4·50
		a. Worn plate (2.84)	70·00	4·50
		b. Perf 12	†	£750
		c. Mixed perf 12 and 12½	†	£750
212	**15**	3d. yellow-orange (13.4.83)	£110	26·00
		a. Dull brownish orange	£110	35·00
213	**32**	4d. rose-red (3.83)	£110	16·00
214	**16**	6d. dull violet-blue (10.11.82)	90·00	6·00
		a. Indigo-blue (11.83)	90·00	6·00
		b. Light ultramarine (8.84)	90·00	8·00

Reprints were made in 1891 of the "Laureated" 1d., 2d., 3d. (in yellow), 4d., 6d., 8d. (in orange-yellow), 10d. (in greenish slate) and 5s. (in blue and red), of the Bell ½d., 1d., 2d. (Die II), 9d. and 1s. and of the Naish 2d. (in brown), 4d. (in pale red) and 2s. With the exception of the Bell 9d., which was watermarked W **19**, all were watermarked W **33** and perforated 12½. Some were from new plates.

THE POST OFFICE ACT OF 1883. Following official concern as to the number of different series of adhesive stamps, both fiscal and postal, used in Victoria it was decided that the system should be unified to the extent that the postage stamps, Stamp Statute fiscals and Stamp Duty fiscals should be replaced by a single series valid for all three purposes. As the Stamp Duty series contained the largest number of values it was adopted as the basis of the new range.

The regulations for the changeover were detailed in the Post Office Act of 1883 which came into force on 1 January 1884. From that date all existing Stamp Statute (first produced in 1871) and Stamp Duty (first produced in 1879) issues became valid for postal purposes, and the previous postage stamps could be used for fiscal fees.

Until matters could be organised printings of some of the existing postage values continued and these will be found included in the listings above.

Printing of the Stamp Statute series was discontinued in early 1884.

The existing Stamp Duty range was initially supplemented by postage stamps overprinted "STAMP DUTY" for those values where the available fiscal design was considered to be too large to be easily used on mail. These overprints were replaced by smaller designs inscribed "STAMP DUTY".

Stamp Statute and Stamp Duty values which became valid for postal purposes on 1 January 1884 have previously been listed in this catalogue as Postal Fiscals. Under the circumstances this distinction appears somewhat arbitrary and all such stamps are now shown in the main listing. Used prices quoted are for examples with postal cancellations. In some instances prices are also provided for fiscally used and these are marked "F.C.".

Nos. 215/92 were extensively used for fiscal purposes. Collectors are warned against the many examples of these stamps which have been cleaned and provided with fake gum or forged cancels.

In practice, many of these stamps are not known to exist in genuine unused or postally used condition and only fiscally cancelled examples are available. This applies especially to stamps of high face value such as Nos. 249/52.

34

35

36

37

(Des and dies eng J. Turner (3d., 2s.6d.), W. Bell (others). Typo from electrotypes)

1884 (1 Jan*). Stamp Statute series. Vert designs as T **34**/**6**, and others showing Queen Victoria within various frames, and T **37**. P 13.

*(a) Wmk single-lined numerals according to face value, as W **11**, (sideways). Paper manufactured by T. H. Saunders unless otherwise stated*

215	1s. blue/*blue*	£200	45·00
	a. Perf 12	£225	50·00
216	2s. blue/*green* (*D.L.R. paper*)	£275	£100
	a. Perf 12	£275	£100
217	2s. deep blue/*green*	£250	
	a. Perf 12	—	£100
	b. Wmk upright		
218	10s. brown-olive/*pink*		
219	10s. red-brown/*pink*	£2250	£400
	a. Wmk upright Perf 12		

*(b) Wmk V over Crown W **19** (sideways). P 13*

220	1d. pale green	£110	65·00
	a. Green (wmk upright) (P 12½)	£160	£100
221	3d. mauve	£1700	£500
222	4d. rose	£1200	£450
	a. Wmk upright	£1300	
223	6d. blue	£190	45·00
	a. Ultramarine	£160	35·00
	ab. Perf 12	£180	38·00
224	1s. blue/*blue*	£170	45·00
	a. Perf 12	£190	50·00
	b. Ultramarine/blue (P 12½)	—	80·00
	ba. Perf 12	—	65·00
	c. Deep blue/blue (P 12½)	£190	45·00
	ca. Perf 12	£200	45·00
225	2s. blue/*green*	£325	£100
	a. Perf 12	£325	
	b. Deep blue/blue-green (glazed paper)	£325	£110
	ba. Perf 12	£325	£120
226	2s.6d. orange	—	£275
	a. Perf 12		
	b. Yellow (glazed paper)	£1300	
	ba. Perf 12	£1300	£300
	c. Orange-yellow (glazed paper) (P 12½)	—	£300
	ca. Perf 12		
227	5s. blue/*yellow*	£650	£120
	a. Perf 12	£650	
	b. Wmk upright		
	ba. Perf 12		
	c. Ultramarine/lemon (glazed paper) (P 12½)	£700	£140
	ca. Wmk upright		
228	10s. brown/*pink*	£2250	£400

	a. Purple-brown/pink	£2250	£400
	ab. Perf 12	£2250	
229	£1 slate-violet/*yellow*	£2500	£425
	a. Wmk upright		
	b. Mauve/yellow		
	ba. Perf 12	£2500	£400
	bb. Perf 12½	£2500	£400
230	£5 black and yellow-green	£18000	
	a. Perf 12		
	b. Wmk upright. Perf 12½ (F.C. £425)	£18000	
	(c) Wmk V over Crown (sideways) W **33**		
231	1d. yellowish green (P 12½)	£120	£110
232	2s.6d. pale orange-yellow (P 12)	£1600	£300
233	£5 black and yellow-green (wmk upright) (P 12) (F.C. £325)	—	

½d

HALF

(**38**)

1884 (1 Jan*). No. 220 surch with T **38** in red.

234	½d. on 1d. pale green	£110	£100

*The dates quoted are those on which the stamps became valid for postal purposes. The ½d., 1d., 4d., 6d., 1s., 5s. and £1 were issued for fiscal purposes on 26 April 1871. The 10s. was added to the series in June 1871, the £5 in September 1871, the 2s.6d. in July 1876 and the 3d. in October 1879.

All values of the Stamp Statute series were reprinted in 1891 on paper watermarked W **19** (5s., 10s., £1) or W **33** (others). The £5 was pulled from the original plate, but the others were produced from new electrotypes taken from the original dies.

39

40

41

42

43

44

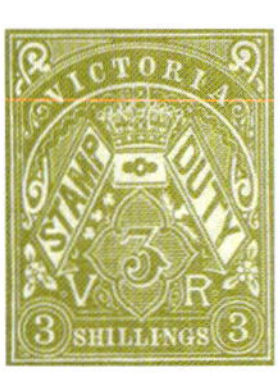

45

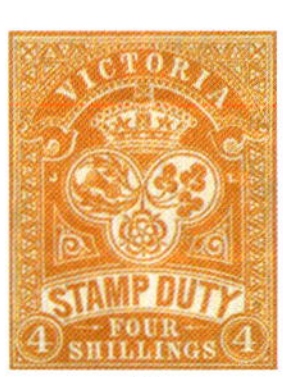

46

47

48

49

50

51

52

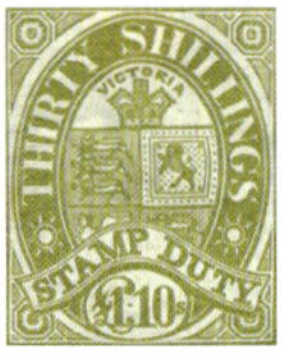

53

54

55

56

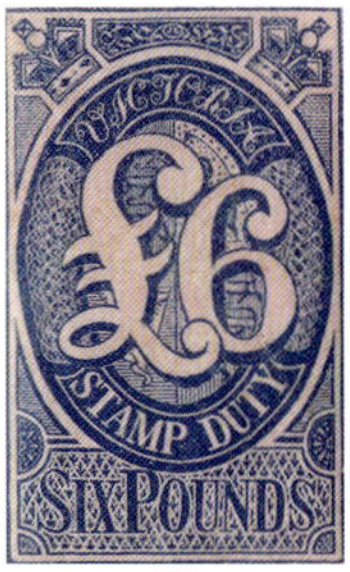

57

58

59

60

61

(Des H. Samson and F. Oxenbould

(T **39**), C. Jackson and L. Lang (all others except T **40**). Dies eng C. Jackson, J. Turner, J. Whipple, A. Williams and other employees of Sands & MacDougall. T **40** die eng C. Naish)

1884 (1 Jan*)–**96**. Existing Stamp Duty series.

(a) Litho. Wmk V over Crown. W **19** *(sideways). P 13*

235	**39**	1d. blue-green	£140	55·00
		a. Perf 12	£140	55·00
		b. Perf 12½		
236	**43**	1s.6d. rosine	£350	60·00
		a. Perf 12	—	70·00
		b. Perf 12½	£350	
237	**45**	3s. purple/*blue*	£850	90·00
		a. Perf 12	£850	90·00
		b. Perf 12½		
238	**46**	4s. orange-red	£170	22·00
		a. Perf 12	£170	22·00
		b. Perf 12½		
239	**48**	6s. apple-green	£500	70·00
		a. Perf 12½	£500	
240	**49**	10s. brown/*rose* (*glazed paper*)	£1600	£120
		a. Perf 12		
		b. Perf 12½		
		c. Wmk upright		
		cb. Perf 12½		
241	**50**	15s. mauve	£5500	£500
242	**51**	£1 red-orange	£1100	£110
		a. Perf 12½	£1100	£110
243	**52**	£1.5s. dull rose (wmk upright)	£4750	£500
244	**53**	£1.10s. deep grey-olive	£6000	£350
		a. Wmk upright	—	£375
245	–	35s. grey-violet (wmk upright) (F.C. £375)	£14000	
246	**54**	£2 blue	—	£225
247	**55**	45s. dull brown-lilac	£9500	£500
248	**56**	£5 rose-red (wmk upright) (F.C. £150)	£14000	£1600
249	**57**	£6 blue/*pink* (wmk upright) (*glazed paper*) (F.C. £200)	—	
250	**58**	£7 violet/*blue* (wmk upright) (F.C. £200)	—	
251	**59**	£8 brownish red/*yellow* (wmk upright) (*glazed paper*) (F.C. £200)	—	
252	**60**	£9 yellow-green/*green* (wmk upright) (*glazed paper*) (F.C. £200)	—	

(b) Typo from electrotypes

(i) Wmk V over Crown. W **19** *(sideways). P 13*

253	**39**	1d. yellowish green	£120	55·00
		a. Perf 12	£120	55·00
		b. Perf 12½	£120	
254	**40**	1d. pale bistre	65·00	12·00
		a. Perf 12	65·00	13·00
		b. Perf 12½		
255	**41**	6d. dull blue	£170	35·00
		a. Perf 12	£170	45·00
		b. Perf 12½		
256	**42**	1s. deep blue/*blue*	£200	7·50
		a. Perf 12	£200	12·00
		b. Perf 12½		
		c. *Bright blue/blue* (*glazed paper*) (P 12½)	£200	8·50
		ca. Perf 12	—	12·00
		d. *Ultramarine/blue* (*glazed paper*) (P 12½) (11.84)	£275	15·00
257		1s. chalky blue/*lemon* (*glazed paper*) (P 12½) (3.3.85)	£250	30·00
258	**44**	2s. deep blue/*green* (*glazed paper*)	£350	32·00
		a. Perf 12	—	42·00
		b. Perf 12½	£350	42·00
		c. *Indigo/green*	£325	42·00
		ca. Perf 12	£400	45·00
		cb. Perf 12½		
259	**45**	3s. maroon/*blue* (*glazed paper*) (P 12½) (8.8.84)	£700	70·00
260	**47**	5s. claret/*yellow* (*glazed paper*)	£110	7·00
		a. Perf 12	£130	19·00
		b. Perf 12½		
		c. *Pale claret/yellow* (P 12½)	£110	19·00
		ca. Perf 12	£140	20·00
		d. *Reddish purple/lemon* (P 12½) (6.87)	£100	14·00
		e. *Brown-red/yellow* (P 12½) (5.93)	£160	50·00
261	**49**	10s. chocolate/*rose* (*glazed paper*)	—	£120
		a. Perf 12		
		b. Perf 12½		
		c. Wmk upright		
262	**51**	£1 yellow-orange/*yellow* (P 12)	£1300	85·00
		a. *Orange/yellow* (P 12½) (8.84)	£1200	60·00
		b. *Reddish orange/yellow* (P 12½) (9.88)	£900	60·00
263	**54**	£2 deep blue (P 12)	—	£180
264	**61**	£10 dull mauve (P 12)		
		a. *Deep red-lilac* (P 12)	£15000	£400

(ii) Wmk V over Crown W **33** *(sideways). P 12½.*

265	**40**	1d. ochre	80·00	20·00
		a. Perf 12	80·00	20·00
266	**41**	6d. ultramarine	£170	38·00
		a. Perf 12	£170	38·00
267	**43**	1s.6d. pink (1.85)	£275	38·00
		a. *Bright rose-carmine* (4.86)	£300	24·00
268	**45**	3s. drab (20.10.85)	£130	16·00
		a. *Olive-drab* (1.93)	£120	16·00
269	**46**	4s. red-orange (5.86)	£130	16·00
		a. *Yellow-orange* (12.94)		
		ab. Wmk upright	£190	15·00
270	**47**	5s. rosine (8.5.96)	£150	20·00
271	**48**	6s. pea-green (12.11.91)	£275	65·00
		a. *Apple-green* (wmk upright)	£375	42·00
272	**49**	10s. dull bluish green (10.85)	£800	70·00
		a. *Grey-green* (5.86)	£700	38·00
273	**50**	15s. purple-brown (12.85)	£1600	£100
		a. *Brown* (wmk upright) (5.95)	£1500	£120
274	**52**	£1.5s. pink (wmk upright) (6.8.90)	£5000	£180
275	**53**	£1.10s. pale olive (6.88)	£5000	£160
276	**54**	£2 bright blue	£2000	£130
		a. *Blue* (7.88)	£1700	£130
277	**55**	45s. lilac (15.8.90)	£9500	£190
278	**56**	£5 rose-pink (P 12)	—	£1400
		a. *Pink* (P 12½)	—	£1500
279	**61**	£10 mauve (3.84)	£15000	£250
		a. *Lilac* (6.85)	—	£250

*This is the date on which the stamps became valid for postal use. The 1d., 6d., 1s., 1s.6d., 2s., 3s., 4s., 5s., 10s., 15s., £1, £1.10s., £2, £5 and £10 were issued for fiscal purposes on 18 December 1879 with the £1.5s., 35s., 45s., £6 and £9 added to the range later the same month and the 6s., £7 and £8 in January 1880.

Used prices for the £1.5s., £1.10s., £2 (No. 276*a*), 45s. and £10 watermarked W **33** are for examples from the cancelled-to-order sets sold to collectors by the Victoria postal authorities between September 1900 and 30 June 1902.

Similar Stamp Duty designs were prepared for 7s., 8s., 9s., 11s., 12s., 13s., 14s., 16s., 17s., 18s., and 19s., but were never issued.

The two different 1d. designs were reprinted in 1891 on W **33** paper. For these designs with later watermarks see Nos. 345/50 and 369/71.

62

(Des C. Jackson and L. Lang. Dies eng C. Jackson)

1884 (1 Jan*)–**00**. High value Stamp Duty series.

(a) Recess-printed direct from the die

(i) Wmk V over Crown W **19** *(sideways). P 12½*

280	**62**	£25 yellow-green (F.C. £140)		
		a. Wmk upright		
		b. Perf 13		
		c. *Deep green* (F.C. £140)		
		ca. Wmk upright		
281		£50 bright mauve (F.C. £200)		
		a. Wmk upright		
		b. Perf 13		
282		£100 crimson-lake (F.C. £300)		
		a. Wmk upright		
		b. Perf 13		

(ii) Wmk V over Crown W **33** *(sideways). P 12½*

283	**62**	£25 yellow-green		
		a. Perf 12		
		b. *Deep green* (1.85) (F.C. £140)	£60000	£1300
		c. *Bright blue-green* (10.90) (F.C. £140)		
		ca. Wmk upright		
284		£50 dull lilac-mauve (wmk upright) (F.C. £180)		
		a. *Black-violet* (10.90) (F.C. £160)	£70000	£1300
		ab. Wmk upright		
285		£100 crimson (F.C. £300)		
		a. Wmk upright		
		b. Perf 12 (F.C. £300)		
		c. *Aniline crimson* (wmk upright) (2.85) (F.C. £300)	£80000	£1600
		d. *Scarlet-red* (5.95)	—	£1600
		da. Wmk upright	—	£1500

(b) Litho. Wmk V over Crown W **33** *(sideways). P 12½*

286	**62**	£25 dull yellowish green (1.86) (F.C. £100)		
		a. Wmk upright (11.87)		
		b. *Dull blue-green* (9.88) (F.C. £100)		
		ba. Wmk upright		
287		£50 dull purple (1.86) (F.C. £120)		
		a. Wmk upright		
		b. *Bright violet* (11.89) (F.C. £120)		
		ba. Wmk upright		
288		£100 rosine (1.86) (F.C. £200)		
		a. Wmk upright		

(c) Typo from electrotyped plates. Wmk V over Crown. W **33**. *P 12½*

289	**62**	£25 dull blue-green (12.97)	—	£500
290		£50 bright mauve (10.97)	—	£600
291		£100 pink-red (10.1900)	—	£950

*This is the date on which the stamps became valid for postal use. All three values were issued for fiscal purposes on 18 December 1879.

Used prices for Nos. 283*b*, 284*a*, 285*c/d* and 289/91 are for examples from the cancelled-to-order sets described beneath No. 279*a*. "F.C." indicates that the price quoted is for a stamp with a fiscal cancellation.

For the £25 and £50 with watermark W **82** see Nos. 351/2.

63

(Des and die eng C. Naish. Typo from electrotyped plates)

1884 (23 Apr)–**92**. New design inscr "STAMP DUTY". Wmk V over Crown, W **33** (sideways). P 12½.

292	**63**	2s.6d. brown-orange	£180	29·00
		a. Yellow (8.85)	£140	15·00
		b. Lemon-yellow (2.92)	£140	23·00

For this design on later watermarks see Nos. 344 and 370.

64

65

66

67

68

(Des and dies eng C. Naish. Typo from electrotyped plates)

1885 (1 Jan)–**95**. New designs inscr "STAMP DUTY". P 12½.

(a) W **19**

293	**68**	8d. rose/*pink*	50·00	11·00
		a. Rose-red/pink (2.88)	50·00	11·00
294	**66**	1s. deep dull blue/*lemon* (11.85)	£170	18·00
		a. Dull blue/yellow (6.86)	£170	19·00
295	**68**	2s. olive/*bluish green* (12.85)	£140	6·50

(b) W **33**

296	**64**	½d. pale rosine	30·00	2·75
		a. Deep rosine (7.85)	35·00	3·25
		b. Salmon (9.85)	35·00	3·25
297	**65**	1d. yellowish green (1.85)	29·00	3·50
		a. Dull pea-green (2.85)	29·00	3·50
298	**66**	2d. lilac	48·00	2·50
		a. Mauve (1886)	48·00	2·50
		b. Rosy-mauve (1886)	55·00	2·50
299	**65**	3d. yellowish brown	55·00	3·50
		a. Pale ochre (9.86)	12·00	2·25
		b. Bistre-yellow (9.92)	12·00	2·25
300	**67**	4d. magenta	£110	7·00
		a. Bright mauve-rose (12.86)	£110	7·50
		b. Error. *Lilac* (12.86)	£7500	£1400
301	**65**	6d. chalky blue (1.85)	£160	9·50
		a. Bright blue (3.85)	£120	8·50
		b. Cobalt (7.85)	£120	4·50
302	**68**	8d. bright scarlet/*pink* (3.95)	32·00	16·00
303		2s. olive-green/*pale green* (1.90)	55·00	7·00
304		2s. apple-green (12.8.95)	32·00	90·00
		a. Blue-green (29.10.95)	22·00	29·00

The plates for the 1d., 6d., 1s. and 2s. were derived from the dies of the 2d. (1s.), 3d. (1d. and 6d.) and 8d. (2s.). In each instance lead moulds of six impressions were taken from the original die and the face values altered by hand creating six slightly different versions.

Two states of the 2d. die exist with the second showing a break in the top frame line near the right-hand corner. This damaged die was used for seven impressions on Plate 1 and all 120 on Plate 2.

No. 300b occurred during the December 1886 printing of the 4d. when about fifty sheets were printed in the colour of the 2d. by mistake. The sheets were issued to Melbourne post offices and used examples are known postmarked between 21 December 1886 and 4 March 1887. Nine unused are also believed to exist.

Reprints of the ½d., 1d., 2d., 4d., 6d. and 1s. values were made in 1891 from the existing plates. The 1s. was watermarked W **19** and the remainder W **33**.

For some of these values used with later watermarks see Nos. 336, 343, 361 and 369.

STAMP DUTY

(69)

1885 (Feb–Nov). Optd with T **69**. P 12½.

(a) W **19**

305	**15**	3d. dull orange-yellow (*glazed paper*) (B.) (Nov)	—	£850
306	**26**	1s. pale blue/*blue* (*glazed paper*) (P 13)	£130	48·00
		a. Deep blue/*blue*	—	50·00
		b. Blue opt (F.C. £350)	£4500	£1800
307	**27**	2s. ultramarine/*green* (*glazed paper*) (Mar)	£180	19·00
		a. Wmk sideways	£200	26·00

(b) W **33**

308	**15**	3d. yellow-orange (B.) (Nov)	70·00	55·00
		a. Dull brownish orange (B.)	75·00	55·00
309	**32**	4d. rose-red (B.) (Nov)	60·00	80·00

Unauthorised reprints of the 4d. and 1s., both with blue overprints and watermarked W **33**, were made during 1895–96. The 4d. reprint, which is in pale red, also exists without the overprint.

70

71

72

73

74

75

76

77

78

79

80

(Des S. Reading (1d.) (No. 313), M. Tannenberg (2½d., 5d.), C. Naish (1s.6d.), P. Astley (others). Dies eng C. Naish (2d., 4d. (both existing dies with lines added behind Queen's head) and 1s.6d.), S. Reading (originally as an employee of Fergusson & Mitchell) (others). Typo from electrotyped plates)

1886 (26 July)–**96**. W **33** (sideways on ½d., 1s., £5, £7 to £9). P 12½.

310	**70**	½d. lilac-grey (28.8.86)	40·00	12·00
		a. Grey-black	—	45·00
311		½d. pink (15.2.87)	38·00	2·25
		a. Rosine (*aniline*) (1889)	18·00	1·25
		b. Rose-red (1891)	14·00	1·00
		c. Vermilion (1896)	18·00	3·00
312	**71**	1d. green	20·00	3·75
		a. Yellow-green (1887)	20·00	3·75

313	**72**	1d. dull chestnut (1.1.90)	29·00	2·50
		a. Deep red-brown (1890)	29·00	2·50
		b. Orange-brown (1890)	29·00	75
		c. Brown-red (1890)	29·00	75
		d. Yellow-brown (1891)	29·00	50
		e. Bright yellow-orange	£110	32·00
		f. Brownish orange (1894)	14·00	40
314	**73**	2d. pale lilac (17.12.86)	35·00	50
		a. Pale mauve (1887)	40·00	30
		b. Deep lilac (1888, 1892)	17·00	30
		c. Purple (1894)	12·00	40
		d. Violet (1895)	12·00	40
		e. Imperf	—	£1000
315	**74**	2½d. red-brown/*lemon* (1.1.91)	38·00	4·00
		a. Brown-red/yellow (1892)	28·00	1·00
		b. Red/yellow (1893)	23·00	70
316	**75**	4d. rose-red (1.4.87)	55·00	1·25
		a. Red (1893)	26·00	1·25
317	**76**	5d. purple-brown (1.1.91)	35·00	3·50
		a. Pale reddish brown (1893)	14·00	3·25
318	**77**	6d. bright ultramarine (27.8.86)	60·00	5·00
		a. Pale ultramarine (1887)	42·00	60
		b. Dull blue (1891)	38·00	75
319	**25**	9d. apple-green (18.10.92)	30·00	15·00
320		9d. carmine-rose (15.10.95)	70·00	26·00
		a. Rosine (aniline) (1896)	70·00	24·00
321	**78**	1s. dull purple-brown (14.3.87)	£120	5·00
		a. Lake (1890)	95·00	6·00
		b. Carmine-lake (1892)	55·00	3·75
		c. Brownish red (1896)	55·00	7·00
322	**79**	1s.6d. pale blue (9.88)	£180	80·00
323		1s.6d. orange (19.9.89)	38·00	25·00
		a. Red-orange (1893)	38·00	13·00
324	**80**	£5 pale blue and maroon (7.2.88)†	£10000	£170
325		£6 yellow and pale blue (1.10.87)†	£11000	£190
326		£7 rosine and black (17.10.89)†	£12000	£225
327		£8 mauve and brown-orange (2.8.90)†	£13000	£275
328		£9 apple-green and rosine (21.8.88)†	£14000	£300

†The used prices provided for these stamps are for cancelled-to-order examples.

Unauthorised reprints of the ½d. lilac-grey and 1s.6d. pale blue were made in 1894–95 on W **33** paper and perforated 12½. These differ in shade from the originals and have rougher perforations. It should be noted that the original printing of No. 322 does not occur with inverted watermark, but the reprint does.

A single example of No. 314e is known postmarked "737" (Foster). A second, postmarked "249" (Mortlake), was reported in 1892. It is known that an imperforate sheet was sold at Mortlake P.O. in 1890. Other examples are believed to be clandestine.

Later printings of the £5 to £9 values, as No. 324/8 but on W **85** paper perforated 12½ or 11, were not valid for postal use (*Unused prices, £275 for £5 value, from £400 for £6 to £9 values*).

A £10 value as Type **80** was prepared, but not issued.

1891 (17 Jun). W **19**. P 12½.

329	**72**	1d. orange-brown/*pink*	17·00	4·50

No. 329 was an emergency printing during a shortage of white W **33** paper.

81

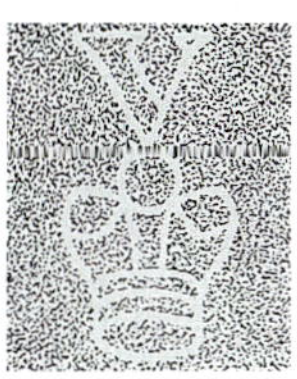
82

(Die eng A. Williams (1½d.). Typo from electrotyped plates).

1896 (11 Jun)–**99**. W **82** (sideways on ½d., 1½d., 1s., 2s.6d. to 15s.). P 12½.

330	**70**	½d. light scarlet (1.7.96)	10·00	5·00
		a. Carmine-rose (1897)	10·00	3·25
		b. Deep carmine-red (coarse impression) (1899)	—	6·50
		c. Wmk upright	£110	65·00
331		½d. emerald (1.8.99)	32·00	8·50
		a. Wmk upright	†	£100
332	**72**	1d. brown-red (13.6.96)	14·00	1·00
		a. Brownish orange (1897)	11·00	10
		b. Wmk sideways	†	—
333	**81**	1½d. apple-green (7.10.97)	3·00	8·00
334	**73**	2d. violet	27·00	50
		a. Wmk sideways	†	90·00
335	**74**	2½d. blue (1.8.99)	25·00	28·00
336	**65**	3d. ochre (11.96)	23·00	2·75
		a. Buff (1898)	13·00	2·75
		b. Wmk sideways	†	—
337	**75**	4d. red (6.97)	50·00	11·00
338	**76**	5d. red-brown (7.97)	38·00	2·25
339	**77**	6d. dull blue (9.96)	35·00	1·25
340	**25**	9d. rosine (8.96)	70·00	7·00
		a. Rose-carmine (1898)	—	7·00
		b. Dull rose (1898)	42·00	7·00
		c. Wmk sideways		
341	**78**	1s. brownish red (3.97)	35·00	4·75
		a. Wmk upright	—	—
342	**79**	1s.6d. brown-orange (8.98)	85·00	60·00
343	**68**	2s. blue-green (4.97)	85·00	16·00
344	**63**	2s.6d. yellow (9.96)	£160	22·00
		a. Wmk upright (1898)	£180	22·00
345	**45**	3s. olive-drab (12.96)	£110	32·00
		a. Wmk upright (1898)	£110	32·00
346	**46**	4s. orange (9.97)	£150	18·00
347	**47**	5s. rosine (2.97)	£160	24·00
		a. Rose-carmine (1897)	£160	24·00
		b. Wmk upright. *Rosine* (1899)	£160	27·00
348	**48**	6s. pale yellow-green (4.99)†	£200	40·00
349	**49**	10s. grey-green (4.97)	£800	48·00
		a. Blue-green (1898)	£800	26·00
350	**50**	15s. brown (4.97)†	£800	85·00
351	**62**	£25 dull bluish green (1897)†	—	£350
352		£50 dull purple (1897)†	—	£500

†The used prices provided for these stamps are for cancelled-to-order examples.

83

84

(Des M. Tannenberg. Dies eng A. Mitchelhill. Typo from electrotyped plates)

1897 (22 Oct). Diamond Jubilee and Hospital Charity Fund. W **82** (sideways). P 12½.

353	**83**	1d. (1s.) blue	20·00	23·00
354	**84**	2½d. (2s.6d) red-brown	£130	80·00
353s/4s		Optd "Specimen" *Set of 2*	£200	

These stamps were sold at 1s. and 2s.6d., but only had postal validity for 1d. and 2½d. with the difference going to the Fund.

1899 (1 Aug). W **33** (sideways). P 12½.

355	**81**	1½d. brown-red/*yellow*	4·75	6·50

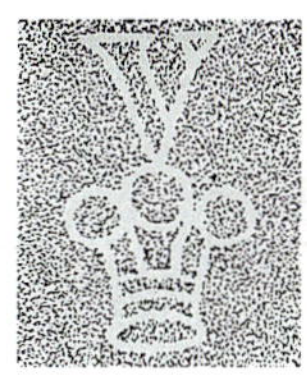
85

1899 (1 Aug)–**1901**. W **85** (sideways on ½d., 1s. and 2s.6d. to 10s.). P 12½.

356	**70**	½d. emerald	5·00	3·50
		a. Deep blue-green	6·50	2·25
		b. Wmk upright	—	13·00
357	**72**	1d. rose-red	15·00	1·00
		a. Rosine (1900)	6·00	10
		b. Wmk sideways	—	—
358		1d. olive (6.6.01)	13·00	4·00
359	**73**	2d. violet	40·00	1·25
		a. Wmk sideways	†	—
360	**74**	2½d. blue (10.99)	48·00	3·00
361	**65**	3d. bistre-yellow (9.99)	7·50	8·50
		a. Wmk sideways	†	—
362		3d. slate-green (20.6.01)	40·00	22·00
363	**75**	4d. rose-red (12.99)	27·00	9·50
364	**76**	5d. red-brown (10.99)	45·00	9·50
365	**77**	6d. dull ultramarine (1.00)	38·00	9·00
366	**25**	9d. rose-red (9.99)	22·00	3·75
		a. Wmk sideways		
367	**78**	1s. brown-red (5.00)	38·00	11·00
368	**79**	1s.6d. orange (2.00)	35·00	60·00
369	**68**	2s. blue-green (6.00)	45·00	45·00
370	**63**	2s.6d. yellow (1.00)	£550	35·00
371	**45**	3s. pale olive (4.00)†	£225	48·00
372	**47**	5s. rose-red (4.00)	£180	48·00
373	**49**	10s. green (3.00)†	£750	48·00

†The used prices provided for these stamps are for cancelled-to-order examples.

From 1 July 1901 stamps inscribed "STAMP DUTY" could only be used for fiscal purposes.

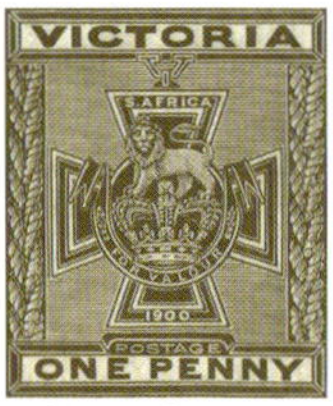

86 Victoria Cross

87 Australian Troops in South Africa

(Des Sands and MacDougall (1d.), J. Sutherland (2d.). Dies eng S. Reading. Typo from electrotyped plates)

1900 (22 May). Anglo-Boer War Patriotic Fund. W **85** (sideways). P 12½.

374	**86**	1d. (1s.) olive-brown	£150	85·00
375	**87**	2d. (2s.) emerald-green	£275	£225

These stamps were sold at 1s. and 2s., but only had postal validity for 1d. and 2d. with the difference going to the Fund.

FEDERATION. The six Australian colonies were federated as the Commonwealth of Australia on 1 January 1901. Under the terms of the Post and Telegraph Act their postal services were amalgamated on 1 March 1901, but other clauses to safeguard the financial position of the individual States provided them with a large degree of independence until 13 October 1910 when issues of each state could be used throughout Australia. Postage stamps for the Commonwealth of Australia did not appear until January 1913.

It was agreed in 1901 that stamp printing should be centralised at Melbourne under J. B. Cooke of South Australia who was appointed Commonwealth Stamp Printer. By 1909 the Commonwealth Stamp Printing Branch in Melbourne was producing stamps for Papua, South Australia, Tasmania and Western Australia in addition to those of Victoria.

On federation it was decided to separate postal and fiscal stamp issues so Victoria needed urgent replacements for the current Stamp Duty series which reverted to fiscal use only on 30 June 1901.

1901 (29 Jan). Re-use of previous designs without "POSTAGE" inscr. W **82** (2s.) or W **85** (others) (sideways on ½d.). P 12×12½.

376	**22**	½d. bluish green	2·50	3·50
		a. "VICTCRIA" (R. 7/19)	42·00	60·00
377	**31**	2d. reddish violet	15·00	4·75
378	**15**	3d. dull orange	15·00	5·00
379	**32**	4d. bistre-yellow	25·00	29·00
380	**16**	6d. emerald	13·00	16·00
381	**26**	1s. yellow	80·00	48·00
382	**27**	2s. blue/*pink*	42·00	75·00
383	**18**	5s. pale red and deep blue	55·00	80·00

88

89

90

91

92

93

94

95

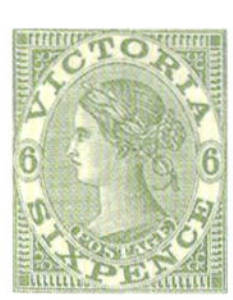

96

97

98

99

100

101

102

I II III

Three die states of ½d.:

I. Outer vertical line of colour to left of "V" continuous except for a break opposite the top of "V". Triangles either end of "VICTORIA" are more or less solid colour.

II. Die re-engraved. Three breaks in outer line of colour left of "V". White lines added to left triangle.

III. Die re-engraved. As II, but equivalent triangle at right also contains white lines.

I

II

III

I and II III

Three die states of 1d.:

I. Thick lines fill top of oval above Queen's head.

II. Die re-engraved. Lines thinner, showing white space between.

III. Die re-engraved. As II, but with bottom left value tablet recut to show full point separated from both "1" and the circular frame.

Two die states of 2d.:

I. Frame line complete at top right corner. Bottom right corner comes to a point.

II. Break in right frame line just below the top corner. Bottom right corner is blunted.

Two types of 1s.:

A. "POSTAGE" 6 mm long (produced by a hand punch applied twice to each impression on the previous 1s. electrotyped plate. Slight variations in position occur).

B. "POSTAGE" 7 mm long (produced from new electrotyped plates incorporating the "POSTAGE" inscriptions).

(Eng S. Reading after photo by W. Stuart (£1, £2))

1901 (29 Jan)–**10**. Previous issues with "POSTAGE" added and new designs (£1, £2). W **85** (sideways on ½d., 1½d., £1, £2).

(a) P 12×12½ (½d. to 2s.) or 12½ (½d., 5s. to £2)

384	**88**	½d. blue-green (I) (26.6.01)	7·50	1·00
		a. Wmk upright (1903)	3·25	3·00
		b. Die state II (6.04)	14·00	2·00
		ba. Wmk upright	14·00	1·75
		c. Die state III (6.05)	24·00	3·25
385	**89**	1d. rose (I)	21·00	1·75
		a. Dull red (12.02)	21·00	1·75
		ab. Wmk sideways	£200	75·00
		b. Die state II (4.01)	6·50	15
		ba. Dull red (12.02)	7·50	15
		bb. Wmk sideways	£200	75·00
		c. Die state III. *Pale rose-red*	6·00	3·00
		ca. Wmk sideways	60·00	60·00
386	**90**	1½d. maroon/*yellow* (9.7.01)	12·00	10·00
		a. Wmk upright. *Brown-red/yellow* (9.01)	4·75	55
		b. Dull red-brown/yellow (1906)	3·00	1·00
		ba. *On yellow-buff back* (1908)	3·75	1·50
387	**91**	2d. lilac (I) (26.6.01)	25·00	2·00
		a. Die state II	50·00	4·50
		b. Reddish violet (1902)	28·00	1·00
		ba. Die state II	55·00	3·25
		c. Bright purple (II) (1905)	9·00	1·25
		d. Rosy mauve (II) (1905)		
		e. Wmk sideways	42·00	
388	**92**	2½d. dull blue	15·00	40
		a. Deep blue (1902)	13·00	40
		b. Wmk sideways	†	£950
389	**93**	3d. dull orange-brown (5.7.01)	17·00	2·75
		a. Chestnut (1901)	19·00	1·00
		b. Yellowish brown (1903)	20·00	1·00
		ba. Wmk sideways	21·00	35·00
390	**94**	4d. bistre-yellow (26.6.01)	9·50	1·00
		a. Brownish bistre (1905)	13·00	2·25
391	**95**	5d. reddish brown	21·00	1·00
		a. Purple-brown (1903)	14·00	1·75
392	**96**	6d. emerald (5.7.01)	12·00	1·00
		a. Dull green (1904)	15·00	2·50
393	**97**	9d. dull rose-red (5.7.01)	28·00	4·00
		a. Wmk sideways (1901)	50·00	35·00
		b. Pale red (1901)	19·00	2·00
		c. Dull brownish red (1905)	38·00	7·00
394	**98**	1s. yellow-orange (A) (5.7.01)	35·00	3·50
		a. Yellow (1902)	24·00	2·75
		b. Type B (4.03)	23·00	3·50
		ba. Orange (1904)	21·00	3·00
		bb. Wmk sideways (1905)	75·00	35·00
395	**99**	2s. blue/*rose* (5.7.01)	30·00	2·00
		a. Wmk sideways	£1200	£1000
398	**100**	5s. rose-red and pale blue (5.7.01)	60·00	25·00
		a. Scarlet and deep blue	70·00	25·00
		b. Rosine and blue (12.04)	70·00	25·00
399	**101**	£1 carmine-rose (18.11.01)	£350	£130
400	**102**	£2 deep blue (2.6.02)	£750	£300

(b) P 11

401	**88**	½d. blue-green (I) (9.02)	22·00	8·50
		a. Wmk upright (1903)	3·25	4·75
		b. Die state II (6.04)	19·00	5·00
		ba. Wmk upright	19·00	7·00
		c. Die state III (6.05)	22·00	6·00
402	**89**	1d. dull red (I) (12.02)	90·00	50·00
		a. Die state II	28·00	11·00
		ab. Pale red (aniline) (3.03)	26·00	4·50
		ac. Pale rose (aniline) (1904)	48·00	9·00
		b. Die state III. *Pale rose-red* (7.05)	90·00	50·00
403	**90**	1½d. dull red-brown/*yellow* (1910)	£160	£100
404	**91**	2d. bright purple (II) (1905)	£750	£300
		a. Rosy mauve (II) (1905)	†	£250
405	**93**	3d. yellowish brown (1903)	5·50	16·00
		a. Wmk sideways	27·00	65·00
406	**96**	6d. emerald (2.03)	12·00	26·00
		a. Dull green (1905)	£1000	£550
407	**101**	£1 rose (5.05)	£375	£170
408	**102**	£2 deep blue (1905)	£2000	£1400

(c) Compound or mixed perfs of 12×12½ or 12½ and 11

409	**88**	½d. blue-green (I) (1901)	60·00	18·00
		a. Wmk upright (1903)	60·00	21·00
		b. Die state II (1904)	60·00	42·00
		ba. Wmk upright	65·00	50·00
410	**89**	1d. dull red (I) (1902)	—	£450
		a. Die state II	£900	£225
411	**90**	1½d. maroon/*yellow* (1903)	£1300	£800
412	**91**	2d. reddish violet (I) (1903)	†	£1200
413	**93**	3d. dull orange-brown (1902)	—	£1400
414	**96**	6d. emerald (1903)	†	£1400
415	**100**	5s. rosine and blue (12.04)	£3500	

Examples of the 1d. Die state II perforated 12×12½ exist with two black lines printed across the face of the stamp. These were prepared in connection with stamp-vending machine trials.

WATERMARK VARIETIES: The attention of collectors is drawn to the note on inverted and reversed watermarks on the stamps of the Australian States at the top of the Australia listings.

1905–**13**. Wmk Crown over A, W w **11** (sideways on ½d., £1, £2).

(a) P 12×12½ (½d. to 1s.) or 12½ (½d., 1d., 2½d., 6d., 5s. to £2)

416	**88**	½d. blue-green (*shades*) (III) (21.10.05).	4·25	1·75
		a. Wmk upright	15·00	8·00
		b. Thin, ready gummed paper (6.12)	5·00	12·00
		ba. Wmk upright	5·00	13·00
417	**89**	1d. rose-red (III) (16.7.05)	5·00	25
		a. Pale rose (1907)	2·00	10
		b. Rose-carmine (1911)	11·00	3·50
		c. Wmk sideways	14·00	10·00
		d. Thin, ready gummed paper (10.12)	4·50	5·00
418	**91**	2d. dull mauve (II) (13.9.05)	6·00	1·75
		a. Lilac (1906)	10·00	1·75
		b. Reddish violet (1907)	9·50	25
		c. Bright mauve (1910)	5·50	1·25
		ca. Thin, ready gummed paper (8.12)	42·00	8·00
419	**92**	2½d. deep dull blue (10.08)	5·00	1·75
		a. Dull blue (11.09)	3·00	40
		b. Indigo (7.09)	27·00	4·75
420	**93**	3d. orange-brown (11.11.05)	22·00	1·25
		a. Yellow-orange (1908)	17·00	3·50
		b. Dull orange-buff (1909)	8·00	1·25
		c. Ochre (1912)	8·00	14·00
421	**94**	4d. yellow-bistre (15.1.06)	8·50	65
		a. Olive-bistre (1908)	8·00	65
		b. Yellow-olive (1912)	7·00	3·75
422	**95**	5d. chocolate (14.8.06)	8·00	8·50
		a. Dull reddish brown (1908)	7·00	6·50
		b. Wmk sideways	†	£850
		c. Thin, ready gummed paper (19.10.12)	13·00	24·00
423	**96**	6d. dull green (25.10.05)	25·00	80
		a. Dull yellow-green (1907)	15·00	80
		b. Emerald (1909)	15·00	1·10
		c. Yellowish green (1911)	18·00	5·50
		d. Emerald. Thin, ready gummed paper (11.12)	35·00	45·00
424	**97**	9d. brown-red (11.12.05)	38·00	9·00
		a. Orange-brown (1906)	32·00	9·00
		b. Red-brown (1908)	48·00	10·00
		c. Pale dull rose (1909)	20·00	10·00
		d. Rose-carmine (1910)	13·00	3·00
		e. Wmk sideways	£325	95·00
425	**98**	1s. orange (B) (13.2.06)	11·00	2·00
		a. Yellow-orange (1906)	11·00	2·00
		b. Yellow (1908)	17·00	2·00
		ba. Thin, ready gummed paper (11.12)	30·00	25·00
		c. Pale orange. Thin, ready gummed paper (1913)	30·00	50·00
430	**100**	5s. rose-red and ultramarine (12.07)	80·00	28·00
		a. Rose-red and blue (1911)	90·00	48·00
		ab. Wmk sideways	£120	50·00
431	**101**	£1 salmon (12.2.07)	£350	£140
		a. Dull rose (1910)	£350	£140
		ab. Wmk upright (1911)	£375	£160
432	**102**	£2 dull blue (18.7.06)	£750	£425

(b) P 11

433	**88**	½d. blue-green (*shades*) (III) (1905)	1·60	30
		a. Wmk upright. Thin, ready gummed paper (1912)	23·00	32·00
434	**89**	1d. rose-red (III) (1905)	8·50	3·00
		a. Pale rose (1907)	4·00	2·75
		b. Rose-carmine (1911)	7·00	8·00
		ba. Wmk sideways	35·00	30·00
		c. Thin, ready gummed paper (10.12)	16·00	5·50
435	**91**	2d. lilac (II) (1906)	†	£375
		a. Reddish violet (1907)	85·00	26·00
		b. Bright mauve (1910)	35·00	26·00
436	**92**	2½d. blue (1908)	60·00	32·00
		a. Indigo (1909)	20·00	25·00
437	**93**	3d. orange-brown (1905)	10·00	19·00
		a. Yellow-orange (1908)	†	£200
		b. Dull orange-buff (1909)	15·00	26·00
		c. Ochre (1912)	9·00	18·00
		d. Wmk sideways	†	£300
438	**94**	4d. yellow-bistre (1906)	15·00	28·00
		a. Olive-bistre (1909)		
		b. Yellow-olive (1912)	8·50	28·00
439	**95**	5d. chocolate (1906)	†	£1400
		a. Dull reddish brown (1908)	†	£1400
440	**96**	6d. emerald (1909)	10·00	26·00
		a. Yellowish green (1911)	21·00	38·00
441	**97**	9d. rose-carmine (1910)	†	£1200
442	**98**	1s. yellow-orange (B) (1906)	†	£375
		a. Orange (1910)	£1400	
443	**100**	5s. rose-red and ultramarine (12.07)	85·00	11·00

444	**101**	£1 salmon (12.2.07)	£475	£170
445	**102**	£2 dull blue (1.07)	£1300	£600
		(c) Compound or mixed perfs of 12×12½ or 12½ and 11		
446	**88**	½d. blue-green (*shades*) (III) (1905)	28·00	18·00
		a. Wmk upright. Thin, ready gummed paper (1912)	£200	£160
447	**89**	1d. rose-red (III) (1905)	95·00	80·00
		a. Pale rose (1907)	—	80·00
		b. Rose-carmine (1911)	—	80·00
448	**91**	2d. reddish violet (II) (1907)	£650	£375
449	**93**	3d. orange-brown (1905)	†	£1200
		a. Ochre (1912)	£650	
450	**94**	4d. bistre (1908)	†	£1500
451	**96**	6d. emerald (1909)	—	£1500
		a. Yellowish green (1911)	†	£850
452	**97**	9d. orange-brown (1906)	†	£1600
		a. Red-brown (1908)	†	£1600
453	**98**	1s. yellow-orange (1906)	£1900	
453*a*		£1 dull rose	†	£12000
		(d) Rotary comb perf 11½×12¼		
454		1d. scarlet-red	4·50	1·75
		a. Thin, ready gummed paper *Rose-carmine*	2·75	4·75
		ab. Rose-red	2·75	4·75
		ac. Wmk sideways	35·00	28·00
455	**91**	2d. lilac (II) (1910)	42·00	2·50

The original Crown over A watermark paper used by Victoria was of medium thickness and had toned gum applied after printing. Stocks of this paper lasted until 1912 when further supplies were ordered from a new papermakers, probably W. Joynson and Son. This paper was much thinner and was supplied with white gum already applied. The first delivery arrived in June 1912 and a second in September of the same year.

The rotary comb perforating machine gauging 11½×12¼ was transferred from South Australia in 1909 when J. B. Cooke moved to Melbourne.

Examples of the 1d. perforated 12½ or 11 exist with two black lines across the face of the stamp. These were prepared in connection with stamp-vending machine trials.

ONE PENNY

(**103**)

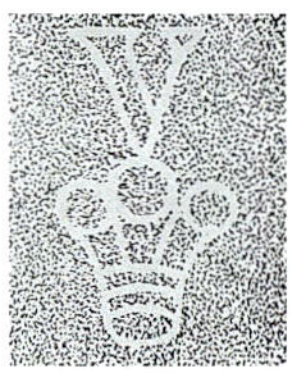

104

1912 (29 June). No. 455 surch with T **103** in red.

456	**91**	1d. on 2d. lilac (II)	1·00	60

1912 (1 Aug–Sept). W **104**.

		(a) P 12½ (½d.) or 12×12½		
457	**88**	½d. bluish green (III)	3·00	9·50
458	**89**	1d. rose-carmine (III)	6·00	6·50
		a. Wmk sideways	50·00	50·00
459	**91**	2d. reddish violet (II) (Sept)	3·00	8·50
		a. Lilac	6·50	13·00
460	**97**	9d. rose-carmine	32·00	45·00
		(b) P 11		
461	**88**	½d. bluish green (III)	20·00	45·00
462	**89**	1d. rose-carmine (III)	50·00	30·00
		a. Wmk sideways	£120	£120
463	**97**	9d. rose-carmine	50·00	75·00
		(c) Compound perfs of 12×12½ or 12½ and 11		
464	**97**	9d. rose-carmine	†	£1700

Nos. 457/64 were emergency printings caused by the non-arrival of stocks of the thin, ready gummed Crown over A watermarked paper. Paper watermarked W **104** had been introduced in 1911 and was normally used for Victoria fiscal stamps. This watermark can be easily distinguished from the previous W **85** by its narrow crown.

STAMP BOOKLETS

There are very few surviving examples of Nos. SB1/4. Listings are provided for those believed to have been issued with prices quoted for those known to still exist.

1904 (Mar)–**09**. Black on red cover as Type B **1** of New South Wales. Stapled.

SB1	£1 booklet containing 240 1d. in four blocks of 30 and two blocks of 60	
	a. Red on pink cover (1909)	£22000
	b. Blue on pink cover	£20000

1904 (Mar). Black on grey cover as No. SB1. Stapled.

SB2	£1 booklet containing 120 2d. in four blocks of 30	

1910 (May). Black on white cover as Type B **2** of New South Wales. Stapled.

SB3	2s. booklet containing 11 ½d. (No. 426), either in block of 6 plus block of 5 or block of 11, and 18 1d. (No. 427), either in three blocks of 6 or block of 6 plus block of 12	£5500
	a. Black on pale green cover	£6000

Unsold stock of No. SB3 was uprated with one additional ½d. in May 1911.

1911 (1 Aug). Red on pink cover as No. SB3. Stapled.

SB4	2s. Booklet containing 12 ½d. (No. 426), either in two blocks of 6 or block of 12, and 18 1d. (No. 427), either in three blocks of 6 or block of 6 plus block of 12	£6000

POSTAGE DUE STAMPS

D **1**

(Dies eng A. Williams (values) and J. McWilliams (frame). Typo)

1890 (1 Nov)–**94**. Wmk V over Crown, W **33**. P 12×12½.

D1	D **1**	½d. dull blue and brown-lake (24.12.90)	8·50	8·50
		a. Dull blue and deep claret	6·50	6·50
D2		1d. dull blue and brown-lake	7·00	2·25
		a. Dull blue and brownish red (1.93)	16·00	2·50
D3		2d. dull blue and brown-lake	14·00	2·25
		a. Dull blue and brownish red (3.93)	27·00	2·50
D4		4d. dull blue and brown-lake	32·00	5·50
		a. Dull blue and pale claret (5.94)	35·00	9·50
D5		5d. dull blue and brown-lake	29·00	3·75
D6		6d. dull blue and brown-lake	23·00	9·00
D7		10d. dull blue and brown-lake	75·00	55·00
D8		1s. dull blue and brown-lake	50·00	11·00
D9		2s. dull blue and brown-lake	£140	70·00
D10		5s. dull blue and brown-lake	£190	£110
D1/10 *Set of 10*			£500	£250
D1as/10s H/S *"Specimen." Set of 10*			£475	

A used example of the 6d. showing compound perforation of 12×12½ and 11 exists in the Royal Collection.

1895 (17 Jan)–**96**. Colours changed. Wmk V over Crown. W **33**. P 12×12½.

D11	D **1**	½d. rosine and bluish green	10·00	2·25
		a. Pale scarlet and yellow-green (3.96)	5·50	3·75
D12		1d. rosine and bluish green	14·00	2·00
		a. Pale scarlet and yellow-green (3.96)	6·00	2·75
D13		2d. rosine and bluish green	27·00	3·00
		a. Pale scarlet and yellow-green (3.96)	25·00	1·50
D14		4d. rosine and bluish green	12·00	1·50
		a. Pale scarlet and yellow-green (3.96)	10·00	2·75
D15		5d. rosine and bluish green	35·00	35·00
		a. Pale scarlet and yellow-green (3.96)	19·00	24·00
D16		6d. rosine and bluish green	24·00	24·00
D17		10d. rosine and bluish green	48·00	10·00
D18		1s. rosine and bluish green	24·00	3·50
D19		2s. pale red and yellowish green (28.3.95)	90·00	26·00
D20		5s. pale red and yellowish green (28.3.95)	£140	40·00
D11/20 *Set of 10*			£350	£120

1897 (1 July)–**99**. Wmk V over Crown. W **82**. P 12×12½.

D21	D **1**	1d. pale scarlet and yellow-green	21·00	2·00
		a. Dull red and bluish green (8.99)	19·00	2·50
D22		2d. pale scarlet and yellow-green	35·00	2·00
		a. Dull red and bluish green (6.99)	35·00	2·00
D23		4d. pale scarlet and yellow-green	55·00	2·50
		a. Dull red and bluish green (8.99)	55·00	2·50
D24		5d. pale scarlet and yellow-green	55·00	7·50
D25		6d. pale scarlet and yellow-green	15·00	7·50
D21/5 *Set of 5*			£160	19·00

1900 (1 Jun)–**04**. Wmk V over Crown. W **85**. P 12×12½.

D26	D **1**	½d. rose-red and pale green	25·00	6·00
		a. Pale red and deep green (8.01)	7·00	5·00
		b. Scarlet and deep green (1.03)	—	30·00
		c. Aniline rosine and green (6.04)	18·00	10·00
D27		1d. rose-red and pale green	24·00	1·75
		a. Pale red and deep green (9.01)	26·00	1·50
		b. Scarlet and deep green (2.02)	26·00	1·00
		c. Aniline rosine and green (9.03)	26·00	1·25
D28		2d. rose-red and pale green (7.00)	16·00	2·25
		a. Pale red and deep green (9.01)	26·00	3·25
		b. Scarlet and deep green (2.02)	26·00	1·25
		c. Aniline rosine and green (9.03)	26·00	2·00

D29		4d. rose-red and pale green (5.01)	50·00	14·00
		a. Pale red and deep green (9.01)	50·00	2·75
		b. Scarlet and deep green (6.03)	50·00	4·50
		c. Aniline rosine and green (6.04)	50·00	4·50
D30		5d. scarlet and deep green (1.03)	24·00	12·00
D31		1s. scarlet and deep green (3.02)	26·00	15·00
D32		2s. scarlet and deep green (1.03)	£180	95·00
D33		5s. scarlet and deep green (1.03)	£200	95·00
D26/33 *Set of 8*			£475	£200

1905 (Dec)–**09**. Wmk Crown over A, W w **11**. P 12×12½.

D34	D **1**	½d. aniline rosine and pale green (1.06)	27·00	21·00
		a. Scarlet and pale yellow-green (7.07)	5·50	12·00
		b. Dull scarlet and pea-green (3.09)	6·50	13·00
		ba. Compound perf 12×12½ and 11	£1600	£1600
D35		1d. aniline rosine and pale green	70·00	9·00
		a. Scarlet and pale yellow-green (5.06)	6·50	2·75
		b. Dull scarlet and pea-green (1.07)	10·00	2·75
D36		2d. aniline scarlet and deep yellow-green (5.06)	45·00	6·00
		a. Dull scarlet and pea-green (11.07)	14·00	3·00
D37		4d. dull scarlet and pea-green (1908)	22·00	26·00
D34*a*/7 *Set of 4*			42·00	40·00
		Prepared for use but not issued		
D38		5d. dull scarlet and pea-green	£2750	£1600

The 5d. value on this paper was prepared in 1907-08 but not put into use. A few examples were subsequently included in presentation sets, either mint or cancelled-to-order.

WESTERN AUSTRALIA

PRICES FOR STAMPS ON COVER

Nos. 1/6	*from* × 6
Nos. 15/32	*from* × 4
Nos. 33/46	*from* × 5
Nos. 49/51	*from* × 6
Nos. 52/62	*from* × 10
Nos. 63/*a*	*from* × 8
No. 67	—
Nos. 68/92*a*	*from* × 10
Nos. 94/102	*from* × 40
Nos. 103/5	*from* × 8
Nos. 107/10*a*	*from* × 12
Nos. 111*a*/*b*	—
Nos. 112/16	*from* × 25
Nos. 117/25	*from* × 10
Nos. 126/8	—
Nos. 129/34	*from* × 8
Nos. 135/6	—
Nos. 138/48	*from* × 12
Nos. 151/63	*from* × 5
Nos. 168/9	*from* × 20
Nos. 170/1	*from* × 4
Nos. 172/3	*from* × 40
Nos. F11/22	*from* × 10
Nos. T1/2	—

SPECIMEN OVERPRINTS. Those listed are from U.P.U. distributions between 1889 and 1892. Further "Specimen" overprints exist, but those were used for other purposes.

1

2

3

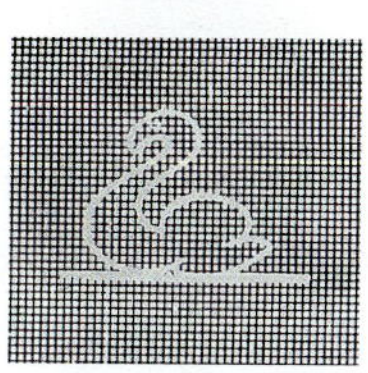
4

GUM. The 1854 and 1857–59 issues are hardly ever seen with gum, so the unused prices quoted are for examples without gum.

(Eng W. Humphrys. Recess P.B.)

1854 (1 Aug). W **4** (sideways).

		(a) Imperf		
1	**1**	1d. black	£1400	£275
		(b) Rouletted 7½ to 14 and compound		
2	**1**	1d. black	£4000	£700

In addition to the supplies received from London a further printing, using the original plate and watermarked paper from Perkins, Bacon, was made in the colony before the date of issue.

The 1d. is also known pin-perforated.

(Litho H. Samson (later A. Hillman), Government Lithographer)

1854 (1 Aug)–**55**. W **4** (sideways).

		(a) Imperf		
3	**2**	4d. pale blue	£375	£200
		a. Blue	£450	£250
		b. Deep dull blue	£2750	£850
		c. Slate-blue (1855)	£4000	£1300
		d. "T" of "POSTAGE" shaved off to a point at foot (R. 7/5, 7/10, 7/15, 7/20)	£2250	£1000
		e. Top of letters of "AUSTRALIA" cut off so that they are barely 1 mm high	†	£30000
		f. "PEICE" instead of "PENCE"	†	£35000
		g. "CE" of "Pence" close together	†	£30000
		h. Frame inverted (R. 8/1, 8/6, 8/11, 8/16)	†	£140000
		i. Tilted border (R. 7/4, 7/9, 7/14, 7/19)	£3000	£1500
		j. "WEST" in squeezed-down letters and "F" of "FOUR" with pointed foot (R. 2/17)	£3500	£1600
		k. "ESTERN" in squeezed-down letters and "U" of "FOUR" squeezed up (R. 3/17)	£5000	£2500
		l. Small "S" in "POSTAGE" (R. 4/17)	£3500	£1600
		m. "EN" of "PENCE" shorter (R. 6/4)	£2750	£1300
		n. "N" of "PENCE" tilted to right with thin first downstroke (R. 6/16)	£2750	£1300
		o. Swan and water above "ENCE" damaged (R. 6/20)	£3750	£1600
		p. "F" of "FOUR" slanting to left (R. 7/17)	£3250	£1500
		q. "WESTERN" in squeezed-down letters only 1½ mm high (R. 8/17)	£3750	£1700
		r. "P" of "PENCE" with small head (R. 9/15)	£3250	£1400
		s. "RALIA" in squeezed-down letters only 1½ mm high (R. 9/16)	£3500	£1500
		t. "PE" of "PENCE" close together (R. 10/15)	£3250	£1400
		u. "N" of "PENCE" narrow (R. 10/16)	£3250	£1400
		v. Part of right cross-stroke and downstroke of "T" of "POSTAGE" cut off (R. 11/15)	£2750	£1300
		w. "A" in "POSTAGE" with thin right limb (R. 11/16)	£3250	£1400
		x. Coloured line above "AGE" of "POSTAGE" (R. 8/6)	£3250	£1500
		y. No outer line above "GE" of "POSTAGE" and coloured line under "FOU" of "FOUR" (R. 8/11)	£3250	£1700
4	**3**	1s. salmon	£25000	£4500
		a. Deep red-brown	£2000	£1100
		b. Grey-brown (1.55)	£650	£375
		c. Pale brown (10.55)	£475	£325
		(b) Rouletted 7½ to 14 and compound		
5	**2**	4d. pale blue	£3750	£700
		a. Blue	—	£700
		b. Slate-blue (1855)	—	£2500
6	**3**	1s. grey-brown (1.55)	£7000	£1200
		a. Pale brown (10.55)	£6500	£1100

Both values are also known pin-perforated.

The 4d. value was prepared by Horace Samson from the Perkins, Bacon 1d. plate. A block of 60 (5×12, cols 16-20) was taken as a "plate to stone" transfer and each frame was then erased. A new lithographic frame, drawn on stone, was transferred 60 times to make up the intermediate stone.

There were a number of transfer varieties, one of the most prominent being the "T" of "POSTAGE" shaved at foot (No. 3d).

Four transfers were taken from the intermediate stone to make printing stone No. I with 240 impressions. Samson printed the initial supply of 100 sheets in deep dull blue (No. 3*b*) in July 1854.

Printing stone No. 1 had three scarce creased transfers whose positions in the sheet have yet to be established (Nos. 3e/g).

Further supplies were printed in January 1855 by Alfred Hillman, Samson's successor. A severe interruption to printing, almost certainly a broken stone, occurred when the fourth sheet was being pulled. On examining the intermediate stone preparatory to making a new printing stone it was found that the frame of R. 8/1 had been damaged and needed replacing.

This was done, but in so doing, Hillman accidentally produced the transfer error "Inverted Frame" (No. 3h). Printing Stone No. 2 was made as before and bore a range of transfer varieties (Nos. 3j/w) along with four "Inverted Frames". This printing was in blue (No. 3*a*). Some time after completion of the required 97 sheets, the "Inverted Frame" was corrected on each of the four positions to make printing stone No. 2A. All four corrections are identifiable and on two of them, traces of the inverted frame remain visible (Nos. 3x/y).

Printing stone No. 2A was used for the third printing undertaken in October 1855, producing 175 sheets of slate-blue (No. 3*c*.) stamps and for the fourth and final printing, totalling 1500 sheets in pale blue (No. 3), undertaken in December 1855.

The 1s. value was produced in much the same way, based on a transfer of cols. 10-14 from the Perkins, Bacon 1d. plate.

5

(Litho A. Hillman, Government Lithographer)

1857 (7 Aug)–**59**. W **4** (sideways).

(a) Imperf

15	5	2d. brown-black/*red* (26.2.58)	£7500	£550
		a. Printed both sides	£9500	£800
16		2d. brown-black/*Indian red* (26.2.58)	£7500	£850
		a. Printed both sides	£9500	£900
17		6d. golden bronze	£20000	£2250
18		6d. black-bronze	£8500	£650
19		6d. grey-black (1859)	£8500	£550

(b) Rouletted 7½ to 14 and compound

20	5	2d. brown-black/*red*	£13000	£1900
		a. Printed both sides	—	£2000
21		2d. brown-black/*Indian red*	—	£1900
22		6d. black-bronze	£13000	£1200
23		6d. grey-black	—	£1300

The 2d. and 6d. are known pin-perforated.

Prices quoted for Nos. 15/23 are for "cut-square" examples. Collectors are warned against "cut-round" copies with corners added.

(Recess in the colony from P.B. plates)

1860 (11 Aug)–**64**. W **4** (sideways on 2d. and 6d.).

(a) Imperf

24	1	2d. pale orange	£130	80·00
25		2d. orange-vermilion	£140	80·00
		a. Wmk upright		
25*b*		2d. deep vermilion	£1900	£800
26		4d. blue (Wmk upright) (21.6.64)	£325	£2250
		a. Wmk sideways	£750	
27		4d. deep blue (Wmk upright)	£325	£2250
28		6d. sage-green (27.7.61)	£2750	£400
28*a*		6d. deep sage-green	—	£550

(b) Rouletted 7½ to 14

29	1	2d. pale orange	£800	£250
30		2d. orange-vermilion	£850	£250
31		4d. deep blue (Wmk upright)	£5500	
32		6d. sage-green	£5500	£700

WATERMARK VARIETIES: On several stamps, Nos. 1 to 46, watermark W **4** exists with the Swan's head to the left or right and reversed in either direction. We do not list these varieties.

PERKINS BACON "CANCELLED". For notes on these handstamps, showing "CANCELLED" between horizontal bars forming an oval, see Catalogue Introduction.

(Recess P.B.)

1861. W **4** (sideways).

(a) Intermediate perf 14–16

33	1	1d. rose	£750	£140
34		2d. blue	£250	40·00
35		4d. vermilion	£1800	£2000
36		6d. purple-brown	£1100	£110
37		1s. yellow-green	£1800	£250

(b) P 14 at Somerset House

38	1	1d. rose	£375	65·00
39		2d. blue	£160	45·00
40		4d. vermilion	£450	£180

(c) Perf clean-cut 14–16

41	1	2d. blue	£110	24·00
		a. Imperf between (pair)	†	—
42		6d. purple-brown	£550	50·00
43		1s. yellow-green	£750	80·00
		a. Wmk upright	£1200	£150

(d) P 14–16 very rough (July)

44	1	1d. rose-carmine (H/S "CANCELLED" in oval £18000)	£350	50·00
45		6d. purple/*blued* (H/S "CANCELLED" in oval £12000)	£4000	£500
46		1s. deep green (H/S "CANCELLED" in oval £11000)	£4250	£375

Perkins, Bacon experienced considerable problems with their perforating machine during the production of these stamps.

The initial printing showed intermediate perforation 14–16. Further supplies were then sent, in late December 1860, to Somerset House to be perforated on their comb 14 machine. The Inland Revenue Board were only able to process the three lower values, although the 6d. purple-brown and 1s. yellow-green are known from this perforation overprinted "SPECIMEN".

The Perkins, Bacon machine was repaired the following month and the 6d., 1s. and a further supply of the 2d. were perforated on it to give a clean-cut 14-16 gauge.

A final printing was produced in July 1861, but by this time the machine had deteriorated so that it produced a very rough 14–16.

(Recess D.L.R. from P.B. plates)

1863 (16 Dec)–**64**. No wmk. P 13.

49	1	1d. carmine-rose	75·00	4·25
50		1d. lake	75·00	4·25
51		6d. deep lilac (15.4.64)	£325	50·00
51*a*		6d. dull violet (15.4.64)	£375	55·00

Both values exist on thin and on thick papers, the former being the scarcer.

Both grades of paper show a marginal sheet watermark, "T H SAUNDERS 1860" in double-lined large and small capitals, but parts of this watermark rarely occur on the stamps.

(Recess D.L.R. from P.B. plates)

1864 (27 Dec)–**79**. Wmk Crown CC (sideways* on 1d.). P 12½.

52	1	1d. bistre	85·00	9·00
		w. Wmk Crown to right of CC	85·00	9·00
		x. Wmk sideways reversed	85·00	9·00
		y. Wmk Crown to right of CC and reversed	90·00	11·00
53		1d. yellow-ochre (16.10.74)	£110	14·00
		w. Wmk Crown to right of CC	£110	14·00
54		2d. chrome-yellow (18.1.65)	95·00	6·50
		x. Wmk reversed	£110	7·50
55		2d. yellow	£100	7·50
		a. Wmk sideways (5.79)	£250	24·00
		aw. Wmk Crown to right of CC	£250	24·00
		b. Error. Mauve (1879)	£20000	£15000
		w. Wmk inverted	£275	42·00
		x. Wmk reversed	£100	6·50
		y. Wmk inverted and reversed	£275	42·00
56		4d. carmine (18.1.65)	£140	7·00
		a. Doubly printed	£30000	
		w. Wmk inverted	£450	42·00
		x. Wmk reversed	£150	8·50
		y. Wmk inverted and reversed	—	60·00
57		6d. violet (18.1.65)	£170	6·00
		a. Doubly printed	†	£22000
		b. Wmk sideways	£800	£325
		bw. Wmk Crown to right of CC		
		w. Wmk inverted	—	60·00
		x. Wmk reversed	£170	6·00
58		6d. indigo-violet	£450	35·00
		w. Wmk inverted		
		x. Wmk reversed	£450	35·00
59		6d. lilac (1872)	£275	6·00
		y. Wmk inverted and reversed	£400	
60		6d. mauve (12.5.75)	£250	6·00
		x. Wmk reversed	£250	6·00
		y. Wmk inverted and reversed	£400	
61		1s. bright green (18.1.65)	£250	19·00
		s. Handstamped "SPECIMEN."	£225	
		w. Wmk inverted		
		y. Wmk inverted and reversed	£300	
62		1s. sage-green (10.68)	£450	35·00

*The normal sideways watermark shows Crown to left of CC, *as seen from the back of the stamp.*

Beware of fakes of No. 55b made by altering the value tablet of No. 60.

7

ONE PENNY

(**8**)

(Typo D.L.R.)

1871 (29 Oct)–**73**. Wmk Crown CC (sideways). P 14.

63	7	3d. pale brown	60·00	5·50
		a. Cinnamon (1873)	60·00	4·50
		s. Handstamped "SPECIMEN."	£150	

1874 (10 Dec). No. 55 surch with T **8** by Govt Printer.

67	1	1d. on 2d. yellow (G.)	£700	55·00
		b. Surch triple	†	£6500
		x. Wmk reversed	£700	60·00
		y. Wmk inverted and reversed	—	£200

Forged surcharges of T **8** are known on stamps wmk Crown CC perf 14, and on Crown CA, perf 12 and 14.

(Recess D.L.R. from P.B. plates)

1876–81. Wmk Crown CC (sideways*). P 14.

68	1	1d. ochre	85·00	3·75
		w. Wmk Crown to right of CC	85·00	3·75
69		1d. bistre (1878)	£160	5·50
		w. Wmk Crown to right of CC	—	6·50
		x. Wmk sideways reversed	£250	20·00
		y. Wmk Crown to right of CC and reversed	£250	20·00
70		1d. yellow-ochre (1879)	95·00	2·75
71		2d. chrome-yellow	£110	1·75
		a. Wmk upright (1877)	£130	3·00
		aw. Wmk inverted	£325	50·00
		ax. Wmk reversed	£275	25·00
		ay. Wmk inverted and reversed		
		bw. Wmk Crown to right of CC	£110	2·00
		by. Wmk Crown to right of CC and reversed	£225	22·00
74		4d. carmine (1881)	£650	£120
		y. Wmk Crown to right of CC and reversed	£650	£150
75		6d. lilac (1877)	£200	4·00
		a. Wmk upright (1879)	£750	15·00
		bw. Wmk Crown to right of CC	£200	4·00
75*c*		6d. reddish lilac (1879)	£225	6·00

*The normal sideways watermark shows Crown to left of CC, *as seen from the back of the stamp.*

(Recess D.L.R. from P.B. plates)

1882 (Mar)–**85**. Wmk Crown CA (sideways*).

(a) P 14

76	1	1d. yellow-ochre	30·00	2·00
		w. Wmk Crown to right of CA	30·00	2·00
		x. Wmk sideways reversed		
		y. Wmk Crown to right of CA and reversed	—	20·00
77		2d. chrome-yellow	42·00	2·00
		a. Wmk upright	†	—
		w. Wmk Crown to right of CA	48·00	2·50
		x. Wmk sideways reversed	—	20·00
		y. Wmk Crown to right of CA and reversed	—	20·00
78		4d. carmine (8.82)	£190	15·00
		a. Wmk upright (1885)	—	£110
		aw. Wmk inverted	—	£200
		ax. Wmk reversed	—	£200
		w. Wmk Crown to right of CA	£190	15·00
		x. Wmk sideways reversed	—	42·00
79		6d. reddish lilac (1882)	£130	3·00
80		6d. lilac (1884)	£130	4·00
		s. Handstamped "SPECIMEN."	£150	
		w. Wmk Crown to right of CA	£140	5·00
		x. Wmk sideways reversed	—	35·00
		y. Wmk Crown to right of CA and reversed	£225	35·00

(b) P 12×14

81	1	1d. yellow-ochre (2.83)	£2750	£170

(c) P 12

82	1	1d. yellow-ochre (2.83)	95·00	5·50
		w. Wmk Crown to right of CA	£110	7·00
83		2d. chrome-yellow (6.83)	£160	5·00
		w. Wmk Crown to right of CA	£160	6·00
		y. Wmk Crown to right of CA and reversed	—	20·00
84		4d. carmine (5.83)	£300	60·00
		w. Wmk Crown to right of CA	£300	60·00
85		6d. lilac (6.83)	£550	55·00
		w. Wmk Crown to right of CA	£550	55·00
		y. Wmk Crown to right of CA and reversed	—	85·00

*The normal sideways watermark shows Crown to left of CA, *as seen from the back of the stamp.*

(Typo D.L.R.)

1882 (July)–**95**. Wmk Crown CA (sideways). P 14.

86	7	3d. pale brown	17·00	3·75
87		3d. red-brown (12.95)	10·00	3·75

The 3d. stamps in other colours, watermark Crown CA and perforated 12, are colour trials dating from 1883.

½ (**9**) **1d.** (**10**) **1d.** (**11**)

1884 (19 Feb). Surch with T **9**, in red, by Govt Printer.

89	1	½d. on 1d. yellow-ochre (No. 76)	30·00	45·00
		a. Thin bar	£110	£160
		w. Wmk Crown to right of CA	30·00	45·00
90		½d. on 1d. yellow-ochre (No. 82)	17·00	19·00
		w. Wmk Crown to right of CA	17·00	29·00

Inverted or double surcharges are forgeries made in London about 1886.

The "Thin bar" varieties occur on R. 12/3, R. 12/8, R. 12/13 and R. 12/18, and show the bar only 0.2 mm thick.

1885 (May). Nos. 63/*a* surch, in green, by Govt Printer.

(a) Thick "1" with slanting top, T **10** *(Horizontal Rows 1/5)*

91		1d. on 3d. pale brown	90·00	30·00
		a. Cinnamon	85·00	29·00
		b. Vert pair. Nos. 91/2	£375	

(b) Thin "1" with straight top, T **11** *(Horizontal Row 6)*

92		1d. on 3d. pale brown	£200	75·00
		a. Cinnamon	£180	75·00

12

13

14

15

(Typo D.L.R.)

1885 (May)–**93**. Wmk Crown CA (sideways). P 14.

94	12	½d. yellow-green	7·00	1·00
		a. Green	4·50	1·00
		w. Wmk Crown to right of CA	—	95·00
95	13	1d. carmine (2.90)	42·00	70
		w. Wmk Crown to right of CA	—	60·00
96	14	2d. bluish grey (6.90)	32·00	3·75
		a. Grey	30·00	3·75
		w. Wmk Crown to right of CA	—	95·00
97	15	2½d. deep blue (1.5.92)	25·00	2·25
		a. Blue	25·00	2·25
		w. Wmk Crown to right of CA	—	95·00
98		4d. chestnut (7.90)	15·00	2·50
99		5d. bistre (1.5.92)	19·00	4·25
100		6d. bright violet (1.93)	20·00	2·00
		w. Wmk Crown to right of CA	—	£130
101		1s. pale olive-green (4.90)	40·00	5·50
102		1s. olive-green	35·00	5·00
94s/101s (ex 1d., 6d.) Handstamped "SPECIMEN." (Nos. 96, 98, 101) or optd "SPECIMEN" *Set of 6*			£550	

The normal sideways watermark shows Crown to left of CA, *as seen from the back of the stamp.*

(Recess D.L.R. from P.B. plates)

1888 (Mar–Apr). Wmk Crown CA (sideways). P 14.

103	1	1d. carmine-pink	32·00	3·50
104		2d. grey	85·00	1·25
		w. Wmk Crown to right of CA	£120	
		y. Wmk Crown to right of CA and reversed	£180	
105		4d. red-brown (April)	80·00	30·00
		x. Wmk sideways reversed	£120	
103s/5s H/S "SPECIMEN." *Set of 3*			£275	

The watermark shows Crown to right of CA on No. 103 and to the left of CA on 104/5, *as seen from the back of the stamp.*

ONE PENNY (**16**) **Half-penny** (**17**)

1893 (Feb). Surch with T **16**, in green, by Govt Printer.

107	7	1d. on 3d. pale brown (No. 63)	15·00	9·00
108		1d. on 3d. cinnamon (No. 63*a*)	15·00	9·00
		a. Double surcharge	£2000	
109		1d. on 3d. pale brown (No. 86)	85·00	14·00

1895 (21 Nov). Surch with T **17** by Govt Printer.

(a) In green

110	7	½d. on 3d. pale brown (No. 63)	10·00	40·00
110*a*		½d. on 3d. cinnamon (No. 63*a*)	10·00	40·00
		b. Surcharge double	£1600	

(b) In red and in green

111*a*	**7**	½d. on 3d. cinnamon (No. 63*a*)	£110	£300
111*b*		½d. on 3d. red-brown (No. 87)	85·00	£180

Green was the adopted surcharge colour but a trial had earlier been made in red on stamps watermarked Crown CC. As they proved unsatisfactory they were given another surcharge in green. The trial stamps were inadvertently issued and, to prevent speculation, a further printing of the duplicated surcharge was made, but on both papers, Crown CC (No. 111*a*) and Crown CA (No. 111*b*).

18

19

20

21

(Typo D.L.R.)

1898 (Dec)–**1907**. Wmk W Crown A, W **18**. P 14.

112	**13**	1d. carmine	9·00	30
		w. Wmk inverted	—	£130
113	**14**	2d. bright yellow (1.99)	32·00	3·00
		w. Wmk inverted	—	£130
114	**19**	2½d. blue (1.01)	16·00	1·25
		w. Wmk inverted	£350	
115	**20**	6d. bright violet (10.06)	42·00	4·50
		w. Wmk inverted	—	£250
116	**21**	1s. olive-green (4.07)	50·00	7·00
		w. Wmk inverted	—	£160

22

23

24

25

26

27

28

29

30

31

32

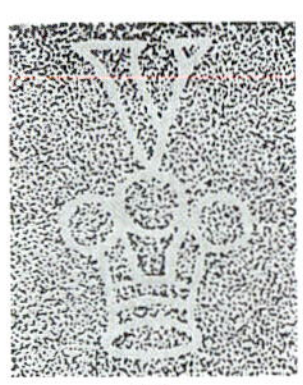

33

(Typo Victoria Govt Printer, Melbourne, Commonwealth Stamp Ptg Branch from March 1909)

1902 (Oct)–**11**. Wmk V and Crown, W **33** (sideways on horiz designs).

(a) P 12½ or 12½×12 (horiz), 12×12½ (vert)

117	**22**	1d. carmine-rose (1.03)	28·00	1·00
		a. Wmk upright (10.02)	25·00	3·00
118	**23**	2d. yellow (4.1.03)	28·00	4·75
		a. Wmk upright (1903)	60·00	8·00
119	**24**	4d. chestnut (4.03)	42·00	4·25
		a. Wmk upright	£600	£600
120	**15**	5d. bistre (4.9.05)	£150	90·00
121	**25**	8d. apple-green (3.03)	21·00	4·50
122	**26**	9d. yellow-orange (5.03)	55·00	32·00
		a. Wmk upright (11.03)	£120	29·00
123	**27**	10d. red (3.03)	32·00	10·00
124	**28**	2s. bright red/*yellow*	85·00	45·00
		a. Wmk sideways	£250	26·00
		b. Orange/yellow (7.06)	55·00	12·00
		c. Brown-red/yellow (5.11)	45·00	27·00
125	**29**	2s.6d. deep blue/*rose*	55·00	21·00
126	**30**	5s. emerald-green	80·00	50·00
127	**31**	10s. deep mauve	£170	£100
		a. Bright purple (1910)	£900	£425
128	**32**	£1 orange-brown (1.11.02)	£425	£190
		a. Orange (10.7.09)	£750	£350

(b) P 11

129	**22**	1d. carmine-rose	£400	50·00
		a. Wmk upright (1905)	†	£500
130	**23**	2d. yellow	£425	60·00
		a. Wmk upright	†	£500
131	**24**	4d. chestnut	£1400	£425
132	**15**	5d. bistre	50·00	75·00
133	**26**	9d. yellow-orange	£180	£180
134	**28**	2s. bright red/*yellow*	£300	£180
		a. Orange/yellow	£425	£225

(c) Perf compound of 12½ or 12½×12 and 11

135	**22**	1d. carmine-rose	£1300	£650
		a. Wmk upright	†	£650
136	**23**	2d. yellow	£1900	£1100
137	**24**	4d. chestnut		

Type **22** is similar to Type **13** but larger.

WATERMARK VARIETIES: The attention of collectors is drawn to the note on inverted and reversed watermarks on the stamps of the Australian States at the top of the Australia listings.

34

35

1905–**12**. Wmk Crown and A, W **34** (sideways).

(a) P 12½ or 12½×12 (horiz), 12×12½ (vert)

138	**12**	½d. green (6.10)	4·50	8·50
139	**22**	1d. rose-pink (10.05)	22·00	3·75
		a. Wmk upright (1.06)	11·00	1·25
		b. Carmine (1909)	13·00	1·25
		c. Carmine-red (1912)	13·00	11·00
140	**23**	2d. yellow (15.11.05)	8·50	2·00
		a. Wmk upright (4.10)	†	£350
141	**7**	3d. brown (2.06)	65·00	4·75
142	**24**	4d. bistre-brown (12.06)	60·00	17·00
		a. Pale chestnut (1908)	45·00	16·00
		b. Bright brown-red (14.10.10)	24·00	5·50
143	**15**	5d. pale olive-bistre (8.05)	35·00	26·00
		a. Olive-green (1.09)	35·00	26·00
		b. Pale greenish yellow (2.12)	60·00	£110
144	**25**	8d. apple-green (20.4.12)	23·00	75·00
145	**26**	9d. orange (11.5.06)	35·00	6·00
		a. Red-orange (6.10)	60·00	6·00
		b. Wmk upright (7.12)	70·00	32·00
146	**27**	10d. rose-orange (16.2.10)	24·00	29·00
148	**30**	5s. emerald-green (wmk upright) (9.07)	£180	£130

(b) P 11

150	**12**	½d. green	£3000	
151	**22**	1d. rose-pink (1908)	50·00	30·00
		a. Carmine-red	60·00	29·00
		b. Wmk upright (2.06)	90·00	29·00
152	**23**	2d. yellow	50·00	45·00
153	**7**	3d. brown	24·00	15·00
154	**24**	4d. yellow-brown	£1200	£275
		a. Pale chestnut	£1500	£400
155	**15**	5d. pale olive-bistre	60·00	11·00
		a. Olive-green	25·00	19·00
157	**26**	9d. orange	£200	£200
		a. Red-orange	—	£200
		b. Wmk upright (1912)	—	£900

(c) Perf compound of 12½ or 12½×12 and 11

161	**22**	1d. rose-pink (wmk upright)	£1200	£500
		a. Wmk sideways	£1500	£800
162	**23**	2d. yellow	£1200	£550
163	**7**	3d. brown	£1500	£1500
163*a*		5d. olive-green	†	£1800
164	**26**	9d. red-orange		

The prices provided for Nos. 154/*a* are for examples perforated "OS".

1912 (25 Mar–9 Apr). Wmk Crown and A W **35** (sideways). P 11½×12.

168	**20**	6d. bright violet (9.4.12)	18·00	27·00
169	**21**	1s. sage-green	32·00	42·00
		a. Perf 12½ (single line)	—	£2500

1912 (7 Aug). Thin, ready gummed paper with white gum (as Victoria*). W **34** (sideways).

170	**7**	3d. brown (P 12½)	75·00	75·00
		a. Wmk upright	£200	£190
171		3d. brown (P 11)		
		a. Wmk upright		

*See note below Victoria No. 455.

ONE PENNY
(**36**)

1912 (6 Nov). Nos. 140 and 162 surch with T **36** in Melbourne.

(a) P 12½ ×12

172	**23**	1d. on 2d. yellow	3·00	3·00
		a. Wmk upright	8·50	15·00

(b) Perf compound of 12½×12 and 11

173	**23**	1d. on 2d. yellow	£750	£450
		a. Wmk upright	£750	

STAMP BOOKLETS

There are very few surviving examples of Nos. SB1/4. Listings are provided for those believed to have been issued with prices quoted for those known to still exist.

1904 (1 Jan)–**09**. Black on red cover as Type B **1** of New South Wales. Stapled.

SB1 £1 booklet containing 240 1d. in four blocks of 30 and two blocks of 60
a. Red on pink cover (1909) £20000
b. blue on pink cover

1904 (1 Jan). Black on grey cover as No. SB1. Stapled.

SB2 £1 Booklet containing 120 2d. in four blocks of 30...

1910 (May). Black on cream cover as Type B **2** of New South Wales. Stapled.

SB3 2s. booklet containing 11 ½d. (No. 138), either in block of 6 plus block of 5 or block of 11, and 18 1d. (No. 139) either in three blocks of 6 or block of 6 plus block of 12 £7500

Unsold stock of No. SB3 was uprated with one additional ½d. in May 1911.

1911 (1 Aug). Red on pink cover as No. SB3. Stapled.

SB4 2s. Booklet containing 12 ½d. (No. 138), either in two blocks of 6 or block of 12, and 18 1d. (No. 139), either in three blocks of 6 or block of 6 plus block of 12 £7500

POSTAL FISCAL STAMPS

By the Post and Telegraph Act of 5 September 1893 the current issue of fiscal stamps up to and including the 1s. value, Nos. F11/15, was authorised for postal use.

These stamps had been initially supplied, for fiscal purposes, in February 1882 and had been preceded by a series of "I R" surcharges and overprints on postage stamps which were in use for a period of about six months. Examples of these 1881–82 provisionals can be found postally used under the terms of the 1893 Act but, as they had not been current for fiscal purposes for over eleven years, we no longer list them.

F **3**

(Typo D.L.R.)

1893 (5 Sept). Definitive fiscal stamps of Feb 1882. Wmk CA over Crown. P 14.

F11	F **3**	1d. dull purple	30·00	7·00
F12		2d. dull purple	£325	80·00
F13		3d. dull purple	£110	10·00
F14		6d. dull purple	£160	17·00
F15		1s. dull purple	£250	28·00

The 1s. value is as Type F **3** but with rectangular outer frame and circular frame surrounding swan.

Higher values in this series were not validated by the Act for postal use.

Two varieties of watermark exist on these stamps. Initial supplies showed an indistinct watermark with the base of the "A" 4 mm wide. From 1896 the paper used showed a clearer watermark on which the base of the "A" was 5 mm wide.

1897. Wmk W Crown A, W **18**. P 14.

F19	F **3**	1d. dull purple	35·00	7·00
F20		3d. dull purple	£110	10·00
F21		6d. dull purple	£150	12·00
F22		1s. dull purple	£250	38·00

The above were invalidated for postal purposes from 1 January 1901.

TELEGRAPH STAMPS

T **1**

1879 (9 Apr). Wmk Crown CC. P 14.

T1	T **1**	1d. bistre	90·00	20·00
		a. Perf 12½	90·00	20·00
T2		6d. lilac	£500	£225

The 1d. Telegraph Stamps were authorised for postal purposes from 25 October 1886. The 6d. is also known postally used but such use was unauthorised.

OFFICIAL STAMPS

From 1 August 1862 stamps of various issues were punched with a circular hole, the earlier size being about 3 mm. in diameter and the latter 4 mm. These were used on official correspondence by the Commissariat and Convict Department, branches of the Imperial administration separate from the colonial government. This system of punching ceased in March 1886. Subsequently many stamps between Nos. 94 and 148 may be found punctured, "PWD", "WA" or "OS".

Western Australia became part of the Commonwealth of Australia on 1 January 1901.

COMMONWEALTH OF AUSTRALIA

On 1 March 1901 control of the postal service passed to the federal administration although it was not until 13 October 1910 that the issues of the various states became valid for use throughout Australia. Postal rates were standardised on 1 May 1911.

The first national postage due stamps appeared in July 1902, but it was not until January 1913 that postage stamps inscribed "AUSTRALIA" were issued.

PRICES FOR STAMPS ON COVER TO 1945

Nos. 1/3	*from* × 10
No. 4	*from* × 4
Nos. 5/12	*from* × 10
Nos. 13/16	—
Nos. 17/19	*from* × 10
Nos. 20/3	*from* × 10
No. 24	*from* × 8
No. 25	*from* × 2
Nos. 26/7	*from* × 8
Nos. 28/30	—
Nos. 35/7	*from* × 5
Nos. 38/9	*from* × 8
Nos. 40/1	*from* × 20
Nos. 42/5	—
No. 47	*from* × 5
Nos. 48/51	*from* × 8
Nos. 52/3	*from* × 5
Nos. 56/7	*from* × 10
Nos. 58/61	*from* × 8
No. 62	*from* × 5
No. 63	*from* × 2
No. 64	*from* × 15
No. 65	*from* × 5
No. 66	—
No. 73	*from* × 20
Nos. 74/5	*from* × 5
Nos. 76/7	*from* × 4
Nos. 78/81	*from* × 8
Nos. 82/4	*from* × 6
Nos. 85/104	*from* × 4
No. 105	*from* × 15
Nos. 106/10	*from* × 6
Nos. 111/14	—
No. 115	*from* × 3
Nos. 116/18	*from* × 5
Nos. 119/20	*from* × 8
Nos. 121/9	*from* × 5
Nos. 130/1	*from* × 25
No. 132	*from* × 3
Nos. 133/5	*from* × 10
Nos. 136/8	*from* × 4
Nos. 139/*a*	*from* × 3
No. 140	*from* × 8
Nos. 141/2	*from* × 4
No. 143	*from* × 6
No. 146	*from* × 20
Nos. 147/8	*from* × 3
Nos. 149	*from* × 6
Nos. 150/2	*from* × 3
Nos. 153/*a*	*from* × 12
No. 154	*from* × 15
No. 155	*from* × 4
No. 156	*from* × 15
Nos. 157/8	*from* × 3
Nos. 159/60	*from* × 6
No. 161	*from* × 10
Nos. 162/3	*from* × 4
Nos. 164/211	*from* × 2
Nos. D1/118	*from* × 8
Nos. O1/3	*from* × 10
Nos. O4/6	*from* × 4
Nos. O7/8	*from* × 10
Nos. O9/15	—
Nos. O16/18	*from* × 10
No. O19	*from* × 3
No. O20	*from* × 15
No. O21	*from* × 3
Nos. O22/3	*from* × 10
No. O24/30	—
Nos. O31/4	*from* × 10
Nos. O35/7	—
Nos. O38/42	*from* × 15
Nos. O43/7	*from* × 10
No. O48	*from* × 30
Nos. O49/53	—
No. O54	*from* × 6
No. O60	*from* × 4
No. O61	*from* × 30
No. O62	—
No. O63	*from* × 5

PRICES FOR STAMPS ON COVER TO 1945

Nos. O64/5	*from* × 15
Nos. O66/7	*from* × 8
No. O68	*from* × 20
No. O69	*from* × 10
Nos. O70/4	*from* × 15
No. O75	—
Nos. O76/7	*from* × 15
No. O78	—
Nos. O79/84	*from* × 8
No. O85	*from* × 6
Nos. O86/7	*from* × 3
No. O88	—
No. O89	*from* × 15
Nos. O90/6	*from* × 6
No. O97	*from* × 20
Nos. O98/110	*from* × 6
Nos. O111	*from* × 10
Nos. O112/17	*from* × 20
Nos. O118/*b*	—
Nos. O119/2	*from* × 20
Nos. O126	*from* × 100
Nos. O127	*from* × 5
Nos. O128	*from* × 200
Nos. O129/31	*from* × 50
Nos. O132/3	*from* × 10
Nos. O134/6	*from* × 40

PRINTERS. Except where otherwise stated, all Commonwealth stamps to No. 581 were printed under Government authority at Melbourne. Until 1918 there were two establishments (both of the Treasury Dept)—the Note Printing Branch and the Stamp Printing Branch. The former printed T **3** and **4**.

In 1918 the Stamp Printing Branch was closed and all stamps were printed by the Note Printing Branch. In 1926 control was transferred from the Treasury to the Commonwealth Bank of Australia, and on 14 January 1960 the branch was attached to the newly established Reserve Bank of Australia.

Until 1942 stamps bore in the sheet margin the initials or names of successive managers and from 1942 to March 1952 the imprint "Printed by the Authority of the Government of the Commonwealth of Australia". After November 1952 (or Nos. D129/31 for Postage Dues) imprints were discontinued.

SPECIMEN OVERPRINTS. These come from Specimen sets, first made available to the public on 15 December 1913. In these sets the lower values were cancelled-to-order, but stamps with a face value of over 5s. or later 50c. were overprinted "SPECIMEN" in different types. These overprints are listed as they could be purchased from the Australian Post Office.

It is, however, believed that examples of No. 112 overprinted "SPECIMEN" were distributed by the U.P.U. in 1929. Supplies of the 1902 and 1902–04 postage due stamps overprinted "SPECIMEN" were supplied to the U.P.U. by some of the states.

1

2

Die I

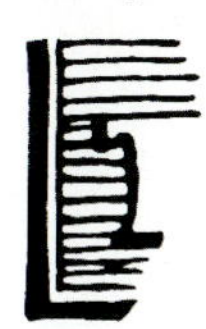

Die II

Dies of Type 1 (mono-coloured values only):—

Die I. Break in inner frame line at lower left level with top of words of value.

Die II. Die repaired showing no break.

Die I was only used for the ½d., 1d., 2d. and 3d. Several plates were produced for each except the 3d. When the second plate of the 3d. was being prepared the damage became aggravated after making 105 out of the 120 units when the die was returned for repair. This gave rise to the *se-tenant* pairs showing the two states of the die.

Die II was used until 1945 and deteriorated progressively with damage to the frame lines and rounding of the corners.

Specialists recognise seven states of this die, but we only list the two most major of the later versions.

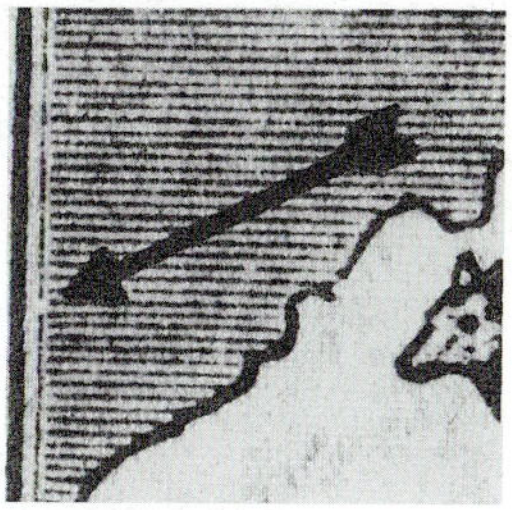

Die IIA. This state is as Die II, but, in addition, shows a break in the inner left-hand frame line, 9 mm from the top of the design (occurs on 1d., 2d. and 6d.).

Die IIB. As Die IIA, but now also showing break in outer frame line above "ST", and (not illustrated) an incomplete corner to the inner frame line at top right (occurs on 3d., 6d., 9d., 1s. and £1 (No. 75)).

No. 9a shows a badly distorted second "E" in "PENCE", which is unmistakable. It occurs on the upper plate right pane R. 10/6 and was replaced by a substitute cliché in Die IIA (No. 9b) in the November 1913 printing.

(Des B. Young. Eng S. Reading. Typo J. B. Cooke)

1913 (2 Jan)–**14**. W **2**. P 12.

1	**1**	½d. green (Die I) (14.1.13)	10·00	6·00
		bw. Wmk inverted	85·00	30·00
		c. Wmk sideways	†	£35000
		cw. Wmk sideways inverted	†	£26000
2		1d. red (Die I)	19·00	1·75
		a. Wmk sideways	£1600	£275
		aw. Wmk sideways inverted	£1800	£300
		b. Carmine	18·00	1·75
		cw. Wmk inverted	85·00	22·00
		d. Die II Red (16.1.13)	16·00	1·00
		da. Wmk sideways	£1600	£325
		daw. Wmk sideways inverted	£1800	£350
		db. Carmine	17·00	1·75
		dw. Wmk inverted	90·00	21·00
		e. Die IIA. *Red* (4.14)	29·00	1·25
		eb. Carmine	29·00	1·75
		ew. Wmk inverted	£170	29·00
3		2d. grey (Die I) (15.1.13)	55·00	6·50
		w. Wmk inverted	£130	35·00
4		2½d. indigo (Die II) (27.1.13)	50·00	20·00
5		3d. olive (Die I) (28.1.13)	80·00	11·00
		a. Imperf three sides (horiz pair)	£75000	
		aa. Imperf three sides (lower stamp of vert pair)	£40000	
		b. in pair with Die II	£1200	£650
		c. Yellow-olive	85·00	11·00
		ca. In pair with Die II	£1200	£650
		dw. Wmk inverted	£190	80·00
		e. Die II *Olive*	£450	90·00
		ea. Yellow-olive	£425	85·00
		ew. Wmk inverted	£950	£375
6		4d. orange (Die II) (19.2.13)	95·00	26·00
		a. Orange-yellow	£475	85·00
8		5d. chestnut (Die II) (18.1.13)	85·00	48·00
9		6d. ultramarine (Die II) (18.1.13)	75·00	20·00
		a. Retouched "E"	£2500	£950
		b. Die IIA (substituted cliché) (11.13)	£5500	£1900
		w. Wmk inverted	£1100	£400
10		9d. violet (Die II) (1.2.13)	80·00	27·00
11		1s. emerald (Die II) (25.1.13)	85·00	27·00
		a. Blue-green	£140	27·00
		w. Wmk inverted	£1500	80·00
12		2s. brown (Die II) (28.1.13)	£275	85·00
13		5s. grey and yellow (Die II) (20.3.13)	£450	£200
14		10s. grey and pink (Die II) (20.3.13)	£900	£700
15		£1 brown and ultramarine (Die II) (20.3.13)	£3000	£2500
16		£2 black and rose (Die II) (8.4.13)	£6500	£4000
1/16 *Set of* 15			£10000	£7000
14s/16s Handstamped *"Specimen" Set of* 3			£1300	

The watermark on Nos. 1c, 2a and 2da shows the Crown pointing to the left and on Nos. 1cw, 2aw and 2daw pointing to the right, *as seen from the back of the stamp.* One example of 1c and two examples of 1cw are known, all used.

The 3d. was printed from two plates, one of which contained 105 stamps as Die I and 15 as Die II. The other plate contained Die I stamps only.

No. 5a is from the top row of a sheet, with perforations at foot only. No. 5aa is from the bottom two rows of a different sheet.

See also Nos. 24/30 (W **5**), 35/45*b* (W **6**), 73/5 (W **6**, new colours), 107/14 (W **7**), 132/8 (W **15**), 212 (2s. re-engraved).

3

4 Laughing Kookaburra

(Des R. A. Harrison. Eng and recess T. S. Harrison)

1913 (9 Dec)–**14**. No wmk. P 11.

17	**3**	1d. red	4·25	5·00
		a. Imperf between (horiz pair)	£5000	
		b. Imperf between (vert pair)	£2500	
		c. Pale rose-red	10·00	15·00
		ca. Imperf between (vert pair)	£3000	
		cb. Imperf between (horiz pair)	£5000	
19	**4**	6d. claret (26.8.14)	75·00	55·00

All printings from Plate 1 of the 1d. were in the shade of No. 17*c*. This plate shows many retouches.

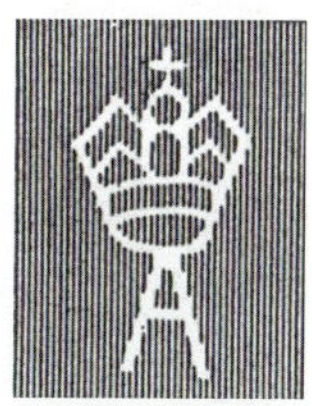

5

5a

Thin "1" in fraction at right (Plate 5 right pane R. 8/1)

Cracked electro (Plate 5 left pane R. 8/4)

1d. Die II

Dot before "1" (Plate 3 right pane R. 4/3)

"Secret mark" (Plate 4 left pane R. 1/1)

Flaw under neck (Plate 4 left pane R. 7/1)

"RA" joined (Plate 4 left pane R. 10/6)

4d. Line through "FOUR PENCE" (Pl. 2 right pane R. 2/6)

1d. Die II. The flaw distinguishing the so-called Die II, a white upward spur to the right of the base of the "1" in the left value tablet, is now known to be due to a defective roller-die. It occurred on all stamps in the second and third vertical rows of upper left plate, right pane. Each of the twenty defective impressions differs slightly; a typical example is illustrated above.

(Dies eng P.B. Typo J. B. Cooke until May 1918, then T. S. Harrison)

1914 (17 July)–**20**. W **5**. P 14¼×14 (comb).

20	**5a**	½d. bright green (22.2.15)	3·75	1·00
		a. Perf 14¼ (line) (12.15)	£11000	£600
		b. Green (1916)	3·75	1·00
		c. Yellow-green (1916)	32·00	13·00
		d. Thin "1" in fraction at right	£21000	£7500
		e. Cracked electro	£8000	£4000
		w. Wmk inverted	23·00	9·50
21		1d. carmine-red (*shades*) (Die I) (P 14¼ (line))	45·00	7·50
		a. Die II	£16000	£3000
		bw. Wmk inverted	†	£13000
		c. Perf 14¼×14 (comb)	12·00	1·00
		ca. Rusted cliché (Pl 2 rt pane R. 6/4 and 5) (9.16)	£17000	£450
		cb. Substituted cliché (Pl 2 right pane R. 6/5) (2.18)	£1900	60·00
		cc. Pale carmine (*shades*) (1917)	13·00	1·00
		cd. Rose-red (1917)	17·00	2·50
		ce. Carmine-pink (1918)	£170	11·00
		cf. Carmine (*aniline*) (1920)	20·00	3·25
		cg. Dot before "1"	95·00	12·00
		ch. "Secret mark"	95·00	12·00
		ci. Flaw under neck	95·00	12·00
		cj. "RA" joined	95·00	12·00
		cw. Wmk inverted	26·00	3·00
		cz. Wmk sideways	†	£50000
		d. Die II *Carmine-red* (*shades*)	£425	6·50
		db. Substituted cliché (Pl 2 right pane R. 6/4) (2.18)	£1900	60·00
		dc. Pale carmine (*shades*)	£425	7·50
		dw. Wmk inverted	£1200	£110
22		4d. orange (6.1.15)	40·00	2·50
		a. Yellow-orange (1915)	40·00	3·25
		b. Lemon-yellow (3.16)	85·00	14·00
		c. Pale orange-yellow (1.17)	£110	12·00
		d. Dull orange (1920)	55·00	3·25
		e. Line through "FOUR PENCE" (*all shades*) *From*	£350	£110
		w. Wmk inverted	42·00	12·00
23		5d. brown (*P* 14¼ (*line*)) (22.2.15)	50·00	7·50
		aw. Wmk inverted	£1400	£950
		b. Perf 14¼×14 (comb)	27·00	2·00
		ba. Yellow-brown (1920)	29·00	2·75
		bw. Wmk inverted	£750	£550

The variety No. 20d was caused by the engraving of a new fraction in a defective electro in 1918.

No. 21ca was caused by rusting on two positions of the steel Plate 2 and shows as white patches on the back of the King's neck and on, and beside, the top of the right frame (right pane R. 6/4) and on the left frame, wattles, head and ears of kangaroo (right pane R. 6/5). These were noticed in December 1916 when the damaged impressions were removed and replaced by a pair of copper electros (Die II for R. 6/4 and Die I for R. 6/5), showing rounded corners and some frame damage, the former also showing a white spot under tail of emu. In time the tops of the crown quickly wore away.

One example of No. 21cz has been recorded. It shows wmk crown to right *(as seen from the back of the stamp)*.

Most of Nos. 20/3 were perforated 14 by a comb machine (exact gauge 14.25×14), but printings of the ½d. in December 1915, of the 1d. in July and August 1914 and of the 5d. until June 1917 were perforated by a line machine measuring 14.2.

See also Nos. 47/k (W 5, rough paper), 48/52 (W 6a), 53/a (1d. Die III), 56/66b and 76/81 (W 5, new colours), 82 (W 6a), 83/4 (no wmk), 85/104 (W 7), 124/31 (W 15).

(Typo J. B. Cooke)

1915 (15 Jan–July). W **5**. P 12.

24	**1**	2d. grey (Die I)	£100	12·00
		w. Wmk inverted	†	£18000
25		2½d. indigo (Die II) (July)	90·00	30·00
26		6d. ultramarine (Die II) (Apr)	£200	22·00
		a. Bright blue	£425	70·00
		b. Die IIA. *Ultramarine* (substituted cliché) (Upper plate right pane R. 10/6)	£7500	£2750
		ba. Bright blue	£9000	£3750
		w. Wmk inverted	†	£40000
27		9d. violet (Die II) (9 July)	£200	45·00
		w. Wmk inverted	£4250	£1800
28		1s. blue-green (Die II) (Apr)	£180	35·00
29		2s. brown (Die II) (Mar)	£700	£120
30		5s. grey and yellow (Die II) (12 Feb)	£1000	£350
		a. Yellow portion doubly printed	£15000	£4000
		w. Wmk inverted	£1300	£500
24/30		*Set of 7*	£2250	£550

6

6a

2d. No. 35a (Upper plate left pane R. 10/1)

6d. Nos. 38da and 73a (Upper plate left pane R. 1/6)

(Typo J. B. Cooke (to May 1918), T. S. Harrison (to February 1926), A. J. Mullett (to June 1927) and thereafter J. Ash).

1915 (8 Oct)–**27**. W **6** (narrow Crown). P 12.

35	**1**	2d. grey (Die I) (11.15)	50·00	8·50
		a. Die IIA substituted cliché (upper plate left pane R. 10/1)*	£10000	£1800
		bw. Wmk inverted	75·00	30·00
		c. Silver-grey (*shiny paper*)	50·00	20·00
		d. Die IIA. *Silver-grey* (*shiny paper*) (3.18)	70·00	22·00
		daw. Wmk inverted	†	£10000
		dba. Grey (1920)	75·00	28·00
36		2½d. deep blue (Die II) (9.17)	27·00	10·00
		aw. Wmk inverted	£130	80·00
		b. Deep indigo (1919)	50·00	9·00
		ba. "1" of fraction omitted (Lower plate left pane R. 6/3)	£55000	£35000
37		3d. yellow-olive (Die I)	40·00	4·75
		a. In pair with Die II	£500	£375
		b. Olive-green (1917)	42·00	4·50
		ba. In pair with Die II	£550	£375
		cw. Wmk inverted	95·00	48·00
		d. Die II *Yellow-olive*	£225	40·00
		da. Olive-green	£250	40·00
		dw. Wmk inverted	£600	£350
		e. Die IIB. *Light olive* (12.22)	60·00	13·00
38		6d. ultramarine (Die II) (15.12.15)	80·00	7·50

a. Die IIA (substituted cliché) (Upper plate rt pane R. 10/6) £6500 £1700
b. Dull blue (6.18) 90·00 11·00
ba. Die IIA (substituted cliché) £6500 £1800
cw. Wmk inverted £450 £100
d. Die IIB. *Bright ultramarine* (23.7.21) 90·00 22·00
da. Leg of kangaroo broken £2250 £700
dw. Wmk inverted £600 £200
39 9d. violet (Die II) (29.7.16) 65·00 11·00
aw. Wmk inverted £325 £100
b. Die IIB. (16.4.19) 75·00 18·00
bw. Wmk inverted £300 95·00
c. Die II (substituted cliché) in pair with Die IIB £700 £550
40 1s. blue-green (Die II) (6.16) 60·00 8·00
aw. Wmk inverted £275 £120
b. Die IIB (11.20) 75·00 8·00
ba. Wmk sideways (13.12.27) 60·00 £400
bw. Wmk inverted £275 £120
41 2s. brown (Die II) (6.16) £275 14·00
a. Imperf three sides (horiz pair) £110000
b. Red-brown (aniline) £3250 £500
w. Wmk inverted £3750 £425
42 5s. grey and yellow (Die II) (4.18) £275 £110
a. Grey and orange (1920) £425 £160
b. Grey and deep yellow £325 £130
ba. Wmk sideways † £80000
c. Grey and pale yellow £275 £100
w. Wmk inverted £1300 £1100
43 10s. grey and pink (Die II) (5.2.17) £550 £350
a. Grey and bright aniline pink (10.18) £500 £325
ab. Wmk sideways £40000 £18000
aw. Wmk inverted £2750 £1600
b. Grey and pale aniline pink (1922) £600 £350
44 £1 chocolate and dull blue (Die II) (7.16) £3000 £1600
a. Chestnut and bright blue (6.17) £3250 £1800
ab. Wmk sideways † £45000
aw. Wmk inverted £4500 £3500
b. Bistre-brown and bright blue (7.19) £3250 £1800
ba. Frame printed double, one albino £8000
45 £2 black and rose (Die II) (12.19) £5000 £3250
a. Grey and crimson (1921) £4750 £3250
b. Purple-black and pale rose (6.24) £4500 £2750
35/45*b Set of* 11 £8000 £4250
43s/5s Optd "SPECIMEN" *Set of* 3 £850

*The Die IIA of No. 35a is a substituted cliché introduced to repair a crack which occurred on R. 10/1 of the upper plate left pane. Its Die IIA characteristics are more pronounced than on the sheet stamps from this die, with the break at left extending to the outer, in addition to the inner, frame line.

One plate of the 3d. contained mixed Die I and Die II stamps as described.

No. 39c comes from six substituted clichés taken from plate 2 (Die II) and inserted in plate 4 (Die IIB) at positions left pane R. 1/3-4, 2/3-4 and 8/6 and right pane R. 2/1 This substitution took place towards the end of the printings on W **6**. The variety can also be found on stamps with W **7** and W **15**, see Nos. 108a and 133a.

All values were printed by both Cooke and Harrison, and the 9d., 1s. and 5s. were also printed by Mullett and Ash.

The watermark on No. 40ba shows the Crown printing to the right, that on Nos. 42ba and 43ab shows the Crown pointing to the left *as seen from the back of the stamp*.

1916 (Nov)–**18**. Rough, unsurfaced paper, locally gummed. W **5**. P 14.

47 **5a** 1d. scarlet (Die I) 28·00 3·00
a. Deep red (1917) 28·00 2·50
b. Rose-red (1918) 35·00 2·75
ba. Substituted cliché (Pl 2 right pane R. 6/5) £1900 75·00
c. Rosine (1918) £400 28·00
ca. Substituted cliché (Pl 2 right pane R. 6/5) £3750 £425
d. Dot before "1" £130 18·00
e. Secret mark £130 18·00
f. Flaw under neck £130 18·00
g. "RA" joined £130 18·00
hw. Wmk inverted 60·00 12·00
i. Die II *Rose-red* (1918) £500 23·00
ia. Substituted cliché (Pl 2 right pane R. 6/4) £1900 75·00
iw. Wmk inverted £1200 £150
j. Die II *Rosine* (1918) £1500 £180
ja. Substituted cliché (Pl 2 right pane R. 6/4) £3750 £425
k. No wmk £6500 £4750

All examples of the 5d. on this paper were perforated "OS" and will be found listed as No. O60.

No. 47k is the result of misplacement of the sheet during printing. To qualify, there should be no trace of the Crown over A or a line watermark.

(Typo J. B. Cooke to May 1918 thereafter T. S. Harrison)

1918 (4 Jan)–**20**. W **6a** (Mult). P 14.

48 **5a** ½d. green (*shades*) 8·50 2·00
a. Thin 1 in fraction at right £100 £140
b. Wmk sideways † £30000
bw. Wmk sideways inverted † £30000
c. Cracked electro £325 £350
w. Wmk inverted 28·00 16·00
49 1d. carmine-pink (Die I) (23.1.18) £250 £140
aw. Wmk inverted † £27000
b. Deep red (1918) £5500 £3000
bw. Wmk inverted † £40000
c. Dot before "1" £1100 £450
d. Secret mark £1100 £450
e. Flaw under neck £1100 £450
f. "RA" joined £1100 £450
50 1d. carmine (10.12.19) 30·00 15·00
aw. Wmk inverted £1400 £3000
b. Deep red (aniline) (1920) £800 £300
c. Dot before "1" £250 90·00
d. Secret mark £250 90·00
e. Flaw under neck £250 90·00
f. "RA" joined £250 90·00
51 1½d. black-brown (30.1.19) 6·00 4·00
a. Very thin paper (2.19) 22·00 17·00
w. Wmk inverted 45·00 35·00
52 1½d. red-brown (4.19) 13·00 2·25
a. Chocolate (1920) 13·00 2·25
w. Wmk inverted £120 70·00

No. 48 was printed by Cooke and Harrison, Nos. 49/*b* by Cooke only and Nos. 50/2*a* by Harrison only. Nos. 49/*b* have rather yellowish gum, that of No. 50 being pure white.

The watermark on No. 48b shows the Crown pointing to the left and on No. 48bw pointing to the right, *as seen from the back of the stamp*. Two examples of No. 48b and two of No. 48bw are known.

1d. Die III

1d. Die III. In 1917 a printing (in sheets of 120) was made on paper originally prepared for printing War Savings Stamps, with watermark T **5**. A special plate was made for this printing, differing in detail from those previously used. The shading round the head is even; the solid background of the words "ONE PENNY" is bounded at each end by a white vertical line; and there is a horizontal white line cutting the vertical shading lines at left on the King's neck.

(Typo J. B. Cooke)

1918 (15 July). Printed from a new Die III plate on white unsurfaced paper, locally gummed. W **5**. P 14.

53 **5a** 1d. rose-red 75·00 35·00
a. Rose-carmine 75·00 35·00
w. Wmk inverted £160 90·00

(Typo T. S. Harrison or A. J. Mullett (1s.4d. from March 1926))

1918 (9 Nov)–**23**. W **5**. P 14.

56 **5a** ½d. orange (8.11.23) 5·50 2·00
w. Wmk inverted 8·50 11·00
57 1d. violet (*shades*) (12.2.22) 8·00 1·50
a. Imperf three sides (horiz pair) £50000
b. Red-violet 10·00 2·25
c. Dot before "1" 65·00 17·00
d. Secret mark 65·00 17·00
e. Flaw under neck 65·00 17·00
f. "RA" joined 65·00 17·00
58 1½d. black-brown 8·50 1·50
w. Wmk inverted 60·00 22·00
59 1½d. deep red-brown (4.19) 15·00 1·00
a. Chocolate (1920) 10·00 60
w. Wmk inverted 65·00 32·00
60 1½d. bright red-brown (20.1.22) 35·00 4·00
61 1½d. green (7.3.23) 5·50 1·00
a. Coarse unsurfaced paper (1923) £425 £170
w. Wmk inverted † £18000
62 2d. brown-orange (9.20) 14·00 1·00
a. Dull orange (1921) 16·00 1·00
w. Wmk inverted † £5500
63 2d. bright rose-scarlet (19.1.22) 18·00 1·50
a. Dull rose-scarlet 18·00 1·50
w. Wmk inverted £19000
64 4d. violet (21.6.21) 17·00 15·00
a. Line through "FOUR PENCE" (Pl 2 right pane R. 2/6) £32000 £8500

		b. "FOUR PENCE" in thinner letters (Pl 2 rt pane R. 2/6)	£475	£300
65		4d. ultramarine (*shades*) (23.3.22)	50·00	7·50
		a. "FOUR PENCE" in thinner letters (Pl 2 right pane R. 2/6)	£475	£170
		b. Pale milky blue	90·00	14·00
		w. Wmk inverted	90·00	£275
66		1s.4d. pale blue (2.12.20)	90·00	32·00
		a. Dull greenish blue	95·00	28·00
		b. Deep turquoise (1922)	£3500	£2750
56/66 *Set of* 11			£225	55·00

In addition to a number of mint pairs of No. 57a from two sheets purchased at Gumeracha, South Australia, with the bottom row imperforate on three sides, a single used example of No. 57 imperforate on three sides is known.

No. 61a was printed on a batch of coarse unsurfaced paper during 1923. Examples may be indentified by a clear vertical mesh in the paper, with mint stamps having a yellowish gum.

The 4d. ultramarine was originally printed from the Cooke plates but the plates were worn in mid-1923 and Harrison prepared a new pair of plates. Stamps from these plates can only be distinguished by the minor flaws which are peculiar to them.

The variety of Nos. 64 and 65 with "FOUR PENCE" thinner, was caused by the correction of the line through "FOUR PENCE" flaw early in the printing of No. 64.

(Typo T. S. Harrison (to February 1926), A. J. Mullett (to June 1927), thereafter J. Ash)

1923 (6 Dec)–**24**. W **6**. P 12.

73	**1**	6d. chestnut (Die IIB)	28·00	1·75
		a. Leg of kangaroo broken (Upper plate lt pane R. 1/6)	75·00	£120
		w. Wmk inverted	†	£22000
74		2s. maroon (Die II) (1.5.24)	75·00	32·00
		w. Wmk inverted	£2250	£1600
75		£1 grey (Die IIB) (1.5.24)	£650	£325
		s. Optd "SPECIMEN"	£100	

The 6d. and 2s. were printed by all three printers, but the £1 only by Harrison.

No. 73a was corrected during the Ash printing.

(Typo T. S. Harrison (to February 1926), thereafter A. J. Mullett)

1924 (1 May–18 Aug). P 14.

(a) W **5**

76	**5a**	1d. sage-green	6·00	1·50
		a. Dot before "1"	50·00	13·00
		b. Secret mark	50·00	13·00
		c. Flaw under neck	50·00	13·00
		d. "RA" joined	50·00	13·00
		w. Wmk inverted	24·00	10·00
77		1½d. scarlet (*shades*)	3·00	40
		a. Very thin paper	£110	50·00
		b. "HALEPENCE" (Pl 22 left pane R. 4/4)	30·00	38·00
		c. "RAL" of AUSTRALIA" thin (Pl 22 Left pane R. 5/4)	32·00	38·00
		d. Curved "1" and thin fraction at left (Pl 24 right pane R. 7/5)	32·00	38·00
		w. Wmk inverted	50·00	24·00
78		2d. red-brown	17·00	7·00
		a. Bright red-brown	22·00	8·00
		w. Wmk inverted	†	£24000
79		3d. dull ultramarine	26·00	2·00
		a. Imperf three sides (horiz pair)	£12000	
80		4d. olive-yellow	35·00	5·50
		a. Olive-green	32·00	6·00
		w. Wmk inverted	†	£17000
81		4½d. violet	24·00	3·50

(b) W **6a**

82	**5a**	1d. sage-green (20.5)	15·00	11·00
		a. Dot before "1"	80·00	75·00
		b. Secret mark	80·00	75·00
		c. Flaw under neck	80·00	75·00
		d. "RA" joined	80·00	75·00
		w. Wmk inverted	†	£18000

(c) No wmk

83	**5a**	1d. sage-green (18.8)	7·50	11·00
		a. Dot before "1"	55·00	75·00
		b. Secret mark	55·00	75·00
		c. Flaw under neck	55·00	75·00
		d. "RA" joined	55·00	75·00
84		1½d. scarlet (14 Aug)	25·00	9·50
76/84 *Set of* 9			£140	45·00

Nos. 78/*a* and 82/4 were printed by Harrison only but the remainder were printed by both Harrison and Mullett.

In the semi-transparent paper of Nos. 51a and 77a the watermark is almost indistinguishable.

Nos. 77b, 77c and 77d are typical examples of retouching of which there are many others in these issues. In No. 77c the letters "RAL" differ markedly from the normal. There is a white stroke cutting the oval frame-line above the "L", and the right-hand outer line of the Crown does not cut the white frame-line above the "A".

It is believed that No. 79a occurs on the bottom row of at least four sheets purchased from post offices in Victoria during 1926.

7

I

II

New Dies

1d.	For differences see note above No. 20.
1½d.	From new steel plates made from a new die. Nos. 87*a* and 96*a* are the Ash printings, the ink of which is shiny.
2d.	Die I. Height of frame 25.6 mm. Left-hand frame-line thick and uneven behind Kangaroo. Pearls in Crown vary in size.
	Die II. Height of frame 25.6 mm. Left-hand frame-line thin and even. Pearls in Crown are all the same size.
	Die III. Height 25.1 mm; lettering and figures of value bolder than Die I.
3d.	Die II has bolder letters and figures than Die I, as illustrated above.
5d.	Die II has a bolder figure "5" with flat top compared with Die I of the earlier issues.

(Typo A. J. Mullett or J. Ash (from June 1927))

1926–**30**. W **7**.

(a) P 14

85	**5a**	½d. orange (10.3.27)	6·50	7·50
		w. Wmk inverted	£110	95·00
86		1d. sage-green (23.10.26)	5·00	1·00
		a. Dot before "1"	65·00	20·00
		b. Secret mark	65·00	20·00
		c. Flaw under neck	90·00	30·00
		d. "RA" joined	90·00	30·00
		w. Wmk inverted	26·00	12·00
87		1½d. scarlet (5.11.26)	12·00	2·50
		a. Golden scarlet (1927)	23·00	2·50
		w. Wmk inverted	30·00	10·00
89		2d. red-brown (Die I) (17.8.27)	40·00	48·00
90		3d. dull ultramarine (12.26)	29·00	5·00
		w. Wmk inverted	†	£12000
91		4d. yellow-olive (17.1.28)	55·00	40·00
92		4½d. violet (26.10.27)	22·00	3·75
93		1s.4d. pale greenish blue (6.9.27)	£130	80·00
		w. Wmk inverted	†	£23000
85/93 *Set of* 8			£375	£170

(b) P 13½×12½

94	**5a**	½d. orange (21.11.28)	2·50	1·00
95		1d. sage-green (Die I) (23.12.26)	5·00	70
		aa. Dot before "1"	£100	40·00
		ab. Secret mark	£130	65·00
		ac. Flaw under neck	£130	55·00
		ad. "RA" joined	£130	55·00
		aw. Wmk inverted	30·00	24·00
		b. Die II (6.28)	50·00	80·00
		bw. Wmk inverted	£1900	£1800
96		1½d. scarlet (14.1.27)	2·75	1·00
		a. Golden scarlet (1927)	5·00	1·00
		w. Wmk inverted	16·00	2·50
97		1½d. red-brown (16.9.30)	6·00	6·50
98		2d. red-brown (Die II) (28.4.28)	17·00	9·50
99		2d. golden scarlet (Die II) (2.8.30)	23·00	2·75
		a. Die III (9.9.30)	8·00	1·00
		ab. No wmk	£1300	£2750
		ac. Tête-bêche (pair)	£200000	
		aw. Wmk inverted (*from booklets*)	9·50	1·60
100		3d. dull ultramarine (Die I) (28.2.28)	38·00	6·50
		aw. Wmk inverted	£180	£3000
		b. Die II *Deep ultramarine* (28.9.29)	20·00	1·40
		bw. Wmk inverted	†	£13000
102		4d. yellow-olive (19.4.29)	32·00	3·25
		w. Wmk inverted	†	£12000
103		4½d. violet Die I* (11.28)	70·00	32·00

103*a*		5d. orange-brown Die II (27.8.30)	45·00	7·00
104		1s.4d. turquoise (30.9.28)	£120	26·00
		w. Wmk inverted	†	£21000
94/104 *Set of* 11			£300	80·00

Owing to defective manufacture, part of the sheet of the 2d. (Die III), discovered in July 1931, escaped unwatermarked; while the watermark in other parts of the same sheet was faint or normal.

Only one example of No. 99ac is known.

*For the 4½d Die II see No. 120a.

8 Parliament House, Canberra

(Des R. A. Harrison. Die eng J. A. C. Harrison (Waterlow, London). Plates and printing by A. J. Mullett)

1927 (9 May). Opening of Parliament House, Canberra. No wmk. P 11.

105	**8**	1½d. brownish lake	50	50
		a. Imperf between (vert pair)	£5500	
		b. Imperf between (horiz pair)	£12000	£12000

(Eng H. W. Bell. Recess J. Ash)

1928 (29 Oct–2 Nov). Fourth National Stamp Exhibition, Melbourne. As T **4**. No wmk. P 11.

106	3d. blue (2 Nov)	4·50	6·50
MS106*a*	65×70 mm. No. 106×4	£110	£200
	ab. Imperf (pane of four)	£200000	

No. **MS**106*a* comes from special sheets of 60 stamps divided into 15 blocks of 4 (5×3) and separated by wide gutters perforated down the middle, printed and sold at the Exhibition.

(Typo J. Ash)

1929 (Feb)–**30**. W **7**. P 12.

107	**1**	6d. chestnut (Die IIB) (25.9.29)	35·00	4·50
108		9d. violet (Die IIB)	42·00	28·00
		a. Die II (substituted cliché) in pair with Die IIB	£600	£475
109		1s. blue-green (Die IIB) (12.6.29)	50·00	10·00
		w. Wmk inverted	†	£22000
110		2s. maroon (Die II) (3.29)	85·00	17·00
111		5s. grey and yellow (Die II) (30.11.29)	£250	£110
112		10s. grey and pink (Die II)	£475	£500
114		£2 black and rose (Die II) (11.30)	£4500	£750
107/14 *Set of* 7			£5000	£1300
112s/14s Optd "SPECIMEN" *Set of* 2			£450	

For No. 108a see note below No. 45*b*.

9 "DH66" Biplane and Pastoral Scene

"Long wing" flaw (R. 2/1 of booklet pane)

(Des R. A. Harrison and H. Herbert. Eng A. Taylor. Recess J. Ash)

1929 (20 May). Air. No wmk. P 11.

115	**9**	3d. green (*shades*)	9·00	4·25
		a. Booklet stamp	30·00	20·00
		b. "Long wing" flaw	£250	£150

No. 115 was originally issued in preparation for the inauguration of the Perth to Adelaide air service on 2 June 1929.

Variations of up to ¾ mm in the design size of No. 115 are due to paper shrinkage on the printings produced by the "wet" process. The last printing, in 1935, was printed by the "dry" method.

Booklet stamps may be identified by a dot in the centre of the horizontal margin between each stamp. The dot may appear above or below the design and is sometimes removed by perforation.

10 Black Swan

11 "Capt. Charles Sturt" (J. H. Crossland)

Re-entry ("T" of "AUSTRALIA" clearly double) (Pl 2 R. 7/4)

(Des G. Pitt Morrison. Eng F. D. Manley. Recess J. Ash)

1929 (28 Sept). Centenary of Western Australia. No wmk. P 11.

116	**10**	1½d. dull scarlet	2·00	2·00
		a. Re-entry	60·00	80·00

(Des R. A. Harrison. Eng F. D. Manley. Recess J. Ash)

1930 (2 June). Centenary of Exploration of River Murray by Capt. Sturt. No wmk. P 11.

117	**11**	1½d. scarlet	1·25	1·00
118		3d. blue	9·00	9·00

No. 117 with manuscript surcharge of "2d. paid P M L H I" was issued by the Postmaster of Lord Howe Island during a shortage of 2d. stamps between 23 August and 17 October 1930 (*Price* £750 *un. or used*). A few copies of the 1½d. value No. 96*a* were also endorsed (*Price* £1700 *un. or used*). These provisionals are not recognized by the Australian postal authorities.

TWO

PENCE

(**12**)

13 Fokker F. VIIa/3m *Southern Cross* above Hemispheres

4½d. Original die

4½d. Redrawn die

1930 (28 July–2 Aug). T **5a** surch as T **12**. W **7**. P 13½×12½.

119	2d. on 1½d. golden scarlet	2·75	1·00
120	5d. on 4½d. violet (2 Aug)	15·00	16·00
	a. Without surcharge	£6000	45·00

No. 120 is from a redrawn die in which the words "FOURPENCE HALFPENNY" are noticeably thicker than in the original die and the figure "4" has square instead of tapering serifs. The redrawn die also shows thin white lines to the left and right of the tablet carrying "FOURPENCE HALFPENNY".

Stamps from the redrawn die without the surcharge were not intended to be issued. Some stamps, *cancelled to order*, were included in sets supplied by the post office. A few mint copies, which escaped the cancellation were found and some may have been used postally.

6d. Re-entry ("FO" and "LD" double) (Pl 1 R. 5/5)

(Des and eng F. D. Manley. Recess John Ash)

1931 (19 Mar). Kingsford Smith's Flights. No wmk. P 11.

		(a) Postage		
121	**13**	2d. rose-red	2·25	1·00
122		3d. blue	8·50	6·50
		(b) Air. Inscr "AIR MAIL SERVICE" at sides		
123	**13**	6d. violet	6·50	17·00
		a. Re-entry	50·00	£110
121/3 *Set of 3*			15·00	22·00

15

17 Superb Lyrebird

(Typo John Ash).

1931–36. W **15**.

		(a) P 13½×12½		
124	**5a**	½d. orange (2.33)	11·00	5·00
125		1d. green (Die I) (10.31)	3·50	20
		w. Wmk inverted	40·00	10·00
		x. Wmk reversed	£2000	£1300
126		1½d. red-brown (10.36)	9·00	14·00
127		2d. golden scarlet (Die III) (18.12.31)	2·50	10
		w. Wmk inverted *(from booklets)*	5·00	50
128		3d. ultramarine (Die II) (30.9.32)	23·00	1·25
		w. Wmk inverted	£16000	£16000
129		4d. yellow-olive (2.33)	23·00	1·25
		w. Wmk inverted	†	£10000
130		5d. orange-brown (Die II) (25.2.32)	22·00	20
		w. Wmk inverted	†	£8000
131		1s.4d. turquoise (18.8.32)	50·00	2·75
		w. Wmk inverted	†	£14000
124/31 *Set of 8*			£130	22·00
		(b) P 12		
132	**1**	6d. chestnut (Die IIB) (20.4.32)	40·00	40·00
133		9d. violet (Die IIB) (20.4.32)	45·00	2·25
		a. Die II (substituted cliché) in pair with Die IIB	£425	£275
134		2s. maroon (Die II) (6.8.35)	12·00	1·00
135		5s. grey and yellow (Die II) (12.32)	£170	20·00
136		10s. grey and pink (Die II) (31.7.32)	£425	£150
137		£1 grey (Die IIB) (11.35)	£650	£275
138		£2 black and rose (Die II) (6.34)	£4250	£600
132/38 *Set of 7*			£5000	£900
136s/8s Optd "SPECIMEN" *Set of 3*			90·00	

Stamps as No. 127, but without watermark and perforated 11, are forgeries made in 1932 to defraud the P.O. (*Price* £400, *unused*).

For re-engraved type of No. 134, see No. 212.

For No. 133a see note below No. 45*b*.

(Des and eng F. D. Manley. Recess John Ash)

1931 (4 Nov). Air Stamp. As T **13** but inscr "AIR MAIL SERVICE" in bottom tablet. No wmk. P 11.

139		6d. sepia	22·00	17·00

1931 (17 Nov). Air. No. 139 optd with Type O **4**.

139*a*		6d. sepia	32·00	60·00

This stamp was not restricted to official use but was on general sale to the public.

(Des and eng F. D. Manley. Recess John Ash)

1932 (15 Feb). No wmk. P 11.

140	**17**	1s. green	45·00	2·75
		a. Yellow-green	55·00	5·00

18 Sydney Harbour Bridge

19 Laughing Kookaburra

(Des R. A. Harrison. Eng F. D. Manley. Printed John Ash)

1932 (14 Mar). Opening of Sydney Harbour Bridge.

		(a) Recess. No wmk. P 11		
141	**18**	2d. scarlet	7·00	4·25
142		3d. blue	10·00	11·00
143		5s. blue-green	£425	£200
		(b) Typo. W **15**. *P 10½*		
144	**18**	2d. scarlet	7·00	2·00
141/44 *Set of 4*			£425	£200

Stamps as No. 144 without wmk and perf 11 are forgeries made in 1932 to defraud the P.O. (*Price* £1000, *unused*).

The used price for No. 143 is for a cancelled to order example. Postally used examples are worth more.

(Des and eng F. D. Manley. Recess John Ash)

1932 (1 June). W **15**. P 13½×12½.

146	**19**	6d. red-brown	18·00	55
		w. Wmk inverted	†	£7000

20 Melbourne and R. Yarra

21 Merino Ram

(Des and eng F. D. Manley. Recess John Ash)

1934 (2 July–Aug). Centenary of Victoria. W **15**. P 10½.

147	**20**	2d. orange-vermilion	4·50	1·75
		a. Perf 11½ (Aug)	14·00	1·75
148		3d. blue	4·50	5·50
		a. Perf 11½ (Aug)	7·00	8·00
149		1s. black	55·00	20·00
		a. Perf 11½ (Aug)	65·00	22·00
147/49 *Set of 3*			55·00	25·00
147a/49a *Set of 3*			75·00	28·00

Stamps were originally issued perforated 10½, but the gauge was subsequently changed to 11½ in August 1934 due to difficulties in separating stamps in the first perforation.

(Des and eng F. D. Manley. Recess John Ash)

1934 (1–26 Nov). Death Centenary of Capt. John Macarthur (founder of Australian sheep farming). W **15**. P 11½.

150	**21**	2d. carmine-red (A)	8·00	1·75
150*a*		2d. carmine-red (B) (26 Nov)	26·00	3·25
151		3d. blue	17·00	18·00
152		9d. bright purple	38·00	50·00
150/52 *Set of 3* (excluding No. 150*a*)			55·00	60·00

Type A of the 2d. shows shading on the hill in the background varying from light to dark (as illustrated). Type B has the shading almost uniformly dark.

22 Hermes

23 Cenotaph, Whitehall

(Des F. D. Manley. Eng E. Broad and F. D. Manley. Recess John Ash until April 1940; W. C. G. McCracken thereafter)

1934 (1 Dec)–**48**.

		(a) No wmk. P 11		
153	**22**	1s.6d. dull purple	50·00	2·00
		(b) W **15**. *Chalk-surfaced paper. P 13½×14*		
153*a*	**22**	1s.6d. dull purple (22.10.37)	11·00	45
		b. Thin rough ordinary paper (12.2.48)	2·25	1·40

(Des B Cottier; adapted and eng F. D. Manley. Recess John Ash)

1935 (18 Mar). 20th Anniv of Gallipoli Landing. W **15**. P 13½×12½ or 11 (1s.).

154	**23**	2d. scarlet	3·25	30
155		1s. black (chalk-surfaced)	50·00	45·00

The 1s. perforated 13½×12½ is a plate proof (*Price* £1600, *unused*).

24 King George V on "Anzac"

3d. Apostrophe after second "E" of "GEORGE" (Sheet C, lower pane R. 4/2)

25 Amphitrite and Telephone Cable

(Des and eng F. D. Manley. Recess John Ash)

1935 (2 May). Silver Jubilee. Chalk-surfaced paper. W **15** (sideways). P 11½.

156	**24**	2d. scarlet	3·25	30
		a. Printed double, one albino	£300	£150
157		3d. blue	10·00	11·00
		a. Apostrophe flaw	£100	£100
158		2s. bright violet	35·00	48·00
156/58 *Set of* 3			42·00	55·00

(Des and eng F. D. Manley. Recess John Ash)

1936 (1 Apr). Opening of Submarine Telephone Link to Tasmania. W **15**. P 11½.

159	**25**	2d. scarlet	2·75	50
160		3d. blue	4·50	2·75

26 Site of Adelaide, 1836; Old Gum Tree, Glenelg; King William St, Adelaide

(Des and eng F. D. Manley. Recess John Ash)

1936 (3 Aug). Centenary of South Australia. W **15**. P 11½.

161	**26**	2d. carmine	4·00	40
162		3d. blue	11·00	3·50
163		1s. green	20·00	13·00
161/63 *Set of* 3			32·00	15·00

27 Wallaroo

28 Queen Elizabeth

28a Queen Elizabeth

29

30 King George VI

30a

31 King George VI

32 Koala

33 Merino Ram

34 Laughing Kookaburra

35 Platypus

36 Superb Lyrebird

38 Queen Elizabeth

39 King George VI

40 King George VI and Queen Elizabeth

Dies of 3d.:

Die I Die Ia Die II

Die I. The letters "TA" of "POSTAGE" at right are joined by a white flaw; the outline of the chin consists of separate strokes.

No. 168a is a preliminary printing made with unsuitable ink and may be detected by the absence of finer details; the King's face appears whitish and the wattles are blank. The greater part of this printing was distributed to the Press with advance notices of the issue.

Die Ia. As Die I, but "T" and "A" have been clearly separated by individual retouches made on the plates.

Die II A completely new die. "T" and "A" are separate and a continuous line has been added to the chin. The outline of the cheek extends to about 1 mm above the lobe of the King's right ear.

Die III. Differs from Dies I and II in the King's left eyebrow which is shaded downwards from left to right instead of from right to left. This die also shows more of the epaulette at the right of the stamp, similar to the 1s.4d. value.

½d. Line to Kangaroo's ear (Right pane R. 6/8)

2d. Medal flaw (Right pane R. 2/5)

6d. "Top hat" flaw (Lower plate, right pane R. 3/3)

1s. Roller flaw over "o" of "one" (Upper plate, right pane R. 1-6/6)

(Des R. A. Harrison (T **28/30**), F. D. Manley (T **27**, **31/6**), H. Barr (T **38/9**), H. Barr and F. D. Manley (T **40**). Eng F. D. Manley and T. C. Duffell (T **34**), T. C. Duffell (revised lettering for T **28a**, **30a**), F. D. Manley and E. Broad (T **38/40**), F. D. Manley (others). All recess with John Ash, W. C. G. McCracken or "By Authority ..." imprints)

1937–49. Chalk-surfaced paper (3d. (No. 168/c), 5s., 10s., £1). W **15** (sideways on 5d., 9d., 5s. and 10s.).

		(a) P 13½×14 (vert designs) or 14×13½ (horiz)		
164	**27**	½d. orange (3.10.38)	2·50	50
165	**28**	1d. emerald-green (10.5.37)	1·00	50
166	**29**	1½d. maroon (20.4.38)	9·00	5·50
167	**30**	2d. scarlet (10.5.37)	1·00	50
168	**31**	3d. blue (Die I) (2.8.37)	65·00	23·00
		a. "White wattles" (from 1st ptg)	£170	85·00
		b. Die Ia	£150	8·50
		c. Die II (3.38)	65·00	7·00
		ca. Bright blue (ordinary thin paper) (20.12.38)	60·00	4·00
170	**32**	4d. green (1.2.38)	7·00	2·25
171	**33**	5d. purple (1.12.38)	2·00	60
172	**34**	6d. purple-brown (2.8.37)	20·00	1·50
173	**35**	9d. chocolate (1.9.38)	8·50	2·50
174	**36**	1s. grey-green (2.8.37)	50·00	2·75
175	**31**	1s. 4d. pale magenta (3.10.38)	3·50	2·50
		a. Deep magenta (1943)	5·50	2·50
		(b) P 13½		
176	**38**	5s. claret (1.4.38)	28·00	2·00
		a. Thin rough ordinary paper (*shades*) (4.2.48)	5·50	3·75
177	**39**	10s. dull purple (1.4.38)	50·00	17·00
		a. Thin rough ordinary paper (11.48)	50·00	35·00
		s. Optd "SPECIMEN"	35·00	
178	**40**	£1 bluish slate (1.11.38)	70·00	35·00
		a. Thin rough ordinary paper (4.4.49)	70·00	75·00
		s. Optd "SPECIMEN"	£800	
164/78 *Set of 14*			£250	65·00
		(c) P 15×14 (vert designs) or 14×15 (horiz) (1d. and 2d. redrawn with background evenly shaded and lettering strengthened)		
179	**27**	½d. orange (28.1.42)	55	60
		a. Line to kangaroo's ear	40·00	30·00
		b. Coil pair (1942)	22·00	38·00
		ba. Coil block of four (1943)	£950	
180	**28a**	1d. emerald-green (1.8.38)	10·00	60
181		1d. maroon (10.12.41)	3·25	80
		a. Coil pair (1942)	14·00	28·00
182	**29**	1½d. maroon (21.11.41)	8·00	17·00
183		1½d. emerald-green (10.12.41)	2·50	2·50
184	**30a**	2d. scarlet (11.7.38)	9·00	20
		a. Coil pair (10.41)	£350	£450
		b. Medal flaw	£325	£110
		w. Wmk inverted (*from booklets*)	15·00	75
185		2d. bright purple (10.12.41)	75	2·00
		a. Coil pair (1942)	50·00	75·00
		b. Medal flaw	80·00	90·00
		w. Wmk inverted (*from coils*)	£170	£130
186	**31**	3d. bright blue (Die III) (11.40)	45·00	3·75
187		3d. purple-brown (Die III) (10.12.41)	1·25	10
188	**32**	4d. green (10.42)	1·00	10
		w. Wmk inverted	£5000	£4000
189	**33**	5d. purple (17.12.45)	65	2·25
190	**34**	6d. red-brown (6.42)	3·50	10
		a. Purple-brown (1944)	1·75	10
		ab. "Top hat" flaw	£1300	£1500
191	**35**	9d. chocolate (12.9.43)	1·00	30
192	**36**	1s. grey-green (29.3.41)	2·75	10
		a. Roller flaw	60·00	23·00
		w. Wmk inverted	£5000	£4000
179/92 *Set of 14*			75·00	27·00

The watermark on No. 191 shows Crown to the left of C of A, on Nos. 171, 173 and 189 it is to the right, *as seen from the back of the stamp*.

For unwmkd issue, see Nos. 228/30*d*.

Thin paper. Nos. 176a, 177a, 178a. In these varieties the watermark is more clearly visible on the back and the design is much less sharp. On early printings of No. 176a the paper appears tinted.

SPECIAL COIL PERFORATION. This special perforation of large and small holes on the narrow sides of the stamps was introduced after 1939 for stamps issued in coils and was intended to facilitate separation. Where they exist they are listed as "Coil pairs".

The following with "special coil" perforation were placed on sale in *sheets*: Nos. 179, 205, 222*a* (1952), 228, 230, 237, 262 (1953), 309, 311, and 314. These are listed as "Coil blocks of four".

Coils with "normal" perforations also exist for Nos. 180 and 184.

41 "Governor Phillip at Sydney Cove" (J. Alcott)

2d. "Tail" flaw (Left pane R. 7/1. Later retouched)

(Des and eng E. Broad and F. D. Manley. Recess J. Ash)

1937 (1 Oct). 150th Anniv of Foundation of New South Wales. W **15**. P 13½×14.

193	**41**	2d. scarlet	3·75	30
		a. "Tail" flaw	£700	£140
194		3d. bright blue	9·50	2·25
195		9d. purple	28·00	14·00
193/95 *Set of 3*			38·00	15·00

42 A.I.F. and Nurse

(Des and eng F. D. Manley from drawing by Virgil Reilly. Recess W. C. G. McCracken)

1940 (15 July). Australian Imperial Forces. W **15** (sideways). P 14×13½.

196	**42**	1d. green	2·50	2·75
197		2d. scarlet	2·00	1·50
198		3d. blue	18·00	11·00
199		6d. brown-purple	35·00	30·00
196/99 *Set of 4*			50·00	40·00

(43) **(44)** **(45)**

(Opts designed by F. D. Manley)

1941 (10 Dec). Nos. 184, 186 and 171 surch with T **43/5**.

200	**30a**	2½d. on 2d. scarlet (V.)	1·00	70
		a. Pair, one without surcharge	£14000	
		b. Medal flaw	£450	£250
201	**31**	3½d. on 3d. bright blue (Y. on Black)	2·50	2·25
202	**33**	5½d. on 5d. purple (V.)	4·25	6·50
200/2 *Set of 3*			7·00	8·50

Nos. 200/2 were prepared in connection with the imposition of a ½d. "war tax" increase on most postage rates.

One sheet of the 2½d. on 2d. was discovered showing the surcharge omitted on R. 1/4 and R. 1/5.

46 Queen Elizabeth

46a Queen Elizabeth

47 King George VI

48 King George VI

49 King George VI

50 Emu

(Des F. D. Maley. Eng F. D. Manley and T. C. Duffell (T **46/a**) or F. D. Manley (others))

1942–50. Recess. W **15**. P 15×14.

203	**46**	1d. brown-purple (2.1.43)	3·00	10
		a. Coil pair (1944)	22·00	42·00

204	**46a**	1½d. green (1.12.42)	3·00	10
		w. Wmk inverted	—	—
205	**47**	2d. bright purple (4.12.44)	1·75	2·00
		b. Coil pair (1.49)	90·00	£120
		ba. Coil block of four (5.50)	£2750	
206	**48**	2½d. scarlet (7.1.42)	60	10
		a. Imperf (pair)*	£6500	
		w. Wmk inverted *(from booklets)*	7·00	2·25
207	**49**	3½d. bright blue (3.42)	3·50	60
		a. Deep blue	2·50	60
208	**50**	5½d. slate-blue (12.2.42)	1·25	20
203/8 *Set of 6*			11·00	2·50

*No. 206a comes in horizontal pair with the right-hand stamp completely imperforate and the left-hand stamp imperforate at right only.

Coils with normal perforations exist for 1d.

For stamps as Nos. 204/5 but without watermark see Nos. 229/30.

The following items are understood to have been the subject of unauthorised leakages from the Commonwealth Note and Stamp Printing Branch and are therefore not listed by us.

It is certain that none of this material was distributed to post offices for issue to the public.

Imperforate all round. 1d. Princess Elizabeth; 1½d. Queen; 2½d. King; 4d. Koala; 6d. Kookaburra; 9d. Platypus; 1s. Lyrebird (small) (also imperf three sides); 1s.6d. Air Mail (Type **22**); 2½d. Mitchell; 2½d. Newcastle (also imperf three sides or imperf vertically).

Also 2½d. Peace, unwatermarked; 2½d. King, *tête-bêche*; 3½d. Newcastle, in dull ultramarine; 2½d. King on "toned" paper.

52 Duke and Duchess of Gloucester

(Des F. D. Manley. Eng F. D. Manley and T. C. Duffell. Recess)

1945 (19 Feb). Arrival of Duke and Duchess of Gloucester in Australia. W **15**. P 14½.

209	**52**	2½d. lake	20	10
210		3½d. ultramarine	40	1·25
211		5½d. indigo	50	1·25
209/11 *Set of 3*			1·00	2·25

A B

1945 (24 Dec). Kangaroo type, as No. 134, but re-engraved as B. W **15**. P 12.

212	**1**	2s. maroon	4·50	7·50
		w. Wmk inverted	†	£24000

No. 134 has two background lines between the value circle and "TWO SHILLINGS"; No. 212 has only one line in this position. There are also differences in the shape of the letters.

53 Star and Wreath

54 Flag and dove

55 Angel and Queensland

56 Sir Thomas Mitchell

(Des F. D. Manley (2½d.), F. D. Manley and G. Lissenden (3½d.), G. Lissenden (5½d.). Eng F. D. Manley. Recess)

1946 (18 Feb). Victory Commemoration. W **15** (sideways on 5½d.). P 14½.

213	**53**	2½d. scarlet	20	10
214	**54**	3½d. blue	75	1·75
215	**55**	5½d. green	75	1·00
213/15 *Set of 3*			1·50	2·50

These designs were re-issued in 1995 with face values in decimal currency.

(Des F. D. Manley. Eng F. D. Manley and T. C. Duffell. Recess)

1946 (14 Oct). Centenary of Mitchell's Exploration of Central Queensland. W **15**. P 14½.

216	**56**	2½d. scarlet	25	10
217		3½d. blue	75	2·00
218		1s. grey-olive	75	75
216/18 *Set of 3*			1·60	2·50

57 Lt. John Shortland R.N.

58 Steel Foundry

59 Coal Carrier/Cranes

(Des and eng G. Lissenden (5½d.), F. D. Manley (others). Recess)

1947 (8 Sept). 150th Anniv of City of Newcastle, New South Wales. W **15** (sideways on 3½d.). P 14½ or 15×14 (2½d.).

219	**57**	2½d. lake	20	10
220	**58**	3½d. blue	60	1·50
221	**59**	5½d. green	60	75
219/21 *Set of 3*			1·25	2·00

60 Queen Elizabeth II when Princess

(Des R. A. Harrison. Eng. F. D. Manley. Recess)

1947 (20 Nov)–**52**. Marriage of Princess Elizabeth. P 14×15.

*(a) W **15** (sideways)*

222	**60**	1d. purple	15	70

(b) No wmk

222*a*	**60**	1d. purple (8.48)	10	10
		b. Coil pair (1.50)	2·25	5·50
		c. Coil block of four (9.52)	5·50	

No. 222 was originally prepared to mark the 21st birthday of Princess Elizabeth, but production delays resulted in it being issued on her wedding day instead.

61 Hereford Bull

61a Hermes and Globe

62 Aboriginal Art

62a Commonwealth Coat of Arms

Roller flaw below "E" of "POSTAGE" (R. 4/1 and 5/1). Later retouched.

(Des G. Sellheim (T **62**), F. D. Manley (others). Eng G. Lissenden (T **62**), F. D. Manley (1s.3d., 1s.6d., 5s.), F. D. Manley and R. J. Becker (10s., £1, £2). Recess)

1948 (16 Feb)–**56**. W **15**.

		(a) Wmk sideways. P 14½		
223	**61**	1s.3d. brown-purple	2·50	1·75
223*a*	**61a**	1s.6d. blackish brown (1.9.49)	1·00	10
224	**62**	2s. chocolate	1·50	10
		(b) Wmk upright. P 14½×13½		
224*a*	**62a**	5s. claret (11.4.49)	4·00	20
		ab. Thin paper (1951)	£100	70·00
224*b*		10s. purple (3.10.49)	20·00	85
		bws. Wmk inverted, optd "SPECIMEN"	£3000	
224*c*		£1 blue (28.11.49)	42·00	4·25
224*d*		£2 green (16.1.50)	85·00	16·00
		da. Roller flaw	£150	£100
223/24*d* *Set of 7*			£140	21·00
224*bs/ds* Optd "SPECIMEN" *Set of 3*			£160	
		(c) No wmk. P 14½		
224*e*	**61a**	1s.6d. blackish brown (2.12.56)	12·00	1·50
224*f*	**62**	2s. chocolate (27.6.56)	8·00	1·25

The frames of Nos. 224*b* and 224*c/d* differ slightly from Type **62a**. No. 224ab is an emergency printing on white Harrison paper instead of the toned paper used for No. 224*a*.

63 William J. Farrer

64 F. von Mueller

65 Boy Scout

(Des and eng F. D. Manley. Recess)

1948 (12 July). William J. Farrer (wheat research) Commemoration. W **15**. P 15×14.

225	**63**	2½d. scarlet	40	10

(Des and eng F. D. Manley. Recess)

1948 (13 Sept). Sir Ferdinand von Mueller (botanist) Commemoration. W **15**. P 15×14.

226	**64**	2½d. lake	30	10

(Des and eng F. D. Manley. Recess)

1948 (15 Nov). Pan-Pacific Scout Jamboree, Wonga Park. W **15** (sideways). P 14×15.

227	**65**	2½d. lake	30	10

See also No. 254.

½d. Sky retouch (normally unshaded near hill) (Rt pane R. 6/8) (No. 228a retouched in 1951)

1s. "Green mist" retouch. A large area to the left of the bird's feathers is recut (Upper plate left pane R. 9/3)

1948–56. No wmk. P 15×14 or 14×15 (9d.).

228	**27**	½d. orange (15.9.49)	20	10
		a. Line to kangaroo's ear	38·00	40·00
		b. Sky retouch	55·00	60·00
		c. Coil pair (1950)	1·00	3·25
		ca. Line to kangaroo's ear	95·00	
		cb. Sky retouch (in pair)	£350	
		d. Coil block of four (1953)	2·75	
229	**46a**	1½d. green (17.8.49)	2·00	2·75
230	**47**	2d. bright purple (20.12.48)	1·75	3·00
		aa. Coil pair	3·50	13·00
230*a*	**32**	4d. green (18.8.56)	2·00	2·25
230*b*	**34**	6d. purple-brown (18.8.56)	8·00	1·00
230*c*	**35**	9d. chocolate (13.12.56)	22·00	4·50
230*d*	**36**	1s. grey-green (13.12.56)	5·00	1·25
		da. "Green mist" retouch	£4250	£3000
		db. Roller flaw	40·00	25·00
228/30*d* *Set of 7*			35·00	13·50

66 "Henry Lawson" (Sir Lionel Lindsay)

67 Mounted Postman and Convair CV 240 Aircraft

(Des F. D. Manley. Eng. E. R. M. Jones. Recess)

1949 (17 June). Henry Lawson (poet) Commemoration. P 15×14.

231	**66**	2½d. maroon	40	10

(Des Sir Daryl Lindsay and F. D. Manley. Eng F. D. Manley. Recess)

1949 (10 Oct). 75th Anniv of Founding of U.P.U. P 15×14.

232	**67**	3½d. ultramarine	60	1·00

68 John, Lord Forrest of Bunbury

69 Queen Elizabeth

70 King George VI

(Des and eng F. D. Manley. Recess)

1949 (28 Nov). John, Lord Forrest of Bunbury (explorer and politician) Commemoration. W **15**. P 15×14.

233	**68**	2½d. lake	60	10

(Des and eng F. D. Manley. Recess)

1950 (12 Apr)–**52**.

		*(a) W **15**. P 15×14*		
234	**70**	2½d. scarlet (12.4.50)	10	10
235		3d. scarlet (28.2.51)	15	25
		aa. Coil pair (4.51)	17·00	50·00
		(b) No wmk		
236	**69**	1½d. green (19.6.50)	1·25	40
237		2d. yellow-green (28.3.51)	15	10
		a. Coil pair	6·50	10·00
		b. Coil block of four (11.52)	13·00	
237*c*	**70**	2½d. purple-brown (23.5.51)	15	50
237*d*		3d. grey-green (14.11.51)	15	10
		da. Coil pair (12.51)	24·00	55·00
234/37*d* *Set of 6*			1·75	1·25

On 14 October 1951 No. 235 was placed on sale in sheets of 144 originally intended for use in stamp booklets. These sheets contain three panes of 48 (16×3) with horizontal gutter margin between.

71 Aborigine

72 Reproduction of First Stamps of New South Wales

73 Reproduction of First Stamps of Victoria

(Des and eng F. D. Manley. Recess)

1950 (14 Aug). W **15**. P 15×14.

238	**71**	8½d. brown	1·00	1·00

For T **71** in a larger size, see Nos. 253/*b*.

(Des and eng G. Lissenden (T **72**), E. R. M. Jones (T **73**). Recess)

1950 (27 Sept). Centenary of First Adhesive Postage Stamps in Australia. P 15×14.

239	**72**	2½d. maroon	50	10
		a. Horiz pair. Nos. 239/40	1·00	1·25
240	**73**	2½d. maroon	50	10

Nos. 239/40 were printed alternately in vertical columns throughout the sheet.

74 Sir Edmund Barton

75 Sir Henry Parkes

76 "Opening First Federal Parliament" (T. Roberts)

77 Federal Parliament House, Canberra

(Des and eng F. D. Manley. Recess)

1951 (1 May). 50th Anniv of Commonwealth of Australia. P 15×14.

241	**74**	3d. lake	1·50	10
		a. Horiz pair. Nos. 241/2	3·00	3·00
242	**75**	3d. lake	1·50	10
243	**76**	5½d. blue	65	2·25
244	**77**	1s.6d. purple-brown	1·25	50
241/44 *Set of 4*			4·50	2·75

Nos. 241/2 were printed alternately in vertical columns throughout the sheet.

78 E. H. Hargraves

79 C. J. Latrobe

(Des and eng F. D. Manley. Recess)

1951 (2 July). Centenaries of Discovery of Gold in Australia and of Responsible Government in Victoria. P 15×14.

245	**78**	3d. maroon	1·10	10
		a. Horiz pair. Nos. 245/6	2·25	3·50
246	**79**	3d. maroon	1·10	10

Nos. 245/6 were printed alternately in vertical columns throughout the sheet.

80

81 King George VI

82

(Des E. R. M. Jones (7½d.), F. D. Manley (others) Eng. F. D. Manley. Recess)

1951–52. W **15** (sideways on 1s.0½d.). P 14½ (1s.0½d.) or 15×14 (others).

247	**80**	3½d. brown-purple (28.11.51)	10	10
		a. Imperf between (horiz pair)	£18000	
248		4½d. scarlet (20.2.52)	15	1·25
249		6½d. brown (20.2.52)	20	1·75
250		6½d. emerald-green (9.4.52)	30	55
251	**81**	7½d. blue (31.10.51)	15	1·25
		a. Imperf three sides (vert pair)	£23000	
252	**82**	1s.0½d. indigo (19.3.52)	1·50	60
247/52 *Set of 6*			2·10	4·75

No. 251a occurs on the left-hand vertical row of one sheet.

(Des F. D. Manley. Eng E. R. M. Jones. Recess)

1952 (19 Mar)–**65**. P 14½.

*(a) W **15** (sideways*)*

253	2s.6d. deep brown	2·25	1·00
	aw. Wmk Crown to left of C of A	£6000	£2750

(b) No wmk

253*b*	2s.6d. deep brown (30.1.57)	4·25	75
	ba. Sepia (10.65)	13·00	14·00

Design:—2s.6d. As T **71** but larger (21×25½ *mm*).

*The normal sideways watermark on No. 253 shows Crown to right of C of A, *as seen from the back of the stamp.*

No. 253*ba* was an emergency printing and can easily be distinguished from No. 253*b* as it is on white Harrison paper, No. 253*b* being on toned paper.

(Des and eng F. D. Manley. Recess)

1952 (19 Nov). Pan-Pacific Scout Jamboree, Greystanes. As T **65**, but inscr "1952–53". W **15** (sideways). P 14×15.

254	3½d. brown-lake	20	10

83 Butter

84 Wheat

85 Beef

(Des P.O. artists; adapted G. Lissenden. Typo)

1953 (11 Feb). Food Production. P 14½.

255	**83**	3d. emerald	30	10
		a. Strip of 3. Nos. 255/7	1·60	2·75
256	**84**	3d. emerald	30	10
257	**85**	3d. emerald	30	10
258	**83**	3½d. scarlet	30	10
		a. Strip of 3. Nos. 258/60	1·60	2·75
259	**84**	3½d. scarlet	30	10
260	**85**	3½d. scarlet	30	10
255/60 *Set of 6*			3·00	55

The three designs in each denomination appear in rotation, both horizontally and vertically, throughout the sheet.

86 Queen Elizabeth II

87 Queen Elizabeth II

(Des F. D. Manley from photograph by Dorothy Wilding Ltd. Eng D. Cameron. Recess)

1953–56. P 15×14.

(a) No wmk

261	**86**	1d. purple (19.8.53)	15	15
261*a*		2½d. blue (23.6.54)	20	15
262		3d. deep green (17.6.53)	20	10
		aa. Coil pair	5·00	8·00
		ab. Coil block of four (9.53)	15·00	
262*a*		3½d. brown-red (2.7.56)	1·00	30
262*b*		6½d. orange (9.56)	1·75	2·50

*(b) W **15***

263	**86**	3½d. brown-red (21.4.53)	20	10
263*a*		6½d. orange (23.6.54)	3·00	50
261/63*a* *Set of 7*			6·00	3·25

(Des and eng F. D. Manley. Recess)

1953 (25 May). Coronation. P 15×14.

264	**87**	3½d. scarlet	40	10
265		7½d. violet	75	1·40
266		2s. dull bluish green	2·50	2·25
264/6 *Set of 3*			3·25	3·25

88 Young Farmers and Calf

(Des P.O. artist; adapted P. E. Morriss. Eng E. R. M. Jones. Recess)

1953 (3 Sept). 25th Anniv of Australian Young Farmers' Clubs. P 14½.

267	**88**	3½d. red-brown and deep green	10	10

89 Lt.-Gov. D. Collins

90 Lt.-Gov. W. Paterson

91 Sullivan Cove, Hobart, 1804

(Des E. R. M. Jones, eng D. Cameron (T **89/90**); des and eng G. Lissenden (T **91**). Recess)

1953 (23 Sept). 150th Anniv of Settlement in Tasmania. P 15×14.

268	**89**	3½d. brown-purple	50	10
		a. Horiz pair. Nos. 268/9	1·00	1·75
269	**90**	3½d. brown-purple	50	10
270	**91**	2s. green	1·25	3·25
268/70 *Set of 3*			2·00	3·25

Nos. 268/9 were printed alternately in vertical columns throughout the sheet.

92 Stamp of 1853

93 Queen Elizabeth II and Duke of Edinburgh

94 Queen Elizabeth II

Re-entry. Vertical lines doubled in "ROYAL VISIT" and "3½ᴰ." (Lower plate left pane R. 8/2)

(Des R. L. Beck; eng G. Lissenden. Recess)

1953 (11 Nov). Tasmanian Postage Stamp Centenary. P 14½.

271	**92**	3d. rose-red	20	40

(Des and eng F. D. Manley; border and lettering on 7½d. des by R. M. Warner. Recess)

1954 (2 Feb). Royal Visit. P 14.

272	**93**	3½d. scarlet	20	10
		a. Re-entry	45·00	21·00
273	**94**	7½d. purple	30	1·25
274	**93**	2s. dull bluish green	60	65
272/74 *Set of 3*			1·00	1·75

95 "Telegraphic Communications"

96 Red Cross and Globe

(Des R. M. Warner. Eng P. E. Morriss. Recess)

1954 (7 Apr). Australian Telegraph System Centenary. P 14.

275	**95**	3½d. brown-red	20	10

(Des B. Stewart. Eng P. E. Morriss. Design recess: cross typo)

1954 (9 June). 40th Anniv of Australian Red Cross Society. P 14½.

276	**96**	3½d. ultramarine and scarlet	20	10

97 Mute Swan

98 Locomotives of 1854 and 1954

(Des R. L. Beck. Eng G. Lissenden. Recess)

1954 (2 Aug). Western Australian Postage Stamp Centenary. P 14½.

277	**97**	3½d. black	20	10

(Des R. M. Warner. Eng G. Lissenden. Recess)

1954 (13 Sept). Australian Railways Centenary. P 14.

278	**98**	3½d. purple-brown	30	10

99 Territory Badge

100 Olympic Games Symbol

101 Rotary Symbol, Globe and Flags

(Des F. D. Manley. Eng G. Lissenden. Recess)

1954 (17 Nov). Australian Antarctic Research. P 14½×13½.

279	**99**	3½d. grey-black	20	10

(Des R. L. Beck. Eng P. E. Morriss. Recess)

1954 (1 Dec)–**55**. Olympic Games Propaganda. P 14.

280	**100**	2s. deep bright blue	1·00	1·00
280*a*		2s. deep bluish green (30.11.55)	2·00	2·50

(Des and eng D. Cameron. Recess)

1955 (23 Feb). 50th Anniv of Rotary International. P 14×14½.

281	**101**	3½d. carmine	10	10

101a Queen Elizabeth II

101b Queen Elizabeth II

102 Queen Elizabeth II

(Des F. D. Manley from bas-relief by W. L. Bowles. Eng D. Cameron (7½d.), G. Lissenden (others). Recess)

1955 (9 Mar)–**57**. P 15×14 (T **101a/b**) or 14½ (T **102**).

*(a) W **15** (sideways)*

282	**102**	1s.0½d. deep blue	1·25	1·25

(b) No wmk

282*a*	**101a**	4d. lake (13.3.57)	40	10

		ab. Booklet pane of 6	7·50	
282*b*	**101b**	7½d. violet (13.11.57)	1·25	1·50
		ba. Double print	£5500	
282*c*	**101a**	10d. deep grey-blue (6.3.57)	60	1·00
282*d*	**102**	1s.7d. red-brown (13.3.57)	1·25	45
282/*d*	*Set of 5*		4·25	3·75

No. 282ab from booklet SB33 has the outer edges of the pane imperforate, producing single stamps with one or two adjacent sides imperforate.

The doubling on No. 282ba affects the lower part of the design only.

103 American Memorial, Canberra

104 Cobb & Co. Coach (from etching by Sir Lionel Lindsay)

(Des R. L. Beck (head by F. D. Manley). Eng F. D. Manley. Recess)

1955 (4 May). Australian–American Friendship. P 14×14½.

283	**103**	3½d. violet-blue	10	10

(Design adapted and eng by F. D. Manley. Recess)

1955 (6 July). Mail-coach Pioneers Commemoration. P 14½×14.

284	**104**	3½d. blackish brown	25	10
285		2s. reddish brown	1·00	1·60

105 Y.M.C.A. Emblem and Map of the World

106 Florence Nightingale and Young Nurse

(Des E. Thake. Eng P. E. Morriss. Design recess; emblem typo)

1955 (10 Aug). World Centenary of Y.M.C.A. P 14½×14.

286	**105**	3½d. deep bluish green and red	20	10
		a. Red (emblem) omitted	£26000	

Only one unused example of No. 286a has been reported. A further defective example exists used on cover.

(Des and eng F. D. Manley. Recess)

1955 (21 Sept). Nursing Profession Commemoration. P 14×14½.

287	**106**	3½d. reddish violet	10	10

107 Queen Victoria

108 Badges of New South Wales, Victoria and Tasmania

(Des and eng D. Cameron. Recess)

1955 (17 Oct). Centenary of First South Australian Postage Stamps. P 14½.

288	**107**	3½d. green	10	10

Imperf pairs of No. 288 are known. They come from die proof blocks of four.

(Des and eng F. D. Manley. Recess)

1956 (26 Sept). Centenary of Responsible Government in New South Wales, Victoria and Tasmania. P 14½×14.

289	**108**	3½d. brown-lake	10	10

109 Arms of Melbourne

110 Olympic Torch and Symbol

111 Collins Street, Melbourne

112 Melbourne across R. Yarra

(Des P. E. Morriss; eng F. D. Manley (4d.). Des and eng F. D. Manley (7½d.) Recess. Des and photo Harrison from photographs by M. Murphy and sketches by L. Coles (1s.). Des and photo Courvoisier from photographs by M. Murphy (2s.))

1956 (31 Oct). Olympic Games, Melbourne. P 14½ (4d.), 14×14½ (7½d., 1s.) or 11½ (2s.).

290	**109**	4d. carmine-red	25	10
291	**110**	7½d. deep bright blue	50	1·40
292	**111**	1s. multicoloured	60	30
293	**112**	2s. multicoloured	1·25	2·25
290/93	*Set of 4*		2·40	3·50

115 South Australia Coat of Arms

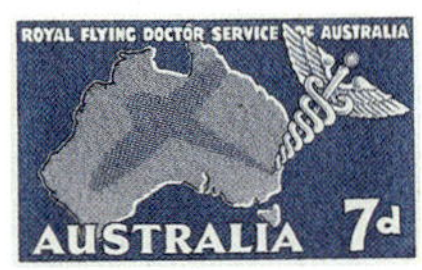

116 Map of Australia and Caduceus

(Des and eng P. E. Morriss. Recess)

1957 (17 Apr). Centenary of Responsible Government in South Australia. P 14½.

296	**115**	4d. red-brown	10	10

(Des J. E. Lyle; adapted B. Stewart. Eng D. Cameron. Recess)

1957 (21 Aug). Flying Doctor Service. P 14½×14.

297	**116**	7d. ultramarine	15	10

117 "The Spirit of Christmas"

Re-entry. "ISTMAS" and "TRALI" double. (Upper plate left pane R. 10/1)

(Des and eng D. Cameron from a painting by Sir Joshua Reynolds. Recess)

1957 (6 Nov). Christmas. P 14½×14.

298	**117**	3½d. scarlet	10	20
		a. Re-entry	9·50	14·00
299		4d. purple	10	10

118 Lockheed L.1049 Super Constellation Airliner

Re-entry on final "A" of "AUSTRALIA" (R. 7/6)

(Des and eng P. E. Morriss. Recess)

1958 (6 Jan). Inauguration of Australian "Round the World" Air Service. P 14½×14.

301	**118**	2s. deep blue	1·00	1·00
		a. Re-entry	48·00	48·00

119 Hall of Memory, Sailor and Airman

120 Sir Charles Kingsford Smith and Fokker F.VIIa/3m *Southern Cross*

(Des and eng G. Lissenden. Recess)

1958 (10 Feb). T **119** and similar horiz design. P 14½×14.

302		5½d. brown-red	60	30
		a. Horiz pair. Nos. 302/303	1·50	5·50
303		5½d. brown-red	60	30

No. 303 shows a soldier and service-woman respectively in place of the sailor and airman. Nos. 302/3 are printed alternately in vertical columns throughout the sheet.

(Des J. E. Lyle. Eng F. D. Manley. Recess)

1958 (27 Aug). 30th Anniv of First Air Crossing of the Tasman Sea. P 14×14½.

304	**120**	8d. deep ultramarine	60	1·00

121 Silver Mine, Broken Hill

122 The Nativity

(Des R. H. Evans; adapted and eng F. D. Manley. Recess)

1958 (10 Sept). 75th Anniv of Founding of Broken Hill. P 14½×14.

305	**121**	4d. chocolate	30	10

(Des D. Cameron. Eng P. E. Morriss. Recess)

1958 (5 Nov). Christmas. P 14½×15.

306	**122**	3½d. deep scarlet	20	30
307		4d. deep violet	20	10

123

124

126

127

128 Queen Elizabeth II

129

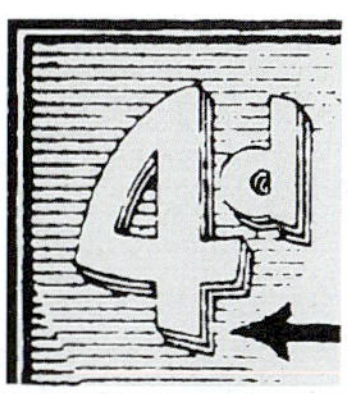

Type I Short break in outer line to bottom right of "4"

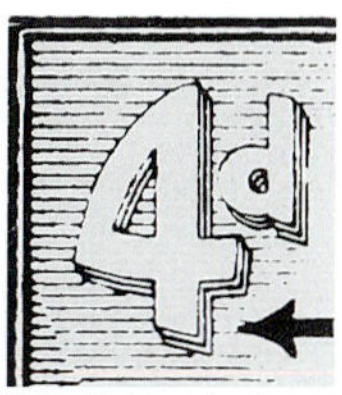

Type II Line unbroken

Type A Four short lines inside "5"

Type B Five short lines inside "5"

1d. Re-entry. Line running through base of "RALIA" (Lower right plate, right pane R. 1/8).

3½d. Re-entry to "E" and left frame (R. 1/10)

(Des G. Lissenden from photographs by Baron Studios. Eng F. D. Manley (2d.), D. Cameron (3d.). P. E. Morriss (others). Recess)

1959–63. P 14×15 (horiz) or 15×14 (vert).

308	**123**	1d. deep slate-purple (2.2.59)	10	10
		a. Deep slate-lilac (1961)	2·00	30
		b. Re-entry	24·00	
309	**124**	2d. brown (21.3.62)	60	20
		a. Coil pair (1962)	4·50	7·00
		b. Coil block of four (1963)	14·00	
311	**126**	3d. blue-green (20.5.59)	15	10
		a. Coil pair (8.59)	4·00	6·50
		b. Coil block of four	14·00	
312	**127**	3½d. deep green (18.3.59)	15	15
		a. Re-entry	24·00	
313	**128**	4d. carmine-lake (Type I) (2.2.59)	3·00	10
		a. Carmine-red	3·00	10
		ab. Booklet pane of 6 (18.3.59)	20·00	
		b. Type II	3·00	10
		ba. Carmine-red	3·00	10
314	**129**	5d. deep blue (Type A or B) (1.10.59)	1·50	10
		a. Vert *se-tenant* pair (A and B)	3·50	6·50
		b. Coil pair (18.7.60)	10·00	15·00
		c. Coil block of four (7.61)	50·00	
		d. Booklet pane of 6 (23.3.60)	11·00	
		da. Imperf between (horiz pair)	£11000	
308/14 *Set of 6*			4·75	65

No. 313. Produced in printer's sheets, of 640 split into sheets of 160 for issue. Type I occurs on the two upper sheets from the printers' sheet and on ten positions from the left pane of the lower right sheet. Type II occurs on all stamps from the lower sheets except for ten positions from the left pane of lower right sheet.

No. 314. Both types occur in alternate horizontal rows in the sheet (Type A in Row 1, Type B in Row 2, and so on), and their value is identical. Booklet pane No. 314d from SB35/6a contains two Type A and four Type B.

Nos. 309a/b, 311a/b and 314b/c have horizontal coil perforations as described after No. 191.

Nos. 313ab from booklets SB34/a and 314d from booklets SB35/6a have the outer edges of the panes imperforate, producing stamps with one or two adjacent sides imperforate.

A single example (imperforate at base) of No.314da is known, apparently from a miscut booklet pane.

Printings of the 2d. (from March 1965) and of the 3d. (from April 1965), both including coils, were on Helecon paper.

131 Numbat

132 Tiger Cat

133 Eastern Grey Kangaroos

134 Common Rabbit-Bandicoot

135 Platypus

136 Thylacine

137 Christmas Bells

138 Flannel Flower

139 Wattle

140 Banksia

141 Waratah

142 Aboriginal Stockman

2s. "T" retouch (Right plate R. 6/8)

(Des Eileen Mayo (6d., 8d., 9d., 11d., 1s., 1s.2d.), B. Stewart (5s.), Margaret Stones (others). Eng P. Morriss (11d.) F. D. Manley (1s.), B. Stewart (others). Recess)

1959–64. T **131/42**. W **15** (5s.), no wmk (others). P 14×15 (1s.2d.), 15×14 (6d. to 1s.), 14½×14 (5s.) or 14½ (others).

316	**131**	6d. brown (30.9.60)	1·75	10
317	**132**	8d. red-brown (11.5.60)	1·00	10
		a. Pale red-brown (9.61)	1·50	10
318	**133**	9d. deep sepia (21.10.59)	2·00	55
319	**134**	11d. deep blue (3.5.61)	1·00	15
320	**135**	1s. deep green (9.9.59)	2·50	40
321	**136**	1s.2d. deep purple (21.3.62)	1·00	15
322	**137**	1s.6d. crimson/*yellow* (3.2.60)	2·25	1·25
323	**138**	2s. grey-blue (8.4.59)	70	10
		a. "T" retouch	45·00	
324	**139**	2s.3d. green/*maize* (9.9.59)	1·00	10
324*a*		2s.3d. yellow-green (28.10.64)	2·50	75
325	**140**	2s.5d. brown/*yellow* (16.3.60)	4·25	1·00
326	**141**	3s. scarlet (15.7.59)	1·75	20
327	**142**	5s. red-brown (26.7.61)	14·00	3·00
		a. White paper. *Brown-red* (17.6.64)	90·00	7·50
316/327		*Set of* 13	32·00	6·50

No. 327 is on toned paper. No. 327a was a late printing on the white paper referred to in the note below No. 360.

An experimental printing of the 11d. was made on Helecon paper in December 1963. See note below No. 362.

All printings of the 8d., 11d., 1s.2d. and 2s.3d. (No. 324*a*) were on Helecon paper from April 1965.

143 Postmaster Isaac Nichols boarding the brig *Experiment*

144 Parliament House, Brisbane, and Arms of Queensland

(Des R. Shackel; adapted and eng F. D. Manley. Recess)

1959 (22 Apr). 150th Anniv of the Australian Post Office. P 14½×14.

331	**143**	4d. slate	15	10

(Des and eng G. Lissenden. Recess and typo)

1959 (5 June). Centenary of Self-Government in Queensland. P 14×14½.

332	**144**	4d. lilac and green	10	10

145 "The Approach of the Magi"

146 Girl Guide and Lord Baden-Powell

(Des and eng F. D. Manley. Recess)

1959 (4 Nov). Christmas. P 15×14.

333	**145**	5d. deep reddish violet	10	10

(Des and eng B. Stewart. Recess)

1960 (18 Aug). 50th Anniv of Girl Guide Movement. P 14½×14.

334	**146**	5d. deep ultramarine	30	15

147 "The Overlanders" (Sir Daryl Lindsay)

148 "Archer" and Melbourne Cup

Two types:

I. Mane rough

II. Mane smooth

Major re-entry below rider's right arm (Lower left plate R. 4/4). This occurs only on Type I.

Type II occurs on Pane A, Row 2 Nos. 8 and 9, Row 4 Nos. 1 to 12, Row 5 Nos. 10 to 12, and on Pane C, Row 4 Nos. 5 to 12, Row 5 Nos. 1 to 9, and Rows 6 to 10 inclusive; the stamps in Row 4 Nos. 5 to 12 and Row 5 Nos. 1 to 9 are considered to be of an intermediate type with the mane as in Type II but the ear and rein being as in Type I. All the rest are Type I.

(Adapted and eng P. E. Morriss. Recess)

1960 (21 Sept). Centenary of Northern Territory Exploration. P 15×14½.

335	**147**	5d. magenta (I)	50	15
		a. Major re-entry	55·00	
		b. Type II	3·50	2·00

(Des F. D. Manley. Eng G. Lissenden. Recess)

1960 (12 Oct). 100th Melbourne Cup Race Commemoration. P 14½.

336	**148**	5d. sepia	20	10

149 Queen Victoria

150 Open Bible and Candle

(Des F. D. Manley. Eng B. Stewart. Recess)

1960 (2 Nov). Centenary of First Queensland Postage Stamp. P 14½×15.

337 **149** 5d. deep myrtle-green 25 10

Re-entry. "19" of "1960" partially double (Lower left plate R. 5/2). On upper left plate R. 10/10 there is a similar partial doubling of "19" but to right of "1" and inside "9". Same price for either variety.

(Des K. McKay. Adapted and eng B. Stewart. Recess)

1960 (9 Nov). Christmas. P 15×14½.

338 **150** 5d. carmine-red 10 10
a. Re-entry .... 20·00

151 Colombo Plan Bureau Emblem

152 Melba (after bust by Sir Bertram Mackennal)

153 Open Prayer Book and Text

(Des and eng G. Lissenden. Recess)

1961 (30 June). Colombo Plan. P 14×14½.

339 **151** 1s. red-brown 30 10

No. 339 was issued on Helecon paper in April 1965. See note after No. 362.

(Des and eng B. Stewart. Recess)

1961 (20 Sept). Birth Centenary of Dame Nellie Melba (singer). P 14½×15.

340 **152** 5d. blue 30 15

(Des G. Lissenden. Eng P. E. Morriss. Recess)

1961 (8 Nov). Christmas. P 14½×14.

341 **153** 5d. brown 10 10

154 J. M. Stuart

155 Flynn's Grave and Nursing Sister

(Des W. Jardine. Eng P. E. Morriss. Recess)

1962 (25 July). Centenary of Stuart's Crossing of Australia from South to North. P 14½×15.

342 **154** 5d. brown-red 40 10

(Des F. D. Manley. Photo)

1962 (5 Sept). 50th Anniv of Australian Inland Mission. P 13½.

343 **155** 5d. multicoloured 30 15
a. Red omitted .... † £1900

The note below No. 372b also applies to No. 343a.

156 "Woman"

157 "Madonna and Child"

(Des D. Dundas. Eng G. Lissenden. Recess)

1962 (26 Sept). "Associated Country Women of the World" Conference, Melbourne. P 14×14½.

344 **156** 5d. deep green 10 10

(Des and eng G. Lissenden. Recess)

1962 (17 Oct). Christmas. P 14½.

345 **157** 5d. violet 15 10

158 Perth and Kangaroo Paw (plant)

159 Arms of Perth and Running Track

(Des R. M. Warner (5d.), G. Hamori (2s.3d.) Photo Harrison)

1962 (1 Nov). Seventh British Empire and Commonwealth Games, Perth. P 14 (5d.) or 14½×14 (2s.3d.).

346 **158** 5d. multicoloured 50 10
a. Red omitted £6500

347 **159** 2s.3d. black, red, blue and green .... 2·00 2·75

160 Queen Elizabeth II

161 Queen Elizabeth II and Duke of Edinburgh

(Des and eng after portraits by Anthony Buckley, P. E. Morriss (5d.), B. Stewart (2s.3d.). Recess)

1963 (18 Feb). Royal Visit. P 14½.

348 **160** 5d. deep green 35 10

349 **161** 2s.3d. brown-lake .... 1·50 3·25

162 Arms of Canberra and W. B. Griffin (architect)

163 Centenary Emblem

(Des and eng B. Stewart. Recess)

1963 (8 Mar). 50th Anniv of Canberra. P 14½×14.

350 **162** 5d. deep green 15 10

(Des G. Hamori. Photo)

1963 (8 May). Red Cross Centenary. P 13½×13.

351 **163** 5d. red, grey-brown and blue 60 10

164 Blaxland, Lawson and Wentworth on Mt. York

(Des T. Alban. Eng P. E. Morriss. Recess)

1963 (28 May). 150th Anniv of First Crossing of Blue Mountains. P 14½×14.

352 **164** 5d. ultramarine 15 10

165 "Export"

166 Queen Elizabeth II

(Des and eng B. Stewart. Recess)

1963 (28 Aug). Export Campaign. P 14½×14.

353	**165**	5d. red	10	10

(Des and eng P. E. Morriss from photograph by Anthony Buckley. Recess)

1963 (9 Oct)–**65**. P 15×14.

354	**166**	5d. deep green	1·00	10
		a. Booklet pane of 6	22·00	
		b. Imperf between (horiz pair) (31.7.64)	1·50	2·50
354*c*		5d. red (30.6.65)	55	10
		ca. Coil pair	19·00	38·00
		cb. Booklet pane of 6	22·00	

The 5d. deep green exists from both sheets and booklets on Helecon paper produced in error.

The 5d. red was issued with or without Helecon added to the ink. All coil and booklet printings included Helecon in the ink, except for a small printing produced in error. Examples of the sheet and booklet printings with Helecon ink have been found on Helecon *paper*.

Nos. 354a and 354cb have the outer edges of the panes imperforate producing single stamps with one or two adjacent sides imperforate. They come from booklets SB37/8a.

No. 354b comes from sheets of uncut booklet panes containing 288 stamps (16×18) with wide margins intersecting the sheet horizontally below each third row, alternate rows of stamps imperforate between vertically and the outer left, right and bottom margins imperforate. This means that in each sheet there are 126 pairs of stamps imperf between vertically, plus a number with wide imperforate margins attached, as shown in the illustration.

A 5d. in a similar design, printed in blue and brown with vertical edges imperforate, was prepared, but not issued.

167 Tasman and *Heemskerk*

168 Dampier and *Roebuck*

169 Captain Cook (after painting by Nathaniel Dance)

170 Flinders and *Investigator*

171 Bass and *Tom Thumb* (whaleboat)

172 Admiral King and *Mermaid (survey cutter)*

£2 Roller flaw, right-hand frame line at top (R. 1/3).

(Des W. Jardine. Eng B. Stewart (4s.), P. E. Morriss (5s., 7s., 6d., £1), M. Jones (10s). Recess)

1963–65. T **167/72**. No wmk (4s.) or W **15** (others), (sideways on 5s., £1). P 14 or 14½ (5s., £1, £2).

355	**167**	4s. ultramarine (9.10.63)	3·00	55
356	**168**	5s. red-brown (25.11.64)	4·75	1·75
357	**169**	7s.6d. olive (26.8.64)	21·00	19·00
358	**170**	10s. brown-purple (26.2.64)	25·00	5·00
		a. White paper. *Deep brown-purple* (14.1.65)	25·00	8·00
359	**171**	£1 deep reddish violet (26.2.64)	38·00	16·00
		a. White paper. *Deep bluish violet* (16.11.64)	48·00	30·00
360	**172**	£2 sepia (26.8.64)	55·00	75·00
		a. Roller flaw	£190	
355/60 *Set of 6*			£120	£110
357s/60s Optd "SPECIMEN" *Set of 4*			£475	

Nos. 358 and 359 were printed on a toned paper but all the other values are on white paper, the unwatermarked paper of the 4s. being rather thicker.

173 "Peace on Earth ..."

174 "Commonwealth Cable"

(Des R. M. Warner. Eng B. Stewart. Recess)

1963 (25 Oct). Christmas. P 14½.

361	**173**	5d. greenish blue	10	10

(Des P. E. Morriss. Photo)

1963 (3 Dec). Opening of COMPAC (Trans-Pacific Telephone Cable). Chalk-surfaced paper. P 13½.

362	**174**	2s.3d. red, blue, black and pale blue	1·50	3·00

HELECON (PHOSPHOR) STAMPS. "Helecon", a chemical substance of the zinc sulphide group, has been incorporated in stamps in two different ways, either in the ink with which the stamps are printed, or included in the surface coating of the stamp paper.

Owing to the difficulty of identification without the use of a U.V. lamp we do not list the Helecon stamps separately but when in stock can supply them after testing under the lamp.

The first stamp to be issued on Helecon was the 11d. Bandicoot (No. 319) from an experimental printing of four million released to the public in December 1963. The next printing, on ordinary paper, was released in September 1964. The experimental printing was coarse, showing a lot of white dots and the colour is slate-blue, differing from both the ordinary and the later Helecon paper.

Further Helecon printings followed from March 1965. Almost all issues from No. 378 onwards were on Helecon paper or paper coated with Derby Luminescence.

175 Yellow-tailed Thornbill

176 Black-backed Magpie

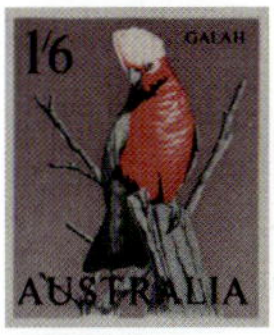

177 Galah

178 Golden Whistler

179 Blue Wren

180 Scarlet Robin

181 Straw-necked Ibis

(Des Betty Temple-Watts. Photo)

1964 (11 Mar)–**65**. Birds. T **175/81** and similar designs. Chalk-surfaced paper. P 13½.

363	**175**	6d. brown, yellow, black and bluish green (19.8.64)	1·50	50
		a. Brown, yellow, black and emerald-green	3·00	2·50
364	**176**	9d. black, grey and pale green	1·00	2·75
365	**177**	1s.6d. pink, grey, dull purple and black	75	1·40
366	**178**	2s. yellow, black and pink (21.4.65)	1·40	50
367	**179**	2s.5d. deep royal blue, light violet-blue, yellow-orange, grey and black	1·75	3·50
		a. Ordinary paper. *Deep blue, light blue, orange-brown, blue-grey and black* (7.65)	6·00	8·00
368	**180**	2s.6d. black, red, grey and green (21.4.65)	2·50	4·50
		a. Red omitted (white breast)	£18000	
369	**181**	3s. black, red, buff and yellow-green (21.4.65)	2·50	2·25
363/69 *Set of 7*			10·00	14·00

No. 367a was from a printing, made in 1962, on unsurfaced Wiggins Teape paper, the rest of the set being on chalk-surfaced Harrison paper. Apart from the differences in shade, the inscriptions, particularly "BLUE WREN", stand out very much more clearly on No. 367a. Although two colours are apparent in both stamps, the grey and black were printed from one cylinder.

The 6d. (No. 363) and 2s.5d. were only issued on ordinary paper. The 9d. and 1s.6d. exist on ordinary or Helecon paper. The 6d. (No. 363*a*), 1s., 2s.6d. and 3s. were issued on Helecon paper only.

182 Bleriot XI Aircraft (type flown by M. Guillaux, 1914)

5d. Re-entry to second "A" of "AUSTRALIA" (Upper right plate, R. 4/4 subsequently retouched)

(Des K. McKay. Adapted and eng P. E. Morriss. Recess)

1964 (1 July). 50th Anniv of First Australian Airmail Flight. P 14½×14.

370	**182**	5d. olive-green	30	10
		a. Re-entry	£275	£180
371		2s.3d. scarlet	1·75	2·75

183 Child looking at Nativity Scene

184 "Simpson and his Donkey"

(Des P. E. Morriss and J. Mason. Photo)

1964 (21 Oct). Christmas. Chalk-surfaced paper. P 13½.

372	**183**	5d. red, blue, buff and black	10	10
		a. Red omitted	£5000	£3250
		b. Black omitted	£3000	

The red ink is soluble and can be removed by bleaching and it is therefore advisable to obtain a certificate from a recognised expert committee before purchasing No. 372a. The used price quoted is for an example on cover.

(Des C. Andrew (after statue, Shrine of Remembrance, Melbourne). Eng E. R. M. Jones. Recess)

1965 (14 Apr). 50th Anniv of Gallipoli Landing. P 14×14½.

373	**184**	5d. drab	50	10
374		8d. blue	75	2·50
375		2s.3d. reddish purple	1·50	2·50
373/75 *Set of 3*			2·50	4·50

185 "Telecommunications"

186 Sir Winston Churchill

(Des J. McMahon and G. Hamori. Photo)

1965 (10 May). I.T.U. Centenary. Chalk-surfaced paper. P 13½.

376	**185**	5d. black, brown, orange-brown and blue	60	10
		a. Black (value and pylon) omitted	£5000	

(Des P. E. Morriss from photo by Karsh. Photo)

1965 (24 May). Churchill Commemoration. Chalk-surfaced paper. P 13½.

377	**186**	5d. black, pale grey, grey and light blue	30	10
		a. Pale grey (facial shading) omitted	£5500	
		b. Grey ("AUSTRALIA") omitted	†	£5500

No. 377a occurred on stamps from the bottom row of one sheet.

No. 377 exists on ordinary or Helecon paper in approximately equal quantities.

HELECON PAPER. All stamps from No. 378 were on Helecon paper, *unless otherwise stated.*

187 General Monash

188 Hargrave and "Multiplane" Seaplane (1902)

(Des O. Foulkes and W. Walters. Photo)

1965 (23 June). Birth Centenary of General Sir John Monash (engineer and soldier). P 13½.

378	**187**	5d. multicoloured	15	10

(Des G. Hamori. Photo)

1965 (4 Aug). 50th Death Anniv of Lawrence Hargrave (aviation pioneer). P 13½.

379	**188**	5d. purple-brown, black, yellow-ochre and purple	25	10
		a. Purple (value) omitted	£500	

189 I.C.Y. Emblem

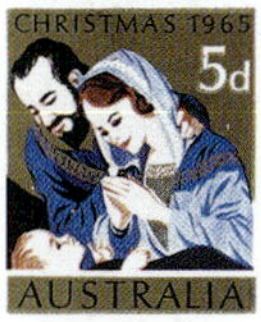

190 "Nativity Scene"

(Des H. Fallu from U.N. theme. Photo)

1965 (1 Sept). International Co-operation Year. P 13½.

380	**189**	2s.3d. emerald and light blue	1·00	1·50

(Des J. Mason. Photo)

1965 (20 Oct). Christmas. P 13½.

381	**190**	5d. multicoloured	15	10
		a. Gold omitted	£5500	
		b. Blue omitted	£1000	
		c. Brown omitted	£5000	

No. 381a comes from the bottom row of a sheet in which the gold is completely omitted, the background appearing as black with "CHRISTMAS 1965" and "AUSTRALIA" omitted. The row above had the gold missing from the lower two-fifths of the stamp.

Pre-decimal stamps, including "states" issues, remained valid for postage until 14 February 1968.

(New Currency. 100 cents = 1 dollar)

191 Queen Elizabeth II

192 Blue-faced Honeyeater

193 White-tailed Dascyllus ("Humbug Fish")

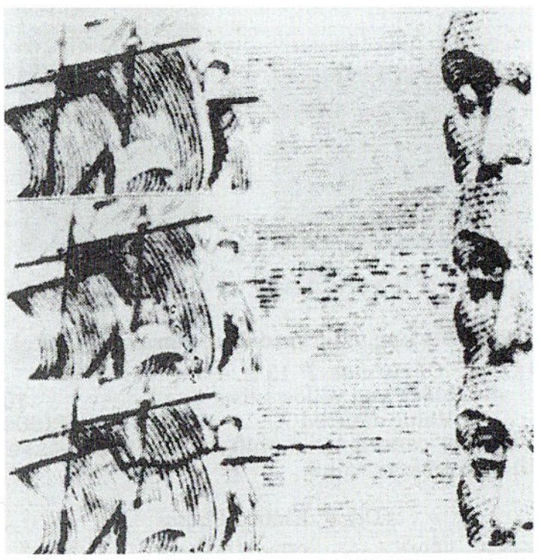

Nos. 401 (top), 401a (centre) and 401b (bottom). No. 401b shows the final form of the variety with a plate crack visible in sky and across sail (Lower sheet left pane. R. 10/1)

(Des Betty Temple-Watts (6c. (No. 387), 13c., 24c.), Eileen Mayo (7c. (No. 388) to 10c.). Recess (T **191**, 40c. to $4). Photo (others))

1966 (14 Feb)–**73**. Decimal currency. T **191/3** and similar designs, some reused from previous issues. P 15×14 (T **191**), 14 (40c., 75c., $1), 14½ (50c., $2, $4) or 13½ (others).

382	**191**	1c. deep red-brown	25	10
383		2c. olive-green	70	10
384		3c. slate-green	70	10
385		4c. red	20	10
		a. Booklet pane. Five stamps plus one printed label	16·00	
386	**175**	5c. brown, yellow, black and emerald-green	25	10
		a. Brown (plumage) omitted	£4500	
		b. Brown, yellow, black and blue-green (1.67)	25	20
386*c*	**191**	5c. deep blue (29.9.67)	70	10
		ca. Booklet pane. Five stamps plus one printed label	8·00	
		cb. Imperf in horiz strip of 3*	£3250	
387	**192**	6c. olive-yellow, black, blue and pale grey	1·00	1·00
		aa. Blue (eye markings) omitted	£3000	
387*a*	**191**	6c. orange (28.9.70)	1·00	10
388	**193**	7c. black, grey, salmon and brown	60	10
388*a*	**191**	7c. purple (1.10.71)	1·00	10
389	–	8c. red, yellow, blue-green and blackish green	60	1·00
390	–	9c. brown-red, purple-brown, black and light yellow-olive	60	20
391	–	10c. orange, blackish brown, pale turquoise blue and olive-brown	60	10
		a. Orange omitted	£5500	
392	–	13c. red black, grey and light turquoise-green	1·00	25
		a. Red omitted	£4250	
		b. Grey (plumage and legs) omitted	£4000	
393	**177**	15c. rose-carmine, black, grey and light bluish green	1·00	2·25
		a. Rose-carmine omitted	£7500	
		b. Grey omitted	£4000	
394	**178**	20c. yellow, black and pink	1·00	15
		a. Yellow (plumage) omitted	£5000	
395	–	24c. ultramarine, yellow, black and light brown	65	1·25
396	**180**	25c. black, red, grey and green	1·00	30
		a. Red omitted	£18000	
397	**181**	30c. black, red, buff and light yellow-green	2·75	1·50
		a. Red omitted	£4250	
398	**167**	40c. ultramarine	2·50	10
399	**168**	50c. red-brown	2·50	10
400	**169**	75c. olive	1·00	1·00
401	**170**	$1 brown-purple (*shades*)	1·50	20
		a. Recut lines in sky	90·00	
		b. Recut lines and plate crack	£130	
		c. Perf 15×14† (5.73)	85·00	22·00
402	**171**	$2 deep reddish violet	5·00	1·00
403	**172**	$4 sepia	6·00	6·50
382/403 *Set of 25*			30·00	15·00
400s/3s Optd "SPECIMEN" *Set of 4*			75·00	

Designs: Vert (as T **193**)—8c. Copper-banded Butterflyfish ("Coral Fish"); 9c. Hermit Crab; 10c. Orange Clownfish ("Anemone Fish"). (As T **192**)—13c. Red-necked Avocet; 15c. Galah; 20c. Golden Whistler; 30c. Straw-necked Ibis. Horiz (as T **192**)—24c. Azure Kingfisher; 25c. Scarlet Robin. As T **167**—75c. Captain Cook; $1 Flinders and *Investigator*. As T **168**—$2 Bass and whaleboat; $4 Admiral King and *Mermaid* (survey cutter).

*This shows two stamps imperforate all round and one imperforate at left only.

†The exact gauge of No. 401c is 14.8×14.1. No. 401 is 14.25×13.95.

Nos. 385a (from booklets SB39/a) and 386ca (from booklets SB42/3a) have the outer edges of the pane imperforate producing single stamps with one or two adjacent sides imperforate.

No. 385 was normally printed in Helecon ink. Early in 1967 experimental printings on different kinds of paper coated with Helecon or Derby Luminescents phosphor were put on sale. These cannot be distinguished by the naked eye.

199 Queen Elizabeth II

200 "Saving Life"

1966 (14 Feb)–**67**. Coil stamps. Photo. P 15×imperf.

404	**199**	3c. black, light brown and green	45	1·25
405		4c. black, light brown and light vermilion	35	1·25
405*a*		5c. black, light brown and new blue (29.9.67)	40	10
404/5*a Set of 3*			1·10	2·25

(Des L. Mason. Photo)

1966 (6 July). 75th Anniv of Royal Life Saving Society. P 13½.

406	**200**	4c. black, bright blue and blue	15	10

201 "Adoration of the Shepherds"

(Des L. Stirling, after medieval engraving. Photo)

1966 (19 Oct). Christmas. P 13½.

407	**201**	4c. black and yellow-olive	10	10
		a. Value omitted	£3750	

No. 407a was caused by a partial omission of the yellow-olive so that there was no colour surrounding the white face value.

202 *Eendracht*

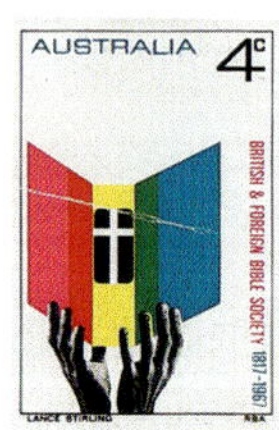

203 Open Bible

(Des F. Eidlitz. Photo)

1966 (24 Oct). 350th Anniv of Dirk Hartog's Landing in Australia. P 13½.

408	**202**	4c. multicoloured	10	10
		a. Red (sphere) omitted	£5000	
		b. Gold omitted	£2750	

(Des L. Stirling. Photo)

1967 (7 Mar). 150th Anniv of British and Foreign Bible Society in Australia. P 13½.

409	**203**	4c. multicoloured	10	10

204 Ancient Keys and Modern Lock

Broken frame between "R" and "S" of "YEARS" (Left-hand pane, R. 8/1)

(Des G. Andrews. Photo)

1967 (5 Apr). 150th Anniv of Australian Banking. P 13½.

410	**204**	4c. black, light blue and emerald	10	10
		a. Broken frame	3·50	

205 Lions Badge and 50 Stars

206 Y.W.C.A. Emblem

(Des M. Ripper. Photo)

1967 (7 June). 50th Anniv of Lions International. P 13½.

411	**205**	4c. black, gold and blue	10	10

(Des H. Williamson. Photo)

1967 (21 Aug). World Y.W.C.A. Council Meeting, Monash University, Melbourne. P 13½.

412	**206**	4c. deep blue, ultramarine, light purple and light blue	10	10

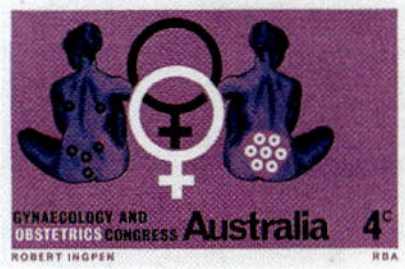

207 Anatomical Figures

5c
(208)

(Des R. Ingpen. Photo)

1967 (20 Sept). Fifth World Gynaecology and Obstetrics Congress, Sydney. P 13½.

413	**207**	4c. black, blue and light reddish violet	10	10

1967 (29 Sept). No. 385 surch with T **208**.

414	**191**	5c. on 4c. red	25	10
		a. Booklet pane. Five stamps plus one printed label	1·00	

No. 414 was only issued in 50c. or $1 booklets, Nos. SB40/1ab, with the outer edges of the pane imperforate so all stamps have one or two adjacent sides imperforate. It only exists printed in Helecon ink.

209 Christmas Bells and Gothic Arches

210 Religious Symbols

(Des M. Ripper (5c.), Erica McGilchrist (25c.). Photo)

1967. Christmas. P 13½.

415	**209**	5c. multicoloured (18.10.67)	20	10
		a. Imperf three sides (vert pair)	£13000	
416	**210**	25c. multicoloured (27.11.67)	1·00	1·90

No. 415a show the stamps perforated at left only.

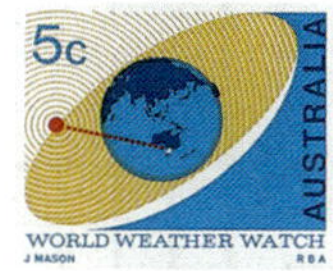

211 Satellite in Orbit

212 World Weather Map

(Des J. Mason. Photo)

1968 (20 Mar). World Weather Watch. P 13½.

417	**211**	5c. orange-brown, pale blue, black and ochre	30	10
418	**212**	20c. orange-brown, blue and black	1·10	3·00
		a. White (radio waves) omitted	£1500	
		b. Orange-brown (triangle) omitted	£4250	

213 Radar Antenna

214 Kangaroo Paw (Western Australia)

(Des R. Ingpen. Photo)

1968 (20 Mar). World Telecommunications via Intelsat II. P 13½.

419	**213**	25c. greenish blue, black and light blue-green	1·00	2·00

Type I.

Type II.

The 30c. was reprinted in 1971 from new cylinders so that Type II shows greater areas of white in the pink tones of the petals.

(Des Nell Wilson (6c., 30c.); R. and P. Warner (13c., 25c.); Dorothy Thornhill (15c., 20c.). Photo)

1968 (10 July)–**71**. State Floral Emblems. T **214** and similar vert designs. Multicoloured. P 13½.

420	6c. Type **214**	45	1·25
421	13c. Pink Heath (Victoria)	50	70
422	15c. Tasmanian Blue Gum (Tasmania)	50	40
423	20c. Sturt's Desert Pea (South Australia)	1·00	75
424	25c. Cooktown Orchid (Queensland)	1·10	75
425	30c. Waratah (New South Wales) (Type I)	50	10
	a. Green (leaves) omitted	£3750	
	b. Type II (29.6.71)	4·75	2·00
420/25	*Set of 6*	3·50	3·50

220 Soil Sample Analysis

(Des R. Ingpen. Photo)

1968 (6 Aug). International Soil Science Congress and World Medical Association Assembly. T **220** and similar horiz design. P 13½.

426	**220**	5c. orange-brown, stone, greenish blue and black	10	10

a. Nos. 426/7 *se-tenant* with gutter margin between .... 6·00 14·00

427 – 5c. greenish blue, dull olive-yellow, rose and black 10 10

Design:—No. 427, Rubber-gloved hands, syringe and head of Hippocrates.

The above were printed in sheets of 100 containing a pane of 50 of each design.

The major shades formerly listed have been deleted as there is a range of intermediate shades.

222 Athlete carrying Torch, and Sunstone Symbol

223 Sunstone Symbol and Mexican Flag

(Des H. Williamson. Photo)

1968 (2 Oct). Olympic Games, Mexico City. P 13½.

428 **222** 5c. multicoloured 30 10

429 **223** 25c. multicoloured .... 40 1·50

a. Green (left-hand panel) omitted £3250

224 Houses and Dollar Signs

225 Church Window and View of Bethlehem

(Des Erica McGilchrist. Photo)

1968 (16 Oct). Building and Savings Societies Congress. P 13½.

430 **224** 5c. multicoloured 10 60

(Des G. Hamori. Photo)

1968 (23 Oct). Christmas. P 13½.

431 **225** 5c. multicoloured 10 10

a. Green window (gold omitted) £850

b. Red (inscr) omitted £2500

226 Edgeworth David (geologist)

(Des Note Ptg Branch (Nos. 432, 434) A. Cook (others). Recess, background litho)

1968 (6 Nov). Famous Australians (1st series). T **226** and similar vert portraits. P 15×14.

432 5c. myrtle-green/*pale green* 25 20

a. Booklet pane. Five stamps plus one printed label .... 1·10

433 5c. black/*pale blue* 25 20

a. Booklet pane. Five stamps plus one printed label .... 1·10

434 5c. blackish brown/*pale buff* 25 20

a. Booklet pane. Five stamps plus one printed label .... 1·10

435 5c. deep violet/*pale lilac* 25 20

a. Booklet pane. Five stamps plus one printed label .... 1·10

432/35 *Set of 4* 90 70

Designs:—No. 432, Type **226**; No. 433, A. B. Paterson (poet); No. 434, Albert Namatjira (artist); No. 435, Caroline Chisholm (social worker).

Nos. 432/5 were only issued in $1 booklets, Nos. SB44/a, with the outer edges of the pane imperforate so all stamps have one or two adjacent sides imperforate.

See also Nos. 446/9, 479/82, 505/8, 537/40, 590/5, 602/7 and 637/40.

230 Macquarie Lighthouse

231 Pioneers and Modern Building, Darwin

(Des and eng Note Ptg Branch. Recess; background litho)

1968 (27 Nov). 150th Anniv of Macquarie Lighthouse. P 14½×13½.

436 **230** 5c. black and pale yellow .... 50 1·00

Used examples are known with the pale yellow background colour omitted.

(Des Marietta Lyon. Photo)

1969 (5 Feb). Centenary of Northern Territory Settlement. P 13½.

437 **231** 5c. blackish brown, yellow-olive and yellow-ochre 10 10

232 Melbourne Harbour

233 Concentric Circles (symbolising Management, Labour and Government)

(Des J. Mason. Photo)

1969 (26 Feb). Sixth Biennial Conference of International Association of Ports and Harbours, Melbourne. P 13½.

438 **232** 5c. multicoloured 20 10

(Des G. Hamori. Photo)

1969 (4 June). 50th Anniv of International Labour Organisation. P 13½.

439 **233** 5c. multicoloured 15 10

a. Gold (middle circle) omitted £3500

234 Sugar Cane

(Des R. Ingpen. Photo)

1969 (17 Sept). Primary Industries. T **234** and similar vert designs. Multicoloured. P 13½.

440 7c. Type **234** .... 50 1·50

441 15c. Timber .... 75 2·50

a. Black ("Australia" and value) omitted £1700

442 20c. Wheat 30 60

443 25c. Wool .... 50 1·50

440/43 *Set of 4* .... 1·90 5·50

238 "The Nativity" (stained-glass window)

240 Edmund Barton

(Des G. Hamori (5c.), J. Coburn (25c.). Photo)

1969 (15 Oct). Christmas. T **238** and similar multicoloured designs. P 13½.

444 5c. Type **238** 20 10

a. Magenta (robe) omitted £1800

b. Yellow omitted £1800

445 25c. "Tree of Life", Christ in Crib and Christmas Star (abstract) .... 1·00 2·00

(Des from drawings by J. Santry. Recess, background litho)

1969 (22 Oct). Famous Australians (2nd series). Prime Ministers. T **240** and similar vert designs each black on pale green. P 15×14.

446	5c. Type **240**	30	20
	a. Booklet pane. Five stamps plus one printed label	1·40	
447	5c. Alfred Deakin	30	20
	a. Booklet pane. Five stamps plus one printed label	1·40	
448	5c. J. C. Watson	30	20
	a. Booklet pane. Five stamps plus one printed label	1·40	
449	5c. G. H. Reid	30	20
	a. Booklet pane. Five stamps plus one printed label	1·40	
446/49 *Set of 4*		1·10	70

Nos. 446/9 were only issued in $1 booklets, Nos. SB45/a, with the outer edges of the pane imperforate so all stamps have one or two adjacent sides imperforate.

244 Capt. Ross Smith's Vickers Vimy, 1919

247 Symbolic Track and Diesel Locomotive

(Des E. Thake. Photo)

1969 (12 Nov). 50th Anniv of First England–Australia Flight. T **244** and similar horiz designs. P 13½.

450	5c. olive-green, pale blue, black and red	15	10
	a. Strip of 3. Nos. 450/2	1·50	2·00
451	5c. black, red and olive-green	15	10
452	5c. olive-green, black, pale blue and red	15	10
450/52 *Set of 3*		1·50	25

Designs:—No. 450, Type **244**; No. 451, Lt. H. Fysh and Lt. P. McGinness on 1919 survey with Ford Model T runabout; No. 452, Capt. Wrigley and Sgt. Murphy in Royal Aircraft Factory B.E.2E taking off to meet the Smiths.

The three designs appear *se-tenant*, both horizontally and vertically, throughout the sheet.

(Des B. Sadgrove. Photo)

1970 (11 Feb). Sydney–Perth Standard Gauge Railway Link. P 13½.

453	**247**	5c. multicoloured	15	10

248 Australian Pavilion, Osaka

251 Australian Flag

(Des J. Copeland (5c.), A. Leydin (20c.). Photo)

1970 (16 Mar). World Fair, Osaka. T **248** and similar horiz design. P 13½.

454	5c. multicoloured	15	10
455	20c. orange-red and black	35	65

Design:—20c. "Southern Cross" and "from the Country of the South with warm feelings" (message).

(Des P.O. Artists (5c.), J. Mason (30c.). Photo)

1970 (31 Mar). Royal Visit. T **251** and similar horiz design. P 13½.

456	5c. black and deep ochre	35	15
457	30c. multicoloured	1·10	2·75

Design:—5c. Queen Elizabeth II and Prince Philip.

252 Lucerne Plant, Bull and Sun

253 Captain Cook and H.M.S. *Endeavour*

5c. (No. 459). Red mark on sail at left (Top pane, R. 5/1)

(Des R. Ingpen. Photo)

1970 (13 Apr). Eleventh International Grasslands Congress, Queensland. P 13½.

458	**252**	5c. multicoloured	10	80

(Des R. Ingpen and "Team" (T. Keneally, A. Leydin, J. R. Smith). Photo)

1970 (20 Apr). Bicentenary of Captain Cook's Discovery of Australia's East Coast. T **253** and similar multicoloured designs. P 13½.

459	5c. Type **253**	30	10
	a. Strip of 5. Nos. 459/63	1·40	1·50
	aa. Black omitted	£16000	
	b. Red mark on sail	3·00	
460	5c. Sextant and H.M.S. *Endeavour*	30	10
461	5c. Landing at Botany Bay	30	10
462	5c. Charting and exploring	30	10
463	5c. Claiming possession	30	10
464	30c. Captain Cook, H.M.S. *Endeavour*, sextant, aborigines and kangaroo (63×30 *mm*)	1·00	2·50
459/64 *Set of 6*		2·25	2·75
MS465	157×129 mm. Nos. 459/64. Imperf	5·00	5·50

The 5c. stamps were issued horizontally *se-tenant* within the sheet, to form a composite design in the order listed.

Several used single 5c. stamps are also known with the black omitted.

50,000 miniature sheets were made available by the Post Office to the organisers of the Australian National Philatelic Exhibition which overprinted them in the white margin at each side of the 30c. stamp with "Souvenir Sheet AUSTRALIAN NATIONAL PHILATELIC EXHIBITION" at left and "ANPEX 1970 SYDNEY 27 APRIL–1 MAY" at right in light red-brown and they were also serially numbered. These were put on sale at the exhibition on the basis of one sheet to each visitor paying 30c. for admission. Although still valid for postage, since the stamps themselves had not been defaced, these sheets were not sold at post offices.

Subsequently further supplies were purchased and similarly overprinted and numbered by a private firm without the authority of the Post Office and ANPEX took successful legal action to stop their further sale to the public. This firm also had the unoverprinted sheets rouletted in colour between the stamps whilst further supplies of the normal sheets were overprinted with reproductions of old coins and others with an inscription commemorating the opening of Melbourne Airport on 1st July 1970, but all these are private productions. Further private productions have been reported.

259 Sturt's Desert Rose

AUSTRALIA I. AUSTRALIA II.

Two types of 2c.

I. "AUSTRALIA" thin: "2c" thin; flower name lightly printed.
II. Redrawn. "AUSTRALIA" thicker; "2c" much more heavily printed; flower name thicker and bolder.

(Des Note Ptg Branch. Photo)

1970–75. Coil Stamps. Vert designs as T **259**. Multicoloured. White fluorescent paper (10c.). Perf 15×imperf.

465*a*	2c. Type **259** (I) (1.10.71)	40	30
	ab. White fluorescent paper	40	
	b. Type II (white fluorescent paper)	1·50	1·25
	ba. Yellow omitted	£2000	
	bb. Grey omitted	£2250	
466	4c. Type **259** (27.4.70)	85	2·25
467	5c. Golden Wattle (27.4.70)	20	10
	aa. Yellow omitted	£2250	
	a. White fluorescent paper	20	
468	6c. Type **259** (28.9.70)	1·25	1·00
	a. Green (leaves) omitted	£3000	

468*b*	7c. Sturt's Desert Pea (1.10.71)	40	70
	ba. Black (berries, "7c." and inscr) omitted	£2000	
	bb. Buff (shadows on flowers) omitted	£225	
	bc. Buff and green (leaves) omitted	80·00	
	bd. White fluorescent paper (10.73)	40	
468*d*	10c. As 7c. (15.1.75)	60	2·00
465*a*/8*d* *Set of* 6		3·25	5·50

Nos. 465*a*/8*d* have horizontal coil perforations described after No. 191.

One used example of No. 468 is known with the magenta omitted.

Examples of No. 468bb also show the green colour displaced downwards.

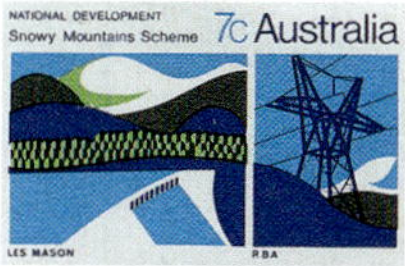

264 Snowy Mountains Scheme

265 Rising Flames

7c. Broken pylon leg (Left pane, R. 7/4).

(Des L. Mason (7c.), R. Ingpen (8c., 9c.), B. Sadgrove (10c.). Photo)

1970 (31 Aug). National Development (1st series). T **264** and similar horiz designs. Multicoloured. P 13½.

469	7c. Type **264**	20	1·75
	a. Broken pylon leg	8·00	
470	8c. Ord River Scheme	10	20
	a. Red omitted	£4250	
471	9c. Bauxite to aluminium	15	20
472	10c. Oil and Natural Gas	30	10
469/72 *Set of* 4		65	2·00

See also Nos. 541/4.

(Des G. Hamori, Photo)

1970 (2 Oct). 16th Commonwealth Parliamentary Association Conference, Canberra. P 13½.

473	**265**	6c. multicoloured	10	10

266 Milk Analysis and Dairy Herd

267 "The Nativity"

(Des R. Honisett. Photo)

1970 (7 Oct). 18th International Dairy Congress, Sydney. P 13½.

474	**266**	6c. multicoloured	10	10

(Des W. Beasley. Photo)

1970 (14 Oct). Christmas. P 13½.

475	**267**	6c. multicoloured	10	10
		a. Yellow omitted	£2250	

268 U.N. "Plant" and Dove of Peace

269 Boeing 707 and Avro 504

(Des Monad Design and Visual Graphics. Photo)

1970 (19 Oct). 25th Anniv of United Nations. P 13½.

476	**268**	6c. multicoloured	15	10

(Des G. Hamori. Photo)

1970 (2 Nov). 50th Anniv of QANTAS Airline. T **269** and similar horiz design. Multicoloured. P 13½.

477	6c. Type **269**	30	10
478	30c. Avro 504 and Boeing 707	70	2·00

270 The Duigan Brothers (Pioneer Aviators)

271 "Theatre"

(Des A. Cook (No. 480), T. Adams (No. 482), Note Ptg Branch (others). Recess (background litho))

1970 (16 Nov). Famous Australians (3rd series). T **270** and similar vert designs. P 15×14.

479	6c. blue	35	20
	a. Booklet pane. Five stamps plus one printed label	1·60	
480	6c. black/*cinnamon*	35	20
	a. Booklet pane. Five stamps plus one printed label	1·60	
481	6c. purple/*pale pink*	35	20
	a. Booklet pane. Five stamps plus one printed label	1·60	
482	6c. brown-lake/*flesh*	35	20
	a. Booklet pane. Five stamps plus one printed label	1·60	
479/82 *Set of* 4		1·25	75

Designs:—No. 479 Type **270**; No. 480 Lachlan Macquarie (Governor of N.S.W.); No. 481 Adam Lindsay Gordon (poet); No. 482 E.J. Eyre (explorer).

Nos. 479/82 were only issued in 60c. or $1.20 booklets, Nos. SB46/8a, with the outer edges of the pane imperforate so all stamps have one or two adjacent sides imperforate.

(Des D. Annand. Photo)

1971 (6 Jan). "Australia-Asia". 28th International Congress of Orientalists, Canberra. T **271** and similar horiz designs. Multicoloured. P 13½.

483	7c. Type **271**	40	40
484	15c. "Music"	60	60
485	20c. "Sea Craft"	60	50
483/5 *Set of* 3		1·40	1·40

272 The Southern Cross

273 Market "Graph"

(Des R. Beck. Photo)

1971 (21 Apr). Centenary of Australian Natives' Association. P 13½.

486	**272**	6c. black, vermilion and bright blue	10	10

(Des Monad Design and Visual Graphics Photo)

1971 (5 May). Centenary of Sydney Stock Exchange. P 13½.

487	**273**	6c. multicoloured	10	10

274 Rotary Emblem

275 Dassault Mirage Jets and de Havilland D.H.9A Biplane

(Des H. Williamson. Photo)

1971 (17 May). 50th Anniv of Rotary International in Australia. P 13½.

488	**274**	6c. multicoloured	15	10

(Des R. Honisett. Photo)

1971 (9 June). 50th Anniv of R.A.A.F. P 13½.

489	**275**	6c. multicoloured	70	10
		a. Black (face value and inscr) omitted	£3000	

276 Draught-horse, Cat and Dog

277 Bark Painting

(Des R. Ingpen. Photo)

1971 (5 July). Animals. T **276** and similar vert designs. Multicoloured. P 13½.

490	6c. Type **276**	20	10
491	12c. Vet and lamb ("Animal Science")	30	20
492	18c. Red Kangaroo ("Fauna Conservation")	1·00	35
493	24c. Guide-dog ("Animals Aid to Man")	70	1·50
490/3 *Set of 4*		2·00	1·90

The 6c. commemorated the Centenary of the Australian R.S.P.C.A., and the others were short-term definitives.

(Des J. Mason. Photo)

1971 (29 Sept)–**74**. Aboriginal Art. T **277** and similar multicoloured designs. P 13½.

494	20c. Type **277**	20	20
	a. White fluorescent paper (12.73)	70	
	ab. Sepia (face value and "Australia") omitted	£2750	
	ac. Blue omitted	£1300	
495	25c. Body decoration	20	55
	a. Black (face value and "Australia") omitted	£1300	
	b. White fluorescent paper (11.73)	70	
496	30c. Cave painting (*vert*)	65	20
	a. White fluorescent paper (12.73)	1·00	
497	35c. Grave posts (*vert*)	30	15
	a. White fluorescent paper (10.74)	75	
	ab. Black (face value and "AUSTRALIA") omitted	£2500	
494/7 *Set of 4*		1·25	1·00

The 35c. exists with either PVA gum or gum arabic.

278 The Three Kings and the Star

279 Andrew Fisher

(Des J. Lee. Photo)

1971 (13 Oct). Christmas. Colours of star and colour of "AUSTRALIA" given. P 13½.

498	**278**	7c. royal blue, pl mauve & pl lake-brn	30	15
		a. Block of 7. Nos. 498/504	12·00	17·00
		ab. Half-pane of 25	24·00	35·00
		b. White fluorescent paper	45	
		ba. Block of 7. Nos. 498b/504b	16·00	22·00
		bb. Half-pane of 25	32·00	42·00
499		7c. pale mauve, pl lake-brown & white	30	15
		b. White fluorescent paper	45	
500		7c. pale mauve, white and black	2·00	80
		b. White fluorescent paper	3·25	
501		7c. black, green and black	30	15
		b. White fluorescent paper	45	
502		7c. lilac, green and lilac	30	15
		b. White fluorescent paper	45	
503		7c. black, pale lake-brown and white	30	15
		b. White fluorescent paper	45	
504		7c. royal blue, pale mauve and green	10·00	2·25
		b. White fluorescent paper	12·00	
498/504 *Set of 7*			12·00	3·50

Nos. 498/504, which also exist on fluorescent paper, were issued in sheets having two panes of 50 stamps. Each half pane had its stamps arranged thus:—

498 499 500 499 498

503 502 501 502 503

504 501 500 501 504

503 502 501 502 503

498 499 500 499 498

FLUORESCENT VERY WHITE CHALK-SURFACED PAPER. As an experiment 10% of the above issue was printed on very white paper which fluoresces back and front under an ultraviolet lamp; it also has a strong coating of chalk on the surface. Late in 1972 this paper began to be introduced more generally and a number of stamps exist on both types. The normal Helecon paper does not fluoresce under the lamp but does react to the chalky test to a lesser degree.

(Des J. Santry. Recess (off-white backgrounds Litho)).

1972 (8 Mar). Famous Australians (4th series). Prime Ministers. T **279** and similar vert designs. P 15×14.

505	7c. ultramarine (Type **279**)	30	20
	a. Booklet pane. Five stamps plus one printed label	1·25	
506	7c. ultramarine (W. M. Hughes)	30	20
	a. Booklet pane. Five stamps plus one printed label	1·25	
507	7c. red (Joseph Cook)	30	20
	a. Booklet pane. Five stamps plus one printed label	1·25	
508	7c. red (S. M. Bruce)	30	20
	a. Booklet pane. Five stamps plus one printed label	1·25	
505/8 *Set of 4*		1·10	70

Nos. 505/8 were only issued in 70c. or $1.40 booklets, Nos. SB49/51a, with the outer edges of the pane imperforate so all stamps have one or two adjacent sides imperforate.

280 Cameo Brooch

281 Fruit

(Des Val Mason. Photo)

1972 (18 Apr). 50th Anniv of Country Women's Association. P 13½.

509	**280**	7c. multicoloured	20	10

(Des D. Annand. Photo)

1972 (14 June). Primary Industries. T **281** and similar horiz designs. Multicoloured. P 13½.

510	20c. Type **281**	1·00	2·50
511	25c. Rice	1·00	4·00
512	30c. Fish	1·00	1·00
513	35c. Beef	1·75	75
510/13 *Set of 4*		4·25	7·50

282 Worker in Wheelchair

283 Telegraph Line

(Des from photographs by Barbara Ardizzone. Photo)

1972 (2 Aug)–**73**. Rehabilitation of the Disabled. T **282** and similar designs. P 13½.

514	12c. yellow-brown and emerald	10	10
	a. White fluorescent paper (12.73)	10	
515	18c. sage-green and yellow-orange	1·00	35
516	24c. blue and yellow-brown	15	10
	a. White fluorescent paper (7.73)	15	
514/16 *Set of 3*		1·10	50

Designs: Horiz—18c. Patient and teacher. Vert—24c. Boy playing with ball.

(Des J. Copeland. Photo)

1972 (22 Aug). Centenary of Overland Telegraph Line. P 13½.

517 **283** 7c. multicoloured 15 15

284 Athletics

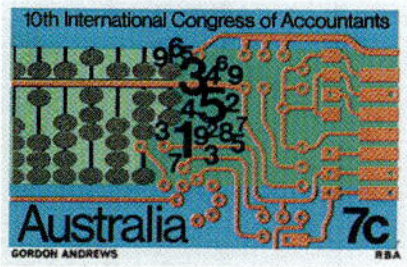

285 Numerals and Computer Circuit

(Des B. Sadgrove. Photo)

1972 (28 Aug). Olympic Games, Munich. T **284** and similar vert designs. Multicoloured. P 13½.

518 7c. Type **284** 25 25
519 7c. Rowing 25 25
520 7c. Swimming 25 25
521 35c. Equestrian .... 1·25 3·50
518/21 *Set of 4* .... 1·75 3·75

(Des G. Andrews. Photo)

1972 (16 Oct). Tenth International Congress of Accountants, Sydney. P 13½.

522 **285** 7c. multicoloured 15 15

286 Australian-built Harvester

(Des R. Ingpen. Photo)

1972 (15 Nov)–**74**. Pioneer Life. T **286** and similar multicoloured designs. P 13½.

523 5c. Pioneer family (*vert*) 10 10
a. White fluorescent paper (11.73) 15
524 10c. Water-pump (*vert*) 20 10
a. White fluorescent paper (5.74) 70
ab. Black (face value and inscr) omitted £1800
525 15c. Type **286** 15 10
a. Black (face value and inscr) omitted £2500
b. White fluorescent paper (12.73) 40
ba. Black (face value and inscr) omitted £1300
526 40c. House 15 30
a. White fluorescent paper (1974) 50
527 50c. Stage-coach 35 20
a. White fluorescent paper (1974) .... 1·25
ab. Black (face value and inscr) omitted £2500
528 60c. Morse key (*vert*) 30 80
a. White fluorescent paper (1974) 40
529 80c. *Gem* (paddle-steamer) 30 80
a. White fluorescent paper (1974) 40
ab. Black (face value and inscr) omitted £1000
523/9 *Set of 7* .... 1·40 1·90

287 Jesus with Children

288 "Length"

(Des from drawing by Wendy Tamlyn (7c.), L. Stirling (35c.). Photo)

1972 (29 Nov). Christmas. T **287** and similar vert design. Multicoloured. White fluorescent paper (7c.). P 15×14 (7c.) or 13½ (35c.).

530 7c. Type **287** 30 10
a. Brown-red ("Australia 7c") omitted £2750
b. Red-brown (inscr) omitted £1000
531 35c. Dove and spectrum motif .... 2·75 4·50

A used example of No. 530 is known with the blue omitted.

(Des Weatherhead & Stitt Pty Ltd. Photo)

1973 (7 Mar). Metric Conversion. T **288** and similar multicoloured designs. White fluorescent paper. P 15×14 (No. 535) or 14×15 (others).

532 7c. Type **288** 35 60
533 7c. "Volume" 35 60
a. Yellow-olive omitted* £1500
b. Pink omitted £1900
534 7c. "Mass" 35 60
a. Yellow-orange omitted £4250
535 7c. "Temperature" (*horiz*) 35 60
532/5 *Set of 4* .... 1·25 2·25

*This results in the man's drink and shorts appearing white, and the colour of the stool being the same as the background.

289 Caduceus and Laurel Wreath

290 William Wentworth (statesman and explorer)

(Des H. Williamson. Photo)

1973 (4 Apr). 25th Anniv of W.H.O. White fluorescent paper. P 15×14.

536 **289** 7c. multicoloured 30 15

(Des J. Santry. Recess and litho)

1973 (16 May). Famous Australians (5th series). T **290** and similar vert designs. P 15×14.

537 7c. yellow-bistre and black 35 50
a. Block of 4. Nos. 537/40 .... 1·25 1·75
538 7c. lilac and black 35 50
539 7c. yellow-bistre and black 35 50
540 7c. lilac and black 35 50
537/40 *Set of 4* .... 1·25 1·75

Designs:—No. 537, Type **290**; No. 538, Isaac Isaacs (first Australian-born Governor-General); No. 539, Mary Gilmore (writer); No. 540, Marcus Clarke (author).

Nos. 537/40 were printed in *se-tenant* blocks of four within the sheet.

291 Shipping

292 Banded Coral Shrimp

(Des J. Copeland. Photo)

1973 (6 June). National Development (2nd series). T **291** and similar vert designs. Multicoloured. P 12.

541 20c. Type **291** .... 1·50 2·75
542 25c. Iron ore and steel .... 1·50 3·25
543 30c. Beef roads .... 1·50 2·75
544 35c. Mapping .... 2·25 2·25
541/4 *Set of 4* .... 6·00 10·00

(Des Printing Bureau artists (1 to 4c.), J. Mason (others). Photo)

1973 (11 July)–**74**. Marine Life and Gemstones. T **292** and similar multicoloured designs. White fluorescent paper. P 14×15 (1 to 4c.) or 15×14 (others).

545 1c. Type **292** 10 10
a. Black (inscr and face value) omitted £450
b. Yellow-brown omitted £1300
546 2c. Fiddler crab 10 10
547 3c. Coral crab 10 10
a. Black (inscr and value) omitted £2250
548 4c. Mauve stinger 15 65
a. Black (face value and inscr) omitted £1300
549 6c. Chrysoprase (*vert*) .... 65 1·50
550 7c. Agate (*vert*) 20 10
a. Black (value and "agate") omitted .... 95·00 95·00
551 8c. Opal (*vert*) 25 10
a. Black (face value and inscr) omitted £425
552 9c. Rhodonite (*vert*) 35 15
552*a* 10c. Star sapphire (*vert*) (16.10.74) 55 10
ab. Black (value, inscr, etc.) omitted £275
ac. Turquoise-blue omitted* £100

ad. Ultramarine omitted £1600
ae. Printed on the gummed side .... 50·00
545/52a *Set of 9* .... 2·00 2·25

*The turquoise-blue occurs on the gemstones, and is normally partly covered by the black.

The 1, 3, 7 and 10c. exist with PVA gum as well as gum arabic.

293 Children at Play

294 John Baptising Jesus

(Des G. Hamori. Photo)

1973 (5 Sept). 50th Anniv of Legacy (Welfare Organisation). P 13½.

553 **293** 7c. cinnamon, deep claret and emerald 30 10

PERFORATIONS. From 1973 to 1975 two different perforating machines were used for some issues, giving gauges of 14½×14 or 15×14 (on horizontal stamps), the exact measurement being 14.4×14.1 or 14.8×14.1. The latter gauge was also used for a reprint of the $1 definitive (No. 401c).

(Des G. Hamori. Photo)

1973 (3 Oct). Christmas. T **294** and similar vert design. Multicoloured. White fluorescent paper. P 14×14½ (7c.) or 13½ (30c.).

554 7c. Type **294** 25 10
a. Perf 14×15 .... 4·50 80
ab. Printed on the gummed side £130
555 30c. The Good Shepherd .... 1·00 2·50

295 Sydney Opera House

296 Wireless Receiver and Speaker

(Des A. Leydin. Photo)

1973 (17 Oct). Architecture. T **295** and similar designs. White fluorescent paper. P 14½×14 (7, 10c.) or 13½ (40, 50c.).

556 7c. pale turquoise-blue and new blue 30 15
a. New blue (building and inscr) omitted. £3000
b. Perf 15×14 .... 4·50 1·60
557 10c. light ochre and sepia 80 70
558 40c. black, drab and dull mauve .... 1·40 2·50
a. Dull mauve (background) omitted £2500
559 50c. multicoloured .... 1·50 3·00
556/9 *Set of 4* .... 3·50 5·75

Designs: Horiz—10c. Buchanan's Hotel, Townsville; 40c. Como House, Melbourne. Vert—50c. St. James' Church, Sydney.

(Des E. Thake. Photo)

1973 (21 Nov). 50th Anniv of Regular Radio Broadcasting. P 13½.

560 **296** 7c. Lt turquoise-blue, brown-red & blk 15 10

297 Common Wombat

298 "Sergeant of Light Horse" (G. Lambert)

(Des R. Bates. Photo)

1974 (13 Feb). Animals. T **297** and similar vert designs. Multicoloured. White fluorescent paper. P 14×15 (20, 30c.) or 13½ (others).

561 20c. Type **297** 25 10
562 25c. Short-nosed Echidna 60 60
563 30c. Brush-tailed Possum .... 1·00 15
a. Carmine-red (face-value, etc) omitted ... £1300
564 75c. Pygmy Glider .... 65 1·00
561/64 *Set of 4* .... 2·25 1·60

The 20c. exists with gum arabic as well as PVA gum.

(Des P.O. artists. Litho Asher & Co, Melbourne ($5, $10). Photo R.B.A. (others))

1974 (24 Apr)–**79**. Paintings. T **298** and similar multicoloured designs. Ordinary paper ($1, $2, $4). P 13½ ($1, $2, $4) or 14½ (others).

565 $1 Type **298** (*shades*) .... 1·00 10
a. Black (face value and inscr) omitted £3250
566 $2 "Red Gums of the Far North" (H. Heysen) (*horiz*) .... 1·25 25
a. Black (face value and inscr) omitted £1600
566*b* $4 "Shearing the Rams" (Tom Roberts) (*horiz*) .... 2·00 1·75
ba. Black (face value and inscr) omitted £3250
567 $5 "McMahon's Point" (Sir Arthur Streeton) (14.3.79) .... 3·00 2·00
s. Optd "Specimen" .... 2·50
567*a* $10 "Coming South" (Tom Roberts) (19.10.77) .... 4·00 3·00
as. Optd "Specimen" .... 2·50
565/7a *Set of 5* .... 10·00 6·50

The $1, $2 and $4 exist with PVA gum as well as gum arabic. Nos. 567/a and 778 optd "Specimen" come from a special "Ausipex 84" Presentation Pack issued on 9 February 1983.

There are considerable variations in the colours of this series.

299 Supreme Court Judge

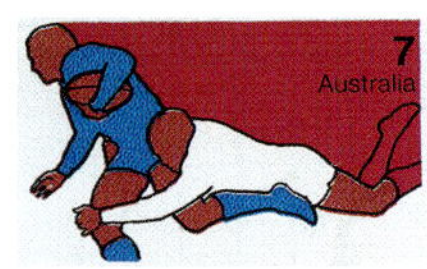

300 Rugby Football

(Des T. Thompson. Photo)

1974 (15 May). 150th Anniv of Australia's Third Charter of Justice. White fluorescent paper. P 14×15.

568 **299** 7c. multicoloured 20 10

(Des A. Leydin from drawings by D. O'Brien. Photo)

1974 (24 July). Non-Olympic Sports. T **300** and similar multicoloured designs. White fluorescent paper. P 15×14 (Nos. 569/70) or 14×15 (others).

569 7c. Type **300** 40 50
570 7c. Bowls 40 50
571 7c. Australian football (*vert*) 40 50
572 7c. Cricket (*vert*) 40 50
573 7c. Golf (*vert*) 40 50
a. Black (face value and inscr) omitted £1800
574 7c. Surfing (*vert*) 40 50
575 7c. Tennis (*vert*) 40 50
a. Light brown (skin colour) omitted £1800
569/75 *Set of 7* .... 2·50 3·25

301 "Transport of Mails"

302 Letter "A" and W. C. Wentworth (co-founder)

(Des J. Copeland. Photo)

1974 (9 Oct). Centenary of Universal Postal Union. T **301** and similar vert design. Multicoloured. White fluorescent paper. P 15×14 (7c.) or 13½ (30c.).

576 7c. Type **301** 40 20
a. Perf 14½×14 .... 1·50 30

577 30c. Three-part version of Type **301** ... 85 2·25

Most examples of the 7c. are on PVA gum; the 30c. was on gum arabic.

(Des I. Dalton. Typo and litho)

1974 (9 Oct). 150th Anniv of First Independent Newspaper, "The Australian". White fluorescent paper. P 14×15.

578 **302** 7c. black/*light cinnamon* ... 30 40
a. Perf 14×14½ ... 1·10 50

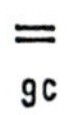

(**303**)

304 "The Adoration of the Magi"

1974 (16 Oct). No. 551 surch with T **303**, in red.

579 9c. on 8c. Opal ... 15 15

(Des, recess and litho R.B.A.)

1974 (13 Nov). Christmas. Woodcuts by Dürer. T **304** and similar vert design. White fluorescent paper. P 14×15.

580 10c. black/*cream* ... 25 10
581 35c. black/*cream* ... 80 1·00

Design:—35c. "The Flight into Egypt".

PROCESS. All the following issues to No. 772 were printed in photogravure, *except where otherwise stated.*

PAPER. The following issues were on white fluorescent paper *unless otherwise stated.* The gum used changed from gum arabic to PVA.

305 "Pre-School Education"

306 "Road Safety"

(Des Vivienne Binns (5c.), Erica McGilchrist (11c.), E. Tanner (15c.), J. Meldrum (60c.))

1974 (20 Nov). Education in Australia. T **305** and similar multicoloured designs. P 13½.

582 5c. Type **305** ... 25 40
583 11c. "Correspondence Schools" ... 25 60
584 15c. "Science Education" ... 40 40
585 60c. "Advanced Education" (*vert*) ... 50 2·00
582/5 *Set of 4* ... 1·25 3·00

(Des G. Andrews)

1975 (29 Jan). Environment Dangers. T **306** and similar horiz designs. Multicoloured. P 14×14½ (No. 586) or 14½×14 (others).

586 10c. Type **306** ... 50 50
a. Printed on the gummed side ... £120
587 10c. "Pollution" ... 50 50
a. Perf 15×14 ... 8·50 3·75
588 10c. "Bush Fires" ... 50 50
a. Perf 15×14 ... 2·50 1·25
586/8 *Set of 3* ... 1·40 1·40

307 Australian Women's Year Emblem

308 J.H. Scullin

(Des Leonora Howlett)

1975 (12 Mar). International Women's Year. P 14×15.

589 **307** 10c. dp violet-blue, green & bluish violet ... 20 15

This stamp exists with either PVA gum or gum arabic.

(Des B. Dunlop)

1975 (26 Mar). Famous Australians (6th series). Prime Ministers. T **308** and similar vert designs. Multicoloured. P 14×15.

590 10c. Type **308** ... 25 35
591 10c. J. A. Lyons ... 25 35
a. Printed on the gummed side ... £130
b. Dark brown omitted ...
592 10c. Earle Page ... 25 35
593 10c. Arthur Fadden ... 25 35
594 10c. John Curtin ... 25 35
595 10c. J. B. Chifley ... 25 35
590/5 *Set of 6* ... 1·40 1·90

Nos. 590/5 exist with either PVA gum or gum arabic.

No. 591b comes from the top row of the sheet on which the darker brown lines of detail on the face and tie are omitted.

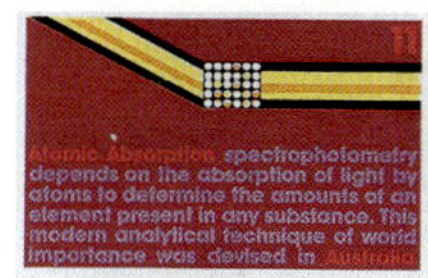

309 Atomic Absorption Spectrophotometry

310 Logo of Australian Postal Commission

(Des Weatherhead & Stitt)

1975 (14 May). Scientific Development. T **309** and similar horiz designs. Multicoloured. P 13½.

596 11c. Type **309** ... 70 75
597 24c. Radio astronomy ... 1·25 2·00
598 33c. Immunology ... 1·25 2·25
599 48c. Oceanography ... 1·50 2·75
596/9 *Set of 4* ... 4·25 7·00

(Des P. Huveneers)

1975 (1 July). Inauguration of Australian Postal and Telecommunications Commissions. T **310** and similar horiz design. P 14½×14.

600 10c. black, rosine and pale grey ... 25 20
a. Pair. Nos. 600/1 ... 1·10 2·00
b. Perf 15×14 ... 25 20
ba. Pair. Nos. 600b/1b ... 1·25 2·25
601 10c. black, orange-yellow and pale grey ... 25 20
b. Perf 15×14 ... 25 20

Design:—No. 601, Logo of Australian Telecommunications Commission.

Nos. 600/1 were printed together, *se-tenant* in horizontal and vertical pairs throughout the sheet.

311 Edith Cowan

312 *Helichrysum thomsonii*

313 "Tambaran" House and Sydney Opera House

(Des D. and J. O'Brien)

1975 (6 Aug). Famous Australians (7th series). Australian Women. T **311** and similar vert designs. Multicoloured. P 14×14½.

602 10c. Type **311** ... 55 80
a. Perf 14×15 ... 55 80
ab. Printed on the gummed side ... £140
603 10c. Louisa Lawson ... 55 80
a. Perf 14×15 ... 80 80
604 10c. Ethel Richardson ... 55 80
a. Perf 14×15 ... 80 80
605 10c. Catherine Spence ... 55 80
a. Perf 14×15 ... 65 80
606 10c. Constance Stone ... 65 80
a. Perf 14×15 ... 55 80
607 10c. Truganini ... 55 80
a. Perf 14×15 ... 55 80
602/7 *Set of 6* ... 3·00 4·25

No. 604 is inscribed with the *nom de plume* "Henry Handel Richardson".

(Des F. Knight)

1975 (27 Aug). Wild Flowers. T **312** and similar multicoloured design. P 15×14 (18c.) or 14×15 (45c.).

608	18c. Type **312**	25	10
	a. Black omitted	42·00	
	b. Grey (stem, etc) omitted	£250	
	c. Green (leaves) omitted	£350	
609	45c. *Callistemon teretifolius* (*horiz*)	50	10
	a. Black (face value and inscr) omitted	£1000	
	b. Yellow-green (twigs) omitted	£500	
	c. Grey (background) omitted	£2000	
	d. Sepia (branch) omitted	£2000	

The 18c. exists with both PVA gum and gum arabic.

(Des D. Annand (18c.) or G. Hamori (25c.))

1975 (16 Sept). Papua New Guinea Independence. T **313** and similar horiz design. Multicoloured. P 13½.

610	18c. Type **313**	20	10
611	25c. "Freedom" (bird in flight)	50	1·50

314 Epiphany Scene

315 Australian Coat of Arms

(Des D. O'Brien (15c.) or J. Milne (45c.))

1975 (29 Oct). Christmas. T **314** and similar horiz design. P 14×15 (15c.) or 13½ (45c.).

612	15c. multicoloured	40	10
613	45c. reddish violet, greenish blue and silver	1·00	3·00

Design:—45c. "Shining Star".

I.

II.

Two types of No. 614:
I. Emu's legs without toes.
II. Emu showing toes.
Other minor differences also occur.

(Des J. Spatchurst)

1976 (5 Jan). 75th Anniv of Nationhood. P 15×14.

614	**315**	18c. multicoloured (I)	40	20
		a. Buff (supporters) omitted	£500	£350
		b. Gold (shield and star) omitted	£350	
		c. Type II	75	40
		cb. Gold (shield and star) omitted	£1300	

316 Telephone-user, *circa* 1878

317 John Oxley

(Des R. Ingpen)

1976 (10 Mar). Telephone Centenary. P 13½.

615	**316**	18c. multicoloured	20	15

(Des B. Dunlop)

1976 (9 June). 19th-Century Explorers. T **317** and similar horiz designs. Multicoloured. P 13½.

616	18c. Type **317**	35	50
617	18c. Hume and Hovell	35	50
618	18c. John Forrest	35	50
619	18c. Ernest Giles	35	50
620	18c. William Gosse	35	50
621	18c. Peter Warburton	35	50
616/21	*Set of* 6	1·90	2·75

318 Measuring Stick, and Computer Tape Graph

319 Football

(Des R. Ingpen)

1976 (15 June). 50th Anniv of Commonwealth Scientific and Industrial Research Organisation. P 15×14.

622	**318**	18c. multicoloured	20	15

(Des A. Leydin)

1976 (14 July). Olympic Games, Montreal. T **319** and similar multicoloured designs. P 13½.

623	18c. Type **319**	15	20
624	18c. Gymnastics (*vert*)	15	20
625	25c. Diving (*vert*)	20	80
626	40c. Cycling	90	1·25
	a. Black (face value and "Australia") omitted	£1600	
623/6	*Set of* 4	1·25	2·25

The 25c. exists with gum arabic as well as PVA gum.

320 Richmond Bridge, Tasmania

321 Blamire Young (designer of first Australian stamp)

(Des O. Borchert)

1976 (23 Aug). Australian Scenes. T **320** and similar designs. Multicoloured. P 14×15 (50c.) or 15×14 (others).

627	5c. Type **320**	20	10
628	25c. Broken Bay, N.S.W.	65	10
629	35c. Wittenoom Gorge, W.A.	45	10
	a. Deep blue omitted	£1750	
630	50c. Mt. Buffalo, Victoria (*vert*)	70	10
631	70c. Barrier Reef	1·00	1·00
	a. Turquoise-green (inscr etc) omitted	£3500	
632	85c. Ayers Rock, N.T.	1·25	2·25
627/32	*Set of* 6	3·75	3·25

(Des R. Honisett)

1976 (27 Sept). National Stamp Week. P 13½.

633	**321**	18c. multicoloured	15	15
MS634		101×112 mm. No. 633×4	60	1·50

The miniature sheet exists with "AUSTRALIAN STAMP PROMOTION COUNCIL" overprinted in red on the margin from a privately produced booklet.

No. **MS**634 contains one stamp coloured as No. 633; the others, showing the different colour separations used in the printing, are each differently coloured.

322 "Virgin and Child" (detail, Simone Cantarini)

323 John Gould

(Des C. Medlycott (15c.), Wendy Tamlyn (45c.))

1976 (1 Nov). Christmas. T **322** and similar horiz design. P 15×14 (15c.) or 13½ (45c.).

635	15c. bright magenta and light azure	20	10
636	45c. multicoloured	50	90

Design:—45c. Toy koala bear and decorations.

(Des B. Weatherhead)

1976 (10 Nov). Famous Australians (8th series). T **323** and similar horiz designs. Multicoloured. P 15×14.

637	18c. Type **323**	35	50
638	18c. Thomas Laby	35	50
	a. Red-brown ("AUSTRALIA" etc.) omitted	£850	

639	18c. Sir Baldwin Spencer	35	50
640	18c. Griffith Taylor	35	50
637/40	*Set of 4*	1·25	1·75

324 "Music"

325 Queen Elizabeth II

(Des W. Tamlyn)

1977 (19 Jan). Performing Arts. T **324** and similar vert designs. Multicoloured. P 14×15.

641	20c. Type **324**	15	15
	a. Olive-green (chairs) omitted	£1000	
642	30c. Drama	15	25
643	40c. Dance	20	30
	a. Black (inscr and face value) omitted	£2500	
644	60c. Opera	1·00	2·00
641/44	*Set of 4*	1·40	2·50

(Des P.O. Artists. Litho Govt Printer, Sydney (2% of supplies) or by Norman J. Field, Melbourne)

1977 (2 Feb). Silver Jubilee. T **325** and similar vert design. Multicoloured. P 14×15.

645	18c. Type **325**	20	10
646	45c. The Queen and Prince Philip	40	90

326 Fielder and Wicket Keeper

327 Parliament House

(Des B. Weatherhead)

1977 (9 Mar). Australia-England Test Cricket Centenary. T **326** and similar vert designs. Multicoloured. P 13½.

647	18c. Type **326**	30	40
	a. Horiz strip of 5. Nos. 647/51	1·40	1·75
	ab. Black (face value, inscr, etc) omitted	£11000	
648	18c. Umpire, batsman and scoreboard	30	40
649	18c. Fielders	30	40
650	18c. Batsman and umpire	30	40
651	18c. Bowler and fielder	30	40
652	45c. Batsman awaiting delivery	40	1·00
647/52	*Set of 6*	1·75	2·75

Nos. 647/51 were printed together, *se-tenant*, in horizontal strips of 5 throughout the sheet, forming a composite design.

No. 647ab shows the black completely omitted from No. 647, but traces of it remain at the top of the other designs. The error occurs on the bottom row of a sheet.

(Des R.B.A.)

1977 (13 Apr). 50th Anniv of Opening of Parliament House, Canberra. P 15×14.

653	**327**	18c. multicoloured	15	10
		a. Yellow (foreground) omitted	£1800	
		b. Bluish grey omitted (white building)	£1300	

328 Trades Union Workers

329 Surfing Santa

(Des D. Lanyon; adapted B. Sadgrove)

1977 (9 May). 50th Anniv of Australian Council of Trade Unions. P 13½.

654	**328**	18c. multicoloured	15	10

(Des R. Roberts (15c.), J. O'Brien (45c.))

1977 (31 Oct). Christmas. T **329** and similar vert design. Multicoloured. P 14×15 (15c.) or 13½ (45c.).

655	15c. Type **329**	25	10
656	45c. Madonna and Child	75	1·25

330 National Flag

331 Harry Hawker and Sopwith Atlantic

(Des Cato Hibberd Design)

1978 (26 Jan). Australia Day. P 13½.

657	**330**	18c. multicoloured	20	15

(Litho Asher and Co, Melbourne)

1978 (19 Apr). Early Australian Aviators. T **331** and similar horiz designs. Multicoloured. P 15½.

658	18c. Type **331**	40	55
	a. Imperf (horiz pair)	£750	
659	18c. Bert Hinkler and Avro Type 581 Avian	40	55
	a. Imperf (horiz pair)	£600	
660	18c. Sir Charles Kingsford Smith and Fokker F311a/3m *Southern Cross*	40	55
	a. Imperf (pair)	£110	
661	18c. Charles Ulm and Fokker F311a/3m *Southern Cross*	40	55
658/61	*Set of 4*	1·40	2·00
MS662	100×112 mm. Nos. 660/1×2. Imperf	75	1·75

Forgeries of No. **MS**662 have been reported. These can be detected, under strong magnification, by the lack of magenta screen on the blue panel at right and by the presence of magenta dots in the yellow background to No. 661.

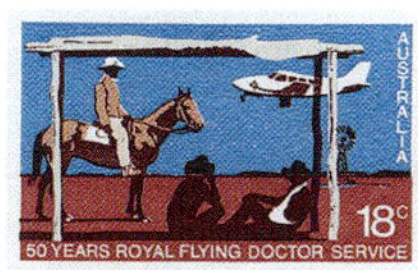

332 Piper PA-31 Navajo landing at Station Airstrip

333 Illawarra Flame Tree

1978 (15 May). 50th Anniv of Royal Flying Doctor Service. P 13½.

663	**332**	18c. multicoloured	20	15

(Des D. Rose)

1978 (1 June). Trees. T **333** and similar vert designs. Multicoloured. P 14×15 (18c.) or 13½ (others).

664	18c. Type **333**	20	15
	a. Black (face value and inscr) omitted	£2500	
665	25c. Ghost Gum	35	1·40
666	40c. Grass Tree	45	2·00
667	45c. Cootamundra Wattle	45	70
664/7	*Set of 4*	1·25	3·75

334 Sturt's Desert Rose and Map

335 Hooded Plover

(Des D. Pitt. Litho Asher and Co, Melbourne)

1978 (19 June). Establishment of State Government for the Northern Territory. P 15½.

668	**334**	18c. multicoloured	20	15

(Des Kay Breeden-Williams. Photo)

1978 (3 July)–**80**. Birds (1st series). Multicoloured designs as T **335**. P 15×14 (20c. (both)), 14×15 (22c.) or 13½ (others).

669	1c. Spotted-sided Finch (17.9.79)	10	20
670	2c. Crimson Finch (17.9.79)	10	20
671	5c. Type **335** (17.7.78)	35	10
	a. Grey-brown (bird's back) omitted	£2750	
672	15c. Forest Kingfisher (*vert*) (17.9.79)	20	20
673	20c. Australian Dabchick ("Little Grebe")	50	10
	a. Yellow (beak and eye) omitted	£190	
674	20c. Eastern Yellow Robin (17.9.79)	55	10
	a. Dull pink (bird's plumage) omitted	£1200	
675	22c. White-tailed Kingfisher (22×29 *mm*) (31.3.80)	30	10
	a. Light brown (rocks) omitted	£2750	—
676	25c. Masked Plover (17.7.78)	75	1·25
677	30c. Pied Oystercatcher (17.7.78)	75	25
678	40c. Variegated Wren (*vert*) (17.9.79)	30	45
679	50c. Flame Robin (*vert*) (17.9.79)	75	1·00
680	55c. Comb-crested Jacana ("Lotus-bird")	1·10	60
669/80	*Set of* 12	4·75	3·75

See also Nos. 734/40.

No. 675a occurred in the left column of a single sheet of 100 (10×10).

336 1928 3d. "National Stamp Exhibition" Commemorative

337 "The Madonna and Child" (after van Eyck)

(Des Cato Hibberd Design. Litho Asher and Co, Melbourne)

1978 (25 Sept). National Stamp Week. 50th Anniv of National Stamp Exhibition, Melbourne. P 15½.

694	**336**	20c. multicoloured	15	15
MS695		78×113 mm. No. 694×4	75	1·50

(Litho Asher and Co, Melbourne)

1978 (3 Oct–1 Nov). Christmas. Paintings. T **337** and similar vert designs. Multicoloured. P 14½.

696	15c. Type **337** (1.11)	25	10
697	25c. "The Virgin and Child" (Marmion)	35	65
698	55c. "The Holy Family" (del Vaga) (1.11)	50	1·00
696/8	*Set of* 3	1·00	1·60

338 "Tulloch"

339 Raising the Flag, Sydney Cove, 26 January 1788

(Des B. Clinton)

1978 (18 Oct). Race-horses. T **338** and similar multicoloured designs. P 15×14 (20c.) or 13½ (others).

699	20c. Type **338**	30	10
700	35c. "Bernborough" (*vert*)	45	85
701	50c. "Phar Lap" (*vert*)	60	1·25
702	55c. "Peter Pan"	60	1·10
699/702	*Set of* 4	1·75	3·00

(Des B. Clinton. Litho Asher and Co, Melbourne)

1979 (26 Jan). Australia Day. P 15½.

703	**339**	20c. multicoloured	15	15
		a. Yellow omitted		

340 *Canberra* (paddle-steamer)

341 Port Campbell, Victoria

(Des O. Borchert)

1979 (14 Feb). Ferries and Murray River Steamers. T **340** and similar horiz designs. Multicoloured. P 15×14 (20c.) or 13½ (others).

704	20c. Type **340**	20	10
705	35c. *Lady Denman*	40	70
706	50c. *Murray River Queen* (paddle-steamer)	50	1·40
707	55c. *Curl Curl* (hydrofoil)	55	1·25
704/7	*Set of* 4	1·50	3·00

(Des M. Robinson. Litho Asher and Co. Melbourne)

1979 (9 Apr). National Parks. T **341** and similar multicoloured designs. P 15½.

708	20c. Type **341**	20	30
	a. Horiz strip of 5. Nos. 708/12	1·00	1·40
709	20c. Uluru, Northern Territory	20	30
710	20c. Royal, New South Wales	20	30
711	20c. Flinders Ranges, South Australia	20	30
712	20c. Nambung, Western Australia	20	30
713	20c. Girraween, Queensland (*vert*)	20	30
	a. Horiz pair. Nos. 713/14	40	60
	ab. Imperf (horiz pair)*	£900	
714	20c. Mount Field, Tasmania (*vert*)	20	30
708/14	*Set of* 7	1·25	1·90

Nos. 708/14 were printed together, *se-tenant*; Nos. 708/12 in horizontal strips of 5 and Nos. 713/14 in horizontal pairs, throughout separate sheets.

*The imperforate error, No. 713ab, involves the two right-hand vertical columns of the sheet only, the left-hand stamp having vertical perforations at left.

342 "Double Fairlie" Type Locomotive, Western Australia

343 Symbolic Swan

(Des R. Honisett)

1979 (16 May). Steam Railways. T **342** and similar horiz designs. Multicoloured. P 14×15 (20c.) or 13½ (others).

715	20c. Type **342**	25	10
	a. Grey-green (face value and inscr) omitted	£2250	
716	35c. Locomotive, Puffing Billy Line, Victoria	45	50
717	50c. Locomotive, Pichi Richi Line, South Australia	55	1·25
718	55c. Locomotive, Zig Zag Railway, New South Wales	70	1·10
715/18	*Set of* 4	1·75	2·75

(Des B. Weatherhead)

1979 (6 June). 150th Anniv of Western Australia. P 13½.

719	**343**	20c. multicoloured	15	15

344 Children playing on Slide

345 Letters and Parcels

(Des Wendy Tamlyn. Litho Asher and Co, Melbourne)

1979 (13 Aug). International Year of the Child. P 13½×13.

720	**344**	20c. multicoloured	15	10

(Des A. Collins. Litho Asher and Co, Melbourne)

1979 (24 Sept–1 Nov). Christmas. T **345** and similar vert designs. Multicoloured. P 13×13½.

721	15c. Christ's Nativity (Eastern European icon) (1.11.79)	15	10
722	25c. Type **345**	15	65
723	55c. "Madonna and Child" (Buglioni) (1.11.79)	25	80
721/3	*Set of 3*	50	1·40

346 Fly-fishing

347 Matthew Flinders

(Des B. Clinton)

1979 (24 Oct). Fishing. T **346** and similar vert designs. P 14×15 (20c.) or 13½ (others).

724	20c. multicoloured	15	10
725	35c. black, deep grey-blue and violet-blue	25	70
726	50c. multicoloured	35	90
727	55c. multicoloured	35	85
724/7	*Set of 4*	1·00	2·25

Designs:—35c. Spinning; 50c. Deep sea game-fishing; 55c. Surf fishing.

(Des B. Weatherhead. Litho Asher and Co, Melbourne)

1980 (23 Jan). Australia Day. P 13½×13.

728	**347**	20c. multicoloured	20	10

348 Dingo

349 Queen Elizabeth II

(Des Marg Towt. Litho Asher and Co, Melbourne)

1980 (20 Feb). Dogs. T **348** and similar horiz designs. Multicoloured. P 13½×13.

729	20c. Type **348**	40	10
730	25c. Border Collie	40	50
731	35c. Australian Terrier	45	70
732	50c. Australian Cattle Dog	80	2·25
733	55c. Australian Kelpie	80	1·40
729/33	*Set of 5*	2·50	4·50

(Des Kay Breeden-Williams. Litho Asher and Co, Melbourne)

1980 (31 Mar)–**82**. Birds (2nd series). Multicoloured designs as T **335**. P 12½.

734	10c. Golden-shouldered Parrot (*vert*) (1.7.80)	50	10
	a. Perf 14½×14 (1982)	1·50	1·50
734*b*	18c. Spotted Catbird (*vert*) (17.11.80)	50	2·50
735	28c. Australian Bee Eater ("Rainbow Bird") (*vert*)	50	20
	a. Pale blue (background) omitted	£200	
736	35c. Regent Bowerbird (*vert*) (1.7.80)	50	10
737	45c. Masked Wood Swallow (1.7.80)	50	10
	a. Perf 14×14½ (1982)	2·00	2·25
738	60c. Australian King Parrot (*vert*)	50	15
739	80c. Rainbow Pitta (1.7.80)	1·00	40
740	$1 Black-backed Magpie (*vert*) (1.7.80)	1·00	10
734/40	*Set of 8*	4·50	3·00

Designs of Nos. 734/40 measure 22×29 mm (*vert*) or 29×22 mm (*horiz*).

(Des B. Weatherhead. Litho Asher and Co, Melbourne)

1980 (21 Apr). Queen Elizabeth II's Birthday. P 13×13½.

741	**349**	22c. multicoloured	30	20

350 "Once a jolly Swagman camp'd by a Billabong"

351 High Court Buildings

(Des R. Roberts. Litho Asher and Co, Melbourne)

1980 (7 May). Folklore. Scenes and Verses from the Folksong *Waltzing Matilda*. T **350** and similar vert designs. Multicoloured. P 13×13½.

742	22c. Type **350**	25	30
	a. Horiz strip of 5. Nos. 742/6	1·10	1·40
743	22c. "And he sang as he shoved that Jumbuck in his Tuckerbag"	25	30
744	22c. "Up rode the Squatter, mounted on his Thoroughbred"	25	30
745	22c. "Down came the Troopers one, two, three"	25	30
746	22c. "And his Ghost may be heard as you pass by that Billabong"	25	30
742/6	*Set of 5*	1·10	1·40

Nos. 742/6 were printed together, *se-tenant*, in horizontal strips of 5 throughout the sheet, forming a composite design.

(Des Cato Hibberd Design. Litho Asher and Co, Melbourne)

1980 (19 May). Opening of High Court Building, Canberra. P 13×13½.

747	**351**	22c. multicoloured	20	20

352 Salvation Army

353 Postbox, *circa* 1900

(Des J. Spatchurst. Litho Asher and Co, Melbourne)

1980 (11 Aug). Community Welfare. T **352** and similar multicoloured designs. P 13½×13 (Nos. 748, 751) or 13×13½ (others).

748	22c. Type **352**	30	30
749	22c. St. Vincent de Paul Society (*vert*)	30	30
750	22c. Meals on Wheels (*vert*)	30	30
751	22c. "Life. Be in it"	30	30
748/51	*Set of 4*	1·10	1·10

(Des B. Weatherhead. Litho Asher and Co, Melbourne)

1980 (29 Sept). National Stamp Week. T **353** and similar vert designs showing postal history, *circa* 1900. Multicoloured. P 13×13½.

752	22c. Type **353**	25	40
	a. Horiz strip of 5. Nos. 752/6	1·10	1·75
753	22c. Postman (facing left)	25	40
754	22c. Ford Model T Mail van	25	40
755	22c. Postman and postbox	25	40
756	22c. Postman (facing right)	25	40
752/6	*Set of 5*	1·10	1·75
MS757	95×130 mm. Nos. 752, 754 and 756	1·10	1·60
	a. Error. Imperf	£3250	

Nos. 752/6 were printed together, *se-tenant*, in horizontal strips of 5 throughout the sheet.

Stamps from No. **MS**757 have different backgrounds to the stamps from normal sheets.

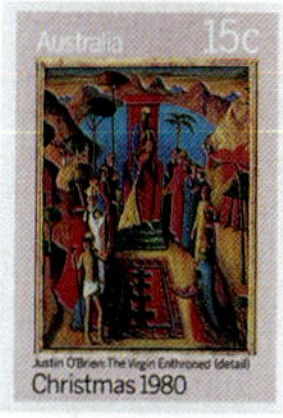

354 "Holy Family" (painting, Prospero Fontana)

355 Commonwealth Aircraft Factory CA-6 Wackett, 1941

(Des B. Weatherhead. Litho Asher and Co, Melbourne)

1980 (1 Oct–3 Nov). Christmas. Works of Art. T **354** and similar vert designs. Multicoloured. P 13×13½.

758	15c. "The Virgin Enthroned" (detail of painting by Justin O'Brien) (3.11)	15	10
759	28c. Type **354**	25	40
760	60c. "Madonna and Child" (sculpture by School of M. Zuern) (3.11)	50	1·10
758/60	*Set of* 3	80	1·40

(Des O. Borchert. Litho Victorian Government Printer, Melbourne (22c.), Asher and Co, Melbourne (others))

1980 (19 Nov). Aircraft. T **355** and similar horiz designs. Multicoloured. P 13½×14 (22c.) or 13½×13 (others).

761	22c. Type **355**	30	10
762	40c. Commonwealth Aircraft Factory CA-25 Winjeel, 1955	50	75
763	45c. Commonwealth Aircraft Factory CA-13 Boomerang, 1944	50	85
764	60c. Government Aircraft Factory N22B Nomad, 1975	65	1·40
761/4	*Set of* 4	1·75	2·75

356 Flag in shape of Australia

357 Caricature of Darby Munro (jockey)

(Des B. Weatherhead. Litho Asher and Co, Melbourne)

1981 (21 Jan). Australia Day. P 13½×13.

765	**356**	22c. multicoloured	20	20

(Des T. Rafty. Litho Cambec Press, Melbourne)

1981 (18 Feb). Sports Personalities. T **357** and similar vert designs showing caricatures. Multicoloured. P 14×13½.

766	22c. Type **357**	20	10
767	35c. Victor Trumper (cricketer)	40	60
768	55c. Sir Norman Brookes (tennis player)	40	1·00
769	60c. Walter Lindrum (billiards player)	40	1·25
766/9	*Set of* 4	1·25	2·75

358 1931 Kingsford Smith's Flights 6d. Commemorative

359 Apex Emblem and Map of Australia

(Des Cato Hibberd Design. Litho Asher and Co, Melbourne)

1981 (25 Mar). 50th Anniv of Official Australia–U.K. Airmail Service. T **358** and similar horiz design showing 1931 Kingsford Smith's Flights 6d. commemorative. P 13×13½ (22c.) or 13½×13 (60c.).

770	22c. blackish lilac, rosine and bright blue	15	10
771	60c. blackish lilac, rosine and ultramarine	40	90

(Des P. Clark)

1981 (6 Apr). 50th Anniv of Apex (young men's service club). P 13½.

772	**359**	22c. multicoloured	20	20

Australia Post first day covers are known, incorrectly dated 6 March 1981.

ASHER AND CO. From April 1981 this firm was known as Leigh-Mardon Ltd, Melbourne.

360 Queen's Personal Standard for Australia

361 "Licence Inspected"

(Litho Leigh-Mardon Ltd, Melbourne)

1981 (21 Apr). Queen Elizabeth II's Birthday. P 13½×13.

773	**360**	22c. multicoloured	20	20

(Des B. Weatherhead. Litho Leigh-Mardon Ltd, Melbourne)

1981 (20 May). Gold Rush Era. Sketches by S. T. Gill. T **361** and similar vert designs. Multicoloured. P 13×13½.

774	22c. Type **361**	20	25
775	22c. "Puddling"	20	25
776	22c. "Quality of washing stuff"	20	25
777	22c. "On route to deposit gold"	20	25
774/7	*Set of* 4	70	90

362 "On the Wallaby Track" (Fred McCubbin)

(Litho Leigh-Mardon Ltd, Melbourne)

1981 (17 June)–**84**. Paintings. T **362** and similar horiz design. Multicoloured. P 15×14½.

778	$2 Type **362** (*shades*)	1·00	20
	s. Optd "Specimen"	2·50	
779	$5 "A Holiday at Mentone, 1888" (Charles Conder) (4.4.84)	2·50	50
	s. Optd "Specimen"	2·50	

363 Thylacine

363a Blue Mountain Tree-Frog

363b *Papilio ulysses* (butterfly)

PRINTINGS OF THE 24C. VALUE. (Nos. 788, 788b). Original printings of this stamp were produced by a combination of printing processes. The centre design was first printed in photogravure by the Note Printing Branch, Reserve Bank of Australia, and then the half-printed sheets were transferred to Leigh-Mardon Ltd for the inscriptions and face value to be added in lithography.

Further supplies of this value were required in late 1981, but these were printed by Leigh-Mardon Ltd entirely in lithography.

The work of the two printers can be identified by the usual differences exhibited by the processes concerned; the lithography version tending to be darker in appearance with much sharper outlines.

Other specific differences are as follows:

On the *photogravure* version the front legs show a diagonal pattern of screening dots which are replaced by vertical and horizontal lines on the *litho* stamp.

The animal's eye is highlighted on the *photogravure* stamp.

The fourth and sixth bands on the animal's back are much longer on the *litho* version.

The end of the right-hand twig is pointed on the *photogravure* and blunt on the *litho*.

Photogravure Centre

Lithography Centre

(Des C. McCubbin (4, 10, 20, 27c. (No. 791), 30c. (No. 792a), 35, 45, 60, 80c., $1), F. Knight (5, 24, 25, 30c. (No. 792), 50, 55c.) or Beverley Bruen (others). Photo Note Ptg Branch, Reserve Bank of Australia and litho Leigh-Mardon (24c. (No. 788)), litho Leigh-Mardon (3, 5, 15, 24c. (No. 788b), 25, 27c. (both), 30c. (both), 40, 50, 55, 65, 75, 90c.), Cambec Press (others))

1981 (15 July)–**83**. Wildlife. Designs as T **363** (5, 24, 25, 30 (No. 792), 50, 55c.), horiz designs as T **363a** (1, 3, 15, 27 (No. 790), 40, 65, 70, 75, 85, 90, 95c.) or vert as T **363b** (others). Multicoloured. P 12½ (unless otherwise stated).

781	1c. Lace Monitor P 13½ (2.2.83)	10	20
782	3c. Corroboree Frog (19.4.82)	10	10
	a. Perf 14×14½ (1983)	2·00	70
783	4c. *Euschemon rafflesio* ("Regent Skipper") (butterfly) (*vert*) P 13½ (15.6.83)	55	80
784	5c. Queensland Hairy-nosed Wombat (*vert*) (15.7.81)	10	10
	a. Perf 14½×14 (12.83)	1·25	2·00
785	10c. *Ornithoptera priamus* ("Cairns Birdwing") (butterfly) (*vert*) P 13½ (15.6.83)	60	10
786	15c. Eastern Snake-necked Tortoise (16.6.82)	1·00	1·00
	a. Perf 14×14½ (12.83)	1·25	2·25
787	20c. *Graphium macleayanus* ("MacLeay's Swallow Tail") (butterfly) (*vert*) P 13½ (15.6.83)	80	35
788	24c. Type **363** (centre photo, inscr litho) P 13½	45	10
	a. Imperf (pair)	£200	
	b. Centre and inscr litho (12.81)	65	1·00
789	25c. Common Rabbit-Bandicoot (*vert*) (15.7.81)	40	1·00
	a. Perf 14×14½ (1982)	1·00	2·75
790	27c. Type **363a** (19.4.82)	1·25	20
	a. Perf 14×14½ (6.82)	1·00	1·00
791	27c. Type **363b** (15.6.83) P 14½×14	1·00	30
	a. Imperf (pair)	£650	
792	30c. Bridle Nail-tailed Wallaby (*vert*) (15.7.81)	90	20
792*a*	30c. *Pseudalmenus chlorinda* ("Chlorinda Hairstreak") (butterfly) (*vert*) P 14½×14 (24.10.83)	1·00	20
793	35c. *Danaus hamata* ("Blue Tiger") (butterfly) (*vert*) P 13½ (15.6.83)	1·00	30
794	40c. Smooth Knob-tailed Gecko (16.6.82)	45	30
	a. Perf 14×14½ (12.83)	2·50	2·00
795	45c. *Cressida cressida* ("Big Greasy") (butterfly) (*vert*) P 13½ (15.6.83)	1·00	30
796	50c. Leadbeater's Possum (15.7.81)	50	10
	a. Perf 14×14½ (1983)	1·50	1·75
797	55c. Stick-nest Rat (*vert*) (15.7.81)	50	30
798	60c. *Delias aganippe* ("Wood White") (butterfly) (*vert*) P 13½ (15.6.83)	1·10	30
799	65c. Yellow-faced Whip Snake (19.4.82)	1·40	1·50
	a. Perf 14×14½ (1983)	1·75	2·50
800	70c. Crucifix Toad P 13½ (2.2.83)	65	1·75
801	75c. Eastern Water Dragon (19.4.82)	1·25	90
	a. Perf 14×14½ (12.83)	1·75	1·50
802	80c. *Ogyris amaryllis* ("Amaryllis Azure") (butterfly) (*vert*) P 13½ (15.6.83)	1·25	2·00
803	85c. Centralian Blue-tongued Lizard P 13½ (2.2.83)	1·10	1·25
804	90c. Freshwater Crocodile (16.6.82)	1·25	1·25
805	95c. Thorny Devil P 13½ (2.2.83)	1·25	2·00
806	$1 *Tisiphone abeona* ("Sword-grass Brown") (butterfly) (*vert*) P 13½ (15.6.83)	1·25	30
781/806	*Set of* 27	19·00	15·00

A late printing of No. 781, issued July 1987, is on thicker paper with a creamier appearance.

364 Prince Charles and Lady Diana Spencer

365 *Cortinarius cinnabarinus*

(Des B. Clinton. Litho Leigh-Mardon Ltd, Melbourne)

1981 (29 July). Royal Wedding. P 13½×13.

821	**364**	24c. multicoloured	20	10
822		60c. multicoloured	55	1·00

(Des Celia Rosser. Litho Leigh-Mardon Ltd, Melbourne)

1981 (19 Aug). Australian Fungi. T **365** and similar vert designs. Multicoloured. P 13×13½.

823	24c. Type **365**	20	10
824	35c. *Coprinus comatus*	30	65
825	55c. *Armillaria luteobubalina*	45	1·00
826	60c. *Cortinarius austrovenetus*	45	1·10
823/6	*Set of* 4	1·25	2·50

366 Disabled People playing Basketball

367 "Christmas Bush for His Adorning"

(Des J. Spatchurst. Litho Cambec Press, Melbourne)

1981 (16 Sept). International Year for Disabled Persons. P 14×13½.

827	**366**	24c. multicoloured	20	20

(Des F. Beck. Litho Leigh-Mardon Ltd, Melbourne)

1981 (28 Sept–2 Nov). Christmas. Scenes and Verses from Carols by W. James and J. Wheeler. T **367** and similar vert designs. Multicoloured. P 13×13½.

828	18c. Type **367** (2 Nov)	20	10
829	30c. "The Silver Stars are in the Sky"	25	25
830	60c. "Noeltime" (2 Nov)	40	1·10
828/30	*Set of* 3	75	1·25

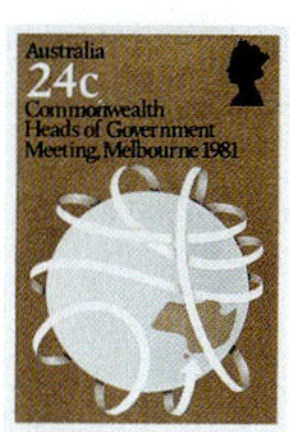

368 Globe depicting Australia

369 *Ragamuffin* (ocean racing yacht)

(Des B. Weatherhead. Litho Leigh-Mardon Ltd, Melbourne)

1981 (30 Sept). Commonwealth Heads of Government Meeting, Melbourne. P 13×13½.

831	**368**	24c. black, pale blue and gold	15	10
832		60c. black, pale blue and silver	45	75

(Des R. Fletcher. Litho Leigh-Mardon Ltd, Melbourne)

1981 (14 Oct). Yachts. T **369** and similar vert designs. Multicoloured. P 13×13½.

833	24c. Type **369**	20	10
834	35c. "Sharpie"	30	55
835	55c. "12 Metre"	40	1·50

836	60c. "Sabot"	50	1·50
833/6	*Set of 4*	1·25	3·25

370 Aborigine, Governor Philip (founder of N.S.W., 1788) and Post-World War II Migrant

371 Humpback Whale

(Des B. Clinton. Litho Cambec Press, Melbourne)

1982 (20 Jan). Australia Day. "Three Great Waves of Migration". P 13½×14.

837	**370**	24c. multicoloured	35	25

(Des R. and Katrina Ingpen. Litho Cambec Press, Melbourne)

1982 (17 Feb). Whales. T **371** and similar multicoloured designs. P 13½×14 (24, 60c.) or 14×13½ (others).

838	24c. Sperm Whale	25	10
839	35c. Black Right Whale (*vert*)	35	50
840	55c. Blue Whale (*vert*)	50	1·25
841	60c. Type **371** (new blue background)	60	1·25
	a. Solid greenish blue background	£250	£225
838/41	*Set of 4*	1·50	2·75

No. 841a comes from a small trial printing, some sheets of which were included amongst normal stock by mistake. The correct version of the 60c. value shows the new blue background streaked with white at top left. On No. 841a the background is in greenish blue and is without the white streaks.

372 Queen Elizabeth II

373 "Marjorie Atherton"

(Des R. Honisett. Litho Cambec Press, Melbourne)

1982 (21 Apr). Queen Elizabeth II's Birthday. P 14×13½.

842	**372**	27c. multicoloured	35	15

(Des Betty Conabere. Litho Leigh-Mardon Ltd, Melbourne)

1982 (19 May). Roses. T **373** and similar vert designs. Multicoloured. P 13×13½.

843	27c. Type **373**	20	10
844	40c. "Imp"	30	50
845	65c. "Minnie Watson"	40	1·75
846	75c. "Satellite"	40	1·00
843/6	*Set of 4*	1·10	3·00

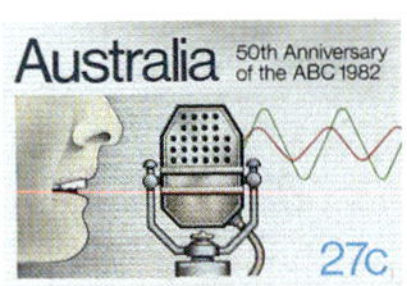

374 Radio Announcer and 1930-style Microphone

375 Forbes Post Office

(Des Cato Hibberd Design. Litho Leigh-Mardon Ltd, Melbourne)

1982 (16 June). 50th Anniv of ABC (Australian Broadcasting Commission). T **374** and similar horiz design. Multicoloured. P 13½×13.

847	27c. Type **374**	30	65
	a. Pair. Nos. 847/8	60	1·25
848	27c. ABC logo	30	65

Nos. 847/8 were printed together, *se-tenant*, in horizontal and vertical pairs throughout the sheet.

(Des F. Beck. Litho Cambec Press, Melbourne)

1982 (4 Aug). Historic Australian Post Offices. T **375** and similar multicoloured designs. P 14×13½ (vert) or 13½×14 (horiz).

849	27c. Type **375**	25	40
850	27c. Flemington Post Office	25	40
851	27c. Rockhampton Post Office	25	40
852	27c. Kingston S.E. Post Office (*horiz*)	25	40
853	27c. York Post Office (*horiz*)	25	40
854	27c. Launceston Post Office	25	40
855	27c. Old Post and Telegraph Station, Alice Springs (*horiz*)	25	40
849/55	*Set of 7*	1·60	2·50

376 Early Australian Christmas Card

377 Boxing

(Des B. Weatherhead. Litho Leigh-Mardon Ltd, Melbourne)

1982 (15 Sept–1 Nov). Christmas. T **376** and similar multicoloured designs. P 14½.

856	21c. Bushman's Hotel, with Cobb's coach arriving (*horiz*) (1.11.82)	25	10
857	35c. Type **376**	40	60
858	75c. Little girl offering Christmas pudding to swagman (1.11.82)	60	1·60
856/8	*Set of 3*	1·10	2·10

(Des R. Carnielye. Litho Leigh-Mardon Ltd, Melbourne)

1982 (22 Sept). Commonwealth Games, Brisbane. T **377** and similar horiz designs. P 14½.

859	27c. stone, lemon and bright carmine	20	25
860	27c. lemon, stone and emerald	20	25
861	27c. stone, lemon and yellow-brown	20	25
862	75c. multicoloured	50	1·25
859/62	*Set of 4*	1·00	1·75
MS863	130×95 mm. Nos. 859/61. P 13½×13	1·00	1·75

Designs:—No. 859, Type **377**; No. 860, Archery; No. 861, Weight-lifting; No. 862, Pole-vaulting.

378 Sydney Harbour Bridge 5s. Stamp of 1932

379 "Yirawala" Bark Painting

(Des Cato Hibberd Design. Litho Cambec Press, Melbourne)

1982 (27 Sept). National Stamp Week. P 13½×14.

864	**378**	27c. multicoloured	35	30

(Des Australia Post Graphic Design Section. Litho Leigh-Mardon Ltd, Melbourne)

1982 (12 Oct). Opening of Australian National Gallery. P 14½.

865	**379**	27c. multicoloured	30	25

380 Mimi Spirits Dancing

381 *Eucalyptus calophylla* "Rosea"

(Des D. Milaybuma (27c.), L. Nabardayal (40c.), J. Galareya (65c.), D. Nguleingulei-Murrumurru (75c.). Litho Cambec Press, Melbourne)

1982 (17 Nov). Aboriginal Culture. Music and Dance. T **380** and similar horiz designs depicting Aboriginal Bark Paintings of Mimi Spirits. P 13½×14.

866	27c. multicoloured	15	10
867	40c. multicoloured	25	60
868	65c. multicoloured	35	1·00
869	75c. multicoloured	35	1·00
866/9	*Set of 4*	1·00	2·40

(Des Elizabeth Conabere. Photo Enschedé)

1982 (17 Nov). Eucalyptus Flowers. T **381** and similar horiz designs. Multicoloured. P 12½×13½.

870	1c. Type **381**		10	40
	a. Booklet pane. Nos. 870/1 and 874 each×2		1·00	
	b. Booklet pane. Nos. 870/1 each×2, 872/3 and 874×3		2·75	
871	2c. *Eucalyptus casia*		10	40
872	3c. *Eucalyptus ficifolia*		1·25	2·50
873	10c. *Eucalyptus globulus*		1·25	2·50
874	27c. *Eucalyptus forrestiana*		30	40
870/4 *Set of 5*			2·75	5·50

Nos. 870/4 only exist from 60c. (pane No. 870a, SB52) and $1 (pane No. 870b, SB53) stamp booklets and the stamps have one or two adjacent sides imperforate. They were printed on Harrison paper which gives a bluish white reaction under U.V. light.

382 Shand Mason Steam Fire Engine, 1891

383 H.M.S. *Sirius*

(Des A. Puckett. Litho Cambec Press, Melbourne)

1983 (12 Jan). Historic Fire Engines. T **382** and similar horiz designs. Multicoloured. P 13½×14.

875	27c. Type **382**	35	10
876	40c. Hotchkiss fire engine, 1914	45	75
877	65c. Ahrens-Fox fire engine, 1929	70	1·60
878	75c. Merryweather manual fire appliance, 1851	70	1·40
875/8 *Set of 4*		2·00	3·50

(Des J. Spatchurst. Litho Leigh-Mardon Ltd, Melbourne)

1983 (26 Jan). Australia Day. T **383** and similar horiz design. Multicoloured. P 14½.

879	27c. Type **383**	40	75
	a. Pair. Nos. 879/80	80	1·50
	ab. Printed on the gummed side	£275	
880	27c. H.M.S. *Supply*	40	75

Nos. 879/80 were printed together, *se-tenant*, in horizontal and vertical pairs throughout the sheet.

384 Stylised Kangaroo and Kiwi

385 Equality and Dignity

(Des G. Emery. Litho Cambec Press, Melbourne)

1983 (2 Feb). Closer Economic Relationship Agreement with New Zealand. P 14×13½.

881	**384**	27c. multicoloured	30	30

(Des G. Emery. Litho Leigh-Mardon Ltd, Melbourne)

1983 (9 Mar). Commonwealth Day. T **385** and similar vert designs. Multicoloured. P 14½.

882	27c. Type **385**	20	25
883	27c. Liberty and Freedom	20	25
884	27c. Social Justice and Co-operation	20	25
885	75c. Peace and Harmony	50	1·50
882/5 *Set of 4*		1·00	2·00

386 R.Y. *Britannia* passing Sydney Opera House

387 "Postal and Telecommunications Services"

(Des J. Richards. Litho Leigh-Mardon Ltd, Melbourne)

1983 (20 Apr). Queen Elizabeth II's Birthday. P 14½.

886	**386**	27c. multicoloured	50	30

(Des B. Sadgrove. Litho Cambec Press, Melbourne)

1983 (18 May). World Communications Year. P 13×13½.

887	**387**	27c. multicoloured	30	30

388 Badge of the Order of St. John

389 Jaycee Members and Badge

(Des T. McCauley. Litho Cambec Press, Melbourne)

1983 (8 June). Centenary of St. John Ambulance in Australia. P 14×13½.

888	**388**	27c. black and deep turquoise-blue	35	30

(Des B. Clinton. Litho Cambec Press, Melbourne)

1983 (8 June). 50th Anniv of Australian Jaycees. P 13½×14.

889	**389**	27c. multicoloured	30	30

390 "The Bloke"

391 Nativity Scene

(Des B. Clinton. Litho Leigh-Mardon Ltd, Melbourne)

1983 (3 Aug). Folklore. "The Sentimental Bloke" (humorous poem by C. J. Dennis). T **390** and similar vert designs. Multicoloured. P 14½.

890	27c. Type **390**	25	50
	a. Horiz strip of 5. Nos. 890/4	1·10	2·25
891	27c. "Doreen—The Intro"	25	50
892	27c. "The Stror' at Coot"	25	50
893	27c. "Hitched"	25	50
894	27c. "The Mooch o'Life"	25	50
890/4 *Set of 5*		1·10	2·25

Nos. 890/4 were printed together, *se-tenant*, in horizontal strips of 5 throughout the sheet.

(Des Holly Alvarez (24c.), Deanne Head (35c.), Justine Jacobi (85c.). Litho Cambec Press, Melbourne)

1983 (14 Sept–2 Nov). Christmas. Children's Paintings. T **391** and similar horiz designs. Multicoloured. P 13½×14.

895	24c. Type **391** (2 November)	20	10
896	35c. Kookaburra	30	45
897	85c. Father Christmas in sleigh over beach (2 November)	60	1·40
895/7 *Set of 3*		1·00	1·75

392 Sir Paul Edmund de Strzelecki

393 Cook Family Cottage, Melbourne

(Des Dianne Quinn. Litho Leigh-Mardon Ltd, Melbourne)

1983 (26 Sept). Explorers of Australia. T **392** and similar vert designs. Multicoloured. P 14½.

898	30c. Type **392**	25	40
899	30c. Ludwig Leichardt	25	40

900	30c. William John Wills and Robert O'Hara Burke	25	40
901	30c. Alexander Forrest	25	40
898/901	*Set of 4*	90	1·40

(Des J. Quinn. Litho Cambec Press, Melbourne)

1984 (26 Jan). Australia Day. P 13½×14.

902	**393**	30c. black and stone	30	35

394 Charles Ulm, Avro Type 618 Ten *Faith in Australia* and Trans-Tasman Cover

(Des G. Beck and J. Quinn. Litho Cambec Press, Melbourne)

1984 (22 Feb). 50th Anniv of First Official Airmail Flights, New Zealand–Australia and Australia–Papua New Guinea. T **394** and similar horiz design. Multicoloured. P 13½.

903	45c. Type **394**	60	1·25
	a. Horiz pair. Nos. 903/4	1·10	2·50
904	45c. As Type **394** but showing flown cover to Papua New Guinea	60	1·25

Nos. 903/4 were printed together, *se-tenant*, in horizontal pairs throughout the sheet.

395 Thomson "Steamer", 1898

396 Queen Elizabeth II

(Des A. Puckett. Litho Leigh-Mardon Ltd, Melbourne)

1984 (14 Mar). Veteran and Vintage Cars. T **395** and similar horiz designs. Multicoloured. P 14½.

905	30c. Type **395**	30	60
	a. Vert strip of 5. Nos. 905/9	1·40	2·75
906	30c. Tarrant two-seater, 1906	30	60
907	30c. Gordon & Co "Australian Six" two-seater, 1919	30	60
908	30c. Summit tourer, 1923	30	60
909	30c. Chic two-seater, 1924	30	60
905/9	*Set of 5*	1·00	2·75

Nos. 905/9 were printed together, *se-tenant*, in vertical strips of 5 throughout the sheet.

(Des B. Weatherhead. Litho Leigh-Mardon Ltd, Melbourne)

1984 (18 Apr). Queen Elizabeth II's Birthday. P 14½.

910	**396**	30c. multicoloured	30	35
		a. Dull mauve (background) omitted	£1600	

397 *Cutty Sark*

398 Freestyle

(Des J. Earl and J. Quinn. Litho Cambec Press, Melbourne)

1984 (23 May). Clipper Ships. T **397** and similar multicoloured designs. P 14×13½ (30c., 85c.) or 13½×14 (others).

911	30c. Type **397**	35	25
912	45c. *Orient* (*horiz*)	45	80
913	75c. *Sobraon* (*horiz*)	60	1·75
914	85c. *Thermopylae*	60	1·25
911/14	*Set of 4*	1·75	3·50

(Des B. Clinton. Litho Leigh-Mardon Ltd, Melbourne)

1984 (6 June). Skiing. T **398** and similar multicoloured designs. P 14½.

915	30c. Type **398**	30	45
916	30c. Downhill racer	30	45
917	30c. Slalom (*horiz*)	30	45
918	30c. Nordic (*horiz*)	30	45
915/18	*Set of 4*	1·10	1·60

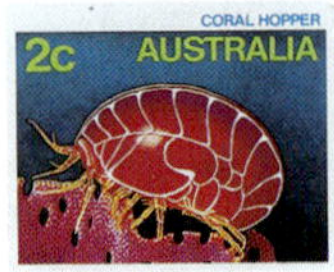

399 Coral Hopper

400 Before the Event

(Des G. Ryan and R. Fletcher (2, 25, 30, 50, 55, 85c.) or G. Ryan (others). Litho Leigh-Mardon Ltd, Melbourne (30, 33c.) or Cambec Press, Melbourne (others))

1984 (18 June)–**86**. Marine Life. T **399** and similar horiz designs. Multicoloured. P 14×14½ (30c., 33c.) or 13½ (others).

919	2c. Type **399**	10	30
920	3c. Jimble (11.6.86)	40	30
921	5c. Tasselled Frogfish ("Anglerfish") (12.6.85)	15	10
922	10c. Rough Stonefish (11.6.86)	1·00	40
923	20c. Red Handfish (12.6.85)	50	30
924	25c. Orange-lipped Cowrie	35	30
925	30c. Choat's Wrasse	35	20
926	33c. Leafy Seadragon (20.3.85)	45	10
927	40c. Red Velvetfish (12.6.85)	70	1·50
928	45c. Textile or Cloth of Gold Cone (11.6.86)	1·50	30
929	50c. Clown Surgeonfish	60	30
930	55c. Bennett's Nudibranch	60	30
	a. New blue ("BENNETT'S NUDIBRANCH") omitted	†	£1500
931	60c. Zebra Lionfish (11.6.86)	1·50	50
932	65c. Banded Stingray (11.6.86)	1·50	2·50
933	70c. Southern Blue-ringed Octopus (11.6.86)	1·50	1·50
934	80c. Pineconefish ("Pineapple Fish") (12.6.85)	1·00	1·50
935	85c. Royal Angelfish	70	50
936	90c. Crab-eyed Goby (12.6.85)	1·25	60
937	$1 Crown of Thorns Starfish (11.6.86)	1·25	40
	s. Optd "Specimen"	50	
919/37	*Set of 19*	13·00	10·50

No. 930a only exists used on maximum card.

Used examples have been reported of both the 33c. and $1 with the face value and inscriptions omitted. The colours involved were dull orange on the 33c. and mauve on the $1.

(Des O. Schmidinger and Christine Stead. Litho Cambec Press, Melbourne)

1984 (25 July). Olympic Games, Los Angeles. T **400** and similar multicoloured designs. P 14×13½ (No. 943) or 13½×14 (others).

941	30c. Type **400**	25	40
942	30c. During the event	25	40
943	30c. After the event (*vert*)	25	40
941/3	*Set of 3*	65	1·10

401 Australian 1913 1d. Kangaroo Stamp

402 "Angel" (stained-glass window, St. Francis' Church, Melbourne)

(Des Ken Cato Design Studio. Litho Cambec Press, Melbourne)

1984 (22 Aug - 21 Sept). Ausipex International Stamp Exhibition, Melbourne. T **401** and similar vert designs. Multicoloured. P 14½.

944	30c. Type **401**	35	30
MS945	126×175 mm. 30c.×7, Victoria 1850 3d. "Half Length"; New South Wales 1850 1d. "Sydney View"; Tasmania 1853 1d.; South Australia 1855 1d.; Western Australia 1854 1d. "Black Swan"; Queensland 1860 6d.; Type **401** (21 Sept)	3·50	4·50

On No. **MS**945 the emblem and inscription on the sheet margin are embossed.

(Des Ken Cato Design Studio. Litho Cambec Press, Melbourne)

1984 (17 Sept–31 Oct). Christmas. Stained-glass Windows. T **402** and similar vert designs. Multicoloured. P 14×13½.

946	24c. "Angel and Child" (Holy Trinity Church, Sydney) (31.10.84)	15	10
947	30c. "Veiled Virgin and Child" (St. Mary's Catholic Church, Geelong) (31.10.84)	20	10
948	40c. Type **402**	30	75

949	50c. "Three Kings" (St. Mary's Cathedral, Sydney) (31.10.84)	40	90
950	85c. "Madonna and Child" (St. Bartholomew's Church, Norwood) (31.10.84)	50	1·60
946/50	*Set of 5*	1·40	3·00

403 "Stick Figures" (Cobar Region)

404 Yellow-tufted Honeyeater

(Des Elizabeth Innes. Litho Leigh-Mardon Ltd, Melbourne)

1984 (7 Nov). Bicentenary of Australian Settlement (1988) (1st issue). The First Australians. T **403** and similar square designs showing aborigine rock paintings. Multicoloured. P 14½.

951	30c. Type **403**	20	45
952	30c. "Bunjil" (large figure), Grampians	20	45
953	30c. "Quikans" (tall figures), Cape York	20	45
954	30c. "Wandjina Spirit and Baby Snakes" (Gibb River)	20	45
955	30c. "Rock Python" (Gibb River)	20	45
956	30c. "Silver Barramundi" (fish) (Kakadu National Park)	20	45
957	30c. Bicentenary emblem	20	45
958	85c. "Rock Possum" (Kakadu National Park)	50	1·40
951/8	*Set of 8*	1·75	4·00

See also Nos. 972/**MS**976, 993/6, 1002/7, 1019/22, 1059/63, 1064/6, 1077/81, 1090/2, 1105/9, 1110, 1137/41, 1145/8 and 1149.

(Des. G. Emery. Litho Leigh-Mardon Ltd, Melbourne)

1984 (19 Nov). 150th Anniv of Victoria. T **404** and similar vert design. Multicoloured. P 14½.

959	30c. Type **404**	40	65
	a. Pair. Nos. 959/60	80	1·25
960	30c. Leadbeater's Possum	40	65

Nos. 959/60 were printed together, *se-tenant*, in horizontal and vertical pairs throughout the sheet.

405 "Musgrave Ranges" (Sir Sidney Nolan)

406 Young People of Different Races, and Sun

(Des Sue Titcher. Litho Leigh-Mardon Ltd, Melbourne)

1985 (25 Jan). Australia Day. Birth Centenary of Dorothea Mackellar (author of poem "My Country"). T **405** and similar horiz design. Multicoloured. P 14½.

961	30c. Type **405**	50	80
	a. *Tête-bêche* (vert pair)	1·75	3·25
	b. Vert pair. Nos. 961/2	1·00	1·60
962	30c. "The Walls of China" (Russell Drysdale)	50	80
	a. *Tête-bêche* (vert pair)	1·75	3·25

Nos. 961/2 were printed together, *se-tenant*, within the sheet of 100 (2 panes 50 (5×10)). In each pane No. 961 occurs in horizontal rows 1, 4, 5, 8 and 9, and No. 962 in rows 2, 3, 6, 7 and 10. Horizontal rows 3/4 and 7/8 are inverted forming *tête-bêche* pairs of the same design in addition to the vertical *se-tenant* pairs containing both designs.

(Des Derryn Vogelnest. Litho Cambec Press, Melbourne)

1985 (13 Feb). International Youth Year. P 14×13½.

963	**406**	30c. multicoloured	40	30

407 Royal Victorian Volunteer Artillery

408 District Nurse of early 1900's

(Des Pam Andrews. Litho Leigh-Mardon Ltd, Melbourne)

1985 (25 Feb). 19th-Century Australian Military Uniforms. T **407** and similar vert designs. Multicoloured. P 14½.

964	33c. Type **407**	35	65
	a. Horiz strip of 5. Nos. 964/8	1·50	3·00
965	33c. Western Australian Pinjarrah Cavalry	35	65
966	33c. New South Wales Lancers	35	65
967	33c. New South Wales Contingent to the Sudan	35	65
968	33c. Victorian Mounted Rifles	35	65
964/8	*Set of 5*	1·50	3·00

Nos. 964/8 were printed together, *se-tenant*, in horizontal strips of 5 throughout the sheet.

(Des Wendy Tamlyn. Litho Leigh-Mardon Ltd, Melbourne)

1985 (13 Mar). Centenary of District Nursing Services. P 14½.

969	**408**	33c. multicoloured	45	35

409 Sulphur-crested Cockatoos

(Des R. Bevers. Litho Leigh-Mardon Ltd, Melbourne)

1985 (13 Mar). Multicoloured, background colour given. P 14½×imperf.

970	**409**	1c. flesh	2·50	5·00
		a. Booklet pane. Nos. 970, and 971×3	3·75	
971		33c. pale turquoise-green	50	55

Nos. 970/1 only exist from $1 stamp booklets, No. SB54. As stamps from these booklets have their outer edges imperforate, the end example of No. 971 is only perforated along one side.

410 Abel Tasman and Journal Entry

411 Sovereign's Badge of Order of Australia

(Des G. Emery. Litho Cambec Press, Melbourne).

1985 (10 Apr). Bicentenary of Australian Settlement (1988) (2nd issue) Navigators. Multicoloured. T **410** and similar square designs. P 13.

972	33c. Type **410**	35	35
973	33c. Dirk Hartog's *Eendracht* (detail, Aert Anthonisz)	35	35
974	33c. "William Dampier" (detail, T. Murray)	35	35
975	90c. Globe and hand with extract from Dampier's journal	65	2·50
972/5	*Set of 4*	1·50	3·25
MS976	150×115 mm. As Nos. 972/5, but with cream coloured margins	1·50	4·00

(Des Elizabeth Innes. Litho Cambec Press, Melbourne)

1985 (22 Apr). Queen Elizabeth II's Birthday. P 14×13½.

977	**411**	33c. multicoloured	40	30

412 Tree, and Soil running through Hourglass ("Soil")

413 *Elves and Fairies* (Annie Rentoul and Ida Rentoul Outhwaite)

(Des L. Whaite and G. Jorgensen. Litho Cambec Press, Melbourne).

1985 (15 May). Conservation. Multicoloured. T **412** and similar vert designs. P 14×13½.

978	33c. Type **412**	25	20
979	50c. Washing on line and smog ("air")	40	75
980	80c. Tap and flower ("water")	50	1·25
981	90c. Chain encircling flames ("energy")	60	1·75
978/81	*Set of 4*	1·60	3·50

(Des P. Leuver. Litho Leigh-Mardon Ltd, Melbourne).

1985 (17 July). Classic Australian Children's Books. T **413** and similar vert designs. Multicoloured. P 14½.

982	33c. Type **413**	25	55
	a. Horiz strip of 5. Nos. 982/6	1·10	2·50
983	33c. *The Magic Pudding* (Norman Lindsay)	25	55
984	33c. *Ginger Meggs* (James Charles Bancks)	25	55
	a. Imperf 3 sides (in horiz pair with No. 985)	£200	—
985	33c. *Blinky Bill* (Dorothy Wall)	25	55
	a. Imperf 3 sides (in horiz pair with No. 986)	£200	—
986	33c. *Snugglepot and Cuddlepie* (May Gibbs)	25	55
982/6	*Set of 5*	1·40	3·00

Nos. 982/6 were printed together, *se-tenant*, in horizontal strips of 5 throughout the sheet.

414 Dish Aerials

415 Angel in Sailing Ship

(Des J. Ostoja-Kotkowski. Litho Leigh-Mardon Ltd, Melbourne)

1985 (18 Sept). Electronic Mail Service. P 14½.

987	**414**	33c. multicoloured	35	30

(Des S. Hartshorne. Litho Leigh-Mardon Ltd, Melbourne)

1985 (18 Sept–1 Nov). Christmas. Multicoloured. T **415** and similar horiz designs. P 14½.

988	27c. Angel with holly wings (1.11)	20	10
989	33c. Angel with bells (1.11)	25	10
990	45c. Type **415**	30	25
991	55c. Angel with star (1.11)	40	75
992	90c. Angel with Christmas tree bauble (1.11)	65	2·25
988/92	*Set of 5*	1·60	3·00

416 Astrolabe (*Batavia*, 1629)

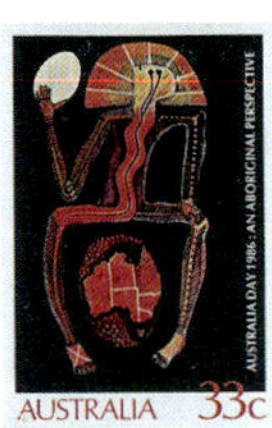

417 Aboriginal Wandjina Spirit, Map of Australia and Egg

(Des G. Emery. Litho Cambec Press, Melbourne)

1985 (2 Oct). Bicentenary of Australian Settlement (1988) (3rd issue). Relics from Early Shipwrecks. T **416** and similar square designs. Multicoloured. P 13.

993	33c. Type **416**	25	10
994	50c. German beardman jug (*Vergulde Draeck*, 1656)	45	80
995	90c. Wooden bobbins (*Batavia*, 1629) and encrusted scissors (*Zeewijk*, 1727)	80	3·75
996	$1 Silver and brass buckle (*Zeewijk*, 1727)	80	2·00
993/6	*Set of 4*	2·10	6·00

(Des R. Meeks. Litho Leigh-Mardon Ltd, Melbourne)

1986 (24 Jan). Australia Day. P 14½.

997	**417**	33c. multicoloured	40	30

418 AUSSAT Satellite, Moon and Earth's Surface

419 H.M.S. *Buffalo*

(Des O. Schmidinger and Christine Stead. Litho Leigh-Mardon Ltd, Melbourne)

1986 (24 Jan). AUSSAT National Communications Satellite System. T **418** and similar vert design. Multicoloured. P 14½.

998	33c. Type **418**	30	10
999	80c. AUSSAT satellite in orbit	70	2·00

(Des I. Kidd. Litho Cambec Press, Melbourne)

1986 (12 Feb). 150th Anniv of South Australia. T **419** and similar horiz design. Multicoloured. P 13½×14.

1000	33c. Type **419**	60	1·25
	a. Pair. Nos. 1000/1	1·10	2·50
1001	33c. "City Sign" sculpture (Otto Hajek), Adelaide	60	1·25

Nos. 1000/1 were printed together, *se-tenant*, in horizontal and vertical pairs throughout the sheet, the background of each horizontal pair showing an extract from the colony's Letters Patent of 1836.

420 *Banksia serrata*

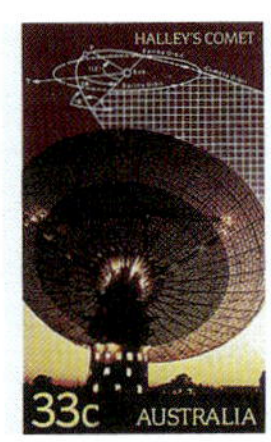

421 Radio Telescope, Parkes, and Diagram of Comet's Orbit

(Des Sue Titcher. Litho Cambec Press, Melbourne)

1986 (12 Mar). Bicentenary of Australian Settlement (1988) (4th issue). Cook's Voyage to New Holland. T **420** and similar horiz designs. Multicoloured. P 13.

1002	33c. Type **420**	50	35
1003	33c. *Hibiscus meraukensis*	50	35
1004	50c. *Dillenia alata*	70	1·10
1005	80c. *Correa reflexa*	1·50	2·75
1006	90c. "Joseph Banks" (botanist) (Reynolds) and Banks with Dr. Solander	2·00	2·75
1007	90c. "Sydney Parkinson" (self-portrait) and Parkinson drawing	2·00	2·75
1002/7	*Set of 6*	6·50	9·00

(Des J. Passmore. Litho Cambec Press, Melbourne)

1986 (9 Apr). Appearance of Halley's Comet. P 14×13½.

1008	**421**	33c. multicoloured	50	35

422 Queen Elizabeth II

423 Brumbies (wild horses)

(Des Fay Plamka. Litho Leigh-Mardon Ltd, Melbourne)

1986 (21 Apr). 60th Birthday of Queen Elizabeth II. P 14½.

1009	**422**	33c. multicoloured	55	35

(Des R. Ingpen. Litho Leigh-Mardon Ltd, Melbourne)

1986 (21 May). Australian Horses. T **423** and similar horiz designs. Multicoloured. P 14½.

1010	33c. Type **423**	60	15
1011	80c. Mustering	1·50	2·25
1012	90c. Show jumping	1·50	2·50
1013	$1 Child on pony	1·75	2·25
1010/13 *Set of 4*		4·75	6·50

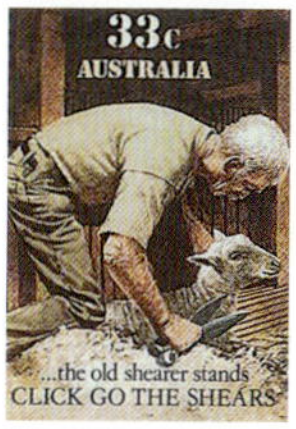

424 "The Old Shearer stands"

425 "King George III" (A. Ramsay) and Convicts

(Des R. Ingpen. Litho Leigh-Mardon Ltd, Melbourne)

1986 (21 July). Folklore. Scenes and Verses from the Folksong "Click go the Shears". T **424** and similar vert designs. Multicoloured. P 14½.

1014	33c. Type **424**	35	70
	a. Horiz strip of 5. Nos. 1014/18	1·60	3·25
1015	33c. "The ringer looks around"	35	70
1016	33c. "The boss of the board"	35	70
1017	33c. "The tar-boy is there"	35	70
1018	33c. "Shearing is all over"	35	70
1014/18 *Set of 5*		1·60	3·25

Nos. 1014/18 were printed together, *se-tenant*, in horizontal strips of 5 throughout the sheet, forming a composite design.

(Des D. Lancashire. Litho Cambec Press, Melbourne)

1986 (6 Aug). Bicentenary of Australian Settlement (1988) (5th issue). Convict Settlement in New South Wales. T **425** and similar horiz designs. Multicoloured. P 13.

1019	33c. Type **425**	40	40
1020	33c. "Lord Sydney" (Gilbert Stuart) and convicts	40	40
1021	33c. "Captain Arthur Phillip" (F. Wheatley) and ship	40	40
1022	$1 "Captain John Hunter" (W. B. Bennett) and aborigines	1·00	4·00
1019/22 *Set of 4*		2·00	4·75

426 Red Kangaroo

427 Royal Bluebell

428 Pink Enamel Orchid

(Des D. Higgins. Litho Leigh-Mardon Ltd, Melbourne)

1986 (13 Aug). Australian Wildlife (1st series). T **426** and similar vert designs. Multicoloured. P 14½×14.

1023	36c. Type **426**	70	95
	a. Horiz strip of 5. Nos. 1023/7	3·00	4·25
1024	36c. Emu	70	95
1026	36c. Laughing Kookaburra	70	95
1025	36c. Koala	70	95
1027	36c. Platypus	70	95
1023/7 *Set of 5*		3·00	4·25

Nos. 1023/7 were printed together, *se-tenant*, in horizontal strips of 5 throughout the sheet.

For 37c. values see Nos. 1072/6.

(Des Betty Conabere. Litho Mercury-Walch Pty, Hobart)

1986 (25 Aug). Alpine Wildflowers. T **427** and similar vert designs. Multicoloured. Roul.

1028	3c. Type **427**	50	75
	a. Booklet pane. Nos. 1028, 1029 and 1031×2	3·00	
	b. Booklet pane. Nos. 1028, 1030 and 1031×2	3·00	
1029	5c. Alpine Marsh Marigold	2·00	3·25
1030	25c. Mount Buffalo Sunray	2·00	3·25
1031	36c. Silver Snow Daisy	45	30
1028/31 *Set of 4*		4·50	6·75

Nos. 1028/31 only exist from 80c. (pane No. 1028a, SB55) and $1 (pane No. 1028b, SB56) stamp booklets. The outer edges of the booklet panes are imperforate.

(Des O. Shmidinger and Christine Stead. Litho Leigh-Mardon Ltd, Melbourne)

1986 (18 Sept). Native Australian Orchids. T **428** and similar vert designs. Multicoloured. P 14½.

1032	36c. Type **428**	55	10
1033	55c. *Dendrobium nindii*	1·00	75
1034	90c. Duck Orchid	1·75	4·25
1035	$1 Queen of Sheba Orchid	1·75	2·25
1032/5 *Set of 4*		4·50	6·50

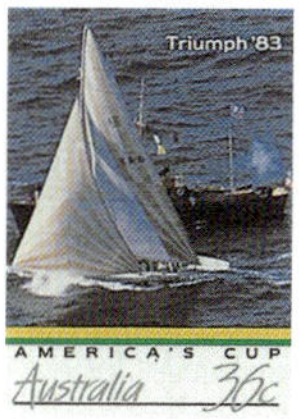

429 *Australia II* crossing Finishing Line

430 Dove with Olive Branch and Sun

(Des J. Passmore and G. Rowan. Litho Cambec Press, Melbourne)

1986 (26 Sept). Australian Victory in America's Cup, 1983. T **429** and similar vert designs. Multicoloured. P 14×13½.

1036	36c. Type **429**	60	75
1037	36c. Boxing kangaroo flag of winning syndicate	60	75
	a. Grey (inscr and face value) omitted	£180	
1038	36c. America's Cup trophy	60	75
	a. Grey (inscr and face value) omitted	£180	
1036/8 *Set of 3*		1·60	2·00

(Des K. Cato. Litho Cambec Press, Melbourne)

1986 (22 Oct). International Peace Year. P 14×13½.

1039	**430**	36c. multicoloured	65	40

Examples with the gutter margin overprinted to commemorate the Papal visit in November 1986 were not produced by the Australian Post Office.

431 Mary and Joseph

432 Australian Flag on Printed Circuit Board

(Des B. Clinton. Litho Leigh-Mardon Ltd, Melbourne)

1986 (3 Nov - Dec). Christmas. T **431** and similar multicoloured designs showing scenes from children's nativity play. P 14½.

1040	30c. Type **431**	30	20
	a. Perf 14×13½ (12.86)	75	75
1041	36c. Three Wise Men leaving gifts	35	10
1042	60c. Angels (*horiz*)	60	1·75
1040/2 *Set of 3*		1·10	1·75
MS1043	147×70 mm. 30c. Three angels and shepherd (*horiz*); 30c. Kneeling shepherds (*horiz*); 30c. Mary, Joseph and three angels; 30c. Innkeeper and two angels; 30c. Three Wise Men (*horiz*)	3·00	4·25

No. 1040a was printed by Cambec Press after stocks of the original printing by Leigh-Mardon Ltd ran short. It is believed that this Cambec Press printing was distributed in New South Wales, Tasmania, Victoria and Western Australia.

(Des J. Passmore. Litho CPE Australia Ltd, Melbourne)

1987 (23 Jan). Australia Day. T **432** and similar horiz design. Multicoloured. P 13½×14.

1044	36c. Type **432**	55	75
1045	36c. "Australian Made" Campaign logos	55	75

433 Aerial View of Yacht

434 Grapes and Melons

(Des O. Schmidinger and Christine Stead. Litho Leigh-Mardon Ltd, Melbourne)

1987 (28 Jan). America's Cup Yachting Championship. T **433** and similar vert designs. Multicoloured. P 14½.

1046	36c. Type **433**	25	10
1047	55c. Two yachts tacking	40	55
1048	90c. Two yachts beating	50	2·50
1049	$1 Two yachts under full sail	55	1·00
1046/9 *Set of 4*		1·50	3·75

(Des Susan Tilley. Litho CPE Australia Ltd, Melbourne)

1987 (11 Feb). Australian Fruit. T **434** and similar vert designs. Multicoloured. P 14×13½.

1050	36c. Type **434**	25	10
1051	65c. Tropical and sub-tropical fruits	50	80
1052	90c. Citrus fruit, apples and pears	80	2·50
1053	$1 Stone and berry fruits	80	1·00
1050/3 *Set of 4*		2·10	4·00

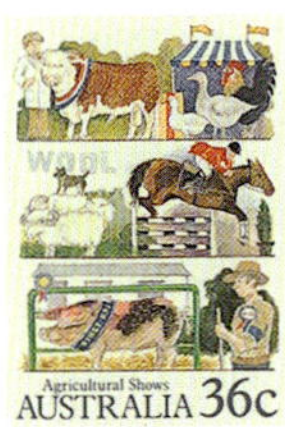

435 Livestock

436 Queen Elizabeth in Australia, 1986

(Des D. Lancashire. Litho CPE Australia Ltd, Melbourne)

1987 (10 Apr). Agricultural Shows. T **435** and similar vert designs. Multicoloured. P 14×13½.

1054	36c. Type **435**	45	20
1055	65c. Produce	80	1·40
1056	90c. Sideshows	1·00	3·00
1057	$1 Competitions	1·10	2·00
1054/7 *Set of 4*		3·00	6·00

(Des Janet Boschen. Litho CPE Australia Ltd, Melbourne)

1987 (21 Apr). Queen Elizabeth II's Birthday. P 13½×14.

1058	**436** 36c. multicoloured	55	40

437 Convicts on Quay

438 "At the Station"

(Des Sue Passmore. Litho CPE Australia Ltd, Melbourne)

1987 (13 May). Bicentenary of Australian Settlement (1988) (6th issue). Departure of the First Fleet. T **437** and similar square designs. Multicoloured. P 13.

1059	36c. Type **437**	45	90
	a. Horiz strip of 5. Nos. 1059/63	2·00	4·00
1060	36c. Royal Marines officer and wife	45	90
1061	36c. Sailors loading supplies	45	90
1062	36c. Officers being ferried to ships	45	90
1063	36c. Fleet in English Channel	45	90
1059/63 *Set of 5*		2·00	4·00

Nos. 1059/63 were printed together, *se-tenant*, in horizontal strips of 5 throughout the sheet.

See also Nos. 1064/6, 1077/81, 1090/2 and 1105/9.

(Des Sue Passmore. Litho CPE Australia Ltd, Melbourne)

1987 (3 June). Bicentenary of Australian Settlement (1988) (7th issue). First Fleet at Tenerife. Square designs as T **437**. Multicoloured. P 13.

1064	36c. Ferrying supplies, Santa Cruz	55	1·00
	a. Horiz pair. Nos. 1064/5	1·10	2·00
1065	36c. Canary Islands fishermen and departing fleet	55	1·00
1066	$1 Fleet arriving at Tenerife	1·40	2·25
	s. Optd "Specimen"	50	
1064/6 *Set of 3*		2·25	3·75

Nos. 1064/5 were printed together, *se-tenant*, in horizontal pairs throughout the sheet, forming a composite design.

(Des C. Lee. Litho CPE Australia Ltd, Melbourne)

1987 (24 June). Folklore. Scenes and Verses from Poem "The Man from Snowy River". T **438** and similar vert designs. Multicoloured. P 14×13½.

1067	36c. Type **438**	65	1·00
	a. Horiz strip of 5. Nos. 1067/71	3·00	4·50
1068	36c. "Mountain bred"	65	1·00
1069	36c. "That terrible descent"	65	1·00
1070	36c. "At their heels"	65	1·00
1071	36c. "Brought them back"	65	1·00
1067/71 *Set of 5*		3·00	4·50

Nos. 1067/71 were printed together, *se-tenant*, in horizontal strips of five throughout the sheet, forming a composite background design of mountain scenery.

(Des D. Higgins. Litho Leigh-Mardon Ltd, Melbourne)

1987 (1 July). Australian Wildlife (2nd series). Vert designs as T **426**. Multicoloured. P 14½×14.

1072	37c. Common Brushtail Possum	55	85
	a. Horiz strip of 5. Nos. 1072/6	2·50	3·75
	ab. Pale orange (top panel) omitted	£4250	
1073	37c. Sulphur-crested Cockatoo	55	85
1074	37c. Common Wombat	55	85
1075	37c. Crimson Rosella	55	85
1076	37c. Echidna	55	85
1072/6 *Set of 5*		2·50	3·75

Nos. 1072/6 were printed together, *se-tenant*, in horizontal strips of 5 throughout the sheet.

(Des Sue Passmore. Litho CPE Australia Ltd, Melbourne)

1987 (6 Aug). Bicentenary of Australian Settlement (1988) (8th issue). First Fleet at Rio de Janeiro. Square designs as T **437**. Multicoloured. P 13.

1077	37c. Sperm Whale and fleet	60	1·10
	a. Horiz strip of 5. Nos. 1077/81	2·75	5·00
1078	37c. Brazilian coast	60	1·10
1079	37c. British officers in market	60	1·10
1080	37c. Religious procession	60	1·10
1081	37c. Fleet leaving Rio	60	1·10
1077/81 *Set of 5*		2·75	5·00

Nos. 1077/81 were printed together, *se-tenant*, in horizontal strips of 5, forming a composite design.

439 Bionic Ear

440 Catching Crayfish

(Des. O. Schmidinger and Christine Stead. Litho Leigh-Mardon Ltd, Melbourne)

1987 (19 Aug). Australian Achievements in Technology. T **439** and similar vert designs. Multicoloured. P 14½.

1082	37c. Type **439**	20	10
1083	53c. Microchips	35	25
1084	63c. Robotics	40	50
1085	68c. Ceramics	40	50
1082/5 *Set of 4*		1·25	1·25

(Des Elizabeth Honey. Litho Leigh-Mardon Ltd, Melbourne)

1987 (16 Sept). "Aussie Kids". T **440** and similar horiz designs. Multicoloured. P 14½.

1086	37c. Type **440**	25	10
1087	55c. Playing cat's cradle	40	40
1088	90c. Young football supporters	65	2·25
1089	$1 Children with kangaroo	65	1·00
	s. Optd "Specimen"	50	
1086/9 *Set of 4*		1·75	3·25

(Des Sue Passmore. Litho CPE Australia Ltd, Melbourne)

1987 (13 Oct). Bicentenary of Australian Settlement (1988) (9th issue). First Fleet at Cape of Good Hope. Square designs as T **437**. Multicoloured. P 13.

1090	37c. Marine checking list of livestock	65	1·00
	a. Horiz pair. Nos. 1090/1	1·25	2·00
1091	37c. Loading livestock	65	1·00
1092	$1 First Fleet at Cape Town	1·50	2·50
	s. Optd "Specimen"	50	
1090/2 *Set of 3*		2·50	4·00

Nos. 1090/1 were printed together, *se-tenant*, in horizontal and vertical pairs throughout the sheet, the former showing a composite design.

441 Detail of Spearthrower, Western Australia

442 Grandmother and Granddaughters with candles

(Des J. Passmore. Litho Leigh-Mardon Ltd, Melbourne)

1987 (13 Oct). Aboriginal Crafts. T **441** and similar horiz designs. Multicoloured. P 15½×imperf.

1093	3c. Type **441**	1·00	1·60
	a. Booklet pane. Nos. 1093 and 1095, each ×2	3·50	
1094	15c. Shield pattern, New South Wales	4·00	10·00
	a. Booklet pane. Nos. 1094, 1096 ×3 and 1097 ×2	7·00	
1095	37c. Basket weave, Queensland	1·00	1·60
1096	37c. Bowl design, Central Australia	70	1·25
1097	37c. Belt pattern, Northern Territory	85	1·60
1093/7 *Set of 5*		6·75	14·50

Nos. 1093/7 only exist from 80c. (pane No. 1093a, SB57) and $2 (pane No. 1094a, SB58) stamp booklets. The vertical edges of the booklet panes are imperforate.

(Des B. Clinton. Litho Leigh-Mardon Ltd, Melbourne (30c.) or CPE Australia Ltd, Melbourne (37c., 63c.))

1987 (2 Nov). Christmas. T **442** and similar multicoloured designs showing carol singing by candlelight. P 14½ (30c.) or 13½×14 (37c., 63c.).

1098	30c. Type **442**	50	70
	a. Horiz strip of 5. Nos. 1098/1102	2·25	3·25
1099	30c. Father and daughters	50	70
1100	30c. Four children	50	70
1101	30c. Family	50	70
1102	30c. Six teenagers	50	70
1103	37c. Choir (*horiz*)	50	20
1104	63c. Father and two children (*horiz*)	85	1·60
1098/104 *Set of 7*		3·50	4·75

Nos. 1098/1102 were printed together, *se-tenant*, in horizontal strips of five throughout the sheet.

(Des Sue Passmore. Litho CPE Australia Ltd, Melbourne)

1988 (26 Jan). Bicentenary of Australian Settlement (10th issue). Arrival of First Fleet. Square designs as T **437**. Multicoloured. P 13.

1105	37c. Aborigines watching arrival of Fleet, Botany Bay	65	95
	a. Horiz strip of 5. Nos. 1105/9	3·00	4·25
1106	37c. Aborigine family and anchored ships	65	95
1107	37c. Fleet arriving at Sydney Cove	65	95
1108	37c. Ship's boat	65	95
1109	37c. Raising the flag, Sydney Cove, 26 January 1788	65	95
1105/9 *Set of 5*		3·00	4·25

Nos. 1105/9 were printed together, *se-tenant*, in horizontal strips of five throughout the sheet, forming a composite design.

443 Koala with Stockman's Hat and Eagle dressed as Uncle Sam

444 "Religion" (A. Horner)

(Des R. Harvey. Litho CPE Australia Ltd, Melbourne)

1988 (26 Jan). Bicentenary of Australian Settlement (11th issue). Joint issue with U.S.A. P 13.

1110 **443**	37c. multicoloured	60	35

NEW PRINTINGS. From the beginning of 1990 new printings of definitive stamps were identified by small koala or kangaroo symbols printed on the vertical sheet margins alongside alternate rows. One koala represented the first printing, two koalas the second and so on. The kangaroo symbol was used once four koalas had been reached.

(Litho Leigh-Mardon Ltd, Melbourne (4, 5, 20, 25, 30, 37, 39, 40, 50, 53, 70, 80, 90c., $1) or CPE Australia Ltd, Melbourne (others))

1988 (17 Feb)–**95**. "Living Together". T **444** and similar square designs showing cartoons. Multicoloured (except 30c.). P 14.

1111	1c. Type **444** (16.3.88)	50	70
1112	2c. "Industry" (P. Nicholson) (16.3.88)	50	60
1113	3c. "Local Government" (A. Collette) (16.3.88)	50	60
1114	4c. "Trade Unions" (Liz Honey)	10	20
1115	5c. "Parliament" (Bronwyn Halls) (16.3.88)	50	50
1116	10c. "Transport" (Meg Williams)	30	50
1117	15c. "Sport" (G. Cook)	1·75	60
1118	20c. "Commerce" (M. Atcherson)	70	1·00
1119	25c. "Housing" (C. Smith)	45	40
	a. Perf 14½ (14.9.95)	4·00	1·50
1120	30c. "Welfare" (R. Tandberg) (black and pale rose-lilac) (16.3.88)	55	1·25
1121	37c. "Postal Services" (P. Viska)	35	50
	a. Booklet pane. No. 1121×10 (1.7.88)	3·00	
1121*b*	39c. "Tourism" (J. Spooner) (28.9.88)	50	50
	ba. Booklet pane. No. 1121b×10	4·50	
1122	40c. "Recreation" (R. Harvey) (16.3.88)	70	70
1123	45c. "Health" (Jenny Coopes)	70	1·25
1124	50c. "Mining" (G. Haddon)	70	50
1125	53c. "Primary Industry" (S. Leahy)	1·75	2·25
1126	55c. "Education" (Victoria Roberts) (16.3.88).	1·25	2·25
1127	60c. "Armed Forces" (B. Green) (16.3.88)	1·50	70
1128	63c. "Police" (J. Russell) (16.3.88)	2·75	1·40
1129	65c. "Telecommunications" (B. Petty) (16.3.88)	1·50	2·75
1130	68c. "The Media" (A. Langoulant) (16.3.88)	2·25	3·75
1131	70c. "Science and Technology" (J. Hook)	1·75	1·75
1132	75c. "Visual Arts" (G. Dazeley) (16.3.88)	1·00	1·00
1133	80c. "Performing Arts" (A. Stitt)	1·25	1·00
1134	90c. "Banking" (S. Billington)	1·50	1·50
1135	95c. "Law" (C. Aslanis) (16.3.88)	1·00	2·75
1136	$1 "Rescue and Emergency" (M. Leunig)	1·10	75
	s. Optd "Specimen"	50	
1111/36 *Set of 27*		24·00	26·00

Although Leigh-Mardon printed the 37c. and 39c. sheet stamps, and some of the 37c. booklets, Nos. 1121a and 1121ba were produced by CPE with the upper and lower edges of the panes imperforate, so that stamps from them exist imperforate at top or bottom. These panes also show margins at both right and left.

Early in 1989 Leigh-Mardon Ltd, whose works were situated at Moorabbin, took over CPE Australia Ltd of Scoresby. Printings of the 45, 55, 60, 75, 80, 95c. and $1 were made at both printing works.

No. 1119a comes from part of the 4 koala printing.

445 "Government House, Sydney, 1790" (George Raper)

446 Queen Elizabeth II (from photo by Tim Graham)

(Des J. Passmore. Litho CPE Australia Ltd, Melbourne)

1988 (13 Apr). Bicentenary of Australian Settlement (12th issue). "The Early Years, 1788-1809". T **445** and similar square designs showing paintings. Multicoloured. P 13.

1137	37c. Type **445**	65	1·00
	a. Horiz strip of 5. No. 1137/41	3·00	4·50
1138	37c. "Government Farm, Parramatta, 1791" ("The Port Jackson Painter")	65	1·00
1139	37c. "Parramatta Road, 1796" (attr Thomas Watling)	65	1·00
1140	37c. "View of Sydney Cove, *c.* 1800" (detail) (Edward Dayes)	65	1·00
1141	37c. "Sydney Hospital, 1803", (detail) (George William Evans)	65	1·00
1137/41 *Set of 5*		3·00	4·50

Nos. 1137/41 were printed together, *se-tenant*, in horizontal strips of 5 throughout the sheet, each strip forming a composite background design from the painting, "View of Sydney from the East Side of the Cove, *c.* 1808" by John Eyre.

(Des Sandra Baker. Litho Leigh-Mardon Ltd, Melbourne).

1988 (21 Apr). Queen Elizabeth II's Birthday. P 14½.

1142	**446**	37c. multicoloured	50	40

447 Expo '88 Logo

448 New Parliament House

(Des G. Emery. Litho CPE Australia Ltd, Melbourne)

1988 (29 Apr). Expo '88 World Fair, Brisbane. P 13.

1143	**447**	37c. multicoloured	50	40

(Des B. Sadgrove. Litho Leigh-Mardon Ltd, Melbourne)

1988 (9 May). Opening of New Parliament House, Canberra. P 14½.

1144	**448**	37c. multicoloured	50	40

449 Early Settler and Sailing Clipper

450 Kiwi and Koala at Campfire

(Des G. Emery. Litho CPE Australia Ltd, Melbourne)

1988 (21 June). Bicentenary of Australian Settlement (13th issue). T **449** and similar square designs. Multicoloured. P 13.

1145	37c. Type **449**	75	1·00
	a. Pair. Nos. 1145/6	1·50	2·00
1146	37c. Queen Elizabeth II with British and Australian Parliament Buildings	75	1·00
1147	$1 W. G. Grace (cricketer) and tennis racquet	1·50	2·25
	a. Pair. Nos. 1147/8	3·00	4·50
1148	$1 Shakespeare, John Lennon (entertainer) and Sydney Opera House	1·50	2·25
1145/8 *Set of 4*		4·00	6·00

Nos. 1145/6 and 1147/8 were printed together, *se-tenant*, in horizontal and vertical pairs throughout the sheets, each horizontal pair showing a background design of the Australian flag.

Stamps in similar designs were also issued by Great Britain.

(Des R. Harvey. Litho Leigh-Mardon Ltd, Melbourne)

1988 (21 June). Bicentenary of Australian Settlement (14th issue). P 14½.

1149	**450**	37c. multicoloured	65	40

A stamp in a similar design was also issued by New Zealand.

451 "Bush Potato Country" (Turkey Tolsen Tjupurrula and David Corby Tjapaltjarri)

452 Basketball

(Des Janet Boschen. Litho CPE Australia Ltd, Melbourne)

1988 (1 Aug). Art of the Desert. Aboriginal Paintings from Central Australia. T **451** and similar square designs. Multicoloured. P 13.

1150	37c. Type **451**	20	10
1151	55c. "Courtship Rejected" (Limpi Puntungka Tjapangati)	35	50
1152	90c. "Medicine Story" (artist unknown)	55	2·50
1153	$1 "Ancestor Dreaming" (Tim Leura Tjapaltjarri)	55	1·25
1150/3 *Set of 4*		1·50	3·75

(Des Sue Passmore. Litho Leigh-Mardon Ltd, Melbourne)

1988 (14 Sept). Olympic Games, Seoul. T **452** and similar horiz designs. Multicoloured. P 14½.

1154	37c. Type **452**	40	25
1155	65c. Athlete crossing finish line	45	1·75
1156	$1 Gymnast with hoop	60	1·75
1154/6 *Set of 3*		1·40	3·25

453 Rod and Mace

(Des K. Christos. Litho Leigh-Mardon Ltd, Melbourne)

1988 (19 Sept). 34th Commonwealth Parliamentary Conference, Canberra. P 14½.

1157	**453**	37c. multicoloured	50	60

454 Necklace by Peter Tully

(Des K. Christos. Litho Mercury-Walch Pty, Hobart)

1988 (28 Sept). Australian Crafts. T **454** and similar horiz designs. Multicoloured. Roulximperf.

1158	2c. Type **454**	3·50	6·50
	a. Booklet pane. Nos. 1158 and 1160×2	3·75	
1159	5c. Vase by Colin Levy	3·50	6·50
	a. Booklet pane. Nos. 1159 and 1160×5	4·75	
1160	39c. Teapot by Frank Bauer	40	35
1158/60 *Set of 3*		6·75	12·00

Nos. 1158/60 only exist from 80c. (pane No. 1158a, SB62) and $2 (pane No. 1159a, SB63) stamp booklets. The vertical edges of the booklet panes are imperforate.

455 Pinnacles Desert

456 "The Nativity" (Danielle Hush)

(Des K. Christos. Litho CPE Australia Ltd, Melbourne)

1988 (17 Oct). Panorama of Australia. T **455** and similar horiz designs. Multicoloured. P 13.

1161	39c. Type **455**	50	10
1162	55c. Flooded landscape, Arnhem Land	65	40
1163	65c. Twelve Apostles, Victoria	80	2·00
1164	70c. Mountain Ash wood	80	2·00
1161/4 *Set of 4*		2·50	4·00

(Des Sandra Baker. Litho CPE Australia Ltd, Melbourne (32, 39c.) or Leigh-Mardon Ltd, Melbourne (63c.))

1988 (31 Oct). Christmas. T **456** and similar square designs. Multicoloured. P 14½ (63c.) or 13 (others).

1165	32c. Type **456**	30	10
1166	39c. "Koala as Father Christmas" (Kylie Courtney)	30	10
1167	63c. "Christmas Cockatoo" (Benjamin Stevenson)	50	1·10
1165/7 *Set of 3*		1·00	1·10

PRINTERS. On 1 April 1989 Leigh-Mardon Ltd took over CPE Australia Ltd. Stamp printing continued at both the Moorabbin (original Leigh-Mardon) and Scoresby (ex-CPE) works with some stamps being printed at one and then perforated at the other. The Scoresby works closed at the end of 1991.

457 Sir Henry Parkes

458 Bowls

(Des R. Bevers. Litho CPE Australia Ltd, Melbourne)

1989 (25 Jan). Australia Day. Centenary of Federation Speech by Sir Henry Parkes (N.S.W. Prime Minister). P 14×13½.

1168	**457**	39c. multicoloured	45	40

(Des Sue Passmore (5, 10, 20, 41, 43, 65c., $1, $1.20), (75, 80, 85, 90c.), G. Cook (others). Litho Printset Cambec Pty Ltd (5c., (No. 1172a), 65c. (No. 1186a) and ptgs of 1c. (No. 1169), 3c., 75c., 80c. (No. 1189) and $1 (No. 1192) from 1993) or Leigh-Mardon Ltd, Melbourne (others))

1989 (13 Feb)–**94**. Sports. T **458** and similar horiz designs. Multicoloured. P 13½ (5, 10, 20, 65c., $1.20) or 14×14½ (others).

1169	1c. Type **458**	10	75
	a. Perf 13½ (4.90)	2·50	2·25
1170	2c. Tenpin-bowling	10	20
	a. Perf 13½ (9.89)	2·25	50
1171	3c. Australian football	1·00	1·50
1172	5c. Kayaking and canoeing (17.1.90)	15	10
	a. Perf 14×14½ (3.94)	2·75	40
1174	10c. Sailboarding (17.1.90)	15	15
	a. Perf 14×14½ (2.92)	5·00	40
1176	20c. Tennis (17.1.90)	20	25
	a. Perf 14×14½ (7.93)	3·50	2·75
1179	39c. Fishing	45	40
	a. Booklet pane. No. 1179×10	5·00	
	b. Perf 13½ (6.89)	1·40	1·50
	ba. Booklet pane. No. 1179b×10	12·00	
1180	41c. Cycling (23.8.89)	40	35
	a. Booklet pane. No. 1180×10	6·00	
	b. Imperf horiz (vert pair)	£170	
1181	43c. Skateboarding (27.8.90)	50	40
	a. Booklet pane. No. 1181×10	6·50	
1184	55c. Kite-flying	50	45
1186	65c. Rock-climbing (17.1.90)	80	70
	a. Perf 14×14½ (2.92)	8·00	4·25
1187	70c. Cricket	1·90	80
1188	75c. Netball (22.8.91)	70	1·50
1189	80c. Squash (22.8.91)	1·00	65
1190	85c. Diving (22.8.91)	1·75	80
1191	90c. Soccer (22.8.91)	1·75	2·00
1192	$1 Fun-run (17.1.90)	1·00	50
	a. Perf 13½ (1.91)	7·50	3·50
1193	$1.10 Golf	4·50	1·00
1194	$1.20 Hang-gliding (27.8.90)	5·50	1·10
1169/94 *Set of 19*		20·00	12·00
1192/4 Optd "Specimen" *Set of 3*		1·75	

The booklet panes come from Nos. SB64/5, SB70/a and have the upper and lower edges imperforate, so that the stamps from them are imperforate at top or bottom, and have margins at both left and right.

No. 1180b occurred in booklet panes, most of which were affixed to first day covers, but not postmarked. Price quoted is for unused pair, without gum. An example also exists used on postmarked cover, together with two mint in booklets.

Nos. 1169a (1 koala ptg), 1170a (all ptgs except the first), 1179b (1st new ptg) and 1192a (1 koala ptg) are Scoresby printings of values originally produced at Moorabbin. Nos. 1174a (2, 3, and 4 koala ptgs) and 1176a (2 and 3 koala) are Moorabbin printings of values originally produced at Scoresby.

No. 1186a (2 koala ptg) was printed by Printset Cambec Pty Ltd. instead of Leigh-Mardon Ltd. There are minor differences in the arrangement of the inscriptions. Further supplies of the 1c. (No. 1169) (2 koala), 3c. (3 and 4 koala), 75c. (1, 2, 3, 4 koala, 1 kangaroo), 80c. (2 koala) and $1 (No. 1192) (2 koala) were also produced by Printset Cambec from 1993.

No. 1172a (4 koala ptg) was printed by McPherson's as were additional supplies of the 65c. (No. 1186a) (3 koala) and $1 (No. 1192) (1 kangaroo + 1 koala and 1 kangaroo + 2 koala ptgs).

For self-adhesive versions of Nos. 1180/1 see Nos. 1259/60a.

WARNING. The coating on a batch of paper used during 1989-90 was defective so that stamps lose parts of their design if immersed in water.

459 Merino

(Des K. McEwan. Litho CPE Australia Ltd, Melbourne)

1989 (27 Feb). Sheep in Australia. T **459** and similar horiz designs. Multicoloured. P 13½×14.

1195	39c. Type **459**	70	50
1196	39c. Poll Dorset	70	50
1197	85c. Polwarth	1·50	3·50
1198	$1 Corriedale	1·50	2·00
	s. Optd "Specimen"	70	
1195/8 *Set of 4*		4·00	6·00

460 Adelaide Botanic Garden

(Des J. Passmore. Eng B. Stewart. Litho Leigh-Mardon Ltd and die-stamped Avon Graphics, both of Melbourne ($20), litho CPE Australia Ltd, Melbourne ($2 later by Leigh-Mardon Ltd) and recess Note Ptg Branch, Reserve Bank of Australia (others))

1989 (12 Apr)–**90**. Botanic Gardens. T **460** and similar horiz designs. Multicoloured. P 14 ($2 to $10) or 14½×14 ($20).

1199	$2 Nooroo, New South Wales (13.9.89)	1·50	30
	a. Perf 13½	10·00	70
1200	$5 Mawarra, Victoria (13.9.89)	3·00	60
	a. Perf 13½	5·50	3·25
1201	$10 Type **460**	5·50	1·00
1201*a*	$20 "A View of the Artist's House and Garden in Mills Plains, Van Diemen's Land" (John Glover) (15.8.90)	20·00	8·00
	b. Gold (value and country name) omitted	£4000	
1199/1201*a* *Set of 4*		27·00	9·00
1199as/1201as Optd "Specimen" *Set of 4*		14·00	

461 "Queen Elizabeth II" (sculpture, John Dowie)

462 Arrival of Immigrant Ship, 1830s

(Des Sandra Baker. Litho Leigh-Mardon Ltd, Melbourne)

1989 (21 Apr). Queen Elizabeth II's Birthday. P 14½.

1202	**461**	39c. multicoloured	55	50

(Des D. Lancashire. Litho Leigh-Mardon Ltd, Melbourne)

1989 (10 May). Colonial Development (1st issue). Pastoral Era, 1810-1850. T **462** and similar square designs. Multicoloured. P 14½.

1203	39c. Type **462**	40	55
	a. Horiz strip of 5. Nos. 1203/7	1·75	2·50
1204	39c. Pioneer cottage and wool dray	40	55
1205	39c. Squatter's homestead	40	55
1206	39c. Shepherd with flock (from Joseph Lycett's "Views of Australia")	40	55
1207	39c. Explorer in desert (after watercolour by Edward Frome)	40	55
1203/7 *Set of 5*		1·75	2·50

Nos. 1203/7 were printed together, *se-tenant*, in horizontal strips of five throughout the sheet.

See also Nos. 1254/8 and 1264/8.

463 Gladys Moncrieff and Roy Rene

464 "Impression" (Tom Roberts)

(Des Sue Passmore. Litho Leigh-Mardon Ltd, Melbourne)

1989 (12 July). Australian Stage and Screen Personalities. T **463** and similar vert designs. Multicoloured. P 14½.

1208	39c. Type **463**	25	25
	a. Perf 14×13½	5·00	6·50
1209	85c. Charles Chauvel and Chips Rafferty	60	2·00
1210	$1 Nellie Stewart and J. C. Williamson	60	1·00
1211	$1.10 Lottie Lyell and Raymond Longford	60	1·25
1208/11	*Set of 4*	1·90	4·00
1210s/11s	Optd "Specimen" *Set of 2*	1·40	

No. 1208a was from a small first printing produced at the Scoresby (ex C.P.E.) plant and used in presentation packs or on first day covers. The rest of the 39c. printing was perforated at the Moorabbin works.

(Des K. Christos. Litho Leigh-Mardon Ltd, Melbourne)

1989 (23 Aug). Australian Impressionist Paintings. T **464** and similar multicoloured designs. P 14×13½ (No. 1214) or 13½×14 (others).

1212	41c. Type **464**	30	40
1213	41c. "Impression for Golden Summer" (Sir Arthur Streeton)	30	40
1214	41c. "All on a Summer's Day" (Charles Conder) (*vert*)	30	40
1215	41c. "Petit Déjeuner" (Frederick McCubbin)	30	40
1212/15	*Set of 4*	1·10	1·40

465 Freeways

(Des Sally Newell and Carolyn Limonta. Litho Leigh-Mardon Ltd, Melbourne)

1989 (1 Sept). The Urban Environment. T **465** and similar horiz designs. P 15½×imperf.

1216	41c. black, maroon and blue-green	65	1·40
	a. Booklet pane. Nos. 1216×2, 1217×3 and 1218×2	4·00	
1217	41c. black, maroon and magenta	65	1·25
1218	41c. black, maroon and bright blue	65	1·40
1216/18	*Set of 3*	1·75	3·75

Designs:—No. 1217, City buildings, Melbourne; No. 1218, Commuter train at platform.

Nos. 1216/18 only exist from $3 stamp booklets, No. SB66, in which the vertical edges of the pane are imperforate.

466 Hikers outside Youth Hostel

467 Horse Tram, Adelaide, 1878

(Des Priscilla Cutter. Litho Leigh-Mardon Ltd, Melbourne)

1989 (13 Sept). 50th Anniv of Australian Youth Hostels. P 14½.

1219	**466**	41c. multicoloured	55	50

(Des I. McKellar. Litho Leigh-Mardon Ltd, Melbourne)

1989 (11 Oct). Historic Trams. T **467** and similar horiz designs. Multicoloured. P 13½×14.

1220	41c. Type **467**	55	80
1221	41c. Steam tram, Sydney, 1884	55	80
1222	41c. Cable tram, Melbourne, 1886	55	80
	a. Perf 14½	1·00	1·75
	ab. Booklet pane. No. 1222a×10	9·00	
1223	41c. Double-deck electric tram, Hobart, 1893	55	80
1224	41c. Combination electric tram, Brisbane, 1901	55	80
1220/4	*Set of 5*	2·50	3·50

The upper and lower edges of booklet pane No. 1222ab from SB67 are imperforate. It was printed and perforated at the Moorabbin plant.

468 "Annunciation" (15th-century *Book of Hours*)

469 Radio Waves and Globe

(Des Lynette Brown. Litho Leigh-Mardon Ltd, Melbourne)

1989 (1 Nov). Christmas. Illuminated Manuscripts. T **468** and similar vert designs. Multicoloured. P 14×13½ (36c.) or 14½ (others).

1225	36c. Type **468**	30	10
	a. Booklet pane. No. 1225×10	3·50	
1226	41c. "Annunciation to the Shepherds" (Wharncliffe Book of Hours, c. 1475)	30	10
1227	80c. "Adoration of the Magi" (15th-century Parisian Book of Hours)	70	1·40
1225/7	*Set of 3*	1·10	1·40

The vertical sides of booklet pane No. 1225a from SB68 are imperforate.

(Des B. Sadgrove. Litho Leigh-Mardon Ltd, Melbourne)

1989 (1 Nov). 50th Anniv of Radio Australia. P 14×13½.

1228	**469**	41c. multicoloured	55	50

470 Golden Wattle

471 Australian Wildflowers

(Des Celia Rosser. Litho Leigh-Mardon Ltd, Melbourne)

1990 (17 Jan). Australia Day. P 14½.

1229	**470**	41c. multicoloured	55	50

(Des Beverley Graham and G. Rogers. Litho Leigh-Mardon Ltd, Melbourne)

1990 (7 Feb–3 Sept). Greetings Stamps. P 14×13½ (41c.) or 14½ (43c.).

1230	**471**	41c. multicoloured	45	65
		a. Booklet pane. No. 1230×10	4·00	
		b. Perf 14½ (May)	1·25	1·50
		ba. Booklet pane. No. 1230b×10	11·00	
1231		43c. multicoloured (3 Sept)	45	50
		a. Booklet pane. No. 1231×10	4·00	

The panes are from booklets SB69/a and SB71 and have the upper and lower edges imperforate.

No. 1230b is a Moorabbin (1 koala) printing which only exists from booklets SB69a. The remainder were printed at the Scoresby works.

472 Dr. Constance Stone (first Australian woman doctor), Modern Doctor and Nurses

473 Greater Glider

(Des Priscilla Cutter. Litho Leigh-Mardon Ltd, Melbourne)

1990 (7 Feb). Centenary of Women in Medical Practice. P 14½.

1232	**472**	41c. multicoloured	50	45

(Des D. Higgins. Litho Leigh-Mardon Ltd, Melbourne)

1990 (21 Feb). Animals of the High Country. T **473** and similar vert designs. Multicoloured. P 14×13½.

1233	41c. Type **473**	60	45
1234	65c. Tiger Cat ("Spotted-tailed Quoll")	90	1·90
1235	70c. Mountain Pygmy-possum	95	1·90
1236	80c. Brush-tailed Rock-wallaby	1·10	1·90
1233/6	*Set of 4*	3·25	5·50

474 "Stop Smoking"

475 Soldiers from Two World Wars

(Des A. Stitt. Litho Leigh-Mardon Ltd, Melbourne)

1990 (14 Mar). Community Health. T **474** and similar vert designs. Multicoloured. P 14×13½.

1237	41c. Type **474**	45	55
1238	41c. "Drinking and driving don't mix"	45	55
1239	41c. "No junk food, please"	45	55
1240	41c. "Guess who's just had a checkup?"	45	55
1237/40	*Set of 4*	1·60	2·00

(Des O. Schmidinger and Christine Stead. Litho Leigh-Mardon Ltd, Melbourne)

1990 (12 Apr). "The Anzac Tradition". T **475** and similar vert designs. Multicoloured. P 14½.

1241	41c. Type **475**	80	40
1242	41c. Fighter pilots and munitions worker	80	40
1243	65c. Veterans and Anzac Day parade	1·25	1·25
1244	$1 Casualty evacuation, Vietnam, and disabled veteran	1·75	1·40
1245	$1.10 Letters from home and returning troopships	1·75	1·50
1241/5	*Set of 5*	5·75	4·50
1244s/5s	Optd "Specimen" *Set of 2*	1·10	

476 Queen at Australian Ballet Performance, London, 1988

477 New South Wales 1861 5s. Stamp

(Des Lynette Brown. Litho Leigh-Mardon Ltd, Melbourne)

1990 (19 Apr). Queen Elizabeth II's Birthday. P 14½.

1246	**476**	41c. multicoloured	1·00	50

(Des J. Passmore. Litho Leigh-Mardon Ltd, Melbourne)

1990 (1 May). 150th Anniv of the Penny Black. T **477** and similar horiz designs showing stamps. Multicoloured. P 13½×14.

1247	41c. Type **477**	75	1·00
	a. Block of 6. Nos. 1247/52	4·00	5·50
1248	41c. South Australia 1855 unissued 1s	75	1·00
1249	41c. Tasmania 1853 4d	75	1·00
1250	41c. Victoria 1867 5s	75	1·00
1251	41c. Queensland 1897 unissued 6d	75	1·00
1252	41c. Western Australia 1855 4d. with inverted frame	75	1·00
1247/52	*Set of 6*	4·00	5·50
MS1253	122×85 mm. Nos. 1247/52	4·00	5·50

Nos. 1247/52 were printed together, *se-tenant*, throughout the sheet of 100 (two panes 5×10). The first and fifth vertical rows contained Nos. 1247 and 1250 alternately, the second and fourth rows Nos. 1248 and 1251, and the third row Nos. 1249 and 1252.

No. **MS**1253 also exists overprinted with the "Stamp World London 90" logo for sale at this international stamp exhibition.

478 Gold Miners on way to Diggings

479 Glaciology Research

(Des B. Weatherhead. Litho Leigh-Mardon Ltd, Melbourne)

1990 (16 May). Colonial Development (2nd issue). Gold Fever. T **478** and similar square designs. Multicoloured. P 13.

1254	41c. Type **478**	85	1·00
	a. Horiz strip of 5. Nos. 1254/8	3·75	4·50
1255	41c. Mining camp	85	1·00
1256	41c. Panning and washing for gold	85	1·00
1257	41c. Gold Commissioner's tent	85	1·00
1258	41c. Moving gold under escort	85	1·00
1254/8	*Set of 5*	3·75	4·50

Nos. 1254/8 were printed together, *se-tenant*, in horizontal strips of five throughout the sheet.

1990 (16 May)–**91**. As Nos. 1180/1, but self-adhesive. P 11½.

(a) Typo Pemara Labels, Victoria

1259	41c. Cycling	1·25	2·25
1260	43c. Skateboarding (27.8.90)	2·25	1·00

(b) Litho Printset-Cambec Pty Ltd, Melbourne

1260*a*	43c. Skateboarding (26.6.91)	1·25	1·50

Nos. 1259/60*a* were only available in rolls of 100, No. 1260*a* also initially in rolls of 200, from major post offices or as strips of three from philatelic counters, each stamp, with die-cut perforations, being separate on the imperforate backing strip.

No. 1260*a* can be identified by its screened colours: on No. 1260 these are solid. The lithography printing also shows a kangaroo on the reverse and is on plain, rather than waxed, backing paper.

Due to the type of adhesive used examples should be retained on piece.

(Des Janet Boschen and Yu Artsimenov. Litho Leigh-Mardon Ltd, Melbourne)

1990 (13 June). Australian-Soviet Scientific Co-operation in Antarctica. T **479** and similar horiz design. Multicoloured. P 14½.

1261	41c. Type **479**	65	40
1262	$1.10 Krill (marine biology research)	1·60	2·00
	s. Optd "Specimen"	55	
MS1263	85×65 mm. Nos. 1261/2	2·25	2·25

Stamps in similar designs were also issued by Russia.

Examples of No. **MS**1263 imperforate originate from the Russian postal archives.

No. **MS**1263 also exists overprinted with the "New Zealand 1990" logo for sale at this international stamp exhibition in Auckland.

480 Auctioning Building Plots

481 "Salmon Gums" (Robert Juniper)

(Des B. Clinton. Litho Leigh-Mardon Ltd, Melbourne)

1990 (12 July). Colonial Development (3rd issue). Boomtime. T **480** and similar square designs. Multicoloured. P 13.

1264	41c. Type **480**	50	45
	a. Horiz strip of 5. Nos. 1264/8	1·75	2·00
1265	41c. Colonial mansion	50	45
1266	41c. Stock exchange	50	45
1267	41c. Fashionable society	50	45
1268	41c. Factories	50	45
1264/8	*Set of 5*	1·75	2·00

Nos. 1264/8 were printed together, *se-tenant*, in horizontal strips of 5 throughout the sheet.

(Des Sandra Baker. Litho Leigh-Mardon Ltd, Melbourne)

1990 (3 Sept). "Heidelberg and Heritage" Art Exhibition. T **481** and similar vert design. Multicoloured. Imperf×P 14½.

1269	28c. Type **481**	2·50	4·50
	a. Booklet pane. Nos. 1269 and 1270 ×4	3·50	
	b. Imperf×P 15½	6·50	9·50
	ba. Booklet pane. Nos. 1269b and 1270a ×4	9·50	
1270	43c. "The Blue Dress" (Brian Dunlop)	40	45
	a. Imperf×P 15½	1·00	1·00

Nos. 1269/70a only exist from $2 stamp booklets in which the horizontal edges of the pane are imperforate.

482 "Adelaide Town Hall" (Edmund Gouldsmith)

483 Laughing Kookaburras and Gifts

(Des Janet Boschen. Litho Leigh-Mardon Ltd, Melbourne)

1990 (31 Oct). 150th Anniv of Local Government. P 14½.

1271	**482**	43c. multicoloured	75	50

(Des Marg Towt. Litho Leigh-Mardon Ltd, Melbourne)

1990 (31 Oct). Christmas. T **483** and similar multicoloured designs. P 14½.

1272	38c. Type **483**	50	15
	a. Booklet pane. No. 1272×10	3·75	
1273	43c. Baby Jesus with Koalas and Wallaby (*vert*)	50	15
1274	80c. Possum on Christmas tree	1·50	3·50
1272/4	*Set of* 3	2·25	3·50

The upper and lower edges of booklet pane No. 1272a from SB73 are imperforate, producing stamps imperforate top or bottom, and there are margins at left and right.

484 National Flag

485 Black-necked Stork

(Des Dianne Cook. Litho Leigh-Mardon Ltd, Melbourne)

1991 (10 Jan). Australia Day. 90th Anniv of Australian Flag. T **484** and similar horiz designs. P 14½.

1275	43c. deep ultramarine, bright scarlet and grey	55	25
1276	90c. multicoloured	1·25	1·25
1277	$1 multicoloured	1·25	1·40
1278	$1.20 brightt scarlet, deep ultramarine and grey	1·60	1·75
1275/8	*Set of* 4	4·25	4·25

Designs:—90c. Royal Australian Navy ensign; $1 Royal Australian Air Force standard; $1.20, Australian Merchant Marine ensign.

(Des P. Margocsy. Litho Leigh-Mardon Ltd, Melbourne)

1991 (14 Feb). Waterbirds. T **485** and similar multicoloured designs. P 14½.

1279	43c. Type **485**	80	60
1280	43c. Black Swan (*horiz*)	80	60
1281	85c. Cereopsis Goose ("Cape Barren Goose")	2·25	3·50
1282	$1 Chestnut-breasted Teal (*horiz*)	2·25	2·50
	s. Optd "Specimen"	55	
1279/82	*Set of* 4	5·50	6·50

486 Recruitment Poster (Womens Services)

487 Queen Elizabeth at Royal Albert Hall, London

(Des Dianne Cook. Litho Leigh-Mardon Ltd, Melbourne)

1991 (14 Mar). Anzac Day. 50th Anniversaries. T **486** and similar horiz designs. P 14½.

1283	43c. multicoloured	60	40
1284	43c. black, brown-olive and pale grey-brown	60	40
1285	$1.20 multicoloured	2·25	2·00
	s. Optd "Specimen"	55	
1283/5	*Set of* 3	3·00	2·50

Designs:—43c. (No. 1284) Patrol (Defence of Tobruk); $1.20, "V-P Day Canberra" (Harold Abbot) (Australian War Memorial).

(Des R. Bulach. Litho Leigh-Mardon Ltd, Melbourne)

1991 (11 Apr). Queen Elizabeth II's Birthday. P 14½.

1286	**487** 43c. multicoloured	1·00	50

488 *Tectocoris diophthalmus* (bug)

489 "Bondi" (Max Dupain)

(Des D. Nelson. Litho Leigh-Mardon Ltd, Melbourne)

1991 (11 Apr). Insects. T **488** and similar horiz designs. Multicoloured. P 14½.

1287	43c. Type **488**	60	45
1288	43c. *Cizara ardeniae* (hawk moth)	60	45
1289	80c. *Petasida ephippigera* (grasshopper)	2·00	2·00
1290	$1 *Castiarina producta* (beetle)	2·00	1·50
1287/90	*Set of* 4	4·75	4·00

(Des Janet Boschen. Litho Leigh-Mardon Ltd, Melbourne)

1991 (13 May). 150 Years of Photography in Australia. T **489** and similar vert designs. P 14½.

1291	43c. black, chestnut and deep ultramarine	80	65
	a. Horiz pair. Nos. 1291/2	1·60	1·25
1292	43c. black, turquoise-green and chestnut	80	65
1293	70c. black, yellow-green and chestnut	1·50	1·10
1294	$1.20 black, light brown and deep blue-green	2·00	1·50
	s. Optd "Specimen"	55	
1291/4	*Set of* 4	4·50	3·50

Designs:—No. 1292, "Gears for the Mining Industry, Vickers Ruwolt, Melbourne" (Wolfgang Sievers); No. 1293, "The Wheel of Youth" (Harold Cazneaux); No. 1294, "Teacup Ballet" (Olive Cotton).

Nos. 1291/2 were printed together, *se-tenant*, in horizontal pairs throughout the sheet.

490 Singing Group

491 Puppy

(Des O. Schmidinger and Christine Stead. Litho Leigh-Mardon Ltd, Melbourne)

1991 (13 June). Australian Radio Broadcasting. T **490** and similar vert designs showing listeners and scenes from radio programmes. Multicoloured. P 14½.

1295	43c. Type **490**	70	45
1296	43c. "Blue Hills" serial	70	45
1297	85c. "The Quiz Kids"	1·40	2·25
1298	$1 "The Argonauts' Club" children's programme	1·60	1·40
	s. Optd "Specimen"	55	
1295/8	*Set of* 4	4·00	4·00

(Des Betina Ogden. Litho Leigh-Mardon Ltd, Melbourne)

1991 (25 July). Domestic Pets. T **491** and similar vert designs. Multicoloured. P 14½.

1299	43c. Type **491**	70	45
1300	43c. Kitten	70	45
1301	70c. Pony	1·40	2·50
1302	$1 Sulphur-crested Cockatoo	1·90	1·50
1299/1302	*Set of* 4	4·25	4·50

492 George Vancouver (1791) and Edward Eyre (1841)

493 *Seven Little Australians* (Ethel Turner)

(Des D. Lancashire. Litho Leigh-Mardon Ltd, Melbourne)

1991 (25 Sept). Exploration of Western Australia. P 14½.

1303 **492** $1.05 multicoloured .... 1·25 1·10
MS1304 100×65 mm. No. 1303 .... 1·25 1·40

No. **MS**1304 also exists overprinted with the "Philanippon '91" logo for sale at this international stamp exhibition in Tokyo.

(Des Dianne Cook. Litho Leigh-Mardon Ltd, Melbourne)

1991 (10 Oct). Australian Writers of the 1890s. T **493** and similar multicoloured designs. P 14½.

1305 43c. Type **493** 50 45
1306 75c. *On Our Selection* (Steele Rudd) .... 80 1·00
1307 $1 "Clancy of the Overflow" (poem, A. B. Paterson) (*vert*) .... 1·10 1·00
1308 $1.20 "The Drover's Wife" (short story, Henry Lawson) (*vert*) .... 1·25 1·60
s. Optd "Specimen" 55
1305/8 *Set of 4* .... 3·25 3·50

494 Shepherd

495 Parma Wallaby

(Des Sue Passmore. Litho Leigh-Mardon Ltd, Melbourne)

1991 (1 Nov). Christmas. T **494** and similar horiz designs. Multicoloured. P 14½.

1309 38c. Type **494** 35 15
a. Booklet pane. No. 1309 ×20 .... 5·50
1310 43c. Infant Jesus 45 15
1311 90c. Wise Man .... 1·50 1·75
1309/11 *Set of 3* .... 2·10 1·90

The vertical edges of booklet pane No. 1309a from SB75 are imperforate, producing stamps imperforate at right or left, and there are margins at top and bottom.

Variations in the shades of all three values were caused by changes in the production method during printing.

(Des Betina Ogden. Litho Leigh-Mardon Ltd, Melbourne)

1992 (2 Jan). Threatened Species. T **495** and similar horiz designs. Multicoloured. P 14×14½.

1312 45c. Type **495** 60 90
a. Block of 6. Nos. 1312/17 .... 3·25 4·75
1313 45c. Ghost Bat 60 90
1314 45c. Long-tailed Dunnart 60 90
1315 45c. Little Pygmy-possum 60 90
1316 45c. Dusky Hopping-mouse 60 90
1317 45c. Squirrel Glider 60 90
1312/17 *Set of 6* .... 3·25 4·75

Nos. 1312/17 were printed together, *se-tenant*, throughout the sheet of 100, giving fifteen blocks of 6 (3×2) and 10 single stamps.

For self-adhesive versions of these designs see Nos. 1321/32.

496 Basket of Wild Flowers

(Des Priscilla Cutter. Litho Leigh-Mardon Ltd, Melbourne)

1992 (2 Jan). Greetings Stamp. P 14½.

1318 **496** 45c. multicoloured 50 50
a. Booklet pane. No. 1318 ×10 .... 4·50

The upper and lower edges of booklet pane No. 1318a from SB77 are imperforate, producing stamps imperforate at top or bottom, and there are margins at left and right.

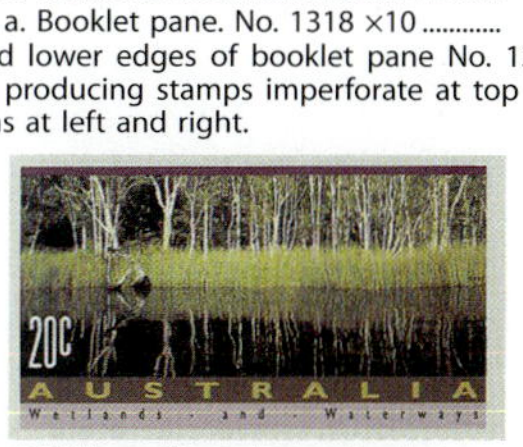

497 Noosa River, Queensland

(Des Sue Passmore. Litho Leigh-Mardon Ltd, Melbourne)

1992 (2 Jan)–**94**. Wetlands and Waterways. T **497** and similar horiz design. P 14½×imperf.

1319 20c. Type **497** .... 1·75 2·50
a. Booklet pane. Nos. 1319 and 1320×4 .... 3·00
b. Perf 14×imperf (3.94) .... 3·00 4·00
ba. Booklet pane. Nos. 1319b and 1320b×4 .... 4·50
1320 45c. Lake Eildon, Victoria 40 45
b. Perf 14×imperf (3.94) 50 55

Nos. 1319/20 only exist from $2 stamp booklets, Nos. SB76/a, in which the vertical edges of the pane are imperforate.

Nos. 1319b/ba and 1320b (2 koala ptg) were printed by McPherson's Ptg Group.

1992 (2 Jan - 22 Apr). As Nos. 1312/17, but self-adhesive.

(a) Typo Pemara Labels, Victoria. Phosphorised paper. P 11

1321 45c. Type **495** 60 70
a. Black (inscr, etc) omitted £200
1322 45c. Squirrel Glider 60 70
a. Black (inscr, etc) omitted £200
1323 45c. Dusky Hopping-mouse 60 70
a. Black (inscr, etc) omitted £200
1324 45c. Little Pygmy-possum 60 70
a. Black (inscr, etc) omitted £200
1325 45c. Long-tailed Dunnart 60 70
a. Black (inscr, etc) omitted £200
1326 45c. Ghost Bat 60 70
a. Black (inscr, etc) omitted £200
1321/6 *Set of 6* .... 3·25 3·75

(b) Litho Printset Cambec Pty Ltd. Phosphorised paper. P 11½

1327 45c. Type **495** 70 90
p. Broad phosphor band at right .... 2·25 2·50
pa. Booklet pane. Nos. 1327p×2, 1328p/9p and 1330p/2p×2 .... 14·00
q. Horiz phosphor bands at top, bottom and on animal (22.4.92) .... 2·25 2·50
qa. Booklet pane. Nos. 1327q×2, 1328q/9q and 1330q/2q×2 .... 14·00
qb. Booklet pane. As No. 1327qa, but imperf £375
1328 45c. Squirrel Glider 70 90
p. Broad phosphor band at right .... 1·75 2·25
pa. Sheetlet of 5. Nos. 1328p/32p .... 6·50
q. Horiz phosphor bands at top, bottom and on animal (22.4.92) .... 1·75 2·25
qa. Sheetlet of 5. Nos. 1328q/32q .... 6·50
1329 45c. Dusky Hopping-mouse 70 90
p. Broad phosphor band at right .... 1·75 2·25
q. Horiz phosphor bands at top, bottom and on animal (22.4.92) .... 1·75 2·25
1330 45c. Little Pygmy-possum 70 90
p. Broad phosphor band at right .... 1·75 2·25
q. Horiz phosphor bands at top, bottom and on animal (22.4.92) .... 1·75 2·25
1331 45c. Long-tailed Dunnart 70 90
p. Broad phosphor band at right .... 1·75 2·25
q. Horiz phosphor bands at top, bottom and on animal (22.4.92) .... 1·75 2·25
1332 45c. Ghost Bat 70 90
p. Broad phosphor band at right .... 1·75 2·25
q. Horiz phosphor bands at top, bottom and on animal (22.4.92) .... 1·75 2·25
1327/32 *Set of 6* .... 3·75 4·75
1327p/32p *Set of 6* .... 10·00 12·50
1327q/32q *Set of 6* .... 10·00 12·50

Nos. 1321/6 were only available in rolls of 100 with Nos. 1327/32 in rolls of 100 or 200, each stamp, with die-cut perforations, being separate on the imperforate backing strip.

Nos. 1321a/6a also show a horizontal red line across the stamp which normally occurs on the reverse. Examples are reported to have been purchased from Buxton, N.S.W., post office.

Booklet panes 1327pa/qb come from Nos. SB78/e.

The booklet panes Nos. 1327pa and 1327qa are arranged as a block of eight and a separate vertical pair with backing card forming the booklet cover. Stamps from these panes and the sheetlet of 5, Nos. 1328pa and 1328qa, differ from the coil printing by retaining the surplus self-adhesive paper around the stamps.

Booklet pane No. 1327pa and sheetlet No. 1328pa have a broad phosphor band, which shows pink under U.V. light, over the right-hand half of each design. Nos. 1327qa and 1328pa show this phosphor as horizontal bands at the top and bottom of each design and also have the animal overprinted in phosphor ink.

No. 1328pa also exists overprinted with the "World Columbian Stamp Expo '92" logo for sale at this international stamp exhibition in Chicago.

498 *Young Endeavour* (cadet brigantine)

499 Bombing of Darwin

(Des Sue Passmore. Litho Leigh-Mardon Ltd, Melbourne)

1992 (15 Jan). Australia Day and 500th Anniv of Discovery of America by Columbus (No. **MS**1337). Sailing Ships. T **498** and similar multicoloured designs. P 14½.

1333	45c. Type **498**	80	50
1334	45c. *Britannia* (yacht) (*vert*)	80	50
1335	$1.05 *Akarana* (cutter) (*vert*)	1·75	2·75
1336	$1.20 *John Louis* (pearling lugger)	2·00	2·00
	s. Optd "Specimen"	55	
1333/6 *Set of 4*		4·75	5·25
MS1337 147×64 mm. Nos. 1333/6		4·75	5·50

No. **MS**1337 also exists overprinted with either the "World Columbian Stamp Expo '92" or "Genova '92" logos for sale at these international stamp exhibitions in Chicago or Genoa.

(Des B. Clinton. Litho Leigh-Mardon Ltd, Melbourne)

1992 (19 Feb). 50th Anniv of Second World War Battles. T **499** and similar horiz designs. Multicoloured. P 14½.

1338	45c. Type **499**	90	45
1339	75c. Anti-aircraft gun and fighters, Milne Bay	1·75	1·90
1340	75c. Infantry on Kokoda Trail	1·75	1·90
1341	$1.05 H.M.A.S. *Australia* (cruiser) and U.S.S. *Yorktown* (aircraft carrier), Coral Sea	2·00	2·25
1342	$1.20 Australians advancing, El Alamein	2·25	2·00
	s. Optd "Specimen"	55	
1338/42 *Set of 5*		7·75	7·75

500 Helix Nebula

501 Hunter Valley, New South Wales

(Des Sandra Harman. Litho Leigh-Mardon Ltd, Melbourne)

1992 (19 Mar). International Space Year. T **500** and similar horiz designs. Multicoloured. P 14½.

1343	45c. Type **500**	65	20
1344	$1.05 The Pleiades	1·40	1·00
1345	$1.20 Spiral Galaxy, NGC 2997	1·50	1·25
	s. Optd "Specimen"	55	
1343/5 *Set of 3*		3·25	2·25
MS1346 133×70 mm. Nos. 1343/5		3·25	3·50

No. **MS**1346 also exists overprinted with the "World Columbian Stamp Expo '92" logo for sale at this international stamp exhibition in Chicago.

(Des P. Blizzard-Allen. Litho McPherson's Ptg Group, Mulgrave)

1992 (9 Apr). Vineyard Regions. T **501** and similar horiz designs. Multicoloured. P 14×14½.

1347	45c. Type **501**	80	1·10
1348	45c. North-east Victoria	80	1·10
1349	45c. Barossa Valley, South Australia	80	1·10
1350	45c. Coonawarra, South Australia	80	1·10
1351	45c. Margaret River, Western Australia	80	1·10
1347/51 *Set of 5*		3·50	5·00

502 3½d. Stamp of 1953

503 Salt Action

(Des Lynette Brown. Litho McPherson's Ptg Group, Mulgrave)

1992 (9 Apr). Queen Elizabeth II's Birthday. P 14×14½.

1352	**502**	45c. multicoloured	1·00	60

(Des J. Wolseley. Litho McPherson's Ptg Group, Mulgrave)

1992 (11 June). Land Conservation. T **503** and similar vert designs. Multicoloured. P 14½×14.

1353	45c. Type **503**	85	1·10
	a. Horiz strip of 5. Nos. 1353/7	3·75	5·00
1354	45c. Farm planning	85	1·10
1355	45c. Erosion control	85	1·10
1356	45c. Tree planting	85	1·10
1357	45c. Dune care	85	1·10
1353/7 *Set of 5*		3·75	5·00

Nos. 1353/7 were printed together, *se-tenant*, in horizontal strips of 5 throughout the sheet.

504 Cycling

505 Echidna

(Des G. Emery. Litho Leigh-Mardon Ltd, Melbourne)

1992 (2 July). Olympic Games and Paralympic Games (No. 1359), Barcelona. T **504** and similar horiz designs. Multicoloured. P 14½.

1358	45c. Type **504**	50	15
1359	$1.20 High jumping	1·10	1·40
1360	$1.20 Weightlifting	1·10	1·40
1358/60 *Set of 3*		2·40	2·75
1359s/60s Optd "Specimen" *Set of 2*		1·10	

(Des Marg Towt (30, 85c., $1.35), Betina Ogden (35, 50, 60, 95c.), S. Morrell (others). Litho McPhersons Ptg Group, Mulgrave)

1992 (13 Aug)–**98**. Australian Wildlife (1st series). T **505** and similar horiz designs. Multicoloured. P 14×14½.

1361	30c. Saltwater Crocodile (10.3.94)	35	20
1362	35c. Type **505**	65	30
1363	40c. Platypus (12.8.93)	2·25	2·00
1364	50c. Koala	60	35
1365	60c. Common Bushtail Possum	1·50	2·00
1366	70c. Laughing Kookaburra ("70 c" and "AUSTRALIA" in orange) (12.8.93)	2·25	1·00
	a. "70c." and "AUSTRALIA" in orange-brown (3.96)	2·25	2·00
1367	85c. Australian Pelican (10.3.94)	1·00	70
1368	90c. Eastern Grey Kangaroo ("90 c" and "AUSTRALIA" in orange) (12.8.93)	3·00	4·00
	a. "90c." and "AUSTRALIA" in orange-brown (4.98)	3·00	4·00
1369	95c. Common Wombat	1·00	2·50
1370	$1.20 Major Mitchell's Cockatoo ("$1.20" and "AUSTRALIA"in orange) (12.8.93)	2·00	1·50
	a. "$1.20" and "AUSTRALIA" in orange-brown (12.98)	2·00	1·40
1371	$1.35 Emu (10.3.94)	2·75	3·50
1361/71 *Set of 11*		15·00	16·00

No. 1366a is from the 3 koala or 1 kangaroo + 1 koala printings, No. 1368a from the 2 koala printing, and No. 1370a from the 1 kangaroo printing.

See also Nos. 1453/1464 and **MS**1626.

Nos. 1372/4 are vacant.

506 Sydney Harbour Tunnel (value at left)

507 Warden's Courthouse, Coolgardie

(Des Sandra Harman. Litho Leigh-Mardon Ltd, Melbourne)

1992 (28 Aug). Opening of Sydney Harbour Tunnel. T **506** and similar vert design. Multicoloured. P 14½.

1375	45c. Type **506**	2·50	3·00
	a. Horiz pair. Nos. 1375/6	5·00	6·00
	b. Perf 15½	1·90	1·90
	ba. Horiz pair. Nos. 1375b/6b	3·75	3·75
1376	45c. Sydney Harbour Tunnel (value at right)	2·50	3·00
	b. Perf 15½	1·90	1·90

Nos. 1375/6 were printed together, *se-tenant*, in horizontal pairs throughout the sheet, each pair forming a composite design.

(Des Janet Boschen. Litho Printset Cambec Pty Ltd)

1992 (17 Sept). Centenary of Discovery of Gold at Coolgardie and Kalgoorlie. T **507** and similar horiz designs. Multicoloured. P 14×14½.

1377	45c. Type **507**	90	50
1378	45c. Post Office, Kalgoorlie	90	50
1379	$1.05, York Hotel, Kalgoorlie	2·00	3·50
1380	$1.20, Town Hall, Kalgoorlie	2·25	2·75
1377/80 *Set of 4*		5·50	6·50

508 Bowler of 1892

509 Children's Nativity Play

(Des Janet Boschen and M. Sofilas. Litho Leigh-Mardon Ltd, Melbourne)

1992 (15 Oct). Centenary of Sheffield Shield Cricket Tournament. T **508** and similar vert design. Multicoloured. P 14½.

1381	45c. Type **508**	1·00	50
1382	$1.20, Batsman and wicket-keeper	2·00	3·00

(Des C. Smith. Litho McPhersons Ptg Group, Mulgrave)

1992 (30 Oct). Christmas. T **509** and similar horiz designs. Multicoloured. P 14×14½.

1383	40c. Type **509**	40	10
	a. Booklet pane. No. 1383×20	6·00	
1384	45c. Child waking on Christmas Day	40	10
1385	$1 Children carol singing	1·60	1·40
1383/5 *Set of 3*		2·25	1·40

The vertical edges of booklet pane No. 1383a from SB79 are imperforate and there are margins at top and bottom.

510 "Ghost Gum, Central Australia" (Namatjira)

511 "Wild Onion Dreaming" (Pauline Nakamarra Woods)

(Des Janet Boschen. Litho McPhersons Ptg Group, Mulgrave)

1993 (14 Jan). Australia Day. Paintings by Albert Namatjira. T **510** and similar horiz design. Multicoloured. P 14×14½.

1386	45c. Type **510**	90	1·40
	a. Pair. Nos. 1386/7	1·75	2·75
1387	45c. "Across the Plain to Mount Giles"	90	1·40

Nos. 1386/7 were printed together, *se-tenant*, in horizontal and vertical pairs throughout the sheet.

(Des C. Atkinson. Litho Printset Cambec Pty Ltd)

1993 (4 Feb). "Dreamings". Paintings by Aboriginal Artists. T **511** and similar multicoloured designs. P 14×14½ (horiz) or 14½×14 (vert).

1388	45c. Type **511**	35	15
1389	75c. "Yam Plants" (Jack Wunuwun) (*vert*)	60	90
1390	85c. "Goose Egg Hunt" (George Milpurrurru) (*vert*)	65	1·40
1391	$1 "Kalumpiwarra-Ngulalintji" (Rover Thomas)	70	1·25
1388/91 *Set of 4*		2·10	3·25

512 Uluru (Ayers Rock) National Park

513 Queen Elizabeth II on Royal Visit, 1992

(Des Lynette Brown. Litho McPhersons Ptg Group, Mulgrave)

1993 (4 Mar). World Heritage Sites (1st series). T **512** and similar horiz designs. Multicoloured. P 14½×14.

1392	45c. Type **512**	60	30
1393	85c. Rain forest, Fraser Island	1·50	1·75
1394	95c. Beach, Shark Bay	1·50	1·75
1395	$2 Waterfall, Kakadu	2·75	3·50
1392/5 *Set of 4*		5·75	6·50

See also Nos. 1582/5.

(Des Dianne Cook. Litho Printset Cambec Pty Ltd)

1993 (7 Apr). Queen Elizabeth II's Birthday. P 14½×14.

1396 **513**	45c. multicoloured	1·00	65

514 H.M.A.S. *Sydney* (cruiser, launched 1934) in Action

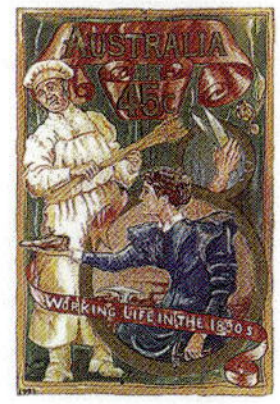

515 "Work in the Home"

(Des R. Shardlow and Sue Passmore. Litho McPhersons Ptg Group, Mulgrave)

1993 (7 Apr). Second World War Naval Vessels. T **514** and similar horiz designs. Multicoloured. P 14×14½.

1397	45c. Type **514**	1·00	45
1398	85c. H.M.A.S. *Bathurst* (minesweeper)	2·25	1·75
1399	$1.05, H.M.A.S. *Arunta* (destroyer)	2·50	2·75
1400	$1.20, *Centaur* (hospital ship) and tug	2·50	2·75
	s. Optd "Specimen"	2·00	
1397/1400 *Set of 4*		7·50	7·00

(Des G. Hogg. Litho McPhersons Ptg Group, Mulgrave)

1993 (7 May). Working Life in the 1890s. T **515** and similar vert designs. Multicoloured. P 14½×14.

1401	45c. Type **515**	30	30
1402	45c. "Work in the Cities"	30	30
1403	$1 "Work in the Country"	60	65
1404	$1.20, Trade Union banner	75	1·10
1401/4 *Set of 4*		1·75	2·10

516 "Centenary Special", Tasmania, 1971

(Des Sue Passmore and J. Richards. Litho Prinset Cambec Pty Ltd)

1993 (1 June). Australian Trains. T **516** and similar horiz designs.

(a) Phosphorised paper. P 14×14½

1405	45c. Type **516**	55	85
	a. Block of 6. Nos. 1405/10	3·00	4·50
1406	45c. "Spirit of Progress", Victoria	55	85
1407	45c. "Western Endeavour", Western Australia, 1970	55	85
1408	45c. "Silver City Comet", New South Wales	55	85
1409	45c. Cairns-Kuranda tourist train, Queensland	55	85
1410	45c. "The Ghan", Northern Territory	55	85
1405/10 *Set of 6*		3·00	4·50

(b) Self-adhesive. Phosphor frame. P 11½

1411	45c. Type **516**	80	1·25
	a. Booklet pane. Nos. 1411/12×2, 1413, 1414/15×2, 1416	6·50	
1412	45c. "Spirit of Progress", Victoria	80	1·25
1413	45c. "Western Endeavour", Western Australia, 1970	80	1·25
1414	45c. "Silver City Comet", New South Wales	80	1·25
1415	45c. Cairns-Kuranda tourist train, Queensland	80	1·25
1416	45c. "The Ghan", Northern Territory	80	1·25
1411/16 *Set of 6*		4·25	6·50

Nos. 1405/10 were printed together, *se-tenant*, in sheets of 100 (2 panes of 50 5×10) each pane providing five blocks of 6 and twenty single stamps.

Nos. 1411/16 occur either in rolls of 100, on which the surplus self-adhesive paper around each stamp was removed, or in $4.50 booklets, No. SB80, containing No. 1411a, on which the surplus paper was retained.

The phosphor on both rolls and booklets, which shows pink under U.V. light, extends from the frame onto sections of the centre design.

517 "Black Cockatoo Feather" (Fiona Foley)

518 Conference Emblem

(Des Lynette Brown. Litho McPhersons Ptg Group, Mulgrave)

1993 (1 July). International Year of Indigenous Peoples. Aboriginal Art. T **517** and similar multicoloured designs. P 14½×14 (vert) or 14×14½ (horiz).

1417	45c. Type **517**	30	20
1418	75c. "Ngarrgooroon Country" (Hector Jandany) (*horiz*)	50	1·25
1419	$1 "Ngak Ngak" (Ginger Riley Munduwalawala) (*horiz*)	65	1·25
1420	$1.05 "Untitled" (Robert Cole)	65	1·75
	s. Optd "Specimen"	2·00	
1417/20 *Set of 4*		1·90	4·00

(Des Dianne Cook. Litho Leigh-Mardon Ltd, Melbourne)

1993 (2 Sept). Inter-Parliamentary Union Conference and 50th Anniv of Women in Federal Parliament. T **518** and similar square design. Multicoloured. P 14½.

1421	45c. Type **518**	50	1·00
	a. Pair. Nos. 1421/2	1·00	2·00
1422	45c. Dame Enid Lyons and Senator Dorothy Tangney	50	1·00

Nos. 1421/2 were printed together, *se-tenant*, in sheets of 25 (5×5) with a block of nine examples of No. 1422 (R. 2/2-4, 3/2-4, 4/2-4) surrounded by sixteen examples of No. 1421 (R. 1/1-5, 2/1, 2/5 3/1, 3/5, 4/1, 4/5, 5/1-5).

These stamps also exist in reverse format showing No. 1421 as the centre block of nine. Such panes were prepared for inclusion in the Eminent Women portfolio which was jointly produced by Note Printing Australia and Australia Post. Examples from the portfolio were numbered in red or black with unnumbered panes also available by mail order.

519 Ornithocheirus

520 "Goodwill"

(Des P. Trusler and Sue Passmore)

1993 (1 Oct). Prehistoric Animals. T **519** and similar multicoloured designs.

(a) Litho McPhersons Ptg Group, Mulgrave. Phosphorised paper. P 14×14½ (Nos. 1423, 1427) or 14½×14 (Nos. 1424/6, 1428)

1423	45c. Type **519**	40	40
1424	45c. Leaellynasaura (25×30 *mm*)	40	40
1425	45c. Timimus (26×38 *mm*)	40	40
1426	45c. Allosaurus (26×38 *mm*)	40	40
1427	75c. Muttaburrasaurus (30×50 *mm*)	70	90
1428	$1.05 Minmi (50×30 *mm*)	80	1·50
1423/8 *Set of 6*		2·75	3·50
MS1429	166×73 mm. Nos. 1423/8. P 14½	3·00	5·50

(b) Litho Printset Cambec Pty Ltd. Self-adhesive. Phosphor background. P 11½

1430	45c. Type **519**	45	80
	a. Booklet pane. Nos. 1430/1, each ×5	4·00	
1431	45c. Leaellynasaura (25×30 *mm*)	45	80

No. **MS**1429 exists overprinted with the logos of "Bangkok '93" or Sydney Stamp and Coin Fair, 1993, for sale at these exhibitions.

Nos. 1430/1 occur either in rolls of 100 and 200, on which the surplus self-adhesive paper around each stamp was removed, or in $4.50 booklets, No. SB81, containing No. 1430a, on which the surplus paper was retained.

The phosphor on both rolls and booklets, which shows pink under U.V. light, covers much of the background of each design.

(Des Sandra Harman. Litho McPhersons Ptg Group, Mulgrave)

1993 (1 Nov). Christmas. T **520** and similar vert designs. Multicoloured. P 14½×14.

1432	40c. Type **520**	35	10
	a. Booklet pane. No. 1432×20	5·50	
1433	45c. "Joy"	40	10
1434	$1 "Peace"	1·10	1·25
1432/4 *Set of 3*		1·75	1·25

The horizontal edges of booklet pane No. 1432a from SB82 are imperforate and there are margins at right and left.

521 "Shoalhaven River Bank – Dawn" (Arthur Boyd)

(Des Lynette Brown. Litho McPhersons Ptg Group, Mulgrave)

1994 (13 Jan). Australia Day. Landscape Paintings. T **521** and similar multicoloured designs. P 14×14½ ($2) or 14½×14 (others).

1435	45c. Type **521**	30	10
1436	85c. "Wimmera" (Sir Sidney Nolan)	50	60
1437	$1.05 "Lagoon, Wimmera" (Nolan)	65	90
1438	$2.00 "White Cockatoos with Flame Trees" (Boyd) (*vert*)	1·25	1·60
1435/8 *Set of 4*		2·40	2·75

522 Teaching Lifesaving Techniques

523 Rose

(Des O. Schmidinger, Christine Stead and Lynette Brown. Litho Printset Cambec Pty Ltd)

1994 (20 Jan). Centenary of Organised Life Saving in Australia. T **522** and similar horiz designs. Multicoloured.

(a) Phosphorised paper. P 14×14½

1439	45c. Type **522**	25	20
1440	45c. Lifeguard on watch	25	20
1441	95c. Lifeguard team	50	70
1442	$1.20 Lifeguards on surfboards	70	80
1439/42 *Set of 4*		1·50	1·75

(b) Self-adhesive. Phosphor frame. P 11½

1443	45c. Type **522**	40	1·00
	a. Booklet pane. Nos. 1443/4, each ×5	3·50	
1444	45c. Lifeguard on watch	40	1·00

Nos. 1443/4 occur either in rolls of 100, on which the surplus self-adhesive paper around each stamp was removed, or in $4.50 booklets, No. SB83, containing No. 1443a, on which the surplus paper was retained.

The phosphor on the rolls and booklets, which shows pink under U.V. light, extends onto the left or right corner of the centre designs.

(Des Sandra Harman. Litho McPhersons Ptg Group, Mulgrave)

1994 (3 Feb). Greetings Stamps. Flower photographs by Lariane Fonseca. T **523** and similar vert designs. Multicoloured. P 14½×14.

1445	45c. Type **523**	40	45
1446	45c. Tulips	40	45
	a. Horiz pair. Nos. 1446/7	80	90
	b. Booklet pane. Nos. 1446/7 each ×5	3·00	
1447	45c. Poppies	40	45
1445/7 *Set of 3*		1·10	1·25

Nos. 1446/7 were printed together, *se-tenant*, in horizontal pairs throughout the sheet.

The vertical edges of booklet pane No. 1446b from SB84 are imperforate, producing stamps imperforate at left (No. 1446) or right (No. 1447), and there are margins at top and bottom.

524 Bridge and National Flags

525 "Queen Elizabeth II" (Sir William Dargie)

(Des W. Crossett and Sue Passmore. Litho McPherson's Ptg Group, Mulgrave)

1994 (8 Apr). Opening of Friendship Bridge between Thailand and Laos. P 14½×14.

1448	**524**	95c. multicoloured	1·25	1·40

(Des Sue Passmore. Litho Leigh-Mardon Ltd, Melbourne)

1994 (8 Apr). Queen Elizabeth II's Birthday. P 14½.

1449	**525**	45c. multicoloured	1·00	70

526 "Family in Field" (Bobbie-Lea Blackmore)

527 Suffragettes

(Des Lynette Brown. Litho Leigh-Mardon Ltd, Melbourne)

1994 (14 Apr). International Year of the Family. Children's Paintings. T **526** and similar horiz designs. Multicoloured. P 14½.

1450	45c. Type **526**	35	10
1451	75c. "Family on Beach" (Kathryn Teoh)	50	65
1452	$1 "Family around Fire" (Maree McCarthy)	60	75
1450/2	*Set of 3*	1·25	1·25

Two types of inscr on Nos. 1453/5:

Type I. "KANGAROO" 9 mm long with spaces between letters.

Type II. "KANGAROO" 7 mm long without spaces between letters.

1994 (12 May)–**97**. Australian Wildlife (2nd series). Horiz designs as T **505**. Multicoloured.

(a) Litho Leigh-Mardon Ltd, Melbourne (Nos. 1453/8) or SNP Cambec (Nos. 1453b/8b, 1453c/8c). Phosphorised paper. P 14×14½

1453	45c. Kangaroo (pale orange inscr) (I)	90	65
	a. Block of 6. Nos. 1453/8	4·75	3·50
	b. Type II. Orange-brown inscr (1.96)	1·25	1·25
	ba. Block of 6. Nos. 1453b/8b	6·50	6·50
	c. Type II. Pale orange inscr (8.97)	1·25	1·25
	ca. Block of 6. Nos. 1453c/5c and 1456/8	6·50	6·50
1454	45c. Female kangaroo with young (pale orange inscr) (I)	90	65
	b. Type II. Orange-brown inscr (1.96)	1·25	1·25
	c. Type II. Pale orange inscr (8.97)	1·25	1·25
1455	45c. Two kangaroos (pale orange inscr) (I)	90	65
	b. Type II. Orange-brown inscr (1.96)	1·25	1·25
	c. Type II. Pale orange inscr (8.97)	1·25	1·25
1456	45c. Family of koalas on branch (pale orange inscr)	90	65
	b. Orange-brown inscr (1.96)	1·25	1·25
1457	45c. Koala on ground (pale orange inscr)	90	65
	b. Orange-brown inscr (1.96)	1·25	1·25
1458	45c. Koala asleep in tree (pale orange inscr)	90	65
	b. Orange-brown inscr (1.96)	1·25	1·25
1453/8	*Set of 6*	4·75	3·50

(b) Litho Printset Cambec Pty Ltd. Self-adhesive. Phosphor frame. P 11½

1459	45c. Kangaroo	50	85
	a. Booklet pane. Nos. 1459/60×2, 1461, 1462/3×2	4·00	
	ab. Imperf pane		
	b. Sheetlet of 5. Nos. 1459 and 1461/4	3·50	
1460	45c. Female kangaroo with young	50	85
1461	45c. Two kangaroos	50	85
1462	45c. Family of koalas on branch	50	85
1463	45c. Koala on ground	50	85
1464	45c. Koala asleep in tree	50	85
1459/64	*Set of 6*	2·75	4·50

(c) Typo Pemara Labels, Victoria. Self-adhesive. Phosphor frame. P 11½

1464*a*	45c. Kangaroo (5.95)	7·50	10·00
	ap. Phosphorised mesh (9.95)	1·25	1·50
1464*b*	45c. Female kangaroo with young (5.95)	7·50	10·00
	bp. Phosphorised mesh (9.95)	1·50	1·75
1464*c*	45c. Two kangaroos (5.95)	7·50	10·00
	cp. Phosphorised mesh (9.95)	1·50	1·75
1464*d*	45c. Family of koalas on branch (5.95)	7·50	10·00
	dp. Phosphorised mesh (9.95)	1·50	1·75
1464*e*	45c. Koala on ground (5.95)	7·50	10·00
	ep. Phosphorised mesh (9.95)	1·50	1·75
1464*f*	45c. Koala asleep in tree (5.95)	7·50	10·00
	fp. Phosphorised mesh (9.95)	1·50	1·75
1464a/f	*Set of 6*	40·00	55·00
1464ap/fp	*Set of 6*	8·00	9·50

Nos. 1453/8 were printed together, *se-tenant*, in sheets of 100 (2 panes of 50 5×10) each pane providing five blocks of 6 and twenty single stamps. They also exist as a *se-tenant* sheetlet of 6 with inscribed margins produced for sale at "Philakorea '94" Stamp Exhibition, Seoul.

The colour of the "AUSTRALIA" inscription and face value is repeated on a horizontal band at the foot of each design.

Nos. 1453b/8b are from the 2 koala printing and Nos. 1453c/5c from the 3 koala printing. Both show "1996" smaller than on the original printing.

Nos. 1459/64 occur either in rolls of 100, rolls of 200, booklets of 10 (Nos. SB85/b) or sheetlets of 5. On all rolls the surplus self-adhesive paper around each stamp was removed, but this was retained on booklet pane No. 1459a and sheetlet No. 1459b.

The phosphor on Nos. 1459/64 and Nos. 1464*a/f*, which shows pink under U.V. light, extends from bars at top and bottom onto sections of the centre designs. On Nos. 1464ap/fp, which come from the 3 koala, 4 koala, 1 kangaroo and 1 kangaroo + 2 koala printings, the phosphor extends over the same area; but is broken up by a mesh pattern into small squares or diamonds.

The Pemara printings were produced in rolls only.

Counter-printed labels, as described beneath No. 1416, in designs as Nos. 1453/64, but 40×28 mm, were issued on 17 November 1994. Possible face values for these labels ranged from 45c. to $100. Machines issuing the labels were located at National Philatelic Centre, Melbourne ("NPC"), Canberra Parliament House post office ("CPH"), Royal Exchange ("REX") and Haymarket ("HAYMKT") post offices, Sydney, and at the General Post Offices in Adelaide ("ADEL GPO"), Brisbane ("BRIS GPO"), Melbourne ("MELB GPO"), Perth ("PERTH GPO") (from 26 June 1995) and Bathurst Street, Hobart ("BTH ST HBT") (from 16 October 1995). Exhibition labels were issued for events both in Australia and overseas from 1994 onwards.

Very similar labels were produced from "Weigh & Pay" machines first used in the Perth area from 20 May 1996. Those from Perth itself were inscribed "GPO PERTH" or "PERTH GPO", but labels from other post offices are without inscription. Exhibition labels were issued at National Stamp Show, Fremantle, 1997 and at "Australia 99". The "Weigh & Pay" machines were withdrawn on 30 June 2000.

For Nos. 1453b, 1454b and 1455b in miniature sheet for "CHINA '96" see No. **MS**1626.

(Des Maire Smith. Litho McPhersons Ptg Group, Mulgrave)

1994 (9 June). Centenary of Women's Emancipation in South Australia. P 14×14½.

1465	**527**	45c. multicoloured	60	60

528 Bunyip from Aboriginal Legend

529 "Robert Menzies" (Sir Ivor Hele)

(Des J. Morrison (No. 1466), D. Lancashire (No. 1467), R. Brooks (No. 1468), Marg Towt (No. 1470). Litho Leigh-Mardon Ltd, Melbourne)

1994 (14 July). The Bunyip (mythological monster). T **528** and similar square designs. Multicoloured. P 14½.

1466	45c. Type **528**	35	70
	a. Pair. Nos. 1466/7	70	1·40
1467	45c. Nature spirit bunyip	35	70
1468	90c. "The Bunyip of Berkeley's Creek" (book illustration)	60	1·25
1469	$1.35 Bunyip as natural history	80	1·50
1466/9	*Set of 4*	1·90	3·75

Nos. 1466/7 were printed together, *se-tenant*, in horizontal or vertical pairs throughout the sheet.

(Des FHA Design. Litho McPhersons Ptg Group, Mulgrave)

1994 (11 Aug). Wartime Prime Ministers. T **529** and similar horiz designs. Multicoloured. P 14×14½.

1470	45c. Type **529**	1·25	1·50
	a. Horiz strip of 5. Nos. 1470/4	5·50	6·75
1471	45c. "Arthur Fadden" (William Dargie)	1·25	1·50
1472	45c. "John Curtin" (Anthony Dattilo-Rubbo)	1·25	1·50
1473	45c. "Francis Forde" (Joshua Smith)	1·25	1·50
1474	45c. "Joseph Chifley" (A. D. Colquhoun)	1·25	1·50
1470/4	*Set of 5*	5·50	6·75

Nos. 1470/4 were printed together, *se-tenant*, in horizontal strips of 5 throughout the sheet.

530 Lawrence Hargrave and Box Kites

531 Scarlet Macaw

(Des Janet Boschen. Eng C. Slania. Recess Royal Swedish Stamp Ptg Office, Stockholm)

1994 (29 Aug). Aviation Pioneers. T **530** and similar vert designs. P 12½.

1475	45c. red-brown, blackish olive and cinnamon	1·25	55
1476	45c. red-brown, deep carmine and lavender	1·25	55
1477	$1.35 red-brown, dp violet & greenish bl	3·00	4·00
1478	$1.80 red-brown, slate-green & sage-grn	3·25	4·00
1475/8	*Set of 4*	8·00	8·25

No. 1475 also exists as a pane of 25 numbered in red or black from a limited issue Hargrave portfolio.

Designs:—No. 1475, Type 530; No. 1476, Ross and Keith Smith with Vickers Vimy (first England-Australia flight); No. 1477, Ivor McIntyre, Stanley Goble and Fairey IIID seaplane (first aerial circumnavigation of Australia); No. 1478, Freda Thompson and de Havilland Moth Major Christopher Robin (first Australian woman to fly solo from England to Australia).

Two types of phosphor on self-adhesive Type **531**;
Type I. Leaf below second tail feather covered by phosphor
Type II. Leaf without phosphor

(Des G. Cook)

1994 (28 Sept). Australian Zoos. Endangered Species. T **531** and similar multicoloured designs.

(a) Litho McPherson's Ptg Group, Mulgrave. Phosphorised paper. P 14×14½ (No. 1479) or 14½×14 (others)

1479	45c. Type **531**	90	55
1480	45c. Cheetah (25×30 *mm*)	90	55
1481	45c. Orang-Utan (27×37 *mm*)	90	55
1482	45c. Fijian Crested Iguana (26×37 *mm*)	90	55
1483	$1.00 Asian Elephants (50×30 *mm*)	2·75	1·60
1479/83	*Set of 5*	6·00	3·50
MS1484	166×73 mm. Nos. 1479/83. P 14½	4·00	4·50

(b) Litho Printset Cambec Pty Ltd. Self-adhesive. Phosphor frame. P 11½

1485	45c. Type **531** (I)	1·10	1·75
	a. Type II	2·25	2·75
	b. Booklet pane. Nos. 1485×4, 1485a×2 and 1486×4	10·00	
1486	45c. Cheetah	1·10	1·75

No. **MS**1484 exists overprinted with the logos of the Sydney Stamp and Coin Fair, Brisbane Stamp and Coin Fair, "Stampshow Melbourne '94" or "Swanpex '94" (including one with overprint inverted) for sale at these Australian exhibitions.

Nos. 1485/6 occur in $4.50 booklets, No. SB86, containing No. 1485b.

The phosphor on the booklets, which shows pink under U.V. light, appears as an irregular frame to each design. Note that the outer part of the design is white on Nos. 1485/6 and coloured on 1479/80.

532 "Madonna and Child" (detail, "The Adoration of the Magi") (Giovanni Toscani)

533 Yachts outside Sydney Harbour

(Des Lisa Christenson. Litho McPhersons Ptg Group, Mulgrave)

1994 (31 Oct). Christmas. T **532** and similar designs showing "The Adoration of the Magi" by Giovanni Toscani. Multicoloured. P 14½×14 (40c., $1.80) or 14×14½ (45c., $1.00).

1487	40c. Type **532**	30	15
	a. Booklet pane. No. 1487×20	5·00	
1488	45c. "Wise Man and Horse" (detail) (*horiz*)	40	10
1489	$1 "Wise Man and St. Joseph" (detail) (*horiz*)	65	60
1490	$1.80 Complete painting (50×30 *mm*)	1·25	2·00
1487/90	*Set of 4*	2·40	2·40

The vertical edges of booklet pane No. 1487a from No. SB87 are imperforate and there are margins at top and bottom.

(Des J. Spatchurst)

1994 (31 Oct). 50th Sydney to Hobart Yacht Race. T **533** and similar horiz design.

(a) Litho Leigh-Mardon Ltd, Melbourne. Phosphorised paper. P 14½

1491	45c. Type **533**	1·00	80
	a. Pair. Nos. 1491/2	2·00	1·60
1492	45c. Yachts passing Tasmania coastline	1·00	80

(b) Litho Printset Cambec Pty Ltd. Self-adhesive. Phosphor frame. P 11½

1493	45c. Type **533** (31×20 *mm*)	80	1·25
1494	45c. Yachts passing Tasmania coastline (31×20 *mm*)	80	1·25

Nos. 1491/2 were printed together, *se-tenant*, in horizontal and vertical pairs throughout the sheet.

Nos. 1493/4 occur in rolls of 100. The phosphor, which shows pink under U.V. light, appears as an irregular frame to each design.

534 Symbolic Kangaroo

535 "Black Verandah" (Russell Drysdale)

(Des Sandra Harman and J. Passmore. Typo (gold die-stamped) Penna Lables, Victoria Labels)

1994 (2 Nov)–**96**. Self-adhesive. Automatic Cash Machine Stamps. Phosphorised paper. P 16½.

1495	**534**	45c. gold, emerald and dull blue-green	55	90
		a. Pane of 20. Nos. 1495/1502	7·00	
		ab. Pane of 20. Nos. 1495/7, 1498a, 1499/1501 and 1502a (11.4.96)	7·00	
1496		45c. gold, emerald and cobalt	55	90
1497		45c. gold, emerald and bright lilac	55	90
1498		45c. gold, emerald and apple-green (grey-brown dots in background)	55	90
		a. Emerald dots in background	55	90
1499		45c. gold, emerald & pale yellow-green	55	90
1500		45c. gold, emerald and pink	55	90
1501		45c. gold, emerald and rose	55	90
1502		45c. gold, emerald and yellow-ochre (grey-brown dots in background)	55	90
		a. Emerald dots in background (11.4.96)	55	90
1495/1502		*Set of 8*	4·00	6·50

Nos. 1495/1502 were issued in panes of 20 from automatic cash machines at Advance Bank branches in Australian Capital Territory, New South Wales and Queensland, and from the National Philatelic Centre, Melbourne. The stamps were arranged, *tête-bêche*, in horizontal rows of 3 or 4 with the pane containing two examples of Nos. 1495, 1497, 1499 and 1501 and three of Nos. 1496, 1498, 1500 and 1502. As originally issued the backing paper carried advertising for the Advance Bank. A second version advertising Postpak packaging was introduced on 11 April 1996 and contained Nos. 1495/7, 1498a, 1499/1501 and 1502a.

St. George Bank took over Advance Bank on 1 April 1998 and the sale of Nos. 1495/1502 through automatic cash machines was discontinued from 11 September 1998.

(Des Allnutt Graphics. Litho Leigh-Mardon Ltd, Melbourne)

1995 (12 Jan). Australia Day. Paintings. T **535** and similar horiz designs. Multicoloured. P 15×14½.

1503	45c. Type **535**	30	30
1504	45c. "Skull Springs Country" (Guy Grey Smith)	30	30
1505	$1.05 "Outcamp" (Robert Juniper)	80	1·00
1506	$1.20 "Kite Flying" (Ian Fairweather)	85	1·00
1503/6	*Set of 4*	2·00	2·40

536 Red Heart and Rose

537 *Endeavour* Replica at Sea

(Des Kim Roberts. Litho Printset Cambec Pty Ltd, (gold die-stamped Avon Graphics))

1995 (30 Jan). St. Valentine's Day. T **536** and similar vert designs. Multicoloured. P 14½×14.

1507	45c. Type **536**	55	55
	a. Horiz strip of 5. Nos. 1507/8×2 and 1509	2·75	3·00
1508	45c. Gold and red heart with rose	55	55
1509	45c. Gold heart and roses	85	1·25
1507/9 *Set of 3*		1·75	2·10

Nos. 1507/9 were printed together, *se-tenant*, in horizontal strips of 5 throughout the sheet each containing two examples of Nos. 1507/8 and one of No. 1509.

(Des Michelle Gauci. Litho McPherson's Ptg Group, Mulgrave)

1995 (9 Feb). Completion of *Endeavour* Replica. T **537** and similar horiz design. Multicoloured.

(a) Sheet stamps, 38×26 mm. P 14×14½

1510	45c. Type **537**	1·50	1·75
	a. Pair. Nos. 1510/11	3·00	3·50
1511	45c. "Captain Cook's *Endeavour*" (detail) (Oswald Brett)	1·50	1·75

(b) Booklet stamps, 44×26 mm. P 14×imperf

1512	20c. Type **537**	1·25	3·25
	a. Booklet pane. Nos. 1512 and 1513×4	2·75	
1513	45c. As No. 1511	45	60

Nos. 1510/11 are printed together, *se-tenant*, in horizontal and vertical pairs throughout the sheet.

The 20c. value was only available from $2 stamp booklets, No. SB88. The vertical edges of pane No. 1512a are imperforate and there are margins at top and bottom.

538 Coalport Plate and Bracket Clock, Old Government House, Parramatta

(Des Janet Boschen. Recess Note Ptg Branch, Reserve Bank of Australia)

1995 (16 Mar). 50th Anniv of Australian National Trusts. T **538** and similar horiz designs. P 14×14½.

1514	45c. deep violet-blue and purple-brown	30	45
	a. Pair. Nos. 1514/15	60	90
1515	45c. deep blue-green and purple-brown	30	45
1516	$1 brown-red and royal blue	70	70
1517	$2 blackish olive and royal blue	1·40	1·90
1514/17 *Set of 4*		2·40	3·25

Designs:—No. 1515, Steiner doll and Italian-style chair, Ayers House, Adelaide; No. 1516, "Advance Australia" teapot and parian-ware statuette, Victoria; No. 1517, Silver bowl and china urn, Old Observatory, Perth.

Nos. 1514/15 were printed together, *se-tenant*, in horizontal and vertical pairs throughout the sheet.

539 Light Opal

(Des Sue Passmore. Litho Printset Cambec Pty Ltd (exelgrams by Avon Graphics))

1995 (5 Apr). Opals. T **539** and similar horiz design. Multicoloured. P 14½×14.

1518	$1.20 Type **539**	3·50	1·25
1519	$2.50 Black opal	4·50	3·75

The opals depicted on Nos. 1518/19 are produced as exelgrams (holographic printing on an ultra thin plastic film) embossed onto the stamps.

540 Queen Elizabeth II at Gala Concert, 1992

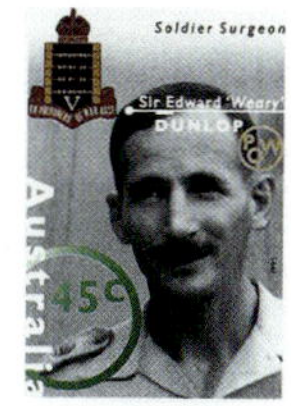

541 Sir Edward Dunlop and P.O.W. Association Badge

(Des Nuttshell Graphics. Litho Leigh-Mardon Ltd, Melbourne)

1995 (20 Apr). Queen Elizabeth II's Birthday. P 14½.

1520	**540**	45c. multicoloured	75	75

Two types of phosphor on Nos. 1527/8:

Type I. Phosphor at right ends level with hat or cap (coils)

Type II. Phosphor at right extends to the ear (No. 1527a) or shoulder (No. 1528a) (booklets).

(Des Sue Passmore)

1995 (20 Apr). Australian Second World War Heroes (1st series). T **541** and similar vert designs. Multicoloured.

(a) Litho McPhersons Ptg Group, Mulgrave. Phosphorised paper. P 14½×14

1521	45c. Type **541**	40	60
	a. Block of 4. Nos. 1521/4	1·40	2·25
1522	45c. Mrs. Jessie Vasey and War Widows' Guild badge	40	60
1523	45c. Sgt. Tom Derrick and Victoria Cross	40	60
1524	45c. Flt. Sgt. Rawdon Middleton and Victoria Cross	40	60
1521/4 *Set of 4*		1·40	2·25

(b) Litho Printset Cambec Pty Ltd. Self-adhesive. Designs 21×32½ mm. Phosphor frame. P 11½

1525	45c. Type **541**	50	1·00
	a. Booklet pane. Nos. 1525×4 and 1526, 1527a/8a, each ×2	4·50	
1526	45c. Mrs. Jessie Vasey and War Widows' Guild badge	50	1·00
1527	45c. Sgt. Tom Derrick and Victoria Cross (I)	50	1·00
	a. Type II	1·00	1·75
1528	45c. Flt. Sgt. Rawdon Middleton and Victoria Cross (I)	50	1·00
	a. Type II	1·00	1·75
1525/8 *Set of 4*		1·75	3·50

Nos. 1521/4 were printed together, *se-tenant*, in sheets of 100 (2 panes of 50 10×5) each pane providing ten blocks of 4 and ten single stamps.

Nos. 1525/8 occur either in rolls of 100, on which the surplus self-adhesive paper around each stamp was removed, or in $4.50 booklets, No. SB89, containing No. 1525a, on which the surplus paper was retained.

The phosphor, which shows pink under U.V. light, covers the designs, with the exception of the portraits and emblems, and the backing paper on both the booklets and the rolls.

See also Nos. 1545/8.

542 Children and Globe of Flags

543 *The Story of the Kelly Gang*

(Des FHA Design. Litho McPherson's Ptg Group, Mulgrave)

1995 (11 May). 50th Anniv of United Nations. P 14×14½.

1529	**542**	45c. multicoloured	75	75

No. 1529 was printed in sheets with *se-tenant* 10×26 mm labels. In rows 1, 3, 5, 7 and 9 these labels occur on the right of each stamp and commemorate either the 50th anniversary or the F.A.O. alternately. On rows 2, 4, 6, 8 and 10 the labels occur on the left of each stamp and are inscribed for either U.N.E.S.C.O. or U.N.I.C.E.F.

(Des J. Spatchurst)

1995 (8 June). Centenary of Cinema. T **543** and similar vert designs showing scenes from films. Multicoloured.

(a) Litho McPhersons Ptg Group, Mulgrave. Phosphorised paper. P 14½×14

1530	45c. Type **543**	1·10	1·50
	a. Horiz strip of 5. Nos. 1530/4	5·00	6·50
1531	45c. *On Our Selection*	1·10	1·50
1532	45c. *Jedda*	1·10	1·50
1533	45c. *Picnic at Hanging Rock*	1·10	1·50
1534	45c. *Strictly Ballroom*	1·10	1·50
1530/4 *Set of 5*		5·00	6·50

(b) Litho Printset Cambec Pty Ltd. Self-adhesive. Designs 19×30½ mm. Phosphor frame. P 11½

1535	45c. Type **543**	1·00	1·50
	a. Booklet pane. Nos. 1535/9 each ×2	9·00	
1536	45c. *On Our Selection*	1·00	1·50
1537	45c. *Jedda*	1·00	1·50
1538	45c. *Picnic at Hanging Rock*	1·00	1·50
1539	45c. *Strictly Ballroom*	1·00	1·50
1535/9 *Set of 5*		4·50	6·50

Nos. 1530/4 were printed together, *se-tenant*, in horizontal strips of 5 throughout the sheet.

Nos. 1535/9 occur either in rolls of 100, on which the surplus self-adhesive paper around each stamp was removed, or in $4.50 booklets, No. SB90, containing No. 1535a, on which the surplus paper was retained.

544 Man in Wheelchair flying kite

545 Koala with Cub

(Des Tracie Grimwood. Litho McPherson's Ptg Group, Mulgrave)

1995 (13 July). People with Disabilities. T **544** and similar vert design. Multicoloured. P 14½×14.

1540	45c. Type **544**	1·00	1·40
	a. Horiz pair. Nos. 1540/1	2·00	2·75
1541	45c. Blind woman playing violin	1·00	1·40

Nos. 1540/1 were printed together, *se-tenant*, in horizontal pairs throughout the sheet.

(Adapted L. Dolan. Recess Note Ptg Branch, Reserve Bank of Australia)

1995 (10 Aug). 50th Anniv of Peace in the Pacific. Designs as 1946 Victory Commemoration (Nos. 213/15) redrawn with new face values. P 14×14½ (horiz) or 14½×14 (vert).

1542	**53**	45c. scarlet	70	70
1543	**54**	45c. green	70	70
1544	**55**	$1.50 blue	1·75	3·00
1542/4 *Set of 3*			2·75	4·00

Designs: Vert—No. 1543, Angel. Horiz—No. 1544, Flag and dove.

(Des Sue Passmore. Litho McPherson's Ptg Group, Mulgrave)

1995 (10 Aug). Australian Second World War Heroes (2nd series). Vert designs as T **541**. Multicoloured. P 14½×14.

1545	45c. Sister Ellen Savage and George Medal	1·25	1·75
	a. Block of 4. Nos. 1545/8	4·50	6·25
1546	45c. Chief Petty Officer Percy Collins and Distinguished Service Medal and Bar	1·25	1·75
1547	45c. Lt-Comm. Leon Goldsworthy and George Cross	1·25	1·75
1548	45c. Warrant Officer Len Waters and R.A.A.F. wings	1·25	1·75
1545/8 *Set of 4*		4·50	6·25

Nos. 1545/8 were printed together, *se-tenant*, in sheets of 100 (2 panes of 50 10×5) each pane providing ten blocks of 4 and ten single stamps.

PRINTERS. Leigh-Mardon Ltd ceased printing Australian stamps in May 1995. On 10 July 1995 Singapore National Printer Pty Ltd took over Printset Cambec and the firm was then known as SNP Cambec.

(Des Xu Yanbo and Lisa Christensen. Litho SNP Cambec (Nos. 1549/50) or Postage Stamp Ptg Works, Peking (No. **MS**1551))

1995 (1 Sept). Australia-China Joint Issue. Endangered Species. T **545** and similar horiz design. Multicoloured. P 14½×14.

1549	45c. Type **545**	70	1·00
	a. Pair. Nos. 1549/50	1·40	2·00
1550	45c. Giant Panda with cubs	70	1·00
MS1551	Two sheets, each 106×70 mm. (a) No. 1549. (b) No. 1550. P 11×11½. *Set of* 2 sheets	2·00	2·25

Nos. 1549/50 were printed together, *se-tenant*, in horizontal and vertical pairs throughout the sheet.

No. **MS**1551a also exists overprinted "AUSTRALIAN STAMP EXHIBITION" and No. **MS**1551b "INTERNATIONAL STAMP & COIN EXPO BEIJING" for sale at these exhibitions in China.

546 Father Joseph Slattery, Thomas Lyle and Walter Filmer (Radiology)

547 Flatback Turtle

(Des O. Schmidinger, Christine Stead and Melinda Whitechurch. Litho McPherson's Ptg Group, Mulgrave)

1995 (7 Sept). Medical Scientists. T **546** and similar multicoloured designs. P 14×14½ (horiz) or 14½×14 (vert).

1552	45c. Type **546**	1·50	1·50
	a. Pair. Nos. 1552/3	3·00	3·00
1553	45c. Dame Jean Macnamara and Sir Macfarlane Burnet (viruses)	1·50	1·50
1554	45c. Fred Hollows (ophthalmology) (*vert*)	1·50	60
1555	$2.50 Sir Howard Florey (antibiotics) (*vert*)	6·00	7·00
1552/5 *Set of 4*		9·50	9·50

Nos. 1552/3 were printed together, *se-tenant*, in horizontal and vertical pairs throughout the sheet.

It was intended that 45c. gutter blocks for philatelic sale would be produced in special sheets, but these were withdrawn just prior to issue when it was found that the gutter pairs contained two examples of the same design, instead of one of each.

No. 1555 also exists as a pane of 10 numbered in red or black from a limited issue Howard Florey portfolio.

Two types of phosphor on self-adhesive Type **547**:

Type I. Outcrop at bottom left completely covered by phosphor (coils)

Type II. Only part of outcrop covered by phosphor (booklets)

(Des G. Ryan. Litho SNP Cambec)

1995 (3 Oct). Marine Life. T **547** and similar horiz designs.

(a) Phosphorised paper. P 14×14½

1556	45c. Type **547**	55	55
	a. Vert pair. Nos. 1556/7	1·10	1·10
1557	45c. Flame Angelfish and Nudibranch	55	55
1558	45c. Potato Grouper ("Potato Cod") and Humpheaded Wrasse ("Maori Wrasse")	55	55
	a. Vert pair. Nos. 1558/9	1·10	1·10
1559	45c. Giant Trevally	55	55
1560	45c. Black Marlin	55	55
	a. Vert pair. Nos. 1560/1	1·10	1·10
1561	45c. Mako and Tiger Sharks	55	55
1556/61 *Set of 6*		3·00	3·00
MS1562	166×73 mm. As Nos. 1556/6, but without lighter frame	3·00	3·00

(b) Self-adhesive. Phosphor frame on three sides. P 11½

1563	45c. Type **547** (I)	55	90
	a. Type II	75	1·50
	ab. Booklet pane Nos. 1563a/6, each×2, and Nos. 1567/8	5·50	
1564	45c. Flame Angelfish and Nudibranch	55	90
1565	45c. Potato Cod and Maori Wrasse	55	90
1566	45c. Giant Trevally	55	90
1567	45c. Black Marlin	55	90
1568	45c. Mako and Tiger Sharks	55	90
1563/8 *Set of 6*		3·00	4·75

Nos. 1556/7, 1558/9 and 1560/1 were printed together, *se-tenant*, in vertical pairs throughout the sheets. Parts of No. **MS**1562 are printed in luminescent ink.

No. **MS**1562 also exists overprinted with the logos of the Adelaide Stamp and Collectables Fair, Sydney Centrepoint 95 National Stamp Exhibition, Brisbane Stamp Show, Melbourne Stamp and Coin Fair and "Swanpex WA", Perth, for sale at these Australian exhibitions.

Nos. 1563/8 occur either in rolls of 100, on which the surplus self-adhesive paper around each stamp was removed, or in $4.50 booklets, No. SB91, containing No. 1563ab, on which the surplus paper was retained.

The phosphor on both rolls and booklets shows pink under U.V. light.

548 "Madonna and Child"

549 "West Australian Banksia" (Margaret Preston)

(Des Dianne Cook. Litho SNP Cambec)

1995 (1 Nov). Christmas. Stained-glass Windows from Our Lady Help of Christians Church, Melbourne. T **548** and similar vert designs.

(a) Phosphorised paper. P 14½×14

1569	40c. Type **548**	80	15
1570	45c. "Angel carrying the Gloria banner"	80	15
1571	$1 "Rejoicing Angels"	3·00	3·25
1569/71	*Set of 3*	4·25	3·25

(b) Self-adhesive. Phosphor frame. P 11½

1572	40c. Type **548**	35	45
	a. Booklet pane. No. 1572×20	6·50	

No. 1572, on which the phosphor shows pink under U.V. light, was only issued in $8 booklets, No. SB92, on which the surplus self-adhesive paper was retained.

(Des Susan Horvath. Litho McPhersons Ptg Group, Mulgrave)

1996 (16 Jan). Australia Day. Paintings. T **549** and similar multicoloured designs. P 14×14½ (vert) or 14½×14 (horiz).

1573	45c. Type **549**	1·00	30
1574	85c. "The Babe is Wise" (Lina Bryans)	2·00	2·50
1575	$1 "The Bridge in Curve" (Grace Cossington Smith) *(horiz)*	2·25	2·00
1576	$1.20 "Beach Umbrellas" (Vida Lahey) *(horiz)*	2·50	3·50
1573/6	*Set of 4*	7·00	7·50

550 Gold Heart and Rose

551 Bristol Type 156 Beaufighter and Curtiss P-40E Kittyhawk I

(Des Kim Roberts and Sandra Harman. Litho SNP Cambec (gold die-stamped Avon Graphics))

1996 (30 Jan). St. Valentine's Day. P 14×14½.

1577	**550** 45c. multicoloured	1·00	1·00

(Des Melinda Whitechurch and N. Clifford. Litho SNP Cambec)

1996 (26 Feb). Military Aviation. T **551** and similar horiz designs. Multicoloured. P 14×14½.

1578	45c. Type **551**	2·00	2·00
	a. Block of 4. Nos. 1578/81	7·25	7·25
1579	45c. Hawker Sea Fury and Fairey Firefly	2·00	2·00
1580	45c. Bell Kiowa helicopters	2·00	2·00
1581	45c. Government Aircraft Factory Hornets	2·00	2·00
1578/81	*Set of 4*	6·25	7·25

Nos. 1578/81 were printed together, *se-tenant*, in different combinations throughout the pane of 25, giving four blocks of 4 and nine single stamps.

552 Tasmanian Wilderness

553 Australian Spotted Cuscus

(Des Dianne Cook. Litho SNP Cambec)

1996 (14 Mar). World Heritage Sites (2nd series). T **552** and similar horiz designs. Multicoloured. P 14½×14.

1582	45c. Type **552**	90	45
1583	75c. Willandra Lakes	2·25	3·00
1584	95c. Naracoorte Fossil Cave	2·50	4·25
1585	$1 Lord Howe Island	2·50	2·25
1582/5	*Set of 4*	7·25	9·00

(Des Rosemary Ganf and Josephine Mure. Litho SNP Cambec)

1996 (22 Mar). Australia–Indonesia Joint Issue. T **553** and similar vert design. Multicoloured. P 14½×14.

1586	45c. Type **553**	90	1·50
	a. Horiz pair. Nos. 1586/7	1·75	3·00
1587	45c. Indonesian Bear Cuscus	90	1·50
MS1588	106×70 mm. Nos. 1586/7	2·25	3·50

Nos. 1586/7 were printed together, *se-tenant*, in horizontal pairs throughout the sheet. No. **MS**1588 also exists overprinted "WORLD PHILATELIC YOUTH EXHIBITION PAMERAN FILATELI REMAJA DUNIA INDONESIA '96" and emblem for sale at this exhibition.

554 Head of Queen Elizabeth II

555 North Melbourne Players

(Des Pendulum Design. Recess and litho Note Ptg Branch, Reserve Bank of Australia and SNP Cambec)

1996 (11 Apr). Queen Elizabeth II's Birthday. P 14×14½.

1589	**554** 45c. multicoloured	1·25	1·00

Numbered gutter strips of ten, overprinted to commemorate the 30th anniversary of decimal currency in Australia, come from a limited issue Queen Elizabeth II portfolio.

(Des Rankin Bevers Design and B. Clinton. Litho SNP Cambec)

1996 (23 Apr). Centenary of Australian Football League. T **555** and similar vert designs each showing players from a different team. Multicoloured.

(a) Phosphorised paper. P 14½×14

1590	45c. Type **555**	50	80
	a. Sheetlet. Nos. 1590/1605	7·00	11·50
1591	45c. Brisbane (red and yellow shirt)	50	80
1592	45c. Sydney (red and white shirt)	50	80
1593	45c. Carlton (black shirt with white emblem)	50	80
1594	45c. Adelaide (black, red and yellow shirt)	50	80
1595	45c. Fitzroy (yellow, red and blue shirt)	50	80
1596	45c. Richmond (black shirt with yellow diagonal stripe)	50	80
1597	45c. St. Kilda (red, white and black shirt)	50	80
1598	45c. Melbourne (black shirt with red top)	50	80
1599	45c. Collingwood (black and white vertical striped shirt)	50	80
1600	45c. Fremantle (green, red, white and blue shirt)	50	80
1601	45c. Footscray (blue, white and red shirt)	50	80
1602	45c. West Coast (deep blue shirt with yellow stripes)	50	80
1603	45c. Essendon (black shirt with red stripe)	50	80
1604	45c. Geelong (black and white horizontal striped shirt)	50	80
1605	45c. Hawthorn (black and yellow vertical striped shirt)	50	80
1590/1605	*Set of 16*	7·00	11·50

(b) Self-adhesive. Phosphor frame at top and left. P 11½

1606	45c. Type **555**	40	90
	a. Booklet pane. No. 1606×10	3·50	
1607	45c. Brisbane	40	90
	a. Booklet pane. No. 1607×10	3·50	
1608	45c. Sydney	40	90
	a. Booklet pane. No. 1608×10	3·50	
1609	45c. Carlton	40	90
	a. Booklet pane. No. 1609×10	3·50	
1610	45c. Adelaide	40	90
	a. Booklet pane. No. 1610×10	3·50	
1611	45c. Fitzroy	40	90
	a. Booklet pane. No. 1611×10	3·50	
1612	45c. Richmond	40	90
	a. Booklet pane. No. 1612×10	3·50	
1613	45c. St. Kilda	40	90
	a. Booklet pane. No. 1613×10	3·50	

1614 45c. Melbourne ... 40 90
a. Booklet pane. No. 1614×10 ... 3·50
1615 45c. Collingwood ... 40 90
a. Booklet pane. No. 1615×10 ... 3·50
1616 45c. Fremantle ... 40 90
a. Booklet pane. No. 1616×10 ... 3·50
1617 45c. Footscray ... 40 90
a. Booklet pane. No. 1617×10 ... 3·50
1618 45c. West Coast ... 40 90
a. Booklet pane. No. 1618×10 ... 3·50
1619 45c. Essendon ... 40 90
a. Booklet pane. No. 1619×10 ... 3·50
1620 45c. Geelong ... 40 90
a. Booklet pane. No. 1620×10 ... 3·50
1621 45c. Hawthorn ... 40 90
a. Booklet pane. No. 1621×10 ... 3·50
1606/21 *Set of 16* ... 6·00 13·00

Nos. 1590/1605 were printed together, *se-tenant*, in sheetlets of 16.

Nos. 1606/21 were only available in $4.50 booklets, Nos. SB93/108. The phosphor shows pink under U.V. light.

556 Leadbeater's Possum

557 Edwin Flack (800 and 1500 metres gold medal winner, 1896)

(Des Rankin Bevers Design. Litho McPherson's Ptg Group, Mulgrave or SNP Ausprint (10c. only))

1996 (9 May). Fauna and Flora (1st series). Central Highlands Forest, Victoria. T **556** and similar multicoloured designs. Phosphorised or ordinary paper (5c., 10c.), phosphorised paper (others). P 14×14½.

1622 5c. Type **556** ... 50 25
1623 10c. Powerful Owl ... 2·50 45
1624 $2 Blackwood Wattle ... 1·60 1·25
1625 $5 Soft Tree Fern and Mountain Ash (30×50 *mm*) ... 14·00 3·75
1622/5 *Set of 4* ... 17·00 5·25

See also Nos. 1679/90, 1854/66, 2126/33, 2200/3a, 2272/80 and 2377/80.

(Des Janet Boschen. Litho McPherson's Ptg Group, Mulgrave)

1996 (18 May). CHINA '96 Ninth Asian International Stamp Exhibition, Peking. Sheet 120×65 mm, containing Nos. 1453b, 1454b and 1455b. Multicoloured. P 14×14½.

MS1626 45c. Kangaroo; 45c. Female kangaroo with young; 45c. Two kangaroos ... 2·00 2·25

(Des Pendulum Design. Eng L. Dolan. Recess and litho Note Ptg Branch, Reserve Bank of Australia and SNP Cambec)

1996 (6 June). Centennial Olympic Games and Tenth Paralympic Games, Atlanta. T **557** and similar horiz designs. Multicoloured. P 14×14½.

1627 45c. Type **557** ... 90 1·00
a. Pair. Nos. 1627/8 ... 1·75 2·00
1628 45c. Fanny Durack (100 metres freestyle swimming gold medal winner, 1912) ... 90 1·00
1629 $1.05 Wheelchair athletes ... 2·25 2·25
1627/9 *Set of 3* ... 3·50 3·75

Nos. 1627/8 were printed together, *se-tenant*, in horizontal and vertical pairs throughout the sheet.

558 *Animalia* (Graeme Base)

559 American Bald Eagle, Kangaroo and Olympic Flame

(Des Pendulum Design. Litho SNP Cambec)

1996 (4 July). 50th Anniv of Children's Book Council Awards. T **558** and similar horiz designs taken from book covers.

(a) Phosphorised paper. P 14×14½

1630 45c. Type **558** ... 60 60
a. Block of 4. Nos. 1630/3 ... 2·25 2·25
1631 45c. *Greetings from Sandy Beach* (Bob Graham) ... 60 60
1632 45c. *Who Sank the Boat?* (Pamela Allen) ... 60 60
1633 45c. *John Brown, Rose and the Midnight Cat* (Jenny Wagner, illustrated by Ron Brooks) ... 60 60
1630/3 *Set of 4* ... 2·25 2·25

(b) Self-adhesive. Phosphor frame. P 11½

1634 45c. Type **558** ... 60 75
a. Booklet pane. Nos. 1634×4 and 1635/7, each ×2 ... 6·00
1635 45c. *Greetings from Sandy Beach* (Bob Graham) ... 60 75
1636 45c. *Who Sank the Boat?* (Pamela Allen) ... 60 75
1637 45c. *John Brown, Rose and the Midnight Cat* (Jenny Wagner, illustrated by Ron Brooks) ... 60 75
1634/7 *Set of 4* ... 2·25 2·75

Nos. 1630/3 were printed together, *se-tenant*, in sheets of 50 (2 panes of 25 5×5) providing ten blocks of 4 and ten single stamps.

Nos. 1634/7 occur either in rolls of 100, on which the surplus self-adhesive paper around each stamp was removed, or in $4.50 booklets, No. SB109, containing No. 1634a, on which the surplus paper was retained.

The phosphor on both rolls and booklets shows pink under U.V. light.

(Des C. Ellett. Litho SNP Cambec (gold die-stamped Avon Graphics))

1996 (22 July). Passing of Olympic Flag to Sydney. P 14×14½.

1638 **559** 45c. multicoloured ... 55 50

560 Margaret Windeyer

561 Pearl

(Des Mad House Design. Litho Canberra Press)

1996 (8 Aug). Centenary of the National Council of Women. T **560** and similar vert design. P 14½×14.

1639 45c. deep reddish purple and lemon ... 40 15
1640 $1 blue and lemon ... 85 1·10

Design:—$1 Rose Scott.

(Des Janet Boschen. Litho SNP Cambec (exelgram (45c.) and hologram ($1.20) Avon Graphics))

1996 (5 Sept). Pearls and Diamonds. T **561** and similar horiz designs. Multicoloured. P 14½×14.

1641 45c. Type **561** ... 60 50
1642 $1.20 Diamond ... 1·40 1·50

The pearl on the 45c. is shown as an exelgram (holographic printing on ultra thin plastic film) and the diamond on the $1.20 as a hologram, each embossed onto the stamp.

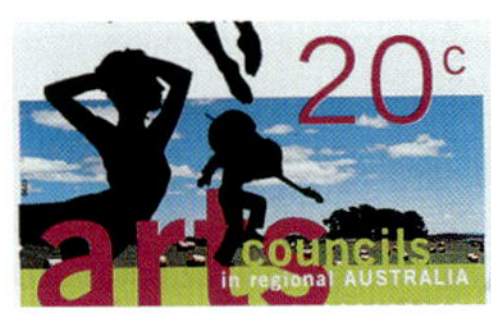

562 Silhouettes of Female Dancer and Musician on Rural Landscape

563 Ginger Cats

(Des A. Ashton. Litho McPherson's Ptg Group, Mulgrave)

1996 (12 Sept)–**2001**. 50th Anniv of Arts Councils. T **562** and similar horiz design. Multicoloured. P 14×imperf.

1643 20c. Type **562** ... 1·40 2·50
a. Booklet pane. Nos. 1643 and 1644×4 ... 2·50
b. Perf 14½×imperf (9.8.01) ... 3·00 4·50
ba. Booklet pane. Nos. 1643b and 1644b×4 ... 4·00
1644 45c. Silhouettes of musician and male dancer on landscape ... 35 45
b. Perf 14½×imperf (9.8.01) ... 40 65

Nos. 1643/4 only exist from $2 stamp booklets, No. SB110, in which the vertical edges of the pane are imperforate.

Nos. 1643b/4b come from the 1 koala printing of the booklet.

(Des Dianne Cooke. Litho SNP Cambec)

1996 (1 Oct). Australian Pets. T **563** and similar multicoloured designs.

(a) Phosphorised paper. P 14×14½ (Nos. 1647, 1650) or 14½×14 (others)

1645 45c. Type **563** ... 65 75
a. Pair. Nos. 1645/6 ... 1·25 1·50
1646 45c. Blue Heeler dogs ... 65 75

1647	45c. Sulphur-crested Cockatoo (30×25 *mm*)	65	75
1648	45c. Duck with ducklings (25×30 *mm*)	65	75
	a. Horiz pair. Nos. 1648/9	1·25	1·50
1649	45c. Dog and cat (25×30 *mm*)	65	75
1650	45c. Ponies (30×50 *mm*)	65	75
1645/50 *Set of 6*		3·50	4·00
MS1651	166×73 mm. Nos. 1645/50. P 14½	3·50	4·00
	(b) Self-adhesive. Phosphor band. P 11½		
1652	45c. Type **563**	75	1·25
	a. Booklet pane. Nos. 1652×4 and 1653×6	6·50	
1653	45c. Blue Heeler dogs	75	1·25

Nos. 1645/6 and 1648/9 were each printed together, *se-tenant*, either in vertical and horizontal pairs (Nos. 1645/6) or in horizontal pairs (Nos. 1648/9) throughout the sheets.

Nos. 1652/3 were printed either in rolls of 100 on which the surplus selfadhesive paper around each stamp was removed, or in $4.50 booklets, No. SB111, containing No. 1652a, on which the surplus paper was retained.

The phosphor on both rolls and booklets shows orange-pink under U. V. light and appears as a bar at the top and on the cats for No. 1652 and as an L-shaped frame for No. 1653.

No. **MS**1651 also exists overprinted with the logos of the ASDA Centrepoint '96 Sydney, St. Peter's Stamp and Coin Fair, "Melbourne '96", "TAIPEI '96", Queensland Stamp and Coin Expo, Stamp Show '96 Claremont and "HONG KONG '97" for sale at these exhibitions.

564 Ferdinand von Mueller

565 Willem de Vlamingh

(Des J. Sellitto and D. Blyth. Litho State Ptg Wks, Berlin)

1996 (9 Oct). Australia—Germany Joint Issue. Death Centenary of Ferdinand von Mueller (botanist). P 14.

1654	**564** $1.20 multicoloured	1·25	2·00

(Des A. Donato. Litho McPherson's Ptg Group, Mulgrave)

1996 (1 Nov). 300th Anniv of the Visit of Willem de Vlamingh to Western Australia. P 14×14½.

1655	**565** 45c. multicoloured	1·00	1·50
	a. Horiz pair. No. 1655 and No. 433 of Christmas Island	2·00	3·00

No. 1655 and No. 433 of Christmas Island were printed together, *se-tenant*, in horizontal pairs throughout the sheet.

566 Madonna and Child

567 "Landscape 74" (Fred Williams)

(Des Vivienne Goodman. Litho SNP Cambec)

1996 (1 Nov). Christmas. T **566** and similar vert designs. Multicoloured.

	(a) Phosphorised paper. P 14½×14		
1656	40c. Type **566**	55	15
1657	45c. Wise man with gift	55	15
1658	$1 Shepherd boy with lamb	1·25	1·50
1656/8 *Set of 3*		2·10	1·60
	(b) Self-adhesive. Phosphor on inscr panel and central figures. P 11½		
1659	40c. Type **566**	75	60
	a. Booklet pane. No. 1659×20	13·00	

No. 1659 on which the phosphor shows pink under U. V. light was only issued in $8 booklets, No. SB112, on which the surplus self-adhesive paper was retained.

(Des Karina Weston. Litho McPhersons Ptg Group, Mulgrave)

1997 (16 Jan). Australia Day. Contemporary Paintings. T **567** and similar horiz designs. Multicoloured. P 14½×14.

1660	85c. Type **567**	60	60
1661	90c. "The Balcony 2" (Brett Whiteley)	60	60
1662	$1.20 "Fire Haze at Gerringong" (Lloyd Rees)	80	80
1660/2 *Set of 3*		1·75	1·75

568 Sir Donald Bradman

569 Red Roses

(Des Sophie Byass. Litho SNP Cambec)

1997 (23 Jan). Australian Legends (1st series). Sir Donald Bradman (cricketer). T **568** and similar square design. Multicoloured. P 14½.

1663	45c. Type **568**	55	55
	a. Horiz pair. Nos. 1663/4	1·10	1·10
1664	45c. Bradman playing stroke	55	55

Nos. 1663/4 were printed together, *se-tenant*, in horizontal pairs throughout the sheet of 10.

For stamps in same design additionally inscribed "1908–2000", see Nos. 2077/8.

See also Nos. 1731/54, 1838/41, 1947/54, 2069/72, 2160/9, 2264/71, 2348/51, 2467/78, 2577/86, 2741/58, 2907/14, 3113/28, 3328/3345, 3533/40, 3587/3916, 3697/712, 4112/21, 4304/14 and 4498/4521..

(Des Kate Linton. Litho SNP Cambec)

1997 (29 Jan). St. Valentine's Day.

	(a) Phosphorised paper. P 14½×14		
1665	**569** 45c. multicoloured	50	50
	(b) Self-adhesive. Phosphor on inscr panel and background. P 11½		
1666	**569** 45c. multicoloured	80	1·25
	a. Booklet pane. No. 1666×10	7·50	

No. 1666, on which the phosphor shows pink under U. V. light, was only issued in $4.50 booklets, No. SB113, on which the surplus self-adhesive paper was retained.

570 Ford Coupe Utility, 1934

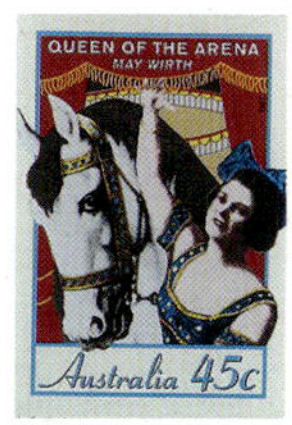

571 May Wirth and Horse

(Des Sandra Harmon. Litho SNP Cambec)

1997 (27 Feb). Classic Cars. T **570** and similar horiz designs. Multicoloured.

	(a) Phosphorised paper. P 14×14½		
1667	45c. Type **570**	50	75
	a. Block of 4. Nos. 1667/70	1·75	2·75
	b. Booklet pane. No. 1667×4 with margins all round	1·75	
1668	45c. Holden 48-215 (FX) sedan, 1948	50	75
	a. Booklet pane. No. 1668×4 with margins all round	1·75	
1669	45c. Austin Lancer sedan, 1958	50	75
	a. Booklet pane. No. 1669×4 with margins all round	1·75	
1670	45c. Chrysler Valiant "R" Series sedan, 1962	50	75
	a. Booklet pane. No. 1670×4 with margins all round	1·75	
1667/70 *Set of 4*		1·75	2·75
	(b) Self-adhesive. Phosphor frames. P 11½		
1671	45c. Type **570**	45	65
	a. Booklet pane. Nos. 1671, 1673 each ×2 and 1672, 1674 each ×3	4·00	
1672	45c. GMH Holden 48-215 (FX), 1948	45	65
1673	45c. Austin Lancer, 1958	45	65
1674	45c. Chrysler Valiant "R" Series, 1962	45	65
1671/4 *Set of 4*		1·60	2·40

Nos. 1667/70 were printed together, *se-tenant*, in sheets of 50 (2 panes 5×5), each sheet providing ten blocks of 4 and ten single stamps. Booklet panes 1667b/70a come from No. SB115.

Nos. 1671/4 occur either in rolls of 100, on which the surplus self-adhesive paper was removed, or in $4.50 booklets, No. SB114, containing No. 1671a, on which the surplus paper was retained. The phosphor on both rolls and booklets shows pink under U. V. light.

(Des Cathleen Bryant. Litho McPherson's Ptg Group, Mulgrave)

1997 (13 Mar). 150th Anniv of the Circus in Australia. T **571** and similar vert designs. Multicoloured. P 14½×14.

1675	45c. Type **571**	55	75
	a. Block of 4. Nos. 1675/8	2·00	2·75
1676	45c. Con Colleano on tightrope	55	75
1677	45c. Clowns	55	75
1678	45c. Acrobats	55	75
1675/8 *Set of 4*		2·00	2·75

Nos. 1675/8 were printed together, *se-tenant*, in sheets of 50 (2 panes of 5×5), each sheet providing ten blocks of 4 and ten single stamps.

(Des Rankin Bevers Design)

1997 (10 Apr–2 Jun). Fauna and Flora (2nd series). Kakadu Wetlands, Northern Territory. Multicoloured designs as T **556**.

(a) Litho SNP Cambec (gold on $10 die-stamped Avon Graphics). Phosphorised paper. P 14½×14 ($10) or 14×14½ (others)

1679	20c. Saltwater Crocodile	60	20
1680	25c. Northern Dwarf Tree Frog	60	25
1681	45c. Comb-crested Jacana (2.6.97)	75	75
	a. Block of 4. Nos. 1681/4	2·75	2·75
1682	45c. Little Kingfisher (2.6.97)	75	75
1683	45c. Brolga (2.6.97)	75	75
1684	45c. Black-necked Stork ("Jabiru") (2.6.97)	75	75
1685	$1 *Cressida cressida* ("Big Greasy Butterfly")	70	75
1686	$10 Kakadu Wetlands (50×30 *mm*)	7·00	5·00
1679/86 *Set of 8*		11·00	8·00
MS1686*a* 106×70 mm. No. 1686		8·00	10·00

Nos. 1681/4 were printed together, *se-tenant*, in sheets of 50 providing ten blocks of 4 and ten single stamps.

Supplies of No. 1685 printed at "Australia '99" showed the exhibition logo on the margin.

No. **MS**1686a was issued in connection with the "Australia 99" International Stamp Exhibition. It also exists overprinted with the "Pacific '97" (San Francisco) "Italia '98" (Milan) or Philanippon 2001 logos for sale at these international stamp exhibitions.

A further miniature sheet containing Nos. 1683/4 was sold at the "International Stamp and Coin Exposition Shanghai 97" and from philatelic outlets.

(b) Self-adhesive. Litho SNP Cambec (Nos. 1687/90) or Pemara (Nos. 1687d/90d). Phosphor frame. P 11½

1687	45c. Comb-crested Jacana (2.6.97)	60	85
	a. Booklet pane. (Nos. 1687 and 1689 each ×3, and Nos. 1688 and 1690, each ×2)	5·50	
	b. Sheetlet. Nos. 1687×2 and 1688/90	2·25	
	c. Booklet pane. Nos. 1687/90, each ×5 (1.9.98)	22·00	
	d. Perf 12½×13 (13.11.97)	1·40	2·00
1688	45c. Little Kingfisher (2.6.97)	60	85
	d. Perf 12½×13 (13.11.97)	1·40	2·00
1689	45c. Brolga (2.6.97)	60	85
	d. Perf 12½×13 (13.11.97)	1·40	2·00
1690	45c. Black-necked Stork (2.6.97)	60	85
	d. Perf 12½×13 (13.11.97)	1·40	2·00
1687/90 *Set of 4*		2·25	3·00

Nos. 1687/90 and 1687d/90d were printed in rolls of 100 or 200 (Nos. 1687/90 only) with the surplus paper around each stamp removed. Nos. 1687/90 also come in $4.50 (SB116) and $9 (SB121) booklets, and also sheetlets of 5, all of which have the surplus paper in place.

The phosphor shows orange-pink under U.V. light and appears as a broken frame around each stamp.

572 Royal Wedding 1d. Stamp of 1947

573 Hand holding Globe and Lions Emblem

(Des Cozzolino Ellett. Recess Note Ptg Branch, Reserve Bank of Australia)

1997 (17 Apr). Queen Elizabeth II's Birthday. P 14×14½.

1691	**572**	45c. blackish purple	1·00	60

(Des Cozzolino Ellett. Recess Note Ptg Branch, Reserve Bank of Australia)

1997 (17 Apr). 50th Anniv of First Australian Lions Club. P 14½×14.

1692	**573**	45c. brt blue, chestnut & blackish pur.	50	50

574 Doll holding Teddy Bear (Kaye Wiggs)

575 Police Rescue Helicopter

(Des Cathleen Bryant. Litho McPherson's Ptg Group, Mulgrave)

1997 (8 May). Dolls and Teddy Bears. T **574** and similar vert designs. Multicoloured. P 14½×14.

1693	45c. Type **574**	40	40
	a. Horiz strip of 5. Nos. 1693/7	1·75	1·75
1694	45c. Teddy bear standing (Jennifer Laing)	40	40
1695	45c. Doll wearing white dress with teddy bear (Susie McMahon)	40	40
1696	45c. Doll in brown dress and bonnet (Lynda Jacobson)	40	40
1697	45c. Teddy bear sitting (Helen Williams)	40	40
1693/7 *Set of 5*		1·75	1·75

Nos. 1693/7 were printed together in sheets of 10, containing two *se-tenant* strips of 5. Sheets exist overprinted for the 1997 Brisbane Stamp and Coin Expo.

(Des B. Sadgrove. Litho McPherson's Ptg Group, Mulgrave)

1997 (10 July). Emergency Services. T **575** and similar horiz designs. Multicoloured. P 14×14½.

1698	45c. Type **575**	1·50	1·00
	a. Horiz pair. Nos. 1698/9	3·00	2·00
1699	45c. Emergency Service volunteers carrying victim	1·50	1·00
1700	$1.05 Fire service at fire	2·75	2·25
1701	$1.20 Loading casualty into ambulance	3·00	2·00
1698/1701 *Set of 4*		8·00	5·50

Nos. 1698/9 were printed together, *se-tenant*, in horizontal pairs throughout the sheet.

Numbered gutter strips of ten of No. 1701, overprinted "Emergency Services", come from a limited issue portfolio.

576 George Peppin Jnr (breeder) Merino Sheep

577 Dumbi the Owl

(Des C. Shurey. Litho SNP Cambec)

1997 (7 Aug). Bicentenary of Arrival of Merino Sheep in Australia. T **576** and similar horiz design. Multicoloured. P 14×14½.

1702	45c. Type **576**	70	1·00
	a. Horiz pair. Nos. 1702/3	1·40	2·00
1703	45c. Pepe chair, cloth and wool logo	70	1·00

Nos. 1702/3 were printed together, *se-tenant*, as horizontal pairs in sheets of 10.

(Des Melinda Coombes. Litho SNP Cambec)

1997 (21 Aug). "The Dreaming". Cartoons from Aboriginal Stories. T **577** and similar square designs. Multicoloured. P 14½.

1704	45c. Type **577**	40	20
1705	$1 The Two Willy-Willies	70	50
1706	$1.20 How Brolga became a Bird	75	1·25
1707	$1.80 Tuggan-Tuggan	1·25	2·75
1704/7 *Set of 4*		2·75	4·25

578 *Rhoetosaurus brownei*

579 Spotted-tailed Quoll

(Des P. Schouten. Litho SNP Cambec)

1997 (4 Sept). Prehistoric Animals. T **578** and similar vert designs. Multicoloured. P 14½×14.

1708	45c. Type **578**	45	60
	a. Horiz strip of 5. Nos. 1708/12	2·00	2·75
1709	45c. *Mcnamaraspis kaprios*	45	60
1710	45c. *Ninjemys oweni*	45	60
1711	45c. *Paracylotosaurus davidi*	45	60
1712	45c. *Woolungasaurus glendowerensis*	45	60
1708/12 *Set of 5*		2·00	2·75

Nos. 1708/12 were printed together, *se-tenant*, as horizontal strips of five in sheets of 10.

(Des P. Gouldthorpe. Litho SNP Cambec)

1997 (1 Oct). Nocturnal Animals. T **579** and similar multicoloured designs.

(a) Phosphorised paper. P 14×14½ (Nos. 1715/17) or 14½×14 (others)

1713	45c. Type **579**	70	90
	a. Pair. Nos. 1713/14	1·40	1·75
1714	45c. Barking Owl	70	90
1715	45c. Platypus (30×25 *mm*)	70	90
	a. Horiz strip of 3. Nos. 1715/17	1·90	2·40
1716	45c. Brown Antechinus (30×25 *mm*)	70	90
1717	45c. Dingo (30×25 *mm*)	70	90
1718	45c. Yellow-bellied Glider (50×30 *mm*)	70	90
1713/18 *Set of 6*		3·75	4·75
MS1719 166×73 mm. Nos. 1713/18. P 14½		4·75	4·75

(b) Self-adhesive. Phosphor frame. P 11½

1720	45c. Type **579** (26×38 *mm*)	80	1·00
	a. Vert pair. Nos. 1720/1	1·60	2·00
	b. Booklet pane. Nos. 1720/1, each ×5	6·00	
1721	45c. Barking Owl (26×38 *mm*)	80	1·00

No. 1713/14 were printed together, *se-tenant*, in horizontal or vertical pairs and Nos. 1715/17 in horizontal strips of three throughout the sheets.

No. **MS**1719 shows a spider and web printed in green phosphor, visible under U.V. light, across much of the sheet.

Nos. 1720/1, on which the phosphor frame appears pink under U.V. light, were printed either in rolls of 100 on which the surplus self-adhesive paper around each stamp was removed or in $4.50 booklets, No. SB117, containing No. 1720b on which the surplus paper was retained.

580 Woman

581 Two Angels

(Des Lynda Warner. Litho SNP Cambec)

1997 (27 Oct). Breast Cancer Awareness Campaign. P 14×14½.

1722	**580**	45c. multicoloured	1·25	60

(Des Cathleen Bryant. Litho SNP Cambec)

1997 (3 Nov). Christmas. Children's Nativity Play. T **581** and similar horiz designs. Multicoloured.

(a) Phosphorised paper. P 14×14½

1723	40c. Type **581**	40	10
1724	45c. Mary	40	10
1725	$1 Three Kings	1·00	1·25
1723/5 *Set of 3*		1·60	1·25

(b) Self-adhesive. Phosphor frame at right and foot. P 11½

1726	40c. Type **581**	30	40
	a. Booklet pane. No. 1726×20	5·50	

No. 1726, on which the phosphor shows pink under U. V. light, was only issued in $8 booklets, No. SB118, on which the surplus self-adhesive paper was retained.

582 *"Flying Cloud"* (clipper) (J. Scott)

583 Betty Cuthbert (1956)

(Des B. Sadgrove. Litho McPherson's Ptg Group, Mulgrave)

1998 (15 Jan). Ship Paintings. T **582** and similar square designs. Multicoloured. P 14½×14.

1727	45c. Type **582**	60	30
1728	85c. *"Marco Polo"* (full-rigged ship) (T. Robertson)	1·00	1·00
1729	$1 *"Chusan I"* (steamship) (C. Gregory)	1·25	1·10
1730	$1.20 *"Heather Belle"* (clipper)	1·50	1·75
1727/30 *Set of 4*		4·00	3·75

No. 1727 was reissued on 17 June 1998 in sheets of 10 (2×5) with inscribed margins publicising "Australia 99" International Stamp Exhibition, Melbourne.

The design of 1728 was utilised in **MS**1851, with perf 13½.

(Des Sophie Byass. Litho SNP Cambec)

1998 (21 Jan). Australian Legends (2nd series). Olympic Gold Medal Winners. T **583** and similar horiz designs.

(a) Phosphorised paper. P 14×14½

1731	45c. Type **583**	30	45
	a. Sheetlet. Nos. 1731/42	3·25	4·75
1732	45c. Betty Cuthbert running	30	45
1733	45c. Herb Elliot (1960)	30	45
1734	45c. Herb Elliot running	30	45
1735	45c. Dawn Fraser (1956, 1960 and 1964)	30	45
1736	45c. Dawn Fraser swimming	30	45
1737	45c. Marjorie Jackson (1952)	30	45
1738	45c. Marjorie Jackson running	30	45
1739	45c. Murray Rose (1956)	30	45
1740	45c. Murray Rose swimming	30	45
1741	45c. Shirley Strickland (1952 and 1956)	30	45
1742	45c. Shirley Strickland hurdling	30	45
1731/42 *Set of 12*		3·25	4·75

(b) Self-adhesive. Two vertical phosphor bands. P 11½

1743	45c. Type **583**	40	80
	b. Booklet pane. Nos. 1743/54	4·25	
1744	45c. Betty Cuthbert running	40	80
1745	45c. Herb Elliot	40	80
1746	45c. Herb Elliot running	40	80
1747	45c. Dawn Fraser	40	80
1748	45c. Dawn Fraser swimming	40	80
1749	45c. Marjorie Jackson	40	80
1750	45c. Marjorie Jackson running	40	80
1751	45c. Murray Rose	40	80
1752	45c. Murray Rose swimming	40	80
1753	45c. Shirley Strickland	40	80
1754	45c. Shirley Strickland hurdling	40	80
1743/54 *Set of 12*		4·25	8·50

Nos. 1731/42 were printed together, *se-tenant*, in sheetlets of 12.

Nos. 1743/54, on which the phosphor bands appear pink under U. V. light, were printed in $5.40 stamp booklets, No. SB119, containing No. 1743b on which the surplus paper around each stamp was retained.

584 Champagne Rose

585 Queen Elizabeth II

(Des Cathleen Bryant. Litho SNP Cambec)

1998 (12 Feb). Greetings Stamp.

(a) P 14½×14

1755	**584**	45c. multicoloured	55	50

(b) Self-adhesive. Phosphor band. P 11½

1756	**584**	45c. multicoloured	45	55
		a. Booklet pane. No. 1756×10	4·00	

No. 1756 was only issued in $4.50 booklets, No. SB120, on which the surplus self-adhesive paper was retained.

The phosphor, which shows pink under U.V. light, covers most of the row of roses to the left of the design.

(Des Hannah Richardson. Litho McPherson's Ptg Group, Mulgrave)

1998 (9 Apr). Queen Elizabeth II's Birthday. P 14×14½.

1757	**585**	45c. multicoloured	70	50

586 Sea Hawk (helicopter) landing on Frigate

587 Sheep Shearer and Sheep

(Des Sandra Harman. Litho McPherson's Ptg Group, Mulgrave)

1998 (9 Apr). 50th Anniv of Royal Australian Navy Fleet Air Arm. P 14×14½.

1758	**586**	45c. multicoloured	1·00	50

(Des C. Shurey. Litho SNP Cambec)

1998 (21 Apr). Farming. T **587** and similar horiz designs. Multicoloured.

(a) Phosphorised paper. P 14×14½

1759	45c. Type **587**	45	50
	a. Horiz strip of 5. Nos. 1759/63	2·00	2·25
1760	45c. Barley and silo	45	50
1761	45c. Farmers herding beef cattle	45	50
1762	45c. Sugar cane harvesting	45	50
1763	45c. Two dairy cows	45	50
1759/63 *Set of 5*		2·00	2·25

(b) Self-adhesive. Phosphor band. P 11½

1764	45c. Type **587**	1·10	1·10
	a. Booklet pane. Nos. 1764/8, each ×2	10·00	
1765	45c. Barley and silo	1·10	1·10
1766	45c. Farmers herding beef cattle	1·10	1·10
1767	45c. Sugar cane harvesting	1·10	1·10
1768	45c. Two dairy cows	1·10	1·10
1764/8 *Set of 5*		5·00	5·00

Nos. 1759/63 were printed together, *se-tenant*, in horizontal strips of 5 throughout the sheet.

On Nos. 1764/8 the phosphor, which shows pink under U. V. light, appears as a horizontal band at the top with an irregular extension to the foot of each design. They were printed in $4.50 stamp booklets, No. SB122, containing No. 1764a on which the surplus paper around each stamp was retained.

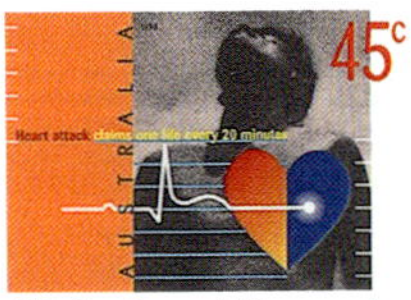

588 Cardiograph Trace and Heart

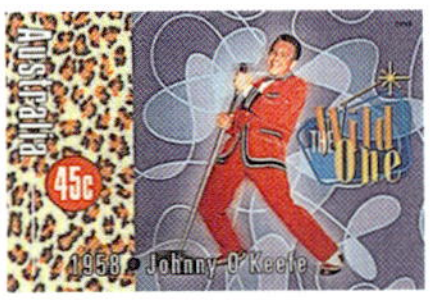

589 Johnny O'Keefe ("The Wild One", 1958)

(Des Lynda Warner. Litho SNP Cambec)

1998 (4 May). Heart Disease Awareness. P 14×14½.

1769	**588**	45c. multicoloured	75	50

(Des Cozzolino Ellett. Litho SNP Cambec)

1998 (26 May). Australian Rock and Roll. T **589** and similar horiz designs. Multicoloured.

(a) Phosphorised paper. P 14×14½

1770	45c. Type **589**	30	40
	a. Sheetlet of 12. Nos. 1770/81	3·25	4·25
1771	45c. Col Joye ("Oh Yeah Uh Huh", 1959)	30	40
1772	45c. Little Pattie ("He's My Blond Headed Stompie Wompie Real Gone Surfer Boy", 1963)	30	40
1773	45c. Normie Rowe ("Shakin all Over", 1965)	30	40
1774	45c. Easybeats ("She's so Fine", 1965)	30	40
1775	45c. Russell Morris ("The Real Thing", 1969)	30	40
1776	45c. Masters Apprentices ("Turn Up Your Radio", 1970)	30	40
1777	45c. Daddy Cool ("Eagle Rock", 1971)	30	40
1778	45c. Billy Thorpe and the Aztecs ("Most People I know Think I'm Crazy", 1972)	30	40
1779	45c. Skyhooks ("Horror Movie", 1974)	30	40
1780	45c. AC/DC ("It's a Long Way to the Top", 1975)	30	40
1781	45c. Sherbet ("Howzat", 1976)	30	40
1770/81 *Set of 12*		3·25	4·25

(b) Self-adhesive. One side phosphor band. P 11½

1782	45c. Sherbet ("Howzat", 1976)	30	60
	a. Horiz strip of 12. Nos. 1782/93	3·25	6·50
1783	45c. AC/DC ("It's a Long Way to the Top", 1975)	30	60
1784	45c. Skyhooks ("Horror Movie", 1974)	30	60
1785	45c. Billy Thorpe and the Aztecs ("Most People I Know Think I'm Crazy", 1972)	30	60
1786	45c. Daddy Cool ("Eagle Rock", 1971)	30	60
1787	45c. The Masters Apprentices ("Turn Up Your Radio", 1970)	30	60
1788	45c. Russell Morris ("The Real Thing", 1969)	30	60
1789	45c. Easybeats ("She's So Fine", 1965)	30	60
1790	45c. Normie Rowe ("Shakin all Over", 1965)	30	60
1791	45c. Little Pattie ("He's My Blond Headed Stompie Wompie Real Gone Surfer Boy", 1963)	30	60
1792	45c. Col Joye ("Oh Yeah Uh Huh", 1959)	30	60
1793	45c. Type **589**	30	60
1782/93 *Set of 12*		3·25	6·50

Nos. 1770/81 were printed together, *se-tenant*, in sheetlets of 12.

Nos. 1782/93, on which the phosphor appears pale purple under U.V. light, shows the band alternating at left or right. They were issued in rolls of 100 on which the surplus paper around each stamp was removed.

590 Yellow-tufted Honeyeater ("Helmeted Honeyeater")

591 French Horn and Cello Players

(Des K. Stead and Melinda Coombes. Litho McPherson's Ptg Group, Mulgrave)

1998 (25 June). Endangered Species. Birds. T **590** and similar horiz designs. Multicoloured. Ordinary paper (Nos. 1794/5). P 14×14½.

1794	5c. Type **590**	45	45
	a. Horiz pair. Nos. 1794/5	90	90
1795	5c. Orange-bellied Parrot	45	45
1796	45c. Red-tailed Cockatoo	80	80
	a. Horiz pair. Nos. 1796/7	1·60	1·60
1797	45c. Gouldian Finch	80	80
1794/7 *Set of 4*		2·25	2·25

Nos. 1794/5 and 1796/7 were each printed together, *se-tenant*, in horizontal pairs throughout the sheets.

(Des Michelle Gauci. Litho SNP Cambec)

1998 (16 July). Youth Arts, Australia. T **591** and similar horiz design. Multicoloured. P 14×14½.

1798	45c. Type **591**	50	50
	a. Horiz pair. Nos. 1798/9	1·00	1·00
1799	45c. Dancers	50	50

Nos. 1798/9 were printed together, *se-tenant*, in horizontal pairs throughout the sheet.

592 *Phalaenopsis rosenstromii*

593 Flying Angel with Teapot (cartoon by Michael Leunig)

(Des Clare Kaegi and Cathleen Cram. Litho SNP Ausprint)

1998 (6 Aug). Australia-Singapore Joint Issue. Orchids. T **592** and similar vert designs. Multicoloured. P 14½×14.

1800	45c. Type **592**	55	25
1801	85c. *Arundina graminifolia*	80	70
1802	$1 *Grammatophyllum speciosum*	1·10	1·00
1803	$1.20, *Dendrobium phalaenopsis*	1·25	1·60
1800/3 *Set of 4*		3·25	3·25
MS1804	138×72 mm. Nos. 1800/3	3·25	3·75

(Des Sandra Harman. Litho SNP Ausprint)

1998 (13 Aug). "The Teapot of Truth" (cartoons by Michael Leunig). T **593** and similar horiz designs. Multicoloured. P 14×14½.

1805	45c. Type **593**	75	80
	a. Booklet pane. No. 1805×4 with margins all round	2·75	
1806	45c. Two birds in heart-shaped tree	75	80
	a. Booklet pane. No. 1806×4 with margins all round	2·75	
1807	45c. Pouring tea	75	80
	a. Booklet pane. No. 1807×4 with margins all round	2·75	
1808	$1 Mother and child (29×24 *mm*)	1·40	1·75
	a. Booklet pane. No. 1808×2 with margins all round	2·75	
1809	$1.20 Cat with smiling face (29×24 *mm*)	1·40	1·75
	a. Booklet pane. No. 1809×2 and stamp-size label	2·75	
1805/9 *Set of 5*		4·50	5·50

Nos. 1805/9 were originally issued in $9.95 stamp booklets No. SB123, but were subsequently made available in a 'collectors pack' sold only by the Bureau. The shades on Nos. 1808/9 differ between the two products.

594 Red Lacewing

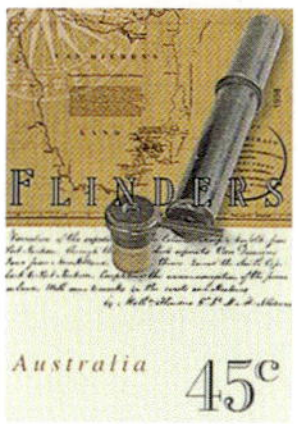

595 Flinders' Telescope and Map of Tasmania

(Des C. Shurey. Litho SNP Ausprint)

1998 (3 Sept). Butterflies. T **594** and similar vert designs. Multicoloured. Phosphorised paper.

(a) P 14½×14

1810	45c. Type **594**	1·40	85
	a. Horiz strip of 5. Nos. 1810/14	6·25	3·75
1811	45c. Dull Oakblue	1·40	85
1812	45c. Meadow Argus	1·40	85
1813	45c. Ulysses Butterfly	1·40	85
1814	45c. Common Red-eye	1·40	85
1810/14	*Set of 5*	6·25	3·75

(b) Self-adhesive. P 11½

1815	45c. Type **594**	75	1·00
	a. Vert strip of 5. Nos. 1815/19	3·25	4·50
1816	45c. Dull Oakblue	75	1·00
1817	45c. Meadow Argus	75	1·00
1818	45c. Ulysses Butterfly	75	1·00
1819	45c. Common Red-eye	75	1·00
1815/19	*Set of 5*	3·25	4·50

Nos. 1810/14 were printed together, *se-tenant*, as horizontal strips of five in sheets of 10.

Nos. 1815/19 come, *se-tenant*, in strips of 5 or rolls of 100 with the surplus self-adhesive paper around each stamp removed.

A miniature sheet containing Nos. 1810/14 was sold at "China '99" International Stamp Exhibition, Beijing, and from philatelic outlets.

(Des Lynda Warner. Litho McPherson's Ptg Group, Mulgrave)

1998 (10 Sept). Bicentenary of the Circumnavigation of Tasmania by George Bass and Matthew Flinders. T **595** and similar vert design. Multicoloured. P 14½×14.

1820	45c. Type **595**	75	65
	a. Vert pair. Nos. 1820/1	1·50	1·25
1821	45c. Sextant and letter from Bass	75	65

Nos. 1820/1 were printed together, *se-tenant*, in vertical pairs throughout the sheet.

596 Weedy Seadragon

597 Rose of Freedom

(Des W. Rankin. Litho SNP Ausprint)

1998 (1 Oct). International Year of the Ocean. T **596** and similar multicoloured designs.

(a) Phosphorised paper. P 14×14½ (Nos. 1825/6) or 14½×14 (others)

1822	45c. Type **596**	55	55
	a. Horiz pair. Nos. 1822/3	1·10	1·10
1823	45c. Bottlenose Dolphin	55	55
1824	45c. Fiery Squid (26×30 *mm*)	55	55
1825	45c. Manta Ray (30×26 *mm*)	55	55
1826	45c. White Pointer Shark (30×50 *mm*)	55	55
1827	45c. Southern Right Whale (50×30 *mm*)	55	55
1822/7	*Set of 6*	3·00	3·00
MS1828	166×73 mm. Nos. 1822/7. P 14½	2·75	2·75

(b) Self-adhesive. Phosphor frame. P 11½

1829	45c. Type **596** (26×38 *mm*)	50	60
	a. Vert pair. Nos. 1829/30	1·00	1·10
	b. Booklet pane. Nos. 1829/30, each ×5	5·00	
1830	45c. Bottlenose Dolphin (24×36 *mm*)	50	60

Nos. 1822/3 were printed together, *se-tenant*, in horizontal or vertical pair throughout the sheet.

Nos. 1829/30, on which the phosphor frame appears pink under U.V. light, were printed either in rolls of 100 on which the surplus self-adhesive paper around each stamp was removed or in $4.50 booklets, No. SB125, containing No. 1826b on which the surplus paper was retained.

(Des Lynda Warner, Litho SNP Ausprint)

1998 (22 Oct). 50th Anniv of Universal Declaration of Human Rights. P 14½×14.

1831 **597**	45c. multicoloured	50	50

598 Three Kings

(Des Sophie Byass and K. Done. Litho SNP Ausprint)

1998 (2 Nov). Christmas. T **598** and similar horiz designs. Multicoloured.

(a) Phosphorised paper. P 14×14½

1832	40c. Type **598**	40	10
1833	45c. Nativity scene	40	10
1834	$1 Mary and Joseph	80	1·00
1832/4	*Set of 3*	1·40	1·00

(b) Self-adhesive. Phosphor frame. P 11½

1835	40c. Type **598**	30	30
	a. Booklet pane. No. 1835×20	5·00	

On Nos. 1832/4 the yellow parts of the designs are printed in fluorescent ink.

No. 1835 was only issued in $8 booklets, No. SB126, on which the surplus self-adhesive paper was retained.

599 Australian Coat of Arms

600 Arthur Boyd

(Des B. Sadgrove. Litho SNP Ausprint)

1999 (14 Jan). 50th Anniv of Australian Citizenship.

(a) Phosphorised paper. P 14×14½

1836 **599**	45c. multicoloured	50	50

(b) Self-adhesive. Phosphor frame around central oval. P 11½

1837 **599**	45c. multicoloured	40	40

No. 1837, on which the phosphor shows pink under U.V. light, was printed in rolls of 100 on which the surplus self-adhesive paper around each stamp was removed.

(Des Lisa Christensen. Litho SNP Ausprint)

1999 (22 Jan). Australian Legends (3rd series). Arthur Boyd (painter). T **600** and similar horiz design. Multicoloured.

(a) Phosphorised paper. P 14×14½

1838	45c. Type **600**	50	50
	a. Horiz pair. Nos. 1838/9	1·00	1·00
1839	45c. "Nebuchadnezzer on fire falling over Waterfall" (Arthur Boyd)	50	50

(b) Self-adhesive. Two phosphor bands over inscr panels. P 11½

1840	45c. Type **600**	50	50
	a. Booklet pane. Nos. 1840/1 each×5	4·25	
1841	45c. "Nebuchadnezzer on fire falling over Waterfall" (Arthur Boyd)	50	50

Nos. 1838/9 were printed together, *se-tenant*, in horizontal pairs throughout the sheet.

Nos. 1840/1 on which the phosphor shows pink under U.V. light, were only issued in $4.50 booklets, No. SB217, on which the surplus self-adhesive paper was retained.

601 Red Roses

602 Elderly Man and Grandmother with Boy

(Des Nicole Bryant. Litho SNP Ausprint)

1999 (4 Feb). Greetings Stamp. Romance.

(a) Phosphorised paper. P 14×14½

1842 **601**	45c. multicoloured	50	50

(b) Self-adhesive. Phosphor background. P 11½

1843 **601**	45c. multicoloured	40	40
	a. Booklet pane. No. 1843×10	3·75	

No. 1843, on which the phosphor shows pink under U.V. light, was only issued in $4.50 booklets, No. SB128, on which the surplus self-adhesive paper was retained.

(Des Lynda Warner. Litho McPherson's Ptg Group, Mulgrave)

1999 (11 Feb). International Year of Older Persons. T **602** and similar horiz design. Multicoloured. P 14×14½.

1844	45c. Type **602**	50	50
	a. Horiz pair. Nos. 1844/5	1·00	1·00
1845	45c. Elderly woman and grandfather with boy	50	50

Nos. 1844/5 were printed together, *se-tenant*, as horizontal pairs in sheets of 10.

603 *Polly Woodside* (barque)

604 Olympic Torch and 1956 7½d. Stamp

(Des Beth McKinlay. Litho SNP Ausprint)

1999 (19 Mar). Sailing Ships. T **603** and similar square designs. Multicoloured. Phosphor background (45c.) or phosphorised paper (others). P 14½×14.

1846	45c. Type **603**	60	35
1847	85c. *Alma Doepel* (topsail schooner)	1·00	1·10
1848	$1 *Enterprize replica* (topsail schooner)	1·25	1·10
1849	$1.05 *Lady Nelson replica* (topsail schooner)	1·40	1·90
1846/9	*Set of 4*	3·75	4·00

No. 1846, on which the phosphor appears pink under U.V. light, was printed in sheets with the stamps horizontally *se-tenant* with half stamp-size labels showing the "Australia '99" International Stamp Exhibition emblem. Examples available at the exhibition could be "personalised" by the addition of a portrait photograph in place of the logo on these labels for the cost of $10 per sheet of ten.

No. 1846 exists as half sheets of 10 numbered in red or black from a limited issue Maritime Heritage portfolio.

No. 1846 was re-issued on 1 September 1999 as part of the personalised Greetings Stamps range. This printing was on phosphorised paper.

No. 1846 was also issued in a sheetlet of 10 for "Encounter 2002".

(Litho SNP Ausprint)

1999 (19 Mar). Australia—Ireland Joint Issue. *Polly Woodside* (barque). Sheet 137×72 mm. Multicoloured. Phosphorised paper. P 14×14½.

MS1850 45c. Type **603**; 30p. Type **374** of Ireland (No. **MS**1850 was sold at $1.25 in Australia)	1·25	1·40

No. **MS**1850 includes the "Australia '99" emblem on the sheet margin and was postally valid in Australia to the value of 45c. The same miniature sheet was also available in Ireland.

(Litho Ashton-Potter Canada)

1999 (19 Mar). Australia–Canada Joint Issue. *Marco Polo* (emigrant ship). Sheet 160×95 mm. Multicoloured. Fluorescent frames. P 13½ (85c.) or 13 (46c.).

MS1851 85c. As No. 1728; 46c. Type **701** of Canada (No. **MS**1851 was sold at $1.30 in Australia)	1·25	1·40

No. **MS**1851, on which the fluorescent frame appears green under U.V. light, includes the "Australia '99" emblem on the sheet margin and was postally valid in Australia to the value of 85c. The same miniature sheet was also available in Canada.

(Litho SNP Ausprint)

1999 (19 Mar). Australia 99 International Stamp Exhibition, Melbourne. Two sheets, each 142×76 mm, containing designs as Nos. 398/403, but printed litho and all with face value of 45c. P 14×14½ (No. **MS**1852a) or 14½×14 (No. **MS**1852b).

MS1852 (a) 45c. deep ultramarine (Type **167**); 45c. grey-olive (Captain Cook); 45c. purple-brown (Flinders). (b) 45c. Indian red (Type **168**); 45c. deep olive-brown (Bass); 45c. deep reddish purple (King). *Set of* 2 sheets	2·50	2·75
c. Imperf. *Set of* 2 sheets	11·00	13·00

Designs in No. **MS**1852a are 37×25 mm and those in No. **MS**1852b 24×29 mm. The imperforate miniature sheets, No. **MS**1852c, could be perforated on machinery at the exhibition which also applied an "A99" perfin. Examples exist showing the perforations inverted or with other perforation varieties.

(Des FHA Image Design. Litho SNP Ausprint)

1999 (22 Mar). Olympic Torch Commemoration. P 14½×14.

1853	**604**	$1.20 multicoloured	1·10	1·10

605 *Correa reflexa* (Native Fuschia)

606 Queen Elizabeth II with Queen Mother

(Des W. Rankin)

1999 (8 Apr–8 Jul). Fauna and Flora (3rd series). Coastal Environment. T **605** and similar horiz designs. Multicoloured.

(a) Litho SNP Ausprint. Phosphorised paper. P 14×14½

1854	45c. Type **605**	50	60
	a. Block of 4. Nos. 1854/7	1·75	2·25
1855	45c. *Hibbertia scandens* (Guinea Flower)	50	60
1856	45c. *Ipomoea pes-caprae* (Beach Morning Glory)	50	60
1857	45c. *Wahlenbergia stricta* (Australian Bluebells)	50	60
1858	70c. Humpback Whales and Zebra Volute shell (8.7.99)	1·00	70
1859	90c. Brahminy Kite and Checkerboard Helmet shell (8.7.99)	90	1·00
	a. Horiz pair. Nos. 1859/60	1·75	2·00
1860	90c. Fraser Island and Chambered Nautilus (8.7.99)	90	1·00
1861	$1.05 Loggerhead Turtle and Melon shell (8.7.99)	1·00	80
1862	$1.20 White-bellied Sea Eagle and Campbell's Stromb shell (8.7.99)	1·25	90
1854/62	*Set of 9*	6·25	5·25

(b) Self-adhesive. Litho SNP Ausprint (Nos. 1863/6) or Pemara (Nos. 1863d/6d). Phosphor frame. P 11½

1863	45c. Type **605**	35	40
	a. Booklet pane. Nos. 1863 and 1865, each ×3, and Nos. 1864 and 1866, each ×2	3·50	
	b. Sheetlet of 5. Nos. 1863, 1864×2 and 1865/6	1·75	
	c. Booklet pane. Nos. 1863/6, each ×5 (8.7.99)	6·00	
	d. Perf 12½×13	35	40
	da. Booklet pane. Nos. 1863d and 1865d, each ×3	3·50	
1864	45c. *Hibbertia scandens* (Guinea Flower)	35	40
	d. Perf 12½×13	35	40
1865	45c. *Ipomoea pes-caprae* (Beach Morning Glory)	35	40
	d. Perf 12½×13	35	40
1866	45c. *Wahlenbergia stricta* (Australian Bluebells)	35	40
	d. Perf 12½×13	35	40
1863/6	*Set of 4*	1·40	1·60
1863d/6d	*Set of 4*	1·40	1·60

Nos. 1854/7 were printed together, *se-tenant*, in sheets of 50 containing ten blocks of 4 and ten single stamps.

Nos. 1859/60 were printed together, *se-tenant*, in horizontal pairs throughout the sheet, each pair forming a composite design.

Nos. 1863/6 and 1863d/6d, on which the phosphor appears pink under U.V. light, were printed in rolls of 100 with the surplus paper around each stamp removed. The SNP Ausprint printing subsequently appeared in rolls of 200. They also come in $4.50 (SB129/ba) and $9 (SB131) booklets or sheetlets of 5, containing Nos. 1863a/c or 1863da, on which the surplus paper was retained.

Nos. 1867/9 are vacant.

(Des A. Christensen. Litho SNP Ausprint)

1999 (15 Apr). Queen Elizabeth II's Birthday. P 14×14½.

1870	**606**	45c. multicoloured	70	50

607 *Here's Humphrey*

608 Obverse and Reverse of 1899 Sovereign

(Des P. Ellett. Litho SNP Ausprint)

1999 (6 May). Children's Television Programmes. T **607** and similar vert designs. Multicoloured.

(a) Phosphorised paper. P 14½×14

1871	45c. Type **607**	40	45
	a. Horiz strip of 5. Nos. 1871/5	1·75	2·00
1872	45c. *Bananas in Pyjamas*	40	45
1873	45c. *Mr. Squiggle*	40	45
1874	45c. *Play School* (teddy bears)	40	45
1875	45c. *Play School* (clock, toy dog and doll)	40	45
1871/5 *Set of 5*		1·75	2·00

(b) Self-adhesive. Phosphor three-sided frame. P 11½×11

1876	45c. Type 607	40	60
	a. Booklet pane. Nos. 1876/80, each ×2	3·50	
1877	45c. *Bananas in Pyjamas*	40	60
1878	45c. *Mr. Squiggle*	40	60
1879	45c. *Play School* (teddy bears)	40	60
1880	45c. *Play School* (clock, toy dog and doll)	40	60
1876/80 *Set of 5*		1·75	2·75

Nos. 1871/5 were printed together, *se-tenant*, as horizontal strips of 5 in sheets of 10.

Nos. 1876/80, on which the phosphor appears pink under U. V. light, were only available in $4.50 booklets, No. SB130, on which the surplus self-adhesive paper was retained.

(Des Janet Boschen. Litho SNP Ausprint (gold embossed Avon Graphics))

1999 (13 May). Centenary of the Perth Mint. P 14½×14.

1881	**608**	$2 gold, ultramarine and grey-green	2·00	1·75

609 Lineout against New Zealand

610 Drilling at Burn's Creek and Rock Bolting in Tumut 2 Power Station Hall

(Des M. Sofilas. Litho SNP Ausprint)

1999 (8 June). Centenary of Australian Test Rugby. T **609** and similar multicoloured designs.

(a) Phosphorised paper. P 14½×14 (45c.) or 14×14½ (others)

1882	45c. Type **609**	40	40
	a. Pair. Nos. 1882/3	80	80
1883	45c. Kicking the ball against England	40	40
1884	$1 Try against South Africa (*horiz*)	80	65
1885	$1.20 Passing the ball against Wales (*horiz*)	90	1·00
1882/5 *Set of 4*		2·25	2·25

(b) Self-adhesive. Phosphor background. P 11½

1886	45c. Type **609**	50	50
	a. Vert pair. Nos. 1886/7	1·00	1·00
1887	45c. Kicking the ball against England	50	50

Nos. 1882/3 were printed together, *se-tenant*, in horizontal or vertical pairs throughout the sheet.

Nos. 1886/7, on which the phosphor appears pink under U.V. light, were only available in rolls of 100 on which the surplus paper around each stamp was removed.

(Des Fragile Design. Litho SNP Ausprint)

1999 (12 Aug). 50th Anniv of Snowy Mountain Scheme (hydro-electric project). T **610** and similar horiz designs. Multicoloured.

(a) Phosphorised paper. P 14×14½

1888	45c. Type **610**	65	65
	a. Block of 4. Nos. 1888/91	2·40	2·40
1889	45c. English class for migrant workers, Cooma	65	65
1890	45c. Tumut 2 Tailwater Tunnel and Eucumbene Dam	65	65
1891	45c. German carpenters and Island Bend Dam	65	65
1888/91 *Set of 4*		2·40	2·40

(b) Self-adhesive. Phosphor frame. P 11½

1892	45c. Type **610**	1·10	1·50
	a. Horiz strip of 4. Nos. 1892/5	4·00	5·50
1893	45c. English class for migrant workers, Cooma	1·10	1·50
1894	45c. Tumut 2 Tailwater Tunnel and Eucumbene Dam	1·10	1·50
1895	45c. German carpenters and Island Bend Dam	1·10	1·50
1892/5 *Set of 4*		4·00	5·50

Nos. 1888/91 were printed together, *se-tenant* in sheets of 50 (2 panes of 5×5), each sheet providing ten blocks of 4 and ten single stamps.

Nos. 1892/5, on which the phosphor shows pink under U.V. light, were printed in rolls of 100 on which the surplus self-adhesive paper around each stamp was removed.

611 Calligraphy Pen and Letter

612 Sydney Olympic Emblem

(Des C. Shurey. Litho SNP Ausprint)

1999 (1 Sept). Greetings Stamps. T **611** and similar square designs. Multicoloured. Phosphorised paper ($1) or phosphor background (others). P 14½×14.

1896	45c. Type **611**	50	55
1897	45c. Wedding rings	50	55
1898	45c. Birthday cake	50	55
1899	45c. Christmas decoration	50	55
1900	45c. Teddy bear	50	55
1901	$1 Koala	1·00	1·25
1896/1901 *Set of 6*		3·25	3·50

Nos. 1896/1901 were each printed in sheets of 20 stamps and 20 *se-tenant* labels inscribed with greetings messages. Labels initially measured 23×30 mm (No. 1899), or 16×30 mm (others), but printings of all designs, including No. 1846, contained 20×30 mm labels from mid-2000 onwards.

No. 1846 was reissued at the same time in a similar format. This printing differs from previous examples of this stamp by being on phosphorised paper instead of having a phosphor background.

Nos. 1896/1901 together with the new printing of No. 1846, were also available with the inscriptions on the *se-tenant* labels replaced by personal photographs. This service was only available by mail order.

Stamps as No. 1897 but on phosphorised paper were issued on 11 May 2002 in premium booklets, No. SP1, sold at $9.95.

See also No. 1921.

See No. 2061 for design as 1901 but International Post.

(Des FHA Image Design. Litho McPherson's Ptg Group, Mulgrave)

1999 (14 Sept). Olympic Games, Sydney (2000) (1st issue). P 14½×14.

1902	**612**	45c. multicoloured	1·50	60

See also Nos. 2005/24.

613 Australia Post Symbol, 1975

614 Magnificent Tree Frog

(Des Lynda Warner. Litho SNP Ausprint)

1999 (16 Sept). Sydney Design '99 International Congress and Exhibition. T **613** and similar horiz designs. Multicoloured. P 14×14½.

1903	45c. Type **613**	35	20
1904	90c. Embryo chair, 1988	65	70
1905	$1.35 Possum skin textile, c 1985	1·00	1·25
1906	$1.50 Storey Hall, R.M.I.T. University, 1995	1·00	1·25
1903/6 *Set of 4*		2·75	3·00

(Des Cathleen Cram and K. Stead. Litho SNP Ausprint)

1999 (1 Oct). National Stamp Collecting Month, Small Pond Life. T **614** and similar multicoloured designs.

(a) Phosphorised paper. P 14×14½ (Nos. 1909/10) or 14½×14 (others)

1907	45c. Type **614**	55	55
	a. Pair. Nos. 1907/8	1·10	1·10
1908	45c. Sacred Kingfisher	55	55
1909	45c. Roth's Tree Frog (29×24 *mm*)	55	55
	a. Pair. Nos. 1909/10	1·10	1·10
1910	45c. Dragonfly (29×24 *mm*)	55	55
1911	50c. Javelin Frog (24×29 *mm*)	65	65
	a. Pair. Nos. 1911/12	1·25	1·25
1912	50c. Northern Dwarf Tree Frog (24×29 *mm*)	65	65
1907/12 *Set of 6*		3·00	3·00
MS1913 166×73 mm. Nos. 1907/12. P 14½		3·00	3·25

(b) Self-adhesive. Phosphor background. P 11½

1914	45c. Type **614**	35	50
	a. Pair. Nos. 1914/15	70	1·00
1915	45c. Sacred Kingfisher	35	50
1916	50c. Javelin Frog (24×29 *mm*)	40	55
	a. Booklet pane. Nos. 1916/17, each ×5	4·00	
1917	50c. Northern Dwarf Tree Frog (24×29 *mm*)	40	55
1914/17 *Set of 4*		1·50	1·90

Nos. 1907/8, 1909/10 and 1911/12 were each printed together, *se-tenant*, in horizontal or vertical pairs throughout the sheets.

On No. **MS**1913 the wings of the dragonfly are printed by silver foil die stamping. The miniature sheet also exists overprinted with either the "Adelaide Stampex 99" or the "Bangkok 2000" logos for sale at these stamp exhibitions.

Nos. 1914/15 were printed in rolls of 100 on which the surplus self-adhesive paper around each stamp was removed. Nos. 1916/17 were printed in $5 booklets, No. SB132, containing No. 1916a on which the surplus paper was retained. All four self-adhesive stamps show large parts of the background overprinted with phosphor which appears pink under U.V. light.

615 Madonna and Child

616 Fireworks and Hologram

(Des J. Coburn. Litho SNP Ausprint)

1999 (1 Nov). Christmas. T **615** and similar multicoloured design.

(a) Phosphorised paper. P 14½×14 (40c.) or 14×14½ ($1)

1918	40c. Type **615**	50	15
1919	$1 Tree of Life (*horiz*)	1·00	1·10

(b) Self-adhesive. Phosphor frame. P 11½

1920	40c. Type **615**	30	35
	a. Booklet pane. No. 1925×20	5·00	

No. 1920 was printed in $8 booklets, No. SB133, containing No. 1920a on which the surplus self-adhesive paper around each stamp was retained.

(Des C. Shurey. Litho SNP Ausprint)

1999 (1 Nov). Millennium Greetings Stamp. P 14½×14.

1921	**616** 45c. multicoloured	50	50

No. 1921 was printed in sheetlets of 10 or 20 with *se-tenant* labels, and was available with the greetings label (16×30 *mm*) replaced by a personal photograph. This and subsequent "personalised" greetings stamps were also produced with the sheet margins, and sometimes also the labels, printed to commemorate various events.

No. 1921 was issued in sheets of 20 with *se-tenant* labels, for "Stamp Show 2000", London and "EXPO '2000" World Stamp Exhibition, Anaheim, USA.

617 Rachael Thomson (college administrator)

618 Walter Parker

(Des Jo Mure. Litho McPherson's Ptg Group, Mulgrave)

2000 (1 Jan). New Millennium. "Face of Australia". T **617** and similar vert designs. Multicoloured. P 14½×14.

1922	45c. Nicholle and Meghan Triandis (twin babies)	30	55
	a. Sheetlet of 25. Nos. 1922/46	7·00	12·00
1923	45c. David Willis (cattleman)	30	55
1924	45c. Natasha Bramley (scuba diver)	30	55
1925	45c. Cyril Watson (Aborigine boy)	30	55
1926	45c. Mollie Dowdall (wearing red hat) (vineyard worker)	30	55
1927	45c. Robin Dicks (flying instructor)	30	55
1928	45c. Mary Simons (retired nurse)	30	55
1929	45c. Peta and Samantha Nieuwerth (mother and baby)	30	55
1930	45c. John Matthews (doctor)	30	55
1931	45c. Edith Dizon-Fitzsimmons (wearing drop earrings) (music teacher)	30	55
1932	45c. Philippa Weir (wearing brown hat) (teacher)	30	55
1933	45c. John Thurgar (in bush hat and jacket) (farmer)	30	55
1934	45c. Miguel Alzona (with face painted) (schoolboy)	30	55
1935	45c. Type **617**	30	55
1936	45c. Necip Akarsu (wearing blue shirt) (postmaster)	30	55
1937	45c. Justin Allan (R.A.N. sailor)	30	55
1938	45c. Wadad Dennaoui (wearing checked shirt) (student)	30	55
1939	45c. Jack Laity (market gardener)	30	55
1940	45c. Kelsey Stubbin (wearing cricket cap) (schoolboy)	30	55
1941	45c. Gianna Rossi (resting chin on hand) (church worker)	30	55
1942	45c. Paris Hansch (toddler)	30	55
1943	45c. Donald George Whatham (in blue shirt and tie) (retired teacher)	30	55
1944	45c. Stacey Coull (wearing pendant) (schoolgirl)	30	55
1945	45c. Alex Payne (wearing cycle helmet) (schoolboy)	30	55
1946	45c. John Lodge (Salvation Army member)	30	55
1922/46 *Set of 25*		7·00	12·00

Nos. 1922/46 were printed together, *se-tenant*, in sheetlets of 25.

(Des Cathleen Cram. Litho SNP Ausprint)

2000 (25 Jan). Australian Legends (4th series). Australia Day. "The Last Anzacs". T **618** and similar horiz designs. Multicoloured.

(a) Phosphorised paper. P 14×14½

1947	45c. Type **618**	55	55
	a. Block of 4. Nos. 1947/50	2·00	2·00
1948	45c. Roy Longmore	55	55
1949	45c. Alec Campbell	55	55
1950	45c. 1914–15 Star (medal)	55	55
1947/50 *Set of 4*		2·00	2·00

(b) Self-adhesive. Two phosphor bands over inscr panels. P 11½

1951	45c. Type **618**	35	40
	a. Booklet pane. Nos. 1951/3×2 and No. 1954×4	3·50	
	ab. Booklet pane. Gold (face value and map) omitted from both examples of No. 1953	£1800	
1952	45c. Roy Longmore	35	40
1953	45c. Alec Campbell	35	40
1954	45c. 1914–15 Star (medal)	35	40
1951/4 *Set of 4*		1·40	1·60

Nos. 1947/50 were printed together, *se-tenant*, in sheets of 50 (2 panes of 5×5), each sheet providing ten blocks of 4 and ten single stamps.

Nos. 1951/4, on which the phosphor shows pink under U.V. light, were only issued in $4.50 booklets, No. SB134, on which the surplus self-adhesive paper was retained.

619 Scenes from *Cloudstreet* (play) (Perth Festival)

620 Coast Banksia, False Sarsaparilla and Swamp Bloodwood (plants)

(Des W. Rankin. Litho McPherson's Ptg Group, Mulgrave)

2000 (24 Feb). Arts Festivals. T **619** and similar vert designs. Multicoloured. P 14½×14.

1955	45c. Type **619**	45	50
	a. Horiz strip of 5. Nos. 1955/9	2·00	2·25
1956	45c. Belgian dancers from Rosas Company (Adelaide Festival)	45	50
1957	45c. "Guardian Angel" (sculpture) and dancer (Sydney Festival)	45	50
1958	45c. Musician and Balinese dancer (Melbourne Festival)	45	50
1959	45c. Members of Vusa Dance Company of South Africa (Brisbane Festival)	45	50
1955/9 *Set of 5*		2·00	2·25

Nos. 1955/9 were printed together, *se-tenant*, in horizontal strips of 5.

(Des Marg Towt. Litho SNP Ausprint)

2000 (23 Mar). Gardens. T **620** and similar vert designs. Multicoloured.

(a) Phosphorised paper. P 14½×14

1960	45c. Type **620**	45	50
	a. Horiz strip of 5. Nos. 1960/4	2·00	2·25
1961	45c. Eastern Spinebill on Swamp Bottlebrush in foreground	45	50

1962	45c. Border of Cannas	45	50
1963	45c. Roses, lake and ornamental bridge	45	50
1964	45c. Hibiscus with bandstand in background	45	50
1960/4 *Set of 5*		2·00	2·25

(b) Self-adhesive. Phosphor frame. P 11½

1965	45c. Type **620**	40	55
	a. Strip of 5. Nos. 1965/9	1·75	2·50
	b. Booklet pane. Nos. 1965/9, each ×2	3·50	
1966	45c. Eastern Spinebill on Swamp Bottlebrush in foreground	40	55
1967	45c. Border of Cannas	40	55
1968	45c. Roses, lake and ornamental bridge	40	55
1969	45c. Hibiscus with bandstand in background	40	55
1965/9 *Set of 5*		1·75	2·50

Nos. 1960/4 were printed together, *se-tenant*, as horizontal strips of 5 in sheets of 10 (5×2).

Nos. 1965/9 are smaller, 26×37 mm, and were issued either as rolls of 100, on which the surplus self-adhesive paper was removed, or in booklets of 10, No. SB135, on which the surplus paper was retained. On both versions the phosphor frame shows pink under U.V. light.

621 Queen Elizabeth II in 1996

622 Medals and Korean Landscape

(Des C. McPartlin. Litho McPherson's Ptg Group, Mulgrave)

2000 (13 Apr). Queen Elizabeth II's Birthday. P 14×14½.

1970	**621**	45c. multicoloured	80	50

(Des B. Sadgrove. Litho McPherson's Ptg Group, Mulgrave)

2000 (18 Apr). 50th Anniv of Korean War. P 14×14½.

1971	**622**	45c. multicoloured	60	50

623 Daisy

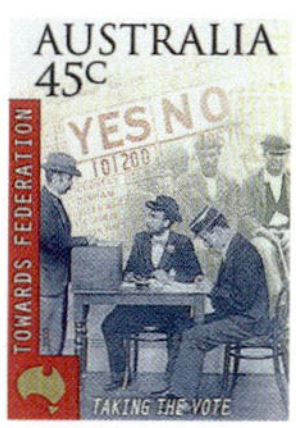

624 Taking the Vote, New South Wales

(Des C. Shurey (Nos. 1972/4), Cozzolino Ellett Design (No. 1975), W. Rankin (No. 1976). Litho SNP Ausprint)

2000 (11 May). "Nature and Nation". Greetings Stamps. T **623** and similar square designs. Multicoloured. Phosphor ink (No. 1972), phosphorised paper (No. 1974) or phosphor frame (others). P 14½×14.

1972	45c. Type **623**	45	50
1973	45c. Australia on globe	45	50
1974	45c. Red Kangaroo and flag	45	50
1975	45c. Sand, sea and sky	45	50
1976	45c. Rainforest	45	50
1972/6 *Set of 5*		2·00	2·25

The phosphor frames on Nos. 1973 and 1975/6 appear pink under U. V. light. On No. 1975 the bands form an incomplete frame.

Nos. 1972/6 were each issued in sheets of 20, each stamp having a *se-tenant* 20×30 mm label attached at the right repeating the title of the design. These sheets occur with or without decorative margins. From 19 June 2000 the sheets with decorative margins could be "personalised" by the addition of a portrait photograph in place of the logos on the labels.

In 2000 and 2001, in conjunction with the Australian Football League, No. 1973 was issued in sheets of 20, the *se-tenant* labels featuring images of each club's players with team logos in the sheet margins.

Seven sheets were also produced in connection with the 2000 Paralympian of the Year award, with the labels in each sheet showing one of the seven category winners.

Nos. 1973 and 1974 were each issued in sheets of 10 or 20 with *se-tenant* labels to celebrate various special events. These sheets were sold at a premium above face value.

No. 1975 was issued in sheets of 20 with *se-tenant* labels in May 2002 for the 20 Australian Football League Clubs.

(Des Asprey Di Donato Design. Litho McPherson's Ptg Group, Mulgrave)

2000 (24 May). Centenary of Commonwealth of Australia Constitution Act. T **624** and similar vert designs. Multicoloured. P 14½×14 (45c.) or 14×14½ ($1.50).

1977	45c. Type **624**	45	40
	a. Pair	90	80
1978	45c. Voters waiting for results, Geraldton, Western Australia	45	40
1979	$1.50 Queen Victoria	1·25	1·40
	a. Pair	2·50	2·75
1980	$1.50 Women dancing ("The Fair New Nation")	1·25	1·40
1977/80 *Set of 4*		3·00	3·25
MS1981 153×89 mm. Nos. 1977/80		3·00	3·25

Nos. 1977/8 and 1979/80 were each printed together, *se-tenant*, both horizontally and vertically within sheets of 50.

No. **MS**1981 also exists overprinted with "The Stamp Show 2000" logo for sale at this international exhibition.

625 Sydney Opera House, New South Wales

626 Tennis Player in Wheelchair

(Des Beth McKinlay. Litho SNP Ausprint)

2000 (20 June). International Stamps. Views of Australia (1st series). T **625** and similar horiz designs. Multicoloured. P 14½×14 (Nos. 1982/6) or 14×14½ (others).

1982	50c. Type **625**	1·00	20
1983	$1 Nandroya Falls, Queensland	1·60	20
1984	$1.50, Sydney Harbour Bridge, New South Wales	2·00	55
1985	$2 Cradle Mountain, Tasmania	2·25	55
1986	$3 The Pinnacles, Western Australia	2·50	1·25
1987	$4.50 Flinders Ranges, South Australia (*51×24 mm*)	3·75	2·00
1988	$5 Twelve Apostles, Victoria (*51×24 mm*)	4·00	1·75
1989	$10 Devil's Marbles, Northern Territory (*51×24 mm*)	8·25	4·50
1982/9 *Set of 8*		23·00	10·00

Nos. 1982/9 were intended for international postage which, under changes in Australian tax laws from 1 July 2000, remained exempt from Goods and Services Tax. From 1 February 2001 only International stamps were valid on overseas mail and from that date could not be used on items posted to Australian addresses.

See also Nos. 2121/5, 2195/9, 2219/22 and 2423/6.

(Des F.H.A. Image Design. Litho SNP Ausprint)

2000 (3 July). Paralympic Games, Sydney (1st issue). T **626** and similar vert designs. Multicoloured.

(a) Phosphorised paper. P 14½×14

1990	45c. Type **626**	40	40
	a. Pair. Nos. 1990/1	80	80
1991	45c. Amputee sprinting	40	40
1992	49c. Basketball player in wheelchair	40	40
	a. Strip of 3. Nos. 1992/4	1·10	1·10
1993	49c. Blind cyclist	40	40
1994	49c. Amputee putting the shot	40	40
	a. Tasmania omitted from map at bottom left (Left pane R. 3/1)	17·00	
1990/4 *Set of 5*		1·75	1·75

(b) Self-adhesive. Phosphor frame. P 11½

1995	45c. Type **626**	50	80
	a. Vert pair. Nos. 1995/670	1·00	1·60
1996	45c. Amputee sprinting	50	80
1997	49c. Basketball player	30	90
	a. Booklet pane. Nos. 1997/8 each×4 and No. 1999×2	3·00	
	b. Perf 11½×11 (31.1.01)	50	90
	ba. Booklet pane. Nos. 1997b/8b each×4 and 1999b ×2	5·00	
1998	49c. Blind cyclist	30	90
	b. Perf 11½×11 (31.1.01)	50	90
1999	49c. Amputee putting the shot	65	2·00
	b. Perf 11½×11 (31.1.01)	80	2·00
1995/9 *Set of 5*		2·00	4·75

Nos. 1990/1 and 1992/4 were each printed together, *se-tenant*, as horizontal or vertical pairs or strips of 3 in sheets of 50.

Nos. 1995/6 were issued *se-tenant* in rolls of 100 on which the surplus self-adhesive paper was removed.

Nos. 1997/9 were only available in $4.90 stamp booklets, No. SB136, on which the surplus self-adhesive paper was retained.

Nos. 1997b/9b come from the 1 koala printing of the booklet.

All self-adhesive stamps show a phosphor frame, which appears pink under U.V. light, at left and foot.

See also Nos. 2053/4.

627 Sir Neville Howse (first Australian recipient of Victoria Cross, 1990)

628 Water Polo

(Des Cathleen Cram. Litho McPherson's Ptg Group, Mulgrave)

2000 (24 July). Centenary of Australia's First Victoria Cross Award. T **627** and similar vert designs. P 14½×14.

2000	45c. multicoloured	70	50
	a. Horiz strip of 5. Nos. 2000/4	3·25	2·25
2001	45c. reddish brown, gold and black	70	50
2002	45c. multicoloured	70	50
2003	45c. multicoloured	70	50
2004	45c. reddish brown, gold and black	70	50
2000/4 *Set of 5*		3·25	2·25

Designs—No. 2000, Type **627**; No. 2001, Sir Roden Cutler, 1941; No. 2002, Victoria Cross; No. 2003, Private Edward Kenna, 1945; No. 2004, Warrant Officer Keith Payne, 1969.

Nos. 2000/4 were printed together, *se-tenant*, as horizontal strips of 5 in sheets of 50.

(Des FHA Image Design. Litho SNP Ausprint)

2000 (17 Aug). Olympic Games, Sydney (2nd issue). T **628** and similar vert designs. Multicoloured.

(a) Phosphorised paper . Competitors highlighted in varnish. P 14½×14

2005	45c. Type **628**	30	30
	a. Sheetlet. Nos. 2005/14	2·75	2·75
2006	45c. Hockey	30	30
2007	45c. Swimming	30	30
2008	45c. Basketball	30	30
2009	45c. Cycling (triathlon)	30	30
2010	45c. Horse riding	30	30
2011	45c. Tennis	30	30
2012	45c. Gymnastics	30	30
2013	45c. Running	30	30
2014	45c. Rowing	30	30
2005/14 *Set of 10*		2·75	2·75

(b) Self-adhesive. Phosphor bands. P 11½*

2015	45c. Swimming	35	40
	a. Booklet pane. Nos. 2015/24	3·00	
2016	45c. Gymnastics	35	40
2017	45c. Basketball	35	40
2018	45c. Cycling (triathlon)	35	40
2019	45c. Running	35	40
2020	45c. Rowing	35	40
2021	45c. Type **628**	35	40
2022	45c. Hockey	35	40
2023	45c. Horse riding	35	40
2024	45c. Tennis	35	40
2015/24 *Set of 10*		3·00	3·50

*On Nos. 2015/20 the phosphor, which shows pink under U.V. light, appears on part of the background, but on Nos. 2021/4 it was applied over the competitors and as a horizontal band.

No. 2005*a* also exists overprinted with the Olymphilex 2000 logo for sale at that exhibition.

Nos. 2005/14 were printed together, *se-tenant*, in sheetlets of 10 with the backgrounds forming a composite design. Nos. 2015/24 were only available in $4.50 stamp booklets, No. SB137, on which the surplus self-adhesive paper was retained.

628a

2000 (Sept). International Mail. As No. 1901 but perf 14×14½, optd with T **628a** in blue.

2024*a*	$1 Koala	5·50	2·25

No. 2024a was first issued as a "personalised" stamp in sheets of 20 with *se-tenant* labels, perf 14×14½ with a printed phosphor background. These sheets were sold at a premium. It was subsequently made generally available, but on phosphorised paper, the *se-tenant* label depicting Australia Post employee, Angela Thom. The earliest recorded date of use of the "general" issue is 8 Sept 2000.

629 Olympic Flag, Flame and Parthenon

630 Ian Thorpe (Men's 400m Freestyle Swimming)

(Des Lynda Warner. Litho SNP Ausprint)

2000 (15 Sept). Transfer of Olympic Flag from Sydney to Athens. Joint issue with Greece. T **629** and similar square design. Multicoloured. Phosphor on flag and white background. P 14½×14.

2025	45c. Type **629**	40	20
2026	$1.50 Olympic Flag, Flame and Sydney Opera House	1·25	1·25

Nos. 2025/6 were each issued with a *se-tenant* label at right (20×30 *mm*), inscribed "Sydney Athens" (45c.) or "International POST" ($1.50), and were also available with the label replaced by a personal photograph. They also exist in sheets overprinted with the Olymphilex logo.

Stamps in similar designs were issued by Greece.

Stamps printed digitally at six different sites. (Nos. 2027A/42A). Under magnification the Australian flag, Olympic rings and inscriptions have blurred outlines, somewhat similar to those found on stamps printed by photogravure. There is a coarse screen, which on areas of colour shows as lines, often diagonal.

Stamps printed in lithography by SNP Ausprint (Nos. 2027B/42B). Australian flag, Olympic and inscriptions show sharp and clear outlines. The screen is very fine and is barely visible under ×10 magnification. There are no lines visible in the areas of colour.

(Des Beth McKinlay)

2000 (17 Sept-3 Oct). Australian Gold Medal Winners at Sydney Olympic Games. T **630** and similar square designs. Multicoloured. P 14.

(a) Printed digitally at six different locations by Fuji Xerox Australia Pty Ltd using Xerox DocuColour 40 colour copiers/printers

2027A	45c. Type **630**	40	45
2028A	45c. Australian team (Men's 4×100 m Freestyle Swimming Relay)	40	45
2029A	45c. Michael Diamond (Men's Trap Shooting) (18 Sept)	40	45
2030A	45c. Australian team (Three Day Equestrian Event) (20 Sept)	40	45

2031A	45c. Susie O'Neill (Women's 200 m Freestyle Swimming) (20 Sept)	40	45
2032A	45c. Australian team (Men's 4 ×200 m Freestyle Swimming Relay) (20 Sept)	40	45
	a. Printing inverted (sheetlet of ten)		
2033A	45c. Simon Fairweather (Men's Individual Archery) (21 Sept)	40	45
2034A	45c. Australian team (Men's Madison Cycling) (22 Sept)	40	45
2035A	45c. Grant Hackett (Men's 1500 m Freestyle Swimming) (24 Sept)	40	45
2036A	45c. Australian team (Women's Water Polo) (24.9)	40	45
2037A	45c. Australian team (Women's Beach Volleyball) (26.9)	40	45
2038A	45c. Cathy Freeman (Women's 400 m Athletics) (26.9)	40	45
2039A	45c. Lauren Burns (Women's under 49 kg Taekwondo) (28.9)	40	45
2040A	45c. Australian team (Women's Hockey) (30.9)	40	45
	a. Printing inverted (sheetlet of ten)		
2041A	45c. Australian crew (Women's 470 Dinghy Sailing) (1.10)	40	45
2042A	45c. Australian crew (Men's 470 Dinghy Sailing) (1.10)	40	45
2027A/42A	*Set of* 16	6·00	6·50

(b) Litho. SNP Ausprint

2027B	45c. Type **630** (19.9)	35	50
2028B	45c. Australian team (Men's 4×100 m Freestyle Swimming Relay) (19.9)	35	50
2029B	45c. Michael Diamond (Men's Trap Shooting) (20.9)	35	50
2030B	45c. Australian team (Three Day Equestrian Event) (22.9)	35	50
2031B	45c. Susie O'Neill (Women's 200 m Freestyle Swimming) (22.9)	35	50
2032B	45c. Australian team (Men's 4×200 m Freestyle Swimming Relay) (22.9)	35	50
2033B	45c. Simon Fairweather (Men's Individual Archery) (23.9)	35	50
2034B	45c. Australian team (Men's Madison Cycling) (24.9)	35	50
2035B	45c. Grant Hackett (Men's 1500 m Freestyle Swimming) (26.9)	35	50
2036B	45c. Australian team (Women's Water Polo) (26.9)	35	50
2037B	45c. Australian team (Women's Beach Volleyball) (28.9)	35	50
2038B	45c. Cathy Freeman (Women's 400m Athletics) (28.9)	35	50
2039B	45c. Lauren Burns (Women's under 49 kg Taekwondo) (30.9)	35	50
2040B	45c. Australian team (Women's Hockey) (2.10)	35	50
2041B	45c. Australian crew (Women's 470 Dinghy Sailing) (3.10)	35	50
2042B	45c. Australian crew (Men's 470 Dinghy Sailing) (3.10)	35	50
2027B/42B	*Set of* 16	5·00	7·00

In an effort to minimise the time between the winning of a medal and the appearance of the commemorative stamp, special arrangements were made for the production of Nos. 2027/42. Each design was in a standard layout and issued in a standard sheet of 10 (2×5) with an enlarged inscribed margin at right.

As soon as a medal had been awarded, a team at Alexandria New South Wales prepared two designs using the standard layout. The selected version was then circulated by ISDN lines to six locations throughout the country where the stamps were produced by Fuji Xerox Australia Pty Ltd using Xerox DocuColour 40 colour printers. Stamps were printed, two sheets at a time, onto pre-gummed and perforated paper.

On "Printing inverted" sheetlets the stamp images are on the opposite side to the perforations.

The location of each digital printing site can be identified by the imprint shown at the bottom right-hand corner of each sheet: Platypus-New South Wales; Possum-Victoria; Koala-Queensland; Swan-Western Australia; Kangaroo-South Australia; Kookaburra-Australian Capital Territory. Supplies for Tasmania were provided by the Victoria site and those for the Northern Territory by South Australia. Sheets from the printing centres were distributed to 67 designated postal outlets by noon of the day following the award of the medal.

Further supplies of each design were produced by SNP Ausprint using lithography, again on to pre-perforated paper. These sheets show a small map of Australia at bottom right. The stamps printed by lithography were available nationwide by noon three days after each medal had been awarded.

A miniature sheet containing Nos. 2027B/42B and 2052 was only issued as part of the 2000 Annual Collection album costing A$87.50.

631 Martian Terrain

632 Cathy Freeman with Olympic Torch and Ring of Flames

(Des Beth McKinlay and O. Schmidinger. Litho SNP Ausprint)

2000 (3 Oct). Stamp Collecting Month. Exploration of Mars. T **631** and similar multicoloured designs.

(a) Phosphorised paper. P 14×14½ (Nos. 2046/7) or 14½×14 (others)

2043	45c. Type **631**	35	35
	a. Pair. Nos. 2043/4	70	70
2044	45c. Astronaut using thrusters	35	35
2045	45c. Spacecraft (50×30 *mm*)	35	35
2046	45c. Flight crew (30×25 *mm*)	35	35
2047	45c. Launch site (30×50 *mm*)	35	35
2048	45c. Robots on kelp rod (25×30 *mm*)	35	35
2043/8	*Set of* 6	1·90	1·90
MS2049	166×73 mm. Nos. 2043/8. P 14½	1·90	2·25

(b) Self-adhesive. Designs 26×37 mm. Phosphor frame. P 11½

2050	45c. Type **631**	45	45
	a. Pair. Nos. 2050/1	90	90
	b. Booklet pane. Nos. 2050/1, each ×5	3·50	
2051	45c. Astronaut using thrusters	45	45

Nos. 2043/4 were printed together, *se-tenant*, as horizontal or vertical pairs throughout the sheet.

Some features on No. **MS**2049 were printed in translucent foil producing a shiny effect.

MS2049 also exists overprinted with the Hong Kong 2001 logo for sale at that exhibition.

Nos. 2050/1 were printed either in rolls of 100, on which the surplus self-adhesive paper around each stamp was removed, or in $4.50 booklets, No. SB138, containing No. 2050b on which the surplus paper was retained. All self-adhesive stamps show a phosphor frame which appears pink under U.V. light.

(Des Janet Boschen. Litho SNP Ausprint)

2000 (10 Oct). Opening Ceremony, Olympic Games, Sydney. P 14.

2052	**632**	45c. multicoloured	1·00	50

633 Blind Athlete carrying Olympic Torch

634 Siobhan Paton (swimmer)

(Des FHA Image Design. Litho SNP Ausprint)

2000 (18 Oct). Paralympic Games, Sydney (2nd issue). T **633** and similar horiz design. Multicoloured. P 14½×14.

2053	45c. Type **633**	55	50
2054	45c. Paralympic Games logo	55	50

Nos. 2053/4 were printed in similar format sheets to Nos. 1896/1901 with *se-tenant* half stamp-sized labels available for "personalised" photographs.

(Des Stacey Zass. Litho SNP Ausprint)

2000 (31 Oct). Siobhan Paton, Paralympian of the Year. P 14½.

2055	**634**	45c. multicoloured	1·25	75

No. 2055 was printed in sheets of 10 (2×5) with enlarged inscribed right margin.

635 "Sleep in Heavenly Peace"

(Des G. Ryan and B. Edwards (40, 45c.), Beth McKinlay (80c.). Litho SNP Ausprint)

2000 (1 Nov). Christmas "Silent Night" (carol).

*(a) T **635** and similar vert design. Multicoloured. Phosphorised paper. P 14½×14*

2056	40c. Type **635**	50	25
2057	45c. "All is Calm, All is Bright"	50	25
MS2058	165×75 mm. Nos. 2056/7	1·00	1·00

(b) Self-adhesive. Phosphor band over figures. P 11½

2059	40c. Type **635**	35	35
	a. Booklet pane. No. 2059×20	6·00	

*(c) International Mail. Horiz design as T **625**, inscr "Season's Greetings". Multicoloured. Phosphorised paper. P 14½ ×14*

2060	80c. Byron Bay, New South Wales	70	85

No. 2059 was only available in $8 stamp booklets, No. SB139, on which the surplus self-adhesive paper was retained. The phosphor band, which shows pink under U.V. light, covers the figures on the design.

The $1 Koala stamp with "International POST" overprint, formerly listed as No.2061 has been renumbered as No. 2024*a*.

Type **636** was left vacant.

637 Parade passing Federation Arch, Sydney

638 Slim Dusty with Guitar in 1940s

(Des A. Di Donato. Litho SNP Ausprint)

2001 (1 Jan). Centenary of Federation. T **637** and similar multicoloured designs.

(a) Phosphorised paper. P 14×14½ (No. 2065) or 14½×14 (others)

2062	49c. Type **637**	50	50
	a. Pair. Nos. 2062/3	1·00	1·00
2063	49c. Edmund Barton (first Federal Prime Minister)	50	50
2064	$2 "Australia For Ever" (song sheet) and Celebration Picnic (50×30 *mm*)	1·50	1·75
2065	$2 State Banquet, Sydney (30×50 *mm*)	1·50	1·75
2062/5 *Set of 4*		3·50	4·00
MS2066	166×73 mm. Nos. 2062/5. P 14½	4·50	5·00

(b) Self-adhesive. Phosphor background. P 11½

2067	49c. Type **637**	45	60
	a. Booklet pane. Nos. 2067/8, each ×5	4·00	
2068	49c. Edmund Barton (first Federal Prime Minister)	45	60

Nos. 2062/3 were printed together, *se-tenant*, in horizontal or vertical pairs throughout the sheet.

Nos. 2067/8, on which the phosphor in the background appears pink under U.V. light, were only issued in $4.90 stamp booklets, No. SB140, on which the surplus self-adhesive paper was retained.

(Des Lisa Christiensen. Litho SNP Ausprint)

2001 (25 Jan). Australian Legends (5th series). Slim Dusty (country music singer). T **638** and similar horiz design. Multicoloured.

(a) Phosphorised paper. P 14×14½

2069	45c. Type **638**	50	50
	a. Horiz pair. Nos. 2069/70	1·00	1·00
2070	45c. Slim Dusty wearing "Sundowner" hat	50	50

(b) Self-adhesive. Two phosphor bands. P 11½

2071	45c. Type **638**	30	55
	a. Booklet pane. Nos. 2071/2, each×5	2·75	
2072	45c. Slim Dusty wearing "Sundowner" hat	30	55

Nos. 2069/70 were printed together, *se-tenant*, as horizontal pairs in sheetlets of 10.

Nos. 2071/2, on which the vertical phosphor bands appear pink under U.V. light, were only available in $4.50 booklets, No. SB141, on which the surplus self-adhesive paper was retained.

639 Light Horse Parade, 1940, and Command Post, New Guinea, 1943

640 Entry Canopy, Skylights and Site Plan

(Des S. Pethick. Litho McPhersons Ptg Group, Mulgrave)

2001 (15 Feb). Centenary of Australian Army. T **639** and similar horiz design. Multicoloured. P 14×14½.

2073	45c. Type **639**	1·40	65
	a. Horiz pair. Nos. 2073/4	2·75	1·25
2074	45c. Soldier carrying Rwandan child and officers on the Commando Selection Course	1·40	65

Nos. 2073/4 were printed together, *se-tenant*, as horizontal pairs in sheets of 10.

(Des Stacey Zass. Litho SNP Ausprint)

2001 (8 Mar). Opening of the National Museum, Canberra. T **640** and similar horiz design. Multicoloured. P 14×14½.

2075	49c. Type **640**	50	50
	a. Pair. Nos. 2075/6	1·00	1·00
2076	49c. Skylights and "Pangk" (wallaby sculpture)	50	50

Nos. 2075/6 were printed together, *se-tenant*, as horizontal or vertical pairs throughout the sheet.

(Des Sophie Byass. Litho SNP Ausprint)

2001 (13 Mar). Sir Donald Bradman (cricketer) Commemoration. Nos. 1663/4 additionally inscribed "1908–2001" in carmine-lake. Multicoloured. P 14½.

2077	45c. Type **568**	50	50
	a. Horiz pair. Nos. 2077/8	1·00	1·00
2078	45c. Bradman playing stroke	50	50

Nos. 2077/8 were printed together, *se-tenant*, as horizontal pairs in sheets of 10 with commemorative inscriptions on the side margins.

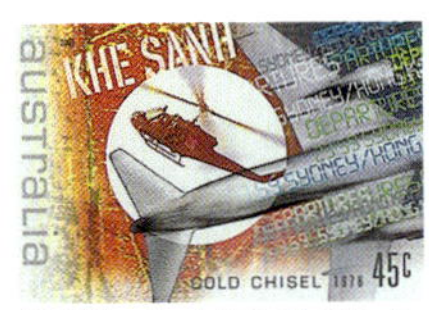

641 "Khe Sanh" (Gold Chisel), 1978

642 Queen Elizabeth II holding Bouquet

(Des Cozzolino Ellett Design. Litho SNP Ausprint)

2001 (20 Mar). Australian Rock and Pop Music. T **641** and similar horiz designs. Multicoloured.

(a) Phosphorised paper. P 14×14½

2079	45c. Type **641**	35	35
	a. Sheetlet. Nos. 2079/88	3·00	3·00
2080	45c. "Down Under" (Men at Work), 1981	35	35
2081	45c. "Power and the Passion" (Midnight Oil), 1983	35	35
2082	45c. "Original Sin" (INXS), 1984	35	35
2083	45c. "You're the Voice" (John Farnham), 1986	35	35
2084	45c. "Don't Dream it's Over" (Crowded House), 1986	35	35
2085	45c. "Treaty" (Yothu Yindi), 1991	35	35
2086	45c. "Tomorrow" (Silverchair), 1994	35	35
2087	45c. "Confide in Me" (Kylie Minogue), 1994	35	35
2088	45c. "Truly, Madly, Deeply" (Savage Garden), 1997	35	35
2079/88 *Set of 10*		3·00	3·00

(b) Self-adhesive. Phosphor frame. P 11½

2089	45c. Type **641**	35	50
	a. Strip of 10. Nos. 2079/88	3·00	4·50
	b. Booklet pane of 10. Nos. 2079/88	3·00	
2090	45c. "Down Under" (Men at Work), 1981	35	50
2091	45c. "Power and the Passion" (Midnight Oil), 1983	35	50
2092	45c. "Original Sin" (INXS), 1984	35	50
2093	45c. "You're the Voice" (John Farnham), 1986	35	50
2094	45c. "Don't Dream it's Over" (Crowded House), 1986	35	50
2095	45c. "Treaty" (Yothu Yindi), 1991	35	50
2096	45c. "Tomorrow" (Silverchair), 1994	35	50
2097	45c. "Confide in Me " (Kylie Minogue), 1994	35	50
2098	45c. "Truly, Madly, Deeply" (Savage Garden), 1997	35	50
2089/98 *Set of 10*		3·00	4·50

Nos. 2079/88 were printed together, *se-tenant*, in sheetlets of 10.

Nos. 2089/98 were available either from rolls of 100, on which the surplus self-adhesive paper was removed, or from $4.50 stamp booklets, No. SB142, on which the paper was retained. In both instances the phosphor, which shows pink under U.V. light, forms a two or three sided frame around each central design.

(Des T. Ledwidge. Litho McPherson's Ptg Group, Mulgrave)

2001 (12 Apr). Queen Elizabeth II's Birthday. P 14½×14.

2099	**642**	45c. multicoloured	1·75	65

643 Party Balloons

644 "Opening of the First Federal Parliament" (Charles Nuttall)

(Des J. Chan (No. 2100), C. Shurey (No. 2101), Janet Boschen (No. 2102), D. Pitt (Nos. 2103/4). Litho SNP Ausprint)

2001 (24 Apr). "Colour My Day". Greetings Stamps. T **643** and similar square designs. P 14½×14.

(a) Domestic Mail

2100	45c. Type **643**	30	35
2101	45c. Smiling Flower	30	35
2102	45c. Hologram and party streamers	30	35

(b) International Mail

2103	$1 Kangaroo and joey	1·00	80
2104	$1.50 The Bayulu Banner	1·40	1·75
2100/4	*Set of 5*	3·00	3·50

Nos. 2100/4 were each printed in sheets of 20 stamps and 20 *se-tenant* labels inscribed with greetings messages. This issue was subsequently available with "personalised" photographs printed on the labels instead of the greetings message.

(Des Sadgrove Design Partners. Litho SNP Ausprint)

2001 (3 May). Centenary of Federal Parliament. Paintings. T **644** and similar square design. Multicoloured. P 14½.

2105	45c. Type **644**	50	25
2106	$2.45 "Prince George opening the First Parliament of the Commonwealth of Australia" (Tom Roberts)	1·50	2·25
MS2107	Two sheets, each 166×75 mm. (a) No. 2105; (b) No. 2106 *Set of 2 sheets*	2·75	3·00

645 Telecommunications Tower

(Des Lynda Warner. Litho SNP Ausprint)

2001 (5 June). Outback Services. T **645** and similar horiz designs. Multicoloured.

(a) Ordinary gum. Phosphorised paper. P 14×14½

2108	45c. Type **645**	1·00	75
	a. Horiz strip of 5. Nos. 2108/12	4·50	3·25
2109	45c. Road train	1·00	75
2110	45c. School of the Air pupil	1·00	75
2111	45c. Outback family and mail box	1·00	75
2112	45c. Royal Flying Doctor Service aircraft and ambulance	1·00	75
2108/12	*Set of 5*	4·50	3·25

(b) Self-adhesive. Phosphor background. P 11½

2113	45c. Type **645**	60	65
	a. Horiz strip of 5. Nos. 2113/17	2·75	3·00
	b. Booklet pane. Nos. 2113/17, each×2	6·50	
2114	45c. Road train	60	65
2115	45c. School of the Air pupil	60	65
2116	45c. Outback family and mail box	60	65
2117	45c. Royal Flying Doctor Service aircraft and ambulance	60	65
2113/17	*Set of 5*	2·75	3·00

Nos. 2108/12 were printed together, *se-tenant*, in horizontal strips of 5 throughout the sheet.

Nos. 2113/17 were issued *se-tenant*, either in rolls of 100 on which the surplus self-adhesive paper was removed or in $4.50 stamp booklets, No. SB143, on which the surplus paper was retained. The phosphor, which shows pink under U.V. light, was applied over the logo and central portion of each design.

646 Dragon Boat and Hong Kong Convention and Exhibition Centre

(Des Kan Tai-keung and Chan Kau On. Litho SNP Ausprint)

2001 (25 June). Joint Issue with Hong Kong. Dragon Boat Racing. T **646** and similar horiz design. Multicoloured. P 14×14½.

(a) Domestic Mail

2118	45c. Type **646**	50	45

(b) International Mail

2119	$1 Dragon boat and Sydney Opera House	1·00	1·00
MS2120	115×70 mm. Nos. 2118/19	1·40	1·40

Stamps in similar designs were issued by Hong Kong.

(Des Stacey Zass and Symone Lambert)

2001 (12 July). International Stamps. Views of Australia (2nd series). Horiz designs as T **625**. Multicoloured.

(a) Litho and die-stamped ($20) or litho (others) McPherson's Ptg Group Mulgrave. PVA gum. Phosphorised paper. P 14×14½ ($20) or 14½×14 (others)

2121	50c. The Three Sisters, Blue Mountains, New South Wales	2·00	40
2122	$1 The Murrumbidgee River, Australian Capital Territory	3·00	40
2123	$1.50 Four Mile Beach, Port Douglas, Queensland	4·00	1·00
2124	$20 Uluru Rock at dusk, Northern Territory (52×24 *mm*)	32·00	16·00
2121/4	*Set of 4*	38·00	16·00

(b) Litho SNP Ausprint. Self-adhesive. One side phosphor band. P 11½×10½

2125	50c. The Three Sisters, Blue Mountains, New South Wales	60	30
	a. Booklet pane. No. 2125×10	5·50	

No. 2125 was only available in $5 stamp booklets, No. SB144, on which the surplus self-adhesive paper was retained. The phosphor, which appears pink under U.V. light, is in a vertical band across the white strip at the right of each stamp.

647 Variegated Wren ("Variegated Fairy-Wren")

648 Daniel Solander (Swedish botanist) and Mango Tree

(Des W. Rankin)

2001 (9 Aug). Fauna and Flora (4th series). Desert Birds. T **647** and similar horiz designs. Multicoloured.

(a) Litho SNP Ausprint. PVA gum. Phosphorised paper. P 14×14½

2126	45c. Type **647**	65	65
	a. Block of 4. Nos. 2126/9	2·40	2·40
2127	45c. Painted Finch ("Painted Firetail")	65	65
2128	45c. Crimson Chat	65	65
2129	45c. Budgerigar	65	65
2126/9	*Set of 4*	2·40	2·40

(b) Litho SNP Ausprint (Nos. 2130/3) or Pemara (Nos. 2130d/3d). Self-adhesive. Phosphor frames. P 11½×11

2130	45c. Type **647**	50	50
	a. Sheetlet of 5. Nos. 2130/2 and 2133×2	2·25	
	b. Booklet pane. Nos. 2130 and 2132, each×2, and Nos. 2131 and 2133, each×3	4·50	
	c. Booklet pane. Nos. 2130/3, each×5	8·50	
	d. Perf 12½ ×13	50	50
2131	45c. Painted Finch ("Painted Firetail")	50	50
	d. Perf 12½×13	50	50
2132	45c. Crimson Chat	50	50
	d. Perf 12½×13	50	50
2133	45c. Budgerigar	50	50
	d. Perf 12½×13	50	50
2130/3	*Set of 4*	1·75	1·75
2130d/3d	*Set of 4*	1·75	1·75

Nos. 2126/9 were printed together, *se-tenant* in sheets of 50 containing ten blocks of 4 and ten single stamps.

Nos. 2130/3 and 2130d/3d, on which the phosphor appears pink under U.V. light, were printed in rolls of 100 or 200 (Nos. 2130d/3d only) with the surplus paper around each stamp removed. The SNP Ausprint stamps also come in sheetlets of 5 or booklet panes of 10 (No. SB145) or 20 (No. SB146) on which the surplus paper was retained.

No. 2130a also exists overprinted with logos of Hafnia 01, Philakorea 2002 and the Beijing Stamp and Coin Expo, for sale at those exhibitions.

(Des Melinda Coombes. Eng C. Slania. Recess and litho Swedish Post Stamp Ptg Works)

2001 (16 Aug). Australia–Sweden Joint Issue. Daniel Solander's Voyage with Captain Cook. T **648** and similar horiz design. Multicoloured. P 12½.

(a) Domestic Mail

2134	45c. Type **648**	1·00	50

(b) International Mail

2135	$1.50 H.M.S. *Endeavour* on reef and Kapok tree	3·75	3·75

649 Christmas Tree

(Des C. Shurey. Litho SNP Ausprint)

2001 (4 Sept). Christmas (1st issue). T **649** and similar square design. Multicoloured. P 14½×14.

(a) Domestic Mail. Part phosphor background

2136	40c. Type **649**	50	20

(b) International Mail. Phosphorised paper

2137	80c. Star	1·50	1·10

Nos. 2136/7 were each printed in sheets of 20 stamps and 20 *se-tenant* labels (20×30 *mm*) inscribed "Season's Greetings" (40c.) or "Peace and Goodwill" (80c.). This issue was also available with the inscriptions on the *se-tenant* labels replaced with personal photographs.

The phosphor on No. 2136, which shows pink under U.V. light, appears to the right and foot of the Christmas tree.

See also Nos. 2157/9.

650 Australia on Globe

(Des C. McPartlin. Litho McPherson's Ptg Group, Mulgrave)

2001 (4 Sept). Commonwealth Heads of Government Meeting (No. 2138) and Commonwealth Parliamentary Conference (No. 2139). T **650** and similar vert design. Multicoloured. P 14½×14.

2138	45c. Type **650**	50	50
	a. Pair. Nos. 2138/9	1·00	1·00
2139	45c. Southern Cross	50	50

Nos. 2138/9 were printed together, *se-tenant*, both horizontally and vertically, in sheets of 10 (5×2). Both designs feature the names of the Commonwealth members with blocks of 4 creating an overall pattern.

651 Wedge-tailed Eagle

652 Cockatoos dancing to Animal Band

(Des P. Trusler. Litho McPherson's Ptg Group, Mulgrave)

2001 (11 Sept). Centenary of Birds Australia (formely Royal Australian Ornithologists Union). Birds of Prey. T **651** and similar multicoloured designs. P 14×14½. (49c.) or 14½×14 (98c.).

2140	49c. Type **651**	1·25	1·00
	a. Pair. Nos. 2140/1	2·50	2·00
2141	49c. Australian Kestrel ("Nankeen Kestrel")	1·25	1·00
2142	98c. Red Goshawk (*vert*)	2·00	2·25
	a. Pair. Nos. 2142/3	4·00	4·50
2143	98c. Spotted Harrier (*vert*)	2·00	2·25
2140/3	*Set of 4*	6·00	6·00

Nos. 2140/1 and 2142/3 were each printed together, *se-tenant*, in pairs both horizontally and vertically in sheets of 50.

(Des R. Harvey and Lisa Christensen. Litho SNP Ausprint)

2001 (2 Oct). National Stamp Collecting Month. "Wild Babies" (cartoons). T **652** and similar vert designs. Multicoloured.

(a) Ordinary gum. Phosphorised paper. P 14½×14

2144	45c. Type **652**	55	45
	a. Horiz strip of 3. Nos. 2144/6	1·50	1·25
2145	45c. Kevin Koala with birthday cake	55	45
2146	45c. Ring-tailed possums eating	55	45
2147	45c. Bilbies at foot of tree	55	45
	a. Horiz strip of 3. Nos. 2147/9	1·50	1·25
2148	45c. James Wombat on rope ladder	55	45
2149	45c. Wallaby, echidna and platypus on rope ladder	55	45
2144/9	*Set of 6*	3·00	2·50
MS2150	Two sheets, each 166×75 mm. (a) Nos. 2144/6. (b) Nos. 2147/9 *Set of 2 sheets*	2·50	2·50

(b) Self-adhesive. Part phosphor background. P 11½

2151	45c. Type **652**	40	45
	a. Vert strip of 6. Nos. 2151/6	2·10	
	b. Booklet pane. Nos. 2151/2 and 2155/6, each×2, and Nos. 2153/4	4·50	
2152	45c. Kevin Koala with birthday cake	40	45
2153	45c. Ring-tailed possums eating	40	45
2154	45c. Bilbies, at foot of tree	40	45
2155	45c. James Wombat on rope ladder	40	45
2156	45c. Wallabies, echidna and platypus on rope ladder	40	45
2151/6	*Set of 6*	2·10	2·50

Nos. 2144/6 and 2147/9 were each printed, *se-tenant*, in sheets of 50 containing ten horizontal strips of 3 and ten additional examples of either Nos. 2144/5 or 2147/8.

Nos. 2151/6 were printed together, in rolls of 100, with the surplus self-adhesive paper around each stamp removed or in booklets of 10, No. SB147, with the paper retained.

The phosphor on Nos. 2151/6, which shows pink under U.V. light, covers an irregular area of the background at the top left or top right of each stamp.

653 "Adoration of the Magi"

654 Sir Gustav Nossal (immunologist)

(Des Beth McKinlay)

2001 (1 Nov). Christmas (2nd issue). Miniatures from "Wharncliffe Hours Manuscript". T **653** and similar vert design. Multicoloured.

(a) Litho McPherson's Ptg Group Mulgrave. Phosphorised paper. P 14½×14

2157	40c. Type **653**	1·10	30
2158	45c. "Flight into Egypt"	1·10	35

(b) Litho SNP Ausprint. Self-adhesive. Phosphor frame. P 11½

2159	40c. Type **653**	40	25
	a. Booklet pane. No. 2159×20 plus 20 "Card Only" labels	7·00	

Booklet pane No. 2159a comes from No. SB148.

(Des Symone Lambert. Litho SNP Ausprint)

2002 (23 Jan). Australian Legends (6th series). Medical Scientists. T **654** and similar horiz designs.

(a) Ordinary gum. Phosphorised paper. P 14×14½

2160	45c. Type **654**	70	80
	a. Vert strip of 5. Nos. 2160/4	3·25	4·00
2161	45c. Nancy Millis (microbiologist)	70	80
2162	45c. Peter Doherty (immunologist)	70	80
2163	45c. Fiona Stanley (epidemiologist)	70	80
2164	45c. Donald Metcalf (haematologist)	70	80
2160/4	*Set of 5*	3·25	4·00

(b) Self-adhesive. Two phosphor bands. P 11½

2165	45c. Type **654**	40	55
	a. Booklet pane. Nos. 2165/9 each×2	3·25	
2166	45c. Nancy Millis (microbiologist)	40	55
2167	45c. Peter Doherty (immunologist)	40	55
2168	45c. Fiona Stanley (epidemiologist)	40	55
2169	45c. Donald Metcalf (haematologist)	40	55
2165/9	*Set of 5*	1·75	2·50

Nos. 2160/4 were printed together, *se-tenant*, as vertical strips of 5, in sheets of 10.

Nos. 2165/9, on which the vertical phosphor bands appear pink under UV light, were only available in $4.50 booklets, No. SB149, on which the surplus self-adhesive paper was retained.

655 Queen Elizabeth in 1953

656 Steven Bradbury (Men's 1000m Short Track Speed Skating)

(Des J. Chong. Litho SNP Ausprint)

2002 (6 Feb). Golden Jubilee. T **655** and similar vert design. Multicoloured. P 15×14.

2170	45c. Type **655**	1·00	35
2171	$2.45 Queen Elizabeth in Italy, 2000	2·25	4·00
MS2172	106×70 mm. Nos. 2170/1	3·25	4·00

(Des Beth McKinlay. Litho SNP Ausprint)

2002 (20–22 Feb). Australian Gold Medal Winners at Salt Lake City Winter Olympic Games. T **656** and similar square design. Multicoloured. P 14½.

2173	45c. Type **656**	95	60
2174	45c. Alisa Camplin (Women's Aerials Freestyle Skiing) (22 Feb)	95	60

657 Austin 7 and Bugatti Type 40, Australian Grand Prix, Phillip Island, 1928

658 Macquarie Lighthouse

(Des Belinda Marshall. Litho SNP Ausprint)

2002 (27 Feb). Centenary of Motor Racing in Australia and New Zealand. T **657** and similar horiz designs. Multicoloured.

(a) Ordinary gum. Phosphorised paper. P 14×14½

2175	45c. Type **657**	60	80
	a. Block of 6 (3×2). Nos. 2175/80	3·25	4·25
2176	45c. Jaguar Mark II, Australian Touring Car Championship, Mallala, 1963	60	80
2177	45c. Repco-Brabham, Tasman Series, Sandown, 1966	60	80
2178	45c. Holden Torana and Ford Falcon, Hardie-Ferodo 500, Bathurst, 1972	60	80
2179	45c. Williams Ford, Australian Grand Prix, Calder, 1980	60	80
2180	45c. Benetton-Renault, Australian Grand Prix, Albert Park, 2001	60	80
2175/80 *Set of 6*		3·25	4·25

(b) Self-adhesive. Part phosphor background. P 11

2181	45c. Type **657**	50	65
	a. Strip of 6. Nos. 2181/6	2·75	3·50
	b. Booklet pane. Nos. 2181/4, each×2, and 2185/6	5·00	
2182	45c. Jaguar Mark II, Australian Touring Car Championship, Mallala, 1963	50	65
2183	45c. Repco-Brabham, Tasman Series, Sandown, 1966	50	65
2184	45c. Holden Torana and Ford Falcon, Hardie-Ferodo 500, Bathurst, 1972	50	65
2185	45c. Williams Ford, Australian Grand Prix, Calder, 1980	50	65
2186	45c. Benetton-Renault, Australian Grand Prix, Albert Park, 2001	50	65
2181/6 *Set of 6*		2·75	3·50

Nos. 2175/80 were printed together, *se-tenant*, in sheets of 50 (2 panes, each 5×5, containing 5 horizontal blocks of 6 and 20 single stamps.

Nos. 2181/6 were issued either as rolls of 100, on which the surplus self-adhesive paper was removed, or in booklets of 10, No. SB150, on which it was retained. On both versions the phosphor, which shows pink under U.V. light, covers parts of the background, always including a strip at foot.

(Des S. Pethick)

2002 (12 Mar). Lighthouses. T **658** and similar vert designs. Multicoloured.

(a) Litho McPherson's Ptg Group Mulgrave. Ordinary gum. Phosphorised paper. P 14½×14

2187	45c. Type **658**	75	35
2188	49c. Cape Naturaliste	90	80
	a. Pair. Nos. 2188/9	1·75	1·60
2189	49c. Troubridge Island	90	80
2190	$1.50 Cape Bruny	2·25	2·25
2187/90 *Set of 4*		4·25	3·75

(b) Litho SNP Ausprint. Self-adhesive. Phosphor frame. P 11½

2191	49c. Cape Naturaliste	55	60
	a. Booklet pane. Nos. 2191/2, each×5	5·50	
2192	49c. Troubridge Island	55	60

Nos. 2188/9 were printed together, *se-tenant*, in horizontal and vertical pairs, throughout the sheets of 50.

Nos. 2187/90 were also issued in premium booklets, No. SP2, sold at $9.95, printed by SNP Ausprint.

Nos. 2191/2, on which the phosphor shows pink under U.V. light, were only available in $4.90 booklets, No. SB151, on which the surplus self-adhesive paper around each stamp was retained.

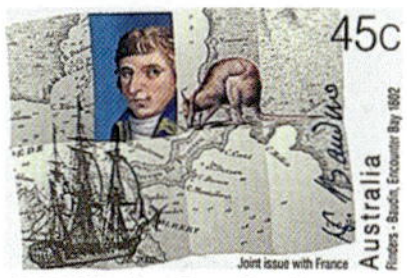

659 Nicolas Baudin, Kangaroo, *Géographe* (ship) and Map

660 Desert Star Flower

(Des B. Sadgrove. Litho SNP Ausprint)

2002 (4 Apr). Australia–France Joint Issue. Bicentenary of Flinders–Baudin Meeting at Encounter Bay. T **659** and similar horiz design. Multicoloured. P 14×14½.

(a) Domestic Mail

2193	45c. Type **659**	60	40

(b) International Mail

2194	$1.50 Matthew Flinders, Port Lincoln Parrot, *Investigator* (ship) and Map	2·00	1·75

(Des Belinda Marshall. Litho SNP Ausprint)

2002 (1 May). International Stamps. Views of Australia (3rd series). Horiz designs as T **625**. Multicoloured.

(a) Ordinary gum. Phosphorised paper. P 14½×14

2195	50c. Walker Flat, River Murray, South Australia	1·00	40
2196	$1 Mt. Roland, Tasmania	1·50	60
2197	$1.50 Cape Leveque, Western Australia	1·75	1·25
2195/7 *Set of 3*		3·75	2·00

(b) Self-adhesive. One side phosphor band. P 11½×10½

2198	50c. Walker Flat, River Murray, South Australia	50	40
	a. Booklet pane. Nos. 2198×6 and 2199×4	6·50	
2199	$1 Mt. Roland, Tasmania	1·10	75

Nos. 2198/9 were only available in $7 stamp booklets, No. SB152, on which the surplus self-adhesive paper was retained. The phosphor band, which appears pink under U.V. light, is at the right hand side of each stamp.

(Des W. Rankin. Litho McPherson's Ptg Group, Mulgrave)

2002 (4 June)–**03** (7 Jan). Fauna and Flora (5th series). Great Sandy Desert. T **660** and similar horiz designs. Multicoloured.

(a) Litho McPhersons. Ordinary gum. Phosphorised paper. P 14½×14 ($2) or 14×14½ (others)

2200	50c. Type **660**	40	35
2201	$1 Bilby	80	65
2202	$1.50 Thorny Devil	1·20	1·60
2203	$2 Great Sandy Desert landscape (50×30 mm)	1·60	1·90
2200/3 *Set of 4*		3·50	4·00

(b) Litho SNP Sprint (No. 2203a) or Pemara (No. 2203ad). Self-adhesive. Phosphor frame. P 11 (7.1.03)

2203*a*	50c. Type **660**	35	50
	ab. Booklet pane. No. 2203a×10	3·50	
	ac. Booklet pane. No. 2203a×20	6·00	
	ad. Perf 12½×13	35	50

No. 2203a (printed by SNP Sprint) was printed in rolls of 100, on which the surplus self-adhesive paper around each stamp was removed, and in booklets of 10 (No. SB157) or 20 (No. SB158) in which it was retained. No. 2203ad (printed by Pemara) comes from rolls of 200 also with the surplus self-adhesive paper removed.

On both stamps the phosphor frame appears pink under U.V. light and is broken where the frame crosses the value tablet.

661 "Ghost Gum, Mt Sonder" (Albert Namatjira)

662 *Nelumbo nucifera*

(Des Cathleen Cram. Litho SNP Ausprint)

2002 (2 July). Birth Centenary of Albert Namatjira (artist). T **661** and similar horiz designs. Multicoloured.

(a) Ordinary gum. Phosphorised paper. P 14×14½

2204	45c. Type **661**	50	50
	a. Block of 4. Nos. 2204/7	1·75	1·75
2205	45c. "Mt Hermannsburg"	50	50
2206	45c. "Glen Helen Country"	50	50
2207	45c. "Simpsons Gap"	50	50
2204/7 *Set of 4*		1·75	1·75
MS2208	133×70 mm. Nos. 2204/7	1·75	1·75

(b) Self-adhesive. Phosphor frame. P 11×11½

2209	45c. Type **661**	40	55
	a. Strip of 4. Nos. 2209/12	1·40	2·00
	b. Booklet pane. Nos. 2209/10, each ×3, and 2211/12, each ×2	3·00	
2210	45c. "Mt Hermannsburg"	40	55
2211	45c. "Glen Helen Country"	40	55
2212	45c. "Simpsons Gap"	40	55
2209/12 *Set of 4*		1·40	2·00

Nos. 2204/7 were printed together, *se-tenant*, in sheets of 50 (2 panes, each 5×5) containing 10 blocks of 4 and 10 single stamps.

Nos. 2209/12 were issued either as rolls of 100, on which the surplus self-adhesive paper was removed, or in booklets of 10, No. SB153, on which it was retained. On both versions the phosphor shows pink under U.V. light.

Nos. 2204/7 were also issued in premium booklets, No. SP3, sold at $9.95.

(Des T. Ponchaiwong. Litho SNP Ausprint)

2002 (6 Aug). Australia–Thailand Joint Issue. 50th Anniv of Diplomatic Relations. Water Lilies. T **662** and similar horiz design. Multicoloured. P 14×14½.

(a) Domestic Mail

2213	45c. Type **662**	60	35

(b) International Mail

2214	$1 *Nymphaea immutabilis*	1·40	75
MS2215	107×70 mm. Nos. 2213/14	2·00	1·75

The phosphorised paper used for Nos. 2213/14 is a new type showing short vertical orange lines.

MS2215 also exists overprinted in celebration of the 50th Anniv of the International Federation of Stamp Dealers' Associations.

663 Star, Presents and Baubles

664 Lilly-pilly

(Des C. Shurey ($1.65), D. Pitt (others). Litho SNP Ausprint)

2002 (23 Aug). International Greetings. T **663** and similar square designs. Multicoloured. P 14½×14.

2216	90c. Type **663**	85	80
2217	$1.10 Koala	1·00	95
2218	$1.65 "Puja" (painting by Ngarralja Tommy May)	1·50	1·40
2216/18 *Set of 3*		3·00	2·75

Nos. 2216/18 were printed in sheets of 20 stamps each with a 20×30 mm *se-tenant* label complementing or extending ($1.65) the design. The stamps were also available with personal photographs on the labels.

Nos. 2217/18 were each issued in sheets of 10 with *se-tenant* labels for Australian Open Tennis Tournament in January 2004 and again in January 2005 (No. 2217 only). These sheets were sold at a premium above face value.

(Des Cathleen Cram. Litho SNP Ausprint)

2002 (23 Aug). International Stamps. Views of Australia (4th series). Horiz designs as T **625**. Multicoloured. P 14½×14.

2219	$1.10 Coonawarra, South Australia	2·75	70
2220	$1.65 Gariwerd (Grampians), Victoria	3·50	1·40
2221	$2.20 National Library, Canberra	4·50	3·75
2222	$3.30 Cape York, Queensland	6·50	6·50
2219/22 *Set of 4*		15·00	11·00

(Des Janet Boschen)

2002 (3 Sept). "Bush Tucker". Edible Plants from the Outback. T **664** and similar vert designs. Multicoloured.

(a) Litho McPherson's Ptg Group Mulgrave. Ordinary gum. Phosphorised paper. P 14½×14

2223	49c. Type **664**	1·10	1·25
	a. *Tête-bêche* pair	2·10	2·50
	b. Horiz strip of 5. Nos. 2223/7	5·00	5·50
	c. *Tête-bêche* block of 10. No. 2223b×2	9·00	10·00
2224	49c. Honey Grevillea	1·10	1·25
	a. *Tête-bêche* pair	2·10	2·50
2225	49c. Quandong	2·10	1·25
	a. *Tête-bêche* pair	2·10	2·50
2226	49c. Acacia seeds	1·10	1·25
	a. *Tête-bêche* pair	2·10	2·50
2227	49c. Murnong	1·10	1·25
	a. *Tête-bêche* pair	2·10	2·50
2223/7 *Set of 5*		5·00	5·50

(b) Litho SNP Ausprint. Self-adhesive. Phosphor background. P 11½

2228	49c. Type **664**	45	55
	a. Booklet pane. Nos. 2228/32, each×2	4·00	
2229	49c. Honey Grevillea	45	55
2230	49c. Quandong	45	55
2231	49c. Acacia seeds	45	55
2232	49c. Murnong	55	55
2228/32 *Set of 5*		2·00	2·50

Nos. 2223/7 were printed together in sheets of 50, two panes (5×5), with the five designs shown as *se-tenant* horizontal strips. In each pane two of the horizontal rows are inverted forming *tête-bêche* pairs.

Nos. 2228/32, on which the phosphor shows pink under U.V. light, were only available in $4.90 stamp booklets, No. SB154, with the self-adhesive paper around each stamp retained.

665 Bunyip

666 "Wakeful"

(Des C. McPartlin. Litho SNP Ausprint)

2002 (25 Sept). Stamp Collecting Month. *The Magic Rainforest* (book by John Marsden). T **665** and similar vert designs. Multicoloured.

(a) Ordinary gum. Phosphorised paper. P 14½×14

2233	45c. Type **665**	50	50
	a. Horiz strip of 3. Nos. 2233/5	1·10	1·40
2234	45c. Fairy on branch	50	50
2235	45c. Gnome with sword	50	50
2236	45c. Goblin with stock whip	50	50
	a. Horiz strip of 3. Nos. 2236/8	1·40	1·40
2237	45c. Wizard	50	50
2238	45c. Sprite	50	50
2233/8 *Set of 6*		2·75	2·75
MS2239	170×90 mm. Nos. 2233/8	3·25	3·00

(b) Self-adhesive. Phosphor frame. P 11½×11

2240	45c. Type **665**	40	60
	a. Strip of 6. Nos. 2240/5	2·25	3·25
	b. Booklet pane. Nos. 2240, 2241/4 each ×2, and 2245	3·50	
2241	45c. Fairy on branch	40	60
2242	45c. Gnome with sword	40	60
2243	45c. Goblin with stock whip	40	60
2244	45c. Wizard	40	60
2245	45c. Sprite	40	60
2240/5 *Set of 6*		2·25	3·25

Nos. 2233/5 and 2236/8 were each printed together in sheets of 50, two panes (5×5), each horizontal row containing a *se-tenant* strip of 3 and two additional examples of either Nos. 2233/4 or 2236/7.

Nos. 2240/5 were issued either as rolls of 100, on which the surplus self-adhesive paper was removed, or in booklets of 10, No. SB155, on which it was retained. On both versions the phosphor shows pink under U.V. light.

(Des O. Schmidinger. Litho McPherson's Ptg Group Mulgrave)

2002 (15 Oct). Champion Racehorses. T **666** and similar horiz designs. Multicoloured. Phosphorised paper. P 14×14½.

2246	45c. Type **666**	1·50	1·50
	a. Horiz strip of 5. Nos. 2247/50	6·75	6·75
2247	45c. "Rising Fast"	1·50	1·50
2248	45c. "Manikato"	1·50	1·50
2249	45c. "Might and Power"	1·50	1·50
2250	45c. "Sunline"	1·50	1·50
2246/50 *Set of 5*		6·75	6·75

Nos. 2246/50 were printed together, *se-tenant*, as horizontal strips of 5 throughout the sheet.

667 Nativity

668 Two Daisies

(Des Tracie Grimwood)

2002 (1 Nov). Christmas. T **667** and similar vert design. Multicoloured.

(a) Litho McPherson's Ptg Group Mulgrave. Ordinary gum. Phosphorised paper. P 14½×14

2251	40c. Type **667**	90	35
2252	45c. The Three Wise Men	90	35

(b) Litho SNP Ausprint. Self-adhesive. Phosphor frame. P 11½×11

2253	40c. Type **667**	35	35
	a. Booklet pane. No. 2253×20 plus 20 "Card Only" labels	6·00	

No. 2253, on which the phosphor shows pink under U.V. light, was only available in $8 stamp booklets, No. SB156, with the surplus self-adhesive paper retained.

(Des Fragile Design (Nos. 2254, 2259, C. Shurey (Nos. 2255, 2257/8, 2263), Symone Lambert (No. 2256), Hannah Mattner (Nos. 2260/1), F. Briggs and Hannah Mattner (No. 2262). Litho SNP Sprint)

2003 (7 Jan). Greetings Stamps. T **668** and similar square designs, some adapted from previous issues. Multicoloured. Phosphorised paper (Nos. 2254/6, 2260/2) or phosphor background (others). P 14½×14.

2254	50c. Type **668**	40	45
	a. Horiz strip of 3. Nos. 2254/6	1·10	1·25
2255	50c. Wedding rings and yellow roses	40	45
2256	50c. Hearts and pink roses	40	45
2257	50c. Birthday cake and present	40	45
	a. Horiz strip of 3. Nos. 2257/9	1·10	1·25
2258	50c. Seated teddy bear	40	45
2259	50c. Balloons	40	45
2260	50c. Red Kangaroo and flag	40	45
	a. Horiz strip of 3. Nos. 2260/2	1·10	1·25
2261	50c. Australia on globe	40	45
2262	50c. Sports car	40	45
2263	$1 Wedding rings and pink rose	80	85
2254/63 *Set of 10*		4·00	4·50

Nos. 2254/6, 2257/9 and 2260/2 were each printed together, *se-tenant*, in sheets of 20 containing ten examples of the first design and five each of the other two. Each stamp, including No. 2263, was accompanied by a *se-tenant* 20×30 mm label showing symbols associated with each design. The stamps also exist in sheets of 20 of one design with decorated margins intended for use with "personalised" photographs.

The phosphor on Nos. 2257/9 and 2263 appears pink under U.V. light and covers an irregular section of the background in each instance.

Nos. 2254/7, 2259 and 2263 were also issued in separate premium stamp booklets, Nos. SP4/9, sold at $20.95 (No. SP9) or $10.95 (others). All designs are on phosphorised paper.

Nos. 2254, 2256, 2259 and 2261 were also issued in $10.95 premium Zodiac booklets; see Nos. SP41/5 and SP47/51.

No. 2259 was also issued in premium booklet No. SP39, sold at $10.95.

No. 2260 was also issued in premium booklets, Nos. SP60/75, sold at $10.95.

Nos. 2260 and 2261 were each issued in sheets of 10 with *se-tenant* labels to celebrate various special events. These sheets were all sold at a premium above face value.

No. 2261 was also issued in premium booklets, Nos. SP109/24, sold for $14.95 each.

669 Margaret Court with Wimbledon Trophy

670 Blue Orchid

(Des Belinda Marshall. Litho SNP Sprint)

2003 (24 Jan). Australian Legends (7th series). Tennis Players. T **669** and similar horiz designs. Multicoloured.

(a) Ordinary gum. Phosphorised paper. P 14×14½

2264	50c. Type **669**	75	50
	a. Block of 4. Nos. 2264/7	2·75	1·75
2265	50c. Margaret Court in action	75	50
2266	50c. Rod Laver with Wimbledon Trophy	75	50
2267	50c. Rod Laver in action	75	50
2264/7 *Set of 4*		2·75	1·75

(b) Self-adhesive. Phosphor bars. P 11

2268	50c. Type **669**	75	65
	a. Booklet pane. Nos. 2268 and 2270, each ×3, and Nos. 2269 and 2271, each ×2	6·00	
2269	50c. Margaret Court in action	75	65
2270	50c. Rod Laver with Wimbledon Trophy	75	65
2271	50c. Rod Laver in action	75	65
2268/71 *Set of 4*		2·75	2·40

Nos. 2264/7 were printed together, *se-tenant*, in sheets of 50 (2 panes 5×5), each sheet providing ten blocks of 4 and ten single stamps.

Nos. 2268/71, on which the phosphor bars each side of the centre design show pink under U.V. light, were only issued in $5 booklets, No. SB159, on which the surplus self-adhesive paper around each stamp was retained.

(Des W. Rankin)

2003 (11 Feb–8 July). Fauna and Flora (6th series). Rainforest, Daintree National Park. T **670** and similar horiz designs. Multicoloured.

(a) Litho SNP Sprint. Ordinary gum. Phosphorised paper. P 14×14½

2272	50c. Orange-thighed Tree Frog (8 July)	1·00	75
	a. Block of 4. Nos. 2272/5	3·50	2·75
2273	50c. Green-spotted Triangle (butterfly) (8 July)	1·00	75
2274	50c. Striped Possum (8 July)	1·00	75
2275	50c. Yellow-bellied Sunbird (8 July)	1·00	75
2276	$1.45 Type **670**	2·50	1·25
2272/6 *Set of 5*		6·00	3·75

(b) Litho SNP Sprint (Nos. 2277/80) or Pemara (Nos. 2277c/80c). Self-adhesive. Phosphor frame. P 11½ (Nos. 2277/80) or 12½×13 (Nos. 2277c/80c) (8 July)

2277	50c. Orange-thighed Tree Frog	55	60
	a. Booklet pane. Nos. 2277/8, each×3, and Nos. 2279/80, each ×2	8·00	
	b. Booklet pane. Nos. 2277/80, each×5	10·00	
	c. Perf 12½×13	55	60
2278	50c. Green-spotted Triangle (butterfly)	55	60
	c. Perf 12½×13	55	60
2279	50c. Striped Possum	55	60
	c. Perf 12½×13	55	60
2280	50c. Yellow-bellied Sunbird	55	60
	c. Perf 12½×13	55	60
2277/80 *Set of 4*		2·00	2·25

On Nos. 2277/80c the phosphor frame is broken where the frame crosses the value tablet.

No. 2281 is left for additions to this series.

Booklet panes Nos. 2277a/b come from Nos. SB162/3.

671 Snapper and Fishing from Beach

(Des E. Guiotto. Litho SNP Sprint)

2003 (11 Feb). Angling in Australia. T **671** and similar horiz designs. Multicoloured. P 14½×14.

2282	50c. Type **671**	60	60
	a. Horiz strip of 5. Nos. 2282/6	2·75	2·75
2283	50c. Murray Cod and flooded wood	60	60
2284	50c. Brown Trout and fly-fishing	60	60
2285	50c. Yellow-finned Tuna and sea-fishing from launch	60	60
2286	50c. Barramundi and anglers in mangrove swamp	60	60
2282/6 *Set of 5*		2·75	2·75

Nos. 2282/6 were printed together, *se-tenant*, as horizontal strips of 5 throughout the sheet.

672 "Hari Withers" Camellia

673 "Ned Kelly" (Sir Sidney Nolan)

(Des Beth McKinlay. Litho SNP Sprint)

2003 (25 Mar). Australian Horticulture. T **672** and similar vert designs. Multicoloured.

(a) Size 26×38 mm. Ordinary gum. Phosphorised paper. P 14½×14

2287	50c. Type **672**	60	60
	a. Horiz strip of 5. Nos. 2287/91	2·75	2·75
2288	50c. "Victoria Gold" rose	60	60
2289	50c. "Superb" grevillea	60	60
2290	50c. "Bush Tango" kangaroo paw	60	60
2291	50c. "Midnight" rhododendron	60	60
2287/91 *Set of 5*		2·75	2·75

(b) Size 26×38 mm. Self-adhesive. Phosphor frame. P 11½×11

2292	50c. Type **672**	50	60
	a. Strip of 5. Nos. 2292/6	2·25	2·75
	b. Booklet pane. Nos. 2292/6, each×2	4·00	
2293	50c. "Victoria Gold" rose	50	60
2294	50c. "Superb" grevillea	50	60
2295	50c. "Bush Tango" kangaroo paw	50	60
2296	50c. "Midnight" rhododendron	50	60
2292/6 *Set of 5*		2·25	2·75

Nos. 2287/91 were printed together, *se-tenant*, as horizontal strips of 5 in small sheets of 10.

Nos. 2292/6 were issued either as rolls of 100 containing the five designs in sequence, on which the surplus self-adhesive paper around each stamp was removed, or in $5 stamp booklets, No. SB160, in which the surplus paper was retained. Both versions have phosphor frames which show pink under U.V. light.

(Des Symone Lambert. Litho SNP Sprint)

2003 (6 May). Australian Paintings. T **673** and similar horiz designs. Multicoloured. P 14½×14.

2297	$1 Type **673**	1·75	2·00
	a. Pair. Nos. 2297/8	3·50	4·00
2298	$1 "Family Home, Suburban Exterior" (Howard Arkley)	1·75	2·00
2299	$1.45 "Cord Long Drawn, Expectant" (Robert Jacks)	2·25	2·25
2300	$2.45 "Girl" (Joy Hester)	3·25	3·75
2297/300 *Set of 4*		8·00	9·00

Nos. 2297/8 were printed together, *se-tenant*, in horizontal and vertical pairs throughout the sheets of 50.

674 Queen Elizabeth II, 1953 (photograph by Cecil Beaton)

(Des Cathleen Cram. Litho SNP Sprint)

2003 (2 June). 50th Anniv of Coronation. T **674** and similar vert designs. Multicoloured.

(a) Ordinary gum. Phosphorised paper. P 14½×14

2301	50c. Type **674**	75	45
2302	$2.45 St. Edward's Crown	2·50	3·50
MS2303	105×70 mm. Nos. 2301/2	3·25	4·25

(b) Self-adhesive. Phosphor background. P 11½×11

2304	50c. Type **674**	1·10	1·25
	a. Booklet pane. No. 2304×10	10·00	

No. 2304, on which the phosphor appears in the pale background at the left of the stamp and in the crown, was only issued in $5 booklets, No. SB161, with the self-adhesive paper around each stamp retained.

675 Untitled Painting by Ningura Napurrula

(Des Beth McKinlay. Litho SNP Sprint)

2003 (17 June). International Stamps. Art of Papunya Tula Movement. T **675** and similar horiz designs showing untitled paintings by Aboriginal artists. Multicoloured. Phosphorised paper. P 14½×14 ($1.10, $1.65) or 14×14½ ($2.20, $3.30).

2305	$1.10 Type **675**	2·25	70
2306	$1.65 Naata Nungurrayi	3·25	1·40
2307	$2.20 Graham Tjupurrula (55×24 *mm*)	3·75	2·00
2308	$3.30 Dini Campbell Tjampitjinpa (55×24 *mm*)	5·50	3·50
2305/8 *Set of 4*		13·00	7·00

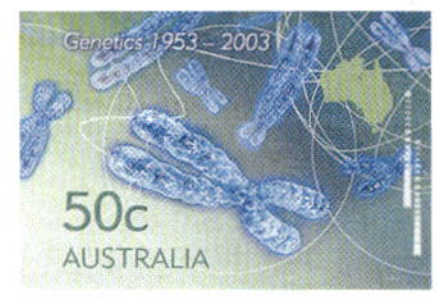

676 Kangaroo Chromosomes

(Des R. Oliver. Litho SNP Sprint)

2003 (8 July). 50th Anniv of Discovery of DNA. T **676** and similar horiz design. Multicoloured. Phosphorised paper. P 14×14½.

2309	50c. Type **676**	1·25	1·25
	a. Pair. Nos. 2309/10	2·50	2·50
2310	50c. DNA double helix	1·25	1·25

Nos. 2309/10 were printed together, *se-tenant*, in horizontal and vertical pairs throughout the sheet.

677 *Oscar W* (paddle-steamer)

(Des C. McGill. Litho SNP Sprint)

2003 (5 Aug). 150th Anniv of Murray River Shipping. T **677** and similar horiz designs. Multicoloured.

(a) Ordinary gum. Phosphorised paper. P 14×14½

2311	50c. Type **677**	80	80
	a. Horiz strip of 5. Nos. 2311/15	3·50	3·50
2312	50c. *Marion* (paddle-steamer)	80	80
2313	50c. *Ruby* (paddle-steamer)	80	80
2314	50c. *Pyap* (cruise vessel)	80	80
2315	50c. *Adelaide* (paddle-steamer)	80	80
2311/15 *Set of 5*		3·50	3·50

(b) Self-adhesive. Phosphor frame. P 11×11½

2316	50c. Type **677**	70	80
	a. Strip of 5. Nos. 2316/20	3·25	3·50
	b. Booklet pane. Nos. 2316/20, each×2	6·25	
2317	50c. *Marion* (paddle-steamer)	70	80
2318	50c. *Ruby* (paddle-steamer)	70	80
2319	50c. *Pyap* (cruise vessel)	70	80
2320	50c. *Adelaide* (paddle-steamer)	70	80
2316/20 *Set of 5*		3·25	3·50

Nos. 2311/15 were printed together, *se-tenant*, in horizontal strips of 5 throughout the sheet.

Nos. 2311/15 were also issued in premium booklets, No. SP10, sold at $10.95.

Nos. 2316/20 were issued either as strips of 5 or rolls of 100 containing the five designs in sequence, on which the surplus self-adhesive paper around each stamp was removed, or in $5 stamp booklets, No. SB164, in which the surplus paper was retained.

678 Christmas Tree

(Des C. Shurey. Litho SNP Sprint)

2003 (5 Aug). Greetings Stamps. Peace and Goodwill. T **678** and similar square design, adapted from Christmas 2001 (1st issue) (Nos. 2136/7). Multicoloured. Phosphor frame. P 14½×14.

(a) Domestic Mail

2321	50c. Type **678**	40	30

(b) International Mail

2322	90c. Star	75	95

679 Sir Samuel Griffith (first Chief Justice)

(Des Janet Boschen. Litho SNP Sprint)

2003 (2 Sept). Centenary of High Court of Australia. T **679** and similar horiz design. P 14×14½.

2323	50c. deep dull purple, black and scarlet-vermilion	55	45
2324	$1.45 scarlet-vermilion, deep rose-red and black	1·50	1·50
MS2325	105×70 mm. Nos. 2323/4	2·50	2·25

Design:—$1.45, "JUSTICE".

680 Ulysses Butterfly

(Des G. Base. Litho SNP Sprint)

2003 (24 Sept). Stamp Collecting Month. Bugs and Butterflies. T **680** and similar horiz designs. Multicoloured. Phosphorised paper.

(a) Ordinary gum. P 14×14½

2326	50c. Type **680**	50	45
	a. Horiz strip of 3. Nos. 2326/8	1·40	1·25
2327	50c. Leichhardt's Grasshopper	50	45
2328	50c. Vedalia Ladybird	50	45
2329	50c. Green Mantid and captured damselfly	50	45
	a. Horiz strip of 3. Nos. 2329/31	1·40	1·25
2330	50c. Emperor Gum Moth Caterpillar	50	45
2331	50c. Fiddler Beetle	50	45
2326/31 *Set of 6*		2·75	2·50
MS2332	170×85 mm. Nos. 2326/31	3·50	3·00

(b) Self-adhesive. P 11×11½

2333	50c. Type **680**	40	45
	a. Strip of 6. Nos. 2333/8	2·25	2·50
	b. Booklet pane. Nos. 2333/6, each×2 and Nos. 2337/8	4·25	
2334	50c. Leichhardt's Grasshopper	40	45
2335	50c. Vedalia Ladybird	40	45
2336	50c. Green Mantid and captured damselfly	40	45
2337	50c. Emperor Gum Moth Caterpillar	40	45
2338	50c. Fiddler Beetle	40	45
2333/8 *Set of 6*		2·25	2·50

Nos. 2326/8 and 2329/31 were each printed together in sheets of 50 with two panes (5×5), each horizontal row containing a *se-tenant* strip of 3 and two additional examples of either Nos. 2326/7 or Nos. 2329/30.

Nos. 2333/8 were issued either as rolls of 100, on which the surplus self-adhesive paper was removed, or in booklets of 10, No. SB165, on which it was retained.

No. **MS**2332 was issued overprinted for "Bangkok 2003" World Philatelic Exhibition.

681 Hands passing Ball and Players

(Des Beth McKinley. Litho McPherson's Ptg Group Mulgrave)

2003 (8 Oct). Rugby World Cup Championship, Australia. T **681** and similar square designs. Multicoloured. *Phosphorised paper*. P 14½×14.

(a) Domestic Mail

2339	50c. Type **681**	55	45

(b) International Mail

2340	$1.10 Trophy (Webb Ellis Cup) and Telstra Stadium	1·10	1·00
2341	$1.65 Hand grasping ball and player taking shot at goal	1·50	2·00
2339/41 *Set of 3*		2·75	3·00
MS2342	115×70 mm. Nos. 2339/41	2·75	3·00

Nos. 2339/41 were also issued in premium booklets, No. SP11, sold at $10.95.

Nos. 2339/41 were each issued in sheets of ten with *se-tenant* labels, in addition to the ordinary sheets of 20. These special event sheets were sold at a premium above face value.

682 "Active with ASTHMA" and Silhouettes of Sportspeople

(Des M. Heine. Litho McPherson's Ptg Group Mulgrave)

2003 (14 Oct). National Asthma Week Campaign. Phosphorised paper. P 14×14½.

2343	**682**	50c. multicoloured	1·00	45

683 Mary, Baby Jesus and Angels

(Des Sally Morgan. Litho SNP Sprint)

2003 (31 Oct). Christmas. T **683** and similar vert designs. Multicoloured.

(a) Ordinary gum. Phosphorised paper. P 14½×14

2344	45c. Type **683**	45	15
2345	50c. Three Wise Men	45	15
2346	90c. Angel appearing to shepherds	80	90
2344/6 *Set of 3*		1·50	1·10

(b) Self-adhesive. Phosphor frame. P 11½×11

2347	45c. Type **683**	45	45
	a. Booklet pane. No. 2347×20 plus 20 "card only" labels	8·00	

No. 2347 was only available in $9 stamp booklets, No. SB166, with the surplus self-adhesive paper retained.

684 Joan Sutherland as Lucia di Lammermoor, 1980

685 Aboriginal shell necklace and bracelet

(Des Lynette Traynor. Litho SNP Sprint)

2004 (23 Jan). Australian Legends (8th series). Dame Joan Sutherland (opera singer). T **684** and similar horiz design. Multicoloured.

(a) Ordinary gum. Phosphorised paper. P 14×14½

2348	50c. Type **684**	90	70
	a. Horiz pair. Nos. 2348/9	1·75	1·40
2349	50c. Joan Sutherland	90	70

(b) Self-adhesive. Phosphor background. P 11×11½

2350	50c. Type **684**	90	80
	a. Booklet pane. Nos. 2350/1, each×5	8·00	
2351	50c. Joan Sutherland	90	80

Nos. 2348/9 were printed together, *se-tenant*, in sheets of ten.

Nos. 2350/1 were only issued in $5 booklets, No. SB167, on which the surplus self-adhesive paper around each stamp was retained.

The phosphor on Nos. 2350/1 covers an irregular area of the background at the sides and top of the stamp (No. 2350) or at the left hand side (No. 2351).

(Des Lynda Warner. Litho SNP Sprint)

2004 (3 Feb). Bicentenary of Settlement of Hobart, Tasmania. T **685** and similar horiz designs. Multicoloured. Phosphorised paper. P 14×14½.

2352	50c. Type **685**	85	70
	a. Pair. Nos. 2352/3	1·60	1·40
2353	50c. Cheshunt House, Deloraine	85	70
2354	$1 "Mount Wellington and Hobart Town from Kangaroo Point" (John Glover)	1·75	1·75
	a. Pair. Nos. 2354/5	3·50	3·50
2355	$1 Mountains, south west Tasmania	1·75	1·75
2352/5 *Set of 4*		4·75	4·50
MS2356 135×72 mm. Nos. 2352/5		4·25	4·25

Nos. 2352/3 and 2354/5 were each printed together, *se-tenant*, in horizontal and vertical pairs in sheets of 50 (containing two panes of 25).

No. **MS**2356 exists overprinted for Salon du Timbre Exhibition, Paris and was subsequently reissued for the China 2004 Stamp and Coin Expo, No. **MS**2459*a*.

686 Ross Bridge, Tasmania, 1836

687 Stylized "Southern Cross"

(Des G. Domoney. Litho SNP Sprint)

2004 (2 Mar). Landmark Bridges. T **686** and similar horiz designs. Multicoloured.

(a) Ordinary gum. Phosphorised paper. P 14×14½

2357	50c. Type **686**	1·25	80
	a. Horiz strip of 5. Nos. 2357/61	5·50	3·50
2358	50c. Lockyer Creek Bridge, Queensland, 1911	1·25	80
2359	50c. Sydney Harbour Bridge, 1932	1·25	80
2360	50c. Birkenhead Bridge, Adelaide, 1940	1·25	80
2361	50c. Bolte Bridge, Melbourne, 1999	1·25	80
2357/60 *Set of 5*		5·50	3·50

(b) Self-adhesive. Phosphor frame. P 11×11½

2362	50c. Type **686**	75	85
	a. Strip of 5. Nos. 2362/6	3·25	3·75
	b. Booklet pane. Nos. 2362/6, each×2	9·00	
2363	50c. Lockyer Creek Bridge, Queensland, 1911	75	85
2364	50c. Sydney Harbour Bridge, 1932	75	85
2365	50c. Birkenhead Bridge, Adelaide, 1940	75	85
2366	50c. Bolte Bridge, Melbourne, 1999	75	85
2362/6 *Set of 5*		3·25	3·75

Nos. 2357/61 were printed together, *se-tenant*, in horizontal strips of 5 throughout the sheet.

Nos. 2357/61 were also issued in Premium booklets, No. SP16, containing five panes of 4, one of each design, each with margins all round. No. SP16 contains stamps with a face value of $10 and was sold for $10.95.

Nos. 2362/6 were issued in rolls of 100 containing the five designs in sequence, on which the surplus self-adhesive paper was removed, and in $5 booklets of 10, No. SB168, on which it was retained.

On Nos. 2362/6 the phosphor frame is broken at bottom left where the designs extend into the white margins of the stamps.

(Des B. Sadgrove. Litho SNP Sprint)

2004 (16 Mar). Greetings Stamp. Phosphorised paper. P 14½×14.

2367	**687**	50c. multicoloured	70	55

No. 2367 was also issued in premium booklets, Nos. SP35, SP40 and SP46, all sold at $10.95.

No. 2367 was issued in sheets of 10 with *se-tenant* labels to celebrate various special events. These sheets were all sold at a premium above face value.

688 Solar Systems CS500 Dish ("solar")

689 Queen Elizabeth II (from photo by Dorothy Wilding)

(Des S. Pethick. Litho SNP Sprint)

2004 (30 Mar). Renewable Energy. T **688** and similar horiz designs. Multicoloured.

(a) Ordinary gum. Phosphorised paper. P 14×14½

2368	50c. Type 688	85	85
	a. Block of 4. Nos. 2368/71	3·00	3·00
2369	50c. Wind turbines ("wind")	85	85
2370	50c. Snowy Mountains Hydro-electric Scheme ("hydro")	85	85
2371	50c. Sugar cane field, bagasse (waste plant fibre) and sugar mill ("biomass")	85	85
2368/71 *Set of 4*		3·00	3·00

(b) Self-adhesive. Phosphor panels. P 11×11½

2372	50c. Type **688**	85	85
	a. Strip of 4. Nos. 2372/5	3·00	3·00
2373	50c. Wind turbines ("wind")	85	85
2374	50c. Snowy Mountains Hydro-electric Scheme ("hydro")	85	85
2375	50c. Sugar cane field, bagasse (waste plant fibre) and sugar mill ("biomass")	85	85
2372/5 *Set of 4*		3·00	3·00

Nos. 2368/71 were printed together, *se-tenant*, in blocks of 4 in sheets of 50 containing two panes of 25.

Nos. 2372/5 were issued in rolls of 100 containing the five designs in sequence and had the surplus self-adhesive paper around each stamp removed.

The phosphor on Nos. 2372/5 appears only on parts of the design including the panel at lower right of each stamp.

(Des Hannah Mattner. Litho SNP Sprint)

2004 (13 Apr). 50th Anniv of Royal Tour to Australia. Phosphorised paper. P 14×14½.

2376	**689**	50c. deep reddish purple, black and olive-grey	1·25	55

No. 2376 was also issued in Premium booklets, No. SP17, containing five panes of four stamps with margins all round. No. SP17 contains stamps with a face value of $10 and was sold for $10.95.

690 Red Lacewing

691 Cockatoos and Aircraft

(Des W. Rankin. Litho SNP Sprint)

2004 (4 May). Fauna and Flora (7th series). Rainforest Butterflies. T **690** and similar horiz designs. Multicoloured. Ordinary paper (5c.) or phosphorised paper (others). P 14½×14 ($2) or 14×14½ (others).

2377	5c. Type **690**	35	20
2378	10c. Blue-banded Eggfly	35	15
	a. Perf 14×13½	7·50	7·50
2379	75c. Cruiser	1·75	50
2380	$2 Ulysses and Red Lacewing butterflies and Daintree Rainforest (50×30 *mm*)	4·00	2·50
2377/80 *Set of 4*		5·75	3·00

(Des M. Heine. Litho SNP Sprint)

2004 (18 May). Australian Innovations. T **691** and similar horiz designs. Multicoloured.

(a) Ordinary gum. Phosphorised paper. P 14×14½

2381	50c. Type **691** (black box flight recorder, 1961)	1·50	1·10
	a. Horiz strip of 5. Nos. 2381/5	6·50	5·00
2382	50c. Pregnant woman (ultrasound imaging equipment, 1976)	1·50	1·10
2383	50c. Driver's hands on wheel (Racecam TV sport coverage, 1979)	1·50	1·10
2384	50c. Kangaroo with joey and car (baby safety capsule, 1984)	1·50	1·10
2385	50c. Portion of banknote and tree (polymer banknotes, 1988)	1·50	1·10
2381/5 *Set of 5*		6·50	5·00

(b) Self-adhesive. Phosphor frame. P 11×11½

2386	50c. Type **691** (black box flight recorder, 1961)	90	1·25
	a. Booklet pane. Nos. 2386/90, each×2	8·00	
2387	50c. Pregnant woman (ultrasound imaging equipment, 1976)	90	1·25
2388	50c. Driver's hands on wheel (Racecam TV sport coverage, 1979)	90	1·25
2389	50c. Kangaroo with joey and car (baby safety capsule, 1984)	90	1·25
2390	50c. Portion of banknote and tree (polymer banknotes, 1988)	90	1·25
2386/90 *Set of 5*		4·00	5·50

Nos. 2381/5 were printed together, *se-tenant*, in horizontal strips of five throughout the sheet.

Nos. 2386/90 were only issued in $5 booklets, No. SB169, on which the surplus self-adhesive paper around each stamp was retained.

Nos. 2386/90 have irregular phosphor frames around the edges of the designs.

692 Shaw Savill Lines *Dominion Monarch*

693 Eureka Flag (Southern Cross)

(Des Melinda Coombs. Litho SNP Sprint)

2004 (1 June)–**05** (22 Feb). "Bon Voyage". Ocean Liners. T **692** and similar vert designs showing advertising posters. Multicoloured. PVA gum.

(a) Phosphorised paper. P 14½×14

2391	50c. Type **692**	1·00	45
2392	$1 Union Steam Ship Co. *Awatea*	1·75	85
2393	$1.45 Orient Line *Ormonde & Orsova*	2·25	2·00
2394	$2 Aberdeen & Commonwealth Line liner passing under bridge	2·75	2·75
2391/4	*Set of 4*	7·00	5·50

(b) Self-adhesive. Partial phosphor frame. P 11½×11

2395	50c. Type **692**	60	80
	a. Booklet pane. No. 2395×10	5·50	
	b. Perf 11½ (interrupted) (22.2.05)	60	80
	ba. Sheetlet of 10	5·50	7·00

No. 2395 was only issued in $5 booklets, No. SB170, on which the surplus self-adhesive paper around each stamp was retained.

No. 2395b was issued in self-adhesive sheetlets of ten. The two horizontal edges of No. 2395b each have two sets of four teeth separated by a straight line.

(Des Janet Boschen. Litho SNP Sprint)

2004 (29 June). 150th Anniv of Eureka Stockade. T **693** and similar horiz design. Multicoloured. Phosphorised paper. P 14½×14.

2396	50c. Type **693**	60	45
2397	$2.45 Peter Lalor (gold diggers leader) and detail from "Swearing allegiance to the Southern Cross 1854" (Alphonse Doudiet)	2·75	3·00
MS2398	106×69 mm. Nos. 2396/7	3·25	3·25

Nos. 2396/8 were also issued in premium booklets, No. SP18, sold at $10.95.

694 Koala

695 Swimming

(Des Belinda Marsh. Litho and foil embossed ($2.45) or litho (others) SNP Sprint)

2004 (13 July). "Impressions". Australian Wildlife and Heritage. T **694** and similar multicoloured designs. Phosphorised paper. P 14×14½ (vert) or 14½×14 (horiz).

2399	$1 Type **694**	2·00	1·75
	a. Pair. Nos. 2399/2400	4·00	3·50
2400	$1 Little Penguin	2·00	1·75
2401	$1.45 Clown Anemonefish (*horiz*)	2·00	1·75
2402	$2.45 Gold Coast (*horiz*)	3·00	3·50
2399/402	*Set of 4*	8·00	8·00

Nos. 2399/2400 were issued together in *se-tenant* pairs throughout the sheet.

(Des C. Shurey. Litho SNP Sprint)

2004 (3 Aug). Olympic Games, Athens. T **695** and similar horiz designs. Multicoloured. Phosphorised paper. P 14×14½.

2403	50c. Type **695**	60	45
2404	$1.65 Sprinting	1·90	1·90
2405	$1.65 Cycling	2·75	1·90
2403/5	*Set of 3*	4·75	3·75

696 Ian Thorpe (Men's 400m Freestyle Swimming)

697 Entrance Beach, Broome, Western Australia

(Des Lisa Christensen. Litho SNP Sprint)

2004 (16 Aug–30 Aug). Australian Gold Medal Winners at Athens Olympic Games. T **696** and similar square designs. Multicoloured. P 14½.

2406	50c. Type **696**	55	65
2407	50c. Women's 4×100m Relay Team (16.8)	55	65
2408	50c. Sara Carrigan (Road Race Cycling) (17.8)	55	65
2409	50c. Petria Thomas (Women's 100m Butterfly Swimming) (17.8)	55	65
2410	50c. Suzanne Balogh (Women's Trap Shooting) (18.8)	55	65
2411	50c. Ian Thorpe (Men's 200m Freestyle Swimming) (18.8)	55	65
2412	50c. Jodie Henry (Women's 100m Freestyle Swimming) (23.8)	55	65
2413	50c. Anna Meares (Women's 500m Time Trial Cycling) (23.8)	55	65
2414	50c. James Tomkins and Drew Ginn (Men's Pair Rowing) (23.8)	55	65
2415	50c. Grant Hacket (Men's 1500m Freestyle Swimming) (23.8)	55	65
2416	50c. Women's 4×100m Medley Relay Swimming Team (23.8)	55	65
2417	50c. Chantelle Newberry (Women's 10m Platform Diving) (24.8)	55	65
2418	50c. Men's 4000m Pursuit Cycling Team (25.8)	55	65
2419	50c. Ryan Bayley (Men's Individual Sprint Cycling) (26.8)	55	65
2420	50c. Graeme Brown and Stuart O'Grady (Men's Madison Cycling) (27 Aug)	55	65
2421	50c. Ryan Bayley (Men's Keirin Cycling) (27.8)	55	65
2422	50c. Men's Hockey Team (30.8)	55	65
2406/22	*Set of 17*	8·50	9·50

Nos. 2406/22 were each issued in a standard sheet of 10 (2×5) with an enlarged inscribed margin at right.

(Des Lynette Traynor. Litho SNP Sprint)

2004 (6 Sept). International Stamps. Views of Australia (5th series). Coastlines. T **697** and similar horiz designs. Multicoloured. Phosphorised paper. P 14½×14.

2423	$1.20 Type **697**	2·50	50
2424	$1.80 Mt. William National Park, Tasmania	3·00	90
2425	$2.40 Potato Point, Bodalla, New South Wales	3·75	1·50
2426	$3.60 Point Gibbon, Eyre Peninsula, South Australia	5·50	2·75
2423/6	*Set of 4*	13·00	5·00

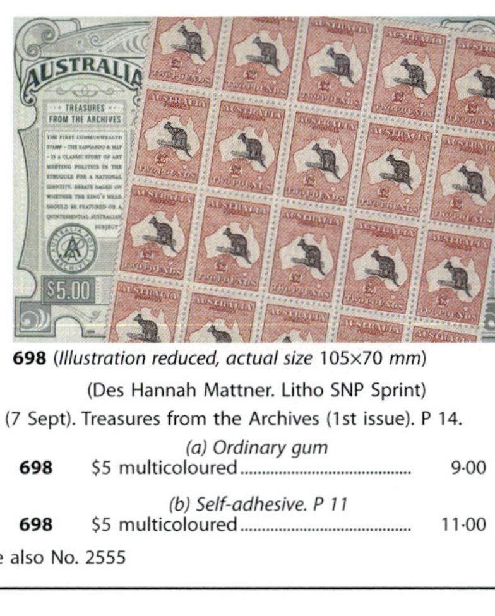

698 (*Illustration reduced, actual size* 105×70 *mm*)

(Des Hannah Mattner. Litho SNP Sprint)

2004 (7 Sept). Treasures from the Archives (1st issue). P 14.

(a) Ordinary gum

2427	**698**	$5 multicoloured	9·00	11·00

(b) Self-adhesive. P 11

2428	**698**	$5 multicoloured	11·00	14·00

See also No. 2555

699 Stephenson 2-4-0 (Melbourne—Sandridge, 1854)

700 "Ezzie" (black and white cat)

(Des N. Culic. Litho SNP Sprint)

2004 (7 Sept). 150th Anniv of Australian Railways. T **699** and similar horiz designs. Multicoloured.

(a) Ordinary gum. Phosphorised paper. P 14×14½

2429	50c. Type **699**	1·00	1·10
	a. Horiz strip of 5. Nos. 2429/33	4·50	5·00
2430	50c. Locomotive No. 1 (Sydney—Parramatta, 1855)	1·00	1·10
2431	50c. B12 Class locomotive (Helidon—Toowoomba, 1867)	1·00	1·10
2432	50c. G Class train (Kalgoorlie—Port Augusta, 1917)	1·00	1·10
2433	50c. The Ghan (Alice Springs—Darwin, 2004)	1·00	1·10
2429/33 *Set of 5*		4·50	5·00

(b) Self-adhesive. Phosphor frame. P 11×11½

2434	50c. Type **699**	75	85
	a. Horiz strip of 5. Nos. 2434/8	3·25	3·75
	b. Booklet pane. Nos. 2434/8, each×2	8·00	
2435	50c. Locomotive No. 1 (Sydney—Parramatta, 1855)	75	85
2436	50c. B12 Class locomotive (Helidon—Toowoomba, 1867)	75	85
2437	50c. G Class train (Kalgoorlie—Port Augusta, 1917)	75	85
2438	50c. The Ghan (Alice Springs—Darwin, 2004)	75	85
2434/8 *Set of 5*		3·25	3·75

Nos. 2429/33 were printed together, *se-tenant*, in horizontal strips of five throughout sheets of 50 stamps.

Nos. 2429/33 were also issued in Premium booklets, No. SP19, containing five panes of four, one of each design, with margins all round. No. SP19 contains stamps with a face value of $10 and was sold for $10.95.

Nos. 2434/8 were issued in rolls of 100 containing the five designs in sequence, on which the surplus self-adhesive paper was removed, and in $5 booklets of 10, No. SB171, on which it was retained.

(Des Jo Muré. Litho SNP Sprint)

2004 (21 Sept). Cats and Dogs. T **700** and similar vert designs. Multicoloured.

(a) Ordinary gum. Phosphorised paper. P 14×14½

2439	50c. Type **700**	1·75	1·75
	a. Pair. Nos. 2439/40	3·50	3·50
2440	50c. "Tinkerbell" (ginger and white kitten)	1·75	1·75
2441	50c. "Max" (Labrador puppy)	1·75	1·75
	a. Pair. Nos. 2441/2	3·50	3·50
2442	50c. "Bridie" and "Lily" (West Highland Terriers)	1·75	1·75
2443	$1 "Edward" (Jack Russell Terrier)	2·50	1·75
2439/43 *Set of 5*		8·50	8·00
MS2444 170×85 mm. Nos. 2439/43		8·50	8·00

(b) Self-adhesive. Irregular phosphor backgrounds. Die-cut perf 11 (interupted on horiz sides)

2445	50c. "Max" (Labrador puppy)	80	1·00
	a. Booklet pane. Nos. 2445/6 both×3, and Nos. 2447/8 both×2	6·50	
	b. Booklet pane. No. 2445×3 and 2447×2	3·50	
2446	50c. Type **700**	80	1·00
	b. Booklet pane. No. 2446×3 and 2448×2	3·50	
2447	50c. "Bridie" and "Lily" (West Highland Terriers)	80	1·00
2448	50c. "Tinkerbell" (ginger and white kitten)	80	1·00
2449	$1 Edward (Jack Russell Terrier)	1·50	1·60
	b. Booklet pane. No. 2449×5	7·00	
2445/9 *Set of 5*		4·25	5·00

Nos. 2439/40 and 2441/2 were each issued together in *se-tenant* pairs throughout the sheet.

Nos. 2439/43 were also issued in Premium booklets, Nos. SP20/1, and sold at $10.95.

Nos. 2445/8 were issued in $5 booklets, No. SB172, on which the surplus self-adhesive paper around each stamp was retained. Nos. 2445b/6b were both issued in $2.50 booklets (Nos. SB173/4) and No. 2449b in $5 booklets (No. SB175).

701 Mick Doohan (Repsol)

702 Mary and Jesus

(Des Symone Lambert. Litho SNP Sprint)

2004 (12 Oct). Heroes of Grand Prix 1 Motorcycle Racing. T **701** and similar horiz designs. Multicoloured. P 14×14½.

(a) Ordinary gum. Phosphorised paper

2450	50c. Type **701**	1·00	1·00
	a. Horiz strip of 5. Nos. 2450/4	4·50	4·50
2451	50c. Wayne Gardner (Racing Honda)	1·00	1·00
2452	50c. Troy Bayliss (Ducati)	1·00	1·00
2453	50c. Daryl Beattie (Team Suzuki)	1·00	1·00
2454	50c. Garry McCoy (Red Bull)	1·00	1·00
2450/4 *Set of 5*		4·50	4·50

(b) Self-adhesive. Irregular phosphor backgrounds. Die-cut perf 11 (interrupted on vert sides)

2455	50c. Type **701**	80	90
	a. Horiz strip of 5. Nos. 2455/9	3·50	4·00
	b. Booklet pane. No. 2455/9, each×2	8·00	
2456	50c. Wayne Gardner (Racing Honda)	80	90
2457	50c. Troy Bayliss (Ducati)	80	90
2458	50c. Daryl Beattie (Team Suzuki)	80	90
2459	50c. Garry McCoy (Red Bull)	80	90
2455/9 *Set of 5*		3·50	4·00

Nos. 2450/4 were printed together, *se-tenant*, as horizontal strips of 5 throughout the sheet.

Nos. 2455/9 were issued in rolls of 100 containing the five designs in sequence, on which the surplus self-adhesive paper was removed, and in $5 booklets of 10, No. SB173, on which it was retained.

2004 (28 Oct). China 2004 Stamp and Coin Expo. No **MS**2356 with inscription in sheet margin.

MS2459*a* 135×72 mm. Nos. 2352/5		4·50	4·75

(Des Jeanette Fallon. Litho SNP Sprint)

2004 (1 Nov). Christmas. T **702** and similar multicoloured designs. Phosphorised paper.

(a) Domestic mail. P 14½×14

2460	45c. Type **702**	40	15
2461	50c. The Angel and the shepherds	45	15

(b) International mail. P 14×14½ ($1)

2462	$1 The Three Wise Men (*horiz*)	80	80
2460/2 *Set of 3*		1·50	1·00

(c) Self-adhesive. Phosphor over design (45c.) or over background ($1). Die-cut perf 11 (interrupted on vert (45c.)or horiz ($1) sides)

2463	45c. Type **702**	40	40
	a. Booklet pane. No. 2463 ×20 plus 20 "card only" labels	7·00	
2464	$1 The Three Wise Men (*horiz*)	90	1·25
	a. Pane. No. 2464 ×5	4·00	

No. 2463 was only available in $9 stamp booklets, No. SB178. No. 2464 was issued in $5 panes of five stamps.

703 Tennis Player and Match, Warehousemen's Cricket Ground, Melbourne, *c.* 1905

704 Prue Acton

(Des Asprey Creative. Litho SNP Sprint)

2005 (11 Jan). Centenary of Australian Open Tennis Championships. T **703** and similar horiz design. Multicoloured. Phosphorised paper. P 14×15.

(a) Domestic Mail

2465	50c. Type **703**	1·50	50

(b) International Post

2466	$1.80 Woman player and match, Melbourne Park, *c.* 2005	3·00	2·75

Nos. 2465/6 were also issued in Premium booklets, No. SP22, sold at $10.95.

(Des A. Pugh. Litho SNP Sprint)

2005 (21 Jan). Australian Legends (9th series). Fashion Designers. T **704** and similar vert designs. Multicoloured. P 15×14.

(a) Ordinary gum. Phosphorised paper

2467	50c. Type **704**	55	80
	a. Horiz pair. Nos. 2467/8	1·10	1·60
2468	50c. Jenny Bannister	55	80
2469	50c. Collette Dinnigan	55	80
	a. Horiz pair. Nos. 2469/70	1·10	1·60
2470	50c. Akira Isogawa	55	80
2471	50c. Joe Saba	55	80
	a. Horiz pair. Nos. 2471/2	1·10	1·60
2472	50c. Carla Zampatti	55	80
2467/72 *Set of 6*		3·00	4·25

(b) Self-adhesive. Irregular phosphor frame (on three sides of each stamp). P 12×11½, interrupted perfs on two sides

2473	50c. Type **704**	90	1·10
	a. Booklet pane. Nos. 2473/4, each×5	8·00	
2474	50c. Jenny Bannister	90	1·10
2475	50c. Collette Dinnigan	90	1·10
	a. Booklet pane. Nos. 2475/6, each×5	8·00	
2476	50c. Akira Isogawa	90	1·10
2477	50c. Joe Saba	90	1·10
	a. Booklet pane. Nos. 2477/8, each×5	8·00	
2478	50c. Carla Zampatti	90	1·10
2473/8 *Set of 6*		4·75	6·00

Nos. 2467/8, 2469/70 and 2471/2 were printed together, *se-tenant*, in horizontal pairs throughout the sheets.

Nos. 2473/4, 2475/6 and 2477/8 were each only issued in $5 booklets, Nos. SB179/81, on which the surplus self-adhesive paper around each stamp was retained.

705 Princess Parrot

706 Sir Donald Bradman's Cap

(Des K. Stead. Litho SNP Sprint)

2005 (6 Feb). Australian Parrots. T **705** and similar vert designs. Multicoloured.

(a) Ordinary gum. Phosphorised paper. P 15×14, interrupted perfs on two sides

2479	50c. Type **705**	1·00	1·00
	a. Horiz strip of 5. Nos. 2479/83	4·50	4·50
2480	50c. Rainbow Lorikeet	1·00	1·00
2481	50c. Green Rosella	1·00	1·00
2482	50c. Red-capped Parrot	1·00	1·00
2483	50c. Purple-crowned Lorikeet	1·00	1·00
2479/83 *Set of 5*		4·50	4·50

(b) Self-adhesive. Irregular phosphor frame. P 12×11½, interrupted perfs on two sides

2484	50c. Type **705**	1·10	1·10
	a. Vert strip of 5. Nos. 2484/8	5·00	5·00
2485	50c. Rainbow Lorikeet	1·10	1·10
2486	50c. Green Rosella	1·10	1·10
2487	50c. Red-capped Parrot	1·10	1·10
2488	50c. Purple-crowned Lorikeet	1·10	1·10
2484/8 *Set of 5*		5·00	5·00

Nos. 2479/83 were printed together, *se-tenant*, in horizontal strips of five throughout the sheet.

Nos. 2484/8 were issued in rolls of 100 containing the five designs in sequence, on which the surplus self-adhesive paper around each stamp was removed.

(Des S. Pethick. Litho SNP Sprint)

2005 (8 Mar). Sporting Treasures. T **706** and similar vert designs. Multicoloured. Phosphorised paper. P 15×14.

2489	50c. Type **706**	1·75	1·25
	a. Pair. Nos. 2489/90	3·50	2·50
2490	50c. Lionel Rose's boxing gloves	1·75	1·25
2491	$1 Marjorie Jackson's running spikes	2·00	1·50
	a. Pair. Nos. 2491/2	4·00	3·00
2492	$1 Phar Lap's racing silks	2·00	1·50
2489/92 *Set of 4*		6·75	5·00

Nos. 2489/90 and 2491/2 were each printed together, *se-tenant*, in horizontal and vertical pairs in sheets of 50 (2 panes of 25).

707 Bumble Bee Toy

708 Greater Blue Mountains Area, New South Wales

(Des Fragile Design. Litho SNP Sprint)

2005 (22 Mar). Greetings Stamps. "Marking the Occasion" (1st series). T **707** and similar vert designs. Multicoloured. Phosphorised paper. P 15×14.

(i) Domestic Mail

2493	50c. Type **707**	1·00	1·10
	a. Horiz strip of 5. Nos. 2493/7	4·50	5·00
2494	50c. Red roses	1·00	1·10
2495	50c. Wrapped presents	1·00	1·10
2496	50c. Kangaroos at sunset	1·00	1·10
2497	50c. Bouquet of white flowers	1·00	1·10
2498	$1 Hand holding bouquet of cream roses	1·75	1·25

(ii) International Post

2499	$1.10 Koala	1·75	1·50
2500	$1.20 Shell on sandy beach	2·00	2·25
2501	$1.80 Sydney Opera House	3·50	3·50
2493/501 *Set of 9*		12·50	12·50

Nos. 2493/7 were printed together, *se-tenant*, in horizontal strips of 5 throughout the sheet.

Self-adhesive designs as Nos. 2493/5 and 2497/501 were also issued in premium stamp booklets, Nos. SP52/8, the $1.80 value having phosphor bands, and the other values from these booklets having irregular phosphor frames. Nos. 2493/5 and 2497/9 were all issued in separate booklets, sold at $10.95 (Nos. 2493/5, 2497), $20.95 (No. 2498) or $12.95 (No. 2499). Nos. 2500/1 were issued together in $12.95 booklets.

See also No. 2556/7

(Des J. Godfrey. Litho SNP Sprint)

2005 (21 Apr). World Heritage Sites. T **708** and similar square designs. Multicoloured. Phosphorised paper. P 14½.

2502	50c. Type **708**	1·50	1·00
	a. Horiz pair. Nos. 2502/3	3·00	2·00
2503	50c. Blenheim Palace, England	1·50	1·00
2504	50c. Wet Tropics, Queensland	1·50	1·00
	a. Horiz pair. Nos. 2504/5	3·00	2·00
2505	50c. Stonehenge, England	1·50	1·00
2506	$1 Purnululu National Park, Western Australia	2·00	1·50
	a. Horiz pair. Nos. 2506/7	4·00	3·00
2507	$1 Heart of Neolithic Orkney, Scotland	2·00	1·50
2508	$1.80 Uluru-Kata Tjuta National Park, Northern Territories	2·75	3·00
	a. Horiz pair. Nos. 2508/9	5·50	6·00
2509	$1.80 Hadrian's Wall, England	2·75	3·00
2502/9 *Set of 8*		14·00	11·50

Nos. 2502/3, 2504/5, 2506/7 and 2508/9 were printed together, *se-tenant*, in horizontal pairs in sheets of 20.

Stamps in similar designs were also issued by Great Britain.

709 *Tribrachidium*

710 Rotary Emblem and Man supporting Globe

(Des P. Trusler and Belinda Marshall. Litho SNP Sprint)

2005 (21 Apr). "Creatures of the Slime" (Ediacaran fossils). T **709** and similar horiz designs. Multicoloured. Phosphorised paper. P 14×15.

2510	50c. Type **709**	1·60	1·00
	a. Horiz strip of 5. Nos. 2510/14	7·00	4·50
2511	50c. *Dickinsonia*	1·60	1·00
2512	50c. *Spriggina*	1·60	1·00
2513	50c. *Kimberella*	1·60	1·00
2514	50c. *Inaria*	1·60	1·00
2515	$1 *Charniodiscus*	2·25	1·50
2510/15 *Set of 6*		9·25	6·00
MS2516	170×210 mm. Nos. 2510/15	6·00	5·50

Nos. 2510/14 were printed together, *se-tenant*, in horizontal strips of 5 in sheets of 50 (2×25).

(Des N. Buchanan. Litho SNP Sprint)

2005 (21 Apr). Centenary of Rotary International.

(a) Ordinary gum. Phosphorised paper. P 15×14

2517	**710**	50c. multicoloured	1·25	85

(b) Self-adhesive. Phosphor over part of design. P 11½ , interrupted perfs on both sides

2518	**710**	50c. multicoloured	70	1·00
		a. Booklet pane. No. 2518×10	6·25	

No. 2517 was issued in sheetlets of ten. A limited number of imperforate sheetlets were sold at face value at the Pacific Explorer International Philatelic Exhibition in April 2005.

No. 2518 was issued either as rolls of 100, on which the surplus self-adhesive paper was removed, or in booklets of ten, No. SB182, on which it was retained.

The two horizontal edges of No. 2518 each have five teeth separated by a straight line. It has phosphor over the Rotary emblem and the top left portion of the yellow part of the design under the globe.

711 Obverse of Coin showing Head of Queen Victoria

712 Queen at Opening Ceremony for Commonwealth Heads of Government Meeting, Queensland, 2002

(Des A. Hogg. Litho or litho and embossed (**MS**2510) SNP Sprint)

2005 (21 Apr). 150th Anniv of First Australian Coin. T **711** and similar horiz design showing one sovereign coin and Sydney Mint building. Multicoloured. Phosphorised paper. P 14×15.

2519	50c. Type **711**	1·50	85
2520	$2.45 Reverse of coin showing olive wreath	4·50	3·25
MS2521	105×69 mm. As Nos. 2519/20 but coins in gold foil	6·00	4·75

(Des Lisa Christensen. Litho SNP Sprint)

2005 (10 May). Queen Elizabeth II's Birthday. Phosphorised paper. P 14×15.

2522	**712**	50c. multicoloured	1·50	60

No. 2522 was also issued in premium stamp booklets, No. SP75, sold at $10.95.

713 Superb Lyrebird

714 Sturt's Desert Pea

(Des K. Stead and Cathleen Cram. Litho SEP Sprint)

2005 (7 June). International Stamps. Bush Wildlife. T **713** and similar horiz designs. Multicoloured.

(a) Ordinary gum. Phosphorised paper. P 14×15

2523	$1 Type **713**	1·50	60
2524	$1.10 Laughing Kookaburra	1·50	65
2525	$1.20 Koala	1·60	80
2526	$1.80 Red Kangaroo	2·50	1·50
2523/6 *Set of 4*		6·25	3·25

*(b) Self-adhesive. Phosphor over *parts of design ($1.10, $1.20) or irregular phosphor frame ($1.80). P 11½, interrupted perfs on two sides*

2527	$1.10 Laughing Kookaburra	1·50	1·75
	a. Booklet pane. No. 2527×5	7·00	
2528	$1.20 Koala	1·60	1·75
	a. Booklet pane. No. 2528×5	7·50	
2529	$1.80 Red Kangaroo	2·25	2·75
	a. Booklet pane. No. 2529×5	10·00	

*No. 2527 has phosphor over the white parts of the kookaburras, No. 2528 has phosphor over the adult koala, and No. 2529 has an irregular phosphor frame at the right and foot of the stamp.

The two vertical edges of Nos. 2527/9 each have two sets of five teeth separated by a straight line.

Nos. 2527/9 were only issued in separate $5.50, $6 and $9 booklets, Nos. SB183/5, on which the surplus self-adhesive paper around each stamp was retained.

(Des Janet Boschen)

2005 (5 July). Australian Wildflowers (1st series). T **714** and similar horiz designs. Multicoloured.

(a) Ordinary gum. Litho SEP Sprint. Phosphorised paper. P 14×14½

2530	50c. Type **714**	1·00	1·00
	a. Horiz strip of 4. Nos. 2530/3	3·50	3·50
2531	50c. Coarse-leaved Mallee	1·00	1·00
2532	50c. Common Fringe Lily	1·00	1·00
2533	50c. Swamp Daisy	1·00	1·00
2530/3 *Set of 4*		3·50	3·50

(b) Self-adhesive. Litho SEP Sprint (Nos. 2534/7) or Pemara (Nos. 2534e/7e). Phosphor over parts of the designs. P 11½ (Nos. 2534/7) or 13 (Nos. 2534e/7e)

2534	50c. Type **714**	85	1·10
	a. Horiz strip of 4. Nos. 2534/7	3·00	4·00
	b. Sheetlet. No. 2534×2 and Nos. 2535/7	3·75	
	c. Booklet pane. Nos. 2534/5, each×3, and Nos. 2536/7, each×2	8·50	
	d. Booklet pane. Nos. 2534/7, each×5	13·00	
	e. Perf 13	85	1·10
	ea. Strip of 4. Nos. 2534e/7e	3·00	4·00
2535	50c. Coarse-leaved Mallee	85	1·10
	e. Perf 13	85	1·10
2536	50c. Common Fringe Lily	85	1·10
	e. Perf 13	85	1·10
2537	50c. Swamp Daisy	85	1·10
	e. Perf 13	85	1·10
2534/7 *Set of 4*		3·00	4·00

Nos. 2530/3 were printed together, *se-tenant*, in horizontal strips of four in sheets of 50.

Nos. 2534/7 come from rolls of 100 (SEP Sprint) or 200 (Pemara) containing the four designs in sequence, and also from self-adhesive sheetlets of five and booklets of ten (SB186) and 20 (SB187). The rolls have the self-adhesive paper around each stamp removed, but the sheetlets and booklets have it retained.

See also Nos. 2590/**MS**2594 and 2759/62.

715 Vineyard

716 Snowgum

(Des A. Hogg. Litho SEP Sprint)

2005 (19 July). Australian Wine. T **715** and similar horiz designs. Multicoloured.

(a) PVA gum. Phosphorised paper. P 14×15

2538	50c. Type **715**	1·50	1·25
	a. Horiz pair. Nos. 2538/9	3·00	2·50
2539	50c. Ripening grapes	1·50	1·25
2540	$1 Harvesting grapes	2·00	2·00
	a. Horiz pair. Nos. 2540/1	4·00	4·00
2541	$1 Casks of wine	2·00	2·00
2542	$1.45 Glasses of red and white wine and cheese	3·00	3·00
2538/42 *Set of 5*		9·00	8·50

(b) Self-adhesive. Phosphor over parts of design. P 11½, interrupted perfs on two sides

2543	50c. Type **715**	80	1·00
	a. Booklet pane. Nos. 2543/4, each×5	7·25	
2544	50c. Ripening grapes	80	1·00

Nos. 2538/9 and 2540/1 were each printed together, *se-tenant*, in horizontal pairs in sheets of 50 (2×25).

Nos. 2538/42 were also issued in premium booklets, No. SP78, sold at $10.95.

The two vertical edges of Nos. 2543/4 each have two sets of five teeth separated by a straight line.

Nos. 2543/4 were only issued in $5 booklets, No. SB188, on which the surplus self-adhesive paper around each stamp was retained.

(Des Lisa Christensen. Litho SEP Sprint)

2005 (8 Aug). Native Trees. T **716** and similar horiz designs. Multicoloured.

(a) PVA gum. Phosphorised paper. P 14×15

2545	50c. Type **716**	90	90
	a. Horiz strip of 5. Nos. 2545/9	4·00	4·00
2546	50c. Wollemi Pine	90	90
2547	50c. Boab	90	90
2548	50c. Karri	90	90
2549	50c. Moreton Bay Fig	90	90
2545/9 *Set of 5*		4·00	4·00

(b) Self-adhesive. Phosphor frame. P 11½ , interrupted perfs on two sides

2550	50c. Type **716**	80	1·00
	a. Horiz strip of 5. Nos. 2550/4	3·50	4·50
2551	50c. Wollemi Pine	80	1·00
2552	50c. Boab	80	1·00
2553	50c. Karri	80	1·00
2554	50c. Moreton Bay Fig	80	1·00
2550/4 *Set of 5*		3·50	4·50

Nos. 2545/9 were printed together, *se-tenant*, in horizontal strips of five in sheets of 50.

Nos. 2550/4 have grey frames, and come from rolls of 100 containing the five designs in sequence, with the surplus self-adhesive paper around each stamp removed. The two vertical edges of Nos. 2550/4 each have two sets of five teeth separated by a straight line.

717 Sheet of 1888 20s. New South Wales Stamps (*Illustration reduced, actual size* 105×70 *mm*)

(Des Hannah Mattner. Litho SEP Sprint)

2005 (6 Sept). Treasures from the Archives (2nd issue). Phosphorised paper. P 14½.

2555	**717**	$5 multicoloured	14·00	16·00

718 Christmas Tree with Lights

719 Chloe the Chicken

(Des Fragile Design. Litho SEP Sprint)

2005 (6 Sept). Greetings Stamps. "Marking the Occasion" (2nd series). T **718** and similar vert design. Multicoloured. Phosphorised paper. P 15×14.

2556	45c. Type **718**	85	85
2557	50c. Map of Australia with stars	85	85

No. 2556 was also issued in premium booklets, No. SP80, sold at $9.95.

(Des J. Tufrey and Beth McKinlay. Litho SEP Sprint)

2005 (4 Oct). Stamp Collecting Month. "Down on the Farm". T **719** and similar horiz designs. Multicoloured.

(a) Ordinary gum. Phosphorised paper. P 14×15

2558	50c. Type **719**	85	85
	a. Horiz strip of 5. Nos. 2558/62	3·75	3·75
2559	50c. Lucy the Lamb	85	85
2560	50c. Gilbert the Goat	85	85
2561	50c. Ralph the Piglet	85	85
2562	50c. Abigail the Cow	85	85
2563	$1 Harry the Horse	1·40	1·40
2558/63	*Set of* 6	5·00	5·00
MS2564	170×85 mm. Nos. 2558/63	5·50	5·50

(b) Self-adhesive. Phosphor frame. P 11½, interrupted perfs on both sides

2565	50c. Type **719**	1·00	1·25
	a. Booklet pane. Nos. 2565/9	6·00	
	b. Booklet pane. Nos. 2565/9, each×2	10·00	
	c. Booklet pane. Nos. 2565/9, each×4	20·00	
2566	50c. Lucy the Lamb	1·00	1·25
2567	50c. Gilbert the Goat	1·00	1·25
2568	50c. Ralph the Piglet	1·00	1·25
2569	50c. Abigail the Cow	1·00	1·25
2570	$1 Harry the Horse	2·25	3·25
	a. Booklet pane. No. 2570×5	10·00	
2565/70	*Set of* 6	6·50	8·50

Nos. 2558/62 were printed together, *se-tenant*, in horizontal strips of five stamps in sheets of 50 (2×25).

Nos. 2558/64 were also issued in premium booklets, No. SP79, sold at $9.95.

The two vertical edges of Nos. 2565/70 each have two sets of five teeth separated by a straight line.

Nos. 2565/9 were only issued in $2.50, $5 or $10 booklets (SB189/90, SB192), and No. 2570 in $5 booklets (SB191), all with the self-adhesive paper around each stamp retained.

720 Madonna and Child

721 Emblem

(Des Ursula Betka. Litho SEP Sprint)

2005 (1 Nov). Christmas. T **720** and similar multicoloured designs.

(a) Ordinary gum. Phosphorised paper. P 15×14 (45c.) or 14×15 ($1)

(i) Domestic Mail

2571	45c. Type **720**	75	15

(ii) International Mail

2572	$1 Adoring angel (*horiz*)	1·50	85

(b) Self-adhesive. Phosphor frame (45c.) or phosphor band at right ($1). P 12×11½ (45c.) or 11½×12 ($1), interrupted perfs on both sides

(i) Domestic Mail

2573	45c. Type **720**	75	15
	a. Booklet pane. No. 2573×20 plus 20 "Card Only" labels	13·00	

(ii) International Post

2574	$1 Adoring angel (*horiz*)	1·50	1·75
	a. Booklet pane. No. 2574×5	7·00	

The two vertical edges of No. 2573 and the two horizontal edges of No. 2574 each have two sets of five teeth separated by a straight line.

No. 2573 was only issued in a $9 booklet and No. 2574 in a $5 booklet.

"IMPRESSIONS". On 10 November 2005 Australia Post released the first in a series of limited-edition products, containing stamps in formats which differ from those of the original issue. As these were only available in limited numbers and lost substantially more than face value, we do not list them.

(Des G. Domoney. Litho SEP Sprint)

2006 (12 Jan). Commonwealth Games, Melbourne (1st issue).

(a) Ordinary gum. Phosphorised paper. P 15×14

2575	**721**	50c. multicoloured	60	45

(b) Self-adhesive. Phosphor over parts of design. P 11½, interrupted perfs on both sides

2576	**721**	50c. multicoloured	60	70

No. 2576 was issued in rolls of 100 and has the surplus self-adhesive paper around each stamp removed. It has irregular phosphor over top, centre and left of design. The two vertical edges each have two sets of five teeth separated by a straight line.

See also Nos. 2596/2600 and **MS**2607/ **MS**2607/ **MS**2623

722 Mrs. Norm Everage, 1969

723 Red Rose

(Des Beth McKinlay. Litho SEP Sprint)

2006 (20 Jan). Australian Legends (10th series). Barry Humphries (satirist and actor). T **722** and similar vert designs. Multicoloured.

(a) Ordinary gum. Phosphorised paper. P 15×14

2577	50c. Type **722**	1·25	1·25
	a. Horiz strip of 5. Nos. 2577/81	5·50	5·50
2578	50c. As Mrs. Edna Everage, 1973	1·25	1·25
2579	50c. As Dame Edna Everage, 1982	1·25	1·25
2580	50c. As Dame Edna Everage, 2004	1·25	1·25
2581	50c. Barry Humphries	1·25	1·25
2577/81	*Set of* 5	5·50	5·50

(b) Self-adhesive. L-shaped phosphor bands. P 11½×11, interrupted perfs on both sides

2582	50c. Type **722**	1·10	1·50
	a. Booklet pane. Nos. 2582×4 and 2583/4, each×3	9·00	
2583	50c. As No. 2578	1·10	1·50
2584	50c. As No. 2579	1·10	1·50

2585 50c. As No 2580 .... 1·10 1·50
a. Booklet pane. No. 2585/6, each×5 .... 9·00
2586 50c. As No. 2581 .... 1·10 1·50
2582/6 *Set of 5* .... 5·00 6·75

Nos. 2577/81 were printed together, *se-tenant*, as horizontal strips of five in sheets of ten.

Nos. 2582/4 and 2585/6 were each printed in separate $5 booklets, Nos. SB195/6.

The two vertical edges of Nos. 2582/6 each have two sets of five teeth separated by a straight line. The surplus self-adhesive paper around each stamp is retained.

(Des Lisa Christensen. SEP Sprint)

2006 (27 Jan). Greetings Stamp. Roses. Litho.

(a) Ordinary gum. Ordinary paper. P 14×15

2587 **723** 50c. multicoloured .... 1·00 45

(b) Self-adhesive. Size 36×25 mm. Phosphor frame. P 11½×11, interrupted perfs on both sides

(i) Litho and typo

2588 **723** 50c. multicoloured 70 70

(ii) Litho

2589 **723** 50c. multicoloured 70 70
a. Booklet pane. No. 2589×10 .... 6·25

No. 2588 has a scented overlay in the centre of the stamp with a rose fragrance. It was printed in sheetlets of ten, sold for $5.

No. 2589 was issued in $5 booklets, No. SB197.

The two vertical edges of Nos. 2588/9 each have five teeth separated by a straight line, and both stamps have the self-adhesive paper around each stamp retained.

724 Pincushion Hakea

725 Dale Begg-Smith

(Des Lynette Traynor. Litho (and embossed **MS**2594) SEP Sprint)

2006 (7 Feb). Australian Wildflowers (2nd series). T **724** and similar horiz designs. Multicoloured. Phosphorised paper. P 14×14½ ($1, $2) or 14½×14 ($5, $10).

2590 $1 Type **724** .... 1·75 50
2591 $2 Donkey orchid .... 3·75 1·25
2592 $5 Mangles kangaroo paw (49×29 *mm*) .... 7·00 4·50
2593 $10 Waratah (49×29 *mm*) .... 13·00 9·00
2590/3 *Set of 4* .... 23·00 14·00
MS2594 105×70 mm. $10 As No. 2593 (49×29 *mm*) .... 11·00 12·00

(Litho SEP Sprint)

2006 (21 Feb). Dale Begg-Smith's Gold Medal for Men's Moguls Skiing at Winter Olympic Games, Turin. Phosphorised paper. P 14½.

2595 **725** 50c. multicoloured .... 1·00 1·00

No. 2595 was printed in sheetlets of ten stamps with enlarged illustrated margins.

726 Athlete at Start

727 Platypus

(Des G. Domoney. Litho SEP Sprint)

2006 (1 Mar). Commonwealth Games, Melbourne (2nd issue). T **726** and similar horiz designs. Multicoloured.

(a) Ordinary gum. Phosphorised paper. P 14×15

(i) Domestic Mail

2596 50c. Type **726** 50 45

(ii) International Post

2597 $1.25 Cyclist .... 2·25 2·00
2598 $1.85 Netball .... 2·75 3·25
2596/8 *Set of 3* .... 5·50 5·50
MS2599 142×75 mm. Nos. 2596/8 .... 5·50 5·50

(b) Self-adhesive. Phosphor over parts of design. P 11½ , interrupted perfs on both sides

2600 50c. Type **726** 75 80
a. Booklet pane. No. 2600×10 .... 7·00

No. 2600 has an irregular block of phosphor at top and left of design. The two vertical edges each have two sets of five teeth separated by a straight line. It was only issued in a $5 booklet, No. SB198.

(Des T. Marriott. Litho SEP Sprint)

2006 (6 Mar). International Post. Native Wildlife. T **727** and similar horiz designs. Multicoloured. Phosphorised paper. P 14×15.

2601 5c. Type **727** 50 45
2602 25c. Short-beaked echidna 80 25
2603 $1.25 Common wombat .... 2·75 70
2604 $1.85 Tasmanian devil .... 3·75 1·40
2605 $2.50 Greater bilby .... 5·00 1·75
2606 $3.70 Dingo .... 7·00 3·25
2601/6 *Set of 6* .... 18·00 7·00

728 Tram with Feathered "Wings" (Opening Ceremony)

729 "Queen Elizabeth II in Garter Robes" (Pietro Annigoni)

2006 (15–28 Mar). Commonwealth Games (3rd issue). Seventeen sheets each 180×200 mm containing horiz designs as T **728** showing opening/closing ceremonies (Nos. **MS**2607, **MS**2622) or Australian gold medal winners (others). Multicoloured. Litho. Phosphorised paper. P 14½×14.

MS2607 50c.×5 No. 1 Opening Ceremony .... 2·50 3·25
MS2608 50c.×5 No. 2 (16.3) .... 2·50 3·25
MS2609 50c.×10 No. 3 (17.3) .... 4·00 6·00
MS2610 50c.×5 No. 4 (18.3) .... 2·50 3·25
MS2611 50c.×10 No. 5 (18.3) .... 4·00 6·00
MS2612 50c.×5 No. 6 (19.3) .... 2·50 3·25
MS2613 50c.×5 No. 7 (20.3) .... 2·50 3·25
MS2614 50c.×10 No. 8 (20.3) .... 4·00 6·00
MS2615 50c.×5 No. 9 (21.3) .... 2·50 3·25
MS2616 50c.×10 No. 10 (21.3) .... 4·00 6·00
MS2617 50c.×5 No. 11 (22.3) .... 2·50 3·25
MS2618 50c.×10 No. 12 (23.3) .... 4·00 6·00
MS2619 50c.×10 No. 13 (24.3) .... 4·00 6·00
MS2620 50c.×10 No. 14 (25.3) .... 4·00 6·00
MS2621 50c.×5 No. 15 (26.3) .... 2·50 3·25
MS2622 50c.×5 No. 16 Closing Ceremony (26 Mar) .... 2·50 3·25
MS2623 50c.×10 No. 17 Most memorable moment Kerryn McCann's Marathon victory (28 Mar) .... 4·00 6·00
MS2607/23 *Set of 17* .... 45·00 60·00

Nos. **MS**2607/23 are numbered from 1 to 17 at the foot of the sheet.

(Des Sally Piskuric. Litho SEP Sprint)

2006 (19 Apr). 80th Birthday of Queen Elizabeth II. T **729** and similar vert design. Multicoloured.

(a) Ordinary gum. Phosphorised paper. P 14½×14

2624 50c. Type **729** .... 1·75 45
2625 $2.45 Queen Elizabeth II (photo by Cecil Beaton) .... 5·00 4·00
MS2626 105×70 mm. Nos. 2624/5 .... 6·75 4·25

(b) Self-adhesive. Phosphor over part of design. P 11½×11, interrupted perfs on both sides

2627 50c. Type **729** .... 75 1·00
a. Booklet pane. No. 2627×10 .... 7·00

No. **MS**2626 also commemorates the 50th anniversary of the portrait by Annigoni.

No. 2627 has phosphor over the Queen and the right hand part and foot of the design. The two vertical edges have two sets of five teeth separated by a straight line.

No. 2627 was only issued in a $5 booklet, No. SB199.

730 Point Lonsdale, Victoria, 1902

731 Koala with Cub

(Des Belinda Witkowski. Litho SEP Sprint)

2006 (2 May). Lighthouses of the 20th Century. T **730** and similar vert designs. Multicoloured.

(a) Ordinary gum. Phosphorised paper. P 14½×14

2628	50c. Type **730**	1·10	1·00
	a. Horiz strip of 5. Nos. 2628/32	5·00	4·50
2629	50c. Cape Don, Northern Territory, 1916	1·10	1·00
2630	50c. Wollongong Head, New South Wales, 1937	1·10	1·00
2631	50c. Casuarina Point, West Australia, 1971	1·10	1·00
2632	50c. Point Cartwright, Queensland, 1979	1·10	1·00
2628/32 *Set of 5*		5·00	4·50

(b) Self-adhesive. Two phosphor bands. P 11½×11, interrupted perfs on both sides

2633	50c. Type **730**	1·10	1·00
	a. Vert strip of 5. Nos. 2633/7	5·00	4·50
2634	50c. As No. 2629	1·10	1·00
2635	50c. As No. 2630	1·10	1·00
2636	50c. As No. 2631	1·10	1·00
2637	50c. As No. 2632	1·10	1·00
2633/7 *Set of 5*		5·00	4·50

Nos. 2628/32 were printed together, *se-tenant*, in horizontal strips of five stamps in sheets of 50.

Nos. 2633/7 come from rolls of 100 containing the five designs in sequence, with the surplus self-adhesive paper around each stamp removed. The two horizontal edges of Nos. 2633/7 each have two sets of five teeth separated by a straight line.

(Des T. Marriott. Litho SEP Sprint)

2006 (2-27 May). International Stamps. "Greetings from Australia". T **731** and similar vert design. Multicoloured.

(a) Ordinary gum. Phosphorised paper. P 14½×14

2638	$1.25 Type **731**	2·75	1·25
2639	$1.85 Royal Exhibition Building, Melbourne	3·75	2·75

(b) Self-adhesive. Phosphor over parts of design. P 11½, interrupted perfs on both sides

2640	$1.25 Type **731**	2·25	1·50
	a. Booklet pane. No. 2640×5	10·00	
	b. As No. 2640a, but Washington 2006 International Stamp Exhibition emblem added to lower right margin of booklet pane (27.5)	11·00	
2641	$1.85 As No. 2639	2·40	3·00
	a. Booklet pane. No. 2641×5	11·00	

Nos. 2640/1 were only issued in $6.25 or $9.25 booklets, Nos. SB200/1.

The two horizontal edges of Nos. 2640/1 each have two sets of five teeth separated by a straight line.

No. 2640 has two irregular patches of phosphor: over the cub and at top left, and over the tree trunk and right middle background.

No. 2641 has phosphor over the building.

732 Boy heading Ball ("PLAY")

733 Kate sorting Mail

(Des V. Frost. Litho SEP Sprint)

2006 (9 May). World Cup Football Championship, Germany. Soccer in Australia. T **732** and similar horiz designs. Multicoloured.

(a) Ordinary gum. Phosphorised paper. P 14×14½

(i) Domestic Mail

2642	50c. Type **732**	70	80
	a. Pair. Nos. 2642/3	1·40	1·60
2643	50c. Player kicking ball ("GOAL")	70	80

(ii) International Post.

2644	$1.25 Goalkeeper ("SAVE")	1·75	1·50
2645	$1.85 Player with ball ("SHOT")	2·40	2·75
2642/5 *Set of 4*		5·00	5·25
MS2646 Circular 170×170 mm. Nos. 2642/5		4·75	4·75

(b) Self-adhesive. Phosphor over parts of design. P 11½, interrupted perfs on both sides

2647	50c. Type **732**	75	90
	a. Booklet pane. Nos. 2647/8, each×5	6·75	
2648	50c. As No. 2643	75	90

Nos. 2642/3 were printed together, *se-tenant*, in horizontal and vertical pairs in sheets of 50. No. **MS**2646 is circular and cut in the shape of a football.

Nos. 2647/8 were only printed in $5 booklets, No. SB202.

The two vertical edges of Nos. 2647/8 each have two sets of five teeth separated by a straight line. They have phosphor over the yellow parts of the design at the left and foot of the stamp.

(Des Jo Mure. Litho SEP Sprint)

2006 (1 June). "Postie Kate". T **733** and similar horiz designs. Multicoloured. Phosphorised paper. P 14×14½.

2649	50c. Type **733**	90	80
	a. Horiz strip of 5. Nos. 2649/53	4·00	3·50
2650	50c. On motorcycle, giving letter to woman	90	80
2651	50c. With van, delivering parcel	90	80
2652	50c. Riding motorcycle. passing mailbox	90	80
2653	50c. With mail satchel on shoulder	90	80
2649/53 *Set of 5*		4·00	3·50

(b) Self-adhesive. Phosphor over parts of designs. P 11½, interrupted perfs on both sides

2654	50c. Type **733**	75	80
	a. Booklet pane. Nos. 2654/8, each×2	7·50	
	b. Booklet pane. Nos. 2654/8, each×4	12·00	
2655	50c. As No. 2650	75	80
2656	50c. As No. 2651	75	80
2657	50c. As No. 2652	75	80
2658	50c. As No. 2653	75	80
2654/8 *Set of 5*		3·25	3·25

Nos. 2649/53 were printed together, *se-tenant*, in horizontal strips of five stamps in sheets of 50.

Nos. 2654/8 were only issued in $5 and $10 booklets, Nos. SB203/4.

The two vertical edges of Nos. 2654/8 each have two sets of five teeth separated by a straight line.

734 Blue Whale

(Des M. Sofilas and Passmore Design. Litho SEP Sprint)

2006 (6 June). Endangered Species. Whales. T **734** and similar horiz design. Multicoloured.

(a) Ordinary gum. Phosphorised paper. P 14×14½

(i) Domestic Mail

2659	50c. Type **734**	75	65
	a. Pair. Nos. 2659/60	1·50	1·25
2660	50c. Humpback Whale	75	65

(ii) International Post

2661	$1.25 Fin Whale	1·75	1·25
2662	$1.85 Southern Bottlenose Whale	2·75	2·75
2659/62 *Set of 4*		5·50	5·00
MS2663 170×92 mm. Nos. 2659/62		5·50	5·00

(b) Self-adhesive. Phosphor frame (50c.) or phosphor band at right (others). P 11½, interrupted perfs on both sides

(i) Domestic Mail

2664	50c. Type **734**	75	90
	a. Horiz pair. Nos. 2664/5	1·50	1·75
2665	50c. As No. 2660	75	90

(ii) International Post

2666	$1.25 As No. 2661	2·25	2·75
	a. Booklet pane. No. 2666×5	10·00	
2667	$1.85 As No. 2662	3·00	4·50
	a. Booklet pane. No. 2667×5	14·00	

Nos. 2659/60 were printed together, *se-tenant*, in horizontal and vertical pairs in sheets of 50 stamps. Nos. 2664/5 come from rolls of 100 containing both designs in sequence. They exist both with the surplus self-adhesive paper around each stamp removed and with it retained.

No. 2666/7 each come from $6.25 or $9.25 booklets, Nos. SB205/6. The two vertical edges of Nos. 2664/7 each have two sets of five teeth separated by a straight line.

2006 (17 June). Le Salon du Timbre Stamp Exhibition, Paris. No. **MS**2646 inscr "LE SALON DU TIMBRE & DE L'ECRIT 17 AU 25 JUIN 2006 PARC FLORAL DE PARIS www.salondutimbre.fr" on sheet margin.

MS2668 Circular 170×170 mm. Nos. 2642/5	4·75	4·75

735 Surfing

(Des Hoyne Design. Litho SEP Sprint)

2006 (18 July). Extreme Sports. T **735** and similar horiz designs. Multicoloured. Phosphorised paper. P 14×14½.

2669	50c. Type **735**	90	50

2670	$1 Snowboarding	1·75	1·25
2671	$1.45 Skateboarding	2·00	2·50
2672	$2 Freestyle motoX	3·50	4·00
2669/72	*Set of 4*	7·25	7·50

736 Ford TT Truck, 1917

737 "Sunbury Rock Festival" (1972)

(Des Melinda Coombes. Litho SEP Sprint)

2006 (15 Aug). Driving through the Years. T **736** and similar horiz designs. Multicoloured.

(a) Ordinary gum. Phosphorised paper. P 14×14½

2673	50c. Type **736**	1·40	1·10
	a. Horiz strip of 5. Nos. 2673/7	6·25	5·00
2674	50c. Holden FE, 1956	1·40	1·10
2675	50c. Morris 850 (Mini Minor), 1961	1·40	1·10
2676	50c. Holden Sandman HX panel van, 1976	1·40	1·10
2677	50c. Toyota LandCruiser FJ60, 1985	1·40	1·10
2673/7	*Set of 5*	6·25	5·00

(b) Self-adhesive. Irregular phosphor frame. P 11½, interrupted perfs on both sides

2678	50c. Type **736**	70	1·00
	a. Imprint date omitted*	4·00	5·00
	b. Booklet pane. No. 2678×10	8·00	
	c. Booklet pane. Nos. 2678/82, each×2	6·50	
2679	50c. As No. (2674)	70	1·00
	a. Booklet pane. No. 2679×10	6·50	
2680	50c. As No. (2675)	70	1·00
	a. Booklet pane. No. 2680×10	6·50	
2681	50c. As No. (2676)	70	1·00
	a. Booklet pane. No. 2681×10	6·50	
2682	50c. As No. (2677)	70	1·00
	a. Booklet pane. No. 2682×10	6·50	
2678/82	*Set of 5*	3·00	4·50

Nos. 2673/7 were printed together, *se-tenant*, in horizontal strips of five stamps in sheets of 50.

Nos. 2678/82 were only printed in $5 booklets, Nos. SB207/12.

The phosphor frame on No. 2678 is broken at top right.

The two vertical edges of Nos. 2678/82 each have two sets of five teeth separated by a straight line.

* The imprint date was omitted from R. 2/2 booklet pane No. 2678b.

(Des Beth McKinlay. Litho SEP Sprint)

2006 (12 Sept). Rock Posters. T **737** and similar vert designs. Multicoloured.

(a) Ordinary gum. Phosphorised paper. P 15×14

2683	50c. Type **737**	1·10	1·10
	a. Sheetlet of 10. Nos. 2683/92	10·00	10·00
2684	50c. "Magic Dirt" (2002)	1·10	1·10
2685	50c. "Masters Apprentices" (1969)	1·10	1·10
2686	50c. "Goanna's Spirit of Place" (1983)	1·10	1·10
2687	50c. "Angels/Sports/Paul Kelly" (*c.* 1979)	1·10	1·10
2688	50c. "Midnight Oil" (c. 1979)	1·10	1·10
2689	50c. "Big Day Out" (2003)	1·10	1·10
2690	50c. "Apollo Bay Music Festival" (1999)	1·10	1·10
2691	50c. "Rolling Stones Australian Tour" (1973)	1·10	1·10
2692	50c. "Mental as Anything" (1990)	1·10	1·10
2683/92	*Set of 10*	10·00	10·00

(b) Self-adhesive. Phosphor frame. P 11½, interrupted perfs on both sides

2693	50c. Type **737**	70	90
	a. Booklet pane. Nos. 2693/702	6·50	
2694	50c. As No. 2684	70	90
2695	50c. As No. 2685	70	90
2696	50c. As No. 2686	70	90
2697	50c. As No. 2687	70	90
2698	50c. As No. 2688	70	90
2699	50c. As No. 2689	70	90
2700	50c. As No. 2690	70	90
2701	50c. As No. 2691	70	90
2702	50c. As No. 2692	70	90
2693/702	*Set of 10*	6·50	8·50

Nos. 2683/92 were printed together, *se-tenant*, in sheetlets of ten stamps.

Nos. 2693/702 were only printed in $5 booklets, No. SB213.

The two vertical edges of Nos. 2693/2702 each have two sets of five teeth separated by a straight line.

738 White Shark

739 "In Melbourne Tonight"

(Des Natalie Leys. Litho SEP Sprint)

2006 (3 Oct). Stamp Collecting Month. Dangerous Australians. T **738** and similar horiz designs. Multicoloured.

(a) Ordinary gum. Phosphorised paper. P 14×15

2703	50c. Type **738**	1·50	1·75
	a. Horiz strip of 5. Nos. 2703/7	6·75	8·00
2704	50c. Eastern Brown Snake	1·50	1·75
2705	50c. Box Jellyfish	1·50	1·75
2706	50c. Saltwater Crocodile	1·50	1·75
2707	50c. Blue-Ringed Octopus	1·50	1·75
2708	$1 Yellow-bellied Sea Snake	2·00	1·75
2703/8	*Set of 6*	8·50	9·50
MS2709	130×90 mm. Nos. 2703/8	6·00	6·00

(b) Self-adhesive. Phosphor over parts of design and partial phosphor frames. P 11½, interrupted perfs on both sides

2710	50c. Type **738**	90	1·10
	a. Horiz strip of 5. Nos. 2710/14	4·00	5·00
	b. Revised phosphor layout	1·25	1·75
	c. Booklet pane. Nos. 2710b/12b and 2713/14	4·50	
2711	50c. As No. 2704	90	1·10
	b. Revised phosphor layout	1·25	1·75
2712	50c. As No 2705	90	1·10
	b. Revised phosphor layout	1·25	1·75
2713	50c. As No. 2706	90	1·10
2714	50c. As No. 2707	90	1·10
2715	$1 As No. 2708	1·40	1·75
	a. Booklet pane. No. 2715×5	6·50	
2710/15	*Set of 6*	5·00	6·50

Nos. 2703/7 were printed together, *se-tenant*, as horizontal strips of five stamps in sheets of 50 (2×25).

Nos. 2710/14 come from rolls of 100 containing the five designs in sequence and from $2.50 booklets, No. SB213. No. 2715 comes from $5 booklets, No. SB214. Stamps from rolls have the surplus self-adhesive paper around each stamp removed, but booklet stamps have it retained.

The two vertical edges of Nos. 2710/15 each have two sets of five teeth separated by a straight line.

Nos. 2710 and 2712 (from rolls) have additional phosphor over the face values at bottom right which is missing from Nos. 2710b and 2712b (from booklets).

No. 2711 (from rolls) has the phosphor at left extending over the "S" of snake, but on No. 2711b (from booklets) the phosphor does not extend over the inscription.

A miniature sheet, imperforate at top and bottom, containing Nos. 2703/7 and a $1 red-back spider stamp was only issued in a $9.95 pack.

(Des M. Heine. Litho SEP Sprint)

2006 (24 Oct). 50th Anniv of Television in Australia. T **739** and similar horiz designs. Multicoloured.

(a) Ordinary gum. Phosphorised paper. P 14×15

2716	50c. Type **739**	70	70
	a. Horiz strip of 5. Nos. 2716/20	3·25	3·25
2717	50c. "Homicide"	70	70
2718	50c. "Dateline"	70	70
2719	50c. "Neighbours"	70	70
2720	50c. "Kath and Kim"	70	70
2716/20	*Set of 5*	3·25	3·25

(b) Self-adhesive. Partial phosphor frame. P 11½, interrupted perfs on both sides

2721	50c. Type **739**	70	85
	a. Horiz strip of 5. Nos. 2721/5	3·25	3·75
	b. Booklet pane. No. 2721×10	6·50	
	c. Booklet pane. Nos. 2721/5, each×2	6·50	
2722	50c. As No. 2717	70	85
2723	50c. As No. 2718	70	85
2724	50c. As No. 2719	70	85
2725	50c. As No. (2720)	70	85
	a. Booklet pane. No. 2725×10	6·50	
2721/5	*Set of 5*	3·25	3·75

Nos. 2716/20 were printed together, *se-tenant*, as horizontal strips of five stamps in sheets of 50.

Nos. 2721/5 come from rolls of 100 containing the five designs in sequence and from $5 booklets, Nos. SB216/18. Stamps from rolls have the surplus self-adhesive paper around each stamp removed, but booklet stamps have it retained.

Nos. 2721/5 have irregular phosphor frames on three sides, broken at left, and on No. 2724 also at top.

The two vertical edges of Nos. 2721/5 each have two sets of five teeth separated by a straight line.

2006 (26 Oct). China 2006 Stamp and Coin Expo. Two sheets, each 110×80 mm containing No. 2638, design on sheet margin given. Phosphorised paper. P 14½×14.

MS2726 **731** (a) $1.25 multicoloured (Great Wall of China). (b) $1.25 multicoloured (Sydney Opera House) ... 6·50 5·50

740 2s. Melbourne across River Yarra Stamp

741 Virgin Mary and Baby Jesus

(Des Lynda Warner. Litho SEP Sprint)

2006 (1 Nov). 50th Anniv of Olympic Games, Melbourne. T **740** and similar horiz designs, showing Australia 1956 Olympic Games stamps and contemporary photographs of Melbourne. Multicoloured. Phosphorised paper. P 14×14½.

2727 50c. Type **740** ... 1·25 1·25
a. Horiz pair. Nos. 2727/8 ... 2·50 2·50
2728 50c. River Yarra, Melbourne ... 1·25 1·25
2729 $11s. Collins Street stamp ... 2·00 2·00
a. Horiz pair. Nos. 2729/30 ... 4·00 4·00
2730 $1 Collins Street, Melbourne ... 2·00 2·00
2727/30 *Set of 4* ... 6·00 6·00

Nos. 2727/8 and 2729/30 were each printed together, *se-tenant*, as horizontal pairs in sheets of 50, each pair forming a composite background design.

(Des Anne Spudvilas. Litho SEP Sprint)

2006 (1 Nov). Christmas. T **741** and similar vert designs. Mult.

(a) Ordinary gum. Phosphorised paper. P 14½×14

(i) Domestic mail

2731 45c. Type **741** ... 80 30
2732 50c. Magi with gift ... 80 35

(ii) International Mail.

2733 $1.05 Young shepherd with lamb ... 1·40 1·10
2731/3 *Set of 3* ... 2·75 1·50

(b) Self-adhesive. Smaller design 22×33 mm. Phosphor frame (45c.) or partial phosphor frame ($1.05). P 11½, interrupted perfs on both sides

(i) Domestic mail

2734 45c. Type **741** ... 70 60
a. Booklet pane. No. 2734×20 plus 20 "CARD ONLY" labels ... 12·00

(ii) International Mail

2735 $1.05 As No. 2733 ... 1·25 1·50
a. Booklet pane. No. 2735×5 ... 7·00

No. 2734 was only issued in a $9 booklet, No. SB220, and No. 2735 was only issued in a $5.25 booklet, No. SB219.

No. 2734 has a complete phosphor frame and No. 2735 has a phosphor frame at top, right and foot of the stamp.

The two horizontal edges of Nos. 2734/5 each have two sets of five teeth separated by a straight line.

742 Victorious Australian Cricketers

743 Scobie Breasley (jockey), 1936

(Des Symone Lambert. Litho SEP Sprint)

2007 (16 Jan). "Australia wins the Ashes". T **742** and similar square designs. Multicoloured.

(a) Ordinary gum. Phosphorised paper. P 14½×14

(i) Domestic Mail

2736 50c. Type **742** ... 2·25 1·00

(ii) International Post

2737 $1.85 Australian team with Ashes Urn ... 6·00 6·00
MS2738 160×80 mm. Nos. 2736/7 ... 8·00 7·00

(b) Self-adhesive. Partial phosphor frame. P 11×11½, interrupted perfs on both sides

(i) Domestic Mail

2739 50c. As No. 2736 ... 1·25 1·25
a. Pane. No. 2739×5 ... 5·00

(ii) International Post

2740 $1.85 As No. 2737 ... 4·00 5·00
a. Pane. No. 2740×5 ... 17·00

Nos. 2739/40 were only printed in separate $2.50 and $9.25 panes of five.

No. 2739 has a phosphor frame at top, left and foot of the stamp. No. 2740 has a phosphor frame at top, right and foot of the stamp.

The two horizontal edges of Nos. 2739/40 each have two sets of six teeth separated by a straight line.

(Des J. Chong. Litho SEP Sprint)

2007 (24 Jan). Australian Legends (11th series). Legends of Australian Horse Racing. T **743** and similar vert designs. Multicoloured.

(a) Ordinary gum. Phosphorised paper. P 14½×14

2741 50c. Type **743** ... 1·50 1·50
a. Block of 4. Nos. 2741/4 ... 5·50 5·50
2742 50c. Scobie Breasley on "Santa Claus" after winning English Derby ... 1·50 1·50
2743 50c. Bart Cummings (trainer) holding binoculars, 1966 ... 1·50 1·50
2744 50c. Bart Cummings holding Melbourne Cup ... 1·50 1·50
2745 50c. Roy Higgins (jockey), 1965 ... 1·50 1·50
a. Block of 4. Nos. 2745/8 ... 5·50 5·50
2746 50c. Roy Higgins riding "Light Fingers" to win Melbourne Cup, 1965 ... 1·50 1·50
2747 50c. Bob Ingham (breeder), *c.* 1972 ... 1·50 1·50
2748 50c. Bob Ingham leading "Lonhro", 2004 ... 1·50 1·50
2749 50c. George Moore (jockey), 1957 ... 1·50 1·50
a. Block of 4. Nos. 2749/52 ... 5·50 5·50
2750 50c. George Moore riding "Tulloch", 1960 ... 1·50 1·50
2751 50c. John Tapp (race commentator), 1972 ... 1·50 1·50
2752 50c. John Tapp at microphone, 1998 ... 1·50 1·50
2741/52 *Set of 12* ... 16·00 16·00

(b) Self-adhesive. Phosphor over parts of design. P 11½, interrupted perfs on both sides

2753 50c. Type **743** ... 1·10 1·25
a. Booklet pane. Nos. 2753/4, each×5 ... 9·00
2754 50c. As No. 2743 ... 1·10 1·25
2755 50c. As No. 2746 ... 1·10 1·25
a. Booklet pane. Nos. 2755/6, each×5 ... 9·00
2756 50c. As No. 2748 ... 1·10 1·25
2757 50c. As No. 2749 ... 1·10 1·25
a. Booklet pane. Nos. 2757/8, each×5 ... 9·00
2758 50c. As No. 2751 ... 1·10 1·25
2753/8 *Set of 6* ... 6·00 6·75

Nos. 2741/4, 2745/8 and 2749/52 were each printed together, *se-tenant*, as blocks of four stamps in sheets of 50.

Nos. 2753/8 were only issued in $5 booklets, Nos. SB223/5.

The two horizontal edges of Nos. 2753/8 each have two sets of five teeth separated by a straight line.

744 Tasmanian Christmas Bell

745 Swimmer

(Des Lynette Traynor)

2007 (13 Feb). Australian Wildflowers (3rd series). T **744** and similar horiz designs. Multicoloured. .

(a) Ordinary gum. Litho SEP Sprint. Phosphorised paper. P 14×14½

2759 50c. Type **744** ... 1·75 2·00
a. Horiz strip of 4. Nos. 2759/62 ... 6·25 7·25
2760 50c. Green spider flower ... 1·75 2·00
2761 50c. Sturt's desert rose ... 1·75 2·00
2762 50c. *Phebalium whitei* ... 1·75 2·00
2759/62 *Set of 4* ... 6·25 7·25

(b) Self-adhesive. Litho SEP Sprint (Nos. 2763/6) or Pemara (Nos. 2763d/6d). Phosphor over parts of the designs. P 11½ (Nos. 2763/6) or 13 (Nos. 2763d/6d)

2763 50c. Type **744** ... 70 90
a. Horiz strip of 4. Nos. 2763/6 ... 2·50 3·25
b. Booklet pane. Nos. 2763/4, each×3 and 2765/6, each×2 ... 6·75
c. Booklet pane. Nos. 2763/6, each×5 ... 12·00
d. Perf 13 ... 70 90
da. Horiz strip of 4. Nos. 2763d/6d ... 2·50 3·25

2764	50c. As No. 2760	70	90
	d. Perf 13	70	90
2765	50c. As No. 2761	70	90
	d. Perf 13	70	90
2766	50c. As No. 2762	70	90
	d. Perf 13	70	90
2763/6 *Set of 4*		2·50	3·25

Nos. 2759/62 were printed together, *se-tenant*, in horizontal strips of four in sheets of 50.

Nos. 2763/6 come from rolls of 100 (SEP Sprint) or 200 (Pemara) containing the four designs in sequence, and also from booklets of ten (SB226) and 20 (SB227). The rolls have the self-adhesive paper around each stamp removed, but the booklets have it retained.

(Des Lisa Christensen. Litho SEP Sprint)

2007 (20 Feb). 12th FINA (Fédération Internationale de Natation) World Championships, Melbourne.

(a) Ordinary gum. Phosphorised paper. P 14½×14

2767	**745**	50c. multicoloured	70	70

(b) Self-adhesive. Phosphor frame. P 11½ , interrupted perfs on both sides

2768	**745**	50c. multicoloured	70	1·00

746 Maria Island, Tasmania

747 Female Lifeguard with Reel

(Des A. Crapp)

2007 (5 Mar). International Post. Island Jewels. T **746** and similar horiz designs. Multicoloured.

(a) Ordinary gum. Litho SEP Sprint. Ordinary paper (10c.) or phosphorised paper (others). P 14×15

2769	10c. Type **746**	15	10
2770	30c. Rottnest Island, West Australia	45	40
2771	$1.30 Green Island, Queensland	2·00	2·10
2772	$1.95 Fraser Island, Queensland	2·50	2·50
2773	$2.60 Kangaroo Island, South Australia	3·25	3·25
2774	$3.85 Lord Howe Island, New South Wales	3·75	4·00
2769/74 *Set of 6*		11·00	11·00

(b) Self-adhesive. Litho Pemara. Phosphor band at right. P 11½ , interrupted perfs on both sides

2775	$1.30 As No. 2771	2·50	3·00
	a. Booklet pane. No. 2775×5	11·00	
2776	$1.95 As No. 2772	3·00	4·25
	a. Booklet pane. No. 2776×5	13·50	

Nos. 2775/6 were only issued in $6.50 and $9.75 booklets, Nos. SB228/9.

The two vertical edges of Nos. 2775/6 each have two sets of five teeth separated by a straight line.

(Des Andrew Hogg Design. Lenticular (**MS**2783 only) and litho SEP Sprint)

2007 (6 Mar). Year of the Surf Lifesaver. T **747** and similar multicoloured designs.

(a) Ordinary gum. Phosphorised paper. P 14×14½

2777	50c. Type **747**	70	90
	a. Pair. Nos. 2777/8	1·40	1·75
2778	50c. Male lifeguards	70	90
2779	$1 Surf boat	2·50	2·25
2780	$2 "Nippers" (life saving club's children's programme)	3·50	4·50
2777/80 *Set of 4*		6·75	7·75

(b) Self-adhesive

(i) Irregular phosphor frame. P 11½ , interrupted perfs on both sides

2781	50c. As No. 2778	70	1·00
	a. Horiz pair. Nos. 2781/2	1·40	2·00
2782	50c. Type **747**	70	1·00

(ii) Phosphor band at left. P 9½

MS2783	160×90 mm. $2.45, Inflatable rescue boat×2.	7·00	8·00

Nos. 2777/8 were printed together, *se-tenant*, in horizontal and vertical pairs in sheets of 50.

Nos. 2781/2 come from rolls of 100 containing both designs in sequence.

Nos. 2781/2 have an irregular phosphor frame around the horizontal pair, giving No. 2781 a phosphor frame at top, left and bottom and No. 2782 a phosphor frame at top, right and bottom.

The two vertical edges of Nos. 2781/2 each have two sets of five teeth interrupted by a straight line.

The two stamps within **MS**2783 each have one phosphor band at left.

748 Aries

749 "At the Beach" (Percy Trompf)

(Des Mitch Vane, Beth McKinlay and Sally Piskuric. Litho SEP Sprint)

2007 (3 Apr). Signs of the Zodiac. T **748** and similar vert designs. Multicoloured.

(a) Ordinary gum. Phosphorised paper. P 15×14

2784	50c. Type **748**	60	80
	a. Block of 4. Nos. 2784/7	2·25	3·00
2785	50c. Taurus	60	80
2786	50c. Gemini	60	80
2787	50c. Cancer	60	80
2788	50c. Leo	2·25	80
	a. Block of 4. Nos. 2788/91	60	3·00
2789	50c. Virgo	60	80
2790	50c. Libra	60	80
2791	50c. Scorpio	60	80
2792	50c. Sagittarius	60	80
	a. Block of 4. Nos. 2792/5	2·25	3·00
2793	50c. Capricorn	60	80
2794	50c. Aquarius	60	80
2795	50c. Pisces	60	80
2784/95 *Set of 12*		6·75	9·00

(b) Self-adhesive. Irregular phosphor frames. P 11½×11, interrupted perfs on horiz edges

2796	50c. Type **748**	60	90
	a. Booklet pane. No. 2796×10	5·50	
2797	50c. As No. 2785	60	90
	a. Booklet pane. No. 2797×10	5·50	
2798	50c. As No. 2786	60	90
	a. Booklet pane. No. 2798×10	5·50	
2799	50c. As No. 2787	60	90
	a. Booklet pane. No. 2799×10	5·50	
2800	50c. As No. 2788	60	90
	a. Booklet pane. No. 2800×10	5·50	
2801	50c. As No. 2789	60	90
	a. Booklet pane. No. 2801×10	5·50	
2802	50c. As No. 2790	60	90
	a. Booklet pane. No. 2802×10	5·50	
2803	50c. As No. 2791	60	90
	a. Booklet pane. No. 2803×10	5·50	
2804	50c. As No. 2792	60	90
	a. Booklet pane. No. 2804 ×10	5·50	
2805	50c. As No. 2793	60	90
	a. Booklet pane. No. 2805×10	5·50	
2806	50c. As No. 2794	60	90
	a. Booklet pane. No. 2806×10	5·50	
2807	50c. As No. 2795	60	90
	a. Booklet pane. No. 2807×10	5·50	
2796/807 *Set of 12*		6·75	9·50

Nos. 2784/7, 2788/91 and 2792/5 were each printed together, *se-tenant*, as blocks of four stamps in sheets of 50.

Nos. 2796/807 were only issued in separate $5 booklets, Nos. SB230/41.

The two horizontal edges of Nos. 2796/807 each have two sets of five teeth separated by a straight line.

Nos. 2796/807 were also issued in seperate premium booklets, Nos. SP135/46, sold at $10.95 each.

(Des Phil Ellett. Litho SEP Sprint)

2007 (10 Apr). Poster Art (2nd series). Nostalgic Tourism. T **749** and similar vert designs showing 1930's tourism posters. Multicoloured. Phosphorised paper. P 14½×14.

2808	50c. Type **749**	70	70
2809	$1 "Fishing" (John Vickery)	1·40	1·25
2810	$2 "Riding in the Country" (James Northfield)	3·00	3·75
2811	$2.45 "Winter Sport" (James Northfield)	3·75	5·50
2808/11 *Set of 4*		8·00	10·00

Nos. 2808/11 were also issued in premium booklets, No. SP125, sold at $10.95.

750 Queen Elizabeth II in Australia, March 2006

751 *Admella* (steamship), 1859

(Des Ern-Mei Lee. Litho SEP Sprint)

2007 (18 Apr). Queen's Birthday. Phosphorised paper. P 14×14½.

2812	**750**	50c. multicoloured	1·50	1·25

(Des Iain MacKellar and Sally Piskuric. Litho SEP Sprint)

2007 (1 May). Historic Shipwrecks. T **751** and similar horiz designs. Multicoloured. Phosphorised paper. P 14×14½.

2813	50c. Type **751**	1·00	70
2814	$1 *Loch Ard* (clipper), 1878	1·75	1·25
2815	$2 *Dunbar* (clipper), 1857	3·00	4·50
2813/15	*Set of* 3	5·25	5·75

752 Yellow-footed Rock-wallaby

753 Sydney Harbour Bridge

(Des Adam Crapp. Litho SEP Sprint)

2007 (8 May). International Post. "Country to Coast". T **752/3**. Multicoloured. Phosphorised paper. P 14½×14.

2816		$1.30 Type **752**	3·75	1·75
2817	**753**	$1.95 Sydney Harbour Bridge	6·00	2·75

A self-adhesive design as No. 2816 was issued in premium booklets, No. SP128, sold at $12.95. This booklet stamp had phosphor over the top and right of the stamp.

For miniature sheets containing T **753**, see **MS**2838.

754 "The Burning Bicycle"

755 Big Golden Guitar, Tamworth, New South Wales

(Des Jim Tsinganos and Sharon Rodziewicz. Litho SEP Sprint)

2007 (15 May). Circus: Under the Big Top. T **754** and similar vert designs. Multicoloured.

(a) Ordinary gum. Phosphorised paper. P 14½×14

2818	50c. Type **754**	85	1·00
	a. Horiz strip of 5. Nos. 2818/22	3·75	4·50
2819	50c. "The Inside-out Man"	85	1·00
2820	50c. "The Dental Trapeze"	85	1·00
2821	50c. "The Banana Lady"	85	1·00
2822	50c. "The Human Cannonball"	85	1·00
2818/22	*Set of* 5	3·75	4·50

(b) Self-adhesive. Irregular phosphor frames. P 11½, interrupted perfs on both sides

2823	50c. Type **754**	80	1·00
	a. Booklet pane. Nos. 2823/7, each×2	7·25	
2824	50c. As No. 2819	80	1·00
2825	50c. As No. 2820	80	1·00
2826	50c. As No. 2821	80	1·00
2827	50c. As No. 2822	80	1·00
2823/7	*Set of* 5	3·50	4·50

Nos. 2818/22 were each printed together, *se-tenant*, as horizontal strips of five in sheets of 50 (2×25).

Nos. 2823/7 were only issued in $5 booklets, No. SB242.

The two horizontal edges of Nos. 2823/7 each have two sets of five teeth separated by a straight line.

Nos. 2818/27 were also sold in premium booklets, No. SP127, sold at $12.95. The self-adhesive stamps as Nos. 2823/7 from this booklet had gold foil stars.

(Des Reg Mombassa. Litho SEP Sprint)

2007 (5 June). "Big Things" (roadside advertising models). T **755** and similar vert designs. Multicoloured.

(a) Ordinary gum. Phosphorised paper. P 14½×14

2828	50c. Type **755**	80	85
	a. Horiz strip of 5. Nos. 2828/32	3·50	3·75
2829	50c. Big lobster, Kingston SE, South Australia	80	85
2830	50c. Big banana, Coffs Harbour, New South Wales	80	85
2831	50c. Big Merino ram, Goulburn, New South Wales	80	85
2832	50c. Big pineapple, Nambour, Queensland	80	85
2828/32	*Set of* 5	3·50	3·75

(b) Self-adhesive. Phosphor frame. P 11½ , interrupted perfs on both sides

2833	50c. Type **755**	80	90
	a. Booklet pane. Nos. 2833/7×2	7·00	
2834	50c. As No. 2829	80	90
2835	50c. As No. 2830	80	90
2836	50c. As No. 2831	80	90
2837	50c. As No. 2832	80	90
2833/7	*Set of* 5	3·50	4·00

Nos. 2828/32 were printed together, *se-tenant*, in horizontal strips of five stamps in sheets of 50 (2×25).

Nos. 2833/7 were only issued in $5 booklets, No. SB243.

The two horizontal edges of Nos. 2833/7 each have two sets of five teeth interrupted by a straight line.

2007 (15 June). International Post. 75th Anniv of Sydney Harbour Bridge. Two sheets, each 130×90 mm and containing Type 753×2. Phosphorised paper. Litho. P 14½×14.

MS2838 **753**	(a) $1.95×2 multicoloured. (b) $1.95×2 multicoloured (emblem and '15 JUNE 2007 SYDNEY NSW 2000' inscr in gold on sheet margin) Set of 2 sheets	11·00	11·00

No. **MS**2838 (a) contains one perforated stamp and one stamp imperforate on three sides (perforated only at right). Both the stamps within No. **MS**2838 (b) are perforated 14½×14 all round. No. **MS**2838 (b) is inscr on the top right sheet margin for Sydney Stamp Expo 2007.

756 Grey-headed Flying-fox

757 Former ICI House, Melbourne, 1973

(Des Ego Guiotto and Simone Sakinofsky. Litho SEP Sprint)

2007 (26 June). Threatened Wildlife. T **756** and similar multicoloured designs. Phosphorised paper. P 14½×14 (vert) or 14×14½ (horiz).

(i) Domestic mail

2839	50c. Type **756**	2·00	1·25
	a. Horiz pair. Nos. 2839/40	4·00	2·50
2840	50c. Mountain Pygmy-possum	2·00	1·25

(ii) International Post

2841	$1.25 Flatback Turtle	3·25	2·50
2842	$1.30 Wandering Albatross	3·75	2·50
2839/42	*Set of* 4	10·00	7·00

Nos. 2839/40 were printed together, *se-tenant*, in horizontal pairs in sheets of 50 containing two panes of 25 (5×5) separated by a horizontal gutter. On the top panes the left-hand stamp in all five horizontal rows is Type **756**, but on the lower panes below the gutter it is No. 2840.

Nos. 2839/42 were also issued in premium booklets, No. SP129, sold at $10.95.

(Des Gary Domoney. Litho SEP Sprint)

2007 (10 July). Landmarks: Modernist Australian Architecture. T **757** and similar horiz designs. Multicoloured. Phosphorised paper. P 14×14½.

2843	50c. Type (**757**)	90	90
	a. Pair. Nos. 2843/4	1·75	1·75
2844	50c. Academy of Science, Canberra, 1958	90	90
2845	$1 Council House, Perth, 1962	1·60	1·25
2846	$2.45 Sydney Opera House, 1973	4·00	4·50
2843/6	*Set of* 4	6·75	6·75
MS2847	90×90 mm. Nos. 2843/6	6·75	6·75

Nos. 2843/6 were printed together, *se-tenant*, in horizontal and vertical pairs in sheets of 50 (2 panes of 25).

The stamps within **MS**2847 are oriented with the top of the design towards the centre of the miniature sheet.

No. 2844 from **MS**2847 is perforated 14½ at top and left of the design and 14 at foot and right. No. 2845 from **MS**2847 is perforated 14½ at top and left of the design and 14 at right and foot.

758 Delicatessen, Dairy Produce Hall, Queen Victoria Market,

759 APEC Logo and Half Melbourne Globe

(Des Adam Crapp. Litho SEP Sprint)

2007 (24 July). Market Feast. T **758** and similar vert designs. Multicoloured.

(a) Ordinary gum. Phosphorised paper. P 14½×14

2848	50c. Type **758**	1·00	1·25
	a. Horiz strip of 5. Nos. 2848/52	4·50	5·50
2849	50c. Banana seller, Rusty's Market, Cairns	1·00	1·25
2850	50c. Sydney Fish Market	1·00	1·25
2851	50c. Vegetable stall, Adelaide Central Market	1·00	1·25
2852	50c. Potato seller, Hume Murray Farmers Market, Albury Wodonga	1·00	1·25
2848/52 *Set of 5*		4·50	5·50

(b) Self-adhesive. Phosphor frame. P 11½, interrupted perfs on both sides

2853	50c. Type **758**	80	1·00
	a. Booklet pane. No. 2853×10	7·25	
2854	50c. As No. 2849	80	1·00
	a. Booklet pane. No. 2854×10	7·25	
2855	50c. As No. 2850	80	1·00
	a. Booklet pane. No. 2855×10	7·25	
2856	50c. As No. 2851	80	1·00
	a. Booklet pane. No. 2856×10	7·25	
2857	50c. As No. 2852	80	1·00
	a. Booklet pane. No. 2857×10	7·25	
2853/7 *Set of 5*		3·50	4·50

Nos. 2848/52 were printed together, *se-tenant*, as horizontal strips of five in sheets of 50 (2 panes of 25).

Nos. 2853/7 were only issued in $5 booklets, Nos. SB244/8.

The two horizontal edges of Nos. 2853/7 each have two sets of five teeth separated by a straight line.

2007 (3 Aug). BANGKOK 2007 International Stamp Exhibition. Sheet as No. **MS**2838 with 'BANGKOK 2007' emblem inscr in gold on sheet margin.

MS2857*b* 130×90 mm. **755** $1.95×2 multicoloured ...... 11·00 9·00

Both stamps within **MS**2857*b* are perforated 14½×14 all round.

(Des Chris Shurey. Litho SEP Sprint)

2007 (28 Aug). Asia-Pacific Economic Cooperation Forum, Australia.

(a) PVA gum. Phosphorised paper. P 14×14½

2858 **759** 50c. multicoloured 70 70

(b) Self-adhesive. Irregular phosphor frame. P 11½, interrupted perfs on both sides

2859 **759** 50c. multicoloured ...... 70 1·00

On No. 2859 the phosphor frame is irregular at left and the two vertical edges have two sets of five teeth separated by a straight line.

760 S.A.S. Soldiers, Helicopter and Parachutist

761 Brisbane Botanic Gardens, Mt. Coot-tha

(Des Passmore Design. Litho SEP Sprint)

2007 (4 Sept). 50th Anniv of the Special Air Service. Phosphorised paper. P 14×14½.

2860 **760** 50c. multicoloured ...... 1·50 1·00

(Des Lynette Traynor. Litho SEP Sprint)

2007 (12 Sept). Australian Botanic Gardens (1st issue). T **761** and similar horiz designs. Multicoloured.

(a) Ordinary gum. Phosphorised paper. P 14×14½

2861	50c. Type **761**	1·75	1·75
	a. Horiz strip of 5. Nos. 2861/5	8·00	8·00
2862	50c. Kings Park and Botanic Garden, Perth	1·75	1·75
2863	50c. Royal Botanic Gardens and Domain, Sydney	1·75	1·75
2864	50c. Royal Botanic Gardens, Melbourne	1·75	1·75
2865	50c. Botanic Gardens of Adelaide	1·75	1·75
2861/5 *Set of 5*		8·00	8·00

(b) Self-adhesive. Phosphor frames. P 11½, interrupted perfs on both sides

2866	50c. Type **761**	80	1·00
	a. Horiz strip of 5. Nos. 2866/70	3·50	4·50
	b. Booklet pane. Nos. 2866/70, each×4	14·00	
2867	50c. As No. 2862	80	1·00
2868	50c. As No. 2863	80	1·00
2869	50c. As No. 2864	80	1·00
2870	50c. As No. 2865	80	1·00
2866/70 *Set of 5*		3·50	4·50

Nos. 2861/5 were printed together, *se-tenant*, as horizontal strips of 5 in sheets of 50 (2 panes of 25).

Nos. 2866/70 come from rolls of 100 containing the five designs in sequence, and also from $10 booklets, No. SB249. The rolls have the self-adhesive paper around each stamp removed, but the booklets have it retained.

The two vertical edges of Nos. 2866/70 each have two sets of five teeth separated by a straight line.

Nos. 2866/70 were also issued in premium booklets, No. SP130, sold at $10.95.

See also Nos. 3973/82

2007 (14 Sept). Collectors International Fair, Prague. No. **MS**2838 inscr 'SBERATEL SAMMLER COLLECTOR' and emblem on sheet margin.

MS2871 130×90 mm. **755** $1.95×2 multicoloured ...... 6·50 5·75

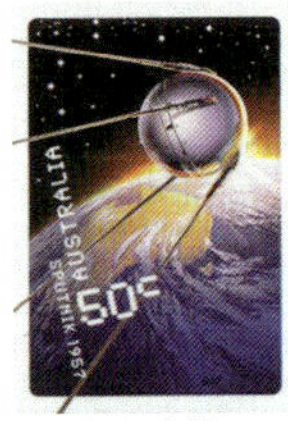

762 *Sputnik* (first satellite), 1957

763 Family Picnic outside Caravan, 1950s

(Des Jamie Tufrey and Spark Studio. Litho SEP Sprint)

2007 (2 Oct). Stamp Collecting Month. Blast Off! 50 Years in Space. T **762** and similar multicoloured designs.

(a) Ordinary gum. Phosphorised paper. P 14½×14

2872	50c. Type **762**	70	80
	a. Horiz strip of 5. Nos. 2872/6	3·25	3·50
2873	50c. Cosmonaut Alexei Leonov on first space walk, 1965	70	80
2874	50c. Neil Armstrong walking on Moon, 1969	70	80
2875	50c. *Voyager* space probe, 1977	70	80
2876	50c. International Space Station, 1998	70	80
2877	$1 Hubble Space Telescope and galaxy, 1990	1·25	1·50
2872/7 *Set of 6*		4·50	5·00
MS2878 160×90 mm. Nos. 2872/7 and as No. 2877 but 51×37 mm		9·00	9·00

(b) Self-adhesive. Phosphor frames. P 11½ (interrupted)

2879	50c. As Type **762**	70	85
	a. Vert strip of 5. Nos. 2879/83	3·25	3·75
	b. Booklet pane. Nos. 2879/83, each×2	7·00	
2880	50c. As No. 2873	70	85
2881	50c. As No. 2874	70	85
2882	50c. As No. 2875	70	85
2883	50c. As No. 2876	70	85
2879/83 *Set of 5*		3·25	3·75

Nos. 2872/6 were printed together, *se-tenant*, as horizontal strips of five stamps in sheets of 50 (2 panes of 25).

Nos. 2872/7 were also issued in premium booklets, No. SP131, sold at $10.95.

Nos. 2879/83 come from rolls of 200 containing the five designs in sequence and $5 booklets, No. SB250.

On No. 2879 the phosphor frame is broken at the top and both sides. No. 2882 has an irregular phosphor frame with phosphor over the left leg and torso of the cosmonaut. The two vertical edges of Nos. 2879/83 each have two sets of five teeth separated by a straight line.

(Des Melinda Coombes. Litho SEP Sprint)

2007 (16 Oct). Caravanning through the Years. T **763** and similar horiz designs. Multicoloured.

(a) Ordinary gum. Phosphorised paper. P 14×14½

2884	50c. Type **763**	1·75	1·75
	a. Horiz strip of 5. Nos. 2884/8	8·00	8·00
2885	50c. Family with kangaroos outside caravan, 1960s	1·75	1·75
2886	50c. Family outside caravan, 1970s	1·75	1·75
2887	50c. Woman and girl outside caravan, 1980s	1·75	1·75
2888	50c. Elderly couple sitting outside caravan, *c.* 2007	1·75	1·75
2884/8 *Set of 5*		8·00	8·00

(b) Self-adhesive. Phosphor over parts of design. P 11½ (interrupted)

2889 50c. As Type **763** 1·00 1·40
a. Booklet pane. No. 2889×10 9·00
b. Booklet pane. Nos. 2889/93, each×2 9·00
2890 50c. As No. 2885 1·00 1·40
a. Booklet pane. No. 2890×10 9·00
2891 50c. As No. 2886 1·00 1·40
a. Booklet pane. No. 2891×10 9·00
2892 50c. As No 2887 1·00 1·40
a. Booklet pane. No. 2892×10 9·00
2893 50c. As No. 2888 1·00 1·40
a. Booklet pane. No. 2893×10 9·00
2889/93 *Set of 5* 4·50 6·25

Nos. 2884/8 were printed together, *se-tenant*, as horizontal strips of five stamps in sheets of 50 (2 panes of 25).

Nos. 2884/8 were also issued in premium booklets, No. SP132, sold at $10.95.

Nos. 2889/93 were only printed in $5 booklets, Nos. SB251/6.

The two horizontal edges of Nos. 2889/93 each have two sets of five teeth separated by a straight line.

764 Surfing Santa Stamp Design by Roger Roberts, 1977

765 Red Rose

(Des Melinda Coombes. Litho Pemara (No. 2899) or SEP Sprint (others)

2007 (1 Nov). Christmas. 50 Years of Christmas Stamps. T **764** and similar multicoloured designs showing Christmas stamp designs from previous years redrawn without the face values.

(a) Ordinary gum. Phosphorised paper. P 14×14½ (horiz) or 14½×14 (vert)

(i) Domestic Mail

2894 45c. Type **764** 80 20
2895 45c. Bush Nativity (Baby Jesus with koalas and wallaby) by Marg Towt, 1990 80 1·00
a. Pair. Nos. 2895/6 1·60 2·00
2896 45c. Madonna and Child by Vivienne Goodman, 1996 80 1·00
2897 50c. 'The Spirit of Christmas' (Infant Samuel from painting by Joshua Reynolds), 1957 (*horiz*) 80 70
2894/7 *Set of 4* 3·00 2·50

(ii) International Post

2898 $1.10 Madonna and Child from stained-glass window, 1984 1·50 1·50

(b) Self-adhesive. Partial phosphor frames. P 11½

(i) Domestic Mail

2899 45c. As Type **764** 65 60
2900 45c. As No. 2895 90 90
a. Booklet pane. No. 2900×20 16·00
2901 45c. As No. 2896 90 90
a. Booklet pane. No. 2901×20 16·00
2902 50c. As No. 2897 90 1·25
a. Booklet pane. No. 2902×5 4·00

(ii) International Post

2903 $1.10 As No. 2898 1·75 2·00
a. Booklet pane. No. 2903×5 8·00
2899/2903 *Set of 5* 4·75 5·00
MS2904 156×100 mm. As No. 2899 and Nos. 2900/3 4·75 4·75

Nos. 2895/6 were printed together, *se-tenant*, in horizontal and vertical pairs throughout the sheets.

No. 2899, printed in sheetlets of ten, has varnish over the stamp design. The varnish is omitted from the miniature sheet stamp of this design.

Nos. 2900/1 were each printed in separate $9 booklets, Nos. SB259/60.

No. 2902/3 were printed in $2.50 and $5.50 booklets, Nos. SB257/8.

The two vertical edges of No. 2902 (horiz design) and the two horizontal edges of Nos. 2899/901 and 2903 each have two sets of five teeth separated by a straight line.

Nos. 2894/7 and **MS**2904 were also issued in premium booklets, No. SP133, sold at $10.95.

(Des Simone Sakinofsky. Litho SEP Sprint, Australia)

2008 (15 Jan). Greetings stamp. 'Love Blooms'.

(a) Ordinary gum. Phosphorised paper. P 14

2905 **765** 50c. multicoloured 80 70

(b) Self-adhesive. Phosphor frame. P 11½ (interrupted)

2906 **765** 50c. multicoloured 70 1·00

No. 2906 was printed in sheetlets of ten with ten *se-tenant* 'Rub & Smell' labels, sold for $5. It has varnish applied to parts of the rose and the stamp and label are scented.

The two horizontal edges of No. 2906 each have five teeth separated by a straight line. Stamps as No. 2906 were also issued in premium booklets, No. SP147, sold for $10.95. The self-adhesive stamps from this booklet did not have the varnish or perfume.

766 Dame Elisabeth Murdoch

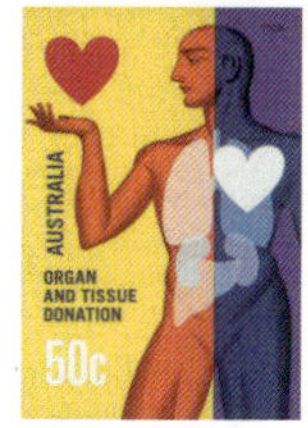

767 Human Body showing Organs

(Des John White. Litho SEP Sprint, Australia)

2008 (23 Jan). Australian Legends (12th series). Philanthropists. T **766** and similar vert designs. Multicoloured.

(a) Ordinary gum. Phosphorised paper. P 14

2907 50c. Type **766** 1·40 1·40
a. Horiz strip of 4. Nos. 2907/10 5·00 5·00
2908 50c. Victor Smorgon and Loti Smorgon 1·40 1·40
2909 50c. Lady (Mary) Fairfax 1·40 1·40
2910 50c. Frank Lowy 1·40 1·40
2907/10 *Set of 4* 5·00 5·00

(b) Self-adhesive. Partial phosphor frame. P 11½ (interrupted)

2911 50c. As No. 2910 80 1·25
a. Vert strip of 4. Nos. 2911/14 3·00 4·50
2912 50c. As No. 2909 80 1·25
2913 50c. As No. 2908 80 1·25
2914 50c. As Type **766** 80 1·25
2911/14 *Set of 4* 3·00 4·50

Nos. 2907/10 were printed together, *se-tenant*, as horizontal strips of four stamps in sheets of 50.

Nos. 2911/14 come from rolls of 100 stamps containing the four designs in sequence. They have a phosphor frame on three sides, at top, left and foot of the stamps. The two horizontal edges of Nos. 2911/14 each have two sets of five teeth separated by a straight line.

(Des Nigel Buchanan. Litho SEP Sprint)

2008 (5 Feb). Organ and Tissue Donation.

(a) Ordinary gum. Phosphorised paper. P 15×14

2915 **767** 50c. multicoloured 75 75

(b) Self-adhesive. Irregular phosphor frame at left. P 11½ (interrupted)

2916 **767** 50c. multicoloured 85 1·00
a. Booklet pane. No. 2916×10 7·50

No. 2916 was only issued in $5 stamp booklets, No. SB135.

The two horizontal edges of No. 2916 have two sets of five teeth separated by a straight line.

768 Scout Camp

769 Hanging Rock, Grose River Gorge, New South Wales

(Des Asprey Creative. Litho SEP Sprint)

2008 (19 Feb). Centenary of Scouting in Australia. T **768** and similar horiz designs. Multicoloured.

(a) Ordinary gum. Phosphorised paper. P 14

(i) Domestic Mail

2917 50c. Type **768** 75 75

(ii) International Post

2918 $1.35 Scouts in circle 1·90 2·00
2919 $2 Lord Baden-Powell (founder) 2·75 3·75
2917/9 *Set of 3* 4·75 6·00

(b) Self-adhesive. Irregular phosphor frame at right. P 11½ (interrupted)

(i) Domestic Mail

2920 50c. As Type **768** 75 1·00

(ii) International Post

2921 $1.35 As No. 2918 4·50 5·50
a. Booklet pane. No. 2921×5 20·00

2922 $2 As No. 2919 ... 6·50 8·50
a. Booklet pane. No. 2922×5 ... 29·00
2920/2 *Set of 3* ... 10·00 13·00

Nos. 2917/9 have been reported perf 14×14½ in used condition, but their source is unknown.

Nos. 2921/2 were only printed in $6.75 and $10 booklets, Nos. SB262/3.

The two vertical edges of Nos. 2920/2 have two sets of five teeth separated by a straight line.

(Des Sally Piskuric)

2008 (3 Mar). International Post. 'Gorgeous Australia'. T **769** and similar multicoloured designs.

(a) Ordinary gum. Litho SEP Sprint. Phosphorised paper. P 14

2923 $1.35 Type **769** ... 1·90 1·90
2924 $2 Walpa Gorge, Northern Territory ... 3·00 2·75
2925 $2.70 Katherine Gorge, Northern Territory (*horiz*) ... 4·00 4·00
2926 $4 Geikie Gorge, West Australia (*horiz*) ... 6·50 6·50
2923/6 *Set of 4* ... 14·00 13·50

(b) Self-adhesive. Litho McKellar. Irregular inverted L-shaped phosphor bands. P 11½ (interrupted)

2927 $1.35 As Type **769** ... 4·50 5·00
a. Booklet pane. No. 2927×5 ... 20·00
2928 $2 As No. 2924 ... 5·50 7·50
a. Booklet pane. No. 2928×5 ... 24·00

Nos. 2927/8 were issued in $6.75 or $10 booklets, Nos. SB264/5.

Nos. 2927/8 have inverted L-shaped phosphor bands, wider at top right, which extend along the top and along the left of the stamps as far as the International Post marker.

The two horizontal edges of Nos. 2927/8 each have two sets of five teeth separated by a straight line.

Nos. 2927/8 were also issued in separate premium booklets, Nos. SP152/3, sold for $10.95 or $16.95.

770 Pope Benedict XVI

771 Bulldogs

(Des Gary Domoney. Litho SEP Sprint)

2008 (4 Mar). World Youth Day, (1st issue) Sydney. T **770** and similar vert designs. Multicoloured.

(a) Ordinary gum. Phosphorised paper. P 14

(i) Domestic Mail

2929 50c. Type **770** ... 1·00 75

(ii) International Post

2930 $1.35 Pope holding crosier ... 2·50 2·50
2931 $2 Pope giving blessing ... 3·00 3·25
2929/31 *Set of 3* ... 6·00 6·00

(b) Self-adhesive. Phosphor frame. P 11½ (interrupted)

(ii) International Post

2932 $1.35 As No. 2930 ... 3·50 4·00
a. Booklet pane. No. 2932×5 ... 16·00
2933 $2 As No. 2931 ... 4·50 6·00
a. Booklet pane. No. 2933×5 ... 20·00

Nos. 2932/3 were only issued in $6.75 or $10 booklets, Nos. SB266/7.

Nos. 2932/3 have phosphor frames broken at the International Post marker at top left. The two horizontal edges of Nos. 2932/3 have two sets of five teeth separated by a straight line.

See also Nos. 3022/6

2008 (14 Mar). Canberra Stamp Show. Sheet 130×90 mm containing No. 2919×2. Multicoloured. Litho. Phosphorised paper. P 14×14½.

MS2934 $2×2 Lord Baden-Powell ... 11·00 9·00

(Des Adam Crapp. Litho SEP Sprint)

2008 (24 Mar). Centenary of Rugby League. T **771** and similar vert designs. Multicoloured.

(a) Ordinary gum. Phosphorised paper. P 14

2935 50c. Type **771** ... 80 90
a. Block of 4. Nos. 2935/8 ... 3·00 3·25
2936 50c. Titans ... 80 90
2937 50c. Sharks ... 80 90
2938 50c. Knights ... 80 90
2939 50c. Cowboys ... 80 90
a. Block of 4. Nos. 2939/42 ... 3·00 3·25
2940 50c. Broncos ... 80 90
2941 50c. Sea Eagles ... 80 90
2942 50c. Storm ... 80 90
2943 50c. Roosters ... 80 90
a. Block of 4. Nos. 2943/6 ... 3·00 3·25
2944 50c. Raiders ... 80 90
2945 50c. Rabbitohs ... 80 90
2946 50c. Panthers ... 80 90
2947 50c. Dragons ... 80 90
a. Block of 4. Nos. 2947/502 ... 3·00 3·25
2948 50c. Eels ... 80 90
2949 50c. Wests Tigers ... 80 90
2950 50c. Warriors ... 80 90
2935/50 *Set of 16* ... 12·00 13·00

(b) Self-adhesive. Phosphor frame. P 11½ (interrupted)

2951 50c. As No. 2942 ... 75 1·00
a. Booklet pane. No. 2951×10 ... 6·50
b. Booklet pane. No. 2951×5 and Nos. 2952/66 ... 14·00
2952 50c. As No. 2937 ... 75 1·00
a. Booklet pane. No. 2952×10 ... 6·50
2953 50c. As No. 2943 ... 75 1·00
a. Booklet pane. No. 2953×10 ... 6·50
2954 50c. As Type **771** ... 75 1·00
a. Booklet pane. No. 2954×10 ... 6·50
2955 50c. As No. 2938 ... 75 1·00
a. Booklet pane. No. 2955×10 ... 6·50
2956 50c. As No. 2939 ... 75 1·00
a. Booklet pane. No. 2956×10 ... 6·50
2957 50c. As No. 2945 ... 75 1·00
a. Booklet pane. No. 2957×10 ... 6·50
2958 50c. As No. 2944 ... 75 1·00
a. Booklet pane. No. 2958×10 ... 6·50
2959 50c. As No. 2948 ... 75 1·00
a. Booklet pane. No. 2959×10 ... 6·50
2960 50c. As No. 2949 ... 75 1·00
a. Booklet pane. No. 2960×10 ... 6·50
2961 50c. As No. 2947 ... 75 1·00
a. Booklet pane. No. 2961×10 ... 6·50
2962 50c. As No. 2941 ... 75 1·00
a. Booklet pane. No. 2962×10 ... 6·50
2963 50c. As No. 2940 ... 75 1·00
a. Booklet pane. No. 2963×10 ... 6·50
2964 50c. As No. 2936 ... 75 1·00
a. Booklet pane. No. 2964×10 ... 6·50
2965 50c. As No. 2946 ... 75 1·00
a. Booklet pane. No. 2965×10 ... 6·50
2966 50c. As No. 2950 ... 75 1·00
a. Booklet pane. No. 2966×10 ... 6·50
2951/66 *Set of 16* ... 10·00 14·00

Nos. 2935/8, 2939/42, 2943/6 and 2947/50 were each printed together, *se-tenant*, as blocks of four stamps in sheets of 50 (2 panes of 25).

Stamps as Nos. 2935/50 but perforated 15×14 were issued in stamp and coin premium booklets, No. SP148, sold at $15.95.

Nos. 2951/66 were issued in separate $5 booklets (Nos. SB268/83) and in $10 booklet (No. SB284). The two horizontal edges of Nos. 2951/66 each have two sets of five teeth separated by a straight line.

772 Face Shovel in Mine

773 Veterans marching

(Des Jamie Tufrey. Litho Pemara (Nos. 2972b/6b) or SEP Sprint (others))

2008 (1 Apr). Heavy Haulers. T **772** and similar vert designs. Multicoloured.

(a) Ordinary gum. Phosphorised paper. P 14

2967 50c. Type **772** ... 2·00 1·50
a. Horiz strip of 5. Nos. 2967/71 ... 9·00 6·75
2968 50c. 200 tonne mine haul truck ... 2·00 1·50
2969 50c. Road train ... 2·00 1·50
2970 50c. Ore train, West Australia ... 2·00 1·50
2971 50c. MS *Berge Stahl* (world's largest bulk carrier) ... 2·00 1·50
2967/71 *Set of 5* ... 9·00 6·75

(b) Self-adhesive. Phosphor over parts of design (Nos. 2972/6). P 11½ (interrupted)

2972 50c. As Type **772** ... 95 1·10
a. Booklet pane. Nos. 2972/6, each×4 ... 17·00
b. White border around design. Phosphor frame ... 95 1·10
ba. White border around design. Vert strip of 5. Nos. 2972b/6b ... 4·25 5·00

2973 50c. As No. 2968 ... 95 1·10
b. White border around design. Phosphor frame ... 95 1·10
2974 50c. As No. 2969 ... 95 1·10
b. White border around design. Phosphor frame ... 95 1·10
2975 50c. As No. 2970 ... 95 1·10
b. White border around design. Phosphor frame ... 95 1·10
2976 50c. As No. 2971 ... 95 1·10
b. White border around design. Phosphor frame ... 95 1·10
2972/6 *Set of 5* ... 4·25 5·00

Nos. 2967/71 were printed together, *se-tenant*, as horizontal strips of five stamps in sheets of 50 (2 panes of 25), each strip forming a composite background design.

Nos. 2972/6 have phosphor over parts of the design and were issued in $10 booklets, No. SB285.

Nos. 2972b/6b all have a white border around the design, and also phosphor frames. They come from rolls of 100 stamps printed by Pemara containing the five designs in sequence.

The two horizontal edges of Nos. 2972/6 and 2972b/6b each have two sets of five teeth separated by a straight line.

(Des Brian Clinton and Sally Piskuric)

2008 (16 Apr). 'Lest We Forget': ANZAC Day. T **773** and similar vert designs. Multicoloured.

(a) Ordinary gum. Litho SEP Sprint. Phosphorised paper. P 14

2977 50c. Type **773** ... 2·00 1·75
a. Horiz strip of 5. Nos. 2977/81 ... 9·00 8·00
2978 50c. Laying wreaths at war memorial ... 2·00 1·75
2979 50c. Playing the *Last Post* ... 2·00 1·75
2980 50c. War veteran and young boy ... 2·00 1·75
2981 50c. Young Australians at Gallipoli ... 2·00 1·75
2977/81 *Set of 5* ... 9·00 8·00
MS2982 160×90 mm. Nos. 2977/81. P 15×14 ... 9·00 8·00

(b) Self-adhesive. Litho SEP Sprint or Pemara. Phosphor frame. P 11½ (interrupted)

2983 50c. As Type **773** ... 1·40 1·50
a. Vert strip of 5. Nos. 2983/7 ... 6·25 6·75
2984 50c. As No. 2978 ... 1·40 1·50
2985 50c. As No. 2979 ... 1·40 1·50
2986 50c. As No. 2980 ... 1·40 1·50
2987 50c. As No. 2981 ... 1·40 1·50
2983/7 *Set of 5* ... 6·25 6·75

Nos. 2977/81 were printed together, *se-tenant*, as horizontal strips of five stamps in sheets of 50 (2 panes of 25).

Stamps as Nos. 2977/81 but perforated 15×14 were issued in premium booklets, No. SP149, sold at $10.95.

Nos. 2983/7 come from rolls of 100 stamps containing the five designs in sequence.

Self-adhesive strips of five printed by Pemara have the sequence of designs in order as No. 2983a, but, strips printed by SEP Sprint have the designs in reverse order.

The two horizontal edges of Nos. 2983/7 each have two sets of five teeth separated by a straight line.

774 Queen Elizabeth II at Official Dinner, Parliament House, Canberra, 2006

775 Balloons over Sydney, New South Wales

(Des Daniel Wenn. Litho SEP Sprint)

2008 (18 Apr). Queen's Birthday. T **774** and similar vert design. Multicoloured. Phosphorised paper. P 14.

(i) Domestic Mail

2988 50c. Type **774** ... 2·00 75

(ii) International Post

2989 $2 Sovereign's badge, Order of Australia ... 6·00 4·00
MS2990 106×70 mm. Nos. 2988/9. P 14½×14 ... 9·00 8·00

(Des Beth McKinlay. Litho Energi Print (Nos. 2991/4) or McKellar Renown (Nos. 2995/8))

2008 (6 May). 'Up Up and Away'. 150th Anniv of First Hot Air Balloon Flight in Australia. T **775** and similar horiz designs. Multicoloured.

(a) Ordinary gum. Phosphorised paper. P 14×15

2991 50c. Type **775** ... 2·00 2·00
a. Horiz strip of 4. Nos. 2991/4 ... 7·25 7·25
2992 50c. Orange and white balloons over Mt. Feathertop, Victoria ... 2·00 2·00
2993 50c. Multicoloured balloons over the Western MacDonnell Ranges, Northern Territories ... 2·00 2·00
2994 50c. Balloons over Canberra, Australian Central Territory ... 2·00 2·00
2991/4 *Set of 4* ... 7·25 7·25

(b) Self-adhesive. Phosphor over parts of design. P 11½ (interrupted)

2995 50c. Type **775** ... 1·40 1·75
a. Booklet pane. No. 2995×4 and Nos. 2996/8, each×2 ... 12·00
2996 50c. As No. 2992 ... 1·40 1·75
2997 50c. As No. 2994 ... 1·40 1·75
2998 50c. As No. 2993 ... 1·40 1·75
2995/8 *Set of 8* ... 5·00 6·00

Nos. 2991/4 were printed together, *se-tenant*, as horizontal strips of four stamps in sheets of 50 (2 panes of 25).

Nos. 2991/4 were also issued in premium booklets, No. SP150, sold at $10.95.

Nos. 2995/8 were only issued in stamp booklets, No. SB286. The two vertical edges of Nos. 2995/8 each have two sets of five teeth separated by a straight line.

2008 (14 May). WSC Israel 2008 World Stamp Championship, Tel-Aviv. Sheet 130×90 mm containing No. 2979×4. Multicoloured. Litho. Phosphorised paper. P 14×14½.

MS2999 50c.× 4 Playing *The Last Post* ... 12·00 9·00

776 German Shepherd Dog

777 Chinese Dragon

(Des Sally Piskuric. Litho Energi)

2008 (10 June). Working Dogs. T **776** and similar vert designs. Multicoloured.

(a) Ordinary gum. Phosphorised paper. P 14½×14

3000 50c. Type **776** ... 2·50 2·25
a. Horiz strip of 5. Nos. 3000/4 ... 11·00 10·00
3001 50c. Australian cattle dog ... 2·50 2·25
3002 50c. Beagle ... 2·50 2·25
3003 50c. Border collie ... 2·50 2·25
3004 50c. Labrador ... 2·50 2·25
3000/4 *Set of 5* ... 11·00 10·00

(b) Self-adhesive. Phosphor over parts of design. P 11½ (interrupted)

3005 50c. As Type **776** ... 1·50 1·75
a. Booklet pane. No. 3005×10 ... 13·00
b. Booklet pane. Nos. 3005/9, each×2 ... 13·00
3006 50c. As No. 3001 ... 1·50 1·75
a. Booklet pane. No. 3006×10 ... 13·00
3007 50c. As No. 3002 ... 1·50 1·75
a. Booklet pane. No. 3007×10 ... 13·00
3008 50c. As No. 3003 ... 1·50 1·75
a. Booklet pane. No. 3008×10 ... 13·00
3009 50c. As No. 3004 ... 1·50 1·75
a. Booklet pane. No. 3009×10 ... 13·00
3005/9 *Set of 5* ... 6·75 8·00

Nos. 3000/4 were printed together, *se-tenant*, as horizontal strips of five stamps in sheets of 50 (2 panes of 25).

Nos. 3000/4 were also issued in premium booklets, No. SP151, sold at $10.95.

Nos. 3005/9 were only issued in $5 booklets, Nos. SB287/92. The two horizontal edges of Nos. 3005/9 each have two sets of five teeth separated by a straight line.

(Des Linda Warner. Litho Energi Print (No. 3010) or Pemara (3011))

2008 (24 June). Olympic Games, Beijing.

(a) Ordinary gum. Phosphorised paper. P 15×14

3010 **777** 50c. multicoloured ... 1·75 1·00

(b) Self-adhesive. Phosphor over parts of design. P 11½ (interrupted)

3011 **777** 50c. multicoloured ... 1·00 1·25

The two vertical edges of No. 3011 has two sets of five teeth separated by a straight line.

778 Watering Can and Rubber Duck ('SAVE WATER')

779 Quarantine Detector Dog and Handler

(Des Hoyne Design)

2008 (8 July). 'Living Green'. T **778** and similar horiz designs. Multicoloured.

(a) Ordinary gum. Litho Energi Print. Phosphorised paper. P 14×15

3012	50c. Type **778**	1·60	1·10
	a. Block of 4. Nos. 3012/15	5·75	4·00
3013	50c. Hand holding bin ('REDUCE WASTE')	1·60	1·10
3014	50c. Bus with legs ('TRAVEL SMART')	1·60	1·10
3015	50c. Crescent moon with light switch ('SAVE ENERGY')	1·60	1·10
3012/15	*Set of 4*	5·50	4·00

(b) Self-adhesive. Litho Pemara (rolls of 100) or McKellar Renown (booklets). Phosphor frame. P 11½ (interrupted)

3016	50c. As Type **778**	90	1·25
	a. Horiz strip of 4. Nos. 3016/19	3·25	4·50
	b. Booklet pane. Nos. 3016/19, each×5	16·00	
3017	50c. As No. 3013	90	1·25
3018	50c. As No. 3014	90	1·25
3019	50c. As No. 3015	90	1·25
3016/19	*Set of 4*	3·25	4·50

Nos. 3012/15 were printed together, *se-tenant*, as blocks of four stamps in sheets of 50.

Nos. 3016/19 were issued in rolls of 100 stamps printed by Pemara containing the four designs in sequence, and also in $10 booklets, No. SB293, printed by McKellar Renown. The two vertical edges of Nos. 3016/19 each have two sets of five teeth separated by a straight line.

Nos. 3016/19 were also issued in premium booklets, No. SP154, sold for $10.95.

(Des Simone Sakinofsky)

2008 (15 July). Centenary of the Quarantine Act.

(a) Ordinary gum. Litho Energi Print. Phosphorised paper. P 14½×14

3020	**779**	50c. multicoloured	1·50	1·00

(b) Self-adhesive. Litho Pemara. Phosphor over parts of design. P 11½ (interrupted)

3021	**779**	50c. multicoloured	1·00	1·25

No. 3020 was issued in sheetlets of ten (5×2).

Stamps as No. 3020 issued in sheetlets of ten stamps and ten labels, and sold in a folder for $9.95, were perforated 14.

The two horizontal edges of No. 3021 each have two sets of five teeth separated by a straight line.

780 Pilgrims with Flags at Barangaroo for Opening Mass

781 Football Game, Melbourne, 1866

2008 (24 July). World Youth Day (2nd issue). T **780** and similar horiz designs. Multicoloured. Litho. P 14½×14.

3022	50c. Type **780**	3·00	2·50
	a. Sheetlet. Nos. 3022/6 ×2	22·00	19·00
3023	50c. Pope Benedict XVI at Barangaroo	3·00	2·50
3024	50c. Re-enactment of Stations of the Cross	3·00	2·50
3025	50c. Start of Pilgrimage Walk at Sydney Harbour Bridge	3·00	2·50
3026	50c. Pope Benedict XVI at Final Mass, Southern Cross Precinct	3·00	2·50
3022/6	*Set of 5*	13·50	11·00

Nos. 3022/6 were printed together, *se-tenant*, in sheetlets of ten stamps containing two of each design. They were sold at $5 per sheetlet.

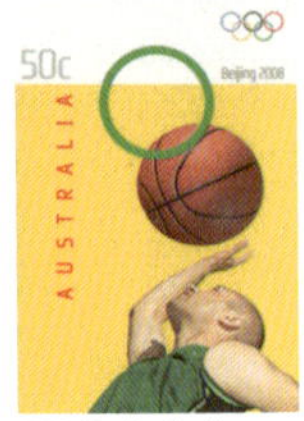

782 Basketball

783 Bristol Tourer

(Des Andrew Hogg. Litho Energi Print)

2008 (29 July). 150th Anniv of Australian Football. Phosphorised paper. P 15×14.

3027	**781**	50c. multicoloured	1·00	1·00

(Des Lynda Warner. Litho Energi Print)

2008 (1 Aug). Olympic Games, Beijing. T **782** and similar vert designs. Multicoloured.

(a) Ordinary gum. Phosphorised paper. P 14½×14

(i) Domestic Mail

3028	50c. Type **782**	2·50	65

(ii) International Post

3029	$1.30 Cycling	4·25	3·00
3030	$1.35 Gymnastics	4·25	3·00
3028/30	*Set of 3*	10·00	6·00

(b) Self-adhesive. Phosphor over parts of design. P 11½ (interrupted)

3031	$1.30 As No. 3029	2·75	3·50
	a. Booklet pane. No. 3031×5	12·00	
3032	$1.35 As No. 3030	2·75	3·50
	a. Booklet pane. No. 3032×5	12·00	

Nos. 3031/2 were issued in separate stamp booklets, Nos. SB294/5. Nos. 3031/2 have irregular partial phosphor frames around the top of the stamps.

No. 3032 also has phosphor over the gymnast.

The two vertical edges of Nos. 3031/2 each have two sets of five teeth separated by a straight line.

(Des Jamie Tufrey and Jonathan Chong. Litho Energi Print)

2008 (5 Aug). Aviation. T **783** and similar horiz designs. Multicoloured.

(a) Ordinary gum. Phosphorised paper. P 14

(i) Domestic mail

3033	50c. Type **783**	1·60	1·60
	a. Horiz strip of 3. Nos. 3033/5	4·25	4·25
3034	50c. Short S.30 Empire flying boat	1·60	1·60
3035	50c. Lockheed Super Constellation	1·60	1·60

(ii) International Post

3036	$2 Airbus A-380	4·75	4·75
3033/6	*Set of 4*	8·50	8·50

(b) Self-adhesive. Irregular partial phosphor frame. P 11½ (interrupted)

3037	$2 As No. 3036	4·50	5·50
	a. Booklet pane. No. 3037×5	20·00	

Nos. 3033/5 were printed together, *se-tenant*, in sheets of 50 (2 panes 5×5), each sheet providing ten strips of three (Nos. 3033/5) and ten pairs (Nos. 3033/4).

Stamps as Nos. 3033/6 but perforated 14×15 were issued in premium booklets, No. SP155, sold for $10.95.

No. 3037 was only issued in $10 stamp booklets, No. SB296. It has an irregular partial phosphor frame at right and foot of the stamp. The two vertical edges have two sets of five teeth separated by a straight line.

784 Stephanie Rice (swimming: women's 400m individual medley)

785 Luna Park, Melbourne

(Des Sally Piskuric)

2008 (11-25 Aug). Australian Gold Medal Winners at Olympic Games, Beijing. T **784** and similar square designs. Multicoloured.

(a) Printed digitally in China by Australia Post. P 14½

3038A	50c. Type **784**	1·75	1·75
3039A	50c. Lisbeth Trickett (swimming: women's 100m butterfly) (12.8)	1·75	1·75
3040A	50c. Leisel Jones (swimming: women's 100m breaststroke) (13.8)	1·75	1·75
3041A	50c. Stephanie Rice (swimming: women's 200m individual medley) (14.8)	1·75	1·75

3042A	50c. Women's 4×200m freestyle relay swimming team (15.8)	1·75	1·75
3043A	50c. Drew Ginn and Duncan Free (rowing: men's pair) (18.8)	1·75	1·75
3044A	50c. David Crawshay and Scott Brennan (rowing: men's double sculls) (18.8)	1·75	1·75
3045A	50c. Women's 4×100m medley relay swimming team (18.8)	1·75	1·75
3046A	50c. Emma Snowsill (women's triathlon) (19.8)	1·75	1·75
3047A	50c. Malcolm Page and Nathan Wilmott (sailing: men's 470) (19.8)	1·75	1·75
3048A	50c. Tessa Parkinson and Elise Rechichi (sailing: women's 470) (19.8)	1·75	1·75
3049A	50c. Ken Wallace (canoe/kayak: men's K-1 500m) (25.8)	1·75	1·75
3050A	50c. Steven Hooker (athletics: men's pole vault) (25.8)	1·75	1·75
3051A	50c. Matthew Mitcham (diving: men's 10m platform) (25.8)	1·75	1·75
3038A/51A *Set of 14*		22·00	22·00

(b) Litho Energi Print. Phosphorised paper. P 14

3038B	50c. Type **784**	90	80
3039B	50c. Lisbeth Trickett (swimming: women's 100m butterfly) (12 Aug)	90	80
3040B	50c. Leisel Jones (swimming: women's 100m breaststroke) (13 Aug)	90	80
3041B	50c. Stephanie Rice (swimming: women's 200m individual medley) (14 Aug)	90	80
3042B	50c. Women's 4×200m freestyle relay swimming team (15 Aug)	90	80
3043B	50c. Drew Ginn and Duncan Free (rowing: men's pair) (18 Aug)	90	80
3044B	50c. David Crawshay and Scott Brennan (rowing: men's double sculls) (18 Aug).	90	80
3045B	50c. Women's 4×100m medley relay swimming team (18 Aug)	90	80
3046B	50c. Emma Snowsill (women's triathlon) (19 Aug)	90	80
3047B	50c. Malcolm Page and Nathan Wilmott (sailing: men's 470) (19 Aug)	90	80
3048B	50c. Tessa Parkinson and Elise Rechichi (sailing: women's 470) (19 Aug)	90	80
3049B	50c. Ken Wallace (canoe/kayak: men's K-1 500m) (25 Aug)	90	80
3050B	50c. Steven Hooker (athletics: men's pole vault) (25 Aug)	90	80
3051B	50c. Matthew Mitcham (diving: men's 10m platform) (25 Aug)	90	80
3038B/51B *Set of 14*		11·50	10·00

Nos. 3038/51 were each printed in sheetlets of ten stamps (2×5) with enlarged right margins.

The dates of issue given were the release dates in Melbourne.

2008 (22 Aug). SunStamp 2008 National Stamp Exhibition, Brisbane. Sheet 130×90 mm containing Nos. 2998 and 3036, each×2. Multicoloured. Litho. Phosphorised paper. P 14×14½.

MS3052	50c.×2 Multicoloured balloons over the Western MacDonnell Ranges, Northern Territories; $2×2 Airbus A320	18·00	18·00

(Des Simone Sakinofsky. Litho Pemara (Nos. 3060c/3c) or McKellar (others))

2008 (8 Sept). Tourist Precincts. T **785** and similar horiz designs. Multicoloured.

(a) Ordinary gum. Phosphorised paper. P 14×14½

3053	55c. Type **785**	90	90
	a. Block of 4. Nos. 3053/6	3·25	3·25
	b. Perf 14×13½		
	ba. Block of 4. Nos. 3053b/6b		
3054	55c. South Bank, Brisbane	90	90
	b. Perf 14×13½		
3055	55c. The Rocks, Sydney	90	90
	b. Perf 14×13½		
3056	55c. Fisherman's Wharf, Fremantle	90	90
	b. Perf 14×13½		
3057	$1.10 Foreshore, Cairns	1·75	1·40
	b. Perf 14×13½		
3058	$1.65 Salamanca Place, Hobart	2·75	2·25
	b. Perf 14×13½		
3059	$2.75 Glenelg, Adelaide (50×30 *mm*)	4·25	4·75
3053/9 *Set of 7*		11·00	11·00

(b) Self-adhesive. Partial phosphor frame (at top, left and bottom). P 11

3060	55c. As Type **785**	80	90
	a. Booklet pane. No. 3060×10	7·00	
	b. Booklet pane. Nos. 3060/3, each×5	14·00	
	c. Perf 12½	80	90
	ca. Vert strip of 4. Nos. 3060c/3c	3·00	3·25
3061	55c. As No. 3054	80	90
	a. Booklet pane. No. 3061×10	7·00	
	c. Perf 12½	80	90
3062	55c. As No. 3055	80	90
	a. Booklet pane. No. 3062×10	7·00	
	c. Perf 12½	80	90
3063	55c. As No. 3056	80	90
	a. Booklet pane. No. 3063×10	7·00	
	c. Perf 12½	80	90
3060/3 *Set of 4*		3·00	3·25

Nos. 3053/6 were printed together, *se-tenant*, as blocks of four stamps in sheets of 50.

Nos. 3060/3 were issued in separate $5 booklets (Nos. SB297/301) and $11 booklet (No. SB301).

Nos. 3060c/3c are perforated 12½ and come from rolls of 100 or 200 printed by Pemara containing the four designs in sequence.

786 Russell Falls, Tasmania

787 Silver Rings

(Des Sally Piskuric. Litho Energi Print)

2008 (8 Sept). International Post. Waterfalls of Australia. T **786** and similar vert designs. Multicoloured.

(a) Ordinary gum. Phosphorised paper. P 14½×14

3064	$1.40 Type **786**	2·00	1·25
3065	$2.05 Jim Jim Falls, Northern Territory	3·00	3·00
3066	$2.80 Spa Pool, Hamersley Gorge, Western Australia	4·00	4·00
3067	$4.10 Mackenzie Falls, Victoria	6·00	6·00
3064/7 *Set of 4*		13·50	13·00

(b) Self-adhesive. Partial phosphor frame. P 11½×11 (interrupted)

3068	$1.40 As Type **786**	2·50	2·75
	a. Booklet pane. No. 3068×5	11·00	
3069	$2.05 As No. 3065	3·00	4·50
	a. Booklet pane. No. 3069×5	13·50	

Nos. 3068/9 were issued in $7 and $10.25 booklets, Nos. SB302/3.

Nos. 3068/9 were also issued in separate premium booklets, Nos. SP156/7, sold at $11.95 and $16.95.

The phosphor frames on Nos. 3068/9 extend along the top of the stamps and also down the left side as far as the International Post marker.

The horizontal edges of Nos. 3068/9 have two sets of five teeth separated by a straight line.

(Des Chris Shurey (No. 3078) or Cathleen Cram (others). Litho Energi Print)

2008 (23 Sept). Greetings Stamps. 'For Every Occasion'. (1st series) T **787** and similar multicoloured designs. Phosphorised paper. P 14½×14.

3070	55c. Type **787**	1·40	1·40
	a. Block of 4. Nos. 3070/3	5·00	5·00
3071	55c. Gold rings	1·40	1·40
3072	55c. Baby's feet	1·40	1·40
3073	55c. Gold heart and pink roses	1·40	1·40
3074	55c. Balloons	1·40	1·40
	a. Block of 4. Nos. 3074/7	5·00	5·00
3075	55c. Bird flying over beach	1·40	1·40
3076	55c. Outline map of Australia as sun and stylised landscape	1·40	1·40
3077	55c. Sparklers	1·40	1·40
3078	55c. Australia and Antarctica on globe (30×30 *mm*)	1·40	1·10
3079	$1.10 Embroidery from wedding dress and pale pink roses	2·00	2·00
3070/9 *Set of 10*		13·00	12·50

Nos. 3070/3 and 3074/7 were each printed together, *se-tenant*, in sheets of 50 (2 panes 5×5), each sheet providing eight blocks of four and eighteen single stamps.

Self-adhesive designs as Nos. 3070/4 and 3077 and 3079 were also issued in separate premium booklets, Nos. SP158/64, sold at $22.95 (No. 3079) or $10.95 (others). Booklet Nos. SP158/9, SP161 and SP164 were printed by McKellar, and Nos. SP160 and SP162/3 by Energi Print.

Stamps from these booklets are all perforated 11½×11, and have phosphor frames (Nos. 3074, 3077) or phosphor over parts of the design (others).

See also Nos. 3148/52

788 Genyornis

789 Matthew Cowdrey (five gold medals, swimming)

(Des Peter Trusler. Litho Energi Print (No. 3087a also Pemara)

2008 (1 Oct). Stamp Collecting Month. Megafauna of Australia. T **788** and similar multicoloured designs.

(a) Ordinary gum. Phosphorised paper. P 14½×14

3080	55c. Type **788**	1·75	1·75
	a. Horiz strip of 4. Nos. 3080/3	6·25	6·25
3081	55c. Diprotodon	1·75	1·75
3082	55c. Thylacoleo	1·75	1·75
3083	55c. Thylacine	1·75	1·75
3084	$1.10 Megalania (52×37 *mm*)	2·25	2·25
	a. Horiz pair. Nos. 3084/5	4·50	4·50
3085	$1.10 Procoptodon (52×37 *mm*)	2·25	2·25
3080/5 *Set of 6*		10·50	10·50
MS3086	170×90 mm. Nos. 3080/5. P 13½×14	9·00	9·00

(b) Self-adhesive. Phosphor over parts of design. P 11½×11 (interrupted)

3087	55c. As Type **788**	1·25	1·25
	a. Vert strip of 4. Nos. 3087/90	4·50	4·50
	b. Booklet pane. Nos. 3087/8, each×3 and Nos. 3089/90, each×2	10·00	
3088	55c. As No. 3081	1·25	1·25
3089	55c. As No. 3082	1·25	1·25
3090	55c. As No. 3083	1·25	1·25
3087/90 *Set of 4*		4·50	4·50

Nos. 3080/3 were printed together, *se-tenant*, as horizontal strips of four stamps in sheets of 50.

Nos. 3084/5 were printed together, *se-tenant*, as horizontal pairs in sheets of 24 stamps.

Nos. 3080/5 were also issued in premium booklets, No. SP165, sold at $13.95.

Nos. 3087/90 were issued in rolls of 100 stamps containing the four designs in sequence, and also in $5.50 booklets, No. SB304.

Self-adhesive strips of four printed by Pemara have the sequence of designs in order as No. 3087a, but strips printed by Energi Print have the designs in reverse order.

The two vertical edges of Nos. 3087/90 each have two sets of five teeth separated by a straight line.

2008 (24 Oct). Beijing Expo. No. **MS**3086 optd with Beijing Expo logo.

MS3091 170×90 mm. Nos. 3080/5 — 7·00 7·00

2008 (24 Oct). Matthew Cowdrey, Paralympian of the Year. P 14.

3092 **789** 55c. multicoloured — 1·50 1·00

No. 3092 was printed in sheets of ten (2×5) with enlarged inscribed right margin.

790 Baubles

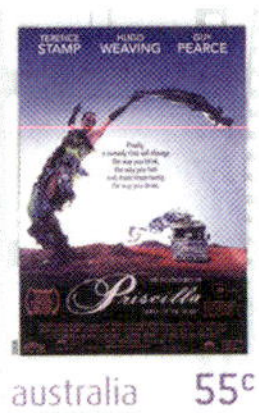

791 *The Adventures of Priscilla, Queen of the Desert*

(Des Adam Crapp (Nos. 3093, 3097/8) or Melinda Coombes (others). Litho Pemara (No. 3098) or McKellar Renown (others))

2008 (31 Oct). Christmas. T **790** and similar vert designs. Multicoloured.

(a) Ordinary gum. Phosphorised paper. P 14½×14

(i) Domestic Mail

3093	50c. Type **790**	75	75
3094	50c. Virgin Mary and baby Jesus	75	75
3095	55c. Angel	75	30

(ii) International Post

3096	$1.20 Wise man carrying gift	1·75	2·50
3093/6 *Set of 4*		3·75	3·75

(b) Self-adhesive. Phosphor over parts of design. P 11½×11 (interrupted)

(i) Domestic Mail

3097	50c. As Type **790**	85	85
	a. Booklet pane. No. 3097×20	15·00	
3098	50c. As Type **790** but gold star on bottom left bauble	85	85
3099	50c. As No. 3094	85	85
	a. Booklet pane. No. 3099×20	15·00	

(ii) International Post

3100	$1.20 As No. 3096	1·75	2·00
	a. Pane. No. 3100×5	8·00	
3097/100 *Set of 4*		4·00	4·00

No. 3098, printed in sheetlets of 10, has varnish over part of the stamp design.

Nos. 3097 and 3099 were each printed in separate $10 booklets, Nos. SB305/6.

No. 3100 was printed in $6 panes of five.

(Des Jo Muré. Litho Pemara (rolls) or Energi Print (others))

2008 (3 Nov). Favourite Australian Films. T **791** and similar vert designs. Multicoloured.

(a) Ordinary gum. Phosphorised paper. P 14½×14

3101	55c. Type **791**	1·75	1·75
	a. Horiz strip of 5. Nos. 3101/5	8·00	8·00
3102	55c. *The Castle*	1·75	1·75
3103	55c. *Muriel's Wedding*	1·75	1·75
3104	55c. *Lantana*	1·75	1·75
3105	55c. *Gallipoli*	1·75	1·75
3101/5 *Set of 5*		8·00	8·00

(b) Self-adhesive. Phosphor frame. P 11½×11 (interrupted)

3106	55c. As Type **791**	85	95
	a. Vert strip of 5. Nos. 3106/10	3·75	4·25
	b. Booklet pane. No. 3106×10	7·50	
	c. Booklet pane. Nos. 3106/10, each×2	7·50	
3107	55c. As No. 3102	85	95
	a. Booklet pane. No. 3107×10	7·50	
3108	55c. As No. 3103	85	95
	a. Booklet pane. No. 3108×10	7·50	
3109	55c. As No. 3104	85	95
	a. Booklet pane. No. 3109×10	7·50	
3110	55c. As No. 3105	85	95
	a. Booklet pane. No. 3110×10	7·50	
3106/10 *Set of 5*		3·75	4·25
MS3110*b*	154×215 mm. As No. 3107×5 and Nos. 3106/10 (8.12.08)	9·50	9·50

Nos. 3101/5 were printed together, *se-tenant*, as horizontal strips of five stamps in sheets of 50.

Nos. 3106/10 were issued in rolls of 100 stamps containing the five designs in sequence, printed by Pemara, and also in $5.50 booklets, Nos. SB307/12.

The two vertical edges of Nos. 3106/10 each have two sets of five teeth separated by a straight line.

No. **MS**3110b contains two vertical strips of self-adhesive stamps separated by a wide gutter. The stamps at left differ from No. 3107 by having the film strips in the background in silver and the aircraft and film title varnished. There are minor differences from Nos. 3106/10 to the stamps in the right-hand strip.

2008 (3 Nov). Discovery of the HMAS *Sydney*. Sheet 130×90 mm containing Nos. 2977/8, each×2. Multicoloured. Litho. Phosphorised paper. P 14.

MS3111 50c.×2 Type **773**; 50c.×2 Laying wreaths at war memorial — 5·00 5·00

2008 (3 Nov). 90th Anniv of the End of World War I. Sheet 160×90 mm containing Nos. 2978/9, each×2. Multicoloured. Litho. Phosphorised paper. P 14.

MS3112 50c.×2 Laying wreaths at war memorial; 50c.×2 Playing the *Last Post* 3.00 — 5·00 5·00

792 Nicole Kidman

(Des Adam Crapp. Litho McKellar)

2009 (22 Jan). Australian Legends (13th series). "Legends of the Screen". T **792** and similar vert designs. Multicoloured.

(a) Ordinary gum. P 14½×14

3113	55c. Type **792**	2·00	1·50
	a. Block of 4. Nos. 3113/16	7·25	5·50
3114	55c. Russell Crowe	2·00	1·50

3115	55c. Geoffrey Rush	2·00	1·50
3116	55c. Cate Blanchett	2·00	1·50
3117	55c. Russell Crowe in *Gladiator*, 2000	2·00	1·50
	a. Block of 4. Nos. 3117/20	7·25	5·50
3118	55c. Nicole Kidman in *Moulin Rouge!*, 2001	2·00	1·50
3119	55c. Cate Blanchett in *Elizabeth: The Golden Age*, 2007	2·00	1·50
3120	55c. Geoffrey Rush in *Shine*, 1996	2·00	1·50
3113/20 *Set of 8*		14·50	11·00

(b) Self-adhesive. Phosphor over upper left part of design (3121/5) or phosphor frame (3125/8). P 11½×11 (interrupted)

3121	55c. As Type **792**	1·00	1·50
	a. Booklet pane. Nos. 3121 and 3126, each×5	9·00	
	b. Booklet pane. Nos. 3121/4, each×3, and Nos. 3125/8, each×2	16·00	
3122	55c. As No. 3114	1·00	1·50
	a. Booklet pane. Nos. 3122 and 3125, each×5	9·00	
3123	55c. As No. 3115	1·00	1·50
	a. Booklet pane. Nos. 3123 and 3128, each×5	9·00	
3124	55c. As No. 3116	1·00	1·50
	a. Booklet pane. Nos. 3124 and 3127, each×5	9·00	
3125	55c. As No. 3117	1·00	1·50
3126	55c. As No. 3118	1·00	1·50
3127	55c. As No. 3119	1·00	1·50
3128	55c. As No. 3120	1·00	1·50
3121/8 *Set of 8*		7·25	11·00

Nos. 3113/20 were also issued in premium booklets, Nos. SP166/9, sold at $10.95 each.

Nos. 3121/8 were only issued in $5 (Nos. SB313/16) or $11 booklets (No. SB317). The two horizontal edges of Nos. 3121/8 each have two sets of five teeth separated by a straight line.

Nos. 3113/16 and 3117/20 were each printed together, se-tenant, in sheets of 50 (2 panes 5×5), each sheet providing eight blocks of four and 18 single stamps (of Nos. 3113, 3115, 3117 or 3119). Nos. 3113/16 have Type 792 as the top left stamp on the top pane and No. 3115 as the top left stamp on the bottom pane. Nos. 3117/20 have No. 3117 as the top left stamp on the top pane and No. 3119 as the top left stamp on the bottom pane.

793 Red Roses

(Des Elise Hurst (3129, 3132), Sally Piskuric (3130, 3133, 3135) or Donna Farquhar (3131, 3134, 3136). Litho McKellar)

2009 (3 Feb). Greetings Stamps. "With Love". T **793** and similar vert designs. Azure (3131, 3134, 3136) or multicoloured (others).

(a) Ordinary gum. P 14½×14

3129	55c. Type **793**	1·25	70
3130	55c. Heart flowers	1·25	1·50
	a. Horiz pair. Nos. 3130/1	2·50	3·00
3131	55c. Filigree heart	1·25	1·50
3129/31 *Set of 3*		3·25	3·25

(b) Self-adhesive. Phosphor frame. P 11½×11 (interrupted)

3132	55c. Type **793**	95	95
	a. Booklet pane. No. 3132×10	8·50	
3133	55c. As No. 3130 but with white border	95	95
	a. Booklet pane. No. 3133×10	8·50	
3134	55c. As No. 3131 but with white border	95	95
	a. Booklet pane. No. 3134×10	8·50	
3135	55c. As No. 3130 but with red foil applied to hearts and white border	95	95
	a. Sheetlet. Nos. 3135/6, each×5	8·50	
3136	55c. As No. 3131 but with flocking applied to filigree heart and white border	95	95
3132/6 *Set of 5*		4·25	4·25

Nos. 3130/1 were printed together, *se-tenant*, in sheets of 50 (2 panes 5×5), each sheet providing 20 horizontal pairs and ten single stamps. On the top pane the left-hand stamp in all five horizontal rows is No. 3130 but on the lower pane it is No. 3131.

Nos. 3132/4 were issued in separate $5.50 booklets, Nos. SB318/20.

Nos. 3135/6 were printed together, *se-tenant*, in sheetlets of ten stamps, each sheetlet providing three horizontal pairs and two vertical pairs.

The two vertical edges of Nos. 3132/6 each have two sets of five teeth separated by a straight line.

794 Esky (coolbox) and Wine Cask

795 Possum ("LIGHTS OUT")

(Des Stuart McLachlan. Litho Energi Print)

2009 (19 Feb). Inventive Australia. T **794** and similar vert designs showing Australian inventions. Multicoloured.

*(a) Ordinary paper. P 14 (***MS***3142) or 14½×14*

3137	55c. Type **794**	1·75	1·60
	a. Horiz strip of 5. Nos. 3137/41	8·00	7·25
3138	55c. Girl swinging on Hills hoist (rotary clothes line)	1·75	1·60
3139	55c. Girl wearing Speedo swimsuit and boy and girl wearing zinc cream	1·75	1·60
3140	55c. Ute and B&D Roll-a-Door (garage door)	1·75	1·60
3141	55c. Victa rotary lawnmower	1·75	1·60
3137/41 *Set of 5*		8·00	7·25
MS3142	170×84 mm. Nos. 3137/41	8·00	7·25

(b) Self-adhesive. Phosphor over parts of design. P 11½×11 (interrupted)

3143	55c. As Type **794**	1·10	1·60
	a. Vert strip of 5. Nos. 3143/7	5·00	7·25
	b. Booklet pane. Nos. 3143/7, each×2	10·00	
3144	55c. As No. 3138	1·10	1·60
3145	55c. As No. 3139	1·10	1·60
3146	55c. As No. 3140	1·10	1·60
3147	55c. As No. 3141	1·10	1·60
3143/7 *Set of 5*		5·00	7·25

Nos. 3137/41 were printed together, *se-tenant*, as horizontal strips of five stamps in sheets of 50.

Nos. 3137/41 were also issued in premium booklets, No. SP170, sold for $12.95.

Nos. 3143/7 were issued in rolls of 200 stamps containing the five designs in sequence, and also in $5.50 booklets, No. SB321.

The two vertical edges of Nos. 3143/7 each have two sets of five teeth separated by a straight line.

(Litho Energi Print)

2009 (2 Mar). Greetings Stamps. "For Every Occasion" (2nd series). As Nos. 3071/2, 3074, 3077 and 3079. Multicoloured. Self-adhesive. Phosphor over parts of design (Nos. 3148 and 3152) or phosphor frame (others). P 11½×11 (interrupted).

3148	55c. Gold rings (3071)	95	95
	a. Booklet pane. No. 3148×10	8·50	
3149	55c. Baby's feet (3072)	95	95
	a. Booklet pane. No. 3149×10	8·50	
3150	55c. Balloons (3074)	95	95
	a. Booklet pane. No. 3150×10	8·50	
3151	55c. Sparklers (3077)	95	95
	a. Booklet pane. No. 3151×10	8·50	
3152	$1.10 Embroidery from wedding dress and pale pink roses (3079)	2·50	2·50
	a. Booklet pane. No. 3152×10	22·00	
3148/52 *Set of 5*		6·00	6·00

Nos. 3148/51 were issued in separate $5.50 booklets, Nos. SB321/4, and No. 3152 in $11 booklet, No. SB325.

The two vertical edges of Nos. 3148/52 each have two sets of five teeth separated by a straight line.

Nos. 3149/51 differ from Nos. 3072, 3074 and 3077 by having white borders.

(Des Hoyne Design. Litho McKellar)

2009 (11 Mar). Earth Hour. T **795** and similar vert designs. Multicoloured.

(a) Ordinary gum. P 14½×14

(i) Domestic Mail

3153	55c. Type **795**	1·00	1·00
	a. Horiz pair. Nos. 3153/4	2·00	2·00
3154	55c. Owl ("SWITCH OFF")	1·00	1·00

(ii) International Post

3155	$2.05 Orang-utan ("SAVE ENERGY")	3·50	3·50
3153/5 *Set of 3*		5·00	5·00

(b) Self-adhesive. Phosphor frame. P 11½×11 (interrupted)

3156	55c. As Type **795**	90	90
	a. Booklet pane. Nos. 3156/7, each×10	16·00	
3157	55c. As No. 3154	90	90

Nos. 3153/4 were printed together, *se-tenant*, in sheets of 50 (2 panes 5×5), each sheet providing 20 horizontal pairs and ten single stamps. On the top pane the left-hand stamp in all five horizontal rows is Type **795**, but on the lower pane it is No. 3157.

Nos. 3156/7 were only issued in $11 booklets, No. SB327.

The two horizontal edges of Nos. 3156/7 each have two sets of five teeth separated by a straight line.

796 Isaac Nicholls, First Postmaster of New South Wales, boarding Ship to Collect Incoming Mail, 1809

797 "Mamu" (Nura Rupert), 2002

(Des Lynette Traynor. Litho Energi Print)

2009 (25 Mar). Bicentenary of Postal Services in Australia (1st issue). T **796** and similar vert designs. Multicoloured.

(a) Ordinary gum. P 14½×14

3158	55c. Type **796**	2·00	1·50
	a. Sheetlet of 10. Nos. 3158/67	18·00	13·50
3159	55c. Menzies Creek Post Office, Victoria, 1900s ("Early post office")	2·00	1·50
3160	55c. Early posting box	2·00	1·50
3161	55c. Australian soldiers reading letters, France, 1918 ("News from home")	2·00	1·50
3162	55c. First Quantas air mail service, Brisbane–Charleville, 1929 ("Early air mail")	2·00	1·50
3163	55c. Home delivery	2·00	1·50
3164	55c. Family reading letter ("Post-war immigration")	2·00	1·50
3165	55c. Retail PostShop	2·00	1·50
3166	55c. Express Post	2·00	1·50
3167	55c. Australia Post lorry ("Part of every day")	2·00	1·50
3158/67 *Set of 10*		18·00	13·50

(b) Self-adhesive. Phosphor frame. P 11½×11 (interrupted)

3168	55c. As Type **796**	1·10	1·50
	a. Vert strip of 10. Nos. 3168/77	10·00	13·00
	b. Booklet pane. Nos. 3168/77	10·00	
3169	55c. As No. 3159	1·10	1·50
3170	55c. As No. 3160	1·10	1·50
3171	55c. As No. 3161	1·10	1·50
3172	55c. As No. 3162	1·10	1·50
3173	55c. As No. 3163	1·10	1·50
3174	55c. As No. 3164	1·10	1·50
3175	55c. As No. 3165	1·10	1·50
3176	55c. As No. 3166	1·10	1·50
3177	55c. As No. 3167	1·10	1·50
3168/77 *Set of 10*		10·00	13·00

Nos. 3158/67 were printed together, *se-tenant*, in sheetlets of ten stamps.

Nos. 3158/67 were also issued in premium booklets, No. SP170, sold for $19.95.

Nos. 3158/67 from both sheets and premium booklets have a simulated "200" watermark.

Nos. 3168/77 were issued in rolls of 100 stamps containing the ten designs in sequence, and also in $5.50 booklets, No. SB328.

The two vertical edges of Nos. 3168/77 have two sets of five teeth separated by a straight line.

See also Nos. 3208/**MS**3217*a* and 3298/3307

(Des Sally Piskuric. Litho McKellar)

2009 (1 Apr). Indigenous Culture. T **797** and similar horiz designs showing aboriginal paintings. Multicoloured.

(a) Ordinary gum. P 14×14½

(i) Domestic Mail

3178	55c. Type **797**	1·00	1·00
	a. Horiz strip of 3. Nos. 3178/80	2·75	2·75
3179	55c. "All the Jila" (Jan Billycan), 2006	1·00	1·00
3180	55c. "Mina Mina" (Judy Napangardi Watson), 2004	1·00	1·00

(ii) International Post

3181	$1.40 Untitled (from the Mission series) (Elaine Russell), 2006	2·75	2·75
3182	$2.05 "Natjula" (Tjuruparu Watson), 2003	3·25	3·25
3178/82 *Set of 5*		8·00	8·00

(b) Self-adhesive. Irregular, broken phosphor frame. P 11×11½ (interrupted)

3183	$1.40 As No. 3181	2·25	2·50
	a. Pane. No. 3183×5	10·00	
3184	$2.05 As No. 3182	3·25	3·25
	a. Pane. No. 3184×5	15·00	

Nos. 3178/80 were printed together, *se-tenant*, in sheets of 50 (2 panes 5×5), each sheet providing ten horizontal strips of three and ten horizontal pairs (Nos. 3178/9).

Nos. 3183/4 were issued in separate panes of five stamps, sold at $7 and $10.25.

The two vertical edges of Nos. 3183/4 each have two sets of five teeth separated by a straight line.

798 Queen Elizabeth II riding Side Saddle at Trooping the Colour

799 Anna Pavlova (ballerina) and Pavlova (meringue, whipped cream and fruit)

(Des Alexandra Hall. Litho Energi Print)

2009 (15 Apr). Queen's Elizabeth II's Birthday. T **798** and similar vert design. Multicoloured. P 14½×14.

3185	55c. Type **798**	2·00	80
3186	$2.05 Queen Elizabeth and Prince Philip riding in carriage at Trooping the Colour	6·50	4·50
MS3187 106×70 mm. Nos. 3185/6		8·50	8·00

Nos. 3185/7 were also issued in premium booklets, No. SP172, sold for $10.95.

2009 (14 May). 23rd Asian International Stamp Exhibition, Hong Kong. Sheet 130×90 mm containing Nos. 3053/6. Multicoloured. Litho. P 14×14½.

MS3188 55c. Type **785**; 55c. South Bank, Brisbane; 55c. The Rocks, Sydney; 55c. Fisherman's Wharf, Fremantle	4·00	4·00

(Des Hoyne Design. Litho McKellar Renown)

2009 (15 May). "Not Just Desserts". T **799** and similar horiz designs. Multicoloured.

(a) Ordinary gum. P 14×14½

3189	55c. Type **799**	2·75	2·50
	a. Horiz strip of 4. Nos. 3189/92	10·00	9·00
3190	55c. Dame Nellie Melba (opera singer) and peach melba	2·75	2·50
3191	55c. Second Baron Lamington (governor of Queensland, 1896–1901), Lady Lamington and lamingtons (sponge cake squares with chocolate and coconut)	2·75	2·50
3192	55c. ANZAC soldiers of 1915 and Anzac biscuits	2·75	2·50
3189/92 *Set of 4*		10·00	9·00

(b) Self-adhesive. Phosphor over parts of design. P 11×11½ (interrupted)

3193	55c. As Type **799**	1·50	2·00
	a. Booklet pane. Nos. 3193/4×3 and 3195/6×2	13·00	
3194	55c. As No. 3190	1·50	2·00
3195	55c. As No. 3191	1·50	2·00
3196	55c. As No. 3192	1·50	2·00
3193/6 *Set of 4*		5·50	7·25

Nos. 3189/92 were printed together, *se-tenant*, in sheets of 50 (2 panes 5×5), each sheet providing ten strips of four and ten single stamps (Type **799**).

Nos. 3189/92 were also issued in premium booklets, No. SP173, sold for $10.95.

Nos. 3193/6 were only issued in $5.50 booklets, No. SB329.

The two vertical edges of Nos. 3193/6 each have two sets of five teeth separated by a straight line.

800 Indian Ocean ("Spotted") Bottlenose Dolphin

801 Queensland Parliament House, Brisbane, Windmill and Outback Red Sands

(Des Ego Guiotto. Litho McKellar Renown)

2009 (26 May). Endangered Species. Dolphins of the Australian Coastline. T **800** and similar horiz designs. Multicoloured.

(a) Ordinary gum. P 14×14½

(i) Domestic Mail

3197	55c. Type **800**	2·00	90

(ii) International Post

3198	$1.35 Hourglass Dolphin	4·25	2·25
3199	$1.40 Southern Right Whale Dolphin	4·25	2·25
3200	$2.05 Dusky Dolphin	6·00	5·50
3197/200	*Set of 4*	15·00	9·75
MS3201	136×70 mm. Nos. 3197/3200	13·00	10·00

(b) Self-adhesive. Partial phosphor frame. P 11×11½ (interrupted)

3202	$1.35 As No. 3198	2·50	2·75
	a. Pane. No. 3202×5	11·00	
3203	$1.40 As No. 3199	2·50	2·75
	a. Pane. No. 3203×5	11·00	
3204	$2.05 As No. 3200	3·75	4·50
	a. Pane. No. 3204×5	17·00	
3202/4	*Set of 3*	8·00	9·00

Nos. 3202/4 were issued in separate panes of five stamps, sold at $6.75, $7 and $10.25.

Nos. 3202/4 have irregular phosphor frames at right and foot of the stamps.

The two vertical edges of Nos. 3202/4 have two sets of five teeth separated by a straight line.

(Des Sally Piskuric. Litho McKellar Renown)

2009 (9 June). 150th Anniv of Queensland. T **801** and similar vert design. Multicoloured. P 14½×14.

3205	55c. Type **801**	1·25	90
3206	$2.75 Great Barrier Reef, Red-Eyed Tree Frog, rainforest and beach	5·50	5·50
MS3207	106×70 mm. Nos. 3205/6	6·00	6·00

802 1913 £2 Kangaroo and Map Stamp

803 Koala (*Phascolarctos cinereus*)

(Des Jo Mure. Litho Energi Print (3208/12) or McKellar Renown or Pemara (3213/17))

2009 (26 June). Bicentenary of Postal Services in Australia (2nd issue). Australia's Favourite Stamps. T **802** and similar horiz designs. Multicoloured.

(a) Ordinary gum. P 14×14½

3208	55c. Type **802**	2·25	2·25
	a. Horiz strip of 5. Nos. 3208/12	10·00	10·00
3209	55c. 1932 5s. Sydney Harbour Bridge stamp	2·25	2·25
3210	55c. 1946 Victory Commemoration 2½d. 'Peace' stamp	2·25	2·25
3211	55c. 1950 8½d. Aborigine stamp	2·25	2·25
3212	55c. 1914 6d. Kookaburra stamp	2·25	2·25
3208/12	*Set of 5*	10·00	10·00

(b) Self-adhesive. Partial phosphor frame. P 11×11½ (interrupted)

3213	55c. As Type **802**	1·10	1·25
	a. Horiz strip of 5. Nos. 3213/17	5·00	5·50
3214	55c. As No. 3209	1·10	1·25
3215	55c. As No. 3210	1·10	1·25
3216	55c. As No. 3211	1·10	1·25
3217	55c. As No. 3212	1·10	1·25
3213/17	*Set of 5*	5·00	5·50

(b) Self-adhesive. Partial phosphor frame. P 11×11½ (interrupted)

MS3217*a*		12·00	12·00

Nos. 3208/12 were printed together, *se-tenant*, as horizontal strips of five stamps in sheets of 50.

Nos. 3208/12 were also issued in $12.95 premium booklets, No. SP174.

Nos. 3208/12 from both sheets and premium booklets have a simulated "200" watermark.

Nos. 3213/17 were issued in rolls of 200 stamps containing the five designs in sequence.

The phosphor frames on Nos. 3213/17 extend along the top and right of the stamps.

The two vertical edges of Nos. 3213/17 have two sets of five teeth separated by a straight line.

(Des Adam Crapp. Litho McKellar)

2009 (1 July). International Post. Australian Bush Babies. T **803** and similar multicoloured designs.

(a) Ordinary gum. P 14½×14 (vert) or 14×14½ (horiz)

3218	$1.45 Type **803**	3·00	1·75
3219	$2.10 Eastern grey kangaroo (*Macropus giganteus*)	5·00	3·00
3220	$2.90 Brushtail possum (*Trichosurus vulpecula*) (horiz)	7·00	5·50
3221	$4.20 Common wombat (*Vombatus ursinus*)	9·50	7·50
3218/21	*Set of 4*	22·00	16·00

(b) Self-adhesive. Inverted L-shaped phosphor bands. Die-cut perf 11½×11 (interrupted)

3222	$1.45 As Type **803**	3·00	3·25
	a. Pane. No. 3222×5	13·00	
3223	$2.10 As No. 3219	4·25	4·75
	a. Pane. No. 3223×5	18·00	

Nos. 3222/3 were issued in separate panes of five stamps, sold at $7.25 and $10.50.

Nos. 3222/3 have L-shaped phosphor bands which extend along the top and left of each stamp as far as the International Post marker.

The two horizontal edges of Nos. 3222/3 each have two sets of five teeth separated by a straight line.

804 Fitzroy Gardens, Melbourne

(Des Simone Sakinofsky. Litho Energi Print/McKellar)

2009 (14 July). Australian Parks and Gardens. T **804** and similar horiz designs. Multicoloured.

(a) Ordinary gum. P 14×14½

3224	55c. Type **804**	2·25	2·25
	a. Horiz strip of 5. Nos. 3224/8	10·00	10·00
3225	55c. Roma Street Parkland, Brisbane	2·25	2·25
3226	55c. St. David's Park, Hobart	2·25	2·25
3227	55c. Commonwealth Park, Canberra	2·25	2·25
3228	55c. Hyde Park, Sydney	2·25	2·25
3224/8	*Set of 5*	10·00	10·00

(b) Self-adhesive. Phosphor frame on three sides. Die-cut perf 11×11½ (interrupted)

3229	55c. As Type **804**	1·50	1·75
	a. Horiz strip of 5. Nos. 3229/33	6·75	8·00
	b. Booklet pane. Nos. 3229/33, each×2	13·00	
3230	55c. As No. 3225	1·50	1·75
3231	55c. As No. 3226	1·50	1·75
3232	55c. As No. 3227	1·50	1·75
3233	55c. As No. 3228	1·50	1·75
3229/33	*Set of 5*	6·75	8·00

Nos. 3224/8 were printed together, *se-tenant*, in horizontal strips of five throughout the sheets.

Nos. 3224/8 were also issued in premium booklets, No. SP175, sold for $12.95.

Nos. 3229/33 were issued in rolls of 100 stamps printed by McKellar Renown containing the five designs in sequence, and in $5.50 booklets, No. SB330.

Nos. 3229/33 have phosphor frames at the top, left and bottom of the stamp.

The two vertical edges of Nos. 3229/33 each have two sets of five teeth separated by a straight line.

2009 (23 July). Melbourne Stampshow 2009 National Stamp Exhibition. Sheet 140×95 mm. Sheet containing Nos. 3192, 3208, 3212 and 3224. Litho. P 14×14½.

MS3234	55c.×4 ANZAC soldiers of 1915 and Anzac biscuits; Type **802**; 1914 6d. Kookaburra stamp; Type **804**	4·50	4·50

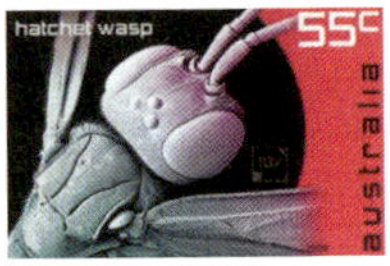

805 Hatchet Wasp

806 Bridled Nailtail Wallaby (Australia)

(Des Wayne Rankin. Litho Energi Print)

2009 (28 July). Micro Monsters. T **805** and similar horiz designs. Multicoloured.

(a) Ordinary gum. P 14×14½

3235	55c. Type **805**	1·10	1·10
	a. Horiz strip of 5. Nos. 3235/9	5·00	5·00
3236	55c. Praying Mantis	1·10	1·10
3237	55c. Ground Beetle	1·10	1·10
3238	55c. Jumping Spider	1·10	1·10
3239	55c. Ant	1·10	1·10
3240	$1.10 Weevil	2·10	2·10
3235/40 *Set of 6*		6·75	6·75
MS3241	160×85 mm. As Nos. 3235/40	6·75	6·75

(b) Self-adhesive. Phosphor frame. Die-cut perf 11×11½ (interrupted)

3242	55c. As Type **805**	1·10	1·10
	a. Vert strip of 5. Nos. 3242/6	5·00	5·00
3243	55c. As No. 3236	1·10	1·10
3244	55c. As No. 3237	1·10	1·10
3245	55c. As No. 3238	1·10	1·10
3246	55c. As No. 3239	1·10	1·10
3242/6 *Set of 5*		5·00	5·00

Nos. 3235/9 were printed together, *se-tenant*, in horizontal strips of five throughout the sheets.

Stamps from **MS**3241 have small blocks of thermochromatic ink applied to them. When rubbed with a thumb these reveal the degree of magnification of each insect.

Nos. 3242/6 were issued in rolls of 100 containing the five designs in sequence.

The two vertical edges of Nos. 3242/6 each have two sets of five teeth separated by a straight line.

(Des Kevin Stead and John White. Litho McKellar)

2009 (4 Aug). Species at Risk. T **806** and similar vert designs. Multicoloured.

(a) Ordinary gum. P 14½×14

3247	55c. Type **806**	2·75	2·75
	a. Horiz strip of 5. Nos. 3247/51	12·00	12·00
3248	55c. Norfolk Island Green Parrot (Norfolk Island)	2·75	2·75
3249	55c. Subantarctic Fur Seal (Australian Antarctic Territory)	2·75	2·75
3250	55c. Christmas Island Blue-Tailed Skink (Christmas Island)	2·75	2·75
3251	55c. Green Turtle (Cocos (Keeling) Islands)	2·75	2·75
3247/51 *Set of 5*		12·00	12·00
MS3252	150×85 mm. As Nos. 3247/51	13·00	13·00

(b) Self-adhesive. Phosphor over parts of design. Die-cut perf 11½×11 (interrupted)

3253	55c. As Type **806**	1·75	2·00
	a. Booklet pane. Nos. 3253/7, each×4	29·00	
3254	55c. As No. 3248	1·75	2·00
3255	55c. As No. 3249	1·75	2·00
3256	55c. As No. 3250	1·75	2·00
3257	55c. As No. 3251	1·75	2·00
3253/7 *Set of 5*		8·00	9·00

Nos. 3247/51 were printed together, *se-tenant*, as horizontal strips of five stamps in sheets of 50.

Nos. 3248 and 3254 were inscr "Australia" at top right but the Green Parrot stamp within **MS**3252 is inscr 'Norfolk Island' at top right.

Stamps in similar designs were issued by Norfolk Island.

Nos. 3253/7 were only issued in $11 booklets, No. SB331.

The two horizontal edges of Nos. 3253/7 each have two sets of five teeth separated by a straight line.

807 Water Tank, Fleurieu Peninsula, South Australia

(Des Andrew Hogg. Litho Energi Print)

2009 (11 Aug). Corrugated Landscapes. T **807** and similar horiz designs. Multicoloured.

(a) Ordinary gum. P 14×14½

3258	55c. Type **807**	1·10	1·10
	a. Horiz strip of 4. Nos. 3258/61	4·00	4·00
3259	55c. Traditional home, Broken Hill, New South Wales	1·10	1·10
3260	55c. Nissen hut converted into shearing shed, Bushy Park Cattle Station, Queensland	1·10	1·10
3261	55c. Magney House, Bingie Bingie Point, New South Wales	1·10	1·10
3258/61 *Set of 4*		4·00	4·00

(b) Self-adhesive. Phosphor frame on three sides. Die-cut perf 11×11½ (interrupted)

3262	55c. As Type **807**	1·00	1·25
	a. Horiz strip of 4. Nos. 3262/5	3·75	4·50
	b. Booklet pane. Nos. 3262/5, each×5	9·50	
3263	55c. As No. 3259	1·00	1·25
3264	55c. As No. 3260	1·00	1·25
3265	55c. As No. 3261	1·00	1·25
3262/5 *Set of 4*		3·75	4·50

Nos. 3258/61 were printed together, *se-tenant*, as horizontal strips of four stamps in sheets of 50 (2 panes of 25).

Nos. 3258/61 were also issued in premium booklets, No. SP176, sold for $10.95.

Nos. 3262/5 were issued in rolls of 200 containing the four designs in sequence, and also in $11 booklets, No. SB332.

The two vertical edges of Nos. 3262/5 each have two sets of five teeth separated by a straight line.

Nos. 3262/5 have a phosphor frame at top, left and right.

808 Sombrero Galaxy M104

809 Green Catbird (*Ailuroedus crassirostris*)

(Des John White. Litho McKellar)

2009 (25 Aug). International Year of Astronomy. Stargazing: The Southern Skies. T **808** and similar horiz designs. Multicoloured. P 14×14½.

(i) Domestic Mail

3266	55c. Type **808**	1·25	1·00

(ii) International Post

3267	$1.45 Reflection nebula M78	2·75	2·75
3268	$2.10 Spiral galaxy M83	3·75	4·00
3266/8 *Set of 3*		7·00	7·00
MS3269	141×75 mm. Nos. 3266/8	7·00	7·00

(Des Christopher Pope. Litho Energi Print)

2009 (9 Sept). Australian Songbirds. T **809** and similar vert designs. Multicoloured.

(a) Ordinary gum. P 14½×14

3270	55c. Type **809**	2·25	60
3271	$1.10 Noisy scrub-bird (*Atrichornis clamosus*)	4·00	1·90
3272	$1.65 Mangrove golden whistler (*Pachycephala melanura*) (male)	5·00	3·50
3273	$2.75 Pair of scarlet honeyeaters (*Myzomela sanguinolenta*)	7·00	7·00
3270/3 *Set of 4*		16·00	11·50

(b) Self-adhesive. Phosphor over part of design. Die-cut perf 11½×11 (interrupted)

3274	55c. As Type **809**	2·00	1·25
	a. Booklet pane. No. 3274×10	17·00	

Nos. 3270/3 were also issued in premium booklets, No. SP177, sold for $12.95, and in a booklet commemorating 300 issues of Stamp Bulletin Australia, sold for $24.95.

No. 3274 was issued in rolls of 100 and also in $5.50 booklets, No. SB333.

No. 3274 has an irregular phosphor frame at right and bottom. Its two horizontal edges each have two sets of five teeth separated by a straight line.

810 Cyclops Pedal Car

811 Australian Rules Football

(Des Jamie Tufrey. Litho McKellar)

2009 (25 Sept). Classic Toys. T **810** and similar vert designs. Multicoloured.

(a) Ordinary gum. Phosphor background. P 14½×14

3275	55c. Type **810**	2·25	2·25
	a. Strip of 5. Nos. 3275/9	10·00	10·00
3276	55c. Test Match board game	2·25	2·25
3277	55c. Barbie doll	2·25	2·25
3278	55c. Malvern Star Dragstar bicycle	2·25	2·25
3279	55c. Cabbage Patch Kids doll	2·25	2·25
3275/9 *Set of 5*		10·00	10·00

(b) Self-adhesive. Phosphor over parts of design. Die-cut perf 11½×11 (interrupted)

3280	55c. As Type **810**	1·25	1·50
	a. Booklet pane. Nos. 3280/4, each×2	11·00	
3281	55c. As No. 3276	1·25	1·50
3282	55c. As No. 3277	1·25	1·50
3283	55c. As No. 3278	1·25	1·50
3284	55c. As No. 3279	1·25	1·50
3280/4 *Set of 5*		5·50	6·75

Nos. 3275/9 were printed together, *se-tenant*, as horizontal strips of five stamps in sheets of 50 (2 panes 5×5).

Nos. 3275/9 were also issued in premium booklets, No. SP178.

No. 3277 was also issued in a sheetlet of ten stamps and ten labels, which were only sold in a pack for $10.95.

Nos. 3280/4 were only issued in $5.50 booklets, No. SB334.

The two vertical edges of Nos. 3280/4 each have two sets of five teeth separated by a straight line.

(Des James Hart. Litho McKellar)

2009 (6 Oct). Stamp Collecting Month. "Let's Get active!" T **811** and similar vert designs. Multicoloured.

(a) Ordinary gum. Phosphor background. P 14½×14

3285	55c. Type **811**	1·10	1·25
	a. Block of 6. Nos. 3285/90	6·00	6·75
3286	55c. Basketball	1·10	1·25
3287	55c. Soccer	1·10	1·25
3288	55c. Netball	1·10	1·25
3289	55c. Cricket	1·10	1·25
3290	55c. Tennis	1·10	1·25
3285/90 *Set of 6*		6·00	6·75
MS3291 160×89 mm. Nos. 3285/90		6·00	6·75

(b) Self-adhesive. Irregular partial phosphor frames. Die-cut perf 11½×11 (interrupted)

3292	55c. As Type **811**	1·00	1·25
	a. Booklet pane. No. 3292×10	9·50	
	b. Booklet pane. Nos. 3292/4 and 3296, each×2, and Nos. 3295 and 3297	9·50	
3293	55c. As No. 3286	1·00	1·25
	a. Booklet pane. No. 3293×10	9·50	
3294	55c. As No. 3287	1·00	1·25
	a. Booklet pane. No. 3294×10	9·50	
3295	55c. As No. 3288	1·00	1·25
	a. Booklet pane. No. 3295×10	9·50	
3296	55c. As No. 3289	1·00	1·25
	a. Booklet pane. No. 3296×10	9·50	
3297	55c. As No. 3290	1·00	1·25
	a. Booklet pane. No. 3297×10	9·50	
3292/7 *Set of 6*		5·50	6·75

Nos. 3285/90 were printed together, *se-tenant*, in sheets of 50 (2 panes 5×5), each sheet providing six blocks of four and 14 single stamps. Each sheet contained ten each of Nos. 3285/6, eight each of Nos. 3287/8 and seven each of Nos. 3289/90. The top pane had its stamps arranged as follows:

3285 3286 3287 3285 3286
3288 3289 3290 3287 3288
3285 3286 3287 3289 3290
3288 3289 3290 3285 3286
3285 3286 3287 3288 3289

The bottom pane had its stamps arranged as follows:

3290 3285 3286 3287 3288
3285 3286 3287 3285 3286
3288 3289 3290 3287 3288
3285 3286 3287 3289 3290
3288 3289 3290 3285 3286

Nos. 3292/7 were only issued in $5.50 booklets, Nos. SB335/41.

The two horizontal edges of Nos. 3292/7 each have two sets of five teeth separated by a straight line.

812 Patrica Crabb

813 Virgin Mary and Infant Jesus

(Des Lynette Traynor. Litho Energi Print)

2009 (13 Oct). Bicentenary of Postal Services in Australia (3rd issue). "Our People Your Post". T **812** and similar vert designs. Multicoloured. Phosphor background. P 14½×14.

3298	55c. Type **812**	2·00	2·00
	a. Sheetlet. Nos. 3298/307	18·00	18·00
3299	55c. Shirley Freeman (behind counter, wearing red blouse)	2·00	2·00
3300	55c. Vinko Romank (carrying box of Express Post)	2·00	2·00
3301	55c. Valda Knott (in front of shelving)	2·00	2·00
3302	55c. Gordon Morgan (in front of Australia Post motorcycles)	2·00	2·00
3303	55c. Vongpradith Phongsavan (wearing striped shirt and fluorescent tabard)	2·00	2·00
3304	55c. Norma Thomas and Australia Post contractor's van	2·00	2·00
3305	55c. John Marsh (wearing pale blue shirt)	2·00	2·00
3306	55c. Anne Brun (behind counter)	2·00	2·00
3307	55c. Russell Price (wearing blue jacket with Australia Post emblem)	2·00	2·00
3298/307 *Set of 10*		18·00	18·00

Nos. 3298/3307 were printed together, *se-tenant*, in sheetlets of ten stamps.

Nos. 3298/307 have a simulated "200" watermark.

(Des Mike Heine. Litho McKellar)

2009 (2 Nov). Christmas (1st issue). T **813** and similar vert design. Multicoloured. P 14½×14.

(a) Ordinary gum. P 14½×14

(i) Domestic mail

3308	50c. Type **813**	95	50

(ii) International Post

3309	$1.25 The Magi	2·40	2·75
MS3310 106×70 mm. Nos. 3308/9		3·25	3·25

(b) Self-adhesive. Phosphor frame. Die-cut perf 11½×11 (interrupted)

(i) Domestic mail

3311	50c. As Type **813**	1·00	1·00
	a. Booklet pane. No. 3311×20	18·00	

(ii) International Post

3312	$1.25 As No. 3309	2·25	2·25
	a. Pane. No. 3312×5	10·00	

No. 3311 was printed in $10 booklets, No. SB342.

No. 3312 was printed in $6.25 panes of five.

814 Candles enclosed in Star

815 Peter Carey

(Des Dong Uong. Litho Pemara (Nos. 3323/7) or Energi Print (others))

2009 (2 Nov). Christmas (2nd issue). T **814** and similar vert designs. Multicoloured.

(a) Ordinary gum. Phosphor background. P 14½×14

3313	50c. Type **814**	95	95
	a. Horiz strip of 5. Nos. 3313/17	4·50	4·50
3314	50c. Decorated Christmas tree	95	95
3315	50c. Wrapped gifts enclosed in Santa hat	95	95
3316	50c. Baubles enclosed in bell	95	95

3317 50c. Candy canes enclosed in stocking 95 95
3313/17 *Set of 5* .... 4·50 4·50

(b) Self-adhesive. Irregular phosphor frame. Die-cut perf 11½×11 (interrupted)

3318 50c. As Type **814** 95 95
a. Booklet pane. Nos. 3318/22, each×2 .... 9·00
3319 50c. As No. 3314 .... 95 95
3320 50c. As No. 3315 .... 95 95
3321 50c. As No. 3316 .... 95 95
3322 50c. As No. 3317 .... 95 95
3318/22 *Set of 5* .... 4·25 4·25

(c) Self-adhesive. Phosphor frame. Die-cut perf 11½×11 (interrupted)

3323 50c. As Type **814** but gold foil star outline .. 1·00 1·00
a. Sheetlet. Nos. 3323/7, each×2 .... 9·25 9·25
3324 50c. As No. 3314 but gold foil Christmas tree outline .... 1·00 1·00
3325 50c. As No. 3315 but gold foil Santa hat outline .... 1·00 1·00
3326 50c. As No. 3316 but gold foil bell outline ... 1·00 1·00
3327 50c. As No. 3317 but gold foil stocking outline .... 1·00 1·00
3323/7 *Set of 5* .... 4·50 4·50

Nos. 3313/17 were printed together, *se-tenant*, as horizontal strips of five stamps in sheets of 50 (2 panes 5×5).

Nos. 3318/22 were only issued in $5 booklets, No. SB343.

Nos. 3323/7 were printed together in self-adhesive sheetlets of ten stamps. These "Merry Christmas" sheetlets were printed using flexographic combination technology, the process images being enhanced with a flexographic spot gloss varnish. The gold foil effect was created with a silver cold foil overprinted with a yellow PMS spot colour.

The two horizontal edges of Nos. 3318/27 each have two sets of five teeth separated by a straight line.

(Des Simone Sakinofsky. Litho McKellar)

2010 (21 Jan). Australian Legends (14th series). "Legends of the Written Word". T **815** and similar vert designs. Multicoloured.

(a) Ordinary gum. P 14½×14

3328 55c. Type **815** .... 1·10 1·10
a. Block of 4. Nos. 3328/31 .... 4·00 4·00
3329 55c. Peter Carey (black/white photo) .... 1·10 1·10
3330 55c. David Malouf (black/white photo) .... 1·10 1·10
3331 55c. David Malouf .... 1·10 1·10
3332 55c. Colleen McCullough .... 1·10 1·10
a. Block of 4. Nos. 3332/5 .... 4·00 4·00
3333 55c. Colleen McCullough (black/white photo) .... 1·10 1·10
3334 55c. Bryce Courtenay (black/white photo) .... 1·10 1·10
3335 55c. Bryce Courtenay .... 1·10 1·10
3336 55c. Thomas Keneally .... 1·10 1·10
a. Block of 4. Nos. 3336/9 .... 4·00 4·00
3337 55c. Thomas Keneally (black/white photo) ... 1·10 1·10
3338 55c. Tim Winton (black/white photo) .... 1·10 1·10
3339 55c. Tim Winton .... 1·10 1·10
3328/39 *Set of 12* .... 12·00 12·00

(b) Self-adhesive. Irregular partial phosphor frame. Die-cut perf 11½×11 (interrupted)

3340 55c. As Type **815** .... 1·00 1·10
a. Booklet pane. Nos. 3340/1 and 3343/5, each×3, and No. 3342×5 .... 18·00
3341 55c. As No. 3331 .... 1·00 1·10
3342 55c. As No. 3332 .... 1·00 1·10
3343 55c. As No. 3335 .... 1·00 1·10
3344 55c. As No. 3336 .... 1·00 1·10
3345 55c. As No. 3339 .... 1·00 1·10
3340/5 *Set of 6* .... 5·50 6·00

Nos. 3328/31, 3332/5 and 3336/9 were each printed together, *se-tenant*, as blocks of four in sheets of 50.

Nos. 3328/39 were also issued in premium booklets, No. SP179.

Nos. 3340/5 were only issued in $11 booklets, No. SB344.

The two horizontal edges of Nos. 3340/5 each have two sets of five teeth separated by a straight line.

816 Governor Macquarie and North View of Sydney

(Des Stacey Zass. Litho McKellar)

2010 (16 Feb). Bicentenary of Arrival of Governor Lachlan Macquarie in New South Wales. T **816** and similar horiz designs. Multicoloured. P 14×14½.

3346 55c. Type **816** .... 2·00 1·50
a. Block of 4. Nos. 3346/9 .... 7·25 5·50
3347 55c. Port Jackson and Sydney Town .... 2·00 1·50
3348 55c. Parramatta Female Penitentiary, 1818 ... 2·00 1·50
3349 55c. Government Stables, Sydney, 1817 .... 2·00 1·50
3346/9 *Set of 4* .... 7·25 5·50

Nos. 3346/9 were printed together, *se-tenant*, as blocks of four in sheets of 50 (2 panes 5×5), giving eight blocks of four and 18 other stamps in each sheet. On the top pane the top left stamp is Type **816**, but on the bottom pane it is No. 3348.

Nos. 3346/9 were also issued in $10.95 premium booklets, No. SP180.

817 Coat of Arms on Reverse of Florin

818 Torah Bright (snowboard – halfpipe)

(Des Disegno. Litho (**MS**3352 also embossed) Energi Print)

2010 (23 Feb). Centenary of First Australian Commonwealth Coins. T **817** and similar horiz design. Multicoloured. P 14×14½.

3350 55c. Type **817** .... 1·25 60
3351 $2.75 King Edward VII on Obverse of Florin .... 6·50 7·00
MS3352 106×70 mm. As Nos. 3350/1 .... 7·50 7·50

(Des Adam Crapp. Litho McKellar Ronown)

2010 (25 Feb). Australian Gold Medallists at Olympic Winter Games, Vancouver. T **818** and similar square design. Multicoloured. P 14.

3353 55c. Type **818** .... 1·10 90
3354 55c. Lydia Lassila (freestyle skiing – aerials). 1·10 90

Nos. 3353/4 were printed in separate sheetlets of ten stamps (2×5) with enlarged right margin.

819 Colin Defries flying modified Wright Model A *The Stella*, Victoria Park Racecourse, Sydney, 9 December 1909

820 Prize Bull

(Des Ethos. Litho McKellar)

2010 (9 Mar). Centenary of Powered Flight. T **819** and similar horiz designs. Multicoloured.

(a) Ordinary gum. P 14×14½

(i) Domestic Mail

3355 55c. Type **819** (first powered flight in Australia) .... 1·75 60

(ii) International Post

3356 $1.45 John Duigan's flight, Mia Mia, Victoria, 7 October 1910 (first flight by Australian in Australian plane) .... 3·50 2·75
3357 $2.10 Harry Houdini flying Voisin aircraft, Diggers Rest, Victoria, 18 March 1910 ... 4·25 5·50
3355/7 Set of 3 .... 8·50 8·00

(b) Self-adhesive. Irregular partial phosphor frames. Die-cut perf 11×11½ (interrupted)

3358 $1.45 As No. 3356 .... 3·25 3·50
a. Pane. No. 3358×6 .... 17·00
3359 $2.10 As No. 3357 .... 4·50 6·00
a. Pane. No. 3359×6 .... 23·00

Nos. 3358/9 were only printed in $7.25 or $10.50 panes of six.

The irregular phosphor frames on Nos. 3358/9 are at the top and left of the stamps.

The two vertical edges of Nos. 3358/9 each have two sets of five teeth separated by a straight line.

2010 (12 Mar). Canberra Stampshow 2010. Sheet 140×95 mm containing Nos. 3346, 3351, and 3355/6. Litho. P 14×14½.

MS3360 55c. Type **816**; 55c. Type **819**; $1.45 John Duigan's flight, Mia Mia, Victoria, 7 October 1910 (first flight by Australian in Australian plane); $2.75 King Edward VII on obverse of florin coin .... 14·00 14·00

(Des Stuart McLachlan and John White. Litho McKellar)

2010 (23 Mar). "Come to the Show". T **820** and similar vert designs. Multicoloured.

(a) Ordinary gum. P 14½×14

3361 55c. Type **820** .... 1·75 1·75
a. Horiz strip of 5. Nos. 3361/5 .... 8·00 8·00

3362	55c. Cake decorating	1·75	1·75
3363	55c. Winning show horse	1·75	1·75
3364	55c. Wood chopping	1·75	1·75
3365	55c. Prizewinning dog	1·75	1·75
3361/5 *Set of 5*		8·00	8·00
MS3366 170×85 mm. Nos. 3361/5		8·00	8·00

(b) Self-adhesive. Phosphor over parts of design. Die-cut perf 11½×11 (interrupted)

3367	55c. As Type **820**	1·25	1·60
	a. Booklet pane. Nos. 3367/71, each×2	11·00	
3368	55c. As No. 3362	1·25	1·60
3369	55c. As No. 3363	1·25	1·60
3370	55c. As No. 3364	1·25	1·60
3371	55c. As No. 3365	1·25	1·60
3367/71 *Set of 5*		6·00	7·25

Nos. 3361/5 were printed together, *se-tenant*, as horizontal strips of five stamps in sheets of 50.

Nos. 3361/5 were also issued in premium booklets, No. SP181.

Nos. 3367/71 were only issued in $5.50 booklets, No. SB345.

The two horizontal edges of Nos. 3367/71 each have two sets of five teeth separated by a straight line.

821 Queen Elizabeth II leaving St. Andrew's Cathedral, Sydney, 2006

822 Australian Soldiers on Kokoda Trail, 1942

(Des John White. Litho McKellar)

2010 (6 Apr). Queen's Birthday.

(a) Ordinary gum. P 14½×14

3372	**821**	55c. multicoloured	1·50	60

(b) Self-adhesive. Irregular partial phosphor frame. Die-cut perf 11½×11 (interrupted)

3373	**821**	55c. multicoloured	1·50	1·00
		a. Booklet pane. No. 3373×10	13·50	

No. 3373 was only issued in $5.50 stamp booklets, No. SB346.

The irregualar partial phosphor frame on No. 3373 is at left and foot of the stamp.

The two horizontal edges of No. 3373 each have two sets of five teeth separated by a straight line.

(Des Brian Clinton and Lynette Traynor. Litho McKellar)

2010 (20 Apr). Kokoda. T **822** and similar vert designs. Multicoloured.

(a) Ordinary gum. P 14½×14

(i) Domestic mail

3374	55c. Type **822**	2·00	1·50
	a. Horiz strip of 4. Nos. 3374/7	7·25	5·50
3375	55c. Papua New Guineans helping wounded soldiers along trail, 1942	2·00	1·50
3376	55c. Kokoda veterans	2·00	1·50
3377	55c. Trekker, guide and memorial	2·00	1·50

(ii) International Post

3378	$1.45 Veterans at Kokoda Isurava Memorial	3·50	3·00
3374/8 *Set of 5*		10·50	8·00
MS3379 160×90 mm. Nos. 3374/8		9·00	8·00

(b) Self-adhesive. Phosphor frame. Die-cut perf 11½×11 (interrupted)

3380	55c. As Type **822**	1·50	1·50
	a. Vert strip of 4. Nos. 3380/3	5·50	5·50
	b. Booklet pane. Nos. 3380 and 3382, each×3, and Nos. 3381 and 3383, each×2	13·50	
3381	55c. As No. 3375	1·50	1·50
3382	55c. As No. 3376	1·50	1·50
3383	55c. As No. 3377	1·50	1·50
3380/3 *Set of 4*		5·50	5·50

Nos. 3374/7 were printed together, *se-tenant*, as horizontal strips of four in sheets of 50, each sheet providing ten strips of four and ten single stamps (Type **822**).

Nos. 3374/8 were also issued in $10.95 premium booklets, No. SP182.

The two horizontal edges of Nos. 3380/3 each have two sets of five teeth separated by a straight line.

Nos. 3380/3 were issued in rolls of 100 containing the four designs in sequence and also in $5.50 booklets, No. SB346.

Stamps in similar designs were issued by Papua New Guinea.

823 The Ghan

824 Queen Victoria

(Des Melinda Coombes. Litho Pemara (No. 3389a) or McKellar Renown)

2010 (7 May). Great Australian Railway Journeys. T **823** and similar horiz designs. Multicoloured.

(a) Ordinary paper

(i) Domestic Mail. P 14×14½

3384	55c. Type **823**	2·00	1·25
3385	55c. West Coast Wilderness Railway, Tasmania	2·00	1·25
3386	55c. 'The Indian Pacific'	2·00	1·25

(ii) International Post. Size 50×30 mm. P 13½×14

3387	$2.10 Kuranda Scenic Railway, Queensland	7·00	4·25
3384/7 *Set of 4*		11·50	7·25
MS3388 140×90 mm. No. 3387		7·00	7·50

(b) Self-adhesive. Phosphor over parts of design

(i) Domestic Mail. Die-cut perf 11×11½ (interrupted)

3389	55c. As Type **823**	1·50	1·50
	a. Horiz strip of 3. Nos. 3389/91	4·50	4·50
	b. Booklet pane. Nos. 3389/90, each×8, and No. 3391×4	27·00	
3390	55c. As No. 3385	1·50	1·50
3391	55c. As No. 3386	1·50	1·50

(ii) International Post. Size 50×30 mm. Die-cut perf 11

3392	$2.10 As No. 3387	7·00	8·00
	a. Pane. No. 3392×5	29·00	
3389/92 *Set of 4*		10·50	11·00

Nos. 3384/6 and **MS**3388 were also issued in premium booklets, No. SP183, sold for $12.95.

Nos. 3389/91 were issued in rolls of 200 containing the three designs in sequence, and also in $11 booklets, No. SB348.

The two vertical edges of Nos. 3389/91 each have two sets of five teeth separated by a straight line.

(Des Ethos. Litho RA Printers/Kemwell Speciality Printing and Energi Print)

2010 (7 May). Colonial Heritage: Empire (1st issue). P 14x13½.

3393	**824**	$5 multicoloured	9·50	12·00
MS3394 140×90 mm. No. 3393			9·50	12·00

MS3394 was also printed in recess and litho and sold in a limited edition presentation pack (selling price $15).

See also Nos. 3622/**MS**3634 and 3795/**MS**3797

(Litho)

2010 (8 May). London 2010 Festival of Stamps. Four sheets, containing Nos. 3355/6×2, containing Nos. 2624, 2988, 3185 and 3372, and as Nos. **MS**3388 and **MS**3394, all overprinted with 'LONDON 2010 FESTIVAL OF STAMPS' logo in gold on margin. Multicoloured. P 14×14½ (**MS**3395), 14½×14 (**MS**3396), 13½×14 (**MS**3397) or 14×13½ (**MS**3398).

MS3395 140×90 mm. Type **819**×2; No. 3356×2	8·50	9·00
MS3396 140×90 mm. Type **821**; Type **774**; Type **798**; Type **729**	8·00	8·50
MS3397 140×90 mm. No. 3387	7·00	7·50
MS3398 140×90 mm. No. 3393	12·00	12·00

825 Peng Peng (Australian kookaburra mascot)

826 Purnululu National Park, Western Australia

(Des Jo Muré. Litho McKellar Renown)

2010 (18 May). Expo 2010, Shanghai, China. T **825** and similar vert design. Multicoloured. P 14½×14.

3399	55c. Type **825**	1·10	1·25
	a. Pair. Nos. 3399/3400	2·10	2·50
3400	55c. Australian pavilion	1·10	1·25

Nos. 3399/3400 were printed, *se-tenant*, as horizontal and vertical pairs in sheetlets of ten (5×2).

(Des Sharon Rodziewicz. Litho McKellar Renown)

2010 (25 May). Australian UNESCO World Heritage Sites. T **826** and similar multicoloured designs.

(a) Ordinary gum. P 14½×14 (vert) or 14×14½ (horiz)

3401	55c. Type **826**	2·00	1·50
	a. Horiz pair. Nos. 3401/2	4·00	3·00
3402	55c. Kakadu National Park, Northern Territory	2·00	1·50
3403	$1.10 Mount Warning, Gondwana Rainforests (*horiz*)	3·25	2·75
	a. Horiz pair. Nos. 3403/4	6·50	5·50
3404	$1.10 Tasmanian Wilderness (*horiz*)	3·25	2·75
3401/4 *Set of 4*		9·50	7·75

(b) Self-adhesive. Partial phosphor frame (at left and foot). Die-cut perf 11½×11 (interrupted)

3405	55c. As No. 3402	1·40	1·40
	a. Vert pair. Nos. 3405/6	2·75	2·75
	b. Booklet pane. Nos. 3405/6, each×5	12·00	
3406	55c. As Type **826**	1·40	1·40

Nos. 3401/2 and 3403/4 were each printed together, *se-tenant*, as horizontal pairs in sheets of 50 containing two panes of 25 (5×5), giving twenty horizontal pairs and ten single stamps.

On the left pane of Nos. 3401/2 the first stamp is Type **826**, but on the right it is No. 3402.

On the top pane of Nos. 3403/4 the first stamp is No. 3403, but on the bottom pane it is No. 3404.

Nos. 3405/6 were issued in rolls of 100 containing the two designs in sequence, and also in $5.50 booklets, No. SB349.

The two horizontal edges of Nos. 3405/6 each have two sets of five teeth separated by a straight line.

827 Coral Rabbitfish

828 Bay of Fires, Tasmania

(Des Simone Sakinofsky. Litho Pemara (3416c/19c) or McKellar Renown (others))

2010 (21–28 June). Fish of the Reef. T **827** and similar horiz designs. Multicoloured.

(a) Ordinary gum. P 14½×14 ($3) or 14×14½ (others)

3407	5c. Type **827**	20	20
3408	60c. Clown Triggerfish	1·25	1·25
	a. Block of 4. Nos. 3408/11	4·50	4·50
3409	60c. Spotted Sweetlips	1·25	1·25
3410	60c. Golden Damselfish	1·25	1·25
3411	60c. Regal Angelfish	1·25	1·25
3412	$1.20 Saddle Butterflyfish (28.6)	2·75	2·50
3413	$1.80 Chevron Butterflyfish (28.6)	3·00	2·75
3414	$3 Orangefin Anemonefish (50×30 *mm*) (28.6)	5·50	6·00
3407/14 *Set of 8*		15·00	15·00

(b) Self-adhesive. Phosphor frame on three sides (except 5c.). Die-cut perf 11

3415	5c. As Type **827**	20	30
	a. Booklet pane. Nos. 3415×20	3·50	
3416	60c. As No. 3408	1·10	1·10
	a. Booklet pane. Nos. 3416/17, each×3 and Nos. 3418/19, each×2	10·00	
	b. Booklet pane. Nos. 3416/19, each×5	20·00	
	c. Perf 12½	1·10	1·10
	ca. Horiz strip of 4. Nos. 3416c/19c	4·25	4·25
3417	60c. As No. 3409	1·10	1·10
	c. Perf 12½	1·10	1·10
3418	60c. As No. 3410	1·10	1·10
	c. Perf 12½	1·10	1·10
3419	60c. As No. 3411	1·10	1·10
	c. Perf 12½	1·10	1·10
3415/19 *Set of 5*		4·25	4·25

Nos. 3408/11 were printed together, *se-tenant*, as blocks of four stamps in sheets of 50 (5×10), each sheet providing ten blocks of four and ten single stamps (Nos. 3408 and 3410).

Nos. 3416/19 have the phosphor frame at top, right and foot of the stamp.

No. 3415 was only issued in $1 stamp booklets, No. SB350.

Nos. 3416/19 were issued in $6 and $12 booklets, Nos. SB351/2.

Nos. 3416c/19c come from rolls of 100 or 200 containing the four designs in seqence.

Nos. 3420/5 are left vacant for possible additions to this series of definitive stamps.

(Des Janet Boschen. Litho McKellar Renown)

2010 (28 June). International Stamps. Australian Beaches. T **828** and similar multicoloured designs.

(a) Ordinary gum. P 14½×14

3426	$1.50 Type **828**	5·00	3·25
3427	$2.20 Cape Tribulation, Queensland	7·00	4·25
3428	$4.30 Hellfire Bay, Western Australia (50×30 *mm*)	12·00	9·00
3426/8 *Set of 3*		22·00	15·00

(b) Self-adhesive. Inverted L-shaped phosphor bands. Die-cut perf 11½×11 (interrupted)

3429	$1.50 As Type **828**	4·00	4·25
	a. Pane. No. 3429×5	17·00	
3430	$2.20 As No. 3427	5·50	6·50
	a. Pane. No. 3430×5	23·00	

Nos. 3429/30 were each printed in panes of five stamps.

The inverted L-shaped phosphor bands on Nos. 3429/30 are at the right and foot of the stamps.

The two vertical edges of Nos. 3429/30 each have two sets of five teeth separated by a straight line.

829 Piper

830 "STAY FOCUSED STAY RELEVANT STAY ON LINE"

(Des Simone Sakinofsky. Litho McKellar Renown)

2010 (29 June). Adopted and Adored. Dogs. T **829** and similar vert designs. Multicoloured.

(a) Ordinary paper. P 14½×14

3431	60c. Type **829**	2·50	2·25
	a. Horiz strip of 5. Nos. 3431/5	11·00	10·00
3432	60c. Jessie	2·50	2·25
3433	60c. Buckley	2·50	2·25
3434	60c. Daisy	2·50	2·25
3435	60c. Tigger	2·50	2·25
3431/5 *Set of 5*		11·00	10·00

(b) Self-adhesive. Phosphor over parts of design. Die-cut perf 11½×11 (interrupted)

3436	60c. As Type **829**	2·00	2·25
	a. Horiz strip of 5. Nos. 3436/40	9·00	10·00
	b. Booklet pane. Nos. 3436/40, each×2	17·00	
3437	60c. As No. 3432	2·00	2·25
3438	60c. As No. 3433	2·00	2·25
3439	60c. As No. 3434	2·00	2·25
3440	60c. As No. 3435	2·00	2·25
3436/40 *Set of 5*		9·00	10·00

Nos. 3431/5 were printed together, *se-tenant*, as horizontal strips of five stamps in sheets of 50 (2 panes of 25).

Nos. 3436/40 were issued in rolls of 100 containing the five designs in sequence, and also in $6 booklets, No. SB353.

The two horizontal edges of Nos. 3436/40 each have two sets of five teeth separated by a straight line.

(Des Andrew Hogg. Litho Pemara (3445a) or McKellar Renown (others))

2010 (13 July). Emergency Services. T **830** and similar vert designs. Multicoloured.

(a) Ordinary gum. P 14½×14

3441	60c. Type **830**	2·25	2·00
	a. Horiz strip of 4. Nos. 3441/4	8·00	7·25
3442	60c. Police helicopter	2·25	2·00
3443	60c. Fire emblem	2·25	2·00
3444	60c. Ambulance service emblem	2·25	2·00
3441/4 *Set of 4*		8·00	7·25

(b) Self-adhesive. Irregular phosphor frame. Die-cut perf 11½×11

3445 60c. As Type **830** 2·25 2·25
a. Vert strip of 4. Nos. 3445/8 8·00 8·00
b. Booklet pane. Nos. 3445/8, each×5 35·00
3446 60c. As No. 3442 2·25 2·25
3447 60c. As No. 3443 2·25 2·25
3448 60c. As No. 3444 2·25 2·25
3445/8 *Set of 4* 8·00 8·00

Nos. 3441/4 were printed together, *se-tenant*, as horizontal strips of four stamps in sheets of 50 (2 panes of 25), each sheet providing ten strips of four and ten single stamps (Type **830**).

Nos. 3445/8 were issued in rolls of 200 containing the four designs in sequence, and also in $12 booklets, No. SB354.

The two horizontal edges of Nos. 3445/8 each have two sets of five teeth separated by a straight line.

831 Gold and White Design

832 Construction Worker, Doctor and Teacher

(Des Jo Muré (3449, 3451, 3458), Dong Uong (3450), Cathleen Cram (3452), Passmore Design (3453), Tracie Grimwood (3454) and Jonathan Chong (3455/7). Litho McKellar Renown)

2010 (19 July). Greetings Stamps. 'For Special Occasions'. T **831** and similar multicoloured designs.

(a) Ordinary gum. P 14½×14

3449 60c. Type **831** 1·25 1·25
a. Block of 4. Nos. 3449/52 4·50 4·50
3450 60c. Pink tulips 1·25 1·25
3451 60c. Cream roses 1·25 1·25
3452 60c. Glasses of champagne 1·25 1·25
3453 60c. Three balloons 1·25 1·25
a. Horiz strip of 3. Nos. 3453/5 3·25 3·25
3454 60c. Teddy bear holding daisy 1·25 1·25
3455 60c. Wattle flowers 1·25 1·25
3456 60c. Southern Cross (deep blue background) (30×30 *mm*) 1·25 1·25
a. Horiz pair. Nos. 3456/7 2·50 2·50
3457 60c. Southern Cross (orange and pink background) (30×30 *mm*) 1·25 1·25
3458 $1.20 Wedding and engagement rings 2·50 2·50
3449/58 *Set of 10* 12·00 12·00

(b) Self-adhesive. Phosphor frame (3462) or irregular partial phosphor frame (others). Die-cut perf 11½×11 (interrupted)

3459 60c. As No. 3450 1·10 1·25
a. Booklet pane. No. 3459×10 10·00
3460 60c. As No. 3451 1·10 1·25
a. Booklet pane. No. 3460×10 10·00
3461 60c. As No. 3453 1·10 1·25
a. Booklet pane. No. 3461×10 10·00
3462 60c. As No. 3454 1·10 1·25
a. Booklet pane. No. 3462×10 10·00
3463 60c. As No. 3455 1·10 1·25
a. Booklet pane. No. 3463×10 10·00
3464 $1.20 As No. 3458 2·50 2·75
a. Booklet pane. No. 3464×10 22·00
3459/64 *Set of 6* 7·25 8·00

Nos. 3449/52 were printed together, *se-tenant*, as blocks of four stamps in sheets of 50 (2 panes of 25), each sheet providing eight blocks of four and 18 single stamps.

Nos. 3453/5 were printed together, *se-tenant*, as horizontal strips of three in sheets of 50 (2 panes of 25), each sheet providing ten strips of three and 20 horiz pairs (Nos. 3453/4).

Nos. 3456/7 were printed together, *se-tenant*, as horizontal pairs in sheets of 50.

Nos. 3459/64 were issued in separate $6 booklets (Nos. SB355/9) and $12 booklet (No. SB360).

The two horizontal edges of Nos. 3459/64 each have two sets of five teeth separated by a straight line.

(Des Hoyne Design. Litho McKellar Renown)

2010 (27 July). Centenary of Australian Taxation Office. P 14×14½.

3465 **832** 60c. multicoloured 1·10 1·10

833 Robert Burke and William Wills

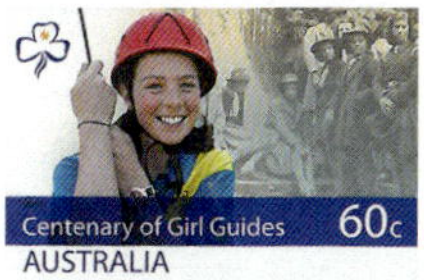

834 Guide

(Des John White. Litho McKellar Renown)

2010 (3 Aug). 150th Anniv of Departure of Burke and Wills Expedition. T **833** and similar horiz designs. Multicoloured.

(a) Ordinary gum. P 14×14½

3466 60c. Type **833** 2·00 1·60
a. Horiz pair. Nos. 3466/7 4·00 3·00
3467 60c. Expedition leaving Melbourne, August 1860 2·00 1·60
3468 $1.20 Return of Burke, Wills and John King from Gulf of Carpentaria to Cooper's Creek, April 1861 3·50 3·25
a. Horiz pair. Nos. 3468/9 7·00 6·50
3469 $1.20 Burke, Wills and King on journey to Mount Hopeless 3·50 3·25
3466/9 *Set of 4* 10·00 8·50

(b) Self-adhesive. Irregular partial phosphor frame. Die-cut perf 11×11½ (interrupted)

3470 60c. As No. 3467 1·60 1·75
a. Horiz pair. Nos. 3470/1 3·00 3·50
3471 60c. As Type **833** 1·60 1·75

Nos. 3466/7 and 3468/9 were each printed together, *se-tenant*, as horizontal pairs in sheets of 50 (2 panes of 25), each sheet providing twenty horizontal pairs and ten single stamps (Type **833** or No. 3468).

Nos. 3466/9 were also issued in $10.95 premium booklets.

Nos. 3470/1 were issued in rolls of 200 containing the two designs in sequence.

The two vertical edges of Nos. 3470/1 each have two sets of five teeth separated by a straight line.

(Litho)

2010 (4 Aug). Bangkok 2010 25th Asian International Stamp Exhibition. Sheet 140×85 mm containing Nos. 3407×2 and 3408/9. Multicoloured. P 14×14½.

MS3472 5c. Coral Rabbitfish×2; 60c. Oriental sweetlips; 60c. Clown triggerfish 7·00 7·00

(Litho)

2010 (20 Aug). Stampex '10 National Stamp Exhibition, Adelaide. Sheet 140×85 mm containing Type **833** and Australian Antarctic Territory No. 191. Multicoloured. P 14×14½.

MS3473 60c. Type **833**; $2.05 Jade iceberg 7·50 7·50

(Des Jo Muré. Litho McKellar Renown)

2010 (31 Aug). Centenary of Girl Guides Australia. T **834** and similar horiz designs. Multicoloured.

(a) Ordinary gum. P 14×14½

(i) Domestic Mail.

3474 60c. Type **834** 1·50 1·50

(ii) International Mail

3475 $1.50 Two guides making guide sign 3·25 2·75
3476 $2.20 Olave Baden Powell (founder) 5·75 5·50
3474/6 *Set of 3* 9·50 8·75

(b) Self-adhesive. Die-cut perf 11×11½

(i) Domestic Mail. Phosphor over parts of design.

3477 60c. As Type **834** 1·50 1·50
a. Booklet pane. No. 3477×20 25·00

(ii) International Post

3478 $1.50 As No. 3475 3·00 4·75
a. Pane. No. 3478×5 13·00
3479 $2.20 As No. 3476 5·25 6·50
a. Pane. No. 3479×5 22·00
3477/9 *Set of 3* 8·75 11·50

No. 3477 was issued in rolls of 200, and also in $12 booklets, No. SB361.

No. 3478/9 were only issued in $7.50 and $12 panes of five stamps.

835 National Service Memorial, Canberra

836 Children on Beach, 1950s

(Des Lynette Traynor. Litho McKellar Renown)

2010 (8 Sept). National Service Memorial, Canberra.

(a) Ordinary gum. P 14×14½

3480 **835** 60c. multicoloured 1·50 1·25

(b) Self-adhesive. Irregular partial phosphor frame. Die-cut perf 11×11½ (interrupted)

3481	60c. multicoloured	1·25	1·40
	a. Booklet pane. No. 3481×10	11·00	

No. 3481 has an irregular partial phosphor frame at right and foot of the stamp.

The two vertical edges of No. 3481 each have two sets of five teeth separated by a straight line.

No. 3481 was issued in $6 booklets, No. SB362.

(Des Melinda Coombes. Litho Pemara (No. 3487a only) or McKellar Renown (others))

2010 (22 Sept). 'Long Weekend'. T **836** and similar horiz designs. Multicoloured.

(a) Ordinary gum. P 14×14½

3482	60c. Type **836**	1·50	1·50
	a. Horiz strip of 5. Nos. 3482/6	6·75	6·75
3483	60c. Family camping, 1960s	1·50	1·50
3484	60c. Surfers on beach, 1970s	1·50	1·50
3485	60c. Family on shore and houseboat on Lake Eildon, Victoria, 1980s	1·50	1·50
3486	60c. Children playing in snow, 1990s	1·50	1·50
3482/6 *Set of 5*		6·75	6·75

(b) Self-adhesive. Phosphor over parts of design. Die-cut perf 11×11½ (interrupted)

3487	60c. As Type **836**	1·75	1·75
	a. Horiz strip of 5. Nos. 3487/91	8·00	8·00
	b. Booklet pane. Nos. 3487/91, each×2	14·00	
3488	60c. As No. 3483	1·75	1·75
3489	60c. As No. 3484	1·75	1·75
3490	60c. As No. 3485	1·75	1·75
3491	60c. As No. 3486	1·75	1·75
3487/91 *Set of 5*		8·00	8·00

Nos. 3482/6 were printed together, *se-tenant*, as horizontal strips of five stamps in sheets of 50 (2 panes of 25).

Nos. 3482/6 were also issued in $13.95 premium booklets, No. SP185.

Nos. 3487/91 were issued in rolls of 100 printed by Pemara containing the five designs in sequence, and also in $6 booklets, No. SB363.

The two vertical edges of Nos. 3487/91 each have two sets of five teeth separated by a straight line.

837 Common Wombat

838 Mary MacKillop

(Des Sharon Rodziewicz. Litho McKellar Renown)

2010 (5 Oct). Wildlife Caring: Rescue to Release. T **837** and similar vert designs. Multicoloured.

(a) Ordinary gum. P 14½×14

3492	60c. Type **837**	2·50	1·75
	a. Horiz strip of 5. Nos. 3492/6	11·00	8·00
3493	60c. Eastern Grey Kangaroo	2·50	1·75
3494	60c. Koala	2·50	1·75
3495	60c. Grey-Headed Flying Fox	2·50	1·75
3496	60c. Southern Boobook Owl	2·50	1·75
3497	$1.20 Ringtail Possum	3·25	3·25
3492/7 *Set of 6*		14·00	11·00
MS3498 170×85 mm. Nos. 3492/7		13·00	11·00

(b) Self-adhesive. Irregular partial phosphor frames. Die-cut perf 11½×11 (interrupted)

3499	60c. As Type **837**	1·60	2·00
	a. Horiz strip of 5. Nos. 3499/3503	7·25	9·00
	b. Booklet pane. Nos. 3499/3503, each×2	12·00	
3500	60c. As No. 3493	1·60	2·00
3501	60c. As No. 3494	1·60	2·00
3502	60c. As No. 3495	1·60	2·00
3503	60c. As No. 3496	1·60	2·00
3499/503 *Set of 5*		7·25	9·00

Nos. 3492/6 were printed together, *se-tenant*, as horizontal strips of five stamps in sheets of 50 (2 panes of 25).

Nos. 3499/3503 were issued in rolls of 200 containing the five designs in sequence, and also in $6 booklets, No. SB364.

(Des Adam Crapp. Litho MacKellar Renown)

2010 (18 Oct). Canonisation of Mary MacKillop (Mother Mary of the Cross, founder of Sisters of St. Joseph of the Sacred Heart). P 14½×14.

3504	**838** 60c. multicoloured	1·50	1·25

839 Red-backed Kingfisher (*Todiramphus pyrrhopygius*)

840 Melbourne Cup, 2010

(Des Christopher Pope and Simone Sakinofsky. Litho McKellar Renown)

2010 (26 Oct). Australian Kingfishers. T **839** and similar vert designs. Multicoloured.

(a) Ordinary gum. P 14½×14

3505	60c. Type **839**	2·50	1·50
3506	$1.20 Sacred Kingfisher (*Todiramphus sanctus*)	3·75	1·75
3507	$1.80 Blue-winged Kookaburra (*Dacelo leachii*)	4·75	3·25
3508	$3 Yellow-billed Kingfisher (*Syma torotoro*)	7·50	8·00
3505/8 *Set of 4*		17·00	13·00

(b) Self-adhesive. Phosphor frame. Die-cut perf 11½×11 (interrupted)

3509	60c. As Type **839**	2·25	1·75
	a. Booklet pane. No. 3509×10	19·00	

No. 3509 was issued in rolls of 100 and also in $6 booklets, No. SB365.

(Des Jonathon Chong. Litho McKellar Renown)

2010 (1 Nov). 150th Anniv of Melbourne Cup Horse Race. T **840** and similar multicoloured designs.

(a) Ordinary gum. P 14½×14 (vert) or 14×14½ (horiz)

3510	60c. Type **840**	2·50	1·25
3511	60c. Carbine, 1890 (*horiz*)	2·50	2·50
	a. Horiz strip of 3. Nos. 3511/13	6·75	6·75
3512	60c. Phar Lap, 1930 (*horiz*)	2·50	2·50
3513	60c. Saintly, 1996 (*horiz*)	2·50	2·50
3510/13 *Set of 4*		9·00	8·00
MS3514 160×85 mm. Nos. 3510/13		9·00	8·00

(b) Self-adhesive. Phosphor frame. Die-cut perf 11×11½ (interrupted)

3515	60c. As No. 3511	2·00	2·25
	a. Booklet pane. Nos. 3515/16, each×7 and No. 3517×6	35·00	
3516	60c. As No. 3512	2·00	2·25
3517	60c. As No. 3513	2·00	2·25
3515/17 *Set of 3*		5·50	6·00

Nos. 3510/13 were printed together, *se-tenant*, as horizontal strips of three stamps in sheets of 50 (2 panes of 25), each sheet providing ten strips of three (Nos. 3511/13) and ten pairs (Nos. 3511/12).

Nos. 3510/13 were also issued in $13.95 premium booklets, No. SP186.

Nos. 3515/17 were only issued in $12 booklets, No. SB366.

841 Young Girl writing Letter

842 Madonna and Child

(Des Mark Sofilas and Jo Muré. Litho McKellar Renown)

2010 (1 Nov). Christmas (1st issue). Dear Santa. T **841** and similar vert design. Multicoloured.

(a) Ordinary gum. P 14½×14

3518	55c. Type **841**	1·25	1·25
	a. Horiz pair. Nos. 3518/19	2·50	2·50
3519	55c. Santa reading letter	1·25	1·25

(b) Self-adhesive. Irregular phosphor frame. Die-cut perf 11½×11 (interrupted)

3520	55c. As No. 3519	1·25	1·25
	a. Booklet pane. Nos. 3520/1, each×10	19·00	
3521	55c. As Type **841**	1·25	1·25
3522	55c. As Type **841** but foil 'AUSTRALIA' and varnish on letter and stocking	1·25	1·25
3523	55c. As No. 3519 but foil 'AUSTRALIA' and varnish on Santa's beard, cuffs and boots	1·25	1·25

3520/3 *Set of 4* .... 4·50 4·50

Nos. 3518/19 were printed together, *se-tenant*, as horizontal pairs in sheets of 50 (2 panes of 25), each sheet providing twenty horizontal pairs and ten single stamps (Type **841**).

Nos. 3520/1 were only issued in $11 stamp booklets, No. SB367.

Nos. 3522/3 come from separate sheetlets of ten.

2010 (1 Nov). Christmas (2nd issue). T **842** and similar vert designs. Multicoloured.

(a) Ordinary gum. P 14½×14

(i) Domestic mail

3524 55c. Type **842** .... 1·25 50

(ii) International Post

3525 $1.30 Angel and shepherds .... 3·00 3·00

(b) Self-adhesive. Phosphor frame. Die-cut perf 11½×11 (interrupted)

(i) Domestic mail

3526 55c. As Type **842** .... 1·25 1·00
a. Booklet pane. No. 3526×20 .... 21·00

(ii) International Post

3527 $1.30 As No. 3525 .... 3·00 3·50
a. Pane. No. 3527×5 .... 12·50

No. 3526 was issued in $11 stamp booklets, No. SB368.

No. 3527 was issued in $6.50 panes of five stamps.

843 "LOVE" and Red Roses

844 Eva Cox (feminist)

2011 (18 Jan). Greetings Stamps. Special Occasions. "LOVE". T **843** and similar vert designs. Multicoloured.

(a) Ordinary gum. P 14½×14

3528 60c. Type **843** .... 1·25 1·25
a. Horiz pair. Nos. 3528/9 .... 2·50 2·50
3529 60c. Pattern of hearts, flowers and vine leaves .... 1·25 1·25

(b) Self-adhesive. Phosphor over part of design (at top right) (3532) or phosphor frame (others). Die-cut perf 11½×11 (interrupted)

3530 60c. As Type **843** .... 1·25 1·50
a. Booklet pane. No. 3530×10 .... 11·00
3531 60c. As No. 3529 .... 1·25 1·50
a. Booklet pane. No. 3531×10 .... 11·00
3532 60c. As No. 3452 .... 1·25 1·50
a. Booklet pane. No. 3532×10 .... 11·00
3530/2 *Set of 3* .... 3·25 4·00

Nos. 3528/9 were printed together, *se-tenant*, as horizontal pairs in sheets of 50 (2 panes of 25), each sheet giving twenty horizontal pairs and ten single stamps (Type **843**).

Nos. 3530/2 were issued in separate $6 booklets, Nos. SB369/71.

The two horizontal edges of Nos. 3530/2 each have two sets of five teeth separated by a straight line.

2011 (20 Jan). Australian Legends (15th series). "Advancing Equality". T **844** and similar vert designs. Multicoloured.

(a) Ordinary gum. P 14½×14

3533 60c. Type **844** .... 1·25 1·25
a. Horiz strip of 4. Nos. 3533/6 .... 4·50 4·50
3534 60c. Germaine Greer (feminist author) .... 1·25 1·25
3535 60c. Elizabeth Evatt (former chief judge) .... 1·25 1·25
3536 60c. Anne Summers (writer and co-founder of first women's refuge) .... 1·25 1·25
3533/6 *Set of 4* .... 4·50 4·50

(b) Self-adhesive. Irregular partial phosphor frame (at right and foot). Die-cut perf 11½×11 (interrupted)

3537 60c. As Type **844** .... 1·25 1·50
a. Booklet pane. Nos. 3537/40, each×5 .... 11·00
3538 60c. As No. 3534 .... 1·25 1·50
3539 60c. As No. 3535 .... 1·25 1·50
3540 60c. As No. 3536 .... 1·25 1·50
3537/40 *Set of 4* .... 4·50 5·50

Nos. 3533/6 were printed together, *se-tenant*, as horizontal strips of four stamps in sheets of 50 (2 panes of 25), giving ten horizontal strips of four and ten single stamps (Type **844**×2 and Nos. 3534/6 on top pane; No. 3533/6, No. 3534×2 on lower pane).

Nos. 3537/40 were issued in $12 booklets, No. SB372.

The two horizontal edges of Nos. 3537/40 each have two sets of five teeth separated by a straight line.

845 Rescuer carrying Baby

846 Women's Eyes

(Des Lynette Traynor and Simone Sakinofsky. Flexography Pemara)

2011 (27 Jan). Premier's Flood Relief Appeal. T **845** and similar vert designs. Multicoloured. Self-adhesive. Phosphor frame. Die-cut perf 11½×11.

3541 60c. Type **845** .... 1·75 1·75
a. Sheetlet. of 10 Nos. 3541/5, each×2 .... 13·00 13·00
3542 60c. House surrounded by floodwater .... 1·75 1·75
3543 60c. Rescuing cat from flooded house .... 1·75 1·75
3544 60c. Wallaby on debris in floodwater .... 1·75 1·75
3545 60c. Aerial view of flooded houses and street .... 1·75 1·75
3541/5 *Set of 5* .... 8·00 8·00

Nos. 3541/5 were printed together, *se-tenant*, in sheetlets of ten stamps containing two of each design.

Each sheetlet was sold at $8, a $2 premium over face value. This premium went to the Premier's Flood Relief Appeal.

Nos. 3546/50 are vacant.

(Des Stacey Zass. Litho RA Printing)

2011 (15 Feb). Centenary of International Women's Day. P 14×14½.

3551 **846** 60c. multicoloured .... 1·40 1·40

847 F-111 ("Pig")

848 Gerbera

(Des Jamie Tufrey and Simone Sakinofsky. Litho RA Printing)

2011 (22 Feb). Royal Australian Air Force (RAAF) Aviation. T **847** and similar horiz designs. Multicoloured.

(a) Ordinary gum. P 14×14½

3552 60c. Type **847** .... 1·75 1·75
a. Horiz pair. Nos. 3552/3 .... 3·50 3·50
3553 60c. F/A -18F .... 1·75 1·75
3554 $1.20 Wedgetail .... 3·50 3·50
3555 $3 C-17 Globemaster III .... 7·00 7·00
3552/5 *Set of 4* .... 12·50 12·50
MS3556 135×72 mm. Nos. 3552/5 .... 13·50 13·50

(b) Self-adhesive. Phosphor over parts of design. Die-cut perf 11×11½ (interrupted on vert sides)

3557 60c. As Type **847** .... 2·00 2·25
a. Booklet pane. Nos. 3557/8, each×5 .... 18·00
3558 60c. As No. 3553 .... 2·00 2·25

Nos. 3552/3 were printed together, *se-tenant*, as horizontal pairs in sheets of 50 (2 panes of 25), each pair forming a composite background design, and each sheet giving 20 horizontal pairs and ten individual stamps (Type **847**).

The stamps and margins of **MS**3556 form a composite design.

Nos. 3557/8 were only issued in $6 booklets, No. SB373.

(Des Adam Crapp. Litho McKellar Renown)

2011 (8 Mar). Floral Festivals Australia. T **848** and similar vert designs. Multicoloured.

(a) Ordinary paper. P 14½×14

3559 60c. Type **848** (Melbourne International Flower and Garden Show) .... 1·50 1·50
a. Horiz strip of 5. Nos. 3559/63 .... 6·50 6·50
3560 60c. Jacaranda (Jacaranda Festival, Grafton) 1·50 1·50
3561 60c. Australian everlasting (Kings Park Festival, Perth) .... 1·50 1·50
3562 60c. Violet (Toowoomba Carnival of Flowers) .... 1·50 1·50
3563 60c. Tulip (Floriade, Canberra) .... 1·50 1·50
3559/63 *Set of 5* .... 6·50 6·50

(b) Self-adhesive. Irregular partial phosphor frame. Die-cut perf 11½×11 (interrupted on horiz sides)

3564 60c. As Type **848** .... 1·50 1·60
a. Vert strip of 5. Nos. 3564/8 .... 6·50 7·00

b. Booklet pane. Nos. 3564/8, each×4 .... 25·00
3565 60c. As No. 3560 .... 1·50 1·60
3566 60c. As No. 3561 .... 1·50 1·60
3567 60c. As No. 3562 .... 1·50 1·60
3568 60c. As No. 3563 .... 1·50 1·60
3564/8 *Set of 5* .... 6·50 7·00

Nos. 3559/63 were printed together, *se-tenant*, as horizontal strips of five stamps in sheets of 50 (2 panes of 25).

Nos. 3559/63 were also issued in $12.95 premium booklets, No. SP187.

Nos. 3564/8 were issued in rolls of 200 containing the five designs in sequence and also in $12 booklets, No. SB374.

849 "A Bunch of Flowers" (Nora Heysen), 1930

850 Salt Pan ("The Dry")

(Des John White. Litho McKellar Renown)

2011 (22 Mar). The Gallery Series. National Gallery of Victoria: Flowers (1st series). T **849** and similar horiz designs. Multicoloured.

(a) Ordinary gum. P 14×14½

3569 60c. Type **849** .... 1·50 1·50
a. Horiz strip of 5. Nos. 3569/73 .... 6·50 6·50
3570 60c. "Camellias" (Arnold Shore), 1937 .... 1·50 1·50
3571 60c. "Fruit and Flowers" (Vida Lahey), *c.* 1924 1·50 1·50
3572 60c. "Still Life, Zinnias" (Roy de Maistre), 1925–30 .... 1·50 1·50
3573 60c. "A Cottage Bunch" (Hans Heysen), 1930 .... 1·50 1·50
3569/73 *Set of 5* .... 6·50 6·50

(b) Self-adhesive. Two phosphor bands. Die-cut perf 11×11½ (interrupted on vert sides)

3574 60c. As Type **849** .... 1·50 1·60
a. Horiz strip of 5. Nos. 3574/8 .... 6·50 7·00
b. Booklet pane. Nos. 3574/8, each×2 .... 12·00
3575 60c. As No. 3570 .... 1·50 1·60
3576 60c. As No. 3571 .... 1·50 1·60
3577 60c. As No. 3572 .... 1·50 1·60
3578 60c. As No. 3573 .... 1·50 1·60
3574/8 *Set of 5* .... 6·50 7·00

Nos. 3569/73 were printed together, *se-tenant*, as horizontal strips of five stamps in sheets of 50 (2 panes of 25).

Nos. 3574/8 were printed in rolls of 100 containing the five designs in sequence, and also in $6 booklets, No. SB375.

See also Nos. 3951/60

(Litho)

2011 (31 Mar). Sydney Stamp Expo 2011. Sheet 130×90 mm containing Nos. 3466, 3468, 3552 and 3554. Multicoloured. P 14×14½.

MS3578*a* 60c. Type **847**; 60c. Type **833**; $1.20 Return of Burke, Wills and John King from Gulf of Carpentaria to Cooper's Creek, April 1861; $1.20 Wedgetail .... 11·00 11·00

(Des Dong Uong. Litho McKellar Renown)

2011 (4 Apr). Lake Eyre. T **850** and similar horiz designs. Multicoloured.

(a) Ordinary gum. P 14½×14

(i) Domestic mail

3579 60c. Type **850** .... 2·25 1·25

(ii) International Post

3580 $1.55 Green land with pools of water ("New Growth") .... 6·00 3·50
3581 $2.25 Australian Pelican flying over breeding colony on island ("Bird Life") .... 8·50 5·50
3582 $3.10 Lake Eyre ("In Flood") .... 9·50 9·00
3580/2 *Set of 4* .... 24·00 17·00

(b) Self-adhesive. Partial phosphor frame (at right and bottom). Die-cut perf 11

3583 $1.55 As No. 3580 .... 4·00 4·00
a. Pane. No. 3583×5 .... 17·00
3584 $2.25 As No. 3581 .... 6·00 7·00
a. Pane. No. 3584×5 .... 25·00

Nos. 3583/4 were only issued in $7.75 or $11.25 panes of five stamps.

851 Queen Elizabeth II, 1984 (Brian Dunlop)

852 Prince William and Miss Catherine Middleton

(Des Lynette Traynor. Litho RA Printing)

2011 (5 Apr). 85th Birthday of Queen Elizabeth II. T **851** and similar vert design showing portrait paintings by Australian artists. Multicoloured. P 14½×14.

(i) Domestic Mail

3585 60c. Type **851** .... 2·25 1·25

(ii) International Post

3586 $2.25 Queen Elizabeth II, 2005 (Rolf Harris) .... 7·50 7·00
MS3587 106×70 mm. Nos. 3585/6 .... 10·00 9·00

(Des Jo Muré. Litho RA Printing)

2011 (12 Apr). Royal Wedding (1st issue). T **852** and similar vert design. Multicoloured.

(a) Ordinary gum P 14½×14

(i) Domestic mail.

3588 60c. Type **852** .... 2·50 1·25

(ii) International Post

3589 $2.25 As Type **852** but white background .... 9·00 9·00
MS3590 .... 11·00 10·00

(b) Self-adhesive. Phosphor over parts of design. Die-cut perf 11½×11 (interrupted on horiz sides)

3591 60c. As Type **852** .... 2·25 1·75
a. Booklet pane. No. 3591×10 .... 19·00

No. 3591 was only issued in $6 stamp booklets, No. SB376.

853 Wedding of Prince William and Miss Catherine Middleton

854 " Madame Melba" (Rupert Bunny)

(Des Jo Muré. Litho McKellar Renown)

2011 (4 May). Royal Wedding (2nd issue).

(a) Ordinary gum. Phosphor frame and phosphor over other parts of design. P 14

3592 **853** 60c. multicoloured .... 2·50 1·50

(b) Self-adhesive. Phosphor frame. Die-cut perf 11½ (interrupted on horiz sides)

3593 60c. multicoloured .... 2·50 1·75
a. Booklet pane. No. 3593×10 .... 19·00

No. 3593 was issued in $6 stamp booklets, No. SB377.

(Des Passmore Design. Litho McKellar Renown)

2011 (10 May). 150th Birth Anniv of Dame Nellie Melba (soprano).

(a) Ordinary paper. P 14½×14

3594 **854** 60c. multicoloured .... 2·25 1·50

(b) Self-adhesive. Partial phosphor frame (at right and foot). Die-cut perf 11½×11 (interrupted on horiz sides)

3595 60c. multicoloured .... 2·50 2·00
a. Booklet pane. No. 3595×20 .... 38·00

No. 3595 was issued in $12 booklets, No. SB378.

855 Eucalyptus Oil and Blue Mallee

856 HMAS *Australia* (I) (1913-22)

(Des Wayne Rankin. Litho McKellar Renown)

2011 (17 May). Farming Australia: Native Plants. T **855** and similar horiz designs. Multicoloured. Phosphor over parts of design.

(a) Ordinary gum. P 14×14½

3596	60c. Type **855**	2·25	2·00
	a. Horiz strip of 4. Nos. 3596/9	8·00	7·25
3597	60c. Eucalyptus flowers and honeycomb ('Australian Honey')	2·25	2·00
3598	60c. Macadamia nuts	2·25	2·00
3599	60c. Tea tree and tea tree oil	2·25	2·00
3596/9	*Set of 4*	8·00	7·25

(b) Self-adhesive. Die-cut perf 11×11½ (interrupted on vert sides)

3600	60c. As Type **855**	2·00	2·25
	a. Horiz strip of 4. Nos. 3600/3	7·25	8·00
	b. Booklet pane. Nos. 3600×4 and 3601/3, each×2	17·00	
3601	60c. As No. 3597	2·00	2·25
3602	60c. As No. 3598	2·00	2·25
3603	60c. As No. 3599	2·00	2·25
3600/3	*Set of 4*	7·25	8·00

Nos. 3596/9 were printed together, *se-tenant*, as horizontal strips of four stamps in sheets of 50 (2 panes of 25), each sheet providing ten strips of four and ten single stamps (Type **855**).

Nos. 3600/3 were issued in rolls of 100 containing the four designs in sequence and also in $6 booklets, No. SB379.

Stamps as Type **855** but with a eucalyptus scented varnish were issued in sheets of ten and only sold in packs at $6.45 per pack.

(Des John White. Litho McKellar Renown)

2011 (14 June). Centenary of Royal Australian Navy. T **856** and similar horiz design. Multicoloured.

(a) Ordinary paper. P 14×14½

3604	60c. Type **856**	2·50	2·25
	a. Horiz pair. Nos. 3604/5	5·00	4·50
3605	60c. HMAS *Sydney* (IV)	2·50	2·25

(b) Self-adhesive. Phosphor bar at top and phosphor at left (3606) or right (3607). Die-cut perf 11×11½ (interrupted on vert sides)

3606	60c. As Type **856**	2·75	2·75
	a. Booklet pane. Nos. 3606/7, each×10	42·00	
3607	60c. As No. 3605	2·75	2·75

Nos. 3604/5 were printed together, *se-tenant*, as horizontal pairs in sheetlets of ten (2×5).

Nos. 3606/7 were issued in $12 booklets, No. SB380.

857 Bilby

858 Man and Dog ("Best Friends")

(Des Simone Sakinofsky. Litho McKellar Renown)

2011 (1 July). Australian Bush Babies. T **857** and similar vert designs. Multicoloured.

(a) Ordinary paper P 14½×14

(i) Domestic mail.

3608	60c. Type **857**	1·75	1·50

(ii) International Post

3609	$1.60 Dingo pup	4·00	4·00
3610	$1.65 Red Kangaroo Joey	4·00	4·00
3611	$2.35 Koala	6·00	6·00
3612	$4.70 Sugar glider	11·00	12·00
3608/12	*Set of 5*	24·00	25·00

(b) Self-adhesive. Irregular partial phosphor frame (at top and left). Die-cut perf 11½×11 (interrupted at top and bottom)

3613	$1.65 As No. 3610	4·50	5·00
	a. Pane. No. 3613×5	17·00	
3614	$2.35 As No. 3611	7·50	8·50
	a. Pane. No. 3614×5	30·00	

Nos. 3613/14 were issued in separate $8.25 and $11.75 panes of five stamps.

See also Nos. 3961/8

(Des Simone Sakinofsky. Litho McKellar Renown)

2011 (5 July). "Living Australian". (1st issue) Winning Entries from Photography Competition. T **858** and similar horiz designs. Multicoloured.

(a) Ordinary paper. P 14×14½

3615	60c. Type **858**	2·25	2·25
	a. Horiz strip of 5. Nos. 3615/19	10·00	10·00
3616	60c. Two girls ("Embrace Friendship")	2·25	2·25
3617	60c. Spectators reflected in sunglasses ("Cricket at the GABBA")	2·25	2·25
3618	60c. Aborigine boy performing Wedge Tail Eagle Dance ("Little Man's Business")	2·25	2·25
3619	60c. Red Kangaroo lying on beach ("This is So Relaxing")	2·25	2·25
3615/19	*Set of 5*	10·00	10·00

(b) Self-adhesive. Partial phosphor frame (at left and foot). Die-cut perf 11×11½ (interrupted on vert edges)

3620	60c. As Type **858**	2·00	2·25
	a. Horiz strip of 5. Nos. 3620/4	9·00	10·00
	b. Booklet pane. Nos. 3620/4, each×2	17·00	
3621	60c. As No. 3616	2·00	2·25
3622	60c. As No. 3617	2·00	2·25
3623	60c. As No. 3618	2·00	2·25
3624	60c. As No. 3619	2·00	2·25
3620/4	*Set of 5*	9·00	10·00

Nos. 3615/19 were printed together, *se-tenant*, as horizontal strips of five stamps in sheets of 50 (2 panes 5×5).

Nos. 3620/4 were issued in rolls of 200 containing the five designs in sequence, and also in $6 booklets, No. SB381.

See also Nos. 3810/9

859 Hand enclosing Candle wrapped in Barbed Wire

860 Child learning to Ski

(Des Nigel Buchanan. Litho RA Printing)

2011 (5 July). 50th Anniv of Amnesty International. P 14½×14.

3625	**859**	60c. black and greenish yellow	1·50	1·50

(Des John White. Litho Pemara (No. 3629) or RA Printing (others))

2011 (19 July). Skiing Australia. T **860** and similar multicoloured designs.

(a) Ordinary paper. P 14½×14 (60c.) or 14×14½ (others)

(i) Domestic mail

3626	60c. Type **860**	1·75	1·50

(ii) International Post

3627	$1.60 Snowboarder (*horiz*)	3·75	3·75
3628	$1.65 Skiier (*horiz*)	4·00	4·25
3626/8	*Set of 3*	8·50	8·50

(b) Self-adhesive Die-cut perf 11½×11 (interrupted on horiz edges) (60c.) or 11×11½ (interrupted vert edges) (others)

(i) Domestic mail. Phosphor over parts of design.

3629	60c. As Type **860**	1·50	1·50

(ii) International Post

3630	$1.60 As No. 3627	3·50	4·00
	a. Pane. No. 3630×5	15·00	
3631	$1.65 As No. 3628	3·75	4·50
	a. Pane. No. 3631×5	16·00	
3629/31	*Set of 3*	8·00	9·00

No. 3629 was issued in rolls of 100.

Nos. 3630/1 were issued in separate $8 and $8.25 panes of five stamps.

(Des Creative Ethos. Litho McKellar Renown)

2011 (28 July). Colonial Heritage: Emerging Identity (2nd issue). Vert designs as T **824**. Multicoloured. P 14×13½.

3632	$2 Kangaroo	5·00	5·00
	a. Pair. Nos. 3632/3	10·00	10·00
3633	$2 Black Swan	5·00	5·00
MS3634	141×90 mm. Nos. 3632/3	9·00	10·00

Nos. 3632/3 were printed together, *se-tenant*, as horizontal and vertical pairs in sheetlets of ten stamps.

(Litho)

2011 (28 July). Phila Nippon '11 World Stamp Exhibition, Yokohama, Japan. Sheet 130×90 mm containing Nos. 3609/10. Multicoloured. P 14½×14.

MS3635	$1.60 Dingo pup; $1.65 Red Kangaroo Joey	7·50	7·50

861 Quokka (*Setonix brachyurus*)

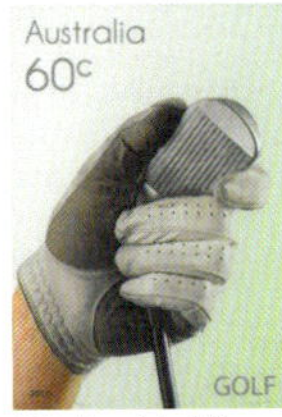

862 Hand holding Golf Club

(Des Kevin Stead. Litho McKellar Renown)

2011 (30 Aug). 50th Anniv of Worldwide Fund for Nature (formerly World Wildlife Fund). T **861** and similar horiz designs. Multicoloured. P 14×14½.

3636	60c. Type **861**	2·75	2·75
	a. Block of 4. Nos. 3636/9	10·00	10·00
3637	60c. Southern Elephant Seal (*Mirounga leonina*) (Australian Antarctic Territory)	2·75	2·75
3638	60c. Dugong (*Dugong dugon*) (Cocos (Keeling) Islands)	2·75	2·75
3639	60c. Christmas Island Shrew (*Crocidura trichura*) (Christmas Island)	2·75	2·75
3636/9 *Set of 4*		10·00	10·00
MS3640 135×72 mm. Nos. 3636/9		10·00	10·00

Nos. 3636/9 were printed together, *se-tenant*, as blocks of four stamps in sheets of 50 (2 panes 5×5) each sheet providing eight blocks of four and 18 single stamps (seven of Nos. 3636 and 3638 and two of Nos. 3637 and 3639).

On the upper pane the top left stamp is No. 3636 but on the lower pane it is No. 3638.

Nos. 3637/9 were all inscr 'AUSTRALIA' and also 'AUSTRALIAN ANTARCTIC TERRITORY' (3637), 'COCOS (KEELING) ISLANDS' (3638) or 'CHRISTMAS ISLAND' (3639).

(Des Jo Muré. Litho McKellar Renown)

2011 (27 Sept). Golf. T **862** and similar vert designs. Multicoloured.

(a) Ordinary paper

(i) Domestic mail. P 14½×14

3641	60c. Type **862**	1·90	1·90
	a. Horiz strip of 3. Nos. 3641/3	5·00	5·00
3642	60c. The President's Cup	1·90	1·90
3643	60c. Golf shoes	1·90	1·90

(ii) International Post. P 14½×14

3644	$1.65 Golf club and ball	4·25	3·25
3645	$2.35 Golf clubs	6·00	6·50
3641/5 *Set of 5*		14·50	14·00
MS3646 170×85 mm. Nos. 3641/5		14·50	14·50

(b) Self-adhesive

(i) Domestic mail. Phosphor over parts of design. Die-cut perf 11½×11 (interrupted on vert edges)

3647	60c. As Type **862**	2·25	2·25
	a. Vert strip of 3. Nos. 3647/9	6·00	6·00
	b. Booklet pane. Nos. 3647/8, each×4, and No. 3649×2	19·00	
3648	60c. As No. 3642	2·25	2·25
3649	60c. As No. 3643	2·25	2·25

(ii) International Post. Phosphor over parts of design. Die-cut perf 11½×11 (interrupted on vert edges)

3650	$1.65 As No. 3644	4·00	4·50
	a. Pane. No. 3650×5	17·00	
3651	$2.35 As No. 3645	6·00	7·50
	a. Pane. No. 3651×5	27·00	
3647/51 *Set of 5*		13·50	16·00

Nos. 3641/3 were printed together, *se-tenant*, as horizontal strips of three in sheets of 50 (2 panes 5×5), each sheet providing ten horizontal strips of three and ten horizontal pairs (Nos. 3641/2).

Nos. 3647/9 were issued in rolls of 100 containing the three designs in sequence, and also in $6 booklets, No. SB382.

Nos. 3650/1 were issued in separate panes of five stamps, sold at $8.25 or $11.75.

863 Fairy

864 Perth Skyline and Southern Cross

(Des Aaron Pocock and Sharon Rodziewicz. Litho McKellar Renown)

2011 (4 Oct). Stamp Collecting Month. Mythical Creatures. T **863** and similar vert designs. Multicoloured.

(a) Ordinary paper. P 14½×14

3652	60c. Type **863**	1·50	1·60
	a. Horiz strip of 5. Nos. 3652/6	6·50	7·00
3653	60c. Troll	1·50	1·60
3654	60c. Mermaid	1·50	1·60
3655	60c. Griffin	1·50	1·60
3656	60c. Unicorn	1·50	1·60
3657	$1.20 Dragon	3·00	3·25
3652/7 *Set of 6*		9·50	10·00
MS3658 170×85 mm. Nos. 3652/7		9·50	10·00

(b) Self-adhesive. Irregular phosphor frame. Die-cut perf 11½×11 (interrupted on horiz edges)

3659	60c. As Type **863**	1·25	1·40
	a. Booklet pane. Nos. 3659/63, each×2	11·00	
	b. Booklet pane. Nos. 3659/63, each×4	22·00	
3660	60c. As No. 3653	1·25	1·40
3661	60c. As No. 3654	1·25	1·40
3662	60c. As No. 3655	1·25	1·40
3663	60c. As No. 3656	1·25	1·40
3659/63 *Set of 5*		5·50	6·25

Nos. 3652/7 were printed together, *se-tenant*, as horizontal strips of five in sheets of 50 (2 panes 5×5).

Nos. 3659/63 were issued in $6 or $12 booklets, Nos. SB383/4.

(Des Rachelle Flynn. Litho RA Printing)

2011 (18 Oct). Commonwealth Heads of Government Meeting, Perth. P 14½×14.

3664	**864**	60c. multicoloured	1·25	1·25

865 Haegeum Musician

866 Virgin Mary and Baby Jesus

(Des Brian Clinton. Litho McKellar Renown)

2011 (31 Oct). Australia - Korea Friendship. T **865** and similar vert design. Multicoloured.

(a) Ordinary gum. P 13

(i) Domestic Mail

3665	60c. Type **865**	1·75	1·25

(ii) International Post

3666	$1.65 Didgeridoo musician	3·75	3·75

(b) Self-adhesive. Phosphor frame on three sides (at top, right and foot). Die-cut perf 11½×11 (interrupted on horiz sides)

3667	$1.65 As No. 3666	3·25	4·00
	a. Pane. No. 3667×5	14·00	

No. 3667 was issued in $8.25 panes of five stamps.

(Des Gavin Ryan. Litho McKellar Renown)

2011 (31 Oct). Christmas. T **866** and similar multicoloured design.

(a) Ordinary gum

(i) Domestic mail. P 14½×14

3668	55c. Type **866**	1·25	50

(ii) International Post. P 14×14½

3669	$1.50 Wise men following Star	3·25	3·75

(b) Self-adhesive. Phosphor frame on three sides (at top, right and foot)

(i) Domestic mail. Die-cut perf 11½×11 (interrupted on horiz edges)

3670	55c. As Type **866**	1·25	1·00
	a. Booklet pane. No. 3670×20	22·00	

(ii) International Post. Die-cut perf 11×11½ (interrupted on vert sides)

3671	$1.50 As No. 3669	3·25	3·25
	a. Pane. No. 3671×5	14·00	

No. 3670 was issued in $11 stamp bookllets, No. SB385.

No. 3671 was issued in $7.50 panes of five panes.

867 Christmas Tree

868 Poppy and Bugler

(Des Gavin Ryan. Litho McKellar Renown)

2011 (31 Oct). Christmas (2nd issue). T **867** and similar vert designs. Multicoloured.

(a) Ordinary gum. P 14½×14

3672	55c. Type **867**	1·60	1·60
	a. Horiz pair. Nos. 3672/3	3·00	3·00
3673	55c. Wrapped present	1·60	1·60
3674	60c. Star and berry decorations	1·60	1·60
3672/4 *Set of 3*		4·25	4·25

(b) Self-adhesive. Irregular partial phosphor frame. Die-cut perf 11½×11 (interrupted on horiz sides)

3675	55c. As Type **867**	1·25	1·25
	a. Booklet pane. Nos. 3675/6, each×10	22·00	
3676	55c. As No. 3673	1·25	1·25
3677	55c. As Type **867** but gold and red foil tree decorations	1·25	1·25
3678	55c. As No. 3673 but gold foil on parcel, silver foil on bow and red foil on star and berry decorations	1·25	1·25
3675/8 *Set of 4*		4·50	4·50

Nos. 3672/3 were printed together, *se-tenant*, as horizontal pairs in sheets of 50 (2 panes 5×5), each sheet providing 20 horizontal pairs and ten single stamps (Type **867**).

Nos. 3675/6 were only issued in $11 booklets, No. SB386.

Nos. 3677/8 come from separate sheetlets of ten.

(Des Tim Hancock. Litho McKellar Renown)

2011 (2 Nov). Remembrance Day. T **868** and similar horiz designs. Multicoloured.

(a) Ordinary gum. P 14×14½

3679	60c. Type **868**	1·50	1·25
3680	$1.20 Two poppies and two soldiers	2·75	3·00
MS3681	Nos. 3679/80	4·25	4·25

(b) Self-adhesive. Partial irregular phosphor frame (broken at left). Die-cut perf 11×11½ (interrupted on vert sides)

3682	60c. As Type **868**	1·25	1·40
	a. Booklet pane. No. 3682×10	12·00	

No. 3682 was issued in rolls of 200 and also in $6 booklets, No. SB387.

(Litho McKellar Renown)

2011 (11 Nov). China 2011 27th Asian International Stamp Exhibition, Wuxi, China. Two sheets, each 130×90 mm. Multicoloured. P 14½×14.

MS3683	No. 3609	4·50	4·50
MS3684	No. 3610	4·50	4·50

869 Lieut-Gen Rowell (Australia), Admiral Radford (US) and Maj-Gen Gentry (New Zealand), 1952

870 Cupcake

(Des Jo Muré. Litho RA Print)

2011 (18 Nov). 50th Anniv of ANZUS Treaty. P 14×14½.

3685	**869**	60c. multicoloured	1·75	1·50

No. 3684 was printed in sheetlets of ten stamps.

(Des Jennifer Scalzo and Jo Muré. Litho McKellar Renown)

2012 (17 Jan). Greetings Stamps. 'Precious Moments'. T **870** and similar vert designs. Multicoloured.

(a) Ordinary gum. P 14½×14

3686	60c. Type **870**	1·75	1·75
3687	60c. Teddy bear and stars within stars	1·75	1·75
3688	60c. Multicoloured balloons	1·75	1·75
3689	60c. 'LOVE' and hearts on strings	1·75	1·75
3690	60c. Love birds, 'with love' and branch of flowering tree	1·75	1·75
3691	$1.20 Pale gold rose	2·75	2·75
3686/91 *Set of 6*		10·50	10·50

(b) Self-adhesive. Irregular partial phosphor frame (3692/4) or phosphor frame (3695/6). Die-cut perf 11½×11 (interrupted on horiz sides)

3692	60c. As Type **870**	1·75	1·75
	a. Booklet pane. Nos. 3692×10	15·00	
3693	60c. As No. 3687	1·75	1·75
	a. Booklet pane. No. 3693×10	15·00	
3694	60c. As No. 3688	1·75	1·75
	a. Booklet pane. No. 3694×10	15·00	
3695	60c. As No. 3689	1·75	1·75
	a. Booklet pane. No. 3695×10	15·00	
3696	60c. As No. 3690	1·75	1·75
	a. Booklet pane. No. 3696×10	15·00	
3692/6 *Set of 5*		8·00	8·00

Nos. 3686/91 were printed together, *se-tenant*, as horizontal strips of five stamps in sheets of 50 (2 panes of 25).

Nos. 3692/6 were issued in separate $6 booklets, Nos. SB388/92.

A self-adhesive stamp as No. 3691 was issued in $24.95 premium booklets, No. SP189.

871 Ron Barassi (Australian rules football)

Des Michaela Gaunt. Lihto McKellar Renown)

2012 (20 Jan). Australian Legends (16th series). Legends of Football. T **871** and similar vert designs. Multicoloured.

(a) Ordinary gum. P 14½×14

3697	60c. Type **871**	1·40	1·40
	a. Vert pair. Nos. 3697/8	2·75	2·75
3698	60c. Gary Ablett (Australian rules football)	1·40	1·40
3699	60c. John Raper (Rugby League)	1·40	1·40
	a. Vert pair. Nos. 3699/3700	2·75	2·75
3700	60c. Billy Slater (Rugby League)	1·40	1·40
3701	60c. David Campese (Rugby Union)	1·40	1·40
	a. Vert pair. Nos. 3701/2	2·75	2·75
3702	60c. David Pocock (Rugby Union)	1·40	1·40
3703	60c. Joe Marston (soccer)	1·40	1·40
	a. Vert pair. Nos. 3703/4	2·75	2·75
3704	60c. Mark Schwarzer (soccer)	1·40	1·40
3697/704 *Set of 8*		10·00	10·00

(b) Self-adhesive. Phosphor at top left and foot of stamp. Die-cut perf 11½×11 (interrupted on horiz sides)

3705	60c. As Type **871**	1·25	1·40
	a. Booklet pane. No. 3705×10	11·00	
3706	60c. As No. 3698	1·25	1·40
	a. Booklet pane. No. 3706×10	11·00	
3707	60c. As No. 3699	1·25	1·40
	a. Booklet pane. No. 3707×10	11·00	
3708	60c. As No. 3700	1·25	1·40
	a. Booklet pane. No. 3708×10	11·00	
3709	60c. As No. 3701	1·25	1·40
	a. Booklet pane. No. 3709×10	11·00	
3710	60c. As No. 3702	1·25	1·40
	a. Booklet pane. No. 3710×10	11·00	
3711	60c. As No. 3703	1·25	1·40
	a. Booklet pane. No. 3711×10	11·00	
3712	60c. As No. 3704	1·25	1·40
	a. Booklet pane. No. 3712×10	11·00	
3705/12 *Set of 8*		9·00	10·00

Nos. 3697/8, 3699/3700, 3701/2 and 3703/4 were printed together, *se-tenant*, as vertical pairs in sheets of 50 (2 panes of 25). On the upper panes the top rows are Nos. 3697, 3699, 3701 or 3703, and on the lower panes the top rows are Nos. 3698, 3700, 3702 or 3704.

Nos. 3697/3704 were also issued in $19.95 premium booklets, No. SP190.

Nos. 3705/12 were issued in separate $6 booklets, Nos. SB393/400.

872 Early Telephone and Modern 4G Phone

(Des Stacey Zass. Litho Pemara (3719a) or McKellar Renown (others))

2012 (7 Feb). Technology - Then and Now. T **872** and similar horiz designs. Multicoloured.

(a) Ordinary gum. P 14×14½

3713	60c. Type **872**	2·00	2·00
	a. Horiz strip of 5. Nos. 3713/17	9·00	9·00
3714	60c. Ice chest and modern refrigerator	2·00	2·00
3715	60c. Early and modern television	2·00	2·00
3716	60c. Record player and digital media player	2·00	2·00
3717	60c. Road map and GPS (global positioning system)	2·00	2·00
3713/17 *Set of* 5		9·00	9·00
MS3718	170×85 mm. Nos. 3713/17	9·00	9·00

(b) Self-adhesive. Phosphor over parts of design. Die-cut perf 11×11½ (interrupted on vert sides)

3719	60c. As Type **872**	2·00	2·25
	a. Horiz strip of 5. Nos. 3719/23	9·00	10·00
	b. Booklet pane. Nos. 3719/23, each×2	17·00	
3720	60c. As No. 3714	2·00	2·25
3721	60c. As No. 3715	2·00	2·25
3722	60c. As No. 3716	2·00	2·25
3723	60c. As No. 3717	2·00	2·25
3719/23 *Set of* 5		9·00	10·00

Nos. 3713/17 were printed together, *se-tenant*, as horizontal strips of five stamps in sheets of 50 (2 panes 5×5).

Nos. 3719/23 were printed in rolls of 200 with the five designs in sequence, and also in $6 booklets, No. SB401.

873 O-Bahn Bus, Adelaide

(Des Jamie Tufrey. Litho McKellar Renown)

2012 (21 Feb). City Transport. T **873** and similar horiz designs. Multicoloured.

(a) Ordinary gum. P 14×14½

3724	60c. Type **873**	2·50	2·50
	a. Horiz strip of 5. Nos. 3724/8	11·00	11·00
3725	60c. *Charlotte* (ferry) passing Luna Park, Sydney	2·50	2·50
3726	60c. Train running alongside roads, Perth	2·50	2·50
3727	60c. W-class tram, Melbourne	2·50	2·50
3728	60c. Double-decker train, Sydney	2·50	2·50
3724/8 *Set of* 5		11·00	11·00

(b) Self-adhesive. Phosphor frame. Die-cut perf 11×11½ (interrupted on vert sides)

3729	60c. As Type **873**	2·25	2·50
	a. Horiz strip of 5. Nos. 3729/33, each×4	30·00	
3730	60c. As No. 3725	2·25	2·50
3731	60c. As No. 3726	2·25	2·50
3732	60c. As No. 3727	2·25	2·50
3733	60c. As No. 3728	2·25	2·50
3724/33 *Set of* 5		10·00	11·00

Nos. 3724/8 were printed together, *se-tenant*, as horizontal strips of five stamps in sheets of 50 (2 panes 5×5).

Nos. 3724/8 were also issued in $12.95 premium booklets, No. SP191.

Nos. 3729/33 were issued in $12 booklets, No. SB402.

874 Radjah Shelduck (*Tadorna radjah*)

(Des Christopher Pope (illustration) and Jo Muré (typography). Litho McKellar Renown)

2012 (6 Mar). Australian Waterbirds. T **874** and similar horiz designs. Multicoloured.

(a) Ordinary gum. P 14×14½

(i) Domestic mail

3734	60c. Type **874**	2·50	2·50
	a. Horiz pair. Nos. 3734/5	5·00	5·00
3735	60c. Pink-eared duck (*Malacorhynchus membranaceus*)	2·50	2·50

(ii) International Post

3736	$1.65 Australian shelduck (*Tadorna tadornoides*)	5·00	3·75
3737	$2.35 Plumed whistling duck (*Dendrocygna eytoni*)	7·50	7·50
3734/37 *Set of* 4		16·00	14·50

(b) Self-adhesive. Die-cut perf 11×11½ (interrupted on vert sides)

(i) Domestic mail. Phosphor frame

3738	60c. As Type **874**	2·50	2·50
	a. Horiz pair. Nos. 3738/9	5·00	5·00
	b. Booklet pane. No. 3738/9, each×5	21·00	
3739	60c. As No. 3735	2·50	2·50

(ii) International Post. Phosphor frame (broken at International Post marker at lower left)

3740	$1.65 As No. 3736	5·00	4·25
	a. Pane. No. 3740×5	21·00	
3741	$2.35 As No. 3737	7·50	8·00
	a. Pane. No. 3741×5	30·00	

Nos. 3734/5 were printed together, *se-tenant*, in horizontal pairs in sheets of 50, giving twenty horizontal pairs and ten single stamps (Type 874). Nos. 3738/9 were issued in rolls of 100 and also in $6 booklets, No. SB403.

Nos. 3740/1 were issued in $8.25 and $11.75 panes of five stamps.

875 Jersey Cattle (Dairy)

(Des Jo Muré. Litho Pemara (3751c/4c) or McKellar Renown (others))

2012 (20 Mar–26 June). Farming Australia (2nd series). T **875** and similar horiz designs . Multicoloured.

(a) Ordinary gum. P 14×14½ (10, 20c., 60c.) or 14½×14 ($1, $3, $5)

3742	10c. Type **875**	35	45
3743	20c. Pineapples	70	80
	a. Uncleared portion of design at left		
3744	60c. Beef cattle (26.6)	1·75	2·00
	a. Block of 4. Nos. 3744/7	6·25	7·25
3745	60c. Oranges (26.6)	1·75	2·00
3746	60c. Sugar cane (26.6)	1·75	2·00
3747	60c. Sheep (Wool) (26.6)	1·75	2·00
3748	$1 Bunch of grapes and vineyard (Wine) (50×30 *mm*)	3·25	2·40
3749	$3 Sunflowers (50×30 *mm*)	8·50	9·50
3750	$5 Apples (50×30 *mm*)	13·00	15·00
3742/50 *Set of* 9		30·00	32·00

(b) Self-adhesive. Partial phosphor frame (at top, left and foot). Die-cut perf 11

3751	60c. As No. 3744 (26.6)	1·40	1·75
	a. Booklet pane. Nos. 3751×2, 3752×4 and 3753/4, each×2	13·00	
	b. Booklet pane. Nos. 3751/4, each×5	22·00	
	c. Perf 12½	1·40	1·75
	ca. Horiz strip of 4. Nos. 3751c/4c	5·50	6·25
3752	60c. As No. 3745 (26.6)	1·40	1·75
	c. Perf 12½	1·40	1·75
3753	60c. As No. 3746 (26.6)	1·40	1·75
	c. Perf 12½	1·40	1·75
3754	60c. As No. 3747 (26 June)	1·40	1·75
	c. Perf 12½	1·40	1·75
3751/54 *Set of* 4		5·50	6·25

Nos. 3744/7 were printed together, se-tenant, as blocks of four in sheets of 50 (2 panes of 25), giving eight blocks of four and eighteen single stamps. Nos. 3751/4 were issued in $6 and $12 booklets (Nos. SB406/7).

No. 3743a occurs on the right-hand four stamps in the bottom row of the sheet of 50, where a portion of the right of the design appears at the left of the stamp. The error was corrected in later printings.

Nos. 3751c/4c come from rolls of 100 or 200 containing the four designs in sequence.

876 "enrol to vote"

(Des Gary Domoney. Litho McKellar Renown)

2012 (27 Mar). Centenary of Compulsory Enrolment to Vote. P 14½×14.

3755	**876**	60c. multicoloured	1·40	1·40

877 Queen Elizabeth II, c. 1952

(Des Jo Muré. Litho McKellar Renown)

2012 (3 Apr). Diamond Jubilee. T **877** and similar vert design. Multicoloured.

(a) Ordinary gum. P 14½×14.

(i) Domestic mail.

3756	60c. Type **877**	2·00	1·40

(ii) International Post

3757	$2.35 Queen Elizabeth II, *c.* 2012	7·50	8·00
MS3758	106×71 mm. Nos. 3756/7	9·50	9·50

(b) Self-adhesive. International Post. Phosphor frame (broken at International Post marker at upper left) . Die-cut perf 11½×11 (interrupted on vert sides)

3759	$2.35 As No. 3757	7·50	8·50
	a. Pane. No. 3751×5	30·00	

No. 3759 was issued in $11.75 panes of five stamps.

878 Professor Chris O'Brien (1952–2009, head and neck surgeon)

(Des Simone Sakinofsky. Litho McKellar Renown (3760/4) or Pemara (3765/9))

2012 (10 Apr). Medical Doctors. T **878** and similar vert designs. Multicoloured.

(a) Ordinary gum. P 14½×14

3760	60c. Type **878**	2·00	2·00
3761	60c. Professor Fred Hollows (1929–93, ophthalmologist)	2·00	2·00
3762	60c. Victor Chang (1936–91, cardiac surgeon)	2·00	2·00
3763	60c. Dame Kate Campbell (1899–1986, paediatrician)	2·00	2·00
3764	60c. Jane Stocks Greig (1872–1939, public health specialist)	2·00	2·00
3760/64	*Set of 5*	9·00	9·00

(b) Self-adhesive. Phosphor band at foot and phosphor over parts of top and left of design. Die-cut perf 11½×11 (interrupted on horiz sides)

3765	60c. As Type **878**	2·00	2·25
	a. Vert strip of 5. Nos. 3765/9	9·00	10·00
3766	60c. As No. 3761	2·00	2·25
3767	60c. As No. 3762	2·00	2·25
3768	60c. As No. 3763	2·00	2·25
3769	60c. As No. 3764	2·00	2·25
3765/3769	*Set of 5*	9·00	10·00

Nos. 3765/9 come from rolls printed by Pemara containing the five designs in sequence.

See also Nos. 3804/9

879 Rising Sun Badge, 1902–4

(Des Lisa Christensen. Litho McKellar Renown)

2012 (17 Apr). Rising Sun Badge (Australian Army General Service badge). T **879** and similar horiz designs. Multicoloured.

(a) Ordinary gum. P 14×14½

3770	60c. Type **879**	2·00	2·00
	a. Horiz strip of 5. Nos. 3770/4	9·00	9·00
3771	60c. Rising Sun badge, 1904–49	2·00	2·00
3772	60c. Rising Sun badge, 1954–69	2·00	2·00
3773	60c. Rising Sun badge, 1969–91	2·00	2·00
3774	60c. Rising Sun badge, from 1991	2·00	2·00
3770/4	*Set of 5*	9·00	9·00
MS3775	130×80 mm. Nos. 3770/4	9·00	9·00

(b) Self-adhesive. Phosphor around right, foot and bottom left of design. Die-cut perf 11×11½ (interrupted on vert sides)

3776	60c. As Type **879**	2·00	2·25
	a. Booklet pane. Nos. 3776/80, each×2	17·00	
3777	60c. As No. 3771	2·00	2·25
3778	60c. As No. 3772	2·00	2·25
3779	60c. As No. 3773	2·00	2·25
3780	60c. As No. 3774	2·00	2·25
3776/80	*Set of 5*	9·00	10·00

Nos. 3770/4 were printed together, *se-tenant*, as horizontal strips of five in sheets of 50 (2 panes 5×5).

Nos. 3776/80 were issued in $6 booklets, No. SB404.

880 *Chromodoris westraliensis*

(Des Simone Sakinofsky. Litho McKellar Renown)

2012 (8 May). Underwater World. Nudibranchs. T **880** and similar horiz designs. Multicoloured.

(a) Ordinary gum. P 14×14½.

3781	60c. Type **880**	1·75	2·00
	a. Horiz strip of 3. Nos. 3781/3	4·75	5·50
3782	60c. *Godiva* sp.	1·75	2·00
3783	60c. *Flabellina rubrolineata*	1·75	2·00
3784	$1.20 *Phyllidia ocellata*	3·00	3·50
	a. Horiz pair. Nos. 3784/5	6·00	7·00
3785	$1.20 *Thorunna florens*	3·00	3·50
3786	$1.80 *Nembrotha purpureolineata*	4·25	4·25
3781/86	*Set of 6*	13·50	15·00
MS3787	170×80 mm. Nos. 3781/6	14·00	15·00

(b) Self-adhesive. Irregular phosphor band at top and phosphor over left portion of design. Die-cut perf 11×11½ (interrupted on vert sides)

3788	60c. As Type **880**	1·75	2·00
	a. Booklet pane. Nos. 3788/9, each×7 and No. 3790×6	30·00	
3789	60c. As No. 3782	1·75	2·00
3790	60c. As No. 3783	1·75	2·00
3788/90	*Set of 3*	4·75	5·50

Nos. 3781/3 were printed together, *se-tenant*, as horizontal strips of three in sheets of 50 (2 panes of 25), each sheet giving ten horizontal strips of three and ten horizontal pairs (Nos. 3781/2). Nos. 3784/5 were printed together, *se-tenant*, as horizontal pairs in sheets of 50 (2 panes of 25), each sheet giving 20 horizontal pairs and ten single stamps (Type 880). Nos. 3781/3 and 3785/6 were also issued in $14.95 premium booklets, No. SP192.

Nos. 3788/90 were issued in $12 booklets, No. SB405.

881 Double-decker Bus, St. Paul's Cathedral, the London Eye and Big Ben

(Des Jonathan Chong. Litho RA Printing)

2012 (5 June). Olympic Games (1st issue). The Road to London.

(a) Ordinary gum. P 14½×14

3791	**881**	60c. multicoloured	1·40	1·40

(b) Self-adhesive. Irregular partial phosphor frame. Die-cut perf 11½×11 (interrupted on horiz sides)

3792 **881** 60c. multicoloured .... 1·75 1·75
a. Booklet pane. No. 3792×10 .... 16·00

No. 3792 was issued in rolls of 100 and also in $6 booklets, No. SB406.

See also Nos. 3804/9

(Litho RA Printing)

2012 (18 June). Indonesia World Stamp Championship, Jakarta. Sheet 130×90 mm containing No. 3611×2. Multicoloured. P 14½×14.

MS3793 $2.35 Koala baby×2 .... 11·00 12·00

(Litho RA Printing)

2012 (18 June). Australia 2013 World Stamp Expo, Melbourne. Sheet 130×90 containing stamp as No. 2639 but 52×37 mm with Australia 2013 World Stamp Expo emblem at left. Multicoloured.

MS3794 $1.85 Australia 2013 Kangaroo on map emblem and Royal Exhibition Building, Melbourne 5·50 5·50

No. **MS**3794 was issued for Indonesia 2012 World Stamp Championship and has the Indonesia 2012 emblem on the lower right sheet margin.

(Des Ethos. Litho McKellar Renown)

2012 (19 June). Colonial Heritage: Visualising Australia (3rd issue). Vert designs as T **824**. P 14×14½ (3795/6) or 14×13½ (**MS**3797).

3795 $2 'Sydney View' (figure of Industry receiving three convicts) .... 4·75 5·00
a. Pair. Nos. 3795/6 .... 9·50 10·00
3796 $2 Hobart .... 4·75 5·00
MS3797 140×90 mm. Nos. 3795/6 .... 9·50 11·00

Nos. 3795/6 were printed together, *se-tenant*, as horizontal and vertical pairs in sheetlets of ten stamps.

No. 3795 is based on the design used for the early stamps of New South Wales (1850–1), and No. 3796 on that used for 1899 2d. stamp of Tasmania.

882 Emblem

(Des Hoyne Design. Litho RA Printing)

2012 (26 June). Olivia Newton-John Cancer and Wellness Centre, Austin Hospital, Melbourne. Self-adhesive. Irregular partial phosphor frame (broken at right and foot). Die-cut perf 11½×11 (interrupted on horiz sides).

3798 **882** 60c. multicoloured .... 2·25 2·25

No. 3798 was issued in sheetlets of ten stamps, each sheetlet sold for $8, the $2 premium over face value going to the Olivia Newton-John Cancer and Wellness Centre Appeal.

883 Blue Mountain Pioneers (engraving by Emile Ulm, from Sydney Mail, 1880)

(Des Craig McGill. Litho McKellar Renown)

2012 (3 July). Inland Explorers. Bicentenary of Gregory Blaxland, William Lawson and William Wentworth's crossing of the Blue Mountains and 150th Anniv of John McDouall Stuart's Overland Crossing of Australia. T **883** and similar horiz designs. Multicoloured. P 14×14½.

3799 60c. Type **883** .... 1·75 2·00
a. Horiz pair. Nos. 3799/3800 .... 3·50 4·00
3800 60c. Gregory Blaxland, William Lawson and William Charles Wentworth .... 1·75 2·00
3801 $1.20 John McDouall Stuart and desert landscape .... 3·25 3·50
a. Horiz pair. Nos. 3801/2 .... 6·50 7·00
3802 $1.20 *Planting the Flag on the Shores of the Indian Ocean Coast* (engraving by George French Angas from *Journals of John McDouall Stuart*, 1865) .... 3·25 3·50
3799/802 *Set of 4* .... 9·00 10·00
MS3803 135×72 mm. Nos. 3799/3802 .... 9·00 10·00

Nos. 3799/800 and 3801/2 were each printed together, *se-tenant*, as horizontal pairs in sheets of 50 (2 panes of 25), each sheet containing 20 horizontal pairs and ten single stamps (Type **883** or No. 3801). Each horizontal pair forms a composite design either of Blaxland, Lawson and Wentworth reaching the westernmost point of their journey in 1813 or of Stuart's overland crossing in 1861–2.

884 Swimming

(Des Jonathan Chong. Litho McKellar Renown)

2012 (17 July). Olympic Games, London (2nd issue). T **884** and similar horiz designs.

(a) Ordinary gum. P 14×14½. Multicoloured

3804 60c. Type **884** .... 1·75 1·40

(ii) International Post. P 14×14½

3805 $1.60 Pole vault .... 4·00 3·75
3806 $2.35 Rowing .... 6·00 6·50
3804/6 *Set of 3* .... 10·50 10·50

(b) Self-adhesive. Domestic mail. Irregular partial phosphor frame (broken at left and right). Die-cut perf 11×11½ (interrupted on vert sides)

3807 60c. As Type **884** .... 1·75 1·40

(ii) International Post

3808 $1.60 As No. 3805 .... 4·00 4·00
a. Pane. No. 3808×5 .... 18·00
3809 $2.35 As No. 3806 .... 6·00 7·00
a. Pane. No. 3809×5 .... 27·00

No. 3807 was issued in rolls of 100.

Nos. 3808/9 were issued in $8 or $11.75 panes of five stamps.

885 *Little Wonders* (Ann Clarke)

(Des Sonia Young. Litho McKellar Renown)

2012 (24 July). Living Australian (2nd issue). Winning Entries from Photography Competition. T **885** and similar horiz designs. Multicoloured.

(a) Ordinary gum. P 14×14½

3810 60c. Type **885** .... 1·75 1·75
a. Horiz strip of 5. Nos. 3810/14 .... 8·00 8·00
3811 60c. Merino sheep ('The Godfathers', Chevelle Williams) .... 1·75 1·75
3812 60c. Rural letter boxes ('Is there a Letter for Me?', Wanda Lach) .... 1·75 1·75
3813 60c. Seagull with chip in beak ('Lunch on the Harbour', Damian Madden) .... 1·75 1·75
3814 60c. Rural service station ('Fuel Ask at the Store across the Road', Ronald Rockman) .... 1·75 1·75
3810/14 *Set of 5* .... 8·00 8·00

(b) Self-adhesive. Phosphor frame on three sides (top, left and foot). Die-cut perf 11×11½ (interrupted on vert sides)

3815 60c. As No. 3814 .... 1·50 1·75
a. Booklet pane. Nos. 3815/19, each×4 .... 27·00
3816 60c. As Type **885** .... 1·50 1·75
3817 60c. As No. 3812 .... 1·50 1·75
3818 60c. As No. 3811 .... 1·50 1·75
3819 60c. As No. 3813 .... 1·50 1·75
3815/19 *Set of 5* .... 7·00 8·00

Nos. 3810/14 were printed together, *se-tenant*, as horizontal strips of five stamps in sheets of 50 (2 panes of 25).

Nos. 3815/19 were issued in $12 booklets, No. SB409.

886 Alicia Coutts, Cate Campbell, Brittany Elmslie and Melanie Schlanger (swimming: women's 4×100m freestyle relay)

(Des Simone Sakinofsky. Litho EGO Print)

2012 (31 July–13 Aug). Australian Gold Medal Winners at Olympic Games, London. T **886** and similar square designs. Multicoloured. P 14.

3820	60c. Type **886**	1·50	1·50
3821	60c. Tom Slingsby (sailing: men's laser)	1·50	1·50
3822	60c. Anna Meares (cycling: women's sprint)	1·50	1·50
3823	60c. Sally Pearson (athletics: women's 100m hurdles)	1·50	1·50
3824	60c. Iain Jensen and Nathan Outteridge (sailing: men's 49er class)	1·50	1·50
3825	60c. Tate Smith, David Smith, Murray Stewart and Jacob Clear (canoe/kayak: men's K4 1000m)	1·50	1·50
3826	60c. Mathew Belcher and Malcolm Page (sailing: men's 470 class)	1·50	1·50
3820/26	*Set of 7*	9·75	9·75

Nos. 3820/6 were each printed in sheetlets of ten stamps (2×5), sold for $6 per sheetlet.

887 *Sir Frank Macfarlane Burnet* (physiology or medicine, 1960) (Clifton Pugh)

(Des Lynette Traynor. Litho McKellar Renown)

2012 (28 Aug). Australian Nobel Prize Winners. T **887** and similar vert designs. Multicoloured.

(a) Ordinary gum. P 14½×14.

3827	60c. Type **887**	1·50	1·50
	a. Horiz strip of 5. Nos. 3827/31	7·00	7·00
3828	60c. *Sir John Carew Eccles* (physiology or medicine, 1963) (Judy Cassab)	1·50	1·50
3829	60c. *Patrick White* (Literature, 1973) (Brett Whiteley)	1·50	1·50
3830	60c. *Sir Howard Walter Florey* (physiology or medicine, 1945) (Allan Gwynne-Jones)	1·50	1·50
3831	60c. *William Lawrence Bragg* (physics, 1915) (Sir William Dargie)	1·50	1·50
3827/31	*Set of 5*	7·00	7·00

(b) Self-adhesive. Phosphor frame. Die-cut perf 11×11½ (interrupted on horiz sides)

3832	60c. As Type **887**	1·50	1·50
	a. Vert strip of 5. Nos. 3832/6	7·00	7·00
	b. Booklet pane. Nos. 3832/6, each×2	13·00	
3833	60c. As No. 3828	1·50	1·50
3834	60c. As No. 3829	1·50	1·50
3835	60c. As No. 3830	1·50	1·50
3836	60c. As No. 3831	1·50	1·50
3832/36	*Set of 5*	7·00	7·00

Nos. 3827/31 were printed together, *se-tenant*, as horizontal strips of five stamps in sheets of 50 (2 panes of 25).

Nos. 3832/6 were issued in rolls of 200 containing the five designs in sequence and also in $6 booklets, No. SB410.

888 Car arriving at Port Arthur

(Des Gavin Ryan. Litho McKellar Renown)

2012 (18 Sept). Road Trip Australia. T **888** and similar square designs. Multicoloured. P 14.

(a) Ordinary gum

(i) Domestic mail

3837	60c. Type **888**	1·75	1·75
	a. Horiz strip of 3. Nos. 3837/9	4·75	4·75
3838	60c. Motor caravan on coast road, diver's goggles and Great Barrier Reef fish and corals	1·75	1·75
3839	60c. Motorcyclists picnicking and vineyard, Margaret River	1·75	1·75

(ii) International Post. P 14

3840	$1.65 Little penguins and laden family car on Phillip Island	3·75	3·75
3841	$2.35 Car and finish of Camel Cup, Alice Springs	5·50	5·50
3837/41	*Set of 5*	13·00	13·00
MS3842	170×80 mm. Nos. 3837/41	13·50	14·50

(b) Self-adhesive. (i) Domestic mail. Phosphor over parts of design. Die-cut perf 11½ (interrupted on horiz sides)

3843	60c. As No. 3838	1·75	2·00
	a. Booklet pane. No. 3843×3, 3844×4 and 3845×3	15·00	
3844	60c. As No. 3839	1·75	2·00
3845	60c. As Type **888**	1·75	2·00

(ii) International Post. Phosphor over parts of design. Die-cut perf 11½ (interrupted on horiz sides)

3846	$1.65 As No. 3840	4·25	4·25
	a. Pane. No. 3846×5	18·00	
3847	$2.35 As No. 3841	6·50	7·50
	a. Pane. No. 3847×5	28·00	
3843/7	*Set of 5*	14·50	16·00

Nos. 3837/9 were printed together, *se-tenant*, as horizontal strips of three in sheets of 50 (2 panes of 25), each sheet giving ten horizontal strips of three and ten horizontal pairs (Nos. 3837/8). Nos. 3843/5 were issued in $6 booklets, No. SB411.

Nos. 3846/7 were issued in $8.25 and $11.75 panes of five stamps.

See also Nos. 4006/16

889 Nullarbor Plain

(Des Janet Boschen. Litho McKellar Renown)

2012 (25 Sept). International Stamps. Wilderness Australia. T **889** and similar vert designs. Multicoloured.

(a) Ordinary gum. P 14½×14

3848	$1.65 Type **889**	3·75	3·75
3849	$2.35 Daintree National Park, Queensland	5·50	5·50
3850	$4.50 Cradle Mountain, Tasmania	10·50	10·50

(b) Self-adhesive. Phosphor band at right and phosphor across centre of stamps. Die-cut perf 11½×11 (interrupted on horiz sides).

3851	$1.65 As Type **889**	4·25	4·25
	a. Pane. No. 3851×5	18·00	
3852	$2.35 As No. 3849	6·50	7·00
	a. Pane. No. 3852×5	28·00	
3843/52	*Set of 5*	27·00	28·00

Nos. 3851/2 were issued in $8.25 and $11.75 panes of five stamps.

890 Black Rhino, Taronga Western Plains Zoo, NSW

(Des Simone Sakinofsky. Litho EGO (**MS**3860) or McKellar Renown (others))

2012 (28 Sept). Stamp Collecting Month. Australian Zoos. T **890** and similar horiz designs. Multicoloured.

(a) Ordinary gum. P 13½×14 (3859) or 14×14½ (others)

3853	60c. Type **890**	1·50	1·50
	a. Horiz pair. Nos. 3853/4	3·00	3·00
3854	60c. Giraffe, Taronga Zoo, New South Wales	1·50	1·50

3855	60c. Giant panda, Adelaide Zoo	1·50	1·50
	a. Horiz pair. Nos. 3855/6	3·00	3·00
3856	60c. Sumatran Orangutan, Perth Zoo	1·50	1·50
3857	60c. Saltwater Crocodile, Australia Zoo, Queensland	1·50	1·50
	a. Horiz pair. Nos. 3857/8	3·00	3·00
3858	60c. Wedge-tailed Eagle, Healesville Sanctuary, Victoria	1·50	1·50
3859	60c. Sumatran Tiger, Melbourne Zoo (*50×30 mm*)	1·50	1·50
3853/59 *Set of 7*		9·75	9·75
MS3860 160×80 mm. Nos. 3853/9		9·75	10·50

(b) Self-adhesive. Irregular partial phosphor frame. Die-cut perf 11×11½ (interrupted on vert sides)

3861	60c. As Type **890**	1·50	1·50
	a. Horiz strip of 6. Nos. 3861/6	8·25	8·25
	b. Booklet pane. Nos. 3861/2, each×4 and Nos. 3863/6, each×3	26·00	
3862	60c. As No. 3854	1·50	1·50
3863	60c. As No. 3855	1·50	1·50
3864	60c. As No. 3856	1·50	1·50
3865	60c. As No. 3857	1·50	1·50
3866	60c. As No. 3858	1·50	1·50
3861/66 *Set of 6*		8·25	8·25

Nos. 3853/4, 3855/6 and 3857/8 were each printed together, *se-tenant*, as horizontal pairs in sheets of 50 (2 panes of 25), each sheet giving 20 horizontal pairs and ten single stamps (Type 890, No. 3855 or 3857). No. 3859 is inscr with emblem and "150 YEARS MELBOURNE ZOO".

Nos. 3861/6 were issued in rolls of 100 containing the six designs in sequence, and also in $12 stamp booklets, No. SB412.

891 Peter Brock's Torana Touring Car

(Des Sean Pethick Xsd. Litho McKellar Renown)

2012 (2 Oct). 50th Anniv (2013) of Bathurst Endurance Race (touring car race). T **891** and similar horiz designs. Multicoloured.

(a) Ordinary gum. P 14×14½

3867	60c. Type **891**	1·50	1·50
	a. Block of 4. Nos. 3867/70	5·50	5·50
3868	60c. Mt. Panorama track	1·50	1·50
3869	60c. Will Davison's Ford	1·50	1·50
3870	60c. Russell Ingall's Holden	1·50	1·50
3867/70 *Set of 6*		5·50	5·50
MS3871 160×80 mm. Nos. 3867/70		5·50	5·50

(b) Self-adhesive. Phosphor bars along top, foot and sides. Die-cut perf 11×11½ (interrupted on vert sides)

3872	60c. As Type **891**	1·50	1·50
	a. Booklet pane. Nos. 3872/4, each×2, and No. 3875×4	13·00	
3873	60c. As No. 3870	1·50	1·50
3874	60c. As No. 3869	1·50	1·50
3875	60c. As No. 3868	1·50	1·50
3872/75 *Set of 4*		5·50	5·50

Nos. 3867/70 were printed together, *se-tenant*, as blocks of four stamps in sheets of 50 (2 panes of 25), each sheet giving eight blocks of four and 18 single stamps. On the top pane the upper left stamp is Type **891**, but on the lower pane the top left stamp is No. 3869.

Nos. 3872/5 were issued in $6 booklets, No. SB413.

892 Susie O'Neill

(Des Jo Muré. Litho McKellar Renown)

2012 (12 Oct). Sporting Legends: Susie O'Neill. T **892** and similar vert design. Multicoloured. P 14½×14.

3876	60c. Type **892**	1·40	1·40
	a. Pair. Nos. 3876/7	2·75	2·75
3877	60c. Susie O'Neill swimming	1·40	1·40

Nos. 3876/7 were printed together, *se-tenant*, as horizontal and vertical pairs in sheetlets of ten (5×2).

893 Ballet Dancer

(Des Jo Muré. Litho McKellar Renown)

2012 (16 Oct). 50th Anniv of the Australian Ballet. T **893** and similar vert designs. Multicoloured.

(a) Ordinary gum. P 14½×14

3878	60c. Type **893**	1·40	1·40
	a. Pair. Nos. 3878/9	2·75	2·75
3879	60c. Two dancers	1·40	1·40

(b) Self-adhesive. Phosphor around parts of design. Die-cut perf 11½×11 (interrupted on horiz sides)

3880	60c. As No. 3879	1·40	1·40
	a. Horiz pair. Nos. 3880/1	2·75	2·75
3881	60c. As Type **893**	1·40	1·40
3878/81 *Set of 4*		5·50	5·50

Nos. 3878/9 were printed together, *se-tenant*, as horizontal and vertical pairs in sheetlets of ten (5×2).

Nos. 3880/1 were issued in rolls of 200 containing the two designs in sequence.

894 Madonna and Christ Child (from tapestry)

(Des Jo Muré. Litho McKellar Renown)

2012 (1 Nov). Christmas (1st issue). T **894** and similar multicoloured designs. P 14½×14.

(a) Ordinary gum

(i) Domestic mail

3882	55c. Type **894**	1·25	50

(ii) International Post. Size 50×30 mm. P 14½×14

3883	$1.60 Adoration of the Magi (tapestry)	3·75	3·75

(b) Self-adhesive

(i) Domestic mail. Phosphor frame. Die-cut perf 11½×11 (interrupted on horiz sides)

3884	55c. As Type **894**	1·25	1·25
	a. Booklet pane. No. 3884×20	22·00	

(ii) International Post. Size 50×30 mm. Phosphor frame (broken upper left at International Post marker). Die-cut perf 11

3885	$1.60 As No. 3883	3·75	4·00
	a. Pane. No. 3885×5	18·00	

No. 3884 was issued in $11 stamp booklets, No. SB414.

No. 3885 was issued in $8 panes of five stamps.

895 Reindeer

(Des Jo Muré. Litho McKellar Renown)

2012 (1 Nov). Christmas (2nd issue). T **895** and similar vert designs. Multicoloured.

(a) Ordinary gum. P 14½×14

3886	55c. Type **895**	1·25	1·25
	a. Horiz pair. Nos. 3886/7	2·50	2·50
3887	55c. Wrapped presents	1·25	1·25
3888	60c. Bells and holly	1·40	1·00
3886/88 *Set of 3*		3·50	3·25

(b) Self-adhesive. Irregular partial phosphor frame (broken at top left and lower left (3889, 3891) or at top (3890, 3892). Die-cut perf 11½×11 (interrupted on horiz sides)

3889	55c. As Type **895**	1·25	1·25
	a. Booklet pane. No. 3889×20	22·00	
3890	55c. As No. 3887	1·25	1·25
3891	55c. As Type **895** but silver foil snowflake and red foil on reindeer's nose and neck ribbon	1·25	1·25
3892	55c. As No. 3890 but red foil ribbon on green parcel	1·25	1·25
3889/92 *Set of* 4		5·00	5·00

Nos. 3886/7 were printed together, *se-tenant*, as horizontal pairs in sheets of 50 (2 panes of 25) giving 20 horizontal pairs and ten single stamps (Type **895**). Nos. 3889/90 were issued in $11 booklets, No. SB415.

Nos. 3891/2 were printed in separate self-adhesive sheetlets of ten stamps.

896 Lawn Bowls

(Des John White. Litho R/A Print)

2012 (1 Nov). Lawn Bowls. T **896** and similar horiz design. Multicoloured. P 14×14½.

3893	60c. Type **896**	1·40	1·40
3894	$1.20 Lawn bowls (men)	2·75	2·75
MS3895	135×80 mm. Nos. 3893/4	4·25	4·25

897 Jacqueline Freney

(Des Simone Sakinofsky. Litho EGO)

2012 (9 Nov). Paralympian of the Year (winner of eight swimming gold medals at Olympic Games, London). P 14.

3896	**897** 60c. multicoloured	1·40	1·40

No. 3896 was printed in sheetlets of ten stamps, sold for $6 per sheetlet.

898 Paul Kelly

(Des Jo Muré. Litho McKellar Renown)

2013 (18 Jan). Australian Legends (17th series). Legends of Music. T **898** and similar vert designs. Multicoloured.

(a) Ordinary gum. P 14½×14

3897	60c. Type **898**	1·50	1·50
	a. Horiz pair. Nos. 3897/8	3·00	3·00
3898	60c. INXS (*Listen Like Thieves* album cover)	1·50	1·50
3899	60c. Kylie Minogue	1·50	1·50
	a. Horiz pair. Nos. 3899/900	3·00	3·00
3900	60c. Ian "Molly" Meldrum	1·50	1·50
3901	60c. Olivia Newton-John	1·50	1·50
	a. Horiz pair. Nos. 3901/2	3·00	3·00
3902	60c. John Farnham	1·50	1·50
3903	60c. AC/DC (*Back in Black* album cover)	1·50	1·50
	a. Horiz pair. Nos. 3903/4	3·00	3·00
3904	60c. Cold Chisel (album cover)	1·50	1·50
3905	60c. Men at Work (*Business as Usual* album cover)	1·50	1·50
	a. Horiz pair. Nos. 3905/6	3·00	3·00
3906	60c. The Seekers (album cover)	1·50	1·50
3897/3906 *Set of* 10		13·50	13·50

(b) Self-adhesive. Phosphor around design. Die-cut perf 11½×11 (interrupted on horiz sides)

3907	60c. As Type **898**	1·50	1·50
	a. Booklet pane. No. 3907	13·00	
3908	60c. As No. 3898	1·50	1·50
	a. Booklet pane. No. 3908	13·00	
3909	60c. As No. 3899	1·50	1·50
	a. Booklet pane. No. 3909×10	13·00	
3910	60c. As No. 3900	1·50	1·50
	a. Booklet pane. No. 3910×10	13·00	
3911	60c. As No. 3901	1·50	1·50
	a. Booklet pane. No. 3911×10	13·00	
3912	60c. As No. 3902	1·50	1·50
	a. Booklet pane. No. 3912×10	13·00	
3913	60c. As No. 3903	1·50	1·50
	a. Booklet pane. No. 3913×10	13·00	
3914	60c. As No. 3904	1·50	1·50
	a. Booklet pane. No. 3914×10	13·00	
3915	60c. As No. 3905	1·50	1·50
	a. Booklet pane. No. 3915×10	13·00	
3916	60c. As No. 3906	1·50	1·50
	a. Booklet pane. No. 3916×10	13·00	

Nos. 3897/8, 3899/3900, 3901/2, 3903/4 and 3905/6 were printed together, *se-tenant*, as horizontal pairs in sheets of 50 (2 panes of 25), each sheet giving 20 horizontal pairs and ten single stamps (Type **898**, No. 3899, 3901, 3903 or 3905). Nos. 3897/3906 were also issued in $24.95 premium booklets, No. SP193.

Nos. 3907/16 were issued in separate $6 booklets, Nos. SB416/25.

899 Sprig of Eucalyptus Leaves

(Des MDM (3917), Lisa Christensen (3918/19) and Sonia Young (2920/2). Litho McKellar Renown)

2013 (5 Feb). Greetings Stamps. Special Occasions. T **899** and similar vert designs. Multicoloured.

(a) Ordinary gum. P 14½×14

3917	60c. Type **899**	2·00	2·00
	a. Horiz strip of 5. Nos. 3917/21	9·00	9·00
3918	60c. Outline map of Australia on globe (green and blue)	2·00	2·00
3919	60c. Outline map of Australia on globe (red and yellow)	2·00	2·00
3920	60c. Rose petal ('Love')	2·00	2·00
3921	60c. Green orchid	2·00	2·00
3922	$1.20 Wedding gift in silver box and two glasses of champagne	3·00	3·00
3917/22 *Set of* 6		11·50	11·50

(b) Self-adhesive. Phosphor over parts of design (3923, 3928), phosphor frame (3924/5) or irregular partial phosphor frame (3926/7). Die-cut perf 11½×11 (interrupted on horiz sides)

3923	60c. As Type **899**	1·75	1·75
	a. Booklet pane. No. 3923×10	15·00	
3924	60c. As No. 3919	1·75	1·75
	a. Booklet pane. No. 3924/8, each×5	15·00	
3925	60c. As No. 3919	1·75	1·75
3926	60c. As No. 3920	1·75	1·75
	a. Booklet pane. No. 3926×10	15·00	
3927	60c. As No. 3921	1·75	1·75
	a. Booklet pane. No. 3927×10	15·00	
3928	$1.20 As No. 3922	2·75	2·75
	a. Booklet pane. No. 3928×10	23·00	
3923/8 *Set of* 6		10·50	10·50

Nos. 3917/21 were printed together, *se-tenant*, as horizontal strips of five stamps in sheets of 50 (2 panes of 25).

Nos. 3923 and 3926/7 were issued in separate $6 booklets (Nos. SB426, SB428/9). Nos. 3924/5 were issued in $6 booklets, No. SB427.

No. 3928 was issued in $12 booklets, No. SB430, and also in $24.95 premium booklets, No. SP194. Booklet panes Nos. 3923a/8a each contain five small circular labels.

900 Women and Surfboards

(Des Andrew Hoyne Design. Litho Pemara (self-adhesive rolls) or McKellar Renown (others))

2013 (12 Feb). 50th Anniv of Surfing Australia. T **900** and similar horiz designs. Multicoloured.

(a) Ordinary paper. P 14×14½

3929	60c. Type **900**	1·50	1·50
	a. Block of 4. Nos. 3929/32	5·50	5·50
3930	60c. Poster of surfer and shore	1·50	1·50
3931	60c. Van carrying surfboards parked on beach	1·50	1·50
3932	60c. Surfer on crest of wave	1·50	1·50
3929/32 *Set of 4*		5·50	5·50
MS3933 130×80 mm. Nos. 3929/32		5·50	5·50

(b) Self-adhesive. Phosphor frame. Die-cut perf 11×11½ (interrupted on vert sides)

3934	60c. As Type **900**	1·50	1·50
	a. Horiz strip of Nos. 3934/7	5·50	5·50
	b. Booklet pane. Nos. 3934×3, 3935/6, each×2 and 3937×3	15·00	
3935	60c. As No. 3930	1·50	1·50
3936	60c. As No. 3931	1·50	1·50
3937	60c. As No. 3932	1·50	1·50
3934/7 *Set of 4*		5·50	5·50

Nos. 3929/32 were printed together, *se-tenant*, as blocks of four stamps in sheets of 50 (2 panes of 25), giving eight blocks of four and 18 single stamps per sheet.

Nos. 3929/32 were also issued in $12.95 premium booklets, No. SP195.

Nos. 3934/7 were issued in rolls of 100 printed by Pemara containing the four designs in sequence, and also in $6 booklets, No. SB431.

901 Miniature Schnauzer

(Des Susan Elliott. Litho McKellar Renown)

2013 (19 Feb). Top Dogs. T **901** and similar vert designs. Multicoloured.

(a) Ordinary paper. P 14½×14

3938	60c. Type **901**	2·25	2·25
	a. Horiz strip of 5. Nos. 3938/42	10·00	10·00
3939	60c. Miniature Dachshund	2·25	2·25
3940	60c. Cavalier King Charles Spaniel	2·25	2·25
3941	60c. Pug	2·25	2·25
3942	60c. Australian Terrier	2·25	2·25
3938/42 *Set of 5*		10·00	10·00

(b) Self-adhesive. Phosphor frame. Die-cut perf 11½×11 (interrupted on horiz sides)

3943	60c. As Type **901**	2·00	2·25
	a. Booklet pane. No. 3943×10	17·00	
3944	60c. As No. 3939	2·00	2·25
	a. Booklet pane. No. 3944×10	17·00	
3945	60c. As No. 3940	2·00	2·25
	a. Booklet pane. No. 3945×10	17·00	
3946	60c. As No. 3941	2·00	2·25
	a. Booklet pane. No. 3946×10	17·00	
3947	60c. As No. 3942	2·00	2·25
	a. Booklet pane. No. 3947×10	17·00	
3943/7 *Set of 5*		9·00	10·00

Nos. 3938/42 were printed together, *se-tenant*, as horizontal strips of five stamps in sheets of 50 (2 panes of 25).

Nos. 3943/7 were issued in separate $6 booklets, Nos. SB432/6. Booklet panes 3943a/7a each have five small circular pawprint labels.

902 National Portrait Gallery, Canberra

(Des Mary Callahan. Litho Pemara (coil stamps) or McKellar Renown (others))

2013 (5 Mar). Centenary of Canberra. T **902** and similar horiz design. Multicoloured.

(a) Ordinary gum

(i) Domestic mail. P 14×14½

3948	60c. Type **902**	1·50	1·00

(ii) International Post. P 14×14½

3949	$2.35 Parliament House, Canberra	5·50	5·50

(b) Self-adhesive. Irregular phosphor frame. Die-cut perf 11×11½ (interrupted on vert sides)

3950	60c. As Type **902**	1·50	1·25
	a. Booklet pane. No. 3950×20	25·00	

Nos. 3948/9 were also issued in $12.95 premium booklets, No. SP196.

No. 3950 was issued in rolls of 200 and also in $12 booklets, No. SB437.

903 *Dandenong Ranges from 'Beleura'* (detail) (Eugene von Guérard), 1870

(Des Lynette Traynor. Litho McKellar Renown)

2013 (19 Mar). The Gallery Series. (2nd series) National Gallery of Australia. Landscape Paintings. T **903** and similar vert designs. Multicoloured.

(a) Ordinary gum. P 14½×14

3951	60c. Type **903**	1·50	1·50
	a. Horiz strip of 5. Nos. 3951/5	6·75	6·75
3952	60c. *In the Flinders – Far North* (detail) (Hans Heysen), 1951	1·50	1·50
3953	60c. *Land of the Golden Fleece* (detail) (Arthur Streeton), 1926	1·50	1·50
3954	60c. *Mr. Robinson's house on the Derwent, Van Diemen's Land* (detail) (John Glover) *c.* 1838	1·50	1·50
3955	60c. *Studley Park at sunrise* (detail) (Nicholas Chevalier), 1861	1·50	1·50
3951/55 *Set of 5*		6·75	6·75

(b) Self-adhesive. Phosphor bands at top and foot of stamps. Die-cut perf 11½×11 (interrupted on horiz sides)

3956	60c. As Type **903**	1·50	1·50
	a. Booklet pane. Nos. 3956/60, each×2	12·00	
3957	60c. As No. 3952	1·50	1·50
3958	60c. As No. 3953	1·50	1·50
3959	60c. As No. 3954	1·50	1·50
3960	60c. As No. 3955	1·50	1·50

Nos. 3951/5 were printed together, *se-tenant*, as horizontal strips of five stamps in sheets of 50 (2 panes 5×5).

Nos. 3956/60 were issued in $6 booklets, No. SB438.

(Des Simone Sakinofsky. Litho McKellar Renown)

2013 (2 Apr). International Post. Bush Babies (2nd issue). Vert designs as T **857**. Multicoloured.

(a) Ordinary paper. P 14½×14

3961	$1.70 Kookaburra	4·00	1·50
3962	$1.75 Wombat Joey	4·00	1·50
3963	$2.60 Echidna	6·00	5·00
3964	$4.65 Platypus	11·00	11·00
3965	$6.45 Brush-tailed Possum	14·00	16·00
3961/5 *Set of 5*		35·00	32·00

(b) Self-adhesive. Irregular partial phosphor frame (broken at right). Die-cut perf 11½×11 (interrupted on horiz sides)

3966	$1.70 As No. 3961	4·00	2·25
3967	$1.75 As No. 3962	4·00	2·25
3968	$2.60 As No. 3963	6·00	6·00
3966/8 *Set of 3*		12·50	9·50

Nos. 3966/8 were printed in separate panes of five stamps sold for $8.50, $8.75 or $13.

905 Gold State Coach

(Des Jo Muré. Litho McKellar Renown)

2013 (9 Apr). 60th Anniv of the Coronation. T **905** and similar multicoloured design.

(a) Ordinary gum

(i) Domestic mail. P 14½×14

3969	60c. Type **905**	2·00	1·00
	(ii) International Post. P 14½×14.		
3970	$2.60 Portrait photograph by Cecil Beaton (*26×37 mm*)	7·50	7·50
MS3971	125×80 mm. Nos. 3969/70	9·50	9·00

(b) Self-adhesive. International Post. Phosphor over parts of design. Die-cut perf 11½×11 (interrupted on horiz sides)

3972	$2.60 As No. 3970	7·50	8·00

No. 3972 was issued in $13 panes of five stamps.

906 Wall and Borders at Royal Tasmanian Botanical Gardens, Hobart

(Des Jennifer Scalzo. Litho EGO Print (3973/7) or Pemara (3978/82))

2013 (23 Apr). Australian Botanic Gardens (2nd issue). T **906** and similar horiz designs. Multicoloured.

(a) Ordinary gum. P 14×14½

3973	60c. Type **906**	2·00	2·00
	a. Horiz strip of 5. Nos. 3973/7	9·00	9·00
3974	60c. Australian National Botanic Gardens, Canberra	2·00	2·00
3975	60c. Blue Mountains Botanic Garden, Mount Tomah, New South Wales	2·00	2·00
3976	60c. George Brown Darwin Botanic Gardens	2·00	2·00
3977	60c. Royal Botanic Gardens, Cranbourne, Victoria	2·00	2·00
3973/77	*Set of 4*	9·00	9·00

(b) Self-adhesive. L-shaped phosphor bands. Die-cut perf 11×11½ (interrupted on vert sides)

3978	60c. As Type **906**	1·75	2·00
	a. Horiz strip of 5. Nos. 3978/82	8·00	9·00
3979	60c. As No. 3974	1·75	2·00
3980	60c. As No. 3975	1·75	2·00
3981	60c. As No. 3976	1·75	2·00
3982	60c. As No. 3977	1·75	2·00

Nos. 3973/7 were printed together, *se-tenant*, as horizontal strips of five stamps in sheets of 50 (2 panes 5×5).

Nos. 3973/7 were also issued in $12.95 premium booklets, No. SP197.

Nos. 3978/82 were issued in rolls of 200 containing the five designs in sequence.

907 Kangaroo and Map of Australia

(Des John White. Litho McKellar Renown)

2013 (10 May). Centenary of First Australian Commonwealth Stamp. P 14½×14.

3983	**907**	$10 scarlet-vermilion	17·00	20·00
MS3984		140×90 mm. No. 3983	17·00	20·00

No. 3983 was issued in sheetlets of 10 (5×2) with a decorative border. A version of this sheetlet was available in which six of the stamps were perforated or overprinted "OS" or overprinted "Specimen". This sold in a pack for $40.45 (*Price* £130).

No. 3983 is based on Type **1**, the design used for the 1913 1d. Australia stamp.

From 10-15 May 2013 personalised stamps with 60c. face value or inscribed "Postage Pre-paid Australia", comprising a bright yellow-green and greenish blue frame and a photograph or image within a "perforated" frame were available at World Stamp Expo 2013 in Melbourne. These stamps were offered in gummed sheetlets of nine (selling price $15) or self-adhesive booklets of 20 (selling price $20). Due to their premium price they are outside the scope of this catalogue.

908 Statue of Australian Light Horseman by Peter Corlett, Beersheva, Israel

(Des Simone Sakinofsky. Litho RA Print)

2013 (10 May). Battle of Beersheba, 1917, T **908** and similar horiz design. Multicoloured. P 13.

(i) Domestic mail

3985	60c. Type **908**	2·00	1·25
	(ii) International Post		
3986	$2.60 Australian Light Horsemen and re-enactment of Battle of Beersheba	7·00	6·50

Similar stamps were issued by Israel.

909 Black Caviar (racehorse)

(Des David Cain, ESP. Litho McKellar Renown)

2013 (10 May). Black Caviar (racehorse).

(a) Ordinary gum. P 14½×14

3987	**909**	60c. multicoloured	2·00	1·00

(b) Self-adhesive. Phosphor over parts of design. Die-cut perf 11½×11 (interrupted on horiz sides)

3988	**909**	60c. multicoloured	2·00	1·75
		a. Booklet pane. No. 3988×10	17·00	

No. 3987 has the design extending to the edge of the stamp. A second version with white borders and in a different shade was available only in sheetlets of ten within 'Expo 2013' packs, sold at a premium above face value.

No. 3988 was issued in $6 booklets, No. SB439.

910 Hon. Judith Denman (Governor-General's daughter) holding First Banknote at Official Numbering Ceremony, Government Printing Works, Melbourne, 1 May 1913

(Des Boschen Design. Litho EGO)

2013 (11 May). Centenary of First Australian Commonwealth Banknote. T **910** and similar vert design. Multicoloured. P 14×13½.

(i) Domestic mail

3989	60c. Type **910**	1·50	1·00

(ii) International Post

3990	$2.60 Australian coat of arms from first banknote (10 shilling with serial number M000001)	6·00	6·50
MS3991	170×80 mm. Nos. 3989/90	7·50	7·50

911 Forty-spotted Pardalote (*Pardalotus quadragintus*)

(Des Christopher Pope. Litho McKellar Renown)

2013 (11 May). Pardalotes. T **911** and similar horiz designs. Multicoloured.

(a) Ordinary gum. P 14×14½

3992	60c. Type **911**	2·50	1·25
3993	$1.20 Spotted Pardalote (*Pardalotus punctatus*)	3·25	2·25
3994	$1.80 Red-browed Pardalote (*Pardalotus rubricatus*)	3·50	3·00
3995	$3 Striated Pardalote (*Pardalotus striatus*)	5·50	7·00
3992/5	*Set of 4*	13·50	12·00

(b) Self-adhesive. Irregular phosphor frame. Die-cut perf 11×11½ (interrupted on vert sides)

3996	60c. As Type **911**	2·50	1·75
3997	$1.20 As No. 3993	3·25	3·25
	a. Pane. No. 3997×5	13·00	

Nos. 3992/5 were also issued in $24.95 premium booklets, No. SP441.

No. 3996 was issued in rolls of 100.

No. 3997 was issued in $6 panes of five stamps.

912 Government House, South Australia

(Des Sonia Young. Litho McKellar Renown)

2013 (11 June). Historical Architecture. Government Houses. T **912** and similar horiz designs. Multicoloured.

(a) Ordinary gum. P 14×14½

3998	60c. Type **912**	1·25	1·25
	a. Block of 4. Nos. 3998/4001	4·50	4·50
3999	60c. Government House, West Australia	1·25	1·25
4000	60c. Government House, New South Wales	1·25	1·25
4001	60c. Government House, Tasmania	1·25	1·25
3998/4001	*Set of 4*	4·50	4·50

(b) Self-adhesive. Partial phosphor frame (at left, right and foot). Die-cut perf 11×11½ (interrupted on vert sides)

4002	60c. As Type **912**	1·25	1·25
	a. Horiz strip of 4. Nos. 4002/5	4·50	4·50
	b. Booklet pane. Nos. 4002/5, each×5	20·00	
4003	60c. As No. 3999	1·25	1·25
4004	60c. As No. 4000	1·25	1·25
4005	60c. As No. 4001	1·25	1·25
4002/5	*Set of 4*	4·50	4·50

Nos. 3998/4001 were printed together, *se-tenant*, as blocks of four stamps in sheets of 50 (2 panes 5×5), each sheet providing 18 blocks of four and eight single stamps.

Nos. 4002/5 were issued in rolls of 100 containing the four designs in sequence, and also in $12 booklets, No. SB440.

(Des Gavin Ryan. Litho McKellar Renown)

2013 (2 July). Road Trip Australia (2nd series). Square designs as T **888**. Multicoloured.

(a) Ordinary gum. P 14

4006	60c. Car laden with canoe, tram and pier, Melbourne	1·25	1·25
4007	60c. Jeep, Sydney Harbour Bridge and Opera House	1·25	1·25
4008	60c. Car towing caravan and carnival, Adelaide	1·25	1·25
4009	60c. Car and caravan at Canberra	1·25	1·25
4010	60c. Car on fairground ride, Gold Coast	1·25	1·25
4006/10	*Set of 5*	5·50	5·50
MS4011	170×80 mm. Nos. 4006/10	5·50	5·50

(b) Self-adhesive. Phosphor over parts of design. Die-cut perf 11½ (interrupted on horiz sides)

4012	60c. As No. 4006	1·25	1·25
	a. Booklet pane. No. 4012/13, each×5	10·00	
4013	60c. As No. 4007	1·25	1·25
4014	60c. As No. 4008	1·25	1·25
	a. Booklet pane. Nos. 4014×7, 4015×6 and 4016×7	18·00	
4015	60c. As No. 4009	1·25	1·25
4016	60c. As No. 4010	1·25	1·25
4012/6	*Set of 5*	5·50	5·50

Nos. 4012/13 were issued in $6 booklets, No. SB441, and Nos. 4014/16 were issued in $12 booklets, No. SB442.

913 Shirley Smith (1921–98)

(Des Lynette Traynor. Litho Pemara (4022/6) or McKellar Renown (others))

2013 (9 July). Indigenous Leaders. T **913** and similar vert designs. Multicoloured.

(a) Ordinary gum. P 14½×14

4017	60c. Type **913**	1·50	1·50
	a. Horiz strip of 5. Nos. 4017/21	6·75	6·75
4018	60c. Neville Bonner (1922–99)	1·50	1·50
4019	60c. Oodgeroo Noonuccal (1920–93)	1·50	1·50
4020	60c. Eddie 'Koiki' Mabo (1936–92)	1·50	1·50
4021	60c. Charles Perkins (1936–2000)	1·50	1·50
4017/21	*Set of 5*	6·75	6·75

(b) Self-adhesive. Phosphor over parts of design. Die-cut perf 11½×11 (interrupted on horiz sides)

4022	60c. As No. 4021	1·50	1·50
	a. Horiz strip of 5. Nos. 4022/6	6·75	6·75
4023	60c. As No. 4020	1·50	1·50
4024	60c. As No. 4019	1·50	1·50
4025	60c. As No. 4018	1·50	1·50
4026	60c. As Type **913**	1·50	1·50
4022/6	*Set of 5*	6·75	6·75

Nos. 4017/21 were printed together, *se-tenant*, as horizontal strips of five stamps in sheets of 50 (2 panes 5×5).

Nos. 4017/21 were also issued in premium booklets, No. SP202.

Nos. 4022/6 were issued in rolls of 200 containing the five designs in sequence.

914 Duke and Duchess of Cambridge with Prince George

(Des Sonia Young. Litho EGO)

2013 (29 July). Birth of Prince George of Cambridge.

(a) Ordinary gum. P 14

4027	60c. Type **914**	1·75	1·00

(b) Self-adhesive. Phosphor frame. Die-cut perf 11½ (interrupted on horiz sides)

4028	60c. As Type **914**	2·00	1·75
	a. Booklet pane. No. 4028×10	17·00	

No. 4027 was issued in sheetlets of ten stamps.

No. 4028 was issued in $6 booklets, No. SB443.

915 "PEACE - WWII OVER!"

(Des Stacey Zass, page 12. Litho McKellar Renown)

2013 (23 July). Headline News. T **915** and similar vert designs. Multicoloured.

(a) Ordinary gum. P 14½×14

4029	60c. Type **915**	1·75	1·75
	a. Block of 4. Nos. 4029/32	6·25	6·25
4030	60c. "A SMALL STEP - A GIANT LEAP"	1·75	1·75
4031	60c. "Tracy Destroys Darwin"	1·75	1·75
4032	60c. "SAILING INTO HISTORY"	1·75	1·75
4029/32	*Set of 4*	6·25	6·25
MS4033	135×72 mm. Nos. 4029/32	6·25	6·25

(b) Self-adhesive. Partial phosphor frame (at left, right and foot). Die-cut perf 11½×11 (interrupted on horiz sides)

4034	60c. As Type **915**	1·75	1·75
	a. Vert strip of 4. Nos. 4034/7	6·25	6·25
	b. Booklet pane. Nos. 4034/7, each×5	22·00	
4035	60c. As No. 4030	1·75	1·75
4036	60c. As No. 4031	1·75	1·75
4037	60c. As No. 4032	1·75	1·75
4034/7	*Set of 4*	6·25	6·25

Nos. 4029/32 were printed together, *se-tenant*, as blocks of four stamps in sheets of 50 (2 panes 5×5), each sheet providing eight blocks of four and eighteen single stamps.

Nos. 4034/7 were issued in rolls of 100 with the four designs in sequence, and also in $12 booklets, No. SB443.

(Recess and litho)

2013 (2 Aug). Thailand 2013 World Stamp Exhibition, Bangkok. As No. **MS**3971 additionally inscr with emblem and "Thailand 2013 World Stamp The Magnificent Heritage" in silver on the upper sheet margin. P 14½×14.

MS4038	125×80 mm. As Nos. 3969/70	7·50	7·50

The Coronation Coach on the 60c. stamp within **MS**4038 was printed in recess and varnished.

916 *Cephalotus follicularis* and Ants

(Des Jo Muré. Litho RA Print (4039/42) or McKellar Renown (4043/6))

2013 (13 Aug). Carnivorous Plants. T **916** and similar vert designs. Multicoloured.

(a) Ordinary gum. P 14½×14

4039	60c. Type **916**	1·25	1·25
	a. Block of 4. Nos. 4039/42	4·50	4·50
4040	60c. *Drosera rupicola*	1·25	1·25
4041	60c. *Drosera lowriei*	1·25	1·25
4042	60c. *Nepenthes rowanae*	1·25	1·25
4039/42	*Set of 4*	4·50	4·50

(b) Self-adhesive. Partial phosphor frame. Die-cut perf 11½×11 (interrupted on horiz sides)

4043	60c. As Type **916**	1·25	1·25
	a. Booklet pane. Nos. 4043×3, 4044×2, 4045×3 and 4046×2	10·00	
4044	60c. As No. 4040	1·25	1·25
4045	60c. As No. 4041	1·25	1·25
4046	60c. As No. 4042	1·25	1·25
4043/6	*Set of 4*	4·50	4·50

Nos. 4039/42 were printed together, *se-tenant*, as blocks of four stamps in sheets of 50 (2 panes of 25), each sheet providing eight blocks of four and 18 single stamps.

Nos. 4043/6 were issued in $6 booklets, No. SB445.

917 Turtle and Coral, Ningaloo Reef

(Des Sharon Rodziewicz. Litho McKellar Renown)

2013 (20 Aug). Coral Reefs. T **917** and similar horiz designs. Multicoloured.

(a) Ordinary gum. P 13½×14

4047	60c. Type **917**	1·00	1·00
	a. Horiz pair. Nos. 4047/8	2·00	2·00
4048	60c. Fish and corals, Great Barrier Reef	1·00	1·00
4049	$1.20 Aerial view of Ningaloo Reef, West Australia	1·75	1·75
	a. Horiz pair. Nos. 4049/50	3·50	3·50
4050	$1.20 Aerial view of Great Barrier Reef, Queensland	1·75	1·75
4047/50	*Set of 4*	5·00	5·00
MS4051	170×80 mm. Nos. 4047/50	5·00	5·00

(b) Self-adhesive. Phosphor band at foot of stamp. Die-cut perf 10½×11 (interrupted on vert sides)

4052	60c. As No. 4048	1·00	1·00
	a. Booklet pane. Nos. 4052/3, each×10	15·00	
4053	60c. As Type **917**	1·00	1·00
4054	$1.20 As No. 4050	1·75	2·00
	a. Pane. Nos. 4054×3 and 4055×2	8·00	
4055	$1.20 As No. 4049	1·75	2·00
4052/5	*Set of 4*	5·00	5·00

Nos. 4047/8 and 4049/50 were each printed together, *se-tenant*, as horizontal pairs in sheets of 40, each sheet giving 16 horizontal pairs and eight single stamps (Type **917** or No. 4049).

Nos. 4052/3 were issued in $12 booklets, No. SB446.

Nos. 4054/5 were issued in $6 panes of five stamps.

918 Australian Game

(Des Kevin Stead (illustration) and Lisa Christensen. Litho EGO)

2013 (3 Sept). Australian Poultry Breeds. T **918** and similar multicoloured designs.

(a) Ordinary gum. P 14×14½ (horiz) or 14×13½ (others)

4056	60c. Type **918**	85	85
4057	60c. Australian Pit Game	85	85
4058	60c. Australorp (37×26 *mm*)	85	85
4056/58	*Set of 3*	2·25	2·25
MS4059	160×80 mm. Nos. 4056/8	2·25	2·25

(b) Self-adhesive. Partial irregular phosphor frame. Die-cut perf 11×11½ (interrupted on vert sides)

4060	60c. As No. 4058	85	85
	a. Booklet pane. No. 4060×10	7·00	

Nos. 4056/8 were also issued in $12.95 premium booklets, SP203.

No. 4060 was issued in $6 booklets, No. SB447.

919 Koolasuchus

(Des James Gurney (illustration) and Sonia Young. Litho McKellar Renown)

2013 (24 Sept). Australia's Age of Dinosaurs. T **919** and similar multicoloured designs.

*(a) Ordinary gum. P 14×14½ (4063/4), 14½ (**MS**4067) or 14½×14 (others)*

4061	60c. Type **919**	1·00	1·00
4062	60c. Serendipaceratops (26×38 *mm*)	1·00	1·00
4063	60c. Timimus (30×50 *mm*)	1·00	1·00
4064	60c. Diamantinasaurus (*horiz*)	1·00	1·00
4065	60c. Qantassaurus (50×30 *mm*)	1·00	1·00
4066	60c. Australovenator (26×38 *mm*)	1·00	1·00
4061/66	*Set of 6*	5·50	5·50
MS4067	166×74 mm. Nos. 4061/6	5·50	5·50

(b) Self-adhesive. Partial irregular phosphor frames. Die-cut perf 11 (4068/9) or 11½×11 (interrupted on horiz sides) (others)

4068	60c. As No. 4064	1·25	1·50
	a. Booklet pane. Nos. 4068/9, each×5	11·00	
4069	60c. As Type **919**	1·25	1·50

4070	60c. As No. 4066	1·00	1·25
	a. Booklet pane. Nos. 4070/1, each×10	15·00	
4071	60c. As No. 4062	1·00	1·25
4068/7	*Set of 4*	4·00	5·00

Nos. 4061/6 were also issued in $12.95 premium booklets, No. SP204.

Nos. 4068/9 were issued in $6 booklets, No. SB448, and Nos. 4070/1 in $12 booklets, No. SB449.

920 Maryborough Railway Station, Victoria

(Des Peter Edgeley (illustration) and John White. Litho McKellar Renown)

2013 (8 Oct). Historic Railway Stations. T **920** and similar horiz designs. Multicoloured.

(a) Ordinary gum. P 14×14½

4072	60c. Type **920**	1·25	1·25
	a. Block of 4. Nos. 4072/5	4·50	4·50
4073	60c. Quorn Railway Station, South Australia	1·25	1·25
4074	60c. Hay Railway Station, New South Wales	1·25	1·25
4075	60c. Normanton Railway Station, Queensland	1·25	1·25
4072/75	*Set of 4*	4·50	4·50

(b) Self-adhesive. Phosphor over parts of design. Die-cut perf 11×11½ (interrupted on vert sides)

4076	60c. As Type **920**	1·50	1·50
	a. Horiz strip of 4. Nos. 4076/9	5·50	5·50
	b. Booklet pane. Nos. 4076/7, each×3, and Nos. 4078/9, each×2	13·00	
4077	60c. As No. 4073	1·50	1·50
4078	60c. As No. 4074	1·50	1·50
4079	60c. As No. 4075	1·50	1·50
4076/9	*Set of 4*	5·50	5·50

Nos. 4072/5 were printed together, *se-tenant*, as blocks of four stamps in sheets of 50 (2 panes 5×5), each sheet providing eight blocks of four and 18 single stamps. On the top pane the top left stamp is Type **920** but on the lower pane it is No. 4074.

Nos. 4076/9 were issued in rolls of 100 with the four designs in sequence, and also in $6 booklets, No. SB450.

921 Ludwig Leichhardt

(Des Melinda Coombes. Litho EGO)

2013 (15 Oct). Birth Bicentenary of Ludwig Leichhardt (German naturalist and explorer, 1813–48). P 14.

4080 **921**	60c. multicoloured	1·00	1·00

Stamps in similar designs were issued by Germany.

(Litho)

2013 (18 Oct). Melbourne International Coin and Banknote Show. Sheet 125×80 mm.

MS4081	As No. 3983 but imperf	19·00	21·00

922 Holey Dollar and Dump

(Des Phil Ellett. Recess and litho (**MS**4084) or litho (others) EGO)

2013 (22 Oct). Bicentenary of Holey Dollar and Dump (first Australian coins, minted New South Wales 1813). T **922** and similar horiz design. Multicoloured. P 14×14½.

4082	60c. Type **922**	1·00	75
4083	$3 Holey dollars	4·50	5·00
MS4084	106×70 mm. As Nos. 4082/3 but silver foil coins	5·50	6·00

Holey Dollars were Spanish real coins with the centres stamped out, value 5 shillings. Dumps were the centres valued at 15 pence.

923 Virgin Mary and Baby Jesus

(Des Paul Newton. Litho McKellar Renown)

2013 (1 Nov). Christmas (1st issue). T **923** and similar vert designs. Multicoloured.

(a) Ordinary gum

(i) Domestic mail. P 14½×14

4085	55c. Type **923**	1·00	40

(ii) International Post. P 14½×14

4086	$2.55 Shepherds and star	3·50	3·50
MS4087	130×80 mm. Nos. 4085/6	4·50	4·50

(b) Self-adhesive

(i) Domestic mail. Phosphor over parts of design. Die-cut perf 11½×11 (interrupted on horiz sides)

4088	55c. As Type **923**	80	50
	a. Booklet pane. No. 4088×20	13·00	

(ii) International Post. Phosphor over parts of design. Die-cut perf 11½×11 (interrupted on horiz sides)

4089	$2.55 As No. 4086	3·50	3·50
	a. Pane. No. 4089×5	14·00	

924 Christmas Tree

(Des Lisa Christensen. Litho EGO)

2013 (1 Nov). Christmas (2nd issue). T **924** and similar vert designs. Multicoloured.

(a) Ordinary gum. Domestic mail. P 14½×14

4090	55c. Type **924**	80	80
	a. Horiz pair. Nos. 4090/1	1·60	1·60
4091	55c. Wrapped gift	80	80
4092	60c. Candle	80	80

(ii) International Post. P 14½×14

4093	$1.70 Bell	2·25	1·75
4090/93	*Set of 4*	4·25	3·50

(b) Self-adhesive

(i) Domestic mail. Phosphor frame. Die-cut perf 11½×11 (interrupted on horiz sides)

4094	55c. As Type **924**	80	80
	a. Booklet pane. Nos. 4094/5, each×10	13·00	
4095	55c. As No. 4091	80	80
4096	55c. As Type **924** but design in green and gold foil and inscriptions in gold foil	80	80
4097	55c. As No. 4091 but design in gold and red foil and inscriptions in red foil	80	80
4094/8	*Set of 5*	5·00	4·75

(ii) International Post. Phosphor frame (interrupted at top left). Die-cut perf 11½×11 (interrupted on horiz sides)

4098	$1.70 As No. 4093	2·25	2·00
	a. Pane. No. 4098×5	10·00	

Nos. 4090/1 were printed together, *se-tenant*, as horizontal pairs in sheets of 50 (2 panes 5×5), each sheet giving 40 horizontal pairs and ten single stamps (Type **924**).

Nos. 4094/5 were issued in $11 booklets, No. SB452. Nos. 4096/7 were printed in separate self-adhesive sheetlets of ten stamps.

No. 4098 was issued in $8.50 panes of five stamps.

925 Duke and Duchess of Cambridge and Prince George

(Des Jo Muré. Litho McKellar)

2014 (7 Jan). Royal Christening. T **925** and similar vert design. Multicoloured.

(a) Ordinary gum

(i) Domestic mail. P 14½×14

4099	60c. Type **925**	1·50	75

(ii) International Post. P 14½×14

4100	$2.60 As Type **925** but with stone background	4·00	4·25
MS4101	106×70 mm. Nos. 4099/4100	5·50	5·00

(b) Self-adhesive

(i) Domestic mail. Phosphor frame. Die-cut perf 11½×11 (interrupted on horiz sides)

4102	60c. Type **925**	1·25	1·25
	a. Booklet pane. No. 4102×10	11·00	

(ii) International Post. Phosphor frame (broken at upper left). Die-cut perf 11½×11 (interrupted on horiz sides)

4103	$2.60 As Type **925** but with stone background	4·00	4·50
	a. Pane. No. 4103×5	16·00	

No. 4102 was issued in $6 booklets, No. SB453.
No. 4103 was issued in $13 panes of five stamps.

926 Golden Rock Orchid

(Des Sonia Young. Litho EGO)

2014 (14 Jan). Native Orchids. T **926** and similar vert designs. Multicoloured.

(a) Ordinary gum. P 14½×14

4104	60c. Type **926**	1·10	1·10
	a. Horiz strip of 4. Nos. 4104/7	4·00	4·00
4105	60c. Bee Orchid	1·10	1·10
4106	60c. Orange Blossom Orchid	1·10	1·10
4107	60c. Shirt Orchid	1·10	1·10
4104/7	*Set of 4*	4·00	4·00

(b) Self-adhesive. Irregular phosphor at top and foot of stamps. Die-cut perf 11½×11 (interrupted on horiz sides)

4108	60c. As Type **926**	1·10	1·10
	a. Booklet pane. Nos. 4108×2, 4109×3, 4110×2 and 4111×3	9·00	
	b. Booklet pane. Nos. 4108/11, each×5	16·00	
4109	60c. As No. 4105	1·10	1·10
4110	60c. As No. 4106	1·10	1·10
4111	60c. As No. 4107	1·10	1·10
4108/11	*Set of 4*	4·00	4·00

Nos. 4104/7 were printed together, *se-tenant*, as horizontal strips of four in sheets of 50, each sheet providing ten strips of four and ten single stamps (Type **926**).

Nos. 4108/11 were issued in $6 and $12 booklets, Nos. SB454/5.

927 Margaret Fulton

(Des Lynette Traynor. Litho McKellar Renown)

2014 (17 Jan). Australian Legends (18th series). Legends of Cooking. T **927** and similar vert designs. Multicoloured.

(a) Ordinary gum. P 14½×14

4112	60c. Type **927**	90	90
4113	60c. Maggie Beer	90	90
4114	60c. Stephanie Alexander	90	90
4115	60c. Neil Perry	90	90
4116	60c. Kylie Kwong	90	90
4112/6	*Set of 5*	4·00	4·00

(b) Self-adhesive. Phosphor frame. Die-cut perf 11½×11 (interrupted on horiz sides)

4117	60c. As Type **927**	90	90
	a. Booklet pane. No. 4117×10	7·50	
4118	60c. As No. 4113	90	90
	a. Booklet pane. No. 4118×10	7·50	
4119	60c. As No. 4114	90	90
	a. Booklet pane. No. 4119×10	7·50	
4120	60c. As No. 4115	90	90
	a. Booklet pane. No. 4120×10	7·50	
4121	60c. As No. 4116	90	90
	a. Booklet pane. No. 4121×10	7·50	
4117/21	*Set of 5*	4·00	4·00

Nos. 4112/16 were also issued in $14.95 premium booklets, No. SP205.

Nos. 4117/21 were issued in separate $6 booklets, Nos. SB456/60.

928 Emblem ("The Urn Returns")

(Des SE Products. Litho McKellar Renown)

2014 (20 Jan). The Urn Returns (Australia's Victory in 2013/14 Ashes Series). T **928** and similar horiz design. Multicoloured.

(a) Ordinary gum

(i) Domestic mail. P 14½×14

4122	60c. Type **928**	90	90

(ii) International Post. P 14½×14

4123	$2.60 Victorious Australian cricket team ('Australia's Ashes Victory')	3·50	3·50
MS4124	170×80 mm. Nos. 4122/3	4·50	4·50

(b) Self-adhesive. Irregular phosphor frame (interrupted at lower left). Die-cut perf 11½×11

4125	$2.60 As No. 4123	4·50	5·00
	a. Booklet pane. No. 4125×5	19·00	

No. 4125 was issued in $13 booklets, No. SB461.

929 Pattern of Hearts

(Des Andrew Hogg (4126, 4128) or Melinda Coombes (Coombes Whitechurch Design) (4127, 4129). Litho EGO)

2014 (4 Feb). Greetings Stamps. Romance. T **929** and similar vert design. Multicoloured.

(a) Ordinary gum. P 14½×14

4126	60c. Type **929**	90	90
	a. Pair. Nos. 4126/7	1·50	1·50
4127	60c. Pink rose	90	90

(b) Self-adhesive. Phosphor over parts of design (4128) or phosphor frame on three sides (at left, right and foot) (4129). Die-cut perf 11½×11 (interrupted on horiz sides)

4128	60c. As Type **929**	90	90
	a. Booklet pane. No. 4128×10	8·00	
4129	60c. As No. 4127	90	90
	a. Booklet pane. No. 4129×20	15·00	

Nos. 4126/7 were printed together, *se-tenant*, as horizontal and vertical pairs in sheetlets of ten stamps (5×2).

930 Tasmanian Blue Gum (Tasmania)

(Des Jo Muré. Litho Pemara (4137c/40c) or McKellar Renown (others))

2014 (24 Mar). Floral Emblems. T **930** and similar vert designs. Multicoloured.

(a) Ordinary gum. P 14½×14

4130	70c. Type **930**	1·00	1·00
	a. Horiz strip of 4. Nos. 4130/3	3·50	3·50
4131	70c. Waratah (New South Wales)	1·00	1·00
4132	70c. Golden Wattle (Australia)	1·00	1·00
4133	70c. Common Heath (Victoria)	1·00	1·00
4134	$1.40 Cooktown Orchid (Queensland)	2·00	2·00
4135	$2.10 Kangaroo Paw (Western Australia)	3·00	3·00
4136	$3.50 Sturt's Desert Pea (South Australia)	5·00	5·00
4130/36	*Set of 7*	13·50	13·50

(b) Self-adhesive. Phosphor frames (broken at left and foot). Die-cut perf 11

4137	70c. As Type **930**	1·00	1·00
	a. Booklet pane. Nos. 4137/8, each×3 and 4139/40, each×2	9·50	
	b. Booklet pane. Nos. 4137/40, each×5	18·00	
	c. Perf 12½	1·00	1·00
	ca. Horiz strip of 4. Nos. 4137c/40c	3·50	3·50
4138	70c. As No. 4131	1·00	1·00
	c. Perf 12½	1·00	1·00
4139	70c. As No. 4132	1·00	1·00
	c. Perf 12½	1·00	1·00
4140	70c. As No. 4133	1·00	1·00
	c. Perf 12½	1·00	1·00
4137/40	*Set of 4*	3·50	3·50

Nos. 4130/3 were printed together, *se-tenant*, as horizontal strips of four stamps in sheets of 50 (5×10), each sheet giving ten horizontal strips of four and ten single stamps (No. 4130). Nos. 4137/40 were issued in rolls of 100 or 200 printed by Pemara containing the four designs in sequence, or $7 or $14 booklets, Nos. SB464/5.

930a Map of Australia in Sand

(Des MDM Design (4140*d*) or John White (4140*e*). Litho RA Printing)

2014 (24 Mar). Concession Post Stamps. T **930a** and similar vert design. Multicoloured. Self-adhesive. Die-cut perf 11½×11 (interrupted on horiz sides).

4140*d*	(60c.) Type **930a**	3·25	1·00
	ab. Pane. Nos. 4140*a*×2 and 4140*b*×3	15·00	
4140*e*	(60c.) Kangaroo on beach at sunset	3·00	1·00

Nos. 4140*d/e* were sold at 60c. each, a discount of 10c. off the standard domestic postage rate, and were only available to Australians on low incomes eligible for a MyPost Concession Account. They were issued in panes of five stamps, each inscr 'Concession POST'.

931 Queen Elizabeth II on Diamond Jubilee Tour

(Des John White. Litho McKellar Renown)

2014 (8 Apr). Queen's Birthday. T **931** and similar vert design. Multicoloured.

(a) Ordinary gum

(i) Domestic mail. P 14½×14

4141	70c. Type **931**	1·00	1·00

(ii) International Post. P 14½×14

4142	$2.60 Queen Elizabeth II at Royal Ascot, 2013	3·50	3·50
MS4143	104×70 mm. Nos. 4141/2	4·50	4·50

(b) Self-adhesive. Phosphor over right-hand part of design. Die-cut perf 11½×11 (interrupted on horiz sides)

4144	$2.60 As No. 4142	3·75	4·00
	a. Pane. No. 4144×5	15·00	

No. 4144 was issued in $13 panes of five.

932 Balloons

(Des Stacey Zass, Lisa Christensen, Gary Domoney, Sean Pethick, Sonia Young or Melinda Coombes. Litho EGO)

2014 (15 Apr). Greetings Stamps. Special Occasions. T **932** and similar vert designs. Multicoloured.

(a) Ordinary gum. P 14½×14

4145	70c. Type **932**	1·00	1·00
4146	70c. Baby mobile	1·00	1·00
4147	70c. Fireworks	1·00	1·00
4148	70c. Map of Australia (blue and green background and blue value tablet)	1·00	1·00
	a. Horiz pair. Nos. 4148/9	2·00	2·00
4149	70c. Map of Australia (yellow, orange and magenta background and magenta value tablet)	1·00	1·00
4150	70c. Red rose	1·00	1·00
4151	70c. Heart-shaped flowers	1·00	1·00
4152	70c. Champage glasses	1·00	1·00
4153	70c. Silver wedding rings and white roses	1·00	1·00
4154	$1.40 Gold wedding rings and filigree pattern	2·00	2·00
4145/54	*Set of 10*	8·50	8·50

(b) Self-adhesive. Phosphor over parts of design. Die-cut perf 11½×11

4155	70c. As Type **932**	1·00	1·00
	a. Booklet pane. No. 4155×10	9·50	
4156	70c. As No. 4146	1·00	1·00
	a. Booklet pane. No. 4156×10	9·50	
4157	70c. As No. 4147	1·00	1·00
	a. Booklet pane. No. 4157×10	9·50	
4158	70c. As No. 4150	1·00	1·00
	a. Booklet pane. No. 4158×10	9·50	
4159	70c. As No. 4151	1·00	1·00
	a. Booklet pane. No. 4159×10	9·50	
4160	70c. As No. 4152	1·00	1·00
	a. Booklet pane. No. 4160×10	9·50	
4161	70c. As No. 4153	1·00	1·00
	a. Booklet pane. No. 4161×10	9·50	
4155/61	*Set of 7*	6·25	6·25

Nos. 4148/9 were printed together, *se-tenant*, as horizontal pairs in sheets of 50 (2 panes 5×5), giving 20 horizontal pairs and ten single stamps (No. 4148).

Nos. 4155/61 were issued in separate $7 booklets, Nos. SB466/72. Self-adhesive stamps as No. 4154 were issued in $28.95 premium booklets, No. SP206.

933 Volunteers queuing to Enlist, Sydney ("War Declared!")

(Des Tim Hancock. Litho EGO)

2014 (22 Apr). Centenary of World War I (1st issue). 1914. T **933** and similar square designs. Multicoloured.

(a) Ordinary gum. P 14

4162	70c. Type **933**	1·50	1·50
4163	70c. Australian Military and Naval Expeditionary Force off Rabaul, German New Guinea ('Australians in Action')	1·50	1·50
4164	70c. Recruits ('Troops Depart')	1·50	1·50
4165	70c. Australian soldiers near the Pyramids, Egypt ('Training Mena Camp')	1·50	1·50
4166	70c. Studio portrait of three soldiers ('Our Boys')	1·50	1·50
4162/66	*Set of 5*	6·75	6·75
MS4167	170×79 mm. Nos. 4162/6	6·75	6·75

(b) Self-adhesive. Phosphor over parts of design. Die-cut perf 11½ (interrupted on horiz sides)

4168	70c. As Type **933**	1·40	1·40
	a. Booklet pane. Nos. 4168/72, each×2	12·50	
4169	70c. As No. 4163	1·40	1·40
4170	70c. As No. 4164	1·40	1·40
4171	70c. As No. 4165	1·40	1·40
4172	70c. As No. 4166	1·40	1·40
4168/72	*Set of 5*	6·25	6·25

Nos. 4168/72 were issued in $7 booklets, No. SB473.

See also Nos. 4350/**MS**4355 and 4559/69

934 Poster for Australian Red Cross

(Des Lisa Christensen. Litho McKellar Renown (4173) or Pemara (4174))

2014 (6 May). Centenary of the Australian Red Cross.

(a) Ordinary gum. P 14×14½

4173	**934**	70c. multicoloured	1·25	1·00

(b) Self-adhesive. Phosphor over parts of design. Die-cut perf 11×11½ (interrupted on vert sides)

4174	**934**	70c. multicoloured	1·50	1·25

No. 4174 was issued in rolls of 200.

935 Clancy of the Overflow

(Des Jamie and Leane Tufrey (illustrations) and John White (typography). Litho McKellar Renown)

2014 (13 May). Bush Ballads by A. B. 'Banjo' Paterson. T **935** and similar horiz designs. Multicoloured.

(a) Ordinary gum. P 14×14½

4175	70c. Type **935**	1·00	1·00
	a. Block of 4. Nos. 4175/8	3·50	3·50
4176	70c. The Man from Snowy River	1·00	1·00
4177	70c. Waltzing Matilda	1·00	1·00
4178	70c. Mulga Bill's Bicycle	1·00	1·00
4175/8	*Set of 4*	3·50	3·50
MS4179	170×80 mm. Nos. 4175/8	3·75	3·75

(b) Self-adhesive. Irregular partial phosphor frames. Die-cut perf 11×11½

4180	70c. As Type **935**	1·00	1·00
	a. Horiz strip of 4. Nos. 4180/3	3·50	
	b. Booklet pane. Nos. 4180×2, 4181/2, each×3 and 4183×2	9·50	
4181	70c. As No. 4176	1·00	1·00
4182	70c. As No. 4177	1·00	1·00
4183	70c. As No. 4178	1·00	1·00
4180/3	*Set of 4*	3·50	3·50

Nos. 4175/8 were printed together, *se-tenant*, as blocks of four stamps in sheets of 50 (2 panes 5×5), each sheet giving eight blocks of four and 18 single stamps. On the upper pane the top left stamp is No. 4175 but on the lower pane it is No. 4177.

Nos. 4175/**MS**4179 were also issued in $16.95 premium booklets, No. SP107.

Nos. 4180/3 were issued in rolls of 100 and also in $7 booklets, No. SB474.

936 Brisbane

(Des MacKillop College. Litho RA Print)

2014 (3 June). G20 Leaders Summit, Brisbane, Queensland. P 14½×14.

4184	**936**	70c. multicoloured	1·00	1·00

937 King George V

(Des John White. Litho (letterpress) EGO (McKellar))

2014 (17 June). Centenary of King George V Stamps. P 14½×14.

4185	**937**	70c. rosine	1·00	1·00
		a. Block of 4. Nos. 4185/8	3·50	3·50
4186		70c. deep claret	1·00	1·00
4187		70c. reddish violet	1·00	1·00
4188		70c. deep green	1·00	1·00
4185/88		*Set of 4*	3·50	3·50
MS4189		135×80 mm. Nos. 4185/8	3·75	3·75

Nos. 4185/8 were printed together, *se-tenant*, as blocks of four stamps in sheets of 50 (2 panes 5×5), each sheet giving eight blocks of four and 18 single stamps.

The design of Nos. 4185/8 is based on Types **3** and **5a**.

Nos. 4185/**MS**4189 were also issued in $16.95 premium booklets, No. SP208.

938 Maurice Guillaux taking off from Melbourne Agricultural Grounds, 16 July 1914

(Des Jo Muré. Litho McKellar Renown)

2014 (1 July). Centenary of First Air Mail. T **938** and similar square design. Multicoloured. P 14.

(i) Domestic mail

4190	70c. Type **938**	1·40	1·40

(ii) International Post

4191	$2.60 Maurice Guillaux and his Bleriot XI Monoplane on Flight from Melbourne to Sydney	6·00	6·00
MS4192	135×80 mm. Nos. 4190/1	7·50	7·50

Nos. 4190/1 were also issued in premium booklets, No. SP209, sold for $19.95.

939 Duke and Duchess of Cambridge

(Des Simone Sakhinofsky. Litho McKellar Renown)

2014 (8 July). Royal Visit. T **939** and similar square design. Multicoloured. (a) Ordinary gum. P 14.

(i) Domestic mail

4193	70c. Type **939**	1·75	1·40

(ii) International Post

4194	$2.60 Duke and Duchess of Cambridge and Prince George	6·50	6·50
MS4195	105×70 mm. Nos. 4193/4	8·00	8·00

(b) Self-adhesive. Die-cut perf 11½ (interrupted on horiz sides)

(i) Domestic mail. Phosphor frame (broken at lower right corner)

4196	70c. As Type **939**	1·40	1·40
	a. Booklet pane. No. 4196×10	12·50	

(iii) International Post. Phosphor frame (broken at upper and lower left). Die-cut perf 11½ (interrupted on horiz sides)

4197	$2.60 As No. 4194	6·50	7·00
	a. Pane. No. 4197×5	26·00	

No. 4196 was issued in $7 booklets, No. SB475.

No. 4197 was issued in $13 panes of five stamps.

940 Dressage

(Des Phil Ellett, Creative Ethos. Llitho Pemara (No. 4203a) or EGO (others))

2014 (15 July). Equestrian Events. T **940** and similar vert designs. Multicoloured.

(a) Ordinary gum. P 14½×14

4198	70c. Type **940**	1·75	1·75
4199	70c. Cross-country	1·75	1·75
4200	70c. Showjumping	1·75	1·75
4201	70c. Polocrosse	1·75	1·75
4202	70c. Pony Club	1·75	1·75
4198/202	*Set of 5*	8·00	8·00

(b) Self-adhesive. Phosphor at right and foot of designs. Die-cut perf 11½×11 (interrupted on horiz sides)

4203	70c. As No. 4202	1·60	1·75
	a. Vert strip of 5. Nos. 4203/7	7·25	8·00
	b. Booklet pane. No. 4203×10	12·50	
4204	70c. As No. 4201	1·60	1·75
	b. Booklet pane. No. 4204×10	12·50	
4205	70c. As No. 4200	1·60	1·75
	b. Booklet pane. No. 4205×10	12·50	
4206	70c. As No. 4199×10	1·60	1·75
	b. Booklet pane. No. 4206×10	12·50	
4207	70c. As Type **940**	1·60	1·75
	b. Booklet pane. No. 4207×10	12·50	
4203/7	*Set of 5*	7·25	7·25

Nos. 4203/7 were issued in rolls of 200 printed by Pemara containing the five designs in sequence, and also in separate $7 booklets, Nos. SB476/80

941 Norfolk Island Pines, Cottesloe Beach, West Australia

(Des Melinda Coombes, Coombes Whitechurch Design. Litho RA Print)

2014 (22 July). Norfolk Island Pine (*Araucaria heterophylla*). T **941** and similar horiz design. Multicoloured. P 14×14½.

4208	70c. Type **941**	1·40	1·40
4209	$1.40 Norfolk Island Pines, Old Military Barracks, Norfolk Island	3·25	3·25

Similar designs were issued on the same date by Norfolk Island.

942 Lt. Eric Harrison flying Bristol Military Biplane CFS-3, 1 March 1914

(Des Jamie and Leanne Tufrey. Litho Ego Print)

2014 (5 Aug). Centenary of Military Aviation and Submarines. T **942** and similar horiz design. Multicoloured.

(a) Ordinary gum. P 14×14½.

4210	70c. Type **942**	1·40	1·40
	a. Vert pair. Nos. 4210/11	2·75	2·75
4211	70c. E-class submarine HMAS *AE2*	1·40	1·40
MS4212	135×72 mm. Nos. 4210/11	2·75	2·75

(b) Self-adhesive. Phosphor over parts of design. Die-cut perf 11×11½

4213	70c. As Type **942**	1·40	1·40
	a. Booklet pane. Nos. 4213/14, each×10	25·00	
4214	70c. As No. 4211	1·40	1·40

Nos. 4210/11 were printed together, *se-tenant*, as vertical pairs in sheetlets of 50 (2 panes 5×5), each sheet giving 20 vertical pairs and ten single stamps. The top left stamp on the upper pane is Type **942**, but on the lower pane it is No. 4211.

Nos. 4213/14 were issued in $14 booklets, No. SB481.

943 Phillip Island Poster, 1930s

(Des Sonia Young. Litho McKellar Renown)

2014 (19 Aug). Nostalgic Advertisements. T **943** and similar vert designs. Multicoloured.

(a) Ordinary gum. P 14½×14.

4215	70c. Type **943**	1·40	1·40
	a. Horiz strip of 5. Nos. 4215/19	7·00	7·00
4216	70c. "Harper's "Empire" self-raising flour, 1920s/1930s	1·40	1·40
4217	70c. 'Fly TAA - the friendly way' (Trans-Australian Airways), *c.* 1954	1·40	1·40
4218	70c. Jacko Shoe Shine poster with kookaburra emblem by James Northfield, 1930s	1·40	1·40
4219	70c. Swallow & Ariell's teddy bear (label for biscuit tin)	1·40	1·40
4215/19	*Set of 5*	7·00	7·00
MS4220	170×80 mm. Nos. 4215/19	7·00	7·00

(b) Self-adhesive. Irregular partial phosphor frame (broken at top). Die-cut perf 11½×11 (interrupted on horiz sides)

4221	70c. As No. 4219	1·40	1·40
	a. Vert strip of 5. Nos. 4221/5	7·00	7·00
4222	70c. As No. 4218	1·40	1·40
4223	70c. As No. 4217	1·40	1·40
4224	70c. As No. 4216	1·40	1·40
4225	70c. As Type **943**	1·40	1·40
4221/5	*Set of 5*	7·00	7·00

Nos. 4215/19 were printed together, *se-tenant*, as horizontal strips of five stamps in sheets of 50 (2 panes 5×5).

Nos. 4221/5 were issued in rolls of 100 containing the five designs in sequence.

944 Southern Lights

(Des Lynda Warner. Llitho McKellar Renown)

2014 (26 Aug). Southern Lights. T **944** and similar horiz designs. Multicoloured.

(a) Ordinary gum. P 14×14½.

4226	70c. Type **944**	1·40	1·40
	a. Horiz pair. Nos. 4226/7	2·75	2·75
4227	70c. Southern lights (green, magenta and purple, iceberg in left foreground)	1·40	1·40
4228	$1.40 Southern lights (pale green, red and purple)	2·75	2·75
	a. Horiz pair. Nos. 4228/9	5·50	5·50
4229	$1.40 Southern lights (green and purple, tussocks of grass in foreground)	2·75	2·75
4226/9	*Set of 4*	8·25	8·25
MS4230	135×80 mm. Nos. 4226/9	8·25	8·25

(b) Self-adhesive. Irregular partial phosphor frame (at left and foot (4231) or right and foot (4232) of design). Die-cut perf 11×11½ (interrupted on vert sides)

4231	70c. As Type **944**	1·40	1·40
	a. Booklet pane. Nos. 4231/2, each×5	13·00	
4232	70c. As No. 4227	1·40	1·40

Nos. 4226/7 and 4228/9 were each printed together, *se-tenant*, as horizontal pairs in sheets of 50 (2 panes 5×5), each sheet giving 20 horizontal pairs and ten single stamps (Nos. 4226 and 4228).

Nos. 4231/2 were issued in $7 booklets, No. SB482. The stamps within **MS**4230 were laid *tête-bêche*.

945 Cruden Farm, Victoria

(Des Simone Sakinofsky. Litho Ego Print)

2014 (2 Sept). Open Gardens. T **945** and similar horiz designs. Multicoloured.

(a) Ordinary gum. P 14×14½.

4233	70c. Type **945**	1·40	1·40
	a. Horiz strip of 5. Nos. 4233/7	7·00	7·00
4234	70c. Mendel Garden, West Australia	1·40	1·40
4235	70c. Niwajiri, South Australia	1·40	1·40
4236	70c. Walcott Garden, Australian Central Territory	1·40	1·40
4237	70c. Wychwood, Tasmania	1·40	1·40
4233/7 *Set of 5*		7·00	7·00

(b) Self-adhesive. Irregular phosphor frame. Die-cut perf 11×11½ (interrupted on vert sides)

4238	70c. As Type **945**	1·40	1·40
	a. Booklet pane. Nos. 4238/42, each×4	25·00	
4239	70c. As No. 4234	1·40	1·40
4240	70c. As No. 4235	1·40	1·40
4241	70c. As No. 4236	1·40	1·40
4242	70c. As No. 4237	1·40	1·40
4238/42 *Set of 5*		6·25	6·25

Nos. 4233/7 were printed together, *se-tenant*, as horizontal strips of five stamps in sheets of 50 (2 panes 5×5).

Nos. 4238/42 were issued in $14 booklets, No. SB483.

946 European Wasp

(Des Sharon Rodziewicz. Litho Ego Print)

2014 (23 Sept). Stamp Collecting Month. Things that Sting. T **946** and similar horiz designs. Multicoloured.

(a) Ordinary gum. P 14×14½.

4243	70c. Type **946**	1·40	1·40
4244	70c. Bull Ant	1·40	1·40
4245	70c. Tiger Snake	1·40	1·40
4246	70c. Stonefish	1·40	1·40
4247	70c. Lionfish	1·40	1·40
4248	70c. Stingray	1·40	1·40
4243/8 *Set of 6*		7·50	7·50
MS4249	170×80 mm. Nos. 4243/8	8·50	8·50

(b) Self-adhesive. Phosphor over parts of design. Die-cut perf 11×11½

4250	70c. As No. 4244	1·40	1·40
	a. Booklet pane. Nos. 4250/1, each×2, 4252, 4253/4, each×2 and 4255	13·00	
	b. Booklet pane. Nos. 4250×3, 4251×4, 4252×3, 4253×4 and 4254/5 each×3	25·00	
4251	70c. As No. 4248	1·40	1·40
4252	70c. As No. As No. 4247	1·40	1·40
4253	70c. As Type **946**	1·40	1·40
4254	70c. As No. 4245	1·40	1·40
4255	70c. As No. 4246	1·40	1·40
4250/5 *Set of 6*		7·50	7·50

Nos. 4250/5 were issued in $7 and $14 booklets, Nos. SB484/5.

947 Alpine National Park, Victoria

(Des Boschen Design. Litho RA Print)

2014 (1 Oct). International Post. Wilderness Australia. T **947** and similar multicoloured designs.

(a) Ordinary gum. P 14½×14.

4256	$2.75 Type **947**	5·50	5·50
4257	$5.35 Blue Mountains National Park, New South Wales	10·50	10·50
4258	$7.40 Judbarra/Gregory National Park, Northern Territory	15·00	15·00
4256/8 *Set of 3*		28·00	28·00

(b) Self-adhesive. Phosphor over parts of design. Die-cut perf 11×11½ (interrupted on vert sides) ($1.85) or 11½×11 (interrupted on horiz sides) ($1.95, $2.75)

4259	$1.85 Tasmanian Devil (*horiz*) (as No. 2604)	3·75	3·75
	a. Pane. No. 4259×5	18·00	
4260	$1.95 Sydney Harbour Bridge (as No. 2817)	4·00	4·00
	a. Pane. No. 4260×5	18·00	
4261	$2.75 As Type **947**	5·50	5·50
	a. Pane. No. 4261×5	25·00	
4259/61 *Set of 3*		12·00	12·00

Nos. 4259/61 were issued in $9.25, $9.75 or $13.75 panes of five stamps.

948 Eagle Farm, Queensland

(Des Sonia Young. Litho Pemara (4266a) or McKellar Renown (others))

2014 (7 Oct). Australian Racecourses. T **948** and similar horiz designs. Multicoloured.

(a) Ordinary gum. P 14×14½.

4262	70c. Type **948**	1·40	1·40
	a. Horiz strip of 4. Nos. 4262/5	5·50	5·50
4263	70c. Royal Randwick, New South Wales	1·40	1·40
4264	70c. Morphettville, South Australia	1·40	1·40
4265	70c. Flemington, Victoria	1·40	1·40
4262/5 *Set of 4*		5·50	5·50

(b) Self-adhesive. Phosphor over parts of design. Die-cut perf 11×11½ (interrupted on vert sides)

4266	70c. As Type **948**	1·40	1·40
	a. Vert strip of 4. Nos. 4266/9	5·50	5·50
	b. Booklet pane. Nos. 4266/7, each×3 and 4268/9, each×2	13·00	
4267	70c. As No. 4263	1·40	1·40
4268	70c. As No. 4264	1·40	1·40
4269	70c. As No. 4265	1·40	1·40
4266/9 *Set of 4*		5·50	5·50

Nos. 4262/5 were printed together, *se-tenant*, as horizontal strips of four stamps in sheets of 50 (2 panes 5×5), each sheet giving ten horizontal strips of four and ten single stamps (Type 948).

Nos. 4266/9 were issued in rolls of 200 printed by Pemara containing the four designs in sequence, and also in $7 booklets, No. SB486.

949 The Royal Australian Navy

(Des Tim Hancock, XSD. Litho Ego Print)

2014 (21 Oct). Centenary of the Australian Defence Force. T **949** and similar square designs. Multicoloured.

(a) Ordinary gum. P 14.

4270	70c. Type **949**	1·40	1·40
4271	70c. The Australian Army	1·40	1·40
4272	70c. The Royal Australian Air Force	1·40	1·40
4273	70c. The Australian Defence Force	1·40	1·40
4270/3 *Set of 4*		5·00	5·00
MS4274 170×80 mm. Nos. 4270/3		5·50	5·50

(b) Self-adhesive. Irregular phosphor frame. Die-cut perf 11½

4275	70c. As Type **949**	1·40	1·40
	a. Booklet pane. Nos. 4275/6, each×2, 4277×4 and 4278×2	13·00	
4276	70c. As No. 4272	1·40	1·40
4277	70c. As No. 4273	1·40	1·40
4278	70c. As No. 4271	1·40	1·40
4275/8 *Set of 4*		5·00	5·00

Nos. 4275/8 were issued in $7 booklets, No. SB487.

950 Virgin Mary and Christ Child

(Des Andrew Hogg Design. Litho McKellar)

2014 (31 Oct). Christmas (1st issue). Stained-glass Windows, St. Patrick's Cathedral, Melbourne. T **950** and similar vert design. Multicoloured.

(a) Ordinary gum.

(i) Domestic Mail. P 14½×14.

4279	65c. Type **950**	1·25	1·25

(ii) International Post. P 14½×14.

4280	$2.55 Angels	5·00	5·00
MS4281 105×70 mm. Nos. 4279/80		6·25	6·25

(b) Self-adhesive.

(i) Domestic Mail. Phosphor frame. Die-cut perf 11½×11 (interrupted on horiz sides)

4282	65c. As Type **950**	1·25	1·25
	a. Booklet pane. No. 4282×20	22·00	

(ii) International Post. Phosphor frame (broken at lower left). Die-cut perf 11½×11 (interrupted on horiz sides)

4283	$2.55 As No. 4280	5·00	5·00
	a. Pane. No. 4283×5	22·00	

No. 4282 was issued in $13 booklets, No. SB488.
No. 4283 was issued in $12.75 panes of five stamps.

951 Christmas Tree

(Des Jo Muré. Litho Ego Print)

2014 (31 Oct). Christmas (2nd issue). T **951** and similar vert designs. Bright green (4284, 4288), rosine (4285, 4289), bright turquoise-green (4286) or bright reddish violet and ultramarine (4287, 4292).

(a) Ordinary gum.

(i) Domestic Mail. P 14½×14.

4284	65c. Type **951**	1·25	1·25
	a. Horiz pair. Nos. 4284/5	2·50	2·50
4285	65c. Gift	1·25	1·25
4286	70c. Dove	1·40	1·40

(ii) International Post. P 14½×14.

4287	$1.70 Bell	3·50	3·50
4284/7 *Set of 4*		7·00	7·00

(b) Self-adhesive.

(i) Domestic Mail. Phosphor frame. Die-cut perf 11½×11 (interrupted on horiz sides)

4288	65c. As Type **951**	1·25	1·25
	a. Booklet pane. Nos. 4288/9, each×10	11·00	
4289	65c. As No. 4285	1·25	1·25
4290	65c. As No. 4288 but emerald foil background	1·25	1·25
4291	65c. As No. 4289 but red foil background	1·25	1·25

(ii) International Post. Phosphor frame (broken at left). Die-cut perf 11½×11 (interrupted on horiz sides)

4292	$1.70 As No. 4287	3·50	3·50
	a. Pane. No. 4292×5	16·00	
4288/92 *Set of 5*		7·75	7·75

Nos. 4284/5 were printed together, *se-tenant*, as horizontal pairs in sheets of 50 (2 panes 5×5), each sheet giving 40 horizontal pairs and ten single stamps (Type **951**).

Nos. 4288/9 were issued in $13 booklets.

No. SB489. Nos. 4290/1 were printed in separate self-adhesive sheetlets of ten stamps.

No. 4292 was issued in $8.50 panes of five stamps.

952 Echidna

(Des Sharon Rodziewicz. Litho Ego Print)

2015 (13 Jan). Native Animals. T **952** and similar horiz designs. Multicoloured.

(a) Ordinary gum. P 14×14½.

4293	70c. Type **952**	1·40	1·40
	a. Block of 4. Nos. 4293/6	5·50	5·50
4294	70c. Common Wombat	1·40	1·40
4295	70c. Eastern Grey Kangaroo	1·40	1·40
4296	70c. Koala	1·40	1·40
4297	$1.40 Numbat	2·75	2·75
	a. Vert pair. Nos. 4297/8	5·50	5·50
4298	$1.40 Tasmanian Devil	2·75	2·75
4293/8 *Set of 6*		11·00	11·00
MS4299 170×80 mm. Nos. 4293/8		11·00	11·00

(b) Self-adhesive. Phosphor over parts of design. Die-cut perf 11×11½ (interrupted on vert sides)

4300	70c. As No. 4295	1·40	1·40
	a. Booklet pane. Nos. 4300/1, each×3 and Nos. 4302/3, each×2	13·00	
	b. Booklet pane. Nos. 4300/3, each×5	25·00	
4301	70c. As No. 4296	1·40	1·40
4302	70c. As No. 4294	1·40	1·40
4303	70c. As Type **952**	1·40	1·40
4300/3 *Set of 4*		5·00	5·00

Nos. 4293/6 were printed together, *se-tenant*, as blocks of four stamps in sheets of 50 (2 panes 5×5), each sheet providing eight blocks of four and 18 single stamps. On the top pane the top left stamp is Type **952** but on the lower pane it is No. 4295.

Nos. 4297/8 were printed together, *se-tenant*, as vertical pairs in sheets of 50 (5×5), each sheet giving 20 vertical pairs and ten single stamps. On the top pane the top left stamp is No. 4297 but on the lower pane it is No. 4298.

Nos. 4300/303 were issued in $7 and $14 stamp booklets, Nos. SB490/1.

953 Keith Payne

(Des Lynette Traynor. Litho McKellar Renown)

2015 (22 Jan). Australian Legends (19th series). The Victoria Cross. T **953** and similar vert designs. Multicoloured.

(a) Ordinary gum. P 14½×14.

4304	70c. Type **953**	1·40	1·40
4305	70c. Mark Donaldson	1·40	1·40
4306	70c. Ben Roberts-Smith	1·40	1·40
4307	70c. Dan Keighran	1·40	1·40
4308	70c. Cameron Baird	1·40	1·40
4304/8 *Set of 5*		6·25	6·25
MS4309 170×85 mm. Nos. 4304/8		7·00	7·00

(b) Self-adhesive. Phosphor at left and top right parts of design. Die-cut perf 11½×11 (interrupted on horiz sides)

4310	70c. As Type **953**	1·40	1·40
	a. Booklet pane. No. 4310×10	13·00	

4311 70c. As No. 4305 .... 1·40 1·40
a. Booklet pane. No. 4311×10 .... 13·00
4312 70c. As No. 4306 .... 1·40 1·40
a. Booklet pane. No. 4312×10 .... 13·00
4313 70c. As No. 4307 .... 1·40 1·40
a. Booklet pane. No. 4313×10 .... 13·00
4314 70c. As No. 4308 .... 1·40 1·40
a. Booklet pane. No. 4314×10 .... 13·00
4310/14 *Set of 5* .... 6·25 6·25

Nos. 4310/14 were printed in separate $7 booklets, Nos. SB492/6.

954 Victoria Cross, 1900

(Des Simone Sakinofsky. Litho McKellar Renown)

2015 (22 Jan). First Victoria Cross awarded to an Australian, 1900. Sheet 135×80 mm containing T **954** and similar vert design. Deep olive (70c.) or deep rose-lilac ($5). P 14×14½.

MS4315 Type **954**; $5 As Type **954** but deep rose-lilac .... 11·50 11·50

955 Heart-shaped Kite

(Des Jonathan Chong. Litho Ego Print)

2015 (3 Feb). Greetings Stamps. 'Love is in the Air'. T **955** and similar vert designs. Multicoloured.

(a) Ordinary gum. P 14½×14.

4316 70c. Type **955** .... 1·40 1·40
a. Horiz strip of 4. Nos. 4316/19 .... 5·50 5·50
4317 70c. Aircraft leaving heart-shaped vapour trail .... 1·40 1·40
4318 70c. Heart-shaped hot air balloon .... 1·40 1·40
4319 70c. Heart-shaped cloud .... 1·40 1·40
4316/19 *Set of 4* .... 5·50 5·50

(b) Self-adhesive. Phosphor frame. Die-cut perf 11½×11 (interrupted on horiz sides)

4320 70c. As No. 4319 .... 1·40 1·40
a. Booklet pane. Nos. 4320/1, each×5 .... 13·00
b. Booklet pane. Nos. 4320/1, each×3 and Nos. 4322/3, each×7 .... 25·00
4321 70c. As No. 4317 .... 1·40 1·40
4322 70c. As No. 4318 .... 1·40 1·40
4323 70c. As Type **955** .... 1·40 1·40
4320/3 *Set of 4* .... 5·00 5·00

Nos. 4316/19 were printed together, *se-tenant*, as horizontal strips of four stamps in sheets of 50 (2 panes 5×5), each sheet giving ten strips of four and ten single stamps (Type 955).

Nos. 4320/1 were issued in $7 booklets, No. SB497, and with Nos. 4322/3 also in $14 booklets, No. SB498.

956 *Frances Henty*

(Des Lisa Christensen. Litho RA Print)

2015 (17 Feb). Era of Sail. Clipper Ships. T **956** and similar horiz designs. Multicoloured. P 14×14½.

4324 70c. Type **956** .... 1·40 1·40
a. Horiz pair. Nos. 4324/5 .... 2·75 2·75
4325 70c. *Phoenician* .... 1·40 1·40
4326 $1.40 *Arabian* .... 2·75 2·75
a. Horiz pair. Nos. 4326/7 .... 5·50 5·50
4327 $1.40 *Monkchester* .... 2·75 2·75
4324/7 *Set of 4* .... 8·25 8·25

Nos. 4324/5 and 4326/7 were each printed together, *se-tenant*, as horizontal pairs in sheets of 50 (2 panes 5×5), each sheet giving 20 horizontal pairs and ten single stamps (Nos. 4324 or 4326).

957 Horse-drawn Tram, Victor Harbor, South Australia

(Des John White. Litho McKellar Renown)

2015 (3 Mar). Tourist Transport. T **957** and similar vert designs. Multicoloured.

(a) Ordinary gum. P 14½×14.

4328 70c. Type **957** .... 1·40 1·40
a. Horiz strip of 4. Nos. 4328/31 .... 5·50 5·50
4329 70c. Seaplane, Whitsunday Islands, Queensland .... 1·40 1·40
4330 70c. Steam train *Puffing Billy*, Dandenong Ranges, Victoria .... 1·40 1·40
4331 70c. Flat-bottomed tourist boat, Katherine Gorge, Northern Territory .... 1·40 1·40
4328/31 *Set of 4* .... 5·50 5·50

(b) Self-adhesive. Phosphor frame. Die-cut perf 11½×11 (interrupted on horiz sides)

4332 70c. As Type **957** .... 1·40 1·40
a. Vert strip of 4. Nos. 4332/5 .... 5·50 5·50
b. Booklet pane. Nos. 4332×3, 4333×2, 4334×3 and 4335×2 .... 13·00
4333 70c. As No. 4329 .... 1·40 1·40
4334 70c. As No. 4330 .... 1·40 1·40
4335 70c. As No. 4331 .... 1·40 1·40
4332/5 *Set of 4* .... 5·50 5·50

Nos. 4328/31 were printed together, *se-tenant*, as horizontal strips of four stamps in sheets of 50 (2 panes 5×5), each sheet giving ten strips of four and ten single stamps (Type **957**).

Nos. 4332/5 were issued in rolls of 100 containing the four designs in sequence, and also in $7 booklets, No. SB499.

958 Lemon-scented Gum

(Des Mary Callahan. Litho McKellar Renown)

2015 (17 Mar). Australian Trees. T **958** and similar horiz designs. Multicoloured. P 14×14½.

4336 70c. Type **958** .... 1·40 1·40
4337 $1.40 Queensland Bottle Tree .... 2·75 2·75
4338 $2.10 Green Fig .... 4·25 4·25
a. Horiz pair. Nos. 4338/9 .... 8·50 8·50
4339 $2.10 Moonah .... 4·25 4·25
4336/9 *Set of 4* .... 11·50 11·50
MS4340 170×80 mm. Nos. 4336/9 .... 12·50 12·50

Nos. 4338/9 were printed together, *se-tenant*, as horizontal pairs in sheets of 50 (2 panes 5×5), each sheet giving 20 horizontal pairs and ten single stamps (Type **958**).

959 Queen Elizabeth II at Ebony Horse Club, Brixton, London, October 2013

(Des Simone Sakinofsky. Litho RA Print)

2015 (7 Apr). Queen's Birthday. T **959** and similar vert design. Multicoloured.

(a) Ordinary gum.

(i) Domestic mail. P 14½×14.

4341 70c. Type **959** .... 1·10 1·10

(ii) International Post. P 14½×14.

4342 $2.75 Queen Elizabeth II wearing blue cashmere picture hat with flower decoration made of feathers, Windsor Castle, April 2014........ 4·25 4·25

MS4343 105×70 mm. Nos. 4341/2........ 5·25 5·25

(b) Self-adhesive. Phosphor over parts of design. Die-cut perf 11½×11 (interrupted on horiz sides)

4344 $2.75 As No. 4342........ 4·25 4·25
a. Pane. No. 4344×5........ 19·00

Nos. 4341/2 were also issued in $14.95 premium booklets, No. SP210.

No. 4344 was issued in $13.75 panes of five.

960 Catafalque Sentry, Bugler, Australian Golden Wattle and Anzac Cove

(Des Sonia Young. Litho McKellar Renown)

2015 (7 Apr). ANZAC Centenary. T **960** and similar vert design. Multicoloured.

(a) Ordinary gum.

(i) Domestic mail. P 14½×14.

4345 70c. Type **960** .... 1·10 1·10

(ii) International Post. P 14½×14.

4346 $1.85 Bugler, catafalque sentry, New Zealand silver fern and ANZAC Cove........ 3·00 3·00

MS4347 105×70 mm. Nos. 4345/6........ 4·00 4·00

(b) Self-adhesive.

(i) Domestic mail. Phosphor over parts of design. Die-cut perf 11½×11 (interrupted on horiz sides)

4348 70c. As Type **960** .... 1·10 1·10
a. Booklet pane. No. 4348×10........ 10·00

(ii) International Post. Phosphor over parts of design. Die-cut perf 11½×11 (interrupted on horiz sides)

4349 $1.85 As No. 4346........ 3·00 3·00
a. Pane. No. 4349×5........ 14·00

No. 4348 was issued in $7 booklets, No. SB500.

No. 4349 was issued in $9.25 panes of five. Similar designs were issued on the same date by New Zealand.

961 Divisional Headquarters Staff come Ashore at Anzac Cove, 25 April 1915 ('The Landing')

(Des Janet Boschen, Boschen Design. Litho Ego Print)

2015 (14 Apr). Centenary of World War I (2nd issue). Gallipoli Campaign. T **961** and similar square designs. Multicoloured.

(a) Ordinary gum. P 14.

4350 70c. Type **961** .... 1·10 1·10
a. Horiz strip of 5. Nos. 4350/4........ 5·50 5·50
4351 70c. LCpl Albert Jacka VC and Victoria Cross 1·10 1·10
4352 70c. Australian soldiers in trench captured at Lone Pine, 6 August 1915........ 1·10 1·10
4353 70c. Private John Simpson Kirkpatrick and his donkey carrying wounded soldier ('Field Medicine')........ 1·10 1·10
4354 70c. Members of 9th Battery, 3rd Field Artillery Brigade loading an 18-pounder gun to expend ammunition before evacuation, 19 December 1915........ 1·10 1·10
4350/4 *Set of 5*........ 5·50 5·50
MS4355 170×80 mm. Nos. 4350/4........ 5·50 5·50

(b) Self-adhesive. Phosphor frame. Die-cut perf 11½ (interrupted on horiz sides)

4356 70c. As Type **961** .... 1·10 1·10
a. Booklet pane. Nos. 4356/60, each×2...... 10·00
4357 70c. As No. 4351........ 1·10 1·10
4358 70c. As No. 4352........ 1·10 1·10
4359 70c. As No. 4353........ 1·10 1·10
4360 70c. As No. 4354........ 1·10 1·10
4356/60 *Set of 5*........ 5·00 5·00

Nos. 4350/4 were printed together, *se-tenant*, as horizontal strips of five stamps in sheets of 50 (2 panes 5×5). Nos. 4350/4 were also issued in $14.95 premium booklets, No. SP211.

Nos. 4356/60 were issued in $7 booklets, No. SB501.

(Litho)

2015 (16 Apr). Sydney Stamp Expo. Anzac Centenary. Sheet as No. **MS**4315 optd '16 - 19 APRIL SYDNEY STAMP EXPO 2015 ANZAC CENTENARY' and emblem in gold on upper left sheet margin. Imperf.

MS4361 135×80 mm. 70c. Type **954**; $5 As Type **954** but deep rose-lilac........ 9·00 9·00

962 Charo

(Des Jonathan Chong. Litho Pemara (4367a) or McKellar Renown (others)

2015 (5 May). Cats. T **962** and similar vert designs. Multicoloured.

(a) Ordinary gum. P 14½×14.

4362 70c. Type **962** .... 1·10 1·10
a. Horiz strip of 5. Nos. 4362/6........ 5·50 5·50
4363 70c. Bubu........ 1·10 1·10
4364 70c. Sweetie........ 1·10 1·10
4365 70c. Cato........ 1·10 1·10
4366 70c. Briony........ 1·10 1·10
4362/5 *Set of 5*........ 5·50 5·50

(b) Self-adhesive. Phosphor over parts of design. Die-cut perf 11½×11 (interrupted on horiz sides)

4367 70c. As Type **962** .... 1·10 1·10
a. Vert strip of 5. Nos. 4367/71........ 5·50 5·50
b. Booklet pane. No. 4367×10........ 10·00
4368 70c. As No. 4366........ 1·10 1·10
b. Booklet pane. No. 4368×10........ 10·00
4369 70c. As No. 4365........ 1·10 1·10
b. Booklet pane. No. 4369×10........ 10·00
4370 70c. As No. 4364........ 1·10 1·10
b. Booklet pane. No. 4370×10........ 10·00
4371 70c. As No. 4363........ 1·10 1·10
c. Booklet pane. No. 4371×10........ 10·00
4367/71 *Set of 5*........ 5·50 5·50

Nos. 4362/6 were printed together, *se-tenant*, as horizontal strips of five stamps in sheets of 50 (2 panes 5×5).

Nos. 4367/71 were issued in rolls of 200 printed by Pemara containing the five designs in sequence, and also in separate $7 booklets, Nos. SB502/6.

963 Model Automatic Totaliser, 1907, Museum of Applied Arts and Sciences

(Des Gary Domoney, Visua. Litho McKellar Renown)

2015 (19 May). Collections Australia. T **963** and similar vert designs. Multicoloured.

(a) Ordinary gum. P 14½×14.

4372 70c. Type **963** ... 1·10 1·10
a. Block of 4. Nos. 4372/5 ... 4·25 4·25
4373 70c. *Turtle* (Ellarose Savage), 2012, Australian Museum ... 1·10 1·10
4374 70c. *Endeavour* anchor, 1770, National Museum of Australia ... 1·10 1·10
4375 70c. Welcome Stranger nugget replica, 1869, Sovereign Hill's Gold Museum ... 1·10 1·10
4372/5 *Set of 4* ... 4·25 4·25
MS4376 135×80 mm. Nos. 4372/5 ... 4·50 4·50

(b) Self-adhesive. Irregular partial phosphor frame. Die-cut perf 11½×11

4377 70c. As No. 4373 ... 1·10 1·10
a. Vert strip of 4. Nos. 4377/80 ... 4·25 4·25
4378 70c. As Type **963** ... 1·10 1·10
4379 70c. As No. 4375 ... 1·10 1·10
4380 70c. As No. 4374 ... 1·10 1·10
4377/80 *Set of 4* ... 4·25 4·25

Nos. 4372/5 were printed together, *se-tenant*, as blocks of four stamps in sheets of 50 (2 panes 5×5), each sheet giving eight blocks of four and 18 single stamps (Nos. 4372 or 4374). On the upper pane the top left stamp is Type **963** but on the lower pane it is No. 4374.

Nos. 4377/80 come from rolls of 100 containing the four designs in sequence.

964 The Pinnacles from Cape Woolamai, Phillip Island, Victoria

(Des Jo Muré. Litho Ego Print)

2015 (2 June). Islands of Australia. T **964** and similar horiz designs. Multicoloured.

(a) Ordinary gum. P 14×14½.

4381 70c. Type **964** ... 1·10 1·10
a. Horiz pair. Nos. 4381/2 ... 2·25 2·25
4382 70c. Lagoon, Lady Musgrave Island, Queensland ... 1·10 1·10
4383 $1.40 View from Truganini's Lookout at The Neck, Bruny Island, Tasmania ... 2·25 2·25
4384 $2.10 Horizontal Falls, Talbot Bay, The Buccaneer Archipelago, West Australia . 3·25 3·25
4381/4 *Set of 4* ... 7·00 7·00

(b) Self-adhesive. Partial phosphor frame (at foot and right). Die-cut perf 11×11½ (interrupted on vert sides)

4385 70c. As Type **964** ... 1·10 1·10
a. Booklet pane. Nos. 4385×3, 4385b×2, 4386×2 and 4386b×3 ... 10·00
b. Phosphor frame at left, right and foot ... 1·10 1·10
4386 70c. As No. 4382 ... 1·10 1·10
b. Phosphor frame at left, right and foot.. 1·10 1·10

Nos. 4381/2 were printed together, *se-tenant*, as horizontal pairs in sheets of 50 (2 panes 5×5, each sheet giving 20 horizontal pairs and ten single stamps (Type **964**).

Nos. 4385/6 were issued in $7 booklets, No. SB507.

965 Dr. Tracy Putoczki and Image in 100

(Des Nicholas Girling. Litho RA Printing)

2015 (30 June). Centenary of Walter and Eliza Hall Institute of Medical Research, Melbourne. P 14½×14.

4387 **965** 70c. multicoloured ... 1·10 1·10

No. 4387 was also issued in $14.95 premium booklets, No. SP212.

966 Cape Byron Lighthouse, New South Wales

(Des Stacey Zass, Page12design. Litho Pemara (4392a) or McKellar Renown (others))

2015 (7 July). Centenary of Commonwealth Management of Lighthouses. T **966** and similar vert designs. Multicoloured.

(a) Ordinary gum. P 14½×14.

4388 70c. Type **966** ... 1·10 1·10
a. Block of 4. Nos. 4388/91 ... 4·25 4·25
4389 70c. Cape Leeuwin, West Australia ... 1·10 1·10
4390 70c. North Reef, Queensland ... 1·10 1·10
4391 70c. Tasman Island, Tasmania ... 1·10 1·10
4388/91 *Set of 4* ... 4·25 4·25

(b) Self-adhesive. Partial phosphor frame (broken at top and lower left). Die-cut perf 11½×11 (interrupted on horiz sides)

4392 70c. As Type **966** ... 1·10 1·10
a. Vert strip of 4. Nos. 4392/5 ... 4·25 4·25
b. Booklet pane. Nos. 4392/5, each×5 ... 10·00
4393 70c. As No. 4389 ... 1·10 1·10
4394 70c. As No. 4390 ... 1·10 1·10
4395 70c. As No. 4391 ... 1·10 1·10
4392/5 *Set of 4* ... 4·25 4·25

Nos. 4388/91 were printed together, *se-tenant*, as blocks of four stamps in sheets of 50 (2 panes of 25), giving eight blocks of four and 18 single stamps per sheet. Nos. 4388/91 were also issued in $14.95 premium booklets, No. SP213.

Nos. 4392/5 were issued in rolls of 200 printed by Pemara containing the four designs in sequence, and also in $14 booklets, No. SB508.

967 National Pass, New South Wales

(Des MDM Design). LItho Bambra McKellar)

2015 (14 July). Great Australian Walks. T **967** and similar horiz designs, each showing silhouette of hiker/s. Multicoloured.

(a) Ordinary gum. P 14×14½.

4396 70c. Type **967** ... 1·10 1·10
a. Horiz strip of 4. Nos. 4396/9 ... 4·25 4·25
4397 70c. Cape to Cape Track, West Australia ... 1·10 1·10
4398 70c. Larapinta Trail, Northern Territory ... 1·10 1·10
4399 70c. Overland Track, Tasmania ... 1·10 1·10
4396/9 *Set of 4* ... 4·25 4·25
MS4400 170×80 mm. Nos. 4396/9 ... 4·50 4·50

(b) Self-adhesive. Phosphor frame. Die-cut perf 11×11½ (interrupted on vert sides)

4401 70c. As Type **967** ... 1·10 1·10
a. Horiz strip of 4. Nos. 4401/4 ... 4·25 4·25
b. Booklet pane. Nos. 4401/2, each×2 and Nos. 4403/4, each×3 ... 10·00
4402 70c. As No. 4397 ... 1·10 1·10
4403 70c. As No. 4398 ... 1·10 1·10
4404 70c. As No. 4399 ... 1·10 1·10
4401/4 *Set of 4* ... 4·25 4·25

Nos. 4396/9 were printed together, *se-tenant*, as horizontal strips of four in sheets of 50 (2 panes 5×5), each sheet giving ten horizontal strips of four and ten single stamps (Type **967**).

Nos. 4396/9 were issued in rolls of 100 containing the four designs in sequence, and also in $7 booklets, No. SB509.

968 Emblem

(Des Jo Muré. Litho Bambra McKellar)

2015 (4 Aug). Netball World Cup, Sydney.

(a) Ordinary gum. Phosphorised paper. P 14½×14.

4405 **968** 70c. multicoloured .... 1·10 1·10

(b) Self-adhesive. Irregular partial phosphor frame at top and right. Die-cut perf 11½×11

4406 **968** 70c. multicoloured .... 1·10 1·10
a. Booklet pane. No. 4406×20 .... 20·00

No. 4406 was issued in $14 booklets, No. SB510.

969 Parliament House, Australia

(Des Sonia Young. Litho RA Printing)

2015 (14 Aug). 50 Years of Bilateral Relations between Singapore and Australia, and Singapore and New Zealand. T **969** and similar horiz designs. Phosphorised paper. P 14.

(a) Domestic mail

4407 **4407** 70c. Type **969** .... 1·10 1·10

(b) International Post

4408 $1.85 Parliament House, New Zealand .... 3·00 3·00
4409 $1.95 Parliament House, Singapore .... 3·00 3·00
4407/9 *Set of 3* .... 6·50 6·50
MS4410 160×80 mm. Nos. 4407/9 .... 7·00 7·00

Similar designs were issued by Singapore and New Zealand.

(Litho)

2015 (14 Aug). Singapore 2015 World Stamp Exhibition. Six sheets, each 120×80 mm and containing Nos. 4407/9. Phosphorised paper. P 14.

MS4411 Nos. 4407/9 (DAY 1) .... 7·00 7·00
MS4412 Nos. 4407/9 (DAY 2) .... 7·00 7·00
MS4413 Nos. 4407/9 (DAY 3) .... 7·00 7·00
MS4414 Nos. 4407/9 (DAY 4) .... 7·00 7·00
MS4415 Nos. 4407/9 (DAY 5) .... 7·00 7·00
MS4416 Nos. 4407/9 (DAY 6) .... 7·00 7·00

Nos. **MS**4411/16 were inscr for the days of the exhibition in a diagonal panel at the bottom right corner of the sheet.

970 Duke and Duchess of Cambridge with Princess Charlotte

(Des Jo Muré. Litho Ego Print)

2015 (25 Aug). Birth of Princess Charlotte.

(a) Ordinary gum. Phosphorised paper. P 14.

4417 **970** 70c. multicoloured .... 1·10 1·10

(b) Self-adhesive. Irregular phosphor frame. Die-cut perf 11½ (interrupted on vert sides)

4418 **970** 70c. multicoloured .... 1·10 1·10
a. Booklet pane. No. 4418×10 .... 20·00

No. 4418 was issued in $7 booklets, No. SB511

971 The Skipping Girl (Little Audrey), Abbotsford, Victoria

(Des John White. Litho Pemara (4423a) or Ego Print (others))

2015 (1 Sept). Signs of the Times (historic neon signs). T **971** and similar vert designs. Multicoloured.

(a) Ordinary gum. Phosphorised paper. P 14½×14.

4419 70c. Type **971** .... 1·10 1·10
4420 70c. The Pink Poodle Motel, Surfers Paradise, Queensland .... 1·10 1·10
4421 $1.40 Dandy Pig, Dandenong, Victoria .... 2·25 2·25
4419/21 *Set of 3* .... 4·00 4·00
MS4422 105×70 mm. Nos. 4419/21 .... 4·50 4·50

(b) Self-adhesive. Irregular phosphor frame. Die-cut perf 11½×11 (interrupted on horiz sides)

4423 70c. As Type **971** .... 1·10 1·10
a. Horiz pair. Nos. 4423/4 .... 2·25 2·25
b. Booklet pane. Nos. 4423/4, each×5 .... 10·00
4424 70c. As No. 4420 .... 1·10 1·10

Nos. 4423/4 were issued in rolls of 200 printed by Pemara containing the two designs in sequence, and also in $7 booklets, No. SB512.

972 Queen Elizabeth II

(Des Sonia Young. Litho RA Print)

2015 (9 Sept). Long May She Reign. T **972** and similar vert designs. Multicoloured.

(a) Ordinary gum.

(i) Domestic mail. P 14½×14.

4425 70c. Type **972** .... 1·10 1·10
a. Horiz strip of 3. Nos. 4425/7 .... 3·25 3·25
4426 70c. Coronation portrait by Cecil Beaton, 2 June 1953 .... 1·10 1·10
4427 70c. Queen Elizabeth II wearing tiara, seated in chair, c. 1970 .... 1·10 1·10

(ii) International Post. P 14½×14.

4428 $2.75 Official Diamond Jubilee portrait (wearing white gloves) .... 4·25 4·25
a. Horiz pair. Nos. 4428/9 .... 8·50 8·50
4429 $2.75 Diamond Jubilee portrait (photo by John Swannell), Buckingham Palace, December 2011 (no gloves) .... 4·25 4·25
4425/9 *Set of 5* .... 11·00 11·00
MS4430 170×80 mm. Nos. 4425/9 .... 11·50 11·50

(b) Self-adhesive. International Post. Partial phosphor frame (at left and foot of stamp). Die-cut perf 11½×11 (interrupted on horiz sides)

4431 $2.75 As No. 4428 .... 4·25 4·25
a. Pane. No. 4431×2 and 4432×3 .... 19·00
4432 $2.75 As No. 4429 .... 4·25 4·25

Nos. 4425/7 were printed together, *se-tenant*, as horizontal strips of three stamps in sheets of 50 (2 panes 5×5), each sheet giving ten horizontal strips of three and ten horizontal pairs (Nos. 4425/6).

Nos. 4428/9 were printed together, *se-tenant*, as horizontal pairs in sheets of 50 (2 panes 5×5), each sheet giving 20 horizontal pairs and ten single stamps (No. 4428).

Nos. 4425/9 were also issued in $19.95 premium booklets, No. SP214.

Nos. 4431/2 were issued in $13.75 panes of five stamps.

973 Mercury

(Des Jo Muré. Litho Ego Print)

2015 (22 Sept). Stamp Collecting Month. Our Solar System. T **973** and similar multicoloured designs.

(a) Ordinary gum. P 14½×14 (4433/4, 4437/8, 4440) or 14×14½ (4435/6, 4439)

4433 35c. Type **973** 55 55
a. Pair. Nos. 4433/4 .... 1·10 1·10
4434 35c. Mars 55 55
4435 70c. Neptune and Pluto (37×26 *mm*) .... 1·10 1·10

4436 70c. Venus (37×26 *mm*) 1·10 1·10
4437 70c. Earth (26×37 *mm*) 1·10 1·10
4438 70c. Uranus (26×37 *mm*) 1·10 1·10
4439 70c. Jupiter (30×50 *mm*) 1·10 1·10
4440 70c. Saturn (50×30 *mm*) 1·10 1·10
4433/40 *Set of* 8 7·00 7·00
MS4441 170×82 mm. As Nos. 4433/40 7·75 7·75

(b) Self-adhesive. Partial phosphor frame. Die-cut perf 11×11½ (interrupted on vert sides) or 11½×11 (interrupted on horiz sides)

4442 70c. As No. 4435 1·10 1·10
a. Booklet pane. Nos. 4442/3, each×5 10·00
4443 70c. As No. 4436 1·10 1·10
4444 70c. As No. 4437 1·10 1·10
a. Booklet pane. Nos. 4444/5, each×10 20·00
4445 70c. As No. 4438 1·10 1·10
4442/5 *Set of* 4 4·00 4·00

Nos. 4433/4 were printed together, *se-tenant*, as horizontal and vertical pairs in sheets of 50 (5×10), each sheet having eight blocks of four containing two horizontal and vertical pairs, four horizontal pairs (at top and foot of sheet), four vertical pairs and two single stamps (at left of sheet).

Stamps from **MS**4441 differ from the sheet stamps in having no white borders. They are perforated 14×14½ (Venus and Neptune) or 14½ (others).

Nos. 4442/3 were issued in $7 booklets, No. SB513.

Nos. 4444/5 were issued in $14 booklets, No. SB514.

(Litho)

2015 (25 Sept). China International Collection Expo, Beijing. Sheet 120×80 mm containing No. 4296×2. Multicoloured. P 14×14½.

MS4446 Koala×2 2·25 2·25

974 Mother Teresa, Honorary AC, 1982

(Des Sonia Young. Litho RA Print)

2015 (5 Oct). Honoured by Australia. T **974** and similar horiz designs. Multicoloured.

(a) Ordinary gum. P 14×14½.

4447 70c. Type **974** 1·10 1·10
4448 70c. Nelson Mandela, Honorary AC, 1999 1·10 1·10
4449 70c. Raoul Wallenberg, Honorary Citizen, 2013 1·10 1·10
4447/9 *Set of* 3 3·00 3·00

(b) Self-adhesive. Phosphor over parts of design. Die-cut perf 11×11½ (interrupted on vert sides)

4450 70c. As Type **974** 1·10 1·10
a. Booklet pane. No. 4450×10 10·00
4451 70c. As No. 4448 1·10 1·10
a. Booklet pane. No. 4451×10 10·00
4452 70c. As No. 4449 1·10 1·10
a. Booklet pane. No. 4452×10 10·00
4450/2 *Set of* 3 3·00 3·00

Nos. 4450/2 were issued in separate $7 booklets, Nos. SB515/17.

975 Bassett & Co Penny-farthing, 1888

(Des Sean Pethick. Litho McKellar Renown)

2015 (13 Oct). Bicycles. T **975** and similar square designs. Multicoloured.

(a) Ordinary gum.

(i) Domestic mail. P 14.

4453 70c. Type **975** 1·10 1·10
a. Horiz pair. Nos. 4453/4 2·25 2·25
4454 70c. Sutherland ladies' safety bike, *c.* 1910 1·10 1·10

(ii) International Post. P 14.

4455 $1.85 Finlay Bros sprung-frame men's safety bike, 1930s 3·00 3·00
4456 $2.75 Contemporary custom-made road bike by Baum cycles, 2015 4·25 4·25
4453/6 *Set of* 4 8·50 8·50

(b) Self-adhesive.

(i) Domestic mail. L-shaped phosphor bands (at left and foot) (4457) or reversed L-shaped phosphor bands (at right and foot) (4458). Die-cut perf 11½ (interrupted on horiz sides)

4457 70c. As Type **975** 1·10 1·10
a. Booklet pane. Nos. 4457/8, each×10 20·00
4458 70c. As No. 4454 1·10 1·10

(ii) International Post. L-shaped phosphor bands (at left and foot). Die-cut perf 11½ (interrupted on horiz sides)

4459 $2.75 As No. 4456 4·25 4·25
a. Pane. No. 4459×5 19·00
4457/9 *Set of* 3 5·75 5·75

Nos. 4453/4 were printed together, *se-tenant*, as horizontal pairs in sheets of 50 (2 panes 5×5), each sheet giving 20 horizontal pairs and ten single stamps (Type **975**).

Nos. 4453/6 were also issued in $14.95 premium booklets, No. SP215.

Nos. 4457/8 were issued in $14 booklets, No. SB518.

No. 4459 was issued in $13.75 panes of five stamps.

976 Soldier with Pack Mule

(Des Lisa Christensen. Litho McKellar Renown)

2015 (27 Oct). Animals in War A Century of Service. T **976** and similar square designs. Multicoloured.

(a) Ordinary gum. P 14.

4460 70c. Type **976** 1·10 1·10
4461 70c. Soldier with dog 1·10 1·10
4462 70c. Two troopers on horseback 1·10 1·10
4463 70c. Imperial Camel Corps soldier riding camel 1·10 1·10
4464 70c. Soldier releasing message-carrying pigeon 1·10 1·10
4460/4 *Set of* 5 5·00 5·00
MS4465 170×80 mm. Nos. 4460/4 4·50 4·50

(b) Self-adhesive. Broad phosphor band at left (4466, 4468/9) or right (4467, 4470). Die-cut perf 11½ (interrupted on horiz sides)

4466 70c. As Type **976** 1·10 1·10
a. Booklet pane. Nos. 4466/70, each×2 10·00
4467 70c. As No. 4461 1·10 1·10
4468 70c. As No. 4462 1·10 1·10
4469 70c. As No. 4463 1·10 1·10
4470 70c. As No. 4464 1·10 1·10
4466/70 *Set of* 5 5·00 5·00

Nos. 4466/70 were issued in $7 booklets, No. SB519.

977 Nativity

(Des Sonia Kretschmar. Litho McKellar)

2015 (30 Oct). Christmas (1st issue). T **977** and similar vert designs. Emerald and grey (4482) or multicoloured (others).

(a) Ordinary gum.

(i) Domestic mail. P 14½×14.

4471 65c. Type **977** 1·00 1·00

(ii) International Post. P 14½×14.

4472 $2.55 Three Wise Men 4·00 4·00
MS4473 130×80 mm. Nos. 4471/2 5·00 5·00

(b) Self-adhesive.

(i) Domestic mail. Phosphor over parts of design. Die-cut perf 11½×11 (interrupted on horiz sides)

4474 65c. As Type **977** 1·00 1·00
a. Booklet pane. No. 4474×20 18·00

(ii) International Post. Phosphor over parts of design. Die-cut perf 11½×11 (interrupted on horiz sides)

4475 $2.55 As No. 4472 4·00 4·00
a. Pane. No. 4475×5 18·00

No. 4474 was issued in $13 booklets, No. SB520.

No. 4475 was issued in $12.75 panes of five stamps.

978 Wrapped Present

(Des John White. Litho Ego Print)

2015 (30 Oct). Christmas (2nd issue). T **978** and similar vert designs. Multicoloured.

(a) Ordinary gum.

(i) Domestic mail. P 14½×14.

4476	65c. Type **978**	1·00	1·00
	a. Horiz pair. Nos. 4476/7	2·00	2·00
4477	65c. Two green peace doves	1·00	1·00

(ii) International Post. P 14½×14.

4478	$1.70 Two blue peace doves	2·75	2·75
4476/8 *Set of 3*		4·25	4·25

(b) Self-adhesive

(i) Domestic mail. Phosphor over parts of design. Die-cut perf 11½×11 (interrupted on horiz sides)

4479	65c. As Type **978**	1·00	1·00
	a. Booklet pane. Nos. 4479/80, each×10	18·00	
4480	65c. As No. 4477	1·00	1·00
4481	65c. As Type **978** but varnish over gift	1·00	1·00
4482	65c. As No. 4480 but green foil over doves, country inscription and face value	1·00	1·00

(ii) International Post. Phosphor over parts of design. Die-cut perf 11½×11 (interrupted on horiz sides)

4483	$1.70 As No. 4478	2·75	2·75
	a. Pane. No. 4483×5	12·50	
4479/83 *Set of 5*		6·00	6·00

Nos. 4476/7 were printed together, *se-tenant*, as horizontal pairs in sheets of 50 (2 panes 5×5), each sheet giving 40 horizontal pairs and ten single stamps (Type **978**).

Nos. 4479/80 were issued in $13 booklets, No. SB521.

Nos. 4481/2 were printed in separate self-adhesive sheetlets of ten stamps.

No. 4483 was issued in $8.50 panes of five stamps.

(Litho)

2015 (20 Nov). Hong Kong 2015 International Stamp Exhibition. Sheet 130×90 mm containing No. 4330×4. Multicoloured. P 14½×14.

MS4484	Steam train *Puffing Billy*, Dandenong Ranges, Victoria×4	1·10	1·10

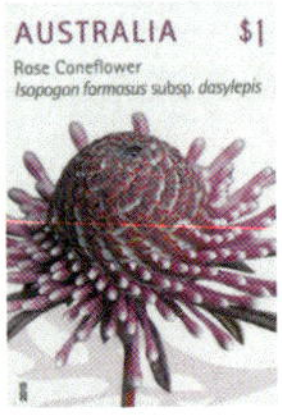

979 Rose Coneflower (*Isopogon formosus* subsp. *dasylepis*)

(Des Simone Sakinofsky. Litho Pemara (4489a) or McKellar Renown (others))

2015 (14 Dec). Wildflowers. T **979** and similar vert designs. Multicoloured.

(a) Ordinary gum. P 14½×14.

4485	$1 Type **979**	1·60	1·60
	a. Horiz strip of 3. Nos. 4485/7	4·75	4·75
4486	$1 Spiny Mirbelia (*Mirbelia spinosa*)	1·60	1·60
4487	$1 Blue Devil (*Eryngium pinnatifidum*)	1·60	1·60
4488	$2 Golden Rainbow (*Drosera microphylla*)	3·25	3·25
4485/8 *Set of 4*		7·25	7·25

(b) Self-adhesive. Phosphor over parts of design. Die-cut perf 11½×11 (interrupted on horiz sides)

4489	$1 As Type **979**	1·60	1·60
	a. Vert strip of 3. Nos. 4489/91	4·75	
	b. Booklet pane. No. 4489×4 and Nos. 4490/1, each×3	14·50	
	c. Booklet pane. No. 4489×8, 4490×5 and 4491×7	29·00	
4490	$1 As No. 4486	1·60	1·60
4491	$1 As No. 4487	1·60	1·60
4489/91 *Set of 3*		4·75	4·75

Nos. 4485/7 were printed together, *se-tenant*, as horizontal strips of three stamps in sheets of 50 (2 panes 5×5), each sheet giving ten horizontal strips of three and ten horizontal pairs (Nos. 4485/6).

Nos. 4489/91 were issued in rolls of 100 or 200 and also in $10 booklets (SB522) and $20 booklets (SB523).

980 Kangaroo

2016 (5 Jan). Counter-printed labels as Type **980**, inscribed 'Adelaide 2016'. Self-adhesive paper. Die-cut perf 11.

4492	30c. Type **980**		
4493	30c. Female Kangaroo with young		
4494	30c. Two Kangaroos		
4495	30c. Family of Koalas on branch		
4496	30c. Koala on ground		
4497	30c. Koala asleep in tree		
4492/7 *Set of 6*			

Nos. 4492/7, in designs as Nos. 1453/8, were supplied to post offices in South Australia during a shortage of 30c. make-up values, following the postal rate increase from 70c. to $1. See notes on counter-printed labels before the design index.

$1 values in the same designs and also inscribed 'Adelaide 2016' were released on 2 February 2016, but were not on general sale at post offices and, as other counter-printed labels, are outside the scope of the catalogue.

981 Pat Cash

(Des Sonia Young. Litho McKellar)

2016 (21 Jan). Australian Legends (20th series). Legends of Singles Tennis. T **981** and similar vert designs. Multicoloured.

(a) Ordinary gum. P 14½×14.

4498	$1 Type **981**	1·60	1·60
	a. Sheetlet. Nos. 4498/4507	16·00	
4499	$1 Ashley Cooper	1·60	1·60
4500	$1 Roy Emerson	1·60	1·60
4501	$1 Neale Fraser	1·60	1·60
4502	$1 Evonne Goolagong Cawley	1·60	1·60
4503	$1 John Newcombe	1·60	1·60
4504	$1 Patrick Rafter	1·60	1·60
4505	$1 Ken Rosewall	1·60	1·60
4506	$1 Frank Sedgman	1·60	1·60
4507	$1 Lleyton Hewitt	1·60	1·60
4508	$1 Tony Roche	1·60	1·60
	a. Vert pair. Nos. 4508/9	3·25	3·25
4509	$1 Fred Stolle	1·60	1·60
4498/509 *Set of 12*		19·00	19·00

(b) Self-adhesive. Irregular phosphor frame. Die-cut perf 11½×11 (interrupted on horiz sides)

4510	$1 As Type **981**	1·60	1·60
	a. Booklet pane. No. 4510×10	14·50	
4511	$1 As No. 4499	1·60	1·60
	a. Booklet pane. No. 4511×10	14·50	
4512	$1 As No. 4500	1·60	1·60
	a. Booklet pane. No. 4512×10	14·50	
4513	$1 As No. 4501	1·60	1·60
	a. Booklet pane. No. 4513×10	14·50	
4514	$1 As No. 4502	1·60	1·60
	a. Booklet pane. No. 4514×10	14·50	
4515	$1 As No. 4503	1·60	1·60
	a. Booklet pane. No. 4515×10	14·50	
4516	$1 As No. 4504	1·60	1·60
	a. Booklet pane. No. 4516×10	14·50	
4517	$1 As No. 4505	1·60	1·60
	a. Booklet pane. No. 4517×10	14·50	
4518	$1 As No. 4506	1·60	1·60
	a. Booklet pane. No. 4518×10	14·50	
4519	$1 As No. 4507	1·60	1·60
	a. Booklet pane. No. 4519×10	14·50	
4520	$1 As No. 4508	1·60	1·60
	a. Booklet pane. No. 4520×10	14·50	

4521 $1 As No. 4509 ... 1·60 1·60
a. Booklet pane. No. 4521×10 ... 14·50

Nos. 4498/507 were printed together, *se-tenant*, in sheetlets of ten stamps.

Nos. 4508/9 were printed together, *se-tenant*, as vertical pairs in sheetlets of ten stamps.

Nos. 4510/21 were printed in separate $10 booklets, Nos. SB524/35.

982 Map of Australia

(Des Sierra Delta. Litho Egotrade Pty Ltd)

2016 (25 Jan). Greetings Stamps. Love to Celebrate. T **982** and similar vert designs. Multicoloured.

(a) Ordinary gum. P 14½×14.

4522 $1 Type **982** ... 1·60 1·60
4523 $1 Flowering gum ... 1·60 1·60
4524 $1 Wattle ... 1·60 1·60
4525 $1 Handprints ... 1·60 1·60
4526 $1 Cake ... 1·60 1·60
4527 $1 Balloons ... 1·60 1·60
4528 $1 White roses ... 1·60 1·60
4529 $1 Champagne glasses ... 1·60 1·60
4530 $1 Heart made from red roses ... 1·60 1·60
4531 $2 Wedding and engagement rings ... 3·25 3·25
4522/31 *Set of 10* ... 16·00 16·00

(b) Self-adhesive. Phosphor frame (4534) or phosphor over parts of design (others). Die-cut perf 11½×11 (interrupted on horiz sides)

4532 $1 As No. 4525 ... 1·60 1·60
a. Booklet pane. No. 4532×10 ... 14·50
4533 $1 As No. 4526 ... 1·60 1·60
a. Booklet pane. No. 4533×10 ... 14·50
4534 $1 As No. 4527 ... 1·60 1·60
a. Booklet pane. No. 4534×10 ... 14·50
4535 $1 As No. 4528 ... 1·60 1·60
a. Booklet pane. No. 4535×10 ... 14·50
4536 $1 As No. 4529 ... 1·60 1·60
a. Booklet pane. No. 4536×10 ... 14·50
4537 $1 As No. 4530 ... 1·60 1·60
a. Booklet pane. No. 4537×10 ... 14·50
4532/7 *Set of 6* ... 8·75 8·75

Stamps as No. 4531 but self-adhesive were issued in $32.95 premium booklets, No. SP216.

Nos. 4532/7 were issued in separate $10 booklets, Nos. SB536/41.

983 One Dollar Coin and Note and Pre-Decimal Australian Pound Note

(Des Melinda Coombes. LItho Egotrade Pty Ltd)

2016 (9 Feb). 50th Anniv of Decimal Currency in Australia. P 14½×14.

4538 **983** $1 multicoloured ... 1·60 1·60

Stamps as No. 4538 but perforated 13½×14 were issued in $20.95 premium booklets, No. SP217.

984 N is for New South Wales, Nipper, Numbat

(Des Gavin Ryan. Litho McKellar)

2016 (1 Mar). Fair Dinkum Aussie Alphabet. T **984** and similar vert designs. Multicoloured.

(a) Ordinary gum. P 14½×14.

4539 $1 Type **984** ... 1·60 1·60
a. Horiz strip of 5. Nos. 4539/43 ... 8·00 8·00
4540 $1 Q is for Queensland, quokka, queue, quoll ... 1·60 1·60
4541 $1 S is for South Australia, shark, sandcastle, surf, starfish, sausage ... 1·60 1·60
4542 $1 V is for Victoria, Victa, vegemite, vegetables, violin ... 1·60 1·60
4543 $1 W is for Western Australia, wombat, wattle, waratah, water hose ... 1·60 1·60
4539/43 *Set of 5* ... 8·00 8·00

(b) Self-adhesive. Irregular partial phosphor frame. Die-cut perf 11½×11 (interrupted on horiz sides)

4544 $1 As Type **984** ... 1·60 1·60
a. Booklet pane. No. 4544×10 ... 14·50
4545 $1 As No. 4540 ... 1·60 1·60
a. Booklet pane. No. 4545×10 ... 14·50
4546 $1 As No. 4541 ... 1·60 1·60
a. Booklet pane. No. 4546×10 ... 14·50
4547 $1 As No. 4542 ... 1·60 1·60
a. Booklet pane. No. 4547×10 ... 14·50
4548 $1 As No. 4543 ... 1·60 1·60
a. Booklet pane. No. 4548×10 ... 14·50
4544/8 *Set of 5* ... 7·50 7·50

Nos. 4539/43 were printed together, *se-tenant*, as horizontal strips of five stamps in sheets of 50 (2 panes 5×5).

Nos. 4544/8 were issued in separate $10 booklets, Nos. SB542/6.

985 Gladesville Bridge, New South Wales

(Des Sean Pethick. Litho EgoTrade Pty Ltd)

2016 (15 Mar). Australian Bridges. T **985** and similar horiz designs. Multicoloured.

(a) Ordinary gum. P 14×14½.

4549 $1 Type **985** ... 1·60 1·60
a. Horiz strip of 3. Nos. 4549/51 ... 4·75 4·75
4550 $1 Story Bridge, Brisbane, Queensland ... 1·60 1·60
4551 $1 Tasman Bridge, Hobart, Tasmania ... 1·60 1·60
4549/51 *Set of 3* ... 4·75 4·75

(b) Self-adhesive. L-shaped phosphor bands (reversed on 4553). Die-cut perf 11×11½ (interrupted on vert sides)

4552 $1 As Type **985** ... 1·60 1·60
a. Booklet pane. Nos. 4552/3, each×7, and 4554×6 ... 28·00
4553 $1 As No. 4551 ... 1·60 1·60
4554 $1 As No. 4550 ... 1·60 1·60
4552/4 *Set of 3* ... 4·25 4·25

Nos. 4549/51 were printed together, *se-tenant*, as horizontal strips of three stamps in sheets of 50 (2 panes 5×5), each sheet giving ten strips of three and ten horizontal pairs (Nos. 4549/50).

Nos. 4552/4 were issued in $20 booklets, No. SB547.

986 Queen Elizabeth II at Garden Party for Not Forgotten Association

(Des Sharon Rodziewicz. Litho RA Printing)

2016 (5 Apr). 90th Birthday of Queen Elizabeth II. T **986** and similar vert design. Multicoloured.

(a) Ordinary gum. P 14½×14 .

(i) Domestic mail

4555 $1 Type **986** ... 1·60 1·60

(ii) International Post

4556	$2.75 Australian Golden Wattle diamond brooch presented to the Queen on inaugural tour of Australia, 1954	4·25	4·25
MS4557	105×70 mm. Nos. 4555/6	5·25	5·25

(b) Self-adhesive. International Post. Irregular partial phosphor frame. Die-cut perf 11½×11 (interrupted on horiz sides)

4558	$2.75 As No. 4556	4·25	4·25
	a. Pane. No. 4558×5	19·00	

No. 4558 was issued in $13.75 panes of five stamps.

987 Soldiers of the 2nd Australian Division in the Bois Grenier sector, June 1916 ('Arrival on the Western Front')

(Des Andrew Hogg Design. Litho McKellar)

2016 (12 Apr). Centenary of World War I (3rd issue). 1916. T **987** and similar square designs. Multicoloured.

(a) Ordinary gum. P 14.

4559	$1 Type **987**	1·60	1·60
4560	$1 Australian machine gunners returning from the frontline near Pozières ('The Somme offensive')	1·60	1·60
4561	$1 Referendum on conscription	1·60	1·60
4562	$1 Matron Grace Wilson (AANS)	1·60	1·60
4563	$1 Soldier of Australian 2nd Battalion writing letter, Flesselles, France, November 1916 ('Ties to home')	1·60	1·60
4559/63	*Set of 5*	7·25	7·25
MS4564	170×80 mm. Nos. 4559/63	7·25	7·25

(b) Self-adhesive. Phosphor over parts of design. Die-cut perf 11½ (interrupted on horiz sides)

4565	$1 As Type **987**	1·60	1·60
	a. Booklet pane. Nos. 4565/9, each×2	14·50	
4566	$1 As No. 4560	1·60	1·60
4567	$1 As No. 4561	1·60	1·60
4568	$1 As No. 4562	1·60	1·60
4569	$1 As No. 4563	1·60	1·60
4565/9	*Set of 5*	7·25	7·25

Nos. 4559/63 were also issued in $20.95 premium booklets, No. SP218.

Nos. 4565/9 were issued in $10 booklets, No. SB548.

MACHINE LABELS

From 22 February 1984 gummed labels in the above design, ranging in value from 1c. to $9.99, were available from seven automatic machines. The postcode at the top of the label indicates the location of the machine from which it was issued; 2000, Sydney; 2601, Canberra (until 1 October 1998) (Canberra subsequently used labels without postcode or code letters); 3000, Melbourne; 4000, Brisbane; 5000, Adelaide; 5790, Darwin (from 29 July 1985 then 0800 from 1 June 1988 until 24 October 1998); 6000, Perth (until 2 November 1998); 7000, Hobart. Labels without postcode numbers appeared on 24 June 1985.

These were replaced by a further series, with a background pattern of Kangaroos, on 22 October 1985. These exist with the same code numbers as before or without code.

On 25 August 1986 a further series, with a background pattern of Platypuses, were issued. The design was again changed on 2 September 1987 to show Echidnas. These were followed by Ringtail Possums on 28 September 1988, Frilled-necked Lizards on 1 September 1989, Koalas on 3 September 1990, Emus on 2 January 1992 and the Waratah (flower) on 8 September 1994.

An overall pattern of geometric shapes, streamers and springs was introduced on 6 June 1996.

A new design using Tiwi aboriginal art was introduced at "Australia 99" where four machines operated producing labels incorporating a line of ship images. Labels in this design, but without the ships, were available nationally from 6 October 1999.

As the number of machines increased only those situated at the State or Capital Territory, General Post Offices showed a postcode. Other machines eventually showed a code, letter followed by numbers at bottom left. Later machines had a top label value of either $10 or $20.

Use of the machines began to decline, however, and due to increasing maintenance costs, Australia Post announced that all machines were to be decommissioned on 1 July 2003. On 13 January 2003 a final label design featuring a pattern of native flora and fauna was introduced, entitled "Farewell Frama".

COUNTER-PRINTED LABELS.

Since 1960 the Australian Post Office used a number of different franking machines at post office counters issuing "POSTAGE PAID" labels. On 21 June 1993 a further type of self-adhesive label was introduced which incorporated Threatened Species designs as Nos. 1312/17 with the machine-printed face value and code. Possible face values of these labels ranged from 45c. to $9,999.99. This was subsequently restricted to a top value of $100.

The labels were initially available at the National Philatelic Centre, Melbourne, showing code "NPC1" and were subsequently available from Canberra Parliament House post office ("ACT 93" and "CPH1") and Royal Exchange, Sydney ("RX1").

DESIGN INDEX

The following index is intended to facilitate the identification of all Australian stamps from 1942 onwards. Portrait stamps are usually listed under surnames views under the name of the town or city and other issues under the main subject or a prominent word and date chosen from the inscription. Simple abbreviations have occasionally been resorted to and when the same design or subject appears on more than one stamp, only the first of each series is indicated.

Machin Watch • Panorama • Catalogue Supplements
Gibbons Stamp Monthly
Large and Small Queens of Canada
Singapore
Queen Victoria Surface-printed Stamps
Creating An Ico
The UK's No.1 stamp magazine

STAMP BOOKLETS

Illustrations of booklet covers are reduced to ½ size, *unless otherwise stated.*

All booklets from 1913 to 1949 were stapled.

1913 (17 Jan). Red on pink cover, 75×60 *mm* as New South Wales Type B **2** (SB1) or blue on pink cover as New South Wales Type B **1** and picture of State G.P.O. on back, 150×175 *mm* (SB2).

SB1 2s. booklet containing twelve ½d. and eighteen 1d. (Nos. 1/2) in blocks of 6 .... £2250

SB2 £1 booklet containing two hundred and forty 1d. (No. 2) in blocks of 30 .... £18000

B **1** *(Illustration reduced. Actual size* 80×60 *mm)*

1914 (6 Oct)–**18**. Red on pink cover, 75×60 *mm* as Type B **1** (Nos. SB2*a*/3), black on red cover, 80×60 *mm* (No. SB4) or blue on pink cover as New South Wales Type B **1** and picture of State G.P.O. on back, 150×175 *mm* (No. SB5).

SB2*a* 2s. booklet containing twelve ½d. and eighteen 1d. (Nos. 1, 21c) in blocks of 6 .... £4000

SB3 2s. booklet containing twelve ½d. and eighteen 1d. (Nos. 20, 21c) in blocks of 6 (1915) £3500

SB4 2s. booklet containing twenty-four 1d. (No. 21c) in blocks of 6 (10.5.17) £3500
- a. Black on green cover £4000
- b. Red on green cover £3750

SB5 £1 booklet containing two hundred and forty 1d. (No. 21c) in blocks of 30 .... £17000
- a. Back cover without G.P.O. picture (1918) £19000

Records show that a £1 booklet containing one hundred and twenty 2d. stamps was issued in very limited quantities during 1914. No examples are known to have survived.

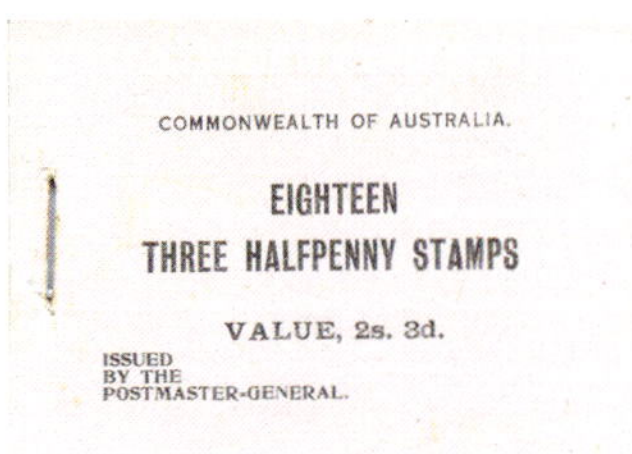

B **1a** *(Illustration reduced. Actual size* 80×60 *mm)*

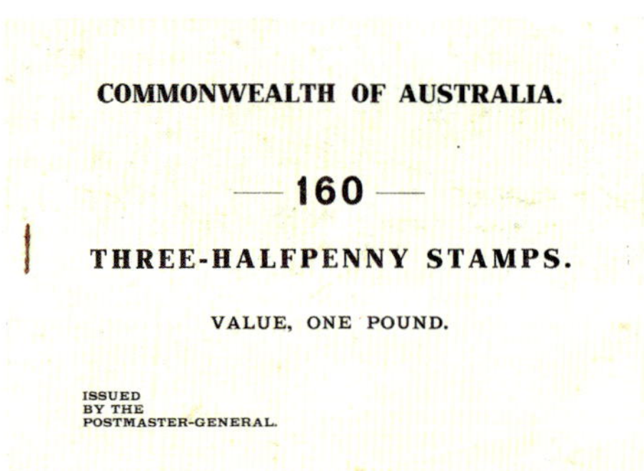

B **1b** *(Illustration reduced. Actual size* 165×120 *mm)*

1919 (Jan–Apr). Black on pink, 80×60 *mm,* as Type B **1a** (Nos. SB6/7), black on green, 80×60 *mm* (Nos. SB8/9b) or black on green, 165×120 *mm* as Type B **1b** (Nos. 9*c*/*d*) covers.

SB6 2s.3d. booklet containing eighteen 1½d. (No. 58) in blocks of 6 .... £3000
- a. Black on green cover £3000

SB7 2s.3d. booklet containing eighteen 1½d. (No. 51) in blocks of 6 .... £3000
- a. Black on green cover £3000

SB8 2s.3d. booklet containing eighteen 1½d. (No. 59) in blocks of 6 (Apr) £3000
- a. Black on pink cover £3000

SB9 2s.3d. booklet containing eighteen 1½d. (No. 52) in blocks of 6 (Apr) £3000
- a. Black on pink cover ....
- b. Black on blue cover £3000

SB9*c* £1 booklet containing one hundred and sixty 1½d. (No. 51) in blocks of 20 .... £19000

SB9*d* £1 booklet containing one hundred and sixty 1½d. (No. 52) in blocks of 20 (Apr) £17000

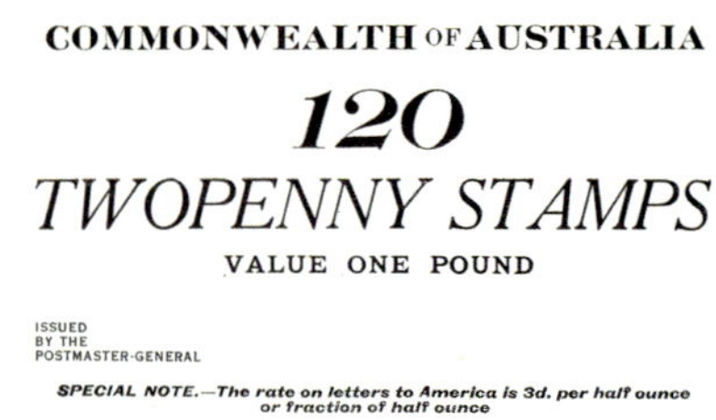

B **1c** *(Illustration reduced. Actual size* 157×90 *mm)*

1920 (Dec)–**22**. Black on blue, 80×60 *mm* (Nos. SB10, SB12), black on white, 157×90 *mm,* as Type B **1c** (No. SB11) or black on brown (No. SB14) covers.

SB10 2s. booklet containing twelve 2d. (No. 62) in blocks of 6 .... £3500
- a. Black on pink cover £3500
- b. Black on orange cover (3.22) £4000

SB11 2s. booklet containing twelve 2d. (No. 63) in blocks of 6 (3.22) £4250
- a. Black on orange cover (7.22) £3750
- b. Black on pink cover £3500
- c. Brown on buff cover £3750
- d. Brown on pink cover £3750

SB12 £1 booklet containing one hundred and twenty 2d. (No. 62) in blocks of 15 (1.21) £18000
- a. Black on pink cover ....

SB13 £1 booklet containing ninety 2d. and fifteen 4d. (Nos. 63, 65) in blocks of 15 (3.22) ....

SB14 £1 booklet containing one hundred and twenty 2d. (No. 63) in blocks of 15 (8.22) £17000

B **1d** *(Illustration reduced. Actual size* 155×90 *mm)*

1923 (Oct)–**24**. Black on rose, 80×60 *mm* (No. SB15), or green on pale green, 80×60 *mm* (No. SB16) or green on pale green, 155×90 *mm,* as Type B **1d** (Nos. 17/18) covers.

SB15 2s.3d. booklet containing eighteen 1½d. (No. 61) in blocks of 6 .... £3000
- a. Black on pale green cover £3000
- b. Green on pale green cover £2500

SB16 2s.3d. booklet containing eighteen 1½d. (No. 77) in blocks of 6 (5.24) £2250

SB17 £1 booklet containing one hundred and sixty 1½d. (No. 61) in blocks of 20 (3.24) £15000

SB18 £1 booklet containing one hundred and sixty 1½d. (No. 77) in blocks of 20 (5.24) £15000

1927 (Jan–June). Green on pale green covers, 82×57 *mm* (Nos. SB19/20) or 150×100 *mm* (No. SB21).

SB19 2s.3d. booklet containing eighteen 1½d. (No. 87) in blocks of 6 .... £1400

SB20 2s.3d. booklet containing eighteen 1½d. (No. 96) in blocks of 6 .... £1400

SB21 £1 booklet containing one hundred and sixty 1½d. (No. 96) in blocks of 20 (June) £13000

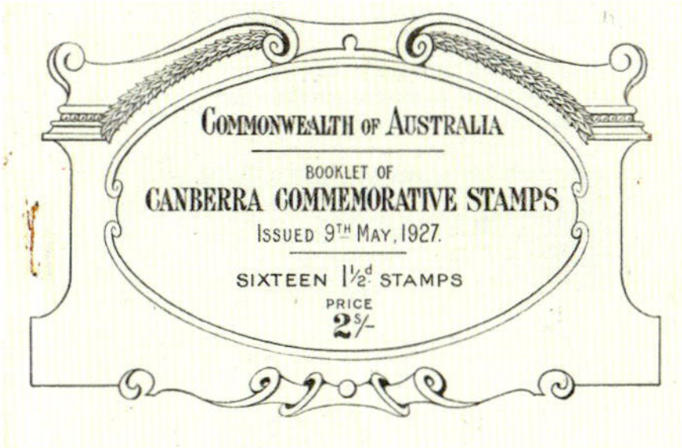

B **1e** *(Illustration reduced. Actual size 115×75 mm)*

1927 (9 May). Opening of Parliament House, Canberra. Green on pale green cover 115×75 *mm,* as Type B **1e** with picture of H.M.S. *Renown* on back (2s.).

SB22 2s. booklet containing sixteen 1½d. (No. 105) in blocks of 8 ..... 90·00

Examples of a 10s. booklet containing eighty 1½d. (No. 105) are known without a front cover and with the back cover blank. There is no record that this was an official issue.

1928 (Nov). Green on pale green cover, 83×58 mm.

SB23 2s.3d. booklet containing eighteen 1½d. (No. 96*a* or 96w) in blocks of 6 ..... £450

B **1f** *(Illustration reduced. Actual size 85×60 mm)*

B **1g** *(Illustration reduced. Actual size 85×60 mm)*

1930 (July)–**35**. Air. Black on blue cover, 85×60 *mm,* as Type B **1f** (No. SB24) or B **1g** (No. SB24a).

SB24 3s. booklet containing twelve 3d. (No. 115a) in blocks of 4 plus two panes of air mail labels £850
a. Black on pale green cover (5.35) £1700

1930 (9 Sep)–**33**. Green on pale green covers inscr "USE THE AIR MAIL" on the back (2s), 83×58 *mm* (Nos. 25/ab), 160×115 *mm* (Nos. 26/*a*).

SB25 2s. booklet containing twelve 2d. (No. 99a or 99aw) in blocks of 6 ..... £425

SB25*a* 2s. booklet containing twelve 2d. (No. 127 or 127w) in blocks of 6 (1.32) £425
ab. Cover with parcel rates on back (1933) £550

SB26 £1 booklet containing one hundred and twenty 2d. (No. 99) in blocks of 20 ..... £11000

SB26*a* £1 booklet containing one hundred and twenty 2d. (No. 99a) in blocks of 20 ..... £11000

1934 (June). Black on cream cover inscr "Address your mail fully..." on front, 81×55 mm.

SB26*b* 2s. booklet containing twelve 2d. (No. 127 or 127w) in blocks of 6 ..... £650

1935–38. Black on green cover with Commonwealth Savings Bank advertisement on front inscr "WHEREVER THERE IS A MONEY ORDER POST OFFICE" 78×55 mm.

SB26*c* 2s. booklet containing twelve 2d. (No. 127 or 127w) in blocks of 6 ..... £475
ca. Front cover inscr "IN MOST MONEY ORDER OFFICES" (1936) £450
cb. Ditto with waxed interleaves (1938) £550

1938 (Dec). Black on green cover as No. SB26*c* but 70×46 mm. Postal rates on interleaves.

SB27 2s. booklet containing twelve 2d. (No. 184 or 184w) in blocks of 6 ..... £500
a. With waxed interleaves. Postal rates on back cover £850
b. Black on buff cover £700

1942 (Aug). Black on buff cover, size 73×47½ mm. Postal rates on interleaves.

SB28 2s.6d. booklet containing twelve 2½d. (No. 206 or 206w) in blocks of 6, upright within the booklet £110
a. With waxed interleaves. Postal rates on back cover £250

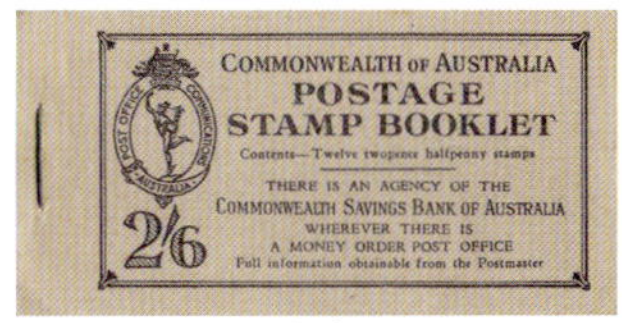

B **1h**

1949 (Sept). Black on buff cover, size 79½×42½ *mm* as Type B **1h**.

SB29 2s.6d. booklet containing twelve 2½d. (No. 206) in blocks of 6, sideways within the booklet ..... 80·00

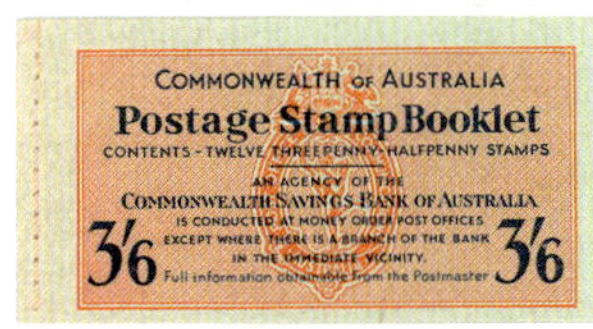

B **1i**

1952 (24 June). Vermilion and deep blue on green cover as Type B **1i**.

SB30 3s.6d. booklet containing twelve 3½d. (No. 247) in blocks of 6 ..... 17·00
a. With waxed interleaves ..... 90·00

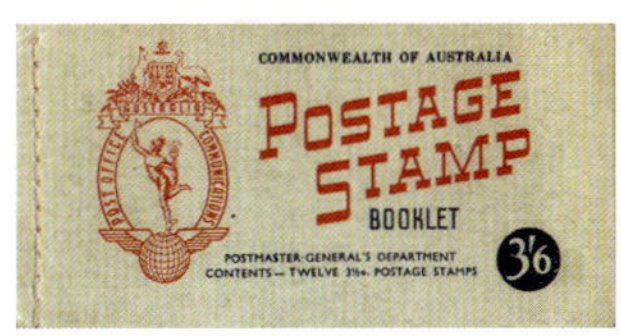

B **1j**

1953 (8 July)–**56**. Vermilion and deep blue on green cover, 80×41 *mm,* as Type B **1j**.

SB31 3s.6d. booklet containing twelve 3½d. (No. 263) in blocks of 6 ..... 11·00
a. With waxed interleaves ..... 30·00

SB32 3s.6d. booklet containing twelve 3½d. (No. 262*a*) in blocks of 6 (7.56) ..... 23·00
a. With waxed interleaves ..... 85·00

B **2**

1957 (13 Mar)–**59**. Vermilion and deep blue on green cover, 80×41 *mm,* as Type B **2**.

SB33 4s. booklet containing two panes of 6×4d. (No. 282ab) ..... 16·00
a. With waxed interleaves ..... 55·00

SB34 4s. booklet containing two panes of 6×4d. (No. 313ab) (18.3.59) ..... 38·00
a. With waxed interleaves ..... 90·00

B **3**

1960 (23 Mar). Vermilion and deep blue on green cover, 80×41 *mm,* as Type B **3**.

SB35 5s. booklet containing two panes of 6×5d. (No. 314d) ... 22·00
a. With waxed interleaves ... 50·00

B **4**

1962 (1 July)–**65**. Rose and emerald on green cover, 80×41 *mm,* as Type B **4**.

SB36 5s. booklet containing two panes of 6×5d. (No. 314d) ... 50·00
a. With waxed interleaves (1963) ... £130

SB37 5s. booklet containing two panes of 6×5d. (No. 354a) (17.6.64) ... 50·00
a. With waxed interleaves ... £120

SB38 5s. booklet containing two panes of 6×5d. (No. 354cb) (13.7.65) ... 60·00
a. With waxed interleaves ... £150

B **5**

1966 (14 Feb). Greenish blue and black on yellow-olive cover, 80×41 *mm,* as Type B **5**.

SB39 60c. booklet containing three panes of 5×4c. and 1 label (No. 385a) ... 45·00
a. With waxed interleaves ... £130

1967 (29 Sept). Greenish blue and black on yellow-olive covers, 80×41 *mm,* as Type B **5**.

(a) Surcharged covers

SB40 50c. booklet containing two panes of 5×5c. on 4c. and 1 label (No. 414a) ... 12·00

SB41 $1 booklet containing four panes of 5×5c. on 4c. and 1 label (No. 414a) ... 4·50
a. Normal cover as Type B **5** ... 5·00
ab. With waxed interleaves ... 65·00

(b) Normal covers

SB42 50c. booklet containing two panes of 5×5c. and 1 label (No. 386ca) ... 17·00

SB43 $1 booklet containing four panes of 5×5c. and 1 label (No. 386ca) ... 23·00
a. With waxed interleaves ... 75·00

Booklets SB40/1ab were intended as provisional issues until supplies of the new 5c. became available in booklet form, but in the event these were put on sale on the same date.

B **6**

1968 (6 Nov). Famous Australians (1st series). Black, red, white and blue cover, 80×41 *mm,* as Type B **6**.

SB44 $1 booklet containing four panes of 5×5c. and 1 label (Nos. 432a, 433a, 434a, 435a) ... 4·00
a. With waxed interleaves ... 55·00

B **7**

1969 (22 Oct). Famous Australians (2nd series). Olive-green, gold and black cover, 80×41 *mm,* as Type B **7**.

SB45 $1 booklet containing four panes of 5×5c. and 1 label (Nos. 446a, 447a, 448a, 449a) ... 5·00
a. With waxed interleaves ... 65·00

B **8**

(Des B. Young. Eng S. Reading. Typo J. B. Cooke)

1970 (16 Nov). Famous Australians (3rd series). Multicoloured on white covers, 41×80 *mm,* as Type B **8**.

SB46 60c. booklet containing two panes of 5×6c. and 1 label (Nos. 479a, 480a) ... 14·00

SB47 60c. booklet containing two panes of 5×6c. and 1 label (Nos. 481a, 482a) ... 14·00

SB48 $1.20 booklet containing four panes of 5×6c. and 1 label (Nos. 479a, 480a, 481a, 482a) ... 7·00
a. With waxed interleaves ... 65·00

1972 (8 Mar). Famous Australians (4th series). Covers (41×80 mm) in reddish violet (No. SB49), yellowish olive (No. SB50) or blue (No. SB51), each with inscr in yellow-brown and black as Type B **7**.

SB49 70c. booklet containing two panes of 5×7c. and 1 label (Nos. 505a, 506a) ... 3·75

SB50 70c. booklet containing two panes of 5×7c. and 1 label (Nos. 507a, 508a) ... 3·75

SB51 $1.40 booklet containing four panes of 5×7c. and 1 label (Nos. 505a, 506a, 507a, 508a) ... 4·50
a. With waxed interleaves ... 5·00

> The Australian Post Office discontinued the general use of stamp booklets in May 1973, but from 30 April 1979 tested two stamp-vending machines in Brisbane which issued 60c. and 80c. folders containing three or four examples of No. 673 taken from sheet stock. These folders were withdrawn on 30 January 1981.

> During 1982 experimental stamp booklet vending machines were under test at the G.P.O.s in Melbourne and Sydney. These machines dispensed a cream card folder, without printing, containing two copies of Nos. 669/70 and 790a. The stamps, from normal sheets, were affixed to the folders by their selvedge. These 60c. trial folders were replaced by booklets Nos. SB52/3 in November 1982.

B **9**

1982 (17 Nov). Eucalyptus Flowers. Covers (79×45 *mm*) in pale greenish yellow with olive-grey (60c.) or rose-red ($1) as Type B **9**.

SB52 60c. booklet containing pane of 6 (No. 870a) .... 1·00
SB53 $1 booklet containing pane of 9 (No. 870b) .... 2·75

Nos. SB52/3 were sold from vending machines.

B **10**

1985 (13 Mar). Turquoise-green on white cover, 78×44 *mm*, as Type B **10**.

SB54 $1 booklet containing pane of 4 (No. 970a) .... 3·75

No. SB54 was sold from vending machines.

B **11**

1986 (25 Aug). Alpine Wildflowers. Apple-green (80c.) or orange-yellow ($1) on white covers, 80×45 *mm*, as Type B **11**.

SB55 80c. booklet containing pane of 4 (No. 1028a) .... 3·00
SB56 $1 booklet containing pane of 4 (No. 1028b) .... 3·00

Nos. SB55/6 were sold from vending machines.

B **12**

1987 (13 Oct). Aboriginal Crafts. Orange-brown (80c.) or orange-yellow ($2) on white covers, 79×45 *mm*, as Type B **12**.

SB57 80c. booklet containing pane of 4 (No. 1093a) .... 3·50
SB58 $2 booklet containing pane of 6 (No. 1094a) .... 7·00

Nos. SB57/8 were sold from vending machines.

Trial versions of both booklets exist which differ considerably from the main supply. On the trial versions the outside back cover is headed "ABORIGINAL CRAFTS", there is no advertisement on the selvedge of the pane and the bottom stamp in each pane is imperforate at foot.

B **13**

1988 (1 July - 28 Sept). Multicoloured covers, 80×60 *mm*, as Type B **13**.

SB59 $3.70 booklet containing 37c. (No. 1121) in block of 10 (printed by Leigh-Mardon Ltd) .... 3·00
SB60 $3.70 booklet containing pane of 10×37c. (No. 1121a) (printed by CPE Australia Ltd) with upper and lower edges of the pane imperf and margins at left and right .... 3·00
SB61 $3.90 booklet containing pane of 10×39c. (No. 1121ba) (28 Sept) .... 4·50

B **14**

1988 (28 Sept). Australian Crafts. Orange-yellow (80c.) or bright purple ($2) on white covers, 79×45 *mm*, as Type B **14**.

SB62 80c. booklet containing pane of 3 (No. 1158a) .... 3·75
SB63 $2 booklet containing pane of 6 (No. 1159a) .... 4·75

Nos. SB62/3 were sold from vending machines.

B **15**

1989 (13 Feb). Multicoloured cover, 77×50 *mm*, as Type B **15**.

SB64 $3.90 booklet containing pane of 10×39c. (No. 1179a) .... 5·00
a. Containing pane No. 1179ba .... 12·00

B **16**

1989 (23 Aug). Multicoloured cover, 77×50 *mm*, as Type B **16**.

SB65 $4.10 booklet containing pane of 10×41c. (No. 1180a) .... 6·00

No. SB65 also exists overprinted with the "Austamp 90" logo for sale at this exhibition.

B **17**

1989 (1 Sept). Urban Environment. Black and grey-brown on white cover, 79×44 *mm*, as Type B **17**.

SB66 $3 booklet containing pane of 7 (No. 1216a) .... 4·00

No. SB66 was sold from vending machines and only contained stamps to a face value of $2.87. A refund of 13c. could, however, be obtained by returning the empty booklet cover to a post office.

No. SB66 also exists overprinted with the "New Zealand 1990" logo for sale at this exhibition.

B **18** (*Illustration reduced. Actual size* 132×54 mm)

1989 (11 Oct). Stampshow '89 National Stamp Exhibition, Melbourne. Multicoloured cover as Type B **18**. Stapled.

SB67 $8 booklet containing pane of 10×41c. (No. 1222ab) .... 9·00

Booklet No. SB67 also contains a Melbourne Metro travel pass and entrance ticket to "Stampshow '89".

B **19**

1989 (1 Nov). Christmas. Reddish brown on toned cover, 94×52 *mm*, as Type B **19**.

SB68 $3.60 booklet containing pane of 10×36c. (No. 1225a) .... 3·50

No. SB68 was also overprinted with the Sydney Stamp and Coin Show, 1989, or "World Stamp Expo", Washington logos for sale at these exhibitions.

B **20**

1990 (7 Feb). Greetings Stamps. Maroon and dull mauve cover, 93×52 *mm*, as Type B **20**.

SB69 $4.10 booklet containing pane of 10×41c. (No. 1230a) and pane of 10 greetings labels .... 4·00
a. Containing pane of 10 (No. 1230ba) and pane of 10 greetings labels (May) .... 11·00

For three months from May 1990 a series of provisional booklets was available from a vending machine at Sydney International Airport. These had plain covers, each handstamped with the airport post office's pictorial cancellation, and exist with the following contents:

70c. (No. 1187)×5 (lemon cover).
75c. (No. 1132)×5 (buff cover).
80c. (No. 1133)×5 (buff cover).
$1 (No. 1192)×5 (buff cover).
$1.10 (No. 1193)×5 (buff cover).

1990 (27 Aug)–**91**. Multicoloured cover, 77×50 *mm*, as Type B **16**.

SB70 $4.30 booklet containing pane of 10×43c. (No. 1181a) .... 6·50
a. Inscription changed and with additional slotted tab attached at right (2.91) .... 12·00

> BARCODES. Barcodes appear on the back cover of booklet No. SB70 and later issues. From 1996 two different barcodes were used on self-adhesive booklets to identify operational from philatelic stock.

1990 (3 Sept). Greetings Stamps. Maroon, brown-olive and pale olive cover, 94×52 *mm*, as Type B **20**.

SB71 $4.30 booklet containing pane of 10×43c. (No. 1231a) and pane of 10 greetings labels .... 4·00

B **21** "Wild Life is Fun" (David Larwill)

1990 (3 Sept). "Heidelberg and Heritage" Art Exhibition. Multicoloured cover, 80×45 *mm*, as Type B **21**.

SB72 $2 booklet containing pane of 5 (No. 1269a) .... 3·50
a. Containing pane of 5 (No. 1269ba) .... 9·50

Nos. SB72/a were sold from vending machines. Both also exist overprinted with the Norpex 91, Newcastle, logo for sale at this exhibition.

B **22** "Parrot unwrapping Parcel"

1990 (31 Oct). Christmas. Multicoloured cover, 94×52 *mm*, as Type B **22**.

SB73 $3.80 booklet containing pane of 10×38c. (No. 1272a) .... 3·75

No. SB73 also exists overprinted with the Sydney Stamp and Coin Show, 1990, logo for sale at this exhibition.

1991 (1 Jan). Red-brown and brown-olive cover, 94×52 *mm*, as Type B **20**, but inscr "8 GREETINGS STICKERS".

SB74 $4.30 booklet containing pane of 10×43c. (No. 1231a) and 8 self-adhesive greetings labels affixed to the inside back cover .... 15·00

B **23**

1991 (1 Nov). Christmas. Multicoloured cover, 76×88 *mm*, as Type B **23**.

SB75 $7.60 booklet containing pane of 20×38c. (No. 1309a) and 20 self-adhesive "Card Only" stickers affixed to the inside back cover .... 5·50

B **24**

1992 (2 Jan)–**94**. Wetlands and Waterways. Multicoloured cover, 80×45 *mm*, as Type B **24**.

SB76 $2 booklet containing pane of 5 (No. 1319a) .... 3·00
a. Containing pane No. 1319ba (3.94) .... 4·50

Nos. SB76/a were sold from vending machines. No. SB76 was also overprinted with "N.P.C. Canberra 14–16 March 1992", "World Columbian Stamp Expo '92", Chicago, "Australian Stamp Exhibition 1993", Kaohsiung, and No. **SB**76 with Queensland Stamp and Coin Show 94 logos for sale at these events.

1992 (2 Jan). "Thinking of You". Orange-yellow, red-orange and grey-black cover, 95×52 *mm*, as Type B **20**, showing wild flowers.

SB77 $4.50 booklet containing pane of 10×45c. (No. 1318a) with 8 self-adhesive greetings labels affixed to the inside back cover.................. 4·50

No. SB77 was also overprinted with "Australian Stamp Exhibition 1993", Taichung, logo for sale at this exhibition.

B **25**

1992 (2 Jan)–**94**. Threatened Species. Multicoloured covers, 58×77 *mm*, as Type B **25**. Self-adhesive.

SB78 $4.50 booklet containing pane of 10×45c. (No. 1327pa) (cover showing No. 1329 on front and Olympic draw details on back)........................ 14·00
a. Containing pane No. 1327qa (cover as Type B **25**, but without Olympic draw flash and with National Philatelic Centre advertisement on back) (22.4.92) .... 14·00
b. Containing pane No. 1327qa (cover as No. SB78a, but Stamp Collecting Kit advertisement on back) (7.11.92) .... 24·00
c. Containing pane No. 1327qa (cover as Type B **25**, but showing larger illustration (46×39 *mm*) of Dusky Hopping-mouse instead of stamp) (1.93) .... 19·00
d. Containing pane No. 1327qa (cover as No. SB78c, but illustration (46×32 *mm*) of Little Pygmy Possum) (7.93).. 24·00
e. Containing pane No. 1327qa (cover as No. SB78c, but illustration (46×32 *mm*) of Ghost Bat) (1.94) .... 24·00

These booklets can also be identified by the new printing symbols (Koalas or Kangaroos) which appear in the margin of the pane. No. SB78a shows 1 or 2 koalas, No. SB78b 3 koalas, No. SB78c 4 koalas, No. SB78d 1 kangaroo and No. SB78e 1 kangaroo and 1 koala.

An example of No. SB78e has been reported showing the printing of the stamps omitted.

No. SB78a (1 koala) was also overprinted with "National Stamp Show '92" logo, No. SB78a (2 koalas) with "Kuala Lumpur '92" and No. SB78c with "Australian Stamp Exhibition 1993", Taipei, logo for sale at these exhibitions.

B **26**

1992 (30 Oct). Christmas. Multicoloured cover, 75×88 *mm*, as Type B **26**.

SB79 $8 booklet containing pane of 20×40c. (No. 1383a) and 20 self-adhesive "Card Only" stickers affixed to the inner cover........................... 6·00

No. SB79 was also overprinted with "Sydney Stamp and Coin Fair "92" logo for sale at this exhibition.

B **27**

1993 (1 June). Trains of Australia. Multicoloured cover as Type B **27**. Self-adhesive.

SB80 $4.50 booklet containing pane of 10×45c. (No. 1411a) .... 6·50

No. SB80 was also overprinted with "Indopex'93", Surabaya, or "Queensland Stamp and Coin Show" logos for sale at these exhibitions.

B **28**

1993 (1 Oct). Prehistoric Animals. Multicoloured cover, 59×77 *mm*, as Type B **28**. Self-adhesive.

SB81 $4.50 booklet containing pane of 10×45c. (No. 1430a) .... 4·00

No. SB81 was also overprinted with the "Sydney Stamp and Coin Show 93" logo for sale at this exhibition.

B **29**

1993 (1 Nov). Christmas. Multicoloured cover, 75×89 *mm*, as Type B **29**.

SB82 $8 booklet containing pane of 20×40c. (No. 1432a) with 20 self-adhesive "Card only" stickers affixed to the inner cover........... 5·50

B **30**

1994 (20 Jan). Centenary of Organised Life Saving in Australia. Multicoloured cover, 60×97 *mm,* as Type B **30**. Self-adhesive.

SB83 $4.50 booklet containing pane of 10×45c. (No. 1443a) .... 3·50

No. SB83 was also overprinted with the "Newcastle Mini-National Exhibition" logo for sale at this event.

B **31** Tulips

1994 (3 Feb). "Thinking of You". Multicoloured cover, 52×95 *mm,* as Type B **31**.

SB84 $4.50 booklet containing pane of 10×45c. (No. 1446b) with 8 self-adhesive greetings stickers affixed to the inner cover .... 3·00

No. SB84 was also overprinted with "Melbourne Stamp and Coin Show" or "Canberra Stamp Show 94" logos for sale at these exhibitions.

B **32** Koala

1994 (12 May)–**96**. Australian Wildlife (2nd series). Multicoloured cover, 58×77 *mm,* as Type B **32**. Self-adhesive.

SB85 $4.50 booklet containing pane of 10×45c. (No. 1459a) .... 4·00
- a. Cover with "BOOKABOUT" advert at foot (1.96) 12·00
- b. Cover with "WIN A TRIP FOR TWO TO THE ATLANTA OLYMPICS" advert at foot (16.3.96) ..... 12·00

No. SB85a is from the 4 koala, 1 kangaroo + 1 koala, 1 kangaroo + 2 koala and 1 kangaroo + 3 koala printings.

No. SB85b is from the 1 kangaroo printing and also exists overprinted "CANBERRA STAMPSHOW 96 16-18 March 1996" in gold on the cover.

B **33**

1994 (28 Sept). Australian Zoos. Endangered Species. Multicoloured cover, 59×77 *mm,* as Type B **33**. Self-adhesive.

SB86 $4.50 booklet containing pane of 10×45c. (No. 1485b) .... 10·00

B **34**

1994 (31 Oct). Christmas. Multicoloured cover, 75×88 *mm,* as Type B **34**.

SB87 $8 booklet containing pane of 20×40c. (No. 1487a) and 20 self-adhesive "CARD ONLY" stickers affixed to the inner cover .... 5·00

B **35**

1995 (9 Feb). Completion of *Endeavour* Replica. Multicoloured cover, 80×45 *mm,* as Type B **35**.

SB88 $2 booklet containing pane of 5 (No. 1512a) .... 2·75

B **36** Sgt. Tom Derrick

1995 (20 Apr). Australian Second World War Heroes. Multicoloured cover, 60×97 *mm,* as Type B **36**. Self-adhesive.

SB89 $4.50 booklet containing pane of 10×45c. (No. 1525a) .... 4·50

B **37** *Picninc at Hanging Rock*

1995 (8 June). Centenary of Cinema. Multicoloured cover, 60×97 *mm,* as Type B **37**. Self-adhesive.

SB90 $4.50 booklet containing pane of 10×45c. (No. 1535a) ..... 9·00

No. SB90 was also overprinted with the "Queensland Stamp and Coin Show 1995" logo for sale at this exhibition.

B **38** Maori Wrasse, Potato Cod and Giant Trevally

B **39**

1995 (3 Oct). Marine Life. Multicoloured cover, 60×97 *mm,* as Type B **38**. Self-adhesive.

SB91 $4.50 booklet containing pane of 10×45c. (No. 1563ab) ..... 5·50

1995 (1 Nov). Christmas. Multicoloured cover, 60×129 *mm,* as Type B **39**. Self-adhesive.

SB92 $8 booklet containing pane of 20×40c. (No. 1572a) and 20 self-adhesive "Card Only" labels affixed to the inner cover ..... 6·50

Booklet No. SB92 shows either an advertisement for B.P. Australia or a selection of Christmas cards available from Australia Post on the back cover.

B **40** North Melbourne

(Des Janet Boschen)

1996 (23 Apr). Centenary of Australian Football League. Multicoloured covers, 60×97 *mm,* as Type B **40** showing team logos. Self-adhesive.

SB93 $4.50 booklet containing pane of 10×45c. (No. 1606a) (Type B **40**) ..... 3·50
SB94 $4.50 booklet containing pane of 10×45c. (No. 1607a) (Brisbane) ..... 3·50
SB95 $4.50 booklet containing pane of 10×45c. (No. 1608a) (Sydney) ..... 3·50
SB96 $4.50 booklet containing pane of 10×45c. (No. 1609a) (Carlton) ..... 3·50
SB97 $4.50 booklet containing pane of 10×45c. (No. 1610a) (Adelaide) ..... 3·50
SB98 $4.50 booklet containing pane of 10×45c. (No. 1611a) (Fitzroy) ..... 3·50
SB99 $4.50 booklet containing pane of 10×45c. (No. 1612a) (Richmond) ..... 3·50
SB100 $4.50 booklet containing pane of 10×45c. (No. 1613a) (St. Kilda) ..... 3·50
SB101 $4.50 booklet containing pane of 10×45c. (No. 1614a) (Melbourne) ..... 3·50
SB102 $4.50 booklet containing pane of 10×45c. (No. 1615a) (Collingwood) ..... 3·50
SB103 $4.50 booklet containing pane of 10×45c. (No. 1616a) (Fremantle) ..... 3·50
SB104 $4.50 booklet containing pane of 10×45c. (No. 1617a) (Footscray) ..... 3·50
SB105 $4.50 booklet containing pane of 10×45c. (No. 1618a) (West Coast) ..... 3·50
SB106 $4.50 booklet containing pane of 10×45c. (No. 1619a) (Essendon) ..... 3·50
SB107 $4.50 booklet containing pane of 10×45c. (No. 1620a) (Geelong) ..... 3·50
SB108 $4.50 booklet containing pane of 10×45c. (No. 1621a) (Hawthorn) ..... 3·50

No. SB94 also exists overprinted with "Queensland Stamp & Coin Expo 1996" for sale at this event.

B **41**

1996 (4 July). 50th Anniv of Children's Book Council Awards. Multicoloured cover, 60×97 *mm,* as Type B **41**. Self-adhesive.

SB109 $4.50 booklet containing panes of 10×45c. (No. 1634a) ..... 6·00

B **42** Silhouettes on Landscape

1996 (12 Sept). 50th Anniv of Arts Councils. Multicoloured cover, 80×44 *mm,* as Type B **42**.

SB110	$2 booklet containing pane of 5 (No. 1643a) (*p* 14×*imperf*)	2·50
	a. Containing pane No. 1643ba (*p* 14½×*imperf*) (9.8.01)	4·00

No. SB110a is from the 1 koala printing.

B **43** Dog and Cat

1996 (1 Oct). Australian Pets. Multicoloured cover, 60×97 *mm,* as Type B **43**. Self-adhesive.

SB111	$4.50 booklet containing pane of 10×45c. (No. 1652a)	6·50

B **44** Madonna and Child

B **45** Rose

1996 (1 Nov). Christmas. Multicoloured cover, 60×129 *mm,* as Type B **44**. Self-adhesive.

SB112	$8 booklet containing pane of 20×40c. (No. 1659a) and 20 self-adhesive "Card Only" labels affixed to the inner cover	13·00

1997 (29 Jan). St. Valentine's Day. Multicoloured cover, 60×88 *mm,* as Type B **45**. Self-adhesive.

SB113	$4.50 booklet containing pane of 10×45c. (No. 1666a) and 12 self-adhesive greetings stickers affixed to the inner cover	7·50

B **46** GMH Holden 48-215 (FX)

1997 (27 Feb). Classic Cars. Multicoloured cover, 60×87 *mm,* as Type B **46**. Self-adhesive.

SB114	$4.50 booklet containing pane of 10×45c. (Nos. 1671a)	4·00

B **47** Classic Cars
(*Illustration reduced. Actual size* 155×105 mm)

1997 (27 Feb). Classic Cars Prestige Booklet. Multicoloured cover as Type B **47**.

SB115	$9.95 booklet containing four panes of 4×45c. (Nos. 1667b/70a), two pre-paid postcards and 16 self-adhesive labels	7·00

B **48** Wetland Birds

1997 (2 June). Flora and Fauna. Multicoloured cover, 58×77 *mm,* as Type B **48**. Self-adhesive.

SB116	$4.50 booklet containing pane of 10×45c. (No. 1687a)	5·50

B **49** Barking Owl

B **50** Two Angels

1997 (1 Oct). Nocturnal Animals. Multicoloured cover, 60×87 *mm*, as Type B **49**. Self-adhesive.

SB117 $4.50 booklet containing pane of 10×45c. (No. 1720b) .... 6·00

1997 (3 Nov). Christmas. Children's Nativity Play. Multicoloured cover, 60×128 *mm*, as Type B **50**. Self-adhesive.

SB118 $8 booklet containing pane of 20×40c. (No. 1726a) and 20 self-adhesive "Card Only" labels affixed to the inner cover .... 5·50

B **51** Australian Athletes

1998 (21 Jan). Australian Legends (2nd series). Olympic Gold Medal Winners. Multicoloured cover, 60×88 *mm*, as Type B **51**. Self-adhesive.

SB119 $5.40 booklet containing pane of 12×45c. (No. 1743b) .... 4·25

B **52** Champagne Rose

B **53** Brolga

1998 (12 Feb). Greetings Stamp. Multicoloured cover, 60×88 *mm*, as Type B **52**. Self-adhesive.

SB120 $4.50 booklet containing pane of 10×45c. (No. 1756a) and 12 self-adhesive greetings stickers affixed to the inner cover .... 4·00

No. SB120 also exists overprinted "Natstamp 98 Canberra 14-16 March 1998" for sale at this exhibition.

1998 (12 Feb). Wetland Birds. Multicoloured cover, 34×75 *mm*, as Type B **53**. Self-adhesive. Stamps loose within cover.

SB121 $9 booklet containing 20×45c. (Nos. 1687d/90d)... 30·00

No. SB121 was introduced as a trial product and was available at a number of Post Offices in Victoria and from Philatelic counters.

B **54** Farmhouse and Fields

1998 (21 Apr). Farming. Multicoloured cover, 60×88 *mm*, as Type B **54**. Self-adhesive.

SB122 $4.50 booklet containing pane of 10×45c. (No. 1764a) .... 10·00

B **55** Pouring Tea (*Illustration reduced. Actual size* 145×103 mm)

1998 (13 Aug). "The Teapot of Truth" Prestige Booklet. Multicoloured cover as Type B **55**. Stapled.

SB123 $9.95 booklet containing three panes of 4×45c. (Nos. 1805a/7a), panes of 2×$1 and $1.20 (Nos. 1808a/9a), pre-paid postcard and 16 self-adhesive labels .... 12·00

B **56**

1998 (1 Sept). Wetland Birds. Multicoloured cover, 79×58 *mm*, as Type B **56**. Self-adhesive.

SB124 $9 booklet containing pane of 20×45c. (No. 1687c) .... 22·00

B **57** Bottlenose Dolphin

1998 (1 Oct). International Year of the Ocean. Multicoloured cover, 60×88 *mm,* as Type B **57**. Self-adhesive.
SB125 $4.50 booklet containing pane of 10×45c. (No. 1829b) .... 5·00

B **58** Christmas Star

1998 (2 Nov). Christmas. Multicoloured cover, 60×129 *mm,* as Type B **58**. Self-adhesive.
SB126 $8 booklet containing pane of 20×40c. (No. 1835a) and 20 self-adhesive "Card Only" labels affixed to the inner cover .... 5·00

B **59**

1999 (22 Jan). Australian Legends (3rd series). Arthur Boyd (painter). Multicoloured cover, 60×87 *mm,* as Type B **59**. Self-adhesive.
SB127 $4.50 booklet containing pane of 10×45c. (No. 1840a) .... 4·25

B **60** Red Roses

B **61** Flowers on Beach

1999 (4 Feb). Greetings Stamp. Romance. Multicoloured cover, 60×88 *mm,* as Type B **60**. Self-adhesive.
SB128 $4.50 booklet containing pane of 10×45c. (No. 1843a) .... 3·75

1999 (8 Apr)–**01**. Coastal Flowers. Multicoloured cover, 58×77 *mm,* as Type B **61**. Self-adhesive.
SB129 $4.50 booklet containing pane of 10×45c. (No. 1863a) .... 3·50
a. Personalised Stamps advertisement on inner cover (8.9.01) .... 7·00
b. Containing booklet pane No. 1863da .... 3·50
ba. Personalised Stamps advertisement on inner cover (8.9.01) .... 7·00

Nos. SB129a and SB129ba, which are from 2 koala printings, show a Personalised Stamps advertisement on the inner cover in place of the Collector's Choice in the original booklets.

B **62** *Bananas in Pyjamas*

B **63** Northern Dwarf Tree Frog

1999 (6 May). Children's Television Programmes. Multicoloured cover, 60×87 *mm,* as Type B **62**. Self-adhesive.
SB130 $4.50 booklet containing pane of 10×45c. (No. 1876a) .... 3·50

1999 (8 July). Flowers. Multicoloured cover, 79×59 *mm,* as Type B **56** showing *Hibbertia scandens*. Self-adhesive.
SB131 $9 booklet containing pane of 20×45c. (No. 1863c) .... 6·00

1999 (1 Oct). National Stamp Collecting Month. Small Pond Life. Multicoloured cover, 58×77 *mm,* as Type B **63**. Self-adhesive.
SB132 $5 booklet containing pane of 10×50c. (No. 1916a) .... 4·00

B **64** Madonna and Child

B **65** Anzac Emblem

1999 (1 Nov). Christmas. Multicoloured cover, 60×129 *mm,* as Type B **64**. Self-adhesive.
SB133 $8 booklet containing pane of 20×40c. (No. 1920a) and 20 "Card Only" labels affixed to the inner cover ..... 5·00

2000 (25 Jan). Australian Legends (4th series). "The Last Anzacs". Multicoloured cover, 61×87 *mm,* as Type B **65**. Self-adhesive.
SB134 $4.50 booklet containing pane of 10×45c. (No. 1951a) ..... 3·50

B **66** Flowers

2000 (23 Mar). Gardens. Multicoloured cover, 61×87 *mm,* as Type B **66**. Self-adhesive.
SB135 $4.50 booklet containing pane of 10×45c. (No. 1965b) ..... 3·50

The cover of No. SB135 is allegedly impregnated with the scent of new mown grass.

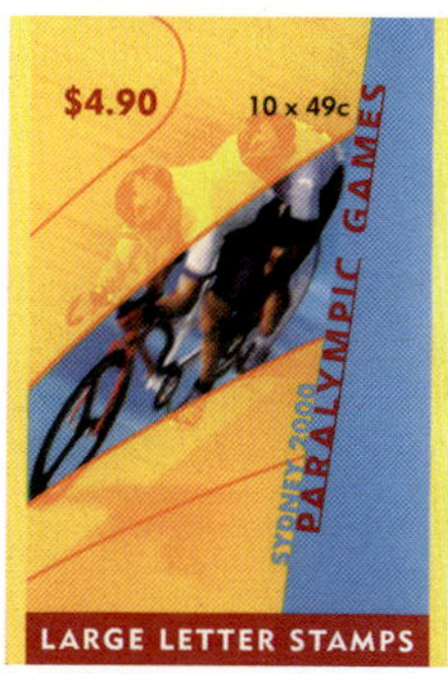

B **67** Cycling

B **68**

2000 (3 July)–**01**. Paralympic Games, Sydney. Multicoloured cover, 61×88 *mm,* as Type B **67**. Self-adhesive.
SB136 $4.90 booklet containing pane of 10×49c. (No. 1997a) (P 11½) ..... 3·00
a. Containing pane No. 1997ba (P 11½×11) (31.1.01) ..... 5·00

No. SB136a is from the 1 koala printing.

2000 (17 Aug). Olympic Games, Sydney. Multicoloured cover, 61×88 *mm,* as Type B **68**. Self-adhesive.
SB137 $4.50 booklet containing pane of 10×45c. (No. 2015a) ..... 3·00

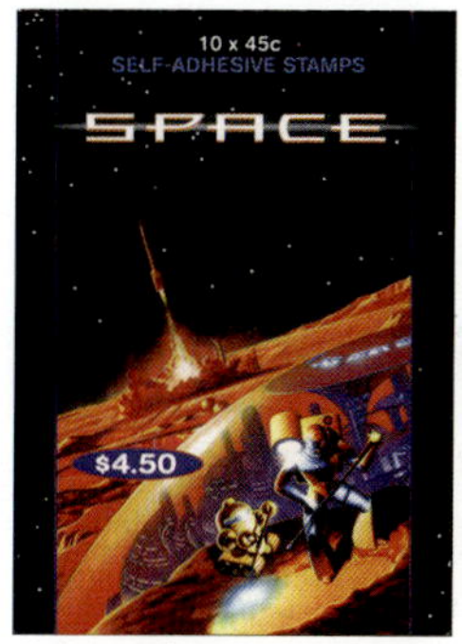

B **69** Launch Site

B **70** The Nativity

2000 (3 Oct). Stamp Collecting Month. Exploration to Mars. Multicoloured cover, 60×87 *mm,* as Type B **69**. Self-adhesive.
SB138 $4.50 booklet containing pane of 10×45c. (No. 2050b) ..... 3·50

2000 (1 Nov). Christmas "Silent Night" (carol). Multicoloured cover, 60×129 *mm,* as Type B **70**. Self-adhesive.
SB139 $8 booklet containing pane of 20×40c. (No. 2059a) and 20 "CARD ONLY" labels affixed to the inner cover ..... 6·00

B **71** Centenial Park Pavilion

B **72** Slim Dusty and Signature

2001 (1 Jan). Centenary of Federation. Black, gold and sage-green cover, 60×88 *mm,* as Type B **71**. Self-adhesive.
SB140 $4.90 booklet containing pane of 10×49c. (No. 2067a) ..... 4·00

2001 (25 Jan). Australian Legends. Slim Dusty (Country music singer). Multicoloured cover, 60×87 *mm,* as Type B **72**. Self-adhesive.
SB141 $4.50 booklet containing pane of 10×45c. (No. 2071a) ..... 2·75

B **73**

B **74** Rural Mail Box

2001 (20 Mar). Australian Rock and Pop Music. Bright carmine, rose-carmine and greenish yellow cover, 60×88 *mm,* as Type B **73**. Self-adhesive.

SB142 $4.50 booklet containing pane of 10×45c. (No. 2089b) .... 3·00

2001 (5 June). Outback Services. Multicoloured cover, 60×87 *mm,* as Type B **74**. Self-adhesive.

SB143 $4.50 booklet containing pane of 10×45c. (No. 2113b) .... 6·50

B **75** The Three Sisters, Blue Mountains

B **76** Crimson Chat

2001 (12 July). International Stamps. Views of Australia. Multicoloured cover, 58×69 *mm,* as Type B **75**. Self-adhesive.

SB144 $5 booklet containing pane of 10×50c. (No. 2125a) .... 5·50

2001 (9 Aug). Fauna and Flora (4th series). Desert Birds. Multicoloured covers as Type B **76**. Self-adhesive.

SB145 $4.50 booklet containing pane of 10×45c. (No. 2130b) (cover 59×73 *mm*) .... 4·50

SB146 $9 booklet containing pane of 20×45c. (No. 2130c) (cover, 79×59 *mm,* showing Variegated Wren) .... 8·50

No. SB145 was issued to post offices bound in bundles of 20 with an illustrated cover.

B **77** Cockatoos dancing

B **78** "Adoration of the Magi"

2001 (2 Oct). National Stamp Collecting Month. "Wild Babies". Multicoloured cover, 60×88 *mm,* as Type B **77**. Self-adhesive.

SB147 $4.50 booklet containing pane of 10×45c. (Nos. 2151b) .... 4·50

2001 (1 Nov). Christmas (2nd issue). Miniatures from "Wharncliffe Hours Manuscript". Multicoloured cover, 60×110 *mm,* as Type B **78**. Self-adhesive.

SB148 $8 booklet containing pane of 20×40c. (No. 2159a) .... 7·00

B **79** Australian Medical Scientists

B **80** Williams Ford, 1980 and Mark II Jaguars, 1963

2002 (23 Jan). Australian Legends (6th series). Medical Scientists. Multicoloured cover, 60×85 *mm,* as Type B **79**. Self-adhesive.

SB149 $4.50 booklet containing pane of 10×45c. (No. 2165a) .... 3·25

2002 (27 Feb). Centenary of Motor Racing in Australia and New Zealand. Multicoloured cover, 60×85 *mm,* as Type B **80**. Self-adhesive.

SB150 $4.50 booklet containing pane of 10×45c. (No. 2181b) .... 5·00

B **81** Lighthouse

2002 (12 Mar). Lighthouses. Multicoloured cover, 61×87 *mm,* as Type B **81**. Self-adhesive.

SB151 $4.90 booklet containing pane of 10×49c. (No. 2191a) .... 5·50

B **82** Mount Roland

B **83** Albert Namatjira

2002 (1 May). International Stamps. Views of Australia (3rd series). Multicoloured cover, 58×69 *mm,* as Type B **82**. Self-adhesive.

SB152 $7 booklet containing pane of 6×50c. and 4×$1 (No. 2198a) .... 6·50

2002 (2 July). Birth Centenary of Albert Namatjira (artist). Multicoloured cover, 60×86 *mm,* as Type B **83**. Self-adhesive.

SB153 $4.50 booklet containing pane of 10×45c. (No. 2209b) .... 3·00

B **84** Seeds and Fruit

B **85** Goblin

2002 (3 Sept). "Bush Tucker". Multicoloured cover, 61×87 *mm,* as Type B **84**. Self-adhesive.

SB154 $4.90 booklet containing pane of 10×49c. (No. 2228a) .... 4·00

2002 (25 Sept). Stamp Collecting Month. The Magic Rainforest. Multicoloured cover, 60×85 *mm,* as Type B **85**. Self-adhesive.

SB155 $4.50 booklet containing pane of 10×45c. (No. 2240b) .... 4·00

B **86** Nativity

2002 (1 Nov). Christmas. Multicoloured cover, 61×110 *mm,* as Type B **86**. Self-adhesive.

SB156 $8 booklet containing pane of 20×40c. (No. 2253a) .... 6·00

B **87** Desert Star Flower

B **88** Margaret Court and Rod Laver

2003 (7 Jan). Flora and Fauna (5th series). Great Sandy Desert. Multicoloured covers as Type B **87**. Self-adhesive.

SB157 $5 booklet containing pane of 10×50c. (No. 2203ab) (cover 57×72 *mm*) .... 3·50

SB158 $10 booklet containing pane of 20×50c. (No. 2203ac) (cover 78×58 *mm*) .... 6·00

2003 (24 Jan). Australian Legends (7th series). Tennis Players. Multicoloured cover, 61×86 *mm,* as Type B **88**. Self-adhesive.

SB159 $5 booklet containing pane of 10×50c. (No. 2268a) .... 6·00

B **89** "Superb" Grevillea

B **90** Queen Elizabeth II in Coronation Robes (photography by Cecil Beaton)

2003 (25 Mar). Australian Horticulture. Multicoloured cover, 60×85 *mm,* as Type B **89**. Self-adhesive.

SB160 $5 booklet containing pane of 10×50c. (No. 2292b) .... 4·00

2003 (2 June). 50th Anniv of Coronation. Multicoloured cover, 60×85 *mm,* as Type B **90**. Self-adhesive.

SB161 $5 booklet containing pane of 10×50c. (No. 2304a) .... 10·00

B **91** Waterfall in Rainforest

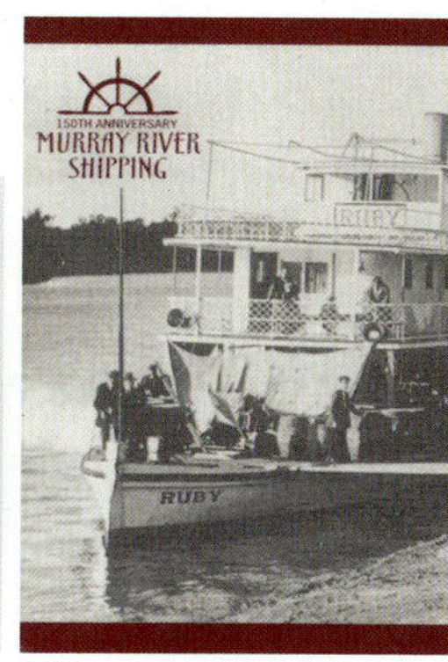

B **92**

2003 (8 July). Fauna and Flora (6th series). Rainforest, Daintree National Park. Multicoloured covers as Type B **91**. Self-adhesive.

SB162 $5 booklet containing pane of 10×50c. (No. 2277a) (cover 57×72 *mm*) .... 8·00

SB163 $10 booklet containing pane of 20×50c. (No. 2277b) (cover 78×58 *mm,* showing rainforest stream) .... 10·00

2003 (5 Aug). 150th Anniv of Murray River Shipping. Black and lake cover as Type B **92**. Self-adhesive.

SB164 $5 booklet containing pane of 10×50c. (No. 2316b) .... 6·25

B **93** Leichhardt's Grasshopper

2003 (24 Sept). Stamp Collecting Month. Bugs and Butterflies. Multicoloured cover, 85×60 *mm,* as Type B **93**. Self-adhesive.

SB165 $5 booklet containing pane of 10×50c. (No. 2333b) .... 4·25

B **94** Mary, Baby Jesus and Angels

B **95** Joan Sutherland as Lucia di Lammermoor

2003 (31 Oct). Christmas. Multicoloured cover, 60×110 *mm,* as Type B **94**. Self-adhesive.

SB166 $9 booklet containing pane of 20×45c. (No. 2347a) .... 8·00

2004 (23 Jan). Australian Legends (8th series). Dame Joan Sutherland (opera singer). Multicoloured cover, 60×85 *mm,* as Type B **95**. Self-adhesive.

SB167 $5 booklet containing pane of 10×50c. (No. 2350a) .... 8·00

B **96** Sydney Harbour Bridge

2004 (2 Mar). Landmark Bridges. Multicoloured cover, 60×86 *mm,* as Type B **96**. Self-adhesive.

SB168 $5 booklet containing pane of 10×50c. (No. 2362b) .... 9·00

B **97** Letters, Ship's Rigging and Bird

B **98** Shaw Savill Lines *Dominion Monarch*

2004 (18 Mar). Australian Innovations. Multicoloured cover, 61×85 *mm,* as Type B **97**. Self-adhesive.

SB169 $5 booklet containing pane of 10×50c. (No. 2386a) .... 8·00

2004 (1 June). "Bon Voyage". Ocean Liners. Multicoloured cover, 60×85 *mm,* as Type B **98**. Self-adhesive.

SB170 $5 booklet containing pane of 10×50c. (No. 2395a) .... 5·50

B **99** The Ghan (Alice Springs-Darwin, 2004)

B **100** Cat and Dog

2004 (7 Sept). 150th Anniv of Australian Railways. Multicoloured cover, 60×85 *mm,* as Type B **99**. Self-adhesive.

SB171 $5 booklet containing pane of 10×50c. (No. 2434b) .... 8·00

2004 (21 Sept). Cats and Dogs. Multicoloured cover, 60×85 *mm,* as Type B **100**. Self-adhesive.

SB172 $5 booklet containing pane of 10×50c. (No. 2445a) .... 6·50

B **101** Dogs

2004 (21 Sept). Cats and Dogs. Multicoloured covers as Type B **101**. Self-adhesive.

SB173 $2.50 booklet containing pane ofx550c (No. 2445b) (cover 62×85 *mm*) .... 3·50

SB174 $2.50 booklet containing pane ofx550c (No. 2446b) (cover 62×85 *mm*) .... 3·50

SB175 $5 booklet containing pane of five $1 (No. 2449b) .... 7·00

B **102** Wayne Gardner (Racing Honda)

2004 (12 Oct). Formula 1 Motorcycle Racing. Multicoloured cover, 60×86 *mm,* as Type B **102**. Self-adhesive.

SB176 $5 booklet containing pane of 10×50c. (No. 2455b) .... 8·00

B **103** Mary and Jesus

2004 (1 Nov). Christmas. Multicoloured cover as Type B **103**. Self-adhesive.

SB178 $9 booklet containing pane of 20×45c. (No. 2463a) .... 7·00

No. SB177 is vacant.

B **104** Open Wardrobe

B **105** Rotary Members on Beach

2005 (21 Jan). Australian Legends. Fashion Designers. Multicoloured covers, 60×85 *mm*, as Type B **104**. Self-adhesive.

SB179 $5 booklet containing pane of 10×50c. (No. 2473a) .... 8·00

SB180 $5 booklet containing pane of 10×50c. (No. 2475a) (cover showing cloth) .... 8·00

SB181 $5 booklet containing pane of 10×50c. (No. 2477a) (cover showing spools of thread) ... 8·00

2005 (21 Apr). Centenary of Rotary International. Multicoloured cover, 60×85 *mm*, as Type B **105**. Self-adhesive.

SB182 $5 booklet containing pane of 10×50c. (No. 2518a) .... 6·25

B **106** Laughing Kookaburra

B **107** Sturt's Desert Pea

2005 (7 June). International Stamps. Bush Wildlife. Multicoloured covers, 62×85 *mm*, as Type B **106**. Self-adhesive.

SB183 $5.50 booklet containing pane of 5×$1.10 (No. 2527a) .... 7·00

SB184 $6 booklet containing pane of 5×$1.20 (No. 2528a) .... 7·50

SB185 $9 booklet containing pane of 5×$1.80 (No. 2529a) .... 10·00

2005 (5 July). Australian Wildflowers. Multicoloured covers as Type B **107**. Self-adhesive.

SB186 $5 booklet containing pane of 10×50c. (No. 2534c) (cover 58×72 *mm*) .... 8·50

SB187 $10 booklet containing pane of twenty 50c. (No. 2534d) (cover 67×87 *mm*, showing Common Fringe Lily) .... 13·00

B **108** Ripening Grapes

B **109** Lucy the Lamb

2005 (19 July). Australian Wine. Multicoloured cover, 60×85 *mm*, as Type B **108**. Self-adhesive.

SB188 $5 booklet containing pane of 10×50c. (No. 2543a) .... 7·25

2005 (4 Oct). Stamp Collecting Month. "Down on the Farm". Multicoloured covers as Type B **109**. Self-adhesive.

SB189 $2.50 booklet containing pane of 5×50c. (No. 2565a) (Type B **109**) (cover 62×85 *mm* folded) .... 6·00

SB190 $5 booklet containing pane of 10×50c. (No. 2565b) (cover 60×85 *mm* folded, showing Ralph the Piglet) .... 10·00

SB191 $5 booklet containing pane of 5×$1 (No. 2570a) (cover 62×85 *mm* folded, showing Harry the Horse) .... 10·00

SB192 $10 booklet containing pane of 20×50c. (No. 2565c) (cover 83×60 *mm* folded, showing Choe the Chicken) .... 20·00

B **110** Adoring Angel

B **111** Barry Humphries as Mrs. Norm Everage, 1969

2005 (1 Nov). Christmas. Multicoloured covers as Type B **110**. Self-adhesive.

SB193 $5 booklet containing pane of 5×$1 (No. 2574a) (cover 62×85 mm) .... 7·00

SB194 $9 booklet containing pane of 20×45c. (No. 2573a) (cover 59×82 *mm* folded, showing Madonna and Child) .... 13·00

2006 (20 Jan). Australian Legends. Barry Humphries (satirist and actor). Multicoloured covers, 60×85 *mm*, as Type B **111**. Self-adhesive.

SB195 $5 booklet containing pane of 10×50c. (No. 2582a) (Type B **111**) .... 9·00

SB196 $5 booklet containing pane of 10×50c. (No. 2585a) (cover showing Barry Humphries) .. 9·00

B **112** Roses

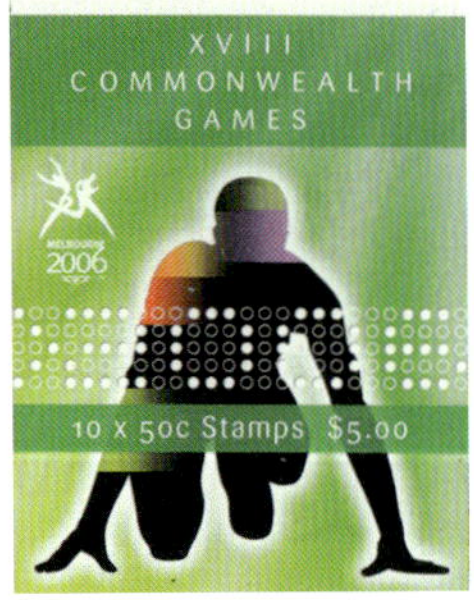

B **113** Athlete at Start

2006 (27 Jan). Greetings Stamp. Roses. Multicoloured cover, 60×85 *mm*, as Type B **112**. Self-adhesive.

SB197 $5 booklet containing pane of 10×50c. (No. 2589a) .... 6·25

2006 (1 Mar). Commonwealth Games, Melbourne. Multicoloured cover, 60×85 *mm*, as Type B **113**. Self-adhesive.

SB198 $5 booklet containing pane of 10×50c. (No. 2600a) .... 7·00

B **114** Garter Badge and Ribbon

B **115** Koala with Cub

2006 (19 Apr). 80th Birthday of Queen Elizabeth II. Multicoloured cover, 60×85 *mm*, as Type B **114**. Self-adhesive.

SB199 $5 booklet containing pane of 10×50c. (No. 2627a) .... 7·00

2006 (2 May). International Stamps. "Greetings from Australia". Multicoloured covers, 62×85 *mm*, as Type B **115**. Self-adhesive.

SB200 $6.25 booklet containing pane of 5×$1.25 (No. 2640a) (Type B **115**) .... 10·00

a. Containing pane No. 2640b (27 May) .... 12·00

SB201 $9.25 booklet containing pane of 5×$1.85 (No. 2641a) (cover showing Royal Exhibition Building, Melbourne) .... 11·00

B **116** Goalkeeper

B **117** Postie Kate on Motorcycle

2006 (9 May). World Cup Football Championship, Germany. Soccer in Australia. Multicoloured cover, 60×85 *mm*, as Type B **116**. Self-adhesive.

SB202 $5 booklet containing pane of 10×50c. (No. 2647a) .... 6·75

2006 (1 June). "Postie Kate". Multicoloured covers as Type B **117**. Self-adhesive.

SB203 $5 booklet containing pane of 10×50c. (No. 2654a) (cover 60×85 *mm*) .... 7·50

SB204 $10 booklet containing pane of 20×50c. (No. 2654b) (cover 85×60 *mm*) .... 12·00

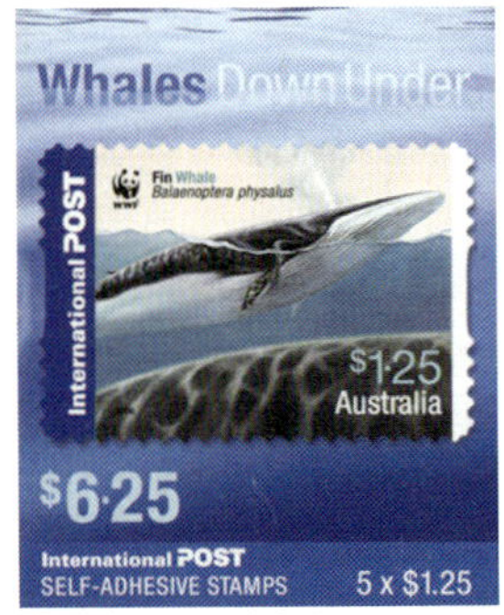

B **118** $1.25 Fin Whale Stamp

2006 (6 June). Endangered Species. Whales. Multicoloured covers, 62×86 *mm*, as Type B **118**. Self-adhesive.

SB205 $6.25 booklet containing pane of 5×$1.25 (No. 2666a) (Type B **118**) .... 10·00

SB206 $9.25 booklet containing pane of 5×$1.85 (No. 2667a) (cover showing $1.85 Southern Bottlenose Whale stamp) .... 14·00

B **119** Car, *c.* 1920

2006 (15 Aug). Driving through the Years. Multicoloured covers, 60×85 *mm*, as Type B **119**. Self-adhesive.

SB207 $5 booklet containing pane of 10×50c. (No. 2678b) (Type B **119**) .... 8·00

SB208 $5 booklet containing pane of 10×50c. (Nos. 2678c) (cover showing car on country road, 1950s) .... 6·50

SB209 $5 booklet containing pane of 10×50c. (No. 2679a) (cover showing Holden car) .... 6·50

SB210 $5 booklet containing pane of 10×50c. (No. 2680a) (cover showing couple with Mini) .. 6·50

SB211 $5 booklet containing pane of 10×50c. (No. 2681a) (cover showing man painting van) 6·50

SB212 $5 booklet containing pane of 10×50c. (No. 2682a) (cover showing Toyota LandCruisers and skiers) .... 6·50

B **120** Rock Guitarists and Drums

B **121** Dangerous Australians Prestige Booklet

2006 (12 Sept). Rock Posters. Multicoloured cover, 60×85 *mm,* as Type B **120**. Self-adhesive.

SB213	$5 booklet containing pane of 10×50c. (No. 2693a)	6·50

2006 (3 Oct). Dangerous Australians. Multicoloured covers, 62×85 *mm,* as Type B **121**. Self-adhesive.

SB214	$2.50 booklet containing pane of 5×50c. (No. 2710c) (Type B **121**)	4·50
SB215	$5 booklet containing pane of 5×$1 (No. 2715a) (cover showing Red-back spider miniature sheet pack)	6·50

B **122** "In Melbourne Tonight"

B **123** "Peace Goodwill Joy"

2006 (24 Oct). 50th Anniv of Television in Australia. Multicoloured covers, 60×85 *mm,* as Type B **122**. Self-adhesive.

SB216	$5 booklet containing pane of 10×50c. (No. 2721b) (Type B **122**)	6·50
SB217	$5 booklet containing pane of 10×50c. (No. 2721c) (cover showing family watching TV)	6·50
SB218	$5 booklet containing pane of 10×50c. (No. 2725a) (cover showing "Kath and Kim")	6·50

2006 (1 Nov). Christmas. Multicoloured covers as Type B **123**. Self-adhesive.

SB219	$5.25 booklet containing pane of 5×$1.05 (No. 2735a) (cover 62×85 mm)	7·00
SB220	$9 booklet containing pane of 20×45c. (No. 2734a) (cover 59×83 *mm* folded)	12·00

Nos. SB221 and SB222 are vacant.

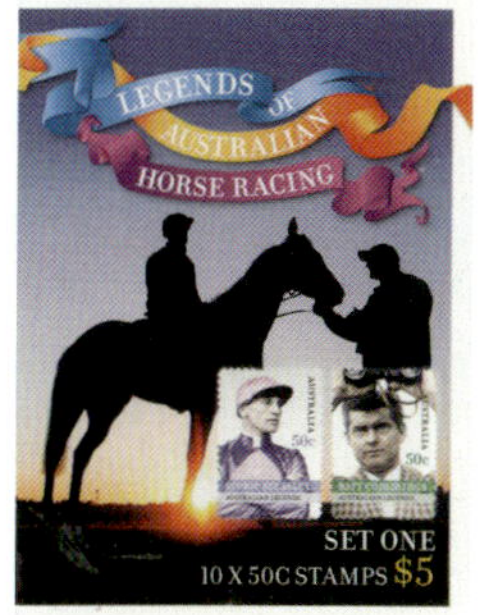

B **125** Horse, Jockey and Trainer at Sunset

B **126** Sturt's Desert Rose

2007 (24 Jan). Legends of Australian Horse Racing. Multicoloured covers, 60×86 *mm,* as Type B **125**. Self-adhesive.

SB223	$5 booklet containing pane of 10×50c. (No. 2753a) (Type B **125**)	9·00
SB224	$5 booklet containing pane of 10×50c. (No. 2755a) (cover showing field rounding corner)	9·00
SB225	$5 booklet containing pane of 10×50c. (No. 2757a) (cover showing race in progress)	9·00

2007 (13 Feb). Australian Wildflowers. Multicoloured covers as Type B **126**. Self-adhesive.

SB226	$5 booklet containing pane of 10×50c. (No. 2763b) (cover 58x72 mm)	6·75
SB227	$10 booklet containing pane of 20×50c. (No. 2763c) (cover 67×87 *mm,* showing Tasmanian Christmas bells)	12·00

B **127** Green Island, Queensland

B **128** Aries

2007 (5 Mar). International Post. Island Jewels. Multicoloured covers, 62×85 *mm,* as Type B **127**. Self-adhesive.

SB228	$6.50 booklet containing pane of 5×$1.30, (No. 2775a) (Type B **127**)	11·00
SB229	$9.75 booklet containing pane of 5×$1.95, (No. 2776a) (cover showing Fraser Island, Queensland)	13·50

2007 (3 Apr). Signs of the Zodiac. Multicoloured covers, 60×85 *mm,* as Type B **128**. Self-adhesive.

SB230	$5 booklet containing pane of 10×50c. (No. 2796a) (Type B **128**)	5·50
SB231	$5 booklet containing pane of 10×50c. (No. 2797a) (Taurus)	5·50
SB232	$5 booklet containing pane of 10×50c. (No. 2798a) (Gemini)	5·50
SB233	$5 booklet containing pane of 10×50c. (No. 2799a) (Cancer)	5·50
SB234	$5 booklet containing pane of 10×50c. (No. 2800a) (Leo)	5·50
SB235	$5 booklet containing pane of 10×50c. (No. 2801a) (Virgo)	5·50
SB236	$5 booklet containing pane of 10×50c. (No. 2802a) (Libra)	5·50
SB237	$5 booklet containing pane of 10×50c. (No. 2803a) (Scorpio)	5·50
SB238	$5 booklet containing pane of 10×50c. (No. 2804a) (Sagittarius)	5·50
SB239	$5 booklet containing pane of 10×50c. (No. 2805a) (Capricorn)	5·50
SB240	$5 booklet containing pane of 10×50c. (No. 2806a) (Aquarius)	5·50
SB241	$5 booklet containing pane of 10×50c. (No. 2807a) (Pisces)	5·50

B **129** Big Top

B **130** Big Banana, Coffs Harbour

2007 (15 May). Circus: Under the Big Top. Multicoloured cover, 60×85 *mm,* as Type B **129**. Self-adhesive.

SB242 $5 booklet containing pane of 10×50c. (No. 2823a) .... 7·25

2007 (5 June). "Big Things" (roadside advertising models). Multicoloured cover, 60×85 *mm,* as Type B **130**. Self-adhesive.

SB243 $5 booklet containing pane of 10×50c. (No. 2833a) .... 7·00

B **131** Produce at Queen Victoria Market

B **132** Tree in Autumn, Royal Botanic Gardens, Melbourne

2007 (24 July). Market Feast. Multicoloured covers, 60×85 *mm,* as Type B **131**. Self-adhesive.

SB244 $5 booklet containing pane of 10×50c. (No. 2853a) (Type B **131**) .... 7·25

SB245 $5 booklet containing pane of 10×50c. (No. 2854a) (cover showing mangoes) .... 7·25

SB246 $5 booklet containing pane of 10×50c. (No. 2855a) (cover showing fish) .... 7·25

SB247 $5 booklet containing pane of 10×50c. (No. 2856a) (cover showing tomatoes) .... 7·25

SB248 $5 booklet containing pane of 10×50c. (No. 2857a) (cover showing red onions and carrots) .... 7·25

2007 (12 Sept). Australian Botanic Gardens. Multicoloured cover, 59×83 *mm,* as Type B **132**. Self-adhesive.

SB249 $10 booklet containing pane of 20×50c. (No. 2866b) .... 14·00

B **133** Earth seen from Space

2007 (2 Oct). Blast Off! 50 Years in Space. Multicoloured cover, 60×85 *mm,* as Type B **133**. Self-adhesive.

SB250 $5 booklet containing pane of 10×50c. (No. 2879b) .... 7·00

B **134** Family Picnic outside Caravan, 1950s

B **135** 'The Spirit of Christmas' Stamp Design, 1957

2007 (16 Oct). Caravanning through the Years. Multicoloured covers, 60×85 *mm,* as Type B **134**. Self-adhesive.

SB251 $5 booklet containing pane of 10×50c. (No. 2889a) (Type B **134**) .... 9·00

SB252 $5 booklet containing pane of 10×50c. (No. 2889b) (cover showing stamps Nos. 2884/8) .... 9·00

SB253 $5 booklet containing pane of 10×50c. (No. 2890a) (cover showing family with kangaroos outside caravan, 1960s) .... 9·00

SB254 $5 booklet containing pane of 10×50c. (No. 2891a) (cover showing family outside caravan, 1970s) .... 9·00

SB255 $5 booklet containing pane of 10×50c. (No. 2892a) (cover showing woman and girl outside caravan, 1980s) .... 9·00

SB256 $5 booklet containing pane of 10×50c. (No. 2893a) (cover showing elderly couple sitting outside caravan, c. 2007) .... 9·00

2007 (1 Nov). Christmas. 50 Years of Christmas Stamps. Multicoloured covers as Type B **135**. Self-adhesive.

SB257 $2.50 booklet containing pane of 5×50c. (No. 2902a) (Type B **135**) (cover 62×85 mm) .... 4·00

SB258 $5.50 booklet containing pane of 5×$1.10 (No. 2903a) (cover showing No. 2903) (62×85 mm) .... 8·00

SB259 $9 booklet containing pane of 20×45c. (No. 2900a) (cover 59×83 *mm* folded, showing No. 2900) .... 16·00

SB260 $9 booklet containing pane of 20×45c. (No. 2901a) (cover 59×83 *mm* folded, showing No. 2901) .... 16·00

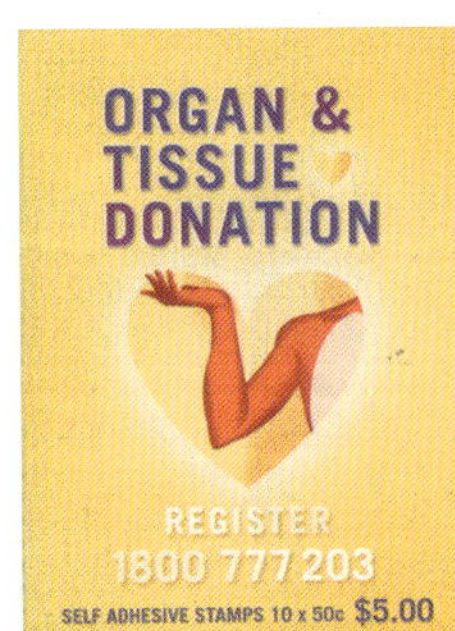

B **136** Outstretched Arm and Heart

2008 (5 Feb). Organ and Tissue Donation. Multicoloured cover, 60×85 *mm,* as Type B **136**. Self-adhesive.

SB261 $5 booklet containing pane of 10×50c. (No. 2916a) .... 7·50

B **137** Scouts in Circle

B **138** Hanging Rock, Grose River Gorge, New South Wales

2008 (19 Feb). Centenary of Scouting. Multicoloured covers, 62×85 *mm,* as Type B **137**. Self-adhesive.

SB262 $6.75 booklet containing pane of 5×$1.35 (No. 2921a) (Type B **137**) .... 20·00

SB263 $10 booklet containing pane of five $2 (No. 2922a) (cover showing Lord Baden-Powell) .... 29·00

2008 (3 Mar). International Post. 'Gorgeous Australia'. Multicoloured covers, 62×85 *mm,* as Type B **138**. Self-adhesive.

SB264 $6.75 booklet containing pane of 5×$1.35 (No. 2927a) (Type B **138**) .... 20·00

SB265 $10 booklet containing pane of five $2 (No. 2928a) (cover showing Walpa Gorge, NT) .... 24·00

B **139** Pope Benedict XVI holding Crozier

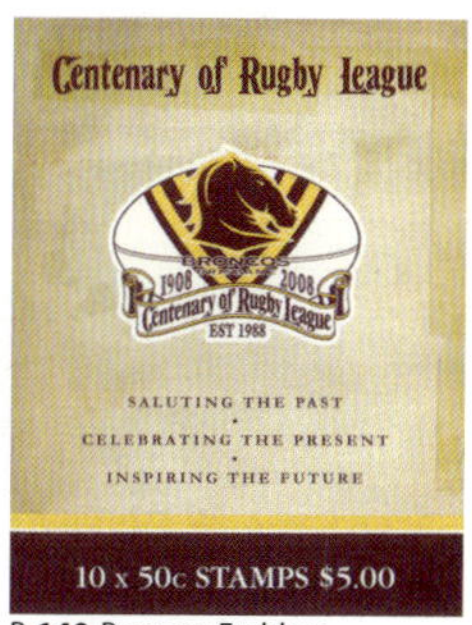

B **140** Broncos Emblem

2008 (4 Mar). International Post. World Youth Day, Sydney. Multicoloured covers, 62×85 *mm,* as Type B **139**. Self-adhesive.

SB266 $6.75 booklet containing pane of 5×$1.35 (No. 2932a) (Type B **139**) .... 16·00

SB267 $10 booklet containing pane of 5×$2 (No. 2933a) (cover showing Pope giving blessing) .... 20·00

2008 (24 Mar). Centenary of Rugby League. Multicoloured covers as Type B **140**. Self-adhesive.

SB268 $5 booklet containing pane of 10×50c. (No. 2951a) (Storm) (cover 60×85 mm) .... 6·50

SB269 $5 booklet containing pane of 10×50c. (No. 2952a) (Sharks) (cover 60×85 mm) .... 6·50

SB270 $5 booklet containing pane of 10×50c. (No. 2953a) (Roosters) (cover 60×85 mm) .... 6·50

SB271 $5 booklet containing pane of 10×50c. (No. 2954a) (Bulldogs) (cover 60×85 mm) .... 6·50

SB272 $5 booklet containing pane of 10×50c. (No. 2955a) (Knights) (cover 60×85 mm) .... 6·50

SB273 $5 booklet containing pane of 10×50c. (No. 2956a) (Cowboys) (cover 60×85 mm) .... 6·50

SB274 $5 booklet containing pane of 10×50c. (No. 2957a) (Rabbitohs) (cover 60×85 mm) .... 6·50

SB275 $5 booklet containing pane of 10×50c. (No. 2958a) (Raiders) (cover 60×85 mm) .... 6·50

SB276 $5 booklet containing pane of 10×50c. (No. 2959a) (Eels) (cover 60×85 mm) .... 6·50

SB277 $5 booklet containing pane of 10×50c. (No. 2960a) (Wests Tigers) (cover 60×85 mm) ... 6·50

SB278 $5 booklet containing pane of 10×50c. (No. 2961a) (Dragons) (cover 60×85 mm) .... 6·50

SB279 $5 booklet containing pane of 10×50c. (No. 2962a) (Sea Eagles) (cover 60×85 mm) .... 6·50

SB280 $5 booklet containing pane of 10×50c. (No. 2963a) (Type B **140**) (cover 60×85 mm) .... 6·50

SB281 $5 booklet containing pane of 10×50c. (No. 2964a) (Titans) (cover 60×85 mm) .... 6·50

SB282 $5 booklet containing pane of 10×50c. (No. 2965a) (Panthers) (cover 60×85 mm) .... 6·50

SB283 $5 booklet containing pane of 10×50c. (No. 2966a) (Warriors) (cover 60×85 mm) .... 6·50

SB284 $10 booklet containing pane of twenty 50c. (No. 2951b) (cover 60×83 *mm* folded, showing centenary emblem) .... 14·00

B **141** Ore Train and Bulk Carrier MS *Berge Stahl*

B **142** Hot Air Balloon

2008 (1 Apr). Heavy Haulers. Multicoloured cover, 60×83 *mm,* as Type B **141**. Self-adhesive.

SB285 $10 booklet containing pane of 20×50c. (No. 2972a) .... 17·00

2008 (6 May). 'Up Up and Away'. 150th Anniv of First Hot Air Balloon Flight in Australia. Multicoloured cover, 60×85 *mm,* as Type B **142**. Self-adhesive.

SB286 $5 booklet containing pane of 10×50c. (No. 2995a) 12·00

B **143** German Shepherd Dog

2008 (10 June). Working Dogs. Multicoloured covers, 61×85 *mm,* as Type B **143**. Self-adhesive.

SB287 $5 booklet containing pane of 10×50c. (No. 3005a) (Type B **143**) .... 13·00

SB288 $5 booklet containing pane of 10×50c. (No. 3005b) (cover showing collar and dog silhouettes) .... 13·00

SB289 $5 booklet containing pane of 10×50c. (No. 3006a) (cover showing Australian cattle dog) .... 13·00

SB290 $5 booklet containing pane of 10×50c. (No. 3007a) (cover showing beagle) .... 13·00

SB291 $5 booklet containing pane of 10×50c. (No. 3008a) (cover showing border collie) .... 13·00

SB292 $5 booklet containing pane of 10×50c. (No. 3009a) (cover showing labrador) .... 13·00

B **144** Green Globe

2008 (8 July). 'Living Green'. Multicoloured cover, 85×61 *mm*, as Type B **144**. Self-adhesive.

SB293 $10 booklet containing double-sided pane of 20×50C. (No. 3016b) .... 16·00

B **145** Olympic Rings

B **146** Qantas Airbus A380

2008 (1 Aug). Olympic Games, Beijing. Multicoloured covers, 62×85 *mm*, as Type B **145**. Self-adhesive.

SB294 $6.50 booklet containing pane of five $1.30 (No. 3031a) .... 12·00

SB295 $6.75 booklet containing pane of 5×$1.35 (No. 3032a) .... 12·00

2008 (5 Aug). Aviation. Multicoloured cover, 70×85 *mm*, as Type B **146**. Self-adhesive.

SB296 $10 booklet containing pane of 5×$2 (No. 3037a)... 20·00

The back cover of No. SB296 is a pane of five airmail labels.

B **147** Luna Park, Melbourne

B **148** Russell Falls, Tasmania

2008 (8 Sept). Tourist Precincts. Multicoloured covers as Type B **147**. Self-adhesive.

SB297 $5.50 booklet containing pane of ten 55c. (No. 3060a) (cover 57×70 mm) (Type B **147**) ..... 7·00

SB298 $5.50 booklet containing pane of ten 55c. (No. 3061a) (cover 57×70 *mm* showing South Bank, Brisbane) .... 7·00

SB299 $5.50 booklet containing pane of ten 55c. (No. 3062a) (cover 57×70 *mm* showing The Rocks, Sydney) .... 7·00

SB300 $5.50 booklet containing pane of ten 55c. (No. 3063a) (cover 57×70 *mm* showing Glenelg, Adelaide) .... 7·00

SB301 $11 booklet containing pane of twenty 55c. (No. 3060b) (cover 67×87 *mm*, showing Nos. 3053/6) .... 14·00

2008 (8 Sept). International Post. Waterfalls of Australia. Multicoloured covers, 62×85 *mm*, as Type B **148**. Self-adhesive.

SB302 $7 booklet containing pane of 5×$1.40 (No. 3068a) (Type B **148**) .... 11·00

SB303 $10.25 booklet containing pane of 5×$2.05 (No. 3069a) (Jim Jim Falls, NT) .... 13·50

B **149** Genyornis

2008 (1 Oct). Stamp Collecting Month. Megafauna of Australia. Multicoloured cover, 58×84 *mm*, as Type B **149**. Self-adhesive.

SB304 $5.50 booklet containing pane of 10×55c. (No. 3087b) .... 10·00

B **150** Bauble

2008 (31 Oct). Christmas. Multicoloured covers as Type B **150**. Self-adhesive.

SB305 $10 booklet containing pane of 20×50c. with twenty "CARD ONLY" labels (No. 3097a) (cover 82×60 *mm* folded)... 15·00

SB306 $10 booklet containing pane of 20×50c. with twenty "CARD ONLY" labels (No. 3099a) (cover 82×60 *mm*, folded, showing star) .... 15·00

B **151** *The Adventures of Priscilla, Queen of the Desert*

2008 (3 Nov). Favourite Australian Films. Multicoloured covers, 60×86 *mm*, as Type B **151**. Self-adhesive.

SB307 $5.50 booklet containing pane of 10×55c. (No. 3106b) (Type B **151**) .... 7·50

SB308 $5.50 booklet containing pane of 10×55c. (No. 3107a) (*The Castle*) .... 7·50

SB309 $5.50 booklet containing pane of 10×55c. (No. 3108a) (*Muriel's Wedding*) .... 7·50

SB310 $5.50 booklet containing pane of 10×55c. (No. 3109a) (*Lantana*) .... 7·50

SB311 $5.50 booklet containing pane of 10×55c. (No. 3110a) (*Gallipoli*) .... 7·50

SB312 $5.50 booklet containing pane of 10×55c. (No. 3106c) (Nos. 3101/5) .... 7·50

B **152** Hexagonal Screen

B **153** Red Roses

2009 (22 Jan). Australian Legends (13th series). "Legends of the Screen". Multicoloured covers as Type B **152**. Self-adhesive.

SB313 $5.50 booklet containing pane of 10×55c. (No. 3121a) (cover 61×85 mm) .... 9·00
SB314 $5.50 booklet containing pane of 10×55c. (No. 3122a) (cover 61×85 mm) .... 9·00
SB315 $5.50 booklet containing pane of 10×55c. (No. 3123a) (cover 61×85 mm) .... 9·00
SB316 $5.50 booklet containing pane of 10×55c. (No. 3124a) (cover 61×85 mm) .... 9·00
SB317 $11 booklet containing pane of twenty 55c. (No. 3121b) (cover 82×60 *mm* folded) .... 16·00

2009 (3 Feb). Greetings Stamps. "With Love". Multicoloured covers, 60×85 *mm*, as Type B **153**. Self-adhesive.

SB318 $5.50 booklet containing pane of 10×55c. (No. 3132a) (Type B **153**) .... 8·50
SB319 $5.50 booklet containing pane of 10×55c. (No. 3133a) (cover showing heart flowers) .... 8·50
SB320 $5.50 booklet containing pane of 10×55c. (No. 3134a) (cover showing filigree heart) .... 8·50

B **154** Mowing Lawn with Victa Rotary Lawnmower

B **155** Gold Rings ("Wedding")

2009 (19 Feb). Inventive Australia. Multicoloured cover, 60×85 *mm*, as Type B **154**. Self-adhesive.

SB321 $5.50 booklet containing pane of 10×55c. (No. 3143b) .... 10·00

2009 (2 Mar). Greetings Stamps. "For Every Occasion". Multicoloured covers, 60×84 *mm*, as Type B **155**. Self-adhesive.

SB322 $5.50 booklet containing pane of 10×55c. (No. 3148a) (Type B **155**) .... 8·50
SB323 $5.50 booklet containing pane of 10×55c. (No. 3149a) (cover showing baby's feet ("BABY")) .... 8·50
SB324 $5.50 booklet containing pane of 10×55c. (No. 3150a) (cover showing balloons ("Party")) . 8·50
SB325 $5.50 booklet containing pane of 10×55c. (No. 3151a) (cover showing sparkler ("CELEBRATE")) .... 8·50
SB326 $11 booklet containing pane of10×$1.10 (No. 3152a) (cover showing bride holding bouquet ("Wedding")) .... 22·00

B **156** Owl in Flight

2009 (11 Mar). Earth Hour. Multicoloured cover, 82×58 *mm* folded, as Type B **156**. Self-adhesive.

SB327 $11 booklet containing pane of 20×55c. (No. 3156a) .... 16·00

B **157** Postman delivering Mail

B **158** Peach Melba

2009 (25 Mar). Bicentenary of Postal Services in Australia. Multicoloured cover, 60×85 *mm*, as Type B **157**. Self-adhesive.

SB328 $5.50 booklet containing pane of 10×55c. (No. 3168b) .... 10·00

2009 (15 May). "Not Just Desserts". Multicoloured cover, 60×85 *mm*, as Type B **158**. Self-adhesive.

SB329 $5.50 booklet containing pane of 10×55c. (No. 3193a) .... 13·00

B **159** Picnic in the Park

2009 (14 July). Australian Parks and Gardens. Multicoloured cover, 60×84 *mm*, as Type B **159**. Self-adhesive.

SB330 $5.50 booklet containing pane of 10×55c. (No. 3229b) .... 13·00

B **160** Bridled Nailtail Wallaby

2009 (4 Aug). Species at Risk. Multicoloured cover, 82×60 *mm* folded, as Type B **160**. Self-adhesive.

SB331 $11 booklet containing pane of 20×55c. (No. 3253a) .... 29·00

B **161** Corrugated Iron

2009 (11 Aug). Corrugated Landscapes. Multicoloured cover, 82×60 *mm* folded, as Type B **161**. Self-adhesive.

SB332 $11 booklet containing pane of 20×55c. (No. 3262b) .... 9·50

B **165**

2009 (2 Nov). Christmas (1st issue). Multicoloured cover, 82×60 *mm* folded, as Type B **165**. Self-adhesive.

SB342 $10 booklet containing pane of 20×50c. with twenty "CARD ONLY" labels (No. 3311a) .... 18·00

B **162** Green Catbird

B **163**

2009 (9 Sept). Australian Songbirds. Multicoloured cover, 61×86 *mm*, as Type B **162**. Self-adhesive.

SB333 $5.50 booklet containing pane of 10×55c. (No. 3274a) .... 17·00

2009 (25 Sept). Classic Toys. Multicoloured cover, 60×85 *mm*, as Type B **163**. Self-adhesive.

SB334 $5.50 booklet containing pane of 10×55c. (No. 3280a) .... 11·00

B **166** Baubles enclosed in Bell

B **167** Author's Names

2009 (2 Nov). Christmas (2nd issue). Multicoloured cover, 61×85 *mm*, as Type B **166**. Self-adhesive.

SB343 $5 booklet containing pane of 10×50c. with ten "Card Only" labels (No. 3318a) .... 9·00

2010 (21 Jan). Australian Legends (14 series). "Legends of the Written Word". Grey, light grey and black cover, 83×118 *mm*, as Type B **167**. Self-adhesive.

SB344 $11 booklet containing pane of 20×55c. (No. 3340a) .... 18·00

B **164** Australian Rules Football

2009 (6 Oct). Stamp Collecting Month. "Let's Get active!". Multicoloured cover, 61×86 *mm*, as Type B **164**. Self-adhesive.

SB335 $5.50 booklet containing pane of 10×55c. (No. 3292a) .... 9·50

SB336 $5.50 booklet containing pane of 10×55c. (No. 3292b) (children playing sports) .... 9·50

SB337 $5.50 booklet containing pane of 10×55c. (No. 3293a) (basketball) .... 9·50

SB338 $5.50 booklet containing pane of 10×55c. (No. 3294a) (soccer) .... 9·50

SB339 $5.50 booklet containing pane of 10×55c. (No. 3295a) (netball) .... 9·50

SB340 $5.50 booklet containing pane of 10×55c. (No. 3296a) (cricket) .... 9·50

SB341 $5.50 booklet containing pane of 10×55c. (No. 3297a) (tennis) .... 9·50

B **168** 'COME TO THE SHOW' and Sun

B **169** Queen Elizabeth II leaving St. Andrew's Cathedral, Sydney, 2006

2010 (23 Mar). 'Come to the Show'. Multicoloured cover, 60×86 *mm*, as Type B **168**. Self-adhesive.

SB345 $5.50 booklet containing pane of 10×55c. (No. 3367a) .... 11·00

2010 (6 Apr). Queen's Birthday. Multicoloured cover, 60×85 *mm*, as Type B **169**. Self-adhesive.

SB346 $5.50 booklet containing pane of 10×55c. (No. 3373a) .... 13·50

B **170** Kokoda Trail

2010 (20 Apr). Kokoda. Multicoloured cover, 61×85 *mm,* as Type B **170**. Self-adhesive.

SB347 $5.50 booklet containing pane of 10×55c. (No. 3380b) .... 13·50

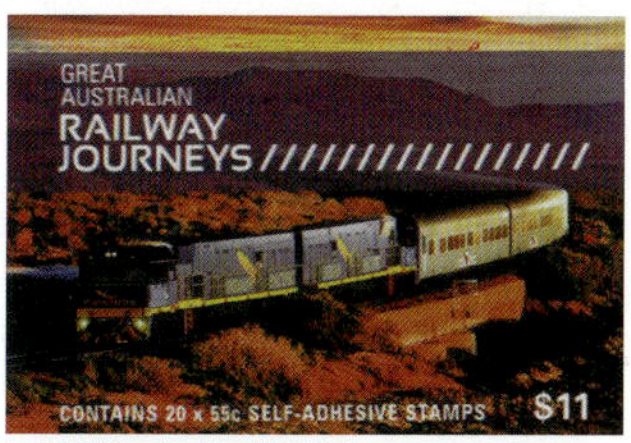

B **171** 'The Indian Pacific'

2010 (7 May). Great Australian Railway Journeys. Multicoloured cover as Type B **171**. Self-adhesive.

SB348 $11 booklet containing pane of 20×55c. (No. 3389b) .... 27·00

B **172** Gorge

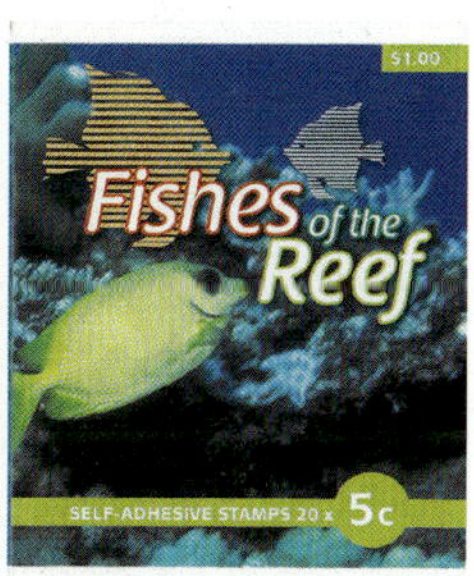

B **173** Coral Rabbitfish

2010 (25 May). Australian World Heritage. Multicoloured cover as Type B **172**. Self-adhesive.

SB349 $5.50 booklet containing pane of 10×55c. (No. 3405b) .... 12·00

2010 (21 June). Fishes of the Reef. Multicoloured covers as Type B **173**. Self-adhesive.

SB350 $1 booklet containing pane of 20×5c. (No. 3415a) (Type B **173**, 69×88 mm) .... 3·50

SB351 $6 booklet containing pane of ten 60c. (No. 3416a) (cover, 57×70 *mm,* showing coral reef, fish silhouettes and diver) .... 10·00

SB352 $12 booklet containing pane of twenty 60c. (No. 3416b) (cover, 68×87 *mm,* showing shoal of fish) .... 20·00

B **174** Tigger sitting in Bowl

2010 (29 June). 'Adopted and Adored'. Dogs. Multicoloured cover as Type B **174**. Self-adhesive.

SB353 $6 booklet containing pane of 10×60c. (No. 3436b) .... 17·00

B **175** 'EMERGENCY SERVICES 000'

2010 (13 July). Emergency Services. Multicoloured cover as Type B **175**. Self-adhesive.

SB354 $12 booklet containing pane of 20×60c. (No. 3445b) .... 35·00

B **176** White Tulips

2010 (19 July). Greetings Stamps. 'For Special Occasions'. Multicoloured covers, 61×85 *mm,* as Type B **176**. Self-adhesive.

SB355 $6 booklet containing pane of 10×60c. (No. 3459a) (cover Type B **176**) .... 10·00

SB356 $6 booklet containing pane of 10×60c. (No. 3460a) (cover showing stamp and red roses) .... 10·00

SB357 $6 booklet containing pane of 10×60c. (No. 3461a) (cover showing stamp, ribbons, crayons and foil stars) .... 10·00

SB358 $6 booklet containing pane of 10×60c. (No. 3462a) (cover showing stamp and teddy bear) .... 10·00

SB359 $6 booklet containing pane of 10×60c. (No. 3463a) (cover showing stamp, butterfly and daisies) .... 10·00

SB360 $12 booklet containing pane of 10×60c. (No. 3464a) (cover showing stamp and rings) ... 22·00

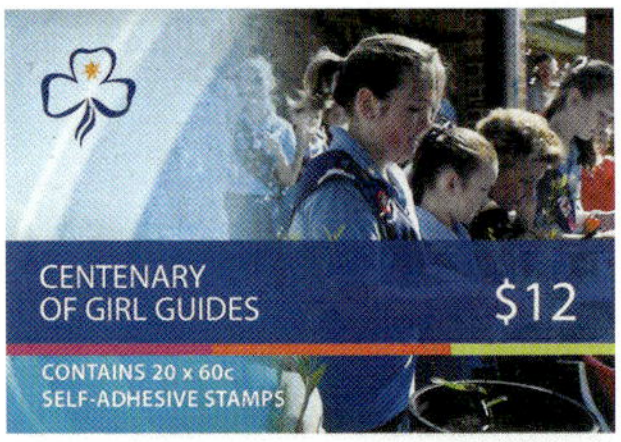

B **177** Girl Guides

2010 (31 Aug). Centenary of Girl Guides Australia. Multicoloured cover as Type B **177**. Self-adhesive.

SB361 $12 booklet containing pane of 20×60c. (No. 3477a) .... 25·00

B **178** National Service Memorial, Canberra

B **179** Boy with Skis and Man by Lakeside

2010 (8 Sept). National Service Memorial, Canberra. Multicoloured cover, 61×85 *mm*, as Type B **178**. Self-adhesive.

SB362 $6 booklet containing pane of 10×60c. (No. 3481a) .... 11·00

2010 (22 Sept). 'Long Weekend'. Multicoloured cover, 60×85 *mm*, as Type B **179**. Self-adhesive.

SB363 $6 booklet containing pane of 10×60c. (No. 3487b) .... 14·00

B **180** Grey-headed Flying Fox

B **181** Red-backed Kingfisher

2010 (5 Oct). Wildlife Caring: Rescue to Release. Multicoloured cover, 61×85 *mm*, as Type B **180**. Self-adhesive.

SB364 $6 booklet containing pane of 10×60c. (No. 3499b) .... 12·00

2010 (26 Oct). Australian Kingfishers. Multicoloured cover, 60×85 *mm*, as Type B **181**. Self-adhesive.

SB365 $6 booklet containing pane of 10×60c. (No. 3509a) .... 19·00

B **182** '150'

2010 (1 Nov). 150th Anniv of Melbourne Cup Horse Race. Multicoloured cover, 82×60 *mm* (folded), as Type B **182**. Self-adhesive.

SB366 $12 booklet containing pane of 20×60c. (No. 3515a) .... 35·00

B **183** Santa reading Letter

2010 (1 Nov). Christmas (1st issue). 'Dear Santa'. Multicoloured cover, 82×60 *mm* (folded), as Type B **183**. Self-adhesive.

SB367 $11 booklet containing pane of 20×55c. with twenty 'Card Only' labels (No. 3520a) .... 19·00

B **184** Stars

2010 (1 Nov). Christmas (2nd issue). Multicoloured cover, 82×60 *mm* (folded), as Type B **184**. Self-adhesive.

SB368 $11 booklet containing pane of 20×55c. with twenty 'CARD ONLY' labels (No. 3526a) .... 21·00

B **185** 'LOVE' and Red Roses

2011 (18 Jan). Greetings Stamps. Special Occasions. 'LOVE'. Multicoloured covers, 60×85 *mm*, as Type B **185**. Self-adhesive.

SB369 $6 booklet containing pane of 10×60c. (No. 3530a) (cover Type B **185**) .... 11·00

SB370 $6 booklet containing pane of 10×60c. (No. 3531a) (cover showing pattern of hearts, flowers and vine leaves) .... 11·00

SB371 $6 booklet containing pane of 10×60c. (No. 3532a) (cover showing champagne glasses and bottle) .... 11·00

B **186** 'ADVANCING EQUALITY'

2011 (20 Jan). Australian Legends. 'Advancing Equality'. Multicoloured cover, 82×60 *mm* folded, as Type B **186**. Self-adhesive.
SB372 $6 booklet containing pane of 10×60c. (No. 3537a) .... 11·00

B **187** F-111 ('Pig')

2011 (22 Feb). Royal Australian Air Force (RAAF) Aviation. Multicoloured cover, 61×85 *mm*, as Type B **187**. Self-adhesive.
SB373 $6 booklet containing pane of 10×60c. (No. 3557a) .... 18·00

B **188** Tulip

2011 (8 Mar). Floral Festivals Australia. Multicoloured cover, 82×59 *mm* folded, as Type B **188**. Self-adhesive.
SB374 $12 booklet containing pane of 20×60c. (No. 3564b) .... 25·00

B **189** Stamps (Nos. 3575 and 3578)

B **190** 'Royal Wedding

2011 (22 Mar). The Gallery Series. National Gallery of Victoria: Flowers (1st series). Multicoloured cover, 61×85 *mm*, as Type B **189**. Self-adhesive.
SB375 $6 booklet containing pane of 10×60c. (No. 3574b) .... 12·00

2011 (12 Apr). Royal Wedding (1st issue). Gold and cream cover, 62×85 *mm*, as Type B **190**. Self-adhesive.
SB376 $6 booklet containing pane of 10×60c. (No. 3591a) .... 19·00

B **191** 'Royal Wedding'

2011 (4 May). Royal Wedding (2nd issue). Gold, pale grey and cream cover, 77×77 *mm*, as Type B **191**. Self-adhesive.
SB377 $6 booklet containing pane of 10×60c. (No. 3593a) .... 19·00

B **192** Dame Nellie Melba

2011 (10 May). 150th Birth Anniv of Dame Nellie Melba (soprano). Multicoloured cover, 83×60 *mm* folded, as Type B **192**. Self-adhesive.
SB378 $12 booklet containing pane of 20×60c. (No. 3595a) .... 38·00

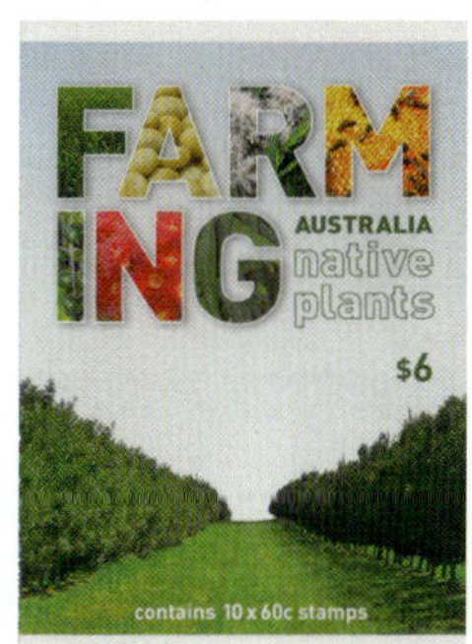

B **193** Plantation

2011 (17 May). Farming Australia: Native Plants. Multicoloured cover, 60×85 *mm*, as Type B **193**. Self-adhesive.
SB379 $6 booklet containing pane of 10×60c. (No. 3600b) .... 17·00

B **194** HMAS *Sydney* (IV)

2011 (14 June). Centenary of Royal Australian Navy. Multicoloured cover, 83×60 *mm* folded, as Type B **194**. Self-adhesive.
SB380 $12 booklet containing pane of 20×60c. (No. 3606a) .... 42·00

B **195** Two Girls

B **196** Golf Course

2011 (5 July). 'Living Australian'. Multicoloured cover, 60×85 *mm*, as Type B **195**. Self-adhesive.

SB381 $6 booklet containing pane of 10×60c. (No. 3620b) .... 17·00

2011 (27 Sept). Golf. Multicoloured cover, 60×85 *mm*, as Type B **196**. Self-adhesive.

SB382 $6 booklet containing pane of 10×60c. (No. 3647b) .... 19·00

B **197** Griffin, Dragon, Unicorn, Fairy, Mermaid and Troll

2011 (4 Oct). Stamp Collecting Month. Mythical Creatures. Multicoloured cover as Type B **197**. Self-adhesive.

SB383 $6 booklet containing pane of 10×60c. (No. 3659a) (cover Type B **197** 60×85 mm) .... 11·00

SB384 $12 booklet containing pane of 20×60c. (No. 3659b) (cover 82×60 *mm* folded) .... 22·00

B **198** Holy Family

2011 (31 Oct). Christmas (1st issue). Multicoloured cover, 82×59 *mm* (folded), as Type B **198**. Self-adhesive.

SB385 $11 booklet containing pane of 20×55c. with twenty 'Card Only' labels (No. 3670a) .... 22·00

B **199** Christmas Decorations

2011 (31 Oct). Christmas. Multicoloured cover, 82×60 *mm* (folded), as Type B **199**. Self-adhesive.

SB386 $11 booklet containing pane of 20×55c. with twenty 'Card Only' labels (No. 3675a) .... 22·00

B **200** Poppy and Bugler

B **201**

2011 (2 Nov). Remembrance Day. Multicoloured cover, 60×85 *mm*, as Type B **200** . Self-adhesive.

SB387 $6 booklet containing pane of 10×60c. (No. 3682a) .... 12·00

2012 (17 Jan). Greetings. Stamps. 'Precious Moments'. Multicoloured covers, 61×85 *mm*, as Type B **201**. Self-adhesive.

SB388 $6 booklet containing pane of 10×60c. (No. 3692a) (cover Type B **201**) .... 15·00

SB389 $6 booklet containing pane of 10×60c. (No. 3693a) (cover showing teddy bear and stars) .... 15·00

SB390 $6 booklet containing pane of 10×60c. (No. 3694a) (cover showing balloons) ... 15·00

SB391 $6 booklet containing pane of 10×60c. (No. 3695a) (cover showing hearts) .... 15·00

SB392 $6 booklet containing pane of 10×60c. (No. 3696a) (cover showing love birds and flowering tree branch) .... 15·00

B **202** Ron Barassi

2012 (20 Jan). Australian Legends. Legends of Football. Multicoloured covers, 61×86 *mm*, as Type B **202**. Self-adhesive.

SB393 $6 booklet containing pane of 10×60c. (No. 3705a) (cover Type B **202**) .... 11·00

SB394 $6 booklet containing pane of 10×60c. (No. 3706a) (Gary Ablett) .... 11·00

SB395 $6 booklet containing pane of 10×60c. (No. 3707a) (John Raper) .... 11·00

SB396 $6 booklet containing pane of 10×60c. (No. 3708a) (Billy Slater) .... 11·00

SB397 $6 booklet containing pane of 10×60c. (No. 3709a) (David Campese) .... 11·00

SB398 $6 booklet containing pane of 10×60c. (No. 3710a) (David Pocock) .... 11·00

SB399 $6 booklet containing pane of 10×60c. (No. 3711a) (Joe Marston) .... 11·00

SB400 $6 booklet containing pane of 10×60c. (No. 3712a) (Mark Schwarzer) .... 11·00

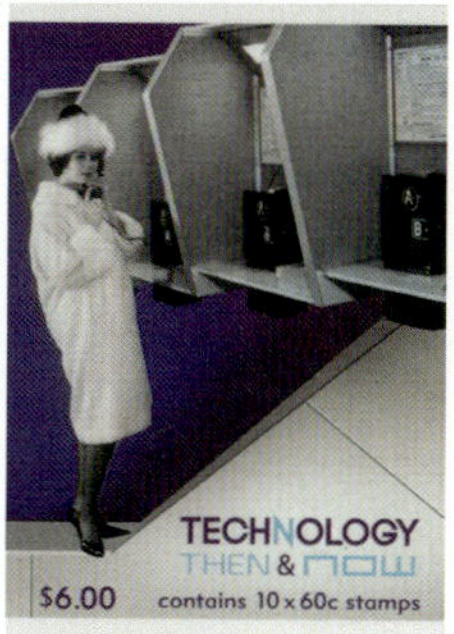

B **203** Telephone

2012 (7 Feb). Technology—Then and Now. Multicoloured cover, 60×85 *mm*, as Type B **203**. Self-adhesive.
SB401 $6 booklet containing pane of 10×60c. (No. 3719b) .... 17·00

B **204** *Charlotte* (ferry) passing Luna Park, Sydney

2012 (21 Feb). City Transport. Multicoloured cover, 82×60 *mm* folded, as Type B **204**. Self-adhesive.
SB402 $12 booklet containing pane of 20×60c. (No. 3729a) .... 30·00

B **205** Radjah Shelduck

B **206** Hat bearing Rising Sun Badge

2012 (6 Mar). Australian Waterbirds. Multicoloured cover, 61×86 *mm*, as Type B **205**. Self-adhesive.
SB403 $6 booklet containing pane of 10×60c. (No. 3738b) .... 21·00

2012 (17 Apr). Rising Sun Badge [(Australian Army General Service badge).] Multicoloured cover, 61×86 *mm*, as Type B **206**. Self-adhesive.
SB404 $6 booklet containing pane of 10×60c. (No. 3776a) .... 17·00

B **207** Coral Reef

2012 (8 May). Underwater World. Nudibranchs. Multicoloured cover, 82×60 *mm* (folded), as Type B **207**. Self-adhesive.
SB405 $20 booklet containing pane of 20×60c. (No. 3788a) .... 30·00

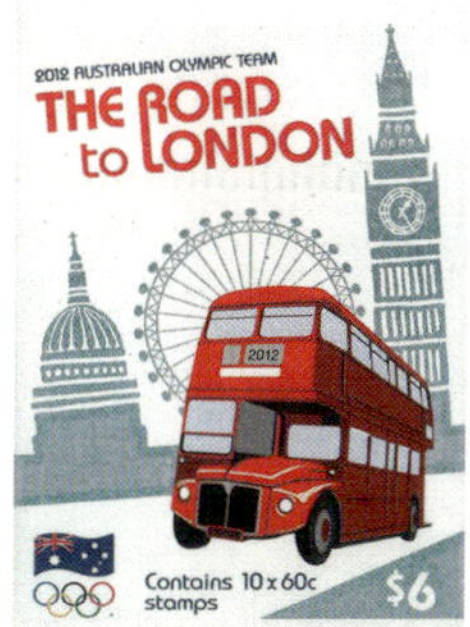

B **208** Double-decker Bus, St. Paul's Cathedral, the London Eye and Big Ben

B **209** Oranges

2012 (5 Jun). Olympic Games. The Road to London. Multicoloured cover, 60×85 *mm*, as Type B **208**. Self-adhesive.
SB406 $6 booklet containing pane of 10×60c. (No. 3792a) .... 16·00

2012 (26 Jun). Farming Australia. Multicoloured covers as Type B **209**. Self-adhesive.
SB407 $6 booklet containing pane of 10×60c. (No. 3751a) (Type B 209) (59×69 *mm*)... 13·00
SB408 $12 booklet containing pane of 20×60c. (No. 3751b) (beef cattle) (67×88 *mm*) ... 22·00

B **210** Photos of Beach Huts and Shore with Sea Stacks

2012 (24 July). Living Australian (2nd issue). Multicoloured cover, 83×60 *mm* (folded), as Type B **210**. Self-adhesive.
SB409 $12 booklet containing pane of 20×60c. (No. 3815a) .... 27·00

B **211** Medal

2012 (28 Aug). Australian Nobel Prize Winners. Gold, green and black cover, 60×86 *mm*, as Type B **211**. Self-adhesive.
SB410 $6 booklet containing pane of 10×60c. (No. 3832b) .... 13·00

B **212** Car arriving at Port Arthur

2012 (18 Sept). Road Trip Australia. Multicoloured cover , 77×78 *mm*, as Type B **212**. Self-adhesive.

SB411 $6 booklet containing pane of 10×60c. (No. 3843a) .... 15·00

B **213** Giraffe

2012 (28 Sept). Stamp Collecting Month. Australian Zoos. Multicoloured cover, 82×60 *mm* (folded), as Type B **213**. Self-adhesive.

SB412 $12 booklet containing pane of 20×60c. (No. 3861b) .... 26·00

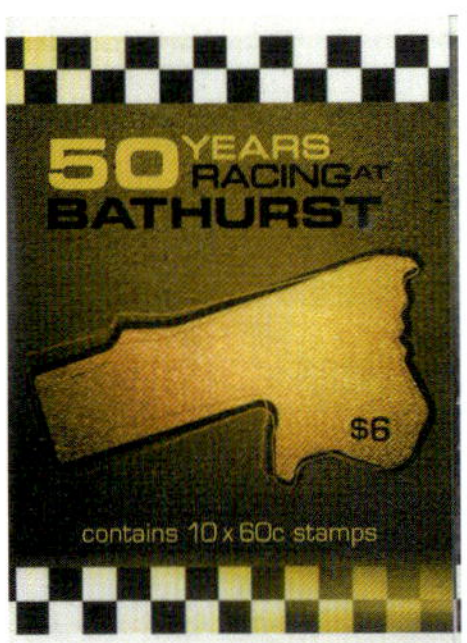

B **214** Outline of Mount Panorama Track

2012 (2 Oct). 50th Anniv (2013) of Bathurst Endurance Race (touring car race). Multicoloured cover, 61×85 *mm*, as Type B **214**. Self-adhesive.

SB413 $6 booklet containing pane of 10×60c. (No. 3872a) .... 13·00-

B **215** Holly Leaves and Snowflakes

2012 (1 Nov). Christmas (1st issue). Red and gold cover, 82×60 *mm* (folded), as Type B **215**. Self-adhesive.

SB414 $11 booklet containing pane of 20×55c. with twenty 'Card Only' labels (No. 3884a) .... 22·00

B **216** Reindeer, Trees and Stars

2012 (1 Nov). Christmas (2nd issue). Multicoloured cover, 82×60 *mm* (folded), as Type B **216**. Self-adhesive.

SB415 $11 booklet containing pane of 20×55c. with twenty 'Card Only' labels (No. 3889a) .... 22·00

B **217** Paul Kelly

2013 (18 Jan). Australian Legends. Legends of Music. Multicoloured covers, 61×86 *mm*, as Type B **217**. Self-adhesive.

SB416 $6 booklet containing pane of 10×60c. (No. 3907a) (cover Type B 217) .... 13·00

SB417 $6 booklet containing pane of 10×60c. (No. 3908a) (INXS) .... 13·00

SB418 $6 booklet containing pane of 10×60c. (No. 3909a) (Kylie Minogue) .... 13·00

SB419 $6 booklet containing pane of 10×60c. (No. 3910a) (Ian "Molly" Meldrum) .... 13·00

SB420 $6 booklet containing pane of 10×60c. (No. 3911a) (Olivia Newton-John) .... 13·00

SB421 $6 booklet containing pane of 10×60c. (No. 3912a) (John Farnham) .... 13·00

SB422 $6 booklet containing pane of 10×60c. (No. 3913a) (AC/DC) .... 13·00

SB423 $6 booklet containing pane of 10×60c. (No. 3914a) (Cold Chisel) .... 13·00

SB424 $6 booklet containing pane of 10×60c. (No. 3915a) (Men at Work) .... 13·00

SB425 $6 booklet containing pane of 10×60c. (No. 3916a) (The Seekers) .... 13·00

B **218** Sprig of Eucalyptus Leaves ('Nature')

B **219** Surfer

2013 (5 Feb). Greetings Stamps. Special Occasions. Multicoloured covers, 60×85 *mm*, as Type B **218**. Self-adhesive.

SB426 $6 booklet containing pane of 10×60c. (No. 3923a) (Type B 218) .... 15·00

SB427 $6 booklet containing pane of 10×60c. (No. 3924a) ('AUSTRALIA') .... 15·00

SB428 $6] booklet containing pane of 10×60c. (No. 3926a) ('LOVE') .... 15·00

SB429 $6 booklet containing pane of 10×60c. (No. 3927a) ('ORCHID') ... 15·00
SB430 $12 booklet containing pane of 10×$1. .20 (No. 3928a) ('CELEBRATION') ... 23·00

2013 (12 Feb). 50th Anniv of Surfing Australia. Multicoloured cover, 60×86 *mm,* as Type B **219**. Self-adhesive.
SB431 $6 booklet containing pane of 10×60c. (No. 3934b) ... 15·00

B **220** Miniature Schnauzer

2013 (19 Feb). Top Dogs. Multicoloured covers, 60×85 *mm,* as Type B **220**. Self-adhesive.
SB432 $6 booklet containing pane of 10×60c. (No. 3943a) (Type B 220) ... 17·00
SB433 $6 booklet containing pane of 10×60c. (No. 3944a) (Miniature Dachshund) ... 17·00
SB434 $6 booklet containing pane of 10×60c. (No. 3945a) (Cavalier King Charles Spaniel) ... 17·00
SB435 $6 booklet containing pane of 10×60c. (No. 3946a) (Pug) ... 17·00
SB436 $6 booklet containing pane of 10×60c. (No. 3947a) (Australian Terrier) ... 17·00

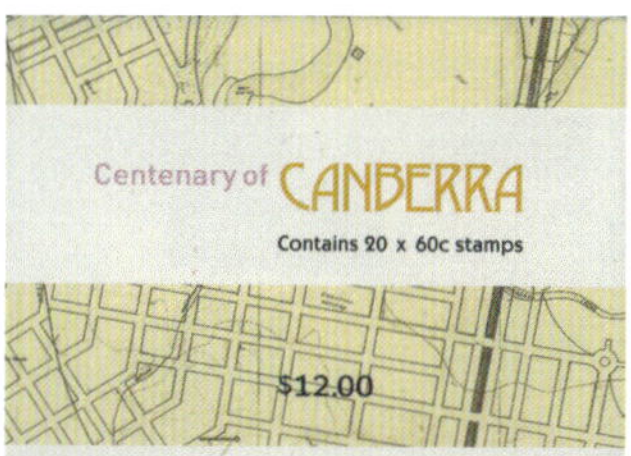

B **221** Plans for Canberra, *c.* 1913

2013 (5 Mar). Centenary of Canberra. Multicoloured cover, 83×60 *mm* (folded) as Type B **221**. Self-adhesive.
SB437 $12 booklet containing pane of 20×60c. (No. 3950a) ... 25·00

B **222** Land of the Golden Fleece and Flinders – Far North Stamps

B **223** Caviar

2013 (19 Mar). The Gallery Series. National Gallery of Australia. Landscape Paintings. Multicoloured cover, 60×86 *mm,* as Type B **222**. Self-adhesive.
SB438 $6 booklet containing pane of 10×60c. (No. 3956a) ... 12·00

2013 (10 May). Black Caviar (racehorse). Multicoloured cover, 60×85 *mm,* as Type B **223**. Self-adhesive.
SB439 $6 booklet containing pane of 10×60c. (No. 3988a) ... 17·00

B **224**

2013 (11 Jun). Historical Architecture. Government Houses. Multicoloured cover, 82×60 *mm* folded, as Type B **224**. Self-adhesive.
SB440 $12 booklet containing pane of 20×60c. (No. 4002b) ... 20·00

B **225** Car laden with Canoe, Melbourne

2013 (2 July). Road Trip Australia (2nd issue). Multicoloured covers as Type B **225**. Self-adhesive.
SB441 $6 booklet containing pane of 10×60c. (No. 4012a) (cover Type B **225**, 78×78 *mm*) ... 10·00
SB442 $12 booklet containing pane of 20×60c. (No. 4014a) (cover showing car and caravan at Adelaide carnival, 78×78 *mm* folded) ... 18·00

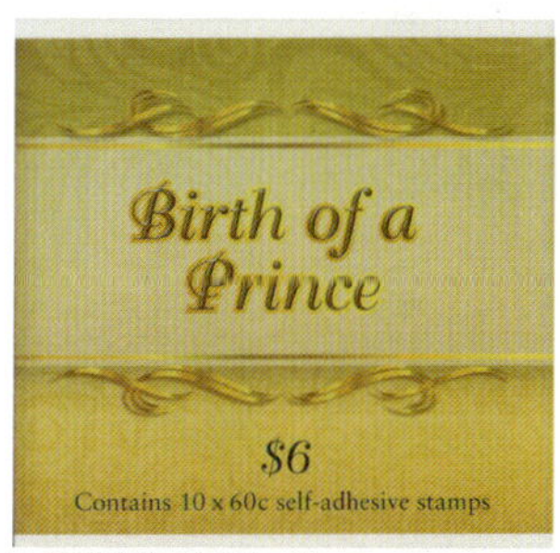

B **226** 'Birth of a Prince'

2013 (22 July). Birth of Prince George of Cambridge. Multicoloured cover, 78×77 *mm,* as Type B **226**. Self-adhesive.
SB443 $6 booklet containing pane of 10×60c. (No. 4028a) ... 17·00

B **227** 'Headline News'

2013 (23 July). Headline News. Multicoloured cover, 82×60 *mm* folded, as Type B **227**. Self-adhesive.

SB444 $12 booklet containing pane of 10×60c. (No. 4034b) .... 22·00

B **228** *Cephalotus follicularis* and Grasshopper

2013 (13 Aug). Carnivorous Plants. Multicoloured cover, 60×85 *mm*, as Type B **228**. Self-adhesive.

SB445 $6 booklet containing pane of 10×60c. (No. 4043a) .... 10·00

B **229** Coral Reef

2013 (20 Aug). Coral Reefs. Multicoloured cover, 109×70 *mm* folded, as Type B **229**. Self-adhesive.

SB446 $12 booklet containing pane of 20×60c. (No. 4052a) .... 15·00

B **230** Australorp

B **231** Diamantinasaurus

2013 (3 Sept). Australian Poultry Breeds. Multicoloured cover, 60×85 *mm*, as Type B **230**. Self-adhesive.

SB447 $6 booklet containing pane of 10×60c. (No. 4060a) .... 7·00

2013 (24 Sept). Australia's Age of the Dinosaurs. Multicoloured covers as Type B **231**. Self-adhesive.

SB448 $6 booklet containing pane of 10×60c. (No. 4068a) (Type B **231**, 58×69 *mm*) .... 11·00

SB449 $12 booklet containing pane of 20×60c. (No. 4070a) (cover 83×60 *mm* folded, showing Serendipaceratops, Australovenator and the monotreme *Kryoryctes*) .... 15·00

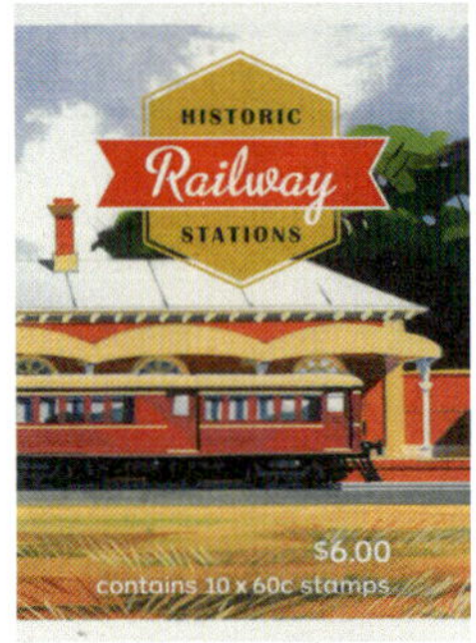

B **232** Hoey Railway station NSW

2013 (8 Oct). Historic Railway Stations. Multicoloured cover, 60×86 *mm*, as Type B **232**. Self-adhesive.

SB450 $6 booklet containing pane of 10×60c. (No. 4076b) .... 13·00

B **233** Nativity

2013 (1 Nov). Christmas. Multicoloured cover, 82×59 *mm* (folded), as Type B **233**. Self-adhesive.

SB451 $11 booklet containing pane of 20×60c. with twenty 'Card Only' labels (No. 4088a) .... 13·00

B **234** 'Merry Christmas'

2013 (1 Nov). Christmas (2nd issue). Multicoloured cover, 82×60 *mm* (folded), as Type B **234**. Self-adhesive.

SB452 $11 booklet containing pane of 20×55c. with twenty 'Card Only' labels (No. 4094a) .... 13·00

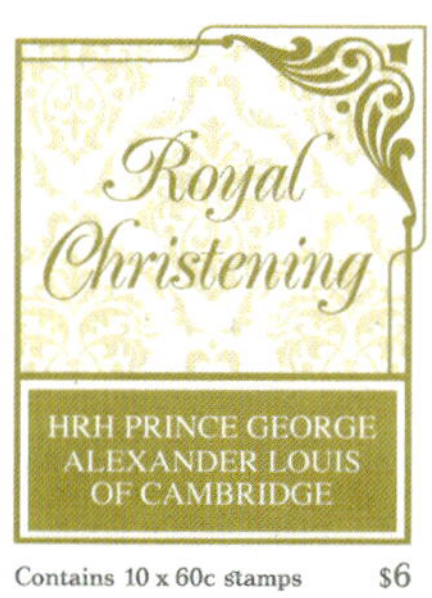

B **235** 'Royal Christening'

B **236** Golden Rock, Bee, Orange Blossom and Shirt Orchids

2014 (7 Jan). Royal Christening. Gold and grey-black cover, 61×85 *mm*, as Type B **235**. Self-adhesive.

SB453 $6 booklet containing pane of 10×60c. (No. 4102a) .... 11·00

2014 (14 Jan). Native Orchids. Multicoloured covers as Type B **236**. Self-adhesive.

SB454 $6 booklet containing pane of 10×60c. (No. 4108a) (60×86 *mm*, Type B **236**) ..... 9·00
SB455 $12 booklet containing pane of 20×60c. (No. 4108b) (cover 82×60 *mm* showing shirt orchid) ..... 16·00

B **237** Margaret Fulton

2014 (17 Jan). Australian Legends. Legends of Cooking. Multicoloured cover, 60×85 *mm*, as Type B **237**. Self-adhesive.

SB456 $6 booklet containing pane of 10×60c. (No. 4117a) (Type B **237**) ..... 7·50
SB457 $6 booklet containing pane of 10×60c. (No. 4118a) (Maggie Beer) ..... 7·50
SB458 $6 booklet containing pane of 10×60c. (No. 4119a) (Stephanie Alexander) ..... 7·50
SB459 $6 booklet containing pane of 10×60c. (No. 4120a) (Neil Perry) ..... 7·50
SB460 $6 booklet containing pane of 10×60c. (No. 4121a) (Kylie Kwong) ..... 7·50

B **238** The Ashes Urn

2014 (20 Jan). The Urn Returns (Australia's Victory in 2013/14 Ashes Series). Multicoloured cover, 82×59 *mm*, as Type B **238**. Self-adhesive.

SB461 $13 booklet containing pane of 5×$2.60 (No. 4125a) ..... 19·00

B **239** Pattern of Hearts

B **240** Tasmanian Blue Gum and Golden Wattle

2014 (4 Feb). Greetings Stamps. Romance. Multicoloured covers as Type B **239**. Self-adhesive.

SB462 $6 booklet containing pane of 10×60c. (No. 4128a) (cover Type B **239**, 60×86 *mm*) ..... 8·00
SB463 $12 booklet containing pane of 20×60c. (cover 82×60 *mm* showing roses, hearts and pink rose in heart) ..... 16·00

2014 (24 Mar). Floral Emblems. Multicoloured covers as Type B **240**. Self-adhesive.

SB464 $7 booklet containing pane of 10×60c. (No. 4137a) (cover Type B **240**, 58×69 *mm*) ..... 9·50
SB465 $14 booklet containing pane of 20×60c. (No. 4137b) (cover showing Waratah, 68×87 *mm*) ..... 18·00

B **241** Balloons

2014 (15 Apr). Greetings Stamps. Special Occasions. Multicoloured covers, 60×86 *mm*, as Type B **241**. Self-adhesive.

SB466 $7 booklet containing pane of 10×70c. (No. 4155a) (Type B **241**) ..... 9·50
SB467 $7 booklet containing pane of 10×70c. (No. 4156a) (baby mobile) ..... 9·50
SB468 $7 booklet containing pane of 10×70c. (No. 4157a) (fireworks) ..... 9·50
SB469 $7 booklet containing pane of 10×70c. (No. 4158a) (red rose) ..... 9·50
SB470 $7 booklet containing pane of 10×70c. (No. 4159a) (heart-shaped flowers) ..... 9·50
SB471 $7 booklet containing pane of 10×70c. (No. 4160a) (champagne glasses) ..... 9·50
SB472 $7 booklet containing pane of 10×70c. (No. 4161a) (silver wedding rings and white roses) ..... 9·50

B **242** Australian Troops

B **243** Mulga Bill's Bicycle

2014 (22 Apr). Centenary of World War I (1st issue). 1914, Multicoloured cover, 78×77 *mm*, as Type B **242**. Self-adhesive.

SB473 $7 booklet containing pane of 10×70c. (No. 4168a) ..... 12·50

2014 (13 May). Bush Ballads by A. B. 'Banjo' Paterson. Multicoloured cover, 61×85 *mm*, as Type B **243**. Self-adhesive.

SB474 $7 booklet containing pane of 10×70c. (No. 4180b) ..... 9·50

B **244** Daffodils

B **245** Pony Club

2014 (8 July). Royal Visit. Multicoloured cover, 78×77 *mm,* as Type B **244**. Self-adhesive.
SB475 $7 booklet containing pane of 10×70c. (No. 4196a) .... 12·50

1914 (15 July). Equestrian Events. Multicoloured covers, 60×85 *mm,* as Type B **245**. Self-adhesive.
SB476 $7 booklet containing pane of 10×70c. (No. 4203b) (Type B 245) .... 12·50
SB477 $7 booklet containing pane of 10×70c. (No. 4204b) (Polocrosse) .... 12·50
SB478 $7 booklet containing pane of 10×70c. (No. 4205b) (Showjumping) .... 12·50
SB479 $7 booklet containing pane of 10×70c. (No. 4206b) (Cross-country) .... 12·50
SB480 $7 booklet containing pane of 10×70c. (No. 4207b) (Dressage) .... 12·50

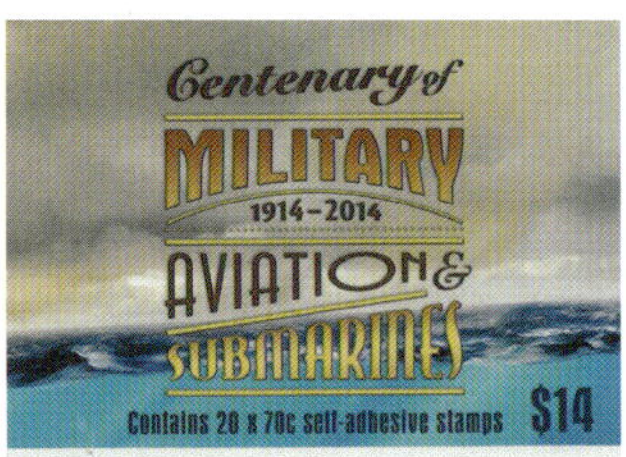

B **246** Sea and Sky

2014 (5 Aug). Centenary of Military Aviation and Submarines. Multicoloured cover, 82×60 *mm* folded, as Type B **246**. Self-adhesive.
SB481 $14 booklet containing pane of 20×70c. (No. 4213a) .... 25·00

B **247** Southern Lights

2014 (26 Aug). Southern Lights. Multicoloured cover, 60×85 *mm,* as Type B **247**. Self-adhesive.
SB482 $7 booklet containing pane of 10×70c. (No. 4231a) .... 13·00

B **248** Footbridge in Garden

2014 (2 Sept). Open Gardens. Multicoloured cover, 82×60 *mm,* as Type B **248**. Self-adhesive.
SB483 $14 booklet containing pane of 20×70c. (No. 4238a) .... 25·00

B **249** Wasp

B **250** Racecourse

2014 (23 Sept). Stamp Collecting Month. Things that Sting. Multicoloured covers as Type B **249**. Self-adhesive.
SB484 $7 booklet containing pane of 10×70c. (No. 4250a) (Type B 249, 60×85 *mm*) .... 13·00
SB485 $14 booklet containing pane of 20×70c. (No. 4250b) (Stingray, 83×60 *mm*) .... 25·00

2014 (7 Oct). Australian Racecourses. Multicoloured cover, 60×85 *mm,* as Type B **250**. Self-adhesive.
SB486 $7 booklet containing pane of 10×70c. (No. 4266b) .... 13·00

B **251** Australian Defence Force

2014 (21 Oct). Centenary of the Australian Defence Force. Multicoloured covers, 79×78 *mm,* as Type B **251**. Self-adhesive.
SB487 $7 booklet containing pane of 10×70c. (No. 4275a) .... 13·00

B **252** Virgin Mary and Christ Child

2014 (31 Oct). Christmas (1st issue). Stained-glass Windows, St. Patrick's Cathedral, Melbourne. Multicoloured cover, 82×59 *mm* (folded), as Type B **252**. Self-adhesive.

SB488 $13 booklet containing pane of 20×65c. with twenty 'Card Only' labels (No. 4282a) .... 22·00

B **253** Christmas Gift

2014 (31 Oct). Christmas (2nd issue). Multicoloured cover, 82×60 *mm* (folded), as Type B **253**. Self-adhesive.

SB489 $13 booklet containing pane of 20×65c. with twenty 'Card Only' labels (No. 4288a) .... 11·00

B **254** Koala

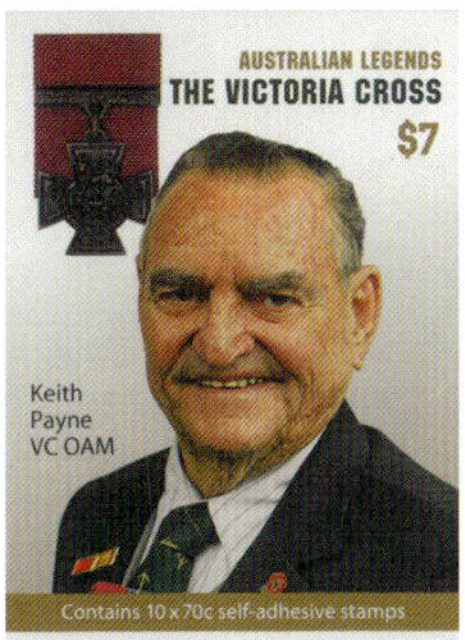

B **255** Keith Payne

2015 (13 Jan). Native Animals. Multicoloured covers as Type B **254**. Self-adhesive.

SB490 $7 booklet containing pane of 10×70c. (No. 4300a) (61×85 *mm*, Type B 254) .... 13·00

SB491 $14 booklet containing pane of 20×70c. (No. 4300b) (cover 82×60 *mm* folded showing Eastern Grey Kangaroo) .... 25·00

2015 (22 Jan). Australian Legends. The Victoria Cross. Multicoloured covers, 60×85 *mm*, as Type B **255**. Self-adhesive.

SB492 $7 booklet containing pane of 10×70c. (No. 4310a) (cover Type B 255) .... 13·00

SB493 $7 booklet containing pane of 10×70c. (No. 4311a) (Mark Donaldson) .... 13·00

SB494 $7 booklet containing pane of 10×70c. (No. 4312a) (Ben Roberts-Smith) .... 13·00

SB495 $7 booklet containing pane of 10×70c. (No. 4313a) (Dan Keighran) .... 13·00

SB496 $7 booklet containing pane of 10×70c. (No. 4314a) (Cameron Baird) .... 13·00

B **256** Aircraft leaving Heart-shaped Vapour Trail

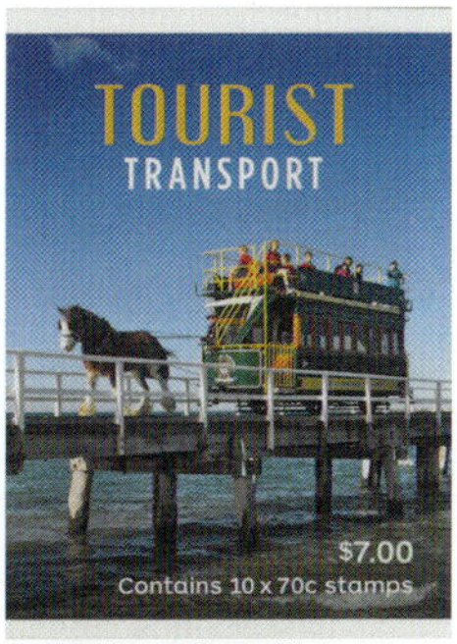

B **257** Horse-drawn Tram

2015 (3 Feb). Greetings Stamps. 'Love is in the Air'. Multicoloured covers, 61×86 *mm*, as Type B **256**. Self-adhesive.

SB497 $7 booklet containing pane of 10×70c. (No. 4320a) (Type B 256) .... 13·00

SB498 $14 booklet containing pane of 20×70c. (No. 4320b) (82×60 *mm* folded, Heart-shaped kite) .... 25·00

2015 (3 Mar). Tourist Transport. Multicoloured cover, 60×85 *mm*, as Type B **257**. Self-adhesive.

SB499 $7 booklet containing pane of 10×70c. (No. 4332b) .... 13·00

B **258** Bugler and Golden Wattle, Anzac Cove

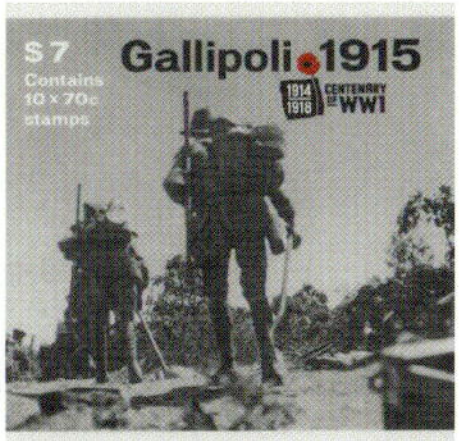

B **259** Anzacs head to Plugge's Plateau, 25 April 1915

2015 (7 Apr). ANZAC Centenary. Multicoloured cover, 60×85 *mm*, as Type B **258**. Self-adhesive.

SB500 $7 booklet containing pane of 10×70c. (No. 4348a) .... 10·00

2015 (14 Apr). Centenary of World War I (2nd issue). Gallipoli Campaign. Grey, black and red cover, 78×77 *mm*, as Type B **259**. Self-adhesive.

SB501 $7 booklet containing pane of 10×70c. (No. 4356a) .... 10·00

B **260** Charo

B **261** Shore of Lagoon, Lady Musgrave Island, Queensland

2015 (5 May). Cats. Multicoloured covers, 60×85 *mm*, as Type B **260**. Self-adhesive.

SB502 $7 booklet containing pane of 10×70c. (No. 4367b) (Type B 260) .... 10·00

SB503 $7 booklet containing pane of 10×70c. (No. 4368b) (Briony) .... 10·00

SB504 $7 booklet containing pane of 10×70c. (No. 4369b) (Cato) .... 10·00

SB505 $7 booklet containing pane of 10×70c. (No. 4370b) (Sweetie) .... 10·00

SB506 $7 booklet containing pane of 10×70c. (No. 4371b) (Bubu) .... 10·00

2015 (2 June). Islands of Australia. Multicoloured cover, 61×86 *mm*, as Type B **261**. Self-adhesive.

SB507 $7 booklet containing pane of 10×70c. (No. 4385a) .... 10·00

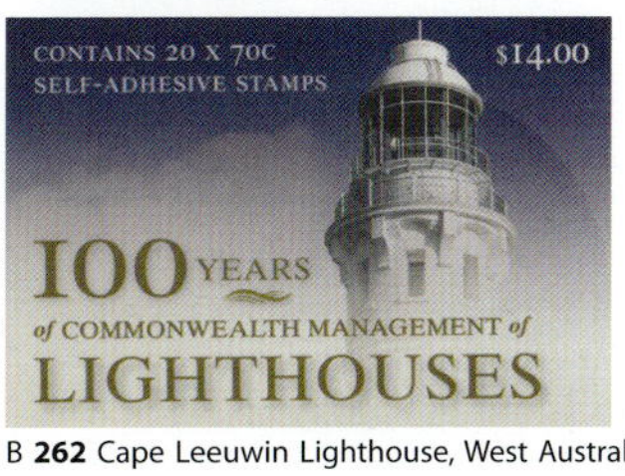

B **262** Cape Leeuwin Lighthouse, West Australia

2015 (7 July). Centenary of Commonwealth Management of Lighthouses. Multicoloured cover, 82×60 *mm* (folded) as Type B **262**. Self-adhesive.
SB508 $14 booklet containing pane of 20×70c. (No. 4392b) .... 10·00

B **263** Trail and Lakes

2015 (14 July). Great Australian Walks. Multicoloured cover, 60×85 *mm*, as Type B **263**. Self-adhesive.
SB509 $7 booklet containing pane of 10×70c. (No. 4401b) .... 10·00

B **264** Emblem

2015 (4 Aug). Netball World Cup, Sydney. Multicoloured cover, 83×59 *mm*, as Type B **264**. Self-adhesive.
SB510 $14 booklet containing pane of 20×70c. (No. 4406a) .... 20·00

B **265** Birth of Princess Charlotte

B **266** Neon Tubes

2015 (25 Aug). Birth of Princess Charlotte. Multicoloured cover, 77×77 *mm*, as Type B **265**. Self-adhesive.
SB511 $7 booklet containing pane of 10×70c. (No. 4418a) .... 20·00

2015 (1 Sept). Signs of the Times (historic neon signs). Multicoloured cover, 60×85 *mm*, as Type B **266**. Self-adhesive.
SB512 $7 booklet containing pane of 10×70c. (No. 4423b) .... 10·00

B **267** Neptune and Pluto

B **268** 'Mother Teresa' Seal

2015 (22 Sept). Stamp Collecting Month. Our Solar System. Multicoloured covers as Type B **267**. Self-adhesive.
SB513 $7 booklet containing pane of 10×70c. (No. 4442a) (Type B 267) (60×85 *mm*) .... 10·00
SB514 $14 booklet containing pane of 20×70c. (No. 4444a) (Earth, 82×118 *mm* folded) .... 20·00

2015 (5 Oct). Honoured by Australia. Multicoloured covers, 60×85 *mm*, as Type B **268**. Self-adhesive.
SB515 $7 booklet containing pane of 10×70c. (No. 4450a) (Type B 268) .... 10·00
SB516 $7 booklet containing pane of 10×70c. (No. 4451a) (Nelson Mandela) .... 10·00
SB517 $7 booklet containing pane of 10×70c. (No. 4452a) (Raoul Wallenberg) .... 10·00

B **269** Penny-farthing Bicycle

B **270** Soldier with Mule

2015 (13 Oct). Bicycles. Multicoloured cover, 76×77 *mm* folded, as Type B **269**. Self-adhesive.
SB518 $14 booklet containing pane of 20×70c. (No. 4457a) .... 20·00

2015 (27 Oct). Animals in War A Century of Service. Multicoloured cover, 77×77 *mm*, as Type B **270**. Self-adhesive.
SB519 $7 booklet containing pane of 10×70c. (No. 4466a) .... 10·00

B **271** Nativity

2015 (30 Oct). Christmas (1st issue). Multicoloured cover, 83×62 *mm* (folded), as Type B **271**. Self-adhesive.
SB520 $13 booklet containing pane of 20×65c. (No. 4474a) with twenty 'Card Only' labels .... 18·00

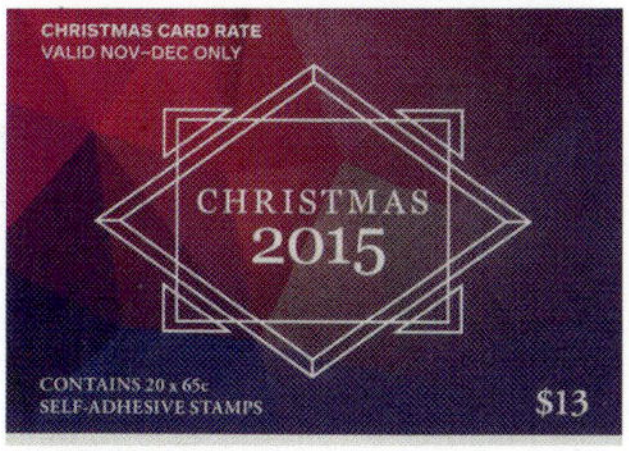

B **272** Christmas

2015 (30 Oct). Christmas (2nd issue). Multicoloured cover, 82×62 *mm* (folded), as Type B **272**. Self-adhesive.

SB521 $13 booklet containing pane of 20×65c. (No. 4479a) with twenty 'Card Only' labels.......... 18·00

B **273** Rose Coneflower

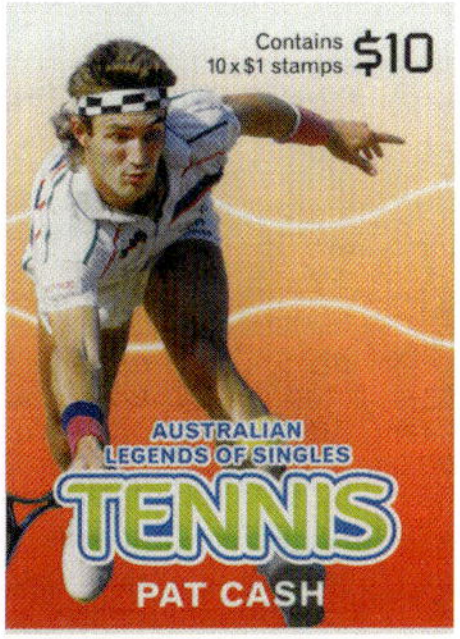

B **274** Pat Cash

2015 (14 Dec). Wildflowers. Multicoloured covers as Type B **273**. Self-adhesive.

SB522 $10 booklet containing pane of 10×$1. (No. 4489b) (Type B 273, 61×85 *mm*)............ 14·50

SB523 $20 booklet containing pane of 20 $1 (No. 4489c) (83×60 *mm* folded)............ 29·00

2016 (21 Jan). Australian Legends (20th series). Legends of Singles Tennis. Multicoloured covers, 60×85 *mm*, as Type B **274**. Self-adhesive.

SB524 $10 booklet containing pane of 10×$1. (No. 4510a) (Type B 274)............ 14·50

SB525 $10 booklet containing pane of 10×$1. (No. 4511a) (Ashley Cooper)............ 14·50

SB526 $10 booklet containing pane of 10×$1. (No. 4512a) (Roy Emerson)............ 14·50

SB527 $10 booklet containing pane of 10×$1. (No. 4513a) (Neale Fraser)............ 14·50

SB528 $10 booklet containing pane of 10×$1. (No. 4514a) (Evonne Goolagong Cawley)............ 14·50

SB529 $10 booklet containing pane of 10×$1. (No. 4515a) (John Newcombe)............ 14·50

SB530 $10 booklet containing pane of 10×$1. (No. 4516a) (Patrick Rafter)............ 14·50

SB531 $10 booklet containing pane of 10×$1. (No. 4517a) (Ken Rosewall)............ 14·50

SB532 $10 booklet containing pane of 10×$1. (No. 4518a) (Frank Sedgman)............ 14·50

SB533 $10 booklet containing pane of 10×$1. (No. 4519a) (Lleyton Hewitt)............ 14·50

SB534 $10 booklet containing pane of 10×$1. (No. 4520a) (Tony Roche)............ 14·50

SB535 $10 booklet containing pane of 10×$1. (No. 4521a) (Fred Stolle)............ 14·50

B **275** Handprints

B **276** N is for New South Wales, Nipper, Numbat

2016 (25 Jan). Greetings Stamps. Love to Celebrate. Multicoloured covers, 61×85 *mm*, as Type B **275**. Self-adhesive.

SB536 $10 booklet containing pane of 10×70c. (No. 4532a) (Type B 275)............ 14·50

SB537 $10 booklet containing pane of 10×70c. (No. 4533a) (Cake)............ 14·50

SB538 $10 booklet containing pane of 10×70c. (No. 4534a) (Balloons)............ 14·50

SB539 $10 booklet containing pane of 10×70c. (No. 4535a) (White roses)............ 14·50

SB540 $10 booklet containing pane of 10×70c. (No. 4536a) (Champagne glasses)............ 14·50

SB541 $10 booklet containing pane of 10×70c. (No. 4537a) (Heart made from red roses)............ 14·50

2016 (1 Mar). Fair Dinkum Aussie Alphabet. Multicoloured cover, 60×84 *mm*, as Type B **276**. Self-adhesive.

SB542 $10 booklet containing pane of 10×$1. (No. 4544a) (Type B 245)............ 14·50

SB543 $10 booklet containing pane of 10×$1. (No. 4545a) (Q)............ 14·50

SB544 $10 booklet containing pane of 10×$1. (No. 4546a) (S)............ 14·50

SB545 $10 booklet containing pane of 10×$1. (No. 4547a) (V)............ 14·50

SB546 $10 booklet containing pane of 10×$1. (No. 4548a) (W)............ 14·50

B **277** Gladesville Bridge, New South Wales

2016 (15 Mar). Australian Bridges. Multicoloured cover, 81×59 *mm* folded, as Type B **277**. Self-adhesive.

SB547 $20 booklet containing pane of 20 $1 (No. 4552a)... 28·00

B **278** Australian Soldiers

2016 (12 Apr). Centenary of World War I (3rd issue). 1916. Multicoloured cover, 76×76 *mm*, as Type B **278**. Self-adhesive.

SB548 $10 booklet containing pane of 10×$1. (No. 4565a) 14·50

PREMIUM BOOKLETS

The following booklets were sold at a premium over the face value of the stamps. All are stapled and have text and illustrations on interleaving pages. All measure 156×104 mm *unless otherwise stated* and are illustrated at one-third actual size *unless otherwise stated.*

P **1**

2002 (11 May). Greetings Stamps. Multicoloured cover as Type P **1**.
SP1 $9.95 booklet containing 20 stamps as No. 1897 but with phosphorised paper in five panes of 4 with margins all round, each stamp accompanied by a half stamp-size *se-tenant* label .... 18·00
No. SP1 has a face value of $9 and contains a pane of 16 self-adhesive labels with a rose design.

P **2**

2002 (12 Mar). Lighthouses. Multicoloured cover as Type P **2**.
SP2 $9.95 booklet containing five panes of No. 2187×4, No. 2188×2, No. 2189×2, No. 2190×2 and Nos. 2187/90, all printed by SNP Ausprint .... 10·00
Face value $9.69.

P **3**

2002 (2 July). Birth Centenary of Albert Namatjira (artist). Multicoloured cover as Type P **3**.
SP3 $9.95 booklet containing four panes of 4 of Nos. 2204/7, one of each design, and a pane as No. **MS**2208, all with margins all round .... 8·50
No. SP3 has a face value of $9 and contains two non-postally valid postcards.

P **4**

2003 (11 Feb). Greetings Stamps. Multicoloured covers as Type P **4**.
SP4 $10.95 booklet containing five panes of No. 2254×4 with four half stamp-size labels .... 24·00
SP5 $10.95 booklet containing five panes of No. 2255×4 with four half stamp-size labels (Weddings cover showing tulips) .... 24·00
SP6 $10.95 booklet containing five panes of No. 2256×4 with four half stamp-size labels (Love cover showing roses) .... 24·00
SP7 $10.95 booklet containing five panes of No. 2257×4 with four half stamp-size labels (Birthdays cover showing candles) .... 24·00
SP8 $10.95 booklet containing five panes of No. 2259×4 with four half stamp-size labels (Celebrations cover showing balloons) .... 24·00
SP9 $20.95 booklet containing five panes of No. 2263×4 with four half stamp-size labels (Weddings cover showing veiled bride) .... 38·00
All designs are on phosphorised paper. All panes from Nos. SP4/9 contain four stamps accompanied by four *se-tenant* stamp-size labels.
The contents of Nos. SP4/8 have a face value of $10, and No. SP9 has a face value of $20.
Nos. SP4/9 each contain a pane of 20 self-adhesive labels.

P **5**

2003 (5 Aug). 150th Anniv of Murray River Shipping. Black and lake cover as Type P **5**. Stapled.
SP10 $10.95 containing five panes of 4 of Nos. 2311/15, one of each design .... 11·00
Face value $10.

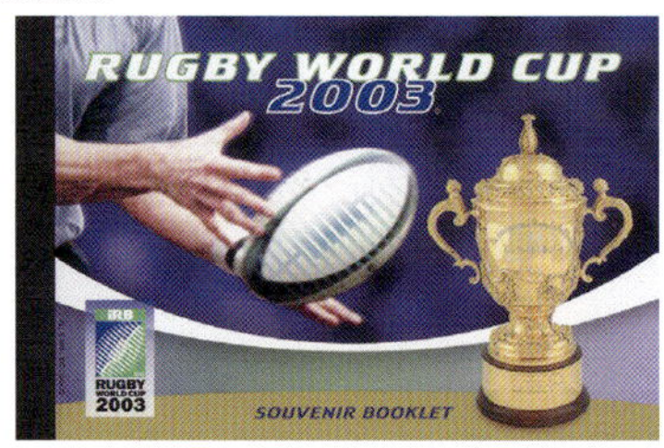

P **6**

2003 (8 Oct). Rugby World Cup Championship, Australia. Multicoloured cover as Type P **6**. Stapled.
SP11 $10.95 booklet containing three panes of 3 of Nos. 2339/41, one of each design .... 10·00
No. SP11 has a face value of $9.75 and contains a non-postally valid postcard.

P **7**

2003 (31 Oct). Greetings Stamps. Multicoloured covers as Type P **7**.
SP12 $9.95 booklet containing five panes of No. 1899×4 with four half stamp-size labels .... 12·50
SP13 $10.95 booklet containing five panes of No. 2258×4 with four half stamp-size labels (My Baby cover showing teddy bears) .... 13·00
SP14 $10.95 booklet containing two panes of No. 2103×4 with four half stamp-size labels (Australian greetings cover showing koala) .... 13·00
SP15 $20.75 booklet containing three panes of No. 2218×4 with four half stamp-size labels which extend the design (Aboriginal Art cover showing painting) .... 26·00
All designs are on phosphorised paper. All panes from Nos. SP12/15 contain four stamps accompanied by four half stamp-size *se-tenant* labels.
Nos. SP12/13 and SP15 each contain a pane of 20 self-adhesive labels.
No. SP14 contains two Air Mail postcards.
The contents of Nos. SP12/15 have face values of $9, $10, $8 and $19.80 respectively.

P **8** Sydney Harbour Bridge

2004 (2 Mar). Landmark Bridges. Multicoloured cover as Type P **8**.
SP16 $10.95 booklet containing five panes of 4 of Nos. 2357/61, one of each design .... 12·00
No. SP16 has a face value of $10.

P **9** Queen Elizabeth II and Wattle

2004 (13 Apr). 50th Anniv of Royal Tour of Australia. Multicoloured cover as Type P **9**.
SP17 $10.95 booklet containing five panes No. 2376×4 .... 12·00
No. SP17 has a face value of $10.

2004 (27 Apr). AFL (Australian Football League) Official Souvenir Booklets. Multicoloured covers as Type P **10**.
SP18 $10.95 booklet containing five panes of No. 2261×4 with labels (Adelaide Crows) .... 8·00
SP19 $10.95 booklet containing five panes of No. 2261×4 with labels (Brisbane Lions) .... 8·00
SP20 $10.95 booklet containing five panes of No. 2261×4 with labels (Carlton) .... 8·00
SP21 $10.95 booklet containing five panes of No. 2261×4 with labels (Collingwood) .... 8·00
SP22 $10.95 booklet containing five panes of No. 2261×4 with labels (Essendon) .... 8·00
SP23 $10.95 booklet containing five panes of No. 2261×4 with labels (Fremantle) .... 8·00
SP24 $10.95 booklet containing five panes of No. 2261×4 with labels (Geelong) .... 8·00
SP25 $10.95 booklet containing five panes of No. 2261×4 with labels (Hawthorn) .... 8·00
SP26 $10.95 booklet containing five panes of No. 2261×4 with labels (Melbourne) .... 8·00
SP27 $10.95 booklet containing five panes of No. 2261×4 with labels (North Melbourne) .... 8·00
SP28 $10.95 booklet containing five panes of No. 2261×4 with labels (Port Adelaide) .... 8·00
SP29 $10.95 booklet containing five panes of No. 2261×4 with labels (Richmond) .... 8·00
SP30 $10.95 booklet containing five panes of No. 2261×4 with labels (St. Kilda) .... 8·00
SP31 $10.95 booklet containing five panes of No. 2261×4 with labels (Sydney Swans) .... 8·00
SP32 $10.95 booklet containing five panes of No. 2261×4 with labels (West Coast Eagles) .... 8·00
SP33 $10.95 booklet containing five panes of No. 2261×4 with labels (Western Bulldogs) .... 8·00
Nos. SP18/33 each contain 20 self-adhesive labels and have a face value of $10.

P **11**

2004 (29 June). 150th Anniv of Eureka Stockade. Multicoloured cover as Type P **11**.
SP34 $10.95 containing two panes of No. 2396×2 and one pane each of No. 2397×2 and No. **MS**2398 .... 12·00
No. SP34 has a face value $9.85.

P **12** Boxing Kangaroo

2004 (3 Aug). BK the Boxing Kangaroo. Multicoloured cover as Type P **12**.
SP35 $10.95 booklet containing five panes of No. 2367×4 with four half stamp-size labels showing BK....... 16·00
No. SP35 also has five airmail postcards (not pre-paid) interleaved with the stamp panes and a pane of 20 self-adhesive labels.
Face value: $10.

P **13**

2004 (7 Sept). 150th Anniv of Australian Railways. Multicoloured cover as Type P **13**.
SP36 $10.95 booklet containing five panes of 4 stamps (Nos. 2413/17), one of each design .... 14·00
No. SP36 has a face value of $10.

P **14**

2004 (21 Sept). Cats and Dogs. Multicoloured covers as Type P **14**.
SP37 $10.95 booklet containing five panes of 4 stamps (Nos. 2439/40) in various combinations .... 14·00

SP38 $10.95 booklet containing four panes of 4 stamps (Nos. 2441/42) in various combinations and one pane of 2 stamps (No. 2443) .... 14·00

Nos. SP37/8 have face values of $10.

P **15** Mickey Mouse

2004 (11 Nov). 75 Years of Mickey Mouse (Disney cartoon character). Multicoloured cover as Type P **15**.

SP39 $10.95 booklet containing five panes of No. 2259×4 with four half stamp-size labels showing Mickey Mouse .... 14·00

No. SP39 has interleaving pages showing scenes from Mickey Mouse cartoon films. Face value: $10.

P **16** Libra

2005 (5 Jan–20 June). Zodiac. Multicoloured covers as Type P **16**.

SP40 $10.95 booklet containing five panes of No. 2367×4 with labels (Capricorn cover showing goat) .... 9·00

SP41 $10.95 booklet containing five panes of No. 2261×4 with labels (Aquarius cover showing water carrier) .... 9·00

SP42 $10.95 booklet containing five panes of No. 2254×4 with labels (Pisces cover showing two fish) .... 9·00

SP43 $10.95 booklet containing five panes of No. 2261×4 with labels (Aries cover showing ram) (8 Mar) ... 9·00

SP44 $10.95 booklet containing five panes of No. 2254×4 with labels (Taurus cover showing bull) (8 Mar) 9·00

SP45 $10.95 booklet containing five panes of No. 2259×4 with labels (Gemini cover showing twins) (8 Mar) .... 9·00

SP46 $10.95 booklet containing five panes of No. 2367×4 with labels (Cancer cover showing crab) (20 June) .... 9·00

SP47 $10.95 booklet containing five panes of No. 2259×4 with labels (Leo cover showing lion) (20 June) .. 9·00

SP48 $10.95 booklet containing five panes of No. 2254×4 with labels (Virgo cover) (20 June) .... 9·00

SP49 $10.95 booklet containing five panes of No. 2254×4 with labels) (20 June) (cover Type P **16**) .... 9·00

SP50 $10.95 booklet containing five panes of No. 2256×4 with labels (Scorpio cover showing scorpion) (20 June) .... 9·00

SP51 $10.95 booklet containing five panes of No. 2259×4 with labels (Sagittarius cover showing archer) (20 June) .... 9·00

All panes from Nos. SP40/51 contain four stamps accompanied by four *se-tenant* half stamp-size labels.

The contents of each Zodiac booklet has a face value of $10.

P **17** Main Stadium at Flinders Park, Melbourne

2005 (11 Jan). Centenary of Australian Open Tennis Championships. Multicoloured cover as Type P **17**.

SP52 $10.95 booklet containing four panes of 2 of Nos. 2465/6, two of each design .... 9·00

Face value $9.20.

P **18** Babies

2005 (22 Mar). Greetings Stamps. "Marking the Occasion". Multicoloured covers as Type P **18**. Self-adhesive.

SP53 $10.95 booklet containing five panes of four self-adhesive stamps as No. 2493 .... 14·00

SP54 $10.95 booklet containing five panes of four self-adhesive stamps as No. 2494 (Roses cover) .... 14·00

SP55 $10.95 booklet containing five panes of four self-adhesive stamps as No. 2495 (Let's Party cover showing wrapped presents) .... 14·00

SP56 $10.95 booklet containing five panes of four self-adhesive stamps as No. 2497 (The Big Day cover showing hands wearing wedding rings)... 14·00

SP57 $12.95 booklet containing two panes of four self-adhesive stamps as No. 2499 (Postcards from Australia cover showing penguins) .... 15·00

SP58 $12.95 booklet containing self-adhesive stamps, two panes of two stamps as No. 2500 and two panes of two stamps as No. 2501 (Destination Australia cover showing coastal cliffs) .... 15·00

SP59 $20.95 booklet containing five panes of four self-adhesive stamps as No. 2498 (Royal Weddings cover showing Princess Margaret) .... 20·00

Stamps from Nos. SP53/7 all have designs as Nos. 2493/5 and 2497/2501, but are self-adhesive. The $1.80 value has phosphor bands at left and foot of stamp and phosphor on the "sails" of Sydney Opera House, and the other values have irregular phosphor frames All are perforated 11½ (interrupted), with the two horizontal edges having two sets of five teeth separated by a straight line.

Booklet Nos. SP53/6 and SP58/9 each contain a pane of self-adhesive labels and No. SP57 contains three non-postally valid postcards.

Face value of contents: SP53/6 $10, SP57 $8.80, SP58 $12, SP59 $20.

P **19** Adelaide Crows

2005 (1 Apr). AFL (Australian Football League) Official Souvenir Booklets. Multicoloured covers as Type P **19**.

SP60 $10.95 booklet containing five panes of No. 2260×4 with labels (cover Type P **19**) .... 10·00

SP61 $10.95 booklet containing five panes of No. 2260×4 with labels (Brisbane Lions) .... 10·00

SP62 $10.95 booklet containing five panes of No. 2260×4 with labels (Carlton) .... 10·00

SP63 $10.95 booklet containing five panes of No. 2260×4 with labels (Collingwood) .... 10·00

SP64 $10.95 booklet containing five panes of No. 2260×4 with labels (Essendon) ..... 10·00
SP65 $10.95 booklet containing five panes of No. 2260×4 with labels (Fremantle) ..... 10·00
SP66 $10.95 booklet containing five panes of No. 2260×4 with labels (Geelong) ..... 10·00
SP67 $10.95 booklet containing five panes of No. 2260×4 with labels (Hawthorn) ..... 10·00
SP68 $10.95 booklet containing five panes of No. 2260×4 with labels (Melbourne) ..... 10·00
SP69 $10.95 booklet containing five panes of No. 2260×4 with labels (North Melbourne) ..... 10·00
SP70 $10.95 booklet containing five panes of No. 2260×4 with labels (Port Adelaide) ..... 10·00
SP71 $10.95 booklet containing five panes of No. 2260×4 with labels (Richmond) ..... 10·00
SP72 $10.95 booklet containing five panes of No. 2260×4 with labels (St. Kilda) ..... 10·00
SP73 $10.95 booklet containing five panes of No. 2260×4 with labels (Sydney Swans) ..... 10·00
SP74 $10.95 booklet containing five panes of No. 2260×4 with labels (West Coast Eagles) ..... 10·00
SP75 $10.95 booklet containing five panes of No. 2260×4 with labels (Western Bulldogs) ..... 10·00

All panes from Nos. SP60/75 contain four stamps accompanied by four se-tenant half stamp-size labels showing players.

Nos. SP60/75 each contain a pane of 20 self-adhesive labels and have a face value of $10.

P **20** Australian Forces at Gallipoli, 1915

2005 (21 Apr). Australia and War. Multicoloured cover as Type P **20**.
SP76 $16.95 booklet containing ten panes: Nos. 2073/4; Nos. 1470 and 1472; Nos. 1397 and 1399; Nos. 1578/9; Nos. 1338/41; Nos. 1521, 1523/4 and 1547; Nos. 374/5 of Victoria; Nos. 1283×4; Nos. 1545 and 1522; Nos. 1243×2 ..... 19·00

No. SP76 contains valid stamps with a face value of $12.92. The Victoria stamps are reproductions of Nos. 374/5 in changed colours and not postally valid.

P **21** Queen at Opening Ceremony for Commonwealth Heads of Government Meeting, Queensland, 2002

2005 (10 May). Commonwealth of Nations. Multicoloured cover as Type P **21**.
SP77 $10.95 booklet containing five panes of No. 2522×4 ..... 11·00
Face value: $10.

P **22** Vineyard in Autumn, Victoria

2005 (19 July). Australian Wine. Multicoloured cover as Type P **22**.
SP78 $10.95 booklet containing four panes: Nos. 2538/9×2, Nos. 2540/1×2, No. 2542×2 and 2538/9×2 ..... 11·00
Face value: $9.90.

P **23** Christmas Decorations

2005 (1 Nov). Christmas. Multicoloured cover as Type P **23**.
SP79 $9.95 booklet containing three panes of No. 2556×4, two panes of Christmas Island No. 579×4 and a pane of 20 self-adhesive labels ..... 23·00
Face value: $9.

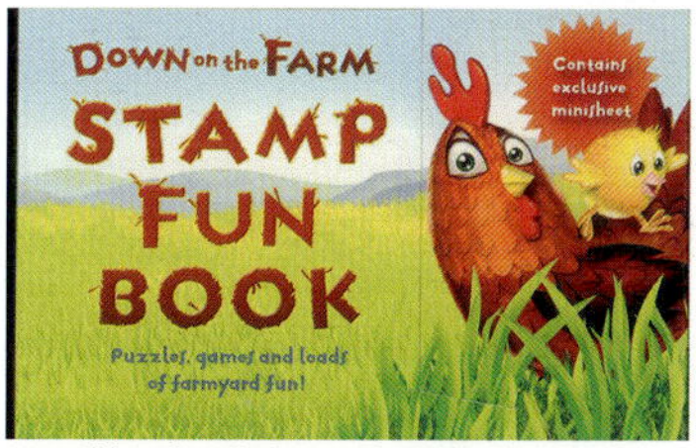

P **24** Chloe the Chicken with Chick

2005 (23 Nov). Stamp Collecting Month. "Down on the Farm Stamp Fun Book". Multicoloured cover, 195×120 *mm,* as Type P **24** containing children's games and puzzles on interleaving pages.
SP80 $9.95 booklet containing Nos. 2558/63 as separate single stamp panes and No. **MS**2564 ..... 24·00

No. SP79 also contains a pane of 12 self-adhesive labels and a non-postally valid postcard.

Face value $7.

P **25** Australian Stamps

2006 (1 Mar). "Australia at the Commonwealth Games". Multicoloured cover as Type P **25**. Booklet contains text and illustrations on panes and interleaving pages.
SP81 $10.95 booklet containing five panes: No. 2575×4; Nos. 346/7; Nos. 859/62; No. 2361×6; As **MS**2599 but 156×105 mm ..... 15·00

Nos. 346/7 are 1962 stamps and not postally valid. Nos. 346/7 and 859/62 are perforated 14×15.
Face value: $10.16.

P **26** Don Elgin (athlete) (*Illustration further reduced. Actual size* 170×118 *mm*)

2006 (15 Mar). "Snapshot!". Commonwealth Games Souvenir Stamp Booklet. Multicoloured cover as Type P **26**. Booklet contains text and illustrations on panes and interleaving pages.

SP82 $19.95 booklet containing six panes: four panes containing self-adhesive No. 2576×4 (two with *se-tenant* labels showing Don Elgin); As **MS**2599 but 156×105 mm; Nos. 1392, 1395, 1582 and 1585 .... 25·00

Face value: $15.50.

No. SP82 also contains three postcards and a pane of 18 small self-adhesive labels.

P **27** Football (*Illustration further reduced. Actual size* 175×117 *mm*)

2006 (20 Mar). AFL (Australian Football League) Official Souvenir Booklets. Multicoloured covers as Type P **27**. Self-adhesive.

SP83 $12.95 booklet containing three panes of four self-adhesive stamps as No. 2557 with labels (Adelaide Crows) .... 10·00

SP84 $12.95 booklet containing three panes of four self-adhesive stamps as No. 2557 with labels (Brisbane Lions) .... 10·00

SP85 $12.95 booklet containing three panes of four self-adhesive stamps as No. 2557 with labels (Carlton) .... 10·00

SP86 $12.95 booklet containing three panes of four self-adhesive stamps as No. 2557 with labels (Collingwood) .... 10·00

SP87 $12.95 booklet containing three panes of four self-adhesive stamps as No. 2557 with labels (Essendon) .... 10·00

SP88 $12.95 booklet containing three panes of four self-adhesive stamps as No. 2557 with labels (Fremantle) .... 10·00

SP89 $12.95 booklet containing three panes of four self-adhesive stamps as No. 2557 with labels (Geelong) .... 10·00

SP90 $12.95 booklet containing three panes of four self-adhesive stamps as No. 2557 with labels (Hawthorn) .... 10·00

SP91 $12.95 booklet containing three panes of four self-adhesive stamps as No. 2557 with labels (Kangaroos, North Melbourne) .... 10·00

SP92 $12.95 booklet containing three panes of four self-adhesive stamps as No. 2557 with labels (Melbourne) .... 10·00

SP93 $12.95 booklet containing three panes of four self-adhesive stamps as No. 2557 with labels (Port Adelaide) .... 10·00

SP94 $12.95 booklet containing three panes of four self-adhesive stamps as No. 2557 with labels (Richmond) .... 10·00

SP95 $12.95 booklet containing three panes of four self-adhesive stamps as No. 2557 with labels (St. Kilda) .... 10·00

SP96 $12.95 booklet containing three panes of four self-adhesive stamps as No. 2557 with labels (Sydney Swans) .... 10·00

SP97 $12.95 booklet containing three panes of four self-adhesive stamps as No. 2557 with labels (West Coast Eagles) .... 10·00

SP98 $12.95 booklet containing three panes of four self-adhesive stamps as No. 2557 with labels (Western Bulldogs) .... 10·00

Stamps from SP83/98 all have design as No. 2557 but are self-adhesive and perforated 11½ (interrupted), with the two horizontal edges having two sets of teeth separated by a straight line.

Booklet Nos. SP83/98 each contain four postcards.

Face value: $6.

P **28**

2006 (19 Apr). 80th Birthday of Queen Elizabeth II. Multicoloured cover as Type P **28**. Booklet contains text and illustrations on interleaving pages.

SP99 $10.95 booklet containing four panes: No. 2624×2 (two panes), No. 2625×2 and **MS**2626 .... 14·00

Face value: $9.85.

P **29**

2006 (2 May). Lighthouses. Multicoloured cover as Type P **29**. Booklet contains text and illustrations on panes and interleaving pages.

SP100 $10.95 booklet containing five panes: Nos. 2628×2 and 2629/30; Nos. 2629×2 and 2631/2; Nos. 2630×2 and 2628/9; Nos. 2631×2, 2630 and 2632; Nos. 2632×2, 2628 and 2631 .... 17·00

No. SP100 has a face value of $10. It also contains a postcard.

P **30**

2006 (2 May). "Greetings from Australia". Australian Animals (SP101) and Heritage Buildings (SP102). Multicoloured covers as Type P **30**. Self-adhesive.

SP101 $12.95 booklet containing five panes of No. 2640×2 .... 15·00

SP102 $14.95 booklet containing four panes of No. 2641×2 (cover showing Royal Exhibition Building, Melbourne) .... 18·00

Both booklets contain a pane of 20 small self-adhesive labels. No. SP102 also contains two postcards.

Face value: $10 (SP101) or $14.80 (SP102).

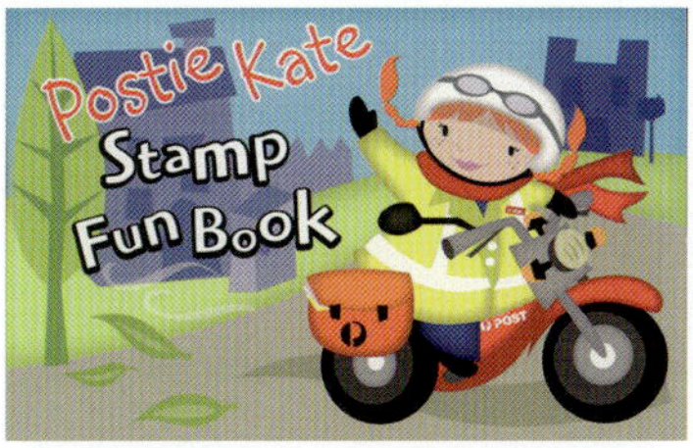

P **31** (*Illustration further reduced. Actual size 195×120 mm*)

2006 (1 June). "Postie Kate Stamp Fun Book". Multicoloured cover as Type P **31**. Booklet contains children's games and puzzles on interleaving pages.

SP103 $9.95 booklet containing Nos. 2649/53 in separate single-stamp panes and Nos. 2654/8 in a *se-tenant* pane .... 12·00

No. SP103 also contains a pane of 12 self-adhesive labels and a 50c. postcard.

Face value: $5.50.

P **32** (*Illustration further reduced. Actual size 170×118 mm)*

2006 (15 Aug). "Driving through the Years". Multicoloured cover as Type P **32**. Booklet contains text and illustrations on panes and interleaving pages.

SP104 $10.95 booklet containing Nos. 2673/7 in separate panes of four .... 15·00

Face value: $10.

P **33**

2006 (12 Sept). Australian Rock Posters. Multicoloured cover as Type P **33**. Booklet contains text and illustrations on panes and front page.

SP105 $10.95 booklet containing Nos. 2683/92 in separate panes of two .... 18·00

No. SP105 also contains ten postcards interleaved with the stamp panes. Face value: $10.

P **34**

2006 (3 Oct). Dangerous Australians. Multicoloured cover as Type P **34**. Booklet contains text and illustrations on panes and interleaving pages.

SP106 $10.95 booklet containing six panes: No. 2703×2; Nos. 2704 and 2708, each×2; No. 2706×2; No. 2705×2; No. 2707×2; No. **MS**2709 .... 16·00

Face value: $10.50.

P **35**

2007 (24 Jan). 10 Years of Australian Legends. Multicoloured cover as Type P **35**. Booklet contains text and illustrations on panes and interleaving pages.

SP107 $22.95 booklet containing fourteen panes: Nos. 1663/4; Nos. 1731/4; Nos. 1735/8; Nos. 1739/42; Nos. 1838/9; Nos. 1947/50; Nos. 2069/70; Nos. 2160/4; Nos. 2264/7; Nos. 2348/9; Nos. 2467/8; Nos. 2469/70; Nos. 2471/2; Nos. 2577/81 .... 24·00

Face value: $20.95.

P **36** Lifeguard on Beach (*Illustration further reduced. Actual size* 170×118 *mm*)

2007 (6 Mar). "Surf's Up!" Multicoloured cover as Type P **36**. Booklet contains text and illustrations on panes and interleaving pages.

SP108 $12.95 booklet containing No. **MS**2783 and Nos. 2777/80 in separate single stamp panes .... 20·00

Face value: $8.90.

P **37** Adelaide Crows Team (*illustration further reduced. Actual size* 170×117 *mm*)

2007 (27 Mar). AFL (Australian Football League) Stamp and Medallion booklets. Multicoloured covers as Type P **37**. Booklet contains text and illustrations on panes and interleaving pages.

SP109 $14.95 booklet containing ten panes of No. 2261×2 with labels (Adelaide Crows) .... 12·00

SP110 $14.95 booklet containing ten panes of No. 2261×2 with labels (Brisbane Lions) .... 12·00

SP111 $14.95 booklet containing ten panes of No. 2261×2 with labels (Carlton) .... 12·00

SP112 $14.95 booklet containing ten panes of No. 2261×2 with labels (Collingwood) .... 12·00

SP113 $14.95 booklet containing ten panes of No. 2261×2 with labels (Essendon) .... 12·00

SP114 $14.95 booklet containing ten panes of No. 2261×2 with labels (Fremantle) .... 12·00

SP115 $14.95 booklet containing ten panes of No. 2261×2 with labels (Geelong) .... 12·00

SP116 $14.95 booklet containing ten panes of No. 2261×2 with labels (Hawthorn) .... 12·00

SP117 $14.95 booklet containing ten panes of No. 2261×2 with labels (Kangaroos, North Melbourne) .... 12·00
SP118 $14.95 booklet containing ten panes of No. 2261×2 with labels (Melbourne) .... 12·00
SP119 $14.95 booklet containing ten panes of No. 2261×2 with labels (Port Adelaide) .... 12·00
SP120 $14.95 booklet containing ten panes of No. 2261×2 with labels (Richmond) .... 12·00
SP121 $14.95 booklet containing ten panes of No. 2261×2 with labels (St. Kilda) .... 12·00
SP122 $14.95 booklet containing ten panes of No. 2261×2 with labels (Sydney Swans) .... 12·00
SP123 $14.95 booklet containing ten panes of No. 2261×2 with labels (West Coast Eagles) .... 12·00
SP124 $14.95 booklet containing ten panes of No. 2261×2 with labels (Western Bulldogs) .... 12·00

All panes from Nos. SP109/24 contain two stamps accompanied by two se-tenant half stamp-size labels showing players.

Nos. SP109/24 each contain a medallion and have a face value of $10.

P **38** Train and Woman carrying Case

2007 (10 Apr). Poster Art. Nostalgic Tourism. Multicoloured cover as Type P **38**. Booklet contains text and illustrations on panes and interleaving pages. Stitched.

SP125 $10.95 booklet containing three panes: Nos. 2808/11; Nos. 2808/9; Nos. 2808 and 2811 .... 13·50

Face value: $10.40.

P **39** Yellow-footed Rock-wallaby

2007 (8 May). Wallabies of Australia. Multicoloured cover as Type P **39**. Booklet contains text and illustrations on panes and interleaving pages. Stitched.

SP126 $12.95 booklet containing four panes of two self-adhesive $1.30 stamps as No. 2816 .... 16·00

Stamps from No. SP126 all have a design as No. 2816 but are self-adhesive, with phosphor over the top and right of the stamp. They are perforated 11½ (interrupted) each horizontal edge having two sets of five teeth separated by a straight line.

No. SP126 has a face value of $10.40. It also contains a pane of 20 small labels.

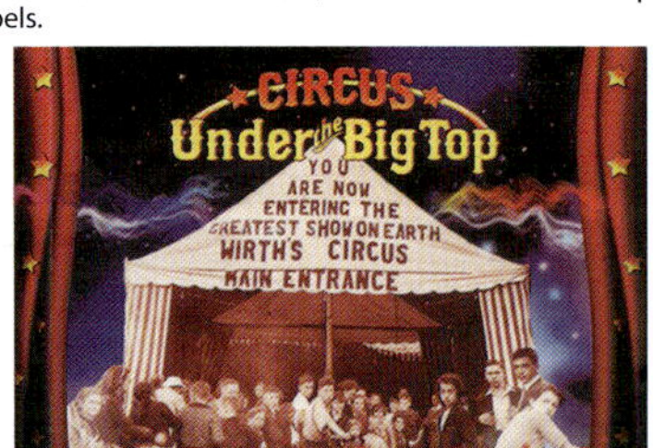

P **40** Entrance to Wirth's Circus Big Top

2007 (15 May). Circus: Under the Big Top. Multicoloured cover as Type P **40**. Booklet contains text and illustrations on panes and interleaving pages. Stitched.

SP127 $12.95 booklet containing six panes: Nos. 2818/22; As Nos. 2823/7; No. 2820×2; No. 2821×2; No. 2819×2; Nos. 2818 and 2822, each×2 .... 16·00

The self-adhesive stamps as Nos. 2823/7 from the booklet all have gold foil stars.

Face value: $10.

P **41** Sydney Harbour Bridge

2007 (15 June). 75th Anniv of Sydney Harbour Bridge. Multicoloured cover as Type P **41**. Booklet contains text and illustrations on panes and interleaving pages. Stitched.

SP128 $14.95 booklet containing self-adhesive $1.95 stamps as Type **755** in three panes of two and one pane containing a single stamp .... 19·00

Stamps from No. SP128 all have a design as Type **755** but are self-adhesive, with phosphor at right of the stamp and over both the bridge piers and underneath the bridge. They are perforated 11½ (interrupted), each horizontal edge having two sets of five teeth separated by a straight line.

No. SP128 has a face value of $13.65. It also contains two airmail postcards.

P **42** Wandering Albatross

2007 (26 June). Threatened Wildlife. Multicoloured cover as Type P **42**. Booklet contains text and illustrations on panes and interleaving pages. Stitched.

SP129 $10.95 booklet containing Nos. 2839/42 in four separate panes of two, and two imperf panes containing Nos. 784, 789, 792 and 797 and two each of Nos. 788 and 796 .... 17·00

All stamps from No. SP129 are on phosphorised paper.

Face value: $9.73.

P **43** Flower Border at Royal Botanical Gardens, Melbourne

2007 (12 Sept). Australian Botanic Gardens. Multicoloured cover as Type P **43**. Booklet contains text and illustrations on panes and interleaving pages. Stitched.

SP130 $10.95 booklet containing five panes of 4 of Nos. 2866/70, one of each design .... 14·50

No. SP130 has a face value of $10. It also contains an airmail postcard (not pre-paid).

P **44** Earth seen from Space

2007 (2 Oct). Blast Off! 50 Years in Space. Multicoloured cover as Type P **44**. Booklet contains text and illustrations on panes and interleaving pages. Stitched.

SP131 $10.95 booklet containing Nos. 2872/7 in separate panes of two and Nos. 2872/6 in *se-tenant* pane .... 14·00

Face value: $9.50.

P **45** Family outside Caravan (*Illustration further reduced. Actual size* 170×118 *mm*)

2007 (16 Oct). Caravanning through the Years. Multicoloured cover as Type P **45**. Booklet contains text and illustrations on panes and interleaving pages. Stitched.

SP132 $10.95 booklet containing Nos. 2884, 2886 and 2888 in separate panes of four and Nos. 2884/5 and 2886/7 in panes containing two of each design 17·00

No. SP132 has a face value of $10. It also contains an airmail postcard (not pre-paid).

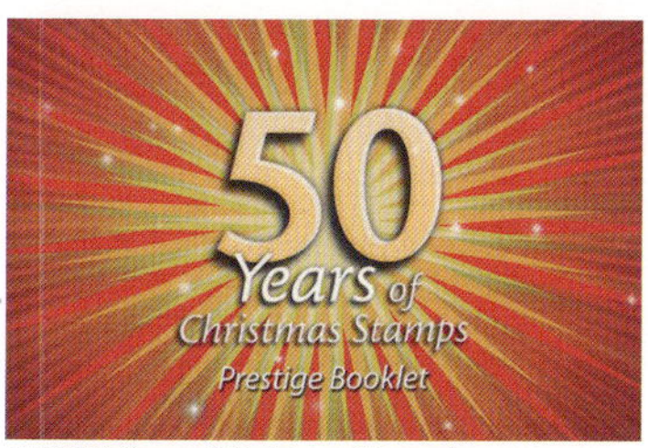

P **46** '50 Years of Christmas Stamps'

2007 (1 Nov). Christmas. 50 Years of Christmas Stamps. Multicoloured cover as Type P **46**. Booklet contains text and illustrations on panes and interleaving pages. Stitched.

SP133 $10.95 booklet containing Nos. 2894/6, each×4, 2897×2, 2898 and **MS**2904 .... 14·00

Face value: $10.45.

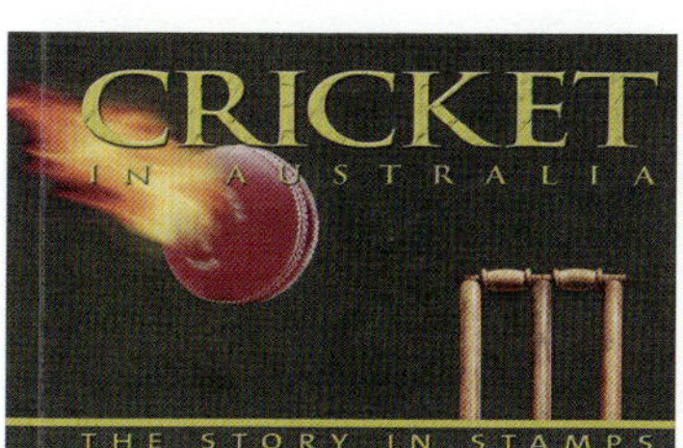

P **47** Cricket Ball and Stumps

2007 (5 Nov). Cricket in Australia. Multicoloured cover as Type P **47**. Booklet contains text and illustrations on panes and interleaving pages. Stitched.

SP134 $14.95 booklet containing seven panes: No. 572; Nos. 647/52; No. 767; As No. 1147 but imperf; Nos. 1381/2 and as No. 1187 but imperf; Nos. 1663/4 and 2489; As No. **MS**2738 but imperf .... 25·00

Stamps from SP134 are perforated 14½×14, with the exception of Nos. 1663/4 from the sixth pane which are perforated 14.

Face value: $9.77.

P **48** Scorpio

2007 (5 Nov)–**08**. Signs of the Zodiac. Multicoloured covers as Type P **48**. Booklet contains text and illustrations on interleaving pages. Stitched.

SP135 $10.95 booklet containing five panes of No. 2803×4 (Type P **48**) .... 15·00

SP136 $10.95 booklet containing five panes of No. 2804×4 (Sagittarius) .... 15·00

SP137 $10.95 booklet containing five panes of No. 2805 (Capricorn) .... 15·00

SP138 $10.95 booklet containing five panes of No. 2806 (Aquarius) .... 15·00

SP139 $10.95 booklet containing five panes of No. 2807 (Pisces) (3.12.07) .... 15·00

SP140 $10.95 booklet containing five panes of No. 2796 (Aries) (3.12.07) .... 15·00

SP141 $10.95 booklet containing five panes of No. 2797 (Taurus) (3.12.07) .... 15·00

SP142 $10.95 booklet containing five panes of No. 2798 (Gemini) (3.12.07) .... 15·00

SP143 $10.95 booklet containing five panes of No. 2799 (Cancer) (7.1.08) .... 15·00

SP144 $10.95 booklet containing five panes of No. 2800 (Leo) (7.1.08) .... 15·00

SP145 $10.95 booklet containing five panes of No. 2801 (Virgo) (7.1.08) .... 15·00

SP146 $10.95 booklet containing five panes of No. 2802 (Libra) (7.1.08) .... 15·00

Booklet Nos. SP135/46 each contain a postcard. They all have a face value of $10.

P **49** Roses 'Imp' and 'Minnie Watson'

2008 (15 Jan). 'Love Blooms'. Multicoloured cover as Type P **49**. Booklet contains text and illustrations on panes and interleaving pages. Stitched.

SP147 $10.95 booklet containing five panes of four self adhesive 50c. stamps as No. 2906 .... 15·00

No. SP147 has a face value of $10. It also contains a pane of 20 small red rose labels.

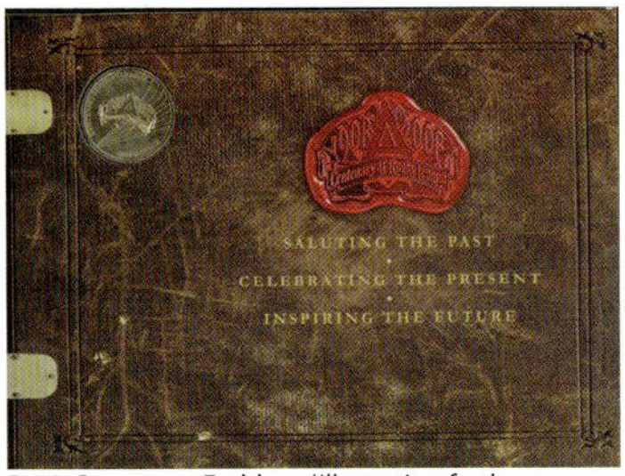

P **50** Centenary Emblem (*Illustration further reduced. Actual size* 170×120 *mm*)

2008 (25 Mar). Centenary of Rugby League. Multicoloured cover as Type P **50**. Booklet contains text and illustrations on panes and interleaving pages. Stitched.

SP148 $15.95 booklet containing stamps as No. 2942×4 and Nos. 2935/8, 2939/42, 2943/6 and 2947/50 .... 20·00

Face value: $12

No. SP148 also contains a $1 commemorative coin.

Stamps from SP148 are all perforated 15×14.

P **51** Playing the *Last Post*

2008 (16 Apr). 'Lest We Forget'. ANZAC Day. Multicoloured cover as Type P **51**. Booklet contains text and illustrations on panes and interleaving pages. Stitched.

SP149 $10.95 booklet containing stamps as Nos. 2977/81, each in panes of four........ 23·00

Face value: $10

Stamps from SP149 are all perforated 15×14.

P **52** Hot Air Balloon over Sydney

2008 (6 May). 'Up Up and Away'. 150th Anniv of First Hot Air Balloon Flight in Australia. Multicoloured cover as Type P **52**. Booklet contains text and illustrations on panes and interleaving pages. Stitched.

SP150 $10.95 booklet containing Nos. 2991/4 in a *se-tenant* pane and in four panes of 4 stamps of each design........ 20·00

Face value: $10.

P **53** Beagle

2008 (10 June). Working Dogs. Multicoloured cover as Type P **53**. Booklet contains text and illustrations on panes and interleaving pages. Stitched.

SP151 $10.95 booklet containing Nos. 3000/4 in five panes of 4 stamps of each design........ 26·00

Face value: $10.

P **54** Hanging Rock, Grose River Gorge, New South Wales

2008 (19 June). Gorgeous Australia. Multicoloured covers as Type P **54**. Booklet contains text and illustrations on panes and interleaving pages. Stitched.

SP152 $10.95 booklet containing No. 2927 in four panes of two........ 23·00

SP153 $16.95 booklet containing No. 2928 in four panes of two (cover showing Walpa Gorge, NT)........ 30·00

Face values: $10.80 (SP152); $16 (SP153).

P **55** Water Droplets on Plants

2008 (8 July). Living Green. Multicoloured cover as Type P **55**. Booklet contains text and illustrations on panes and interleaving pages. Stitched.

SP154 $10.95 booklet containing Nos. 3016/19 in three panes containing all four designs and four panes containing the four designs in panes of two of the same design........ 18·00

No. SP154 has six stamp panes, one being double-sided with four stamps on each side.

Face value: $10.

P **56** Lockheed Super Constellation

2008 (5 Aug). Aviation. Multicoloured cover as Type P **56**. Booklet contains text and illustrations on panes and interleaving pages. Stitched.

SP155 $10.95 booklet containing five panes: As No. 3033×2; As No. 3034×2; As Nos. 3033/6; As No. 3035×2; As No. 3036........ 25·00

Stamps from SP155 are perforated 14×15.

Face value: $8.50.

P **57** Russell Falls, Tasmania

2008 (15 Sept). Waterfalls of Australia. Multicoloured covers as Type P **57**. Booklets contain text and illustrations on panes and interleaving pages.

SP156 $11.95 booklet containing four panes of No. 3068×2.... 17·00
SP157 $16.95 booklet containing four panes of No. 3069×2.... 22·00

Face values: SP156 $11.20; SP157 $16.40.

P **58** Megalania

2008 (1 Oct). Megafauna in Australia. Grey, black and deep rose-red cover as Type P **58**. Booklet contains text and illustrations on panes and interleaving pages. Stitched.

SP158 $13.95 booklet containing eight panes: No. 3081×2; No. 3082×2; No. 3086×2; No. 3085×2; No. 3083×2; No. 3084×2; Nos. 3081/4; Nos. 3085/6 .... 18·00

Face value: $13.20.

P **59** Bride and Groom on Shore of Sydney Harbour ('love is...')

2008 (2–28 Oct). Greetings Stamps. 'Special Occasions'. Multicoloured covers as Type P **59**. Booklets contain text and illustrations on panes and interleaving pages.

SP159 $11.95 booklet containing five panes of four self-adhesive 55c. stamps as No. 3070 (Type P **59**).. 15·00
SP160 $11.95 booklet containing five panes of four self-adhesive 55c. stamps as No. 3071 ('Tying the knot')........ 15·00
SP161 $11.95 booklet containing five panes of four self-adhesive 55c. stamps as No. 3072 ('Babies') (28.10)........ 15·00
SP162 $11.95 booklet containing five panes of four self-adhesive 55c. stamps as No. 3073 ('love') .... 15·00
SP163 $11.95 booklet containing five panes of four self-adhesive 55c. stamps as No. 3074 ('HAPPY BIRTHDAY!') (28.10)........ 15·00
SP164 $11.95 booklet containing five panes of four self-adhesive 55c. stamps as No. 3077 ('CeLeBRaTe!') (28.10)........ 15·00
SP165 $22.95 booklet containing five panes of four self-adhesive [$1.10] stamps as No. 3079 ('A day to remember')........ 30·00

Stamps from Nos. SP158/64 all have designs as Nos. 3070/4, 3077 and 3079, but are self-adhesive. Stamps from SP162/3 have phosphor frames; stamps from the other booklets have phosphor over parts of the design. All are perforated 11½×11 (interrupted), with the two horizontal edges having two sets of five teeth separated by a straight line.

Nos. SP158/9, SP161 and SP164 each contain a pane of 20 small self-adhesive labels.

Nos. SP158/9, SP161 and SP164 were printed by McKellar, and Nos. SP160 and SP162/3 by Energi Print.

Face value: SP158/63 $11; SP164 $22.

P **60** Nicole Kidman

2009 (22 Jan). Australian Legends. "Legends of the Screen". Multicoloured covers as Type P **60**. Booklets contain text and illustrations on panes and interleaving pages.

SP166 $10.95 booklet containing four panes: No. 3113×4; No. 3118×4; Nos. 3113 and 3118, each×2; Nos. 3113/16........ 15·00
SP167 $10.95 booklet containing four panes: No. 3114×4; No. 3117×4; Nos. 3114 and 3117, each×2; Nos. 3113/16........ 15·00
SP168 $10.95 booklet containing four panes: No. 3115×4; No. 3120×4; Nos. 3115 and 3120, each×2; Nos. 3113/16........ 15·00
SP169 $10.95 booklet containing four panes: No. 3116×4; No. 3119×4; Nos. 3116 and 3119, each×2; Nos. 3113/16........ 15·00

Face value: $8.80.

P **61** Children playing around Rotary Clothes Line

2009 (19 Feb). Inventive Australia. Multicoloured cover as Type P **61**. Booklet contains text and illustrations on panes and interleaving pages.

SP170 $12.95 booklet containing five panes of Nos. 3137/41, each design in panes of four stamps .... 18·00

Face value: $11.

P **62** Australia Post Lorry

2009 (25 Mar). Bicentenary of Postal Services in Australia (1st issue). Multicoloured cover, 155×207 *mm*, as Type P **62**. Booklet contains text and illustrations on interleaving pages. Stitched.

SP171 $19.95 booklet containing Nos. 3158/67 in three panes containing all ten designs, one pane imperforate........ 42·00

Face value: $16.50.

P **63** Queen Elizabeth II at Trooping the Colour

2009 (15 Apr). Queen's Birthday. Multicoloured cover as Type P **63**. Booklet contains text and illustrations on interleaving pages.

SP172 $10.95 booklet containing four panes: No. 3185×2; No. 3186×2; No. 3185×2; No. **MS**3187 .... 25·00

Face value: $8.90.

P **64** Wooden Spoon and Recipes

2009 (15 May). "Not Just Desserts". Multicoloured cover as Type P **64**. Booklet contains text and illustrations on panes and interleaving pages.

SP173 $10.95 booklet containing four panes of Nos. 3189/92, each design in panes of four stamps .... 15·00

Face value: $8.80.

P **65** Aborigine and Kangaroo Stamps and Letter

2009 (26 June). Bicentenary of Postal Services in Australia (2nd issue). Australia's Favourite Stamps. Grey, black and scarlet cover as Type P **65**. Booklet contains text and illustrations on panes and interleaving pages. Stitched.

SP174 $12.95 booklet containing Nos. 3208/12 in separate panes of four .... 26·00

Face value: $11.

P **66** Children playing in Park

2009 (14 July). Australian Parks and Gardens. Multicoloured cover as Type P **66**. Booklet contains text and illustrations on panes and interleaving pages.

SP175 $12.95 booklet containing five panes of Nos. 3224/8, each design in panes of four stamps .... 21·00

Face value: $11.

A similar booklet containing imperforate panes was issued on 23 July 2009 for the Melbourne Stamp Show.

P **67** *White Garden* (Rosalie Gascoigne), 1995

2009 (11 Aug). Corrugated Landscapes. Multicoloured cover as Type P **67**. Booklet contains text and illustrations on panes and interleaving pages.

SP176 $10.95 booklet containing Nos. 3258/61 in separate panes of four .... 15·00

Face value: $8.80.

P **68** Pair of Blue-faced Honeyeaters

2009 (9 Sept). "Birds of a feather". John Gould (ornithologist) and the Gould League. Multicoloured cover as Type P **68**. Booklet contains text and illustrations on panes and interleaving pages.

SP177 $12.95 booklet containing four panes of two stamps in vertical pairs: Nos. 3272 and 3271; Nos. 3271 and 3270; Nos. 3270 and 3272; Nos. 3273 and 3270 .... 27·00

Face value: $9.90.

A similar booklet with commemorative inscription added for 300 issues of *Stamp Bulletin Australia* was issued on 15 Sept 2009 in limited quantities. This booklet included a pane of four containing Nos. 3270/4 and was sold for $24.95.

P **69** Young Girls playing with Pedal Car

2009 (25 Sept). Classic Toys. Multicoloured cover as Type P **69**. Booklet contains text and illustrations on panes and interleaving pages.

SP178 $12.95 booklet containing Nos. 3275/9 in separate panes of four .... 21·00

Face value: $11.

P **70** Author's Names

2010 (22 Jan). Australian Legends. "Legends of the Written Word". Grey, light grey and black cover, 158×208 *mm,* as Type P **70**. Booklets contain text and illustrations on interleaving pages.
SP179 $24.95 booklet containing Nos. 3328/31, 3332/5 and 3336/9 in blocks of four and in panes with two horizontal pairs .... 35·00
Face value: $13.20.

P **71** Governor Lachlan Macquarie and Windsor, New South Wales, 1813

2010 (16 Feb). Bicentenary of Arrival of Governor Lachlan Macquarie in New South Wales. Multicoloured cover as Type P **71**. Booklet contains text and illustrations on panes and interleaving pages. Stitched.
SP180 $10.95 booklet containing Nos. 3346/9 in separate panes of four .... 22·00
A similar booklet containing imperforate panes was issued on 12 March 2010 for the Canberra Stamp Show.

P **72** Carousel Horse, Hot Dog and Ticket

2010 (23 Mar). "Come to the Show". Multicoloured cover as Type P **72**. Booklet contains text and illustrations on panes and interleaving pages.
SP181 $12.95 booklet containing Nos. 3361/5 in separate panes of four .... 20·00
Face value: $11.

P **73** Kokoda Trail, 1942

2010 (20 Apr). Kokoda. Multicoloured cover as Type P **73**. Stitched.
SP182 $10.95 booklet containing three panes: Nos. 3374/5, each×2; Nos. 3376 and 3378, each×2; No. 3377×4 .... 27·00
Face value: $8.40.

P **74** Steam Train, West Coast Wilderness Railway, Tasmania

2010 (7 May). Great Australian Railways. Multicoloured cover as Type P **74**.
SP183 $12.95 booklet containing four panes: Nos. 3384/5 and 3386×2; No. 3384×2 and 3385/6; As **MS**3388 but 156×104 mm; Nos. 3384, 3385×2 and 3386 .... 22·00
No. SP183 also contains four postcards.
Face value: $8.70.

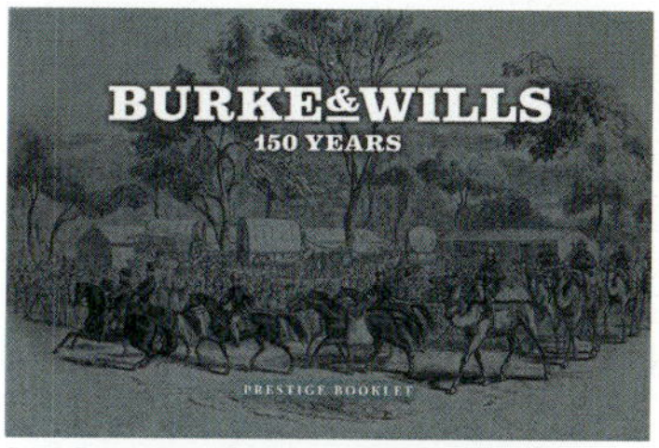

P **75** Departure of Burke and Wills Expedition from Royal Park, Melbourne, August 1860

2010 (3 Aug). 150th Anniv of Departure of Burke and Wills Expedition from Melbourne. Black and bluish grey cover as Type P **75**. Booklet contains text and illustrations on panes and interleaving pages.
SP184 $10.95 booklet containing Nos. 3466/9 in separate panes of four (3466/7) or two (3468/9) .... 20·00
Face value: $9.60.
A similar booklet containing imperforate panes was issued on 3 August 2010 for Adelaide Stampex.

P **76** 'LONG WEEKEND' (*Illustration reduced. Actual size* 157×105 *mm*)

2010 (22 Sept). 'Long Weekend'. Multicoloured cover, 157×105 *mm,* as Type P **76**. Booklet contains text and illustrations on panes and interleaving pages.
SP185 $13.95 booklet containing Nos. 3482/6 in separate panes of four .... 19·00
No. SP185 also contains five postcards.
Face value: $12.

P **77** Early Melbourne Cup Race

2010 (1 Nov). 150th Anniv of Melbourne Cup Horse Race. Multicoloured cover, 159×104 *mm*, as Type P **77**.

SP186 $13.95 booklet containing Nos. 3510/13 in separate panes of four .... 28·00

No. SP186 also contains reproductions of Nos. 336, 701/2, 2247 and 2249 in separate panes of two.

Face value: $9.60.

P **78** Flowers

2011 (8 Mar). Floral Festivals Australia. Multicoloured cover, 157×105 *mm*, as Type P **78**. Booklet contains text and illustrations on panes and interleaving pages.

SP187 $12.95 booklet containing Nos. 3559/63 in separate panes of four .... 17·00

Face value: $12.

P **79** Griffin, Dragon, Mermaid, Troll, Fairy and Unicorn

2011 (4 Oct). Mythical Creatures. Multicoloured cover, 156×209 *mm*, as Type P **79**. Booklet contains text and illustrations on panes and interleaving pages.

SP188 $19.95 booklet containing Nos. 3652/7 in separate panes of four .... 28·00

Face value: $16.80

P **80** Couple Holding Bouquet

2012 (17 Jan). Greetings Stamps. 'Precious Moments'. Multicoloured cover, 157×105 *mm*, as Type P **80**. Booklet contains text and illustrations on panes and interleaving pages.

SP189 $24.95 booklet containing self-adhesive design as No. 3691 in five panes of four .... 35·00

Stamps from SP189 are as No. 3691 but self-adhesive, have irregular partial phosphor frames and die-cut perforations 11½×11 (interrupted on horiz sides).

No. SP189 contains a pane of 20 small circular self-adhesive labels.

Face value: $24.

P **81** Legends of Football'

2012 (20 Jan). Australian Legends. Legends of Football. Multicoloured cover, 155×209 *mm*, as Type P **81**. Booklet contains text and illustrations on panes and interleaving pages.

SP190 $19.95 booklet containing Nos. 3697/704 in separate panes of four .... 28·00

Face value: $19.20.

P **82** *Charlotte* (ferry) passing Luna Park, Sydney

2012 (21 Feb). City Transport. Multicoloured cover, 158×105 *mm*, as Type P **82**. Booklet contains text and illustrations on panes and interleaving pages.

SP191 $12.95 booklet containing Nos. 3724/8 in panes of four .... 23·00

Face value: $12

P **83** *Chromodoris westraliensis*

2012 (8 May). Underwater World. Nudibranchs. Multicoloured cover, 159×106 *mm*, as Type P **83**. Booklet contains text and illustrations on panes and interleaving pages.

SP192 $14.95 booklet containing five panes of four stamps as follows: No.3781×4; No. 3782×4; No. 3783×4; Nos. 3781/3 and 3785; Nos. 3781/3 and 3786.... 21·00

Face value: $13.80

P **84** Concert Audience

2012 (18 Jan). Australian Legends. Legends of Music. Multicoloured cover, 156×208 *mm,* as Type P **84**. Booklet contains text and illustrations on panes and interleaving pages.

SP193 $24.95 booklet containing Nos. 3897/906 in separate panes of four .... 35·00

Face value: $24

P **85** 'Wedding Greetings'

2013 (5 Feb). Greetings Stamps. Wedding Greetings. Multicoloured cover, 104×156 *mm,* as Type P **85**. Booklet contains illustrations on panes and interleaving pages.

SP194 $24.95 booklet containing No. 3928 in five panes of four
Face value: $24 .... 35·00

No. SP194 contains a pane of 20 circular self-adhesive labels.

P **86** Surfer

2013 (12 Feb). 50th Anniv of Surfing Australia. Multicoloured cover, 157×104 *mm,* as Type P **86**. Booklet contains text and illustrations on panes and interleaving pages.

SP195 $24 95 booklet containing Nos. 3929/32 in separate panes of four and in *se-tenant* pane .... 35·00

Booklet contains text and illustrations on panes and interleaving pages.

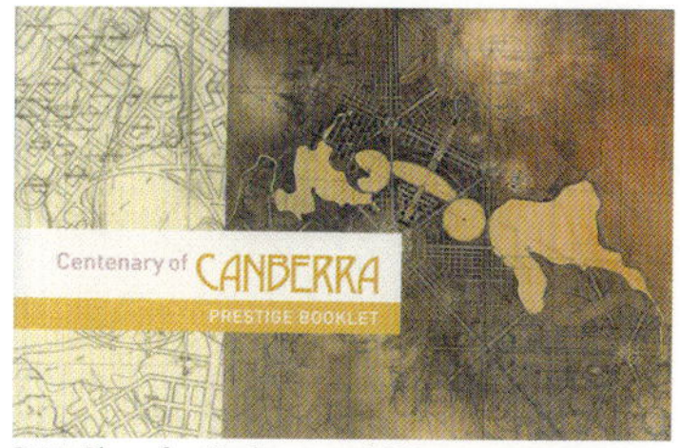

P **87** Plans for Canberra, *c.* 1913

2013 (5 Mar). Centenary of Canberra. Multicoloured cover, 158×104 *mm,* as Type P **87**. Booklet contains text and illustrations on panes and interleaving pages.

SP196 $12.95 booklet containing six panes as follows: Nos. 3948/9, each×2; No. 3480×4; No. 3227×2; No. 2994×2; No. 2844×2; Nos. 2075/6 .... 18·00

Face value: $12.38

P **88** Pond, Bridge and Borders at Royal Tasmanian Botanical Gardens

2013 (23 Apr). Australian Botanic Gardens (2nd issue). Multicoloured cover, 158×104 *mm,* as Type P **88**. Booklet contains text and illustrations on panes and interleaving pages.

SP197 $12.95 booklet containing five panes of 4 of Nos. 3973/7, one of each design, each pane with two central stamp-size labels .... 18·00

Face value: $12

P **89** Kangaroos

2013 (10 May). Story of the Kangaroo. Multicoloured cover, 158×105 *mm,* as Type P **89**. Booklet contains text and illustrations on panes and interleaving pages.

SP198 $12.95 booklet containing: Nos. 164 and 318; Nos. 492, 881, 977 and 1037; Nos. 1368 and 1453/5; Nos. 1273, 2496, 3219 and 3610 .... 13·00

No. SP198 contains valid stamps with a face value of $8.07.

Nos. 164 and 318 are in pre-decimal currency and not postally valid.

Stamps from booklet No. SP198 are perforated 14×14½ (third pane) or 14½×14 (others).

P **90** Kangaroo and Map of Australia

2013 (10 May). Centenary of First Australian Commonwealth Stamp. Kangaroo and Map 1913 - 2013. Multicoloured cover, 156×208 *mm*, as Type P **90**.
SP199 $24.95 booklet containing two panes: No. 3983; As No. 3983 but imperf .... 35·00

P **91** Spotted Pardalote (*Illustration further reduced*)

2013 (11 May). Australian Birds. Multicoloured cover, 210×145 *mm*, as Type P **91**. Booklet contains text and illustrations on panes and interleaving pages.
SP200 $24.95 booklet containing: Nos. 3992/5, 3734/7, 3505/8, 3270/3 .... 38·00
Face value: $24.45

P **92** Royal Jubilees

2013 (18 Jun). Royal Jubilees Stamp and Coin booklet. Multicoloured cover, 172×119 *mm*, as Type P **92**. Booklet contains text and illustrations on panes and interleaving pages.
SP201 $19.95 booklet containing two panes of No. 3969, two panes of No. 3970×3 and one pane of No. 3970 .... 30·00
Face value: $19.40

P **93**

2013 (9 July). Indigenous Leaders. Multicoloured cover, 159×105 *mm*, as Type P **93**. Booklet contains text and illustrations on panes and interleaving pages.
SP202 $12.95 booklet containing Nos. 4017/21 in panes of four .... 15·00
Face value: $12

P **94** Australian Langshan

2013 (3 Sept). Australian Poultry Breeds. Multicoloured cover, 156×104 *mm*, as Type P **94**. Booklet contains text and illustrations on panes and interleaving pages.
SP203 $12.95 booklet containing the following panes: No. 4056×4; No. 4057×4; No. 4058×4; Nos. 4056/7, each×2; No. 4058×4 .... 15·00
Face value: $12

P **95** Australovenator, Qantassaurus and Timimus (*Illustration further reduced*)

2013 (24 Sept). Australia's Age of the Dinosaurs. Multicoloured cover, 196×121 *mm*, as Type P **95**. Booklet contains text and illustrations on panes and interleaving pages.
SP204 $12.95 booklet containing Nos. 4061/2, 4064 and 4066 in separate panes of four and Nos. 4063 and 4065 in separate panes of two .... 17·00
Face value: $12

P **96** Cook's Knife, Wooden Spoon and Spatula

2014 (17 Jan). Australian Legends. Legends of Cooking. Multicoloured cover, 156×208 *mm*, as Type P **96**. Booklet contains text and illustrations on panes and interleaving pages.
SP205 $14.95 booklet containing Nos. 4112/16 in separate panes of four .... 16·00
Face value: $12

P **97** Couple holding Hands

2014 (15 Apr). Greetings Stamps. Wedding Day. Multicoloured cover, 105×157 *mm,* as Type P **97**. Booklet contains illustrations on panes and interleaving pages.

SP206 $28.95 booklet containing self-adhesive design as No. 4154 in five panes of four .... 40·00

Stamps from SP105 are as No. 4154 but self-adhesive, with phosphor frames at left, right and foot of the stamp and die-cut perforations 11½×11 (interrupted on horiz sides). No. SP105 contains a pane of 20 small circular self-adhesive labels.

Face value $28

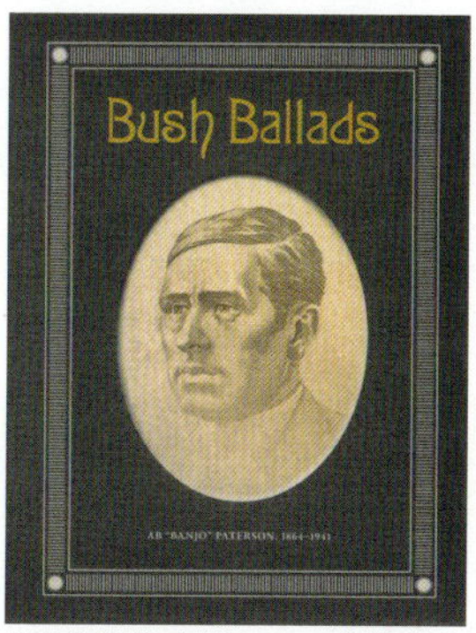

P **98** A. B. 'Banjo' Paterson, 1864–1941

2014 (13 May). Bush Ballads by A. B. 'Banjo' Paterson. Multicoloured cover, 156×209 *mm,* as Type P **98**. Booklet contains text and illustrations on panes and interleaving pages.

SP207 $16.95 booklet containing Nos. 4175/8 in *se-tenant* pane and in separate panes of four, and pane as **MS**4179 but 156×209 mm....................................... 20·00

Face value: $16.80

P **99** King George V, *c.* 1935 and Australia 1914 1d. Red Stamp

2014 (17 Jun). Centenary of King George V Stamps. Multicoloured cover, 158×208 *mm,* as Type P **99**. Booklet contains text and illustrations on panes and interleaving pages.

SP208 $16.95 booklet containing Nos. 4185/8 in separate panes of four and in *se-tenant* pane, and pane as **MS**4189 but 158×208 *mm* and imperf............ 22·00

Face value: $16.80

P **100** Maurice Guillaux and Bleriot XI Monoplane

2014 (1 July). Centenary of First Air Mail. Multicoloured cover, 172×119 *mm,* as Type P 100. Booklet conatines text and illustrations on panes and interleaving pages.

SP209 $19.95 booklet containing four panes as follows: Nos. 4190/1; two panes of No. 4190×4; No. 4191×4.............................. 32·00 30·00

Face value: $19.30

No. SP209 contains a pane of eight air mail labels inscribed '100 Years of Air Mail in Australia'.

P **101** Queen Elizabeth II at Liège, Belgium, May 1966

2015 (7 Apr). Queen's Birthday. The Queen's Hats. Multicoloured cover, 106×158 *mm,* as Type P **101**. Booklet contains text and illustrations on interleaving pages.

SP210 $14.95 booklet containing Nos. 4341/2, two panes of No. 4341×4 and No. 4342×2...................................... 24·00

Face value: $14.55

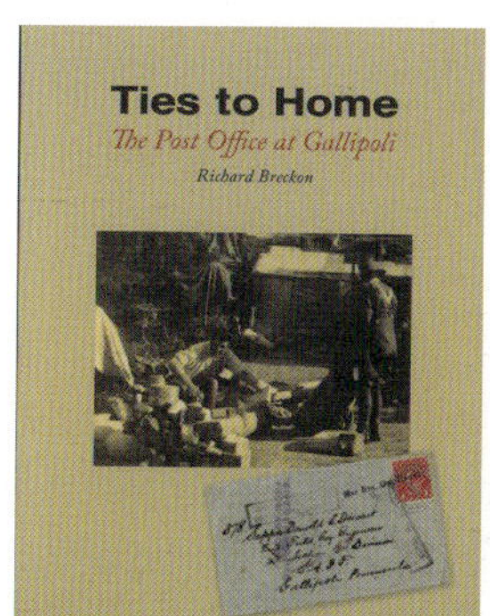

P **102** Sorting Parcels for the 1st Australian Light Horse Regiment and Inward Letter

2015 (14 Apr). Centenary of World War I. Gallipoli Campaign. Ties to Home. The Post Office at Gallipoli. Multicoloured cover, 156×208 *mm,* as Type P **102**. Booklet contains text and illustrations on panes and interleaving pages.

SP211 $14.95 booklet containing Nos. 4356/60 in separate panes of four .... 24·00

Face value: $14

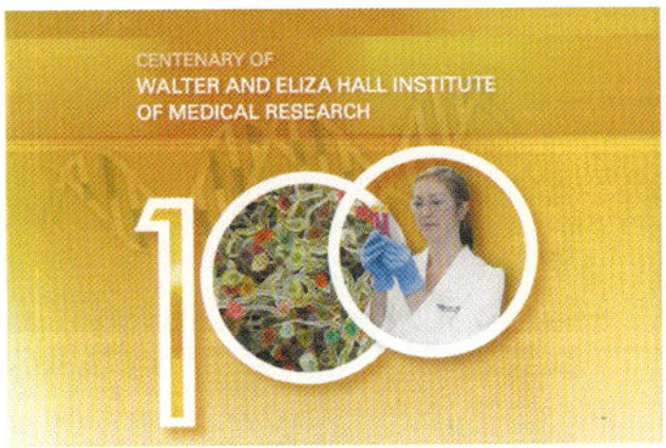

P **103** Dr. Tracy Putoczki and B Cells in Fibrous Network of a Lymph Node

2015 (30 June). Centenary of Walter and Eliza Hall Institute of Medical Research, Melbourne. Multicoloured cover, 156×104 *mm,* as Type P **103**. Booklet contains text and illustrations on panes and interleaving pages.

SP212 $14.95 booklet containing No. 4387 in five panes of four .... 24·00

Face value: $14

P **104** Tasman Island, Tasmania

2015 (7 July). Centenary of Commonwealth Management of Lighthouses. Multicoloured cover, 156×104 *mm,* as Type P **104**. Booklet contains text and illustrations on panes and interleaving pages.

SP213 $14.95 booklet containing Nos. 4388/91 in separate panes and in *se-tenant* pane .... 24·00

Face value: $14

P **105** Queen Elizabeth II

2015 (9 Sept). Long May She Reign. Multicoloured cover, 157×207 *mm,* as Type P **105**. Booklet contains text and illustrations on panes and interleaving pages.

SP214 $19.95 booklet containing Nos. 4425/7 in separate panes of four and Nos. 4428/9 in separate panes of two .... 32·00

Face value: $19.40

P **106** Cyclist

2015 (13 Oct). Bicycles. Multicoloured cover, 157×104 *mm,* as Type P **106**. Booklet contains text and illustrations on panes and interleaving pages.

SP215 $14.95 booklet containing Nos. 4453/6 as separate panes of four (4453/4) or two (4455/6) .... 24·00

Face value: $14.80

P **107** 'I DO!'

2016 (25 Jan). Weddings 2016. Multicoloured cover, 171×120 *mm,* as Type P **107**. Booklet contains illustrations on panes and interleaving pages.

SP216 $32.95 booklet containing self-adhesive design as No. 4531 in four panes of four .... 50·00

Stamps from SP216 are as No. 4531 but self-adhesive, with phosphor frames at left, right and foot of the stamp and die-cut perforations 11½×11 (interrupted on *horiz* sides). No. SP216 contains a pane of 20 small circular self-adhesive labels.

Face value $32

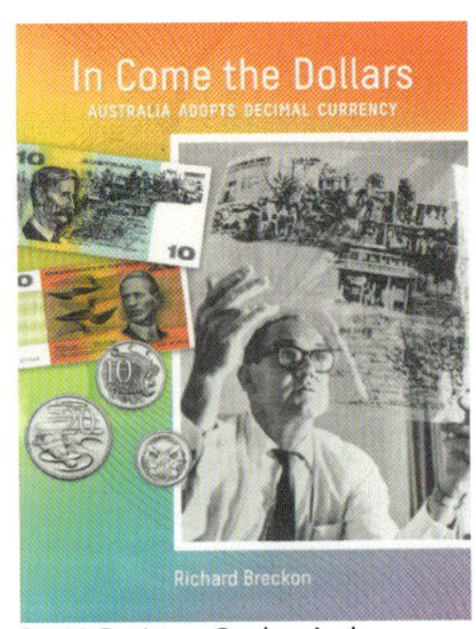

P **108** Designer Gordon Andrews checking Transparency of Ten Dollar Note Artwork, *c.* 1965, and Decimal Notes and Coins

2016 (9 Feb). 50th Anniv of Decimal Currency in Australia. 'In Come the Dollars'. Multicoloured cover, 150×207 *mm,* as Type P **108**. Booklet contains text and illustrations on panes and interleaving pages.

SP217 $20.95 booklet containing stamps as No. 4538 but P. 13½×14 in five panes of four .... 32·00

Face value: $20

P **109** Soldier of Australian 2nd Battalion writing letter, Flesselles, France, November 1916

2016 (12 Apr). Centenary of World War I. The Western Front. Ties to Home. Multicoloured cover, 155×207 *mm*, as Type P **109**. Booklet contains text and illustrations on panes and interleaving pages.

SP218	$20.95 booklet containing Nos. 4559/62 in five panes of four	32·00

Face value: $20

Military Post Booklets

Issued for the use of Australian Forces in Vietnam

MB **1**

1967 (30 May–Sept). Yellow-green and black on white cover as Type MB **1**. Pane attached by selvedge.

MB1	50c. booklet containing 5c. (No. 386) in block of 10	80·00
	a. Containing No. 386*b* (Sept)	80·00

1968 (1 Mar). Yellow-green and black on white cover as Type MB **1**. Pane attached by selvedge.

MB2	50c. booklet containing 5c. (No. 386*c*) in block of 10	50·00

POSTAGE DUE STAMPS

POSTAGE DUE PRINTERS. Nos. D1/62 were typographed at the New South Wales Government Printing Office, Sydney. They were not used in Victoria.

D **1**

D **2**

D **3**

Type D **1** adapted from plates of New South Wales Type D **1**. No letters at foot.

1902 (1 July). Chalk-surfaced paper. Wmk Type D **2** (inverted on 1d., 3d. and 4d.).

(a) P 11½, 12

D1	D **1**	½d. emerald-green or dull green	3·50	6·50
D2		1d. emerald-green	25·00	13·00
		w. Wmk upright	45·00	26·00
D3		2d. emerald-green	65·00	15·00
		w. Wmk inverted	£130	
D4		3d. emerald-green	50·00	30·00
		w. Wmk upright	55·00	38·00
D5		4d. emerald-green	50·00	14·00
		w. Wmk upright	65·00	25·00
D6		6d. emerald-green	60·00	12·00
		w. Wmk inverted	55·00	12·00
D7		8d. emerald-green or dull green	£100	85·00
D8		5s. emerald-green or dull green	£200	75·00
D1/8 *Set of* 8			£475	£200
D1s/7s Opt "SPECIMEN" *Set of* 7			£350	

(b) P 11½, 12, compound with 11

D9	D **1**	1d. emerald-green	£350	£160
		w. Wmk upright	£375	£150
D10		2d. emerald-green	£500	£180
		w. Wmk inverted	£600	£225

(c) P 11

D12	D **1**	1d. emerald-green (*wmk upright*)	£2500	£900

Stamps may be found showing portions of the marginal watermark "NEW SOUTH WALES POSTAGE".

1902 (July)–**04**. Type D **3** (with space at foot filled in). Chalk-surfaced paper. Wmk Type D **2** (inverted on 3d., 4d., 6d., 8d. and 5s.).

(a) P 11½, 12

D13	D **3**	1d. emerald-green (10.02)	£275	£130
D14		2d. emerald-green (3.03)	—	£170
D15		3d. emerald-green (3.03)	£350	£100
D17		5d. emerald-green	70·00	18·00
D18		10d. emerald-green *or* dull green	95·00	23·00
D19		1s. emerald-green	80·00	19·00
D20		2s. emerald-green	£130	18·00

(b) P 11½, 12, compound with 11

D22	D **3**	½d. emerald-green *or* dull green (3.04)	21·00	17·00
		w. Wmk inverted	23·00	19·00
D23		1d. emerald-green *or* dull green (10.02)	20·00	4·50
		w. Wmk inverted	20·00	4·50
D24		2d. emerald-green *or* dull green (3.03)	50·00	3·00
		w. Wmk inverted	50·00	3·00
D25		3d. emerald-green *or* dull green (3.03)	90·00	17·00
		w. Wmk upright	£120	32·00
D26		4d. emerald-green *or* dull green (5.03)	75·00	22·00
		w. Wmk upright	75·00	24·00
D27		5d. emerald-green	65·00	23·00
D28		6d. emerald-green (3.04)	75·00	11·00
D29		8d. emerald-green (3.04)	£140	55·00
D30		10d. emerald-green *or* dull green	£120	19·00
D31		1s. emerald-green	£110	28·00
D32		2s. emerald-green	£190	27·00
D33		5s. emerald-green *or* dull green (5.03)	£450	24·00

(c) P 11

D34	D **3**	½d. emerald-green *or* dull green (wmk inverted) (3.04)	£550	£300
D35		1d. emerald-green *or* dull green (10.02)	£160	30·00
		w. Wmk inverted	£200	40·00
D36		2d. emerald-green (3.03)	£225	29·00
		w. Wmk inverted	£225	29·00
D37		3d. emerald-green *or* dull green (3.03)	£150	60·00
		w. Wmk upright	£160	60·00
D38		4d. emerald-green *or* dull green (5.03)	£250	70·00
		w. Wmk upright	£250	70·00
D39		5d. emerald-green	£375	55·00
D40		6d. emerald-green (3.04)	£110	16·00
D41		1s. emerald-green	£475	30·00
D42		5s. emerald-green (5.03)	£1600	£275
D43		10s. dull green (10.03)	£2000	£1800
D44		20s. dull green (10.03)	£4250	£2250
D13/44 *Set of* 14			£6500	£4000
D13s/44s Opt "SPECIMEN" *Set of* 14			£1100	

The 10s. and 20s. values were only issued in New South Wales.

The used prices quoted for Nos. D43/4 are for cancelled to order examples.

D **4**

D **6**

1906 (Jan)–**08**. Chalk-surfaced paper. Wmk Type D **4**.

(a) P 11½, 12, compound with 11

D45	D **3**	½d. green (1.07)	15·00	17·00
		w. Wmk inverted	15·00	17·00
D46		1d. green	27·00	5·00
		w. Wmk inverted	27·00	6·00
D47		2d. green	75·00	9·00
		w. Wmk inverted	75·00	9·00
D48		3d. green (7.08)	£700	£325

D49		4d. green (4.07)	70·00	23·00
		w. Wmk inverted	70·00	23·00
D50		6d. green (3.08)	£300	25·00
		w. Wmk inverted	£300	25·00
D45/50 *Set of* 6			£1000	£350

(b) P 11

D51	D **3**	1d. dull green	£3000	£1100
		aw. Wmk inverted	£3000	£1100
D51*b*		2d. green	†	£4750
D52		4d. dull green (4.07)	£5500	£3250

No. D51*b* is only known pen-cancelled.
Shades exist.

1907 (July–Sept). Chalk-surfaced paper. Wmk Type w **11** (Crown over double lined A) (inverted on ½d.). P 11½×11.

D53	D **3**	½d. dull green	35·00	75·00
		w. Wmk upright	55·00	£100
D54		1d. dull green (Aug)	£140	75·00
		w. Wmk inverted	£140	75·00
D55		2d. dull green (Sept)	£275	£160
		w. Wmk inverted	£300	£180
D56		4d. dull green (Sept)	£275	£150
		w. Wmk inverted	£275	£160
		y. Wmk inverted and reversed	£700	
D57		6d. dull green (Sept)	£325	£225
		w. Wmk inverted	—	£375
D53/7 *Set of* 5			£900	£600

1908 (Sept)–**09**. Stroke after figure of value. Chalk-surfaced paper. Wmk Type D **4** (inverted on 10s.).

(a) P 11½×11

D58	D **6**	1s. dull green (1909)	£120	16·00
D59		5s. dull green	£250	48·00

(b) P 11

D60	D **6**	2s. dull green (1909)	£1000	£17000
D61		10s. dull green (1909)	£2500	£26000
D62		20s. dull green (1909)	£7000	£50000

Nos. D61/2 were only issued in New South Wales. The used prices quoted for Nos. D60/2 are for examples with verified postal cancellations from the period of issue.

D **7**

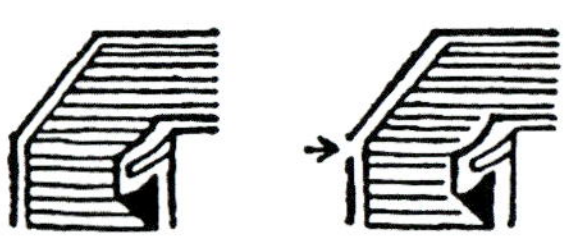

1d.

2d.

(Typo J. B. Cooke, Melbourne)

1909 (1 July)–**10**. Wmk Crown over A, Type w **11**.

*(a) P 12×12½ (comb)**

D63	D **7**	½d. rosine and yellow-green (8.09)	16·00	32·00
D64		1d. rosine and yellow-green (I)	14·00	4·00
		b. Die II (7.10)	35·00	2·00
D65		2d. rosine and yellow-green (I)	38·00	5·50
		a. Die II (8.10)	48·00	2·00
		aw. Wmk inverted	†	£5500
D66		3d. rosine and yellow-green (9.09)	40·00	19·00
D67		4d. rosine and yellow-green (8.09)	42·00	5·00
D68		6d. rosine and yellow-green (8.09)	27·00	2·75
D69		1s. rosine and yellow-green (8.09)	30·00	3·25
D70		2s. rosine and yellow-green (8.09)	70·00	10·00
D71		5s. rosine and yellow-green (10.09)	90·00	12·00
D72		10s. rosine and yellow-green (11.09)	£250	£150
D73		£1 rosine and yellow-green (11.09)	£500	£300
D63/73 *Set of* 11			£950	£475

(b) P 11 (line)

D74	D **7**	1d. rose and yellow-green (II)	£3750	£1400
D74*a*		2d. rose and yellow-green (II)	£24000	£15000
D75		6d. rose and yellow-green	£35000	£24000

*Nos. D64/b and D65a are also known perf 12½ (line).

Only one unused example, without gum, and another pen-cancelled are known of No. D74*a*.

The 1d. of this printing (No. D74) is distinguishable from No. D78 by the colours, the green being very yellow and the rose having less of a carmine tone. The paper is thicker and slightly toned, that of No D78 being pure white; the gum is thick and yellowish, No. D78 having thin white gum.

All later issues of the 1d. and 2d. are Die II.

(Typo J.B. Cooke (later ptgs by T.S. Harrison))

1913 (July)–**23**. Thin paper. White gum. W w **11**.

(a) P 12½ (line)

D76	D **7**	½d. scarlet and pale yellow-green (7.13)	32·00	27·00
		w. Wmk inverted	£110	£110

(b) P 11

D77	D **7**	½d. rosine and bright apple-green (10.14)	20·00	20·00
		a. Wmk sideways	6·50	13·00
D78		1d. rosine and bright apple-green (8.14)	22·00	3·75
		a. Wmk sideways	28·00	2·50
		w. Wmk inverted	£100	75·00

(c) P 14

D79	D **7**	½d. rosine and bright apple-green (11.14)	£225	£275
		a. Carmine and apple-green (Harrison) (1919)	9·00	17·00
D80		1d. rosine and bright apple-green (9.14)	£170	16·00
		a. Scarlet and pale yellow-green (2.18)	20·00	15·00
		aw. Wmk inverted	†	£1400
		b. Carmine and apple-green (Harrison) (1919)	18·00	3·75
D81		2d. scarlet and pale yellow-green (11.17)	17·00	11·00
		a. Carmine and apple-green (Harrison) (11.18)	29·00	6·00
D82		3d. rosine and apple-green (5.16)	85·00	32·00
		a. Wmk sideways	£7500	£4500
D83		4d. carmine and apple-green (Harrison) (4.21)	£110	55·00
		b. Carmine and pale yellow-green	£110	50·00
		ba. Wmk sideways	£1000	£475
D85		1s. scarlet and pale yellow-green (6.23)	25·00	15·00
D86		10s. scarlet and pale yellow-green (5.21)	£1400	
D87		£1 scarlet and pale yellow-green (5.21)	£950	£2750
D79*a*/87 *Set of* 8			£2250	

(d) Perf 14 compound with 11

D88	D **7**	1d. carmine and apple-green	£12000	

(Typo T. S. Harrison (to Feb 1926), A. J. Mullett (to June 1927) and J. Ash (thereafter))

1922 (Feb)–**30**. W **6**.

(a) P 14

D91	D **7**	½d. carmine and yellow-green (17.5.23)	3·50	8·00
D92		1d. carmine and yellow-green	4·00	1·00
		w. Wmk inverted	£6000	
D93		1½d. carmine and yellow-green (3.25)	1·50	9·00
		w. Wmk inverted	†	£6000
D94		2d. carmine and yellow-green	3·50	2·25
D95		3d. carmine and yellow-green	9·50	4·75
D96		4d. carmine and yellow-green	35·00	22·00
D97		6d. carmine and yellow-green (8.22)	26·00	16·00

(b) P 11

D98	D **7**	4d. carmine and yellow-green (22.9.30)	16·00	7·00
D91/98 *Set of* 8			90·00	60·00

All values perforated 14 were printed by Harrison and all but the 1d. by Mullett and Ash. The 4d. perforated 11 was produced by J. Ash. There is a wide variation of shades in this issue.

(Typo J. Ash)

1931 (Oct)–**36**. W **15**.

(a) P 14

D100	D **7**	1d. carmine and yellow-green (10.31)	7·00	11·00
		a. Imperf between (horiz pair)	†	£20000
D102		2d. carmine and yellow-green (19.10.31)	7·00	11·00

(b) P 11

D105	D **7**	½d. carmine and yellow-green (4.34)	12·00	19·00
D106		1d. carmine and yellow-green (21.11.32)	7·50	3·25
D107		2d. carmine and yellow-green (1933)	16·00	2·00
D108		3d. carmine and yellow-green (5.36)	75·00	70·00
D109		4d. carmine and yellow-green (23.5.34)	16·00	4·75
D110		6d. carmine and yellow-green (4.36)	£375	£325
D111		1s. carmine and yellow-green (8.34)	55·00	35·00

D105/11	*Set of 7*	£475	£400

D **8**

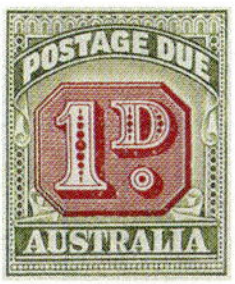

D **9**

A.

B.

C.

Type A. Solid rectangle inside "D" (ptgs of ½d., 1d., 2d., 4d. and 6d. from 1909 to 1945)

Type B. Shaded area inside "D" (ptgs of 3d. from 1909 to 1945)

Type C. Solid segment of circle inside "D" (ptgs of all values below 1s. from 1946)

D.

E.

Type D. Six lines of shading above numeral and four below (ptgs of 1s. from 1909 to 1945)

Type E. Larger "1" with only three background lines above; hyphen more upright (ptgs of 1s. from 1946 to 1953)

(Frame recess. Value typo J. Ash (to 1940, then W. C. G. McCracken))

1938 (July–Sept). W **15**. P 14½×14.

D112	D **8**	½d. carmine and green (A) (Sept)	3·00	6·00
D113		1d. carmine and green (A)	16·00	1·75
D114		2d. carmine and green (A)	24·00	3·25
D115		3d. carmine and green (B) (Aug)	65·00	26·00
D116		4d. carmine and green (A) (Aug)	9·00	1·00
D117		6d. carmine and green (A) (Aug)	75·00	48·00
D118		1s. carmine and green (D) (Aug)	40·00	12·00
D112/18		*Set of 7*	£200	85·00

Shades exist.

1946–57. Redrawn as Type C and E (1s). W **15**. P 14½×14.

D119	D **9**	½d. carmine and green (9.56)	1·50	4·00
D120		1d. carmine and green (17.6.46)	1·25	80
		w. Wmk inverted	£6500	
D121		2d. carmine and green (9.46)	6·00	1·25
		w. Wmk inverted	†	£6500
D122		3d. carmine and green (6.8.46)	6·50	1·25
D123		4d. carmine and green (30.7.52)	8·50	2·50
D124		5d. carmine and green (16.12.48)	21·00	12·00
D125		6d. carmine and green (19.8.47)	13·00	2·00
D126		7d. carmine and green (26.8.53)	2·75	1·50
D127		8d. carmine and green (24.4.57)	4·50	15·00
D128		1s. carmine and green (9.47)	17·00	1·75
D119/28		*Set of 10*	70·00	38·00

There are many shades in this issue.

D **10**

1953 (26 Aug)–**59**. W **15**. P 14½×14.

D129	1s. carmine and yellow-green (17.2.54)	8·50	1·50
	a. *Carmine and deep green*	12·00	5·50
D130	2s. carmine and yellow-green	14·00	5·00
	a. *Carmine and deep green*	£400	£130
D131	5s. carmine and green	14·00	2·25
	a. *Carmine and deep green* (6.59)	12·00	1·00
D129/31	*Set of 3*	32·00	8·00
D129a/31a	*Set of 3*	£350	£120

A new die was introduced for No. D131a. This differs from the original in having a distinct gap between the two arms of the "5". On No. D131 these two features are joined.

Two Dies of ½d.:
Die I. Six dots in base of "2"
Die II. Seven dots in base of "2"

I.

II.

Two Dies of 1d. to 10d.:
Die I. Numeral, "D" and stop, generally unoutlined.
Die II. Clear white line separates numeral, etc. from background.

1958–60. No wmk. P 14½×14.

D132	½d. carmine and dp green (I) (27.2.58)	4·75	4·75
	a. Die II (6.59)	2·50	1·25
D133	1d. carmine and deep green (I) (25.2.58)	2·50	3·00
	a. Die II (6.59)	2·50	75
D134	3d. carmine and deep green (II) (25.5.60)	2·00	3·00
D135	4d. carmine and deep green (I) (27.2.58)	9·00	7·00
	a. Die II (6.59)	2·75	4·00
D136	5d. carmine and deep green (I) (27.2.58)	11·00	21·00
	a. Die II (6.59)	60·00	70·00
D137	6d. carmine and deep green (II) (25.5.60)	2·50	2·00
D138	8d. carmine and deep green (II) (25.2.58)	6·00	28·00
D139	10d. carmine and deep green (II) (9.12.59)	3·50	1·75
D140	1s. carmine and deep green (6.5.58)	5·50	1·50
	a. *Deep carmine and deep green* (6.59)	6·50	1·00
D141	2s. dp carmine and deep green (8.3.60)	12·00	2·00
D132a/41	*Set of 10*	45·00	60·00

Nos. D140*a* and D141. Value tablets are re-engraved and have thicker and sharper printed lines than before.

The use of Postage Due stamps ceased on 13 January 1963.

OFFICIAL STAMPS

From 1902 the departments of the Commonwealth government were issued with stamps of the various Australian States perforated "OS" to denote official use. These were replaced in 1913 by Commonwealth of Australia issues with similar perforated initials as listed below.

During the same period the administrations of the Australian States used their own stamps and those of the Commonwealth perforated with other initials for the same purpose. These States issues are outside the scope of this catalogue.

Most shades listed under the postage issues also exist perforated "OS". Only those which are worth more than the basic colours are included below.

(O **1**)

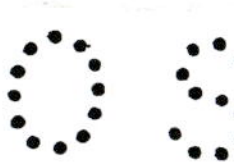

(O **2**) (11 holes in "S". Examples with 12 holes in "S" are N.S.W. state issues)

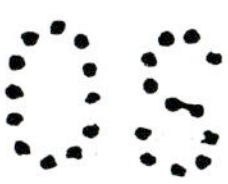

(O **3**)

1913 (Jan–Apr). Nos. 1/16 punctured as Type O **1**. W **2**. P 12.

O1	**1**	½d. green (Die I)	27·00	19·00
		w. Wmk inverted	†	£150
O2		1d. red (Die I)	16·00	4·75
		cw. Wmk inverted	£150	25·00
		d. Die II	40·00	15·00
		da. Wmk sideways	†	£1100
		dw. Wmk inverted	£150	25·00
O3		2d. grey (Die I)	55·00	22·00
O4		2½d. indigo (Die II)	£325	£140
O5		3d. olive (Die I)	£190	50·00
		ca. In pair with Die II	£1800	
		dw. Wmk inverted	£325	£130
		e. Die II	£700	£250
		ew. Wmk inverted	£1600	£425
O6		4d. orange (Die II)	£275	22·00
		a. Orange-yellow	£650	£180
O7		5d. chestnut (Die II)	£250	50·00
O8		6d. ultramarine (Die II)	£200	20·00
		w. Wmk inverted	£1700	£600
O9		9d. violet (Die II)	£300	65·00
		w. Wmk inverted	†	£10000
O10		1s. emerald (Die II)	£325	28·00
		w. Wmk inverted	£2500	£1000
O11		2s. brown (Die II)	£600	£160
		a. Double print	†	£5000
O12		5s. grey and yellow	£1500	£700
O13		10s. grey and pink	£5500	£3000
O14		£1 brown and ultramarine	£9500	£7500

O15		£2 black and rose	£48000	£40000

1914. Nos. 1/16 punctured as Type O **2**. W **2**. P 12.

O16	**1**	½d. green (Die I)	25·00	10·00
		w. Wmk inverted	†	£160
O17		1d. red (Die I)	50·00	26·00
		d. Die II	42·00	3·75
		e. Die IIA	40·00	3·75
O18		2d. grey (Die I)	85·00	4·50
		w. Wmk inverted	£190	50·00
O19		2½d. indigo (Die II)	£375	£150
O20		3d. olive (Die I)	£160	16·00
		dw. Wmk inverted	£375	75·00
		e. Die II	£750	£275
		ew. Wmk inverted	£1300	£450
O21		4d. orange (Die II)	£425	95·00
		a. Orange-yellow	£900	£300
O22		5d. chestnut (Die II)	£325	60·00
O23		6d. ultramarine (Die II)	£225	14·00
		w. Wmk inverted	†	£900
O24		9d. violet (Die II)	£300	50·00
O25		1s. emerald (Die II)	£300	22·00
O26		2s. brown (Die II)	£950	£140
O27		5s. grey and yellow		
O28		10s. grey and pink	£11000	£8000
O29		£1 brown and ultramarine	£16000	£11000
O30		£2 black and rose	£42000	

1915. Nos. 24 and 26/30 punctured as Type O **2**. W **5**. P 12.

O31	**1**	2d. grey (Die I)	£200	12·00
O33		6d. ultramarine (Die II)	£425	18·00
		b. Die IIA	£7000	£3500
O34		9d. violet (Die II)	£900	£110
O35		1s. blue-green (Die II)	£900	£110
O36		2s. brown (Die II)	£1800	£160
O37		5s. grey and yellow	£1900	£225
		a. Yellow portion doubly printed	†	£4750
		w. Wmk inverted	£2000	£325

1914–21. Nos. 20/3 punctured as Type O **2**. W **5**. P 14¼x14 (comb).

O38	**5a**	½d. bright green	22·00	2·75
		a. Perf 14¼ (line)	†	£3500
		w. Wmk inverted	30·00	9·50
O39		1d. carmine-red (I) (No. 21c)	15·00	1·00
		gw. Wmk inverted	30·00	6·00
		h. Die II	£550	65·00
O41		4d. orange	85·00	3·50
		a. Yellow-orange	95·00	7·50
		b. Pale orange-yellow	£190	18·00
		c. Lemon-yellow	£650	95·00
		w. Wmk inverted	£130	28·00
O42		5d. brown (P 14¼ (line))	85·00	4·50
		aw. Wmk inverted	£1300	£700
		b. Printed on the gummed side (wmk inverted)	£8500	
		c. Perf 14¼x14 (comb)	85·00	4·00
		cw. Wmk inverted	£1200	£700

1915–28. Nos. 35/45 punctured as Type O **2**. W **6**. P 12.

O43	**1**	2d. grey (Die I)	60·00	12·00
		bw. Wmk inverted	£160	75·00
		d. Die IIA	85·00	25·00
		da. Printed double	†	£3500
O44		2½d. deep blue (Die II)	95·00	30·00
		w. Wmk inverted	†	£140
O45		3d. yellow-olive (Die I)	65·00	5·50
		cw. Wmk inverted	£120	60·00
		d. Die II	£350	£120
		dw. Wmk inverted	£550	£250
		e. Die IIB	80·00	29·00
		ew. Wmk inverted	£225	£110
O46		6d. ultramarine (Die II)	80·00	10·00
		a. Die IIA	£5500	£1700
		d. Die IIB	£150	42·00
		dw. Wmk inverted	£700	£250
O47		9d. violet (Die II)	95·00	30·00
		b. Die IIB	85·00	35·00
		bw. Wmk inverted	†	£140
O48		1s. blue-green (Die II)	50·00	3·50
		aw. Wmk inverted	£1200	£800
		b. Die IIB	55·00	5·50
O49		2s. brown (Die II)	£475	17·00
		b. Red-brown (aniline)	£2250	£750
		w. Wmk inverted	£4000	£850
O50		5s. grey and yellow	£700	70·00
		w. Wmk inverted	£2000	£1300
O51		10s. grey and pink	£1200	75·00
O52		£1 chocolate and dull blue	£8500	£5500
		ab. Wmk sideways. *Chestnut and bright blue*	£160000	
		aw. Wmk inverted	£9500	£6500
O53		£2 black and rose	£5000	£2500

1916–20. Nos. 47/f and 5d. as No. 23 punctured as Type O **2**. Rough paper. W **5**. P 14.

O54	**5a**	1d. scarlet (Die I)	45·00	7·00
		a. Deep red	45·00	7·00
		b. Rose-red	45·00	7·00
		c. Rosine	£130	22·00
		dw. Wmk inverted	£100	21·00
		e. Die II. *Rose-red*	£475	38·00
		f. Die II. *Rosine*	£750	£120
		gw. Die II. Wmk inverted	£1000	£150
O60		5d. bright chestnut (P 14¼ (line)) (9.20)	£5000	£180

All examples of the 5d. on this paper were perforated "OS".

1918–20. Nos. 48/52 punctured as Type O **2**. W **6a**. P 14.

O61	**5a**	½d. green	29·00	2·00
		w. Wmk inverted	50·00	20·00
O62		1d. carmine-pink (I)	†	£2000
O63		1d. carmine (I)	£200	75·00
O64		1½d. black-brown	20·00	12·00
		a. Very thin paper	£150	65·00
		w. Wmk inverted	£110	55·00
O65		1½d. red-brown	40·00	2·50
		w. Wmk inverted	£130	60·00
O61/5 *Set of 4*			£250	80·00

1918–23. Nos. 56/9 and 61/6 punctured as Type O **2**. W **5**. P 14.

O66	**5a**	½d. orange	17·00	10·00
O67		1d. violet	50·00	15·00
		w. Wmk inverted	†	£25000
O68		1½d. black-brown	48·00	6·00
		w. Wmk inverted	£110	35·00
O69		1½d. deep red-brown	50·00	2·50
		aw. Wmk inverted	£130	60·00
O69*b*		1½d. bright red-brown	—	£120
O70		1½d. green	40·00	3·75
O71		2d. brown-orange	16·00	3·25
		w. Wmk inverted	£325	85·00
O72		2d. bright rose-scarlet	40·00	4·00
		w. Wmk inverted	£1300	£200
O73		4d. violet	90·00	13·00
O74		4d. ultramarine	80·00	11·00
O75		1s.4d. pale blue	£110	18·00
		b. Deep turquoise	£4250	£3500
O66/75 *Set of 10*			£450	75·00

1923–24. Nos. 73/5 punctured as Type O **2**. W **6**. P 12.

O76	**1**	6d. chestnut (Die IIB)	45·00	2·50
O77		2s. maroon (Die II)	£180	12·00
O78		£1 grey (Die IIB)	£1800	£1000
O76/8 *Set of 3*			£1900	£1000

1924. Nos. 76/84 punctured as Type O **2**. P 14.

(a) W **5**

O79	**5a**	1d. sage-green	23·00	5·00
O80		1½d. scarlet	14·00	1·00
		w. Wmk inverted	£130	30·00
		wa. Printed on the gummed side	£375	
O81		2d. red-brown	24·00	18·00
		a. Bright red-brown	75·00	35·00
O82		3d. dull ultramarine	55·00	6·00
O83		4d. olive-yellow	60·00	6·00
O84		4½d. violet	£275	17·00
		w. Wmk inverted	†	£15000

(b) W **6a**

O85	**5a**	1d. sage-green	40·00	30·00

(c) No wmk

O86		1d. sage-green	85·00	85·00
O87		1½d. scarlet	90·00	85·00
O79/87 *Set of 9*			£550	£225

1926–30. Nos. 85/104 punctured as Type O **2**. W **7**.

(a) P 14

O88	**5a**	½d. orange	£400	£160
O89		1d. sage-green	12·00	3·00
O90		1½d. scarlet	40·00	4·50
		a. Golden scarlet	50·00	8·00
		w. Wmk inverted	60·00	11·00
O92		2d. red-brown (Die I)	£250	45·00
O93		3d. dull ultramarine	£100	13·00
		w. Wmk inverted	£120	90·00
O94		4d. yellow-olive	£275	50·00
O95		4½d. violet	£275	40·00
O96		1s.4d. pale greenish blue	£750	£250
O88/96 *Set of 8*			£1800	£475

(b) P 13½x12½

O97	**5a**	½d. orange	11·00	1·25
O98		1d. sage-green (Die I)	7·00	1·75
		b. Die II	£160	£160
O100		1½d. scarlet	18·00	2·50
		a. Golden scarlet	18·00	4·75
		w. Wmk inverted	20·00	5·50
O102		1½d. red-brown	35·00	5·00
O103		2d. red-brown (Die II)	55·00	16·00

O104		2d. golden scarlet (Die II)	22·00	4·50
		a. Die III	27·00	6·00
		aw. Wmk inverted	35·00	11·00
O106		3d. dull ultramarine (Die I)	50·00	6·00
		b. Die II. *Deep ultramarine*	22·00	1·50
		bw. Wmk inverted	£16000	£13000
O108		4d. yellow-olive	38·00	3·75
O109		4½d. violet	£250	£170
O110		5d. orange-brown (Die II)	90·00	7·00
O111		1s.4d. turquoise	£500	35·00
O97/111		*Set of* 11	£850	£225

1927 (9 May). Opening of Parliament House, Canberra. No. 105 punctured as Type O **3**.

O112	**8**	1½d. brownish lake	24·00	9·00

1928 (29 Oct). National Stamp Exhibition, Melbourne. No. 106 punctured as Type O **2**.

O113		3d. blue	13·00	9·00

1929–30. Nos. 107/14 punctured as Type O **2**. W **7**. P 12.

O114	**1**	6d. chestnut (Die IIB)	42·00	6·50
O115		9d. violet (Die IIB)	90·00	7·00
O116		1s. blue-green (Die IIB)	25·00	9·00
O117		2s. maroon (Die II)	£200	8·50
O118		5s. grey and yellow	£750	45·00
O118*a*		10s. grey and pink	£13000	£13000
O118*b*		£2 black and rose	£30000	£28000

1929 (20 May). Air. No. 115 punctured as Type O **3**.

O119	**9**	3d. green	32·00	12·00

1929 (28 Sept). Centenary of Western Australia. No. 116 punctured as Type O **3**.

O120	**10**	1½d. dull scarlet	26·00	22·00

1930 (2 June). Centenary of Exploration of River Murray by Capt. Sturt. Nos. 117/18 punctured as Type O **2**.

O121	**11**	1½d. scarlet	23·00	8·50
O122		3d. blue	29·00	8·50

(O **4**)

1931 (4 May). Nos. 121/2 optd with Type O **4**.

O123	**13**	2d. rose-red	85·00	27·00
O124		3d. blue	£275	27·00

For No. 139 overprinted with Type O **4**, see No. 139*a*.

1932 (Feb)–**33**. Optd as Type O **4**.

(a) W **7**

(i) P 13½×12½

O125	**5a**	2d. golden scarlet (Die III)	26·00	1·50
		a. Opt inverted	†	£70000
		w. Wmk inverted	£4500	£3000
O126		4d. yellow-olive (3.32)	24·00	3·00

(ii) P 12

O127	**1**	6d. chestnut (3.32)	55·00	55·00

(b) W **15**

(i) P 13½×12½

O128	**5a**	½d. orange (11.7.32)	10·00	1·50
		a. Opt inverted	£28000	£20000
O129		1d. green (3.32)	4·25	45
		w. Wmk inverted	£1300	£800
		x. Wmk reversed	£2250	£900
O130		2d. golden scarlet (Die III)	24·00	55
		a. Opt inverted	†	£45000
O131		3d. ultramarine (Die II) (2.33)	7·50	4·75
O132		5d. orange-brown (7.32)	50·00	27·00

(ii) P 12

O133	**1**	6d. chestnut (9.32)	40·00	20·00
		a. Opt inverted	†	£70000

(c) Recess. No wmk. P 11

O134	**18**	2d. scarlet (3.32)	11·00	2·00
O135		3d. blue (3.32)	18·00	5·00
O136	**17**	1s. green (4.32)	50·00	30·00

No. O128a and probably the other inverted overprints were caused by the insertion of a stamp upside down into sheets repaired before surcharging.

Issue of overprinted official stamps ceased in February 1933 and remaining supplies were withdrawn from sale on 1 October 1935, Thereafter mail from the federal administration was carried free.

BRITISH COMMONWEALTH OCCUPATION FORCE – JAPAN

Nos. J1/7 were used by the Australian forces occupying Japan after the Second World War. Initially their military post offices supplied unoverprinted Australian stamps, but it was decided to introduce the overprinted issue to prevent currency speculation.

B.C.O.F.
JAPAN
1946
(1)

B.C.O.F.
JAPAN
1946
(2)

1946 — Wrong fount "6" (left pane R. 9/4)

O.F. AN — Normal

O.F. AN — Narrow "N" (right pane R. 1/8)

1946 (12 Oct)–**47**. Stamps of Australia optd as T **1** (1d., 3d.,) or T **2** (others) at Hiroshima Printing Co, Japan.

J1	**27**	½d. orange (No. 179)	9·00	14·00
		a. Wrong fount "6"	£190	£200
		b. Narrow "N"	£200	£225
		c. Stop after "JAPAN" (right pane R.5/5)	£300	£325
J2	**46**	1d. brown-purple (No. 203)	7·00	8·50
		a. Blue-black overprint	60·00	£110
J3	**31**	3d. purple-brown (No. 187)	3·00	5·00
		a. Opt double	£1200	
J4	**34**	6d. purple-brown (No. 190*g*) (8.5.47)	29·00	23·00
		a. Wrong fount "6"	£300	£325
		b. Stop after "JAPAN" (right pane R. 5/5)	£425	£425
		c. Narrow "N"	£300	£325
J5	**36**	1s. grey-green (No. 192) (8.5.47)	20·00	25·00
		a. Wrong fount "6"	£350	£425
		b. Stop after "JAPAN" (right pane R. 5/5)	£550	£600
		c. Narrow "N"	£350	£425
		d. Roller flaw	£200	£225
J6	**1**	2s. maroon (No. 212) (8.5.47)	45·00	65·00
J7	**38**	5s. claret (No. 176) (8.5.47)	£140	£180
		a. Thin rough paper (No. 176a)	£110	£180
J1/7a *Set of* 7			£190	£275

The ½d., 1d. and 3d. values were first issued on 12 October 1946, and withdrawn two days later, but were re-issued together with the other values on 8 May 1947.

The following values with T **2** in the colours given were from proof sheets which, however, were used for postage: ½d. (red) 1d. (red or black) and 3d. (gold, red or black). (*Prices for black opts* £100, *each, and for red or gold from* £325 each, *all un*).

The use of B.C.O.F. stamps ceased on 12 February 1949.

AUSTRALIAN ANTARCTIC TERRITORY

For use at the Antarctic bases of Casey (opened early 1969: used Wilkes postmark until early 1970), Davis (closed from 1965 until early 1969), Heard Island (seasonal occupation only), Macquarie Island, Mawson and Wilkes (closed January 1969). Stamps of Australia were used from the bases before 27 March 1957 and remained valid for use there after the introduction of Australian Antarctic Territory issues.

The following are also valid for use in Australia, where they are put on sale for a limited period when first issued.

DATES OF ISSUE. The dates given refer to release dates in Australia. Local release dates are usually later and where known they are given in footnotes.

1 1954 Expedition at Vestfold Hills and Map

(Des. T. Lawrence: adapted by artist of the Printing Branch. Recess)

1957 (27 Mar). P 14½.

1	**1**	2s. ultramarine	1·00	65

Issued Macquarie Island 11.12.57, Davis 6.2.58, Mawson 18.2.58, Wilkes 1.2.59.

2 Members of Shackleton Expedition at South Magnetic Pole, 1909

3 Weazel and Team

4 Dog team and iceberg

5 Map of Antarctica and Emperor Penguins

1959 (16 Dec). T **2/4.** T **3**. Recess; new values surch typo (5d., 8d.). P 14½ (5d.), 14½×14 (8d.) or 14×14½ (others).

2	**2**	5d. on 4d. black and sepia	60	15
3	**3**	8d. on 7d. black and indigo	1·75	2·25
4	**4**	1s. deep green	2·25	2·00
5	**5**	2s.3d. green	7·00	3·00
2/5 *Set of* 4			10·50	6·75

Issued Macquarie Island 26.12.59, Davis 30.1.60, Mawson 10.2.60, Wilkes 13.2.60.

6

7 Sir Douglas Mawson (Expedition leader)

Normal

Weak entry

Weak entry at left (R. 1/5 and 2/5)

1961 (5 July). Recess. P 14½.

6	**6**	5d. deep blue	1·60	20
		a. Weak entry	30·00	

Issued Macquarie Island 6.12.61, Wilkes 10.1.62, Davis 20.1.62, Mawson 30.1.62.

1961 (18 Oct). 50th Anniv of 1911–14 Australasian Antarctic Expedition. Recess. P 14½.

7	**7**	5d. myrtle-green	55	20

Issued Macquarie Island 6.12.61, Wilkes 10.1.62, Davis 20.1.62, Mawson 30.1.62.

(New Currency. 100 cents = 1 Australian dollar)

8 Aurora and Camera Dome

9 Bell 47G Trooper Helicopter

(Des J. Mason. Photo)

1966 (28 Sept)–**68**. Vert designs as T **8** (1c. to 15c.) or horiz as T **9** (20c. to $1). Multicoloured. Helecon paper (5c.). P 13½.

8	1c. Type **8** (*shades*)	70	30
9	2c. Emperor Penguins (*shades*)	3·00	80
10	4c. Ship and iceberg	1·00	90
11	5c. Banding Elephant-seals (25.9.68)	2·25	1·75
12	7c. Measuring snow strata	80	80
13	10c. Wind gauges	1·25	1·10
14	15c. Weather balloon	5·00	2·00
15	20c. Type **9**	9·50	2·50
16	25c. Radio operator	1·75	2·25
17	50c. Ice compression tests	2·50	4·00
18	$1 Parahelion ("mock sun")	19·00	12·00
8/18 *Set of* 11		42·00	25·00

Nos. 13/15 and 17 have parts of the designs printed in bright orange fluorescent ink.

Nos. 8/10 and 12/18 placed on sale locally at Macquarie Island on 11.12.66, Wilkes 9.2.67 and Mawson 16.2.67.

No. 11 issued Macquarie Island 4.12.68, Mawson 13.1.69, Wilkes/Casey 9.2.69 and Davis 20.2.69.

11 Sastrugi (Snow Ridges)

12 Capt. Cook, Sextant and Compass

(Des J. Mason. Photo)

1971 (23 June). Tenth Anniv of Antarctic Treaty. T **11** and similar horiz design. P 13½.

19	**11**	6c. blue and black	75	1·00
20		30c. multicoloured (Pancake ice)	2·75	7·00

Issued Macquarie Island 23.11.71, Mawson 27.12.71, Davis 13.1.72 and Casey 17.1.72.

(Des J. Mason. Photo)

1972 (13 Sept). Bicentenary of Cook's Circumnavigation of Antarctica. T **12** and similar horiz design. Multicoloured Helecon paper (7c.). P 13½.

21	7c. Type **12**	1·25	75
22	35c. Chart and H.M.S. *Resolution*	2·75	1·25

Issued Macquarie Island 19.11.72, Mawson 24.12.72, Davis 3.1.73 and Casey 22.1.73.

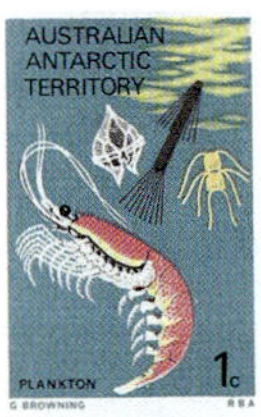

13 Plankton

14 Admiral Byrd (expedition leader), Ford 4-AT-B Trimotor *Floyd Bennett* and Map of South Pole

(Des G. Browning (1, 7, 9, 10, 20c., $1), R. Honisett (others). Photo)

1973 (5 Aug). T **13** and similar multicoloured designs. Helecon paper. P 13½.

23	1c. Type **13**	30	20
24	5c. Mawson's de Havilland DH.60G Gipsy Moth, 1931	55	1·00
25	7c. Adélie Penguin	1·50	1·25
26	8c. Rymill's de Havilland DH.83 Fox Moth, 1934-7	60	1·25
27	9c. Leopard Seal (*horiz*)	40	1·25
28	10c. Killer Whale (*horiz*)	2·25	2·00
	a. Buff (overlay on seals) omitted	£1800	
29	20c. Wandering Albatross (*horiz*)	1·50	1·00
30	25c. Wilkins's Lockheed X-3903 *San Francisco*, 1928 (*horiz*)	55	1·25
31	30c. Ellsworth's Northrop Gamma *Polar Star*, 1935	55	1·25
32	35c. Christensen's Avro Type 581 Avian, 1934 (*horiz*)	55	1·25
33	50c. Byrd's Ford 4-AT-B Trimotor *Floyd Bennett*, 1929	55	1·40
34	$1 Sperm Whale	75	1·40
23/34 *Set of* 12		9·00	13·00

The red ink used on the 1c. and $1 is fluorescent.

Issued Macquarie Island 29.11.73, Mawson 30.12.73, Davis 10.1.74 and Casey 31.1.74.

(Des R. Honisett. Litho Asher and Co, Melbourne)

1979 (20 June). 50th Anniv of First Flight over South Pole. T **14** and similar horiz design. Multicoloured. P 15½.

35	20c. Type **14**	25	60
36	55c. Admiral Byrd, Ford 4-AT-B Trimotor *Floyd Bennett* and Antarctic terrain	50	1·25

Issued Macquarie Island 24.10.79, Davis 3.1.80, Mawson 13.1.80 and Casey 9.2.80.

15 *Thala Dan* (supply ship)

16 Sir Douglas Mawson in Antarctic Terrain

(Des R. Honisett, Litho Asher and Co, Melbourne)

1979 (29 Aug)–**81**. Ships. Multicoloured designs as T **15**. P 13½×13 (horiz) or 13×13½ (vert).

37	1c. *Aurora* (*horiz*) (21.5.80)	15	10
38	2c. *Penola* (Rymill) (9.9.81)	40	10
39	5c. Type **15**	30	40
40	10c. H.M.S. *Challenger* (survey ship) (*horiz*) (9.9.81)	50	1·50
41	15c. *Morning** (bow view) (whaling ship) (*horiz*) (21.5.80)	2·00	3·00
42	15c. *Nimrod* (stern view) (Shackleton) (*horiz*) (9.9.81)	1·40	3·00
43	20c. *Discovery II* (supply ship) (*horiz*)	1·50	1·50
44	22c. *Terra Nova* (Scott) (21.5.80)	1·00	1·25
45	25c. *Endurance* (Shackleton)	1·00	1·00
46	30c. *Fram* (Amundsen) (*horiz*)	60	1·75
47	35c. *Nella Dan* (supply ship) (*horiz*) (21.5.80)	80	1·75
48	40c. *Kista Dan* (supply ship) (9.9.81)	1·25	2·75
49	45c. *L'Astrolabe* (D'Urville) (*horiz*) (9.9.81)	70	1·50
50	50c. *Norvegia* (supply ship) (*horiz*) (9.9.81)	70	1·00
51	55c. *Discovery* (Scott)	1·00	2·00
52	$1 H.M.S. *Resolution* (Cook) (21.5.80)	1·90	2·50
37/52 *Set of* 16		12·50	22·00

*No. 41 is incorrectly inscribed "S.Y. *Nimrod*".

On No. 46 the S.S. *Fram* is shown flying the Icelandic ensign, instead of the Norwegian.

Nos. 37, 41, 44, 47 and 52 issued Macquarie Island 27.10.80, Casey 1.12.80, Mawson 5.12.80 and Davis 11.12.80.

Nos. 38, 40, 42 and 48/50 issued Macquarie Island 21.10.81, Mawson 25.11.81, Davis 11.1.82 and Casey 25.1.82.

Nos. 39, 43, 45/6 and 51 issued Macquarie Island 24.10.79, Davis 3.1.80, Mawson 13.1.80 and Casey 9.2.80.

(Des R. Honisett. Litho Cambec Press, Melbourne)

1982 (5 May). Birth Centenary of Sir Douglas Mawson (Antarctic explorer). T **16** and similar vert design. Multicoloured. P 14×13½.

53	27c. Type **16**	25	25
54	75c. Sir Douglas Mawson and map of Australian Antarctic Territory	75	1·50

Issued Macquarie Island 26.10.82, Casey 16.1.83, Davis 10.2.83 and Mawson 2.3.83.

17 Light-mantled Sooty Albatross

18 Antarctic Scientist

(Des R. Honisett. Litho Leigh-Mardon Ltd, Melbourne)

1983 (6 Apr). Regional Wildlife. T **17** and similar vert designs. Multicoloured. P 14½.

55	27c. Type **17**	60	90
	a. Horiz strip of 5. Nos. 55/9	2·75	4·00
56	27c. King Cormorant	60	90
57	27c. Southern Elephant-Seal	60	90
58	27c. Royal Penguin	60	90
59	27c. Dove Prion	60	90
55/9 *Set of 5*		2·75	4·00

Nos. 55/9 were issued together, *se-tenant*, in horizontal strips of five, forming a composite design.

Issued Macquarie Island 21.10.83, Mawson 9.12.83, Casey 1.1.84 and Davis 2.1.84.

(Des R. Honisett. Litho Leigh-Mardon Ltd, Melbourne)

1983 (7 Sept). 12th Antarctic Treaty Consultative Meeting, Canberra. P 14½.

60	**18** 27c. multicoloured	55	1·00

Issued Macquarie Island 21.10.83, Mawson 9.12.83, Casey 1.1.84 and Davis 2.1.84.

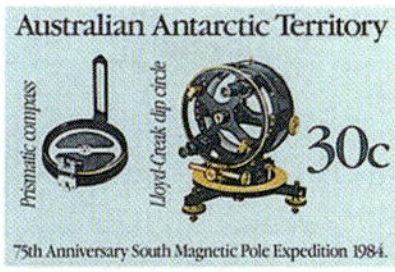

19 Prismatic Compass and Lloyd-Creak Dip Circle

20 Dog Team pulling Sledge

(Des R. Fletcher. Litho Leigh-Mardon Ltd, Melbourne)

1984 (16 Jan). 75th Anniv of Magnetic Pole Expedition. T **19** and similar horiz design. Multicoloured. P 14½.

61	30c. Type **19**	30	30
62	85c. Aneroid barometer and theodolite	70	1·25

Issued Macquarie Island 23.10.84, Mawson 15.11.84, Casey 16.11.84 and Davis 1.2.85.

(Des G. Emery. Litho Leigh-Mardon Ltd (2, 10, 20, 36, 60c.) or Cambec Press (others), both of Melbourne)

1984 (18 July)–**87**. Antarctic Scenes. T **20** and similar multicoloured designs. P 14½ (2c., 10c., 20c., 36c., 60c.), 14×13½ (45c., 90c.) or 13½×14 (others).

63	2c. Summer afternoon, Mawson Station (11.3.87)	20	1·25
64	5c. Type **20**	20	40
65	10c. Late summer evening, MacRobertson Land (11.3.87)	20	40
66	15c. Prince Charles Mountains (7.8.85)	20	1·25
67	20c. Summer morning, Wilkes Land (11.3.87)	20	1·75
68	25c. Sea-ice and iceberg	60	1·75
69	30c. Mount Coates	25	50
70	33c. "Iceberg Alley", Mawson (7.8.85)	25	1·25
71	36c. Early winter evening, Casey Station (11.3.87)	1·25	50
72	45c. Brash ice (*vert*) (7.8.85)	70	2·00
73	60c. Midwinter shadows, Casey Station (11.3.87)	50	65
74	75c. Coastline	2·25	3·00
75	85c. Landing strip	2·50	3·00
76	90c. Pancake ice (*vert*) (7.8.85)	75	80
77	$1 Emperor Penguins (7.8.85)	3·00	1·75
	s. Optd "Specimen"	50	
63/77 *Set of 15*		11·50	18·00

Nos. 63, 65, 67, 71 and 73 issued Macquarie Island 6.10.87, Davis 25.11.87, Mawson 1.1.88 and Casey 13.1.88.

Nos. 64, 68/9 and 74/5 issued Macquarie Island 23.10.84, Mawson 15.11.84, Casey 16.11.84 and Davis 1.2.85.

Nos. 66, 70, 72 and 76/7 issued Heard Island 1.11.85, Casey 31.11.85, Mawson 6.12.85, Macquarie Island 6.12.85 and Davis 11.12.85.

21 Prince Charles Mountains near Mawson Station

22 Hourglass Dolphins and *Nella Dan*

(Des A. McGregor. Litho Cambec Press, Melbourne)

1986 (17 Sept). 25th Anniv of Antarctic Treaty. P 14×13½.

78	**21** 36c. multicoloured	1·25	1·10

Issued Mawson 9.11.86, Davis 15.11.86, Casey 23.11.86 and Macquarie Island 7.12.86.

(Des Trish Hart. Litho CPE Australia Ltd, Melbourne)

1988 (20 July). Environment, Conservation and Technology. T **22** and similar square designs. Multicoloured. P 13.

79	37c. Type **22**	1·25	1·40
	a. Horiz strip of 5. Nos. 79/83	5·50	6·00
80	37c. Emperor Penguins and Davis Station	1·25	1·40
81	37c. Crabeater Seal and Hughes 500D helicopters	1·25	1·40
82	37c. Adélie Penguins and tracked vehicle	1·25	1·40
83	37c. Grey-headed Albatross and photographer	1·25	1·40
79/83 *Set of 5*		5·50	6·25

Nos. 79/83 were printed together, *se-tenant*, in horizontal strips of five throughout the sheet.

Issued Macquarie Island 29.10.88, Casey 14.12.88, Mawson 21.12.88 and Davis 29.12.88.

23 "Antarctica"

24 Aurora Australis

(Des Janet Boschen. Litho CPE Australia Ltd, Melbourne)

1989 (14 June). Antarctic Landscape Paintings by Sir Sidney Nolan. T **23** and similar vert designs. Multicoloured. P 14×13½.

84	39c. Type **23**	1·50	1·75
85	39c. "Iceberg Alley"	1·50	1·75
86	60c. "Glacial Flow"	2·00	2·75
87	80c. "Frozen Sea"	2·50	3·25
84/7 *Set of 4*		6·75	8·50

Issued Casey 28.10.89, Davis 29.10.89, Mawson 17.11 89 and Macquarie Island 24.11.89.

Supplies of Australia Nos. 1261/3 were sent to the Antarctic and were issued at Macquarie Island on 24.11.90, Mawson 10.12.90, Davis 14.12.90 and Casey 19.12.90.

(Des Lynette Brown. Litho Leigh-Mardon Ltd, Melbourne)

1991 (20 June). 30th Anniv of Antarctic Treaty (43c.) and Maiden Voyage of *Aurora Australis* (research ship) ($1.20). T **24** and similar horiz design. Multicoloured. P 14½.

88	43c. Type **24**	75	60
89	$1.20 *Aurora Australis* off Heard Island	2·75	4·25
	s. Optd "Specimen"	55	

Issued Mawson 12.11.91, Casey 22.12.91, Macquarie Island 17.1.92 and Davis 9.2.92.

25 Adélie Penguin and Chick

26 Head of Husky

(Des Janet Boschen. Litho McPherson's Ptg Group, Mulgrave ($1, $1.40, $1.50) or Printset Cambec Pty Ltd (others))

1992 (14 May)–**93**. Antarctic Wildlife. T **25** and similar multicoloured designs. P 14½×14 ($1.20, $1.50) or 14×14½ (others).

90	45c. Type **25**	1·00	50
91	75c. Elephant Seal with pup	1·40	90
92	85c. Hall's Giant Petrel on nest with fledgeling	2·00	1·00
93	95c. Weddell Seal and pup	1·75	1·00
94	$1 Royal Penguin (14.1.93)	2·00	1·00
95	$1.20 Emperor Penguins with chicks (*vert*)	2·50	1·40
	s. Optd "Specimen"	55	
96	$1.40 Fur Seal (14.1.93)	2·00	1·75
97	$1.50 King Penguin (*vert*) (14.1.93)	2·50	2·25
90/7	*Set of* 8	13·50	9·00

Nos. 90/3 and 95 issued Mawson 2.11.92, Davis 11.11.92, Casey 27.11.92 and Macquarie Island 10.12.92.

Nos. 94 and 96/7 issued Mawson 28.10.93, Casey 13.11.93, Davis 2.12.93 and Macquarie Island 19.12.93.

Nos. 98/103 are vacant.

(Des FHA Design. Litho Leigh-Mardon Ltd, Melbourne)

1994 (13 Jan). Departure of Huskies from Antarctica. T **26** and similar multicoloured designs. P 14½.

104	45c. Type **26**	1·75	75
105	75c. Dogs pulling sledge (*horiz*)	2·00	2·25
106	85c. Husky in harness	2·25	2·50
107	$1.05 Dogs on leads (*horiz*)	2·50	3·00
104/7	*Set of* 4	7·75	7·75

Issued Casey 31.10.94, Davis 11.11.94, Mawson 14.11.94 and Macquarie Island 4.12.94.

27 Humpback Whale with Calf

28 "Rafting Sea Ice" (Christian Clare Robertson)

(Des D. Nelson. Litho Leigh-Mardon Ltd, Melbourne)

1995 (15 June). Whales and Dolphins. T **27** and similar multicoloured designs. P 14½.

108	45c. Type **27**	1·50	80
109	45c. Pair of Hourglass Dolphins (*vert*)	1·50	2·00
	a. Horiz pair. Nos. 109/10	3·00	4·00
110	45c. Pair of Minke Whales (*vert*)	1·50	2·00
111	$1 Killer Whale	2·50	3·00
108/11	*Set of* 4	6·25	7·00
MS112	146×64 *mm*. Nos. 108/111	8·00	8·00

Nos. 109/10 were printed together, *se-tenant*, in horizontal pairs throughout the sheet, with the background forming a composite design.

Issued Macquarie Island 18.11.95, Casey 5.12.95, Mawson 16.12.95 and Davis 20.12.95.

No. **MS**112 also exists overprinted "Singapore 95 World Stamp Exhibition", "Philately and Collections Fair, Hong Kong '95" or "CAPEX '96 WORLD PHILATELIC EXHIBITION EXPOSITION PHILATELIQUE MONDIALE" for sale at these exhibitions.

(Des Melinda Whitechurch. Litho McPherson's Ptg Group, Mulgrave)

1996 (16 May). Paintings by Christian Clare Robertson. T **28** and similar vert designs. Multicoloured. P 14½×14.

113	45c. Type **28**	90	1·60
	a. Horiz pair. Nos. 113/14	1·75	3·00
114	45c. "Shadow on the Plateau"	90	1·60
115	$1 "Ice Cave"	1·90	2·00
116	$1.20 "Twelve Lake"	2·25	2·75
113/16	*Set of* 4	5·50	7·00

Nos. 113/14 were printed together, *se-tenant*, in horizontal pairs throughout the sheet.

Issued Macquarie Island 28.11.96, Mawson 23.12.96, Davis 29.12.96 and Casey 11.1.97.

29 Apple Huts

30 *Aurora Australis* (research ship)

(Des Sophie Byass. Litho McPherson's Ptg Group, Mulgrave)

1997 (15 May). 50th Anniv of Australian National Antarctic Research Expeditions (A.N.A.R.E.). T **29** and similar horiz designs. Multicoloured. P 14×14½.

117	45c. Type **29**	1·00	1·25
	a. Pair. Nos. 117/18	2·00	2·50
118	45c. Tuning a radio receiver	1·00	1·25
119	95c. Summer surveying	1·60	2·25
120	$1.05 Scientists in cage above sea ice	1·75	2·25
121	$1.20 Scientists and tents	1·90	2·50
117/21	*Set of* 5	6·50	8·50

Nos. 117/18 were printed together, *se-tenant*, in horizontal and vertical pairs throughout the sheet.

Issued Macquarie Island 18.11.97, Davis 22.12.97, Mawson 26.12.97 and Casey 7.1.98.

(Des Sandra Harman. Litho McPherson's Ptg Group, Mulgrave)

1998 (5 Mar). Antarctic Transport. T **30** and similar multicoloured designs. P 14×14½ (45c.) or 14½×14 (others).

122	45c. Type **30**	2·25	2·50
	a. Pair. Nos. 122/3	4·50	5·00
123	45c. Skidoo	2·25	2·50
124	$1 Helicopter lifting quad motorcycle (*vert*)	5·00	3·50
125	$2 Hagglunds tractor and trailer (*vert*)	5·50	7·00
122/5	*Set of* 4	13·50	14·00

Nos. 122/3 were printed together, *se-tenant*, in horizontal and vertical pairs throughout the sheet.

Issued Davis 18.11.98, Macquarie Island 21.11.98, Casey and Mawson 1.12.98.

31 Sir Douglas Mawson (expedition leader, 1911-14) and *Aurora* (research ship)

32 Emperor Penguin

(Des Janet Boschen. Litho SNP Ausprint)

1999 (13 May). Restoration of Mawson's Huts, Cape Denison. T **31** and similar horiz designs, each including a background drawing of a hut. Multicoloured. P 14×14½.

126	45c. Type **31**	2·25	2·50
	a. Pair. Nos. 126/7	4·50	5·00
127	45c. Huts in blizzard	2·25	2·50
128	90c. Husky team	3·50	4·00
129	$1.35 Conservation in progress	3·50	4·00
126/9	*Set of* 4	10·50	11·50

Nos. 126/7 were printed together, *se-tenant*, in horizontal or vertical pairs throughout the sheet.

Nos. 126/9 were spot-coated with U.V. varnish to simulate ice.

Issued Macquarie Island 14.11.99, Casey 22.11.99, Davis 28.12.99 and Mawson 5.1.2000.

(Des Janet Boschen. Litho McPherson's Ptg Group, Mulgrave)

2000 (24 July). Penguins. T **32** and similar horiz design. Multicoloured. P 14×14½.

130	45c. Type **32**	4·00	4·00
	a. Pair, Nos. 130/1	8·00	8·00
131	45c. Adélie Penguins	4·00	4·00

Nos. 130/1 were printed together, *se-tenant*, as horizontal or vertical pairs in sheets of 50.

33 Adélie Penguins with Egg

34 Female Leopard Seal and Pup

(Des Janet Boschen. Litho SNP Ausprint)

2001 (17 May). Centenary of Australian Antarctic Exploration. T **33** and similar vert designs. Multicoloured. P 14½×14.

132	5c. Type **33**	1·25	1·40
	a. Sheetlet of 20. Nos. 132/51	24·00	26·00
133	5c. Louis Bernacchi (physicist)	1·25	1·40
134	5c. *Nimrod* (Shackleton)	1·25	1·40
135	5c. Mackay, Edgeworth David and Mawson at South Magnetic Pole, 1909.	1·25	1·40
136	5c. Taylor and Debenham (geologists)	1·25	1·40

137	10c. Early radio set	1·25	1·40
138	10c. Lockheed-Vega aircraft and husky team	1·25	1·40
139	10c. Sir Douglas Mawson	1·25	1·40
140	10c. Members of BANZARE. Expedition, 1929–31	1·25	1·40
141	10c. Hoisting Union Jack	1·25	1·40
142	25c. Hoisting Australian flag, 1948	1·40	1·50
143	25c. Hagglund vehicle and helicopter	1·40	1·50
144	25c. Aurora australis over Casey	1·40	1·50
145	25c. Scientist with weather balloon	1·40	1·50
146	25c. Modern Antarctic clothing and "apple" hut	1·40	1·50
147	45c. *Nella Dan* (supply ship) and Emperor Penguins	1·40	1·50
148	45c. Male and female scientists taking ice sample	1·40	1·50
149	45c. Scientist using satellite phone	1·40	1·50
150	45c. Weddell Seal and tourists	1·40	1·50
151	45c. Satellite photograph of Antarctica	1·40	1·50
132/51	*Set of* 20	24·00	26·00

Nos. 132/51 were printed together, *se-tenant*, in sheets of 20 with the backgrounds of each horizontal row forming composite designs which continue onto the sheet margins. Each stamp carries an inscription on the reverse, printed over the gum.

(Des P. Walton. Litho SNP Ausprint)

2001 (11 Sept). Endangered Species. Leopard Seal. T **34** and similar horiz designs. Multicoloured. P 14×14½.

152	45c. Type **34**	2·25	2·75
	a. Block of 4. Nos. 152/5	8·00	10·00
153	45c. Male seal on ice floe chasing penguins	2·25	2·75
154	45c. Female seal and pup swimming underwater	2·25	2·75
155	45c. Adult seal chasing Adélie Penguins underwater	2·25	2·75
152/5	*Set of* 4	8·00	10·00

Nos. 152/5 were printed together, *se-tenant*, as blocks of four in sheets of 50 containing ten blocks and ten single stamps.

35 Light Detection and Ranging Equipment, Davis Base

36 *Kista Dan* in Heavy Seas

(Des Lynda Warner. Litho SNP Ausprint)

2002 (2 July). Antarctic Research. T **35** and similar horiz designs. Multicoloured. P 14×14½.

156	45c. Type **35**	3·00	3·25
	a. Block of 4. Nos. 156/9	11·00	11·50
157	45c. Magnified diatom and coastline, Casey Base	3·00	3·25
158	45c. Wandering Albatross, Macquarie Base	3·00	3·25
159	45c. Adèlie Penguin, Mawson Base	3·00	3·25
156/9	*Set of* 4	11·00	11·50

Nos. 156/9 were printed together, *se-tenant*, in sheets of 50 (2 panes, each 5×5) containing 10 blocks of 4 and 10 single stamps.

(Des P. Gouldthorpe. Litho SNP Sprint)

2003 (15 Apr). Antarctic Supply Ships. T **36** and similar multicoloured designs. P 14×14½ (50c.) or 14½×14 (others).

160	50c. Type **36**	3·50	3·75
	a. Pair. Nos. 160/1	7·00	7·50
161	50c. *Magga Dan* entering pack ice	3·50	3·75
162	$1 *Thala Dan* and iceberg (*vert*)	5·00	3·00
163	$1.45 *Nella Dan* unloading in Antarctic (*vert*).	6·00	7·00
160/3	*Set of* 4	16·00	16·00

Nos. 160/1 were printed together, *se-tenant*, in horizontal and vertical pairs throughout the sheets of 50.

37 Naming Ceremony, 1954

38 Hughes 500 Helicopter

(Des S. Pethick. Litho SNP Sprint)

2004 (13 Feb). 50th Anniv of Mawson Station. T **37** and similar horiz designs. Multicoloured. Phosphorised paper. P 14×14½.

164	50c. Type **37**	3·00	3·50
	a. Horiz pair. Nos. 164/5	6·00	7·00
165	50c. Mawson Station, 2004	3·00	3·50
166	$1 Accomodation "caravan", 1950s	3·75	3·00
167	$1.45 Emperor Penguin rookery	5·00	6·00
164/7	*Set of* 4	13·00	14·50

Nos. 164/5 were printed together, *se-tenant*, in horizontal pairs in sheets of 50 (containing two panes of 25).

(Des Lynda Warner. Litho SEP Sprint)

2005 (6 Sept). Aviation in the Australian Antarctic Territory. T **38** and similar horiz designs. Multicoloured. Phosphorised paper. P 14×15.

168	50c. Type **38**	2·50	2·50
	a. Pair. Nos. 168/9	5·00	5·00
169	50c. de Havilland DHC-2 Beaver	2·50	2·50
170	$1 Pilatus PC-6 Porter	3·25	2·50
171	$1.45 Douglas DC-3/Dakota C-47	4·00	4·50
168/71	*Set of* 4	11·00	11·00

Nos. 168/9 were printed together, *se-tenant*, in horizontal and vertical pairs in sheets of 50.

39 Mackerel Icefish

40 Royal Penguins

(Des Janet Matthews. Litho SEP Sprint)

2006 (1 Aug). Fish of the Australian Antarctic Territory. T **39** and similar horiz designs. Multicoloured. Phosphorised paper. P 14×15.

172	50c. Type **39**	2·25	2·50
	a. Horiz pair. Nos. 172/3	4·50	5·00
173	50c. Lanternfish	2·25	2·50
174	$1 Eaton's Skate	2·75	3·00
	a. Horiz pair. Nos. 174/5	5·50	6·00
175	$1 Patagonian Toothfish	2·75	3·00
172/5	*Set of* 4	9·00	10·00

Nos. 172/3 and 174/5 were each printed together, *se-tenant*, in horizontal pairs in sheets of 50.

(Des Doug Pitt. Litho SEP Sprint)

2007 (7 Aug). Endangered Species. Royal Penguins (*Eudyptes schlegeli*). T **40** and similar multicoloured designs. Phosphorised paper. P 14½×14 (50c.) or 14×14½ ($1).

176	50c. Type **40**	3·00	3·00
	a. Pair. Nos. 176/7	6·00	6·00
177	50c. Penguin with egg	3·00	3·00
178	$1 Two penguins sparring	3·25	3·25
	a. Pair. Nos. 178/9	6·50	6·50
179	$1 Pair snuggling together	3·25	3·25
176/9	*Set of* 4	11·50	11·50

Nos. 176/7 and 178/9 were each printed together, *se-tenant*, in horizontal and vertical pairs in sheets of 50 (2 panes of 25).

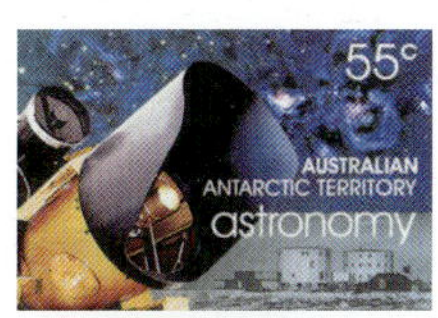

41 Telescope, AASTINO Observatory, Stars and Gas Cloud (Astronomy from the Polar Plateaus)

42 Unloading *Nimrod*

(Des Chris Shurey. Litho Energi Print)

2008 (16 Sept). International Polar Year 2007–08. T **41** and similar horiz designs. Multicoloured. P 14×15.

180	55c. Type **41**	3·25	3·25
	a. Pair. Nos. 180/1	6·50	6·50
181	55c. Scientists drilling through sea ice (Sea Ice Physics and Ecosystem Experiment)	3·25	3·25
182	$1.10 Pteropod, Pelagic Snail *Limacina helicina* and Emperor Penguin (marine biology)	4·50	4·50
	a. Pair. Nos. 182/3	9·00	9·00
183	$1.10 CTD (conductivity-temperature-depth) probe and ocean (Climate of Antarctica and the Southern Ocean project)	4·50	4·50

180/3 *Set of 4* .... 14·00 14·00
MS184 160×90 *mm.* Nos. 180/3 .... 15·00 15·00

Nos. 180/1 and 182/3 were each printed together, *se-tenant*, as horizontal and vertical pairs in sheets of 50.

(Des Disegno. Litho Energi Print)

2009 (8 Jan). Centenary of the First Expedition to the South Magnetic Pole. T **42** and similar vert designs. Each black, grey and pale blue. P 14½×14.

185 55c. Type **42** .... 2·75 2·75
a. Horiz pair. Nos. 185/6 .... 5·50 5·50
186 55c. Arroll-Johnston car towing provisions on sledge .... 2·75 2·75
187 $1.10 Northern Party camp .... 4·00 4·00
a. Horiz pair. Nos. 187/8 .... 8·00 8·00
188 $1.10 Alistair Mackay, Douglas Mawson and Edgeworth David raising Union Jack at South Magnetic Pole .... 4·00 4·00
185/8 *Set of 4* .... 12·00 12·00
MS189 170×85 *mm.* Nos. 185/8 .... 12·00 12·00

Nos. 185/6 and 187/8 were each printed together, *se-tenant*, in sheets of 50, each sheet providing 20 pairs and ten single stamps (Type **42** or No. 187).

43 Snow Petrel

44 *Pleurophyllum hookeri*

(Des Doug Pitt. Litho Energi Print)

2009 (4 Mar). Preserve the Polar Regions and Glaciers. T **43** and similar horiz design. Multicoloured. P 14×14½.

(i) Domestic Mail

190 55c. Type **43** .... 3·50 1·75

(ii) International Post

191 $2.05 Jade iceberg .... 8·50 10·00
MS192 120×80 *mm.* Nos. 190/1 .... 12·00 12·00

(Des Adam Crapp. Litho McKellar Renown)

2010 (26 Oct). Macquarie Island. T **44** and similar square designs. Multicoloured. P 14.

193 60c. Type **44** .... 3·00 3·00
a. Horiz pair. Nos. 193/4 .... 6·00 6·00
194 60c. Southern Elephant Seal .... 3·00 3·00
195 $1.20 Mawson Point Stacks .... 4·50 4·50
a. Horiz pair. Nos. 195/6 .... 9·00 9·00
196 $1.20 Caroline Cove .... 4·50 4·50
193/6 *Set of 4* .... 13·50 13·50
MS197 159×85 *mm.* Nos. 193/6 .... 13·50 13·50

Nos. 193/4 and 195/6 were each printed together, *se-tenant*, in horizontal pairs in sheets of 50 containing two panes of 25 (5×5) separated by a horizontal gutter, each pane of 25 giving ten horizontal pairs and five single stamps.

For Nos. 193/4 on the top pane the left hand stamp in all five horizontal rows is Type **44**, but on the lower pane below the gutter it is No. 194.

For Nos. 195/6 on the top pane the left hand stamp in all five horizontal rows is No. 195, but on the lower pane below the gutter it is No. 196.

45 Greenish Iceberg with Pinnacle

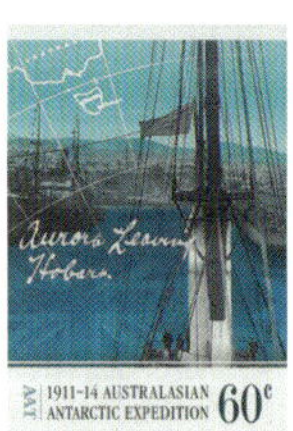

46 SY *Aurora* leaving Hobart, December 1911

(Des Lynette Traynor. Litho RA Printing)

2011 (7 June). Icebergs. T **45** and similar horiz designs. Multicoloured.

(a) Ordinary gum. P 14 ×14½

198 60c. Type **45** .... 2·50 2·50
a. Block of 4. Nos. 198/201 .... 9·00 9·00
199 60c. Flat-topped iceberg with overhang at left .... 2·50 2·50
200 60c. Dark iceberg with fluted sides .... 2·50 2·50
201 60c. Iceberg with low ridge in foreground and higher ridge with pinnacle at right .... 2·50 2·50
198/201 *Set of 4* .... 9·00 9·00
MS202 135×72 *mm.* Nos. 198/201 .... 9·00 9·00

(b) Self-adhesive, Phosphor frame. Die-cut perf 11×11½ (interrupted on vert edges)

203 60c. As Type **45** .... 2·00 2·50
a. Booklet pane. Nos. 203/4, each×3, and Nos. 205/6, each×2 .... 16·00
204 60c. As No. 199 .... 2·00 2·50
205 60c. As No. 200 .... 2·00 2·50
206 60c. As No. 201 .... 2·00 2·50
203/6 *Set of 4* .... 7·00 9·00

Nos. 198/201 were printed together, *se-tenant*, as blocks of four stamps in sheets of 50 (2 panes 5×5), each sheet giving eight blocks of four and 18 single stamps. The top left stamp on the upper pane is Type **45** and on the lower pane it is No. 200.

Nos. 202/5 were issued in $6 booklets, No. SB1.

(Des Andrew Hogg Design. Litho RA Printing)

2011 (2 Aug). Centenary of the Australasian Antarctic Expedition, 1911-14 (1st issue). T **46** and similar vert designs. Multicoloured. P 14½×14.

207 60c. Type **46** .... 2·50 2·50
a. Horiz strip of 5. Nos. 207/11 .... 11·50 11·50
208 60c. Captain John King Davis of the SY *Aurora* .... 2·50 2·50
209 60c. SY *Aurora* on Antarctic voyage .... 2·50 2·50
210 60c. Landing at Macquarie Island .... 2·50 2·50
211 60c. Birdlife on Macquarie Island .... 2·50 2·50
207/11 *Set of 5* .... 11·50 11·50
MS212 169×85 *mm.* Nos. 207/11 .... 11·50 11·50

Nos. 207/11 were printed together, *se-tenant*, as horizontal strips of five stamps in sheets of 50 (2 panes 5×5), each horizontal strip forming a composite background design of sea and coast.

See also Nos. 218/**MS**5234 and 229/**MS**5234 and 235/**MS**240.

47 *(Actual size* 135×71 *mm)*

(Des Kevin Stead. Litho McKellar Renown)

2011 (30 Aug). 50th Anniv of Worldwide Fund for Nature (formerly World Wildlife Fund). Sheet 135×72 mm. Multicoloured. P 14×14½.

MS213 **47** 60c.×4 Southern Elephant Seal (*Mirounga leonina*) (Australian Antarctic Territory); Dugong (*Dugong dugon*) (Cocos (Keeling) Islands); Christmas Island Shrew (*Crocidura trichura*) (Christmas Island); Type **861** of Australia .... 7·50 8·50

No. **MS**213 differs from **MS**3640 of Australia in the sheet margins and in the order of the stamps within the miniature sheet (top left stamp, Australian Antarctic Territory; top right, Cocos (Keeling) Islands; bottom left, Christmas Island; bottom right, Australia).

48 Phillip Law

(Des Gary Domoney. Litho McKellar Renown)

2012 (6 Mar). Birth Centenary of Dr. Phillip Law (Antarctic explorer). T **48** and similar vert designs. Multicoloured. P 14½×14.

214 60c. Type **48** .... 2·50 1·75
215 $1.20 Phillip Law in Antarctic snow, landed helicopter and map of Antarctic .... 6·00 5·00
216 $1.80 Researchers, Australian flag and map of Antarctica .... 7·00 7·50
214/6 *Set of 3* .... 14·00 13·00
MS217 160×90 *mm.* Nos. 214/16 .... 14·00 14·00

(Des Andrew Hogg Design. Litho RA Printing)

2012 (4 Sept). Centenary of the Australasian Antarctic Expedition, 1911-14 (2nd issue). Arrival and Exploration. Vert designs as T **46**. Multicoloured. P 14½×14.

218	60c. Main Hut, Cape Denison	2·50	2·50
	a. Horiz strip of 3. Nos. 218/20	6·75	6·75
219	60c. Xavier Mertz and dog team	2·50	2·50
220	60c. Dog handler Belgrave Ninnis and sled..	2·50	2·50
221	$1.20 SY *Aurora* anchored off Cape Denison, January 1912	4·00	4·00
	a. Horiz pair. Nos. 221/2	8·00	8·00
222	$1.20 Unloading supplies from SY *Aurora*	4·00	4·00
218/22 *Set of 5*		14·00	14·00
MS223 171×86 *mm*. Nos. 218/22		14·00	14·00

Nos. 218/20 were printed together, *se-tenant*, as horizontal strips of three stamps in sheets of 50 (2 panes 5×5), each sheet providing ten strips of three and ten horiz pairs (Nos. 218/19). Nos. 218/20 form a composite background design.

Nos. 221/2 were printed together, *se-tenant*, as horizontal pairs in sheets of 50 (2 panes 5×5), each sheet providing 20 horizontal pairs and ten single stamps (No. 221). Nos. 221/2 form a composite background design.

49 Mt. Parsons

(Des Sharon Rodziewicz. Litho RA Printing)

2013 (12 Mar). Mountains. T **49** and similar horiz designs. Multicoloured. P 14×14½.

224	60c. Type **49**	2·25	2·25
	a. Horiz pair. Nos. 224/5	4·50	4·50
225	60c. Mawson Escarpment	2·25	2·25
226	$1.20 South Masson Range	3·25	3·25
227	$1.80 David Range	4·00	4·00
224/7 *Set of 4*		10·50	10·50
MS228 135×72 *mm*. Nos. 224/7		10·50	10·50

Nos. 224/5 were printed together, *se-tenant*, as horizontal pairs in sheets of 50 (2 panes 5×5), each sheet giving 20 horizontal pairs and ten single stamps (Type **49**).

(Des Andrew Hogg Design. Litho RA Print)

2013 (10 Sept). Centenary of the Australasian Antarctic Expedition 1911–14 (3rd issue). Disaster and Isolation. Vert designs as T **46**. Multicoloured. P 14½×14.

229	60c. Two men in winter blizzard near base camp	2·00	2·00
	a. Horiz strip of 3. Nos. 229/31	5·50	5·50
230	60c. Recording wind speed	2·00	2·00
231	60c. Weddell Seal and Cape Petrel	2·00	2·00
232	$1.20 Wireless operator Walter Hannam ('Mawson Returns')	3·50	3·50
	a. Horiz pair. Nos. 232/3	7·00	7·00
233	$1.20 Frank Wild (leader of the Western Party)	3·50	3·50
229/33 *Set of 5*		11·00	11·00
MS234 170×85 *mm*. Nos. 229/33		11·50	11·50

Nos. 229/31 were printed together, *se-tenant*, as horizontal strips of three stamps in sheets of 50 (2 panes 5×5), each sheet providing ten strips of three and ten horiz pairs (Nos. 229/30). Nos. 232/3 were printed together, *se-tenant*, as horizontal pairs in sheets of 50 (2 panes 5×5), each sheet providing 20 horizontal pairs and ten single stamps (No. 232).

Nos. 229/31 and 232/3 form composite background designs of Antarctic landscapes.

MS234 was also sold in uncut imperf panes of 15 sheets, available only from Australia Post at above face value.

(Des Andrew Hogg design. Litho RA Print)

2014 (18 Feb). Centenary of the Australasian Antarctic Expedition 1911–14 (4th issue). Homeward Bound 1914 Vert designs as T **46**. Multicoloured. P 14½×14.

235	60c. Mawson and others with large circular net ('Scientific Research')	2·25	2·25
	a. Horiz strip of 3. Nos. 235/7	6·00	6·00
236	60c. Returning expedition members on board S.Y. *Aurora*	2·25	2·25
237	60c. Douglas Mawson	2·25	2·25
238	$1.20 Douglas Mawson and Adélie Penguin sitting on motor launch at ice front	4·00	4·00
	a. Horiz pair. Nos. 238/9	8·00	8·00
239	$1.20 Frank Hurley (onshore) filming S.Y. *Aurora* off Antartic ice front with cinema camera	4·00	4·00
235/39 *Set of 5*		13·00	13·00
MS240 170×85 *mm*. Nos. 235/9		13·00	13·00

Nos. 235/7 were printed together, *se-tenant*, as horizontal strips of three stamps in sheets of 50 (2 panes 5×5), each sheet providing ten strips of three and ten horiz pairs (Nos. 235/6).

Nos. 238/9 were printed together, *se-tenant*, as horizontal pairs in sheets of 50 (2 panes 5×5), each sheet providing 20 horizontal pairs and ten single stamps (No. 238).

Nos. 235/7 and 238/9 form composite background designs.

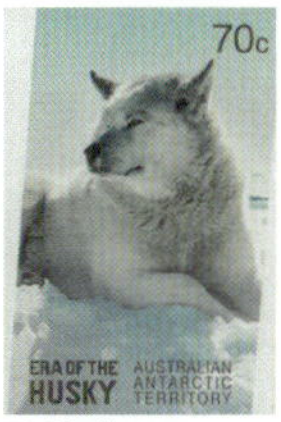

50 Husky

(Des Jo Muré. Litho McKellar Renown)

2014 (9 Sept). Era of the Husky. T **50** and similar multicoloured designs.

(a) Ordinary gum. P 14½×14 (vert) or 14×14½ (horiz)

241	70c. Type **50**	1·40	1·40
	a. Horiz pair. Nos. 241/2	2·75	2·75
242	70c. Black and tan husky	1·40	1·40
243	$1.40 Husky team pulling sledge (blue background) (*horiz*)	2·75	2·75
	a. Horiz pair. Nos. 243/4	5·50	5·50
244	$1.40 Husky team pulling sledge (white background) (*horiz*)	2·75	2·75
241/4 *Set of 4*		8·25	8·25
MS245 170×80 *mm*. Nos. 241/4		8·25	8·25

(b) Self-adhesive. Phosphor over parts of design. Die-cut perf 11½×11 (interrupted on horiz sides)

246	70c. As Type **50**	1·40	1·40
	a. Booklet pane. Nos. 246/7, each ×5	13·00	
247	70c. As No. 242	1·40	1·40

Nos. 241/2 and 243/4 were each printed together, *se-tenant*, as horizontal pairs in sheets of 50 (2 panes 5×5), each sheet giving 20 horizontal pairs and ten single stamps (Nos. 241 or 243).

Nos. 246/7 were issued in $7 booklets, No. SB2.

51 Sunset

(Des Jo Muré. Litho RA Printing)

2015 (26 May). Colours of the Australian Antarctic Territory. T **51** and similar horiz designs. Multicoloured.

248	70c. Type **51**	1·40	1·40
	a. Horiz pair. Nos. 248/9	2·75	2·75
249	70c. Research station and sunset	1·40	1·40
250	$1.40 Sunrise over research station	2·75	2·75
	a. Horiz pair. Nos. 250/1	5·50	5·50
251	$1.40 Sun pillars	2·75	2·75
248/51 *Set of 4*		7·50	7·50
MS252 136×80 *mm*. Nos. 248/51		8·25	8·25

Nos. 248/9 and 250/1 were each printed together, *se-tenant*, as horizontal pairs in sheets of 50 (2 panes 5×5), each sheet giving 20 horizontal pairs and ten single stamps (Nos. 248 or 250).

52 Springer Spaniel and Penguins

(Des Simone Sakinofsky. Litho RA Print)

2015 (9 Sept). The Dogs that Saved Macquarie Island (campaign for eradication of cats, rabbits, rats and mice). T **52** and similar horiz designs. P 14×14½.

253	70c. Type **52**	1·40	1·40
	a. Horiz pair. Nos. 253/4	2·75	2·75
254	70c. Labrador and handler searching for surviving Rabbits	1·40	1·40
255	$1.40 Flowers and handler with Labrador and Springer Spaniel	2·75	2·75
	a. Horiz pair. Nos. 255/6	5·50	5·50

256	$1.40 Springer Spaniel, Labrador and handler in snow	2·75	2·75
253/6 *Set of* 4		7·50	7·50
MS257 170×80 *mm*. Nos. 253/6		8·25	8·25

Nos. 253/4 and 255/6 were printed together, *se-tenant*, as horizontal pairs in sheets of 50 (5×5), each sheet containing twenty horizontal pairs and ten single stamps (Nos. 254 or 256) at left of sheet.

STAMP BOOKLETS

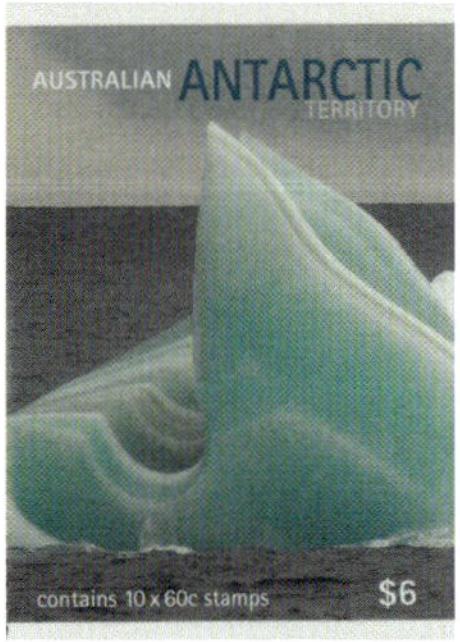

B **1** Iceberg

2011 (7 June). Icebergs. Multicoloured cover, 61×85 mm, as Type B **1**. Self-adhesive.

SB1	$6 booklet containing pane of 10×60c. (Nos. 203a)	16·00

B **2** Dog Sledge

2014 (9 Sept). Era of the Husky. Multicoloured cover, 61×86 mm, as Type B **2**. Self-adhesive.

SB2	$7 booklet containing pane of 10×70c. (No. 246a).	13·00

CHRISTMAS ISLAND

Formerly a part of the Straits Settlements and then of the Colony of Singapore, Christmas Island was occupied by the Japanese from 31 March, 1942, until September, 1945. It reverted to Singapore after liberation, but subsequently became an Australian territory on 15 October 1958.

> Stamps of the STRAITS SETTLEMENTS were used on Christmas Island from 1901 until 1942. Following liberation issues of MALAYA (BRITISH MILITARY ADMINISTRATION) and then SINGAPORE were used from 1946 to 1958.

(Currency. 100 cents = 1 Malayan dollar)

1 Queen Elizabeth II

(Des G. Lissenden. Recess with name and value typo in black. Note Printing Branch, Commonwealth Bank, Melbourne)

1958 (15 Oct). No wmk. P 14½.

1	**1**	2c. yellow-orange	55	80
2		4c. brown	60	30
3		5c. deep mauve	60	50
4		6c. grey-blue	1·00	30
5		8c. black-brown	1·75	50
6		10c. violet	1·00	30
7		12c. carmine	1·75	1·75
8		20c. blue	1·00	1·75
9		50c. yellow-green	2·00	1·75
10		$1 deep bluish green	2·00	1·75
1/10 *Set of* 10			11·00	8·75

> **PRINTERS**. Nos. 11/32 were printed by the Note Printing Branch, Reserve Bank of Australia, Melbourne. Nos. 33/82 were printed in photogravure by Harrison and Sons, Ltd, London.

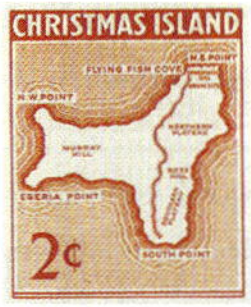

2 Map

3 Moonflower

4 Robber crab

5 Island scene

6 Phosphate train

7 Raising phosphate

8 Flying Fish Cove

9 Loading cantilever

10 Christmas Island Frigate Bird

11 White-tailed Tropic Bird

(Des G. Lissenden (2, 8c.), P. Morriss (4, 5, 10, 20c.), B. Stewart (others). Recess)

1963 (28 Aug). T **2/11**. P 14½×14 ($1) or 14½ (others).

11	**2**	2c. orange	1·25	35
12	**3**	4c. red-brown	50	15
13	**4**	5c. purple	50	20
14	**5**	6c. indigo	30	35
15	**6**	8c. black	2·50	35
16	**7**	10c. violet	40	15
17	**8**	12c. brown-red	40	25
18	**9**	20c. blue	1·00	20
19	**10**	50c. green	1·00	20
20	**11**	$1 yellow	1·75	35
11/20 *Set of* 10			8·50	2·25

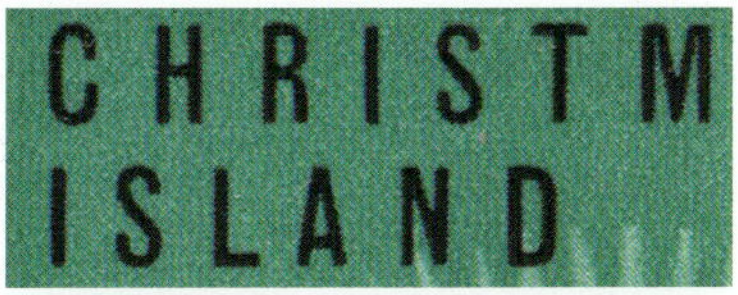

I Thick lettering

II Thinner lettering

1965. (14-24 Apr). 50th Anniversary of Gallipoli Landing. As T **184** of Australia but slightly larger (22×34½ *mm*) and colour changed. Photo. P 13½.

21	10c. sepia, black and emerald (I) (14.4)	30	1·75
	a. *Black-brown, black and light emerald* (II) (24.4)	2·50	2·75

(New Currency. 100 cents = 1 Australian dollar)

12 Golden-striped Grouper

13 "Angel" (mosaic)

(Des G. Hamori. Photo)

1968 (6 May)–**70**. Fish. T **12** and similar horiz designs. Multicoloured. P 13½.

22	1c. Type **12**	45	45
23	2c. Moorish Idol	60	20
24	3c. Long-nosed Butterflyfish	60	30
25	4c. Pink-tailed Triggerfish	60	20
	a. Deep blue (face value) omitted	£3000	
26	5c. Regal Angelfish	60	20
27	9c. White-cheeked Surgeonfish	60	40
28	10c. Lionfish	60	20
28*a*	15c. Saddle Butterflyfish (14.12.70)	3·50	2·50
29	20c. Ornate Butterflyfish	1·50	55
29*a*	30c. Giant Ghost Pipefish (14.12.70)	3·50	2·50
30	50c. Clown Surgeonfish	2·75	2·75
31	$1 Meyer's Butterflyfish	2·75	2·75
22/31	*Set of* 12	16·00	11·50

(Des G. Hamori. Photo)

1969 (10 Nov). Christmas. P 13½.

32	**13**	5c. red, deep blue and gold	20	30

14 "The Ansidei Madonna" (Raphael)

15 "The Adoration of the Shepherds" (ascr to the school of Seville)

(Des Harrison)

1970 (26 Oct). Christmas. Paintings. T **14** and similar vert design. Multicoloured. P 14×14½.

33	3c. Type **14**	20	15
34	5c. "The Virgin and Child, St. John the Baptist and an Angel" (Morando)	20	15

(Des Harrison)

1971 (4 Oct). Christmas. T **15** and similar vert design. Multicoloured. W w **12**. P 14.

35	6c. Type **15**	30	50
36	20c. "The Adoration of the Shepherds" (Reni)	70	1·00

16 H.M.S. *Flying Fish*, 1887

17 Angel of Peace

(Des V. Whiteley)

1972 (7 Feb)–**73**. Ships. Horiz designs as T **16**. Multicoloured. P 14×13½.

37	1c. *Eagle* (merchantman), 1714 (5.6.72)	25	60
38	2c. H.M.S. *Redpole* (gunboat), 1890 (5.6.72)	30	70
39	3c. *Hoi Houw* (freighter), 1959 (5.6.72)	30	70
40	4c. *Pigot* (sailing ship), 1771 (6.2.73)	40	75
41	5c. *Valetta* (cargo-liner), 1968 (6.2.73)	40	75
42	6c. Type **16**	40	75
43	7c. *Asia* (merchantman), 1805	40	75
44	8c. *Islander* (freighter), 1929-60	45	80
45	9c. H.M.S. *Imperieuse* (armoured cruiser), 1888 (6.2.73)	65	70
46	10c. H.M.S. *Hecate* (coast defence turret ship), 1871 (4.6.73)	50	80
47	20c. *Thomas* (galleon), 1615	50	1·00
48	25c. Royal Navy sail sloop, 1864 (4.6.73)	50	1·75
49	30c. *Cygnet* (flute), 1688 (4.6.73)	50	1·00
50	35c. *Triadic* (freighter), 1958 (4.6.73)	50	1·00
51	50c. H.M.S. *Amethyst* (frigate), 1857 (6.2.73)	50	1·50
52	$1 *Royal Mary* (warship), 1643 (5.6.72)	70	1·75
37/52	*Set of* 16	6·50	13·50

No. 45 is inscribed "H.M.S. *Imperious*", No. 46 "H.M.S. *Egeria*" and No. 48 "H.M.S. *Gordon*", all in error.

(Des Jennifer Toombs)

1972 (2 Oct). Christmas. T **17** and similar vert design. Multicoloured. P 14.

53	3c. Type **17**	15	40
	a. Pair. Nos. 53/4	30	80
54	3c. Angel of Joy	15	40
55	7c. Type **17**	20	50
	a. Pair. Nos. 55/6	40	1·00
56	7c. As No. 54	20	50
53/6	*Set of* 4	65	1·60

Nos. 53/4 and 55/6 have the two designs printed horizontally *se-tenant* within the sheet.

18 Virgin and Child, and Map

19 Mary and Holy Child within Christmas Star

(Des P. Law)

1973 (2 Oct). Christmas. P 14×13.

57	**18**	7c. multicoloured	25	35
58		25c. multicoloured	75	1·00

(Des Jennifer Toombs)

1974 (2 Oct). Christmas. P 13×14½.

59	**19**	7c. mauve and grey-black	25	60
60		30c. light orange, bright yellow and grey-black	75	2·50

20 "The Flight into Egypt"

21 Dove of Peace and Star of Bethlehem

(Des Jennifer Toombs)

1975 (2 Oct). Christmas. P 14×13.

61	**20**	10c. light greenish yellow, agate and gold	25	35
62		35c. bright rose, deep blue and gold	75	1·75

(Des R. Bates)

1976 (2 Oct). Christmas. P 13½.

63	**21**	10c. cerise, lemon and bright mauve	15	45
		a. Pair. Nos. 63/4	30	90
64	–	10c. cerise, lemon and bright mauve	15	45
65	**21**	35c. reddish violet, light greenish blue and light yellow-green	20	55
		a. Pair. Nos. 65/6	40	1·10
66	–	35c. reddish violet, light greenish blue and light yellow-green	20	55
63/6 *Set of 4*			65	1·75

Nos. 64 and 66 are "mirror-images" of T **21**, the two designs of each value being printed horizontally *se-tenant* throughout the sheet.

22 William Dampier (explorer)

23 Australian Coat of Arms on Map of Christmas Island

(Des V. Whiteley Studio)

1977 (30 Apr)–**78**. Famous Visitors. Horiz designs as T **22** in black, vermilion and greenish yellow (45c.) or multicoloured (others). P 14×13.

67	1c. Type **22**	15	80
68	2c. Capt. de Vlamingh (explorer) (22.2.78)	20	1·00
69	3c. Vice-Admiral MacLear (22.2.78)	30	80
70	4c. Sir John Murray (oceanographer) (22.2.78)	30	90
71	5c. Admiral Aldrich (31.5.78)	30	40
72	6c. Andrew Clunies Ross (first settler)	30	60
73	7c. J.J. Lister (naturalist) (31.5.78)	30	40
74	8c. Admiral of the Fleet Sir William May (1.9.78)	35	70
75	9c. Henry Ridley (botanist)	30	1·75
76	10c. George Clunies Ross (phosphate miner) (1.9.78)	55	55
77	20c. Capt. Joshua Slocum (yachtsman) (1.9.78)	40	75
78	45c. Charles Andrews (naturalist) (31.5.78)	50	45
79	50c. Richard Hanitsch (biologist) (31.5.78)	1·00	2·00
80	75c. Victor Purcell (scholar) (1.9.78)	40	1·25
81	$1 Fam Choo Beng (educator)	40	1·25
82	$2 Sir Harold Spencer-Jones (astronomer) (22.2.78)	45	2·00
67/82 *Set of 16*		5·50	14·00

(Des Mrs S. Muir. Litho Harrison)

1977 (2 June). Silver Jubilee. P 14½×13½.

83	**23**	45c. multicoloured	45	55

24 "A Partridge in a Pear Tree"

25 Abbott's Booby

(Des Jennifer Toombs. Litho Questa)

1977 (20 Oct)–**78**. Christmas. T **24** and similar vert designs depicting the carol *The Twelve Days of Christmas*. Multicoloured. P 14.

A. No wmk

84A	10c. Type **24**	10	20
	a. Sheetlet. Nos. 84A/95A	1·10	2·25
85A	10c. "Two Turtle Doves"	10	20
86A	10c. "Three French Hens"	10	20
87A	10c. "Four calling birds"	10	20
88A	10c. "Five gold rings"	10	20
89A	10c. "Six geese a-laying"	10	20
90A	10c. "Seven swans a-swimming"	10	20
91A	10c. "Eight maids a-milking"	10	20
92A	10c. "Nine ladies dancing"	10	20
93A	10c. "Ten lords a-leaping"	10	20
94A	10c. "Eleven pipers piping"	10	20
95A	10c. "Twelve drummers drumming"	10	20
84A/95A *Set of 12*		1·10	2·25

B. W w **14** (27.1.78)

84B	10c. Type **24**	15	25
	a. Sheetlet of 12. Nos. 84B/95B	1·60	2·75
85B	10c. "Two Turtle Doves"	15	25
86B	10c. "Three French Hens"	15	25
87B	10c. "Four calling birds"	15	25
88B	10c. "Five gold rings"	15	25
89B	10c. "Six geese a-laying"	15	25
90B	10c. "Seven swans a-swimming"	15	25
91B	10c. "Eight maids a-milking"	15	25
92B	10c. "Nine ladies dancing"	15	25
93B	10c. "Ten lords a-leaping"	15	25
94B	10c. "Eleven pipers piping"	15	25
95B	10c. "Twelve drummers drumming"	15	25
84B/95B *Set of 12*		1·60	2·75

Nos. 84/95 were printed as a *se-tenant* block within a sheetlet 142×170 mm.

(Des Jennifer Toombs. Litho Questa)

1978 (21 Apr). 25th Anniv of Coronation. T **25** and similar vert designs. P 15.

96	45c. black and bright ultramarine	40	60
	a. Sheetlet of 6. Nos. 96/8×2	1·75	2·75
97	45c. multicoloured	40	60
98	45c. black and bright ultramarine	40	60
96/8 *Set of 3*		1·00	1·60

Designs:—No. 96, White Swan of Bohun; No. 97, Queen Elizabeth II; No. 98, Type **25**.

Nos. 96/8 were printed together in small sheets of 6, containing two *se-tenant* strips of 3 with horizontal gutter margin between.

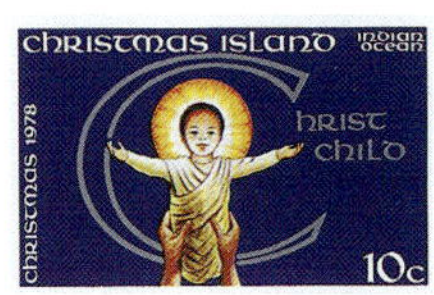

26 "Christ Child"

27 Chinese Children

(Des Jennifer Toombs. Litho J.W.)

1978 (2 Oct). Christmas. Scenes from "The Song of Christmas". T **26** and similar horiz designs. Multicoloured. P 14.

99	10c. Type **26**	15	20
	a. Sheetlet. Nos. 99/107	1·25	1·60
100	10c. "Herald Angels"	15	20
101	10c. "Redeemer"	15	20
102	10c. "Israel"	15	20
103	10c. "Star"	15	20
104	10c. "Three Wise Men"	15	20
105	10c. "Manger"	15	20
106	10c. "All He Stands For"	15	20
107	10c. "Shepherds Came"	15	20
99/107 *Set of 9*		1·25	1·60

Nos. 99/107 were printed together, *se-tenant*, in a small sheet of nine.

(Des Jennifer Toombs. Litho Questa)

1979 (20 Apr). International Year of the Child. T **27** and similar vert designs showing children of different races. Multicoloured, colour of inscr given. P 14.

108	20c. apple-green (Type **27**)	25	45
	a. Horiz strip of 5. Nos. 108/12	1·00	2·00
109	20c. turquoise-green (Malay children)	25	45
110	20c. lilac (Indian children)	25	45
111	20c. rose (European children)	25	45
112	20c. orange-yellow ("Oranges and Lemons")	25	45
108/12 *Set of 5*		1·00	2·00

Nos. 108/12 were printed together, *se-tenant*, in horizontal strips of five throughout the sheet, forming a composite design.

28 1958 2c. Definitive

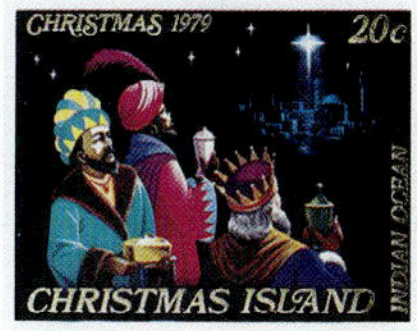

29 Wise Men following Star

(Des J. W. Litho Questa)

1979 (27 Aug). Death Centenary of Sir Rowland Hill. T **28** and similar horiz designs showing stamps and Sir Rowland Hill. Multicoloured. P 13½.

113	20c. Type **28**	25	40
	a. Horiz strip of 5. Nos. 113/17	1·10	1·75
114	20c. 1963 2c. Map definitive	25	40
115	20c. 1965 50th anniversary of Gallipoli Landing 10c. commemorative	25	40
116	20c. 1968 4c. Pink-tailed Triggerfish definitive	25	40
117	20c. 1969 5c. Christmas issue	25	40
113/17 *Set of 5*		1·10	1·75

Nos. 113/17 were printed together, *se-tenant*, in horizontal strips of five throughout the sheet.

(Des L. Curtis. Litho Walsall)

1979 (22 Oct). Christmas. T **29** and similar horiz design. Multicoloured. P 14×14½.

118	20c. Type **29**	20	30
119	55c. Virgin and Child	45	70

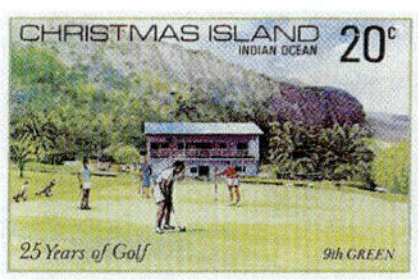

30 9th Green

31 Surveying

(Des R. Granger Barrett. Litho Format)

1980 (12 Feb). 25th Anniv of Christmas Island Golf Club. T **30** and similar horiz design. Multicoloured. P 14½×14.

120	20c. Type **30**	35	50
121	55c. Clubhouse	40	1·00

(Des L. Curtis. Litho Walsall)

1980 (6 May). Phosphate Industry (1st issue). T **31** and similar horiz design. Multicoloured. P 14.

122	15c. Type **31**	15	30
123	22c. Drilling for samples	15	35
124	40c. Sample analysis	20	55
125	55c. Mine planning	25	60
122/5 *Set of 4*		65	1·60

See also Nos. 126/9, 136/9 and 140/3.

(Des L. Curtis. Litho Walsall)

1980 (14 July). Phosphate Industry (2nd issue). Horiz designs as T **31**. Multicoloured. P 14.

126	15c. Jungle clearing	15	15
127	22c. Overburden removal	15	20
128	40c. Open cut mining	20	25
129	55c. Restoration	20	30
126/9 *Set of 4*		65	80

32 Angel with Harp

33 *Cryptoblepharus egeriae*

(Des Jennifer Toombs. Litho Walsall)

1980 (6 Oct). Christmas. T **32** and similar vert designs. Multicoloured. P 13½×13.

130	15c. Type **32**	10	25
	a. Sheetlet of 6. Nos. 130/5	75	1·50
131	15c. Angel with wounded soldier	10	25
132	22c. Virgin and Child	15	30
133	22c. Kneeling couple	15	30
134	60c. Angel with harp (*different*)	20	30
135	60c. Angel with children	20	30
130/5 *Set of 6*		75	1·50

Nos. 130/5 were printed together in small sheets of six containing two *se-tenant* strips of three (Nos. 130, 132, 134 and 131, 133, 135) with horizontal gutter margin between.

(Des L. Curtis. Litho Walsall)

1981 (9 Feb). Phosphate Industry (3rd issue). Horiz designs as T **31**. Multicoloured. P 14.

136	22c. Screening and stockpiling	15	15
137	28c. Train loading	20	20
138	40c. Railing	25	25
139	60c. Drying	25	25
136/9 *Set of 4*		75	75

(Des L. Curtis. Litho Walsall)

1981 (4 May). Phosphate Industry (4th issue). Horiz designs as T **31**. Multicoloured. P 14.

140	22c. Crushing	20	20
141	28c. Conveying	25	25
142	40c. Bulk storage	30	30
143	60c. *Consolidated Venture* (bulk carrier) loading	35	35
140/3 *Set of 4*		1·00	1·00

(Des L. Curtis. Litho Walsall)

1981 (10 Aug). Reptiles. T **33** and similar horiz designs. Multicoloured. P 13.

144	24c. Type **33**	20	20
145	30c. *Emoia nativitata*	25	25
146	40c. *Lepidodactylus listeri*	30	30
147	60c. *Cyrtodactylus sp. nov.*	35	35
144/7 *Set of 4*		1·00	1·00

34 Scene from Carol *Away in a Manger*

35 Reef Heron

(Des Jennifer Toombs. Litho Questa)

1981 (19 Oct). Christmas. T **34** and similar horiz designs showing scenes from carol *Away in a Manger*. P 14½×14.

148	18c. silver, deep blue and turquoise-blue	30	50
	a. Sheetlet of 4. Nos. 148/51	1·25	2·25
149	24c. multicoloured	30	55
150	40c. multicoloured	35	65
151	60c. multicoloured	40	75
148/51 *Set of 4*		1·25	2·25

Nos. 148/51 were printed together, *se-tenant*, in sheetlets of four.

(Des N. Arlott. Litho Questa)

1982 (8 Mar)–**83**. Birds. Multicoloured designs as T **35**. P 14.

152	1c. Type **35**	50	30
153	2c. Common Noddy	50	30
154	3c. White-tailed Swiftlet (14.6.82)	50	70
155	4c. Christmas Island Imperial Pigeon (14.6.82)	50	70
156	5c. Christmas Island White Eye (21.2.83)	60	70
157	10c. Island Thrush (14.6.82)	60	70
158	25c. Red-tailed Tropic Bird	1·25	60
159	30c. Emerald Dove (21.2.83)	60	70
160	40c. Brown Booby (23.8.82)	60	55
161	50c. Red-footed Booby (23.8.82)	60	55
162	65c. Christmas Island Frigate Bird (23.8.82)	60	55
163	75c. White-tailed Tropic Bird (23.8.82)	70	65
164	80c. Australian Kestrel (*vert*) (21.2.83)	1·50	2·75
165	$1 Moluccan Hawk Owl (*vert*) (21.2.83)	2·00	3·25
166	$2 Australian Goshawk (*vert*) (14.6.82)	1·50	4·00
167	$4 Abbott's Booby (*vert*)	1·50	2·00
152/67 *Set of 16*		12·50	17·00

36 Joseph

37 "Mirror" Dinghy and Club House

(Des Jennifer Toombs. Litho and embossed Walsall)

1982 (18 Oct). Christmas. Origami Paper Sculptures. T **36** and similar vert designs. Multicoloured. P 14½×14.

168	27c. Type **36**	30	30
	a. Horiz strip of 3. Nos. 168/70	1·00	1·25
169	50c. Angel	35	45
170	75c. Mary and baby Jesus	45	65
168/70 *Set of 3*		1·00	1·25

Nos. 168/70 were printed together, *se-tenant*, in horiz strips of three throughout the sheet.

(Des L. McCombie. Litho Format)

1983 (2 May). 25th Anniv of Christmas Island Boat Club. T **37** and similar multicoloured designs. P 14×14½ (27, 35c.) or 14½×14 (others).

171	27c. Type **37**	20	30
172	35c. Ocean-going yachts	20	35
173	50c. Fishing launch and cargo ship (*horiz*)	25	40
174	75c. Dinghy-racing and cantilever (*horiz*)	25	60
171/4 *Set of 4*		80	1·50

38 Maps of Christmas Island and Australia, Eastern Grey Kangaroo and White-tailed Tropic Bird

39 Candle and Holly

(Des A. Theobald. Litho Questa)

1983 (1 Oct). 25th Anniv of Christmas Island as an Australian Territory. T **38** and similar horiz designs. Multicoloured. P 14.

175	24c. Type **38**	60	40
176	30c. Christmas Island and Australian flag	70	70
177	85c. Maps of Christmas Island and Australia, with Boeing 727	1·50	2·25
175/7 *Set of 3*		2·50	3·00

(Des J. W. Litho Walsall)

1983 (31 Oct). Christmas. Candles. T **39** and similar vert designs. Multicoloured. P 13.

178	24c. Type **39**	20	20
179	30c. Six gold candles	30	40
180	85c. Candles	70	1·50
178/80 *Set of 3*		1·10	1·90

40 Feeding on Leaf

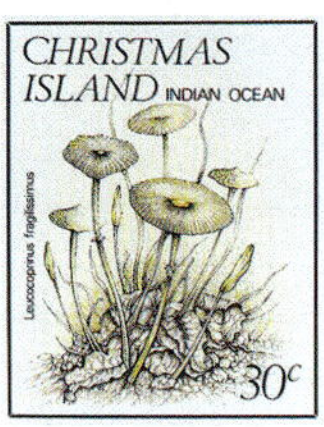

41 *Leucocoprinus fragilissimus*

(Des L. Curtis. Litho Questa)

1984 (20 Feb). Red Land Crab. T **40** and similar horiz designs showing various aspects of crab's life. Multicoloured. P 14×14½.

181	30c. Type **40**	25	30
182	40c. Migration	30	40
183	55c. Development stages	30	50
184	85c. Adult female and young	45	70
181/4 *Set of 4*		1·10	1·75

(Des I. Loe. Litho Format)

1984 (30 Apr). Fungi. T **41** and similar vert designs. Multicoloured. P 14×14½.

185	30c. Type **41**	20	55
186	40c. *Microporus xanthopus*	25	70
187	45c. *Hydropus anthidepas* ("*Trogia anthidepas*")	30	80
188	55c. *Haddowia longipes*	30	90
189	85c. *Phillipsia domingensis*	35	1·25
185/9 *Set of 5*		1·25	3·75

42 Run-out

43 Arrival of Father Christmas

(Des A. Theobald. Litho J. W.)

1984 (23 July). 25th Anniversary of Cricket on Christmas Island. T **42** and similar horiz designs. Multicoloured. P 14.

190	30c. Type **42**	30	85
191	40c. Bowled-out	30	1·10
192	55c. Batsman in action	35	1·50
193	85c. Fielder diving for catch	55	1·75
190/3 *Set of 4*		1·40	4·75

(Des D. Slater. Litho B.D.T.)

1984 (21 Sept). Christmas and Ausipex International Stamp Exhibition, Melbourne. Sheet 100×100 mm containing T **43** and similar horiz designs. Multicoloured. P 13½.

MS194	30c. Type **43**; 55c. Distribution of presents; 85c. Departure of Father Christmas	2·00	2·75

No. **MS**194 also contains three labels horizontally *se-tenant* with the stamps and forming composite designs with them.

44 Robber Crab

45 "Once in Royal David's City"

(Des L. Curtis. Litho Walsall)

1985 (30 Jan). Crabs (1st series). T **44** and similar horiz designs. Multicoloured. P 13×13½.

195	30c. Type **44**	70	70
196	40c. Horn-eyed Ghost Crab	80	1·10
197	55c. Purple Hermit Crab	1·00	1·60
198	85c. Little Nipper	1·50	2·50
195/8 *Set of 4*		3·50	5·50

See also Nos. 199/202 and 203/6.

(Des L. Curtis. Litho Walsall)

1985 (29 Apr). Crabs (2nd series). Horiz designs as T **44**. Multicoloured. P 13×13½.

199	33c. Blue Crab	80	65
200	45c. Tawny Hermit Crab	1·00	1·25
201	60c. Red Nipper	1·10	2·00
202	90c. Smooth-handed Ghost Crab	1·75	3·00
199/202 *Set of 4*		4·25	6·25

(Des L. Curtis. Litho Walsall)

1985 (22 July). Crabs (3rd series). Horiz designs as T **44**. Multicoloured. P 13×13½.

203	33c. Red Crab	1·00	60
204	45c. Mottled Crab	1·40	1·40
205	60c. Rock Hopper Crab	1·90	2·50
206	90c. Yellow Nipper	2·50	3·50
203/6 *Set of 4*		6·00	7·25

(Des Jennifer Toombs. Litho Harrison)

1985 (28 Oct). Christmas. Carols. T **45** and similar vert designs. Multicoloured. P 14×14½.

207	27c. Type **45**	1·10	1·40
	a. Horiz strip of 5. Nos. 207/11	6·50	7·75
208	33c. "While Shepherds Watched Their Flocks by Night"	1·25	1·50
209	45c. "Away in a Manger"	1·50	1·75
210	60c. "We Three Kings of Orient Are"	1·60	1·90
211	90c. "Hark the Herald Angels Sing"	1·75	2·00
207/11 *Set of 5*		6·50	7·75

Nos. 207/11 were printed together, *se-tenant*, in horizontal strips of five throughout the sheet.

46 Halley's Comet over Christmas Island

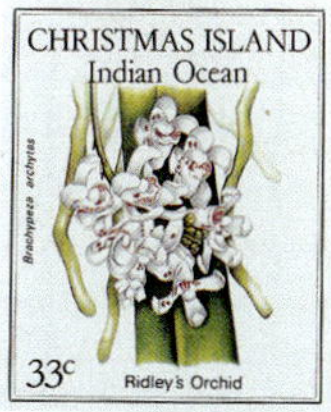

47 Ridley's Orchid

(Des L. Curtis. Litho Format)

1986 (30 Apr). Appearance of Halley's Comet. T **46** and similar horiz designs. Multicoloured. P 14.

212	33c. Type **46**	30	80
213	45c. Edmond Halley	35	1·10
214	60c. Comet and *Consolidated Venture* (bulk carrier) loading phosphate	40	2·25
215	90c. Comet over Flying Fish Cove	50	2·50
212/15	*Set of* 4	1·40	6·00

(Des I. Loe. Litho Format)

1986 (23 June). Native Flowers. T **47** and similar vert designs. Multicoloured. P 14.

216	33c. Type **47**	50	55
217	45c. Hanging Flower	30	85
218	60c. Hoya	30	1·50
219	90c. Sea Hibiscus	35	2·00
216/19	*Set of* 4	1·25	4·50

47a Prince Andrew and Miss Sarah Ferguson

48 Father Christmas and Reindeer in Speedboat

(Des D. Miller. Litho Walsall)

1986 (23 July). Royal Wedding. T **47a** and similar horiz designs. Multicoloured. P 14½×14.

220	33c. Type **47a**	25	35
221	90c. Prince Andrew piloting helicopter, Digby, Canada, 1985	75	1·40

(Des G. Vasarhelyi. Litho Walsall)

1986 (30 Sept). Christmas. T **48** and similar horiz designs. Multicoloured. P 13×13½.

222	30c. Type **48**	85	60
223	36c. Father Christmas and reindeer on beach	1·00	60
224	55c. Father Christmas fishing	1·50	1·50
225	70c. Playing golf	2·75	3·50
226	$1 Sleeping in hammock	2·75	4·00
222/6	*Set of* 5	8·00	9·00

49 H.M.S. *Flying Fish* and Outline Map of Christmas Island

(Des L. Curtis. Litho Format)

1987 (21 Jan). Centenary of Visits by H.M.S. *Flying Fish* and H.M.S. *Egeria*. T **49** and similar horiz design. Multicoloured. P 14½.

227	36c. Type **49**	40	75
228	90c. H.M.S. *Egeria* and outline map	70	2·50

50 Blind Snake

51 Children Watching Father Christmas in Sleigh

(Des G. Drummond. Litho Questa)

1987 (25 Mar)–**89**. Wildlife. T **50** and similar horiz designs. Multicoloured. P 14.

229	1c. Type **50**	40	90
	a. Sheetlet of 16. Nos. 229/37 and 238/44 (1.3.88)	32·00	
230	2c. Blue-tailed Skink	40	90
231	3c. Insectivorous Bat (24.6.87)	90	90
232	5c. Grasshopper (1.3.88)	1·50	90
233	10c. Christmas Island Fruit Bat (24.6.87)	90	90
234	25c. Gecko	1·00	1·00
235	30c. *Mantis religiosa* (mantis) (1.3.88)	1·25	1·25
236	36c. Moluccan Hawk Owl (24.6.87)	3·00	1·75
237	40c. Bull-mouth Helmet (*Cypraecassis rufa*) (26.8.87)	1·75	2·75
237*a*	41c. Nudibranch (*Phidiana* sp) (1.9.89)	1·25	70
238	50c. Textile or Cloth of Gold Cone (*Conus textile*) (26.8.87)	1·75	2·75
239	65c. Brittle Stars (26.8.87)	1·40	1·25
240	75c. Regal Angelfish (26.8.87)	1·40	1·75
241	90c. *Appias paulina* (butterfly) (1.3.88)	1·50	3·25
242	$1 *Hypolimnas misippus* (butterfly) (1.3.88)	1·50	3·25
243	$2 Shrew (*Crocidura attenuata trichura*) (24.6.87)	1·50	7·00
244	$5 Green Turtle	2·00	7·00
229/44	*Set of* 17	20·00	32·00

No. 229a was originally only available from a presentation pack, but was, subsequently, sold separately by the Christmas Island Post Office. Stamps from it show "1988" imprint date. Examples from the ordinary sheets are without imprint date.

(Des D. Miller. Litho CPE Australia Ltd, Melbourne)

1987 (7 Oct). Christmas. Sheet 165×65 mm, containing T **51** and similar multicoloured designs. P 13½.

MS245	30c. Type **51**; 37c. Father Christmas distributing gifts (48×22 *mm*); 90c. Children with presents (48×22 *mm*); $1 Singing carols	4·00	4·00
	a. Imperf between 37c. and 90c.		

The stamps within No. **MS**245 form a composite design of a beach scene.

(Des Sue Passmore. Litho CPE Australia Ltd, Melbourne)

1988 (26 Jan). Bicentenary of Australian Settlement. Arrival of First Fleet. Square designs as Nos. 1105/9 of Australia, but each inscribed "CHRISTMAS ISLAND Indian Ocean" and "AUSTRALIA BICENTENARY".

246	37c. Aborigines watching arrival of Fleet, Botany Bay	1·50	1·90
	a. Horiz strip of 5. Nos. 246/50	6·75	8·50
247	37c. Aboriginal family and anchored ships	1·50	1·90
248	37c. Fleet arriving at Sydney Cove	1·50	1·90
249	37c. Ship's boat	1·50	1·90
250	37c. Raising the flag, Sydney Cove, 26 January 1788	1·50	1·90
246/50	*Set of* 5	6·75	8·50

Nos. 246/50 were printed together, *se-tenant*, in horizontal strips of five throughout the sheet, forming a composite design.

52 Captain William May

53 Pony and Trap, 1910

(Des Josephine Martin. Litho Questa)

1988 (8 June). Centenary of British Annexation. T **52** and similar vert designs. Multicoloured. P 14½×14.

251	37c. Type **52**	40	40
252	53c. Annexation ceremony	55	55
253	95c. H.M.S. *Imperieuse* (armoured cruiser) firing salute	1·50	95
254	$1.50 Building commemorative cairn	1·25	1·50
251/4 *Set of* 4		3·25	3·00

(Des L. Curtis. Litho Walsall)

1988 (24 Aug). Centenary of Permanent Settlement. T **53** and similar horiz designs. Multicoloured. P 14×14½.

255	37c. Type **53**	1·25	40
256	55c. Phosphate mining, 1910	1·50	55
257	70c. Steam locomotive, 1914	2·00	85
258	$1 Arrival of first aircraft, 1957	2·50	1·25
255/8 *Set of* 4		6·50	2·75

54 Beach Toys

55 Food on Table ("Good Harvesting")

(Des N. Shewring. Litho Format)

1988 (15 Nov). Christmas. Toys and Gifts. T **54** and similar vert designs. Multicoloured. P 14.

259	32c. Type **54**	40	35
260	39c. Flippers, snorkel and mask	45	40
261	90c. Model soldier, doll and soft toys	80	1·10
262	$1 Models of racing car, lorry and jet aircraft	90	1·25
259/62 *Set of* 4		2·25	2·75

(Des D. Miller. Litho Questa)

1989 (31 Jan). Chinese New Year. T **55** and similar horiz designs. Multicoloured. P 14×14½.

263	39c. Type **55**	45	40
264	70c. Decorations ("Prosperity")	80	70
265	90c. Chinese girls ("Good Fortune")	1·10	90
266	$1 Lion dance ("Progress Every Year")	1·25	1·00
263/6 *Set of* 4		3·25	2·75

56 Sir John Murray

57 Four Children

(Des S. Noon. Litho Walsall)

1989 (16 Mar). 75th Death Anniv of Sir John Murray (oceanographer). T **56** and similar horiz designs. Multicoloured. P 14×14½.

267	39c. Type **56**	50	50
268	80c. Map of Christmas Island showing Murray Hill	1·25	95
269	$1 Oceanographic equipment	1·50	1·25
270	$1.10 H.M.S. *Challenger* (survey ship), 1872	1·75	1·50
267/70 *Set of* 4		4·50	3·75

(Des C. Burke. Litho Questa)

1989 (31 May). Malay Hari Raya Festival. T **57** and similar vert designs. Multicoloured. P 14.

271	39c. Type **57**	30	50
272	55c. Man playing tambourine	50	70
273	80c. Girl in festival costume	65	1·00
274	$1.10 Christmas Island Mosque	80	1·40
271/4 *Set of* 4		2·00	3·25

58 *Huperzia phlegmaria*

59 Virgin Mary and Star

(Des Kerrie Rockett. Litho Walsall)

1989 (16 Aug). Ferns. T **58** and similar vert designs. Multicoloured. P 14.

275	41c. Type **58**	50	60
276	65c. *Asplenium polydon*	70	85
277	80c. Common Bracken	80	1·00
278	$1.10 Birds-nest Fern	95	1·40
275/8 *Set of* 4		2·75	3·50

(Des G. Maynard. Litho Leigh-Mardon Ltd, Melbourne)

1989 (4 Oct). Christmas. T **59** and similar vert designs. Multicoloured. P 14½.

279	36c. Type **59**	60	40
280	41c. Christ Child in manger	60	45
281	80c. Shepherds and Star	1·50	80
282	$1.10 Three Wise Men following Star	1·60	1·10
279/82 *Set of* 4		3·75	2·50

(60)

61 First Sighting, 1615

1989 (18 Oct). Melbourne Stampshow '89. No. 237a and as No. 242, but with imprint date, optd with T **60**.

283	41c. Nudibranch (*Phidiana* sp.)	1·75	45
284	$1 *Hypolimnas misippus*	4·00	1·25

Designs:—No. 96, White Swan of Bohun; No. 97, Queen Elizabeth II; No. 98, Type 25.

(Des R. Honisett. Litho Note Ptg Branch, Reserve Bank of Australia)

1990 (31 Jan). 375th Anniv of Discovery of Christmas Island. T **61** and similar vert design. Multicoloured. P 14×15.

285	41c. Type **61**	2·00	50
286	$1.10 Second sighting and naming, 1643	3·00	1·40

62 Miniature Tractor pulling Phosphate

63 Male Abbott's Booby

(Des C. Lee. Litho Leigh-Mardon Ltd, Melbourne)

1990 (18 Apr–22 Aug). Christmas Island Transport. T **62** and similar multicoloured designs. P 13½×14 (horiz) or 14×13½ (vert).

287	1c. Type **62**	15	20
288	2c. Phosphate train (22.8)	40	40
289	3c. Diesel railcar No. 8802 (*vert*)	20	20
290	5c. Loading Road train (22.8)	40	40
291	10c. Trishaw (*vert*)	30	30
292	15c. Terex truck (22.8)	65	65
293	25c. Articulated bus	30	30
294	30c. Cable passenger carriage (*vert*)	30	35
295	40c. Passenger barge (*vert*)	35	40
296	50c. Kolek (outrigger canoe)	55	55
297	65c. Flying Doctor aircraft and ambulance (22.8)	3·50	1·50

298	75c. Toyota truck (22.8)	1·25	1·50
299	90c. Vintage truck (22.8)	1·25	1·75
300	$1 Water tanker (22.8)	1·25	1·75
301	$2 Traction engine (22.8)	1·25	3·00
302	$5 Steam locomotive No. 1	2·00	3·75
287/302	*Set of* 16	12·50	16·00

(Des N. Shewring. Litho Questa)

1990 (6 June). Abbott's Booby. T **63** and similar vert designs. Multicoloured. P 13½×14.

303	10c. Type **63**	60	30
304	20c. Juvenile male	80	40
305	29c. Female with egg	85	50
306	41c. Pair with chick	1·10	55
303/6	*Set of* 4	3·00	1·60
MS307	122×68 *mm.* Male with wings spread; 41c. Male on branch; 41c. Female with fledgling. P 14½	4·75	3·00

The three stamps within No. **MS**307 form a composite design and are without the W.W.F. logo.

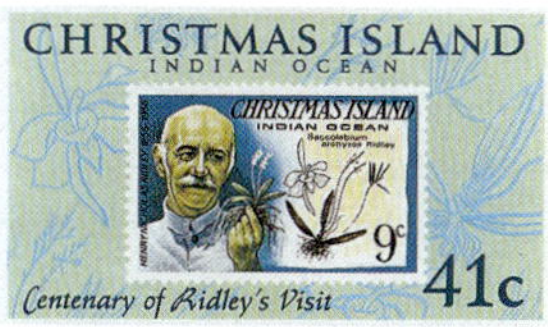

64 1977 Famous Visitors 9c. Stamp

(Des Elizabeth Innes. Litho Leigh-Mardon Ltd, Melbourne)

1990 (11 July). Centenary of Henry Ridley's Visit. T **64** and similar multicoloured design. P 15×14½ (41c.) or 14½×15 (75c.).

308	41c. Type **64**	55	75
309	75c. Ridley (botanist) in rainforest (*vert*)	85	2·00

1990 (24 Aug). "New Zealand 1990" International Stamp Exhibition, Auckland. No. **MS**307 optd "NZ 1990 WORLD STAMP EXHIBITION AUCKLAND, NEW ZEALAND, 24 AUGUST – 2 SEPTEMBER 1990" in purple on the sheet margins.

MS310	122×68 *mm.* 41c. Male with wings spread; 41c. Male on branch; 41c. Female with fledgling	8·00	9·00
	a. Error Imperf	£1200	

65 *Corymborkus veratrifolia*

66 *Islander* (freighter), 1898

(Litho Leigh-Mardon Ltd, Melbourne)

1990 (3 Oct). Christmas. Flowers. T **65** and similar horiz designs. Multicoloured. P 14½.

311	38c. Type **65**	1·10	70
312	43c. *Hoya aldrichii*	1·25	75
313	80c. *Quisqualis indica*	1·75	2·75
314	$1.20 *Barringtonia racemosa*	2·25	3·50
311/14	*Set of* 4	5·50	7·00

1990 (6 Dec). "Birdpex '90" Stamp Exhibition, Christchurch. No. **MS**307 optd "BIRDPEX '90 NATIONAL PHILATELIC EXHIBITION UNIVERSITY OF CANTERBURY CHRISTCHURCH NZ 6–9 DEC 1990 IN CONJUNCTION WITH THE 20th INTERNATIONAL ORNITHOLOGICAL CONGRESS" in green on the sheet margins.

MS315	122×68 *mm.* 41c. Male with wings spread; 41c. Male on branch; 41c. Female with fledgling	12·00	11·00

(Des C. Lee. Litho Leigh-Mardon Ltd, Melbourne)

1991 (13 Feb). Centenary of First Phosphate Mining Lease. T **66** and similar vert designs. Multicoloured. P 14½.

316	43c. Type **66**	1·00	90
	a. Horiz strip of 5. Nos. 316/20	6·50	6·00
317	43c. Miners loading tipper wagons, 1908	1·00	90
318	85c. Shay steam locomotive No. 4, 1925	1·40	1·25
319	$1.20 Extracting phosphate, 1951	1·75	1·60
320	$1.70 Land reclamation, 1990	2·00	1·90
316/20	*Set of* 5	6·50	6·00

Nos. 316/20 were printed together, *se-tenant*, in horizontal strips of five throughout the sheet, the background forming a composite forest design.

67 Teaching Children Road Safety

68 Map of Christmas Island, 1991

(Des R. Honisett. Litho Leigh-Mardon Ltd, Melbourne)

1991 (17 Apr). Christmas Island Police Force. T **67** and similar horiz designs. Multicoloured. P 14½.

321	43c. Type **67**	1·50	1·00
322	43c. Traffic control	1·50	1·00
323	90c. Airport customs	2·25	3·25
324	$1.20 Police launch *Fregata Andrews* towing rescued boat	3·00	3·00
321/4	*Set of* 4	7·50	7·50
MS325	135×88 *mm.* Nos. 321/4	7·50	7·50

(Des D. Miller. Litho Questa)

1991 (19 June). Maps of Christmas Island. T **68** and similar vert designs. Multicoloured. P 14×13½.

326	43c. Type **68**	1·00	65
327	75c. Goos Atlas, 1666	1·75	1·10
328	$1.10 De Manevillette, 1745	2·25	1·60
329	$1.20 Comberford, 1667	2·25	1·90
326/9	*Set of* 4	6·50	4·75

69 *Bruguiera gymnorrhiza*

70 "Family round Christmas Tree", (S'ng Yen Luiw)

(Des Jane Moore. Litho Leigh-Mardon Ltd, Melbourne)

1991 (21 Aug). Local Trees. T **69** and similar horiz designs. Multicoloured. P 14.

330	43c. Type **69**	1·00	65
331	70c. *Syzygium operculatum*	1·50	1·00
332	85c. *Ficus microcarpa*	1·75	1·25
333	$1.20 *Arenga listeri*	2·00	1·60
330/3	*Set of* 4	5·75	4·00

(Des Liz Innes. Litho Leigh-Mardon Ltd, Melbourne)

1991 (2 Oct). Christmas. Children's Paintings. T **70** and similar horiz designs. Multicoloured. P 14½.

334	38c. Type **70**	75	55
	a. Horiz strip of 5. Nos. 334/8	3·25	2·50
335	38c. "Opening Presents" (Liew Ann Nee)	75	55
336	38c. "Beach Party" (Foo Pang Chuan)	75	55
337	38c. "Christmas Walk" (Too Lai Peng)	75	55
338	38c. "Santa Claus and Christmas Tree" (Jesamine Wheeler)	75	55
339	43c. "Santa Claus fishing" (Ho Puay Ha)	75	60
340	$1 "Santa Claus in Boat" (Ng Hooi Hua)	1·50	1·50
341	$1.20 "Santa Claus surfing" (Yani Kawi)	1·75	1·75
334/41	*Set of* 8	7·00	6·00

Nos. 334/8 were printed together, *se-tenant*, in horizontal strips of five throughout the sheet.

71 Discussing Evacuation, 1942

72 Snake's-head Cowrie (*Cypraea caputserpentis*)

(Des C. Lee. Litho Leigh-Mardon Ltd, Melbourne)

1992 (19 Feb). 50th Anniv of Partial Evacuation. T **71** and similar vert designs. Multicoloured. P 14½.

342	45c. Type **71**	1·50	1·50
343	45c. Families waiting to embark	1·50	1·50
344	$1.05 Ferrying evacuees to *Islander*	3·25	3·50
345	$1.20 Departure of *Islander* (freighter)	3·75	4·00
342/5 *Set of 4*		9·00	9·50

(Des G. Ryan. Litho Leigh-Mardon Ltd, Melbourne)

1992 (15 Apr–19 Aug). Shells. T **72** and similar vert designs. Multicoloured. P 14½.

346	5c. Tiger Cowrie (*Cypraea tigris*) (19.8)	60	70
347	10c. Type **72**	80	70
348	15c. Scorpion Conch (*Lambis scorpius*) (19.8)	1·50	70
349	20c. Royal Oak Scallop (*Cryptopecten pallium*)	1·25	70
350	25c. Striped Engina (*Engina mendicaria*) (19.8)	1·25	70
351	30c. Prickly Pacific Drupe (*Drupa ricinus*)	1·25	70
352	40c. Reticulate Distorsio (*Distorsio recticulata*) (19.8)	1·25	75
353	45c. Tapestry Turban (*Turbo petholatus*)	1·25	75
354	50c. Beautiful Goblet (*Pollia puchra*) (19.8)	1·25	75
355	60c. Captain Cone (*Conus capitaneus*)	1·50	80
356	70c. Lajonkaire's Turban (*Turbo lajonkairii*) (19.8)	2·50	90
357	80c. Chiragra Spider Conch (*Lambis chiragra chiragra*)	1·75	1·00
358	90c. Common Delphina (*Angaria delphinus*) (19.8)	1·75	1·25
359	$1 Ceramic Vase (*Vasum ceramicum*)	1·75	1·50
360	$2 Pacific Partridge Tun (*Tonna perdix*)	1·40	1·75
361	$5 Strawberry Drupe (*Drupa rubusidaeus*) (19.8)	3·50	3·75
346/61 *Set of 16*		22·00	16·00

73 Torpedoing of *Eidsvold*

(**74**)

(Des R. Watton. Litho Enschedé)

1992 (17 June). 50th Anniv of Sinkings of *Eidsvold* and *Nissa Maru*. T **73** and similar horiz designs. Multicoloured. P 14×13½.

362	45c. Type **73**	2·75	1·25
363	80c. *Eidsvold* sinking	3·50	3·25
364	$1.05 *Nissa Maru* under attack	4·00	5·00
365	$1.20 *Nissa Maru* beached	4·25	5·00
362/5 *Set of 4*		13·00	13·00

1992 (1 Sept). "Kuala Lumpur '92" International Philatelic Exhibition. No. 361 optd with T **74** in red.

366	$5 Strawberry Drupe (*Drupa rubusidaeus*)	9·00	7·00

75 Jungle

76 Abbott's Booby

(Des Jane Moore and Elizabeth Innes. Litho Leigh-Mardon Ltd, Melbourne)

1992 (7 Oct). Christmas. T **75** and similar vert designs. Multicoloured. P 14½.

367	40c. Type **75**	90	1·25
	a. Horiz strip of 5. Nos. 367/71	5·50	6·50
368	40c. Seabirds over rock	90	1·25
369	45c. Brown Boobies on headland	90	1·25
370	$1.05 Seabirds and cliffs	1·60	1·75
371	$1.20 Cliffs	1·60	1·75
367/71 *Set of 5*		5·50	6·50

Nos. 367/71 were printed together, *se-tenant*, in horizontal strips of five throughout the sheet, each strip forming a composite coastal design.

On 2 March 1993 responsibility for the Christmas Island postal service passed from the territorial administration to Australia Post. In consequence Nos. 372/7 and all subsequent issues are valid for postal purposes in both Christmas Island and Australia. From the same date the stamps of Australia became valid for use on Christmas Island

(Des D. Nelson and Janet Boschen. Litho McPherson's Ptg Group, Mulgrave)

1993 (4 Mar). Seabirds. T **76** and similar vert designs. Multicoloured. P 14½×14.

372	45c. Type **76**	60	85
	a. Horiz strip of 5. Nos. 372/6	2·75	3·75
373	45c. Christmas Island Frigate Bird	60	85
374	45c. Common Noddy	60	85
375	45c. White-tailed Tropic Bird ("Golden Bosunbird")	60	85
376	45c. Brown Booby	60	85
372/6 *Set of 5*		2·75	3·75
MS377	140×70 *mm*. Nos. 372/6	2·75	4·50

Nos. 372/6 were printed together, *se-tenant*, in horizontal strips of five throughout the sheet, forming a composite design.

No. **MS**377 also exists overprinted with the "Indopex '93" or "Taipei '93" logos for sale at these stamp exhibitions in Surabaya, Indonesia, and Taiwan.

77 Dolly Beach

78 Turtle on Beach

(Des Jane Moore and Janet Boschen. Litho McPherson's Ptg Group, Mulgrave)

1993 (1 June). Scenic Views of Christmas Island. T **77** and similar horiz designs. Multicoloured. P 14×14½.

378	85c. Type **77**	1·75	1·75
379	95c. Blow Holes	2·00	2·25
380	$1.05 Merrial Beach	2·25	2·50
381	$1.20 Rainforest	2·25	2·50
378/81 *Set of 4*		7·50	8·00

(Des B. Wood and Sandra Harman. Litho McPherson's Ptg Group, Mulgrave)

1993 (2 Sept). Christmas. T **78** and similar vert designs. Multicoloured. P 14½×14.

382	40c. Type **78**	1·00	70
383	45c. Crabs and wave	1·00	70
384	$1 Christmas Island Frigate Bird and rainforest	2·25	3·25
382/4 *Set of 3*		3·75	4·25

79 Map of Christmas Island

80 Pekingese

(Des Betina Ogden. Litho McPherson's Ptg Group, Mulgrave)

1993 (1 Dec). 350th Anniv of Naming of Christmas Island. P 14×14½.

385	**79**	$2 multicoloured	3·00	3·50

(Des Yen Lau. Litho McPherson's Ptg Group, Mulgrave)

1994 (20 Jan). Chinese New Year ("Year of the Dog"). T **80** and similar horiz design. P 14×14½.

386	45c. Type **80**	1·00	1·40
	a. Pair. Nos. 386/7	2·00	2·75
387	45c. Mickey (Christmas Island dog)	1·00	1·40
MS388	106×70 *mm*. Nos. 386/7	3·00	4·00

Nos. 386/7 were printed together, *se-tenant*, in horizontal or vertical pairs throughout the sheet.

No. **MS**388 also exists overprinted with "Melbourne Stamp & Coin Show 11–13 February 1994", "Hong Kong '94 Stamp Exhibition", "Canberra Stamp Show 94" or "Queensland Stamp and Coin Show 94" logos for sale at these exhibitions.

81 Shay Locomotive No. 4

82 *Brachypeza archyas*

(Des J. Richards. Litho McPherson's Ptg Group, Mulgrave)

1994 (19 May). Steam Locomotives. T **81** and similar horiz designs. Multicoloured. P 14×14½.

389	85c. Type **81**	1·75	1·75
390	95c. Locomotive No. 9	1·75	2·00
391	$1.20 Locomotive No. 1	2·00	2·25
389/91	*Set of 3*	5·00	5·50

(Des Celia Rosser. Litho McPherson's Ptg Group, Mulgrave)

1994 (16 Aug). Orchids. T **82** and similar vert designs. Multicoloured. P 14½×14.

392	45c. Type **82**	1·10	1·40
	a. Horiz strip of 5. Nos. 392/6	5·00	6·25
393	45c. *Thelasis capitata*	1·10	1·40
394	45c. *Corymborkis veratrifolia*	1·10	1·40
395	45c. *Flickingeria nativitatis*	1·10	1·40
396	45c. *Dendrobium crumenatum*	1·10	1·40
392/6	*Set of 5*	5·00	6·25

Nos. 392/6 were printed together, *se-tenant*, in horizontal strips of five throughout the sheet.

83 Angel blowing Trumpet

84 Pig

(Des Tracie Grimwood. Litho McPherson's Ptg Group, Mulgrave)

1994 (8 Sept). Christmas. T **83** and similar horiz designs. Multicoloured. P 14×14½.

397	40c. Type **83**	70	60
398	45c. Wise Man holding gift	70	60
399	80c. Star over Bethlehem	1·40	2·50
397/9	*Set of 3*	2·50	3·25

(Des J. Chan. Litho McPherson's Ptg Group, Mulgrave)

1995 (12 Jan). Chinese New Year ("Year of the Pig"). T **84** and similar horiz design showing a different pig. P 14×14½.

400	45c. multicoloured	75	60
401	85c. multicoloured	1·25	1·75
MS402	106×71 *mm*. Nos. 400/1	2·25	2·75

No. **MS**402 also exists overprinted with "Melbourne Stamp & Coin Show 10–12 February 1995" logo for sale at this exhibition.

85 Golfer playing Shot

86 Father Christmas with Map on Christmas Island Frigate Bird

(Des N. Buchanan. Litho McPherson's Ptg Group, Mulgrave)

1995 (11 May). 40th Anniv of Christmas Island Golf Course. P 14×14½.

403	**85** $2.50 multicoloured	4·25	4·25

(Des B. Wood and Sophie Newman. Litho McPherson's Ptg Group, Mulgrave)

1995 (14 Sept). Christmas. T **86** and similar horiz designs. Multicoloured. P 14×14½.

404	40c. Type **86**	70	60
405	45c. Father Christmas distributing presents	70	60
406	80c. Father Christmas waving goodbye	1·40	2·50
404/6	*Set of 3*	2·50	3·25

87 de Havilland DH.98 Mosquite on Reconnaissance

88 Lemon-peel Angelfish

(Des B. Sadgrove. Recess and litho Note Ptg Branch, Reserve Bank of Australia)

1995 (12 Oct). 50th Anniv of End of Second World War. T **87** and similar horiz design. Each black, stone and vermilion. P 14×14½.

407	45c. Type **87**	95	95
	a. Pair. Nos. 407/8	1·90	1·90
408	45c. H.M.S. *Rother* (frigate)	95	95

Nos. 407/8 were printed together, *se-tenant*, in horizontal and vertical pairs throughout the sheet.

(Des Lisa Christensen (85c., 95c., $1.20), Josephine Muré (others). Litho SNP Cambec (75c., $1) or McPherson's Ptg Group, Mulgrave (others))

1995 (12 Oct)–**97**. Marine Life. T **88** and similar horiz designs. Multicoloured. P 14×14½.

412	20c. Pink-tailed Triggerfish (18.4.96)	35	35
413	30c. Japanese Inflator-filefish ("Longnose Filefish") (18.4.96)	50	50
414	45c. Princess Anthias (18.4.96)	65	50
415	75c. Type **88**	1·00	2·00
416	85c. Moon Wrasse (17.7.97)	2·50	2·50
417	90c. Spotted Boxfish (18.4.96)	1·25	1·00
418	95c. Moorish Idol (17.7.97)	2·50	3·00
419	$1 Emperor Angelfish	1·25	2·25
420	$1.20 Glass-eyed Snapper ("Glass Bigeye") (17.7.97)	2·75	3·50
412/20	*Set of 9*	11·50	14·00

Nos. 421/4 are vacant.

89 Rat with Drum

90 Christmas Island White Eye

(Des L. Chiang. Litho SNP Cambec (gold die-stamped Avon Graphics))

1996 (9 Jan). Chinese New Year ("Year of the Rat"). T **89** and similar horiz design. Multicoloured. P 14×14½.

425	45c. Type **89**	1·40	1·75
	a. Pair. Nos. 425/6	2·75	3·50
426	45c. Rat with tambourine	1·40	1·75
MS427	106×70 *mm*. Nos. 425/6	1·25	1·75

Nos. 425/6 were printed together, *se-tenant*, in horizontal and vertical pairs throughout the sheet.

No. **MS**427 also exists overprinted with the logo of the Melbourne Stamp and Coin Fair for sale at this Australian exhibition.

(Des T. Pridham and Susan Horvath. Litho McPherson's Ptg Group, Mulgrave)

1996 (11 July). Christmas Island Land Birds. T **90** and similar vert design. Multicoloured. P 14½×14.

428	45c. Type **90**	75	50
429	85c. Moluccan Hawk Owl	1·75	2·00

91 Three Ships approaching Island

92 Ox facing Right

(Des P. Gifford. Litho McPherson's Ptg Group, Mulgrave)

1996 (12 Sept). Christmas. "I saw Three Ships" (carol). T **91** and similar square designs. Multicoloured. P 14½.

430	40c. Type **91**	90	75

431	45c. Madonna and Child with ships at anchor	90	75
432	80c. Ships leaving	1·75	2·25
430/2	*Set of 3*	3·25	3·25

(Des A. Donato. Litho McPherson's Ptg Group, Mulgrave)

1996 (1 Nov). 300th Anniv of Willem de Vlaming's Discovery of Christmas Island. As No. 1655 of Australia. P 14×14½.

433	45c. multicoloured	1·25	1·75

No. 433 and No. 1655 of Australia were printed together, *se-tenant*, in horizontal pairs throughout the sheet which are listed as No. 1655a of Australia.

(Des L. Chiang. Litho SNP Cambec (gold die-stamped Avon Graphics))

1997 (6 Jan). Chinese New Year ("Year of the Ox"). T **92** and similar horiz design. Multicoloured. P 14×14½.

434	45c. Type **92**	1·25	1·25
	a. Pair. Nos. 434/5	2·50	2·50
435	45c. Ox facing left	1·25	1·25
MS436	106×70 *mm*. Nos. 434/5	3·00	3·75

Nos. 434/5 were printed together, *se-tenant*, in horizontal and vertical pairs throughout the sheet.

93 Father Christmas reading Letter

94 Tiger

(Des A. Hopgood. Litho McPherson's Ptg Group, Mulgrave)

1997 (11 Sept). Christmas. T **93** and similar horiz designs. Multicoloured. P 14×14½.

437	40c. Type **93**	90	70
438	45c. Father Christmas carving wooden boat	90	70
439	80c. Father Christmas in sleigh	1·90	2·50
437/9	*Set of 3*	3·25	3·50

(Des L. Chiang. Litho SNP Cambec)

1998 (5 Jan). Chinese New Year ("Year of the Tiger"). T **94** and similar horiz design. Multicoloured. P 14×14½.

440	45c. Type **94**	2·25	2·25
	a. Pair. Nos. 440/1	4·50	4·50
441	45c. Tiger with head facing left	2·25	2·25
MS442	106×70 *mm*. Nos. 440/1	4·50	4·75

Nos. 440/1 were printed together, *se-tenant*, in horizontal and vertical pairs throughout the sheet.

95 Christmas Island Frigate Bird

96 Orchid Tree

(Des Lisa Christensen. Litho SNP Cambec)

1998 (12 Mar). Marine Life. T **95** and similar horiz designs. Multicoloured. P 14×14½.

443	5c. Type **95**	40	45
	a. Sheetletof 20. Nos. 443/62	9·00	10·00
444	5c. Four Ambon Chromis	40	45
445	5c. Three Ambon Chromis	40	45
446	5c. One Pink Anemonefish	40	45
447	5c. Three Pink Anemonefish	40	45
448	10c. Reef Heron ("Eastern Reef Egret")	40	45
449	10c. Whitelined Cod	40	45
450	10c. Pyramid Butterflyfish	40	45
451	10c. Dusky Parrotfish	40	45
452	10c. Spotted Garden Eel	40	45
453	25c. Sooty Tern	55	60
454	25c. Stripe-tailed Damselfish ("Scissortail Sergeant")	55	60
455	25c. Thicklip Wrasse	55	60
456	25c. Blackaxil Chromis	55	60
457	25c. Orange Anthias	55	60
458	45c. Brown Booby	65	70
459	45c. Green Turtle	65	70
460	45c. Pink Anemonefish	65	70
461	45c. Blue Sea Star	65	70
462	45c. Kunie's Chromodoris	65	70
443/62	*Set of 20*	9·00	10·00

Nos. 443/62 were printed together, *se-tenant*, in sheetlets of 20 with the backgrounds forming a composite design.

(Des Clare Kaegi. Litho McPherson's Ptg Group, Mulgrave)

1998 (3 Sept). Christmas. Flowering Trees. T **96** and similar vert designs. Multicoloured. P 14½×14.

463	40c. Type **96**	60	50
464	80c. Flame Tree	1·40	1·40
465	95c. Sea Hibiscus	1·40	2·00
463/5	*Set of 3*	3·00	3·50

97 Leaping Rabbit

98 Carnival Dragon (Fong Jason) (Community Arts Festival)

(Des L. Chiang. Litho SNP Ausprint)

1999 (14 Jan). Chinese New Year ("Year of the Rabbit"). T **97** and similar horiz design. Multicoloured. P 14×14½.

466	45c. Type **97**	1·50	1·75
	a. Pair. Nos. 466/7	3·00	3·50
467	45c. Rabbit with pestle and mortar	1·50	1·75
MS468	106×70 *mm*. Nos. 466/7	4·00	4·50

Nos. 466/7 were printed together, *se-tenant*, in horizontal and vertical pairs throughout the sheet.

(Des A. Christensen. Litho McPherson's Ptg Group, Mulgrave)

1999 (15 July). Festivals. Children's Paintings. T **98** and similar multicoloured designs. P 14×14½ (45c.) or 14½×14 (others).

469	45c. Type **98**	70	70
	a. Pair. Nos. 469/70	1·40	1·40
470	45c. Red crab holding Easter egg (Community Arts Festival, Siti Zanariah Zainal)	70	70
471	85c. Ghost and child (Tan Diana) (Hungry Ghost Festival) (*vert*)	1·25	1·25
472	$1.20 Walls of Mecca (Anwar Ramlan) (Hari Raya Haji Festival) (*vert*)	1·40	1·60
469/72	*Set of 4*	3·50	3·75

Nos. 469/70 were printed together, *se-tenant*, in horizontal and vertical pairs throughout the sheet.

99 Santa Claus in Hammock

100 Chinese Dragon

(Des N. Buchanan and Jo Mure. Litho McPherson's Ptg Group, Mulgrave)

1999 (9 Sept). Christmas. T **99** and similar horiz designs. Multicoloured. P 14×14½.

473	40c. Type **99**	80	70
474	45c. Santa Claus with Christmas pudding	80	70
475	95c. Santa Claus in sleigh pulled by Abbott's Boobies	1·75	2·00
473/5	*Set of 3*	3·00	3·00

(Des L. Chiang. Litho SNP Ausprint)

2000 (13 Jan). Chinese New Year ("Year of the Dragon"). T **100** and similar horiz design. Multicoloured. P 14×14½.

476	45c. Type **100**	1·50	1·75
	a. Pair. Nos. 476/7	3·00	3·50
477	45c. Chinese dragon facing left	1·50	1·75
MS478	106×70 *mm*. Nos. 476/7	3·75	4·25

Nos. 476/7 were printed together, *se-tenant*, in horizontal and vertical pairs throughout the sheet.

101 Yeow Jian Min

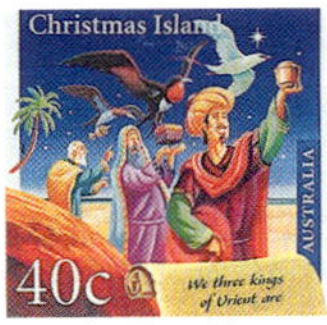

102 The Three Kings

(Des C. McPartlin. Litho SNP Ausprint)

2000 (13 Apr). New Millennium. "Face of Christmas Island". T **101** and similar vert designs. Multicoloured. P 14½×14.

479	45c. Type **101**	1·40	1·40
	a. Horiz strip of 5. Nos. 479/83	6·00	6·00
480	45c. Ida Chin (school girl)	1·40	1·40
481	45c. Ho Tak Wah (elderly man)	1·40	1·40
482	45c. Thomas Faul and James Neill (young boys)	1·40	1·40
483	45c. Siti Sanniah Kawi (mother of three)	1·40	1·40
479/83 *Set of 5*		6·00	6·00

Nos. 479/83 were printed together, *se-tenant*, as horizontal strips of 5 in sheets of 50 (2×25).

(Des B. Wood. Litho SNP Ausprint)

2000 (5 Sept). Christmas. "We Three Kings" (carol). T **102** and similar square designs. Multicoloured. Phosphorised paper. P 14½×14.

484	40c. Type **102**	65	75
	a. Pair. Nos. 484/5	1·25	1·50
485	40c. Birds with Three Gifts	65	75
486	45c. Crabs with Three Gifts	65	75
484/6 *Set of 3*		1·75	2·00

Nos. 484/5 were printed together, *se-tenant*, in horizontal or vertical pairs throughout the sheet.

103 Green Snake

104 *Chaetocalathus semisupinus*

(Des L. Chiang. Litho SNP Ausprint.)

2001 (8 Jan). Chinese New Year ("Year of the Snake"). T **103** and similar horiz design. Multicoloured. P 14×14½.

487	45c. Type **103**	1·75	1·50
488	$1.35 Silver Snake	3·00	3·75
MS489 106×70 *mm.* Nos. 487/8		4·75	5·50

(Des Belinda Marshall and Celia Rosser. Litho SNP Ausprint)

2001 (25 Oct). International Stamps. Fungi. T **104** and similar horiz design. Phosphorised paper. P 14×14½.

490	$1 Type **104**	1·75	1·25
491	$1.50 *Pycnoporus sanguineus*	2·25	2·50

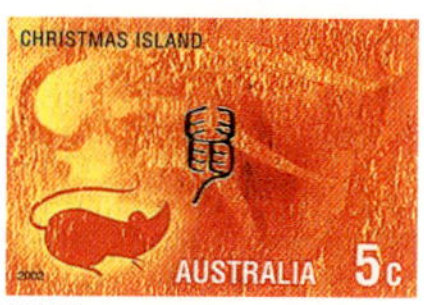

105 Rat

106 Imperial Pigeon

(Des L. Chiang. Litho SNP Ausprint)

2002 (8 Jan). Chinese New Year ("Year of the Horse"). T **105** and similar horiz designs. Multicoloured. P 14×14½.

492	5c. Type **105**	70	80
	a. Sheetlet. Nos. 492/505	9·50	11·00
493	5c. Ox	70	80
494	5c. Tiger	70	80
495	5c. Rabbit	70	80
496	15c. Dragon	70	80
497	15c. Snake	70	80
498	15c. Horse (gold)	70	80
499	15c. Goat	70	80
500	25c. Monkey	70	80
501	25c. Cock	70	80
502	25c. Dog	70	80
503	25c. Pig	70	80
504	45c. Horse (purple)	90	1·00
505	$1.35 Horse (gold)	1·25	1·50
492/505 *Set of 14*		9·50	11·00
MS506 106×70 *mm.* Nos. 504/5		4·00	4·50

Nos. 492/505 were printed together, *se-tenant*, as a sheetlet containing the 5c. to 25c. values as a block of 12 (4×3) and the 45c. plus $1.35 as a separate horizontal pair within margins similar to No. **MS**506. Nos. 504/5 were also printed in sheets of 50.

(Des Stacey Zass. Litho McPhersons)

2002 (1 May). Endangered Species. Christmas Island Birds. T **106** and similar vert designs. Multicoloured. P 14½×14.

507	45c. Type **106**	1·50	1·50
	a. Pair. Nos. 507/8	3·00	3·00
508	45c. Christmas Island Hawk Owl	1·50	1·50
509	$1 Goshawk	2·00	2·00
510	$1.50 Thrush	2·50	2·50
507/10 *Set of 4*		6·75	6·75

Nos. 507/8 were printed together *se-tenant*, as vertical and horizontal pairs, throughout the sheets of 50.

107 Yellow Goat

108 Santa riding on Whale Shark

(Des L. Chiang. Litho SNP Sprint)

2003 (7 Jan). Chinese New Year ("Year of the Goat"). T **107** and similar horiz design plus designs as Nos. 492/503 with backgrounds in magenta and some values changed. Multicoloured. P 14×14½.

511	10c. Type **107**	70	80
	a. Sheetlet. Nos. 511/24	9·75	11·00
512	10c. Ox	70	80
513	10c. Tiger	70	80
514	10c. Rabbit	70	80
515	15c. Dragon	70	80
516	15c. Snake	70	80
517	15c. Horse	70	80
518	15c. Goat (animal in gold)	70	80
519	25c. Monkey	70	80
520	25c. Cock	70	80
521	25c. Dog	70	80
522	25c. Pig	70	80
523	50c. Type **107**	70	80
524	$1.50 Blue goat	1·75	2·00
511/24 *Set of 14*		9·75	11·00
MS525 105×70 *mm.* Nos. 523/4		4·25	4·50

Nos. 511/24 were printed together, *se-tenant*, as a sheetlet containing the 10c. to 25c. values as a block of 12 (4×3) and the 50c. plus $1.50 as a separate horizontal pair within margins similar to No. **MS**525. Nos. 523/4 were also printed in separate sheets of 50.

Nos. 492/503 have vermilion backgrounds.

(Des B. Wood. Litho SNP Sprint)

2003 (31 Oct). Christmas. T **108** and similar square design. Multicoloured. P 14½×14.

526	45c. Type **108**	1·40	1·40
527	50c. Santa sitting on green turtle and distributing gifts	1·40	1·40

109 Yellow Monkey

110 Meyer's Butterflyfish

(Des L. Chiang. Litho SNP Sprint)

2004 (6 Jan). Chinese New Year ("Year of the Monkey"). T **109** and similar horiz design plus designs as Nos. 492/503 in turquoise and blue with some values changed. Multicoloured. P 14×14½.

528	10c. Rat	70	70
	a. Sheetlet. Nos. 528/41	9·50	10·00
529	10c. Ox	70	70
530	10c. Tiger	70	70
531	10c. Rabbit	70	70
532	15c. Dragon	70	70
533	15c. Snake	70	70
534	15c. Horse	70	70
535	15c. Goat	70	70
536	25c. Monkey (animal in gold)	70	70
537	25c. Cock	70	70
538	25c. Dog	70	70
539	25c. Pig	70	70
540	50c. Type **109**	70	75
541	$1.45 Orange-brown monkey	1·60	1·90
528/41 *Set of 14*		9·50	10·00
MS542 105×70 *mm.* Nos. 540/1		5·50	6·00

Nos. 528/41 were printed together, *se-tenant*, as a sheetlet containing Nos. 528/39 as a block of 12 (4×3) and Nos. 540/1 as a separate horizontal pair within margins similar to No. **MS**542. Nos. 540/1 were also printed in separate sheets of 50.

No. **MS**542 was also issued overprinted "HONG KONG Stamp Expo 2004" sold only at this exhibition and by mail order from the Australian Philatelic Bureau.

(Des J. Muré. Litho SNP Sprint)

2004 (13 July). Christmas Island Underwater. T **110** and similar vert designs. Multicoloured. P 15×14.

543	10c. Type **110**	50	60
	a. Sheetlet of 20. Nos. 543/62	10·00	12·00
544	10c. Whale Shark	50	60
545	10c. Saddle Butterflyfish	50	60
546	10c. Racoon Butterflyfish	50	60
547	10c. Green Turtles	50	60
548	25c. Clown Triggerfish	55	65
549	25c. Pair of Emperor Angelfish	55	65
550	25c. False Moorish Idols	55	65
551	25c. Emperor Angelfish (juvenile)	55	65
552	25c. Pyramid Butterflyfish	55	65
553	25c. Bennett's Butterflyfish	55	65
554	25c. Parrotfish with blue and yellow stripes	55	65
555	25c. Dotty Triggerfish	55	65
556	25c. Divers observing fish	55	65
557	25c. Pair of Butterflyfish	55	65
558	50c. Coral Cod and Powder-blue Surgeonfish	75	85
559	50c. Emperor Angelfish (adult)	75	85
560	50c. Harlequin Filefish	75	85
561	50c. Pink Anemonefish	75	85
562	50c. Nudibranch	75	85
543/62 *Set of* 20		10·00	12·00

Nos. 543/62 were printed together, *se-tenant*, in sheetlets of 20, with the background forming a composite design showing a coral reef and schools of fish.

111 Rooster

(**112**)

(Des L. Chiang. Litho SNP Sprint)

2005 (4 Jan). Chinese New Year ("Year of the Rooster"). T **111** and similar horiz design plus designs as Nos. 492/503 with backgrounds in carmine-vermilion and yellow with some values changed. Multicoloured. P 15×14.

563	10c. Rat	70	80
	a. Sheetlet of 14. Nos. 563/76	10·00	11·50
564	10c. Ox	70	80
565	10c. Tiger	70	80
566	10c. Rabbit	70	80
567	15c. Dragon	70	80
568	15c. Snake	70	80
569	15c. Horse	70	80
570	15c. Goat	70	80
571	25c. Monkey	70	80
572	25c. Cock (animal in red foil)	70	80
573	25c. Dog	70	80
574	25c. Pig	70	80
575	50c. Type **111**	1·00	1·10
576	$1.45 Rooster (with right foot raised under body)	1·75	2·00
563/76 *Set of* 14		10·00	11·50
MS577 105×70 *mm*. Nos. 575/6		4·75	5·50

Nos. 563/74 were printed together, *se-tenant*, as a sheetlet containing Nos. 563/74 as a block of 12 (4×3) and Nos. 575/6 as a separate horizontal pair within margins similar to No. **MS**577.

Nos. 575/6 were also printed in separate sheets of 50.

2005 (19 Aug). Taipei 2005 International Stamp Exhibition. No. **MS**577 optd with T **112** in gold on sheet margin at top left.

MS578 105×70 *mm*. Nos. 575/6		3·50	4·00

113 Santa and Decorated Palm Tree

114 Purple Dog

(Des Tracie Grimwood. Litho SEP Sprint)

2005 (1 Nov). Christmas. T **113** and similar square design. Multicoloured. Phosphorised paper. P 14½×14.

579	45c. Type **113**	1·25	1·00
580	90c. Santa in sleigh drawn by crabs	2·25	2·50

Nos. 579/80 were also issued in Australia premium booklets, No. SP80, sold at $9.95.

(Des L. Chiang. Litho SEP Sprint)

2006 (5 Jan). Chinese New Year ("Year of the Dog"). T **114** and similar horiz designs. Multicoloured. Phosphorised paper. P 14×15.

581	10c. Rat	90	90
	a. Sheetlet. Nos. 581/94	12·50	12·50
582	10c. Ox	90	90
583	10c. Tiger	90	90
584	10c. Rabbit	90	90
585	15c. Dragon	90	90
586	15c. Snake	90	90
587	15c. Horse	90	90
588	15c. Goat	90	90
589	25c. Monkey	90	90
590	25c. Cock	90	90
591	25c. Dog (animal in copper foil)	90	90
592	25c. Pig	90	90
593	50c. Type **114**	1·10	1·10
594	$1.45 Leaping dog (in copper foil)	2·00	2·00
581/94 *Set of* 14		12·50	12·50
MS595 106×70 *mm*. Nos. 593/4		5·50	6·00

Nos. 581/92 were printed together, *se-tenant*, in a sheetlet containing Nos. 581/92 as a block of 12 (4×3) and Nos. 593/4 as a separate horizontal pair within margins similar to No. **MS**595.

Nos. 593/4 were also printed in separate sheets of 50 (2 panes of 25).

115 Mosque

116 Orange Pig running

(Des N. Buchanan. Litho SEP Sprint)

2006 (13 June). Heritage Buildings. T **115** and similar vert designs. Multicoloured. Phosphorised paper. P 14½×14.

596	50c. Type **115**	1·40	1·00
597	$1 Tai Pak Kong Temple	2·25	2·75
	a. Horiz pair. Nos. 597/8	4·50	5·50
598	$1 Soon Tian Temple	2·25	2·75
599	$1.45 Tai Jin House	3·00	3·50
596/9 *Set of* 4		8·00	9·00

Nos. 597/8 were printed together, *se-tenant*, in horizontal pairs in sheets of 50.

(Des Luis Chiang. Litho SEP Sprint)

2007 (9 Jan). Chinese New Year ("Year of the Pig"). T **116** and similar horiz designs plus designs as Nos. 492/503 with composite backgrounds showing pigs. Multicoloured.

(a) PVA gum. P 14×14½

600	10c. Rat	85	85
	a. Sheetlet of 14. Nos. 600/13	12·00	12·00
601	10c. Ox	85	85
602	10c. Tiger	85	85
603	10c. Rabbit	85	85
604	15c. Dragon	85	85
605	15c. Snake	85	85
606	15c. Horse	85	85
607	15c. Goat	85	85
608	25c. Monkey	85	85
609	25c. Cock	85	85
610	25c. Dog	85	85
611	25c. Pig (animal in gold foil)	85	85
612	50c. Type **116**	1·25	1·25
613	$1.45 Yellow pig standing	2·00	2·00
600/13 *Set of* 14		12·00	12·00
MS614 106×70 *mm*. Nos. 612/13		6·50	6·50

(b) Circular sheet 170×170 mm containing designs as Nos. 426, 434, 440, 466, 476, 487, 504, 523, 540, 575, 593 and 612 but smaller, 33×23 mm, with some values changed. Self-adhesive. Partial phosphor frames (50c.) or phosphor frame ($1). P 12½×13 (50c.) or 10½ ($1) (circular 37 mm diameter)

MS615 50c.×12 Rat with tambourine; As Type **92**; As Type **94**; As Type **97**; As Type **100**; As Type **103**; Horse (purple); As Type **107**; As Type **109**; As Type **111**; As Type **114**; As Type **116**; $1 Frieze of zodiac animals		11·00	13·00

Nos. 600/11 were printed together, *se-tenant*, in a sheetlet containing Nos. 600/11 as a block of 12 (4×3) and Nos. 612/13 as a separate horizontal pair within margins similar to No. **MS**614.

Nos. 612/13 were also printed in separate sheets of 50. No. **MS**615 commemorates the end of the 12-year cycle of Chinese New Year stamps.

The 50c. designs within No. **MS**615 were also issued in premium stamp booklets, No. SP1, sold at $12.95.

117 Santa arriving by Speedboat

118 Rat

(Des Lloyd Foye and Sally Piskuric. Litho SEP Sprint)

2007 (1 Nov). Christmas. T **117** and similar horiz designs. Multicoloured. Phosphorised paper. P 14×14½.

	(i) Domestic Mail		
616	45c. Type **117**	1·00	1·00
617	50c. Santa unloading net full of presents	1·10	1·10
	(ii) International Post		
618	$1.10 Santa on beach distributing presents	2·50	2·75
616/618	*Set of 3*	4·25	4·25

(Des Dani Poon. Litho SEP Sprint, Australia)

2008 (8 Jan). Chinese New Year ('Year of the Rat'). T **118** and similar vert designs. Multicoloured. Phosphorised paper. P 14½×14.

619	10c. Rat (11.01pm–1.00am) (animal in gold foil)	80	90
	a. Sheetlet of 14. Nos. 619/31 and 632	11·00	12·50
620	10c. Ox (1.01am–3.00am)	80	90
621	10c. Dragon (7.01am–9.00am)	80	90
622	10c. Snake (9.01am–11.00am)	80	90
623	15c. Tiger (3.01am–5.00am)	80	90
624	15c. Rabbit (5.01am–7.00am)	80	90
625	15c. Horse (11.01am–1.00pm)	80	90
626	15c. Pig (9.01pm–11.00pm)	80	90
627	25c. Goat (1.01pm–3.00pm)	80	90
628	25c. Monkey (3.01pm–5.00pm)	80	90
629	25c. Cock (5.01pm–7.00pm)	80	90
630	25c. Dog (7.01pm–9.00pm)	80	90
631	50c. Type **118**	1·00	1·10
	a. Perf 14	1·25	1·25
632	$1.45 Calligraphy (in gold foil)	1·90	1·90
619/32	*Set of 14*	11·00	12·50
MS633	136×70 *mm.* Nos. 631 and 632	6·50	7·00

Nos. 619/30 were printed together, *se-tenant*, in a sheetlet containing Nos. 619/30 as a block of 12 (6×2) and Nos. 631 and 632 as a separate horizontal pair within margins similar to **MS**633. Nos. 619/30 show the zodiac's ruling hours.

No. 631a was only printed in separate sheets of 50. No. 632 was also printed in separate sheets of 50.

119 *Gecarcoidea natalis* (red crab)

120 Christmas Tree with Red Crabs and Seashells

(Des Brian Sadgrove. Litho Energi Print)

2008 (18 June). 50th Anniv of Christmas Island as an Australian Territory. T **119** and similar square designs. Multicoloured. P 14½.

634	50c. Type **119**	1·25	1·40
	a. Horiz strip of 3. Nos. 634/6	3·25	3·75
635	50c. *Papasula abbotti* (Abbott's Booby)	1·25	1·40
636	50c. *Asplenium listeri* (Christmas Island Spleenwort)	1·25	1·40
637	$1.45 Seal of Union of Christmas Island Workers	2·75	3·25
638	$2.45 Christmas Island flag	4·75	5·00
634/8	*Set of 5*	10·00	11·00

Nos. 634/6 were printed together, *se-tenant*, as horizontal strips of three in sheets of 50.

2008 (8 Aug). Olympex the Olympic Expo, Beijing. Sheet 130×90 mm containing designs as Nos. 631/2. Multicoloured. Litho. P 14½×14.

MS639	50c. Type **118**; $1.45 Calligraphy (in gold foil).	3·25	3·75

(Des Rob Kiely and John White. Litho McKellar Renown)

2008 (31 Oct). Christmas. T **120** and similar vert designs. Multicoloured. P 14½×14.

	(a) PVA gum		
	(i) Domestic Mail		
640	50c. Type **120**	1·00	1·00
	(ii) International Post		
641	$1.20 Robber crab stealing Christmas presents	2·50	2·50
	(b) Self-adhesive. Phosphor over upper left parts of design. P 11½×11 (interrupted)		
	(i) Domestic Mail		
642	50c. As Type **120**	1·10	1·25
	a. Booklet pane. No. 642×10	10·00	
	(ii) International Post		
643	$1.20 As No. 641	2·50	2·75
	a. Pane. No. 643×5	11·00	

No. 642 was issued in panes of ten sold for $5, and also in $5 booklets with five "Card Only" stickers, No. SB2.

No. 643 was only issued in panes of ten sold for $6.

The two vertical edges of Nos. 642/3 each have two sets of five teeth separated by a straight line.

121 Ox

(Des Dani Poon. Litho Energi Print)

2009 (8 Jan). Chinese New Year ("Year of the Ox"). T **121** and similar vert designs. Multicoloured. P 14½×14.

644	10c. Rat	75	80
	a. Sheetlet of 14. Nos. 644/57	11·00	10·00
645	10c. Ox (animal in foil)	75	80
646	10c. Dragon	75	80
647	10c. Snake	75	80
648	20c. Tiger	75	80
649	20c. Rabbit	75	80
650	20c. Horse	75	80
651	20c. Pig	75	80
652	25c. Goat	75	80
653	25c. Monkey	75	80
654	25c. Cock	75	80
655	25c. Dog	75	80
656	55c. Ox	1·00	1·10
657	$1.65 Calligraphic symbol for ox	2·25	2·50
644/57	*Set of 14*	11·00	12·00
MS658	135×70 *mm.* Nos. 656/7	6·00	6·50

Nos. 644/57 were printed together, *se-tenant*, as a sheetlet containing Nos. 644/55 as a block of 12 (6×2) and Nos. 656/7 as a separate horizontal pair within margins similar to No. **MS**658.

Nos. 656/7 were also printed in separate sheets of 50.

A souvenir stamp sheet issued on 14 May 2009 for the 23rd Asian International Stamp Exhibition contained stamps as Nos. 644/55 with *se-tenant* "HONG KONG 2009" labels. This sheet contained stamps with a face value of $2.20 but was sold at $9.95.

(Des Rob Kiely. Litho Energi Print)

2009 (2 Nov). International Post. Christmas. Vert design as T **120**. Multicoloured. P 14½×14.

	(a) Ordinary gum		
659	$1.25 Christmas Island Frigate Bird with presents	2·50	2·25
	(b) Self-adhesive. Die-cut perf 11½		
660	$1.25 As No. 659	2·25	2·50
	a. Pane. No. 660×5	10·00	

122 Tiger

(Des Dani Poon. Litho McKellar)

2010 (12 Jan). Chinese New Year. Year of the Tiger. T **122** and similar vert designs. Multicoloured. P 14½×14.

661	10c. Rat (+dragon "Best-arranged union")	80	80
	a. Sheetlet of 14. Nos. 661/74	12·50	12·50
662	10c. Ox (+rooster "Stable relationship")	80	80
663	10c. Dragon (+rat "Highly compatible")	80	80
664	10c. Snake (+rooster "Love connection")	80	80
665	20c. Tiger (gold foil surround) (+dog "Harmonic match")	80	80
666	20c. Rabbit (+ram "Fruitful union")	80	80
667	20c. Horse (+dog "Mutual love")	80	80
668	20c. Pig (+ram "Happiest couple")	80	80
669	25c. Ram (+pig "Best combination")	80	80
670	25c. Monkey (+rat "Long-lasting relationship")	80	80
671	25c. Rooster (+ox "Prosperous union")	80	80
672	25c. Dog (+tiger "Favourable relationship")	80	80
673	55c. Tiger (animal in gold foil)	1·25	1·25
674	$1.65 Calligraphic symbol for tiger (in gold foil)	3·25	3·25
661/74 *Set of 14*		12·50	12·50
MS675 136×70 *mm*. Nos. 673/4		6·00	6·50

Nos. 661/74 were printed together, *se-tenant*, as a sheetlet containing Nos. 661/72 as a block of 12 (6×2) and Nos. 673/4 as a separate horizontal pair within margins similar to **MS**675.

Nos. 673/4 were also printed in separate sheets of 50.

Nos. 661/74 were also issued in premium booklets, No. SP3, sold for $12.95.

123 Male Frigatebird

124 White-tailed Tropic Bird carrying Christmas Gift

(Des Ego Guiotto and Simone Sakinofsky. Litho McKellar Renown)

2010 (17 Aug). Endangered Species. Christmas Island Frigate Bird (*Fregata andrewsii*). T **123** and similar square designs. Multicoloured. P 14.

676	60c. Type **123**	2·50	2·50
	a. Horiz pair. Nos. 676/7	5·00	5·00
677	60c. Pair and fledgling	2·50	2·50
678	$1.80 Large fledgling and adult perched on branch	5·50	5·50
	a. Horiz pair. Nos. 678/9	11·00	11·00
679	$1.80 Adult male in flight	5·50	5·50
676/9 *Set of 4*		14·50	14·50
MS680 150×85 *mm*. Nos. 676/9		14·50	14·50

Nos. 676/7 and 678/9 were each printed together, *se-tenant*, as horizontal pairs in sheets of 50 (2 panes of 25), each sheet providing ten strips of four and ten single stamps (Type **123** or No. 678).

(Des Rob Kiely. Litho McKellar Renown)

2010 (1 Nov). Christmas. T **124** and similar vert design. Multicoloured.

(a) Ordinary gum. P 14½×14

(i) Domestic mail

681	60c. Type **124**	1·75	1·50

(ii) International Post

682	$1.30 Gift bound with vine *Hoya aldrichii* and Ridley's Orchid (*Brachypeza archytas*)	3·50	3·75

(b) Self-adhesive. Phosphor over parts of design (60c.) or partial irregular phosphor frame (at right and foot) ($1.30). Die-cut perf 11½×11 (interrupted)

(i) Domestic mail

683	60c. As Type **124**	1·25	1·40
	a. Booklet pane. No. 683×10	10·00	

(ii) International Post

684	$1.30 As No. 682	3·50	4·00
	a. Pane. No. 684×5	14·00	

No. 683 was issued in $6 booklets, No. SB3.

No. 684 was issued in $6.50 panes of five stamps.

The two horizontal edges of Nos. 683/4 each have two sets of five teeth separated by a straight line.

125 Rabbit

126 Red Crab (*Gecarcoidea natalis*)

(Des Dani Poon. Litho McKellar Renown)

2011 (11 Jan). Chinese New Year. Year of the Rabbit. T **125** and similar vert designs. Multicoloured. P 14½×14.

685	15c. Rat–Sagittarius	80	80
	a. Sheetlet of 14. Nos. 685/98	12·00	12·00
686	15c. Ox–Capricorn	80	80
687	15c. Dragon–Aries	80	80
688	15c. Snake–Taurus	80	80
689	20c. Tiger–Aquarius	80	80
690	20c. Rabbit–Pisces (in silver foil disc)	80	80
691	20c. Horse–Gemini	80	80
692	20c. Pig–Scorpio	80	80
693	25c. Goat–Cancer	80	80
694	25c. Monkey–Leo	80	80
695	25c. Rooster–Virgo	80	80
696	25c. Dog–Libra	80	80
697	60c. Type **125**	1·00	1·00
698	$1.80 Calligraphic symbol for rabbit	2·50	2·50
685/98 *Set of 14*		12·00	12·00
MS699 136×70 *mm*. Nos. 697/8		5·50	6·00

Nos. 685/98 were printed together, *se-tenant*, as a sheetlet containing Nos. 685/96 as a block of 12 (6×2) and Nos. 697/8 as a separate horizontal pair within margins similar to **MS**699.

Nos. 697/8 were also printed in separate sheets of 50 (2 panes of 25).

Nos. 685/98 were also issued in premium booklets, No. SP4, sold for $14.95.

(Des Jo Muré. Litho McKellar Renown)

2011 (7 June). Christmas Island Crabs. T **126** and similar vert designs. Multicoloured. P 14½×14.

700	60c. Type **126**	2·00	2·00
	a. Horiz pair. Nos. 700/1	4·00	4·00
701	60c. Robber crab (*Birgus latro*)	2·00	2·00
702	$1.20 Jackson's crab (*Karstarma jacksoni*)	3·75	3·75
	a. Horiz pair. Nos. 702/3	7·50	7·50
703	$1.20 Blue crab (*Discoplax hirtipes*)	3·75	3·75
700/703 *Set of 4*		10·50	10·50

Nos. 700/1 and 702/3 were each printed together, *se-tenant*, as horizontal pairs in sheets of 50 (2 panes of 25), giving twenty horizontal pairs and ten single stamps (Type **126** or No. 702) in each sheet.

127 (*Actual size* 135×71 *mm*)

(Des Kevin Stead. Litho McKellar Renown)

2011 (30 Aug). 50th Anniv of Worldwide Fund for Nature (formerly World Wildlife Fund). Sheet 135×72 mm as **MS**3640 of Australia. Multicoloured. P 14×14½.

MS704 **127** 60c.×4 Christmas Island Shrew (*Crocidura trichura*) (Christmas Island); Type **861** of Australia; Southern Elephant eal (*Mirounga leonina*) (Australian Antarctic Territory); Dugong (*Dugong dugon*) (Cocos (Keeling) Islands)		8·50	8·50

No. **MS**704 differs from **MS**3640 of Australia in the sheet margins and in the order of the stamps within the miniature sheet (top left stamp Christams Island; top right. Australian; bottom left, Australia Antarctic Territory; bottom right Cocos (Keeling) Islands.

128 Father Christmas pulling Cracker with Red Crab

(Des Andrew Hopgood and Jennifer Scalzo. Litho RA Printing)

2011 (31 Oct). Christmas. T **128** and similar horiz design. Multicoloured.

(a) Ordinary gum. P 14×14½

(i) Domestic mail

705	55c. Type **128**	1·50	1·00

(ii) International Post

706	$1.50 Father Christmas coming ashore	3·50	4·00

(b) Self-adhesive. Phosphor over parts of design. Die-cut perf 11×11½ (interrupted on vert sides)

707	55c. As Type **128**	1·50	1·50
	a. Booklet pane. No. 707×10	12·00	
708	$1.50 As No. 706	3·50	4·25
	a. Booklet. No. 708×5	14·00	

No. 707 was issued in $5.50 booklets, No. SB4.

No. 708 was issued in $7.50 panes of five stamps.

129 Dragon (animal outlined in gold foil)

2012 (10 Jan). Chinese New Year. Year of the Dragon. T **129** and similar vert designs. Multicoloured. P 14½×14.

709	15c. Rat (1st)	80	80
	a. Sheetlet. Nos. 709/22	12·00	12·00
710	15c. Ox (2nd)	80	80
711	15c. 'Dragon' in gold disc and gold flames (5th)	80	80
712	15c. Snake (6th)	80	80
713	20c. Tiger (3rd)	80	80
714	20c. Rabbit (4th)	80	80
715	20c. Horse (7th)	80	80
716	20c. Pig (12th)	80	80
717	25c. Goat (8th)	80	80
718	25c. Monkey (9th)	80	80
719	25c. Rooster (10th)	80	80
720	25c. Dog (11th)	80	80
721	60c. Type **129**	1·25	1·25
722	$1.80 Chinese symbol for dragon (in gold foil)	2·50	2·50
709/22 *Set of* 14		12·00	12·00
MS723 136×70 *mm*. Nos. 721/2		6·00	6·50

Nos. 709/22 were printed together, *se-tenant*, as a sheetlet containing Nos. 709/20 as a block of of 12 (6×2) and Nos. 621/2 as a separate horizontal pair within margins similar to **MS**723.

Nos. 721/2 were also printed in separate sheets of 50.

Nos. 709/22 were also issued in premium booklets, No. SP5, sold for $12.95.

130 *Tectaria devexa* var minor

(Des Jenny Phillips (illustration) and John White (typography). Litho RA Printing)

2012 (1 May). Christmas Island Ferns. T **130** and similar horiz designs. Multicoloured. P 14×14½.

724	60c. Type **130**	2·00	2·00
	a. Horiz pair. Nos. 724/5	4·00	4·00
725	60c. *Asplenium listeri* (Christmas Island Spleenwort)	2·00	2·00
726	$1.20 *Bolbitis heteroclita*	3·25	3·50
	a. Horiz pair. Nos. 726/7	6·50	7·00
727	$1.20 *Pteris tripartita* (Giant Brake Fern)	3·25	3·50
724/7 *Set of* 4		9·50	10·00

Nos. 724/5 and 726/7 were each printed together, *se-tenant*, as horizontal pairs in sheets of 50 (2 panes of 25), giving 20 horizontal pairs and ten single stamps (Type **130** or No. 726).

131 Santa Sand Sculpture

(Des Andrew Hopgood (illustration) and John White (typography). Litho RA Print)

2012 (1 Nov). Christmas. T **131** and similar vert design. Multicoloured.

(a) Ordinary gum

(i) Domestic mail. P 14½×14

728	55c. Type **131**	1·50	1·00

(ii) International Post. P 14½×14

729	$1.60 Santa decorating sand sculpture Christmas tree	3·50	4·00
MS730 135×80 *mm*. Nos. 728/9		5·00	5·50

(b) Self-adhesive

731	$1.60 As No. 729	3·50	4·00

No. 731 was issued in $8 panes of five stamps.

(Litho)

2012 (2 Nov). Beijing Stamp and Coin Expo 2012. No. **MS**723 additionally inscr with emblem and BEIJING INTERNATIONAL STAMP AND COIN EXPO. 2012 2 - 4 NOVEMBER 2012 in gold. Multicoloured. P 14½×14.

MS732 Nos. 721/2	4·75	5·50

132 Snake and Calligraphic Symbol (outlined in dark blue foil)

(Des Dani Poon. Litho McKellar Renown)

2013 (8 Jan). Chinese New Year. Year of the Snake. T **132** and similar vert designs. Multicoloured. P 14½×14.

733	15c. Rat (apple)	80	80
	a. Sheetlet of 14. Nos. 733/46	12·00	12·00
734	15c. Ox (cherry)	80	80
735	15c. Dragon (tomato)	80	80
736	15c. Snake (animal in dark blue foil) (egg)	80	80
737	20c. Tiger (fish)	80	80
738	20c. Rabbit (orange)	80	80
739	20c. Horse (banana)	80	80
740	20c. Pig (spinach)	80	80
741	25c. Ram (onion)	80	80
742	25c. Monkey (grapes)	80	80
743	25c. Cock (pumpkin)	80	80
744	25c. Dog (milk)	80	80
745	60c. Type **132**	1·25	1·25
746	$1.80 Calligraphic symbol for snake (in dark blue foil)	2·50	2·50
733/46 *Set of* 14		12·00	12·00
MS747 136×70 *mm*. Nos. 745/6		6·00	6·50

Nos. 733/46 were printed together, *se-tenant*, as a sheetlet containing Nos. 733/44 as a block of 12 (6×2) and Nos. 745/6 as a separate horizontal pair within margins similar to **MS**747. Nos. 745/6 were also printed in separate sheets of 50.

Nos. 733/46 were also issued in premium booklets, No. SP6, sold for $12.95.

133 Cocos Angelfish (*Centropyge joculator*)

(Des Ego Guiotto. Litho EGO)

2013 (21 May). Fish of Christmas Island. T **133** and similar horiz designs. Multicoloured. P 14×14½.

748	60c. Type **133**	1·75	1·75
	a. Horiz pair. Nos. 748/9	3·50	3·50
749	60c. Ladder Wrasse (*Thalassoma trilobatum*)	1·75	1·75
750	$1.20 Redtooth Triggerfish (*Odonus niger*)	2·75	2·75
751	$1.80 Red-striped Pigfish (*Bodianus opercularis*)	3·50	3·50
748/51 *Set of 4*		8·75	8·75

Nos. 748/9 were printed together, *se-tenant*, as horizontal pairs in sheets of 50 (2 panes 5×5), each sheet providing 20 horizontal pairs and ten single stamps (Type **133**).

134 *Colubrina pedunculata*

(Des Dierdre Bean (illustration) and Simone Sakhinofsky (typography). Litho McKellar Renown)

2013 (18 June). Flowering Shrubs. T **134** and similar vert designs. Multicoloured.

(a) Ordinary gum. P 14½×14

752	60c. Type **134**	1·75	1·75
	a. Horiz pair. Nos. 752/3	3·50	3·50
753	60c. *Abutilon listeri*	1·75	1·75
754	$1.20 *Urena lobata* var. *sinuata*	3·00	3·25
	a. Horiz pair. Nos. 754/5	6·00	6·50
755	$1.20 *Indigofera hirsuta*	3·00	3·25
752/22 *Set of 4*		8·50	9·00

(b) Self-adhesive. Phosphor frame (broken at left) (756) or irregular partial phosphor frame (broken at top) (757). Die-cut perf 11½×11 (interrupted on horiz sides)

756	60c. As Type **134**	1·75	2·00
	a. Booklet pane. Nos. 756/7, each ×5	14·00	
757	60c. As No. 753	1·75	2·00

Nos. 752/3 and 754/5 were each printed together, *se-tenant*, as horizontal pairs in sheets of 50 (2 panes 5×5), each sheet providing 20 horizontal pairs and ten single stamps (Type **134** or No. 754).

Nos. 756/7 were issued in $6 booklets, No. SB5.

2013 (26 Sept). China International Collection Expo 2013, Beijing. No. **MS**747 optd with exhibition emblem and "CHINA INTERNATIONAL COLLECTION EXPO" in gold on the upper sheet margin. P 14½×14.

MS758 136×70 *mm*. Nos. 745/6		4·75	5·50

135 Santa riding on Frigatebird

(Des Andrew Hopgood. Litho RA Print)

2013 (1 Nov). Christmas. T **135** and similar horiz design. Multicoloured. P 14×14½.

(i) Domestic mail

759	55c. Type **135**	1·50	1·00

(ii) International Post

760	$1.85 Frigatebird and Red Crab in hot-air balloon with load of presents **MS**761 135×80 *mm*. Nos. 759/60	4·75	5·00

(b) Self-adhesive

762	$1.80 As No. 760	3·75	4·25
763	$1.80 As No. 762 but green foil on "Merry" and red foil on "Christmas Island" and on balloon stripes	3·75	4·25

No. 762 was issued in $9 panes of five stamps.

No. 763 was issued in $18 sheetlets of ten.

136 Horse

(Des Dani Poon. Litho McKellar)

2014 (7 Jan). Chinese New Year. Year of the Horse. T **136** and similar vert designs. Multicoloured. P 14½×14.

764	15c. Rat (Water)	75	75
	a. Sheetlet of 12. Nos. 764/75	12·00	12·00
765	15c. Ox (Earth)	75	75
766	15c. Dragon (Earth)	75	75
767	15c. Snake (Fire)	75	75
768	20c. Tiger (Wood)	75	75
769	20c. Rabbit (Wood)	75	75
770	20c. Horse (Fire)	75	75
771	20c. Pig (Water)	75	75
772	25c. Goat (Earth)	75	75
773	25c. Monkey (Metal)	75	75
774	25c. Rooster (Metal)	75	75
775	25c. Dog (Earth)	75	75
776	60c. Horse (outlined in gold foil)	1·50	1·50
777	$1.80 Calligraphic symbol for horse (in gold foil)	3·00	3·00
764/77 *Set of 14*		12·00	12·00
MS778 136×70 *mm*. Nos. 746/77		5·50	6·00

Nos. 764/77 were printed together, *se-tenant*, as a sheetlet containing Nos. 764/75 as a block of 12 (6×2) and Nos. 776/7 as a separate horizontal pair within margins similar to **MS**778. Nos. 776/7 were also printed in separate sheets of 50.

Nos. 764/77 were also issued in premium booklets, No. SP7, sold for $12.95.

137 Forest

(Des Sharon Rodziewicz. Litho RA Print)

2014 (17 June). Christmas Island National Park. T **137** and similar horiz designs. Multicoloured. P 14×14½.

779	70c. Type **137**	2·00	2·00
	a. Horiz pair. Nos. 779/80	4·00	4·00
780	70c. Beach	2·00	2·00
781	$1.40 Sea cliffs	3·25	3·25
782	$2.10 Wetlands	3·75	3·75
779/82 *Set of 4*		10·00	10·00

Nos. 779/80 were printed together, *se-tenant*, as horizontal pairs in sheets of 50 (2 panes 5×5), each sheet giving 20 horizontal pairs and ten single stamps (No. 779).

138 Red Crab

(Des Sonia Young. Litho RA Print)

2014 (12 Aug). Red Crab (*Gecarcoidea natalis*) Migration. T **138** and similar horiz design. Multicoloured. P 14×14½.

783	70c. Type **138**	1·60	1·60
784	$2.10 Migrating Red Crabs on road	4·75	4·75

139 Santa holding Crab

(Des Gavin Ryan. Litho RA Print)

2014 (31 Oct). Christmas. T **139** and similar vert designs. Multicoloured.

(a) Ordinary gum.

(i) Domestic Mail. P 14½×14.

785	65c. Type **139**	1·40	1·40

(ii) International Post. P 14½×14.

786	$1.80 Crab with Santa hat carrying bauble in claws	4·25	4·25
MS787	135×80 *mm.* Nos. 785/6	6·75	6·75

(b) Self-adhesive.

(i) Domestic Mail. Phosphor over parts of design. Die-cut perf 11½×11

788	65c. As Type **139**	1·40	1·40

(ii) International Post. Phosphor over parts of design. Die-cut perf 11½×11

789	$1.80 As No. 786	4·25	4·25
	a. Pane. No. 789×5	19·00	

No. 788 was issued in $6.50 sheetlets of ten stamps with ten 'Card Only' labels.

No. 789 was issued in $9 panes of five stamps.

140 Goat (outlined in turquoise-blue foil)

(Des Dani Poon. Litho McKellar Renown)

2015 (8 Jan). Chinese New Year. Year of the Goat. T **140** and similar vert designs. Multicoloured. P 14½×14.

790	15c. Rat (Garnet)	35	35
	a. Sheetlet of 14. Nos. 790/803	12·50	12·50
791	15c. Ox (Aquamarine)	35	35
792	15c. Dragon (Amethyst)	35	35
793	15c. Snake (Opal)	35	35
794	25c. Goat (Emerald)	60	60
795	25c. Monkey (Peridot)	60	60
796	25c. Rooster (Citrine)	60	60
797	25c. Dog (Diamond)	60	60
798	30c. Tiger (Sapphire)	70	70
799	30c. Rabbit (Pearl)	70	70
800	30c. Horse (Topaz)	70	70
801	30c. Pig (Ruby)	70	70
802	70c. Type **140**	1·60	1·60
803	$2.10 Chinese symbol for goat (in turquoise-blue foil)	4·75	4·75
790/803	*Set of* 14	12·50	12·50
MS804	136×70 *mm.* Nos. 802/3	13·00	13·00

Nos. 790/803 were printed together, *se-tenant*, as a sheetlet containing Nos. 790/801 as a block of 12 (6×2) and Nos. 802/3 as a separate horizontal pair within margins similar to **MS**804. Nos. 802/3 were also printed in separate sheets of 50.

Nos. 790/803 were also issued in premium booklets, No. SP8, sold for $14.95.

141 Red Crabs forming a Christmas Tree

(Des Stuart McLachlan. Litho RA Print)

2015 (30 Oct). Christmas. T **141** and similar vert design. Multicoloured.

(a) Ordinary gum.

(i) Domestic mail. P 14½×14.

805	65c. Type **141**	1·00	1·00

(ii) International Post. P 14½×14.

806	$1.80 Red crabs hailing 'snowman' made from coconuts	3·00	3·00
MS807	135×80 *mm.* Nos. 805/6	4·00	4·00

(b) Self-adhesive. Phosphor over parts of design. Die-cut perf 11½×11 (interrupted on horiz sides)

(i) Domestic mail

808	65c. As Type **141** but with red foil on crabs	1·00	1·00

(ii) International Post

809	$1.80 As No. 806	3·00	3·00
	a. Pane. Nos. 809×5	13·50	

No. 808 was printed in a self-adhesive sheetlet of ten stamps and ten 'CARD ONLY' labels.

No. 809 was issued in $9 panes of five stamps.

142 Monkey and Calligraphic Symbol (outlined in gold foil)

(Des Dani Poon. Litho RA Printing)

2016 (3 Feb). Chinese New Year. Year of the Monkey. T **142** and similar vert designs. Multicoloured. P 14½×14.

810	20c. Rat	30	30
	a. Sheetlet. Nos. 810/23	12·00	12·00
811	20c. Rabbit	30	30
812	20c. Goat	30	30
813	20c. Goat	30	30
814	30c. Ox	45	45
815	30c. Dragon	45	45
816	30c. Monkey (in gold foil)	45	45
817	30c. Pig	45	45
818	50c. Tiger	80	80
819	50c. Snake	80	80
820	50c. Horse	80	80
821	50c. Rooster	80	80
822	$1 Type **142**	1·50	1·50
823	$3 Chinese symbol for monkey (in gold foil)	4·50	4·50
810/23	*Set of* 14	12·00	12·00
MS824	135×70 *mm.* Nos. 822/3	6·00	6·00

Nos. 810/23 were printed together, *se-tenant*, as a sheetlet containing Nos. 810/21 as a block of 12 (6×2) and Nos. 822/3 as a separate horizontal pair within margins similar to **MS**824. Nos. 822/3 were also printed in separate sheets of 50.

Nos. 810/23 were also issued in premium booklets, No. SP9, sold for $20.95.

143 Robber Crab on Palm Tree Trunk

(Des Sharon Rodziewicz. Litho RA Printing)

2016 (26 Apr). Robber Crabs (*Birgus latro*). T **143** and similar horiz designs. Multicoloured. P 14×14½.

825	$1 Type **143**	1·50	1·50
	a. Horiz pair. Nos. 825/6	3·00	3·00
826	$1 Robber Crab on beach	1·50	1·50
827	$2 Four Robber Crabs on beach	3·00	3·00
825/7	*Set of* 3	5·50	5·50

Nos. 825/6 were printed together, *se-tenant*, as horizontal pairs in sheets of 50 (2 panes 5×5), each sheet giving 20 horizontal pairs and ten single stamps (Type 143).

STAMP BOOKLETS

Between mid-1995 and 25 June 1996 the Christmas Island Postmaster produced stamp booklets utilising card from surplus Presentation Packs. These booklets contained blocks of ten 45c. stamps from whichever issue was currently available
.

1996 (26 June). Black on red cover, 95×150 mm, inscr "CHRISTMAS ISLAND POST OFFICE STAMP BOOKLET", often with Christmas Island postmark on the front. Stapled.

SB1 $4.50 Booklet containing 45c. (No. 414) in block of 10 .... £160

a. Containing 45c. (No. 353) £650

All examples of No. SB1a are postmarked 23 June 1996.

B **1** Christmas Tree with Red Crabs and Seashells

2008 (31 Oct). Christmas. Multicoloured covers, 62×85 mm, as Type B **1**. Self-adhesive.

SB2 $5 booklet containing pane of 10×50c. with five "Card Only" labels (No. 642a) .... 10·00

B **2** White-tailed Tropic Bird carrying Christmas Gift

2010 (1 Nov). Christmas. Multicoloured cover, 60×85 mm, as Type B **2**. Self-adhesive.

SB3 $6 booklet containing pane of ten 60c. (No. 683a) 10·00

B **3** Father Christmas pulling Cracker with Red Crab

2011 (31 Oct). Christmas. Multicoloured cover, 61×85 mm, as Type B **3**. Self-adhesive.

SB4 $5.50 booklet containing pane of ten 55c. (No. 707a) .... 12·00

PREMIUM BOOKLETS

The following booklet was sold at a premium over the face value of the stamps.

P **1** Boy

2007 (9 Jan). Chinese New Year ("Year of the Pig"). Multicoloured cover, 156×104 mm, as Type P **1**. Booklet contains text and illustrations on panes and interleaving pages. Self-adhesive.

SP1 $12.95 booklet containing six panes of four self-adhesive stamps, each pane containing two of each design: As Nos. 426 and 434; As Nos. 440 and 466; As Nos. 476 and 487; As Nos. 504 and 523; As Nos. 540 and 575; As Nos. 593 and 612 .... 22·00

Stamps from No. SP1 all have designs as Nos. 426, 434, 440, 466, 476, 487, 504, 523, 540, 575, 593 and 612, but they are self-adhesive p 12½×13 (interrupted) with partial phosphor frames as the 50c. stamps within **MS**615. Face value: $12.

P **2** Zodiac Animals in Stylized Landscape

2008 (8 Jan). Chinese New Year ('Year of the Rat'). Multicoloured cover, 156×104 mm, as Type P **2**. Booklet contains text and illustrations on panes and interleaving pages. Stitched.

SP2 $10.95 booklet containing six panes of four stamps as follows: Nos. 619/20 and 632×2; Nos. 623/4 and as No. 631×2; Nos. 621/2 and as No. 631×2; Nos. 625, 627 and as No. 631×2; Nos. 628/9 and as No. 631×2; Nos. 626, 630 and as No. 631×2 .... 16·00

All stamps from SP2 are perforated 14½×14.
Face value: $9.80.

P **3** Tiger and Flower Petals

2010 (12 Jan). Chinese New Year. Year of the Tiger. Multicoloured cover, 154×105 mm, as Type P **3**. Booklet contains text and illustrations on panes and interleaving pages. Stitched.

SP3 $12.95 booklet containing six panes of four stamps as follows: Nos. 665/6 and 674×2; Nos. 663/4 and 673×2; Nos. 667, 669 and 673×2; Nos. 670/1 and 673×2; Nos. 668, 672 and 673×2; Nos. 661/2 and 673×2 .... 17·00

Face value: $11.

P **4** Rabbit

2011 (11 Jan). Chinese New Year. Year of the Rabbit. Multicoloured cover, 157×104 mm, as Type P **4.** Booklet contains text and illustrations on interleaving pages. Stitched.

SP4 $14.95 booklet containing six panes of four stamps as follows: Nos. 689/90 and 697×2; Nos. 687/8 and 698×2; Nos. 691, 693 and 697×2; Nos. 694/5 and 697×2; Nos. 692, 696 and 697×2; Nos. 685/6 and 697×2 .... 19·00

P **5** Chinese Zodiac

2012 (10 Jan). Chinese New Year. Year of the Dragon. Multicoloured cover, 158×104 mm, as Type P **5.** Booklet contains text and illustrations on panes and interleaving pages. Stitched.

SP5 $12.95 booklet containing six panes of four stamps as follows: Nos. 711/12 and 722×2; Nos. 715, 717 and 721×2; Nos. 718/19 and 721×2; Nos. 716, 720 and 721×2; Nos. 709/10 and 721×2; Nos. 713/14 and 721×2 .... 19·00

P **6** 'long life' and Zodiac Animals

2013 (8 Jan). Chinese New Year. Year of the Snake. Multicoloured cover, 157×106 mm, as Type P **6**. Booklet contains text and illustrations on panes and interleaving pages.

SP6 $12.95 booklet containing six panes of four stamps as follows: Nos. 736, 739 and 746×2; Nos. 741/2 and 745×2; Nos. 743/4 and 745×2; Nos. 733, 740 and 745×2; Nos. 734, 737 and 745×2; Nos. 735, 738 and 745×2 .... 19·00

Face value: $12

P **7** Horse and the Five Elements

2014 (7 Jan). Chinese New Year. Year of the Horse. Multicoloured cover, 157×104 mm, as Type P **7**. Booklet contains text and illustrations on panes and interleaving pages.

SP7 $12.95 booklet containing six panes of four stamps as follows: Nos. 770, 772 and 777×2; Nos. 773/4 and 776×2; Nos. 771, 775 and 776×2; Nos. 764/5 and 776×2; Nos. 768/9 and 776×2; Nos. Nos. 766/7 and 776×2 .... 19·00

Face value: $12

P **8** Roses and Gemstones

2015 (8 Jan). Chinese New Year. Year of the Goat. Multicoloured cover, 156×104 mm, as Type P **8**. Booklet contains text and illustrations on panes and interleaving pages.

SP8 $14.95 booklet containing six panes of four stamps as follows: Nos. 794/5 and 803×2; Nos. 796/7 and 802×2; Nos. 790, 801 and 802×2; Nos. 791, 798 and 802×2; Nos. 792, 799 and 802×2; Nos. 793, 800 and 802×2 .... 24·00

Face value: $14

P **9** Monkey

2016 (3 Feb). Chinese New Year. Year of the Monkey. Multicoloured cover, 150×103 mm, as Type P **9**. Booklet contains text and illustrations on panes and interleaving pages

SP9 $20.95 booklet containing six panes of four stamps as follows: Nos. 810, 814 and 822/3; Nos. 811, 818 and 822×2; Nos. 815, 819 and 822×2; Nos. 812, 820 and 822/3; Nos. 816, 821 and 822×2; Nos. 813, 817 and 822×2 .... 32·00

Face value: $20

COCOS (KEELING) ISLANDS

The Cocos (Keeling) Islands, which had been settled by the Clunies Ross family in the 1820s, were annexed by Great Britain in 1857. In 1878 the group was attached to Ceylon, but was transferred to the Straits Settlements on 7 February 1886. During the Second World War the islands were under British military control exercised from Ceylon. At the end of hostilities administration from Singapore was continued until the islands were transferred to Australia on 23 November 1955.

The stamps of the STRAITS SETTLEMENTS were used by a postal agency operating on Cocos (Keeling) Islands from 1 April 1933 until 1 March 1937. The postal agency reopened on 2 September 1952 and used the stamps of SINGAPORE until the islands were transferred to Australia in 1955. From 1955 until 1963 stamps of AUSTRALIA were in use.
Nos. 1/31 were also valid for use in Australia.

PRINTERS. All the following stamps to No. 31 were printed by the Note Printing Branch, Reserve Bank of Australia, Melbourne.

1 Copra Industry

2 "Super Constellation"

3 Map of islands

4 Palms

5 Dukong (sail boat)

6 White Tern

(Des K. McKay and E. Jones (5d.), E. Jones (others). Eng E. Jones. Recess)

1963 (11 June). T **1/6**. P 14½×14 (5d., 2s.3d.) or 14½ (others).

1	3d. chocolate	1·50	1·50
2	5d. ultramarine	2·00	80
3	8d. scarlet	1·00	1·75
4	1s. green	1·00	75
5	2s. deep purple	8·00	2·00
6	2s.3d. deep green	9·00	1·75
1/6 *Set of 6*		20·00	7·50

I Thick lettering

II Thinner lettering

1965 (14 Apr). 50th Anniv of Gallipoli Landing. As T **184** of Australia, but slightly larger (22×34½ *mm*) and colour changed. Photo. P 13½.

7	5d. sepia, black and emerald (I)	60	45
	a. Black-brown, black and light emerald (II)	3·00	2·25

No. 7a comes from a second printing, using a new black cylinder, which was available from the end of April.

With the introduction of decimal currency on 14 February 1966, Australian stamps were used in Cocos Islands, until the appearance of the new definitives on 9 July 1969.

(New Currency. 100 cents = 1 Australian dollar)

7 Reef Clam (*Tridacna derasa*)

8 Great Frigate Bird

(Des L. Annois (1c. to 6c.), P. Jones (10c. to $1). Photo)

1969 (9 July). Decimal Currency. T **8** or designs as T **7**. Multicoloured. P 13½.

8	1c. Lajonkaines Turbo shell (*Turbo lajonkairii*) (*vert*)	30	60
9	2c. Elongate or Small Giant Clam (*Tridacna maxima*) (*vert*)	75	80
10	3c. Type **7**	40	20
11	4c. Floral Blenny (fish)	30	50
	a. Salmon-pink omitted	£2750	
12	5c. *Porites cocosensis* (coral)	35	30
13	6c. Atrisignis Flyingfish	75	75
14	10c. Buff-banded Rail	75	70
15	15c. Java Sparrow	75	30
16	20c. Red-tailed Tropic Bird	75	30
17	30c. Sooty Tern	75	30
18	50c. Eastern Reef Heron (*vert*)	75	30
19	$1 Type **8**	1·50	75
8/19 *Set of 12*		7·25	5·25

9 *Dragon*, 1609

10 Map of Cocos (Keeling) Island Union Flag, Stars and Trees

(Des R. Honisett. Photo)

1976 (29 Mar). Ships. Multicoloured designs as T **9**. P 13½.

20	1c. Type **9**	30	40
21	2c. H.M.S. *Juno*, 1857	30	40
22	5c. H.M.S. *Beagle*, 1836	30	40
23	10c. H.M.A.S. *Sydney*, 1914	35	40
24	15c. S.M.S *Emden*, 1914	60	55
25	20c. *Ayesha*, 1907	60	65
26	25c. T.S.S. *Islander*, 1927	60	75
27	30c. M.V. *Cheshire*, 1951	60	75
28	35c. *Jukong* (sailboat)	60	75
29	40c. C.S. *Scotia*, 1900	60	75
30	50c. R.M.S. *Orontes*, 1929	60	75
31	$1 Royal Yacht *Gothic*, 1954	75	1·00
20/31 *Set of 12*		5·50	6·75

The 2c. to 20c., 35c. and 40c. are horizontal designs.

(Des Marg Towt. Litho Asher and Co, Melbourne)

1979 (3 Sept). Inauguration of Independent Postal Service (20c.) and Establishment of First Statutory Council (50c.). T **10** and similar horiz design. Multicoloured. P 15½×15.

32	20c. Type **10**	20	40
33	50c. Council seal and jukong (sailboat)	25	85

11 Forceps Fish

(Des Marg Towt. Litho Asher and Co, Melbourne)

1979 (3 Sept)–**80**. Fish. Horiz designs as T **11**. Multicoloured. P 13½×13 (22c., 28c., 60c.) or 15½×15 (others).

34	1c. Type **11**	30	1·00
35	2c. Ornate Butterflyfish (19.11.79)	30	30
36	5c. Barbier	50	1·25
37	10c. Meyer's Butterflyfish (18.2.80)	30	1·25
38	15c. Pink Wrasse (19.11.79)	30	30
39	20c. Clark's Anemonefish (19.11.79)	40	30
39*a*	22c. Undulate Triggerfish (1.7.80)	45	30
40	25c. Red-breasted Wrasse (18.2.80)	40	1·25
40*a*	28c. Guineafowl Wrasse (1.7.80)	35	35
41	30c. Madagascar Butterflyfish (19.11.79)	40	45
42	35c. Cocos-Keeling Angelfish	40	1·75
43	40c. Coral Hogfish (19.11.79)	45	1·00
44	50c. Clown Wrasse (19.11.79)	85	75
45	55c. Yellow-tailed Tamarin (18.2.80)	50	1·50
45*a*	60c. Greasy Grouper (1.7.80)	50	75
46	$1 Palette Surgeonfish	60	2·50
47	$2 Melon Butterflyfish (18.2.80)	70	2·50
34/47 *Set of 17*		7·00	15·00

12 "Peace on Earth"

(Des D. Pitt. Litho Asher & Co, Melbourne)

1979 (22 Oct). Christmas. T **12** and similar multicoloured design. P 15×15½ (25c.) or 15½×15 (55c.).

48	25c. Type **12**	25	40
49	55c. "Goodwill Toward Men" (*horiz*)	40	70

13 Star, Map of Cocos (Keeling) Islands and Island Landscape

14 "Administered by the British Government, 1857"

(Des P. Arnold. Litho Asher and Co, Melbourne)

1980 (22 Oct). Christmas. T **13** and similar horiz designs. Multicoloured. P 13.

50	15c. Type **13**	10	10
51	28c. Map and Wise Men following star	15	15
52	60c. Map and Nativity scene	40	40
50/2 *Set of 3*		60	60

(Des Sue Wilson. Litho Asher and Co, Melbourne)

1980 (24 Nov). 25th Anniv of Cocos (Keeling) Islands as an Australian Territory. T **14** and similar horiz designs. Multicoloured. P 13½×13.

53	22c. Type **14**	15	15
	a. Horiz strip of 5. Nos. 53/7	70	70
54	22c. "Administered by the Government of Ceylon, 1878, 1942-6"	15	15
55	22c. "Administered by the Straits Settlements, 1886"	15	15
56	22c. "Administered by the Colony of Singapore, 1946"	15	15
57	22c. "Administered by the Australian Government, 1955"	15	15
53/7 *Set of 5*		70	70

Nos. 53/7 were printed together, *se-tenant*, in horizontal strips of five throughout the sheet, forming a composite design.

15 *Eye of the Wind* and Map of Cocos (Keeling) Islands

16 Aerial View of Animal Quarantine Station

(Des Sue Wilson. Litho Asher and Co, Melbourne)

1980 (18 Dec). "Operation Drake" (round the world expedition) and 400th Anniv of Sir Francis Drake's Circumnavigation of the World. T **15** and similar multicoloured designs. P 13.

58	22c. Type **15**	25	15
59	28c. Map showing voyage routes (*horiz*)	25	15
60	35c. Sir Francis Drake and *Golden Hind*	25	15
61	60c. Prince Charles and *Eye of the Wind* (brigantine)	45	30
58/61 *Set of 4*		1·10	65

(Des Cato Hibberd Design. Litho Leigh-Mardon Ltd, Melbourne)

1981 (12 May). Opening of Animal Quarantine Station. T **16** and similar horiz designs. Multicoloured. P 13½×13.

62	22c. Type **16**	15	15
63	45c. Unloading livestock	20	30
64	60c. Livestock in pen	20	35
62/4 *Set of 3*		50	70

17 Consolidated "Catalina" *Guba II* Flying

18 Prince Charles and Lady Diana Spencer

(Des R. Honisett. Litho Leigh-Mardon Ltd, Melbourne)

1981 (23 June). Aircraft. T **17** and similar horiz designs. Multicoloured. P 13½×13.

65	22c. Type **17**	25	25
	a. Horiz strip of 5. Nos. 65/9	1·10	1·10
66	22c. Consolidated "Liberator" and Avro "Lancastrian"	25	25
67	22c. Douglas "DC4 (Skymaster)" and Lockheed "Constellation"	25	25
68	22c. Lockheed "Electra"	25	25
69	22c. Boeing "727" airliners	25	25
65/9 *Set of 5*		1·10	1·10

Nos. 65/9 were printed together, *se-tenant*, in horizontal strips of five throughout the sheet.

(Des B. Clinton. Litho Leigh-Mardon Ltd, Melbourne)

1981 (29 July). Royal Wedding. P 13½×13.

70	**18** 24c. multicoloured	25	20
71	60c. multicoloured	35	60

19 "Angels we have heard on High"

20 *Pachyseris speciosa* and *Heliofungia actiniformis*

(Des B. Weatherhead. Litho Leigh-Mardon Ltd, Melbourne)

1981 (22 Oct). Christmas. Scenes and Lines from Carol "Angels we have heard on High". T **19** and similar horiz designs. Multicoloured. P 13½×13.

72	18c. Type **19**	10	10
73	30c. "Shepherds why this Jubilee?"	20	20
74	60c. "Come to Bethlehem and see Him"	35	35
72/4 *Set of 3*		60	60

(Des B. Weatherhead. Litho Leigh-Mardon Ltd, Melbourne)

1981 (28 Dec). 150th Anniv of Charles Darwin's Voyage. T **20** and similar horiz designs. Multicoloured. P 13½×13.

75	24c. Type **20**	25	15
76	45c. Charles Darwin in 1853 and *Pavona cactus* (coral)	40	30

77	60c. H.M.S. *Beagle*, 1832, and *Lobophyllia hemprichii* (coral)	45	35
75/7	*Set of 3*	1·00	70
MS78	130×95 *mm.* 24c. Cross-section of West Island; 24c. Cross-section of Home Island	75	85

21 Queen Victoria

22 Lord Baden-Powell

(Des B. Weatherhead. Litho Cambec Press, Melbourne)

1982 (31 Mar). 125th Anniv of Annexation of Cocos (Keeling) Islands to British Empire. T **21** and similar horiz designs. Multicoloured. P 13½×14.

79	24c. Type **21**	15	15
80	45c. Union flag	25	25
81	60c. Capt. S. Fremantle (annexation visit, 1857)	30	35
79/81	*Set of 3*	65	65

(Des B. Clinton. Litho Cambec Press, Melbourne)

1982 (21 July). 75th Anniv of Boy Scout Movement. T **22** and similar multicoloured design. P 13½×14 (27c.) or 14×13½ (75c.).

82	27c. Type **22**	20	25
83	75c. "75" and map of Cocos (Keeling) Islands (*vert*)	50	1·25

23 *Precis villida*

24 "Call His Name Immanuel"

(Des B. Hargreaves. Litho Harrison)

1982 (6 Sept)–**83**. Butterflies and Moths. T **23** and similar multicoloured designs. P 14.

84	1c. Type **23**	1·00	60
85	2c. *Cephonodes picus* (*horiz*) (6.1.83)	40	40
86	5c. *Macroglossum corythus* (*horiz*)	1·50	70
87	10c. *Chasmina candida* (6.1.83)	40	40
88	20c. *Nagia linteola* (*horiz*) (6.4.83)	40	65
89	25c. *Eublemma rivula* (1.7.83)	40	75
90	30c. *Eurrhyparodes tricoloralis* (6.4.83)	40	65
91	35c. *Hippotion boerhaviae* (*horiz*)	1·75	75
92	40c. *Euploea core* (6.4.83)	40	80
93	45c. *Psara hipponalis* (*horiz*) (6.4.83)	40	80
94	50c. *Danaus chrysippus* (*horiz*) (1.7.83)	50	1·25
95	55c. *Hypolimnas misippus* (6.1.83)	50	70
96	60c. *Spodoptera litura* (1.7.83)	55	1·75
97	$1 *Achaea janata*	2·25	2·75
98	$2 *Panacra velox* (*horiz*) (1.7.83)	1·25	2·75
99	$3 *Utetheisa pulchelloides* (*horiz*) (6.1.83)	1·50	2·75
84/99	*Set of 16*	12·00	17·00

(Des G. Hamori. Litho Cambec Press, Melbourne)

1982 (25 Oct). Christmas. T **24** and similar horiz designs. Multicoloured. P 13½×14.

100	21c. Type **24**	25	30
101	35c. "I bring you good tidings"	40	40
102	75c. "Arise and flee into Egypt"	1·00	1·25
100/2	*Set of 3*	1·50	1·75

25 "God will look after us" (*Matt.* 1:20)

26 Hari Raya Celebrations

(Des R. Roberts. Litho Cambec Press, Melbourne)

1983 (25 Oct). Christmas. Extracts from the New Testament. T **25** and similar vert designs. Multicoloured. P 14×13½.

103	24c. Type **25**	30	45
	a. Horiz strip of 5. Nos. 103/7	1·40	2·00
104	24c. "Our baby King, Jesus" (*Matthew* 2:2)	30	45
105	24c. "Your Saviour is born" (*Luke* 2:11)	30	45
106	24c. "Wise men followed the Star" (*Matthew* 2:9-10)	30	45
107	24c. "And worship the Lord" (*Matthew* 2:11)	30	45
103/7	*Set of 5*	1·40	2·00

Nos. 103/7 were printed together, *se-tenant*, in horizontal strips of five throughout the sheet.

(Des Marg Towt. Litho Cambec Press, Melbourne)

1984 (24 Jan). Cocos-Malay Culture. (1st series). Festivals. T **26** and similar vert designs. Multicoloured. P 13½×13.

108	45c. Type **26**	25	35
109	75c. Melonggok dancing	40	50
110	85c. Cocos-Malay wedding	45	55
108/10	*Set of 3*	1·00	1·25

See also Nos. 126/8.

27 Unpacking Barrel

28 Captain William Keeling

(Des R. Honisett. Litho Cambec Press, Melbourne)

1984 (20 Apr). 75th Anniv of Cocos Barrel Mail. T **27** and similar horiz designs. Multicoloured. P 13½×14.

111	35c. Type **27**	40	25
112	55c. Jukong awaiting mail ship	75	50
113	70c. P. & O. mail ship *Morea*	85	55
111/13	*Set of 3*	1·75	1·10
MS114	125×95 *mm.* $1 Retrieving barrel	1·00	1·25

(Des B. Clinton. Litho Cambec Press, Melbourne)

1984 (10 July). 375th Anniv of Discovery of Cocos (Keeling) Islands. T **28** and similar vert designs. Multicoloured. P 14.

115	30c. Type **28**	45	40
116	65c. Keeling's ship *Hector*	1·00	90
117	95c. Mariner's astrolabe	1·10	1·25
118	$1.10 Map *circa* 1666	1·40	1·50
115/18	*Set of 4*	3·50	3·50

29 Malay Settlement, Home Island

30 "Rainbow" Fish

(Des E. Roberts. Litho Cambec Press, Melbourne)

1984 (21 Sept). "Ausipex" International Stamp Exhibition, Melbourne. T **29** and similar horiz designs. Multicoloured. P 13½×14.

119	45c. Type **29**	60	50
120	55c. Airstrip, West Island	65	60
MS121	130×95 *mm.* $2 Jukongs (native craft) racing	1·25	1·40

(Des R. Roberts. Litho Cambec Press, Melbourne)

1984 (31 Oct). Christmas. T **30** and similar horiz designs. Multicoloured. P 13½×14.

122	24c. Type **30**	40	50
123	35c. "Rainbow" butterfly	80	1·10
124	55c. "Rainbow" bird	1·00	1·50
122/4	*Set of 3*	2·00	2·75

31 Cocos Islanders

32 Jukong Building

(Des B. Weatherhead. Litho Cambec Press, Melbourne)

1984 (30 Nov). Integration of Cocos (Keeling) Islands with Australia. Sheet 90×52 mm containing T **31** and similar horiz design. Multicoloured. P 13½×14.

MS125 30c. Type **31**; 30c. Australian flag on island ...... 1·10 1·25

(Des Marg Towt. Litho Cambec Press, Melbourne)

1985 (30 Jan). Cocos-Malay Culture (2nd series). Handicrafts. T **32** and similar vert designs. Multicoloured. P 14×13½.

126	30c. Type **32**	45	35
127	45c. Blacksmithing	65	55
128	55c. Woodcarving	75	65
126/8	*Set of 3*	1·75	1·40

33 C.S. *Scotia*

34 Red-footed Booby

(Des B. Clinton. Litho Cambec Press, Melbourne)

1985 (24 Apr). Cable-laying Ships. T **33** and similar horiz designs. Multicoloured. P 13½×14.

129	33c. Type **33**	1·50	40
130	65c. C.S. *Anglia*	2·25	1·60
131	80c. C.S. *Patrol*	2·25	2·25
129/31	*Set of 3*	5·50	3·75

(Des Marg Towt. Litho Cambec Press, Melbourne)

1985 (17 July). Birds of Cocos (Keeling) Islands. T **34** and similar multicoloured designs. P 13½.

132	33c. Type **34**	1·50	2·50
	a. Block of 3. Nos. 132/4	4·75	7·25
	ab. Imperf vert (block of 3)	£1000	
133	60c. Nankeen Night Heron (juvenile) (*horiz*)	1·75	2·75
134	$1 Buff-banded Rail (*horiz*)	2·00	2·75
132/4	*Set of 3*	4·75	7·25

Nos. 132/4 were printed together, *se-tenant*, in blocks of three throughout the sheet, each block forming a composite design.

35 Mantled Top (*Trochus maculatus*)

36 Night Sky and Palm Trees

(Des G. Ryan. Litho Cambec Press, Melbourne)

1985 (18 Sept)-**86**. Shells and Molluscs. T **35** and similar horiz designs. Multicoloured. P 13½×14.

135	1c. Type **35**	60	1·25
136	2c. Rang's Nerite (*Smaragdia rangiana*) (29.1.86)	60	1·25
137	3c. Jewel Box (*Chama* sp) (29.1.86)	60	1·25
138	4c. Money Cowrie (*Cypraea moneta*) (30.7.86)	1·00	1·25
139	5c. Purple Pacific Drupe (*Drupa morum*)	60	1·25
140	10c. Soldier Cone (*Conus miles*) (29.1.86)	70	1·50
141	15c. Marlin-spike Auger (*Terebra maculata*) (30.4.86)	2·00	1·25
142	20c. Pacific Strawberry Cockle (*Fragum fragum*) (30.4.86)	2·00	1·50
143	30c. Lajonkaire's Turban (*Turbo lajonkairii*) (30.4.86)	2·00	1·50
144	33c. Reticulate Mitre (*Scabricola fissurata*)	2·00	1·50
145	40c. Common Spider Conch (*Lambis lambis*) (30.4.86)	2·00	1·50
146	50c. Fluted Giant Clam or Scaled Tridacna (*Tridacna squamosa*) (30.7.86)	2·00	1·75
147	60c. Minstrel Cowrie (*Cypraea histrio*) (30.7.86)	2·00	2·25
148	$1 Varicose Nudibranch (*Phyllidia varicosa*)	2·50	3·25
149	$2 Tesselated Nudibranch (*Halgerda tessellata*) (30.7.86)	2·50	4·25
150	$3 *Haminoea cymballum* (29.1.86)	2·50	4·75
135/50	*Set of 16*	23·00	28·00

(Des D. Goodwin. Litho Cambec Press, Melbourne)

1985 (30 Oct). Christmas. Sheet 121×88 mm, containing T **36** and similar horiz designs. P 13½×14.

MS151 27c.×4 multicoloured ...... 1·50 2·50

The stamps within **MS**151 show a composite design of the night sky seen through a grove of palm trees. The position of the face value on the four stamps varies. Type **36** shows the top left design. The top right stamp shows the face value at bottom right, the bottom left at top left and the bottom right at top right.

37 Charles Darwin, *c* 1840

38 Coconut Palm and Holly Sprigs

(Des B. Clinton. Litho Cambec Press, Melbourne)

1986 (1 Apr). 150th Anniv of Charles Darwin's Visit. T **37** and similar vert designs. Multicoloured. P 14×13½.

152	33c. Type **37**	70	60
153	60c. Map of H.M.S. *Beagle's* route Australia to Cocos Islands	1·25	2·25
154	$1 H.M.S. *Beagle*	1·50	2·75
152/4	*Set of 3*	3·00	5·00

(Des S. Hartshorne. Litho Cambec Press, Melbourne)

1986 (29 Oct). Christmas. T **38** and similar horiz designs. Multicoloured. P 13½×14.

155	30c. Type **38**	60	70
156	90c. Nautilus Shell and Christmas tree bauble	2·00	3·00
157	$1 Tropical fish and bell	2·00	3·00
155/7	*Set of 3*	4·25	6·00

39 Jukong

40 Beach, Direction Island

(Des J. Earl. Litho Cambec Press, Melbourne)

1987 (28 Jan). Sailing Craft. T **39** and similar horiz designs. Multicoloured. P 13½×14.

158	36c. Type **39**	1·00	1·60
	a. Horiz strip of 4. Nos. 158/61	3·50	6·00
159	36c. Ocean racing yachts	1·00	1·60
160	36c. *Sarimanok* (replica of early dhow)	1·00	1·60
161	36c. *Ayesha* (schooner)	1·00	1·60
158/61	*Set of 4*	3·50	6·00

Nos. 158/61 were printed together, *se-tenant*, in horizontal strips of five throughout the sheet, each strip forming a composite background design.

(Des H. Missingham and R. Fletcher. Litho CPE Australia Ltd, Melbourne)

1987 (8 Apr). Cocos Islands Scenes. T **40** and similar horiz designs. Multicoloured. P 13½×14.

162	70c. Type **40**	1·25	1·40
163	90c. Palm forest, West Island	1·40	2·00
164	$1 Golf course	2·75	3·00
162/4	*Set of 3*	4·75	5·75

41 Radio Transmitter and Palm Trees at Sunset

42 Batik Printing

(Des R. Fletcher. Litho CPE Australia Ltd, Melbourne)

1987 (29 July). Communications. T **41** and similar horiz designs. Multicoloured. P 13½×14.

165	70c. Type **41**	1·00	1·50
166	75c. Airliner at terminal	1·25	1·75
167	90c. "Intelsat 5" satellite	1·50	2·25
168	$1 Airmail letter and globe	1·75	2·25
165/8 *Set of 4*		5·00	7·00

(Des B. Clinton. Litho CPE Australia Ltd, Melbourne)

1987 (16 Sept). Cocos (Keeling) Islands Malay Industries. T **42** and similar horiz designs. Multicoloured. P 13½×14.

169	45c. Type **42**	1·00	1·50
170	65c. Jukong building	1·10	2·00
171	75c. Copra production	1·25	2·25
169/71 *Set of 3*		3·00	5·25

43 Hands Releasing Peace Dove and Map of Islands

44 Coconut Flower

(Des Marg Towt. Litho CPE Australia Ltd, Melbourne)

1987 (28 Oct). Christmas. T **43** and similar vert designs. Multicoloured. P 14×13½.

172	30c. Type **43**	30	40
173	90c. Local children at Christmas party	1·00	1·90
174	$1 Island family and Christmas star	1·25	1·90
172/4 *Set of 3*		2·25	3·75

(Des Sue Passmore. Litho CPE Australia Ltd, Melbourne)

1988 (26 Jan). Bicentenary of Australian Settlement. Arrival of First Fleet. Square designs as Nos. 1105/9 of Australia but each inscribed "COCOS (KEELING) ISLANDS" and "AUSTRALIA BICENTENARY".

175	37c. Aborigines watching arrival of Fleet, Botany Bay	2·00	2·00
	a. Horiz strip of 5. Nos. 175/9	9·00	9·00
176	37c. Aboriginal family and anchored ships	2·00	2·00
177	37c. Fleet arriving at Sydney Cove	2·00	2·00
178	37c. Ship's boat	2·00	2·00
179	37c. Raising the flag, Sydney Cove, 26 January 1788	2·00	2·00
175/9 *Set of 5*		9·00	9·00

Nos. 175/9 were printed together, *se-tenant*, in horizontal strips of five throughout the sheet, forming a composite design.

(Des Celia Rosser. Litho CPE Australia Ltd, Melbourne)

1988 (13 Apr). Life Cycle of the Coconut. T **44** and similar vert designs. Multicoloured. P 14×13½.

180	37c. Type **44**	40	40
181	65c. Immature nuts	60	90
182	90c. Coconut palm and mature nuts	75	1·50
183	$1 Seedlings	80	1·50
180/3 *Set of 4*		2·25	3·75
MS184 102×91 *mm*. Nos. 180/3		2·25	3·75

45 Copra 3d. Stamp of 1963

46 *Pisonia Grandis*

(Des R. Fletcher. Recess and litho Note Printing Branch, Reserve Bank of Australia, Melbourne)

1988 (15 June). 25th Anniv of First Cocos (Keeling) Islands Stamps. T **45** and similar vert designs, each showing stamp from 1963 definitive set. P 15×14.

185	37c. chocolate, black and azure	90	1·00
186	55c. green, black and pale drab	1·25	1·50
187	65c. ultramarine, black and pale grey-lilac	1·40	2·25
188	70c. scarlet, black and bluish grey	1·40	2·25
189	90c. deep purple, black and greenish grey	1·50	2·50
190	$1 deep green, black and light brown	1·50	2·50
185/90 *Set of 6*		7·00	11·00

Designs:—55c. Palms 1s.; 65c. "Super Constellation" 5d.; 70c. Map 8d.; 90c. Jukong (sailboat) 2s.; $1 White Tern 2s.3d.

(Des R. Fletcher. Litho CPE Australia Ltd, Melbourne)

1988 (29 July)–**89**. Flora. T **46** and similar vert designs. Multicoloured. P 14×13½.

191	1c. Type **46**	50	80
192	2c. *Cocos nucifera* (18.1.89)	50	80
193	5c. *Morinda citrifolia*	1·00	90
194	10c. *Cordia subcordata* (18.1.89)	70	90
195	30c. *Argusia argentea* (18.1.89)	1·00	1·25
196	37c. *Calophyllum inophyllum*	1·50	1·00
197	40c. *Barringtonia asiatica* (19.4.89)	1·00	1·25
198	50c. *Caesalpinia bonduc* (19.4.89)	1·25	3·00
199	90c. *Terminalia catappa* (19.4.89)	1·75	4·00
200	$1 *Pemphis acidula* (19.4.89)	1·75	2·50
201	$2 *Scaevola sericea* (18.1.89)	2·50	2·50
202	$3 *Hibiscus tiliaceus*	3·50	3·75
191/202 *Set of 12*		15·00	20·00

(Des R. Fletcher. Litho CPE Australia Ltd, Melbourne)

1988 (30 July). "Sydpex '88" National Stamp Exhibition, Sydney. Sheet 70×85 mm. Multicoloured. P 14×13½.

MS203 $3 As No. 202	3·00	5·00

47 Beach at Sunset

48 Capt. P. G. Taylor

(Des T. Bland. Litho CPE Australia Ltd, Melbourne)

1988 (12 Oct). Christmas. P 13½×14.

204	**47**	32c. multicoloured	50	50
205		90c. multicoloured	1·00	2·25
206		$1 multicoloured	1·00	2·25
204/6 *Set of 3*			2·25	4·50

(Des B. Clinton. Litho CPE Australia Ltd, Melbourne)

1989 (19 July). 50th Anniv of First Indian Ocean Aerial Survey. T **48** and similar vert designs. P 14×13½.

207	40c. multicoloured	80	60
208	70c. multicoloured	1·75	2·50
209	$1 multicoloured	2·00	2·50
210	$1.10 deep ultramarine, pale lilac and black	2·25	2·75
207/10 *Set of 4*		6·00	7·50

Designs:—70c. Consolidated Catalina "PBY2" *Guba II* and crew; $1 *Guba II* over Direction Island; $1.10, Unissued Australia 5s. stamp commemorating flight.

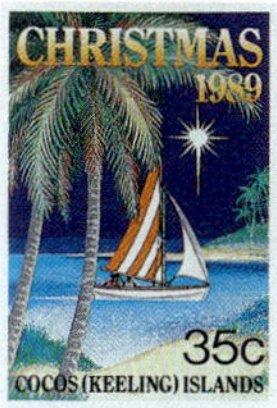

49 Jukong and Star

50 H.M.A.S *Sydney* (cruiser)

(Des T. Bland. Litho Leigh-Mardon Ltd, Melbourne)

1989 (18 Oct). Christmas. P 14×13½.

211	**49** 35c. multicoloured	80	60
212	80c. multicoloured	2·00	2·50
213	$1.10 multicoloured	2·00	2·50
211/13	*Set of 3*	4·25	5·00

(Des PCS Studios. Litho Leigh-Mardon Ltd, Melbourne)

1989 (9 Nov). 75th Anniv of Destruction of German Cruiser *Emden*. T **50** and similar horiz designs. Multicoloured. P 13½×14.

214	40c. Type **50**	1·75	1·75
	a. Horiz strip of 4, Nos. 214/17, with central label	7·50	7·50
215	70c. *Emden* (German cruiser)	2·00	2·00
216	$1 *Emden's* steam launch	2·25	2·25
217	$1.10 H.M.A.S. *Sydney* (1914) and crest	2·25	2·25
214/17	*Set of 4*	7·50	7·50
MS218	145×90 *mm*. Nos. 214/17	7·50	7·50

Nos. 214/17 were printed together, *se-tenant*, in horizontal strips of four stamps and one label throughout the sheet.

51 Xanthid Crab

52 Captain Keeling and *Hector*, 1609

(Des Jill Ruse. Litho Leigh-Mardon Ltd, Melbourne)

1990 (31 May). Cocos Islands Crabs. T **51** and similar multicoloured designs. P 14½.

219	45c. Type **51**	2·00	75
220	75c. Ghost Crab	2·75	2·00
221	$1 Red-backed Mud Crab	3·00	2·25
222	$1.30 Coconut Crab (*vert*)	3·25	3·00
219/22	*Set of 4*	10·00	7·25

(Des Elizabeth and R. Innes. Litho Note Ptg Branch, Reserve Bank of Australia)

1990 (24 Aug). Navigators of the Pacific. T **52** and similar horiz designs. P 14½.

223	45c. dull mauve	2·75	1·25
224	75c. dull mauve and pale azure	3·00	3·25
225	$1 dull mauve and pale stone	3·50	3·75
226	$1.30 dull mauve and pale buff	4·25	5·00
223/6	*Set of 4*	12·00	12·00
MS227	120×95 *mm*. As Nos. 223/6, but imperf	7·50	9·00

Designs:—75c. Captain Fitzroy and H.M.S. *Beagle*, 1836; $1 Captain Belcher and H.M.S. *Samarang*, 1846; $1.30, Captain Fremantle and H.M.S. *Juno*, 1857.

(**53**)

(**54**)

(Des Elizabeth Innes (No. **MS**229) Litho Western Australian Govt Ptg Division, Perth)

1990 (3 Sept). "New Zealand 1990" International Stamp Exhibition, Auckland. No. 188 optd with T **53** in red and miniature sheet containing designs as Nos. 194, 199 and 201.

228	70c. scarlet, black and bluish grey	4·25	4·50
MS229	127×90 *mm*. As Nos. 194, 199 and 201, but self-adhesive. Roul 9	8·00	9·50

Nos. 228/9 were available at the Exhibition from 24 August 1990, but were not sold locally until 3 September.

1990 (11 Dec). No. 187 surch with T **54** in deep ultramarine by Western Australian Govt Ptg Division, Perth.

230	$5 on 65c. ultramarine, black and pale grey-lilac	17·00	19·00

55 Coco Atoll from West and Star

(Des Stylegraphics, Perth. Litho Scott Four-Colour Print, Perth)

1990 (12 Dec). Christmas. T **55** and similar square designs. Multicoloured. Roul 5.

231	40c. Type **55**	80	1·25
	a. Booklet pane. No. 231×4 and No. 232×2 plus 6 labels	13·00	
	b. Booklet pane. No. 231×10 plus 2 labels	16·00	
232	70c. Cocos atoll from south	1·75	2·75
233	$1.30 Cocos atoll from east	3·00	4·00
231/3	*Set of 3*	5·00	7·25

Booklet panes Nos. 231a/b have the upper and lower edges imperforate, producing stamps imperforate at top or bottom, and there are margins at left and right.

(**56**)

(**57**)

1990 (12 Dec)–**91**. Nos. 140/1, 143 and 146/7 surch by Western Australian Govt Ptg Division.

*(a) With T **56** in blue*

234	(43c.) on 10c. Soldier Cone (*Conus miles*)	35·00	4·00

(b) No. 234 with additional cross-hatching overprinted on the original face value in blue

235	(43c.) on 10c. Soldier Cone (*Conus miles*) (7.3.91)	2·75	2·00

*(c) As T **57** with original face value obliterated*

236	(1c.) on 30c. Lajonkaire's Turban (*Turbo lajonkairii*) (Type **57**) (B.) (21.1.91)	2·00	2·75
237	70c. on 60c. Minstrel Cowrie (*Cypraea histrio*) ("ZONE 1") (7.3.91)	2·75	2·75
238	80c. on 50c. Fluted Giant Clam or Scaled Tridacna (*Tridacna squamosa*) ("ZONE 2") (7.3.91)	3·00	3·50
239	$1.20 on 15c. Marlin-spike Auger (*Terebra maculata*) ("ZONE 5") (7.3.91)	3·50	3·75
234/9	*Set of 6*	45·00	17·00

58 Beaded Sea Star

59 Cocos Islands

(Des Jill Ruse. Litho Leigh-Mardon Ltd, Melbourne)

1991 (28 Feb). Starfish and Sea Urchins. T **58** and similar horiz designs. Multicoloured. P 14½.

240	45c. Type **58**	1·25	75
241	75c. Feather Star	2·00	2·25
242	$1 Slate Pencil Urchin	2·00	2·25
243	$1.30 Globose Sea Urchin	2·75	3·25
240/3	*Set of 4*	7·25	7·75

(Des P. Cunningham. Litho Leigh-Mardon Ltd, Melbourne)

1991 (16 Apr). Malay Hari Raya Festival. T **59** and similar horiz designs. Multicoloured. P 14½.

244	45c. Type **59**	1·00	65
245	75c. Island house	1·75	2·25
246	$1.30 Islands scene	2·50	3·25
244/6	*Set of 3*	4·75	5·50

60 Child Praying

61 *Lybia tessellata*

(Des R. Honisett. Litho Leigh-Mardon Ltd, Melbourne)

1991 (6 Nov). Christmas. T **60** and similar vert designs. Multicoloured. P 15½.

247	38c. Type **60**	1·00	80
248	43c. Child dreaming of Christmas Day	1·00	80
249	$1 Child singing	1·75	2·50
250	$1.20 Child fascinated by decorations	1·75	4·00
247/50	*Set of* 4	5·00	7·25
MS251	118×74 *mm.* 38c., 43c., $1, $1.20, Local children's choir	5·00	8·00

The four values in **MS**251 form a composite design.

(Des Jane Moore. Litho Leigh-Mardon Ltd, Melbourne)

1992 (28 Feb–11 Aug). Crustaceans. T **61** and similar multicoloured designs. P 14½.

252	5c. Type **61**	1·25	1·60
253	10c. *Pilodius areolatus* (11.8)	1·75	1·75
254	20c. *Trizopagurus strigatus*	2·00	2·00
255	30c. *Lophozozymus pulchellus* (11.8)	2·50	2·50
256	40c. *Thalamitoides quadridens*	2·50	2·50
257	45c. *Calcinus elegans* (*vert*)	2·50	2·50
258	50c. *Clibarius humilis* (11.8)	2·75	2·75
259	60c. *Trapezia rufopunctata* (*vert*)	3·00	3·00
260	80c. *Pylopaguropsis magnimanus* (*vert*) (11.8)	3·50	4·00
261	$1 *Trapezia ferruginea* (*vert*) (11.8)	3·50	4·00
262	$2 *Trapezia guttata* (*vert*) (11.8)	4·50	5·50
263	$3 *Trapezia cymodoce* (*vert*)	4·75	5·50
252/63	*Set of* 12	32·00	35·00

62 *Santa Maria*

63 Banded Rail Searching for Food

(Des Philatelic Studios, Melbourne. Litho Leigh-Mardon Ltd, Melbourne)

1992 (22 May). 500th Anniv of Discovery of America by Columbus. P 14½.

264	**62** $1.05 multicoloured	3·75	4·25

(Des G. Drummond. Litho Questa)

1992 (11 June). Endangered Species. Banded Rail. T **63** and similar horiz designs. Multicoloured. P 14.

265	10c. Type **63**	70	85
	a. Strip of 4. Nos. 265/8	4·00	4·50
266	15c. Banded Rail with chick	90	1·10
267	30c. Two Rails drinking	1·25	1·40
268	45c. Rail and nest	1·50	1·60
265/8	*Set of* 4	4·00	4·50
MS269	165×78 *mm.* 45c. Two Rails by pool; 85c. Chick hatching; $1.20, Head of Rail	12·00	12·00

Nos. 265/8 were printed together, *se-tenant*, in horizontal or vertical strips of four throughout the sheet.

64 R.A.F Spitfires on Island Airstrip

65 Waves breaking on Reef

(Des Philatelic Studios, Melbourne. Litho Leigh-Mardon Ltd, Melbourne)

1992 (13 Oct). 50th Anniv of Second World War. T **64** and similar horiz designs. Multicoloured. P 14½.

270	45c. Type **64**	3·00	1·50
271	85c. Japanese aircraft bombing Kampong	4·00	3·75
272	$1.20 R.A.F. Sunderland (flying boat)	5·00	5·50
270/2	*Set of* 3	11·00	9·75

(Des Philatelic Studios, Melbourne. Litho Leigh-Mardon Ltd, Melbourne)

1992 (11 Nov). Christmas. T **65** and similar vert designs. Multicoloured. P 14½.

273	40c. Type **65**	1·50	80
274	80c. Direction Island	3·25	3·50
275	$1 Moorish Idols (fish) and coral	3·25	3·50
273/5	*Set of* 3	7·25	7·00

One imperforate sheet of No. 275 has been reported. Its status is uncertain.

66 *Lobophyllia hemprichii*

67 Plastic 5r. Token

(Litho Leigh-Mardon Ltd, Melbourne)

1993 (28 Jan). Corals. T **66** and similar vert designs. Multicoloured. P 14½.

276	45c. Type **66**	55	55
277	85c. *Pocillopora eydouxi*	80	1·75
278	$1.05 *Fungia scutaria*	1·25	2·00
279	$1.20 *Sarcophyton* sp	1·25	2·25
276/9	*Set of* 4	3·50	6·00

One imperforate sheet of Nos. 277 has been reported. It's status is uncertain.

(Des Sandra Harman. Litho Leigh-Mardon Ltd, Melbourne)

1993 (30 Mar). Early Cocos (Keeling) Islands Currency. T **67** and similar vert designs. Multicoloured. P 14½.

280	45c. Type **67**	1·60	80
281	85c. 1968 1r. plastic token	2·25	2·50
282	$1.05 1977 150r. commemorative gold coin	2·75	3·00
283	$1.20 1910 plastic token	2·75	3·50
280/3	*Set of* 4	8·50	8·75

One imperforate sheet of No. 283 has been reported. Its status is uncertain.

68 Primary School Pupil

69 Lifeboat and Crippled Yacht

(Des Philatelic Studios. Litho Leigh-Mardon Ltd, Melbourne)

1993 (1 June). Education. T **68** and similar vert designs. Multicoloured. P 14½.

284	5c. Type **68**	50	85
285	45c. Secondary school pupil	1·25	60
286	85c. Learning traditional crafts	2·25	2·25
287	$1.05 Learning office skills	2·75	3·50
288	$1.20 Seaman training	3·25	3·75
284/8	*Set of* 5	9·00	9·75

(Des Philatelic Studios. Litho Leigh-Mardon Ltd, Melbourne)

1993 (17 Aug). Air-Sea Rescue. T **69** and similar horiz designs. Multicoloured. P 14½.

289	45c. Type **69**	3·00	1·60
290	85c. *Westwind Seascan* (aircraft)	4·50	4·50
291	$1.05 *R.J. Hawke* (ferry)	5·00	6·00
289/91	*Set of* 3	11·00	11·00
MS292	135×61 *mm.* Nos. 289/91	12·00	13·00

70 Peace Doves

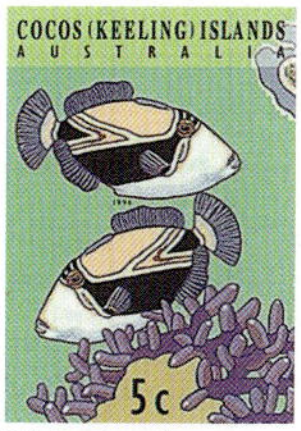

71 Rectangle Triggerfish and Coral

(Des Philatelic Studios. Litho Leigh-Mardon Ltd, Melbourne)

1993 (26 Oct). Christmas. P 14½.

293	**70**	40c. multicoloured	1·75	80
294		80c. multicoloured	3·00	3·50
295		$1 multicoloured	3·00	3·50
293/5 *Set of 3*			7·00	7·00

On 1 January 1994 responsibility for the Cocos (Keeling) Islands postal service passed from the territorial administration to Australia Post. In consequence Nos. 296/315 and all subsequent issues are valid for postal purposes in both Cocos (Keeling) Islands and Australia. The stamps of Australia also became valid for use from Cocos (Keeling) Islands.

(Des Sue Passmore. Litho McPherson's Ptg Group, Mulgrave)

1994 (17 Feb). Transfer of Postal Service to Australia Post. T **71** and similar vert designs. Multicoloured. P 14½×14.

296	5c. Type **71**	35	45
	a. Sheetlet of 20. Nos. 296/315	8·50	10·00
297	5c. Three Rectangle Triggerfish and map section	35	45
298	5c. Two Rectangle Triggerfish and map section	35	45
299	5c. Two Rectangle Triggerfish, map section and red coral	35	45
300	5c. Rectangle Triggerfish with red and brown corals	35	45
301	10c. Green Turtles on beach	35	45
302	10c. Two Green Turtles	35	45
303	10c. Crowd of young Green Turtles	35	45
304	10c. Green Turtle and map section	35	45
305	10c. Green Turtle, Pyramid Butterflyfish and map section	35	45
306	20c. Three Pyramid Butterflyfish and map section	55	65
307	20c. Pyramid Butterflyfish with brown coral	55	65
308	20c. Two Pyramid Butterflyfish and coral	55	65
309	20c. Three Pyramid Butterflyfish and coral	55	65
310	20c. Coral, Pyramid Butterflyfish and map section	55	65
311	45c. Jukongs with map of airport	60	70
	a. Horiz strip of 5. Nos. 311/15	2·75	3·25
312	45c. Two jukongs with red or blue sails and map section	60	70
313	45c. Jukong in shallows	60	70
314	45c. Two jukongs with red or yellow sails and map section	60	70
315	45c. Two jukongs, one with blue jib, and map section	60	70
296/315 *Set of 20*		8·50	10·00

Nos. 296/315 were printed together, *se-tenant*, in sheetlets of 20 with inscriptions on the sheet margins and the backgrounds forming a composite map. Nos. 311/15 were also available printed together, *se-tenant*, in horizontal strips of five in sheets of 100.

72 Prabu Abjasa Puppet

73 Angel Playing Harp

(Des Josephine Muré. Litho McPherson's Ptg Group, Mulgrave)

1994 (16 June). Shadow Puppets. T **72** and similar vert designs. Multicoloured. P 14½×14.

316	45c. Type **72**	40	40
317	90c. Prabu Pandu	70	1·00
318	$1 Judistra	80	1·00
319	$1.35 Abimanju	95	2·25
316/19 *Set of 4*		2·50	4·25

(Des Tracie Grimwood. Litho McPherson's Ptg Group, Mulgrave)

1994 (31 Oct). Seasonal Festivals. T **73** and similar horiz designs. Multicoloured. P 14×14½.

320	40c. Type **73**	50	50
321	45c. Wise Man holding gift	55	50
322	80c. Mosque at night	1·00	1·75
320/2 *Set of 3*		1·90	2·50

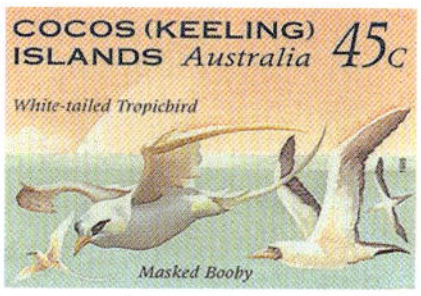

74 White-tailed Tropic Bird and Blue-faced Booby

75 Yellow Crazy Ant

(Des Lisa Christensen and B. Wood. Litho McPherson's Ptg Group, Mulgrave)

1995 (16 Mar). Sea-birds of North Keeling Island. T **74** and similar horiz design. Multicoloured. P 14×14½.

323	45c. Type **74**	75	50
324	85c. Great Frigate Bird and White Tern	1·00	1·50
MS325	106×70 *mm*. Nos. 323/4	1·75	2·50

No. **MS**325 also exists overprinted with the "JAKARTA 95" logo for sale at this exhibition.

(Des Sue Maddern. Litho McPherson's Ptg Group, Mulgrave)

1995 (13 July). Insects. T **75** and similar vert designs. Multicoloured. P 14½×14.

326	45c. Type **75**	1·00	1·25
	a. Horiz strip of 5. Nos. 326/30	4·50	5·50
327	45c. Aedes Mosquito	1·00	1·25
328	45c. Hawk Moth	1·00	1·25
329	45c. Scarab Beetle	1·00	1·25
330	45c. Lauxaniid Fly	1·00	1·25
331	$1.20 Common Eggfly (butterfly)	1·50	1·75
326/31 *Set of 6*		6·00	7·00

Nos. 326/30 were printed together, *se-tenant*, in horizontal strips of five throughout the sheet, with the backgrounds forming a composite design.

76 Saddle Butterflyfish

77 Members of Malay Community

(Des M. Baker and Sandra Harman (5c., 75c., 90c., $1, $1.20), M. Baker and Dianne Cook (70c., 95c., $5), M. Baker and Sophie Byass (others). Litho SNP Cambec (40c., 80c., $1.05) or McPherson's Ptg Group, Mulgrave (others))

1995 (1 Nov)–**2001**. Marine Life. T **76** and similar horiz designs. Multicoloured. P 14×14½.

332	5c. Redspot Wrasse (14.8.97)	25	40
333	30c. Blue-throated Triggerfish ("Gilded Triggerfish") (15.8.96)	50	65
334	40c. Type **76**	1·75	70
335	45c. Arc-eyed Hawkfish (15.8.96)	1·00	1·00
335*a*	45c. Wideband Fusilier (8.2.01)	1·00	1·25
	ab. Block of 4. Nos. 335*a/d*	3·50	4·50
335*b*	45c. Striped Surgeonfish (8.2.01)	1·00	1·25
335*c*	45c. Orangeband Surgeonfish (8.2.01)	1·00	1·25
335*d*	45c. Indo-Pacific Sergeant (8.2.01)	1·00	1·25
335*e*	70c. Crowned Squirrelfish (13.8.98)	1·00	1·25
336	75c. Orangespine Unicornfish (14.8.97)	1·00	1·25
337	80c. Blue Tang	2·50	1·00
338	85c. Juvenile Twin-spotted Wrasse ("Humphead Wrasse") (15.8.96)	1·00	1·00
339	90c. Threadfin Butterflyfish (14.8.97)	1·00	1·50
339*a*	95c. Sixstripe Wrasse (13.8.98)	1·00	1·25
340	$1 Bluestripe Snapper (14.8.97)	1·25	1·25
341	$1.05 Longnosed Butterflyfish	2·50	1·50
342	$1.20 Freckled Hawkfish (14.8.97)	1·25	1·50
343	$2 Powder-blue Surgeonfish (15.8.96)	1·75	2·25
343*a*	$5 Goldback Anthias (13.8.98)	3·50	4·50
332/43*a* *Set of 19*		23·00	23·00

(Des Melinda Whitechurch and Jacqui Young. Litho McPherson's Ptg Group, Mulgrave)

1996 (19 Feb). Hari Raya Puasa Festival. T **77** and similar square designs. Multicoloured. P 14½.

344	45c. Type **77**	55	50
345	75c. Beating drums	1·10	1·75
346	85c. Preparing festival meal	1·10	1·75
344/6	*Set of* 3	2·50	3·50

78 Black Rhinoceros with Calf

79 Dancers and Tambourine

(Des Kerry Argent and Lisa Christensen. Litho Canberra Press)

1996 (13 June). Cocos Quarantine Station. T **78** and similar vert designs. Multicoloured. P 14½×14.

347	45c. Type **78**	2·50	1·25
348	50c. Alpacas	1·25	1·50
349	$1.05 Boran cattle	2·00	2·50
350	$1.20 Ostrich with chicks	3·00	3·00
347/50	*Set of* 4	8·00	7·50

(Des MYD Graphic. Litho SNP Cambec)

1997 (6 Jan). Hari Raya Puasa Festival. T **79** and similar square designs. Multicoloured. P 14½.

351	45c. Type **79**	55	50
352	75c. Girl clapping and sailing dinghies	80	1·40
353	85c. Dancers on beach and food	1·00	1·40
351/3	*Set of* 3	2·10	3·00

80 "Wrapped Present" (Lazina Brian)

81 Preparing Food on Beach

(Adapted Dianne Cook. Litho SNP Cambec)

1998 (22 Jan). Hari Raya Puasa Festival. T **80** and similar vert designs showing paintings by children. Multicoloured. P 14½×14.

354	45c. Type **80**	90	1·10
	a. Horiz strip of 5. Nos. 354/8	4·00	5·00
355	45c. "Mosque" (Azran Jim)	90	1·10
356	45c. "Cocos Malay Woman" (Kate Gossage)	90	1·10
357	45c. "Yacht" (Matt Harber)	90	1·10
358	45c. "People dancing" (Rakin Chongkin)	90	1·10
354/8	*Set of* 5	4·00	5·00

Nos. 354/8 were printed together, *se-tenant*, in horizontal strips of five throughout the sheet.

(Des Jacqui Young and Sandra Harman. Litho SNP Ausprint)

1999 (11 Feb). Hari Raya Puasa Festival. T **81** and similar vert designs. Multicoloured. P 14½×14.

359	45c. Type **81**	70	85
	a. Horiz strip of 5. Nos. 359/63	3·25	3·75
360	45c. Woman with child and jukongs on beach	70	85
361	45c. Jukongs and palm fronds	70	85
362	45c. Two men watching jukongs	70	85
363	45c. Jukong and white flowers	70	85
359/63	*Set of* 5	3·25	3·75

Nos. 359/63 were printed together, *se-tenant*, in horizontal strips of five throughout the sheet.

82 Jukong (Cocos sailing boat)

83 Ratma Anthoney

(Des Melinda Coombes. Litho SNP Ausprint)

1999 (17 June). Island Wildlife. T **82** and similar horiz designs. Multicoloured. P 14×14½.

364	5c. Type **82**	75	85
	a. Sheetlet of 20. Nos. 364/83	15·00	17·00
365	5c. Bennett's and Ornate Butterflyfish	75	85
366	5c. Green and Hawksbill Turtles	75	85
367	5c. Yellow-tailed Anemonefish and various Butterflyfish	75	85
368	5c. Hump-headed Wrasse	75	85
369	10c. Yacht, Direction Island	75	85
370	10c. Black-backed Butterflyfish	75	85
371	10c. Moorish Idols	75	85
372	10c. *Pseudoanthias cooperi* (fish)	75	85
373	10c. Red-tailed Tropic Birds	75	85
374	25c. Blue-faced Booby	85	95
375	25c. Lesser Wanderer (butterfly)	85	95
376	25c. Lesser and Greater Frigate Birds	85	95
377	25c. *Hippotion velox* (moth)	85	95
378	25c. Common Eggfly (butterfly)	85	95
379	45c. White Tern	95	1·10
380	45c. Red-tailed Tropic Bird and Great Frigate Bird	95	1·10
381	45c. Chinese Rose	95	1·10
382	45c. Meadow Argus (butterfly)	95	1·10
383	45c. Sea Hibiscus	95	1·10
364/83	*Set of* 20	15·00	17·00

Nos. 364/83 were printed together, *se-tenant*, in sheetlets of 20 with the backgrounds forming a composite design.

(Des Lisa Christensen. Litho SNP Ausprint)

2000 (13 Apr). New Millennium. "Face of Cocos (Keeling) Islands". T **83** and similar horiz designs. Multicoloured. P 14×14½.

384	45c. Type **83**	70	90
	a. Horiz strip of 5. Nos. 384/8	3·25	4·00
385	45c. Nakia Haji Dolman (schoolgirl)	70	90
386	45c. Muller Eymin (elderly man)	70	90
387	45c. Courtney Press (toddler)	70	90
388	45c. Mhd. Abu-Yazid (schoolboy)	70	90
384/8	*Set of* 5	3·25	4·00

Nos. 384/8 were printed together, *se-tenant*, as horizontal strips of five in sheets of 50 (2×25).

84 Little Nipper (crab)

85 Loggerhead Turtle

(Des Deidre Hunt. Litho SNP Ausprint)

2000 (20 June). Endangered Species. Crabs of Cocos (Keeling) Islands. T **84** and similar horiz designs. Multicoloured. P 14×14½.

389	5c. Type **84**	75	85
	a. Horiz pair. Nos. 389/90	1·50	1·60
390	5c. Purple Crab	75	85
391	45c. Smooth-handed Ghost Crab	1·00	1·25
	a. Horiz pair. Nos. 391/2	2·00	2·50
392	45c. Horn-eyed Ghost Crab	1·00	1·25
389/92	*Set of* 4	3·25	3·75

Nos. 389/90 and 391/2 were each printed together, *se-tenant*, in horizontal pairs throughout the sheets.

(Des E. Guiotto. Litho McPhersons)

2002 (1 Oct). Turtles. T **85** and similar horiz designs. Phosphorised paper. Multicoloured. P 14×14½.

393	45c. Type **85**	1·75	1·75
	a. Block of 4. Nos. 393/6	6·25	6·25
394	45c. Hawksbill Turtle	1·75	1·75
395	45c. Leatherback Turtle	1·75	1·75
396	45c. Green Turtle	1·75	1·75
393/6	*Set of* 4	6·25	6·25

Nos. 393/6 were printed together in sheets of 50, two panes (5×5), containing ten *se-tenant* blocks of four and ten single stamps.

86 Eastern Reef Egret

87 Queen Elizabeth II and Cocos Malay Musicians

(Des K. Stead. Litho SNP Sprint)

2003 (17 June). Shoreline Birds. T **86** and similar horiz designs. Multicoloured. P 14×14½.

397	50c. Type **86**	2·75	2·25
	a. Horiz strip of 4. Nos. 397/400	10·00	8·00
398	50c. Sooty Tern	2·75	2·25
399	50c. Ruddy Turnstone	2·75	2·25
400	50c. Whimbrel	2·75	2·25
397/400 *Set of* 4		10·00	8·00

Nos. 397/400 were printed together, *se-tenant*, in horizontal strips of four throughout the sheet, each strip forming a composite background design of a shoreline.

(Des Melinda Coombes. Litho SNP Sprint)

2004 (16 Mar). 50th Anniv of Royal Tour to Australia. Visit of Queen Elizabeth II to Cocos (Keeling) Islands. T **87** and similar horiz designs. Multicoloured. P 14×14½.

401	50c. Type **87**	1·75	1·75
	a. Pair. Nos. 401/2	3·50	3·50
402	50c. Queen and *Gothic* (liner acting as Royal Yacht)	1·75	1·75
403	$1 Queen and Clunies Ross (Oceania) House	2·75	2·75
404	$1.45 Queen and model jukong (Cocos sailing boat)	3·00	3·00
401/4 *Set of* 4		8·25	8·25
MS405 135×72 *mm.* Nos. 401/4		8·25	8·75

Nos. 401/2 were printed together, *se-tenant*, in horizontal and vertical pairs throughout the sheet.

No. **MS**405 also exists overprinted for World Stamp Championship 2004 Singapore.

88 Blacktip Reef Shark

89 Frigate Bird

(Des E. Guiotto. Litho SEP Sprint)

2005 (21 June). Reef Sharks. T **88** and similar horiz designs. Multicoloured. Phosphorised paper. P 14½×14.

406	50c. Type **88**	2·00	2·00
	a. Horiz pair. Nos. 406/7	4·00	4·00
407	50c. Two Grey Reef Sharks	2·00	2·00
408	$1 Two Blacktip Reef Sharks near atoll	3·25	3·25
409	$1.45 Grey Reef Shark	3·50	3·50
406/9 *Set of* 4		9·75	9·75

Nos. 406/7 were printed together, *se-tenant*, in horizontal pairs in sheets of 50 (2 panes of 25).

(Des Ego Guiotto and Trevor Marriot. Litho SEP Sprint)

2006 (13 June). Coral Reefs. T **89** and similar vert designs. Multicoloured. P 14½×14.

410	10c. Type **89**	1·00	1·00
	a. Sheetlet of 20. Nos. 410/29	22·00	22·00
411	10c. Booby	1·00	1·00
412	10c. Sooty Terns	1·00	1·00
413	10c. White Terns	1·00	1·00
414	10c. Rupous Night-heron	1·00	1·00
415	25c. Threadfin Butterflyfish	1·10	1·10
416	25c. Saddley Butterflyfish	1·10	1·10
417	25c. Orangehand Surgeonfish	1·10	1·10
418	25c. Manta Ray	1·10	1·10
419	25c. Scrawled Butterflyfish	1·10	1·10
420	25c. Blue Tang	1·10	1·10
421	25c. Picasso Triggerfish and Wrasse	1·10	1·10
422	25c. Turtle	1·10	1·10
423	25c. Moorish Idol	1·10	1·10
424	25c. Longnose Butterflyfish	1·10	1·10
425	50c. Seychelles Butterflyfish	1·60	1·60
426	50c. Powderblue Surgeonfish	1·60	1·60
427	50c. Orange-lined Triggerfish and Starfish	1·60	1·60
428	50c. Evan's Anthias and Sea |Cucumber	1·60	1·60
429	50c. Yellow and Blue Damselfish	1·60	1·60
410/29 *Set of* 20		22·00	22·00

Nos. 410/29 were printed together, *se-tenant*, in sheetlets of 20, each sheetlet forming a composite background design showing a coral reef and atoll.

90 Oriental Moonsnail

91 Chinese Pond Heron

(Des Lisa Christensen. Litho SEP Sprint)

2007 (20 Mar). Living Shells. T **90** and similar horiz designs. Multicoloured. P 14×14½.

430	50c. Type **90**	3·25	3·25
	a. Horiz pair. Nos. 430/1	6·50	6·50
431	50c. Pearly Nautilus	3·25	3·25
432	$1 Partridge Tun	5·50	4·25
433	$1.45 Giant Clam	7·00	8·00
430/3 *Set of* 4		17·00	17·00

Nos. 430/1 were printed together, *se-tenant*, in horizontal pairs in sheets of 50.

(Des Christopher Pope and Jo Muré. Litho SEP Sprint, Australia)

2008 (26 Feb). Visiting Birds. T **91** and similar vert designs. Multicoloured. P 14.

434	50c. Type **91**	3·25	3·25
	a. Pair. Nos. 434/5	6·50	6·50
435	50c. Black-winged Stilt	3·25	3·25
436	$1 White-breasted Waterhen	5·50	4·25
437	$1.45 Saunders' Tern	7·00	8·00
434/7 *Set of* 4		17·00	17·00

Nos. 434/5 were printed together, *se-tenant*, as horizontal and vertical pairs in sheets of 50 (2 panes 5×5).

92 Early 17th-century English East Indiaman

(Des Stacey Zass. Litho Energi Print)

2009 (21 Apr). 400th Anniv of First European Sighting of Cocos (Keeling) Islands by Captain William Keeling. T **92** and similar square designs. Multicoloured. P 14.

438	55c. Type **92**	3·00	3·00
	a. Horiz pair. Nos. 438/9	6·00	6·00
439	55c. Detail from Darwin's notebooks and sketch of fish (Charles Darwin's visit, 1836)	3·00	3·00
440	$1.10 Coconut labourer	4·75	4·25
441	$1.65 Dugong	6·00	7·00
438/41 *Set of* 4		15·00	15·00

Nos. 438/9 were printed together, *se-tenant*, as horizontal pairs in sheets of 50 containing two panes of 25 (5×5). On the top pane the left-hand stamp in all five horizontal rows is Type **92**, but on the lower pane it is No. 439.

93 *Hibiscus tiliaceus*

94 Jukongs

(Des Jo McAlpine. Litho McKellar Renown)

2010 (15 Sept). Flowers of Cocos (Keeling) Islands. T **93** and similar vert designs. Multicoloured. P 14½×14.

442	60c. Type **93**	3·25	3·25
	a. Horiz pair. Nos. 442/3	6·50	6·50
443	60c. *Ipomoea pes-caprae*	3·25	3·25
444	$1.20 *Morinda citrifolia*	5·00	5·00
	a. Horiz pair. Nos. 444/5	10·00	10·00
445	$1.20 *Suriana maritima*	5·00	5·00

442/5 *Set of 4*		15·00	15·00

Nos. 442/3 and 444/5 were each printed together, *se-tenant*, as horizontal pairs in sheets of 50.

(Des Rachelle Flynn. Litho RA Printing)

2011 (18 Jan). Boats. T **94** and similar vert designs. Multicoloured. P 14½×14.

446	60c. Type **94**	2·50	2·00
447	$1.20 Dinghy on beach	4·00	3·25
448	$1.80 Glass-bottom boat with canopy	5·00	5·00
449	$3 Catamaran	7·00	8·50
446/9 *Set of 4*		17·00	17·00

95 (*Actual size* 135×71 *mm*)

(Des Kevin Stead. Litho McKellar Renown)

2011 (30 Aug). 50th Anniv of Worldwide Fund for Nature (formerly World Wildlife Fund). Sheet 135×72 mm as **MS**360 of Australia. Multicoloured. P 14×14½.

MS450	**95** 60c.×4 Dugong (*Dugong dugon*) (Cocos (Keeling) Islands); Christmas Island Shrew (*Crocidura trichura*) (Christmas Island); Type **861** of Australia; Southern Elephant Seal (*Mirounga leonina*) (Australian Antarctic Territory)	7·50	8·50

No. **MS**450 differs from **MS**3640 of Australia in the sheet margins and in the order of the stamps within the miniature sheet (top left stamp Cocos (Keeling) Islands; top right Christmas Island; bottom left, Australia; bottom right, Australian Antarctic Territory).

96 Sea Cucumber
(*Theleriota ananas*)

(Des Lynette Traynor. Litho McKellar Renown)

2011 (6 Sept). 'Colours of Cocos (Keeling) Islands' (marine life). T **96** and similar vert designs. Multicoloured. P 14.

451	60c. Type **96**	1·75	1·75
	a. Sheetlet of 20. Nos. 451/70	32·00	32·00
452	60c. Fan Coral (*Melithaea* sp.) (bright blue background)	1·75	1·75
453	60c. Sea Cucumber (*Thelenota ananas*) (pink)	1·75	1·75
454	60c. Pink Anemonefish (*Amphiprion perideraion*) and coral	1·75	1·75
455	60c. Christmas Tree Worm (*Spirobranchus* sp.) (in close up)	1·75	1·75
456	60c. Mushroom Coral (*Fungia* sp.)	1·75	1·75
457	60c. Giant Clam (*Tridacna maxima*) in soft coral (*Sinularia* sp.)	1·75	1·75
458	60c. Spotfin Lionfish (*Pterois antennata*)	1·75	1·75
459	60c. Scribbled Filefish (*Aluterus scriptus*)	1·75	1·75
460	60c. Neon Fusilier (*Pterocaesio tile*)	1·75	1·75
461	60c. Fan Coral (*Melithaea* sp.) (dark blue background)	1·75	1·75
462	60c. Nudibranch (*Phyllidia* cf. *varicosa*)	1·75	1·75
463	60c. Pink Anemonefish (*Amphiprion peridiraeon*) (in close up)	1·75	1·75
464	60c. Two Christmas Tree Worms (*Spirobranchus* sp.)	1·75	1·75
465	60c. Forster's Hawkfish (*Paracirrhites forsteri*)	1·75	1·75
466	60c. Foliaceous Coral (*Echinopora lamellosa*)	1·75	1·75
467	60c. Durban Dancing Shrimp (*Rhinchocinetes durbanensis*)	1·75	1·75
468	60c. Magnificent Sea Anemone (*Heteractis magnifica*)	1·75	1·75
469	60c. Brain Coral (*Platygyra sinensis*)	1·75	1·75
470	60c. Crown of Thorns Sea Star (*Acanthaster planci*)	1·75	1·75
451/70 *Set of 20*		32·00	32·00

Nos. 451/70 were printed together, *se-tenant*, in sheets of 20.

97 Pier at Sunrise

(Des Jennifer Scalzo. Litho McKellar Renown)

2012 (22 May). Skies of Cocos. T **97** and similar horiz designs. Multicoloured. P 14×14½.

471	60c. Type **97**	1·75	1·40
472	$1.20 Sunrise over seashore	3·25	2·75
473	$1.80 Sunset over sandy beach with palm trees	4·75	4·75
474	$3 Sunset, two palm trees in foreground	7·50	8·50
471/4 *Set of 4*		16·00	16·00

98 Meadow Argus

(Des Sharon Rodziewicz. Litho RA Printing)

2012 (2 Aug). Butterflies. T **98** and similar horiz designs. Multicoloured. P 14×14½.

475	60c. Type **98**	2·25	2·25
	a. Horiz pair. Nos. 475/6	4·50	4·50
476	60c. Common Crow	2·25	2·25
477	$1.20 Australian Painted Lady	4·00	4·00
	a. Horiz pair. Nos. 477/8	8·00	8·00
478	$1.20 Varied Eggfly	4·00	4·00
475/8 *Set of 4*		11·50	11·50

Nos. 475/6 and 477/8 were each printed together, *se-tenant*, as horizontal pairs in sheets of 50 (2 panes of 25), giving 20 horizontal pairs and ten single stamps (Type **98** or No. 477).

99 Turtle and Diver

(Des John White. Litho RA Printing)

2013 (4 June). 50th Anniv of First Cocos (Keeling) Islands Stamps. T **99** and similar vert designs. Multicoloured. P 14½×14.

479	5c. Type **99**	30	75
480	60c. Canoe	1·75	1·00
481	$1 Windsurfer	2·75	2·25
482	$1.20 Coconut	3·00	2·75
483	$2 Heron	5·00	6·50
479/83 *Set of 5*		11·50	12·00
MS484	170×210 *mm*. Nos. 479/83	11·50	12·00

100 Landing Barrel Mail
and Barrel Mail Cancellation

(Des Melinda Coombes. Litho EGO)

2013 (6 Aug). Barrel Mail (c. 1909–54). T **100** and similar square design. Multicoloured. P 14.

485	60c. Type **100**	2·25	1·50
486	$3 Mail barrels, barrel mail cancellation and mailmen signalling passing ship	7·50	8·50

101 Cocos Islands on 17th-century Map

(Des Boschen Design. Litho RA Print)

2014 (24 June). Maps of Cocos Islands. T **101** and similar horiz designs. Multicoloured. P 14.

487	70c. Type **101**	2·50	2·50
488	70c. 18th-century map showing Nouvelle Hollande and Isles des Cocos	2·50	2·50
489	$1.40 19th-century map of Cocos or Keeling Islands	4·25	4·25
490	$2.10 Home Island on 20th-century map	6·00	6·00
487/90	*Set of 4*	14·00	14·00

Nos. 487/8 were printed together, *se-tenant*, as horizontal pairs in sheets of 50.

102 Australian Cruiser HMAS *Sydney*

(Des Stacey Zass, page12. Litho RA Print)

2014 (14 Oct). Centenary of the *Sydney/Emden Engagement* (Battle of Cocos). T **102** and similar square design. Multicoloured. P 14.

491	70c. Type **102**	1·90	1·90
492	$3.50 German cruiser SMS *Emden*	9·50	9·50

103 Herald Petrel (*Pterodroma heraldica*)

(Des Owen Bell (illustration) and John White (typography). Litho RA Printing)

2015 (24 Mar). Visiting Birds. T **103** and similar square designs. Multicoloured. P 14.

493	70c. Type **103**	1·10	1·10
494	70c. Oriental Pratincole (*Glareola maldivarum*)	1·10	1·10
495	70c. Little Curlew (*Numenius minutus*)	1·10	1·10
496	70c. Indian Yellow-nosed Albatross (*Thalassarche carteri*)	1·10	1·10
493/6	*Set of 4*	4·00	4·00

104 Island

(Des Lisa Christensen. Litho Bambra McKellar)

2015 (25 Aug). Islands of Cocos. T **104** and similar vert designs. Multicoloured. P 14½×14.

497	70c. Type **104**	1·10	1·10
	a. Horiz pair. Nos. 497/8	2·25	2·25
498	70c. Beach (in foreground) and island	1·10	1·10
499	$1.40 Island at sunset	2·25	2·25
	a. Horiz pair. Nos. 499/500	4·50	4·50
500	$1.40 Island (*different*)	2·25	2·25
497/500	*Set of 4*	6·00	6·00

Nos. 497/8 and 499/500 were each printed together, *se-tenant*, as horizontal pairs in sheets of 50 (2 panes 5×5), each sheet giving 20 horizontal pairs and ten single stamps (Type **104** or No. 499).

STAMP BOOKLETS

B **1** Prison Island

1990 (12 Dec). Christmas. Multicoloured cover, 92×74 mm, as Type B **1**. Panes attached by selvedge.

SB1	$3 booklet containing *se-tenant* pane of 6 (No. 231a)	13·00
SB2	$4 booklet containing pane of 10 (No. 231b)	16·00

B **2**

2013 (4 June). 50th Anniv of First Cocos (Keeling) Islands Stamps. Green cover, 160×70 mm, as Type B**2**. Panes attached by selvedge.

SB3	$3 booklet containing strip of 5 (No. 480)	£100

OFFICIAL STAMP

OFFICIAL PAID
MAINLAND
(O **1**)

1991 (25 Jan). No. 182 surch with Type O **1** in deep violet-blue.

O1	(43c.) on 90c. Coconut palm and mature nuts	†	90·00

No. O1 was only sold to the public cancelled-to-order and not in unused condition.

NAURU

Stamps of MARSHALL ISLANDS were used in Nauru from the opening of the German Colonial Post Office on 14 July 1908 until 8 September 1914.

Following the occupation by Australian forces on 6 November 1914 the "N.W. PACIFIC ISLANDS" overprints on Australia (see NEW GUINEA) were used from 2 January 1915.

PRICES FOR STAMPS ON COVER TO 1945		
Nos.	1/12	*from*×10
Nos.	13/16	*from*×4
Nos.	17/25	—
Nos.	26/39	*from*×6
Nos.	40/3	*from*×10
Nos.	44/7	*from*×15

BRITISH MANDATE

NAURU (1) NAURU (2) NAURU (3)

1916 (2 Sept)–**23**. Stamps of Great Britain (1912–22) over-printed at Somerset House.

(a) With T **1** *(12½ mm long) at foot*

1	½d. yellow-green	2·25	11·00
	a. "NAUP.U"	£450	
	b. Double opt, one albino	60·00	
	c. Triple opt, two albino	£400	
2	1d. bright scarlet	2·50	14·00
	a. "NAUP.U"	£700	£1300
	b. Double opt, one albino	£325	
2*c*	1d. carmine-red	21·00	
	cb. Double opt, one albino	£225	
3	1½d. red-brown (1923)	55·00	85·00
4	2d. orange (Die I)	2·00	13·00
	a. "NAUP.U"	£425	£950
	b. Double opt, one albino	£110	
	c. Triple opt, two albino	£425	
	y. Wmk inverted and reversed	£120	
5	2d. orange (Die II) (1923)	70·00	£100
6	2½d. blue	2·75	7·00
	a. "NAUP.U"	£475	£1000
	b. Double opt, one albino	£225	
7	3d. bluish violet	2·00	6·00
	a. "NAUP.U"	£475	£1000
	b. Double opt, one albino	£350	
8	4d. slate-green	2·00	8·50
	a. "NAUP.U"	£200	£1600
	b. Double opt, one albino	£225	
9	5d. yellow-brown	2·25	10·00
	a. "NAUP.U"	£2250	
	b. Double opt, one albino	£180	
10	6d. purple (*chalk-surfaced paper*)	7·50	10·00
	a. "NAUP.U"	£1600	
	b. Double opt, one albino	£350	
11	9d. agate	8·50	23·00
	a. Double opt, one albino	£375	
12	1s. bistre-brown	7·00	19·00
	a. Double opt, one albino	£400	
	s. Optd "Specimen"	£130	
1/12 *Set of 11*		85·00	£190

(b) With T **2** *(13½ mm long) at centre (1923)*

13	½d. green	4·00	55·00
14	1d. scarlet	19·00	45·00
15	1½d. red-brown	28·00	55·00
	a. Double opt, one albino	£225	
16	2d. orange (Die II)	30·00	80·00
13/16 *Set of 4*		70·00	£200

The "NAUP.U" errors occur on R. 6/2 from Control I 16 only. The ink used on this batch of overprints was shiny jet-black.

There is a constant variety consisting of short left stroke to "N" which occurs at R. 1/8 on Nos. 1, 2, 4 (£30 *each*); 2*c* (£75); 3 (£175); 5 (£200); 6, 7 (£40 *each*); 8, 9, 10 (£60 *each*); 11, 12 (£85 *each*). All unused prices.

(c) With T **3**

(i) Waterlow printing

17	5s. rose-carmine	£2500	£2250
	s. Optd "Specimen"	£1800	
18	10s. indigo-blue (R.)	£10000	£5000
	a. Double opt, one albino	£13000	£7000
	s. Optd "Specimen"	£1000	
	sa. Ditto "NAURU" double, one albino	£2500	

(ii) De La Rue printing

19	2s.6d. sepia-brown (*shades*)	£600	£1600
	a. Double opt, one albino	£1700	
	b. Treble opt, two albino	£1800	
	s. Optd "Specimen"	£350	
20	2s.6d. yellow-brown (*shades*)	70·00	£120
21	2s.6d. brown (*shades*)	70·00	£120
	a. Re-entry (R. 2/1)	£6000	
22	5s. bright carmine (*shades*)	£100	£150
	a. Treble opt, two albino	£1500	
	s. Optd "Specimen"	£325	
	sa. Ditto "NAURU" double, one albino	£1500	£700
23	10s. pale blue (R.)	£250	£325
	a. Treble opt (Blk.+R.+albino)	£3750	
	b. Double opt, one albino	£1600	
	c. Treble opt, two albino	£1700	
23*d*	10s. deep bright blue (R.)	£500	£700

(iii) Bradbury, Wilkinson printing (1919)

24	2s.6d. chocolate-brown	90·00	£200
	b. Double opt, one albino	£500	
25	2s.6d. pale brown	80·00	£190
	a. Double opt, one albino	£500	

The initial printing of the 2s.6d. to 10s. values, made in Sept 1915 but not known to have been issued before 2 Sept 1916, comprised 1½ sheets each of the 2s.6d. (No. 19) and 10s. (No. 18) and 3 sheets of the 5s. (No. 17), as well as the supply of "Specimens", where the 5s. value was mostly from the De La Rue printing (No. 22).

The original supply of the 2s.6d. value (No. 19) included distinct shade variants, covered by "sepia-brown (*shades*)". The "Specimens" are mostly in a deeper shade than the issued stamp. One half-sheet of 20 was quite deep, and only appears to exist cancelled "SE 2 16", apart from a mint block of four in the Royal Collection. The full sheet of 40 was in a slightly paler shade and included 12 double, one albino and eight treble, two albino varieties. A few sheets in sepia-brown shades were also included in later supplies of the 2s.6d. value, but these were mostly in shades of yellow-brown (No. 20) and brown (No. 21).

Examples of most values between Nos. 1 and 25 are known showing a forged P.O. Pleasant Island postmark dated "NO 2 21".

AUSTRALIAN MANDATE

4 *Century* (freighter)

(Des R. A. Harrison. Eng T. S. Harrison. Recess Note Printing Branch of the Treasury, Melbourne and from 1926 by the Commonwealth Bank of Australia)

1924–48. No wmk. P 11.

A. Rough surfaced, greyish paper (1924–34)

26A	4	½d. chestnut	2·55	2·75
27A		1d. green	3·50	2·75
28A		1½d. scarlet	4·00	4·00
29A		2d. orange	4·00	19·00
30A		2½d. slate-blue	6·00	25·00
		c. Greenish blue (1934)	17·00	30·00
31A		3d. pale blue	4·00	13·00
32A		4d. olive-green	7·50	27·00
33A		5d. brown	4·25	7·00
34A		6d. dull violet	4·75	20·00
35A		9d. olive-brown	9·50	19·00
36A		1s. brown-lake	6·50	13·00
37A		2s.6d. grey-green	32·00	55·00
38A		5s. claret	50·00	£110
39A		10s. yellow	£130	£190
26A/39A *Set of 14*			£225	£450

B. Shiny surfaced, white paper (1937–48)

26B	4	½d. chestnut	4·00	13·00
		c. Perf 14 (1947)	1·60	10·00
27B		1d. green	2·50	3·00
28B		1½d. scarlet	1·00	1·50
29B		2d. orange	5·50	8·00
30B		2½d. dull blue (1948)	4·50	4·00
		a. Imperf between (vert pair)	£17000	£18000
		b. Imperf between (horiz pair)	£17000	£18000
31B		3d. greenish grey (1947)	6·50	22·00
32B		4d. olive-green	6·50	13·00
33B		5d. brown	12·00	4·00
34B		6d. dull violet	11·00	5·00
35B		9d. olive-brown	12·00	21·00
36B		1s. brown-lake	13·00	2·75
37B		2s.6d. grey-green	32·00	35·00
38B		5s. claret	38·00	50·00
39B		10s. yellow	85·00	£100
26B/39B *Set of 14*			£200	£225

(5)

6

1935 (12 July). Silver Jubilee. T **4** (shiny surfaced, white paper) optd with T **5**.

40	1½d. scarlet	75	80
41	2d. orange	1·50	4·25
42	2½d. dull blue	1·50	1·50
43	1s. brown-lake	5·00	3·50
40/3	*Set of* 4	8·00	9·00

2½d. Re-entry (R. 4/4)

(Recess John Ash, Melbourne)

1937 (10 May). Coronation. P 11.

44	**6**	1½d. scarlet	45	1·75
45		2d. orange	45	2·75
46		2½d. blue	45	1·75
		a. Re-entry	35·00	35·00
47		1s. purple	65	2·00
44/7		*Set of* 4	1·75	7·25

Japanese forces invaded Nauru on 26 August 1942 and virtually all the inhabitants were removed to Truk in the Caroline Islands.

The Australian army liberated Nauru on 13 September 1945. After an initial period without stamps Australian issues were supplied during October 1945 and were used from Nauru until further supplies of Nos. 26/39 became available. The deportees did not return until early in 1946.

7 Nauruan Netting Fish

8 Anibare Bay

15 Map of Nauru

(Recess Note Printing Branch, Commonwealth Bank, Melbourne, and from 1960 by Note Ptg Branch, Reserve Bank of Australia, Melbourne)

1954 (6 Feb)–**65**. T **7/8**, **15** and similar designs. Toned paper. P 13½×14½ (horiz) or 14½×13½ (vert).

48	½d. deep violet	20	2·00
	a. Violet (8.5.61)	20	80
49	1d. bluish green	30	2·00
	a. Emerald-green (8.5.61)	20	40
	b. Deep green (1965)	3·25	2·75
50	3½d. scarlet	1·75	75
	a. Vermilion (1958)	8·50	75
51	4d. grey-blue	2·50	2·00
	a. Deep blue (1958)	18·00	4·00
52	6d. orange	70	20
53	9d. claret	60	20
54	1s. deep purple	30	30
55	2s.6d. deep green	2·75	1·00
56	5s. magenta	8·00	2·25
48/56	*Set of* 9	15·00	7·00

Designs: *Horiz*—3½d. Loading phosphate from cantilever; 4d. Great Frigate Bird; 6d. Nauruan canoe; 9d. Domaneab (meeting-house); 2s.6d. Buada lagoon. *Vert*—1s. Palm trees.

Nos. 48*a*, 49*a*/*b*, 50*a* and 51*a* are on white paper.

16 Micronesian Pigeon

17 Poison Nut

20 Capparis

21 White Tern

(Recess (10d., 2s.3d.) or photo (others) Note Ptg Branch, Reserve Bank of Australia, Melbourne)

1963–65. T **16/17**, **20/1** and similar designs. P 13½×13 (5d.), 13×13½ (8d.), 14×13½ (10d.), 15×14½ (1s.3d.) or 13½ (others).

57	2d. black, blue, red-brown and orange-yellow (3.5.65)	75	2·25
58	3d. multicoloured (16.4.64)	40	35
59	5d. multicoloured (22.4.63)	40	75
60	8d. black and green (1.7.63)	1·75	80
61	10d. black (16.4.64)	40	30
62	1s.3d. blue, black and yellow-green (3.5.65)	2·00	4·75
63	2s.3d. ultramarine (16.4.64)	2·75	55
64	3s.3d. multicoloured (3.5.65)	1·00	2·75
57/64	*Set of* 8	7·00	12·50

Designs: Vert—5d. "Iyo" (*calophyllum*). Horiz—8d. Black Lizard; 2s.3d. Coral pinnacles; 3s.3d. Finsch's Reed Warbler.

22 "Simpson and his Donkey"

(Des C. Andrew (after statue, Shrine of Remembrance, Melbourne. Photo Note Ptg Branch, Reserve Bank of Australia, Melbourne))

1965 (14 Apr). 50th Anniv of Gallipoli Landing. P 13½.

65	**22**	5d. sepia, black and emerald	15	10

(New Currency. 100 cents = 1 Australian dollar)

24 Anibare Bay

25 "Iyo" (*calophyllum*)

(Recess (1, 2, 3, 5, 8,19, 25c. and $1) or photo (others))

1966 (14 Feb–25 May). Decimal Currency. Various stamps with values in cents and dollars as T **24/5** and some colours changed. Recess printed stamps on helecon paper.

66	**24**	1c. deep blue	15	10
67	**7**	2c. brown-purple (25.5)	15	40
68	–	3c. bluish green (as 3½d.) (25.5)	30	2·00
69	**25**	4c. multicoloured	20	10
70	–	5c. deep ultramarine (as 1s.) (25.5)	25	60
71	–	7c. black and chestnut (as 8d.)	30	10
72	**20**	8c. olive-green	20	10
73	–	10c. red (as 4d.)	40	10
74	**21**	15c. blue, black and yellow-green (25.5)	60	2·00
75	–	25c. deep brown (as 2s.3d.) (25.5)	30	1·00
76	**17**	30c. multicoloured	45	30
77	–	35c. multicoloured (as 3s.3d.) (25.5)	75	35
78	**16**	50c. multicoloured	1·50	80

79	–	$1 magenta (as 5s.)	75	1·00
66/79 *Set of 14*			5·50	8·00

The 25c. is as No. 63, but larger, 27½×24½ mm.

Naru became independent on 31 January 1968.

Later issues will be found listed in the Stanley Gibbons *Western Pacific Catalogue*.

NEW GUINEA

German New Guinea

On 16 November 1884, ten days after the south-eastern part of New Guinea became a British protectorate, the north-eastern part of the island was declared to be a German protectorate and was named Kaiser-Wilhelms-Land. At the same time a German protectorate was declared over the Bismarck archipelago, consisting of New Pomerania (now New Britain), New Mecklenburg (now New Ireland) and New Hanover; and also over the Admiralty Islands and the northern Solomon Islands. On 14 November 1899 these Solomon Islands, except Bougainville and Buka, were ceded to the United Kingdom in return for the renunciation of British claims in Samoa.

Postal agencies were opened at Finschhafen on 15 February 1888 (closed 19 March 1891 but re-opened 15 July 1904); Hatzfeldthafen on 1 April 1888 (closed 30 September 1891); Kerawara on 4 April 1888 (used "Matupi" cancellation until May 1888, closed June 1890); Konstantinhafen on 15 May 1888 (closed 30 September 1891); Stephansort on 14 December 1889 (closed between 30 July 1892 and 14 February 1893); Herbertshöhe in June 1890 (used "Kerawara" cancellation until December 1890); Friedrich-Wilhelmshafen on 1 March 1892; Matupi on 1 November 1894 (closed 31 January 1906); and Berlinhafen on 22 May 1898. Unoverprinted stamps of Germany were used from these dates.

PRICES. Prices for Nos. Z1 and Z2/7 are for Finschhafen postmarks, those of most other postal agencies being worth more. Prices for Nos. Z1a and Z8/13 are for the cheapest cancel found on each stamp, prices varying according to post office and type of postmark. Prices for No. Z8 are however for cancellations before 1899; cancellations after this date are worth about 50% less.

Stamps of Germany used in German New Guinea

5

6

7

8

9

1888–98. Stamps of Germany cancelled with circular postmarks of German New Guinea postal agencies.

(a) Nos. 38c/d (Numeral inscr "DEUTSCHE REICHS-POST")

Z1	**7**	2m. mauve (1890)	£3500
		a. Deep claret (1891)	£600

(b) Nos. 39/44 (Numeral or Eagle inscr "DEUTSCHE REICHS-POST")

Z2	**5**	3pf. green (24.1.90)	£5000
Z3		5pf. mauve (29.4.88)	£700
Z4	**6**	10pf. carmine (16.4.88)	£600
Z5		20pf. bright blue (16.2.88)	£300
Z6		25pf. deep chestnut (1890)	—
Z7		50pf. dull olive-green (21.2.88)	£450

(c) Nos. 46/51 (Numeral or Eagle inscr "REICHSPOST")

Z8	**8**	3pf. brown (23.6.91)	£170
		a. Grey-brown (1892)	£100
		b. Orange-brown (1898)	£140
Z9		5pf. green (30.1.91)	£225
		a. Yellow-green (1891)	£120
Z10	**9**	10pf. rose (2.5.90)	£120
		a. Carmine (1894)	70.00
Z11		20pf. ultramarine (2.9.90)	£225
		a. Dull blue (1892)	70.00
Z12		25pf. orange-yellow (23.6.91)	£450
		a. Orange (1894)	£350
Z13		50pf. lake-brown (24.1.90)	£1200
		a. Chocolate (1891)	90.00

Dates are those of earliest known use.

Nos. Z2/7 were valid until 31 January 1891 and Nos. Z1 and Z8/13 until 30 September 1901.

(**1**)

1897 (22 Sept)–**99**. Stamps of Germany, 1889, optd with T **1**.

1	**8**	3pf. bistre-brown (7.98)	44.00	80.00
		a. Grey-brown (1899)	11.50	15.00
		b. Reddish brown (1899)	£200	£350
2		5pf. green	5.75	7.50
3	**9**	10pf. carmine	9.25	12.50
4		20pf. ultramarine	12.50	18.00
5		25pf. orange (7.98)	40.00	75.00
6		50pf. chocolate	46.00	70.00
1/6 *Set of 6 (cheapest)*			£110	£180

The above stamps also exist with the Type **1** overprint deeply impressed into the stamp and showing clearly on the back. These overprints were made officially to supply the U.P.U. (*Price* £1500 *per set of 6*). The shades of the special reprints also differ markedly from the issued stamps, especially the 3pf.

A

B

"YACHT" KEY TYPES. Types A and B, representing the ex-Kaiser's yacht *Hohenzollern*, were in use throughout the German colonies, inscribed with the name of the particular colony for which they were issued. Type A was printed by typography and Type B was recess-printed, both by Imperial Printing Office, Berlin.

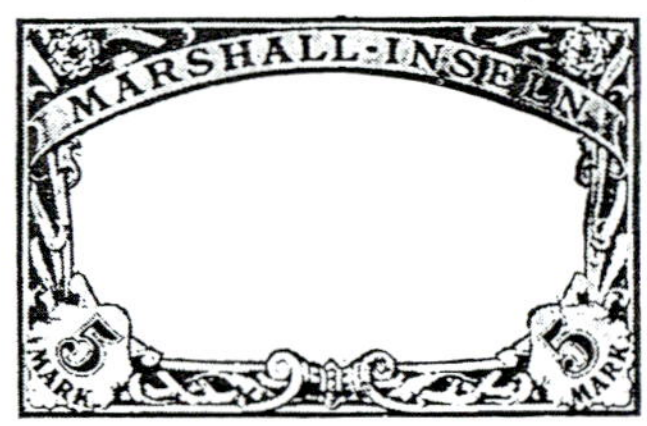

Frame Type I

Centre Type I

Centre Type II

Plates. Two types of centre plate were used for the 5m. value, as illustrated. In the lists which follow "(I)" means that both the frame and centre plate were Type I. Nos. 23b/c have a combination of frame plate I and centre plate II.

Perforations. Type A (low values) is perforated 14. In Type B (high values) there are two types of perforation, both measuring about 14½. They are distinguishable by the number of holes along the horizontal and down the vertical sides of the stamps thus:—

(*a*) 26×17 holes

(*b*) 25×17 holes

Wmk Lozenges

(Typo (Type A) or Recess (Type B), Imperial Printing Office, Berlin)

1901 (Jan–15 Mar). No wmk. P 14 (A) or 14½ (B).

7	A	3pf. brown	1.70	1.70
8		5pf. green	9.50	1.70
9		10pf. carmine	32.00	4.50
10		20pf. ultramarine	2.30	4.50
11		25pf. black and red/*yellow*	2.30	23.00
12		30pf. black and orange/*buff*	2.30	29.00
13		40pf. black and carmine	2.30	32.00
14		50pf. black and purple/*buff*	3.00	28.00
15		80pf. black and carmine/*rose*	5.25	39.00
16	B	1m. carmine (*a*) (15.3)	11.50	75.00
17		2m. blue (*a*) (15.3)	11.50	£110
18		3m. violet-black (*a*) (15.3)	16.00	£225.
19		5m. carmine and black (I) (*a*) (15.3)	£225	£700
7/19 *Set of* 13			£300	£1100
7/19s Optd "Specimen" *Set of* 13			£600	

2pf. grey is a proof.

1914–19. Wmk Lozenges.

20	A	3pf. brown (1919)	1.20
21		5pf. green	2.30
22		10pf. carmine	2.30
23	B	5m. carmine and black (I) (*a*)	70.00
		a. Ditto, but perf (*b*)	£1200
		b. Frame I, Centre II (*a*)	50.00
		c. Ditto, but perf (*b*)	46.00

No. 20 is inscribed "DEUTSCH-NEU GUINEA" (as Nos. 7/19); Nos. 21/3 "DEUTSCH-NEU-GUINEA".

Nos. 20/23 were only on sale in Berlin.

On 11 September 1914, Australian forces landed in New Pomerania and the German forces in New Guinea surrendered ten days later. On 17 December 1920 Australia received a Mandate of the League of Nations to administer the territories of the former German protectorate.

Stamps of Germany and later of GERMAN NEW GUINEA were used in New Guinea from 1888 until 1914.

During the interim period between the "G.R.I." surcharges and the "N.W. PACIFIC ISLANDS" overprints, stamps of AUSTRALIA perforated "OS" were utilised.

PRICES FOR STAMPS ON COVER

Nos. 1/30	*from*×3
Nos. 31/2	—
Nos. 33/49	*from*×3
Nos. 50/9	*from*×2
Nos. 60/2	—
Nos. 63/4	*from*×2
Nos. 64*c*/*q*	—
Nos. 65/81	*from*×5
Nos. 83/5	—
Nos. 86/97	*from*×5
No. 99	—
Nos. 100/16	*from*×4
Nos. 117/18	—
Nos. 119/24	*from*×4
Nos. 125/203	*from*×2
Nos. 204/5	—
Nos. 206/11	*from*×8
Nos. 212/25	*from*×2
Nos. O1/54	*from*×8

AUSTRALIAN OCCUPATION

Stamps of German New Guinea surcharged

(1) (2) (3)

SETTINGS. The "G.R.I" issues of New Guinea were surcharged on a small hand press which could only accommodate one horizontal row of stamps at a time. In addition to complete sheets the surcharges were also applied to multiples and individual stamps which were first lightly affixed to plain paper backing sheets. Such backing sheets could contain a mixture of denominations, some of which required different surcharges.

Specialists recognise twelve settings of the low value surcharges (1d. to 8d.):

Setting 1	(Nos. 1/4, 7/11) shows the bottom of the "R" 6 *mm* from the top of the "d"
Setting 2	(Nos. 16/19, 22/6) shows the bottom of the "R" 5 *mm* from the top of the "d"
Setting 3	was used for the Official stamps (Nos. O1/2)
Setting 4, and Setting 5	which included the 2½d. value for the first time, showed individual stamps with either 6 *mm* or 5 *mm* spacing.

These five settings were for rows of ten stamps, but the remaining seven, used on odd stamps handed in for surcharging, were applied as strips of five only. One has, so far, not been reconstructed, but of the remainder three show the 6 mm spacing, two the 5 mm and one both.

On the shilling values the surcharges were applied as horizontal rows of four and the various settings divide into two groups, one with 3½ to 4½ mm between the bottom of the "R" and the top of numeral, and the second with 5½ mm between the "R" and numeral. The first group includes the very rare initial setting on which the space is 4 to 4½ mm.

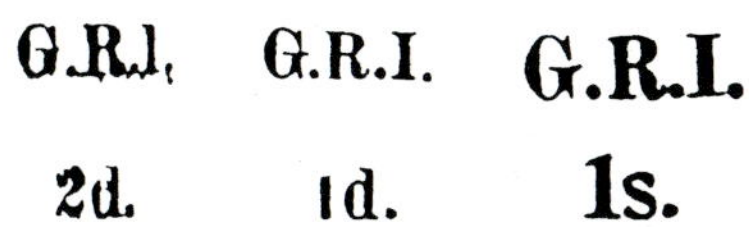

"1" for "I" (Setting 1) — Short "1" (Setting 1) — Large "S" (Setting 1)

1914 (17 Oct)–**15**. Stamps of 1901 surch.

(a) As T **1**. *"G.R.I." and value 6 mm apart*

1	1d. on 3pf. brown	£750	£850
	a. "1" for "I"	£2000	£2250
	b. Short "1"	£2000	
	c. "1" with straight top serif (Setting 6)	£2000	
	d. "I" for "1" (Setting 12)	£3500	
2	1d. on 5pf. green	85·00	£110
	a. "1" for "I"	£350	£425
	b. Short "1"	£350	£425
	c. "1" with straight top serif (Settings 6 and 9)	£475	£550
3	2d. on 10pf. carmine	90·00	£120
	a. "1" for "I"	£400	£500
4	2d. on 20pf. ultramarine	90·00	£110
	a. "1" for "I"	£375	£425
	e. Surch double, one "G.R.I." albino	£5500	
	f. Surch inverted	£16000	
5	2½d. on 10pf. carmine (27.2.15)	95·00	£200
	a. Fraction bar omitted (Setting 9)	£3500	£3500
6	2½d. on 20pf. ultramarine (27.2.15)	£110	£225
	a. Fraction bar omitted (Setting 9)	†	£9500
7	3d. on 25pf. black and red/*yellow*	£375	£450
	a. "1" for "I"	£1100	£1300
8	3d. on 30pf. black and orange/*buff*	£475	£500
	a. "1" for "I"	£1300	£1500
	e. Surch double	£15000	£15000
9	4d. on 40pf. black and carmine	£475	£500
	a. "1" for "I"	£1500	
	e. Surch double	£4000	£4750
	f. Surch inverted	£16000	
10	5d. on 50pf. black and purple/*buff*	£850	£1000
	a. "1" for "I"	£2250	£3000
	e. Surch double	£16000	
	f. Surch inverted		
11	8d. on 80pf. black and carmine/*rose*	£1000	£1500
	a. "1" for "I"	£3250	£4250
	d. No stop after "d"	£4250	
	e. Error. Surch "G.R.I. 4d."	£15000	

(b) As T **2**. *"G.R.I." and value 3½ to 4 mm apart*

12	1s. on 1m. carmine	£3500	£4250
	a. Large "s"	£13000	£13000
13	2s. on 2m. blue	£3250	£4000
	a. Large "s"	£12000	£14000

No.	Description	Unused	Used
	c. Error. Surch "G.R.I. 5s."	£45000	
	d. Error. Surch "G.R.I. 2d." corrected by handstamped "S"	£50000	
14	3s. on 3m. violet-black	£5500	£7000
	a. Large "s"	£16000	
	b. No stop after "I" (Setting 3)	£13000	£13000
15	5s. on 5m. carmine and black	£14000	£16000
	a. Large "s"	£29000	
	b. No stop after "I" (Setting 3)	£18000	£20000
	c. Error. Surch "G.R.I. 1s."	£85000	

G.R.I.

3d.

Thick "3"
(Setting 2)

G.R.I.

5d.

Thin "5"
(Setting 2)

1914 (16 Dec)–**15**. Stamps of 1901 surch.

(a) As T **1**. *"G.R.I." and value 5 mm apart*

No.	Description	Unused	Used
16	1d. on 3pf. brown	95·00	£100
	a. "I" for "1" (Setting 11)	£750	
	b. Short "1" (Setting 2)	£325	
	c. "1" with straight top serif (Settings 2 and 6)	£140	£170
	e. Surch double	£1500	£1800
	f. Surch double, one inverted	£8000	
	g. Surch inverted	£6000	
	h. Error. Surch "G.R.I. 4d."	£17000	
17	1d. on 5pf. green	35·00	50·00
	b. Short "1" (Setting 2)	£130	£190
	c. "1" with straight top serif (Setting 2)	50·00	80·00
	e. "d" inverted	†	£3750
	f. "1d" inverted	†	£11000
	g. "G.R.I." without stops or spaces	£11000	
	ga. "G.R.I." without stops, but with normal spaces	—	£11000
	h. "G.I.R." instead of "G.R.I."	£13000	£14000
	i. Surch double	£5000	
18	2d. on 10pf. carmine	48·00	60·00
	e. No stop after "d" (Setting 2)	£180	£250
	f. Stop before, instead of after, "G" (Settings 4 and 5)	£11000	
	g. Surch double	£16000	£16000
	h. Surch double, one inverted	—	£13000
	i. In vert pair with No. 20	£20000	
	j. In horiz pair with No. 20	£28000	
	k. Error. Surch ".GR.I. 1d."	£12000	£11000
	l. Error. Surch "G.I.R. 3d."	£13000	
19	2d. on 20pf. ultramarine	50·00	70·00
	e. No stop after "d" (Setting 2)	£130	£190
	f. No stop after "I" (Setting 11)	£1500	
	g. "R" inverted (Settings 4 and 5)	—	£9000
	h. Surch double	£3500	£4500
	i. Surch double, one inverted	£4750	£6000
	j. Surch inverted	£10000	
	k. Albino surch (in horiz pair with normal)	£23000	
	l. In vert pair with No. 21	£18000	£21000
	m. Error. Surch "G.R.I. 1d."	£13000	£14000
20	2½d. on 10pf. carmine (27.2.15)	£225	£350
21	2½d. on 20pf. ultramarine (27.2.15)	£2000	£2500
	a. Error. Surch "G.R.I. 3d." (in vert pair with normal)	£40000	
22	3d. on 25pf. black and red/*yellow*	£190	£250
	e. Thick "3"	£600	£750
	f. Surch double	£11000	£13000
	g. Surch inverted	£11000	£13000
	h. Surch omitted (in horiz pair with normal)	£13000	
	i. Error. Surch "G.R.I. 1d."	£20000	
23	3d. on 30pf. black and orange/*buff*	£170	£200
	e. No stop after "d" (Setting 2)	£800	
	f. Thick "3"	£550	
	g. Surch double	£4000	£4500
	h. Surch double, one inverted	£4500	£5500
	i. Surch double, both inverted	£13000	£14000
	j. Surch inverted	£10000	
	k. Albino surch	£12000	
	l. Surch omitted (in vert pair with normal)	£13000	
	m. Error. Surch "G.R.I. 1d."	£12000	£15000
24	4d. on 40pf. black and carmine	£180	£275
	e. Surch double	£3500	
	f. Surch double, one inverted	£5000	
	g. Surch double, both inverted	£13000	
	h. Surch inverted	£9500	
	i. Error. Surch "G.R.I. 1d."	£9000	
	ia. Surch "G.R.I. 1d." inverted	£19000	
	j. Error. Surch "G.R.I. 3d." double	£27000	
	k. No stop after "I" (Setting 11)	£3250	
25	5d. on 50pf. black and purple/*buff*	£325	£400
	e. Thin "5"	£1100	£2500
	f. Surch double	£4500	£5500
	g. Surch double, one inverted	£10000	£10000
	h. Surch double, both inverted	£13000	£14000
	i. Surch inverted	£10000	
	j. Error. Surch "G.I.R. 3d."	£22000	
26	8d. on 80pf. black and carmine/*rose*	£425	£600
	e. Surch double	£7000	£8000
	f. Surch double, one inverted	£7000	£8000
	g. Surch triple	£9500	£10000
	h. Surch inverted	£14000	
	i. Error. Surch "G.R.I. 3d."	£18000	

(b) As T **2**. *"G.R.I." and value 5½ mm apart*

No.	Description	Unused	Used
27	1s. on 1m. carmine	£5000	£7000
	a. No stop after "I" (Setting 7)	£12000	
28	2s. on 2m. blue	£5000	£8000
	a. No stop after "I" (Setting 7)	£12000	
29	3s. on 3m. violet-black	£10000	£15000
	a. "G.R.I." double	£45000	
30	5s. on 5m. carmine and black	£40000	£45000

1915 (1 Jan). Nos. 18 and 19 further surch with T **3**.

No.	Description	Unused	Used
31	1d. on 2d. on 10pf.	£28000	£28000
32	1d. on 2d. on 20pf.	£28000	£17000

German New Guinea Registration Labels surcharged

4

4a

G.R.I.

3d.

Sans serif "G"
and different "3"

1915 (Jan). Registration Labels surch "G.R.I. 3d." in settings of five or ten and used for postage. Each black and red on buff. Inscr "(Deutsch Neuguinea)" spelt in various ways as indicated. P 14 (No. 43) or 11½ (others).

I. With name of town in sans-serif letters as T **4**

No.	Description	Unused	Used
33	**Rabaul** "(Deutsch Neuguinea)"	£275	£325
	a. "G.R.I. 3d." double	£5000	£6500
	b. No bracket before "Deutsch"	£900	£1300
	ba. No bracket and surch double	£16000	
	d. "(Deutsch-Neuguinea)"	£425	£550
	da. "G.R.I. 3d." double	£16000	£16000
	db. No stop after "I"	£900	
	dc. "G.R.I. 3d" inverted	£16000	
	dd. No bracket before "Deutsch"	£1500	£2000
	de. No bracket after "Neuguinea"	£1500	£2000
34	**Deulon** "(Deutsch Neuguinea)"	£26000	£28000
35	**Friedrich-Wilhelmshafen** "(Deutsch Neuguinea)"	£250	£800
	a. No stop after "d"	£450	
	b. "G" omitted	£7500	
	c. Sans-serif "G"	£16000	
	d. Sans-serif "G" and different "3"	£14000	
	e. Surch inverted	†	£16000
	f. "(Deutsch-Neuguinea)"	£275	£800
	fa. No stop after "d"	£475	
36	**Herbertshohe** "(Deutsch Neuguinea)"	£300	£750
	a. No stop after "d"	£500	
	b. No stop after "I"	£900	£1800
	c. "G" omitted	£8500	
	d. Surch omitted (in horiz pair with normal)	£18000	
	e. "(Deutsch Neu-Guinea)"	£500	£1000
	f. "(Deutsch-Neuguinea)"		
37	**Kawieng** "(Deutsch-Neuguinea)"	£1000	
	a. No bracket after "Neuguinea"	£3750	
	b. "Deutsch Neu-Guinea"	£325	£650
	ba. No stop after "d"	£550	
	bb. "G.R.I." double	£8000	

bc. "3d." double £8000
bd. "G" omitted £8500
38 **Kieta** "(Deutsch-Neuguinea)" £450 £800
a. No bracket before "Deutsch" £1600 £2750
b. No stop after "d" £850
c. Surch omitted (right hand stamp of horiz pair) £16000
e. No stop after "I" £1300
f. "G" omitted £8000
39 **Manus** "(Deutsch Neuguinea)" £325 £900
a. "G.R.I. 3d." double £9000
b. No bracket before "Deutsch" £1500 £2500
40 **Stephansort** "(Deutsch Neu-Guinea)" — £4250
a. No stop after "d" † £8500

*II. With name of town in letters with serifs as T **4a***

41 **Friedrich Wilhelmshafen** "(Deutsch-Neuguinea)" £275 £750
b. No stop after "d" £450 £1100
c. No stop after "I" £850 £1600
d. No bracket before "Deutsch" £1600 £2250
e. No bracket after "Neuguinea" £1600 £2250
42 **Kawieng** "(Deutsch Neuguinea)" £250 £650
a. No stop after "d" £475
b. No stop after "I"
43 **Manus** "(Deutsch-Neuguinea)" £4250 £5000
a. No stop after "I" £8500 £8000

Examples of Nos. 33db, 36b, 38e, 41c and 43a also show the stop after "R" either very faint or missing completely.

Stamps of Marshall Islands surcharged

SETTINGS. The initial supply of Marshall Islands stamps, obtained from Nauru, was surcharged with Setting 2 (5 *mm* between "R" and "d") on the penny values and with the 3½ to 4 setting on the shilling stamps.

Small quantities subsequently handed in were surcharged, often on the same backing sheet as German New Guinea values, with Settings 6, 7 or 12 (all 6 *mm* between "R" and "d") for the penny values and with a 5½ mm setting for the shilling stamps.

1914 (16 Dec). Stamps of 1901 surch.

*(a) As T **1**. "G.R.I." and value 5 mm apart*

50 1d. on 3pf. brown £110 £170
c. "1" with straight top serif (Setting 2) £180 £300
d. ".GR.I." and "1" with straight top serif (Settings 4 and 5) † £14000
e. Surch inverted £9000
51 1d. on 5pf. green 80·00 85·00
c. "1" with straight top serif (Settings 2 and 11) £140 £160
d. "I" for "1" (Setting 11) £1200
e. "1" and "d" spaced £300 £325
f. Surch double £3750
g. Surch inverted £5000
52 2d. on 10pf. carmine 27·00 48·00
e. No stop after "G" (Setting 2) £850
f. Surch double £3750
g. Surch double, one inverted £5500
h. Surch inverted £7000
i. Surch sideways £10000
53 2d. on 20pf. ultramarine 27·00 50·00
e. No stop after "d" (Setting 2) 70·00 £110
g. Surch double £4000 £5000
h. Surch double, one inverted £10000 £10000
i. Surch inverted £11000 £11000
54 3d. on 25pf. black and red/*yellow* £450 £550
e. No stop after "d" (Settings 2 and 11) £850 £1100
f. Thick "3" £1000 £1400
g. Surch double £4250 £4750
h. Surch double, one inverted £4750
i. Surch inverted £13000
55 3d. on 30pf. black and orange/*buff* £475 £600
e. No stop after "d" (Setting 2) £900 £1200
f. Thick "3" £1100
g. Surch inverted £9000 £9500
h. Surch double £7000
56 4d. on 40pf. black and carmine £170 £250
e. No stop after "d" (Setting 2) £425 £650
f. "d" omitted (Setting 2) † £7000
g. Surch double £7000 £8000
h. Surch triple £14000
i. Surch inverted £10000
j. Error. Surch "G.R.I. 1d." £17000
k. Error. Surch "G.R.I. 3d." £17000
57 5d. on 50pf. black and purple/*buff* £300 £375
e. Thin "5" £3750
f. "d" omitted (Setting 2) £2000
g. Surch double £10000
h. Surch inverted £16000
58 8d. on 80pf. black and carmine/*rose* £475 £700
e. Surch double £10000
f. Surch double, both inverted £13000 £14000
g. Surch triple £16000
h. Surch inverted £11000

*(b) As T **2**. "G.R.I." and value 3½–4 mm apart*

59 1s. on 1m. carmine £4000 £5000
b. No stop after "I" £6000 £8500
e. Surch double £45000
f. Error. Additional surch "1d." £45000
60 2s. on 2m. blue £1900 £4000
b. No stop after "I" £3500 £6000
e. Surch double £45000
f. Surch double, one inverted £42000 £42000
61 3s. on 3m. violet-black £6500 £9500
b. No stop after "I" £8500
e. Surch double £40000 £45000
62 5s. on 5m. carmine and black £14000 £15000
e. Surch double, one inverted † £65000

1915 (Jan). Nos. 52 and 53 further surch with T **3**.

63 1d. on 2d. on 10pf. carmine £200 £275
a. "1" double £16000
b. "1" inverted £19000 £19000
c. Small "1" £650
64 1d. on 2d. on 20pf. ultramarine £4000 £2500
a. On No. 53e £9000 £4000
b. "1" inverted £19000 £19000

The surcharged "1" on No. 63c is just over 4 mm tall. Type **3** is 6 mm tall.

1915. Stamps of 1901 surch.

*(a) As T **1**. "G.R.I." and value 6 mm apart*

64c 1d. on 3pf. brown £3500
cc. "1" with straight top serif (Setting 6)
cd. "I" for "1" (Setting 12) £4250
ce. Surch inverted £16000
64d 1d. on 5pf. green £3500
dc. "1" with straight top serif (Setting 6) £4250
dd. "I" for "1" (Setting 12) £4250
de. Surch inverted £16000
df. Surch double £16000
64e 2d. on 10pf carmine £4500
ea. Surch sideways £16000
64f 2d. on 20pf. ultramarine £4000
fe. Surch inverted £16000
64g 2½d. on 10pf. carmine £27000
64h 2½d. on 20pf. ultramarine £40000
64i 3d. on 25pf. black and red/*yellow* £6500
64j 3d. on 30pf. black and orange/*buff* £6500
je. Error. Surch "G.R.I. 1d." £18000
64k 4d. on 40pf. black and carmine £6500
ke. Surch double £18000
kf. Surch inverted £18000
64l 5d. on 50pf. black and purple/*buff* £6000
le. Surch double £18000
64m 8d. on 80pf. black and carmine/*rose* £7500
me. Surch inverted £18000

*(b) As T **2**. "G.R.I." and value 5½ mm apart*

64n 1s. on 1m. carmine £17000
na. Large "s" (Setting 5) £21000
nb. No stop after "I" (Setting 7) £21000
64o 2s. on 2m. blue £14000
a. Large "s" (Setting 5) £19000
b. Surch double, one inverted £55000
64p 3s. on 3m. violet-black £27000
pa. Large "s" (Setting 5) £38000
pb. No stop after "I" (Setting 7) £38000
pe. Surch inverted £65000
64q 5s. on 5m. carmine and black £38000
qa. Large "s" (Setting 5) £50000

Stamps of Australia overprinted

N. W. PACIFIC ISLANDS.	N. W. PACIFIC ISLANDS.	N. W. PACIFIC ISLANDS.
(a)	(b)	(c)

(6)

1915–16. Stamps of Australia optd in black as T **6** (a), (b) or (c).

*(i) T **5a**. W **5** of Australia. P 14¼×14 (4 Jan–15 Mar 1915)*

65 ½d. green 3·00 9·00
a. Bright green 3·00 10·00
aw. Wmk inverted £2250 £2500
67 1d. pale rose (Die I) (4.1) 7·00 6·50
a. Dull red 7·00 6·50
b. Carmine-red 7·00 6·50
ba. Substituted cliché (Pl 2 rt pane R. 6/5). £1900 £1500
bb. Dot before "1" £110 £120
bc. "Secret mark" £110 £120
bd. Flaw under neck £110 £120
be. "RA" joined £110 £120
c. Die II. *Carmine-red* £110 £140
ca. Substituted cliché (Pl 2 rt pane R. 6/4). £1900 £1500
70 4d. yellow-orange 4·00 15·00
a. Pale orange-yellow 30·00 55·00

	b. Chrome-yellow	£250	£275
	c. Line through "FOUR PENCE" (PL 2 rt pane R. 2/6) (*all shades*) *from*	£425	£700
72	5d. brown (P 14¼ (line))	3·00	17·00
	(ii) T **1**. *W* **2** *of Australia. P 12 (4 Jan 1915–March 1916)*		
73	2d. grey (Die I)	20·00	65·00
74	2½d. indigo (Die II) (4.1.15)	2·75	16·00
76	3d. yellow-olive (Die I)	21·00	55·00
	a. Die II	£350	£550
	ab. In pair with Die I	£800	£1200
	c. Greenish olive	£200	£275
	ca. Die II	£1300	
	cb. In pair with Die I	£2250	
78	6d. ultramarine (Die II)	£110	£120
	a. Retouched "E"	£7500	£8500
	w. Wmk inverted	£300	£400
79	9d. violet (Die II)	55·00	65·00
81	1s. green (Die II)	60·00	70·00
83	5s. grey and yellow (Die II) (3.16)	£2750	£3750
84	10s. grey and pink (Die II) (12.15)	£150	£180
85	£1 brown and ultramarine (Die II) (12.15)	£550	£700
	(iii) T **1**. *W* **5** *of Australia. P 12 (Oct 1915–July 1916)*		
86	2d. grey (Die I)	18·00	48·00
87	2½d. indigo (Die II) (7.16)	£28000	£28000
88	6d. ultramarine (Die II)	10·00	12·00
89	9d. violet (Die II) (12.15)	16·00	21·00
90	1s. emerald (Die II) (12.15)	11·00	24·00
91	2s. brown (Die II) (12.15)	£110	£130
92	5s. grey and yellow (Die II) (12.15)	75·00	£110
	(iv) T **1**. *W* **6** *of Australia. P 12 (Dec 1915–1916)*		
94	2d. grey (Die I)	6·50	32·00
96	3d. yellow-olive (Die I)	5·50	11·00
	a. Die II	£110	£170
	ab. In pair with Die I	£325	
97	2s. brown (Die II) (8.16)	35·00	50·00
	w. Wmk inverted	30·00	90·00
99	£1 chocolate and dull blue (Die II) (8.16)	£350	£450

Dates for Nos. 67 and 74 are issue dates at Rabaul. The stamps were in use from 2 January 1915 on Nauru. All other dates are those of despatch. Nos. 65/6, 68/73, 76/81 were despatched on 15 March 1915.

For Die IIA of 2d. see note below Australia No. 45.

SETTINGS. Type **6** exists in three slightly different versions, illustrated above as (*a*), (*b*), and (*c*). These differ in the letters "S" of "ISLANDS" as follows:

(*a*) Both "SS" normal.
(*b*) First "S" with small head and large tail and second "S" normal.
(*c*) Both "SS" with small head and large tail.

Type **11**, which also shows the examples of "S" as the normal version, can be identified from Type **6** (*a*) by the relative position of the second and third lines of the overprint. On Type **6** (*a*) the "P" of "PACIFIC" is exactly over the first "S" of "ISLANDS". On Type **11** the "P" appears over the space between "I" and "S".

It has been established, by the study of minor variations, that there are actually six settings of the "N.W. PACIFIC ISLANDS" overprint, including that represented by T **11**, but the following are the different arrangements of Type **6** (*a*), (*b*), and (*c*) which occur.

A. Horizontal rows 1 and 2 all Type (*a*). Row 3 all Type (*b*). Rows 4 and 5 all Type (*c*).
B. (½d. green only). As A, except that the types in the bottom row run (*c*) (*c*) (*c*) (*c*) (*b*) (*c*).
C. As A, but bottom row now shows types (*a*) (*c*) (*c*) (*c*) (*b*) (*c*).

Horizontal strips and pairs showing varieties (*a*) and (*c*), or (*b*) and (*c*) *se-tenant* are scarce.

The earliest printing of the 1d. and 2½d. values was made on sheets with margin attached on two sides, the later printings being on sheets from which the margins had been removed. In this printing the vertical distances between the overprints are less than in later printings, so that in the lower horizontal rows of the sheet the overprint is near the top of the stamp.

The settings used on King George stamps and on the Kangaroo type are similar, but the latter stamps being smaller the overprints are closer together in the vertical rows.

PURPLE OVERPRINTS. We no longer differentiate between purple and black overprints in the above series. In our opinion the two colours are nowadays insufficiently distinct to warrant separation.

PRICES. The prices quoted for Nos. 65 to 101 apply to stamps with opts Types **6** (*a*) or **6** (*c*). Stamps with opt Type **6** (*b*) are worth a 25 per cent premium. Vertical strips of three, showing (*a*), (*b*) and (*c*), are worth from four times the prices quoted for singles as Types **6** (*a*) or **6** (*c*).

One Penny
(**10**)

N. W.
PACIFIC
ISLANDS.
(**11**)

1918 (23 May). Nos. 72 and 81 surch locally with T **10**.

100	1d. on 5d. brown	90·00	80·00
101	1d. on 1s. green	£100	80·00

Types **6** (*a*), (*b*), (*c*) occur on these stamps also.

1918–22. Stamps of Australia optd with T **11** ("P" of "PACIFIC" over space between "I" and "S" of "ISLANDS").

	(i) T **5a**. *W* **5** *of Australia. P 14¼×14*		
102	½d. green	1·75	3·50
	w. Wmk inverted	£3500	
103	1d. carmine-red (Die I)	3·75	1·60
	a. Substituted cliché (Pl 2 rt pane R. 6/5)	£1000	£650
	ab. Dot before "1"	80·00	70·00
	ac. "Secret mark"	80·00	70·00
	ad. Flaw under neck	80·00	70·00
	ae. "RA" joined	80·00	70·00
	b. Die II	£110	80·00
	ba. Substituted cliché (Pl 2 rt pane R. 6/4)	£1000	£650
104	4d. yellow-orange (1919)	4·25	16·00
	a. Line through "FOUR PENCE" (Pl 2 rt pane R. 2/6)	£850	£1300
105	5d. brown (1919)	4·00	12·00
	(ii) T **1**. *W* **6** *of Australia. P 12*		
106	2d. grey (Die I) (1919)	7·50	25·00
	a. Die II	12·00	50·00
107	2½d. indigo (Die II) (1919)	5·50	16·00
	a. "1" of "½" omitted	£14000	£17000
	b. Blue (1920)	15·00	48·00
109	3d. greenish olive (Die I) (1919)	23·00	26·00
	a. Die II	75·00	85·00
	ab. In pair with Die I	£425	£650
110	6d. ultramarine (Die II) (1919)	4·75	14·00
	a. Greyish ultramarine (1922)	42·00	65·00
	b. Die IIB. Greyish ultramarine	—	£750
112	9d. violet (Die IIB) (1919)	9·00	50·00
113	1s. emerald (Die II)	6·50	30·00
	a. Pale blue-green (Die IIB)	14·00	32·00
115	2s. brown (Die II) (1919)	21·00	38·00
116	5s. grey and yellow (Die II) (1919)	65·00	70·00
117	10s. grey and bright pink (Die II) (1919)	£170	£250
118	£1 bistre-brown and grey-blue (Die II) (1922)	£4500	£5500
	(iii) T **5a**. *W* **6a**. *of Australia (Mult Crown A). P 14*		
119	½d. green (1919)	5·00	7·00
	w. Wmk inverted	£130	£275
	(iv) T **5a**. *W* **5** *of Australia. Colour changes and new value*		
120	1d. violet (*shades*) (1922)	2·50	6·50
	a. Dot before "1"	65·00	£120
	b. "Secret mark"	65·00	£120
	c. Flaw under neck	65·00	£120
	d. "RA" joined	65·00	£120
121	2d. orange (1921)	8·50	2·50
122	2d. rose-scarlet (1922)	9·50	2·00
123	4d. violet (1922)	20·00	40·00
	a. "FOUR PENCE" in thinner letters (Pl 2 rt pane R. 2/6)	£800	£1400
124	4d. ultramarine (1922)	11·00	60·00
	a. "FOUR PENCE" in thinner letters (Pl 2 rt pane R. 2/6)	£900	£1800
120/24	*Set of 5*	45·00	£100

Type **11** differs from Type **6** (*a*) in the position of the "P" of "PACIFIC", which is further to the left in Type **11**.

For 1d. rosine Dies I and II on rough unsurfaced paper see Nos. O16/b.

MANDATED TERRITORY OF NEW GUINEA

A civil administration for the Mandated Territory of New Guinea was established on 9 May 1921.

PRINTERS. See note at the beginning of Australia.

12 Native Village

(**13**)

(Des R. Harrison. Eng T. Harrison. Recess Note Printing Branch, Treasury, Melbourne, from 1926 Note Ptg Branch, Commonwealth Bank of Australia, Melbourne)

1925 (23 Jan)–**27**. P 11.

125	**12**	½d. orange	2·50	7·00
126		1d. green	2·50	5·50
126*a*		1½d. orange-vermilion (1926)	3·25	2·75
127		2d. claret	7·00	4·50
128		3d. blue	7·50	4·00
129		4d. olive-green	13·00	24·00
130		6d. brown-ochre	20·00	50·00
		a. Bistre (1.25)	6·00	50·00
		b. Yellow-brown (7.27)	13·00	48·00
131		9d. dull purple (*to violet*)	13·00	45·00
132		1s. dull blue-green (6.4.25)	15·00	27·00
133		2s. brown-lake (6.4.25)	30·00	48·00
134		5s. bistre (6.4.25)	50·00	65·00

135		10s. dull rose (6.4.25)	£120	£180
136		£1 dull olive-green (6.4.25)	£190	£300
125/36 *Set of* 13			£400	£650

1931 (8 June). Air. Optd with T **13**. P 11.

137	**12**	½d. orange	1·50	9·00
138		1d. green	1·60	5·00
139		1½d. orange-vermilion	1·25	7·50
140		2d. claret	1·25	7·00
141		3d. blue	1·75	13·00
142		4d. olive-green	1·25	9·00
143		6d. light brown	1·75	14·00
144		9d. violet	3·00	17·00
145		1s. dull blue-green	3·00	17·00
146		2s. brown-lake	7·00	48·00
147		5s. olive-bistre	20·00	65·00
148		10s. bright pink	85·00	£110
149		£1 olive-grey	£160	£250
137/49 *Set of* 13			£250	£500

14 Raggiana Bird of Paradise (Dates either side of value)

AIR
MAIL

(**15**)

(Recess John Ash, Melbourne)

1931 (2 Aug). Tenth Anniv of Australian Administration. T **14** (with dates). P 11.

150	**14**	1d. green	4·25	6·50
151		1½d. vermilion	5·00	10·00
152		2d. claret	5·00	2·25
153		3d. blue	5·00	4·75
154		4d. olive-green	6·50	29·00
155		5d. deep blue-green	8·00	22·00
156		6d. bistre-brown	5·00	19·00
157		9d. violet	8·50	19·00
158		1s. pale blue-green	6·00	15·00
159		2s. brown-lake	10·00	48·00
160		5s. olive-brown	42·00	55·00
161		10s. bright pink	£120	£140
162		£1 olive-grey	£250	£275
150/62 *Set of* 13			£425	£550

1931 (2 Aug). Air. Optd with T **15**.

163	**14**	½d. orange	3·25	3·25
164		1d. green	4·00	7·00
165		1½d. vermilion	3·75	10·00
166		2d. claret	3·75	3·00
167		3d. blue	6·00	6·50
168		4d. olive-green	6·00	6·00
169		5d. deep blue-green	6·00	11·00
170		6d. bistre-brown	7·00	26·00
171		9d. violet	8·00	15·00
172		1s. pale blue-green	7·50	15·00
173		2s. dull lake	16·00	50·00
174		5s. olive-brown	42·00	70·00
175		10s. bright pink	80·00	£120
176		£1 olive-grey	£150	£250
163/76 *Set of* 14			£300	£500

1932 (30 June)–**34**. T **14** (redrawn without dates). P 11.

177	1d. green	7·00	20
178	1½d. claret	7·00	19·00
179	2d. vermilion	5·50	20
179*a*	2½d. green (14.9.34)	6·50	27·00
180	3d. blue	7·50	1·25
180*a*	3½d. aniline carmine (14.9.34)	13·00	21·00
181	4d. olive-green	6·50	6·50
182	5d. deep blue-green	7·00	70
183	6d. bistre-brown	7·50	4·75
184	9d. violet	9·50	26·00
185	1s. blue-green	6·50	10·00
186	2s. dull lake	5·00	17·00
187	5s. olive	32·00	48·00
188	10s. pink	55·00	70·00
189	£1 olive-grey	£120	£100
177/89 *Set of* 15		£250	£300

The ½d. orange redrawn without dates exists without overprint, but it is believed that this was not issued (*Price* £100 *un*).

1932 (30 June)–**34**. Air. T **14** (redrawn without dates), optd with T **15**. P 11.

190	½d. orange	60	1·50
191	1d. green	1·25	3·25
192	1½d. claret	1·75	11·00
193	2d. vermilion	1·75	30
193*a*	2½d. green (14.9.34)	8·50	2·50
194	3d. blue	3·25	3·00
194*a*	3½d. aniline carmine (14.9.34)	4·75	3·25
195	4d. olive-green	4·50	10·00
196	5d. deep blue-green	7·00	7·50
197	6d. bistre-brown	4·50	15·00
198	9d. violet	6·00	9·00
199	1s. pale blue-green	6·00	12·00
200	2s. dull lake	13·00	50·00
201	5s. olive-brown	50·00	60·00
202	10s. pink	95·00	85·00
203	£1 olive-grey	85·00	55·00
190/203 *Set of* 16		£250	£275

16 Bulolo Goldfields

(Recess John Ash, Melbourne)

1935 (1 May). Air. P 11.

204	**16**	£2 bright violet	£350	£140
205		£5 emerald-green	£750	£450

HIS MAJESTY'S
JUBILEE.
1910 — 1935

(**17**)

18

1935 (27 June). Silver Jubilee. As Nos. 177 and 179, but shiny paper. Optd with T **17**.

206	1d. green	1·00	65
207	2d. vermilion	3·50	65

Re-entry (design completely duplicated) (Pl 2a R. 5/2)

(Recess John Ash, Melbourne)

1937 (18 May). Coronation. P 11.

208	**18**	2d. scarlet	50	1·50
209		3d. blue	50	1·75
210		5d. green	50	1·75
		a. Re-entry	75·00	£130
211		1s. purple	50	2·25
208/11 *Set of* 4			1·75	6·50

(Recess John Ash, Melbourne)

1939 (1 Mar). Air. Inscr "AIRMAIL POSTAGE" at foot. P 11.

212	**16**	½d. orange	4·00	9·00
213		1d. green	3·25	4·50
214		1½d. claret	4·00	18·00
215		2d. vermilion	9·00	3·50
216		3d. blue	18·00	18·00
217		4d. yellow-olive	15·00	8·50
218		5d. deep green	14·00	4·00
219		6d. bistre-brown	45·00	30·00
220		9d. violet	45·00	45·00
221		1s. pale blue-green	45·00	32·00
222		2s. dull lake	90·00	75·00
223		5s. olive-brown	£190	£160
224		10s. pink	£600	£425
225		£1 olive-green	£140	£150
212/25 *Set of* 14			£1100	£850

OFFICIAL STAMPS

O. S.
G.R.I.
1d.

(O **1**)

O S

(O **2**)

O S

(O **3**)

1915 (27 Feb). Stamps of 1901 surch as Type O **1**. "G.R.I." and value 3½ mm apart.

O1	1d. on 3pf. brown	35·00	75·00
	a. "1" and "d" spaced	85·00	£170
	b. Surch double	£5500	
O2	1d. on 5pf. green	£100	£140
	a. "1" and "d" spaced	£200	£300

1919–23. Stamps of Australia optd with T **11** and punctured "O S" (8×15½ *mm* with eleven holes in the perforated "S").

(i) T **5a**. *of Australia. W* **5**. *P 14¼×14*

O3	1d. carmine-red (Die I)	£250	55·00
	ab. Dot before "1"	—	£275
	ac. "Secret mark"	—	£275
	ad. Flaw under neck	£850	£275
O4	4d. yellow-orange (19.5.19)	£325	£100
	a. Line through "FOUR PENCE" (Pl 2 rt pane R. 2/6)	—	£4250
O5	5d. brown (1921)	£425	£100

(ii) T **1** *of Australia. W* **6**. *P 12*

O6	2d. grey (Die I)	£400	80·00
O7	2½d. indigo (Die II)	£600	£425
O8	3d. greenish olive (Die I) (1921)	£650	£140
O9	6d. ultramarine (Die II) (1921)	£700	£200
	a. Greyish ultramarine	£600	£200
	b. Die IIB. Greyish ultramarine	—	£250
O10	9d. violet (Die IIB) (1921)	£275	£150
O11	1s. emerald (Die II) (1921)	£375	£160
	a. Pale blue-green	£425	£170
O12	2s. brown (Die II) (1922)	£700	£350
O13	5s. grey and yellow (Die II) (1922)	—	£1500
O14	10s. grey and bright pink (Die II) (1921)		

(iii) T **5a** *of Australia. W* **5**. *Rough unsurfaced paper, locally gummed. P 14*

O16	1d. rosine (Die I) (1920)	£1100	£190
	b. Die II	£4750	£950

(iv) T **5a** *of Australia. W* **5**. *Colour changes and new value. P 14*

O17	1d. violet (*shades*) (1923)	£350	50·00
O18	2d. orange (1921)	£150	48·00
O19	2d. rose-scarlet (1923)	£350	35·00
O20	4d. violet (23.7.21)	£225	£110
	a. "FOUR PENCE" in thinner letters (Pl 2 rt pane R. 2/6)	—	£4250
O21	4d. ultramarine (1.23)	£350	£150

Dates quoted for Nos. O3/21 are those of despatch from Australia. The earliest postmark date recorded is 2 April 1919 on No. O3. Their continued use on mail from government departments after the establishment of the civil administration is confirmed by a notice in the official *New Guinea Gazette* of 1 August 1921.

Australian postal archives indicate that nine sheets of the £1 Type **1** perforated "O S" were sent to New Guinea in September 1921. There is a pane of 30 of this stamp in the Royal Collection, but as no other examples are known it may not have been issued for postal purposes.

1925 (6 Apr)–**31**. Optd with Type O **2**. P 11.

O22	**12**	1d. green	4·75	4·50
O23		1½d. orange-vermilion (1931)	5·50	17·00
O24		2d. claret	3·00	3·75
O25		3d. blue	6·00	10·00
O26		4d. olive-green	4·50	8·50
O27		6d. bistre	27·00	35·00
		a. Yellow-brown (4.31)	7·50	35·00
O28		9d. violet	4·25	35·00
O29		1s. dull blue-green	5·50	35·00
O30		2s. brown-lake	42·00	65·00
O22/30 *Set of* 9			75·00	£190

1931 (2 Aug). Optd with Type O **3**. P 11.

O31	**14**	1d. green	12·00	13·00
O32		1½d. vermilion	12·00	12·00
O33		2d. claret	12·00	7·00
O34		3d. blue	7·00	6·00
O35		4d. olive-green	7·50	8·50
O36		5d. deep blue-green	10·00	12·00
O37		6d. bistre-brown	14·00	17·00
O38		9d. violet	16·00	28·00
O39		1s. pale blue-green	16·00	28·00
O40		2s. brown-lake	40·00	70·00
O41		5s. olive-brown	£110	£180
O31/41 *Set of* 11			£225	£350

1932 (30 June)–**34**. T **14** (redrawn without dates), optd with Type O **3**. P 11.

O42	1d. green	19·00	20·00
O43	1½d. claret	19·00	20·00
O44	2d. vermilion	19·00	3·25
O45	2½d. green (14.9.34)	10·00	12·00
O46	3d. blue	11·00	42·00
	a. Double opt, one albino	£1000	
O47	3½d. aniline carmine (14.9.34)	9·00	9·00
O48	4d. olive-green	20·00	32·00
O49	5d. deep blue-green	9·00	30·00
O50	6d. bistre-brown	25·00	55·00
O51	9d. violet	15·00	48·00
O52	1s. pale blue-green	15·00	30·00
O53	2s. dull lake	30·00	75·00
O54	5s. olive-brown	£120	£180
O42/54 *Set of* 13		£275	£475

Civil Administration in New Guinea was suspended in 1942, following the Japanese invasion.

Various New Guinea stamps exist overprinted with an anchor and three Japanese characters in a style similar to the Japanese Naval Control Area overprints found on the stamps of Netherlands Indies. These overprints on New Guinea are bogus. Two different versions are known, one produced in Japan during 1947 and the other in Australia during the late 1980s.

On resumption, after the Japanese defeat in 1945, Australian stamps were used until the appearance of the issue for the combined territories of Papua & New Guinea.

NORFOLK ISLAND

Norfolk Island, first settled in 1788 from New South Wales, was transferred to Tasmania on 29 September 1844. It became a separate settlement on 1 November 1856 under the control of the Governor of New South Wales. The island was declared an Australian Territory on 1 July 1914. Unlike the other External Territories it retains an independent postal administration.

A Post Office was opened on Norfolk Island in 1832. The stamps of TASMANIA were used on Norfolk Island from July 1854 until May 1855, such use being identified by the "72" numeral cancellation. Stamps of NEW SOUTH WALES were first used on the island in 1877, but were not regularly available until 1898. The first "NORFOLK ISLAND" cancellation was supplied in 1892, but not used until 1898. Stamps of AUSTRALIA were in use from 1913 to 1947.

1 Ball Bay

(Des and eng F. Manley. Recess Note Printing Branch, Reserve Bank of Australia)

1947 (10 June)–**59**. Toned paper. P 14.

1	**1**	½d. orange	85	60
		a. White paper (11.56)	2·50	10·00
2		1d. bright violet	50	60
		a. White paper (8.57)	5·00	24·00
3		1½d. emerald-green	50	70
		a. White paper (11.56)	9·00	24·00
4		2d. reddish violet	55	40
		a. White paper (11.56)	£100	£160
5		2½d. scarlet	80	30
6		3d. chestnut	70	70
6*a*		3d. emerald-green (*white paper*) (6.7.59)	12·00	8·50
7		4d. claret	1·75	40
8		5½d. indigo	70	30
9		6d. purple-brown	70	30
10		9d. magenta	1·25	40
11		1s. grey-green	70	40
12		2s. yellow-bistre	1·00	1·25
12*a*		2s. deep blue (*white paper*) (6.7.59)	14·00	9·00
1/12*a* *Set of* 14			32·00	21·00

Stamps as Type **1**, some in different colours, perforated 11 were prepared in 1940 but never issued. Examples exist from sheets stolen prior to the destruction of these stocks.

2 Warder's Tower

3 Airfield

(Des B. Stewart, eng. G. Lissenden (3½d.), D. Cameron (7½d.). Des and eng D. Cameron (6½d.), P. Morriss (8½d., 10d.) or G. Lissenden (5s.))

1953 (10 June). T **2/3** and similar designs. P 14½×15 (vert) or 15×14½ (horiz).

13	3½d. brown-lake	1·00	90
14	6½d. deep green	2·25	3·50
15	7½d. deep blue	1·50	3·00
16	8½d. chocolate	1·75	4·75
17	10d. reddish violet	1·00	75
18	5s. sepia	35·00	8·50
13/18 *Set of* 6		38·00	19·00

Designs: *Horiz* (*as T* **3**)—7½d. Old Stores (Crankmill); 5s. Bloody Bridge. *Vert* (*as T* **2**)—8½d. Barracks entrance; 10d. Salt House.

8 Norfolk Island Seal and Pitcairners Landing

Two types of 2s.:

Type I

Type II

Alternate stamps on each horizontal row are with or without a dot in bottom right corner.

(Des and eng F. Manley)

1956 (8 June). Centenary of Landing of Pitcairn Islanders on Norfolk Island. P 15×14½.

19	**8**	3d. deep bluish green	75	40
20		2s. violet (I)	1·25	1·00
		a. Type II	1·25	1·00
		b. Deep violet (I)	2·75	1·75
		ba. Type II	2·75	1·75

(**9**) (**10**) (**11**)

1958 (1 July). Nos. 15/16 surch with T **9**/**10**.

21	7d. on 7½d. deep blue	1·25	1·00
22	8d. on 8½d. chocolate	1·25	1·00

1959 (7 Dec). 150th Anniv of Australian Post Office. No. 331 of Australia surch with T **11**.

23	5d. on 4d. slate (R.)	35	30

12 *Hibiscus insularis*

14 White Tern

16 Red Hibiscus

17 Queen Elizabeth II and Cereus

21 Rose Apple

22 Red-tailed Tropic Bird

(Des G. Lissenden, eng P. Morriss (5s.). Des and eng G. Lissenden (10s.), P. Morriss (others). Recess and typo (2s.8d.), recess (others))

1960–62. T **12**, **14**, **16**/**17**, **21**/**2** and similar designs. P 14½ or 14½×14 (10s.).

24	1d. bluish green (23.5.60)	15	10
25	2d. rose and myrtle-green (23.5.60)	20	10
26	3d. green (1.5.61)	70	15
27	5d. bright purple (20.6.60)	55	20
28	8d. red (20.6.60)	80	50
29	9d. ultramarine (23.5.60)	80	45
30	10d. brown and reddish violet (as No. 17) (27.2.61)	1·25	1·00
31	1s. on 1d. carmine-red (16.10.61)	80	35
32	2s. sepia (1.5.61)	4·00	1·00
33	2s.5d. deep violet (5.2.62)	1·00	40
34	2s.8d. cinnamon and deep green (9.4.62)	2·25	55
35	5s. sepia and deep green (as No. 18) (27.2.61)	2·75	75
36	10s. emerald-green (14.8.61)	26·00	32·00
	s. Optd "Specimen"	42·00	
24/36	*Set of* 13	38·00	32·00

Designs: *Vert* (*as T* **12**)—2d. *Lagunaria patersonii*; 5d. Lantana. (*As T* **21**); 1s.1d. Fringed Hibiscus; 2s.5d. Passion flower. (*As T* **14**)—2s. Solander's Petrel.

Nos. 30 and 35 are redrawn.

The Specimen overprint on No. 36 is from sets sold by the Australian Post Office.

For Nos. 25 and 28 with face values in decimal currency see Nos. 600/1.

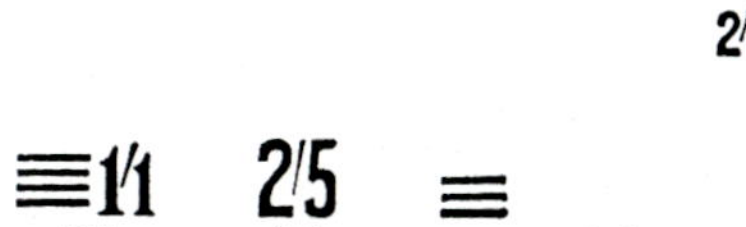

(**23**) (**24**) (**25**)

1960. As Nos. 13/15 but colours changed, surch with T **23**/**5**.

37	1s.1d. on 3½d. deep ultramarine (26.9.60)	2·00	1·00
38	2s.5d. on 6½d. bluish green (26.9.60)	3·00	1·00
39	2s.8d. on 7½d. sepia (29.8.60)	7·00	6·00
37/9	*Set of* 3	11·00	7·25

26 Queen Elizabeth II and Map

27 Open Bible and Candle

(Des and eng P. Morriss)

1960 (24 Oct). Introduction of Local Government. P 14.

40	**26**	2s. on 8d. reddish purple	4·50	6·50

(Des K. McKay. Adapted and eng B. Stewart. Recess)

1960 (21 Nov). Christmas. P 15×14½.

41	**27**	5d. bright purple	40	50

28 Open Prayer Book and Text

29 Stripey (*Atypichthys latus*)

(Des G. Lissenden. Eng P. Morriss. Recess)

1961 (20 Nov). Christmas. P 14½×14.

42	**28**	5d. slate-blue	30	70

PRINTERS. All the following issues to No. 233 were printed in photogravure by Harrison and Sons, Ltd, London, except where otherwise stated.

1962–63. Fishes. Horiz designs as T **29**. P 14½×14.

43	6d. sepia, yellow and deep bluish green (16.7.62)	60	25
44	11d. red-orange, brown and blue (25.2.63)	1·00	80
45	1s. blue, pink and yellow-olive (17.9.62)	60	25
46	1s.3d. blue, red-brown and green (15.7.63)	1·00	2·00
47	1s.6d. sepia, violet and light blue	1·25	80
48	2s.3d. deep blue, red and greenish yellow (23.9.63)	2·50	80
43/8	*Set of* 6	6·25	4·50

Designs:—11d. Gold-mouthed Emperor (*Lethrinus chrysostomus*); 1s. Surge Wrasse ("Po'ov"); 1s.3d. Seachub ("Dreamfish"); 1s.6d. Giant Grouper (*Promicrops lanceolatus*); 2s.3d. White Trevally (*Carangidae*).

30 "Madonna and Child"

31 "Peace on Earth..."

(Des and eng G. Lissenden. Recess Note Ptg Branch, Reserve Bank of Australia)

1962 (19 Nov). Christmas. P 14½.

49	**30**	5d. ultramarine	45	80

(Des R. Warner. Eng B. Stewart. Recess Note Ptg Branch, Reserve Bank of Australia)

1963 (11 Nov). Christmas. P 14½.

50	**31**	5d. red	40	70

32 Overlooking Kingston

33 Norfolk Pine

1964 (24 Feb). Views. Horiz designs as T **32**. Multicoloured. P 14½×14.

51		5d. Type **32**	60	60
52		8d. Kingston	1·00	1·50
53		9d. The Arches (Bumboras) (11.5)	1·00	30
54		10d. Slaughter Bay (28.9)	1·00	30
51/4		*Set of* 4	3·25	2·50

(Photo Note Ptg Branch, Reserve Bank of Australia, Melbourne)

1964 (1 July). 50th Anniv of Norfolk Island as Australian Territory. P 13½.

55	**33**	5d. black, red and orange	40	15
56		8d. black, red and grey-green	40	1·10

34 Child looking at Nativity Scene

35 Nativity Scene

(Des P. Morriss and J. Mason. Photo Note Ptg Branch, Reserve Bank of Australia)

1964 (9 Nov). Christmas. P 13½.

57	**34**	5d. green, blue, buff and violet	30	40

1965 (14 Apr). 50th Anniv of Gallipoli Landing. As T **22** of Nauru. P 13½.

58		5d. sepia, black and emerald	15	10

(Des J. Mason. Photo Note Ptg Branch, Reserve Bank of Australia)

1965 (25 Oct). Christmas. Helecon paper. P 13½.

59	**35**	5d. multicoloured	15	10

(New Currency. 100 cents = 1 Australian dollar)

38 *Hibiscus insularis*

39 Headstone Bridge

1966 (14 Feb). Decimal currency. Various stamps surch in black on silver tablets, which vary slightly in size, obliterating old value as in T **38**. Surch typo.

60	**38**	1c. on 1d. bluish green (*value tablet* 4×5 *mm*)	20	10
		a. Value tablet larger, 5½×5½ *mm*	40	30
61	**13**	2c. on 2d. rose and myrtle-green (No. 25)	20	10
62	**14**	3c. on 3d. green	75	90
		a. Silver tablet omitted	£550	
63	**15**	4c. on 5d. bright purple (No. 27)	25	10
64	**16**	5c. on 8d. red	30	10
65	**6**	10c. on 10d. brown and reddish violet (No. 30)	1·00	15
66	**18**	15c. on 1s.1d. carmine-red (No. 31)	50	1·00
67	**19**	20c. on 2s. sepia (No. 32)	2·75	3·00
68	**20**	25c. on 2s.5d. deep violet (No. 33)	1·00	40
69	**21**	30c. on 2s.8d. cinnamon and deep green	1·00	50
70	**7**	50c. on 5s. sepia and deep green (No. 35)	1·75	75
71	**22**	$1 on 10s. emerald-green (*value tablet 7×6½ mm*)	2·50	2·50
		a. Value tablet smaller, 6½×4 *mm*	2·00	3·25
60/71a		*Set of* 12	10·50	8·50

1966 (27 June). Horiz designs as T **39**. Multicoloured. P 14½×14.

72		7c. Type **39**	40	15
73		9c. Cemetery Road	40	15

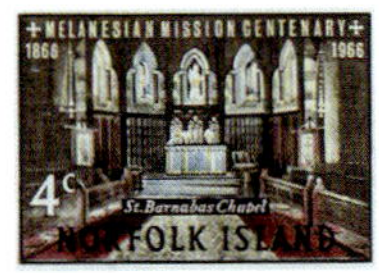

41 St. Barnabas' Chapel (interior)

42 St. Barnabas' Chapel (exterior)

1966 (23 Aug). Centenary of Melanesian Mission. P 14×14½.

74	**41**	4c. multicoloured	10	10
75	**42**	25c. multicoloured	20	20

43 Star over Philip Island

44 H.M.S. *Resolution*, 1774

(Des B. G. W. McCoy)

1966 (24 Oct). Christmas. P 14½.

76	**43**	4c. multicoloured	10	10

(Des V. Whiteley)

1967 (17 Apr)–**68**. T **44** and similar horiz designs showing ships. Multicoloured. P 14×14½.

77		1c. Type **44**	10	10
78		2c. *La Boussole and L'Astrolabe*, 1788	15	10
79		3c. H.M.S. *Supply*, 1788	15	10
80		4c. H.M.S. *Sirius*, 1790	75	10
81		5c. *Norfolk* (sloop), 1798 (14.8.67)	20	10
82		7c. H.M.S. *Mermaid* (survey cutter), 1825 (14.8.67)	20	10
83		9c. *Lady Franklin*, 1853 (14.8.67)	20	10
84		10c. *Morayshire*, 1856 (14.8.67)	20	50
85		15c. *Southern Cross*, 1866 (18.3.68)	50	30
86		20c. *Pitcairn*, 1891 (18.3.68)	60	40
87		25c. *Black Billy* (Norfolk Island whaleboat), 1895 (18.3.68)	1·50	75
88		30c. *Iris* (cable ship), 1907 (18.6.68)	1·50	2·00
89		50c. *Resolution*, 1926 (18.6.68)	2·50	2·75
90		$1 *Morinda*, 1931 (18.6.68)	3·00	2·75
77/90		*Set of* 14	10·50	9·00

45 Lions Badge and 50 Stars

46 Prayer of John Adams and Candle

(Des M. Ripper. Photo Note Ptg Branch, Reserve Bank of Australia)

1967 (7 June). 50th Anniv of Lions International. P 13½.

91	**45**	4c. black, bluish green and olive-yellow	10	10

(Des B. G. W. McCoy)

1967 (16 Oct). Christmas. P 14.

92	**46**	5c. black, light yellow-olive and red	10	10

47 Queen Elizabeth II

(Photo Note Ptg Branch, Reserve Bank of Australia)

1968 (5 Aug)–**71**. Coil stamps. P 15×imperf.

93	**47**	3c. black, light brown and vermilion	10	10
94		4c. black, light brown and blue-green	10	10
95		5c. black, light brown and deep violet	10	10
95*a*		6c. black, light brown and lake-brown (25.8.71)	30	60
93/5*a* *Set of 4*			55	80

59 Avro Type 691 Lancastrian and Douglas DC-4 Aircraft

60 Bethlehem Star and Flowers

(Des Harrison)

1968 (25 Sept). 21st Anniv of QANTAS Air Service, Sydney-Norfolk Island. P 14.

96	**59**	5c. bluish black, carmine-red and light blue	15	10
97		7c. blackish brown, carmine-red and turquoise	15	10

(Des Betty Laing)

1968 (24 Oct). Christmas. P 14×14½.

98	**60**	5c. multicoloured	10	10

61 Captain Cook, Quadrant and Chart of Pacific Ocean

62 Van Diemen's Land, Norfolk Island and Sailing Cutter

(Des V. Whiteley from sketch by J. Cowap)

1969 (3 June). Captain Cook Bicentenary (1st issue). Observation of the transit of Venus across the Sun, from Tahiti. P 14.

99	**61**	10c. multicoloured	10	10

See also Nos. 118/19, 129, 152/5, 200/2 and 213/14.

(Des Mrs. A. Bathie and Mrs. M. J. McCoy)

1969 (29 Sept). 125th Anniv of the Annexation of Norfolk Island to Van Diemen's Land. P 14×14½.

100	**62**	5c. multicoloured	10	10
101		30c. multicoloured	50	1·00
		a. Inscr "VAN DIFMEN'S LAND" (R. 8/5)	13·00	

63 "The Nativity" (carved mother-of-pearl plaque)

64 New Zealand Grey Flyeater

(Des J. Cowap)

1969 (27 Oct). Christmas. P 14½×14.

102	**63**	5c. multicoloured	10	10

(Des G. Mathews)

1970–71. Birds. T **64** and similar multicoloured designs. Chalk-surfaced paper. P 14.

103	1c. Scarlet Robins (22.7.70)	30	10
104	2c. Golden Whistler (24.2.71)	30	40
105	3c. Type **64** (25.2.70)	30	10
106	4c. Long-tailed Koels (25.2.70)	60	10
107	5c. Red-fronted Parakeet (24.2.71)	1·50	60
108	7c. Long-tailed Triller (22.7.70)	45	10
109	9c. Island Thrush (25.2.70)	70	10
110	10c. Boobook Owl (22.7.70)	1·75	3·00
111	15c. Norfolk Island Pigeon (24.2.71)	1·25	65
112	20c. White-chested White Eye	6·00	3·50
113	25c. Norfolk Island Parrots (22.7.70)	1·25	40
	a. Error. Glazed, ordinary paper	£400	
114	30c. Collared Grey Fantail (16.6.71)	6·00	2·00
115	45c. Norfolk Island Starlings (25.2.70)	1·00	80
116	50c. Crimson Rosella (24.2.71)	1·25	2·00
117	$1 Sacred Kingfisher (16.6.71)	7·00	10·00
103/17 *Set of 15*		27·00	21·00

Nos. 105, 106, 109, 112, 114, 115 and 117 are horizontal, and the remainder vertical designs.

It is believed that only one sheet of No. 113a was issued.

65 Capt. Cook and Map of Australia

66 First Christmas Service, 1788

(Des R. Bates)

1970 (29 Apr). Captain Cook Bicentenary (2nd issue). Discovery of Australia's East Coast. T **65** and similar horiz design. Multicoloured. P 14.

118	5c. Type **65**	15	10
119	10c. H.M.S. *Endeavour* and aborigine	40	10

(Des R. Bates)

1970 (15 Oct). Christmas. P 14.

120	**66**	5c. multicoloured	10	10

67 Bishop Patteson and Martyrdom of St. Stephen

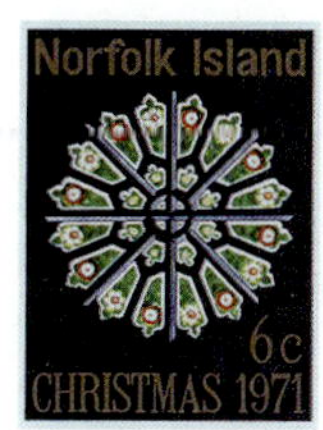

68 Rose Window, St. Barnabas Chapel, Kingston

(Des R. Bates)

1971 (20 Sept). Death Centenary of Bishop Patteson. T **67** and similar horiz designs. Multicoloured. P 14×14½.

121	6c. Type **67**	10	35
	a. Pair. Nos. 121/2	15	70
122	6c. Bible, Martyrdom of St. Stephen and knotted palm-frond	10	35
123	10c. Bishop Patteson and stained-glass	10	35
	a. Pair. Nos. 123/4	20	70
124	10c. Cross and Bishop's Arms	10	35
121/4 *Set of 4*		30	1·25

Nos. 121/2 and 123/4 were printed in *se-tenant* pairs throughout the sheet.

(Des G. Hitch. Photo Heraclio Fournier, Spain)

1971 (25 Oct). Christmas. P 14×13½.

125	**68**	6c. multicoloured	10	10

69 Map and Flag

70 "St. Mark" (stained-glass window, All Saints, Norfolk Is)

(Des G. Hitch)

1972 (7 Feb). 25th Anniv of South Pacific Commission. P 14×14½.

126	**69**	7c. multicoloured	15	20

(Des Mrs. M. J. McCoy)

1972 (16 Oct). Christmas. P 14.

127	**70**	7c. multicoloured	10	10

71 Cross and Pines (stained-glass window, All Saints Church)

72 H.M.S. *Resolution* in the Antarctic

(Des Harrison)

1972 (20 Nov). Centenary of First Pitcairner-built Church. P 14.

128	**71**	12c. multicoloured	10	10
		a. Purple (background to dates) omitted	£1800	

No. 128a occurred on the top row of one sheet.

(Des G. Hitch)

1973 (17 Jan). Captain Cook Bicentenary (3rd issue). Crossing of the Antarctic Circle. P 14.

129	**72**	35c. multicoloured	1·75	1·75

73 Child and Christmas Tree

74 Protestant Clergyman's Quarters

(Des B. G. W. McCoy (T **73**), R. Westwood (35c.))

1973 (22 Oct). Christmas. T **73** and similar vert design. Multicoloured. P 14.

130	7c. Type **73**	20	10
131	12c. Type **73**	25	10
132	35c. Fir trees and star	70	90
130/2	*Set of* 3	1·00	1·00

(Des G. Hitch)

1973 (19 Nov)–**75**. Historic Buildings. T **74** and similar horiz designs. Multicoloured. P 14×14½.

133	1c. Type **74**	10	10
134	2c. Royal Engineers' Office (1.5.74)	10	10
135	3c. Double Quarters for Free Overseers (19.2.75)	20	1·00
136	4c. Guard House (12.7.74)	15	20
137	5c. Entrance to Pentagonal Gaol	20	15
138	7c. Pentagonal Gaol (1.5.74)	25	25
139	8c. Prisoners' Barracks (19.2.75)	75	2·25
140	10c. Officers' Quarters, New Military Barracks	25	45
141	12c. New Military Barracks (1.5.74)	25	30
142	14c. Beach Stores (12.7.74)	25	50
143	15c. The Magazine (19.2.75)	75	35
144	20c. Entrance, Old Military Barracks (12.7.74)	30	1·00
145	25c. Old Military Barracks (19.2.75)	75	1·50
146	30c. Old Stores (Crankmill) (1.5.74)	30	40
147	50c. Commissariat Stores	30	1·50
148	$1 Government House (12.7.74)	75	2·75
133/48	*Set of* 16	5·00	11·50

75 Royal Couple and Map

(Des Harrison)

1974 (8 Feb). Royal Visit. P 14×14½.

149	**75**	7c. multicoloured	40	20
150		25c. multicoloured	70	80

76 Chichester's de Havilland DH.60G Gipsy Moth Seaplane *Madame Elijah*

(Des B. G. W. McCoy. Litho State Bank Note Printing Works, Helsinki)

1974 (28 Mar). First Aircraft Landing on Norfolk Island. P 14.

151	**76**	14c. multicoloured	75	70

77 "Captain Cook" (engraving by J. Basire)

78 Nativity Scene (pearl-shell pew carving)

(Des C.I. Buffett. Litho Questa)

1974 (8 Oct). Captain Cook Bicentenary (4th issue). Discovery of Norfolk Is. T **77** and similar vert designs. Multicoloured. P 14.

152	7c. Type **77**	45	50
153	10c. "H.M.S. *Resolution*" (H. Roberts)	80	90
154	14c. Norfolk Island Pine	50	90
155	25c. "Norfolk Island flax" (G. Raper)	50	1·25
152/5	*Set of* 4	2·00	3·25

(Des G. Hitch)

1974 (18 Oct). Christmas. P 14½.

156	**78**	7c. multicoloured	15	10
157		30c. multicoloured	60	75

79 Norfolk Pine

(Manufactured by Walsall)

1974 (16 Dec). Centenary of Universal Postal Union. T **79** and similar "island"-shaped designs. Multicoloured. Imperf (backing paper roul 20). Self-adhesive.

158	10c. Type **79**	35	50
159	15c. Offshore islands	45	50

160	35c. Crimson Rosella and Sacred Kingfisher.	1·00	85
	a. Backing paper inverted	£100	
161	40c. Pacific map	1·00	95
158/61	*Set of 4*	2·50	2·50
MS162	106×101 *mm*. Map of Norfolk Is. cut-to-shape with reduced-size replicas of Nos. 158/61	15·00	24·00

80 H.M.S. *Mermaid* (survey cutter)

(Manufactured by Walsall)

1975 (18 Aug). 150th Anniv of Second Settlement. T **80** and similar "island" shaped-design. Multicoloured. Imperf (backing paper roul 20). Self-adhesive.

163	10c. Type **80**	40	1·10
164	35c. Kingston, 1835 (from painting by T. Seller)	60	1·25

81 Star on Norfolk Island Pine

82 Memorial Cross

(Des Harrison)

1975 (6 Oct). Christmas. P 14.

165	**81**	10c. multicoloured	15	10
166		15c. multicoloured	20	10
167		35c. multicoloured	30	35
165/7		*Set of 3*	60	45

(Des Harrison)

1975 (24 Nov). Centenary of St. Barnabas Chapel. T **82** and similar horiz design. Multicoloured. P 14.

168	30c. Type **82**	20	15
169	60c. Laying foundation stone and Chapel in 1975	40	40

83 Launching of *Resolution*

84 Whaleship *Charles W. Morgan*

(Des Harrison)

1975 (1 Dec). 50th Anniv of Launching of Schooner "Resolution". T **83** and similar horiz design. Multicoloured. P 14.

170	25c. Type **83**	25	40
171	45c. *Resolution* at sea	40	70

(Des Harrison)

1976 (5 July). Bicentenary of American Revolution. T **84** and similar horiz designs. Multicoloured. P 14.

172	18c. Type **84**	20	35
173	25c. Thanksgiving Service	20	35
174	40c. Boeing B-17 Flying Fortress over Norfolk Is	30	85
175	45c. California Quail	45	85
172/5	*Set of 4*	1·00	2·25

85 Antarctic Tern and Sun

86 *Vanessa ita*

(Des Harrison)

1976 (4 Oct). Christmas. P 14.

176	**85**	18c. multicoloured	25	15
177		25c. multicoloured	35	20
178		45c. multicoloured	50	50
176/8		*Set of 3*	1·00	75

(Des B. Hargreaves)

1976 (17 Nov)–**77**. Butterflies and Moths. T **86** and similar horiz designs. Multicoloured. P 14.

179	1c. Type **86**	10	40
180	2c. *Utetheisa pulchelloides* (moth) (22.2.77)	10	40
181	3c. *Agathia asterias* (moth) (5.7.77)	10	20
182	4c. *Cynthia kershawi* (5.7.77)	10	60
183	5c. *Leucania loreyimima* (moth)	15	1·10
184	10c. *Hypolimnas bolina*	30	1·10
185	15c. *Pyrrhorachis pyrrhogona* (moth) (22.2.77)	30	30
186	16c. *Austrocarea iocephala* (moth)	30	30
187	17c. *Pseudocoremia christiani* (moth) (10.5.77)	35	30
188	18c. *Cleora idiocrossa* (moth)	35	30
189	19c. *Simplicia caeneusalis* (moth) (10.5.77)	35	30
190	20c. *Austrocidaria ralstonae* (moth) (10.5.77)	35	30
191	30c. *Hippotion scrofa* (moth) (22.2.77)	40	75
192	40c. *Papilio amynthor* (*ilioneus*) (10.5.77)	40	40
193	50c. *Tiracola plagiata* (moth) (22.2.77)	40	1·00
194	$1 *Precis villida*	50	75
195	$2 *Cepora perimale* (5.7.77)	65	1·40
179/95	*Set of 17*	4·50	8·50

87 Queen's View, Kingston

(Des Harrison)

1977 (10 June). Silver Jubilee. P 14.

196	**87**	25c. multicoloured	35	30

88 Hibiscus Flowers and Oil Lamp

89 Captain Cook (from a portrait by Nathaniel Dance)

(Des Marguerite M. J. McCoy)

1977 (4 Oct). Christmas. P 14×14½.

197	**88**	18c. multicoloured	15	10
198		25c. multicoloured	15	10
199		45c. multicoloured	30	35
197/9		*Set of 3*	55	50

(Des Harrison)

1978 (18 Jan). Captain Cook Bicentenary (5th issue). Discovery of Hawaii. T **89** and similar horiz designs. Multicoloured. P 14½.

200	18c. Type **89**	30	20
201	25c. Discovery of Northern Hawaiian islands	30	30
202	80c. British flag against island background	60	70
200/2	*Set of 3*	1·10	1·10

90 Guide Flag and Globe

(Manufactured by Walsall)

1978 (22 Feb). 50th Anniv of Girl Guides. T **90** and similar "island" shaped-designs. Multicoloured. Imperf (backing paper roul 20). Self-adhesive.

203	18c. Type **90**	25	50
204	25c. Emblem and scarf badge	30	60
	a. Horiz roul omitted (vert pair)		
205	35c. Emblem and Queen Elizabeth	45	85
	a. Horiz roul omitted (vert pair)		
206	45c. Emblem and Lady Baden-Powell	55	85
203/6 *Set of 4*		1·40	2·50

Nos. 204a and 205a each come from sheets of 20 on which all the horizontal roulettes were omitted.

91 St. Edward's Crown

(Des Harrison)

1978 (29 June). 25th Anniv of Coronation. T **91** and similar horiz design. Multicoloured. P 14½.

207	25c. Type **91**	15	15
208	70c. Coronation regalia	40	45

92 View of Duncombe Bay with Scout at Camp Fire

(Des S. Jensen. Manufactured by Walsall)

1978 (22 Aug). 50th Anniv of Boy Scouts. T **92** and similar "island"-shaped designs. Multicoloured. Imperf (backing paper roul 20). Self-adhesive.

209	20c. Type **92**	30	45
210	25c. View from Kingston and emblem	35	55
211	35c. View of Anson Bay and Link Badge	50	90
212	45c. Sunset scene and Lord Baden-Powell	55	95
209/12 *Set of 4*		1·50	2·50

93 Chart showing Route of Arctic Voyage

94 Poinsettia and Bible

(Des G. Hitch)

1978 (29 Aug). Captain Cook Bicentenary (6th issue). Northern most Voyages. T **93** and similar horiz design. Multicoloured. P 14½.

213	25c. Type **93**	30	30
214	90c. "H.M.S. *Resolution* and H.M.S. *Discovery* in Pack Ice" (painting by Webber)	80	80

(Des Marie L. McCoy)

1978 (3 Oct). Christmas. T **94** and similar vert designs. Multicoloured. P 14½×14.

215	20c. Type **94**	15	10
216	30c. Native Oak and Bible	20	15
217	55c. Hibiscus and Bible	30	30
215/17 *Set of 3*		60	50

95 Cook and Village of Staithess near Marton

(Des Harrison)

1978 (27 Oct). 250th Birth Anniv of Captain Cook. T **95** and similar horiz design. Multicoloured. P 14½.

218	20c. Type **95**	30	25
219	80c. Cook and Whitby Harbour	70	1·25

96 H.M.S. *Resolution*

97 Assembly Building

(Des G. Hitch)

1979 (14 Feb). Death Bicentenary of Captain Cook. T **96** and similar horiz designs. Multicoloured. P 14.

220	20c. Type **96**	25	30
	a. Pair. Nos. 220/1	50	60
221	20c. Cook (statue)	25	30
222	40c. Cook's death	30	50
	a. Pair. Nos. 222/3	60	1·00
223	40c. Cook's death (*different*)	30	50
220/23 *Set of 4*		1·00	1·60

The 20c. designs depict the *Resolution* and Cook's statue on a map showing the last voyage. The 40c. designs show Cook's death from an aquatint by John Clevely.

Nos. 220/1 and 222/3 were each printed together, *se-tenant*, in horizontal pairs throughout the sheets, forming composite designs.

1979 (10 Aug). First Norfolk Island Legislative Assembly. P 14½×14.

224	**97**	$1 multicoloured	50	50

98 Tasmania 1853 1d. Stamp and Sir Rowland Hill

1979 (27 Aug). Death Centenary of Sir Rowland Hill. T **98** and similar horiz designs showing stamps and Sir Rowland Hill. P 14×14½.

225	20c. new blue and sepia	20	10
226	30c. brown-red and olive-grey	20	15
227	55c. violet and indigo	30	30
225/7 *Set of 3*		60	50
MS228	142×91 *mm*. No. 227. P 14	55	1·25

Designs:—30c. Penny Red; 55c. 1d. "Ball Bay".

99 I.Y.C. Emblem and Map of Pacific showing Norfolk Island as Pine Tree

(Des Claire Walters. Litho Asher and Co, Melbourne)

1979 (25 Sept). International Year of the Child. P 15.

229	**99**	80c. multicoloured	40	45

100 Emily Bay

101 Lions International Emblem

1979 (5* Nov). Christmas. T **100** and similar horiz designs showing different aspects of Emily Bay. P 12½×13.

230	15c. multicoloured	15	15
	a. Horiz strip of 3. Nos. 230/2	40	40
231	20c. multicoloured	15	15
232	30c. multicoloured	15	15
230/2	*Set of* 3	40	40
MS233	152×83 *mm*. Nos. 230/2. P 14×14½	1·00	1·40

Nos. 230/2 were printed together, *se-tenant*, in horizontal strips of 3 throughout the sheet, forming a composite design.

*Although released by the Crown Agents in London on 2 October the stamps were not released locally until 5 November.

(Des Norfolk Island Lions Club. Litho Asher and Co, Melbourne)

1980 (25 Jan). Lions Convention. P 15.

234	**101**	50c. multicoloured	35	30

102 Rotary International Emblem

(Des E. Lenthall. Litho Asher and Co, Melbourne)

1980 (21 Feb). 75th Anniv of Rotary International. P 15.

235	**102**	50c. multicoloured	35	30
		a. Black (face value and "NORFOLK ISLAND") omitted	£12000	

103 de Havilland DH.60G. Gipsy Moth Seaplane *Madame Elijah*

(Des G. Hitch and B. G. W. McCoy. Litho Harrison)

1980 (25 Mar)–**81**. Aeroplanes. Horiz designs as T **103**. Multicoloured. P 14½×14.

236	1c. Hawker Siddeley H.S.748 (3.3.81)	10	20
237	2c. Type **103**	10	20
238	3c. Curtiss P.40E Kittyhawk I	10	20
239	4c. Chance Vought F4U-1 Corsair (19.8.80).	15	30
240	5c. Grumman TBF Avenger (19.8.80)	15	30
241	15c. Douglas SBD-5 Dauntless (19.8.80)	25	30
242	20c. Cessna 172D Skyhawk	25	30
243	25c. Lockheed 414 Hudson (3.3.81)	25	35
244	30c. Lockheed PV-1 Ventura (13.1.81)	40	2·00
245	40c. Avro Type 685 York (3.3.81)	40	45
246	50c. Douglas DC-3 (13.1.81)	50	55
247	60c. Avro Type 691 Lancastrian (13.1.81)	65	65
248	80c. Douglas DC-4 (13.1.81)	1·00	1·00
249	$1 Beech 200 Super King Air (3.3.81)	1·00	1·00
250	$2 Fokker F.27 Friendship (19.8.80)	1·75	2·50
251	$5 Lockheed C-130 Hercules	1·75	1·50
236/51	*Set of* 16	7·75	10·50

104 Queen Elizabeth the Queen Mother

(Des K. Williams. Litho Harrison)

1980 (4 Aug). 80th Birthday of Queen Elizabeth the Queen Mother. P 14.

252	**104**	22c. multicoloured	20	20
253		60c. multicoloured	35	40

105 Red-tailed Tropic Birds

(Des K. Williams. Litho Harrison)

1980 (28 Oct). Christmas. Birds. T **105** and similar horiz designs. Multicoloured. P 14×14½.

254	15c. Type **105**	30	25
	a. Horiz strip of 3. Nos. 254/6	80	80
255	22c. White Terns	30	25
256	35c. White-capped Noddys	30	25
257	60c. White Terns (*different*)	40	45
254/7	*Set of* 4	1·10	1·10

Nos. 254/6 were printed together, *se-tenant*, in horizontal strips of 3 throughout the sheet.

106 *Morayshire* and view of Norfolk Island

107 Wedding Bouquet from Norfolk Island

(Des Jennifer Toombs. Litho Harrison)

1981 (5 June). 125th Anniv of Pitcairn Islanders' Migration to Norfolk Island. T **106** and similar horiz designs. Multicoloured. P 14½.

258	5c. Type **106**	15	15
259	35c. Islanders arriving ashore	40	30
260	60c. View of new settlement	60	45
258/60	*Set of* 3	1·00	80
MS261	183×127 *mm*. Nos. 258/60	1·00	1·25

(Des J.W. Litho Harrison)

1981 (22 July). Royal Wedding. T **107** and similar vert designs. Multicoloured. P 14.

262	35c. Type **107**	15	15
263	55c. Prince Charles at horse trials	25	25
264	60c. Prince Charles and Lady Diana Spencer	25	35
262/4	*Set of* 3	60	65

108 Uniting Church in Australia

109 Pair of White-chested White Eyes

(Des K. Williams. Litho Harrison)

1981 (15 Sept). Christmas. Churches. T **108** and similar horiz designs. Multicoloured. P 14½×14.

265	18c. Type **108**	10	10
266	24c. Seventh Day Adventist Church	15	15
267	30c. Church of the Sacred Heart	15	20
268	$1 St. Barnabas Chapel	35	70
265/8	*Set of* 4	65	1·00

(Des P. Slater. Litho Questa)

1981 (10 Nov). White-chested White Eye ("Silvereye"). T **109** and similar horiz designs. Multicoloured. P 14×14½.

269	35c. Type **109**	25	30
	a. Horiz strip of 5. Nos. 269/73	1·10	1·40
270	35c. Bird on nest	25	30
271	35c. Bird with egg	25	30
272	35c. Parents with chicks	25	30
273	35c. Fledglings	25	30
269/73	*Set of* 5	1·10	1·40

Nos. 269/73 were printed together, *se-tenant*, in horizontal strips of five throughout the sheet.

110 Aerial View of Philip Island

(Des local artist. Litho Harrison)

1982 (12 Jan). Philip and Nepean Islands. T **110** and similar horiz designs. Multicoloured. P 14×13½.

274	24c. Type **110**	15	15
	a. Horiz strip of 5. Nos. 274/8	65	65
275	24c. Close-up view of Philip Island landscape	15	15
276	24c. Gecko (*Phyllodactylus guentheri*), Philip Island	15	15
277	24c. Sooty Tern (*Sterna fuscata*), Philip Island	15	15
278	24c. Philip Island Hibiscus (*Hibiscus insularis*)	15	15
279	35c. Aerial view of Nepean Island	20	20
	a. Horiz strip of 5. Nos. 279/83	90	90
280	35c. Close-up view of Nepean Island landscape	20	20
281	35c. Gecko (*Phyllodactylus guentheri*), Nepean Island	20	20
282	35c. Blue-faced Boobies (*Sula dactylatra*), Nepean Island	20	20
283	35c. *Carpobrotus glaucescens* (flower), Nepean Island	20	20
274/83	*Set of* 10	1·50	1·50

The five designs of each value were printed together, *se-tenant*, in horizontal strips of five throughout the sheet.

111 Sperm Whale

(Des Jennifer Toombs. Litho Harrison)

1982 (23 Feb). Whales. T **111** and similar horiz designs. P 14½.

284	24c. multicoloured	40	35
285	55c. multicoloured	55	95
286	80c. black, mauve and stone	65	2·25
284/6	*Set of* 3	1·40	3·25

Designs:—55c. Black Right Whale; 80c. Humpback Whale.

112 *Diocet*, Wrecked 20 April 1873

(Litho Harrison)

1982 (18 May–27 July). Shipwrecks. T **112** and similar horiz designs. Multicoloured. P 14½×14.

287	24c. H.M.S. *Sirius*, wrecked 19 March 1790 (27.7)	50	75
288	27c. Type **112**	50	50
289	35c. *Friendship*, wrecked 17 May 1835 (27.7)	90	1·50
290	40c. *Mary Hamilton*, wrecked 6 May 1873	90	1·25
291	55c. *Fairlie*, wrecked 14 February 1840 (27.7)	1·25	1·75
292	65c. *Warrigal*, wrecked 18 March 1918	1·25	2·25
287/92	*Set of* 6	4·75	7·00

C-KURITY PAPER. The following issues up to No. 342 were all printed on this type of security paper, *unless otherwise stated*. It shows a pattern of blue fluorescent markings, resembling rosettes, on the reverse beneath the gum.

113 R.N.Z.A.F. Lockheed 414 Hudson dropping Christmas Supplies, 1942

114 50th (Queen's Own) Regiment

(Des A. Theobald. Litho Walsall)

1982 (7 Sept). Christmas. 40th Anniv of first Supply-plane Landings on Norfolk Island (Christmas Day 1942). T **113** and similar horiz designs. Multicoloured. P 14.

293	27c. Type **113**	80	35
294	40c. Lockheed 414 Hudson landing Christmas supplies, 1942	1·00	70
295	75c. Christmas, 1942	1·25	2·25
293/5	*Set of* 3	2·75	3·00

(Des W. Fenton. Litho Questa)

1982 (9 Nov). Military Uniforms. T **114** and similar vert designs. Multicoloured. P 14½×14.

296	27c. Type **114**	25	35
297	40c. 58th (Rutlandshire) Regiment	30	75
298	55c. 80th (Staffordshire Volunteers) Battalion Company	35	95
299	65c. 11th (North Devonshire) Regiment	40	1·25
296/9	*Set of* 4	1·10	3·00

115 *Panaeolus papilionaceus*

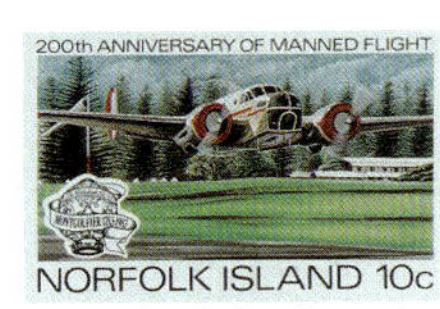

116 Beech 18 Aircraft

(Des Jane Thatcher, Litho Enschedé)

1983 (29 Mar). Fungi. T **115** and similar vert designs. Multicoloured. P 13½×13.

300	27c. Type **115**	25	35
301	40c. *Coprinus domesticus*	30	50
302	55c. *Marasmius niveus*	40	70
303	65c. *Cymatodermu elegans var lamellatum*	45	85
300/3	*Set of* 4	1·25	2·25

(Des Walsall. Litho Format)

1983 (12 July). Bicentenary of Manned Flight. T **116** and similar horiz designs. Multicoloured. P 14½×14.

304	10c. Type **116**	15	15
305	27c. Fokker F.28 Fellowship	25	35
306	45c. French military Douglas C-54	40	60
307	75c. Sikorsky S-61N helicopter	60	95
304/7	*Set of* 4	1·25	1·90
MS308	105×100 *mm*. Nos. 304/7	1·40	2·50

117 St. Matthew

118 Cable Ship *Chantik*

(Des McCombie-Skinner Studio. Litho Format)

1983 (13 Sept). Christmas. 150th Birth Anniv of Sir Edward Burne-Jones. T **117** and similar vert designs showing stained-glass windows from St. Barnabas Chapel, Norfolk Island. Multicoloured. P 14.

309	5c. Type **117**	10	10
310	24c. St. Mark	15	30
311	30c. Jesus Christ	20	40
312	45c. St. Luke	30	55
313	85c. St. John	40	1·10
309/13 *Set of 5*		1·00	2·25

(Des G. Drummond. Litho Format)

1983 (15 Nov). World Communications Year. ANZCAN Cable. T **118** and similar horiz designs. Multicoloured. Ordinary paper. P 14½×14.

314	30c. Type **118**	25	40
315	45c. *Chantik* during in-shore operations	30	55
316	75c. Cable ship *Mercury*	40	95
317	85c. Diagram of cable route	40	1·10
314/17 *Set of 4*		1·10	2·75

119 Popwood

120 Morwong

(Des I. Loe. Litho B.D.T.)

1984 (10 Jan). Flowers. T **119** and similar vert designs. Multicoloured. P 14.

318	1c. Type **119** (27.3)	30	70
319	2c. Strand Morning Glory	35	70
320	3c. Native Phreatia	35	70
321	4c. Philip Island Wisteria (27.3)	35	70
322	5c. Norfolk Island Palm (27.3)	40	70
323	10c. Evergreen	40	70
324	15c. Bastard Oak (27.3)	40	70
325	20c. Devil's Guts	40	70
326	25c. White Oak	40	80
327	30c. Ti (27.3)	40	1·00
328	35c. Philip Island Hibiscus (27.3)	40	1·00
329	40c. Native Wisteria	40	1·25
330	50c. Native Jasmine	45	1·25
331	$1 Norfolk Island Hibiscus (27.3)	50	1·75
332	$3 Native Oberonia (27.3)	70	3·00
333	$5 Norfolk Island Pine	1·00	3·50
318/33 *Set of 16*		6·50	17·00

(Des Marg Towt. Litho Cambec Press, Melbourne)

1984 (17 Apr). Reef Fish. T **120** and similar horiz designs. Multicoloured. Ordinary paper. P 13½×14.

334	30c. Type **120**	20	45
335	45c. Black-spotted Goatfish (*Pseudopeneus signatus*)	25	65
336	75c. Surgeonfish (*Acanthuridae*)	30	1·10
337	85c. Three-striped Butterflyfish (*Chaeton ancinetus*)	35	1·40
334/7 *Set of 4*		1·00	3·25

121 Owl with Eggs

122 1953 7½d. and 1974 Cook Bicent 10c. Stamps

(Des P. Slater. Litho Questa)

1984 (17 July). Boobook Owl. T **121** and similar vert designs. Multicoloured. P 14.

338	30c. Type **121**	45	80
	a. Horiz strip of 5. Nos. 338/42	2·00	3·50
339	30c. Fledgling	45	80
340	30c. Young owl on stump	45	80
341	30c. Adult on branch	45	80
342	30c. Owl in flight	45	80
338/42 *Set of 5*		2·00	3·50

Nos. 338/42 were printed together, *se-tenant*, in horizontal strips of 5 throughout the sheet.

(Des D. Miller. Litho Harrison)

1984 (18 Sept). Ausipex International Stamp Exhibition, Melbourne. T **122** and similar horiz designs. Multicoloured. W w **14** (sideways). P 14.

343	30c. Type **122**	25	35
344	45c. John Buffett commemorative postal stationery envelope	35	75
345	75c. Design from Presentation Pack for 1982 Military Uniforms issue	50	1·75
343/5 *Set of 3*		1·00	2·50
MS346 151×93 *mm*. Nos. 343/5. P 14½		2·75	5·00

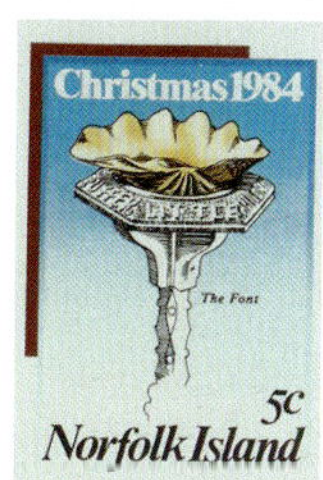

123 Font, Kingston Methodist Church

124 The Revd. Nobbs teaching Pitcairn Islanders

(Des R. Murphy. Litho Questa)

1984 (9 Oct). Christmas. Centenary of Methodist Church on Norfolk Island. T **123** and similar vert designs. Multicoloured. W **14**. P 14.

347	5c. Type **123**	10	30
348	24c. Church service in Old Barracks, Kingston, late 1800's	20	40
349	30c. The Revd. & Mrs. A. H. Phelps and sailing ship	20	45
350	45c. The Revd. A. H. Phelps and First Congregational Church, Chester, USA	25	65
351	85c. Interior of Kingston Methodist Church	40	1·40
347/51 *Set of 5*		1·00	2·75

(Des D. Hopkins. Litho B.D.T.)

1984 (6 Nov). Death Centenary of the Revd. George Hunn Nobbs (leader of Pitcairn community). T **124** and similar vert designs. Multicoloured. W **14**. P 14×15.

352	30c. Type **124**	20	45
353	45c. The Revd. Nobbs with sick islander	25	65
354	75c. Baptising baby	35	1·10
355	85c. Presented to Queen Victoria, 1852	45	1·40
352/5 *Set of 4*		1·10	3·25

125 *Fanny Fisher*

126 The Queen Mother (from photo by Norman Parkinson)

(Des D. Hopkins. Litho Cambec Press, Melbourne)

1985 (19 Feb). 19th-Century Whaling Ships (1st series). T **125** and similar horiz designs. Multicoloured. P 13½×14.

356	5c. Type **125**	30	1·25
357	33c. *Costa Rica Packet*	60	55
358	50c. *Splendid*	1·00	1·50
359	90c. *Onward*	1·25	3·25
356/9 *Set of 4*		2·75	6·00

See also Nos. 360/3.

(Des D. Hopkins. Litho Cambec Press, Melbourne)

1985 (30 Apr). 19th-Century Whaling Ships (2nd series). Horiz designs as T **125**. Multicoloured. P 13½×14.

360	15c. *Waterwitch*	50	1·10
361	20c. *Canton*	55	1·10
362	60c. *Aladdin*	1·00	2·00
363	80c. *California*	1·00	2·50
360/3 *Set of 4*		2·75	6·00

(Des A. Theobald ($1), C. Abbott (others). Litho Questa)

1985 (6 June). Life and Times of Queen Elizabeth the Queen Mother. T **126** and similar vert designs. Multicoloured. W **16**. P 14½×14.

364	5c. The Queen Mother (from photo by Dorothy Wilding)	10	40
365	33c. With Princess Anne at Trooping the Colour	25	25
366	50c. Type **126**	40	55
367	90c. With Prince Henry at his christening (from photo by Lord Snowdon)	60	1·00
364/7 *Set of 4*		1·25	2·00
MS368 91×73 *mm*. $1 With Princess Anne at Ascot Races. Wmk sideways		1·75	2·25

127 "Swimming"

128 Prize-winning Cow and Owner

(Des from Children's paintings. Litho Cambec Press, Melbourne)

1985 (9 July). International Youth Year. T **127** and similar horiz design. Multicoloured. P 13½×14.

369	33c. Type **127**	40	40
370	50c. "A Walk in the Country"	70	85

(Des Flett Henderson & Arnold. Litho Cambec Press, Melbourne)

1985 (10 Sept). 125th Anniv of Royal Norfolk Island Agricultural and Horticultural Show. T **128** and similar horiz design. Multicoloured. P 13½×14.

371	80c. Type **128**	50	80
372	90c. Show exhibits	50	90
MS373 132×85 *mm*. Nos. 371/2		2·00	3·25

129 Shepherds with flock

130 Long-spined Sea Urchin

(Des R. Murphy. Litho Cambec Press, Melbourne)

1985 (3 Oct). Christmas. T **129** and similar vert designs. Multicoloured. P 13½.

374	27c. Type **129**	20	30
375	33c. Mary and Joseph with donkey	20	30
376	50c. The Three Wise Men	30	65
377	90c. The Nativity	55	1·25
374/7 *Set of 4*		1·10	2·25

(Des L. Curtis. Litho Cambec Press, Melbourne)

1986 (14 Jan). Marine Life. T **130** and similar horiz designs. Multicoloured. P 13½×14.

378	5c. Type **130**	10	10
379	33c. Blue Starfish	25	35
380	55c. Southern Eagle Ray	40	85
381	75c. Snowflake Moray	55	1·50
378/81 *Set of 4*		1·10	2·50
MS382 100×95 *mm*. Nos. 378/81		1·75	4·00

131 *Giotto* Spacecraft

132 Isaac Robinson (U.S. Consul 1887-1908)

(Des G. Revell. Litho Leigh-Mardon Ltd, Melbourne)

1986 (11 Mar). Appearance of Halley's Comet. T **131** and similar vert design. Multicoloured. P 14½×15.

383	$1 Type **131**	50	1·50
	a. Horiz pair. Nos. 383/4	1·00	3·00
384	$1 Halley's Comet	50	1·50

Nos. 383/4 were printed together, *se-tenant*, in horizontal pairs throughout the sheet, each pair forming a composite design.

(Des G. Revell. Litho Cambec Press, Melbourne)

1986 (22 May). Ameripex '86 International Stamp Exhibition, Chicago. T **132** and similar multicoloured designs. P 13½.

385	33c. Type **132**	30	35
386	50c. Ford "Model T" (first vehicle on island) (*horiz*)	40	50
387	80c. Statue of Liberty	40	1·10
385/7 *Set of 3*		1·00	1·75
MS388 125×100 *mm*. Nos. 385/7		1·00	2·25

No. 387 also commemorates the Centenary of the Statue of Liberty.

133 Princess Elizabeth and Dog

134 Stylized Dove and Norfolk Island

(Des Allison Ryves. Litho Cambec Press, Melbourne)

1986 (12 June). 60th Birthday of Queen Elizabeth II. T **133** and similar vert designs. Multicoloured. P 13½.

389	5c. Type **133**	20	40
390	33c. Queen Elizabeth II	40	35
391	80c. Opening Norfolk Island Golf Club	2·25	1·60
392	90c. With Duke of Edinburgh in carriage	1·25	1·60
389/92 *Set of 4*		3·50	3·50

(Des Lyn Studham. Litho Cambec Press, Melbourne)

1986 (23 Sept). Christmas. P 13½×14.

393	**134** 30c. multicoloured	25	30
394	40c. multicoloured	30	45
395	$1 multicoloured	70	1·50
393/5 *Set of 3*		1·10	2·00

135 British Convicts, 1787

136 Stone Tools

(Des Josephine Martin. Litho Cambec Press, Melbourne)

1986 (14 Oct–16 Dec). Bicentenary of Norfolk Island Settlement (1988) (1st issue). Governor Phillip's Commission. T **135** and similar vert designs. Multicoloured. P 14×13½.

396	36c. Type **135**	50	35
397	55c. Judge passing sentence of transportation	1·00	85
398	90c. Governor Phillip meeting Home Secretary (inscr "Home Society")	2·00	3·75
399	90c. As No. 398, but correctly inscr "Home Secretary" (16.12)	2·00	3·75
400	$1 Captain Arthur Phillip	2·00	2·75
396/400 *Set of 5*		6·75	10·50

See also Nos. 401/4, 421/4, 433/5, 436/7 and 438/43.

(Des B. Clinton. Litho Cambec Press, Melbourne)

1986 (16 Dec). Bicentenary of Norfolk Island Settlement (1988) (2nd issue). Pre-European Occupation. T **136** and similar horiz designs. Multicoloured. P 13½.

401	36c. Type **136**	30	85
402	36c. Bananas and Taro	30	85
403	36c. Polynesian outrigger canoe	30	85
404	36c. Maori chief	30	85
401/4 *Set of 4*		1·00	3·00

137 Philip Island from Point Ross

138 Male Red-fronted Parakeet

(Des C. Abbott. Litho CPE Australia Ltd, Melbourne)

1987 (17 Feb)–**88**. Norfolk Island Scenes. T **137** and similar square designs. Multicoloured. P 13½.

405	1c. Cockpit Creek Bridge (17.5.88)	50	2·00
406	2c. Cemetery Bay Beach (17.5.88)	50	2·00
407	3c. Island guesthouse (17.5.88)	50	2·00
408	5c. Type **137**	30	1·00
409	15c. Cattle in pasture (27.7.87)	80	2·00
410	30c. Rock fishing (7.4.87)	30	1·25
411	37c. Old Pitcairner-style house (27.7.87)	1·40	2·00
412	40c. Shopping centre (7.4.87)	35	1·25
413	50c. Emily Bay	45	1·25
414	60c. Bloody Bridge (27.7.87)	2·00	3·00
415	80c. Pitcairner-style shop (7.4.87)	1·75	2·75
416	90c. Government House	1·25	2·25
417	$1 Melanesian Memorial Chapel	1·00	1·75
418	$2 Convict Settlement, Kingston (7.4.87)	1·25	3·50
419	$3 Ball Bay (27.7.87)	2·00	5·00
420	$5 Northern cliffs (17.5.88)	2·50	7·00
405/20 *Set of 16*		15·00	35·00

(Des Josephine Martin. Litho CPE Australia Ltd, Melbourne)

1987 (13 May). Bicentenary of Norfolk Island Settlement (1988) (3rd issue). The First Fleet. Vert designs as T **135**. Multicoloured. P 14×13½.

421	5c. Loading supplies, Deptford	50	1·50
422	55c. Fleet leaving Spithead	2·00	2·50
	a. Horiz pair. Nos. 422/3	4·00	5·00
423	55c. H.M.S. *Sirius* leaving Spithead	2·00	2·50
424	$1 Female convicts below decks	2·25	3·00
421/4 *Set of 4*		6·00	8·50

Nos. 422/3 were printed together, *se-tenant*, in horizontal pairs throughout the sheet, forming a composite design.

(Des P. Slater. Litho CPE Australia Ltd, Melbourne)

1987 (16 Sept). Endangered Species. Red-fronted Parakeet ("Green Parrot"). T **138** and similar vert designs. Multicoloured. P 14×13½.

425	5c. Type **138**	2·00	2·00
	a. Horiz strip of 4. Nos. 425/8	10·00	10·00
426	15c. Adult with fledgeling and egg	2·50	2·50
427	36c. Young parakeets	2·75	2·75
428	55c. Female parakeet	3·75	3·75
425/8 *Set of 4*		10·00	10·00

Nos. 425/8 were printed together, *se-tenant*, in horizontal strips of four throughout the sheet.

139 Christmas Tree and Restored Garrison Barracks

140 Airliner, Container Ship and Sydney Harbour Bridge

(Des T. Bland and Alison Ryves. Litho CPE Australia Ltd, Melbourne)

1987 (13 Oct). Christmas. T **139** and similar horiz designs. Multicoloured. P 13½×14.

429	30c. Type **139**	25	25
430	42c. Children opening presents	35	45
431	58c. Father Christmas with children	50	90
432	63c. Children's party	60	1·10
429/32 *Set of 4*		1·50	2·40

(Des Josephine Martin. Litho CPE Australia Ltd, Melbourne)

1987 (8 Dec). Bicentenary of Norfolk Island Settlement (1988) (4th issue). Visit of La Perouse (navigator). Vert designs as T **135**. Multicoloured. P 14×13½.

433	37c. La Perouse with King Louis XVI	95	55
434	90c. *L'Astrolabe* and *La Boussole* off Norfolk Island	2·75	3·00
435	$1 *L'Astrolabe* wrecked in Solomon Islands	2·75	3·00
433/5 *Set of 3*		5·75	6·00

(Des Josephine Martin. Litho CPE Australia Ltd, Melbourne)

1988 (25 Jan). Bicentenary of Norfolk Island Settlement (5th issue). Arrival of First Fleet at Sydney. Vert designs as T **135**. Multicoloured. P 14×13½.

436	37c. Ship's cutter approaching Port Jackson	1·50	75
437	$1 Landing at Sydney Cove	2·75	3·75

(Des Josephine Martin. Litho CPE Australia Ltd, Melbourne)

1988 (4 Mar). Bicentenary of Norfolk Island Settlement (6th issue). Foundation of First Settlement. Vert designs as T **135**. Multicoloured. P 14×13½.

438	5c. Lt. Philip Gidley King	20	50
439	37c. Raising the flag, March 1788	85	75
440	55c. King exploring	1·50	1·50
441	70c. Landing at Sydney Bay, Norfolk Island	1·75	2·50
442	90c. H.M.S. *Supply* (brig)	2·00	2·75
443	$1 Sydney Bay settlement, 1788	2·00	2·75
438/43 *Set of 6*		7·50	9·75

(Des Janet Boschen. Litho CPE Australia Ltd, Melbourne)

1988 (30 July). Sydpex '88 National Stamp Exhibition, Sydney. T **140** and similar multicoloured designs. P 14×13½ (vert) or 13½×14 (horiz).

444	37c. Type **140**	45	1·00
445	37c. Exhibition label under magnifying glass (*horiz*)	45	1·00
446	37c. Telephone and dish aerial	45	1·00
444/6 *Set of 3*		1·25	2·75
MS447 118×84 *mm*. Nos. 444/6		6·00	7·00

In No. **MS**447 the horizontal design is perforated 14 at foot and 13½ on the other three sides.

141 Flowers and Decorations

142 Pier Store and Boat Shed

(Des Sue Pearson. Litho CPE Australia Ltd, Melbourne)

1988 (27 Sept). Christmas. T **141** and similar vert designs. Multicoloured. P 14×13½.

448	30c. Type **141**	25	30
449	42c. Flowers	30	50
450	58c. Fish and beach	40	85
451	63c. Norfolk Island	45	1·00
448/51	*Set of 4*	1·25	2·40

(Des R. Murphy. Litho CPE Australia Ltd, Melbourne)

1988 (6 Dec). Restored Buildings from the Convict Era. T **142** and similar horiz designs. Multicoloured. P 13½×14.

452	39c. Type **142**	40	35
453	55c. Royal Engineers Building	50	50
454	90c. Old Military Barracks	70	1·40
455	$1 Commissariat Store and New Military Barracks	75	1·40
452/5	*Set of 4*	2·10	3·25

143 *Lamprima aenea*

144 H.M.S. *Bounty* off Tasmania

(Des T. Nolan. Litho CPE Australia Ltd, Melbourne)

1989 (14 Feb). Endemic Insects. T **143** and similar horiz designs. Multicoloured. P 13½×14.

456	39c. Type **143**	50	40
457	55c. *Insulascirtus nythos*	75	75
458	90c. *Caedicia araucariae*	1·10	2·25
459	$1 *Thrincophora aridela*	1·25	2·25
456/9	*Set of 4*	3·25	5·00

(Des C. Abbott. Litho CPE Australia Ltd, Melbourne (Nos. 460/3), B.D.T. (No. **MS**464))

1989 (28 Apr). Bicentenary of the Mutiny on the *Bounty*. T **144** and similar horiz designs. Multicoloured. P 13½.

460	5c. Type **144**	60	60
461	39c. Mutineers and Polynesian women, Pitcairn Island	1·75	1·25
462	55c. Lake Windermere, Cumbria (Christian's home county)	2·25	2·25
463	$1.10 "Mutineers casting Bligh adrift" (Robert Dodd)	3·50	4·50
460/3	*Set of 4*	7·25	7·75
MS464	110×85 *mm*. 39c. No. 461; 90c. Isle of Man 1989 Mutiny 35p., No. 414; $1 Pitcairn Islands 1989 Settlement Bicent 90c., No. 345. P 14	7·50	8·50

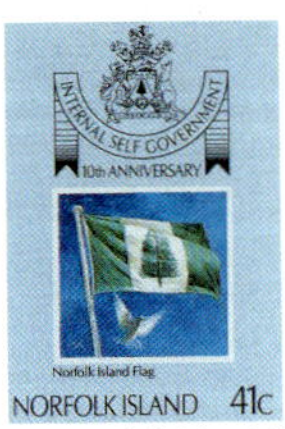

145 Norfolk Island Flag

146 Red Cross

(Des R. Fletcher. Litho CPE Australia Ltd, Melbourne)

1989 (10 Aug). Tenth Anniv of Internal Self-Government. T **145** and similar vert designs. Multicoloured. P 14×13½.

465	41c. Type **145**	90	55
466	55c. Old ballot box	95	65
467	$1 Norfolk Island Act, 1979	1·40	2·25
468	$1.10 Island crest	1·40	3·25
465/8	*Set of 4*	4·25	6·00

(Des E. Lenthall. Litho CPE Australia Ltd, Melbourne)

1989 (25 Sept). 75th Anniv of Red Cross on Norfolk Island. P 13½.

469	**146**	$1 bright rose-red and ultramarine	2·50	3·25

147 "Gethsemane"

148 John Royal (first announcer)

(Des Sue Pearson, Litho CPE Australia Ltd, Melbourne)

1989 (19 Oct). Christmas. T **147** and similar horiz designs showing opening lines of hymns and local scenes. Multicoloured. P 13½×14.

470	36c. Type **147**	80	40
471	60c. "In the Sweet Bye and Bye"	1·50	2·00
472	75c. "Let the Lower Lights Be Burning"	1·75	3·25
473	80c. "The Beautiful Stream"	1·75	3·25
470/3	*Set of 4*	5·25	8·00

(Des Philatelic Studios. Litho Leigh-Mardon Ltd, Melbourne)

1989 (21 Nov). 50th Anniv of Radio Australia. T **148** and similar vert designs each showing Kingston buildings. Multicoloured. P 14×13½.

474	41c. Type **148**	70	50
475	65c. Radio waves linking Australia and Norfolk Island	1·25	2·00
476	$1.10 Anniversary Kookaburra logo	2·00	4·50
474/6	*Set of 3*	3·50	6·25

149 H.M.S. *Bounty* on fire, Pitcairn Island, 1790

150 H.M.S. *Sirius* striking Reef

(Des G. Hitch. Litho Leigh-Mardon Ltd, Melbourne)

1990 (23 Jan). History of the Norfolk Islanders (1st series). Settlement on Pitcairn Island. T **149** and similar vert design. Multicoloured. P 14½.

477	70c. Type **149**	2·50	3·00
478	$1.10 Arms of Norfolk Island	2·50	3·50

See also Nos. 503/4 and 516/17.

(Des Maree Edmiston. Litho Leigh-Mardon Ltd, Melbourne)

1990 (19 Mar). Bicentenary of Wreck of H.M.S. *Sirius*. T **150** and similar horiz designs. Multicoloured. P 13½.

479	41c. Type **150**	1·50	2·00
	a. Horiz pair. Nos. 479/80	3·00	4·00
480	41c. H.M.S. *Sirius* failing to clear bay	1·50	2·00
481	65c. Divers at work on wreck	2·00	3·00
482	$1 Recovered artifacts and chart of site	2·25	3·25
479/82	*Set of 4*	6·50	9·25

Nos. 479/80 were printed together, *se-tenant*, in horizontal pairs throughout the sheet, each pair forming a composite design.

151 Unloading Lighter, Kingston

152 *Ile de Lumiere* (freighter)

(Des Philatelic Studios. Litho Leigh-Mardon Ltd, Melbourne)

1990 (17 July)–**91**. Ships. T **151** and horiz designs as T **152**. P 14×14½ (5, 10c.) or 14½ (others).

483	**151**	5c. purple-brown	20	50
484		10c. ochre	20	50

485	–	45c. multicoloured (19.2.91)	1·00	60
486	–	50c. multicoloured (19.2.91)	1·00	1·00
487	–	65c. multicoloured (19.2.91)	1·00	1·25
488	**152**	70c. multicoloured	1·00	1·25
489	–	75c. multicoloured (13.8.91)	1·50	2·00
490	–	80c. multicoloured (13.8.91)	1·50	2·25
491	–	90c. multicoloured (13.8.91)	1·50	2·25
492	–	$1 multicoloured (13.8.91)	1·50	2·00
493	–	$2 multicoloured	1·50	3·50
494	–	$5 multicoloured (19.2.91)	2·50	7·00
483/94 *Set of* 12			13·00	21·00

Designs: Horiz (as *T* **152**)—45c. *La Dunkerquoise* (French patrol vessel): 50c. *Dmitri Mendeleev* (Russian research vessel); 65c. *Pacific Rover* (tanker); 75c. *Norfolk Trader* (freighter); 80c. *Roseville* (transport); 90c. *Kalia* (container ship); $1 *Bounty* (replica); $2 H.M.A.S. *Success* (supply ship); $5 H.M.A.S. *Whyalla* (patrol vessel).

153 Santa on House Roof

154 William Charles Wentworth

(Des G. Hitch, adapted Philatelic Studios. Litho Leigh-Mardon Ltd, Melbourne)

1990 (25 Sept). Christmas. T **153** and similar multicoloured designs. P 14½.

499	38c. Type **153**	60	35
500	43c. Santa at Kingston Post Office	65	40
501	65c. Santa over Sydney Bay, Kingston (*horiz*)	1·25	2·00
502	85c. Santa on Officers' Quarters (*horiz*)	1·50	2·50
499/502 *Set of* 4		3·50	4·75

(Des G. Hitch. Litho Leigh-Mardon Ltd, Melbourne)

1990 (11 Oct). History of the Norfolk Islanders (2nd series) The First Generation. T **154** and similar vert design. P 14½.

503	70c. reddish brown and pale cinnamon	1·00	1·50
504	$1.20 reddish brown and pale cinnamon	1·50	2·50

Designs:—$1.20 Thursday October Christian.

155 Adult Robin and Chicks in Nest

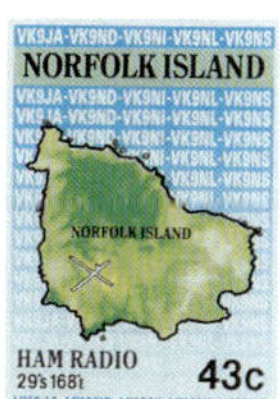

156 Map of Norfolk Island

(Des E. Monks. Litho Leigh-Mardon Ltd, Melbourne)

1990 (3 Dec). "Birdpex '90" Stamp Exhibition, Christchurch, New Zealand. Scarlet Robin. T **155** and similar vert designs. Multicoloured. P 14½.

505	65c. Type **155**	1·25	1·50
506	$1 Hen on branch	1·75	2·00
507	$1.20 Cock on branch	1·75	2·25
505/7 *Set of* 3		4·25	5·25
MS508 70×90 *mm.* $1 Hen; $1 Cock and hen		4·50	4·75

(Des Philatelic Studios. Litho Leigh-Mardon Ltd, Melbourne)

1991 (9 Apr). Ham Radio Network. T **156** and similar vert designs. Multicoloured. P 14½.

509	43c. Type **156**	1·25	70
510	$1 Globe showing Norfolk Island	2·00	3·00
511	$1.20 Map of South-west Pacific	2·25	4·00
509/11 *Set of* 3		5·00	7·00

157 Display in *Sirius* Museum

158 H.M.S. *Pandora* wrecked on Great Barrier Reef

(Des Philatelic Studios. Litho Leigh-Mardon Ltd, Melbourne)

1991 (16 May). Norfolk Island Museums. T **157** and similar multicoloured designs. P 14½.

512	43c. Type **157**	60	50
513	70c. 19th-century sitting room, House Museum (*horiz*)	1·00	2·25
514	$1 Carronade, *Sirius* Museum (*horiz*)	1·25	2·50
515	$1.20 Reconstructed jug and beaker, Archaeological Museum	1·25	3·50
512/15 *Set of* 4		3·50	8·00

(Des Philatelic Studios. Litho Leigh-Mardon, Melbourne)

1991 (2 July). History of the Norfolk Islanders (3rd series). Search for the *Bounty*. T **158** and similar horiz design. Multicoloured. P 13½×14.

516	$1 Type **158**	2·75	2·50
517	$1.20 H.M.S. *Pandora* leaving bay	2·75	3·00

159 Hibiscus and Island Scene

160 Tank and Soldier in Jungle

(Des Philatelic Studios. Litho Leigh-Mardon Ltd, Melbourne)

1991 (23 Sept). Christmas. P 14½.

518	**159**	38c. multicoloured	50	40
519		43c. multicoloured	60	45
520		65c. multicoloured	1·00	1·75
521		85c. multicoloured	1·10	2·25
518/21 *Set of* 4			3·00	4·25

(Des Philatelic Studios. Litho Leigh-Mardon Ltd, Melbourne)

1991 (9 Dec). 50th Anniv of Outbreak of Pacific War. T **160** and similar horiz designs. Multicoloured. P 14½.

522	43c. Type **160**	1·25	65
523	70c. Boeing B-17 Flying Fortress on jungle airstrip	2·25	2·75
524	$1 Warships	2·75	3·50
522/4 *Set of* 3		5·50	6·25

161 Coat of Arms

162 Deployment Map

(Des Philatelic Studios. Litho Leigh-Mardon Ltd, Melbourne)

1992 (11 Feb). 500th Anniv of Discovery of America by Columbus. T **161** and similar vert designs. Multicoloured. P 14½.

525	45c. Type **161**	85	55
526	$1.05 *Santa Maria*	2·00	2·75
527	$1.20 Columbus and globe	2·50	3·25
525/7 *Set of* 3		4·75	6·00

(Des Philatelic Studios. Litho Leigh-Mardon Ltd, Melbourne)

1992 (4 May). 50th Anniv of Battle of the Coral Sea. T **162** and similar vert designs. Multicoloured. P 14½.

528	45c. Type **162**	1·25	60
529	70c. H.M.A.S. *Australia* (cruiser)	2·00	2·50
530	$1.05 U.S.S. *Yorktown* (aircraft carrier)	2·75	3·50
528/30 *Set of* 3		5·50	6·00

(Des Philatelic Studios. Litho Leigh-Mardon Ltd, Melbourne)

1992 (4 May). 50th Anniv of Battle of Midway. Vert designs as T **162**. Multicoloured. P 14½.

531	45c. Battle area	1·25	60
532	70c. Consolidated PBY-5 Catalina flying boat over task force	2·00	2·50
533	$1.05 Douglas SBD Dauntless dive bomber and *Akagi* (Japanese aircraft carrier) burning	2·75	3·50
531/3 *Set of 3*		5·50	6·00

(Des Philatelic Studios. Litho Leigh-Mardon Ltd, Melbourne)

1992 (6 Aug). 50th Anniv of Battle of Guadalcanal. Multicoloured designs as T **162**, but horiz. P 14½.

534	45c. American troops landing	1·25	60
535	70c. Machine-gun crew	2·00	2·50
536	$1.05 Map of Pacific with Japanese and American flags	5·00	5·00
534/6 *Set of 3*		7·50	7·25

163 Norfolk Pines above Ball Bay

164 Boat Shed and Flaghouses, Kingston

(Des Philatelic Studios. Litho Leigh-Mardon Ltd, Melbourne)

1992 (29 Oct). Christmas. T **163** and similar vert designs. Multicoloured. P 14½.

537	40c. Type **163**	70	40
538	45c. Headstone Creek	75	45
539	75c. South side of Ball Bay	1·25	2·25
540	$1.20 Rocky Point Reserve	1·75	3·00
537/40 *Set of 4*		4·00	5·50

(Des Philatelic Studios. Litho Leigh-Mardon Ltd, Melbourne)

1993 (23 Feb). Tourism. Historic Kingston. T **164** and similar horiz designs. Multicoloured. P 14½.

541	45c. Type **164**	70	1·00
	a. Horiz strip of 5. Nos. 541/5	3·25	4·50
542	45c. Old Military Barracks	70	1·00
543	45c. All Saints Church	70	1·00
544	45c. Officers' Quarters	70	1·00
545	45c. Quality Row	70	1·00
541/5 *Set of 5*		3·25	4·50

Nos. 541/5 were printed together, *se-tenant*, in horizontal strips of five forming a composite design.

165 Bedford Fire Engine

166 Blue Sea Lizard (*Glaucus atlanticus*)

(Des Philatelic Studios, Melbourne. Litho Leigh-Mardon Ltd, Melbourne)

1993 (18 May). Emergency Services. T **165** and similar horiz designs. Multicoloured. P 14½.

546	45c. Type **165**	1·00	60
547	70c. Cliff rescue squad	1·10	1·75
548	75c. Ford Ambulance	1·40	1·90
549	$1.20 Toyota Landcruiser 4WD Police car	2·50	3·00
546/9 *Set of 4*		5·50	6·50

(Des Philatelic Studios. Litho Leigh-Mardon Ltd, Melbourne)

1993 (7 July). Nudibranchs. T **166** and similar horiz designs. Multicoloured. P 14½.

550	45c. Type **166**	60	55
551	45c. Ocellate Nudibranch (*Phyllidia ocellata*)	60	55
552	75c. *Bornella* sp	80	1·00
553	85c. *Glossodoris rubroannolata*	80	1·75
554	95c. *Halgerda villeyi*	80	2·00
555	$1.05 *Ceratosoma amoena*	80	2·00
550/5 *Set of 6*		4·00	7·00

167 Christmas Wreath

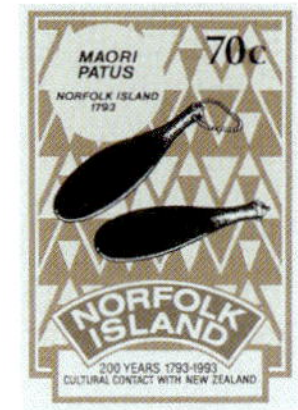

168 Maori Stone Clubs

(Des Philatelic Studios. Litho Leigh-Mardon Ltd, Melbourne)

1993 (28 Oct). Christmas. P 14½.

556	**167** 40c. multicoloured	50	40
557	45c. multicoloured	50	40
558	75c. multicoloured	75	1·25
559	$1.20 multicoloured	1·25	2·75
556/9 *Set of 4*		2·75	4·25

(Des Philatelic Studios. Litho Leigh-Mardon Ltd, Melbourne)

1993 (28 Oct). Bicentenary of Contact with New Zealand. T **168** and similar vert design. Multicoloured. P 14½.

560	70c. Type **168**	75	1·25
561	$1.20 First Maori map of New Zealand, 1793	1·25	2·25

169 Alvaro de Saavedra, Route Map and Florida

170 Sooty Tern

(Des G. Hitch and Philatelic Consultative Services. Litho Leigh-Mardon Ltd, Melbourne)

1994 (8 Feb). Pacific Explorers. T **169** and similar multicoloured designs. P 14½.

562	5c. Vasco Nunez de Balboa, map and *Barbara* (3.5)	1·25	1·75
563	10c. Ferdinand Magellan, map and *Vitoria* (3.5)	1·50	2·00
564	20c. Juan Sebastian del Cano, map and *Vitoria* (3.5)	2·00	1·50
565	50c. Type **169**	2·00	1·25
566	70c. Ruy Lopez de Villalobos, map and *San Juan*	2·50	1·50
567	75c. Miguel Lopez de Legaspi, map and *San Lesmes*	2·50	2·00
568	80c. Sir Francis Drake, map and *Golden Hind* (26.7)	3·00	2·00
569	85c. Alvaro de Mendana, map and *Santiago* (26.7)	2·50	2·00
570	90c. Pedro Fernandes de Quiros, map and *San Pedro y Pablo* (26.7)	2·50	2·00
571	$1 Luis Baez de Torres, map and *San Pedrico* (26.7)	2·50	2·00
572	$2 Abel Tasman, map and *Heemskerk*	3·25	5·00
573	$5 William Dampier, map and *Cygnet* (3.5)	5·50	8·50
562/73 *Set of 12*		27·00	28·00
MS574	100×80 *mm*. $1.20 *Golden Hind* (Drake) (32×52 *mm*). P 13	5·00	5·50

(Des Philatelic Studios. Litho Leigh-Mardon Ltd, Melbourne)

1994 (17 Aug). Sea Birds. T **170** and similar vert designs. Multicoloured. P 14½.

575	45c. Type **170**	95	1·25
	a. Horiz strip of 5. Nos. 575/9	4·25	5·50
576	45c. Red-tailed Tropic Bird	95	1·25
577	45c. Australian Gannet	95	1·25
578	45c. Wedge-tailed Shearwater	95	1·25
579	45c. Blue-faced Booby	95	1·25
575/9 *Set of 5*		4·25	5·50

Nos. 575/9 were printed together, *se-tenant*, in horizontal strips of five throughout the sheet with the backgrounds forming a composite design.

171 House and Star

172 Chevrolet "Woody", 1926

(Des Olive Gregory. Litho Walsall)

1994 (27 Oct). Christmas. T **171** and similar vert designs. Multicoloured. Roul 9×imperf*. Self-adhesive.

580	45c. Type **171**	80	55
581	75c. Figures from stained-glass windows	1·50	2·00
582	$1.20 Rainbow and *The Church of God* (missionary sailing ship)	2·50	3·50
580/2 *Set of* 3		4·25	5·50

*Nos. 580/2 were separated horizontally by roulette and vertically by rotary knife cuts which produce straight edges with two teeth between stamps.

(Litho McPherson's Ptg Group, Mulgrave)

1995 (7 Feb). Vintage Motor Vehicles. T **172** and similar horiz designs. Multicoloured. P 14×14½.

583	45c. Type **172**	60	55
584	75c. Ford Model A utility, 1928	80	1·25
585	$1.05 Ford Model AAC truck, 1929	1·00	1·60
586	$1.20 Ford Model A sedan, 1930	1·25	2·00
583/6 *Set of* 4		3·25	4·75

173 Tail Flukes of Humpback Whale

174 Dot-and-Dash Butterflyfish

(Des Mary Butterfield. Litho McPherson's Ptg Group, Mulgrave)

1995 (11 May). Humpback Whale Conservation. T **173** and similar multicoloured designs. P 14½×14 ($1.05) or 14×14½ (others).

587	45c. Type **173**	1·00	55
588	75c. Mother and calf	1·25	2·00
589	$1.05 Whale breaching (*vert*)	1·50	2·50
587/9 *Set of* 3		3·25	4·50
MS590	107×84 *mm.* $1.20, Humpback Whale (29×49 *mm*). P 14×14½	2·75	4·00

(Des Mary Butterfield. Litho Leigh-Mardon Ltd, Melbourne)

1995 (15 June). Butterflyfish. T **174** and similar square designs. Multicoloured. P 14×14½.

591	5c. Type **174**	30	75
592	45c. Blue-spotted Butterflyfish (*Chaetodon plebeius*)	85	50
593	$1.20 Three-belted Butterflyfish (*Chaetodon tricinatus*)	2·00	2·75
594	$1.50 Thread-finned Butterflyfish (*Chaetodon auriga*)	2·25	3·25
591/4 *Set of* 4		4·75	6·50

1995 (19 July). JAKARTA '95 Stamp Exhibition, Indonesia. No. **MS**590 optd "Selamat Hari Merdeka" and emblem on sheet margin in gold.

MS595	107×84 *mm.* $1.20, Humpback Whale	2·25	2·75

175 International 4×4 Refueller, 1942

176 Servicing Fighter

(Des G. Douran. Litho Southern Colour Print, Dunedin)

1995 (8 Aug). Second World War Vehicles. T **175** and similar horiz designs. Multicoloured. P 14×14½.

596	5c. Type **175**	30	75
597	45c. Ford Sedan, 1942	75	45
598	$1.20 Ford 3 ton tipper truck, 1942	2·00	2·50
599	$2 D8 caterpillar with scraper	3·00	4·00
596/9 *Set of* 4		5·50	7·00

NORFOLK ISLAND INTERNAL POSTAL SERVICE. Nos. 600/1 and subsequent locally-produced booklet stamps were primarily intended for use in the island postal service which collects mail from letter boxes and sorts it into boxes at the main post office for residents to pick up. Such issues are, however, also valid for postage on mail sent overseas.

(Litho Photopress International, Norfolk Island)

1995 (1 Sept). Flower designs as 1960 issues, but with face values in decimal currency. Roul 7.

600	5c. bright rose and deep blue-green (as No. 25)	20	65
	a. Booklet pane. No. 600×18	2·75	
601	5c. bright rose-red (as No. 28)	20	65
	a. Booklet pane. No. 601×18	2·75	

Nos. 600/1 were only issued in $1.80 stamp booklets, No. SB7, containing panes of 18 (two blocks of nine separated by a horizontal gutter and with margins all round).

The original printing of Nos. 600a/1a had black inscriptions beneath each pane. These were subsequently changed to deep blue-green (No. 600a) or bright rose-red (No. 601a).

(Des Mary Butterfield (Nos. 602/5). Litho and die-stamped ($10) or litho (others) Southern Colour Print, Dunedin)

1995 (18 Sept). 50th Anniv of End of Second World War in the Pacific. T **176** and similar multicoloured designs. P 12.

602	5c. Type **176**	55	1·00
603	45c. Sgt. Tom Derrick, V.C. (*vert*)	85	45
604	75c. Gen. Douglas MacArthur (*vert*)	1·50	1·50
605	$1.05 Girls celebrating victory	2·25	2·25
606	$10 Pacific War medals (50×30 *mm*)	20·00	25·00
602/6 *Set of* 5		23·00	27·00

The $10 also includes the "Singapore '95" International stamp exhibition logo.

177 Peace Dove and Anniversary Emblem

178 Skink on Bank

(Des Mary Butterfield. Litho SNP Cambec)

1995 (7 Nov). Christmas. 50th Anniv of United Nations. T **177** and similar vert designs, each including U.N. anniversary emblem. P 14½×14.

607	45c. gold and new blue	40	35
608	75c. gold and bright violet	60	60
609	$1.05 gold and bright rose-red	70	2·00
610	$1.20 gold and light green	80	2·00
607/10 *Set of* 3		2·25	4·50

Designs:—75c. Star of Bethlehem; $1.05, Symbolic candles on cake; $1.20, Olive branch.

(Des Doreen McGuiness. Litho Questa)

1996 (6 Feb). Endangered Species. Skinks and Geckos. T **178** and similar horiz designs. Multicoloured. P 14½×15.

611	5c. Type **178**	60	85
	a. Strip of 4 Nos. 611/14	2·50	3·00
612	5c. Gecko on branch	60	85
613	45c. Skink facing right	80	85
614	45c. Gecko on flower	80	85
611/14 *Set of* 4		2·50	3·00

Nos. 611/14 were printed together, *se-tenant*, in horizontal and vertical strips of four throughout sheets of 16.

179 Sopwith Pup Biplane and Emblem

(Des B. McCoy and B. Klemke. Litho Southern Colour Print, Dunedin)

1996 (22 Apr). 75th Anniv of Royal Australian Air Force. T **179** and similar vert designs showing aircraft. Multicoloured. P 14.

615	45c. Type **179**	60	60
616	45c. Wirraway fighter	60	60
617	75c. F-111C jet fighter	1·00	1·50
618	85c. F/A-18 Hornet jet fighter	1·10	1·60
615/18	*Set of* 4	3·00	3·75

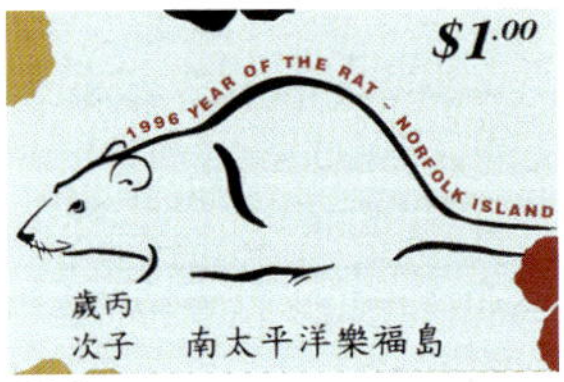

180 Rat

(Des G. Douran. Litho Southern Colour Print, Dunedin)

1996 (18 May). Chinese New Year ("Year of the Rat"). Sheet 100×75 mm. P 12.

MS619	**180** $1 black, rosine and brown-ochre	1·50	2·25
	a. With "CHINA '96" 9th Asian International Stamp	1·60	2·25

181 *Naticarlus oncus*

182 Shopping

(Des Mary Butterfield. Litho Southern Colour Print, Dunedin)

1996 (2 July). Shells. T **181** and similar square designs. Multicoloured. P 14.

620	45c. Type **181**	60	85
621	45c. *Janthina janthina*	60	85
622	45c. *Cypraea caputserpentis*	60	85
623	45c. *Argonauta nodosa*	60	85
620/3	*Set of* 4	2·25	3·00

(Des G. Douran. Litho Southern Colour Print, Dunedin)

1996 (17 Sept). Tourism. T **182** and similar horiz designs. Multicoloured. P 13½×14.

624	45c. Type **182**	50	50
625	75c. Celebrating Bounty Day	1·00	1·00
626	$2.50 Horse riding	3·50	4·50
627	$3.70 Unloading lighter	4·00	5·75
624/7	*Set of* 4	8·00	10·50

183 The Nativity

184 Coat of Arms

(Des Mary Duke. Litho Questa)

1996 (5 Nov). Christmas. T **183** and similar vert designs. Multicoloured. P 14½.

628	45c. Type **183**	40	40
629	45c. Star and boat sheds	40	40
630	75c. Star, bungalow and ox	75	1·25
631	85c. Star, fruit, flowers and ox	85	1·50
628/31	*Set of* 4	2·25	3·25

(Litho Photopress International, Norfolk Island)

1997 (22 Jan). T **184** and similar vert design. Roul 7.

632	**184**	5c. turquoise-blue and pale lemon	25	65
		a. Booklet pane of 10 with margins all round	2·25	
633	–	5c. orange-brown	25	65
		a. Booklet pane of 10 with margins all	2·25	

Design:—No. 633, Great Seal of Norfolk Island.

Nos. 632/3 were only issued in $2 stamp booklets, No. SB8.

185 Calf

186 *Cepora perimale*

(Des G. Douran. Litho Southern Colour Print, Dunedin)

1997 (11 Feb). Beef Cattle. Sheet 67×67 mm. P 13½×13.

MS634	$1.20 multicoloured	2·00	2·75

1997 (12 Feb). HONG KONG '97 International Stamp Exhibition. As No. **MS**634, but with exhibition emblem on sheet margin.

MS635	**185** 67×67 *mm.* $1.20 multicoloured	3·25	4·00

(Des Tracey Yager. Litho and gold die-stamped Southern Colour Print, Dunedin)

1997 (28 Mar). Butterflies. T **186** and similar horiz designs. Multicoloured. P 14½.

636	75c. Type **186**	1·10	1·00
	a. Gold (country name and value) omitted	£425	
637	90c. *Danaus chryspippus*	1·40	1·60
638	$1 *Donaus hamata*	1·40	1·60
639	$1.20 *Danaus plexippus*	1·50	2·25
636/9	*Set of* 4	4·75	5·75

187 Dusky Dolphins

(Des Mary Butterfield. Litho Southern Colour Print, Dunedin)

1997 (29 May). Dolphins. T **187** and similar horiz designs. Multicoloured. P 14.

640	45c. Type **187**	75	60
641	75c. Common Dolphin and calf	1·25	1·40
MS642	106×80 *mm.* $1.05, Dolphin	2·75	3·25

1997 (29 May). Pacific '97 International Stamp Exhibition, San Francisco. As No. **MS**642, but with exhibition emblem on sheet margin.

MS643	106×80 *mm.* $1.05 Dolphin	5·50	6·00

188 Ball Bay, Norfolk Island

188a Queen Elizabeth

(Litho Southern Colour Print, Dunedin)

1997 (30 June). 50th Anniv of Norfolk Island Stamps. T **188** and similar multicoloured designs. P 12.

644	$1 Type **188**	1·25	2·25
	a. Horiz pair. Nos. 644/5	2·50	4·50
645	$1.50 1947 2d. stamp	1·25	2·25

646 $8 Ball Bay and 1947 2s. yellow-bistre stamp (90×45 *mm*) 6·50 12·00
644/6 *Set of* 3 8·00 15·00

Nos. 644/5 were printed together, *se-tenant*, in horizontal pairs with the backgrounds forming a composite design.

(Des N. Shewring (No. **MS**651), D. Miller (others). Litho Questa)

1997 (12 Aug). Golden Wedding of Queen Elizabeth and Prince Philip. T **188a** and similar horiz designs. Multicoloured. P 14½×14.

647 20c. Type **188a** 50 60
a. Horiz pair. Nos. 647/648 1·00 1·10
648 25c. Prince Philip in carriage-driving trials 50 60
649 25c. Prince Philip 55 65
a. Horiz pair. Nos. 649/50 1·25 1·40
650 50c. Queen in phaeton at Trooping the Colour 70 80
647/50 *Set of* 4 2·00 2·40
MS651 110×70 *mm*. $1.50 Queen Elizabeth and Prince Philip in landau (*horiz*). P 14×14½ 2·25 2·75

Nos. 647/8 and 649/50 were each printed together, *se-tenant*, in horizontal pairs throughout the sheets with the backgrounds forming composite designs.

189 Royal Yacht *Britannia* leaving Hong Kong

190 Christmas Tree

1997 (16 Sept). Return of Hong Kong to China. Sheet 126×91 mm. Litho. P 14.

MS652 **189** 45c. multicoloured 1·00 1·50

No. **MS**652 is inscribed "Brittania" in error.

(Des Sue Wickison. Litho Southern Colour Print, Dunedin)

1997 (4 Nov). Annual Festivals. T **190** and similar vert designs. Multicoloured. P 13½.

653 45c. Type **190** 60 45
654 75c. Fireworks (New Year's Eve) 90 1·25
655 $1.20 Rose (Valentine's Day) 1·40 2·00
653/5 *Set of* 3 2·50 3·25

191 Oriental Pearl T.V. Tower, Shanghai

192 Tiger Mask

(Litho Questa)

1997 (18 Nov). Shanghai '97 International Stamp and Coin Exhibition, Shanghai. Sheet 103×138 mm. P 14½.

MS656 **191** 45c. multicoloured 1·00 1·50

(Des Ren Yu. Litho Southern Colour Print, Dunedin)

1998 (12 Feb). Chinese New Year ("Year of the Tiger"). Sheet 75×95 mm. P 12.

MS657 **192** 45c. multicoloured 1·00 1·50

193 "Pepper"

194 Entrance to Pentagonal Gaol

(Des Mary Butterfield. Litho Southern Colour Print, Dunedin)

1998 (26 Feb). Cats. T **193** and similar vert designs. Multicoloured. P 14½.

658 45c. Type **193** 65 65
659 45c. "Tabitha" at window 65 65
660 75c. "Midnight" 85 1·25
661 $1.20 "Rainbow" with flower pot 1·25 1·75
658/61 *Set of* 4 3·00 3·75

(Des B. Hilder. Litho Photopress International, Norfolk Island)

1998 (27 Feb). T **194** and similar horiz design. Roul 7.

662 **194** 5c. black and azure 25 65
a. Booklet pane of 10 with margins all round 2·25
663 – 5c. black and turquoise-green 25 65
a. Booklet pane of 10 with margins all round 2·25

Design:—No. 663, Ruined First Settlement cottage.

Nos. 662/3 were only issued in $2 stamp booklets, No. SB9.

194a Princess Diana with Bouquet, 1991

195 Tweed Trousers

(Des D. Miller. Litho Questa)

1998 (28 Apr). Diana, Princess of Wales Commemoration. T **194a** and similar vert designs. Multicoloured. P 14½×14.

664 45c. Type **194a** 60 60
MS665 145×70 *mm*. 45c. Wearing blue and white dress, 1989; 45c. Wearing pearl earrings, 1990; 45c. No. 664; 45c. Wearing striped dress (sold at $1.80+45c. charity premium) 1·25 2·00

(Des Mary Butterfield. Litho Questa)

1998 (5 May). Reef Fish. T **195** and similar multicoloured designs. P 14½.

666 10c. Type **195** 30 55
667 20c. Conspicuous Angelfish (29.6) 55 65
668 30c. Moon Wrasse 65 65
669 45c. Wide-striped Clownfish (29.6) 75 50
670 50c. Raccoon Butterflyfish 80 80
671 70c. Artooti (juvenile) (29.6) 1·00 1·00
672 75c. Splendid Hawkfish 1·00 1·00
673 85c. Scorpion Fish (29.6) 1·25 1·25
674 90c. Orange Fairy Basslet 1·75 1·25
675 $1 Sweetlips (29.6) 1·25 1·25
676 $3 Moorish Idol (29.6) 2·75 4·00
677 $4 Gold-ribbon Soapfish 3·75 4·75
666/77 *Set of* 12 14·00 16·00
MS678 110×85 *mm*. $1.20, Shark (29×39 *mm*). P 14×14½ 1·50 2·00

Nos. 672 and 675 are incorrectly inscribed "Splendid Hawkefish" and "Sweetlip".

196 Hammer Throwing

197 *Norfolk* (sloop)

(Des Tracey Yager. Litho Southern Colour Print, Dunedin)

1998 (23 July). 16th Commonwealth Games, Kuala Lumpur. T **196** and similar designs. P 14½.

679	75c. orange-vermilion and black	50	65
680	95c. bluish violet and black	55	1·00
681	$1.05 deep mauve and black	60	1·10
679/81	*Set of* 3	1·50	2·50
MS682	80×100 *mm.* 85c. brt blue-green and black	1·00	1·75

Designs: Horiz—95c. Trap shooting. Vert—85c. Flag bearer; $1.05, Lawn bowls.

(Des Mary Butterfield. Litho Cartor)

1998 (24 Sept). Bicentenary of the Circumnavigation of Tasmania by George Bass and Matthew Flinders. P 13.

683	**197** 45c. multicoloured	1·90	1·25
MS684	101×69 *mm.* **197** $1.20 multicoloured	4·25	4·75

198 Blue Whale

(Des Mary Butterfield. Litho Questa)

1998 (23 Oct). Whales of the Southern Oceans (joint issue with Namibia and South Africa). Sheet 103×70 mm. P 13½×14.

MS685	**198** $1.50 multicoloured	1·90	2·75

199 "*Peace* on Earth"

200 Short S.23 Sandringham (flying boat)

(Des Mary Butterfield. Litho Cartor)

1998 (10 Nov). Christmas. T **199** and similar horiz designs. Multicoloured. P 13×13½.

686	45c. Type **199**	50	50
687	75c. "Joy to the World"	80	80
688	$1.05 "A Season of Love"	1·00	1·75
689	$1.20 "Light of the World"	1·00	1·75
686/9	*Set of* 4	3·00	4·25

(Des Mary Duke. Litho Photopress International, Norfolk Island)

1999 (28 Jan). Booklet Stamps. Aircraft. T **200** and similar horiz design. Each brown-lake and deep grey-green. Roul 7.

690	5c. Type **200**	30	75
	a. Booklet pane of 10 with margins all round	2·75	
691	5c. DC-4 *Norfolk Trader*	30	75
	a. Booklet pane of 10 with margins all round	2·75	

Booklet panes 690a/1a come from No. SB10.

201 Soft Toy Rabbit

202 Hull of *Resolution* under Construction

(Des K. Partridge. Litho Questa)

1999 (9 Feb). Chinese New Year ("Year of the Rabbit"). Sheet 80×100 mm. P 14.

MS692	**201** 95c. multicoloured	1·00	1·75

(Des R. Pennycuick. Litho Cartor)

1999 (19 Mar). Australia '99 International Stamp Exhibition, Melbourne. Schooner *Resolution*. T **202** and similar horiz designs. Multicoloured. P 13×13½.

693	45c. Type **202**	1·60	2·00
	a. Booklet pane. Nos. 693/7 plus printed label	7·00	
694	45c. After being launched	1·60	2·00
695	45c. In Emily Bay	1·60	2·00
696	45c. Off Cascade	1·60	2·00
697	45c. Alongside at Auckland	1·60	2·00
693/7	*Set of* 5	7·00	9·00

Nos. 693/7 were only available in stamp booklets, No. SB11, sold for $2.50.

203 Pacific Black Duck

204 Solander's Petrel in Flight

(Des Tracey Yager. Litho Southern Colour Print, Dunedin)

1999 (27 Apr). IBRA '99 International Stamp Exhibition, Nuremberg. Sheet 80×100 mm. P 14½.

MS698	**203** $2.50 multicoloured	6·50	7·50

(Des Patricia Altman. Litho Southern Colour Print, Dunedin)

1999 (27 May). Endangered Species. Solander's Petrel ("Providence Petrel"). T **204** and similar multicoloured designs. P 14½.

699	75c. Type **204**	2·75	1·75
700	$1.05 Head of Solander's Petrel (*horiz*)	3·00	2·50
701	$1.20 Adult and fledgling (*horiz*)	3·50	3·50
699/701	*Set of* 3	8·50	7·00
MS702	130×90 *mm.* $4.50, Solander's Petrel in flight (35×51 *mm*). P 13	10·00	12·00

For No. 701 in miniature sheet see No. **MS**738.

205 "Cecile Brunner" Rose

206 Pottery

(Litho Questa)

1999 (30 July). Roses. T **205** and similar vert designs. Multicoloured. P 14½×14.

703	45c. Type **205**	50	40
704	75c. Green rose	70	90
705	$1.05 "David Buffett" Rose	1·00	1·75
703/5	*Set of* 3	2·00	2·75
MS706	60×81 *mm.* $1.20, "A Country Woman" Rose	1·10	2·00

No. **MS**706 also commemorates the 50th anniversary of the Country Women's Association on Norfolk Island.

(Des K. Partridge. Litho Questa)

1999 (23 Aug). China '99 International Stamp Exhibition, Beijing. No. **MS**692 with "China '99" logo optd on the margin in carmine. P 14.

MS707	80×100 *mm.* 95c. Type **201**	2·25	2·75

(Des G. Douran. Litho B.D.T.)

1999 (16 Sept). Handcrafts of Norfolk Island. T **206** and similar vert designs. Multicoloured. P 14×15.

708	45c. Type **206**	70	70
709	45c. Woodcarving	70	70
710	75c. Quilting	1·25	1·25
711	$1.05 Basket-weaving	1·50	2·25
708/11	*Set of* 4	3·75	4·50

206a Inspecting bomb damage, Buckingham Palace, 1940

(Des D. Miller. Litho Cartor)

1999 (12 Oct). "Queen Elizabeth the Queen Mother's Century". T **206a** and similar horiz designs. Multicoloured (except $1.20). P 13½.

712	45c. Type **206a**	70	70
713	45c. At Abergeldy Castle sale of work, 1955	70	70
714	75c. Queen Mother, Queen Elizabeth and Prince William, 1994	95	95
715	$1.20 Inspecting the King's Regiment (black).	1·50	1·75
712/15	*Set of 4*	3·25	3·75

MS716 145×70 *mm.* $3 Queen Elizabeth, 1937, and Amy Johnson's flight to Australia, 1930 ... 3·50 4·00

207 Bishop George Augustus Selwyn

208 Basket of Food (Thanksgiving)

(Des Tracey Yager. Litho B.D.T.)

1999 (10 Nov). Christmas. 150th Anniv of Melanesian Mission. T **207** and similar vert designs. Multicoloured (except 75c.). P 14.

717	45c. Type **207**	1·50	1·75
	a. Horiz strip of 5. Nos. 717/21	8·00	9·00
718	45c. Bishop John Coleridge Patteson	1·50	1·75
719	75c. "150 YEARS MELANESIAN MISSION" (black)	1·75	1·90
720	$1.05 Stained-glass windows	2·00	2·25
721	$1.20 *Southern Cross* (missionary ship) and religious symbols	2·25	2·50
717/21	*Set of 5*	8·00	9·00

Nos. 717/21 were printed together, *se-tenant*, in horizontal strips of five throughout the sheet with the backgrounds forming a composite design.

(Des R. Pennycuick. Litho Photopress International, Norfolk Island)

2000 (31 Jan). Festivals. T **208** and similar horiz design. Roul 5½.

722	5c. black and ultramarine	40	80
	a. Booklet pane. Nos. 722/3 each ×20	8·00	
723	5c. black and ultramarine	40	80

Design—No. 723, Musician playing guitar (Country Music Festival).

Nos. 722/3 were only issued in $2 stamp booklets, No. SB12, containing four panes of 10 (2×5) showing the two designs *se-tenant* horizontally.

209 Dragon

210 Domestic Goose

(Des Mary Butterfield. Litho B.D.T.)

2000 (7 Feb). Chinese New Year ("Year of the Dragon"). Sheet 106×86 mm. P 13×13½.

MS724 **209** $2 multicoloured ... 3·00 3·75

(Des Tracey Yager. Litho Southern Colour Print, Dunedin)

2000 (18 Feb). Ducks and Geese. T **210** and similar square designs. Multicoloured. P 14½.

725	45c. Type **210**	1·50	70
726	75c. Pacific Black Duck	2·00	1·25
727	$1.05 Mallard Drake	2·25	2·50
728	$1.20 Aylesbury Duck	2·50	2·50
725/8	*Set of 4*	7·50	6·25

211 Honour Roll for First World War

212 Young Boy, Shipwright and Whaleboat

(Des Photopress International. Litho Questa)

2000 (25 Apr). Anzac Day. T **211** and similar vert design. Multicoloured. P 14×15.

729	45c. Type **211**	1·50	1·00
730	75c. Honour rolls for Second World War and Korea	2·00	1·75

(Des G. Douran. Litho B.D.T.)

2000 (1 May). "Whaler Project 2000". Two sheets, each 96×76 mm, containing T **212**. Multicoloured. P 14 (No. **MS**731) or imperf (No. **MS**732).

MS731	**212** $4 multicoloured	8·00	9·50
MS732	$4 mult ("THE STAMP SHOW 2000" and Crown Agents logos added in gold)	8·00	9·50

213 Captain William Bligh and *Bounty*

214 Turtle

(Des Tracey Yager. Litho Questa)

2000 (8 June). Bounty Day. T **213** and similar square design. Multicoloured. P 14½.

733	45c. Type **213**	2·00	1·50
734	75c. Fletcher Christian and Tahiti	2·25	2·00

(Des Alison Ryves. Litho B.D.T.)

2000 (19 June). Eighth Festival of Pacific Arts, New Caledonia. T **214** and similar vert designs. Multicoloured.

(a) Size 24×29 mm. Self-adhesive. P 9

735 45c. Urn and swat ... 1·50 1·50

(b) Sheet 130×70 mm. P 13½

MS736 75c. Type **214**; $1.05, Traditional mosaic; $1.20 Mask and spearhead; $2 Decorated utensils... 7·50 8·50

215 Malcolm Champion (Olympic Gold Medal Winner, Stockholm, 1912)

216 Sun over Pines

(Litho Questa)

2000 (15 Sept). Olymphilex 2000 International Stamp Exhibition, Sydney. Sheet 120×70 mm. P 14.

MS737 **215** $3 multicoloured ... 7·00 8·00

(Des R. Pennycuick. Litho Questa)

2000 (5 Oct). Canpex 2000 National Stamp Exhibition, Christchurch, New Zealand. Sheet 120×90 mm. P 14½.

MS738 $2.40 No. 701×2 ... 9·00 9·50

(Des R. Pennycuick. Litho Cartor)

2000 (20 Oct). Christmas. T **216** and similar vert designs. Multicoloured. P 13½×13.

739	45c. Type **216**	1·50	55
740	75c. Candle over pines	2·00	85
741	$1.05 Moon over pines	2·50	3·00
742	$1.20 Star over pines	2·75	3·00
739/42	*Set of* 4	8·00	6·75

217 "Norfolk Island in 1825 and 2001" (Jessica Wong and Mardi Pye)

(Litho Southern Colour Print, Dunedin)

2000 (31 Dec). New Millennium. T **217** and similar horiz designs showing children's drawings. Multicoloured. P 14½×15.

743	45c. Type **217**	2·25	2·00
744	45c. "Seabirds over Norfolk Island" (Roxanne Spreag)	2·25	2·00
745	75c. "Trees and Clothes" (Tara Grube)	3·50	3·25
746	75c. "Underwater Scene" (Thomas Greenwood)	3·50	3·25
743/6	*Set of* 4	10·50	9·50

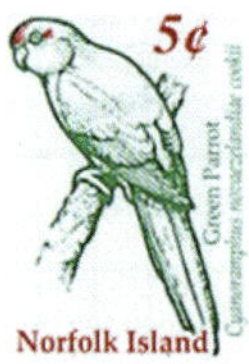

218 Red-fronted Parakeet ("Green Parrot")

219 Purple Swamphen

(Litho Photopress International, Norfolk Island)

2001 (26 Jan). Red-fronted Parakeet. Roul 6.

747	**218**	5c. scarlet and emerald	40	80
		a. Booklet pane of 10 with margins all round	3·50	

No. 747 was only issued in $2 stamp booklets, No. SB13, containing four panes.

(Litho Cartor)

2001 (1 Feb). Chinese New Year ("Year of the Snake") and International Stamp Exhibition. P 13.

748	**219**	45c. multicoloured	2·00	2·25
		a. Sheetlet of 5 and 1 label	9·00	

MS749 **219** 110×70 *mm*. $2.30 Norfolk Island Eel and Purple Swamphen (as Type **219**, but without country inscr and face value). Imperf ..... 3·25 4·00

No. 748 was printed in sheetlets of five stamps and one *se-tenant* label showing the exhibition logo.

220 "Old Clothes"

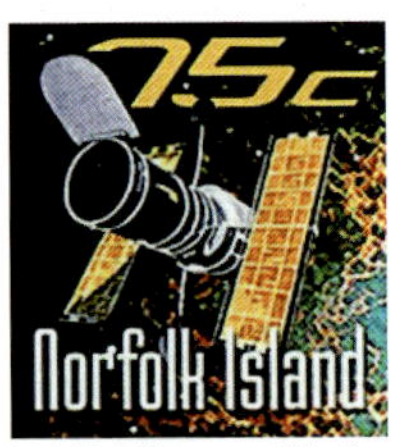

221 "Satellite over China"

(Des Photopress International. Litho Questa)

2001 (12 Mar). Centenary of Australian Federation. Cartoons from *The Bulletin Magazine*. T **220** and similar vert designs. Multicoloured. P 14×14½.

750	45c. Type **220**	70	80
751	45c. "Tower of Babel"	70	80
752	45c. "The Political Garotters"	70	80
753	45c. "Promises, Promises!"	70	80
754	45c. "The Gout of Federation"	70	80
755	45c. "The Federal Spirit"	70	80
756	75c. "Australia Faces the Dawn"	1·00	1·00
757	$1.05 "The Federation Capital Question"	1·25	1·60
758	$1.20 "The Imperial Fowl-Yard"	1·40	1·75
750/8	*Set of* 9	7·00	8·00

(Des Beth McKinlay. Litho Cartor)

2001 (16 May). Invercargill Stamp Odyssey 2001 National Stamp Exhibition, New Zealand. Sheet 136×105 mm, containing T **221** and similar vert designs. Multicoloured. P 13.

MS759 75c. Type **221**; 75c. Satellite over Pacific; 75c. Satellite over Australia ..... 4·00 5·00

222 Woman and Child in Victorian Dress

223 *Jasminium simplicifolium*

(Litho Photopress International, Norfolk Island)

2001 (8 June). Bounty Day. Roul 5½.

760	**222**	5c. black and emerald	30	70
		a. Booklet pane of 10 with margins all round	2·50	

No. 760 was only issued in $2 stamp booklets, No. SB14.

(Des Photopress International, Norfolk Island. Litho Cartor)

2001 (9–29 June). Perfume from Norfolk Island. T **223** and similar vert designs. Multicoloured. P 13½.

761	45c. Type **223** (29.6)	50	35
762	75c. Girl's face in perfume bottle (29.6)	70	70
763	$1.05 Girl and roses (29.6)	90	1·25
764	$1.20 Taylor's Road, Norfolk Island (29.6)	90	1·50
765	$1.50 Couple shopping for perfume (29.6)	1·00	1·75
761/5	*Set of* 5	3·50	5·00

MS766 145×98 *mm*. $3 Girl and perfume bottle (60×72 *mm*) ..... 3·00 4·00

Nos. 761/6 were printed on paper impregnated with the Jasmine fragrance.

Nos. 761/6 were also issued in premium booklets, No. SP1, sold at $10. The $3 pane from booklet SP1 is imperf and also differs from **MS**766 by showing "NORFOLK ISLAND" at top left and face value at bottom right, instead of on the perforated portion of the miniature sheet.

224 Whaleboat

225 Australian Soldiers playing Cards

(Des Tracey Yager)

2001 (1 Aug). Local Boats. T **224** and similar multicoloured designs. P 14½.

(a) Litho Questa. PVA gum

768	45c. Type **224**	1·50	50
769	$1 Motor launch	2·50	3·00
770	$1 Family rowing boat (*horiz*)	2·50	3·00
771	$1.50 Sailing cutter (*horiz*)	3·00	3·50
768/71	*Set of* 4	8·50	9·00

(b) Litho Southern Colour Print, Dunedin. Self-adhesive

772	45c. Type **224**	1·25	1·25

No. 772 was printed in rolls of 50 on which the self-adhesive paper around each stamp was removed.

(Litho Questa)

2001 (9 Sept). Centenary of Australian Army. B.C.O.F. Japan. T **225** and similar horiz designs. P 14½.

773	45c. grey-brown and royal blue	1·75	1·75
774	45c. grey-brown and royal blue	1·75	1·75
775	$1 grey-brown and deep green	3·75	3·75
776	$1 grey-brown and deep green	3·75	3·75
773/6	*Set of* 4	10·00	10·00

Designs:—No. 773, Type **225**; No. 774, Christmas float; No. 775, Birthday cake; No. 776, Australian military policeman directing traffic.

Nos. 773 and 775, and 774 and 776, were both printed together in sheets containing two panes, one of each design, separated by vertical illustrated gutters.

226 Miamiti (cartoon owl) holding Island Flag

227 Strawberry Guava

(Des Tracey Yager. Litho Photopress International, Norfolk Island)

2001 (1 Oct). Sixth South Pacific Mini Games (1st issue). Roul 5½.

777	**226**	10c. grey-brown and emerald	40	75
		a. Booklet pane of 10 with margins all round	3·75	

No. 777 was only issued in $2 stamp booklets, No. SB15.
See also Nos. 794/5.

(Des Mary Butterfield. Litho Cartor)

2001 (26 Oct). Christmas. Island Plants. T **227** and similar square designs each incorporating carol music. Multicoloured. P 12½.

778	45c. Type **227**	1·25	1·25
779	45c. Poinsettia	1·25	1·25
780	$1 Christmas Croton	2·00	2·00
781	$1 Hibiscus	2·00	2·00
782	$1.50 Indian Shot	2·50	2·50
778/82	*Set of 5*	9·00	9·00

No. 779 is inscribed "Pointsettia" in error.

228 Sacred Kingfisher

229 Red-tailed Tropic Bird

(Des R. Pennycuick. Litho Photopress International, Norfolk Island)

2002 (15 Jan). "Nuffka" (Sacred Kingfisher). Roul 5½.

783	**228**	10c. royal blue and greenish blue	75	1·00
		a. Booklet pane of 10 with margins all round	6·50	

No. 783 was only issued in $2 stamp booklets, No. SB16.

(Des Patricia Altman. Litho Cartor)

2002 (21 Jan). Cliff Ecology. T **229** and similar horiz designs. Multicoloured. P 13.

784	45c. Type **229**	2·00	1·00
785	$1 White Oak blossom	2·75	2·75
786	$1 White Oak tree	2·75	2·75
787	$1.50 Eagle Ray	3·00	3·25
784/7	*Set of 4*	9·50	8·75

Nos. 784/7 were each printed in sheets of 20 containing two panes (2×5) separated by vertical illustrated gutters.

229a Elizabeth, Duchess of York with Princesses Elizabeth and Margaret, 1930

(Des A. Robinson. Litho Questa)

2002 (6 Feb). Golden Jubilee. T **229a** and similar designs. W w **14** (*sideways*). P 14½.

788	45c. brownish black, claret and gold	1·25	55
789	75c. multicoloured	1·40	1·00
790	$1 brownish black, claret and gold	1·75	1·25
791	$1.50 multicoloured	2·25	2·75
788/91	*Set of 4*	6·00	5·00
MS792	162×95 *mm*. Nos. 788/91 and $3 multicoloured. P 13½ ($3) or 14½ (others)	6·50	7·50

Designs: Horiz —75c. Queen Elizabeth in multicoloured hat, 1977; $1 Queen Elizabeth wearing Imperial State Crown, Coronation, 1953; $1.50, Queen Elizabeth at Windsor Horse Show, 2000. Vert (38×51 *mm*)—$3 Queen Elizabeth after Annigoni.

Designs as Nos. 788/91 in No. **MS**792 omit the gold frame around each stamp and the "Golden Jubilee 1952-2002" inscription.

230 Derelict Steam Engine

231 Miamiti (cartoon owl) running

(Des R. Pennycuick. Litho Questa)

2002 (21 Mar). Restoration of Yeaman's Mill Steam Engine. P 14½.

793	**230**	$4.50 multicoloured	8·50	10·00

No. 793 was printed in sheets of ten containing two panes separated by an illustrated horizontal gutter.

(Des Tracey Yager. Litho Questa)

2002 (21 Mar). Sixth South Pacific Mini Games (2nd issue). T **231** and similar vert design. Multicoloured. P 13½×14.

794	50c. Type **231**	1·50	1·00
795	$1.50 Miamiti playing tennis	2·75	3·25

Two miniature sheets, both inscr 'SIXTH SOUTH PACIFIC GAMES' on sheet margins, were printed but never officially issued. They were 4×45c. depicting bodybuilding, netball, lawn bowls and shooting, and 4×$1 showing squash, golf, triathlon and athletics.

232 Lawn Bowls Player

233 *Streblorrhiza speciosa*

(Des and litho Photopress International, Norfolk Island)

2002 (6 May). Bounty Bowls Tournament. Roul 5½.

796	**232**	10c. black and emerald	30	70
		a. Booklet pane of 10 with margins all round	2·25	

No. 796 was only issued in $2 stamp booklets, No. SB17.

Two miniature sheets, one comprising 4×45c., the other with 4×$1 stamps, depicting different sports, were prepared but withdrawn prior to issue. A small number were, however, distributed to dealers.

(Des Mary Butterfield. Litho Southern Colour Print, Dunedin)

2002 (21 May–18 Sept). Phillip Island Flowers. T **233** and similar vert designs. Multicoloured. P 14½.

797	10c. Type **233** (18.9)	1·00	1·00
798	20c. *Plumbago zeylanica*	55	45
799	30c. *Canavalia rosea* (18.9)	1·50	65
800	40c. *Ipomea pes-caprae*	60	60
801	45c. *Hibiscus insularis*	60	45
802	50c. *Solanum laciniatum* (18.9)	2·00	55
803	95c. *Phormium tenax*	1·00	1·25
804	$1 *Lobelia anceps* (18.9)	3·00	1·50
805	$1.50 *Carpobrotus glaucescens* (18.9)	4·50	4·25
806	$2 *Abutilon julianae*	2·50	4·25
807	$3 *Wollastonia biflora* (18.9)	6·00	6·50
808	$5 *Oxalis corniculata*	7·00	8·50
797/808	*Set of 12*	27·00	27·00

No. 797 is inscribed "specioca" in error.

234 Running

235 Adult Sperm Whale and Calf

(Des G. Doran. Litho Southern Colour Print, Dunedin)

2002 (25 July). 17th Commonwealth Games, Manchester. T **234** and similar multicoloured designs. P 14½.

809	10c. Type **234**	55	75
810	45c. Cycling (*horiz*)	3·50	1·25
811	$1 Lawn bowls	2·00	2·00
812	$1.50 Shooting (*horiz*)	3·00	3·50
809/12	*Set of 4*	8·00	6·75

(Des J-R Lisiak. Litho Southern Colour Print, Dunedin)

2002 (18 Sept). Opération Cétacés (marine mammal study). T **235** and similar horiz design. Multicoloured. P 14.

813	$1 Type **235**	3·00	3·00
	a. Horiz strip of 3. Nos. 813/14 plus label.	6·00	6·00
814	$1 Sperm Whale attacked by Giant Squid	3·00	3·00

Nos. 813/14 were printed together, in sheetlets of 10, as vertical strips of 5 with the backgrounds extending onto a central gutter of stamp-sized labels showing the project logo.

A similar set was issued by New Caledonia.

236 White Tern incubating Egg

(Des R. Pennycuick. Litho Southern Colour Print, Dunedin)

2002 (12 Nov). Christmas. White Tern. T **236** and similar horiz designs. Multicoloured. P 14.

815	45c. Type **236**	1·50	1·25
816	45c. White Tern chick	1·50	1·25
817	$1 Two White Terns in flight	2·50	1·75
818	$1.50 White Tern landing	3·50	5·00
815/18 *Set of 4*		8·00	8·00

237 Horses in Riding School

(Des G. Douran. Litho Southern Colour Print, Dunedin)

2003 (14 Jan). Horses on Norfolk Island. T **237** and similar horiz designs. Multicoloured. P 14.

819	45c. Type **237**	1·40	1·50
	a. Horiz strip of 5. Nos. 819/23	6·75	7·25
820	45c. Mares and foals in paddock	1·40	1·50
821	45c. Showjumpers	1·40	1·50
822	75c. Racehorses	1·60	1·75
823	75c. Draught horses	1·60	1·75
819/23 *Set of 5*		6·75	7·25

Nos. 819/23 were printed together, *se-tenant*, in horizontal strips of 5 throughout the sheet.

238 Old Warehouse Buildings at Seashore

(Des Mary Butterfield. Litho Southern Colour Print, Dunedin)

2003 (18 Mar). Photographic Scenes of Norfolk Island (1st series). T **238** and similar horiz designs. Multicoloured. P 14×14½.

824	50c. Type **238**	1·50	75
825	95c. Beached boat (with rainbow markings) and sandy shore	2·50	2·25
826	$1.10 Grazing cattle and pine trees	2·75	2·25
827	$1.65 Sandy shore and headland with single pine tree	3·75	5·50
824/7 *Set of 4*		9·50	9·50

See also Nos. 859/62

239 "Southern Prize"

240 Maeve and Gil Hitch

(Des Mary Butterfield. Litho Southern Colour Print, Dunedin)

2003 (10 June). Day Lilies. T **239** and similar horiz designs. Multicoloured. P 14½.

828	50c. Type **239**	65	75
	a. Block of 10. Nos. 828/37	5·75	
	b. Booklet pane. Nos. 828/37	37·00	
829	50c. "Becky Stone"	65	75
830	50c. "Cameroons"	65	75
831	50c. "Chinese Autumn"	65	75
832	50c. "Scarlet Orbit"	65	75
833	50c. "Ocean Rain"	65	75
834	50c. "Gingerbread Man"	65	75
835	50c. "Pink Corduroy"	65	75
836	50c. "Elizabeth Hinrichsen"	65	75
837	50c. "Simply Pretty"	65	75
828/37 *Set of 10*		5·75	6·75

Nos. 828/37 were printed together, *se-tenant*, in blocks of ten (2×5) with the two horizontal panes separated by a gutter. They were also available as a pane of ten from $5 stamp booklets (No. SB18).

(Des Bronwyn Tofts. Litho Southern Colour Print, Dunedin)

2003 (21 July). First Norfolk Island Writers' Festival. T **240** and similar vert designs. Black, bluish violet and lilac (Nos. 838/9 and 844/5) or multicoloured (Nos. 840/3). P 14½.

838	10c. Type **240**	60	75
	a. Block of 4. Nos. 838/41	2·25	2·75
839	10c. Alice Buffett	60	75
840	10c. Nan Smith	60	75
841	10c. Archie Bigg	60	75
842	50c. Colleen McCullough	60	75
	a. Block of 4. Nos. 842/5	2·25	2·75
843	50c. Peter Clarke	60	75
844	50c. Bob Tofts	60	75
845	50c. Merval Hoare	60	75
838/45 *Set of 8*		4·50	5·50

Nos. 838/41 and 842/5 were each printed together, *se-tenant*, in blocks of four throughout sheets of 40 made up of four panes of ten, separated by illustrated stamp-size labels. The top of the sheet contains four blocks of Nos. 838/41 and one gutter pair, and the bottom contains four blocks of Nos. 842/5 and one gutter pair.

241 Seashore with Trees and Stream

242 Queen Elizabeth II wearing Imperial State Crown

(Des Sue Draper. Litho Southern Colour Print, Dunedin)

2003 (21 July). Island Landscapes. T **241** and similar square designs. Multicoloured. P 14.

846	50c. Type **241**	2·00	2·25
	a. Horiz strip of 4. Nos. 846/9 and four labels	7·25	8·00
847	50c. Sandy shore with wooden post and small boat	2·00	2·25
848	50c. Rocky bay with pine trees on headland	2·00	2·25
849	50c. Grazing cattle, pine trees and ruined building	2·00	2·25
846/9 *Set of 4*		7·25	8·00

Nos. 846/9 were printed together, *se-tenant*, in horizontal strips of 4, each stamp accompanied by a blank half stamp-size *se-tenant* label, within sheetlets of 20. The sheetlets could be personalised with a photograph printed on the labels. A limited number were sold with a photograph of author Dr. Colleen McCullough on the labels. Stamps and sheetlets with blank labels were sold at face value and personalised sheetlets at $20 each.

(Des G. Douran. Litho Southern Colour Print, Dunedin)

2003 (29 July). 50th Anniv of Coronation. T **242** and similar horiz design. P 14½.

MS850	115×85 *mm.* 10c. Type **242** (black, deep violet and violet); $3 Queen wearing flowered hat and dress (multicoloured)	4·50	5·50

243 Globe ("Peace on Earth")

244 de Havilland DH.60G Gipsy Moth Floatplane (first aircraft at Norfolk Island, 1931)

(Litho Southern Colour Print, Dunedin)

2003 (21 Oct). Christmas. T **243** and similar vert designs. Multicoloured. P 14½×14.

851	50c. Type **243**	1·25	1·00
852	50c. Bird and rainbow ("Joy to the World")	1·25	1·00
853	$1.10 Heart-shaped Christmas present ("Give the gift of Love")	2·25	1·75
854	$1.65 Candle ("Trust in Faith")	3·00	4·50
851/4	*Set of* 4	7·00	7·50

(Des R. Pennycuick. Litho Southern Colour Print, Dunedin)

2003 (2 Dec). Centenary of Powered Flight. T **244** and similar horiz designs. Multicoloured (except Type **244**). P 14×14½.

855	50c. Type **244** (black, reddish brown and deep violet)	2·25	85
856	$1.10 Boeing 737 (Norfolk Island—Australia service)	3·50	2·25
857	$1.65 Douglas DC-4 (passenger service 1949–1977)	5·00	7·50
855/7	*Set of* 3	9·75	9·75
MS858	110×83 *mm.* $1.65 Wright *Flyer I*, 1903 (47×29 *mm*)	6·00	6·50

245 Timbers from Prow of Boat and Houses

246 Whale Shark

(Des Mary Butterfield. Litho Southern Colour Print, New Zealand)

2004 (10 Feb). Photographic Scenes of Norfolk Island (2nd series). T **245** and similar vert designs. Multicoloured. P 14½×14.

859	50c. Type **245**	1·50	1·00
860	95c. Waterfall	2·75	2·50
861	$1.10 Cattle and pine trees	2·75	2·50
862	$1.65 Beach and headland at sunset	4·00	6·00
859/62	*Set of* 4	10·00	11·00

(Des Mary Butterfield. Litho Southern Colour Print, New Zealand)

2004 (6 Apr). Sharks. T **246** and similar horiz designs. Multicoloured. P 15.

863	10c. Type **246**	75	1·25
864	50c. Hammerhead Shark	2·00	70
865	$1.10 Tiger Shark	3·50	2·75
866	$1.65 Bronze Whale Shark	5·00	6·50
863/6	*Set of* 4	10·00	10·00

247 Golden Orb Spider

(Des Mary Butterfield. Litho Southern Colour Print, Dunedin)

2004 (1 June). Spiders. T **247** and similar horiz designs. Multicoloured. P 14½.

867	50c. Type **247**	1·00	1·00
868	50c. Community Spider	1·00	1·00
869	$1 St. Andrews Cross Spider	1·60	1·60
870	$1.65 Red-horned Spider	2·50	3·75
867/70	*Set of* 4	5·50	6·50
MS871	120×80 *mm.* $1.50 Red-horned Spider (48×40 *mm*). P 14½×14	2·50	3·50

248 Loading Cargo into Light Craft

(Des Tracey Yager. Litho Southern Colour Print, Dunedin)

2004 (13 July). "Werken Dar Shep". T **248** and similar horiz designs. Multicoloured. P 15×14½.

872	50c. Type **248**	1·25	70
873	$1.10 Transporting cargo	2·00	2·00
874	$1.65 Two light craft	2·25	4·00
872/4	*Set of* 3	5·00	6·00
MS875	130×85 *mm.* $1.65 Craft moored alongside dock	3·25	4·00

249 Apple Blossom

250 Three Children

(Des Mary Butterfield. Litho Southern Colour Print, Dunedin)

2004 (16 Aug). Hippeastrums. T **249** and similar horiz designs. Multicoloured. P 14½.

876	50c. Type **249**	80	95
	a. Block of 10. Nos. 876/85	7·00	8·50
	b. Booklet pane. Nos. 876/85	9·00	
877	50c. Carnival	80	95
878	50c. Cherry Blossom	80	95
879	50c. Lilac Wonder	80	95
880	50c. Millennium Star	80	95
881	50c. Cocktail	80	95
882	50c. Milady	80	95
883	50c. Pacific Sunset	80	95
884	50c. Geisha Girl	80	95
885	50c. Lady Jane	80	95
876/85	*Set of* 10	7·00	8·50

Nos. 876/85 were printed together, *se-tenant*, in blocks of ten (2×5) with the two horizontal rows separated by a gutter. They were also available as a block of ten from $5 stamp booklets (No. SB19).

(Des Mary Butterfield. Litho Southern Colour Print, Dunedin)

2004 (16 Aug). 25th Anniv of Quota International (humanitarian organisation). Sheet 135×73 mm containing T **250** and similar horiz designs. Multicoloured. P 14½.

MS886	50c. Type **250**; $1.10 Feet painted with "WE CARE"; $1.65 Boy drawing "Quota" in sand	5·00	6·50

(Des Mary Butterfield. Litho Southern Colour Print, Dunedin)

2004 (28 Sept). Perfume from Norfolk Island. Special Edition. No. **MS**766 optd with "SPECIAL EDITION". P 14½.

MS887	145×98 *mm.* $3 Girl and perfume bottle	3·00	4·00

251 Tree Fern

252 Tree and "Twas the Night Before Christmas"

(Des Sue Draper. Litho Photopress International, Norfolk Island)

2004 (28 Sept). Norfolk Island Palm and Fern. T **251** and similar square designs. Rouletted.

888	10c. pale turquoise-green and black	25	75
	a. Booklet pane. No. 888×10	2·00	
889	10c. pale greenish yellow and black	25	75
	a. Booklet pane. No. 889×10	2·00	

Designs—No. 888, Type **251**; No. 889, Palm.

Nos. 888/9 were only issued in $2 stamp booklets (No. SB21) containing two panes of 10.

(Des J. Godward. Litho Southern Colour Print, Dunedin)

2004 (26 Oct). Christmas. T **252** and similar vert designs showing Christmas tree and excerpt of carol. P 14½.

890	50c. yellow-green and silver	75	70
891	50c. deep rose-lilac and silver	75	70
892	$1.10 carmine and silver	1·50	1·40
893	$1.65 dull orange and silver	2·25	3·75
890/3 *Set of 4*		4·75	6·00

Designs—No. 890, Type **252**; No. 891, "Silent Night"; No. 892, "Twelve Days of Christmas"; No. 893, "Oh Holy Night".

253 Sacred Kingfisher

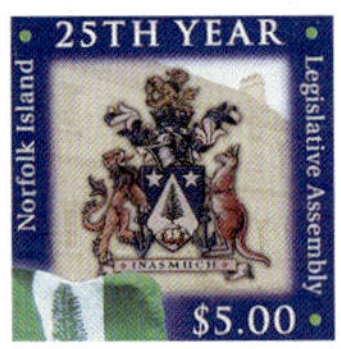

254 Coat of Arms and Flag

(Des R. Gorringe. Litho Southern Colour Print, Dunedin)

2004 (14 Dec). Sacred Kingfisher. T **253** and similar horiz designs. Multicoloured. P 14.

894	50c. Type **253**	1·60	1·50
895	50c. Two Sacred Kingfishers	1·60	1·50
896	$1 Sacred Kingfisher perched	2·75	2·00
897	$2 Sacred Kingfisher from back	4·00	5·00
894/7 *Set of 4*		9·00	9·00
MS898	130×158 *mm*. Nos. 894/7, each×2	14·00	17·00

(Des J. Godward. Litho Southern Colour Print, Dunedin)

2004 (14 Dec). 25th Anniv of Self-Government. P 14.

899	**254** $5 multicoloured	7·50	9·00

255 Boat Race

256 Tea Cup, 1856

(Des R. Pennycuick. Litho Southern Colour Print, Dunedin)

2005 (23 Feb). Centenary of Rotary International (humanitarian organisation). T **255** and similar multicoloured designs. P 14½.

900	50c. Type **255**	75	75
901	50c. Tree planting (*vert*)	75	75
902	$1.20 Paul Harris (founder)	1·50	1·40
903	$1.80 Rotary Youth Leadership Awards (*vert*)	2·25	4·25
900/3 *Set of 4*		4·75	6·50
MS904	110×80 *mm*. $2 District 9910 (Rotary community). P 14	3·00	4·25

(Des Louise Donald. Litho Southern Colour Print, New Zealand)

2005 (5 Apr). Norfolk Island Museum, Kingston. T **256** and similar horiz designs. Multicoloured. P 14½×15.

905	50c. Type **256**	1·25	1·00
906	50c. Salt cellar from HMS *Bounty*, 1856	1·25	1·00
907	$1.10 Medicine cups, 1825–55	2·00	1·75
908	$1.65 Stoneware jar, 1825–55	2·75	3·75
905/8 *Set of 4*		6·50	6·75

257 Polynesian Explorer and Voyaging Canoe

258 Branka House

(Des Tracy Yager. Litho Southern Colour Print, New Zealand)

2005 (21 Apr). Pacific Explorers. T **257** and similar vert designs. Multicoloured. P 14.

909	50c. Type **257**	70	50
910	$1.20 *Vitoria* (Magellan)	1·75	1·60
911	$1.80 Captain Cook ashore at Norfolk Island and HMS *Resolution*	2·50	4·00
909/11 *Set of 3*		4·50	5·50
MS912	140×85 *mm*. $2 Early map of Pacific (45×31 *mm*). P 15	2·75	3·50

No. **MS**912 also commemorates Pacific Explorer 2005 World Stamp Expo, Sydney.

(Des Sue Draper. Litho Southern Colour Print, New Zealand)

2005 (16 June). Old Island Houses. T **258** and similar horiz designs. Multicoloured. P 14½×15.

913	50c. Type **258**	60	55
914	50c. Greenacres	60	55
915	$1.20 Ma Annas	1·40	1·40
916	$1.80 Naumai	2·00	3·50
913/16 *Set of 4*		4·25	5·50

259 Red-tailed Tropic Bird

260 "Marjory Brown"

(Des R. Pennycuick. Litho Southern Colour Print, New Zealand)

2005 (9 Aug)–**06**. Seabirds of Norfolk Island. T **259** and similar multicoloured designs. P 14½×15 (**MS**922) or 15×14½ (others).

917	10c. Type **259**	40	60
918	25c. White Tern (9.8.06)	75	55
919	40c. Sooty Tern (9.8.06)	1·00	60
920	50c. Australasian Gannet	1·00	40
921	70c. Black-winged Petrel (9.8.06)	1·40	1·25
922	$1 Black Noddy (9.8.06)	1·75	1·25
923	$1.50 Grey Ternlet	2·25	1·75
924	$2 Masked Booby	3·25	3·50
925	$3 Wedge-tailed Shearwater (9.8.06)	4·25	4·50
926	$5 White-necked Petrel	6·50	7·50
917/26 *Set of 10*		20·00	20·00
MS927	(a) 65×90 *mm*. $2 Sooty tern in flight (9.8.06). (b) 100×70 *mm*. $4 Red-tailed tropic bird (*horiz*) *Set of 2 sheets*	9·00	10·00

(Des Mary Butterfield. Litho Southern Colour Print, New Zealand)

2005 (30 Aug). Hibiscus Varieties. T **260** and similar horiz designs. Multicoloured. P 14½×14.

928	50c. Type **260**	60	75
	a. Block of 12. Nos. 928/39	6·50	8·00
929	50c. "Aloha"	60	75
930	50c. "Pulau Tree"	60	75
931	50c. "Ann Miller"	60	75
932	50c. "Surfrider"	60	75
933	50c. "Philip Island"	60	75
934	50c. "Rose of Sharon"	60	75
935	50c. "D.J. O'Brien"	60	75
936	50c. "Elaine's Pride"	60	75
937	50c. "Castle White"	60	75
938	50c. Skeleton Hibiscus	60	75
939	50c. "Pink Sunset"	60	75
928/39 *Set of 12*		6·50	8·00

Nos. 928/39 were printed together, *se-tenant*, in blocks of 12 (6×2), making sheets of 48 containing two panes of 24 separated by an illustrated gutter.

261 Anson Bay

(Des Mary Butterfield. Litho Southern Colour Print, New Zealand)

2005 (25 Oct). Christmas. T **261** and similar horiz designs. Multicoloured. P 14½×14.

940	50c. Type **261**	75	50
941	$1.20 Cascade Bay	1·60	1·40
942	$1.80 Ball Bay	2·25	4·00
940/2	*Set of* 3	4·25	5·50

262 Drummer

264 Shooting

263 Baton and Norfolk Island Pines

(Des Jodie Williams. Litho Southern Colour Print, New Zealand)

2005 (6 Dec). Norfolk Island Jazz Festival. T **262** and similar vert designs. Multicoloured. P 14×14½.

943	50c. Type **262**	75	50
944	$1.20 Saxophone player	1·60	1·40
945	$1.80 Guitarist and pine tree	2·25	3·75
943/5	*Set of* 3	4·25	5·00

(Des Mary Butterfield. Litho Southern Colour Print, New Zealand)

2006 (16 Jan). Commonwealth Games Queen's Baton Relay on Norfolk Island. T **263** and similar horiz design. Multicoloured. P 14½.

946	50c. Prow of ship and girl carrying baton	2·25	2·75
	a. Horiz pair. Nos. 946/7	5·50	6·50
947	$1.50 Type **263**	3·25	3·75

Nos. 946/7 were printed together, *se-tenant*, in horizontal pairs in sheets of 48 stamps (2 panes of 24).

(Des Mary Butterfield. Litho Southern Colour Print, New Zealand)

2006 (14 Mar). Commonwealth Games. T **264** and similar vert designs. Multicoloured. P 14½.

948	50c. Type **264**	70	50
949	$1.50 Lawn bowls	1·50	1·50
950	$2 Squash	2·00	3·50
948/50	*Set of* 3	3·75	5·00

265 HMS *Bounty* at Portsmouth, 1789

(Des Tracey Yager. Litho Southern Colour Print, New Zealand)

2006 (4 May). 150th Anniv of Migration of Pitcairn Islanders to Norfolk Island (1st issue). Departure from Pitcairn Island. T **265** and similar horiz designs showing scenes from cyclorama on Norfolk Island depicting the *Bounty* story. Multicoloured. P 14×14½.

951	50c. Type **265**	2·25	2·25
952	50c. Collecting breadfruit at Tahiti	2·25	2·25
953	$1.20 Capt. Bligh cast adrift in *Bounty's* launch	4·00	3·00
954	$1.50 Burning of HMS *Bounty* at Pitcairn Island	4·75	5·50
955	$1.80 Pitcairn Islanders arriving at Norfolk Island, 1856	5·00	6·00
951/5	*Set of* 5	16·00	17·00

266 Re-enactment Procession

(Des Tracey Yager. Litho Southern Colour Print, New Zealand)

2006 (7 June). 150th Anniv of Migration of Pitcairn Islanders to Norfolk Island (2nd issue). Arrival on Norfolk Island. T **266** and similar horiz designs showing Bounty Day re-enactment and celebrations. Multicoloured. P 14×14½.

956	10c. Type **266**	75	1·00
957	30c. Laying wreath at war memorial	1·25	1·00
958	50c. Honouring ancestors	1·50	1·50
959	50c. Community picnic	1·50	1·50
960	$4 Bounty ball	9·00	13·00
956/60	*Set of* 5	12·50	16·00

267 Hat with Decorated Brim

268 "Wal"

(Des Sue Draper. Litho Southern Colour Print, New Zealand)

2006 (7 June). Traditional Hats. T **267** and similar vert designs. Multicoloured, colour of panel at foot of stamp given. P 15.

961	50c. Type **267** (turquoise-blue)	1·50	2·00
	a. Horiz pair. Nos. 961/2	3·00	4·00
962	50c. Hat with pale woven band (turquoise-blue)	1·50	2·00
963	50c. Hat with flowers on brim (yellow-green)	1·50	2·00
	a. Horiz pair. Nos. 963/4	3·00	4·00
964	50c. Plain hat (yellow-green)	1·50	2·00
965	50c. Hat with white decoration around brim (violet)	1·50	2·00
	a. Horiz pair. Nos. 965/6	3·00	4·00
966	50c. Plain hat (different) (violet)	1·50	2·00
961/6	*Set of* 6	8·00	11·00

Nos. 961/2, 963/4 and 965/6 were each printed together, *se-tenant*, in horizontal pairs throughout the sheets.

(Des Jodie Williams. Litho Southern Colour Print, New Zealand)

2006 (12 Sept). Dogs of Norfolk Island ("Year of the Dog"). T **268** and similar horiz designs. Multicoloured. P 14½.

967	10c. Type **268**	1·00	1·25
968	50c. "Axel"	2·25	75
969	$1 "Wag"	3·25	2·00
970	$2.65 "Gemma"	8·50	11·00
967/70	*Set of* 4	13·50	13·50

269 Norfolk Island Central School, Middlegate, *c.* 1906

(Des Photopress International, Norfolk Island. Litho Southern Colour Print, New Zealand)

2006 (3 Oct). Centenary of Norfolk Island Central School, Middlegate. T **269** and similar horiz design. Multicoloured. P 14½.

971	$2 Type **269**	7·00	8·00

972 $2 Norfolk Island Central School, Middlegate, 2006 ... 7·00 8·00

270 Adult and Juvenile Boobies enclosed in Bauble

271 *Lantana camara*

(Des Mary Butterfield. Litho Southern Colour Print, New Zealand)

2006 (21 Nov). Christmas. T **270** and similar vert designs. Multicoloured. P 14½.

973 50c. Type **270** ... 1·50 1·00
974 50c. Prow of boat and houses in bauble and fish decoration ... 1·50 1·00
975 $1.20 Old Military Barracks, Kingston, in bauble and star decoration ... 3·00 2·00
976 $1.80 Hibiscus flower in bauble and bird decoration ... 4·50 6·50
973/6 *Set of 4* ... 9·50 9·50

(Litho Southern Colour Print, New Zealand)

2007 (6 Feb). Weed Flowers. T **271** and similar vert designs. Multicoloured. P 14½×14.

977 50c. Type **271** ... 2·00 1·75
978 50c. *Ageratina riparia* (Crofton weed) ... 2·00 1·75
979 $1.20 *Ipomoea cairica* (morning glory) ... 4·00 2·75
980 $1.80 *Solanum mauritianum* (wild tobacco) ... 5·50 8·00
977/80 *Set of 4* ... 12·00 13·00

272 Sea Kayaking

(Des Rob Nisbet. Litho Southern Colour Print, New Zealand)

2007 (3 Apr). Adventure Sports. T **272** and similar horiz designs. Multicoloured. Litho. P 14½.

981 50c. Type **272** ... 1·50 1·25
982 50c. Wind surfing ... 1·50 1·25
983 $1.20 Mountain biking ... 3·00 2·25
984 $1.80 Surfing ... 4·50 6·50
981/4 *Set of 4* ... 9·50 10·00

273 Kentia Palms

274 The Violin Teacher and Government House

(Des Mary Butterfield. Litho Southern Colour Print, New Zealand)

2007 (29 May). Kentia Palm Seed Harvest. Sheet 82×82 mm containing T **273** and similar multicoloured designs and one label. Litho. P 14.

MS985 50c. Type **273**; 50c. Dog guarding buckets of palm seeds (*horiz*); 50c. Emptying bucket into wooden crates (*horiz*); 50c. Kentia palm tree laden with seeds ... 4·25 5·25

The vertical and horizontal stamps within **MS**985 are arranged around a small central label.

(Des Emily Ryves. Litho Southern Colour Print, New Zealand)

2007 (26 June). Ghosts of Norfolk Island. T **274** and similar vert designs. Multicoloured. P 14½.

986 10c. Type **274** ... 50 1·00
987 50c. Ghosts in graveyard ... 1·50 75
988 $1 Emily (lady in white) at Kingston Pier ... 3·00 2·25
989 $1.80 Officer on guard at entrance to Barracks ... 5·00 6·50
986/9 *Set of 4* ... 9·00 9·50

275 Queen Victoria

276 Squash player

(Litho Southern Colour Print, New Zealand)

2007 (31 July). 120th Anniv of Queen Victoria Scholarship at Norfolk Island Central School. Self-adhesive. Die-cut.

(a) Booklet stamp

990 **275** 10c. multicoloured ... 30 70
a. Booklet pane. No. 990×10 ... 2·50

(b) Sheet stamp. Size 25×32 mm

991 **275** $5 multicoloured ... 14·00 17·00

No. 990 was only issued in $1 booklets, No. SB22.

(Des Tracey Yager. Litho Southern Colour Print, New Zealand)

2007 (28 Aug). South Pacific Games, Samoa. T **276** and similar vert designs. Multicoloured. P 14½×14.

992 50c. Type **276** ... 1·25 75
993 $1 Golf ... 2·50 1·75
994 $1.20 Netball player ... 2·00 2·00
995 $1.80 Athlete running ... 3·50 5·50
992/5 *Set of 4* ... 8·25 9·00
MS996 115×90 *mm*. $2 Emblem ... 3·00 4·25

277 HMS *Sirius* and *Supply* off Kingston

278 Two Children ('friendship')

(Des Photopress International. Litho Southern Colour Print, New Zealand)

2007 (13 Nov). Bicentenary of Transfer of First Convict Settlement to Tasmania. T **277** and similar horiz designs. Multicoloured. Litho. P 14×14½.

997 10c. Type **277** ... 1·00 1·25
998 50c. Shipping Signal, Kingston ... 2·25 75
999 $1.20 First Settlement, Kingston ... 4·00 3·00
1000 $1.80 *Lady Nelson* leaving for Tasmania, 1807 ... 6·00 7·00
997/1000 *Set of 4* ... 12·00 11·00

(Des Cristina Rose and Alice Rogers. Litho Southern Colour Print, New Zealand)

2007 (27 Nov). 30th Anniv of Banyan Park Play Centre. T **278** and similar horiz designs. Multicoloured. P 14×14½.

1001 50c. Type **278** ... 1·75 1·00
1002 $1 Four children ('Community') ... 2·50 2·00
1003 $1.20 Three children playing ('Play grow learn together') ... 2·75 2·75
1004 $1.80 Two children reading book ('read books') ... 4·50 7·00
1001/4 *Set of 4* ... 10·50 11·50

279 Young Norfolk Island Pine

(Des Rob Nisbet. Litho Southern Colour Print, New Zealand)

2007 (27 Nov). Christmas. "Fairy Lights". T **279** and similar horiz designs. Multicoloured. P 14×14½.

1005 50c. Type **279** ... 1·75 75
1006 $1.20 Back of Melanesian Chapel ... 3·25 2·25
1007 $1.80 Old lighter on Kingston foreshore ... 4·75 6·50
1005/7 *Set of 3* ... 8·75 8·50

280 Ford Falcon XP, 1965

281 Andre Nobbs

(Des Mary Butterfield. Litho Southern Colour Print, New Zealand)

2008 (5 Feb). Classic Cars. T **280** and similar horiz designs, each showing car and photograph of Norfolk Island scene. Multicoloured. P 14×14½.

1008	50c. Type **280**	2·00	1·00
1009	$1 Chevrolet Styleline, 1952	3·25	2·00
1010	$1.20 Pontiac Silver Arrow, 1953	3·25	3·00
1011	$1.80 Rolls Royce Silver Shadow, 1971	5·00	7·00
1008/11	*Set of 4*	12·00	11·50

(Des Adam Jauczius. Litho Southern Colour Print, New Zealand)

2008 (4 Apr). Faces of Norfolk Island. T **281** and similar vert designs showing portraits by Adam Jauczius. Multicoloured. P 15×14½.

1012	50c. Type **281**	1·50	1·00
1013	$1 Darlene Buffett	2·25	2·00
1014	$1.20 Colin Lindsay Buffett ('Boonie')	2·75	2·75
1015	$1.80 Tania Grube and her baby son	3·50	5·00
1012/15	*Set of 4*	9·00	9·75

282 Limousin Cross Calf

283 Gravestone

(Des Haylee Fieldes. Litho Southern Colour Print, New Zealand)

2008 (30 May). Norfolk Island Cattle (1st series) Calves. T **282** and similar horiz designs. Multicoloured. P 14×14½.

1016	50c. Type **282**	1·25	1·00
1017	$1 Murray Grey	2·25	2·00
1018	$1.20 Poll Hereford	2·50	2·50
1019	$1.80 Brahman Cross	3·50	5·00
1016/19	*Set of 4*	8·50	9·50

See also Nos. 1052/**MS**1056

(Des Tracey Yager. Litho Southern Colour Print, New Zealand)

2008 (14 May). "A Jewish Resting Place". T **283** and similar vert designs showing Jewish gravestones. Multicoloured. P 14½.

1020	**283** 50c. multicoloured	2·50	1·00
1021	– $1.20 multicoloured	3·75	2·75
1022	– $1.80 multicoloured	5·00	7·00
1020/22	*Set of 3*	10·00	9·75

2008 (14 May). Israel 2008 World Stamp Championship, Tel-Aviv. Sheet 103×80 mm containing stamp as T **283** but 30×40 mm, optd **World Stamp Championship Israel 2008 Tel-Aviv 14–21 May** and emblem on right-hand sheet margin. P 13½.

MS1023	$2 Jewish gravestone	12·00	11·00

284 Past and Present Members

285 Netted Brakefern

(Des Robin Nisbet. Litho Southern Colour Print, New Zealand)

2008 (27 June). 25th Anniv of St. John's Ambulance in Norfolk Island. T **284** and similar horiz designs. Multicoloured. P 14½.

1024	30c. Type **284**	1·25	75
1025	40c. Re-enactment: putting casualty in recovery position	1·40	1·00
1026	95c. Re-enactment: loading casualty into ambulance	3·00	2·00
1027	$4 Re-enactment: taking casualty into hospital	11·00	13·00
1024/7	*Set of 4*	15·00	15·00

(Des Mary Butterfield. Litho Southern Colour Print, New Zealand)

2008 (1 Aug). Rare Endemic and Indigenous Ferns. T **285** and similar horiz designs. Multicoloured. P 14.

1028	20c. Type **285**	90	1·25
	a. Horiz pair. Nos. 1028/9	1·75	2·50
1029	20c. *Pteris zahlbruckneriana*	90	1·25
1030	50c. Robinsonia	1·75	2·00
	a. Horiz pair. Nos. 1030/1	3·50	4·00
1031	50c. *Asplenium australasicum f. robinsonii*	1·75	2·00
1032	80c. Hanging fork fern	2·25	2·50
	a. Horiz pair. Nos. 1032/3	4·50	5·00
1033	80c. *Tmesipteris norfolkensis*	2·25	2·50
1034	$2 King fern	4·25	4·50
	a. Horiz pair. Nos. 1034/5	8·50	9·00
1035	$2 *Marattia salicina*	4·25	4·50
1028/35	*Set of 8*	16·00	18·00

Nos. 1028/9, 1030/1, 1032/3 and 1034/5 were printed together, *se-tenant*, in horizontal pairs throughout the sheets.

286 *Norfolk* (sloop), 1798

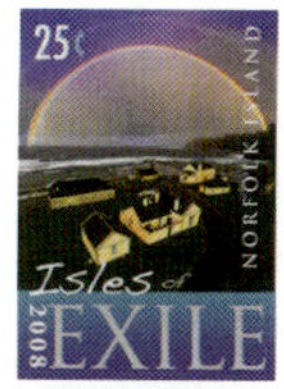

287 Royal Engineers Cottage, Store and Guard Houses from Second Settlement

(Des Tracey Yager. Litho Southern Colour Print, New Zealand)

2008 (2 Sept). Ships built on Norfolk Island. T **286** and similar square designs. Multicoloured. P 14.

1036	50c. Type **286**	2·75	1·00
1037	$1.20 *Resolution* (schooner), 1925	4·50	3·25
1038	$1.80 *Endeavour* (schooner), 1808	7·00	9·00
1036/8	*Set of 3*	13·00	12·00

(Des Robin Nisbet. Litho Southern Colour Print, New Zealand)

2008 (27 Oct). "Isles of Exile". T **287** and similar vert designs. Multicoloured. P 14½.

1039	25c. Type **287**	1·25	1·00
1040	55c. Commissariat Stores	2·00	80
1041	$1.75 Cemetery	4·50	4·75
1042	$2.50 Aerial view of Pentagonal Gaol from the Second Settlement	6·50	10·00
1039/42	*Set of 4*	13·00	15·00

288 Child at Prayer

289 Fish Mosaic

(Des Tracey Yager. Litho Southern Colour Print, New Zealand)

2008 (7 Nov). Christmas. T **288** and similar vert designs. Multicoloured. P 14.

1043	55c. Type **288**	1·25	80
1044	$1.40 Virgin Mary and baby Jesus	2·75	2·25
1045	$2.05 Three Magi carrying gifts	4·25	6·50
1043/5	*Set of 3*	7·50	8·50

(Des Mary Butterfield. Litho Southern Colour Print, New Zealand)

2009 (16 Feb). Norfolk Island Mosaics. T **289** and similar horiz designs. Multicoloured.

(a) Ordinary gum. P 14

1046	5c. Type **289**	20	80
1047	15c. Lily	50	1·00
1048	55c. Red-tailed Tropic Bird	1·50	1·00
1049	$1.40 Tree	2·50	3·25
1046/9	*Set of 4*	4·25	5·50

(b) Self-adhesive. Die-cut perf 9½×10

1050	15c. Sea Turtle (Jasmine Kiernan)	50	80
	a. Booklet pane. Nos. 1050/1, each×6	5·50	
1051	15c. Starfish on urn (Jeannie Sheridan)	50	80

Nos. 1050/1 were only issued in $1.80 booklets, No. SB23.

(Des Haylee Fieldes. Litho Southern Colour Print, New Zealand)

2009 (24 Apr). Norfolk Island Cattle (2nd series). Cattle Breeds. Horiz designs as T **282**. Multicoloured. P 14.

1052	15c. Shorthorn	35	70
1053	55c. South Devon	1·25	85
1054	$1.40 Norfolk Blue	2·75	2·75
1055	$2.05 Lincoln Red	3·75	5·50
1052/5	*Set of* 4	7·25	9·00
MS1056	110×84 *mm*. $5 Young cattle in pasture	8·50	10·00

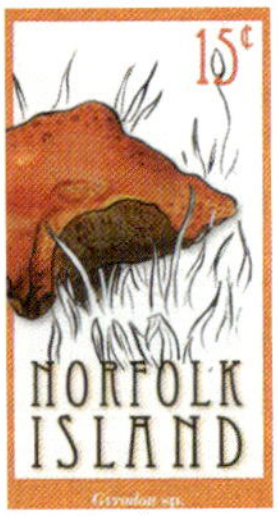

290 *Gyrodon* sp.

291 Bridled Nailtail Wallaby

(Des Haylee Fieldes. Litho Southern Colour Print, New Zealand)

2009 (30 May). Fungi of Norfolk Island. T **290** and similar vert designs. Multicoloured. P 14½×14.

1057	15c. Type **290**	35	70
1058	55c. *Stereum ostrea*	1·25	85
1059	$1.40 *Cymatoderma elegans* var *lamellatum*	2·75	2·75
1060	$2.05 *Chlorophyllum molybdites*	3·75	5·50
1057/60	*Set of* 4	7·25	9·00
MS1061	130×71 *mm*. Nos. 1057/60	7·25	9·00

Des Kevin Stead. Litho McKellar)

2009 (4 Aug)–**2010**. Species at Risk. T **291** and similar vert designs. Multicoloured. P 14½×14.

1062	55c. Type **291**	3·00	3·00
	a. Horiz strip of 5. Nos. 1062/6	13·50	13·50
1063	55c. Norfolk Island Green Parrot	3·00	3·00
1064	55c. Subantarctic Fur Seal	3·00	3·00
1065	55c. Christmas Island Blue-tailed Skink	3·00	3·00
1066	55c. Green Turtle	3·00	3·00
1062/6	*Set of* 5	13·50	13·50
MS1067	150×85 *mm*. Nos. 3247 and 3249/51 of Australia and No. 1063	13·00	13·00

Nos. 1062/6 were printed together, *se-tenant*, as horizontal strips of five in sheets of 50 (2 panes 5×5).

Similar designs were issued by Australia.

No. **MS**1067 is identical to No. **MS**3252 of Australia.

Nos. 1062/**MS**1067 of Norfolk Island and Nos. 3247/**MS**3252 of Australia were all issued on 4 August 2010.

292 Grey Fantail

(Des Tracey Yager. Litho Southern Colour Print, New Zealand)

2009 (18 Aug). Bush Birds. T **292** and similar multicoloured designs. P 14½.

1068	15c. Type **292**	70	1·00
1069	55c. Pacific Robin	1·75	90
1070	$1.40 Golden Whistler	3·50	3·25
1071	$2.05 Sacred Kingfisher	4·50	6·50
1068/71	*Set of* 4	9·50	10·50

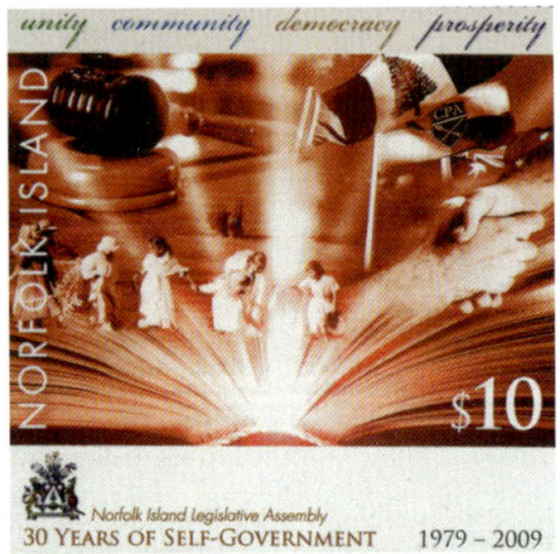

293 Children in Bounty Day Dress, Gavel, Handshake and Flags of Norfolk Island, Commonwealth Parliamentary Association and Australia

(Des Rob Nisbet. Litho Southern Colour Print, New Zealand)

2009 (19 Aug). 30th Anniv of Self-Government (Norfolk Island Legislative Assembly). P 14.

1072	**293**	$10 multicoloured	20·00	23·00

294 St. Mathew, St. Barnabas Chapel

295 Pottery from Second Convict Settlement

(Des Mary Butterfield. Litho Southern Colour Print, New Zealand)

2009 (2 Nov). Christmas. Stained Glass Windows from St. Barnabas Chapel and All Saints Church. T **294** and similar vert designs. Multicoloured. P 14.

1073	15c. Type **294**	45	45
1074	50c. Rose window, St. Barnabas Chapel	1·25	85
1075	$1.45 Christ in Glory, All Saints Church, Kingston	3·00	2·75
1076	$2.10 Memorial window to missionaries at St. Barnabas Chapel	4·25	6·00
1073/6	*Set of* 4	8·00	9·00

(Des Mary Butterfield. Litho Southern Colour Print, New Zealand)

2010 (22 Feb). Artefacts from Norfolk Island's Museums (1st series). T **295** and similar horiz designs. Multicoloured. P 14½.

1077	5c. Type **295**	20	75
1078	55c. Polynesian ivory fish hook, c.1450	1·50	1·00
1079	$1.10 Regimental badge	2·50	1·50
1080	$1.45 Brass wall fitting from wreck of HMS *Sirius*	3·00	2·50
1081	$1.65 Bottles from Convict Settlement's hospital	3·50	4·25
1082	$2.10 The Bounty Ring	4·25	6·50
1077/82	*Set of* 6	13·50	15·00

See also Nos. 1104/9

296 *Pacific Jewel*

297 Pitcairn Island Girls on Norfolk Island, 1857

(Des Mary Butterfield. Litho Southern Colour Print, New Zealand)

2010 (26 Mar). Cruise Ships to Norfolk Island. T **296** and similar horiz designs. Multicoloured. P 14×14½.

1083	55c. Type **296**	2·25	1·25
1084	$1.45 *Pacific Sun*	2·75	1·75
1085	$1.65 *Pacific Pearl*	4·00	4·00
1086	$1.75 *Pacific Dawn*	4·25	4·50
1087	$2.10 RMS *Strathaird*	4·75	6·00
1083/7	*Set of* 5	16·00	16·00

(Des Mary Butterfield. Litho Southern Colour Print, New Zealand)

2010 (15 June). 'They came aboard the *Morayshire*'. T **297** and similar horiz designs showing Pitcairn Islanders who emigrated to Norfolk Island in 1856. Multicoloured. P 13½.

1088	55c. Type **297**	1·60	1·00
1089	$1.10 Pitcairn Islanders aboard the *Morayshire*, 1856	2·00	1·40
1090	$1.45 Pitcairn Island men on Norfolk Island, 1861	3·00	2·75
1091	$2.75 Naomi and Jane Nobbs	5·50	8·00
1088/91	*Set of* 4	11·00	12·00

298 Blessing of the Boats

299 Crimson Rosella

(Des Tracey Yager. Litho Southern Colour Print, New Zealand)

2010 (16 Aug). History of Whaling in Norfolk Island. T **298** and similar horiz designs. Multicoloured. P 14.

1092	60c. Type **298**	1·25	1·00
1093	60c. Launching boat from shore	1·25	1·00
1094	$1.20 Women on cliff tops burning fires to guide boats back to shore	2·50	1·75
1095	$3 Whale products	6·00	8·00
1092/5	*Set of* 4	10·00	10·50

(Des Mary Butterfield. Litho Southern Colour Print, New Zealand)

2010 (18 Oct). Christmas. Parrots. T **299** and similar vert design. Multicoloured. P 13½.

1096	15c. Type **299**	80	60
1097	55c. Crimson Rosella and Norfolk Island Green Parrot	2·00	1·00
1098	60c. Norfolk Island Green Parrot and wrapped present	2·25	1·10
1099	$1.30 Crimson Rosella with ribbon and bauble in beak	4·75	6·25
1096/9	*Set of* 4	9·00	8·00

2010 (7 Nov). 'Beijing 2010' International Stamp and Coin Expo, Beijing, China. No. **MS**1061 inscr 'INTERNATIONAL STAMP & COIN EXPO BEIJING 7th-10th NOVEMBER 2010' and BEIJING 2010 emblem on sheet margins. P 14½×14.

MS1099*a*	130×71 *mm*. Nos. 1057/60	6·50	8·50

300 Bowler holding Trophy

301 Construction of St Barnabas Chapel, 1880

(Des Tracey Yager. Litho Southern Colour Print, New Zealand)

2010 (23 Nov). World Bowls Champion of Champions. T **300** and similar horiz designs. Multicoloured. P 14.

1100	60c. Type **300**	1·75	1·00
1101	$1.50 Bowler	3·25	2·75
1102	$2.20 Bowls and jack	5·00	7·00
1100/2	*Set of* 3	9·00	9·75

(Des Mary Butterfield. Litho Southern Colour Print, New Zealand)

2010 (7 Dec). 130th Anniv of St Barnabas Chapel. Sheet 100×65 mm containing T **301** and similar horiz designs. Multicoloured. P 14½×14.

MS1103	60c.×3 Type **301**; St. Barnabas Chapel and congregation; Chapel wall and builders	7·50	7·50

2011 (22 Feb). Artefacts from Norfolk Island's Museums (2nd series). Horiz designs as T **295**. Multicoloured. P 14½.

1104	15c. Iron from No. 10 Quality Row	60	60
1105	60c. Mug with personal scratch mark of Thursday October Christian	1·60	1·00
1106	$1.20 Bone dominoes from Convict Settlement	3·00	2·00
1107	$1.50 Clay pipes and ceramics from the civil Hospital	3·50	3·00
1108	$1.80 Doll fragments from privies, Quality Row	4·25	4·25
1109	$3 Wooden and shell hair items from the Melanesian Mission	7·00	9·50
1104/9	*Set of* 6	18·00	18·00

302 *Cirsotrema zelebori* (Zelebor Wentletrap) and *Canarium labiatum* (Plicate Conch)

303 Norfolk Island Abutilon (*Abutilon julianae*)

(Des Mary Butterfield. Litho Southern Colour Print, New Zealand)

2011 (21 Apr). Shells of Norfolk Island. T **302** and similar vert designs. Multicoloured. P 14½.

1110	15c. Type **302**	70	60
1111	60c. *Janthina janthina* (violet snail) and *Spirula spirula* (ram's horn)	2·00	1·50
1112	$1.50 *Conus capitaneus* (captain cone) and *Conus ebraeus* (Hebrew cone)	3·75	3·75
1113	$1.80 *Cypraea vitellus* (Pacific dear cowrie) and *Cypraea caputserpentis* (serpent's head cowrie)	4·50	4·75
1114	$3 *Nerita atramentosa* (black nerite) and *Nerita turrita* (turreted nerite)	7·50	8·50
1110/14	*Set of* 5	16·00	17·00

(Des 2899 Design. Litho Southern Colour Print, New Zealand)

2011 (24 June). 25th Anniv of Norfolk Island National Park. T **303** and similar horiz designs. Multicoloured. P 13½.

1115	25c. Type **303**	1·25	1·00
1116	60c. Phillip Island Hibiscus (*Hibiscus insularis*)	2·25	1·60
1117	$1.55 Popwood (*Myoporum obscurum*)	4·75	4·50
1118	$2.25 Broad-leaved Meryta (*Meryta latifolia*)	7·00	8·00
1115/18	*Set of* 4	13·50	13·50

304 Guard House, 1796-1826

305 Bounty Day, *c.* 1933

(Des 2899 Design. Litho Southern Colour Print, New Zealand)

2011 (1 Aug). World Heritage. Kingston and Arthur's Vale Historic Area. T **304** and similar horiz designs, each showing arrow carved in stone (convict symbol). Multicoloured. Self-adhesive. Die-cut perf 9½×10.

1119	60c. Type **304**	1·50	1·75
	a. Booklet. Nos. 1119/30		
1120	60c. The Graveyard, 1790s/1825	1·50	1·75
1121	60c. Government House, 1804/28	1·50	1·75
1122	60c. Pier Store, 1825	1·50	1·75
1123	60c. The Crank Mill, 1827	1·50	1·75
1124	60c. Bloody Bridge, 1835	1·50	1·75
1125	60c. Commissariat Store, 1835	1·50	1·75
1126	60c. Kingston Pier, 1839	1·50	1·75
1127	60c. No. 9 Quality Row, 1839	1·50	1·75
1128	60c. Flaghouses, 1840s	1·50	1·75
1129	60c. New Gaol, 1847	1·50	1·75
1130	60c. Royal Engineers Office, 1851	1·50	1·75
1119/30	*Set of* 12	16·00	18·00

Nos. 1119/30 commemorate the first anniversary of the declaration of Kingston and Arthur's Vale Historical Area as a world heritage site.

Nos. 1119/30 were only issued in $7.20 stamp booklets, No. SB25.

(Des 2899 Design. Litho Southern Colour Print, New Zealand)

2011 (14 Oct). 80th Anniv of the Norfolk Island Police Force (NIPF). T **305** and similar horiz designs. Multicoloured. P 13.

1131	60c. Type **305**	3·00	1·50
1132	$1.55 Police car, 1970s	5·00	4·50
1133	$2.25 Modern policeman watching ship ('Watching the seas')	7·00	8·00
1131/3	*Set of* 3	13·50	12·50

306 Protea

(Des Mary Butterfield. Litho Southern Colour Print, New Zealand)

2011 (14 Oct). Christmas. Flowers. T **306** and similar vert designs. Multicoloured. P 14½.

1134	15c. Type **306**	55	50
1135	55c. Frangipani	1·60	1·40
1136	60c. Cordyline	1·75	1·50
1137	$1.35 Orchid	3·50	5·00
1134/7 *Set of 4*		6·75	7·75

(307)

2012 (13 Feb). No. 917 surch with T **307**.

1138	$4on Type **259** 10c.	11·00	12·00

308

(Des 2899 Design, Norfolk Island. Litho Southern Colour Print, New Zealand)

2012 (10 Apr). Iconic Activities. T **308** and similar horiz designs. Multicoloured. Self-adhesive. Die-cut.

1139	60c. Type **308**	2·00	1·40
1140	75c. Collecting Whale Bird eggs	2·25	2·00
1141	$1.55 Fishing off the rocks	4·50	5·00
1142	$2.75 Clifftop barbecue	8·00	9·50
1139/1142 *Set of 4*		15·00	16·00

Nos. 1139/42 were each cut around in the shape of an outline map of Norfolk Island. The backing paper is divided into rectangles by lines of rouletting.

309

(Des Robin Nisbet, 2899 Design. Litho Southern Colour Print, New Zealand)

2012 (20 Aug). Diamond Jubilee. Sheet, 130×100 mm, containing T **309** and similar vert designs. Multicoloured. P 14½.

MS1143	$1.60×3 Type **309**; Beacon at Queen Elizabeth Lookout; Illuminated pine tree at Government House	11·00	11·00

310 Dishes from *Norfolk Island Cookery Book*

(Des Emily Ryves. Litho Southern Colour Print, New Zealand)

2012 (19 Oct). 51st Anniv of the Sunshine Club (assists senior citizens and people needing offshore medical treatment). T **310** and similar horiz designs. Multicoloured. P 14.

1144	60c. Type **310**	1·60	1·40
1145	$1.60 Wicker basket lined with patchwork containing fruit, sugar and flour	4·00	4·00
1146	$1.65 Ingredients, flan case and *Norfolk Island Cookery Book*	4·00	4·00
1147	$2.35 Cupped hands and sunset	6·00	7·00
1144/1147 *Set of 4*		14·00	15·00

311 Pearl Inlay and Lyrics from Carol 'Silent Night'

(Des Jodie Williams, Studio Monarch. Litho Southern Colour Print, New Zealand)

2012 (1 Nov). Christmas. Pearl Inlays from Pews at St. Barnabas Chapel and Lyrics from Carols and Hymns. T **311** and similar horiz designs. Multicoloured. P 14.

1148	15c. Type **311**	50	45
1149	55c. Three pearl inlays and lyrics from 'O Come All Ye Faithful'	1·50	1·25
1150	$1.55 Pearl inlay with square surrounded by four triangles design and hymn lyrics	3·75	3·75
1151	$2.35 Pearl inlay with geometric flower design and hymn lyrics	6·00	8·00
1148/51 *Set of 4*		10·50	12·00

312 RNZAF Hudson Bomber

(Des Robin Nisbet, 2899 Design. Litho Southern Colour Print, New Zealand)

2012 (24 Dec). 70th Anniv of First Aircraft Landing on Norfolk Island. T **312** and similar horiz designs. Multicoloured. Self-adhesive. Die-cut perf 9½×10.

1152	60c. Type **312**	1·75	2·00
	a. Booklet pane. Nos. 1152/63	18·00	
1153	60c. DC-3	1·75	2·00
1154	60c. Lancastrian	1·75	2·00
1155	60c. DC-4 Skymaster	1·75	2·00
1156	60c. Fokker F27 Friendship	1·75	2·00
1157	60c. Beechcraft Super King Air 200	1·75	2·00
1158	60c. Fokker F28 Fellowship	1·75	2·00
1159	60c. C-130 Hercules	1·75	2·00
1160	60c. BAe 146	1·75	2·00
1161	60c. Boeing 737-300	1·75	2·00
1162	60c. F/A 18 Hornet	1·75	2·00
1163	60c. Airbus A320	1·75	2·00
1152/63 *Set of 12*		18·00	22·00

Nos. 1152/63 were issued in $7.20 stamp booklets, No. SB26.

313 Bell, All Saints Church, Kingston

(Des Mary Pavicich. Litho Southern Colour Print, New Zealand)

2013 (9 Apr). "Church Bell", Norfolk Island. P 14.

1164	**313**	$5 multicoloured	7·75	8·25

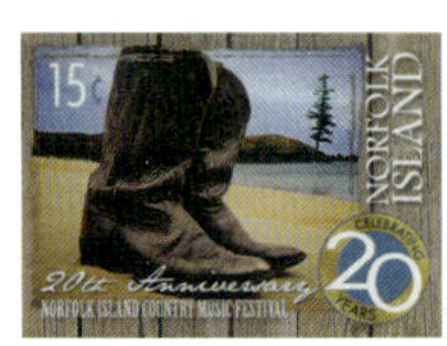

314 Boots on Sands of Emily Bay

(Des Robin Nisbet, 2899 Design. Litho Southern Colour Print, New Zealand)

2013 (20 May). 20th Anniv (2014) of Norfolk Island Country Music Festival. T **314** and similar horiz designs. Multicoloured. P 14.

1165	15c. Type **314**	50	40
1166	60c. Adam Harvey	1·50	1·00
1167	$1.60 Guitar	2·75	3·25
1168	$1.65 Dennis Marsh	2·75	3·25
1169	$2.35 Guitar player on main street of Burnt Pine	3·25	4·00
1165/69	*Set of 5*	9·75	10·50

315 Ball Bay

(Des Mary Pavicich. Litho Southern Colour Print, New Zealand)

2013 (30 Sept)–**2014**. Shorelines of Norfolk Island. T **315** and similar horiz designs. Multicoloured. P 13½.

1170	5c. Cemetery Beach (7.5.14)	50	40
1171	10c. Beefsteak (7.5.14)	1·25	75
1172	15c. Type **315**	1·75	1·25
1173	25c. Crystal Pool (7.5.14)	2·00	1·50
1174	60c. Second Sands	2·25	2·50
1175	70c. Cascade Bay (7.5.14)	2·10	2·50
1176	95c. Anson Bay	1·75	1·25
1177	$1.20 Slaughter Bay	2·00	1·50
1178	$1.70 Bumboras	2·25	2·50
1179	$1.75 Garnet Point (7.5.14)	2·75	2·75
1180	$1.85 Emily Bay	2·25	2·50
1181	$2.60 Duncombe Bay (7.5.14)	4·00	4·00
1170/81	*Set of 12*	17·00	16·00

316 Driftwood Wreath

(Des Mary Pavicich. Litho Southern Colour Print, New Zealand)

2013 (1 Nov). Christmas. Items made from Driftwood. T **316** and similar square designs. Multicoloured. P 14½.

1182	15c. Type **316**	50	40
1183	55c. Driftwood pine tree and beach	1·00	50
1184	$1.10 Seabird driftwood sculpture and sea	1·50	1·10
1185	$1.65 Three driftwood stars and beach	2·00	3·00
1182/5	*Set of 4*	4·50	4·50

317 Joe McNaughton

(Des Mary Pavicich. Litho Southern Colour Print, New Zealand)

2013 (18 Dec). Trans Tasman FMX (Freestyle Motor Cross) Challenge. T **317** and similar horiz designs. Multicoloured. P 13½.

1186	50c. Type **317**	1·25	60
1187	$1 Joe McNaughton (holding back of bike)	2·00	1·10
1188	$1.50 Joe McNaughton (in air above bike)	2·50	3·00
1189	$1.60 Callum Shaw	2·50	3·00
1186/9	*Set of 4*	7·50	7·00

318 *Fishing for the Groom* (Wayne Boniface)

(Des Mary Pavicich. Litho Southern Colour Print, New Zealand)

2014 (26 May). Artwear. T **318** and similar vert designs. Multicoloured. P 13½×14.

1190	15c. Type **318**	25	25
1191	70c. *Pasta Bella* (Wayne Boniface)	1·10	1·10
1192	$1.40 *Flora Abunda Metallica* (Tony Gazzard)	2·25	2·25
1193	$1.50 *Romeo and Julieta* (Julie Paris)	2·40	2·40
1194	$3.50 *Bamboo Princess Warrior* (Robyn Butterfield)	5·50	5·50
1190/4	*Set of 5*	10·50	10·50

319 Norfolk Island Pines, Cottesloe Beach, West Australia

(Litho Australia Post/Sprintpak)

2014 (22 July). Norfolk Island Pine (Araucaria heterophylla). T **319** and similar horiz design. Multicoloured. P 14×14½.

1195	20c. Type **319**	30	30
1196	70c. Norfolk Island Pines, Old Military Barracks, Norfolk Island	1·10	1·10

Nos. 1195/6 commemorate the Centenary of Norfolk Island becoming an External Territory of Australia.

Similar designs were issued by Australia.

320 Picnic Table provided by Quota Club, Emily Bay

(Des Mary Pavicich. Litho Southern Colour Print, New Zealand)

2014 (15 Aug). 35th Anniv of Quota Club International on Norfolk Island. T **320** and similar horiz designs. Multicoloured. P 14.

1197	15c. Type **320**	25	25
1198	70c. Seecoast Telescope Mark 1 installed by Quota Club at Queen Elizabeth Lookout in 2009	1·10	1·10
1199	$3.20 Family sitting on Memorial Seat overlooking the Landing Place and Sydney Bay provided by Norfolk Island Quota Club in 2000	5·00	5·00
1197/9	*Set of 3*	5·75	5·75

321 Red Cross Poster

(Des Mary Pavicich. Litho Southern Colour Print, New Zealand)

2014 (29 Sept). Centenary of Red Cross on Norfolk Island. Sheet 108×70 mm. P 14.

MS1200	**321** $3.50 multicoloured	5·50	5·50

322 Young Norfolk Island Pine

(Des Mary Pavicich. Litho Southern Colour Print, New Zealand)

2014 (29 Sept). Norfolk Island Pine Trees (*Araucaria heterophylla*). T **322** and similar vert designs. Multicoloured. Self-adhesive. Die-cut perf 10½×10.

1201	70c. Type **322**	1·10	1·10
	a. Booklet pane. Nos. 1201/10	10·00	
1202	70c. Young bulbous pine cone	1·10	1·10
1203	70c. Norfolk Pine seedling on shoreline	1·10	1·10
1204	70c. Norfolk Pine forest	1·10	1·10
1205	70c. Burst Pine cone scattering seeds	1·10	1·10
1206	70c. Uniform Norfolk Pine branches	1·10	1·10
1207	70c. Pine needles	1·10	1·10
1208	70c. Inside old hollow Pine tree	1·10	1·10
1209	70c. Four old Norfolk Pines on coastline	1·10	1·10
1210	70c. Norfolk Pine tree (with multiple shoots at top) at sunset	1·10	1·10
1201/10	*Set of* 10	10·00	

Nos. 1201/10 were issued in $7 booklets, No. SB27.

323 *Quillow* Memory Quilt (Julie South)

(Des Mary Pavicich. Litho Southern Colour Print, New Zealand)

2014 (17 Oct). Quilts. T **323** and similar vert designs. Multicoloured. P 14½.

1211	15c. Type **323**	25	25
1212	70c. *Norfolk Island Inspirations* sampler (Kay Greenbury, Raewyn Maxwell, Rowena Massicks, Barbara Solomon)	1·10	1·10
1213	$1.40 *Sunset at Puppy's Point* wall hanging (Kay Greenbury)	2·25	2·25
1214	$1.50 *Southern Cross Shared* (Kay Greenbury)	2·40	2·40
1215	$3.50 Miniature wall hanging in traditional *Storm at Sea* pattern (Rowena Massicks)	5·50	5·50
1211/15	*Set of* 5	10·50	10·50

324 Breadfruit Pattern

(Des Mary Pavicich. Litho Southern Colour Print, New Zealand)

2014 (3 Nov). Christmas. Hand Printed Fabrics by Sue Pearson. T **324** and similar horiz designs. Multicoloured. P 14.

1216	15c. Type **324**	25	25
1217	65c. Passionflower pattern	1·00	1·00
1218	$1.70 Pattern with turtle shell	2·75	2·75
1219	$1.80 Taro pattern	2·75	2·75
1220	$2.55 Hibiscus pattern	4·00	4·00
1216/20	*Set of* 5	9·75	9·75

325 Diver and Underwater Memorial at Wreck Site

(Des Mary Pavicich. Litho Southern Colour Print, New Zealand)

2015 (19 Mar). 225th Anniv of Wrecking of HMS Sirius (Flagship of the First Fleet) on Reef at Norfolk Island. T **325** and similar horiz designs. Multicoloured. Self-adhesive. Die-cut perf 10×10½.

1221	70c. Type **325**	1·10	1·10
	a. Booklet pane. Nos. 1221/30	10·00	
1222	70c. HMS *Sirius* in full sail (John Alcott)	1·10	1·10
1223	70c. HMS *Sirius* on reef, Sydney Bay, Norfolk Island (Midshipman George Raper)	1·10	1·10
1224	70c. Goss Belt Plate	1·10	1·10
1225	70c. Captain John Hunter	1·10	1·10
1226	70c. Anchor of HMS *Sirius* on sea bed	1·10	1·10
1227	70c. Model of HMS *Sirius* in Sirius Museum, Norfolk Island	1·10	1·10
1228	70c. Carronades from HMS *Sirius*	1·10	1·10
1229	70c. Bronze shackles from HMS *Sirius*	1·10	1·10
1230	70c. Pantograph from HMS *Sirius*	1·10	1·10
1221/30	*Set of* 10	10·00	10·00

Nos. 1221/30 were issued in $7 booklets, No. SB28.

326 War Memorial/ Cenotaph on Norfolk Island

(Des Mary Pavicich. Litho Southern Colour Print, New Zealand)

2015 (24 Apr). Centenary of Norfolk Islanders Landing at Gallipoli. Sheet 147×70 mm. P 13½.

MS1231	**326** $5 multicoloured	7·75	7·75

(Litho Southern Colour Print, New Zealand)

2015 (1 June). As Nos. 1201/10 but revalued. Multicoloured. Self-adhesive. Die-cut perf 10½×10.

1232	15c. Type **322**	25	25
	a. Booklet pane. Nos. 1232/41	2·25	2·25
1233	15c. Young bulbous pine cone	25	25
1234	15c. Norfolk Pine seedling on shoreline	25	25
1235	15c. Norfolk Pine forest	25	25
1236	15c. Burst pine cone scattering seeds	25	25
1237	15c. Uniform Norfolk Pine branches	25	25
1238	15c. Pine needles	25	25
1239	15c. Inside old hollow Pine tree	25	25
1240	15c. Four old Norfolk Pines on coastline	25	25
1241	15c. Norfolk Pine tree (with multiple shoots at top) at sunset	25	25
1232/41	*Set of* 10	2·25	2·25

Nos. 1201/10 were issued in $7 booklets, No. SB29.

327 John Rowles (singer)

(Des Mary Pavicich. Litho Southern Colour Print, New Zealand)

2015 (13 July). Christmas in July Festival. T **327** and similar square designs. Multicoloured. P 14.

1242	25c. Type **327**	40	40
1243	35c. Suzanne Prentice (singer)	55	55
1244	45c. Normie Rowe (singer)	70	70
1245	$1.40 Glenn A. Baker (Master of Ceremonies)	2·25	2·25
1246	$1.95 Colleen McCullough (writer, 1937–2015)	3·00	3·00
1242/6	*Set of* 5	6·25	6·25

328 Bird woven from Kentia Palm Frond Leaf

(Des Mary Pavicich. Litho Southern Colour Print, New Zealand)

2015 (1 Oct). Christmas. Weaving. T **328** and similar horiz designs. Multicoloured. P 14½.

1247	15c. Type **328**	25	25
1248	65c. Star woven from Kentia Palm	1·00	1·00
1249	$1.30 Candle and Kentia Palm weaving	2·00	2·00
1250	$1.70 Sennet plait forming two fish	2·75	2·75
1251	$2.55 Glass ball covered in netting woven from Routi plant	4·00	4·00
1247/51	*Set of* 5	9·00	9·00

329 Outrigger Canoe

(Des Mary Pavicich. Litho Southern Colour Print, New Zealand)

2016 (14 Jan). Inaugural Norfolk Ocean Challenge Outrigger Canoe Race. T **329** and similar horiz designs. Multicoloured. P 14×14½.

1252	$1 Type **329**	1·60	1·60
1253	$1 Outrigger canoe (bow facing camera)	1·60	1·60
1254	$1.85 Outrigger canoe off coast	3·00	3·00
1255	$2.75 Outrigger canoes at start of race	4·25	4·25
1252/5	*Set of* 4	9·50	9·50

330 Dwelling on Phillip Island

(Des Tim Murphy. Litho Southern Colour Print, New Zealand)

2016 (22 Feb). Diverse Phillip Island. T **330** and similar horiz designs. Multicoloured. P 14½.

1256	15c. Type **330**	25	25
1257	20c. Hut on rocky ground	40	40
1258	$1 Cabin in trees	1·60	1·60
1259	$1 Owen and Beryl Evans outside their cabin on Phillip Island	1·60	1·60
1260	$1.85 Dwelling on rocky seashore	3·00	3·00
1261	$2 Norfolk Pines growing on bare sandstone	3·00	3·00
1256/61	*Set of* 6	8·75	8·75

MACHINE LABELS

A Hytech weighing and label printing machine was introduced by the Norfolk Island Post Office in 1996 for use on parcels. This machine produced adhesive labels as illustrated with face values of $1.40 or above to reflect current parcel rates. The earliest recorded date is 5 November 1996.

STAMP BOOKLETS

A $4.10 booklet containing No. 465 in block of ten was prepared in 1989, but not issued.

B **1**

1991 (9 Apr). Ham Radio Network. Emerald on cinnamon cover as Type B **1**. Stamps attached by selvedge.

SB1	$4.30 booklet containing 43c. (No. 509) in block of 10	8·00

B **2**

1991 (Dec). Ships. Emerald on bluish grey (No. SB2) or cinnamon (No. SB3) covers as Type B **2**. Stamps attached by selvedge.

SB2	$4.50 booklet containing 45c. (No. 485) in block of 10 (cover 89×55 *mm*)	8·50
SB3	$7 booklet containing 70c. (No. 488) in block of 10 (cover 55×89 *mm*)	8·50

B **3**

1993 (23 Feb). Tourism. Emerald on white cover, 90×56 mm, as Type B **3**. Stamps attached by selvedge.

SB4	$4.50 booklet containing five different 45c. (Nos. 541/5) in block of 10	10·00

1993 (20 Aug). Nudibranchs. Emerald on white cover, 89×55 mm, as Type B **3** showing illustration of No. 550. Stamps attached by selvedge.

SB5	$4.50 booklet containing 45c. (No. 550) in block of 10	15·00

1994 (17 Aug). Sea Birds. Emerald on white cover, 93×60 mm, as Type B **3**, but showing illustration of No. 577. Stamps attached by selvedge.

SB6	$4.50 booklet containing horiz gutter strip of 10×45c. (No. 575a×2)	12·00

B **4**

1995 (1 Sept). Flowers. Rose and blue-green cover, 96×130 mm, as Type B **4**. Stamps attached by selvedge.

SB7 $1.80 booklet containing two different panes of eighteen 5c. (Nos. 600a/1a) .... 5·50

No. SB7 also exists with either the "Singapore '95" International Stamp Exhibition or Australian Stamp Dealers' Association logos shown on the front cover at bottom left.

B **5** (*Illustration reduced. Actual size* 170×80 *mm*)

1997 (22 Jan). Multicoloured cover as Type B **5**. Stamps attached by selvedge.

SB8 $2 booklet containing four panes of 10×5c. (Nos. 632a/3a, each×2) .... 8·50

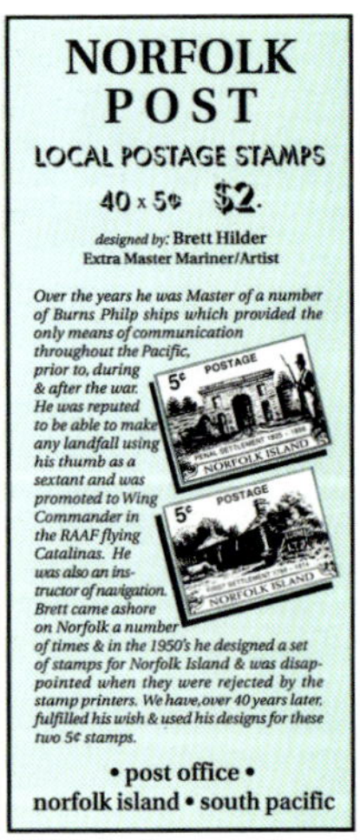

B **6** (*Illustration reduced. Actual size* 87×178 *mm*)

1998 (27 Feb). Black and turquoise-green cover as Type B **6**. Stamps attached by selvedge.

SB9 $2 booklet containing four panes of 10×5c. (Nos. 662a/3a, each×2) .... 8·50

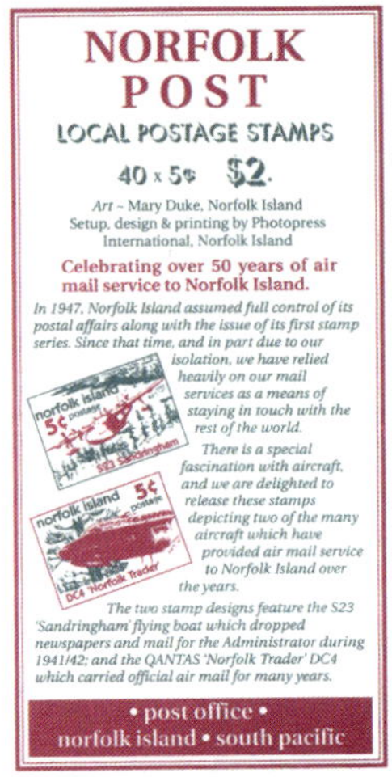

B **7** (*Illustration reduced. Actual size* 90×177 *mm*)

1999 (28 Jan). Aircraft. Brown-lake and deep grey-green on white cover as Type B **7**. Stamps attached by selvedge.

SB10 $2 booklet containing four panes of 10×5c. (Nos. 690a/1a, each×2) .... 10·00

B **8** Emily Bay (*Illustration reduced. Actual size* 170×75 *mm*)

1999 (19 Mar). "Australia'99" International Stamp Exhibition, Melbourne. Schooner Resolution. Multicoloured cover as Type B **8**. Stamps attached by selvedge.

SB11 $2.50 booklet containing pane of five 45c. and label (No. 693a) .... 7·00

B **9** (*Illustration reduced. Actual size* 92×168 *mm*)

2000 (31 Jan). Festivals. Bright ultramarine and bright carmine cover as Type B **9**. Stamps attached by selvedge.

SB12 $2 booklet containing four panes of 10×5c. (No. 722a) .... 8·00

B **10** (*Illustration reduced. Actual size 168×92 mm*)

2001 (26 Jan). Green Parrot. Scarlet and emerald cover as Type B **10**. Stamps affixed by selvedge.

SB13 $2 booklet containing four panes of 10×5c. (No. 747a) .... 12·00

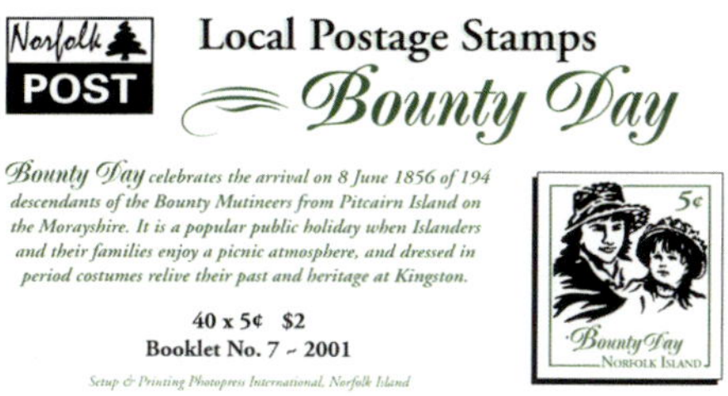

B **11** (*Illustration reduced. Actual size 179×95 mm*)

2001 (8 June). Bounty Day. Black and emerald cover as Type B **11**. Stamps affixed by selvedge.

SB14 $2 booklet containing four panes of 10×5c. (No. 760a) .... 9·00

B **12** (*Illustration reduced. Actual size 185×93 mm*)

2001 (1 Oct). 6th South Pacific Mini Games. Grey-brown and emerald cover as Type B **12**. Stamps affixed by selvedge.

SB15 $2 booklet containing two panes of 10×10c. (No. 777a) .... 7·50

B **13** (*Illustration reduced. Actual size 185×93 mm*)

2002 (15 Jan). "Nuffka" (Sacred Kingfisher). Royal blue and greenish blue cover as Type B **13**. Stamps affixed by selvedge.

SB16 $2 booklet containing two panes of 10×10c. (No. 783a) .... 13·00

B **14** (*Illustration reduced. Actual size 186×93 mm*)

2002 (6 May). Bounty Bowls Tournament. Black and emerald cover as Type B **14**. Stamps affixed by selvedge.

SB17 $2 booklet containing two panes of 10×10c. (No. 796a) .... 4·25

B **15** (*Illustration reduced. Actual size 210×75 mm*)

2003 (10 June). Day Lilies. Multicoloured cover as Type B **15**. Stamps affixed by selvedge.

SB18 $5 booklet containing pane of 10×50c. (No. 828a) .... 5·75

B **16** (*Illustration reduced. Actual size 210×75 mm*)

2004 (16 Aug). Hippeastrums. Multicoloured cover as Type B **16**. Stamps attached by selvedge.

SB19 $5 booklet containing pane of 10×50c. (No. 876b) .... 9·00

B **17** (*Illustration reduced. Actual size 185×93 mm*)

2004 (20 Sept). Norfolk Island Palm and Fern. Pale turquoise-green and black on white cover as Type B **17**. Stamps attached by selvedge.

SB20 $2 booklet containing two panes of 10×10c. (Nos. 888a/9a) .... 4·00

B **18** Hibiscus Flowers (*Illustration reduced. Actual size 116×85 mm*)

2005 (30 Aug). Hibiscus Varieties. Multicoloured cover as Type B **18**. Stamps attached by selvedge.

SB21 $6 booklet containing pane of 12×50c. (Nos. 928/39) .... 7·50

B **19** Queen Victoria

2007 (31 July). 120th Anniv of Queen Victoria Scholarship at Norfolk Island Central School. Multicoloured cover, 84×60 mm, as Type B **19**. Self-adhesive.
SB22 $1 booklet containing pane of 10×10c. (No. 990a) .... 2·50

B **20** Sea Turtle Mosaic (Jasmine Kiernan)

2009 (16 Feb). Norfolk Island Mosaics. Multicoloured cover, 77×72 mm, as Type B **20**. Self-adhesive.
SB23 $1.80 booklet containing pane of 12×15c. (No. 1050a) .... 5·50

B **21** Pacific Robin (*illustration reduced. Actual size* 185×93 *mm*)

2009 (18 Aug). Bush Birds. Multicoloured cover, 185×93 mm, as Type B **21**. Stamps attached by selvedge.
SB24 $5.50 booklet containing 55c. (No. 1069) in gutter block of ten........ 16·00

B **22** Arrow carved in Stone (convict symbol)

2011 (1 Aug). World Heritage. Kingston and Arthur's Vale Historic Area. Multicoloured cover as Type B **22**, 78×68 mm. Self-adhesive.
SB25 $7.20 booklet containing pane of 12×60c. (No. 1119a) .... 16·00

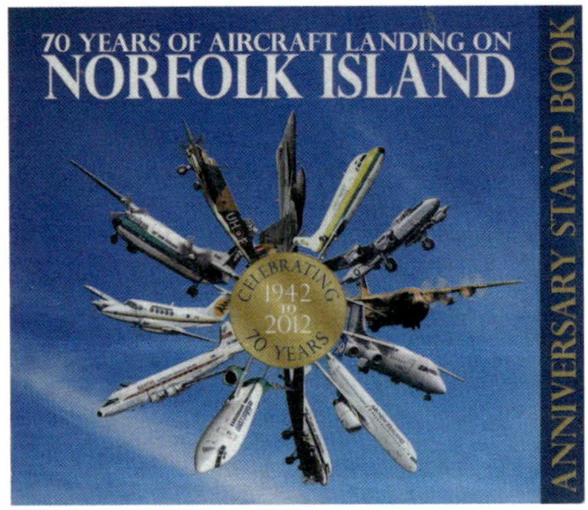

B **23** Aircraft

2012 (24 Dec). 70th Anniv of First Aircraft Landing on Norfolk Island. Multicoloured cover, 77×68 mm, as Type B **23**. Self-adhesive.
SB26 $7.20 booklet containing pane of 12×60c. (No. 1152a) .... 18·00

B **24** Norfolk Island Pine Trees

2014 (29 Sept). Norfolk Island Pine Trees. Multicoloured cover as Type B **24**. Self-adhesive.
SB27 $7 booklet containing pane of 10×70c. (No. 1201a) .... 10·00

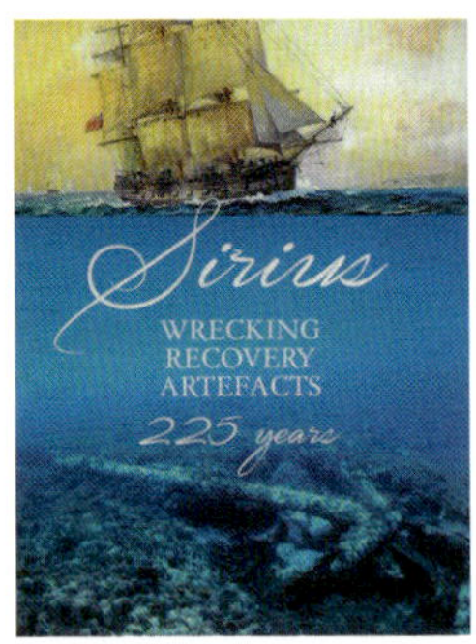

B **25** HMS *Sirius* and Anchor on Sea Bed

2015 (19 Mar). 225th Anniv of Wrecking of HMS Sirius (Flagship of the First Fleet) on Reef at Norfolk Island. Multicoloured cover as Type B **25**. Self-adhesive.
SB28 $7 booklet containing pane of 10×70c. (No. 1221a) .... 10·00

2015 (1 June). Norfolk Island Pine Trees. Multicoloured cover as Type B **24**. Self-adhesive.
SB29 $1.50 booklet containing pane of 10×15c. (No. 1232a) .... 2·25

PREMIUM BOOKLET

P **1** Girl and Ruined Building (*Illustration reduced. Actual size* 155×96 *mm*)

2001 (29 June). Perfume from Norfolk Island. Multicoloured cover as Type P **1**. Booklet contains text and illustrations on panes and interleaving pages. Stitched.

SP1	$10 booklet containing four panes: Nos. 761/2, Nos. 763/4, No. 765 and pane as No. **MS**766 together with a pre-paid postal stationery card	9·50
	a. With "Belgica 2001" International Stamp Exhibition, Brussels logo on cover	9·50

The panes containing Nos. 761/2, 763/4 and No. 765 each have one stamp-size label showing flowers.

The $3 pane from booklet SP1 is imperf and also differs from **MS**766 by showing "NORFOLK ISLAND" at top left and face value at bottom right.

The contents of No. SP1 have a face value of $7.95 but the booklet was sold at $10.

It is printed on paper impregnated with Jasmine fragrance.

PAPUA (BRITISH NEW GUINEA)

Stamps of QUEENSLAND were used in British New Guinea (Papua) from at least 1885 onwards. Post Offices were opened at Daru (1894), Kulumadau (Woodlarks) (1899), Nivani (1899), Port Moresby (1885), Samarai (1888), Sudest (1899) and Tamata (1899). Stamps were usually cancelled "N.G." (at Port Moresby from 1885) or "BNG" (without stops at Samarai or with stops at the other offices) from 1888. Queensland stamps were replaced in Papua by the issue of 1901.

PRICES FOR STAMPS ON COVER

Nos. 1/7	*from*×15
No. 8	—
Nos. 9/15	*from*×20
No. 16	—
Nos. 17/27	*from*×6
No. 28	—
Nos. 34/45a	*from*×5
Nos. 47/71	*from*×8
Nos. 72/4	—
Nos. 75/92*a*	*from*×8
Nos. 93/103	*from*×6
Nos. 104/5	—
Nos. 106/11	*from*×10
Nos. 112/14	*from*×6
No. 115	—
Nos. 116/28	*from*×5
Nos. 130/53	*from*×4
Nos. 154/7	*from*×12
Nos. 158/67	*from*×4
No. 168	*from*×3
Nos. O1/54	*from*×10
Nos. O55/66*a*	*from*×7
No. F1	*from*×8

1 Lakatoi (trading canoe) with Hanuabada Village in Background

2 (Horizontal)

Normal

Thin "d" at left (R. 4/2)

Deformed "d" at left (R. 4/3)

(Recess D.L.R.)

1901 (1 July)–**05**. Wmk Mult Rosettes, W **2**. P 14.

		A. Wmk horizontal. Thick paper. Line perf		
1	**1**	½d. black and yellow-green	24·00	26·00
		a. Thin paper	£350	£250
2		1d. black and carmine	20·00	19·00
3		2d. black and violet	27·00	9·00
4		2½d. black and ultramarine	40·00	10·00
		a. Thin paper	£400	£225
		ab. Black and dull blue	£900	£475
		b. Thin "d" at left	£375	£130
5		4d. black and sepia	65·00	35·00
		a. Deformed "d" at left	£750	£475
6		6d. black and myrtle-green	65·00	35·00
7		1s. black and orange	75·00	70·00
8		2s.6d. black and brown (1.1.05)	£650	£550
1/8 *Set of* 8			£850	£650
		B. Wmk vertical. Medium to thick paper. Line or comb perf		
9	**1**	½d. black and yellow-green	23·00	3·75
		a. Thin paper (*comb perf*) (1905)	28·00	40·00
10		1d. black and carmine	12·00	2·00
11		2d. black and violet	13·00	4·25
		a. Thin paper (*comb perf*) (1905)	65·00	16·00
12		2½d. black and ultramarine (*shades*)	35·00	12·00
		a. Thin "d" at left	£325	£140
13		4d. black and sepia	42·00	55·00
		a. Deformed "d" at left	£600	£750
		b. Thin paper (*comb perf*) (1905)	£350	£1300
		ba. Deformed "d" at left	£3250	
14		6d. black and myrtle-green	65·00	90·00
		a. Thin paper (*comb perf*) (1905)	£1200	
15		1s. black and orange	65·00	£100
		a. Thin paper (*comb perf*) (1905)	£950	£4250
16		2s.6d. black and brown (1905)	£5500	£3750
		a. Thin paper (*comb perf*)	£600	£1300
9/16a *Set of* 8 (*cheapest*)			£750	£1400

The paper used for Nos. 1/8 is white, of consistent thickness and rather opaque. The thin paper used for the horizontal watermark printings is of variable thickness, readily distinguishable from the thick paper by its greater transparency and by the gum which is thin and smooth.

Nos. 9/16 were initially printed on the same thick paper as the stamps with horizontal watermark and were line perforated. Values from ½d. to 2½d. were subsequently printed on medium paper on which the watermark was more visible. These were comb perforated. The thin paper with vertical watermark, produced in 1905, is much more transparent and has smooth gum. Printings were made on this paper for all values except the 2½d., but only the ½d. and 2d. were issued in Papua although used examples of the 4d., 1s. and 2s.6d. are also known. The entire printing of the 1d. on thin paper with vertical watermark was used for subsequent overprints.

The sheets of the ½d., 2d. and 2½d. show a variety known as "white leaves" on R. 4/5, while the 2d. and 2½d. (both R. 6/2) and the ½d. and 1s. (both R. 6/3) show what is known as the "unshaded leaves" variety.

Papua. (3) Papua. (4)

1906 (8 Nov). I. Optd with T **3** (large opt), at Port Moresby.

		A. Wmk horizontal. Thick paper. Line perf		
16*b*		2½d. black and ultramarine	†	—
17	**1**	4d. black and sepia	£250	£170
		a. Deformed "d" at left	£2000	£1600
18		6d. black and myrtle-green	60·00	48·00
19		1s. black and orange	26·00	48·00
20		2s.6d. black and brown	£170	£190

B. Wmk vertical. Thin paper (½d., 1d., 2d.) or medium to thick paper (others). Comb perf (½d. to 2½d.) or line perf (others)

21	1	½d. black and yellow-green	11·00	20·00
22		1d. black and carmine	19·00	19·00
23		2d. black and violet	18·00	5·00
24		2½d. black and ultramarine	11·00	15·00
		a. Thin "d" at left	£120	£150
25		4d. black and sepia	£225	£160
		a. Deformed "d" at left	£1900	£1500
26		6d. black and myrtle-green	45·00	60·00
27		1s. black and orange	£1800	£1400
28		2s.6d. black and brown	£17000	£12000
19/26 *Set of 8*			£450	£450

1907 (May–June). Optd with T **4** (small opt), at Brisbane.

A. Wmk horizontal. Thick paper. Line perf

34	1	½d. black and yellow-green	—	
		a. Thin paper	75·00	90·00
35		2½d. black and ultramarine	£2000	
		a. Thin paper	80·00	85·00
		ac. Black and dull blue	£325	£325
		b. Thin "d" at left	£700	£750
36		1s. black and orange	£325	£400
37		2s.6d. black and brown	50·00	75·00
		a. Opt reading downwards	£7500	
		c. Opt double *(horiz)*	†	£6000
		d. Opt triple *(horiz)*	†	£4500

B. Wmk vertical. Thin paper (½d., 1d., 2d., 4d., 6d.) or medium to thick paper (2½d., 1s., 2s.6d.). Line or comb perf (2½d.), line perf (1s., 2s.6d.) or comb perf (others)

38	1	½d. black and yellow-green	23·00	28·00
		a. Opt double	£3500	
39		1d. black and carmine	11·00	5·00
		a. Opt reading upwards	£7500	£4500
40		2d. black and violet	7·50	2·25
		a. Opt double	£4250	
41		2½d. black and ultramarine	20·00	20·00
		a. Thin "d" at left	£180	£200
42		4d. black and sepia	50·00	70·00
		a. Deformed "d" at left	£650	£750
43		6d. black and myrtle-green	50·00	45·00
		a. Opt double	£7000	£13000
44		1s. black and orange	80·00	90·00
		b. Thin paper *(comb perf)*	48·00	42·00
		ba. Opt double, one diagonal	£21000	£14000
45		2s.6d. black and brown	£18000	£10000
		a. Thin paper *(comb perf)*	55·00	90·00
38/45a *Set of 8*			£225	£250

In the setting of this overprint Nos. 10, 16, and 21 have the "p" of "Papua" with a defective foot or inverted "d" for "p", and in No. 17 the "pua" of "Papua" is a shade lower than the first "a".

No. 37a comes from a single sheet on which the overprints were sideways. Examples exist showing one, two or four complete or partial overprints.

PRINTERS. All the following issues were printed at Melbourne by the Stamp Ptg Branch (to 1928) or Note Ptg Branch.

WATERMARK VARIETIES. The lithographed issues Nos. 47/83 were printed using a "print-and-turn" technique. Thus, after one half of the sheet had been printed it was turned 180 degrees and the second half printed. As a result, upright and inverted (or sideways and sideways-inverted) watermarks were produced in equal quantities. Nos. 51/3, 55, 57, 62 and 69 are known with watermark reversed and others may well exist.

5 Large "PAPUA"

B

C

Three types of the 2s.6d.:—

A. Thin top to "2" and small ball. Thin "6" and small ball. Thick uneven stroke.

B. Thin top to "2" and large, round ball. Thin "6" and large ball. Very thick uneven stroke. Every stamp in Type B varies slightly.

C. Thick uniform figures with large oval balls Thin even stroke.

Type A is not illustrated as the stamp is distinguishable by perf and watermark.

The litho stones were prepared from the engraved plates of the 1901 issue, value for value except the 2s.6d. for which the original plate was mislaid. No. 48 containing Type A was prepared from the original ½d. plate with the value inserted on the stone and later a fresh stone was prepared from the 1d. plate and this contained Type B. Finally, the original plate of the 2s.6d. was found and a third stone was prepared from this, and issued in 1911. These stamps show Type C.

6 Small "PAPUA"

(Litho Stamp Ptg Branch, Melbourne, from transfers taken from original engraved plates)

1907–10. A. Large "PAPUA". Wmk Crown over A, W w **11**.

(a) Wmk upright. P 11

47	5	½d. black and yellow-green (11.07)	4·50	3·50

(b) Wmk sideways. P 11

48	5	2s.6d. black and chocolate (A) (12.09)	75·00	90·00
		a. "POSTAGIE" at left (R.1/5)	£1500	£1700

B. Small "PAPUA" I. Wmk upright

(a) P 11 (1907–8)

49	6	1d. black and rose (6.08)	6·50	5·00
50		2d. black and purple (10.08)	26·00	4·50
51		2½d. black and bright ultramarine (7.08)	30·00	35·00
		a. Black and pale ultramarine	17·00	7·00
		b. Thin "d" at left	£150	85·00
52		4d. black and sepia (20.11.07)	7·00	16·00
		a. Deformed "d" at left	£130	£225
53		6d. black and myrtle-green (4.08)	15·00	16·00
54		1s. black and orange (10.08)	55·00	20·00

(b) P 12½ (1907–9)

55	6	2d. black and purple (10.08)	40·00	9·00
56		2½d. black and bright ultramarine (7.08)	£180	£190
		a. Black and pale ultramarine	65·00	85·00
		b. Thin "d" at left	£550	£650
57		4d. black and sepia (20.11.07)	9·00	8·00
		a. Deformed "d" at left	£160	£150
58		1s. black and orange (1.09)	75·00	£100

II. Wmk sideways

(a) P 11 (1909–10)

59	6	½d. black and yellow-green (12.09)	2·50	3·00
		a. Black and deep green (1910)	28·00	42·00
60		1d. black and carmine (1.10)	9·50	8·00
61		2d. black and purple (1.10)	26·00	8·00
62		2½d. black and dull blue (1.10)	4·50	26·00
		a. Thin "d" at left	85·00	£170
63		4d. black and sepia (1.10)	4·75	9·00
		a. Deformed "d" at left	£130	£160
64		6d. black and myrtle-green (11.09)	10·00	22·00
65		1s. black and orange (3.10)	55·00	75·00

(b) P 12½ (1909–10)

66	6	½d. black and yellow-green (12.09)	3·75	4·00
		a. Black and deep green (1910)	32·00	45·00
67		1d. black and carmine (12.09)	7·50	12·00
68		2d. black and purple (1.10)	9·50	13·00
69		2½d. black and dull blue (1.10)	10·00	45·00
		a. Thin "d" at left	£130	£275
70		6d. black and myrtle-green (11.09)	£5500	£14000
71		1s. black and orange (3.10)	19·00	65·00

(c) Perf compound of 11 and 12½

72	6	½d. black and yellow-green	£5000	£5000
73		2d. black and purple	£1700	

(d) Mixed perfs 11 and 12½

74	6	4d. black and sepia	£16000	

Compound perforations on the 4d. are fakes.

The only known examples of No. 74 come from the top row of a sheet perforated 11 and with an additional line perf 12½ in the top margin.

(Litho Stamp Ptg Branch, Melbourne, by J. B. Cooke, from new stones made by fresh transfers)

1910 (Sept)–**11**. Large "PAPUA". W w **11** (upright). P 12½.

75	5	½d. black and green (12.10)	4·50	14·00
76		1d. black and carmine	13·00	15·00
77		2d. black and dull purple *(shades)* (12.10)	6·50	5·00
		a. "C" for "O" in "POSTAGE" (R. 4/3)	£140	£130
78		2½d. black and blue-violet (10.10)	12·00	18·00
		a. Thin "d" at left	£120	£170
79		4d. black and sepia (10.10)	11·00	11·00
		a. Deformed "d" at left	£190	£190
80		6d. black and myrtle-green	8·50	12·00
81		1s. black and deep orange (12.10)	12·00	20·00
82		2s.6d. black and brown (B)	60·00	60·00
83		2s.6d. black and brown (C) (1911)	75·00	75·00
75/82 *Set of 8*			£110	£140

A variety showing a white line or "rift" in clouds occurs on R. 5/3 in Nos. 49/74 and the "white leaves" variety mentioned below No. 16 occurs on the 2d. and 2½d. values in both issues. They are worth about three times the normal price.

8

ONE PENNY

(9)

(Eng S. Reading. Typo J. B. Cooke)

1911–15. Printed in one colour. W **8** (sideways*).

		(a) P 12½ (1911–12)		
84	**6**	½d. yellow-green	2·00	3·75
		a. Green	70	2·25
		w. Wmk Crown to right of A	23·00	
85		1d. rose-pink	2·00	75
		w. Wmk Crown to right of A	65·00	65·00
86		2d. bright mauve	3·75	75
		w. Wmk Crown to right of A	£160	£110
87		2½d. bright ultramarine	6·50	8·50
		a. Dull ultramarine	8·00	8·50
		aw. Wmk Crown to right of A	£160	
88		4d. pale olive-green	2·25	11·00
		w. Wmk Crown to right of A	£190	£150
89		6d. orange-brown	3·75	5·00
		w. Wmk Crown to right of A	£225	
90		1s. yellow	9·50	15·00
		w. Wmk Crown to right of A	£250	
91		2s.6d. rose-carmine	42·00	50·00
		w. Wmk Crown to right of A	£450	
84/91 *Set of 8*			60·00	85·00
		(b) P 14		
92	**6**	1d. rose-pink (6.15)	38·00	7·00
		a. Pale scarlet	21·00	2·00
		w. Wmk Crown to right of A	—	£160

*The normal sideways watermark shows Crown to left of A, *as seen from the back of the stamp.*

(Typo J. B. Cooke (1916–18), T. S. Harrison (1918–26), A. J. Mullett (No. 95*b* only) (1926–27), or John Ash (1927–31))

1916 (Aug)–**31**. Printed in two colours. W **8** (sideways*). P 14.

93	**6**	½d. myrtle and apple green (Harrison and Ash) (1919)	80	1·00
		a. Myrtle and pale olive-green (1927)	1·75	3·00
		w. Wmk Crown to right of A	26·00	28·00
94		1d. black and carmine-red	1·75	1·25
		aw. Wmk Crown to right of A		
		b. Grey-black and red (1918)	1·75	1·25
		bw. Wmk Crown to right of A	5·50	50
		c. Intense black and red (Harrison) (*wmk Crown to right of A*) (1926)	2·50	2·50
95		1½d. pale grey-blue (*shades*) and brown (1925)	1·50	80
		aw. Wmk Crown to right of A	22·00	8·00
		b. Cobalt and light brown (Mullett) (*wmk Crown to right of A*) (1927)	9·50	3·25
		c. Bright blue and bright brown (1929)	3·00	2·00
		d. "POSTACE" at right (R.1/1) (all printings) *From*	40·00	40·00
96		2d. brown-purple and brown-lake (1919)	1·75	75
		a. Deep brown-purple and lake (1931)	25·00	1·75
		aw. Wmk Crown to right of A	42·00	5·00
		b. Brown-purple and claret (1931)	2·00	75
97		2½d. myrtle and ultramarine (1919)	4·75	12·00
98		3d. black and bright blue-green (12.16)	4·50	1·75
		a. Error. Black and deep greenish Prussian blue†	£1300	£1300
		b. Sepia-black and bright blue-green (Harrison)	22·00	19·00
		c. Black and blue-green (1927)	4·50	8·00
99		4d. brown and orange (1919)	2·50	5·00
		a. Light brown and orange (1927)	20·00	18·00
		aw. Wmk Crown to right of A	17·00	30·00
100		5d. bluish slate and pale brown (1931)	4·25	16·00
101		6d. dull and pale purple (*wmk Crown to right of A*) (1919)	4·50	9·50
		aw. Wmk Crown to left of A	32·00	
		b. Dull purple and red-purple (*wmk Crown to left of A*) (1927)	16·00	24·00
		c. "POSTACE" at left (R. 6/2) (all printings) *From*	95·00	£140
102		1s. sepia and olive (1919)	5·50	7·00
		a. Brown and yellow-olive (1927)	8·50	14·00
103		2s.6d. maroon and pale pink (1919)	23·00	40·00
		a. Maroon and bright pink (*shades*) (1927)	20·00	50·00
104		5s. black and deep green (12.16)	55·00	48·00
105		10s. green and pale ultramarine (1925)	£180	£190
93/105 *Set of 13*			£250	£300

*The normal sideways watermark shows Crown to left of A, *as seen from the back of the stamp.*

†Beware of similar shades produced by removal of yellow pigment. No 98a is a colour trial, prepared by Cooke, of which, it is believed, five sheets were sold in error.

The printers of various shades can be determined by their dates of issue. The Ash printings are on whiter paper.

For 9d. and 1s.3d. values, see Nos. 127/8.

1917 (Oct). Nos. 84, 86/9 and 91 surch with T **9** by Govt Ptg Office, Melbourne.

106	**6**	1d. on ½d. yellow-green	1·50	1·60
		a. Green	1·00	1·25
		w. Wmk Crown to right of A	8·00	11·00
107		1d. on 2d. bright mauve	12·00	15·00
		w. Wmk Crown to right of A	£275	
108		1d. on 2½d. ultramarine	1·25	3·75
109		1d. on 4d. pale olive-green	1·75	4·50
		w. Wmk Crown to right of A	£160	£130
110		1d. on 6d. orange-brown	8·50	23·00
111		1d. on 2s.6d. rose-carmine	3·25	6·00
		a. Wmk upright (inverted)	£2250	
106/11 *Set of 6*			25·00	48·00

AIR MAIL

(10) (11)

1929 (Oct)–**30**. Air. Optd with T **10** by Govt Printer, Port Moresby.

		(a) Cooke printing. Yellowish paper		
112	**6**	3d. black and bright blue-green	2·75	18·00
		a. Opt omitted in vert pair with normal	£8000	
		(b) Harrison printing. Yellowish paper		
113	**6**	3d. sepia-black and bright blue-green	50·00	75·00
		a. Opt double	£4500	
		b. Opt double, one albino	£2500	
		(c) Ash printing. White paper		
114	**6**	3d. black and blue-green	2·00	10·00
		aa. Opt double (one albino)	£2500	
		a. Opt omitted (in horiz pair with normal)	£8000	
		b. Ditto, but vert pair	£7500	
		c. Opt vertical, on back	£6000	
		d. Opts *tête-bêche* (vert pair)	£12000	

1930 (15 Sept). Air. Optd with T **11**, in carmine by Govt Printer, Port Moresby.

		(a) Harrison printings. Yellowish paper		
115	**6**	3d. sepia-black and bright blue-green	£3750	£5500
116		6d. dull and pale purple (Wmk Crown to right of A)	3·00	12·00
		a. "POSTACE" at left (R. 6/2)	80·00	£150
117		1s. sepia and olive	7·00	20·00
		a. Opt inverted	£15000	
		(b) Ash printings. White paper		
118	**6**	3d. black and blue-green	2·25	6·00
119		6d. dull purple and red purple	5·50	19·00
		a. "POSTACE" at left (R. 6/2)	£100	£180
120		1s. brown and yellow-olive	4·75	13·00
118/20 *Set of 3*			11·00	35·00

The rare Harrison printing with this overprint, No. 115, should not be confused with examples of the Ash printing, No. 118, which have been climatically toned.

5d.

TWO PENCE (12)

FIVE PENCE (13)

1931 (1 Jan). Surch with T **12** by Govt Printer, Port Moresby.

		(a) Mullett printing		
121	**6**	2d. on 1½d. cobalt and light brown	12·00	24·00
		a. "POSTACE" at right (R. 1/1)	£150	£225
		(b) Ash printing		
122	**6**	2d. on 1½d. bright blue and bright brown	1·00	2·00
		a. "POSTACE" at right (R. 1/1)	28·00	42·00

1931. Surch as T **13** by Govt Printer, Port Moresby.

		(a) Cooke printing		
123	**6**	1s.3d. on 5s. black and deep green	6·50	13·00
		(b) Harrison printing. Yellowish paper		
124	**6**	9d. on 2s.6d. maroon and pale pink (Dec)	6·00	27·00

(c) Ash printings. White paper

125	6	5d. on 1s. brown and yellow-olive (26.7)	1·25	2·00
126		9d. on 2s.6d. maroon and bright pink	5·50	9·00

(Typo J. Ash)

1932. W **15** of Australia (Mult "C of A"). P 11.

127	5	9d. lilac and violet	8·00	38·00
128		1s.3d. lilac and pale greenish blue	10·00	38·00
127s/8s Optd "SPECIMEN" *Set of 2*			£700	

15 Motuan girl

16 A Chieftain's son

17 Tree houses

18 Raggiana Bird of Paradise

19 Papuan dandy

20 Native mother and child

21 Masked dancer

22 Papuan motherhood

23 Papuan shooting fish

24 *Dubu*—or ceremonial platform

25 "Lakatoi"

26 Papuan art

27 Pottery making

28 Native policeman

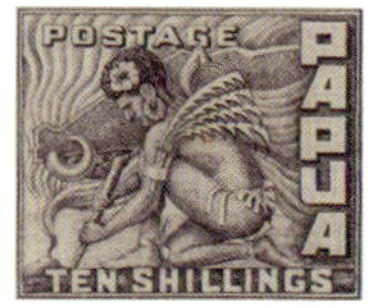

29 Lighting a fire

30 Delta house

(Des F. E. Williams (2s., £1 and frames of other values), E. Whitehouse (2d., 4d., 6d., 1s., and 10s.); remaining centres from photos by Messrs F. E. Williams and Gibson. Recess J. Ash (all values) and W. C. G. McCracken (½d., 1d., 2d., 4d.))

1932 (14 Nov)–**40**. T **15/30**. No wmk. P 11.

130	15	½d. black and orange	4·00	3·75
		a. Black and buff (McCracken) (1940)	19·00	38·00
131	16	1d. black and green	3·50	60
132	17	1½d. black and lake	4·00	8·00
133	18	2d. red	12·00	30
134	19	3d. black and blue	4·00	6·50
135	20	4d. olive-green	12·00	9·50
136	21	5d. black and slate-green	6·50	3·00
137	22	6d. bistre-brown	7·50	5·50
138	23	9d. black and violet	11·00	21·00
139	24	1s. dull blue-green	9·00	8·50
140	25	1s.3d. black and dull purple	18·00	28·00
141	26	2s. black and slate-green	15·00	24·00
142	27	2s.6d. black and rose-mauve	25·00	38·00
143	28	5s. black and olive-brown	70·00	55·00
144	29	10s. violet	£150	£120
145	30	£1 black and olive-grey	£275	£180
130/145 *Set of 16*			£550	£450

31 Hoisting the Union Jack

32 Scene on H.M.S. *Nelson*

(Recess J. Ash)

1934 (6 Nov). 50th Anniv of Declaration of British Protectorate. P 11.

146	31	1d. green	2·50	3·50
147	32	2d. scarlet	2·25	3·00
148	31	3d. blue	2·50	3·00
149	32	5d. purple	11·00	22·00
146/49 *Set of 4*			16·00	28·00

HIS MAJESTY'S JUBILEE.

1910 1935

(33)

HIS MAJESTY'S
JUBILEE.
1910 — 1935

(34)

MAJESTY'S
Normal

MAJESTY'S
"Accent" flaw (R.5/4)

1935 (9 July). Silver Jubilee. Nos. 131, 133/4 and 136 optd with T **33** or **34** (2d.).

150	1d. black and green	1·50	3·25
	a. "Accent" flaw	45·00	75·00
151	2d. scarlet	7·50	6·50
152	3d. black and blue	4·50	3·50
	a. "Accent" flaw	85·00	95·00
153	5d. black and slate-green	4·50	3·50
	a. "Accent" flaw	90·00	£110
150/53 *Set of 4*		16·00	15·00

35

36 Port Moresby

(Recess J. Ash)

1937 (14 May). Coronation. P 11.

154	**35**	1d. green	45	20
155		2d. scarlet	45	1·25
156		3d. blue	45	1·25
157		5d. purple	45	1·75
154/57 *Set of 4*			1·60	4·00

Some covers franked with these stamps and posted on 2 June 1937 were postmarked 2 April 1937 in error.

(Recess J. Ash)

1938 (6 Sept). Air. 50th Anniv of Declaration of British Possession. P 11.

158	**36**	2d. rose-red	3·00	3·50
159		3d. bright blue	3·00	2·50
160		5d. green	3·00	3·75
161		8d. brown-lake	6·00	24·00
162		1s. mauve	25·00	27·00
158/62 *Set of 5*			35·00	55·00

37 Natives poling Rafts

(Recess J. Ash)

1939 (6 Sept). Air. P 11.

163	**37**	2d. rose-red	4·00	8·50
164		3d. bright blue	4·00	14·00
165		5d. green	3·50	2·50
166		8d. brown-lake	8·00	6·00
167		1s. mauve	14·00	10·00

(Recess W. C. G. McCracken)

1941 (2 Jan). Air. P 11½.

168	**37**	1s.6d. olive-green	30·00	42·00
163/168 *Set of 6*			55·00	75·00

OFFICIAL STAMPS

1908 (Oct). Punctured "OS".

O1	**1**	2s.6d. black and brown (No. 37)	£1200	38·00
O2		2s.6d. black and brown (No. 45)	£6000	£3750
		a. Thin paper (No. 45a)	£1600	£1600

1908 (Dec)–**10**. Nos. 49/71 punctured "OS".

I. Wmk upright

(a) P 11

O4	**6**	1d. black and rose	50·00	14·00
O5		2d. black and purple	60·00	5·00
O6		2½d. black and bright ultramarine	95·00	40·00
		a. Black and pale ultramarine	55·00	5·00
		b. Thin "d" at left	£500	£110
O7		4d. black and sepia	55·00	5·00
		a. Deformed "d" at left	£500	£130
O8		6d. black and myrtle-green	£130	55·00
O9		1s. black and orange	£130	21·00
O4/9 *Set of 6*			£450	95·00

(b) P 12½

O10	**6**	2d. black and purple	£100	28·00
O11		2½d. black and bright ultramarine	£325	£140
		a. Black and pale ultramarine	£170	95·00
		b. Thin "d" at left	£1200	£700
O12		4d. black and sepia	£110	9·50
		a. Deformed "d" at left	£850	£190
O13		1s. black and orange	£300	£100
O10/13 *Set of 4*			£650	£200

II. Wmk sideways

(a) P 11

O14	**6**	½d. black and yellow-green	50·00	4·75
		a. Black and deep green	85·00	38·00
O15		1d. black and carmine	£100	28·00
O16		2d. black and purple	30·00	2·50
O17		2½d. black and dull blue	70·00	6·00
		a. Thin "d" at left	£600	£100
O18		4d. black and sepia	50·00	11·00
		a. Deformed "d" at left	£475	£225
O19		6d. black and myrtle-green	90·00	6·00
O20		1s. black and orange	£300	90·00
O14/20 *Set of 7*			£600	£130

(b) P 12½

O21	**6**	½d. black and yellow-green	45·00	2·25
		a. Black and deep green	75·00	32·00
O22		1d. black and carmine	90·00	4·25
O23		2d. black and purple	55·00	3·25
O24		2½d. black and dull blue	95·00	15·00
		a. Thin "d" at left	£800	£160
O25		6d. black and myrtle-green	—	£1400
O26		1s. black and orange	£130	35·00

No. O7 is known with watermark reversed.

1910. Nos. 47/8 punctured "OS".

O27	**5**	½d. black and yellow-green (wmk upright)	50·00	16·00
O28		2s.6d. black and chocolate (wmk sideways)	£300	£140

1910–11. Nos. 75/83 punctured "OS".

O29	**5**	½d. black and green	50·00	25·00
O30		1d. black and carmine	£110	20·00
O31		2d. black and dull purple	50·00	25·00
		a. "C" for "O" in "POSTAGE"	£475	£250
O32		2½d. black and blue-violet	70·00	8·00
		a. Thin "d" at left	£550	£140
O33		4d. black and sepia	70·00	7·00
		a. Deformed "d" at left	£700	£150
O34		6d. black and myrtle-green	80·00	7·00
O35		1s. black and deep orange	£120	10·00
O36		2s.6d. black and brown (B)	£150	35·00
O37		2s.6d. black and brown (C)	£170	80·00
O29/36 *Set of 8*			£650	£120

1911–12. Nos. 84/91 punctured "OS".

O38	**6**	½d. yellow-green	30·00	2·25
		w. Wmk Crown to right of A	—	75·00
O39		1d. rose-pink	35·00	1·50
O40		2d. bright mauve	35·00	1·50
		w. Wmk Crown to right of A	—	£100
O41		2½d. bright ultramarine	45·00	24·00
O42		4d. pale olive-green	60·00	30·00
O43		6d. orange-brown	60·00	7·00
O44		1s. yellow	90·00	18·00
O45		2s.6d. rose-carmine	£150	£110
O38/45 *Set of 8*			£450	£160

1930. Nos. 93/6*a* and 98*c*/103 punctured "OS".

O46	**6**	½d. myrtle and apple green	24·00	35·00
O47		1d. intense black and red	40·00	11·00
O48		1½d. bright blue and bright brown	27·00	38·00
		a. "POSTACE" at right	£250	£300
O49		2d. deep brown-purple and lake	45·00	55·00
O50		3d. black and blue-green	£120	£140
O51		4d. light brown and orange	65·00	65·00
O52		6d. dull purple and pale purple	35·00	55·00
		a. "POSTACE" at left	£400	£600
O53		1s. brown and yellow-olive	90·00	95·00
O54		2s.6d. maroon and pale pink	£200	£250
O46/54 *Set of 9*			£600	£650

O S

(O **1**)

(Typo T. S. Harrison (1d. and 2s.6d.) and J. Ash)

1931 (29 July)–**32**. Optd with Type O **1**. W **7** or W **15** of Australia (9d., 1s.3d.). P 14 or 11 (9d., 1s.3d.).

O55	**6**	½d. myrtle and apple-green	3·00	4·75
O56		1d. Intense black and red	9·00	18·00
O57		1½d. bright blue and bright brown	2·00	12·00
		a. "POSTACE" at right	75·00	£200
O58		2d. brown-purple and claret	9·00	20·00
O59		3d. black and blue-green	2·75	22·00
O60		4d. light brown and orange (No. 99aw)	3·25	20·00
		w. Wmk Crown to left of A		
O61		5d. bluish slate and pale brown	6·00	38·00
O62		6d. dull purple and red-purple	4·50	8·50
		a. "POSTACE" at left	£170	£325
O63		9d. lilac and violet (1932)	30·00	48·00
O64		1s. brown and yellow-olive	9·00	30·00
O65		1s.3d. lilac and pale greenish blue (1932)	30·00	48·00
O66		2s.6d. maroon and pale pink (Harrison)	48·00	95·00
		a. Maroon and bright pink (Ash)	55·00	95·00
O55/66 *Set of 12*			£130	£325

Civil Administration in Papua was suspended in 1942. On resumption, after the Japanese defeat in 1945, Australian stamps were used until the appearance of the issue of the combined territories of Papua & New Guinea.

POSTAL FISCAL STAMP

Stamp Duty.

F **1**

1912 (May) No. 85 Optd with T F **1** by Govt Printer, Port Moresby.

F1	1d. rose-pink	50·00	65·00
	a. Pair, one without opt	£4000	
	b. Opt double	£1500	£1500
	c. "Samp" for "Stamp" (R. 1/1)	£1100	

The use of No. F1 was authorised at Samarai in May 1912 and in early 1913 during shortages of 1d. stamps. Other values, including the 1d. with a curved sans-serif overprint are known used at other offices and at other times, but such use was not authorised.

PAPUA NEW GUINEA

AUSTRALIAN TRUST TERRITORY

Stamps of Australia were used in the combined territory following the defeat of the Japanese in 1945. They remained valid for postal purposes from Papua and New Guinea until 1 March 1953.

The name of the combined territory was changed from "Papua and New Guinea" to "Papua New Guinea" at the beginning of 1972.

SPECIMEN OVERPRINTS. These come from specimen sets in which the lower values were cancelled-to-order, but stamps above the value of 10s. were overprinted "SPECIMEN". These overprints are listed as they could be purchased from the Post Office.

1 Matschie's Tree Kangaroo

2 Buka Head-dresses

3 Native Youth

4 Greater Bird of Paradise

5 Native policeman

6 Papuan Head-dress

7 Kiriwana Chief house

8 Kiriwana Yam house

9 Copra making

10 Lakatoi

11 Rubber tapping

12 Sepik dancing masks

13 Native shepherd and flock

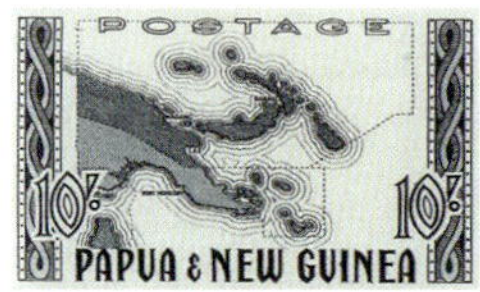
14 Map of Papua and New Guinea

15 Papuan shooting Fish

(Recess Note Printing Branch, Commonwealth Bank, Melbourne)

1952 (30 Oct)–**58**. T **1/15**. P 14.

1	**1**	½d. emerald	30	10
2	**2**	1d. deep brown	20	10
3	**3**	2d. blue	35	10
4	**4**	2½d. orange	3·00	50
5	**5**	3d. deep green	50	10
6	**6**	3½d. carmine-red	50	10
6a		3½d. black (2.6.58)	5·00	1·00
7	**7**	6½d. dull purple	1·25	10
		a. Maroon (1956)	9·00	25
8	**8**	7½d. blue	2·50	1·00
9	**9**	9d. brown	2·50	40
10	**10**	1s. yellow-green	1·50	10
11	**11**	1s.6d. deep green	2·75	60
12	**12**	2s. indigo	2·50	10
13	**13**	2s.6d. brown-purple	2·50	40
14	**14**	10s. blue-black	32·00	13·00
15	**15**	£1 deep brown	42·00	15·00
1/15 *Set of* 16			90·00	29·00
14s/15s Optd "SPECIMEN" *Set of* 2			90·00	

(16)

(17)

1957 (29 Jan). Nos. 4 and 10 surch with T **16** or T **17**.

16	4d. on 2½d. orange	1·25	10
17	7d. on 1s. yellow-green	40	10

18 Cacao Plant

19 Klinki Plymill

20 Cattle

21 Coffee Beans

(Recess Note Ptg Branch, Commonwealth Bank, Melbourne)

1958 (2 June)–**60**. New values. P 14.

18	**18**	4d. vermilion	60	10

19		5d. green (10.11.60)	60	10
20	**19**	7d. bronze-green	2·00	10
21		8d. deep ultramarine (10.11.60)	60	1·00
22	**20**	1s.7d. red-brown	6·00	3·00
23		2s.5d. vermilion (10.11.60)	1·50	1·00
24	**21**	5s. crimson and olive-green	2·50	1·00
18/24 *Set of 7*			12·50	5·50

(**22**)

23 Council Chamber, Port Moresby

1959 (1 Dec). No. 1 surch with T **22**.

25	**1**	5d. on ½d. emerald	75	10

(Photo Harrison)

1961 (10 Apr). Reconstitution of Legislative Council. P 15×14.

26	**23**	5d. deep green and yellow	75	25
27		2s.3d. deep green and light salmon	2·00	2·25

24 Female, Goroka, New Guinea

25 Tribal elder, Tari, Papua

26 Female Dancer

27 Male Dancer

28 Traffic Policeman

(Des Pamela M. Prescott, Recess Note Ptg Branch, Reserve Bank of Australia, Melbourne)

1961 (26.7)–**62**. T **24/8**. P 14½×14 (1d., 3d., 3s.) or 14×14½ (others).

28	**24**	1d. lake	70	10
29	**25**	3d. indigo	30	10
30	**26**	1s. bronze-green	1·00	15
31	**27**	2s. maroon	45	15
32	**28**	3s. deep bluish green (5.9.62)	1·00	2·00
28/32 *Set of 5*			3·00	2·25

29 Campaign Emblem

30 Map of South Pacific

(Recess Note Ptg Branch, Reserve Bank of Australia, Melbourne)

1962 (7 Apr). Malaria Eradication. P 14.

33	**29**	5d. carmine-red and light blue	30	15
34		1s. red and sepia	50	25
35		2s. black and yellow-green	60	1·25
33/35 *Set of 3*			1·25	1·50

(Des Pamela M. Prescott. Recess Note Ptg Branch, Reserve Bank of Australia, Melbourne)

1962 (9 July). Fifth South Pacific Conference, Pago Pago. P 14½×14.

36	**30**	5d. scarlet and light green	50	15
37		1s.6d. deep violet and light yellow	85	1·40
38		2s.6d. deep green and light blue	85	1·40
36/38 *Set of 3*			2·00	2·75

31 Throwing the Javelin

33 Runners

(Des G. Hamori. Photo Courvoisier)

1962 (24 Oct). Seventh British Empire and Commonwealth Games, Perth. T **31**, **33** and similar design. P 11½.

39	**31**	5d. brown and light blue	20	10
		a. Pair. Nos. 39/40	40	50
40		5d. brown and orange	20	10
41	**33**	2s.3d. brown and light green	70	75
39/41 *Set of 3*			1·00	85

Design: (As T **31**)—5d. High jump.

Nos. 39/40 are arranged together *se-tenant* in sheets of 100.

34 Raggiana Bird of Paradise

35 Common Phalanger

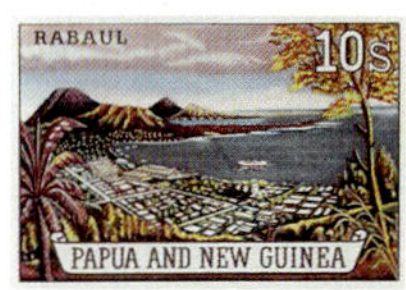

36 Rabaul

37 Queen Elizabeth II

(Des S. T. Cham (10s.), A. Buckley (photo) (£1). Photo Harrison (£1), Courvoisier (others))

1963 (13 Feb–3 July). P 14½ (£1) or 11½ (others).

42	**34**	5d. yellow, chestnut and sepia (27.3)	70	10
43	**35**	6d. red, yellow-brown and grey (27.3)	50	1·00
44	**36**	10s. multicoloured (13.2)	8·50	4·50
45	**37**	£1 sepia, gold and blue-green (3.7)	1·25	1·75
		a. Gold ptd double		
42/45 *Set of 4*			10·00	6·50
44s/5s Optd "SPECIMEN" *Set of 2*			90·00	

38 Centenary Emblem

39 Waterfront, Port Moresby

39a Piaggio P-166B Portofino aircraft landing at Tapini

(Des G. Hamori. Photo Note Ptg Branch, Reserve Bank of Australia, Melbourne)

1963 (1 May). Red Cross Centenary. P 13½×13.

46	**38**	5d. red, grey-brown and bluish green	75	10

(Des J. McMahon (8d.), Pamela M. Prescott (2s.3d.). Recess Note Ptg Branch, Reserve Bank of Australia, Melbourne)

1963 (8 May). T **39** and similar horiz design. P 14×13½.

47	**39**	8d. green	30	15
48	**39a**	2s.3d. ultramarine	30	30

40 Games Emblem

41 Watam Head

(Des Pamela M. Prescott. Recess Note Ptg Branch, Reserve Bank of Australia, Melbourne)

1963 (14 Aug). First South Pacific Games, Suva. P 13½×14½.

49	**40**	5d. bistre	10	10
50		1s. deep green	30	60

(Des Pamela M. Prescott. Photo Courvoisier)

1964 (5 Feb). Native Artefacts. T **41** and similar vert designs. Multicoloured. P 11½.

51	11d. Type **41**	25	10
52	2s.5d. Watam Head *(different)*	30	1·75
53	2s.6d. Bosmun Head	30	10
54	5s. Medina Head	35	20
51/54 *Set of 4*		1·10	1·75

45 Casting Vote

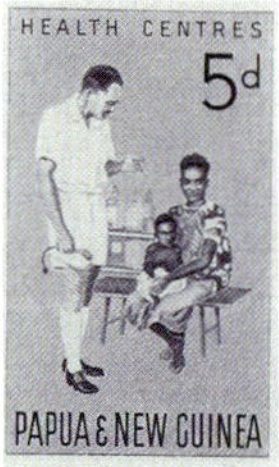

46 "Health Centres"

(Photo Courvoisier)

1964 (4 Mar). Common Roll Elections. P 11½.

55	**45**	5d. brown and drab	10	10
56		2s.3d. brown and pale blue	20	25

(Recess Note Ptg Branch, Reserve Bank of Australia, Melbourne)

1964 (5 Aug). Health Services. T **46** and similar vert designs. P 14.

57	5d. violet	10	10
58	8d. bronze-green	10	10
59	1s. blue	15	10
60	1s.2d. brown-red	20	35
57/60 *Set of 4*		50	60

Designs: 8d. "School health"; 1s. "Infant, child and maternal health"; 1s.2d. "Medical training".

50 Striped Gardener Bowerbird

51 Emperor of Germany Bird of Paradise

(Photo Courvoisier)

1964 (28 Oct)–**65**. Vert designs as T **50** (1d. to 8d.) or **51** (others). Multicoloured; background colours given. P 11½ (1d. to 8d.) or 12×11½ (1s. to 10s.).

61	**50**	1d. pale olive-yellow (20.1.65)	50	10
62		3d. light grey (20.1.65)	50	30
63		5d. pale red (20.1.65)	55	10
64		6d. pale green	60	10
65		8d. lilac	1·00	20
66	**51**	1s. salmon	1·50	10
67		2s. light blue (20.1.65)	60	30
68		2s.3d. light green (20.1.65)	60	85
69		3s. pale yellow (20.1.65)	60	1·25
70		5s. cobalt (20.1.65)	6·00	1·00
71		10s. pale drab	1·75	6·50
		s. Optd "SPECIMEN"	85·00	
61/71 *Set of 11*			13·00	9·50

Designs: 3d. Adelbert Bowerbird; 5d. Blue Bird of Paradise; 6d. Lawes's Parotia; 8d. Black-billed Sicklebill; 2s. Brown Sicklebill; 2s.3d. Lesser Bird of Paradise; 3s. Magnificent Bird of Paradise; 5s. Twelve-wired Bird of Paradise; 10s. Magnificent Riflebird.

61 Canoe Prow

(Des Pamela M. Prescott. Photo Courvoisier)

1965 (24 Mar). Sepik Canoe Prows in Port Moresby Museum. T **61** and similar horiz designs showing carved prows. P 11½.

72	4d. multicoloured	30	10
73	1s.2d. multicoloured	1·00	1·75
74	1s.6d. multicoloured	30	10
75	4s. multicoloured	40	50
72/75 *Set of 4*		1·75	2·25

1965 (14 Apr). 50th Anniv of Gallipoli Landing. As T **22** of Nauru. P 13½.

76	2s.3d. sepia, black and emerald	20	10

65 Urban Plan and Native House

(Des G. Hamori. Photo Courvoisier)

1965 (7 July). Sixth South Pacific Conference, Lae. T **65** and similar horiz design. P 11½.

77	6d. multicoloured	10	10
78	1s. multicoloured	10	10

No. 78 is similar to T **65** but with the plan on the right and the house on the left. Also "URBANISATION" reads downwards.

66 Mother and Child

67 Globe and U.N. Emblem

(Photo Courvoisier)

1965 (13 Oct). 20th Anniv of U.N.O. T **66/7** and similar vert design. P 11½.

79	**66**	6d. sepia, blue and pale turquoise-blue	10	10
80	**67**	1s. orange-brown, blue and reddish violet	10	10
81		2s. blue, blue-green and light yellow-olive	10	10
79/81 *Set of 3*			25	25

Design:—2s. U.N. Emblem and globes.

(New Currency. 100 cents = 1 Australian dollar)

69 *Papilio ulysses*

71 *Ornithoptera priamus*

$1 Plate I

Black line through left blue patch on wing consists of two dots only. There are two blue lines extending from upper right edge of right wing towards two small patches of blue.

$1 Plate II

The black line through left blue patch on wing is continuous. Blue lines at upper right edge of wing are omitted. There is an extra short faint blue line extending from edge of lower right wing which is absent in Plate I.

$2 Plate I

In the lower left of the butterfly there are two short black lines from the edge to the yellow part.

In the lower part of the upper right wing there is a series of indeterminate short lines and dots.

$2 Plate II

The two black lines at lower left are lacking.

There are clear fine lines of shading in place of the thicker lines.

There are numerous other minor differences between the two plates of each value and also slight variations in the shades.

(Photo Courvoisier)

1966 (14 Feb)–**67**. Decimal Currency. Butterflies. Vert designs as T **69** (1 to 5c.), or horiz as T **71** (others). Multicoloured. P 11½.

82	1c. Type **69**	40	1·00
83	3c. *Cyrestis acilia*	40	1·00
84	4c. *Graphium weiskei*	40	1·00
85	5c. *Terinos alurgis*	40	10
86	10c. Type **71**	50	30
86*a*	12c. *Euploea callithoe* (12.10)	4·50	2·25
87	15c. *Papilio euchenor*	1·00	80
88	20c. *Parthenos sylvia*	50	25
89	25c. *Delias aruna*	70	1·25
90	50c. *Apaturina erminea*	10·00	1·25
91	$1 *Doleschallia dascylus* (Plate I)	2·75	2·50
	a. Plate II (8.67)	4·50	2·50
92	$2 *Ornithoptera paradises* (Plate I)	4·00	10·00
	a. Plate II (8.67)	8·50	10·00
82/92	*Set of* 12	23·00	19·00

80 "Molala Harai"

84 Throwing the Discus

(Des Rev. H. A. Brown. Photo Courvoisier)

1966 (8 June). Folklore. Elema Art (1st series). T **80** and similar vert designs. P 11½.

93	2c. black and carmine	10	10
94	7c. black, light yellow and light blue	10	65
95	30c. black, carmine and apple-green	15	15
96	60c. black, carmine and yellow	40	65
93/96	*Set of* 4	65	1·40

Designs: 7c. "Marai"; 30c. "Meavea Kivovia"; 60c. "Toivita Tapaivita".

Nos. 93/6 were supplementary values to the decimal currency definitive issue.

See also Nos. 152/5. A further set was issued in 1977.

(Photo Courvoisier)

1966 (31 Aug). South Pacific Games, Nouméa. T **84** and similar vert designs. Multicoloured. P 11½.

97	5c. Type **84**	10	10
98	10c. Football	15	10
99	20c. Tennis	20	40
97/99	*Set of* 3	40	55

(Des Mrs. D. Pearce. Photo Courvoisier)

1966 (7 Dec). Flowers. T **87** and similar vert designs. Multicoloured. P 11½.

100	5c. Type **87**	15	10
101	10c. *Tecomanthe dendrophila*	15	10
102	20c. *Rhododendron macgregoriae*	20	10
103	60c. *Rhododendron konori*	50	1·40
100/3	*Set of* 4	90	1·50

87 *Mucuna novoguineensis*

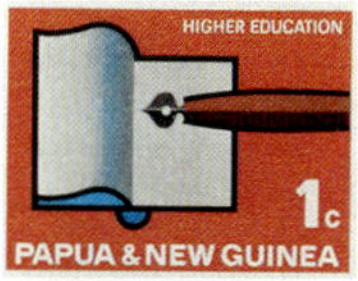

91 "Fine Arts"

(Des G. Hamori. Photo Courvoisier)

1967 (8 Feb). Higher Education. T **91** and similar horiz designs. Multicoloured. P 12½×12.

104	1c. Type **91**	10	10
105	3c. "Surveying"	10	15
106	4c. "Civil Engineering"	10	15
107	5c. "Science"	10	10
108	20c. "Law"	15	10
104/8	*Set of* 5	45	45

96 *Sagra speciosa*

100 Laloki River

(Des Pamela M. Prescott. Photo Courvoisier)

1967 (12 Apr). Fauna Conservation (Beetles). T **96** and similar vert designs. Multicoloured. P 11½.

109	5c. Type **96**	15	10
110	10c. *Eupholus schoenherri*	15	10
111	20c. *Sphingnotus albertisi*	25	10
112	25c. *Cyphogastra albertisi*	25	10
109/12	*Set of* 4	70	35

(Des G. Wade. Photo Courvoisier)

1967 (28 June). Laloki River Hydro-Electric Scheme, and "New Industries". T **100** and similar vert designs. Multicoloured. P 12½.

113	5c. Type **100**	10	10
114	10c. Pyrethrum	10	10
115	20c. Tea Plant	15	10
116	25c. Type **100**	15	10
113/16	*Set of* 4	45	35

103 Air Attack at Milne Bay

107 Papuan Lory

(Des R. Hodgkinson (2c.), F. Hodgkinson (5c.), G. Wade (20c., 50c.). Photo Courvoisier)

1967 (30 Aug). 25th Anniv of the Pacific War. T **103** and similar multicoloured designs. P 11½.

117	2c. Type **103**	10	50
118	5c. Kokoda Trail (*vert*)	10	10
119	20c. The Coast Watchers	25	10
120	50c. Battle of the Coral Sea	80	70
117/20	*Set of* 4	1·10	1·25

(Des T. Walcot. Photo Courvoisier)

1967 (29 Nov). Christmas. Territory Parrots. T **107** and similar vert designs. Multicoloured. P 12½.

121	5c. Type **107**	20	10
122	7c. Pesquet's Parrot	25	90
123	20c. Dusky Lory	30	10
124	25c. Edward's Fig Parrot	35	10
121/24	*Set of* 4	1·00	1·10

111 Chimbu Head-dresses

112

(Des P. Jones. Photo Courvoisier)

1968 (21 Feb). "National Heritage". T **111/12** and similar multicoloured designs. P 12×12½ (5, 60c.) or 12½×12 (10, 20c.).

125	5c. Type **111**	10	10
126	10c. Southern Highlands Head-dress (*horiz*)	15	10
127	20c. Western Highlands Head-dress (*horiz*)	15	10
128	60c. Type **112**	40	45
125/28	*Set of* 4	70	65

115 *Hyla thesaurensis*

119 Human Rights Emblem and Papuan Head-dress (abstract)

(Des and photo Courvoisier)

1968 (24 Apr). Fauna Conservation (Frogs). T **115** and similar horiz designs. Multicoloured. P 11½.

129	5c. Type **115**	15	10
130	10c. *Hyla iris*	15	20
131	15c. *Ceratobatrachus guentheri*	15	30
132	20c. *Nyctimystes narinosa*	20	60
129/32	*Set of* 4	60	1·10

(Des G. Hamori. Litho Enschedé)

1968 (26 June). Human Rights Year. T **119** and similar horiz design. Multicoloured. P 13½×12½.

133	5c. Type **119**	10	10
134	10c. Human Rights in the World (abstract)	10	10

121 Leadership (abstract)

123 Common Egg Cowrie (*Ovula ovum*)

(Des G. Hamori. Litho Enschedé)

1968 (26 June). Universal Suffrage. T **121** and similar horiz design. Multicoloured. P 13½×12½.

135	20c. Type **121**	15	20
136	25c. Leadership of the community (abstract)	15	30

(Des P. Jones. Photo Courvoisier)

1968–69. Sea Shells. Multicoloured designs as T **123**. P 12×12½ ($2), 12½×12 (1c. to 20c.) or 11½ (others).

137	1c. Type **123** (29.1.69)	10	10
138	3c. Laciniate Conch (*Strombus sinuatus*) (30.10.68)	30	1·25
139	4c. Lithograph Cone (*Conus litoglyphus*) (29.1.69)	20	1·25
140	5c. Marbled Cone (*Conus marmoreus marmoreus*) (28.8.68)	25	10
141	7c. Episcopal Mitre (*Mitra mitra*) (29.1.69)	35	10
142	10c. *Cymbiola rutila ruckeri* (30.10.68)	45	10
143	12c. Checkerboard Bonnet (*Phalium areola*) (29.1.69)	1·25	2·00
144	15c. Scorpion Conch (*Lambis scorpius*) (30.10.68)	60	1·00
145	20c. Fluted Giant Clam or Scale Tridacna (*Tridacna sqamosa*) (28.8.68)	70	10
146	25c. Camp Pitar Venus (*Lioconcha castrensis*) (28.8.68)	70	1·75
147	30c. Ramose Murex (*Murex ramosus*) (28.8.68)	70	1·00
148	40c. Chambered or Pearly Nautilus (*Nautilus pompilius*) (30.10.68)	75	1·25
149	60c. Trumpet Triton (*Charonia tritonis*) (28.8.68)	70	50
150	$1 Manus Green Papuina (*Papuina pulcherrima*) (30.10.68)	1·00	60
151	$2 Glory of the Sea Cone (*Conus gloriamaris*) (*vert*) (29.1.69)	8·00	1·50
137/51	*Set of* 15	14·00	11·00

The 1, 5, 7, 15, 40, 60c. and $1 exist with PVA gum as well as gum arabic.

138 Tito Myth

139 Iko Myth

140 Luvuapo Myth

141 Miro Myth

(Des from native motifs by Revd. H. A. Brown. Litho Enschedé)

1969 (9 Apr). Folklore. Elema Art (2nd series). P 12½×13½×Roul 9 between *se-tenant* pairs.

152	**138**	5c. black, yellow and red	10	60
		a. Pair. Nos. 152/3	20	1·10
153	**139**	5c. black, yellow and red	10	60
154	**140**	10c. black, grey and red	15	60
		a. Pair. Nos. 154/5	30	1·10
155	**141**	10c. black, grey and red	15	60
152/55 *Set of 4*			45	2·00

Nos. 152/3 and 154/5 were issued in vertical *se-tenant* pairs, separated by a line of roulette.

142 "Fireball" class Dinghy

145 *Dendrobium ostrinoglossum*

(Des J. Fallas. Recess Note Ptg Branch, Reserve Bank of Australia)

1969 (25 June). Third South Pacific Games, Port Moresby. T **142** and similar designs. P 14×14½ (5c.) or 14½×14 (others).

156	5c. black	10	10
157	10c. deep bluish violet	10	20
158	20c. myrtle-green	15	30
156/58 *Set of 3*		30	50

Designs: Horiz—10c. Swimming pool, Boroko; 20c. Games arena, Konedobu.

(Des P. Jones. Photo Courvoisier)

1969 (27 Aug). Flora conservation (Orchids). T **145** and similar vert designs. Multicoloured. P 11½.

159	5c. Type **145**	25	10
160	10c. *Dendrobium lawesii*	25	70
161	20c. *Dendrobium pseudofrigidum*	30	90
162	30c. *Dendrobium conanthum*	30	70
159/62 *Set of 4*		1·00	2·25

149 Bird of Paradise

150 Native Potter

(Des G. Hamori. Photo Note Ptg Branch, Reserve Bank of Australia)

1969 (24 Sept)–**71**. Coil stamps. P 15×imperf.

162*a*	**149**	2c. blue, black and red (1.4.71)	10	65
163		5c. bright green, brown and red-orange	10	10

(Des G. Hamori. Photo Courvoisier)

1969 (24 Sept). 50th Anniv of International Labour Organization. P 11½.

164	**150**	5c. multicoloured	10	10

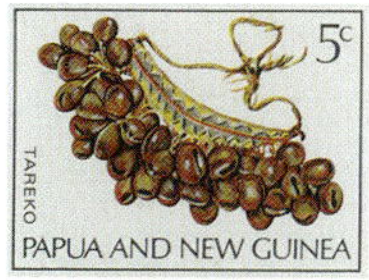

151 Tareko

155 Prehistoric Ambun Stone

(Des G. Hamori. Photo Courvoisier)

1969 (29 Oct). Musical Instruments. T **151** and similar horiz designs. P 12½×12.

165	5c. multicoloured	10	10
166	10c. black, olive-green and pale yellow	10	10
167	25c. black, yellow and brown	15	15
168	30c. multicoloured	25	15
165/68 *Set of 4*		55	45

Designs: 10c. Garamut; 25c. Iviliko; 30c. Kundu.

(Des R. Bates. Photo Courvoisier)

1970 (11 Feb). "National Heritage". T **155** and similar horiz designs. Multicoloured. P 12½×12.

169	5c. Type **155**	10	10
170	10c. Masawa canoe of Kula circuit	10	10
171	25c. Torres' Map, 1606	40	15
172	30c. H.M.S. *Basilisk* (paddle-sloop), 1873	65	25
169/72 *Set of 4*		1·10	55

159 King of Saxony Bird Paradise

(Des T. Walcot. Photo Courvoisier)

1970 (13 May). Fauna Conservation (Birds of Paradise). T **159** and similar vert designs. Multicoloured. P 12.

173	5c. Type **159**	40	15
174	10c. King Bird of Paradise	40	45
175	15c. Raggiana Bird of Paradise	55	80
176	25c. Sickle-crested Bird of Paradise	65	50
173/76 *Set of 4*		1·75	1·75

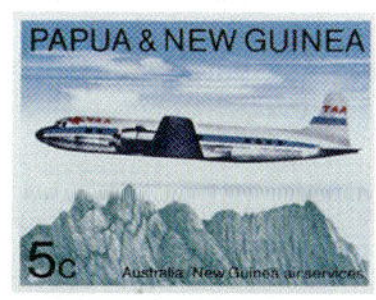

163 Douglas Dc-6B and Mt Wilhelm

164 Lockheed L.188 Electra and Mt. Yule

165 Boeing 727-100 and Mt. Giluwe

166 Fokker F.27 Friendship and Manam Island

(Des D. Gentleman. Photo Harrison)

1970 (8 July). Australian and New Guinea Air Services. T **163/6** and similar horiz designs. Multicoloured. P 14½×14.

177	5c. Type **163**	25	30
	a. Block of 4. Nos. 177/80	1·00	2·00
178	5c. Type **164**	25	30
179	5c. Type **165**	25	30
180	5c. Type **166**	25	30
181	25c. Douglas DC-3 and Matupi Volcano	35	40
182	30c. Boeing 707 and Hombrom's Bluff	35	60
177/82 *Set of 6*		1·50	2·50

Nos. 177/80 were issued together, *se-tenant*, in blocks of four throughout the sheet.

169 N. Miklouho-Maclay (scientist) and Effigy

170 Wogeo Island Food Bowl

(Des D. Gentleman. Photo Courvoisier)

1970 (19 Aug). 42nd ANZAAS (Australian—New Zealand Association for the Advancement of Science) congress, Port Moresby. T **169** and similar horiz designs. P 11½.

183	5c. multicoloured	10	10
184	10c. multicoloured	20	10
185	15c. multicoloured	70	25
186	20c. multicoloured	40	25
183/86 *Set of 4*		1·25	60

Designs: 10c. B. Malinowski (anthropologist) and native hut; 15c. T. Salvadori (ornithologist) and Double-wattled Cassowary; 20c. F.R.R. Schlechter (botanist) and flower.

(Des P. Jones. Photo Courvoisier)

1970 (28 Oct). Native Artefacts. T **170** and similar multicoloured designs. P 12½×12 (30c.) or 12×12½ (others).

187	5c. Type **170**	10	10
188	10c. Lime Pot	20	10
189	15c. Aibom Sago Storage Pot	20	10
190	30c. Manus Island Bowl (*horiz*)	25	30
187/90 *Set of 4*		65	55

171 Eastern Highlands Dwelling

172 Spotted Phalanger

(Des G. Wade. Photo Courvoisier)

1971 (27 Jan). Native Dwellings. T **171** and similar vert designs showing dwellings from the places given. Multicoloured. P 11½.

191	5c. Type **171**	10	10
192	7c. Milne Bay	15	90
193	10c. Purari Delta	15	10
194	40c. Sepik	25	90
191/4 *Set of 4*		60	1·75

(Des R. Bates. Photo Courvoisier)

1971 (31 Mar). Fauna Conservation. T **172** and similar multicoloured designs. P 11½.

195	5c. Type **172**	25	10
196	10c. Long fingered Possum	25	10
197	15c. Feather-tailed Possum	35	80
198	25c. Long-nosed Echidna (*horiz*)	45	80
199	30c. Ornate Tree Kangaroo (*horiz*)	45	50
195/9 *Set of 5*		1·60	2·00

173 "Basketball"

174 Bartering Fish for Vegetables

(Des G. Hamori, Litho D.L.R.)

1971 (9 June). Fourth South Pacific Games, Papeete, Tahiti. T **173** and similar horiz designs. Multicoloured. P 13½×14.

200	7c. Type **173**	10	10
201	14c. "Sailing"	15	20
202	21c. "Boxing"	15	30
203	28c. "Athletics"	15	40
200/3 *Set of 4*		50	85

(Des G. Wade. Photo Courvoisier)

1971 (18 Aug). Primary Industries. T **174** and similar vert designs. Multicoloured. P 11½.

204	7c. Type **174**	10	10
205	9c. Man stacking yams	15	30
206	14c. Vegetable market	25	10
207	30c. Highlanders cultivating garden	45	65
204/7 *Set of 4*		85	1·00

175 Sia Dancer

176 Papuan Flag over Australian Flag

(Des Bette Hays. Photo Courvoisier)

1971 (27 Oct). Native Dancers. T **175** and similar multicoloured designs. P 11½.

208	7c. Type **175**	15	10
209	9c. Urasena dancer	15	20
210	20c. Siassi Tubuan dancers (*horiz*)	40	75
211	28c. Sia dancers (*horiz*)	55	90
208/11 *Set of 4*		1·10	1·75

(Des R. Bates. Photo Courvoisier)

1972 (26 Jan). Constitutional Development. T **176** and similar horiz design. P 12½×12.

212	**176**	7c. multicoloured	30	10
		a. Pair. Nos. 212/13	60	1·00
213		7c. multicoloured	30	10

Design:—No. 213, Crest of Papua New Guinea and Australian coat of arms.

Nos. 212/13 were printed vertically *se-tenant* within the sheet.

177 Map of Papua New Guinea and Flag of South Pacific Commission

178 Turtle

(Des R. Bates. Photo Courvoisier)

1972 (26 Jan). 25th Anniv of South Pacific Commission. T **177** and similar horiz design. P 12½×12.

214	**177**	15c. multicoloured	45	55
		a. Pair. Nos. 214/15	90	1·75
215	–	15c. multicoloured	45	55

Design:—No. 215, Man's face and flag of the Commission.

Nos. 214/15 were printed vertically *se-tenant* within the sheet.

(Des R. Bates. Photo Courvoisier)

1972 (17 Mar). Fauna Conservation (Reptiles). T **178** and similar horiz designs. Multicoloured. P 11½.

216	7c. Type **178**	35	10
217	14c. Rainforest Dragon	50	1·25
218	21c. Green Python	55	1·50
219	30c. Salvador's Monitor	60	1·25
216/19 *Set of 4*		1·75	3·50

179 Curtiss MF-6 Seagull Aircraft and *Eureka* (schooner)

180 New National Flag

(Des Major L. G. Halls. Photo Courvoisier)

1972 (7 June). 50th Anniv of Aviation. T **179** and similar horiz designs. Multicoloured. P 11½.

220	7c. Type **179**	40	10
221	14c. De Havilland D.H.37 and native porters	60	1·25
222	20c. Junkers G.31 and gold dredger	70	1·25
223	25c. Junkers F-13 and mission church	70	1·25
220/3 *Set of 4*		2·25	3·50

(Des R. Bates. Photo Courvoisier)

1972 (16 Aug). National Day. T **180** and similar vert designs. Multicoloured. P 11½.

224	7c. Type **180**	20	10
225	10c. Native drum	20	25
226	30c. Trumpet Triton	35	50
224/6	*Set of* 3	65	70

181 Rev. Copland King

182 Mt Tomavatur Station

(Des G. Wade. Photo Courvoisier)

1972 (25 Oct). Christmas (Missionaries). T **181** and similar horiz designs. Multicoloured. P 11½.

227	7c. Type **181**	20	40
228	7c. Rev. Dr. Flierl	20	40
229	7c. Bishop Verjus	20	40
230	7c. Pastor Ruatoka	20	40
227/30	*Set of* 4	70	1·40

(Des R. Bates. Photo Courvoisier)

1973 (24 Jan). Completion of Telecommunications Project, 1968–72. T **182** and similar horiz designs. Multicoloured. P 12½ (Nos. 231/4) or 11½ (others).

231	7c. Type **182**	15	20
	a. Block of 4. Nos. 231/4	55	70
232	7c. Mt Kerigomma Station	15	20
233	7c. Sattelburg Station	15	20
234	7c. Wideru Station	15	20
235	9c. Teleprinter (36×26 *mm*)	15	20
236	30c. Network Map (36×26 *mm*)	35	50
231/6	*Set of* 6	1·00	1·40

Nos. 231/4 were printed in *se-tenant* blocks of four within the sheet.

183 Queen Carola's Parotia

184 Wood Carver

(Des W. Cooper. Photo Courvoisier)

1973 (30 Mar). Birds of Paradise. T **183** and similar vert designs. Multicoloured. P 11½.

237	7c. Type **183**	80	35
238	14c. Goldie's Bird of Paradise	1·50	1·00
239	21c. Ribbon-tailed Bird of Paradise (18×49 *mm*)	1·60	1·50
240	28c. Princess Stephanie's Bird of Paradise (18×49 *mm*)	1·60	2·00
237/40	*Set of* 4	5·00	4·25

(Des R. Bates. Photo Courvoisier)

1973 (13 June)–**74**. T **184** and similar horiz designs. Multicoloured. P 11½.

241	1c. Type **184**	10	10
242	3c. Wig-makers (23.1.74)	30	10
243	5c. Mt Bagana (22.8.73)	55	10
244	6c. Pig Exchange (7.8.74)	80	1·50
245	7c. Coastal village	20	10
246	8c. Arawe mother (23.1.74)	25	30
247	9c. Fire dancers	20	20
248	10c. Tifalmin hunter (23.1.74)	40	10
249	14c. Crocodile hunters (22.8.73)	35	70
250	15c. Mt Elimbari	50	30
251	20c. Canoe-racing, Manus (23.1.74)	60	40
252	21c. Making sago (22.8.73)	30	1·00
253	25c. Council House	30	45
254	28c. Menyamya bowmen (22.8.73)	30	1·00
255	30c. Shark-snaring (22.8.73)	50	50
256	40c. Fishing cancel, Madang	30	40
257	60c. Tapa cloth-making (23.1.74)	40	50
258	$1 Asaro Mudmen (23.1.74)	45	1·10
259	$2 Enga "Sing Sing" (7.8.74)	1·75	6·00
241/59	*Set of* 19	7·50	13·00

185 Stamps of German New Guinea, 1897

(Des R. Bates. Photo (1c.), litho and recess (6c.) or litho (7c.) State Printing Works, Berlin. Photo and recess D.L.R. (9c.). Recess and typo Reserve Bank of Australia (25 and 30c.))

1973 (24 Oct). 75th Anniv of Papua New Guinea Stamps. T **185** and similar horiz designs. Chalky paper (25, 30c.). P 13½ (1, 6, 7c.), 14×13½ (9c.) or 14×14½ (25, 30c.).

260	1c. multicoloured	10	15
261	6c. indigo, new blue and silver	15	30
262	7c. multicoloured	15	30
263	9c. multicoloured	15	30
264	25c. orange and gold	30	80
265	30c. plum and silver	30	90
260/65	*Set of* 6	1·00	2·50

Designs: *As T* **185**—6c. 2 mark stamp of German New Guinea, 1900; 7c. Surcharged registration label of New Guinea, 1914. 46×35 mm—9c. Papua 1s. stamp, 1901. 45×38 mm—25c. ½d. stamp of New Guinea, 1925; 30c. Papua 10s. stamp, 1932.

SELF-GOVERNMENT

186 Native Carved Heads

187 Queen Elizabeth II (from photograph by Karsh)

(Des G. Wade. Photo Courvoisier)

1973 (5 Dec). Self-Government. P 11½.

266	**186**	7c. multicoloured	30	15
267		10c. multicoloured	50	65

(Des and photo Harrison)

1974 (22 Feb). Royal Visit. P 14×14½.

268	**187**	7c. multicoloured	25	15
269		30c. multicoloured	75	1·50

188 Blyth's Hornbill

189 *Dendrobium bracteosum*

(Des T. Nolan. Photo Courvoisier)

1974 (12 June). Birds' Heads. T **188** and similar multicoloured designs. P 11½ (10c.) or 12 (others).

270	7c. Type **188**	1·00	70
271	10c. Double-wattled Cassowary (33×49 *mm*)	1·50	3·00
272	30c. New Guinea Harpy Eagle	3·00	7·50
270/2	*Set of* 3	5·00	10·00

(Des T. Nolan. Photo Courvoisier)

1974 (20 Nov). Flora Conservation. T **189** and similar vert designs. Multicoloured. P 11½.

273	7c. Type **189**	25	10
274	10c. *D. anosmum*	30	50

275	20c. *D. smillieae*	40	1·10
276	30c. *D. insigne*	45	1·75
273/6	*Set of 4*	1·25	3·00

190 Motu Lakatoi

191 1-toea Coin

(Des G. Wade. Photo Courvoisier)

1975 (26 Feb). National Heritage—Canoes. T **190** and similar horiz designs. Multicoloured. P 11½.

277	7c. Type **190**	30	10
278	10c. Tami two-master morobe	30	55
279	25c. Aramia racing canoe	60	3·00
280	30c. Buka Island canoe	60	1·00
277/80	*Set of 4*	1·60	4·25

(New Currency. 100 toea = 1 kina)

(Des G. Wade. Photo Courvoisier)

1975 (21 Apr). New Coinage. T **191** and similar multicoloured designs. P 11½.

281	1t. Type **191**	10	30
282	7t. New 2t. and 5t. coins (45×26 *mm*)	20	10
283	10t. New 10t. coin	20	30
284	20t. New 20t. coin	30	70
285	1k. New 1k. coin (45×26 *mm*)	90	4·00
281/5	*Set of 5*	1·50	4·75

192 *Ornithoptera alexandrae*

193 Boxing

(Des R. Bates. Photo Courvoisier)

1975 (11 June). Fauna Conservation (Birdwing Butterflies). T **192** and similar vert designs. Multicoloured. P 11½.

286	7t. Type **192**	25	10
287	10t. *O. victoriae*	25	45
288	30t. *O. allottei*	50	1·50
289	40t. *O. chimaera*	65	3·00
286/9	*Set of 4*	1·50	4·50

(Des R. Bates. Photo Courvoisier)

1975 (2 Aug). Fifth South Pacific Games, Guam. T **193** and similar vert designs. Multicoloured. P 11½.

290	7t. Type **193**	10	10
291	20t. Running	15	30
292	25t. Basketball	30	45
293	30t. Swimming	30	50
290/3	*Set of 4*	70	1·10

Papua New Guinea became fully independent on 16 September 1975. Later issues will be found in the *Stanley Gibbons Western Pacific Catalogue*.

STAMP BOOKLETS

B **1**

1970 (28 Jan). Green on olive-yellow cover as Type B **1**, but *"POSTAGE STAMP"* in seriffed type. Stamps attached by selvedge.

SB1	50c. booklet containing 5c. (No. 140) in block of 10	£375

1970 (25 May). Green on cream cover, 121×53 mm, as Type B **1** with *"POSTAGE STAMP"* without serifs. Stamps attached by selvedge.

SB2	50c. booklet containing 5c. (No. 140) in block of 10	18·00

No. SB2 shows "GP-P&NG/B1112" imprint on reverse.

An example of No. SB2 has been reported containing No. 187 in block of 10.

B **2**

1971 (1 Apr). Red and green printed cover, 120×60 mm, as Type B **2**. Stamps attached by selvedge.

SB3	70c. booklet containing 7c. (No. 141) in block of 10	13·00

B **3**

1972 (14 Feb). Orange and black printed cover as Type B **3**. Stamps attached by selvedge.

SB4	70c. booklet containing 7c. (Nos. 212/13) in block of 10	14·00

1973 (16 Feb). Orange and black printed cover, 122×58 mm, as Type B **3**. Stamps attached by selvedge.

SB5	70c. booklet containing 7c. (Nos. 231/4) in block of 10	10·00
	a. Cover optd for "INTERPEX" Stamp Exhibition	£120

An example of No. SB5 has been reported containing No. 229 in block of 10.

POSTAGE DUE STAMPS

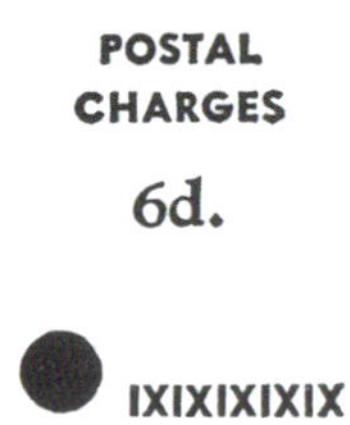

(D **1**)

(D **2**)

1960 (1 Mar). Postage stamps surcharged.

(a) No. 8 with Type D **1**

D1	6d. on 7½d. blue (R.)	£800	£425
	a. Surch double	£4000	£2000

(b) Nos. 1, 4, 6a, 7/8 as Type D **2**

D2	1d. on 6½d. maroon	2·50	4·00
D3	3d. on ½d. emerald (B.)	3·00	1·25
	a. Surch double	£850	
D4	6d. on 7½d. blue (R.)	32·00	5·50
	a. Surch double	£900	
D5	1s.3d. on 3½d. black (O.)	2·50	1·25
D6	3s. on 2½d. orange	10·00	2·25
D2/6	*Set of 5*	45·00	13·00

Genuine used examples of No. D1a should be postmarked at Goroko or Kawieng.

Examples of Nos. D1, D1a, D3a and D4a should only be purchased if accompanied by an expert committee's certificate.

D **3**

(Typo Note Ptg Branch, Reserve Bank of Australia, Melbourne)

1960 (2 June). W **15** of Australia. P 14.

D7	D **3**	1d. orange	65	75
D8		3d. yellow-brown	70	75
D9		6d. blue	75	40
D10		9d. deep red	75	1·75
D11		1s. light emerald	75	50
D12		1s.3d. violet	1·00	1·25
D13		1s.6d. pale blue	3·50	5·50
D14		3s. yellow	1·50	50
D7/14 *Set of* 8			8·75	10·00

The use of Postal Charge stamps was discontinued on 12 February 1966, but they remained on sale at the Philatelic Bureau until 31 August 1966.

Papua New Guinea became independent on 16 September 1975.

Est 1856

STANLEY GIBBONS

Dear Catalogue User,

As a collector and Stanley Gibbons catalogue user for many years myself, I am only too aware of the need to provide you with the information you seek in an accurate, timely and easily accessible manner. Naturally, I have my own views on where changes could be made, but one thing I learned long ago is that we all have different opinions and requirements.

I would therefore be most grateful if you would complete the form overleaf and return it to me. Please contact Lorraine Holcombe (lholcombe@stanleygibbons.com) if you would like to be emailed the questionnaire.

Very many thanks for your help.

Yours sincerely,

Hugh Jefferies,
Editor.

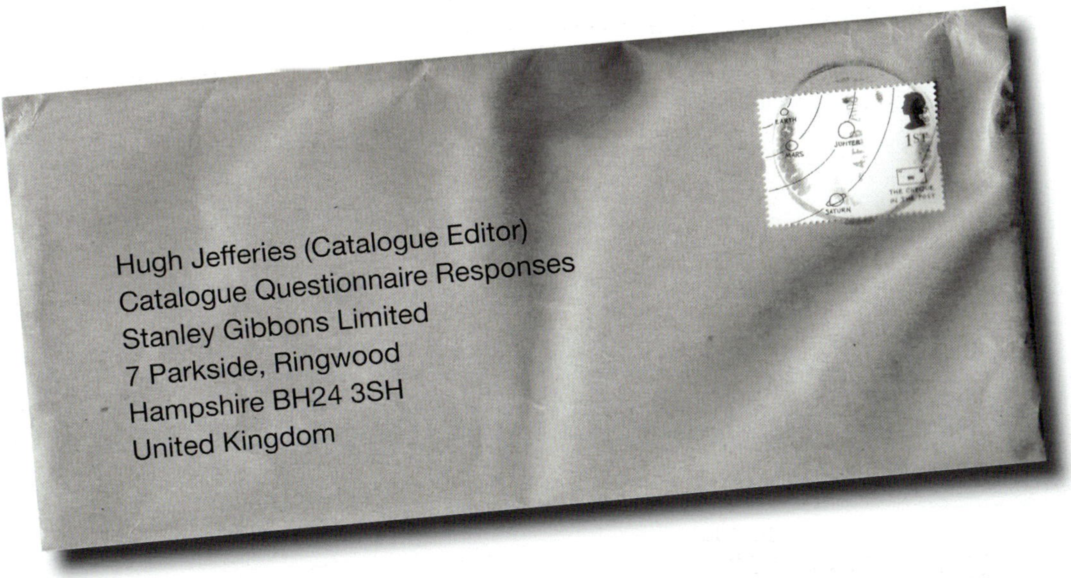

Questionnaire

2016 Australia

1. Level of detail
   Do you feel that the level of detail in this catalogue is:
   a. too specialised ○
   b. about right ○
   c. inadequate ○

2. Frequency of issue
   How often would you purchase a new edition of this catalogue?
   a. Annually ○
   b. Every two years ○
   c. Every three to five years ○
   d. Less frequently ○

3. Design and Quality
   How would you describe the layout and appearance of this catalogue?
   a. Excellent ○
   b. Good ○
   c. Adequate ○
   d. Poor ○

4. How important to you are the prices given in the catalogue:
   a. Important ○
   b. Quite important ○
   c. Of little interest ○
   d. Of no interest ○

5. Would you be interested in an online version of this catalogue?
   a. Yes ○
   b. No ○

6. Do you like the new format?
   a. Yes ○
   b. No ○

7. What changes would you suggest to improve the catalogue? E.g. Which other indices would you like to see included?
   ....
   ....
   ....
   ....

8. Which other Stanley Gibbons Catalogues do you buy?
   ....
   ....
   ....
   ....

9. Would you like us to let you know when the next edition of this catalogue is due to be published?
   a. Yes ○
   b. No ○

   If so please give your contact details below.
   Name: ....
   Address:...
   ....
   ....
   ....
   Email: ....
   Telephone:..

10. Which other Stanley Gibbons Catalogues are you interested in?
    a. ....
    b. ....
    c. ....

Many thanks for your comments.

Please complete and return it to: Hugh Jefferies (Catalogue Editor)
Stanley Gibbons Limited, 7 Parkside, Ringwood, Hampshire BH24 3SH, United Kingdom
or email: lholcombe@stanleygibbons.com to request a soft copy

Est 1856 STANLEY GIBBONS

Australia Order Form

YOUR ORDER

Stanley Gibbons account number

Condition (mint/UM/ used)	Country	SG No.	Description	Price	Office use only
			POSTAGE & PACKING	£3.60	
			TOTAL		

The lowest price charged for individual stamps or sets purchased from Stanley Gibbons Ltd, is £1.

Payment & address details

Name

Address (We cannot deliver to PO Boxes)

Postcode

Tel No.

Email

PLEASE NOTE Overseas customers MUST quote a telephone number or the order cannot be dispatched. Please complete ALL sections of this form to allow us to process the order.

Cheque (made payable to Stanley Gibbons)

I authorise you to charge my

Mastercard Visa Diners Amex Maestro

Card No. (Maestro only)

Valid from Expiry date Issue No. (Maestro only) CVC No. (4 if Amex)

CVC No. is the last three digits on the back of your card (4 if Amex)

Signature Date

4 EASY WAYS TO ORDER

Post to
Lesley Mourne, Stamp Mail Order Department, Stanley Gibbons Ltd, 399 Strand, London, WC2R 0LX, England

Call
020 7836 8444
+44 (0)20 7836 8444

Fax
020 7557 4499
+44 (0)20 7557 4499

Click
lmourne@stanleygibbons.com

Handy Auction Selection Guide...

REW PROMOTING PHILATELY ON ALAN TITCHMARSH SHOW ITV

When I was in my teens I attended my 1st auction which, frankly, I found intimidating – now, a few years (!) further on, with so few stamp shops, buying stamps at auction has become an essential tool of the collector's armoury ... so here are a few tips of what to look for ... *and* here's the reason why to do it now:

Collectors buy stamps from dealers
Dealers buy stamps from auctions
Therefore Collectors benefit buying from auction too ...

So How to Choose an Auction ?

Check/Keep these Key Questions to ask: Features to Look for...

	Name of Auction: *UNIVERSAL PHILATELIC AUCTIONS*		Name of Auction: (Insert Here) ?	
	IMPORTANT BIDDER CHECKLIST			
	U P A 1st £55 WINNINGS FREE	✓	***Introductory Offer .... ?***	☐
1	NO Buyer's Premium ?	✓		☐
2	NO Risk ?	✓		☐
3	ALL Lots Guaranteed ?	✓		☐
4	Reducing Estimate System ?	✓		☐
5	Lots £10 to £100,000 ?	✓		☐
6	Describers: 295 years Total Experience?	✓		☐
7	Massive Philatelic Choice ? (20,000+/- lot auctions)	✓		☐
8	£1.5 to £2 Million Auctions ?	✓		☐
9	Prices Realised (transparency) ?	✓		☐
10	FREE highest quality catalogues ? (to New Clients & Regular Clients)	✓		☐
11	6,000+/- Catalogues Distributed Worldwide?	✓		☐
12	FREE On-line Catalogue ?	✓		☐
13	'Keyword' Searchable on-line ?.	✓		☐
14	3,000+ 300/600 DPI photos ?	✓		☐
15	Colour-corrected 300/600 DPI images ?	✓		☐
16	1,900+/- Different Bidders in each auction?	✓		☐
17	90%+/- Bidders Successful ?	✓		☐
18	Low Bid Steps ?	✓		☐
19	Conventional Bidding NO charge ?	✓		☐
20	Electronic Bidding NO charge ?	✓		☐
21	'Live' bidding NO charge ?	✓		☐
22	Limit Bidders accepted NO charge ?	✓		☐
23	Payment Instalments NO charge ?	✓		☐
24	NO Credit Card Charges ?	✓		☐
25	NO Paypal Charges ?	✓		☐
26	NO on-line bidding charges ? (Eg. TheSaleRoom.com)	✓		☐
27	No charge for scans ? (Reasonable requests)	✓		☐
28	NO charge photocopies ? (Reasonable requests)	✓		☐
29	FREE Expert Condition Reports	✓		☐
30	Low Delivery Charges ?	✓		☐
31	Free Delivery Insurance ?	✓		☐
32	Generous ***NO Quibble Refund Policy ?.***	✓		☐
33	Reduced UNSOLD LOTS SERVICE ?	✓		☐
34	Expert, Welcoming Friendly Service ?	✓		☐
35	Andrew's ***FREE* 'TIPS OF THE TRADE'**	✓		☐

NEW POST-FREE UPA Loyalty Bonus ✓

Request UPA Catalogue? ☐ **Request Catalogue?** ☐
Thank you, You're literally requesting The Collectors' Secret Weapon so

SPACE FOR NOTES:
COMPARISON

£55 1st Winnings Free **?**
No buyer's premium **?**
All lots guaranteed **?**
Unique reducing Estimate system **?**
Loyalty Post Free **?**

Australia Lots included ✓

"This is My Promise to YOU"